GRAPPLING WITH THE CHRONOLOGY OF THE GENESIS FLOOD

GRAPPLING WITH THE
CHRONOLOGY OF THE
GENESIS FLOOD

Navigating the Flow of Time in Biblical Narrative

A RESEARCH INITIATIVE OF THE

THE CATACLYSM CHRONOLOGY
RESEARCH GROUP

Steven W. Boyd & Andrew A. Snelling, *Editors*

Master
Books®

A Division of New Leaf Publishing Group
www.masterbooks.net

Third printing: January 2015

Master Books®, P.O. Box 726, Green Forest, AR 72638
Master Books® is a division of the New Leaf Publishing Group, Inc.

ISBN: 978-0-89051-709-3
Library of Congress Number: 2014945606

Cover by Diana Bogardus
CCRG logo design by Luke Bugbee

Frontispiece used by permission of The J. Paul Getty Museum, Los Angeles
Jan Brueghel the Elder, *The Entry of the Animals into Noah's Ark*, 1613, oil on panel, unframed: 54.6 × 83.8 cm (21½ × 33 in.), framed: 86.4 × 118.7 × 9.5 cm (34 × 46¾ × 3¾ in.)

Please consider requesting that a copy of this volume be purchased by your local library system.

Printed in the United States of America

Please visit our website for other great titles:
www.masterbooks.net

For information regarding author interviews,
please contact the publicity department at (870) 438-5288

To two faithful servants of God,
who were the great pioneers
of Young-Earth Creation research,
in memory of the late Dr. Henry M. Morris, Jr.
and in honor of Dr. John C. Whitcomb, Jr.,
whose groundbreaking work made this book
and the others that will follow it possible.

It is our hope that our book,
Grappling with the Chronology of the Genesis Flood,
shall have a modicum of the impact of its namesake,
their *magnum opus*, *The Genesis Flood*.

So all shall turn degenerate, all deprav'd,
Justice and Temperance, Truth and Faith forgot;
One Man except, the onely Son of light
In a dark Age, against example good,
Against allurement, custom, and a World
Offended; fearless of reproach and scorn,
Or violence, hee of thir wicked wayes
Shall them admonish, and before them set
The paths of righteousness, how much more safe,
And full of peace, denouncing wrauth to come
On thir impenitence; and shall returne
Of them derided, but of God observed
The one just Man alive; by his command
Shall build a wondrous Ark, as thou beheldst,
To save himself and household from amidst
A World devote to universal rack.
No sooner hee with them of Man and Beast
Select for life shall in the Ark be lodg'd
And shelterd round, but all the Cataracts
Of Heav'n set open on the Earth shall powre
Raine day and night, all fountains of the Deep
Broke up, shall heave the Ocean to usurp
Beyond all bounds, till inundation rise
Above the highest Hills:

....

He lookd, and saw the Ark hull on the floud,
Which now abated, for the Clouds were fled,
Drivn by a keen North-winde, that blowing drie
Wrinkl'd the face of Deluge, as decai'd;
And the cleer Sun on his wide watrie Glass
Gaz'd hot, and of the fresh Wave largely drew,
As after thirst, which made thir flowing shrink
From standing lake to tripping ebbe, that stole
With soft foot towards the deep, who now had stopt
His Sluces, as the Heav'n his windows shut.
The Ark no more now flotes, but seems on ground
Fast on the top of som high mountain fixt.
And now the tops of Hills as Rocks appeer;
With clamor thence the rapid Currents drive
Towards the retreating Sea thir furious tyde.
Forthwith from out the Arke a Raven flies,
And after him, the surer messenger,
A Dove sent forth once and agen to spie
Green Tree or ground whereon his foot may light;
The second time returning, in his Bill
An Olive leafe he brings, pacific signe;
Anon drie ground appeers, and from his Arke
The ancient Sire descends with all his Train;
Then with uplifted hands, and eyes devout,
Grateful to Heav'n, over his head beholds
A dewie Cloud, and in the Cloud a Bow
Conspicuous with three listed colours gay,
Betok'ning peace from God, and Cov'nant new.

—Milton, from *Paradise Lost*

CONTENTS

PART I.   CHARTING THE COURSE: INTRODUCTION

PART II.   TAKING OUR BEARINGS: RELEVANT ISSUES

PART III.   THE VOYAGE BEGINS: INVESTIGATION

FOREWORD

Certain important issues regarding the integrity, credibility, and relevance of the Bible never go away and need fresh visitation in every generation. This is eminently true of the narrative of the Noah Flood and its literary, hermeneutical, and scientific dimensions. Usually the matter is pursued by the solitary exegete or geologist but seldom by both in one publication, particularly when the two are acknowledged to be among the top in their respective disciplines. *Grappling with the Chronology of the Genesis Flood* breathes the rarefied air of precisely that collaboration in the persons of Steven W. Boyd and Andrew A. Snelling, editors of essays by six scholars adept in the subject matter of the various topics with which they engage. Professor Boyd is a recognized Hebrew language scholar who controls many of the cognate languages as well as the history and literature of the ancient Near East. Dr. Snelling is not just a theorist but a hands-on geologist who has worked on such projects as the RATE (Radioisotopes and the Age of the Earth). His well-known two-volume work *Earth's Catastrophic Past* (Dallas, TX: Institute for Creation Research, 2009) speaks for itself as an authoritative work on the physical history of the earth.

In a day when once again the "Bible-science" wars have flared up, this time primarily with regard to the literary nature of the accounts of early biblical events such as Creation and the Flood, the gauntlet must once more be taken up to readdress issues that keep arising though in different forms and shapes. This alone is sufficient justification for the present work. But the case made here is almost unprecedented because of the assemblage of experts who have pooled their efforts under the watchful eyes of Boyd and Snelling. Without doubt, the world of skepticism and cynicism will be shaken by it while the confidence of those who already believe the written Word to be reliable will be renewed and strengthened by this bold new venture.

Eugene H. Merrill, Ph.D.
Distinguished Professor of Old Testament Studies,
Dallas Theological Seminary

FOREWORD

Seldom does a book appear that has such great potential to "change the world" as this book does, for it addresses some seminal questions of today: How old is the earth? What was its history? Did life evolve? Was the earth shaped by catastrophe? As all honest investigators know, scientific, historical, and theological questions such as these involve presuppositions within which the data are studied and the solutions derived. Every individual has deeply held presuppositions that inform his or her thinking, whether or not they admit or even know it. But not every presupposition set can be correct—in fact, some are mutually exclusive.

Thinkers of today often adopt a naturalistic worldview and interpret everything within present-day natural law. No matter how different observations are to what is predicted by natural law, these individuals only consider naturalistic explanations to be acceptable because allowing supernatural input is unthinkable. Conversely, Christians today believe in the supernatural, that God does exist and has been involved on earth. This doesn't mean they think that miracles regularly occur, but that they are possible and were certainly operating on the specific occasions mentioned in Scripture. Present-day observations of data are interpreted within this worldview. Both sides are "religious" in this fashion, relying on a different bias about the unseen past.

Scientists and theologians have long recognized that the great Flood of Noah's day holds the key to resolving the raging creation/evolution conflict. The Bible obviously teaches that the great Flood was global in extent and catastrophic in nature, and this book adopts that perspective. No place on earth escaped the Flood's wrath, and thus everywhere you look you would see its results. Every rock unit, every mountain chain, every animal or plant population, and every fossil would have been affected. If one attempts an interpretation of any of these without including the Flood in his thinking, he will fail to arrive at truth. But these systems in nature are the very systems used by evolutionists to support evolution. Their conclusions, dictated by an assumption of uniformitarian and naturalistic thinking have—if this book is correct—led them to error.

Several previous treatments of the Flood's geological effects have been undertaken, especially by author Dr. Andrew Snelling. His thinking is now partnered with and supplemented by Dr. Steven Boyd's understanding of the details of the Hebrew text. Carefully working out the chronology and details of the Flood given in authoritative Scripture gives us a much clearer understanding of the Flood's geologic consequences.

Both editors of this book are careful scholars, one a geologist and the other a theologian/Hebrew expert. They share an insistence on careful observation and interpretation, but do so within a biblical framework. The result is a clear elucidation of biblical thinking and an expansion of our knowledge into truly difficult realms. Together, they have produced a presentation like no other.

May the Creator of all things in the beginning, the Judge of man's sin in the great Flood, and the Redeemer of sinful man on the cross, be pleased to grant this treatment a wonderful ministry, to His great glory.

John D. Morris, Ph.D.
President, Institute for Creation Research,
Dallas

PREFACE

Welcome aboard! You have just embarked on our exploration vessel on our voyage of discovery—the chronology of the Genesis Flood. This book, the first deliverable of our research team, tells this story of discovery so far. You are holding in your hands our ship's log—it records the squalls we have braved, the contrary currents we have crossed by days of long, hard rowing. Now the voyage is well under way. In fact, according to our most reliable charts, we are about one-third of the way toward our destination. The destination is not obscure, whose coordinates are unknown. Quite the contrary. The chronology of the Genesis Flood lies within the text, within easy reach. Nevertheless, it has proved to be an elusive quarry. Many have tried to reach its fabled shores, only to fail, shipwrecked on its reefs or forced to turn back because of shoal water. It may even be the case that no one has ever made landfall there. We hope to be among the first to set foot on those golden sands.

The History of the Voyage

The story behind this voyage began in the fertile mind of Steve Austin. He knew me as a fellow member of the RATE (Radioisotopes and the Age of the Earth) team. I joined the team in 2001 after the initial RATE book was published, and contributed to the team's final publication a chapter presenting my statistical analysis of the genre of the Genesis Creation account, which showed that it is statistically indefensible to argue that it is poetry. The following year, 2006, Steve asked me to join a new project that he had devised, FAST (Flood Activated Sedimentation and Tectonics), as their Hebrew consultant and also as a principle investigator for a research project on the Hebrew text which would shed light on the physical processes being investigated by the geologists on the team.

    The goal of FAST was to investigate the Genesis Flood with the same kind of concerted effort which led to the extraordinary findings of the RATE project. I started reading the text of the Flood narrative with the singular purpose of helping the geologists on the team—who did not know Hebrew—understand the niceties of the Hebrew text. I decided that I should do some kind of project about the chronology of the Flood, because geological processes are time-dependent. Countless times I read the text, analyzing it ever more closely on each pass. I printed it up and started to colorize it as is my custom with any text I am meticulously studying. In the midst of this examination what stood out to me was the need to more precisely clarify the chronology of the Flood. There seemed to be some kind of chronological conundrum that demanded immediate resolution.

Specifically, my attention was drawn to the portion of the narrative from Genesis 7:24 to 8:4, in particular the one hundred fifty days mentioned in verse twenty-four and the date the Ark ran aground, which was five months after the Flood began. I realized that five months was one hundred fifty days, if a schematic calendar of thirty days is assumed.

I had always thought and taught my students that God remembered Noah at the middle of the Flood (8:1), and that "God remembered Noah" chronologically followed 7:24. But there were seven verbs involving processes in between the two aforementioned chronological pieces of information, which both appeared to point to the same or nearly the same time. How would there be time in between these virtually identical instants of time for all the events represented by these verbs? Could 8:1 be at a different time than is conventionally thought? Sequential *wayyiqtol* indicating temporal sequence did not permit that, however. For years I had taught my students that *wayyiqtols*, as well as being the backbone of biblical Hebrew narrative, whenever in sequence represented sequential eventualities—a principle almost universally embraced by Hebraists.

Since the text cannot be compromised, our understanding of the grammar must be mistaken. As a grammarian, this was a hard pill to swallow. But there is no other alternative. The long-standing concept that sequential *wayyiqtols necessarily* represent temporally sequential eventualities is wrong. Thus, because it is replete with *wayyiqtols*, at that point I began to question the conventional understanding of the chronology of the entire Flood narrative. I proposed a project for FAST to examine the chronology, which included an investigation of sequential *wayyiqtol*.

In the course of time my involvement with FAST ended, but encouraged by one of my students at the college (one of the contributors to this book), I decided to pursue the research on my own. Every voyage in the days of the tall-masted ships had a financier—whether a monarch, a wealthy merchant, a joint-stock company, or some other entity. The present voyage is no different. I needed a backer, a team (or crew) to help me, and a publisher (or shipwright). Answers in Genesis became the backer (or if you will, the joint-stock company), with the encouragement of their Director of Research, Andrew Snelling. I hand-picked the crew from among my best former students in my Hebrew classes, who are now pursuing doctoral studies. And Master Books became the publisher who would build the ship for the voyage. In the process, Andrew Snelling became my co-editor (or chief officer).

My original idea was to have a multidisciplinary research team, but it was decided that it would be a Hebrew project, with Andrew as our geological consultant. I met regularly with the team. We pored over the text and isolated the grammatical, linguistic, and literary issues that had to be resolved to ascertain the chronology of the Flood narrative. Each crewman compiled four lists concerning the chronology: those things certain, those things more certain than uncertain, those things more uncertain than certain, and those things about which he did not have a clue.

Each team member dug vigorously into the project. We knew what was at stake: an opportunity to develop a viable chronology of the Flood (we will argue in **Chapters 1–3** that this happy circumstance has never before obtained). This book, repeating what we said earlier, is in fact the log of our voyage of discovery up till now.

The key to the project was the *wayyiqtol*. A preliminary sweep of the literature revealed that a few others had recognized that temporally sequential *wayyiqtol* was problematic. At that time, as I read other Hebrew texts, I began increasingly finding dischronologized *wayyiqtols*, that is, where the order of the eventualities represented by the verbs was not the same as the linear order of the verbs in the text. It was obvious: we needed to focus on this issue.

Once our research showed that we could not assume temporal progression just because of the presence of *wayyiqtol*, we were left with a perplexity: in narrative, how then is temporal progression ascertained? All this time the team and I had been perusing the linguistic literature to answer this question. The answer was clear: the semantics of the text. There are countless articles on situational aspect, which focus on the temporal characteristics of *individual verbs* or verbs phrases. There are also an equal number of treatments of the temporal relations *between verbs* and verb phrases. There are far fewer—a handful in fact—dealing directly with *compatibility versus incompatibility* of eventualities as determinative of temporal progresssion. More linguists discuss *the place of attachment* between verbs. And a few others, *temporal breaks*.

We realized that we needed to consider all of these in developing a methodology to be applied to the Flood narrative in order to arrive at a cogent chronology of the cataclysm. It also became readily apparent that the presentation of the methodology was so extensive that it would be a book on its own, an essential prequel to the book we had intended to write on the chronology of the Flood.

The Maiden Voyage

Passenger Orientation

We recognized that the esoteria of Hebrew grammar, which is the "bread and butter" of Hebraists, would not be understood by or appeal to all readers. So we decided to link our research presentation to the sea voyages of discovery, adventure, profit, etc., which began with the Age of Discovery in the fifteenth century and continued commercially until fully supplanted by steam.

The names of sea captains are well known: such as Magellan, De Gama, Columbus, Drake, Cabrillo. Even ships are famous: the *Nina, Pinta* and *Santa Maria, Mayflower, U.S.S. Constitution, HMS Victory* (Lord Nelson's flagship), the *Flying Cloud* (whose record run around the Horn from New York to San Francisco of eighty-nine days, eight hours in 1853 stood for one hundred forty-six years), and the *Cutty Sark*. The whalers too had their part, so poignantly told by Herman Melville in *Moby Dick*. And fast clippers with their cargo of tea and gold brought great wealth to their owners during the California gold rush.

Each chapter of the book, therefore, begins with an "analogy and orientation," a story of sailing ships and an orientation to the topic to be covered in the chapter.

The Description of the Voyage

The entries in the ship's log are as follows: The destination of the voyage before us is clear and we are well aware of the obstacles that confront us (**Chapter 1**). We understand the importance of this voyage (**Chapter 2**). We have been informed of the treacherous waters encountered by previous expeditions which have run aground (**Chapter 3**). Details are given of how we will adjust our course so as to obtain a different outcome (**Chapter 4**). Before these specifics however, our formative, fundamental assumptions are stated, that the text is inspired, inerrant, authoritative, historical, literary, and theological. The glass indicates that heavy weather looms ahead as geological, geophysical, and paleontological challenges (**Chapters 5–7**). We weigh anchor! As we set out, we cull and synthesize the waves of opinion on the Flood (from the propitious tradewinds of the Reformation through the turbulent seas of the Enlightenment, to the becalmed Horse Latitudes of current Evangelical treatments), which have preceded our investigation (**Chapter 8**), and we chart the textual waters, determining the best reading for the five fixed dates and the entire narrative (**Chapter 9**). We are out of port and under sail! We are looking at the issue of temporal progression in biblical narrative. This is a crucial point in our voyage, the core of the book. We can see the Charybdis of morphology ahead. We successfully avoided it, thereby challenging the idea of temporal progression in *wayyiqtol* (**Chapter 10**). Out of view of land. On the open sea we investigate the factors that determine the temporal profile of texts on three different levels: we take a turn at the verbal tiller of individual verbs (the *micro level*) (**Chapter 11**), we tack with the text between verbs (the *macro level*) (**Chapter 12**), and we read the literary currents considering the purposes for the narrative as a whole (the *mega level*) (**Chapter 13**). We have to batten down the hatches, for we expect heavy seas ahead: applying our model to the complex Flood narrative. We are taking soundings of the structural depths to segment the narrative and to discover possible temporal discontinuities within it (**Chapter 14**). We need to understand the navigation points in the Flood narrative (the crucial *wayᵉhî*), which we are encountering (**Chapter 15**). One by one all of us climbed the mast-head and surveyed the sea all around the ship far and near. We looked far aft and saw whence we came. We looked around close to the ship and saw where we are. And we looked far fore and saw whither we go (**Chapter 16**).

That is the content of the ship's log so far. We will be making more entries in the near future.

Instructions to Passengers

The most important leg of the voyage comprises log entries **Chapters 10–13**. Certain chapters are easier to read. Everyone should read all of **Chapters 1–5**; as well as **Chapter 6**, **Sections 1** (introduction), **2** (historical background), and **8** (conclusion); **Chapter 7**, **Sections 1** (introduction), **2–3** (overview of the fossil record), **4** (burial order of the Flood), and **9** (conclusion); all of **Chapter 8**; **Chapter 9**, **Sections 1** (introduction) and **3** (conclusion); **Chapter 10**, **Sections 1** (introduction), **4** (biblical examples of dischronologization), and **5** (conclusion); **Chapter 11**, **Sections 1** (introduction) and **5** (conclusion); **Chapter 12**, **Sections 1** (introduction), **4** (issues pertaining to text, eventualities, and time), and **5** (final summation); all of **Chapter 13**; **Chapter 14**, **Sections 1**, **2** (introductory material), and **5** (conclusion); **Chapter 15**, **Sections 1** (introduction) and **7** (conclusion); and all of **Chapter 16**. Those who wish to delve into the particulars of the Hebrew grammar and general linguistics are encouraged to read the rest.

The Vessel

Ship's Regulations

All translations of the biblical Hebrew are by the authors unless indicated otherwise.

The Crew

Captain Steven W. Boyd, M.S., Th.M., Ph.D. in Hebraic and Cognate Studies, Hebrew Union College-Jewish Institute of Religion
Director of CCRG (Cataclysm Chronology Research Group)
Professor of Old Testament and Semitic Languages
The Master's College
Santa Clarita, California

Chief Officer Andrew A. Snelling, Ph.D. in Geology, University of Sydney
Geologist and Director of Research
Answers in Genesis
Hebron, Kentucky

Specialists (All pursuing doctoral studies)
Thomas L. Stroup, M.Div., Th.M.
Drew G. Longacre, M. Div., Ph.D. candidate at University of Birmingham, UK
Kai M. Akagi, M.Div., Th.M., Ph.D. candidate at University of St. Andrews, UK
Lee A. Anderson Jr., M.A.

S. W. B.

Castaic, California
February 20th, 2014

ACKNOWLEDGMENTS

The editors and authors would like to thank the following individuals and groups for their indispensable help on making this project and our first publication possible:

Ken Ham, *President* of Answers in Genesis, for AiG's financial support for this research project.

Tim Dudley, President, Master Books and his staff. Special thanks to Laurel Hemmings in Australia working for Answers in Genesis, for her meticulous formatting and typesetting of the entire manuscript.

The reviewers, whose comments challenged us and transformed the rough product we sent them into the much better work you see before you. The improvement is due to them. Any deficiencies are ours. Specifically, we acknowledge: Stephen A. Kaufman, *Professor Emeritus of Bible and Cognate Literature*, Hebrew Union College-Jewish Institute of Religion, Cincinnati, whose focused response caused us to properly align our ideas on the temporality of sequential *wayyiqtol*. Alice ter Meulen, *Professor of Linguistics*, University of Geneva, Switzerland, whose idea of temporal reasoning informed the entire study. Also we thank her for her insightful comments on **Chapters 10, 11**, and **13**, and for her and Susan Rothstein's (*Professor of Linguistics*, Bar Ilan University, Israel) evaluation of sample *wayyiqtol* chains (which can be seen in **Chapter 12, Appendix A**) we sent them. Jan Joosten, *Professeur d'Ancien Testament, Faculté de Théologie Protestante*, Université de Strasbourg, France, for his enthusiasm and encouragement with our project and findings and for his helpful input on **Chapters 10–13**. Sebastian Floor, *Director of Wycliffe Regional Translation Services, Bible translation consultant*, for his detailed perusal of **Chapter 14**, which was based on his dissertation, and his encouragement to its author. Saburo Matsumoto, *Professor of Mathematics (Topology)*, College of the Canyons, Santa Clarita, California, for his one-on-one interaction with the author of **Chapter 12** on first-order set theory and topology, which was needed to develop a mathematical model of time (**subsection 3.4** of **Chapter 12**). William Barrick, *Professor of Old Testament, Director of Th.D. Studies*, The Master's Seminary, for his extremely thorough interaction with **Chapters 10, 11, 13**, and **14**. Robert Holmstead, *Associate Professor, Ancient Hebrew and Northwest Semitic*

Languages, Department of Near and Middle Eastern Civilization, University of Toronto, Canada, for looking at **Chapter 15**. Andrew Bowling, *Professor of Applied Linguistics*, Summer Institute of Linguistics, Dallas, for sharing his and Robert Longacres's manuscript on the biblical Hebrew verb with us and looking at **Chapters 10** and **11**. Cameron Baxter, for his thorough copy editing of **Chapter 12**. Joelle MacKenzie, Amy Throop, Princess Amontos, and Rachel Castaneda, *Biblical Studies Department TAs*, and Megan Low *Administrative Assistant of Biblical Studies*, for their careful proofreading of **Chapter 12**.

Eugene Merrill and John Morris for their thoughtful forewords.

Luke Bugbee for his talented artwork for the part and section dividers, which are based upon Anna Anderson's tracings.

The administration, faculty and staff of The Master's College. Specifically: John MacArthur, *President*. Alexander Granados, *Vice President of Academic Affairs*, for his encouragement. My colleagues in Biblical Studies for their encouragement, especially: Dennis Hutchison, Brian Morley, Paul Thorsell, William Varner, and Daniel Wong. Amy Kidder, *Administrative Assistant of Biblical Studies*. The librarians at the college. In particular, the interlibrary loan librarians, Peg Westphalen and Grace Bater, and Reference Librarian, Janet Tillman.

Steven William Boyd would like to thank his team, Thomas Laney Stroup, Drew Glenn Longacre, Kai Matthew Akagi, and Lee Allen Anderson Jr. for their hard work, brilliant research, and compelling writing in their contributions in the book. Special additional thanks to Laney for technical support, Kai for keeping and synthesizing all the meeting minutes, and Lee for editing and compiling the manuscript from the time the manuscript was submitted to the publisher until it was printed. He was an indispensable help in bringing the book to fruition.

Steven Boyd is especially grateful to his co-editor and contributor, Andrew A. Snelling, for his contributions to the book, liaison work with the publisher, and for keeping the project going.

Finally, Steven Boyd would like to express his deepest and sincerest gratitude to his son, Hugh, for carefully editing **Chapter 12** to bring it into its final form, for transforming the preface, and much more—for working side-by-side with him after the manuscript was submitted as his de facto editorial assistant in many aspects of the production of the final manuscript.

Our wives, families, and friends. Steven Boyd: "I thank my wife, Janette, and son Hugh, for their love, patience, and unfailing support during a long ongoing project." Andrew Snelling: "I am exceedingly grateful to my wife,

Kym, for her unfailing support, love, and patience during this project." Thomas Stroup: "I thank Sarah, Noelle (3), and Tyndale (1), my beautiful wife, joyful daughter, and playful son, who have borne the brunt of this sacrifice with me." Drew Longacre: "I would like to thank my wife, Michelle, and daughters Victoria and Gloria, for their patience and support during this project, since they have had to sacrifice much time for my research." Kai Akagi: "I would like to offer special thanks to Anna Kroll and Oliver Schulz at The Master's Seminary Library and Grace Bater at the Powell Library of The Master's College for their assistance in obtaining various materials for research for **Chapter 11**. I would also like to thank the library staff at the Charles E. Young Research Library of the University of California, Los Angeles; the Dabney Humanities Library at the California Institute of Technology; the David Allan Hubbard Library of Fuller Theological Seminary; and the Oviatt Library of California State University, Northridge. Lee Anderson: "I thank my wife, Anna, for her enduring, faithful love, support, and encouragement throughout the length of the project. I would also like to thank the many friends who aided me in my research."

Our greatest acknowledgement is to the Triune God: Father, Son, our Lord and Savior Jesus Christ, and Holy Spirit.

Sola Scriptura
Sola Fide
Sola Gratia
Solus Christus
Soli Deo Gloria

PSALM 29:10

יְהוָה לַמַּבּוּל יָשָׁב וַיֵּשֶׁב יְהוָה מֶלֶךְ לְעוֹלָם׃

General Abbreviations & Technical-Term Conventions

ANE   Ancient Near East

BH   Biblical Hebrew

ESV   English Standard Version

GNV   Geneva Bible

KJV   King James Version

LXX   Septuagint

MT   Masoretic Text (Hebrew)*

NAS   New American Standard Bible

NIV   New International Version

NJB   New Jerusalem Bible

NKJ   New King James

NRS   New Revised Standard

NT   New Testament

OT   Old Testament

TNK   The New Jewish Publication Society of America Tanakh†

VP   verb phrase

All translations, unless otherwise noted, are those of the authors.

---

* The oldest complete manuscript of the MT is L, The Leningrad Codex B19a, which is in St. Petersburg, Russia. It was copied and corrected from a text printed by Aaron ben Moses ben Asher. It was written in Old Cairo in AD 1009 by the scribe Samuel ben Jacob

† Published in 1985, this version is a modern Jewish translation of the Masoretic Text of the Hebrew Bible into English.

General technical terms are italicized on first usage only
      example: *cohesion*

Types of Discourse Modes are capitalized, bolded, and italicized on first usage only
      Narration
      Description
      Report
      Information
      Argument

Names of Biblical Hebrew finite verb forms are italicized
      qatal
      wᵊqatal
      yiqtol
      wayyiqtol

Names of Biblical Hebrew verb stems are italicized and capitalized
      Qal
      Niphal
      Piel
      Pual
      Hithpael
      Hiphil
      Hophal

Members of the set of ***coherence relations*** are italicized and capitalized
      Serialation
      Result/Cause/Explanation
      Contrast/Comparison
      Introductory Encapsulation/ Elaboration/ Summation/Restatement
      Background

Temporal relations are bolded
      precedence
      inclusion
      superposition
      abutment

Semantic levels of the text are bolded and italicized
> ***micro-level***
> ***macro-level***
> ***mega-level***

Semantic factors on the ***macro-level*** are bolded and italicized
> ***coherence relations***
> ***compatibility/incompatibility***
> ***connectivity/connection/attachment***
> ***continuity/discontinuity***

PART I

CHARTING THE COURSE:

INTRODUCTION

Map of the world by Flemish cartographer Jodocus Hondius in the Mercator projection *Atlas* of 1630.

GEOLOGISTS STUDY THE RESULTS OF
THE MOST DESTRUCTIVE FORCES
UNLEASHED UPON THE EARTH.

THEOLOGIANS STUDY THEIR CAUSES.

THE HEBREW TEXT LINKS THE TWO:
DELINEATING THE FIRST
AND SPECIFYING THE SECOND.

CHAPTER 1

Destination Specified and Challenges Identified: Research Objectives and Obstacles

Steven W. Boyd and Andrew A. Snelling

Analogy and Orientation. As in any sea voyage, this voyage of research of the Cataclysm Chronology Research Group (CCRG) has a clear destination: ascertaining the chronology of the Genesis Flood—a goal easily stated but not easily achieved, because there are significant challenges to correctly doing so. Succinctly put, the ideal chronology of the Flood would be a description that gives the absolute time of the beginning and end of the events of the Flood recorded in Scripture. Or, alternatively, the time of their beginnings and their durations would secure the chronology. We are not given these absolute dates, but rather, relative dates. So, for us, this voyage is a pursuit of the sequence of the beginning of events and their duration. And, as in the heyday of the great sailing ships, the prospect of a voyage caused those so engaged to anticipate the challenges and dangers that would test the mettle of the most competent of hardy seamen, we must do the same, because challenges and danger lie before us, seven challenges to ascertaining the temporal sequences and thus avoiding the one ever present danger in biblical studies, arriving at an incorrect interpretation of Scripture. These seven are the challenge of the theological bent of the narrative, the challenge of the interaction of the structures in Genesis as a whole with those of the narrative itself, the challenge of the text, the challenges of the grammar, the challenges of the semantics, the challenge of the calendar, and the challenge of the nature of time itself. We will take these up in turn briefly in this chapter, but they will be taken up in great detail in the subsequent chapters. We will also consider how the chronology sets the parameters of the geology, geophysics, and paleontology of the Flood with the main crucial questions and issues being raised by these earth scientists.

Outline

1. Resolving the Chronology of the Flood Narrative
2. Setting the Parameters of Flood Geology, Geophysics, and Paleontology

1. Resolving the Chronology of the Flood Narrative

The seven challenges to resolving the chronology of the Flood, mentioned above and discussed below, are innate to the Flood narrative itself, but most are not confined to this narrative. In fact, all but one challenge are incumbent to every narrative; only the challenge of the calendar is uniquely pertinent to this narrative. We will now take these up in order, starting with the theological.

1.1   The Theological Bent of the Narrative
1.2   The Structures
1.3   The Text
1.4   Grammar
1.5   Semantics
1.6   Calendar
1.7   Time

1.1 *The Theological Bent of the Narrative*

Arguably, the extended narrative spans from Genesis 5:28 through 9:29. And clearly the central human character is Noah. Furthermore, it is obvious that the center of this extended narrative is 8:1, "God remembered Noah," in that this focal point is marked by several chiastic structures. There is the concentric structure of the numbers seven, forty, and one hundred fifty before this verse and one hundred fifty, forty, and seven after it; an inlusio of almost identical syntactic structures in 6:17 and 9:9, with 1cs (first common singular) ipp (independent personal pronoun) *hinneh* (indicates imminence) +1cs, "come" or "enter" *Hiphil* (causative verb stem) ptc. (participle) *'et* (definite direct object marker) *Hammabbûl*, "the Flood," in the former and 1cs ipp *hinneh*+1cs *qûm* "rise up," *Hiph* ptc. *'et bᵊrît*, "covenant," +1cs in the latter; and Noah building the Ark before the Flood and an altar afterwards—to mention a few. Such theological centralization makes it difficult to determine the sequence of the beginning of events, which is one of two hallmarks of chronology; the other being their duration. Specifically, the aforementioned centralization clouds the issue of the sequence of the events in 7:24 with those in 8:1. Also, of interest is the striking lexical change seen in the narrative. The root *bw'* occurs fifteen times before 8:11 but not at all after this.

1.2 *The Structures*

The Flood narrative evidences five structures, which complicates ascertaining the temporal sequence. First, the extended narrative is an atypical member of a ten-part genealogy beginning in Genesis 5:1, with generations two through six and eight exhibiting the typical formula and one, seven, nine, and ten being atypical. Moreover, second, intertwined with this is the Über-structure of Genesis, the *tol^edot* formulae, which separates the book into eleven parts, beginning with Genesis 2:4, with Genesis 1:1–2:3 serving as a prologue to the whole. A third structure is the interchange between God's dealings with the world and His dealings with Noah. A fourth is a recapitulation/ elaboration structure, which occurs several times in the narrative. Fifth, and finally, are the chiastic structures, which are mentioned above.

1.3 *The Text*

Just as whenever ancient sailors ventured out on the high seas, they found their whereabouts on the featureless expanse of the oceans on clear nights by orienting themselves to the "fixed stars," so we must base any chronology of the Flood on the so-called fixed dates from the life of Noah, which anchor crucial moments of the cataclysm: its beginning, the day the Ark ran aground, the day the mountain tops reappeared, the day the ground appeared to be dry and Noah removed the cover of the Ark, and the day the land was completely dry, the end of the Flood. These "fixed dates" are not sure cynosures, however: the Hebrew Masoretic Text (MT), Jubilees and 4Q252 of the Dead Sea Scrolls, the Greek Septuagint (LXX), the Latin Vulgate, and other important witnesses to the text, differ on these dates. Longacre will unravel the tangled skein in **Chapter 3**, **Section 3**; **Chapter 4**, **Sub-subsection 2.1.2**; and in **Chapter 9**.

1.4 *Grammar*

There are two main grammatical issues pertaining to temporal sequence in the narrative and two lesser ones. As for the main issues, in question is the temporal sequence of the chain of events represented by the chain of *wayyiqtols*,[1] the most common verb forms in Hebrew narrative; and the temporal significance of *wayʾhî*. The former of these will be discussed by Stroup—briefly in **Chapter 3, Subsection 4.2**, and in great detail in **Chapter 10**. And the latter of these will be introduced by Longacre in **Chapter 4, Sub-subsection 3.3.3**; and covered in more detail in **Chapter 15**. As for the lesser issues, which are the meanings of the three double infinitive absolutes and the meaning of all the verbs describing the transgression and regression of the water, these will be taken up by Stroup and by Akagi, respectively. The importance of the first is discussed in **Subsection 3.1**, but Stroup will present his findings in the next book. Akagi discusses the second in **Chapter 4, Sub-subsection 3.3.1** and **Chapter 11**.

1.5 *Semantics*

Although we are interested in the semantics of all parts of speech, the semantics of verbs and verb phrases is most germane to our study. We will be looking at the *semantic relations **between verbs*** and the *semantic characteristics of **individual verbs***, both of which are keys to unlocking the temporal sequence of the events represented by the verbs. The former, which Boyd will briefly elucidate in **Chapter 3, Subsection 4.1** and **Chapter 4, Subsection 3.2** and **Sub-subsection 3.3.2**, and discuss in great detail in **Chapter 12**, are variously termed logical semantics, rhetorical relations, discourse relations, conjunctive relations, and coherence relations (our preference). The latter, which Akagi will briefly address in **Chapter 4, Sub-subsection 3.3.1**, and greatly expand on in **Chapter 11**, also have their share of nomenclature: lexical semantics, situational aspect, and *Aktionsart*, among others.

1.6 *Calendar*

Calendrical issues abound in this chronological undertaking, which can be roughly divided into two multi-faceted groups, issues pertaining to points of time and those pertaining to duration of time. But what complicates any analysis of the chronology and seemingly defies our efforts is that when the text gives us the point in time, such as the date the Ark ran aground, six hundred years seven months seventeen days (the six hundredth year of the life of Noah, the seventh month of this year and the seventeenth day of this month), the accompanying durations are unknown. If we did know them, we could easily calculate how many days after the beginning of the Flood (six

---

1. The *wayyiqtol* verb is elsewhere called the preterite or the *waw*-consecutive imperfect.

hundred years two months seventeen days) the Ark ran aground. For the sake of argument let us suppose that months have thirty days. Then the number of days in question would have been the number of days remaining in the second month (thirty minus seventeen) plus the number of days in four months (four times thirty) plus the seventeen days of the seventh month, which yields a grand total of one hundred fifty days. But the fact of the matter is that we do not know. Nevertheless, since the author of the narrative gives us dates, it is natural to ask: what calendar did the author use for this detailed chronological record? Noah's or his? How many days were in a year? Was it three hundred sixty-five, that is, a solar calendar? Or was it three hundred fifty-four—a lunar calendar? Or, perhaps three hundred sixty—a schematic calendar? Or even the three hundred sixty-four day calendar, which is found in the Book of Jubilees? This triggers the next round of questions. How many days were in a month? How many months in a year? What—if any—adjustments were made to the calendar to bring it into line with the real passage of time? Were intercalary months inserted? Or, alternatively, were epagomenal days added at the end of the calendar year? Or was the method apparently employed in Jubilees used, the insertion of inter-seasonal days after the third, sixth, ninth, and twelfth months? Conversely, when we are given the length of intervals of time, we do not know to what point of time they attach. Should we count the one hundred fifty days from the beginning of the Flood, from after the first forty days, or from a different point in time?

1.7 *Time*

Finally, time itself is against us. Time is mysterious. Philosophers have striven to understand it; physicists have tried to explain how it works; and linguists discuss the relationship between time and events. Among the first group there are those who argue that time does not exist at all. Aristotle and Newton are two of the better known of these. Plato argued for the reality of time. Augustine, contemplating the experience and perception of time, concluded that we only experience the present; the past and the future are in our minds.

Physicists understand time to be a fourth dimension like the three spatial dimensions. In Einstein's theories of special relativity and general relativity time intervals change with velocity and acceleration, respectively. This is known as time dilation, the amount of which can be calculated according to the theory but is difficult if not impossible to conceptualize. But providentially we do not have to look at time relativistically in the Flood narrative. Nevertheless, we must ask some probing questions with respect to events, which linguists ask, such as: is time to be understood as discrete or continuous; are we dealing with points of time, intervals, or both; can we go from points to intervals and vice-versa; and how does time depend on different kinds of events, and conversely, how do different kinds of events depend on time? The first three of these are of a more theoretical nature, but the fourth is quite practical for our purposes, because the duration of time in an event is one of two components of the situational aspect of verbs—the other being dynamic (or not). Both *states* (e.g., The sky was overcast all day) and *activities* (e.g., John ran) involve duration in time. On the other hand *achievements*, which are instantaneous changes of state (e.g., Bob arrived at the house), and *accomplishments* (e.g., Bob built his house in three months) do not. In addition, states have the property that during any point in the interval of time the referent will be in that state (called right downward monotonicity); whereas, with action events the time interval is controlled by the event (called upward monotonicity)

So the voyage is ahead of us, a fascinating study to be sure in its own right; but it is also vitally significant to our understanding of Flood geology, to which we now turn.

2. Setting the Parameters of Flood Geology, Geophysics, and Paleontology

Resolving the chronology of the Flood from the Genesis narrative is crucial to setting the parameters for the geology, geophysics, and paleontology of the Flood. In particular, the timing in the development of the geologic record needs to be correlated with the various stages of the Flood so that the catastrophic Flood model for earth history can be firmly reestablished as a credible scientific alternative to the reigning secular gradualistic model. Furthermore, there are potential descriptions of the actions of the Floodwaters and other features that might possibly be gleaned from the Hebrew text that would be very helpful to aligning details of the geologic record with the outcomes of the Flood event. These geological, geophysical, and paleontological issues are discussed in detail by Snelling in **Chapters 5, 6**, and **7**, respectively, but some of the main questions being asked are briefly elaborated on here.

2.1   What were "the Fountains of the Great Deep" and "the Windows of Heaven"?

2.2   When did the Floodwater Level Reach its Peak?

2.3   Did the Floodwaters and their Levels Fluctuate and Oscillate during their Prevailing?

2.4   When were the "Fountains" Stopped and the "Windows" Closed?

2.5   Did the Floodwaters also Fluctuate and Oscillate during their Abating?

2.6   Does the Hebrew Indicate when all Life had Perished?

2.7   Does the Description in the Hebrew of the Mountains Appearing Refer to Only the Waters Abating, or did the Mountains also Rise?

2.1 *What were "the Fountains of the Great Deep" and "the Windows of Heaven"?*

These two descriptions of significant physical realities have long puzzled biblical scholars and Flood geologists alike. Knowing exactly what the Hebrew text allows these to be is very important for our understanding of the geology and physics of the Flood. It has been suggested that these "fountains" breaking up to initiate the Flood event could be supersonic steam jets produced by the rifting of the earth's crust around the globe into tectonic plates, which then sprinted around the globe, colliding to form mountains and more as the Flood event continued. And these "windows" could be a description of the intense global rainfall resulting from the ocean waters entrained in those supersonic steam jets cascading back to the earth's surface.

2.2 *When did the Floodwater Level Reach Its Peak?*

Did the waters only lift the Ark off the ground on the fortieth day of the Flood, or did the waters actually peak on that day? Or did it take until the one hundred fiftieth day for the waters to peak? Or did they peak before the one hundred fiftieth day? This is crucial to know, because the waters peaking would correlate with the apparent relative sea level inferred from the geologic record and with the deposition of the sediments carrying and burying marine creatures in rock layers right across all the continents. This seems to have been achieved early in the geologic record of the Flood event, after sediment-laden waters advanced rapidly onto the continents eroding off the pre-Flood land surface.

2.3 *Did the Floodwaters and their Levels Fluctuate and Oscillate during their Prevailing?*

The usual mental image of the Flood is that the waters steadily rose, peaked, and then subsided. Such an erroneous perception has readily facilitated the tranquil flood and local flood compromises. However, the fossil-bearing sedimentary rock layers that record the passage of the Floodwaters across the continents are stacked in distinctive megasequences that seem to record fluctuating water levels as the ocean waters oscillated across the continents, first advancing (transgressing) and then retreating (regressing). So does the Hebrew text of the Flood account allow for this? Specifically, does the Hebrew describe the waters' actions as oscillating forwards then backwards, and the water levels rising and falling while the "fountains" and the "windows" were open? The physical realities of daily tidal fluctuations and water surges due to earthquake-generated tsunamis would require such a description of the Floodwaters. It may be that the Hebrew text doesn't specify such details but would accommodate them.

2.4 *When were the "Fountains" Stopped and the "Windows" Closed?*

The answer to this question is very critical. If the "fountains" are to be equated with supersonic steam jets produced by the rifting of the earth's crust driven by upwelling and convecting molten mantle rock material, then the timing of their stopping potentially implies the start of the cessation of rifting and the deceleration of both mantle convection and the sprinting of the continental plates. This in turn would allow correlation of that point in the geologic record coinciding with the final phase of the plate movements with that point in the chronology of the Flood event (presumably the one hundred fiftieth day). This would have profound implications for our understanding of the timing of the mechanics of the Flood and the alignment of its geologic record with the Hebrew text. Equally important is to know whether the "windows" were closed at the same time as the "fountains" were stopped, as that would potentially confirm a causal link between them, namely, the supersonic steam jets as they shot up into the atmosphere entraining ocean waters that cascaded back to the earth's surface as intense global rainfall. But what if the intense global rainfall described as the "windows" ended after the first forty days?

2.5 *Did the Floodwaters also Fluctuate and Oscillate during their Abating?*

As stated above, the usual mental image of the Flood is that the waters steadily rose, peaked, and then subsided. But the realities of the physical movements of waters due to almost twice daily global tides and earthquake-generated tsunamis, and of the resultant deposition of the fossil-bearing rock layers, strongly imply water level oscillations and fluctuating currents and surges throughout the accumulation of the geologic record. A fluctuating relative sea level is inferred in the geologic record, even after the continent-covering waters apparently peaked high up in the rock record. So again, it is important to know whether the Hebrew words used in the Flood account can accommodate such descriptions of the waters also during the abating stage of the Flood event, even if such details are not directly specified.

2.6 *Does the Hebrew Indicate when all Life had Perished?*

One obvious evidence of the Flood as God's judgment on the earth and its inhabitants is the billions of dead animals and plants found buried and fossilized in sedimentary rock layers that have been rapidly deposited by water all over the continents. However, not only are the fossilized bodies of animals found in the rock record, but their fossilized trails and footprints. This means that these animals were alive and moving around during the advance of the Floodwaters. That would have been facilitated by fluctuating water levels, particularly because it would allow land vertebrates caught up in the Floodwaters to have left behind their footprints and tracks on any temporarily exposed soft sediment surfaces they were "beached" on. But once the waters peaked globally it would be assumed all land life had perished, just as the Genesis account describes, and maybe from then on only carcasses were buried. If the Hebrew text can shed some light on this question, then it will help Flood geologists in their interpretation of the fossil record, especially on the issue of where in the record is the location of the Flood/post-Flood boundary.

2.7 *Does the Description in the Hebrew of the Mountains Appearing Refer to Only the Waters Abating, or did the Mountains also Rise?*

This at first might appear to be a somewhat obscure question. But to Flood geologists this is very relevant. No one contests the view that today's highest mountains were formed only recently from the last tectonic plate collisions. Earthquakes and volcanic eruptions in recorded history are testimony to the fact that slow plate movements are still ongoing today. The Genesis account records that the Ark landed on the mountains of Ararat, apparently on the one hundred fiftieth day of the Flood event, perhaps even on the same day as the Floodwaters peaked and the "fountains" were stopped. So if the Floodwaters were peaking, the grounding of the Ark *at the same time* only makes sense if these mountains were in the process of being formed and therefore rose up from under the waters to intersect with the Ark. And even though the Floodwaters apparently then began to abate and levels presumably started falling, when seventy-four days later the tops of surrounding mountains became visible, perhaps those mountains were also being formed and thus also were rising up through the Floodwaters. This question may be asking for elaboration from the Hebrew text which it cannot provide. If that were the case, then at least the Flood geologists and geophysicists would be free to adopt mountain-building models consistent and compatible with the geologic record without violating the Hebrew text of the Flood account.

The foregoing is just a summary of the main vital questions Flood geologists, geophysicists, and paleontologists are asking of the Hebrew text that an in-depth study of the Genesis Flood narrative might resolve as the Flood's chronology is unravelled and the meanings of key words are elucidated. As the Hebraists and biblical scholars dissect the Genesis narrative using linguistic and other tools to unpack the chronology of the Flood, it is hoped that many, if not all, of these and other questions might be resolved. Yet it is also guaranteed that as these biblical scholars provide the needed feedback to the Flood geologists, geophysicists, and paleontologists, other issues and questions relevant to the geology, geophysics, and paleontology of the Flood will undoubtedly arise, that will sorely test us researchers in this voyage together.

Only with God's Word in our hands, the Holy Spirit's guidance of our minds, and God preserving our hearts steadfastly resolved on His calling to this task, will we have any assurance of safely reaching the destination we covet—a coherent chronology of the Flood event that successfully informs, elucidates, and constrains the parameters for understanding and building a robust, consistent model for the Flood's geology, geophysics, and paleontology that is defendable with integrity.

CHAPTER 2

The Profit of the Venture:
The Significance of Flood Chronology

Steven W. Boyd and Andrew A. Snelling

*Analogy and Orientation. The Age of Exploration (or Discovery) is
the historical period spanning from the early fifteenth century to the
seventeenth century, in which the western European nations discovered
(some would say rediscovered) new lands (the so-called New World among
them) and circumnavigated the globe, conclusively demonstrating what
had been known in theory since the days of Pythagoras, whose observations
of ships as they came into port led him to conclude that the earth is a
sphere, and the days of Eratosthenes, the Ancient Greek mathematician
and geographer (among other things), who calculated the circumference
of the earth. These western European explorers were set apart from earlier
ones by their undertaking of ocean voyages, not land expeditions, in the
face of the fear of the unknown and of the real uncertainty of returning
home.*

*Pride of place among them goes to Prince Henry the Navigator, of
the royal family of Portugal, the third son of John I and Philippa, sister
of Henry IV of England. Being barred from the royal succession by the
order of his birth, he turned his interests to the exploration of the west
coast of Africa, abandoned the comfortable life of the royal court and
set up his base of operations at the remote, forbidding escarpment of
Sagres, assiduously studied the navigators of the past, their techniques
and charts, and drew to himself the celebrated navigators, cartographers,*

*ship designers and builders and those who would command and man them
of his day. Of his accomplishments it has been said, "Until his day the
pathways of the human race had been the mountain, the river, and the
plain, the strait, the lake, and the inland sea. It was he who first conceived
the thought of opening a road through the unexplored ocean—a road
replete with danger but abundant in promise" (Encyclopedia Britannica,
ninth edition).*

*Funded by his governorship of the affluent Military Order of Christ,
by the exclusive rights given to him by his brother Eduard to trade revenues
from lands he discovered and by monopolies in the Algarve, granted at
his brother's behest exclusive control of all expeditions exploring the west
coast of Africa, and further motivated by the hope of meeting and uniting
with the forces of the legendary Prester John against those he called the
infidel, Henry sponsored many maritime missions. Under his auspices, the
Portuguese ship designers and shipbuilders developed and built a fleet of
new, faster, and more maneuverable craft, with a shallower keel and rigged
with lateen sails, the caravel, which enabled his captains to sail south along
the west coast of Africa, braving ceaseless, strong northeast winds, which
threatened to blow them out into the open sea and out of sight of land; to
eventually round the then dreaded and still treacherous Cape Bojador off
the coast of the western Sahara, whose underwater reef extends offshore
for 3mi (4.8km), producing unpredictable currents and dangerous shoals
only 7ft (2.1m) deep, upon which many ships had foundered; to venture ever
farther southward to circumvent the Islamic sphere of mercantile control
and gain direct access to the lucrative gold trade; and eventually, after his
death, to round the Cape of Good Hope, and thereby to reach India and all
points east and their coveted spices and other goods.*

*It is with a similar hope of great gain—linguistic, hermeneutical, and
spiritual, not financial—that we pursue our study, and we trust, with equal or
greater enterprise, energy, exactitude, effort, and effect. To the elucidation
of the significance and benefits of our study we now turn.*

Outline

1. Historicity and Credibility Issues
2. Geological, Geophysical, and Paleontological Issues

1. Historicity and Credibility Issues

For over four years now a team of Hebraists, the Cataclysm Chronology Research Group (CCRG), has been engaged in a crucial research project under the auspices of *Answers in Genesis* (AiG), with assistance and input from AiG's geologist and Director of Research, Dr. Andrew Snelling. The team is conducting an exhaustive linguistic and literary study of the Hebrew narrative of the Genesis Flood in order to ascertain its chronology and thereby provide the only solid foundation for research on the geological record of the Flood. Why is this research so vital? To answer this question we must go back almost five hundred years to Wittenberg, Germany.

    1.1   Scripture Supreme: The Perspective of the Reformation
    1.2   Scripture Dethroned: The Effect of the -Isms

1.1 *Scripture Supreme: The Perspective of the Reformation*

On October 31, 1517, Martin Luther nailed his ninety-five theses to the door of that city's cathedral, the standard procedure in that day to invite other scholars to a debate. He had only wanted to purify the Roman Catholic Church, being convinced that his arguments against the abuses of the Church were compelling and would provoke reform, but because of his stand, *Sola Scriptura* (Scripture alone) and *Sola Fide* (faith alone)—along with *Solus Christus* (Christ alone), *Sola Gratia* (grace alone) and *Soli Deo Gloria* (the glory of God alone)—and the intransigence of the Pope, Luther finally broke with the Roman Catholic Church, launching the Protestant Reformation.

The Solas were the five pillars of the Reformation, of which *Sola Scriptura*—our Faith must be based on Scripture only—was arguably the source of the rest. *Sola Scriptura* was the watchword of all the Reformers. For example, to Luther, Scripture was "through itself most certain, most easily accessible, comprehensible, interpreting itself, proving, judging all the words of all men" (Frei 1974, 19). It remained so with their successors for several generations. Scripture, not the traditions of men, was believed to be authoritative, because "all Scripture is *Theopneustos* 'God-breathed'" (2 Tm 3:16a). Scripture was believed to be truthful and accurate in all things whereof it speaks—including the content of the first eleven chapters of Genesis. In the sixteenth century it was believed that Creation, the Fall, the decline of man into depravity, the Flood and the dispersion of mankind and origin of the language families of the world at the Tower of Babel happened as Scripture describes. This situation obtained even at the beginning of the seventeenth century.

1.2 *Scripture Dethroned: The Effect of the -Isms*

Something happened in the seventeenth century, which challenged Scripture's authority—at first in matters of history, but eventually in general—until truthfully, albeit astonishingly, it can be stated that it was dethroned as the authority.[1] How was this possible only one hundred years after the inauguration of the Reformation? Moreover, what happened that by the eighteenth century (the 1700s) the beloved Word of God was subjected to scathing vitriol, such as the following by Thomas Paine?

> Whenever we read the obscene stories, the voluptuous debaucheries, the cruel and torturous executions, the unrelenting vindictiveness, with which more than half the Bible is filled, it would be more consistent that we called it the word of a demon than the word of God. It is a history of wickedness that has served to corrupt and brutalize mankind and, for my part I sincerely detest it, as I detest everything that is cruel....[2]

What was the origin, focus, and strategy of the attack on Scripture—for that is what it was and remains to this day—to bring it into such disrepute?[3] Who was this enemy, who vehemently, viciously, and viscerally attacked? What were his tactics? What did he concentrate on? And who carried out his biddings?

The enemy who has sworn to destroy Scripture is the Old Foe, whose mission was (and still is) to defeat the purposes and plan of God, the people of God, and God Himself. His strategy was and remains simple but brilliant: penetrate the defense lines of orthodoxy and then attack them from the rear, attacking what he perceived to be a point of weakness in the enemy's (that is, the people of God's) lines. Consequently, he focused on the early chapters of Genesis,[4] not immediately upon the carefully guarded miracles

---

1. From K. Scholder, *Ursprünge und Probleme der Bibelkritik im 17. Jahrhundert* (1966) as quoted in Reventlow, (1985, 3).

2. Excerpt from *Age of Reason* as quoted in Hayes (1977, 50).

3. The perspective of liberal biblical interpretation, of course, is that this was a rebellion against heavy handed orthodoxy: "The preeminence of a literal and historical reading of the most important biblical stories was never wholly lost in western Christendom. It actually received new impetus in the era of the Renaissance and the Reformation when it became the regnant mode of biblical reading. From it modern biblical interpretation began its quest in continuity as well as *rebellion*. Most important were three elements in the traditional realistic interpretation of the biblical stories, which also served as the foci for the *rebellion* against it" (Frei 1974, 1, emphasis added).

4. "The earlier parts of the Pentateuch, especially what scholars were pleased to call the biblical cosmogony, together with the original literary shape of the gospels, were topics of particular critical concern" (Frei 1974, 17).

of Jesus and the reality of the Resurrection—although, that too would come in time. And his minions were the philosophers and fledgling scientists of that day, who, as it were, forged a list of counterfeit *Solas*, which are the -isms of today: *Sola Natura* (nature alone—naturalism), *Solum Indicium* (empirical evidence alone—empiricism), *Solus Ratio Hominis* (human reason alone—rationalism), *Solus Labor* (effort alone—pragmatism) and *Soli Homi Gloria* (glory to man alone—humanism). His tactics were to feint charge after charge, probing for a soft spot he could exploit. Sadly, he found one: the wobbly defense of the historicity, feasibility, and manner and means of the Flood (which included its chronology), which was offered in the Renaissance.[5]

The blame for an incorrect analysis of the chronology of the Flood cannot be laid at the feet of any one person; rather, it can be traced to linguistic naïveté (quite understandable, centuries before the rise of modern linguistics!) It was assumed—and still is in many quarters—that the sequence of verbs of a particular form (namely, the sequence of *wayyiqtols*, which makes up the "backbone" of a BH narrative) mirrors the order of the events depicted in the text, so that the sequence of events can be read off of the sequence of verbs.[6] But now we know that temporal sequence is not marked in the verb form; that assumption, therefore, can lead to incoherent chronology. And that is what happened with the understanding of the chronology of the Flood: the guardians of Scripture were left defending an incoherent chronology, a battle they could not win. They fought valiantly, but inevitably were forced to give ground to the enemy. At first it was an orderly retreat, but then it turned into a rout.

That battle was lost. The enemy took the hill. And how costly was the defeat. The historicity of the text was questioned from then on, and its integrity impugned. Previously, truth had been determined at the bar of Scripture; but, from that point on Scripture had to stand before the bar of

5. These are documented by Allen (1963, 66–91), whose liberal perspective is evinced as he explains why he studied the history of the interpretation of the Flood narrative: "I have selected the Noah story, however, because its vicissitudes at the hands of commentators are less known, and because the attempt to provide it with a reasonable explanation led to other investigations that did much to stimulate other sciences of great modern value. The progress of mankind often depends more on glorious failures than brilliant successes, and the attempt to provide a rational explanation of the Noah story is one of the glorious failures" (1963, 66). Also see Allen for a discussion of the specific chronological issues swirling around at that time (1963, 74, 82–84).

6. The study of the event sequence represented by the *wayyiqtols* in sequence in the text is crucial to determining the chronology of the Flood, because there are seven *wayyiqtols* in a row in Genesis 7:17–18 (the first being וַיְהִי [*wayᵉhî*]) and twelve in a row in 7:23–8:4.

human reason.[7] Furthermore, a text that could not be trusted opened the door to destructive biblical criticism. And finally, a Flood whose chronology could not be cogently explained led to Lyellian slow-and-gradual, millions-of-years geology (1830–1833) and Darwinian evolution (1859).

But now we have the opportunity to turn back the clock. We can revisit the battlefield, join the battle again and take back the hill that was lost. How? Armed with the findings of modern linguistics and literary theory, the CCRG is attempting to develop a coherent Flood chronology. Even as we study the BH text, it is imperative that we document what others have understood about the chronology of the Flood; and to that end, one of our team members is conducting a thorough study of the history of interpretation of the Flood from the Patristic period to the present. The team as a whole is looking at the BH text of the Flood narrative from a micro perspective, individual verbs, up to a mega perspective, the structure of the whole narrative—and everything in between. That is, we must both ascertain the order of the events described in the Flood narrative, which are depicted by the verbs, and segment the overall narrative into its hierarchy of episodes, scenes, and paragraphs.[8] We now turn to explain these two extremes.

Let us start with the verbs. The verbs are in sequence, but were the events they represent? We must ask this question, because it is no longer linguistically tenable to assume that verbal sequence determines event sequence. Instead, event sequence is determined by the lexical semantics of individual verbs and the logical semantics between verbs.

Lexical semantics focuses on the types of actions represented by individual verbs. Consequently, we are studying the types of actions represented by the individual verbs in the Flood narrative. Linguists recognize that there are four basic types: *states* ("John was tired"), *activities* ("John ran"), *achievements* ("John won the race"), and *accomplishments* ("John built a house"). The first and second of these have no natural endpoint (the technical term for this property is *atelic*); and, therefore, for verbs of these types, time does not

---

7. Kant said of the eighteenth century, "Our age is the age of criticism, to which everything must be subjected. The sacredness of religion, and the authority of legislation, are by many regarded as grounds of exemption from the examination of this tribunal. But if they are exempted, they become the subjects of just suspicion, and cannot lay claim to sincere respect, which reason accords only to that which has stood the test of a free and public examination" (quoted in Hayes and Prussner 1985, 53). Hayes and Prussner call Kant's statements "the most clear-cut descriptions of the entire century to be found anywhere" (1985, 53).

8. The largest sub-units of narratives are episodes. These in turn may contain one or more scenes. Finally, scenes are composed of the smallest sub-units, paragraphs.

necessarily advance in a narrative. That is, the event depicted by the next verb may have occurred at the same time as the event depicted by the verb in question, or the two events may have occurred in a different order (called *dischronologization*). On the other hand, the third and fourth types do have an endpoint (called *telic*). So, time must advance.

Logical semantics, however, is concerned with the interactions between verbs. The most germane for us are compatibility and rhetorical relations. As for the first, compatibility, time must advance if actions are incompatible; there is no advance if they are compatible. For example, in the sentence, "John ran and sat down," John must stop running before he can sit down. The two verbal actions are incompatible. They cannot occur at the same time. But with the sentence, "John ran and whistled," John does not have to stop running before he can whistle. These verbal actions are compatible. They can occur at the same time.

As for the second interaction, rhetorical relations are the ways the events depicted by sequential verbs can relate temporally. Seven have been suggested. Here are five of them. The most common we have coined *Serialation*. This obtains when the events depicted by the verbs are in the same order as the verbs, and, moreover, are not related causally. An example would be "John went to the store and bought some milk." Another way is *Explanation*. In this case, the second verbal action explains the first, and may be its cause. "John fell. Bill pushed him" would be an example. A third way is *Elaboration*, such as "John wrote an email to his friend. He booted up his computer, opened his browser, went to the college webpage, moused down to email, entered his password, clicked on new, and typed out the message." In this sequence of verbs, "wrote an email" is an *introductory encapsulation*, elaborated by the verbs following it.[9] That is, all the events depicted by the verbs after "wrote an email" are parts of the overall event of emailing. *Result* is a fourth way events represented by verbs can relate temporally, which may be illustrated by "John turned off the light. It was pitch black." This is in contrast to a fifth way, *Background,* as in the following: "The basement was dark. John cautiously descended the stairs."

Now let us turn to the issue of the structure of the narrative. We must divide the narrative into its constituent parts, because temporal discontinuities are not uncommon between episodes, scenes, and even paragraphs, with the degree of temporal dislocation corresponding to the level in the narrative hierarchy. To that end the CCRG is employing

---

9. The CCRG suspects that Genesis 7:17a, "The Flood was on the earth for forty days," is such an *introductory encapsulation*, with the subsequent verses elaborating the particulars.

information theory involving activation levels, topic and focus, and theme analysis. Also we are investigating the syntactic and discourse function of a particular BH verbal form, וַיְהִי (way°hî), which occurs at critical points of the narrative, and may mark discontinuities.[10]

We of the CCRG are confident that with the Lord's help and by approaching the Hebrew text in the multifaceted way delineated above, we can resolve the chronology of the Genesis Flood.

In conclusion, we turn to a Lutherian-like quote. Its words give us our marching orders:

> If I profess with the loudest voice and clearest exposition every portion of the truth of God except precisely that little point which the world and the devil are at that moment attacking, I am not confessing Christ, however boldly I may be professing Christ. Where the battle rages, there the loyalty of the soldier is proved, and to be steady on all the battlefield besides, is mere flight and disgrace if he flinches at that point.[11]

With this clarion call, it is clear what we must do: retake the hill so that the godless -isms of most biblical scholarship of yesterday and today and of most of science will lose their foothold and down they will come; and their counterfeit solas will be replaced by the genuine. With the chronology of the Flood firmly established, and with a better understanding of the Hebrew description of the Flood and its processes, geologists committed to the authority of Scripture will be able to reclaim geology, returning it to its original biblical foundations, and thus be able to better construct and constrain their comprehensive model of the Flood event, and the strata and structures it produced. To the issues raised by these earth scientists we now turn.

2. Geological, Geophysical, and Paleontological Issues

2.1   Scripture Dethroned: The Genesis Flood Relegated to being Geologically Irrelevant

2.2   Anchoring the Geology, Geophysics and Paleontology of the Flood in Scripture

---

10. Of the ten וַיְהִי (way°hîs) in Genesis 5:28–9:29, the most important for resolving the chronology of the Flood are the fourth through the eighth, found in 7:10, 12, 17; 8:6, 13, respectively.

11. From a nineteenth century novel about the Reformation, *The Chronicles of the Schoenberg Cotta Family*, by Elizabeth Rundle Charles. Although these exact words were not stated by Luther all on one occasion, it appears that it accurately represents a compilation of his thoughts and sensibilities.

2.1 *Scripture Dethroned: The Genesis Flood Relegated to being Geologically Irrelevant*

Early in man's quest to understand the world around him, to satisfy his curiosity and to utilize the earth's resources to improve his living standards, the fossils were a puzzle. Though there were those who recognized them and the sedimentary rock layers containing them as testimony to the Flood event recorded in the Bible, most thought they were freaks of nature.

However, by the time of the Reformation and the two centuries following it many who delved into theorizing about the earth and its rock layers insisted the fossils represented creatures washed away and buried in the Genesis Flood. Nevertheless, there was also a swelling tide of rationalism demanding that human reasoning should also be utilized in any investigation of the earth's past history. After all, current geologic processes could be observed, so why could they not be simply extrapolated back in time and be used to explain the earth's past history? So increasingly only natural explanations were to be preferred (naturalism) when they could be found via observations in the present coupled with human reasoning. This tide of rationalism and naturalism increasingly spurred outright disdain of the Scriptures, which were progressively being dethroned as the final and absolute authority.

The turning point in relation to the overthrow of the Genesis Flood has having any relevance to geology was the work of James Hutton (1788, 1795) and Charles Lyell (1830–1833). By 1850 the rout was complete. The ruling paradigm in geology had become uniformitarianism, the belief in the uniformity of natural processes in space and time, or the present is the key to past, as being the *only* tool for interpreting the earth's past history. If there had been a Genesis Flood, it must have been tranquil or local, as it apparently left no evidence and was therefore irrelevant to the earth sciences.

So total was the rout that the publication of a book in 1859 by a Bible-believing geologist proposing the catastrophic break-up of a supercontinent followed by the sprinting of the resultant continents into their positions today, all during the year-long Genesis Flood, was not even noticed. Yet there has always been a faithful remnant of Bible-believing scientists who have fought to have the Genesis Flood reinstated as the key to understanding the earth's past history and the geologic record it produced. Thankfully today their ranks are growing. However, since Scripture is their final, absolute authority in which they desire to anchor their earth science, they need help from the Hebraists and biblical scholars to elucidate the chronology and details of the Flood from the Genesis narrative, so they can then firmly constrain their modelling of the Flood and thereby robustly and coherently recalibrate the geologic record, and can again defend it with integrity. And it is imperative that this battle be fought and won, because the centrality of God's Word in all human endeavors is at stake, but more so the eternal destiny of countless souls.

2.2 Anchoring the Geology, Geophysics and Paleontology of the Flood in Scripture

Based on the description in the Hebrew narrative of the Genesis Flood event, it is abundantly clear that the Flood engulfed the whole earth. Since water flows under gravity to seek a uniform level, if *all* the high hills under the *whole* heaven were covered, and the *mountains* were covered, then the Floodwaters had a global reach. As the Apostle Peter wrote, "the world that then was, being overflowed with water, perished" (2 Pt 3:6; KJV). All flesh died that moved on the earth, and all living things on the face of the ground were destroyed, and as the waters abated, the tops of the mountains were exposed.

These statements have implications. After all, if the Genesis Flood really occurred as described, what evidence of it would we expect to find today? Surely we would find billions of dead animals and plants buried in rock layers deposited rapidly by water all over the earth? And we do—billions of fossils in sedimentary rock layers deposited rapidly across all the continents. Even marine creatures are found fossilized in contorted and buckled rock layers in high mountains. These are testimony to the ocean waters having totally flooded all the continents. Thus Scripture informs and guides our understanding of the earth's geology, geophysics, and paleontology. Scientific investigations continue to uncover myriads of details that need systematizing into an overall scheme which pieces together the progressive building of today's continents with their fossil-bearing sedimentary layers and their landscapes. The Flood event provides such an overarching scheme or model. The fossil-bearing rock layers are stacked in catalogued sequences that have been matched from region to region across continents and between continents into the so-called geologic column. Its reality provides the record of the outcomes of the Flood event.

The model of a pre-Flood supercontinent being catastrophically broken up and the fragments sprinting across the globe to become today's continents, as proposed by Antonio Snider-Pellegrini in 1859, has been further developed into the catastrophic plate tectonics model of Steve Austin et al. in 1994. It has become a powerful Flood model of earth history that explains all that the secular slow-and-gradual plate tectonics model does, but a lot more that the secular model does not. Yet it is a model that still needs further refinement, not least by the need to understand the identity and nature of what the Hebrew text describes as "the fountains of the great deep" and "the windows of heaven." These have been interpreted respectively as supersonic steam jets produced by the catastrophic rifting of the earth's crust all around the globe, and the global torrential rainfall produced by the ocean waters entrained in those supersonic steam jets cascading back to the earth's surface. This catastrophic plate tectonics model then explains how the newly-erupted hot ocean crust expanded to push sea level up by over a mile, so that the ocean waters flooded the continental fragments as they sprinted across the globe, tidal surges and earthquake-generated tsunamis sweeping sediments and progressively entombed animals and plants into stacked rock layers across those continental plates, which when they collided produced mountain belts.

Flood geologists have a handle on the location in the geologic record where the evidence for the Flood begins, namely, near and at the continent-wide catastrophic erosion surface that marks the landwards advance of the Floodwaters, above which the fossils of myriads of shallow-water marine invertebrates begin to be found. However, it is the pinning down of the location of the Flood/post-Flood boundary that is much debated. The puzzle is complicated by finding higher in the fossil record up to the present more and more land-dwelling vertebrate fossils that have extant (currently living) representatives who are obviously descended from the Ark survivors. Additionally, the fossilized footprints of many of these vertebrates are found in the rock record at the levels where all land-dwelling vertebrates outside the Ark should have perished in the Floodwaters, rather than still being alive running around on wet sediment surfaces. So the Hebraists need to tell us when during the Flood all land-dwelling creatures had perished, because after that only carcasses should have been buried and fossilized.

There is thus no doubt about the profit of this venture, this voyage of unravelling the chronology of the Flood, because it will provide the remaining anchor points in what should then be a comprehensive, coherent, robust, and fully defendable Genesis Flood model for the formation of the geologic record and the earth's current landscapes. Some of the questions being asked of the biblical scholars by Flood geologists, geophysicists, and paleontologists have already been alluded to, while others have been specifically discussed previously. When did the Floodwater level reach its peak, and when were the "fountains" stopped and the "windows" closed? Did the Floodwaters and their levels fluctuate and oscillate during their prevailing, and did the Floodwaters also fluctuate and oscillate during their abating? And does the description in the Hebrew of the mountains appearing refer to only the waters abating, or did the mountains also rise?

The answers to these questions will enable alignment of that point in the geologic record where the relative sea level appears to have been at its highest, before eventually falling to its present level, with the day of the Flood when the waters are said to have peaked. Elucidation of the actions of the Floodwaters would confirm how their fluctuating and oscillating levels were responsible for stacking the fossil-bearing sediment layers across the continents as they prevailed, and then the subsequent erosion and deposition during their abating. Today's mountains were formed by the buckling of fossil-bearing sedimentary rock layers in plate collision zones, many very late in the earth's history, almost into the period in the geologic record which all Flood geologists would agree represents the post-Flood Ice Age. Yet mountains are mentioned when the Ark ran aground on the one hundred fiftieth day of the Flood, and then again seventy-four days later during the abating of the waters. Indeed, the mountains of Ararat on which the Ark ran aground persisted into the post-Flood world, so answering this question about the timing of the rising of the mountains during the Flood would seem to anchor the latest phase of mountain-building in the geologic record there in the Flood's chronology.

Only with the Lord's help can the research team of Hebraists resolve the chronology of the Genesis Flood and mine key Hebrew words for the nuggets that will shed light on the issues and questions raised by the Flood geologists, geophysicists, and palaeontologists. Likewise, with the Lord's help alone, the earth scientists who must then apply what the Hebraists provide them to their understanding of the geologic record will be able to have new insights that will complete the comprehensive, coherent, and robust Flood model they desire to have so as to defend the integrity of the Scriptures in explaining the formation of the geologic record and the earth's current landscapes.

Yet the bottom line is, as it always must be, that the ultimate profit of this venture is to remove the millions of years that are perhaps for many today the greatest stumbling block to their listening to and receiving the Gospel message, as well as being the source of so much compromise and lukewarmness in so many churches around the world. After all, the eternal destiny of countless souls is at stake in a spiritual battle we must be involved in, until He comes.

References

Allen, D. C. 1963. *The legend of Noah: Renaissance rationalism in art, science, and letters*. Urbana, IL: University of Illinois Press.

Austin, S. A., J. R. Baumgardner, D. R. Humphreys, A. A. Snelling, L. Vardiman, and K. P. Wise. 1994. Catastrophic plate tectonics: A global Flood model of earth history. In *Proceedings of the third International Conference on Creationism*. Ed. R. E. Walsh, 609–621. Pittsburgh, PA: Creation Science Fellowship.

Frei, H. W. 1974. *The eclipse of biblical narrative: A study in eighteenth and nineteenth century hermeneutics*. New Haven and London, England: Yale University Press.

Hayes, J. 1977. History of the study of Israelite and Judean history. In *Israelite and Judean history*. Ed. J. H. Hayes and J. M. Miller. Philadelphia, PA: Westminster Press.

Hayes, J. H., and F. Prussner. 1985. *Old Testament theology: Its history and development*. Atlanta, GA: John Knox Press.

Hutton, J. 1788. Theory of the earth: or an investigation of the laws observable in the composition, dissolution, and restoration of land on the globe. In *Transactions of the Royal Society of Edinburgh* 1: 109–304.

Hutton, J. 1795. *Theory of the earth, with proofs and illustrations*. 2 vols. Edinburgh, Scotland: W. Creech.

Lyell, C. 1830–1833. *Principles of geology*. 3 vols. London, England: J. Murray.

Reventlow, H. G. 1985. *The authority of the Bible and the rise of the modern world*. Trans. J. Bowden. Philadelphia, PA: Fortress Press.

Snider-Pellegrini, A. 1859 (early release 1858). *La création et ses mystères dévoilés*. Paris, France: A. Frank et E. Dentu.

PART II

TAKING OUR BEARINGS:
RELEVANT ISSUES

FIRST SECTION

ROUGH SEAS:
ISSUES OF TEXT AND TIME

PSALM 107:23–26A

יוֹרְדֵי הַיָּם בָּאֳנִיּוֹת עֹשֵׂי מְלָאכָה בְּמַיִם רַבִּים: ז ²⁴ הֵמָּה רָאוּ מַעֲשֵׂי יְהוָה וְנִפְלְאוֹתָיו
בִּמְצוּלָה: ז ²⁵ וַיֹּאמֶר וַיַּעֲמֵד רוּחַ סְעָרָה וַתְּרוֹמֵם גַּלָּיו: ז
²⁶ יַעֲלוּ שָׁמַיִם יֵרְדוּ תְהוֹמוֹת

Those who go down to the sea in ships, who do business on many waters.

They themselves have seen the works of Yнwн and His wonders in the deep.

He said and He caused the storm wind to stand and it raised up the rollers.

They went up to the sky and down into the oceans . . . .

Who hath desired the Sea?—the sight of salt water unbounded—

The heave and the halt and the hurl and the crash of the comber wind-hounded?

The sleek-barrelled swell before storm, grey, foamless, enormous, and growing—

Stark calm on the lap of the Line or the crazy-eyed hurricane blowing—

. . .

Who hath desired the Sea?—the immense and contemptuous surges?

The shudder, the stumble, the swerve, as the star-stabbing bow-sprit emerges?

The orderly clouds of the Trades, the ridged, roaring sapphire thereunder—

Unheralded cliff-haunting flaws and the headsail's low-volleying thunder—

. . .

—Kipling from *The Sea and the Hills*

CHAPTER 3

Treacherous Waters:
The Necessity for a New Approach

Steven W. Boyd, Thomas L. Stroup,
Drew G. Longacre, Kai M. Akagi,
and Lee A. Anderson Jr.

Analogy and Orientation. At the southern tip of South America lie two sea passages. The first, discovered in 1520 by Ferdinand Magellan in his circumnavigation of the globe, is known as the Straits of Magellan, and the second, happened upon by Sir Francis Drake in 1578 and later confirmed by Isaac Le Maire in 1616, is known as Drake's Passage. The Straits of Magellan travel westward between mainland South America and the island of Terra Del Fuego before winding northward through Smyth Channel off the western coast, and Drake's Passage rounds the southernmost tip of Cape Horn, reaching an incredible 55°58.46 0' latitude, the farthest south of any shipping route in the world. Prior to the building of the Panama Canal (and besides the lesser-used Beagle Passage) these were the two options for sailing westward from the Atlantic to the Pacific Ocean.

Because of the narrowness of the Straits of Magellan, reaching less than two miles at one point, the unpredictability of the winds, and the exposed granite on either side, the passage was risky at best: pleasant enough when the skies were clear, but hazardous for sailing ships if any storm should arise. For these reasons, Drake's Passage became the route of choice upon its discovery for sailing ships.

But Drake's Passage featured its own hazards as well. The winds below 40° south blow around the globe largely unhindered by landmasses, earning the names the "roaring forties" at 40-50°, the "furious fifties" at 50-60° (where Cape Horn lies), and the "screaming sixties" below 60°. Furthermore, the Andes Mountains to the north and the continent of Antarctica to the south create a funneling effect through this passage that further exacerbates the wind. Not only were these winds often strong enough to blow a ship far off course, they blew from west to east, requiring significant skill to make any sort of headway against them. Likewise, the currents flow largely unhindered by landmasses at this latitude, also flowing eastward with the winds. All of these factors contribute to very large waves through the channel, some of which can reach up to one hundred feet (30.5 m) in height. If one approaches from the west, there is even a "False Cape Horn" that has tricked sailors into turning eastward too soon, thinking they had rounded the horn, only to be driven by the winds into the Wollaston Islands.

Thus the attempt to round the tip of South America was no trivial matter; it required a thorough understanding of the hazards it entailed as well as a study of the mistakes that had caused the shipwrecks before. In like manner, the study of Flood chronology must be approached with extreme care. In order to have any chance of success, one must understand the challenges of this study and the reasons for the failures of those who have gone before. To this end, the present chapter will explore the various reasons underlying the general failure to understand the chronology of the Flood. These include indifference concerning the chronology, failure to reconcile the disparate witnesses to the text, and contestable assumptions of temporal sequence, Hebrew verb forms, and narrative theory in general. [TLS]

Outline

1.   Indifference Concerning the Chronology
2.   Lack of Consensus in Understanding the Chronology
3.   Failure to Reconcile the Disparate Witnesses to the Text
4.   Contestable Assumptions
5.   Serious Consequences of the Regnant Chronologies

1. Indifference Concerning the Chronology

The Genesis Flood has been the focal point of much study in the last half century. Sparked by the publication of the groundbreaking book *The Genesis Flood* by John Whitcomb and Henry Morris in 1961, biblical scholarship saw what was essentially a rebirth of conservative young-earth creationism in higher academic circles. No longer could young-earth creationism (and the accompanying global Flood view) be viewed as a position held only by unenlightened fundamentalists. Consequently, in the last fifty years the Flood narrative has been given increased consideration from multiple angles. Hebraists have marveled at the elaborate structure it employs. Theologians have been awestruck by the powerful message of judgment and salvation it communicates. Geologists and paleontologists have been amazed by the ramifications it bears for their respective fields of study. Conservative scholars who hold unswervingly to the inerrancy and historical accuracy of Scripture (cf. Ps 119:160; Jn 17:17) have certainly been at the forefront of the continuing investigation of the Flood narrative; however, even the most liberal critics have been forced to pay attention and interact with the growing stream of material written concerning it.

Despite the greatly increased amount of attention that has surrounded the Flood narrative in recent decades, relatively little serious study has addressed the chronological issues connected with the narrative. Most commentaries, articles, and other sources focus mainly (if not almost exclusively) on the theological message of the narrative. This problem is particularly noticeable among (often well-meaning) conservative commentators. Granted, the Flood narrative was indeed intended to convey a theological point; however, that message is embedded in the account's description of a historical event and cannot ultimately be divorced from how that event unfolded in time. Accordingly, a complete study of the Flood narrative must include a careful consideration of the chronology it presents. This argument, however, has been largely overlooked.

The problem is equally troublesome in more liberal circles, but for entirely different reasons. Since the introduction of Wellhausen's Documentary Hypothesis, the mode in academia has been to divide the book of Genesis (along with the rest of the Pentateuch) into multiple source texts. The Flood narrative itself, spanning from Genesis 6 to Genesis 9, is commonly regarded as the work of two, if not three, different individuals writing over a span of multiple centuries that have been cleverly compiled by a redactor. This redactor, however, allegedly failed to reconcile the differing chronological accounts found in the source texts. What supposedly is left, therefore, is a confused text—one that actually contains two chronologies that are in conflict with each other. For this reason, many scholars holding to a form of the Documentary Hypothesis have been reluctant to devote much effort to the study of the matter.[1]

Although it is not possible to quantify the degree of neglect that there has been of the chronology of the Flood, some numbers can help put the concern into perspective. One of the goals of this book was to examine historical views on the chronology by consulting prior literature on the Genesis Flood. Due to the sheer volume of literature on the subject, it was impossible to document, within the space of a single chapter, all views and arguments ever made on the issue. However, it was possible to conduct an expansive study on the views and arguments prevalent since the time of the Reformation. In total, one hundred sixty-seven sources dating from the early days of the Reformation to the present were consulted. Of these sources, eighty-six (over half) failed to give any genuinely useful information on the chronology beyond the five fixed dates explicitly stated in the text. While this total does reflect the contents of a number of lighter devotional commentaries, the fact that over fifty percent of the sources consulted (many written specifically on the book of Genesis) did not regard the chronology of the Flood important enough to comment on is most unfortunate. Martin Luther, though briefly arguing in favor of a peak on the one hundred fiftieth day of the Flood, provides a disheartening insight about the unspoken consensus on the chronology of the Flood. He writes in his comment on the time of the grounding of the Ark, "At this point the Jews argue about the number of months [of the Flood], *but it is useless to bother about things that do not matter*" (Luther 1958, 152, emphasis added).

No critic could have summed up any better the outlook on the chronology of the Flood. Simply stated, the chronology is not viewed as important enough to warrant attention. Luther's statement is a sad one, especially coming from someone who was generally a solid defender of biblical authority. In view of his statement, however, the following question deserves to be asked: If the chronology is not important, then what is? More specifically, if the historical facts of biblical narrative are minimized, what can be said for the theological, salvific, and moral material that is rooted in those

---

1. See especially the works of Harland (1996), Lemche (1980), and von Rad (1973). Note that the classic Documentary Hypothesis has been largely dismissed; however, many scholars still adopt some variant of the view and consequently question the legitimacy of the Flood's chronology.

same narratives? It appears that the unfortunate unintended consequence of neglecting the historical matters of Scripture in favor of the more distinctly theological aspects is that, in time, biblical history is greatly minimized or discarded altogether, leaving the theology without any basis whatsoever. If attention is not given to the careful study and teaching of biblical history, there can be no basis for the study and teaching of the theology engrained in that history. In neglecting the study of the chronology of the Flood, there is a definite risk of minimizing the historical event itself and failing to grasp the significance and authority of the theological message it conveys.

2. Lack of Consensus in Understanding the Chronology

Not only has there been a terrible lack of consideration of the chronology of the Genesis Flood, there is also among those who *have* written on the subject a notable lack of consensus. Virtually all sources consulted, with the exception of the liberal proponents of a conflicting chronological record, argue that the Flood lasted approximately one year in total from the time Noah entered the Ark to the time God commanded him to disembark. Such can be easily determined from the first and last of the five dates listed in the narrative (Gn 7:11; 8:14). The exact number of days spanning these two points varies only slightly due to differing assumptions concerning the calendar employed. Beyond this matter, however, there is considerable disagreement. The most notable area of disagreement (which, incidentally, is the primary chronological consideration in most sources) surrounds the date of the peak of the Flood. The study conducted in **Chapter 8** finds (besides the untenable liberal position of two conflicting chronologies) three major positions, as well as a handful of other unique and unusual views on this issue.

The most popular of the major positions contends that the peak occurred on the one hundred fiftieth day of the Flood. According to proponents of this position, the "springs of the deep" and the "windows of heaven" were open for *at least* the initial forty days of the Flood but may have remained active beyond that point. By virtue of some mechanism (concerning which multiple theories have been given), the Floodwaters continued to rise until the one hundred fiftieth day of the Flood when the Ark ran aground on the mountains of Ararat; then the waters began slowly receding. Generally speaking, proponents of this view see the narrative as strictly sequential, with the description of events in the text laid out exactly in the order of their occurrence during the course of the event itself.[2]

---

2. See Barrick and Sigler (2003) for the most detailed explanation and defense of this position.

The second view holds that the Floodwaters rose rapidly until the fortieth day of the Flood, at which point the mechanisms driving the Flood ceased. The waters then began their descent. The Ark ran aground not at the highpoint of the Flood, but only after the waters had been receding for over three and one-half months. Proponents of this position tend to see temporal overlap between the various scenes contained within the Flood, with the narrative constructed schematically, not necessarily chronologically.[3]

The third major position presents a scenario that is something of a hybrid of the two previous views. According to proponents of this position, the Floodwaters rose for the initial forty days of the Flood and then remained roughly stagnate, thereby maintaining their peak for the next one hundred ten days of the Flood until the Ark ran aground on the one hundred fiftieth day. Undoubtedly, this view was an attempt to reconcile two very pointed statements in the text, one which notes that the Flood was on the earth for forty days (Gn 7:17), and the second which states that the Floodwaters "prevailed" for one hundred fifty days (Gn 7:24).[4]

A discussion of the assumptions, merits, and potential problems associated with each view is beyond the scope of this chapter (see **Chapter 8**, as well as the bibliography contained in the chapter's appendix for further information on these and other views). However, the point remains that there is a general lack of consensus on the chronology of the Flood. While this is an area of Scripture where there may be room for disagreement and discussion, such should be based upon careful observation and detailed study. Unfortunately, these have lacked, engendering two problems. The first problem is that many sources have merely assumed the accuracy of a particular chronological model without assessing the potential problems it might present. While this may not initially appear to bear any ramifications for theology, it does impact the work of young-earth geologists and paleontologists who are basing their models on the biblical record. The second (and far more serious problem) is that the lack of detailed study on the chronology of the Flood has left the door open for the advancement of the liberal argument that the Flood narrative contains conflicting chronological records. This perspective naturally undermines the authority and inerrancy of Scripture. However, until there is more careful investigation of the chronological issues (and, presumably, a greater consensus on the correct understanding of those issues) the liberal position will remain insufficiently answered. [LAA]

---

3. On this point, see especially Cassuto (1997) and Chisholm (2003).
4. On this view, see especially Keil and Delitzsch (1976).

3. Failure to Reconcile the Disparate Witnesses to the Text

As readers examine the critical literature about the chronology of the Genesis Flood narrative, they are immediately immersed in a wash of redaction criticism, literary criticism, and a whole host of other methods of inquiry. The overwhelming majority of such studies simply assume with little or no comment the fixed dates of the Masoretic text as preserved in the medieval Hebrew Jewish manuscript tradition. But, unrecognized by many, there lies a lurking danger that threatens to undermine much of their work before it even begins.

At key chronological points in the narrative, careful analysis of the ancient witnesses reveals that there are great discrepancies between many of the texts. In particular, the fixed dates for the beginning of the Flood (7:11), the setting aground of the Ark (8:4), the appearance of the mountaintops (8:5), and the end of the Flood (8:14) are all textually questionable. Furthermore, some traditions include additional dates not mentioned in the Masoretic text. If any of these alternative dates are actually original to the Hebrew text of Genesis, they have the potential to invalidate the results of many previous studies based on the dates of the Masoretic text.

Recent studies, particularly those of Hendel (1995; 1998) and those responding to him (e.g., Zipor 1997; Rösel 1998a), have reopened serious consideration of the variant textual traditions, but there is still much work to be done to resolve the issue. Even so, many studies of the Flood narrative continue to assume the dates of the Masoretic text without text-critical examination and defense. The lack of extensive text-critical engagement with the different traditions has weakened the results of critical analysis of the text and demands a remedy. Whatever dates are preferred in the end, no dates can be uncritically assumed. [DGL]

4. Contestable Assumptions and Understanding

4.1   Temporal Sequentiality in Texts
4.2   Temporal Sequentiality of *Wayyiqtol*
4.3   The Nature of Hebrew Narrative

4.1 *Temporal Sequentiality in Texts*

It is tempting to think that the temporal sequence of events can be read off a text's sequence of verbs. For example, in Genesis 42:24, the first three verbs present three events clearly in the order of their occurrence: "He [Joseph] went away from them, wept and returned to them." This is particularly the case when the verbs are *wayyiqtol* forms, which form the backbone of BH narrative. But thoughtful reflection on the physical linearity of texts, their semantic nature, and the limits of morphology will disabuse us of this idea. For example, look at the following text with the *wayyiqtols* italicized and translated in the linear order of the text: "Jacob gave to Esau his brother, bread and lentil stew. And he [Esau] *ate, drank, arose,* and *went.* Esau *despised* his birthright" (Gn 25:34). In this passage does the sequence *ate* and *drank* mean that he ate the entire bowl of stew and then drank, or does it indicate the more natural situation that he ate, then drank, ate, then drank, etc.? Also, the last verb in the verse is part of a summary statement and not in chronological order. We now turn to briefly examine the issues raised by this text and others.

4.1.1 The Physical Linearity of Texts
4.1.2 The Semantic Properties of Texts
4.1.3 The Morphological Properties of Texts

4.1.1 The Physical Linearity of Texts

What is a text physically but a linear sequence of words, which is molded into columns or pages by the physical limits of the scroll or page? Viewed from this perspective, texts are not two-dimensional but one-dimensional. Admittedly, it might be considered strange to look at a text apart from its meaning; but, not so, it is quite instructive in this way: the physical one-dimensionality of texts introduces a peculiar constraint on the textual presentation of simultaneous events: they are forced into a linear sequence. Thus, linear sequence does not necessarily imply temporal sequence. For example, the sentence, "Pete laughed and jumped for joy when handed the puppy," does not imply that Pete laughed and then jumped; they likely occurred at the same time.

A clear example from Scripture is found in Numbers 22:25. This text recounts the reactions of Balaam's donkey to the presence of the Angel of Yhwh, who had a drawn sword in His hand. At one point the Angel stationed Himself where the road narrowed between the vineyards. Stone walls were on both sides. To get by the Angel the donkey had to press up against one of the walls, painfully squeezing Balaam's foot against the wall in the process. The donkey's moving up against the wall and the squeezing of Balaam's foot happened at the same time. They were simultaneous events, even using the same verbal root לחץ (*lḥs*) for both, in the *Niphal* for the donkey's movement and in the *Qal* for the squeezing of Balaam's foot. Nevertheless, the text must report these simultaneous actions in textual sequence.

In the Flood narrative, a similar situation obtains when the rapid rise of the water is described: "(The water) lifted the Ark, and it rose up above the land" (Gn 7:17). In fact, in this case we appear to be looking at the same event from two vantage points.

4.1.2 The Semantic Properties of Texts

Departing for the moment from considering the significance of the physical aspect of texts, let us look at them in the usual way, as imbued with meaning, semantically multi-dimensional, conveying participants (or referents) doing something, undergoing something, or being something in particular times and places. For example, the fabricated sentence, "Mike hit Max's thumb with a hammer when he missed the nail the latter was holding, while the two of them were working on John's roof last summer," has six referents (seven, if we count the roof): Mike, Max, his thumb, a hammer, a nail, and John. It has an event: the smashing of Max's thumb. It has a location where the event took place: John's roof. It has a time when it took place: last summer. This sentence illustrates that place is conveyed lexically. Time, however, is not always indicated this way. When it is, it is by absolute time words, such as "last summer"; or relative time words, such as "while." In the absence of such words, time is indicated alexically, as in the reworking of the above sentence: "Mike hit Max's thumb with a hammer. He missed the nail the latter was holding. The two of them were working on John's roof." Moreover, even though these three sentences lack time words, the time information is clear: the "hitting," "missing," "holding," and "working" all occurred at the same time. In addition, the semantic relationship between the first two of these sentences is evident (the "missing" caused the "hitting"), lest we think there was some malevolent premeditation on Mike's part.

The above makes it evident that we must start with two caveats specifying what is *not* the focus of our study: those cases in which the text explicitly signals the temporal sequence (such as with "then," "after this," etc.) and, therefore—at the risk of tautologizing—the temporal sequence is known; and similarly, those instances in which the semantic relation is explicitly given (such as with "because," "for example," etc.), because in these the temporal sequence of the events that are depicted by the verbs is also known. On the contrary, *our* focus is on those many instances in which the temporal relations are not explicitly indicated. This naturally leads us to the final consideration: morphology.

4.1.3 The Morphological Properties of Texts

Finally let us briefly examine the limits of morphology, posing the question: what, if any, information about temporal sequence does verbal morphology supply to us? Linguists used to think that temporal sequence was marked morphologically. But their findings almost univocally indicate that this is not the case. Similarly, Hebraists assumed—and still do in many quarters—that the sequence of *wayyiqtols* mirrors the order of the events depicted in the text, such that the sequence of events can be read off of the sequence of verbs. The linguistic evidence suggests, however, that *wayyiqtol* is also a temporally underspecified form. This is germane to BH narrative in general, in which *wayyiqtols* make up over fifty percent of the finite verb forms,[5] and especially so for the Flood narrative, which contains two long chains of *wayyiqtols*.[6] In BH, explicit relative temporal sequence is usually construed by the collocation of a preposition with the infinitive construct form of a verb.

As another illustration of temporal non-sequentiality in a biblical text, consider the following sequence of verbs, which evinces non-sequentiality of *wayyiqtol* in the movement from the third to the fourth instances of this verb form: "Joseph *dreamed* a dream and *told* it to his brothers, and they *hated* him even more. And he *said* to them, 'Please listen to this dream I have dreamt'..." (Gn 37:5–6). At the end of verse five the telling has already happened and its results are described, but in verse six the narrator retreats in time and relates the details of what Joseph said. Thus, verbs three and four are clearly not in chronological order. It would appear, then, that factors other than linear sequence can determine temporal sequence.

If neither linear position nor morphology is a certain indicator of temporal sequence, what is? There are six: the semantic characteristics of individual verbs; the semantic relationships between verbs (described in terms of textual coherence); the role of simultaneity; the connectedness of verbs; the possible presence, or not, of chronological discontinuities; and the purposes of the larger narrative. Akagi will handle the first of these in **Chapters 4** and **11**. I will discuss the next three, cursorily treating them in **Chapter 4** and extensively in **Chapter 12**, where I will also give some biblical examples of the fifth factor. But this important factor largely will be handled by Anderson, briefly in **Chapter 4**, but extensively in **Chapter 14**, with a full segmentation of the Flood narrative. The last factor will be taken up by Stroup in **Chapter 13**. As for now, we turn to Stroup's introductory thoughts on the temporal sequentiality of *wayyiqtol*. [SWB]

---

5. To be precise, the median relative frequency in a stratified random sample is fifty-two percent. See Chapter 9 in the RATE study on the distribution of *wayyiqtols* in narrative versus poetry.

6. The study of the event sequence represented by the *wayyiqtols* in sequence in the text is crucial to determining the chronology of the Flood, because there are seven *wayyiqtols* in a row in Gn 7:17–18 (the first being וַיְהִי [*wayʰî*]) and twelve in a row in 7:23–8:4.

4.2 *Temporal Sequentiality of* Wayyiqtol

One of the primary pitfalls for the study of Flood chronology has been the assumption of the temporal sequentiality of the *wayyiqtol*. In short, the *wayyiqtol* is the mainline verb form of past tense Hebrew narrative. Thus, when a Hebrew narrative wishes to relate a simple sequence of events it will normally use the *wayyiqtol* (e.g., "He went to the store, and bought a loaf of bread"). In contrast, almost any time a Hebrew narrative relates an event out of sequence, it will resort to the *qatal* instead (e.g., "He had run out of sandwich supplies").

This usage produces a very strong correlation, easily ninety percent or more (Cook 2012, 256), between the *wayyiqtol* and temporal sequence. Because of this correlation between the *wayyiqtol* and temporal sequence, there is no doubt that the *wayyiqtol* is used frequently to convey temporal sequence in Hebrew narrative. However, many have made the mistake of assuming that the *wayyiqtol* itself somehow indicates temporal sequence, making it the cause of this correlation.

This assumption has created significant problems for the study of Flood chronology. For example, if one assumes the temporal sequence of the forty days given in Genesis 7:17 and the floating of the Ark in 7:18, then the Ark does not rise from the earth until forty days into the Flood; surely those outside the Ark would have had time to construct their own vessels or even to break into the Ark if given that much time before the Floodwaters rose. Similarly, if one assumes the temporal sequence of the time periods given in Genesis 7:12 and 24, then the Ark did not come to rest until one hundred ninety days after the rains begin. However, the two fixed dates in 7:11 and 8:4 limit this time period to about one hundred fifty days. Moreover, if one adds together all of the time periods given in the course of the narrative, the result is a total of four hundred thirty-four days (cf. Gn 7:12, 17, 24; 8:3, 6, 10, 12); this is about seventy days too long, given the fixed dates in Genesis 7:11 and 8:14. And lastly, if one assumes the temporal sequence of the *wayyiqtols* in Genesis 7:5, 7:7, 7:13, and 7:15, then one must explain how Noah and his family could have entered the Ark as many as three or four times.

Because of these problems, there has been very little consensus on the duration of the rainfall, the peak of the Floodwaters, or the time frame required for the draining of the waters afterwards. In fact, the difficulty of reconciling the time periods with the fixed dates, along with the seemingly repeat entrances of Noah into the Ark, has led many to conclude that the story of Genesis 6–8 reflects the preexistence of several disparate textual traditions in accordance with the higher criticism of the JEPD theory. Thus, any study of the Flood's chronology must reckon with the true significance of the *wayyiqtol* and reexamine its function within Hebrew narrative.

4.3 *The Nature of Hebrew Narrative*

Another assumption that has played a subtle but significant role in the study of Flood chronology is the nature of narrative in general. As an example of this assumption, consider the following definitions for the English word "story" from *Webster's New Universal Unabridged Dictionary* (1996, 1877):

> "The plot or succession of incidents of a novel, poem, drama etc."
>
> "A narration of an incident or a series of events or an example of these that is or may be narrated, as an anecdote, joke, etc."

As these definitions underscore, the majority of people tend to equate a narrative with a retelling of a series or succession of events in chronological sequence.

This assumption may be accurate to a degree, especially when following a simple narrative with a single character plot (e.g., *Robinson Crusoe*); things become more complicated, however, with the addition of other characters separated from the main character (e.g., *The Lord of the Rings*), with the addition of plots and subplots possessing their own sequence of events, or with the addition of other purposes (e.g., historical, theological) besides story telling that can affect the order of presentation.

This assumption encounters problems when applied to the Flood story as well. As already mentioned above in relation to the *wayyiqtol*, a strictly sequential reading of Genesis 7:5, 7, 13, and 15 results in Noah entering the Ark as many as three or four times. In addition, a strictly sequential reading of Genesis 8:1 suggests that God only remembered Noah halfway through the Flood. And the chiasmic arrangement of the forty and one hundred fifty days around the statement in Genesis 8:1 (cf. Gn 7:17, 24; 8:3, 6) has led some to conclude that Genesis 8:1 marks the peak of the Flood.

Observations like these invite us to consider the nature of Hebrew narrative in general. Does a narrative always relate a series of events in chronological sequence? What happens when the narrator has several characters or several plots to follow? What happens when multiple purposes begin to overlap (i.e., historical and theological), influencing the order of presentation? And could the overlap of these purposes account for the apparent rearrangement and repetition of certain events within the Flood narrative? [TLS]

5. Serious Consequences of the Regnant Chronologies

As we consider the metaphorical voyage ahead of us, we must make a few course corrections at the outset so that later we do not run aground, become scuttled on the rocks, or be swamped in treacherous seas. Let it be said that the corrections need only be slight if made at the beginning of the journey, but nevertheless they are significant. Slight because we follow a train of stalwart venturers, who for the most part steered a straight course: embracing the literalness and historicity of the Flood and pointing to abundant evidence of the global inundation. But significant because—despite their noblest efforts—they did not attain the goal: the articulation of a tenable chronology, which can withstand the relentless onslaught of literal biblical criticism. Our heading therefore must be different from theirs or we must expect no different result. So we must reject the assumptions that would take us inevitably into dangerous waters, namely, 1) that linear textual sequence necessarily implies temporal sequence; and 2) that temporal sequence is morphologically marked, in particular, that *wayyiqtol* is marked for temporal sequence. Moreover, we must study linguistic theory to ascertain what *actually* determines temporal sequence, such as logical semantics, situation aspect, incompatibility, and the identification of possible temporal discontinuities through text segmentation, among other things. And finally, we must apply the linguistic theory to the Flood narrative. In the next chapter we will look at this new heading in some detail. [SWB]

References

Barrick, W. D., and R. Sigler. 2003. Hebrew and geologic analyses of the chronology and parallelism of the flood: Implications for interpretation of the geologic record. In *Proceedings of the fifth International Conference on Creationism*. Ed. R. L. Ivey Jr., 397–408. Pittsburgh, PA: Creation Science Fellowship.

Cassuto, U. 1997. *A commentary on the book of Genesis, part II—from Noah to Abraham*. Trans. I. Abrahams. Jerusalem, Israel: The Magnes Press.

Chisholm, R. B. Jr. 2003. History or story? The literary dimension in narrative texts. In *Giving the sense: Understanding and using Old Testament historical texts*. Ed. D. M. Howard Jr., and M. A. Grisanti. Grand Rapids, MI: Kregal Publications.

Cook, J. A. 2012. *Time and the biblical Hebrew verb: The expression of tense, aspect, and modality in biblical Hebrew*. Winona Lake, IN: Eisenbrauns.

Harland, J. P. 1996. *The value of human life: A study of the story of the Flood (Genesis 6–9)*. Leiden, Netherlands: Brill.

Hendel, R. S. 1995. 4Q252 and the Flood chronology of Genesis 7–8: A text-critical solution. *Dead Sea Discoveries* 2.1: 72–79.

Hendel, R. S. 1998. *The text of Genesis 1–11: Textual studies and critical edition.* New York, NY: Oxford University Press.

Keil, C. F., and F. Delitzsch. 1976. *Commentary on the Old Testament.* Vol. 7. Trans. J. Martin. Grand Rapids, MI: William B. Eerdmans Publishing Company. (Orig. pub. 1878.)

Lemche, N. P. 1980. The chronology in the story of the flood. *Journal for the Study of the Old Testament* 18: 52–62.

Luther, M. 1958. *Luther's commentary on Genesis.* Vol. 1. Trans. J. T. Mueller. Grand Rapids, MI: Zondervan Publishing House.

Rösel, M. 1998. Die chronologie der Flut in Gen 7–8: Keine neuen textkritischen losungen. *Zeitschrift fur die alttestamentliche Wissenschaft* 110.4: 590–93.

von Rad, G. 1973. *Genesis: A commentary.* Trans. J. H. Marks. Philadelphia, PA: Westminster.

Zipor, M. A. 1997. The Flood chronology: Too many an accident? *Dead Sea Discoveries* 4.2: 207–210.

CHAPTER 4

Adjusting our Heading: Delineating the New Approach

Steven W. Boyd, Thomas Laney Stroup,
Drew G. Longacre, Kai M. Akagi,
and Lee A. Anderson Jr.

Analogy and Orientation. When boarding a vessel, a passenger may give little more than a passing thought to the extensive planning and preparation leading to that moment. The captain and his officers, however, anticipate the implementation of a detailed voyage plan which they have been long preparing. From berth to berth, they have charted a carefully designed route, considered currents and potential hazards along with the real possibility of encountering foul weather or being becalmed, calculated distances between each waypoint, and ensured the proper preparation of all necessary documents for port entries, among many other particulars. Others have ensured that the ship is seaworthy, and still others that there are adequate stores for all on board for a potentially long and arduous journey. And finally, others have made provision for the cargo, which will be delivered to distant lands for a handsome sum.

Having surveyed previous related work and the necessity of extensive consideration of the chronology of the Genesis Flood with a new approach, such a "voyage plan" may now prepare for engaging the various facets of the project. As in any study, a set of relevant assumptions underlies inquiry and research. While these cannot receive extensive discussion and defense here, they require mention and brief explanation, much as captain and crew accept reports of the condition of a ship from others as sufficient demonstration of the vessel's readiness for a voyage. A specification of the starting point and a sketch of the strategy of the project, detailing the course, distances, and waypoints of its route, may then follow in anticipation of departure. We begin by outlining our assumptions. [KMA]

Outline

1. Assumptions
2. Starting Point
3. Strategy
4. Setting Sail

1. Assumptions

As we stated above in different words, many previous efforts to establish the chronology of the Flood started out with the right assumptions, which we will specify here. These are the fundamental presuppositions we bring to this study with regard to the ***inspiration, inerrancy, and authority of Scripture; its three-fold nature***; and ***the coherence of this particular narrative***—as well as the implications for this study, which stem from them. These broadly pertain to the text and to time in its various manifestations under the following rubrics:

1.1   The Text as Scripture
1.2   The Nature of Biblical Narratives
1.3   The Unity and Coherence of the Flood Narrative
1.4   Summation

1.1 *The Text as Scripture: Inspiration and its Implications*

Our first assumption pertains to the Divine origin of Scripture. Scripture is ***inspired***. In no way are we attempting to advance rigorous theological arguments; that is for others to do at another time. What follows are more in the way of assertions, both affirmations and denials, with various Scriptures adduced to support them. The biblical basis of inspiration is found in two verses, 2 Timothy 3:16 and 2 Peter 1:21. The first of these asserts that *all* Scripture is given by inspiration of God. There is no question that Scripture was recognized to be inspired, such as we see in Isaiah 8:20; Ezra 3:2; Nehemiah 8:1, 3, 8–9, to name a few. Also, note the following statement from the Chicago Statement on Biblical Inerrancy (CSBI), which supports this: "We affirm that the written Word in its entirety is revelation given by God" (Article III).

In addition, 2 Timothy 3:16 refers to what is *written* as being inspired, not the human authors. Thus, the very words themselves, not just the ideas behind them, are inspired. The Old Testament is replete with thousands of instances in which the authors claim to be transmitting the very words of God—for example the ubiquitous "The Word of YHWH came to me" intoned by Jeremiah and Ezekiel. The writing of Scripture is referred to in Exodus 17:14; Deuteronomy 31:24–26; and Joshua 24:25–26. Again we add to this the support of the CSBI: "We affirm that the whole of Scripture and all its parts, down to the very words of the original, were given by divine inspiration" (Article VI).

Moreover, the word translated "inspiration" in 2 Timothy 3:16 means "God breathed," that is, *God* is the source of His written Word, as is affirmed by Exodus 31:18; 32:15–16; Jeremiah 36; Ezra 1:1 referring to Jeremiah 25:11, for example.

From 2 Peter 1:21 comes the explanation of the interaction between the Divine Author and the human authors: authors of Scripture were superintended by the Holy Spirit so as to preserve their style and at the same time to write the very words God wanted to be written. This is well stated by the CSBI: "We affirm that God in His work of inspiration utilized the distinctive personalities and literary styles of the writers whom He had chosen and prepared" (Article VIII).

Drawing from all of the above, inspiration may be defined as

The Holy Spirit superintending the writing of Scripture so that the very words God wanted to be written were written.

The implication of this understanding of inspiration is that Scripture is **inerrant**, as well as truthful and reliable. Jesus speaks of these qualities in John 10:34–35 and Matthew 5:18. The CSBI also affirms this:

We affirm that inspiration, though not conferring omniscience, guaranteed true and trustworthy utterance on all matters of which the biblical authors were moved to speak or write.

We deny that the finitude or fallenness of these writers, by necessity or otherwise, introduced distortion or falsehood into God's Word (Article IX).

And further

We affirm that Scripture in its entirety is inerrant, being free from all falsehood, fraud, or deceit.

We deny that biblical infallability and inerrancy are limited to spiritual, religious, or redemptive themes, exclusive of assertions in the fields of history and science. We further deny that scientific hypotheses about earth history may properly be used to overturn the teaching of Scripture on creation and the flood (Article XII).

Finally, because of its Divine authorship, Scripture is **authoritative**, as stated in the CSBI:

> We affirm that the Scriptures are the supreme written norm by which God binds the conscience, and that the authority of the church is subordinate to that of Scripture (Article II).

The biblical basis for this consists in *its claim to authority*, its *use as an authoritative source*, and *its credibility*. The first of these is found in passages such as Psalms 19:7; 119:142, 144, etc. As far as the second is concerned, Jesus appealed to the Old Testament as the final authority on marriage and divorce (Mt 19:4–5, quoting Gn 2:23–24); when answering the question, what is the greatest commandment (Lk 10:25–27; 18:18–20); and as the decisive point proving His Deity, when He elucidated Psalm 110:1 (Mk 12:36). Finally, the third is evinced in its historical and scientific accuracy, and most extraordinarily, in the exactness of fulfilled prophecy.

1.2 *The Three-fold Nature of Biblical Narratives*

The second assumption concerns the nature of biblical narratives. We affirm that they are **historically accurate accounts, magisterial literary compositions**, and **profound theological treatises**. We deny the not uncommon idea that these three are mutually exclusive and label such notions as false dichotomies. I have extensively written on this elsewhere, but here I want to focus on the chronological implications of this three-fold characteristic of the Flood narrative.

Because the narrative describes a flood of almost unimaginable proportions and effects and what is more, we assert the **historicity of this account**, we expect to and do find unmistakable evidence of it in the rock record. Snelling has adduced an enormous amount of evidence, arguing that the nature of the rock record can only be explained by a global inundation (2010). In addition, the historical accuracy of the account provides the *raison d'etre* for this study: the chronology affects the geology.

This perspective on the Flood account has not been without its detractors. An idea has been advanced among evangelicals, namely, that the early chapters of Genesis have the genre of myth. By myth is meant non-historical, fictitious stories that resemble the ANE Creation and Flood accounts, not just mythical language. We assert that this idea could lead to a compromise of the integrity and trustworthiness of Scripture. At this time I would like to respond briefly by offering the following two arguments that the Flood account is *not* myth.

First, ANE myths are written in *poetry*; the Flood account is *not*. It is written in *prose*. The language of the ANE myths is so radically different from that of other texts that von Soden, who wrote the definitive reference grammar of Akkadian, wrote a separate grammar for the hymnic-epic dialect. Furthermore, Hebraists have noticed the uniqueness of the Old Testament Creation and Flood accounts with respect to this very thing: they are *not* written in *poetry*, but in *prose*. And to carry this point further, unlike the radical literary and grammatical differences between the ANE Creation and Flood myths vis-à-vis narrative texts, the biblical Creation and Flood accounts bear numerous literary and grammatical similarities to other BH narrative texts. Westermann comments: "The average reader who opens his Bible to Genesis 1 and 2 receives the impression that he is reading a sober account of Creation which relates facts in much the same manner as does the story of the rise of the Israelites monarchy, that is, as straightforward history" (1964, 5).

By choosing to write in narrative prose, therefore, the author chose the genre that most clearly conveys that his document was relating an accurate historical account. Moreover, BH narratives are highly historiological—to coin a term—not just history-like, the usual description. The problem with the latter term is that, just as saying that this jam has a blueberry-like flavor, implies it does not contain blueberries, saying that the Flood narrative is history-like implies that it is not history. But it most certainly is. The authors of biblical narratives believed that they were relating real history. Because we believe that the text is inspired, we must accept the authors' assessment and agree with them. Elsewhere, I have extensively argued this point as well.

My second argument is an assembly of the opinions of a few of the world's top Hebraists and specialists on Genesis on the matter. E. A. Speiser's comments on Genesis 1 are typical of this group: "What we have here is not primarily a description of events or a reflection of unique experience. Rather, we are given the barest sequence of facts resulting from the fiat of the supreme and absolute master of the universe" (1964, 8). And secondly, consider Nahum Sarna's thoughts. After discussing the Babylonian Creation account, *Enūma Elish*, he contrasts Genesis 1:1–2:3 to it and other extra-biblical versions of Creation: "Genesis is but a prologue of the historical drama that unfolds in the ensuing pages of the Bible," and, furthermore, "The outstanding peculiarity of the biblical account is the *complete absence of mythology* in the classic pagan sense of the term" and, finally, "Nowhere is the *non-mythological outlook* better illustrated than in the Genesis narrative. The Hebrew account is matchless in its solemn and majestic simplicity" (1966, 9–10, emphasis mine). Thirdly, Gordon Wenham comments forcefully on the anti-mythical, polemical nature of the text: "Gen. 1 is a deliberate statement of [the] Hebrew view of creation over against rival views. It is *not merely a demythologization of oriental creation myths*, whether Babylonian or Egyptian; rather *it is polemical repudiation of such myths*" (1987, 9, emphasis added). And fourthly, ponder the poignant words of Meir Sternberg:

Suppose the Creation narrative elicited from the audience the challenge "But the Babylonians tell a different story!"...Would the biblical narrator just shrug his shoulders as any self-respecting novelist would do? *One inclined to answer in the affirmative would have to make fictional sense of all the overwhelming evidence to the contrary; and I do not see how even a confirmed anachronist would go about it with any show of reason. This way madness lies— and I mean interpretive, teleological as well as theological madness* (1985, 32, emphasis added).

We will let the matter rest for now,[1] but be assured we will answer this idea in full in the next book. Our working assumption for *this* book is that the Flood narrative is **not a myth**. Now we must turn to the second characteristic of biblical narratives.

The second characteristic is its **literary nature**. As such, it has purposeful structure. Above, I discussed the various structures in the narrative, but let me zero in on two that affect ascertaining the chronology: *interchange* and *recapitulation*. The former is consistently employed to show the contrast between YHWH's treatment of men at large and His treatment of Noah. So, for example, after the text recounts the corruption of mankind and YHWH pronouncing their doom (Gn 6:1–7), we find, "But Noah found favor with God" (6:8). Also YHWH Himself makes the distinction in His speeches to Noah: "I even I am about to bring the *Mabbûl* [unique word for the Flood] of water on the earth to destroy all flesh in which there is the breath of life.... But I will make my covenant with you..." (6:17–18). The realization that the author is using this literary device puts us on guard lest we attribute temporal sequence to linear textual sequence.

The second structure, *recapitulation*, has been at times responsible for scholars maintaining that the Flood narrative is confused, is a conflation

---

1. For similar thoughts on this see Gerhard F. Hasel, The significance of the cosmology in Gen 1 in relation to Ancient Near Eastern parallels, *AUSS* 10 (1972): 19–20; idem., The Polemical Nature of the Genesis Cosmology, *EvQ* 46 (1974): 81–102.

of contradictory sources, and certainly is not a unified account. The most striking example is the three-fold telling of the entrance of Noah and his family into the Ark (7:1, 7, 13). The first of these is implied, because God commanded Noah to enter and the text also says that he did everything God commanded him to do (7:5), which would include entering into the Ark. The last two are straightforward reporting, although the first uses *wayyiqtol* (the verb in BH that carries the main line of the narrative; it must be first in a clause), whereas the second uses *qatal* (the verb in BH that is used when something other than the verb is first in the clause; also it is used in relative clauses). Assuming—as seems likely—that these are not three different entries, what sense can be made out of this repetition? Upon closer inspection it is clear that each serves its own purpose, but each is referring to the same event. And so accompanying recapitulation is a resetting of the time; a fact that must be kept in mind when attempting to ascertain the chronology.

Moving to the third characteristic, I pointed out above that the ***theological nature of the text*** is an obstacle to ascertaining the chronology. But in another sense, the realization that the text is—not surprisingly— profoundly theological and that its literary composition is at least in part if not entirely directed to that end, alerts us against deriving eventuality (i.e., state or event) sequence exclusively from text sequence apart from other factors. Forewarned is forearmed, as it were. In fact, every instance of temporal sequence based on text sequence must be met with the healthy suspicion that the textual juxtaposition may be there to advance a theological point and not to indicate the advancement of time. As a case in point, consider two *wayyiqtol* sequences, the last verb of Genesis 7:20, "The mountains *were covered*," with the first verb of 7:21, "All flesh which moved on the earth...*expired*"; and the only verb in 7:24 "The water *was powerful* upon the earth for one hundred fifty days," with the first verb in 8:1, "God *remembered* Noah...." As for the first, are we to suppose that the extermination of all life did not occur until *after* the mountains were covered, a conclusion to which we are led by assuming an iconic text, or that the extermination of all life occurred *at the time* the mountains were being covered, and that the juxtaposition is due to the linear nature of text? As for the second, is it reasonable to conclude that God did not remember Noah for one hundred fifty days and that only after this number of days did He do so, or that He remembered him all along and what is being emphasized is the contrast between how God treated Noah and his family with the way He dealt with the rest of mankind?

1.3 *Cogency/Unity of the Flood Narrative*

The third assumption concerns the **coherence of the narrative**. At this point in the project, we assume that the text is coherent and the chronology, when properly understood, is sensible. Furthermore, we assert that understandings to the contrary might stem from an unfamiliarity with the three-fold nature of biblical narrative and the complexities of temporal sequence in texts in general—and in the Flood narrative in particular.

But we are not satisfied with just assuming this. The coherence and unity of the text can be proven by rigorous methodology. The concept of coherence in discourse is widely discussed in the linguistic literature and beyond, and there is a general consensus as to what it is and to whether a text exhibits it. A coherent text manifests the following characteristics: cohesion, coherence (the technical term), intentionality, acceptability, informativity, situationality, and intertextuality. We will take up the gauntlet to establish the unity and coherence of this text in the next book.

1.4 *Summation*

With these assumptions regarding the text in place, we are ready to begin our investigation. We start with what the text gives us.

2. Starting Point

As we pointed out above, the Genesis Flood narrative comprises literary and theological structures, which complicate our chronological efforts. We do not have to start our quest for the chronology of the Flood from zero, however. The text gives us chronological information and calendrical information, both of which aid us in overcoming the difficulties imposed by these structures. Thus, the following headings constitute our starting point and organize our discussion below.

    2.1   Embedded Chronological Information
    2.2   Embedded Calendrical Information
    2.3   Summation

2.1 *Embedded Chronological Information*

    2.1.1   Introduction
    2.1.2   Determining the Text: Extracting the Chronological Information

2.1.1 Introduction

The starting point for ascertaining the chronology of the Flood is the **explicit chronological information that the text gives us**. There are two kinds of temporal data supplied: *intervals of time* and *instants of time*. The former are periods of seven days, forty days, and one hundred fifty days. The latter are the so-called five fixed dates of the Flood narrative. The aforementioned periods of time form a chiastic structure around the central theological passage of the narrative: "God remembered Noah." The points of time are not so "fixed," however, inasmuch as there are disparate textual witnesses, which must be weighed to determine the best reading for these dates. Longacre in **Chapter 9** has taken this task upon himself. [SWB]

2.1.2 Determining the Text: Extracting the Chronological Information

The first step in any critical study of the Genesis Flood narrative must be to establish the text to be studied. If one given textual tradition is preferred without engaging in preliminary text-critical studies, researchers run the risk of studying the wrong text and invalidating their results because of elementary methodological flaws. Establishing a reliable critical text of Genesis 6:5–9:17 is especially essential to this study for two primary reasons.

First, among the numerous ancient textual witnesses to the Genesis Flood narrative are vastly disparate dating and chronological systems. In particular, the fixed dates for the beginning of the Flood (7:11), the setting aground of the Ark (8:4), the appearance of the mountaintops (8:5), and the end of the Flood (8:14) are all textually questionable. Furthermore, a number of other key dates are identified in the witnesses, which also deserve serious consideration. The significance of the differing fixed dates should be immediately obvious for a study on the chronology of the Flood narrative. Any such study will be greatly affected by the researchers' choices between variant readings at contested locations.

Second, this study proposes to examine the text of the Genesis Flood narrative with a linguistic precision that demands an established text on even some of the minutest of details that are normally overlooked. Simple variants such as conjunctions, articles, personal pronouns, temporal adjuncts, word order, glosses, and explicit character references can have a profound effect on how readers follow the flow of the narrative. Where uncertainty does obtain, it is incumbent upon researchers to acknowledge the doubt and incorporate that complicating factor into their analysis of the linguistic phenomena. The critical text and apparatus will provide the textual foundation upon which the results of this study will be based. Researchers will not be bound to follow the editor's decisions where they disagree, but they will do so in full cognizance of the textual data.

In order to accomplish the goal of establishing a reliable critical text, this project will proceed along the lines of standard text-critical methodology. This will consist of two primary phases. Longacre will first collate all of the significant ancient witnesses to the text of the Genesis Flood narrative. He will then evaluate the noteworthy variant readings and construct a critical text in his view most nearly approximating the original Hebrew text of the canonical Genesis Flood narrative, including textual apparatus and textual commentary explaining his decisions on chronological variants. [DGL]

2.2 *Calendrical Information: The Reckoning of Time*

2.2.1 Introduction: Addressing the Ancient Calendar
2.2.2 Is There a Calendar?
2.2.3 What Calendar Is It?

2.2.1 Introduction: Addressing the Ancient Calendar

Once having determined the five fixed dates, in order to develop a chronology, we must know the time span between them. This depends on how many days there are in a month and how many months in a year. In short, *we need to understand the calendar used in the Flood account*.

This issue will be taken up in detail in the *next* book, because the focus of *this* book is the development of linguistic methodologies to address the general problem of how to ascertain temporal sequence in BH narrative. These will then be applied to delineating the chronology dictated by the Flood narrative. At this point we will just frame the calendrical quandaries with a series of questions and brief discussions.

2.2.2 Is There a Calendar?

By this question we mean is the reckoning of the five fixed dates in the Flood account according to a known calendar or—because these dates are correlated to the life of Noah—to Noah's personal pseudo-calendar, nothing more, and thus nothing more can be said about the calendar. But the fact that in the reckoning the dates advance from the sixtieth year, second month, seventeenth day to the six hundred first year, second month, twenty-seventh day of Noah's life entails that his calendar has a cyclical nature because the year advanced when a certain day of a month was passed. This invites a related question: are the months numbered from an independent calendar or just from Noah's life? In other words is the second month the second month of a year starting at a particular time independent of the life of Noah or is it the second month of Noah's sixtieth year, with the year starting at his birthday? Of course we could always ask: is this a determinative issue?

2.2.3 What Calendar Is It?

Given that Moses authored Genesis and the Flood account in particular, which calendar did he use? The answer to this does not depend on the answer to the first question, because whether he used Noah's personal calendar or an independent calendar, the calendar is cylical.

(1) **Noah's Personal Calendar.** If it is Noah's personal calendar, what can we deduce from the text about it? It has at least ten months, because the date six hundred years ten months one day is given in the text (Gn 8:5). Also we can be certain that a month has at least twenty-seven days, because Genesis 8:14 records that the Flood ended in the six hundred first year, in the second month, on the twenty-seventh day.

What do we *not* know? Much. How many days are in this personal year? How many months are in it? And how many days are in a month?

(2) **An Independent Calendar.** The second possibility is that the calendar is a known calendar, either from Noah's day or Moses' day.

(a) *An Independent Calendar from Noah's Day.* We know the same things about this calendar as we do about Noah's personal calendar; and we are ignorant of the same things about the former as we are about the latter.

Having briefly considered the issues pertaining to a Noahic calendar, his own or from his day, we are moved to pose the following question: in light of the background of Moses and his audience, would it make sense for him to use such a calendar? My tentative answer at this point is that although it is possible that Moses would have employed a Noahic calendar, it is not very plausible, because that would be orienting his audience to the Flood with a calendar *inaccessible* and *unknown* to them. For that is what Noah's personal calendar or a calendar from Noah's day would be. It is much more likely that Moses employed a calendar *known* to his readers, an independent calendar from *his* day. To that possibility we now turn.

(b) *An Independent Calendar from Moses' Day.* There are at least four different possibilities for this type of calendar (each with subtypes): a solar calendar of three hundred sixty-five days; a lunar calendar of three hundred fifty-four days; a three hundred sixty-four day calendar as is seen in the Book of Jubilees; and a schematic calendar of three hundred sixty days. There is evidence for each type, the specifics of which will be the topic of the next book. But a few comments and/or questions are in order.

The first comment is that all of these require calendrical corrections to make them line up with the solar year—the first and third, the least; the second, the most, an intercalary month; and, the last, the insertion of five epagomenal days—because regardless of the calendrical system there are not a whole number of solar days in a solar year and thus a particular date will precess. If adjustments were not made for this, the dates of important yearly festivals would drift, if unchecked, into a different season. Today we follow the Gregorian Calendar, which is designed with a leap year every four years to correct for precession. The pertinent question then is: what was the means of correction in the calendar of the Flood account? And, what is more, how does this apply to the Flood dates?

A second comment and/or question pertains to the provenance of the calendar. Was it Egyptian, Amorite, Sumerian, Babylonian, Assyrian, Hittite, or other? Does it matter?

A third concerns the calendar in the Book of Jubilees. What is its connection to that of the Flood account? Also there is the Qumran version of the Flood narrative, 4Q252, which embellishes the text with chronological commentary.

2.3 Summation

We have surveyed above the textual issues and numerous calendrical issues. It is imperative that we answer these questions, because they all impinge on our chronological research. All our work on developing methodologies for ascertaining temporal progression in texts—which we will introduce below—will be for naught if we have not interacted with the five fixed dates. We pledge ourselves, therefore, to be fully conversant with the ancient calendar from this text.

3. Strategy

Having established the five fixed dates and the entire critical text of the Flood narrative and fully aware of the importance of understanding the Flood narrative calendar, we pause to reflect on the grammatical challenges presented by the text and how we have met these and will continue to do so as the project continues. Below is a précis of the linguistic methodologies we developed to wrestle the chronology from this complex narrative. These will be presented in detail in **Chapters 10–15**.

> 3.1 Introduction: Identifying the Grammatical and Linguistic Issues
> 3.2 The Nature of Temporal Sequentiality: Text, Eventualities, and Time
> 3.3 Determining Sequentiality

3.1 Introduction: Identifying the Grammatical and Linguistic Issues

Four grammatical issues in the text must be addressed to ascertain the chronology of the Flood narrative. This must be accompanied by a consideration of the not-unrelated general linguistic studies on the factors that affect temporal sequence. The former are the *sequentiality of wayyiqtol*, the *possibility of chronological breaks, the significance of the eight* וַיְהִי (*way°hî*), and *the meaning of the double infinitive absolutes*. The latter are semantic characteristics of verbs and verb phrases (VPs) (we call this the *micro-level*), semantic relationships between VPs (the *macro-level*), and the overall semantic structure of the narrative (the *mega-level*).

The grammatical issues have been tackled in the following ways. The last of these, Stroup's findings on the *double infinitive absolutes*, will appear in the second book, since they are not germane to the main focus of this book: the investigation of the factors which contribute to temporal progression in a narrative. Nevertheless, the findings are very important to the success of the overall research project, in that they are used to describe the movement of the water and are thus an essential part of the understanding of the geology of the Flood.

The first three of these, however, are the focus of this book. We challenge the commonly held view that *wayyiqtol* marks temporal sequence. Stroup in **Chapter 10** investigates this issue thoroughly and presents quite a few examples of dischronologized *wayyiqtol*. Additional biblical passages evincing dischronologization are found in **Chapter 12**. We conclude, therefore, that *wayyiqtol* does not mark temporal progression. We suspect, however, that *wayyiqtol* is *necessary* if temporal sequence is to be conveyed, even though it is *not sufficient* to indicate it. This leads us into a major investigation of *the factors that* do *convey temporal progression*. We will look at these below and in detail in **Chapters 11–15**.

In addition, the possible presence of temporal gaps in the narrative is extremely relevant to its chronology. To this end, Anderson in **Chapter 14** identifies locations in the text where there might be chronological discontinuities. He does this by first segmenting the Flood narrative.

The last issue that must be considered is the discourse-level function of וַיְהִי (*waye°hî*)—along with its other significations. Longacre lays out the issues in **Chapter 15** and will conclude his study in the next book.

Before we talk about these factors that affect temporal sequence, however, we must first present a brief primer on temporal sequentiality.

3.2 *The Nature of Temporal Sequentiality: Text, Eventualities, and Time*

3.2.1 Defining Sequentiality
3.2.2 Delimiting Sequentiality

3.2.1 Defining Sequentiality: Texts, Eventualities, and Time

There are three dimensions, as it were, to sequentiality: that of text, that of eventuality, and that of time. The last two are more important to this study, but only the first is immediately accessible and beyond debate. Nevertheless, the three work together. We define them as follows and illustrate them with examples translated without temporal connectors:

(1) **Textual Sequence.** This is a sequence of the same type of verbs, with no other types intervening except those in speeches, which are the "content" of a verb of speaking. A famous example of textual sequence is Julius Caesar's *veni, vidi, vici,* "I came, I saw, I conquered."

In BH narrative this is most often a sequence of *wayyiqtols*, since these, as mentioned above and as can be seen in Genesis 44:11–14 below, form the backbone of Hebrew narrative. [NB in the following example and from hereon in the chapter the *wayyiqtols* are in bold-face in the text and the translation].

וַיְמַהֲר֗וּ **וַיּוֹרִ֡דוּ** אִ֣ישׁ אֶת־אַמְתַּחְתּ֞וֹ אַ֗רְצָה **וַיִּפְתְּח֖וּ** אִ֥ישׁ אַמְתַּחְתּֽוֹ׃
וַיְחַפֵּ֕שׂ בַּגָּד֣וֹל הֵחֵ֔ל וּבַקָּטֹ֖ן כִּלָּ֑ה **וַיִּמָּצֵא֙** הַגָּבִ֔יעַ בְּאַמְתַּ֖חַת בִּנְיָמִֽן׃ [12]
[13] **וַיִּקְרְע֖וּ** שִׂמְלֹתָ֑ם **וַֽיַּעֲמֹס֙** אִ֣ישׁ עַל־חֲמֹר֔וֹ **וַיָּשֻׁ֖בוּ** הָעִֽירָה׃ [14] **וַיָּבֹ֨א**
יְהוּדָ֤ה וְאֶחָיו֙ בֵּ֣יתָה יוֹסֵ֔ף וְה֖וּא עוֹדֶ֣נּוּ שָׁ֑ם **וַיִּפְּל֥וּ** לְפָנָ֖יו אָֽרְצָה׃

Each man **hastily lowered** his sack to the ground. Each man **opened** his sack. He began **searching** with the eldest and finished with the youngest. The goblet **was found** in Benjamin's sack. They **tore** their clothes. Each man **loaded** [his sack] onto his donkey. They **returned** to the city. Judah and his brothers **entered** into the house of Joseph. (Now he was still there.) They **fell** before him onto the ground.

(2) **Eventuality Sequence.** This is the actual sequence in time of the eventualities represented by the verbs. Let us consider the examples from the preceding paragraph. In terms of eventualities, Caesar could not conquer until he saw, and he could not see until he came. Consequently, he has to come, then see, then conquer.

In the example from the Joseph story, the brothers had to **lower** their sacks and **open** them for Joseph's majordomo to **search** them. Thus, the event represented by the last-mentioned verb is the cause of the first two actions (represented by three *wayyiqtols*), although the actual search took place after they lowered and opened their sacks. Subsequently, the brothers tore their clothes because the goblet was found in Benjamin's sack. Because of their oath to the head of Joseph's house and their support of Benjamin, Joseph's older brothers prepared to return to Joseph's house—they thought— to deliver Benjamin to slavery (or worse), in spite of the fact that Joseph's man had graciously changed the agreement, making it more favorable for both the guilty one and the non-guilty ones (lowering the penalty for the guilty from death to slavery and setting the innocent free). As a result, they loaded their sacks onto their donkeys and trudged back to the city where Joseph was waiting for them and fell on the ground before him. The order of the eventualities in time is now clear: they lowered their sacks, then opened their sacks, then Joseph's man searched their sacks, the goblet was found at the end of the search, then they tore their clothes, then they loaded up their donkeys, then they returned to the city, then they entered into Joseph's house, then they did obeisance to him.

(3) **Time.** From an everyday perspective, eventualities and time are inexorably linked together and a simple calculus explains them. But their relationship can be mathematically established, which we do in **Chapter 12**. Our interest here, however, is the intersection of time and eventualities insofar as their possibility of simultaneity is concerned. To this end we must consider the significance of the compatibility of eventualities.

Compatible eventualities can occur at the same time. Incompatible cannot. This means the latter happen before or after each other (this is because the structure of time has the property of *linearity*)—hence, incompatible eventualities must form a temporal sequence: time advances. Time must advance if actions are incompatible; but there is no necessary advance if they are compatible. I will not go into the types of eventualities here and how they affect sequence; Akagi will be covering that below. A couple of simple sentences will illustrate what I am trying to say at this point. For example, in the sentence, "John ran and sat down," John must stop running before he can sit down. The two verbal actions are incompatible. They cannot occur at the same time. But with the sentence, "John ran and whistled," John does not have to stop running before he can whistle. These verbal actions are compatible. They can occur at the same time. Nevertheless, they are not constrained to happen at the same time: John could refrain from whistling until after he stops running.

3.2.2 Delimiting Sequentiality

Although for the most part in narrative the three sequences (text, eventuality, and time) line up, this is not always the case. And therefore, whether in language in general or in BH in particular, text sequence is not a certain determiner of eventuality sequence. Two examples of each will have to suffice at this juncture; I will discuss this extensively in **Chapter 12**. In the English sentences, "Bob fell. Al pushed him," the order of the verbs does not correspond to the most likely order of the eventualities, which is that Al's pushing caused Bob's falling.

Here is a second: "Harry took his family on a great day trip. He drove them up the coast, explored a state park with them, treated them to a nice seafood dinner, and drove them back home tired but happy." This is a classic example of *introductory encapsulation* followed by *Elaboration* with the details. The *day trip* lasted all day. It did not conclude until he pulled into his garage. Within that time all the other eventualities occurred, which happen to be in sequential order.

Similarly, in BH just because verbs are in sequence does not necessarily mean that the eventualities they represent are in the same sequence—although usually they are (because this is a characteristic of narrative). Consider, for example, Genesis 43:30:

וַיְמַהֵר יוֹסֵף כִּי־נִכְמְרוּ רַחֲמָיו אֶל־אָחִיו וַיְבַקֵּשׁ לִבְכּוֹת וַיָּבֹא הַחַדְרָה
וַיֵּבְךְּ שָׁמָּה:

Joseph **hurried** because his inner being warmed toward his brother. He **sought** to weep. He **entered** an inner chamber and **wept** there.

In this case the order of eventualities is clear. Either **hurried** is an *introductory encapsulation* followed by an *Elaboration* of the details of his hurrying or his hurrying is *caused* by the fact that he needed to find a place to weep out of sight of his brothers so that his charade could continue. But hurrying could not *cause* him to seek to weep or be the occasion of him seeking to weep. It appears that the sequence of the verbs does *not* reflect the order of the eventualities.

Exodus 1:22–2:2 is a second example. Keep in mind that the chapter divisions were added later.

וַיְצַו פַּרְעֹה לְכָל־עַמּוֹ לֵאמֹר כָּל־הַבֵּן הַיִּלּוֹד הַיְאֹרָה תַּשְׁלִיכֻהוּ וְכָל־
הַבַּת תְּחַיּוּן: ס ²:¹ וַיֵּלֶךְ אִישׁ מִבֵּית לֵוִי וַיִּקַּח אֶת־בַּת־לֵוִי: ² וַתַּהַר
הָאִשָּׁה וַתֵּלֶד בֵּן וַתֵּרֶא אֹתוֹ כִּי־טוֹב הוּא וַתִּצְפְּנֵהוּ שְׁלֹשָׁה יְרָחִים:

Pharaoh **commanded** his people: "Every son who is born, into the Nile you will throw him, but every daughter you may spare."

A man from the house of Levi **went** and **took** a daughter from the house of Levi. The woman **became pregnant** and **gave birth** to a son. She **saw** him that he was good. She **hid** him three months.

The question is the order of Pharaoh's command and the Levites' marriage. If the marriage followed the command—which is the sequence in the text—then no children were born until after the command. But this is impossible, because two children were born to this Levite, Amram, and his wife, Jochebed, *before* Moses was born, namely Aaron, who was three years older than his brother,[2] and Miriam, who was older still.[3]

3.3 *Determining Sequentiality*

As we discussed above, but stated in a different way, temporal sequence manifests itself on the **micro-level** (*intrinsic* to each VP), the **macro-level** (relationships *between* verbs/clauses), in the transition between levels (the interface between the **macro-** and **mega-levels**), and on the **mega-level** (the effect of the narrative purposes as a whole). We will introduce the first two of these and the fourth below and deal with them extensively in **Part Three**, **Second Section** of the book. The third comprises a consideration of *temporal discontinuity* and *structural chronological markers*, which will be examined carefully in **Part Four** and briefly below. We consider these last two to be in the transition between levels, because not only is the local level in view but also the global. Inasmuch as they look at the whole narrative, they serve as a transition to the **mega-level**.

3.3.1 The Micro-level of Determination

Our concern here is the advancement of time *within* eventualities. Situation aspect, as it is commonly called, focuses on the types of actions represented by VPs. Consequently, we are studying the types of actions represented by the *individual verbs* in the Flood narrative.

Just a brief orientation before Akagi's more detailed introduction. Linguists commonly acknowledge five basic types: *states* ("John was tired"), *activities* ("John ran"), *achievements* ("John won the race"), *accomplishments* ("John built a house"), and *semelfactives* ("John sneezed"). The first, second, and fifth of these have no natural endpoint resulting in a change of state (the technical term for this property is *atelic*) . . . and, therefore, although other factors are often involved, for verbs of these types, time often does not advance in a narrative. That is, the eventuality depicted by the next verb may have occurred at the same time as the eventuality depicted by the verb in question, or the two eventualities may have occurred in a different order (called *dischronologization*). On the other hand, the third and fourth types do have an endpoint resulting in a change of state (called *telic*). So time often advances. [SWB]

---

2. "Now Moses was eighty years old and Aaron eighty-three years old when they spoke with Pharaoh" (Ex 7:7).

3. Miriam's interaction with Pharaoh's daughter indicates that she was at least six years old (if she was precocious) and probably older.

Determining sequentiality at the **micro-level** in a narrative discourse requires consideration of the semantic properties of individual verbs and verb phrases (VPs), particularly those of situation aspect. While tense concerns the relative placement of situations in time, whether past, present, or future, aspect concerns the internal temporal properties of situations (alternatively, "eventualities")[4] as verbs and VPs represent them. Two classes of aspect receive primary attention in linguistic literature: viewpoint aspect (also called grammatical aspect or *Aspekt*) and situation aspect (also called lexical aspect or *Aktionsart*). The former class encompasses formally marked distinctions and refers to the speaker or writer's portrayal of temporal properties according to viewpoints relative to situations. Such distinctions include those between "perfective" and "imperfective" viewpoint aspect, as between "Mary ate" and "Mary was eating" in English and as featured prominently in Slavic languages. Situation aspect refers to temporal properties of the representation of situations due to inherent semantic properties of verbs along with their accompanying modifiers. Two VPs, such as "Jim ran" and "Jim stopped," although syntactically identical, may portray events with different temporal properties. The former VP portrays an event taking place over a duration of time without any indication of a stopping point inherent in the VP, whereas the latter represents an event taking place only at a moment in time.

Zeno Vendler (1957; 1967) offered a pioneering system of classification for situation aspect. In his original system, four classes of VPs exist: state terms, achievement terms, activity terms, and accomplishment terms. This system has provided the foundation for much subsequent research, such that state, achievement, activity, and accomplishment remain standard designations for situation types. Simplistically, these classes differ in durativity, telicity (the presence or absence of an inherent point of completion), and inherent change (dynamicity). VPs representing states denote continuing, unaltered conditions, and thus are negative according to the three variables. In the examples concerning Jim above, the VP of the first sentence is dynamic and durative, but it includes no inherent point of completion. Such a VP denotes an "activity." Addition of a modifier such as "to the store" or "a mile" would result in a change of class through adding the property of telicity; the VPs including these modifiers would denote "accomplishments," having properties of both durativity and telicity. Other verbal lexemes may represent accomplishments without the additional modifiers as part of their

---

4. "Eventuality" and "situation" are used interchangeably in this book. Hereafter in this sub-subsection of the chapter, the latter term will be used.

VPs. Finally, dynamic VPs without properties of either durativity or telicity receive the label of "achievement." Achievements equate to momentary events, such as that represented by the second example concerning Jim above, or even, ironically, by the sentence, "She died." Later writers have further developed this system of classification, increasing precision and proposing additional classes, such as "semelfactive," which may refer to a momentary event resulting in no change of state or also to the repeated occurrence of such an event, depending on the linguist. Examples of verbs representing semelfactives include "knock" and sometimes "sneeze." **Chapter 11** will present subclasses of states differing in these variables but all having negative dynamicity values. Increased precision in study of situation aspect has resulted in the classification of various kinds of scales. VPs may, to provide an example of one kind of variation, represent eventualities occurring according to a scale of theoretically infinite gradation ("The balloon rose") or one with only two points ("She closed her eyes").

The correlation of various kinds of verb modifiers, such as objects and prepositional phrases, within VPs to their situation aspect has also invited inquiry. The addition of a singular direct object, for example, to a VP consisting only of a verb representing an activity ("He wrote") may result in a VP representing an accomplishment ("He wrote a book"), whereas a plural form of that object may return the VP to representing an activity ("He wrote books"). The presence of other modifiers in VPs may have similar effects, and a single VP may denote situations of differing classes due to varying contexts.

Within the development and application of situation aspect theory, Alice G. B. ter Meulen (1995) significantly related situation aspect to the temporal relation of situations to one another in narrative and offered a system of representation, Dynamic Aspect Trees (DATs), drawn from mathematical tree diagrams. Ter Meulen's observations indicate that aspectual properties of situations, particularly telicity, often correspond to particular temporal relations between situations in the absence of opposing presupposed knowledge or explicit indicators to the contrary. Temporal sequence in narrative, therefore, frequently corresponds to particular successions of situation types. This correspondence allows for predictable representation of temporal relations of situations in narrative through DATs. DATs subsequently have provided an instrument for representing aspectual properties and temporal relationships outside of English.

Despite the abundance, particularly in the past two decades, of material proceeding from situation aspect research and despite attempts to relate the language's system of verb forms to viewpoint aspect, few significant studies have extensively applied situation aspect research to BH. The aspectual properties of VPs in the Genesis Flood narrative therefore require attention in attempting to establish the chronology of the situations they represent. VPs may represent situations that take place over time, occur at points in time, overlap, occur within the temporal duration or as part of other situations, transpire simultaneously, or occur sequentially. Analysis of the particular VPs in the narrative assists in determining which of these and other possibilities may match the writer's intended portrayal of temporal relationships between situations.

The process of such an analysis requires determining the common properties of verbs appearing in the narrative from their usage elsewhere in the corpus of BH literature. Analysis of many occurrences of these verbs in a variety of VPs throughout that corpus may establish through comparison the most likely aspectual properties of VPs within the narrative. Likely consequent temporal relations between the VPs of the narrative may then emerge. Of particular significance in the Flood narrative are those VPs describing the progress of the Flood and its effects from the record of the onslaught of water in Genesis 7:17 through the clear end of Flood processes and conditions in 8:14. Sample analyses of a few selected portions of BH narrative portraying more obvious temporal relationships between situations provide demonstration of the general consistency of temporal relationships determined through analysis of situation aspect and those understood merely through the clarity of these portions of narrative.

However, not only the likely aspectual properties of situations VPs represent require consideration, but also, more fundamentally, the general semantic significance of VPs. The precise meaning of the verb גבר (gbr) in the Qal stem, for instance, which occurs crucially four times between Genesis 7:18 and 7:24 but appears with various renderings in translations, and the distinction between יבש (ybš) and חרב (ḥrb) in the same stem, two verbs relating to dryness or the drying process, pertain to the chronology of the narrative's situations. The need for analyzing these verbs extends not only to determining relations to time, but also to establishing more broadly the nature of the situations or conditions they depict. Thus, in establishing the chronology of the situations of the Flood narrative, lexical semantic analysis, while primarily concerning the situation aspectual properties of verbs in their VPs, must secondarily address the significance of verbs with precisely established meaning according to traditional lexicography.

When combined with considering dictates from logical semantics, analysis of the situation aspect of VPs within BH narrative moves toward greater precision in establishing the presence, absence, and nature of sequentiality between the smallest elements of discourse. These relationships between individual VPs combine to form the temporal structure throughout segments above the **micro-level** within narratives. As a result, analysis of situation aspect may contribute to understanding the complete chronological framework of a narrative by providing foundational blocks on which that framework is constructed. [KMA]

3.3.2 The Macro-level of Determination

Our concern at this level is the relationships *between* verbs/clauses, which are factors in determining temporal progression. Three of these, **coherence relations**, **compatibility/incompatibility** issues, and **connection** issues, I will discuss briefly here and in great detail in **Chapter 12**. An additional two, **continuity/discontinuity** issues and **structural chronological** issues, are mentioned here inasmuch as they bridge between the **macro-level** and the **mega-level**, but will be covered under a separate sub-subsection (**3.3.3**), because of their transitional nature. But now we turn to consider *coherence relations*.

(1) **Coherence Relations.** Scores of linguists, psycho-linguists, artificial intelligence researchers, language development specialists, and others have offered their sets of **coherence relations** (also called discourse relations, conjunctive relations, rhetorical relations, and even inter-segmental relations) to explain the interaction between verbs/clauses. The number of relations in these sets runs from zero of the minimalist approach to over seventy in the maximalist approach. Also, the content of the sets vary. Drawing on the previous work on discourse relations, we would propose the following set of discourse relations: *Serialation, Result* (and its antitheses *Cause* and *Explanation*), *Elaboration* (and its converses *Summation* and *Restatement*), *Comparison/Contrast*, and (possibly) *Background*. These represent an intersection of a sizable cross section of scholars' choices for **coherence relations** that should be included to explain inter-clausal semantic relations. I will now briefly define these.

(a) *Serialation.* This **coherence relation** is a coined term for the most common discourse relation in narration. This is also called elsewhere continuation, contiguity, occasion, consequential, and even narration itself. This relation obtains when the eventualities depicted by the verbs are in the same order as the verbs, and, moreover, are not related causally. An example would be "John went to the store. He bought some milk." In this pair of sentences, going to the store does not cause the buying of milk, but provides the necessary circumstances for the milk to be bought. The milk cannot be bought any other way.

(b) *Result/Cause.* This is a relation in which the second verb or clause is the cause/result of the first verb. *Cause* is different from *Explanation* (also called *Solutionhood*). The former answers the question *what?* The latter answers *why?* Nevertheless, they are not necessarily mutually exclusive, as the following example illustrates: "As for them, they did not know that Joseph was hearing (and understanding), because an interpreter was between them" (Gn 42:23). Why did Joseph's brothers not know that he was hearing their belated confessions? Only because they assumed he could not understand them. Why did they assume this? Because he was using an interpreter. But also it could be said that the presence of the interpreter caused Joseph's brothers to think that he could not understand them. And they spoke therefore in an unguarded manner.

Result is illustrated by "John turned off the light. It was pitch black." The first sentence implies that the light originally was on and the initial state therefore could not be darkness. The darkness was the state that ensued when and because the light was turned off. This is quite different from the relation *Background*, as in, "The basement was dark. John cautiously descended the stairs," in which the initial state persists during the second action.

(c) *Contrast (also Concession and Qualification)/Comparison.* These are included in most sets, although some see them merely as a difference in semantic polarity. It may be defined as follows: one of the text segments raises expectations, which are contradicted/violated by the other. In order to understand *Contrast* we must introduce the concepts of *violated expectation* and *denial of preventer*. An example of the first is the following pair based on Genesis 44:30: Joseph wanted to exhibit an impassive front before his brothers (in order to prolong the charade to accomplish his purposes); nevertheless when he saw his full brother, he rushed away from all of his brothers in an emotional state. An example of the second concept comes from the grand irony in the Book of Esther, that Haman was forced to personally give the highest honors to Mordecai, whom he hated and wanted to kill.

(d) *Elaboration.* This last relation is frequently included in **coherence relation** sets. Also referred to as additive, expansion, and resemblance, *Elaboration* may be defined as follows: given two text segments, the second expands on the first by specifying it in greater detail or in other words, in the following ways: set to member, process to step, part to whole, object to attribute, abstract to instance, and general to specific. *Restatement* and *Summary* go in the opposite direction: member to set, part to whole, etc. An artificial example of *Elaboration* is "John wrote an email to his friend. He booted up his computer, opened his browser, went to the college webpage, moused down to email, entered his password, clicked on new, and typed out the message." In this sequence of verbs, "wrote an email" is an *introductory encapsulation*, elaborated by the verbs following it.[5] That is, all the eventualities depicted by the verbs after "wrote an email" are parts of the overall eventuality of emailing.

(2) **Compatibility/Incompatibility.** To define these I want to show how the *micro-* and *macro-levels* complement each other at times to move time forward and stop it at others. For the former, consider the sentence pair "Bob ran. He sat down." The first verb is an atelic activity verb; the second, a telic achievement verb. The actions are incompatible. So the sitting down must follow the running. In fact, the sitting brings an end to the running. What if the second verb is atelic as well, will the eventuality it represents follow the running? It depends on the verb. If it is "climbed," also an activity, the actions could be compatible: he is running on a hilly course. On the other hand, if it is different activity verb, "swam," they are incompatible: swimming cannot coincide with running. It appears that the *compatability/incompatability* factor is decisive when the first verb is atelic.

(3) **Connection.** We will be discussing *connection* issues in **Chapter 12**. The following is a domestic example:

a.   John took his family to church on Sunday.
b.   They piled into their SUV.
c.   John drove down the highway.
d.   They parked in the lot.
e.   They walked to the church.
f.   They sat in their usual pew.
g.   They enjoyed the organ prelude.
h.   They sang four hymns.
i.   The pastor preached a great sermon.
j.   They returned home.
k.   John swerved to avoid a box dropped in his lane.
l.   They ate lunch.
m.   They all took naps in the afternoon.

It is obvious that (a) is an *introductory encapsulation* of (b)–(d) (perhaps (e) could be included here as well), which in turn elaborate on "took his family to church." We cannot insert after (d) another detail about the ride to church. Swerving to miss a box in his lane (k), cannot be attached to any

---

5. The CCRG suspects that Genesis 7:17a, "The Flood was on the earth for forty days," is such an *introductory encapsulation,* with the subsequent verses elaborating the particulars.

of (d)–(i) (parking, walking, and (f)–(i) [activities during the service]). But it can be connected to (j) as an elaboration on what happened on the drive home. Similarly, neither (d) nor (e) could happen after (f). On the other hand, (l)–(m) are part of the bigger narrative: (a), (d)–(j), (l)–(m).

For a biblical example of **connection** and the temporal complexity of narrative, consider Exodus 19:1–3a.

בַּחֹ֙דֶשׁ֙ הַשְּׁלִישִׁ֔י לְצֵ֥את בְּנֵֽי־יִשְׂרָאֵ֖ל מֵאֶ֣רֶץ מִצְרָ֑יִם בַּיּ֣וֹם הַזֶּ֔ה **בָּ֖אוּ**
מִדְבַּ֥ר סִינָֽי׃ ² **וַיִּסְע֣וּ** מֵרְפִידִ֗ים **וַיָּבֹ֙אוּ֙** מִדְבַּ֣ר סִינַ֔י **וַֽיַּחֲנ֖וּ** בַּמִּדְבָּ֑ר **וַיִּֽחַן־**שָׁ֥ם
יִשְׂרָאֵ֖ל נֶ֥גֶד הָהָֽר׃ ³ וּמֹשֶׁ֥ה עָלָ֖ה אֶל־הָאֱלֹהִ֑ים וַיִּקְרָ֨א אֵלָ֤יו יְהוָה֙ מִן־הָהָ֣ר

In the third month of the coming out of the Sons of Israel from the Land of Egypt, on this day, they *arrived* at the wilderness of Sinai. They **journeyed** from Rephidim, **arrived** at Sinai, and **camped** in the wilderness. Israel **camped** there opposite the mountain. Now Moses *went* up to God. Yhwh **called** to him from the mountain....

In this account the arrival at Sinai is described using a *qatal*. This serves as an *introductory encapsulation* for the actions that follow. The next four verbs are *wayyiqtols*. The first actually goes back in time to explain from where Israel journeyed to get to Sinai. The second records their arrival *again*. This is a time advance from the preceding verb, but merely brings us back to the time that obtained after the arrival mentioned in the first verse. The third *wayyiqtol* relates that they **camped** in the wilderness. The fourth that they **camped** there again, but with the additional information supplied that it was "opposite the mountain." There is obviously no temporal progression here. Moreover, we can observe the following about **connection**. This second "camped" clearly does not temporally follow the previous verb, "camped," since it refers to the same action, but rather follows "arrived." With verse three the narrative continues with the activities of Moses and the call of Yhwh.

We have encountered above—albeit, briefly—three **macro-level** factors. Now, however, we turn to the two factors that are at the interface between levels.

3.3.3 Transition between the Macro-Level and the Mega-Level
Anderson will introduce his study on segmentation briefly below (to be developed fully in **Chapter 14**). After which, Longacre will introduce his study of וַיְהִי (*wayʾhî*) (greatly expanded in **Chapter 15**). Anderson will be exposing the possible locations of temporal discontinuities in the Flood narrative in his chapter, in which he discusses the issues involved

in the segmentation of texts into narratives, episodes, scenes, and thematic paragraphs. Longacre will explain the importance of the study of וַיְהִי (*wayᵊhî*) to ascertaining the chronology of the Flood narrative. [swb]

(1) **Continuity/Discontinuity.** A thorough analysis of the text of the Flood narrative includes more than just grammatical studies; in order to gain a comprehensive understanding of the chronology embedded in the narrative, the text must be segmented. Text segmentation, simply defined, is the process of methodologically dividing a document into concise, meaningful units of text in accordance with a set of predetermined factors.

This warrants two questions: First, how is the text to be segmented (that is, what methodology should be employed to ensure that the text is divided in a consistent, cogent, and useful fashion)? Second, how will segmentation aid in understanding chronology?

With regard to the first question, it must be stated that there have been multiple approaches to the segmentation of Hebrew narrative texts, some of which have been more useful and comprehensive than others. After giving due consideration to previous models, S. J. Floor, in his dissertation, *From Information Structure, Topic and Focus, to Theme in Biblical Hebrew Narrative* (2004), refined a model of text segmentation Hebrew narrative based upon a careful analysis of theme, which Floor defined as "the developing and coherent core or thread of a discourse in the mind of the speaker-author and hearer-reader, functioning as the prominent macrostructure of the discourse" (243). Notably, while the narrative as a whole expresses an expansive, universal theme, each unit of text in a narrative is involved in advancing a more localized theme. The transitions in local theme from one unit of text to the next are key to determining the boundaries between segments of text. As **Chapter 14** will discuss, a variety of textual features are involved in tracing the development of theme throughout the course of a narrative and are thus vital to segmentation. These features include syntactically marked configurations in the text (e.g., fronting, left- and right-dislocation, end weight, explicit pronouns, focus particles, and spatio-temporal orientations), as well as syntactically unmarked but still cognitively prominent configurations (e.g., relexicalization).

Concerning the second question, because transitions in theme indicate the boundaries between segments of text in a narrative, each segment of text is therefore marked, to some degree and in one or more of a variety of ways, by discontinuities from the preceding segment (e.g., discontinuities in such things as place, time, participants, and action; cf. Runge 2007, 126).

A single type of discontinuity may serve to mark a minor or subtle break between segments, while a greater number of discontinuities may signal a far more drastic break. Generally speaking, the more drastic a given break in a narrative is, the greater likelihood that there may be severe chronological disjunction in the actual sequence of eventualities described at that point in the narrative. Consequently, by segmenting the text of the Flood narrative and by analyzing the thematic breaks between segments, it may be possible to gain a clearer understanding of the chronology embedded in the Flood narrative. [LAA]

(2) **The Role of וַיְהִי** *Wayᵊhî.* Readers are guided along through a narrative by significant structural markers. One of the most important of these in Hebrew narrative is the verb וַיְהִי (*wayeᵊhî*). וַיְהִי varies greatly in its functions in Hebrew text on a number of levels, and its proper contextual analysis is hotly debated. Extensive consideration of the nature of וַיְהִי is necessary for our research because of the key role that it plays in the Genesis Flood narrative. Occurring at significant points in the text (7:10, 12, 17; 8:6, 13), וַיְהִי is found introducing temporal information and describing key events, often at the beginning of new sections of the narrative. The functions of וַיְהִי of sometimes providing temporal orientation and sometimes predicating repetitive chronological information (e.g., "forty days" in 7:12, 17) increase the likelihood of temporal discontinuities in the course of the narrative at these points. Research on the structure of the Flood narrative, therefore, will have to give adequate attention to וַיְהִי. This, of course, must be done in the broader context of the various theories of the Hebrew verbal system of which וַיְהִי is one important part, but in **Chapter 15** we will seek to isolate the linguistic questions which must be answered when incorporating our understanding of וַיְהִי into our theory and reading of Hebrew narrative.

Lexically, וַיְהִי is a *Qal*-stem verb from the root היה (*hyh*) meaning "to be," which is normally used to predicate existence, description, or equation. It is normally analyzed as a stative verb indicating a state of being, but it may also be a dynamic stative indicating a change of state or an entrance into a state of being, with the resulting meaning "to become." In some cases, וַיְהִי may even cease to behave verbally at all. The lexical semantics of וַיְהִי must be further studied in order to determine which meaning is appropriate in any given contexts.

Morphologically, וַיְהִי is a *wayyiqtol*-form third person masculine singular verb. A number of questions will need to be answered with regard to the form of וַיְהִי. What is the relationship between וַיְהִי and other verbs of its *wayyiqtol*-form pattern? Once the nature of the *wayyiqtol* verb form has been determined, researchers must examine how closely וַיְהִי conforms to this usage and where (if ever) it departs from that normal usage. For example, does וַיְהִי (as is commonly maintained for *wayyiqtol*-form verb chains in general) function on the mainline of narrative events, or does it provide background information? Does וַיְהִי indicate any sort of temporal or logical sequence or progression? Is it marked for a tense value? These and many similar questions about the relationship between וַיְהִי and other *wayyiqtol*-form verbs need to be resolved for a proper analysis of the structure of Hebrew narrative.

Syntactically, וַיְהִי is used in a variety of grammatical combinations that complicate its analysis. A step in the right direction would be to distinguish temporal and verbal uses of וַיְהִי, the former introducing a temporal clause dependent on the following main clause and the latter functioning as the main verb of an independent clause. A related question is who or what (if anything) is the subject of temporal וַיְהִי? Furthermore, what is the significance of each of the various verb-forms observed to follow dependent clauses introduced by temporal וַיְהִי? Also what (if anything) is the difference between temporal clauses initiated by וַיְהִי and those not so initiated? The complicated syntax of וַיְהִי still requires much more examination.

Structurally, וַיְהִי commonly occurs at key points in the overall discourse structure of Hebrew narratives, normally at the beginning of paragraphs, scenes, episodes, and narratives. By examining its position within these various levels—particularly when consistent patterns emerge—researchers can gain a better idea of how וַיְהִי is used at key points to mark and/or shape the structure of Hebrew narrative.

Pragmatically, וַיְהִי can be shown to perform various discourse-pragmatic roles in Hebrew narratives. It will be important, for instance, to note the possible ways in which it is used to advance the narrative, provide background orientation to the narrative, give temporal information, summarize, and a whole host of other categories. Only when researchers identify the pragmatic function of וַיְהִי in a given narrative can they fully assess its *raison d'être* in the text.

The study of וַיְהִי from these perspectives will provide a firmer foundation for understanding the role of וַיְהִי in the Hebrew verbal system and Hebrew narrative. Once this nuanced understanding of וַיְהִי has been delineated, the results can be applied to the cases in the Genesis Flood narrative to determine how they are functioning in the narrative and how they influence the information structure and flow of the narrative. [DGL]

3.3.4 The Mega-level of Determination

We could say that the four factors we have briefly examined concern the *what* of temporal sequence. By way of contrast and conclusion let us look at the **mega-level**. This level does not so much explore *what* causes temporal dischronologization so much as *why* it is there. Stroup will engage in a fascinating discussion of this topic in **Chapter 13**. [SWB]

As foreign as the idea of temporal discontinuity may seem, it is surprisingly commonplace in narrative literature, both English and Hebrew. An investigation of the **mega-level** helps to understand the reasons for this frequency by identifying three main factors that can affect the representation of time in narrative: the level of complexity, the mode of discourse, and the purposes of the narrator.

(1) **The Level of Complexity.** The first factor is the level of complexity. Whereas a simple narrative with a single character plot (e.g., *Robinson Crusoe*) will generally progress in temporal sequence, where there are one or more characters involved in multiple plots and subplots, the issue becomes more complex. Unlike visual art forms like painting and film that can portray multiple events at once, narrative is a linear art form, and is therefore limited to portraying events one at a time in narrative sequence, regardless of the order that they occur in actual time. This requires the narrator to switch back and forth between the different characters, progressing and regressing in time sequence as he does so, to keep the various plots and subplots moving forward with the appearance of simultaneity.

An excellent example of the above is *The Lord of the Rings* trilogy by J. R. R. Tolkien. In this narrative, there are several major plots and subplots, the most prominent two being Frodo and Sam's journey to Mordor, and the rest of the Fellowship's journey to Minas Tirith. Because of these two plots, and because of the linearity of narrative, Tolkien is forced to switch back and forth between these two groups of characters in his books, much like the game of leap frog, in order to keep both plots progressing together. This complexity produces multiple dischronologizations in the narrative, which will be explored further in **Chapter 13**.

(2) **The Mode of Discourse.** The second factor is the mode of discourse. Carlota Smith's *Modes of Discourse* (2003) defines five types of discourse that are instructive for understanding temporal continuity: *Narrative, Report, Description, Information,* and *Argument* (these will be further discussed in **Chapter 13**). Whereas narrative generally relates events and states dynamically through cause and effect, the others do not

necessarily do so, and therefore will often relate events and states out of temporal sequence. Therefore, where a text consists of one of these other modes of discourse, or where these other modes of discourse are embedded within a narrative, they can cause temporal discontinuity.

Examples of each of these modes of discourse embedded within a larger narrative can be seen in J. R. R. Tolkien's *The Hobbit*. In Tolkien's opening chapter, for example, one finds a description of Bilbo's hobbit hole embedded within the narrative:

> It had a perfectly round door like a porthole, painted green, with a shiny yellow brass knob in the exact middle. The door opened on to a tube-shaped hall like a tunnel: a very comfortable tunnel without smoke, with paneled walls, and floors tiled and carpeted, provided with polished chairs, and lots and lots of pegs for hats and coats—the hobbit was fond of visitors. The tunnel wound on and on, going fairly but not quite straight into the side of the hill....

As explained by Smith, a description often progresses spatially rather than temporally, and therefore the absence of temporal sequence in this sample is simply a consequence of the mode of discourse at hand. This and other examples will be explored in **Chapter 13**.

(3) The Purposes of the Narrator. The last factor is the purposes of the narrator. Besides the purpose of entertainment, a narrative can possess any number of purposes including historical documentation, behavioral instruction, social reform, and theological argument. The combination of these purposes can affect the portrayal of time sequence in the text, as they determine which events are included, which events are omitted, and even the order in which the events are conveyed.

An excellent example of this is *Uncle Tom's Cabin*, where the author plunges the reader directly into the climatic sale of Uncle Tom and Eliza's son Harry, subsequently regressing in time to fill in the details of Eliza's blissful marriage and confident trust in her mistress. In doing so, the narrator employs gapping, retrospection, suspense, and gradual characterization in order to highlight the horror and treachery of the deed at hand. This and other examples will be further explored in **Chapter 13**. [TLS]

3.3.4 Summation
The interaction of the eventualities represented by the verbs and the temporal dimension of eventualities ensues in six factors which determine temporal sequence: the advancement of time within eventualities, the advancement

of time between eventualities, the temporal displacement of eventualities due to incompatibility, the temporal attachment of eventualities, the possibility of temporal discontinuity of eventualities, and the reasons on the narrative level for dischronologization. Consequently, in order to ascertain the temporal sequence of eventualities represented by the verbs in a text, we must examine these factors to ascertain the temporal profile of a text, that is, to see the flow of time in the narrative.

4. Setting Sail

With the stated assumptions of the supernatural character of Scripture, its unique combination of history, literature, and theology, and the unity and coherence of the Flood narrative in place, we know whence we have come in this voyage of discovery.

Furthermore, with confidence in the five fixed dates, with a trustworthy text of the narrative in place, and with a commitment to understanding the Flood narrative calendar, we are ready to commence our investigation of temporal progression in BH. Moreover, with a strategy on the chart table, which will look at temporal sequence from the **micro-**, **macro-**, and **mega-levels**, we know our course hence. We will be ready to set sail as soon as we check on the specifics of the gale warnings we have heard about: the geological, geophysical, and paleontological issues that pertain to the chronology of the Flood. These will be addressed by Snelling in **Chapters 5–7**. [SWB]

References

Floor, S. J. 2004. *From information structure, topic and focus, to theme in biblical Hebrew narrative.* Ph.D. Diss. University of Stellenbosch.

Runge, S. E. 2007. *A discourse-functional description of participant reference in biblical Hebrew narrative.* Ph.D. Diss. University of Stellenbosch.

Sarna, N. 1966. *Understanding Genesis.* New York, NY: Schocken Books.

Smith, C. S. 2003. *Modes of discourse: The local structure of texts.* Cambridge, England: Cambridge University Press.

Snelling, A. A. 2010. *Earth's catastrophic past: Geology, Creation & the Flood.* 2 Vols. Dallas, TX: Institute for Creation Research.

Speiser, E. A. 1964. *Genesis: Introduction, translation and notes.* Garden City, NY: Doubleday and Company.

Sternberg, M. 1985. *The poetics of biblical narrative: Ideological literature and the drama of reading.* Bloomington, IN: Indiana University Press.

ter Meulen, A. 1995. *Representing time in natural language: The dynamic interpretation of tense and aspect.* Cambridge, MA: MIT Press.

Vendler, Z. 1957. Verbs and times. *Philosophical Review* 66.2: 143–160.

Vendler, Z. 1967. *Linguistics in philosophy*. Cornell, NY: Cornell University Press.

Wenham, G. 1987. *Genesis 1–15* (Word Biblical Commentary). Vol. 1. Waco, TX: Word Books, Publisher.

Westermann, C. 1964. *The Genesis account of Creation*. Trans. N. Wagner. Philadelphia, PA: Fortress Press.

PART II

TAKING OUR BEARINGS:
RELEVANT ISSUES

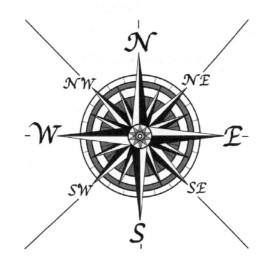

SECOND SECTION

GALE WARNINGS:
GEOLOGICAL GEOPHYSICAL,
AND PALEONTOLOGICAL ISSUES

Down they crash on the sea, the Eastwind, Southwind,

all as one with the Southwest's squalls in hot pursuit,

heaving up from the ocean depths huge killer-breakers

rolling toward the beaches.

—Virgil from *The Aeneid* (trans. Robert Fagles)

CHAPTER 5

Geological Issues: Charting a Scheme for Correlating the Rock Layers with the Biblical Record

Andrew A. Snelling

> ***Analogy and Orientation.*** *As both maritime history and recent events have shown, failures by ships' captains to know where rock layers should be based on their navigation charts have ended in disasters. It's all too easy to take one's eyes off the navigation charts where the positions of the rock layers are clearly marked, and instead think one can rely on one's own ability to easily figure out where the rock layers are by visual surveillance and then steer the ship accordingly. However, changing tides and weather conditions can mislead and hamper one's judgment. This analogy mirrors the history of geologic thought as to the role of the Genesis Flood in accounting for the earth's fossil-bearing sedimentary layers. As men have taken their eyes off the eyewitness account of earth history God has provided in His Word and relied only on their own reasoning, their thinking has eliminated the Flood altogether as a geologic agent, which has spiritually shipwrecked many lives. That's why it is crucial to develop a biblically and geologically defensible Flood model that accounts for these rock layers. The goal of this chapter is to provide a brief overview of the development of geologic thinking in relation to the Genesis Flood, especially focusing on Flood modeling in recent decades that is pinpointing where in the rock record the Flood began and ended, as well as highlighting issues that may be resolved by study of the Hebrew text of the Genesis Flood account.*

Abstract. Throughout history debate has raged over the role of the Genesis Flood in shaping the earth's geology. The majority view for more than two centuries has been that the earth's past history should only be deciphered in terms of presently observed geologic processes ("the present is the key to the past"), so the Flood has been deemed geologically irrelevant. However, the latter half of the twentieth century saw a revival of Flood geology among Bible-believing Christian scholars and scientists, including geologists, so that much effort is now focused on building a coherent, robust Flood model for the world's geology. The current consensus is that the location of the Flood's beginning in the geologic record is in some uppermost Precambrian strata consisting of debris from avalanches and at the widespread erosional Precambrian/Cambrian unconformity. The rising Floodwaters advanced over the continents, levels fluctuating as they deposited five megasequences of fossil-bearing sediment layers. The highest peaking of the Floodwaters was in the upper Cretaceous, after which they dramatically fell and retreated, soon thereafter marking the Flood/post-Flood boundary in the geologic record, with continuing local catastrophic deposition before the onset of the Pleistocene Ice Age. There is an urgent need for the chronology of the Flood, the timing of the peaking of the Floodwaters, and their actions to be more clearly understood from the Hebrew text of the Genesis Flood account so as to further our understanding of the Flood's geologic record.

Outline

1. Introduction: The World's Geology Is Established

Ever since God issued the "dominion mandate" (Gn 1:28–30), man has explored and investigated his earthly home, that was created by God during the six literal days of Creation (Gn 1:1–2:3; Ex 20:11, 31:17). God's command assumed even more urgency and significance after Adam and Eve were expelled from the Garden of Eden where God's provision for them had been bountiful. Now they faced a cursed world, where toil would be hard. To maintain their survival and improve their living standards necessitated understanding the world around them and therefore how the forces that affect the earth's surface operate (for example, climate and rainfall, rivers, and erosion).

In the pre-Flood world, agriculture and animal husbandry flourished (Gn 4:2, 20). Men began to build cities, and also to make musical instruments, and tools of brass and iron (Gn 4:17, 21–22). Gold was available in the land of Havilah (Gn 2:11). Men had therefore begun to explore the world's geology and had successfully located the required metal ores in suitable host rocks. And man had used his God-given ingenuity to devise the technology to mine these ores and to smelt them to extract the needed metals.

However, the global cataclysmic Flood (Gn 7–8) destroyed the pre-Flood world, its biosphere and human civilization, apart from Noah, his family, and the animals (plus food) on the Ark, and reshaped the world's geology. So after the Flood Noah and his descendants had a whole new world to explore and had to investigate its new rocks for the new resources they needed to reestablish human civilization.

It did not take long for Noah to plant a vineyard (Gn 9:20). Then about one hundred years after the Flood his descendants came together at Babel on the Plain of Shinar to make bricks and mortar in order to build a city and a tower, in defiance of God's command to spread out across the earth's surface and inhabit it (Gn 11:1–4). So God confused their language and scattered them. Close to Babel, civilization still flourished in Egypt and across the Fertile Crescent of Mesopotamia. The Egyptians eventually found, mined, and smelted copper at Timna, now in southern Israel.

2. Man Begins His Quest to Understand the World's Geology: Who or What Was Responsible?

The quest had thus begun to understand the geology of the post-Flood world so as to exploit its resources for man's benefit. Unfortunately, even though successive empires and all the scattered tribes found and exploited the rocks, metals, and gems for their needs, the people soon forgot that it was the Flood that had reshaped the earth and rebuilt its geology. Even though the Sumerians, Babylonians, Hindus, and Greeks all made remarkable discoveries in mathematics and astronomy, they regarded the phenomena of "nature" (for example, tempests, thunderbolts, and volcanoes) as manifestations of power by mythological pagan deities who were thought to behave like irresponsible men of highly uncertain temper (Typhon, Zeus, and Vulcan, respectively).

A notable exception was Thales of Miletus (about 624–565 BC) who regarded the activities of nature not as indications of supernatural intervention, but as natural and orderly events which could be investigated in the light of observation and reason (Berry 1968). Yet even though Plato (427–347 BC) and Aristotle (384–322 BC) induced from their observations of nature's processes that the existing positions of land and sea were not permanent, but that certain land areas had been covered by sea at one time, they unwittingly revived the idea that the earth, sun, and planets were all deities (Holmes 1965). Similarly, Herodotus (484–426 BC), who was a great traveler and made significant geological observations, speculated about the effect of earthquakes on landscapes, suggesting it was quite reasonable to ascribe the earthquakes themselves to Poseidon. Much later, Pliny the Elder (AD 23–79), who lost his life while investigating and then getting too close to a volcano while rescuing people from its effects, explained earthquakes as an expression of the earth's resentment against those who mutilated and plundered her skin by mining for gold, silver, and iron.

Even though the Greeks as early as the sixth century BC had begun to record and analyze data in a way that could be described as the beginning of science (recorded knowledge), scientific thought was limited until well into the sixteenth century AD. Notable exceptions were the activities of a few scholars, such as Roger Bacon (1210–1294) and Leonardo da Vinci (1452–1519) (Berry 1968). Around 1500, da Vinci observed the fossil seashells in sedimentary rocks of the Italian Apennines. He deduced that those fossils were the remains of animals that had lived in a sea that once covered the area. He noted that rivers erode their valleys and deposit fine muds at their mouths, and that animals and plants tend to be buried in the muds. He therefore reasoned that river muds from Alpine lands had been transported into the sea and had buried the shells of marine animals, which were preserved as the mud hardened to rock. Areas of such rock had then risen, or been shoved upwards, above sea level to become land.

During da Vinci's time and soon after it, two opposing views concerning earth history confronted one another. One was the biblical view from the book of Genesis, in which it was maintained that the complete formation of the earth occurred only a few thousand years ago during a literal Creation week. Only one catastrophe had subsequently wrought any major change on the earth, and that had been the Noachian Deluge. After that, the earth had been in a relatively stable state. Thus any major changes in the sea's position had to be related to the Deluge. In opposition was the stand taken in the writings of the Greeks and Romans that changes were always taking place on the earth's surface by more gradual processes. Da Vinci renewed this idea with his observations concerning the deposition of muds by rivers and the conclusion that the muds harden to rock and become land over long periods of time.

Along with this difference of opinion concerning the timing and nature of changes on the surface of the earth, another controversy raged, a controversy over the nature of the remains found in rocks that closely resembled the shells of animals then living along the existing shorelines (Berry 1968). That the remains were some of the shells of living marine animals was quite apparent, but how did the shells get into the rocks? To many it seemed that they must have been formed there during the Creation, or had been transported there during the Deluge. For those who attempted to express some doubt, there was the example of Giordano Bruno who was burned at the stake in Rome in 1600 for stating that there had never been a Deluge and that the positions of land and sea had changed many times. Bernard Palissy was another who was denounced as a heretic for his statements that fossils were the remains of once-living animals and plants. But gradually over the next two centuries it was firmly established that fossils were the remains of once-living organisms.

In the years following da Vinci's observations and conclusions concerning natural processes, a number of observant investigators began to study natural processes and to discuss their effects on the earth's crust. Among them were Nicolaus Steno, Thomas Burnet, John Woodward, and Robert Hooke.

Steno began investigating the fossil-bearing strata around Rome and traveled widely studying the rocks in northern Italy (Berry 1968). On the basis of his studies, he made the first known attempt to place strata in some kind of positional order. He summed up his geologic observations and conclusions in 1669 in the book *De Solido Intra Solidum Naturaliter Contento Dissertationis Prodromus*, which became a classic in the geologic literature. He postulated that in any sequence of flat-lying strata, the oldest layers are at the bottom and the youngest at the top, a concept now referred to as the principle of superposition. He also proposed the principle of original horizontality, which states that beds are always deposited initially in a nearly horizontal position, even though they may later be found dipping steeply. He suggested that tilted and deformed strata are the result of displacement by earth movements after their initial deposition. All geologists still use these principles today.

Like Steno, Burnet was a firm believer in the biblical view of Creation and the Flood. His major work was *The Sacred Theory of the Earth*, published in four volumes between 1680 and 1690 (Palmer 1999). He started with the assumption that the biblical record was essentially true, and then sought natural explanations for the events described. Just as Isaac Newton thought that gravitational forces must be supernatural in origin, yet operated in an unchanging fashion according to physical laws, so Burnet believed that God set natural laws in motion at the time of creation. Yet he noted that in time all the mountains of the earth could be washed into the sea by the everyday processes of rainfall and run-off, and wind abrasion. So he attacked those who needed to call upon miraculous interventions to explain certain events. Hence, as Burnet saw it, the waters causing the Flood must have come from somewhere, as he was not prepared to accept that they had been miraculously created by God, and the interior of the earth seemed the most likely possibility. Instead of relying on just rain and subsidence to cause the Flood, Burnet invoked the appearance of wide cracks in the earth's surface to cause the release of waters from beneath. He even believed this sudden release of water might have shaken the earth on its axis and produced the present tilt.

Other cosmogonists proposed systems similar to that of Burnet. The most influential was John Woodward's *Essay Toward a Natural History of the Earth* (1695). In his model, materials carried by or released from the waters of the Flood sedimented according to their specific gravities to form horizontal strata, which were later dislocated by depressions and elevations of unspecified origin to form the patterns his contemporaries could observe (Palmer 1999). Woodward was a great field investigator and collector, who paid close attention to strata and fossils (Vaccari 2001). For this reason his *Essay Toward a Natural History of the Earth* was of particular interest to European scholars who continued in the Steno heritage. They reinforced the link with biblical chronology and elaborated upon the main episodes of Genesis within a general theory of the formation of the earth's surface which adopted Woodward's idea of the universal dissolution of the original earth's crust (with its primitive mountains) by the waters of the Deluge. According to Woodward, that catastrophic event had deposited regular strata, which later cracked to form new relief and mountain chains, and after that all the water had flowed back into the central abyss of the earth.

On the other hand, Hooke was unconvinced that Noah's Flood could have lasted long enough to account for all the world's fossil-bearing strata (Berry 1968). He pointed out that such commonplace events as a river's washing sediment into the sea, the sea's pounding upon a shore, and the wind's abrading the land all wrought changes on the earth's surface. He regarded earthquakes and volcanic eruptions as the most powerful forces operative in changing the surface of the earth, including sometimes sudden redistribution of land and sea. Hooke was also a firm advocate of the theory that the fossils in rocks are the remains of once-living organisms. So because he considered that extinctions and appearances of new life forms had taken place, he suggested that fossil forms might be used to determine a record of past ages.

Close to a century after Hooke's time, the French naturalist Georges Louis LeClerc, Comte de Buffon, in his *Natural History*, the first volume of which appeared in 1749, attempted to explain the earth as a system of matter in continual motion. Buffon tried to keep within the biblical account, but substituted epochs of unspecified length for the creation days, suggesting the latter were not meant to be taken literally (Palmer 1999). He calculated that the earth, from an incandescent beginning, could have cooled within thirty-five thousand years to allow condensation of atmospheric water vapor to form a universal ocean. Further cooling caused cavities to appear in the earth's surface through which seawater drained until it reached its present level. He thought that the earth's surface had thus been formed beneath the sea by tidal and current action. Volcanoes began to erupt, the continents appeared, and valleys were gouged out by ocean currents. More cooling took place and there was gradual erosion of the mountains, until the earth assumed its present form. He thus emphasized that commonplace natural events, not catastrophic ones, were the fundamental causes of the surface features of the earth.

In the latter part of the eighteenth century, a considerable background of observations and conclusions pertaining to uniformity in natural processes through time had been recorded. Up to this time, most of the conclusions took into account the biblical record of earth history, even though many naturalists only paid lip service to the biblical record. Instead, they preferred to only want to use human reasoning apart from the Bible to interpret their observations of geologic processes. Therefore, a number of writers, among them Voltaire, were questioning theological tenets, pointing out in their opinion that geology was nothing but the handmaiden of the book of Genesis, so consistent were geologists in paying obeisance to the history of the earth as given there.

3. James Hutton (1788 and 1795): Only Present Processes Responsible

By this time many scientific societies had sprung up in Britain. The first had been founded in London. Another was the Royal Society of Edinburgh. Late in March 1785, James Hutton, a gentleman farmer and avid student of rocks and minerals, strode into the weekly meeting of that society to present to the gathered group the results of several years of his intensive collecting, sifting, and synthesizing of observations concerning earth's processes. The fundamental principle involved in reading the meanings of the rocks as pages in the book of earth history Hutton enunciated when he declared that "the present is the key to the past," meaning that "the past history of our globe must be explained by what can be seen happening now" (Holmes 1965). His talk, in printed version, which appeared in 1788 under the title *Theory of the Earth: or an Investigation of the Laws Observable in the Composition, Dissolution, and Restoration of Land upon the Globe*, encompassed in conclusive form the principle that natural laws may be derived from studying the present processes, and that understanding of nature's past operations may be obtained from observations of present natural relationships (Hutton 1788).

Hutton had been educated as a physician, but turned to agriculture before devoting his full attention to the study of the earth and its rocks and minerals. He read widely and traveled extensively about the British Isles, always observing the rocks and the natural processes acting upon the earth's surface. Hutton offered many proofs for his hypothesis that past changes of the earth had been brought about only by the agency of everyday, observable processes. He noted that layered rocks were composed of detrital fragments, grains from preexisting layered rocks, or bodies of even greater antiquity. Running water sculpted the surface of the earth and ultimately deposited the detritus it had carved from the land into the sea. Pressure and subterranean heat caused the formation of stratified rocks from the original deposits of loose detritus on the seafloor. Then, by the operation of great forces, the layers were cast up to form new lands. Once the lands had emerged from the sea, the destructive agents—running water, tides, and winds—conspired to carry particles of it back to the sea. Hutton maintained: "Time, which measures every thing in our idea, and is often deficient to our schemes, is to nature endless and as nothing.... If the succession of worlds is established in the system of nature, it is vain to look for anything higher in the origin of the earth.... No powers are to be employed that are not natural to the globe, no action admitted except those of which we know the principle. The result, therefore, of our present enquiry is that we find no vestige of a beginning— no prospect of an end" (Holmes 1965; Palmer 1999).

Among Hutton's listeners was John Playfair, Professor of Mathematics at the University of Edinburgh. He and the other listeners had heard many of his thoughts before, and some had even been on excursions with him to see proofs of his hypothesis. It seems they did not think that Hutton had shaken the foundations of the history of the earth given in the book of Genesis. Yet Hutton's most breathtaking point was the immensity of time he envisaged, which was diametrically opposed to the biblical chronology of earth history of only about six thousand years. But to many people the thought of a much longer time was inconceivable, and out of step with Scripture. Even though it was not until nearly five years after his theory was published that it was attacked, when criticism came it was sharp and cutting, and pointed primarily to divergences from the Scriptures. Thus his critics branded the entire hypothesis as anti-theological, and Hutton as an atheist. However, Hutton apparently did not doubt that the world had been carefully designed by a wise and benevolent Creator, but he was a deist, not a Christian, and from his religious views was predisposed toward a system that God could allow to operate without interference (Palmer 1999).

To set forth his evidence more fully, Hutton expanded his original talk into a two-volume book, *Theory of the Earth*, which was published in 1795 (Hutton 1795). Hutton died only two years after his volumes appeared, so his friend and colleague John Playfair undertook the task of amplifying and defending Hutton's views. Hutton's work was difficult to read and encumbered with excessive verbiage. However, Playfair was able to summarize and elucidate Hutton's hypothesis brilliantly, so because of his clear, concise style, Hutton's views became widely known. Playfair published his summary of Hutton's work as *Illustrations of the Huttonian Theory of the Earth* in 1802 (Playfair 1802)

4. Charles Lyell (1830–1833): Victory for Uniformitarianism ("The Present Is the Key to the Past")

Hutton's ideas began to be used by a number of naturalists, but none had so broad an influence on the thought of his time, and since, as Charles Lyell, a lawyer turned geologist. Lyell's *Principles of Geology*, published in three volumes that appeared in 1830, 1832, and 1833, covered the complete scope of geology, and not only supported but also amplified the principle of the uniformity of natural processes through time by extensive coverage of erosional and depositional processes (Lyell 1830–1833). Indeed, Lyell was adamant that only present observable processes at their current rates of operation were to be used to explain the development of the rock record, a principle he called uniformitarianism, which echoed Hutton's view that "the present is the key to the past." This automatically ruled out catastrophism, and especially the global Genesis Flood catastrophe. Lyell insisted that all geologic processes had been very gradual in the past, and utterly abhorred anything suggestive of sudden catastrophes: "For this reason all theories are rejected which involve the assumption of sudden and violent catastrophes and revolutions of the whole earth, and its inhabitants" (Lyell 1830–1833). By his own admission, he saw himself as "the spiritual saviour of geology, freeing it from the old dispensation of Moses" (Mortenson 2004). So he sought to explain the whole rock record by only slow gradual processes in order to reduce the Genesis Flood to a geologic non-event.

Lyell's *Principles of Geology* went through many editions and was widely read by nineteenth-century naturalists. More than any other work, and the avalanche it generated, it swept away almost all vestiges of a biblical view of earth history as the basis for geology. So emphatic was Lyell's victory that it can now be claimed "all phenomena that are related to the past history of the earth are dependent upon the principle of uniformity in nature's processes through time for their interpretation.... Hutton's conclusions and Lyell's amplification of them are the heart and soul of geology" (Berry 1968). There is no question that Hutton and Lyell sweeping away the last vestiges of the biblical Flood in geology paved the way for Charles Darwin's theory of evolution in his *On the Origin of Species*. Indeed, Darwin acknowledged his debt of gratitude to Lyell, when he pointed out: "He who can read Sir Charles Lyell's grand work on the *Principles of Geology*, which the future historian will recognize as having produced a revolution in natural science, and yet does not admit how incomprehensibly vast have been the past periods of time, may at once close this volume" (Darwin 1859). After all, what could not be conceived of happening in a human lifetime could be imagined to have happened over millions of years. "Time is the hero of the plot.... what we regard as impossible on the basis of human experience is meaningless here." Given so much time, the "impossible becomes possible, the possible probable, and the probable virtually certain. One has only to wait: time itself performs the miracles" (Wald 1954, 48).

5. One Hundred Thirty Years of Lone Voices Defending Flood Geology against the Tide of Compromise in the Church

During the first half of the nineteenth century, while this paradigm shift in geology was occurring, there was also much debate over the age of the earth and the Flood within the church. On the one hand there were those who sought to find a way to fit the new geological paradigm of slow and gradual geologic processes on an older earth into the Scriptures by proposing the gap theory (proposed by Thomas Chalmers in 1814), the tranquil Flood (proposed by John Fleming in 1826), a local Flood (proposed by John Pye Smith in 1839), and the day-age theory (proposed by Hugh Miller in 1857) (Whitcomb and Morris 1961). On the other hand, various individuals, some who were clergymen who had varying amounts of geological training and experience, mounted personal writing campaigns to defend the book of Genesis as the real literal account of the earth's history, the recent six-day Creation of the universe, and the global cataclysmic Flood. Collectively, these men became known as the Scriptural geologists (Mortenson 2004). While they mounted a valiant campaign, they were unable to stem the tide of compromise with the new old-age geology within the church as a result of the influence of Lyell's *Principles of Geology*.

By the late nineteenth century there were virtually no voices of any note inside or outside the church attempting to champion the literal record of Genesis 1–11 as a framework for understanding the earth's geology, including the effects of the global cataclysmic Flood. So complete was the paradigm shift that there was hardly any vestige of catastrophism left in the geological establishment and their science. The commitment to Lyell's uniformitarianism was complete. The earth's past geology had to be understood only in terms of present geological processes and their current rates of operation. Of course, there were those in the church who still held to a literal Genesis Flood, but they were not high-profile enough to make any impact either inside or outside the church.

Early in the twentieth century, the main voices defending the early chapters of Genesis by seeking to explain the earth's geology in terms of the global cataclysmic Flood were scientists in the Seventh Day Adventist Church, most notably George McCready Price. Their influence was minimal, because they were not in the Christian mainstream. Nevertheless, their written works influenced hydraulic engineer Dr. Henry Morris, who in mid-century began writing and speaking out against the compromise in the church with evolutionary biology and uniformitarian geology. He teamed up with theologian Dr. John Whitcomb to co-author and publish in 1961 the book *The Genesis Flood: The Biblical Record and its Scientific Implications*. There can be no doubt that it was this book that led to the modern revival in creation science and Flood geology. It brought together the founders of the Creation Research Society in 1963 and led to the establishment of the Institute for Creation Research in 1970 (Morris 1993).

6. Towards the Building of a Coherent, Robust Flood Model for the World's Geology

In the last fifty years since publication of *The Genesis Flood* book there have been numerous attempts to construct a coherent understanding and explanation of the earth's geology and the development of its rock record, with fossil-bearing sedimentary strata, granite intrusions and volcanic rocks, metamorphic terranes and ore deposits, within the biblical framework of a literal six-day Creation week about six thousand years ago followed about one thousand six hundred fifty years later by the year-long global cataclysmic Flood. The difficulties of achieving such a synthesis have always been two-fold. On the one hand is the secular interpretation of the geologic record, involving the slow-and-gradual geologic processes of the present which it is claimed have built this geologic record over four and a half billion years. Of course, the modern uniformitarian geologic synthesis is an ongoing work in progress as the world's geology continues to be explored, new laboratory research and analyses are undertaken, and new ideas and compilations are tested against the field evidence.

On the other hand, the Bible's account of earth history is fixed and final, having been provided by the divine eyewitness and author, the Creator Himself (Gn 1:1, 4, 10, 12, 18, 21, 25, 31; Jn 1:1–3; Col 1:15–17; 2 Tm 3:16; 2 Pt 1:20–21). However, the details provided in Genesis 1–11 that cover the bulk of the earth's history when its geology was mostly developed are minimal and sketchy at best. Of course, the Bible is not a geology textbook, and never was intended to be such. Yet it does provide details of the events in the earth's history that shaped the earth's geology, namely, the Creation week (especially Days 1–3) and the Flood. Exhaustive details are not given, but just a broad overview, so based on the Hebrew text informed inferences can be made that help us build a model for the development of the geologic record that is consistent with Scripture. Thus there have been various attempts to build a biblical geological model that is faithful to both Scripture and science. Refinement of those models has been necessitated by new insights and better understanding of the biblical text, due to increased knowledge of the earth's geology, and new insights into the operation of geologic processes.

6.1   Whitcomb and Morris (1961)
6.2   Coffin (1983)
6.3   Walker (1994)
6.4   Austin et al. (1994)
6.5   Brand (1997)
6.6   Barrick and Sigler (2003)
6.7   Snelling (2009)

6.1 *Whitcomb and Morris (1961)*

In their book *The Genesis Flood*, Whitcomb and Morris (1961) focused on demonstrating that the fossil-bearing sedimentary rock layers could be adequately explained by the catastrophic geologic processes operating during the global cataclysmic Genesis Flood. The genius of their book was their comprehensive treatment of the geologic evidence consistent with the Flood, as well as their biblical defense of the Flood against the many critics and compromisers who over the years have tried to reinterpret Scripture to fit in with uniformitarian geological science. They did not attempt to meticulously align the various strata of the uniformitarian geologic column with the various stages of the Flood as outlined in the Scriptures. Nevertheless, in broad terms they outlined the scriptural framework for historical geology, in which they regarded the Precambrian rocks as pre-Flood, largely due to the events of the Creation week, and thus providing a basement foundation on which the Cambrian-Tertiary fossil-bearing sedimentary rocks were deposited by the waters of the Flood, which were sent by God to destroy all land-dwelling, air-breathing animals and man, except those on the Ark. They suggested that the Floodwaters reached their maximum height after only the first forty days, and then maintained that height until Day 150 when the Ark landed on the mountains of Ararat (Figure 1). The next two hundred twenty-one days after Day 150 were required for the waters to recede sufficiently for Noah and the animals to leave the Ark.

They did note, however, that the order of strata and fossils in the geologic record could be explained by the actions of the Floodwaters, with the early burial of marine creatures matching the record in the uniformitarian's lower Paleozoic strata, and the higher mobility of vertebrates leading to the eventual burial of land animals and plants as the Floodwaters rose over the continents, hydrodynamically sorting both sediments and fossils as they were deposited and buried respectively. They viewed the so-called Tertiary strata as the final Flood deposits, with the uplift of many of today's high mountain ranges occurring as the Flood ended, in accordance with the description in Psalm 104:8–9 of the mountains rising and the valleys sinking so that the waters could drain off the continents into the newly formed ocean basins, with their boundaries set which the waters would never again cross. The end result of the Flood was that the earth's climate system had to readjust itself, the initially warmer ocean waters and barren landscape triggering the onset of the post-Flood Ice Age. Thus they placed the Flood/post-Flood boundary more or less coinciding with the boundary between the Tertiary and Quaternary of the uniformitarian geologic column.

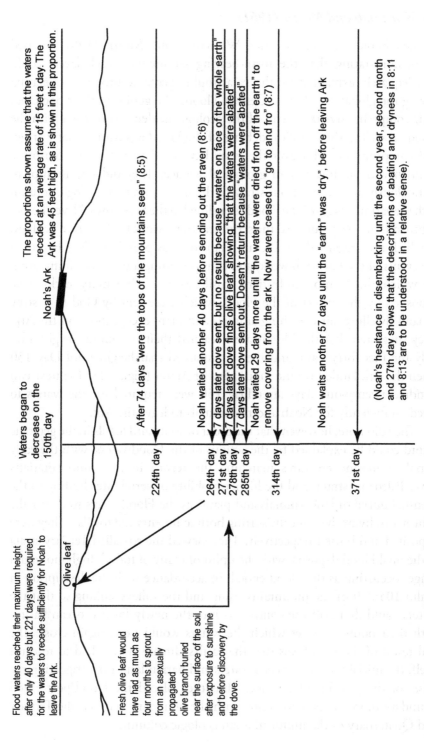

The proportions shown assume that the waters receded at an average rate of 15 feet a day. The Ark was 45 feet high, as shown in this proportion.

Flood waters reached their maximum height after only 40 days but 221 days were required for the waters to recede sufficiently for Noah to leave the Ark.

Waters began to decrease on the 150th day

Noah's Ark

After 74 days "were the tops of the mountains seen" (8:5)

Noah waited another 40 days before sending out the raven (8:6)

7 days later dove sent, but no results because "waters on face of the whole earth"

7 days later dove finds olive leaf, showing "that the waters were abated"

7 days later dove sent out. Doesn't return because "waters were abated"

Noah waited 29 days more until "the waters were dried from off the earth" to remove covering from the ark. Now raven ceased to "go to and fro" (8:7)

Noah waits another 57 days until the "earth" was "dry", before leaving Ark

(Noah's hesitance in disembarking until the second year, second month and 27th day shows that the descriptions of abating and dryness in 8:11 and 8:13 are to be understood in a relative sense).

Olive leaf

Fresh olive leaf would have had as much as four months to sprout from an asexually propagated olive branch buried near the surface of the soil, after exposure to sunshine and before discovery by the dove.

224th day

264th day
271st day
278th day
285th day

314th day

371st day

Figure 1. The Whitcomb and Morris (1961) time line for the prevailing and abating of the Floodwaters.

6.2 *Coffin (1983)*

This general framework for fitting the world's geology to a biblical Flood model has more or less been followed since, with minor adjustments and further additional details. Building on the earlier work of George McCready Price, it is hardly surprising that there has been a stream of scientists of Adventist persuasion who have similarly defended the geologic plausibility of the Genesis Flood and contributed to the building of a biblical Creation-Flood model for the earth's geology. Coffin's Genesis Flood model (Figure 2) closely followed the framework established by Whitcomb and Morris (Coffin 1983; Coffin et al. 2005). He also regarded the Precambrian rocks of the continental basement as pre-Flood, the Flood beginning with the breaking-up of the earth's crust, corresponding closely with the boundary between the Precambrian and Cambrian. But he noted that there were some uppermost Precambrian sedimentary rocks consisting of broken remnants of other older rocks which also record this initial upheaval marking the beginning of the Flood. Coffin envisaged that the earthquakes resulting from the breaking up of "the fountains of the great deep" (Gn 7:11) in the ocean basins would have generated tsunamis that swept landwards eroding pre-Flood ocean floor sediments and depositing them with marine creatures as fossils up on the continental margins initially, and then farther inland as the Floodwaters continued to rise. Furthermore, he pointed out the striking similarity between the groups of fossils at the various levels in the strata record and the creatures and plants to be found in various ecological zones, from bottom-dwelling and swimming marine animals, through seashore animals and plants to lowland swamps and forests, and then upland forests and animals, equating this order of these fossil "communities" to the order we would expect from the progressive inundation and burial of different pre-Flood ecological zones by the rising Floodwaters, an idea first noted by the Adventist pioneer Harold W. Clark (Clark 1946).

Unlike Whitcomb and Morris, who suggested the Floodwaters reached their maximum height after the first forty days (Figure 1), Coffin suggested that the Floodwaters rose continually through the first one hundred fifty days before reaching their maximum on Day 150 when the rain stopped, with sufficient water to float the Ark by Day 40 (Figure 3). Coffin roughly equated the high point of the Floodwaters on Day 150 as coinciding with the end of the Permian period and Paleozoic era of the uniformitarian geologic timescale (Figure 2). However, having suggested this benchmark when the Floodwaters would have covered all the land, Coffin equated the mountain-building beginning in the Mesozoic as coinciding with the mountains rising and being seen (Gn 8:5) when the waters had started to recede. However, he failed to explain how the reptiles and mammals would have survived after the Floodwaters reached their zenith on Day 150 (equivalent to the end of the Permian), to subsequently be buried during the Mesozoic and Tertiary when the Floodwaters were receding. Like Whitcomb and Morris though, he had the Ark being abandoned by Noah and the animals at the end of the Pliocene epoch of the Tertiary period to begin colonizing the post-Flood world with its climatic changes that resulted in the Pleistocene Ice Age.

Genesis Flood Model

Geological Column		Genesis Flood Narrative	Comparisons and Comments
Precambrian		Pre-Flood	Breakup of earth's crust
Cambrian			Erosion and deposition of pre-Flood ocean sediments
	Beginning Storm	Heavy rain (Gn 7:11, 12)	Formation of the great Precambrian/Cambrian unconformity
Ordovician	Beginning Storm	Subterranean waters released (Gn 7:11)	Burial of benthonic animals
Silurian	Beginning Storm	Rising water (Gn 7:20)	Upward coarse to fine grading of sediments
Devonian	Standing Water	High water (Gn 7:24)	Deposition of thick shale and limestone
Mississippian	Standing Water	Tidal and wave action (Gn 8:3)	Cyclothems—rhythmic deposition of sediments
Pennsylvanian	Standing Water	Water covers all land (Gn 7:20)	Formation of coal; burial of lowland forests, trees of greater density and/or less buoyancy
Permian			
Triassic		Rain stops, wind starts (Gn 8:1, 2)	Crossbedded sandstones
			Moving continents
Jurassic	Windstorm	Mountains rise (Gn 8:5)	Mountain building (tectonic) activities
Cretaceous	Windstorm	Waters start to recede (Gn 8:5)	Major erosion of emerging mountains; guyots
Paleocene			Burial of reptiles
Eocene		Birds released (Gn 8:8–12)	Formation of coal; burial of upland forests, trees of less density and/or more buoyancy
			Burial of mammals
Oligocene	Receding Water	Water continues to drop (Gn 8:13)	Sediments accumulate along continental margins
Miocene	Receding Water		Less dense and less well indurated strata Major volcanic activity
Pliocene	Receding Water	Ark abandoned (Gn 8:14, 15)	Localized sediments and valley fills
Pleistocene			Post-Flood erosional reworking of surface sediment Post-Flood climatic changes (glaciation)
Recent		Post-Flood	

Figure 2. The Coffin (1983) model for correlating the geologic record with the Genesis Flood.

6.3 Walker (1994)

A different approach was taken by Walker (1994). He disregarded the uniformitarian geologic column as a general description of the strata sequence of the Flood, and instead built his "biblical geologic model" exclusively from the framework of earth history described primarily in Genesis. In this model (Figure 4) he had the Floodwaters reaching their zenith between thirty and sixty days after the fountains of the great deep broke open, with the rain stopping on Day 40. He considered that the first sixty days of the Flood were the inundatory stage, with the remaining three hundred days representing the recessive stage. In a subsequent version of this model (Walker 2011) (Figure 5), he corrected his model to align it more with the Scriptural benchmarks, placing the first forty days of heavy rainfall in his "eruptive phase" of the inundatory stage, with the Floodwaters reaching their zenith in the sixty days leading to Day 150 of the Flood. This left his recessive stage to cover the remaining two hundred twenty days of the Flood.

Walker made no effort to connect the various strata of the uniformitarian geologic column with his biblical geologic model, instead laying down criteria by which specific

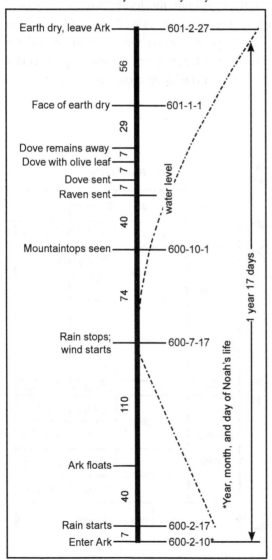

Figure 3. The Coffin (1983) time line for the prevailing and abating of the Floodwaters.

strata could be classified within his biblical geologic model. However, his subsequent work has demonstrated the shortcomings of his criteria and his approach, because specific strata he has assigned, for example, in Australia to the beginning of the Flood event can easily be demonstrated from the bigger picture of world geology very clearly fitting physically to later in the Flood. This has only served to confuse efforts to unravel the world's geology and realign it from a Flood perspective. Nevertheless, many have still adopted his biblical geologic model (Figure 5) as a useful Flood stage classification and naming scheme, as well as a scheme useful for describing when in the Flood specific strata were deposited and for cross-correlating specific physical rock layers from a biblical perspective with the strata sequence of the uniformitarian geologic column.

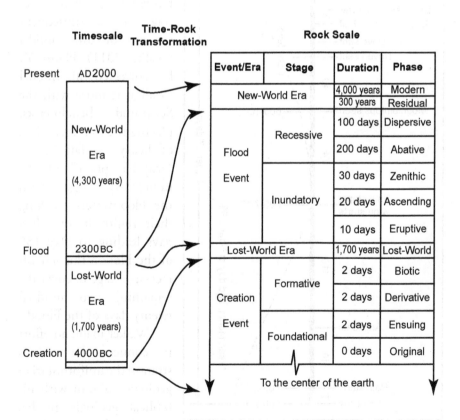

Figure 4. The Walker (1994) biblical geologic model for redefining rock units in terms of the biblical framework of earth history.

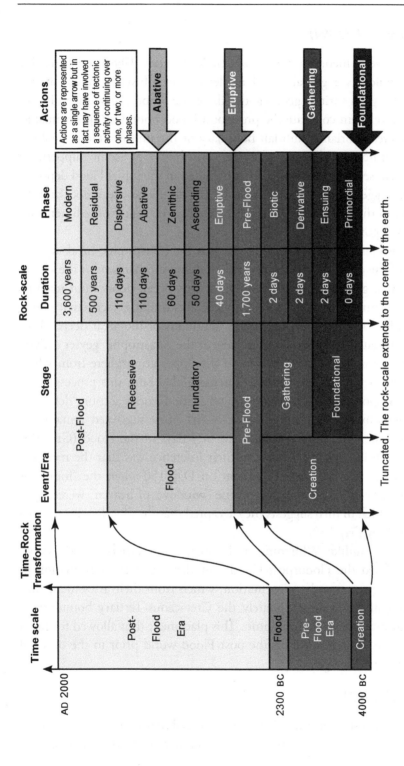

Figure 5. The Walker (2011) revised biblical geologic model for redefining rock units in terms of the biblical framework of earth history.

6.4 Austin et al. (1994)

A parallel development was the proposal by Austin et al. (1994) of catastrophic plate tectonics as a global Flood model of earth history. While mainly concentrating on various geologic details of the Flood event, they did like others before them correlate the pre-Flood/Flood boundary approximately with the Precambrian/Cambrian boundary of the uniformitarian geologic column, although allowing for the possibility of some uppermost Precambrian sedimentary layers being included in the initial Flood deposits. They also suggested that the sediments on the pre-Flood ocean floor and the chemistry of the pre-Flood ocean contributed to the source of sediments for the strata deposited during the Flood.

The primary feature of their model was the catastrophic break-up and shifting of the earth's crustal plates as the driving mechanism for the Flood, coupled with generation and spreading of new ocean floors from magmas upwelling from the mantle, coinciding with catastrophic geyser activity along the spreading centers equating to the "fountains of the great deep." They postulated that the supersonic steam jets of the catastrophic geyser activity entrained ocean water, carrying it into the upper atmosphere from where it fell back to the earth's surface as intense global rain, this process being primarily responsible for the rain from what the Genesis account described as the "windows of heaven" opening, which they suggested remained a source of water for up to one hundred fifty days of the Flood (Gn 7:11; 8:2). Though not specifically stated, their inference was that the recession of the Floodwaters began at this point on Day 150 when the "fountains of the great deep" were stopped and the "windows of heaven" were closed (Gn 8:2), which in turn suggests they accepted that the Floodwaters reached their zenith by Day 150.

However, unlike Whitcomb and Morris, and others, Austin et al. (1994) defined the Flood/post-Flood boundary as at the termination of global-scale erosion and sedimentation, which from their assessment they placed tentatively at approximately the Cretaceous/Tertiary boundary of the uniformitarian geologic column. This placement thus allowed for rapid residual local catastrophism in the post-Flood world prior to the onset of the Pleistocene Ice Age.

6.5 Brand (1997)

Because of focusing on the science and not elaborating on the Scriptures, Brand (1997, 2009) does not comment on any correlation between the biblical account of the Flood and its chronology with the uniformitarian geologic column, apart from the beginning and end points of the Flood. Like so many others before him, Brand correlated the beginning of the Flood with the bottom of the Paleozoic, but allowed for some of the uppermost Precambrian sedimentary strata to be part of the initial Flood deposits, as also suggested by Austin and Wise (1994). Brand thus regarded the Paleozoic strata to represent early Flood deposits, while the Mesozoic strata belonged to the middle to late Flood deposits. Whether he meant that the Paleozoic ended around Day 150 is not stated. However, he acknowledged that the Flood/post-Flood boundary is especially difficult to determine, but he regarded it as probably being somewhere between the Cretaceous and the Pliocene. Like Austin et al. (1994), this allows for rapid residual local catastrophism to have occurred in the immediate post-Flood period prior to the onset of the Pleistocene Ice Age.

The rationale used by Brand can be seen in Figure 6, which depicts the preserved rock record between major unconformities across the North American continent, coupled with what uniformitarian geologists interpret as major mass extinctions. Preserved rock strata across the North American continent represent megasequences or large packages of sediment layers deposited as the Floodwaters spread right across the continent, the unconformities being due to fluctuations in water levels. It should be noted that after the Cretaceous there is no longer any continental-wide sedimentation, which obviously must coincide with the final full retreat of the Floodwaters.

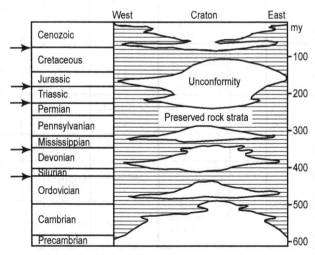

Figure 6. The preserved rock record between major unconformities and mass extinctions (arrowed) across the North American continent (Brand 1997).

6.6 *Barrick and Sigler (2003)*

Barrick and Sigler (2003) and Barrick (2008) carefully looked at the Hebrew text of the Flood in Genesis 7–8 to determine the chronology of the Flood, which they summarized in a table (Figure 7). They divided the chronology of the Flood into one hundred fifty days of destructive prevailing waters, followed by two hundred twenty-one days of subsiding/regressive waters. This chronological framework is of course determined by the fixed dates given in the Hebrew text and the descriptions of what was happening in relation to the Floodwaters in association with those fixed dates (see Figure 7). Thus they suggested that the Floodwaters rose until they were high enough to lift the Ark off the ground on Day 40, which they showed diagrammatically (Figure 8). The Floodwaters continued to rise so the Ark moved about on the water surface, and then the waters prevailed until Day 150 (Figure 7).

150 Days of Destructive Prevailing Waters				221 Days of Subsiding/Regressive Waters			
Passage	Date	Day	Stage	Passage	Date	Day	Stage
Gn 7:24	7/16/600	150	Waters prevail through this day	Gn 8:1–4 ↓	**7/17/600**	151	Commencement of subsiding waters; sources are stopped; Ark grounded
Gn 7:21–23	?	?	All the creatures of the dry land died	Gn 8:5 ↓	**10/1/600**	225	Mountaintops appear
				Gn 8:6 ↓	11/11/600	265	Noah opens hatch
Gn 7:19–20 ↑	?	?	Waters prevail even more so that the pre-Flood mountains were overwhelmed	Gn 8:7 ↓	11/12/600	266	Raven released
Gn 7:18 ↑	?	?	Waters rise more and Ark moves about on the water surface	Gn 8:8–9 ↓	11/19/600	273	Dove released
Gn 7:12, 17 ↑	03/26/600	40	Rising waters lift the Ark off the ground	Gn 8:10–11 ↓	11/26/600	280	Dove released and returns with olive leaf
				Gn 8:12 ↓	12/3/600	287	Dove released and did not return
Gn 7:11	**02/17/600**	1	Commencement of prevailing waters by upheavals of the earth's crust (mostly oceanic) and torrential rain	Gn 8:13 ↓	**01/01/601**	315	Ground surface free of excess water
				Gn 8:14	**02/27/601**	371	Earth dry enough to leave the Ark

↑ Rising waters   ↓ Falling waters   Dates in **bold** are given in Scripture

Figure 7. The Barrick and Sigler (2003) chronology of the Flood.

However, in their diagram (Figure 8) they have the Floodwaters peaking sometime soon after Day 40 and then prevailing at that maximum level until Day 150 when the Ark was grounded on "the mountains of Ararat."

Even though Barrick and Sigler (2003) and Barrick (2008) do not attempt to link the chronology of the Flood (Figure 7) to the uniformitarian geologic column, assigning which strata belonged to which part of the Flood event, they nonetheless made a number of geologic inferences, as shown in their diagram (Figure 8). The most significant of their geologic inferences is with respect to the level of the Floodwaters, which they equated to a progressively rising sea level that peaked and then maintained that highest sea level until the waters began to subside after Day 150, though more rapidly after Day 225 when the tops of the mountains were first seen. In parallel with this sea level curve they envisaged submarine deposition progressively increasing on the continents as the Floodwaters rose to produce a global ocean (Figure 8).

They did allow for some fluctuations in the sea level due to the back and forth nature of the ocean tides that would have temporarily exposed land surfaces during both the prevailing phase and the subsiding stage of the Flood, but this is not reflected in their diagram, which essentially has the sea level at its highest and therefore exclusively submarine deposition from about Day 60 or so until beyond Day 150. Of course, this is relevant to the nature of the sedimentary strata of the geologic record and the fossils contained within them. However, their sea level curve does not match that suggested by the secular interpretation of that part of the geologic record that creationist geologists would equate with the Flood (Figures 9 and 10). Though there is some semblance of agreement, the secular sea level curve initially rose sharply from the Flood/pre-Flood boundary at the end of the so-called Precambrian, quickly reached a peak, from which sea level progressively declined with several fluctuations almost back to the present sea level, before quickly rising again during the Cretaceous to its highest level recorded in the geologic record, and then declining rapidly to its current level. Of course, there are a lot of factors involved in interpreting what the relative sea level was in the past, based on examining the character of the various strata of the geologic record, but nonetheless, on the gross scale the secular interpreted relative sea level curve does not altogether match that of Barrick and Sigler (2003). Thus as the geology of the Flood is unraveled more specifically in relation to the physical rock record of the Flood, such fluctuations in the relative sea level, or rather the relative level of the Floodwaters on a global scale, will have to be taken into account in conjunction with both the chronology of the Flood and the descriptions of the actions of the Floodwaters in the Hebrew text.

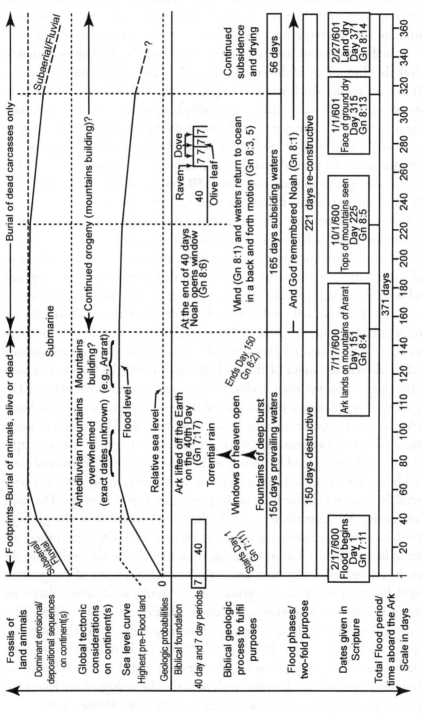

Figure 8. The Barrick and Sigler (2003) diagrammatic representation of the chronology of the Flood and the prevailing and abating of the Floodwaters.

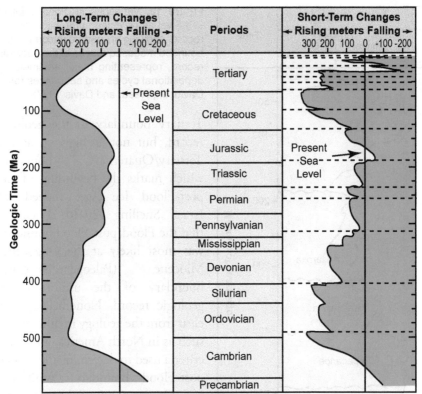

Figure 9. Postulated long- and short-term changes in sea level through the Phanerozoic (Flood) geologic record (modified after Vail and Mitchum 1979).

6.7 *Snelling (2009)*

In the most recent effort to tie together the rock layers and fossils of the geologic record of the Flood with the biblical account of earth history, Snelling (2009) followed the basic model suggested by Whitcomb and Morris (1961), but modified it according to later contributions by Austin et al. (1994), Austin and Wise (1994), and Brand (1997). He correlated the pre-Flood/Flood boundary and the beginning of the Flood with disrupted strata and catastrophic erosion on an almost global scale coinciding in most places with the base of the Cambrian, but in other places with some uppermost Precambrian strata consisting of tectonically disrupted blocks and debris from underlying Precambrian (pre-Flood) rock units that appeared to have been deposited by catastrophic avalanches around the margins of the pre-Flood supercontinent (Austin and Wise 1994; Sigler and Wingerden 1998; Wingerden 2003).

Furthermore, like Austin et al. (1994) and Brand (1997), he correlated the Flood/post-Flood boundary as being somewhere above the Cretaceous/

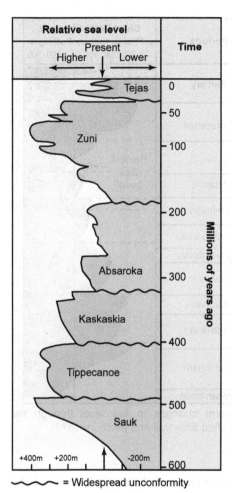

Figure 10. Variations in global relative sea level as reflected in the sedimentary record, showing six named unconformity-bounded megasequences of the geologic record, representing major sedimentary depositional cycles and sequences (after Davidson, Reed, and Davis 1997).

Tertiary boundary in the geologic record, but not as high up as the Tertiary/Quaternary boundary which marks the beginning of the post-Flood Ice Age. Indeed, in Israel, Snelling (2010) concluded that the Flood/post-Flood boundary was most likely at the Oligocene/ Miocene (Paleogene/Neogene) boundary of the uniformitarian geologic record. Nonetheless, it is clear from the geology in other areas, such as in North America, and from criteria used to determine the Flood/ post-Flood boundary (Whitmore and Garner 2008; Whitmore and Wise 2008), that this boundary in the geologic record might vary from place to place according to the stage at which the Floodwaters had retreated from the emerging post-Flood land surfaces. In other places, apart from the area around the mountains of Ararat where Noah and his companions alighted from the Ark at the end of the Flood according to Genesis 8:18, the Floodwaters are likely to have taken longer to retreat completely.

Otherwise, Snelling (2009) like others regarded the description in Genesis 7–8 as implying that the Floodwaters rose rapidly during the first forty days of the Flood to cover the earth's surface globally, and then reached their peak by Day 150 or earlier, as they progressively prevailed in destroying the land, and all air-breathing, land-dwelling creatures outside the Ark. He also agreed with Austin et al. (1994) that catastrophic plate tectonics was the driving force for the Flood, providing a good working model for how the geologic record of the Flood accumulated, and explaining not only all that conventional slow-and-gradual plate tectonics does, but much more.

7. Discussion: Where to from Here?

There is thus clearly a lack of consensus among Flood geologists as to how the geologic record can be directly correlated with the biblical account of the Flood. Whitcomb and Morris (1961), Brand (1997, 2009), and Snelling (2009) have each presented powerful evidences to show how the various sedimentary strata had to have been catastrophically deposited during the Flood, but an exact correlation between the various levels in the physical geologic record and the various stages of the Flood as described in Genesis has not been attempted. The primary reason would appear to be that Flood geologists have not been provided with sufficient biblical constraints from the Hebrew text upon which they are seeking to base their geologic model of the Flood and their correlations with the physical rock record.

In particular, the chronology of the Flood needs to be more clearly understood. Were the fountains of the great deep, which opened at the commencement of the Flood, shut on Day 150 as Genesis 8:2 appears to be saying happened on Day 150? Similarly, did the rainfall, which started at the beginning of the Flood, last until Day 150, as the text in the same verse (Gn 8:2) appears to be saying? Or did the sources of the Floodwaters shut off after forty days (forty days and nights of rain), one hundred ninety days (forty + one hundred fifty), or some other time? And what was the duration of the rise and fall of the Floodwaters? When did the peak in the level of the Floodwaters occur? Was it on Day 150, or earlier? Opinions differ among biblical scholars. Barrick (2008) and Barrick and Sigler (2003) maintained that Day 40 only marked the lifting of the Ark off the earth by the Floodwaters, which then peaked sometime soon thereafter and maintained that level until Day 150, whereas Whitcomb and Morris (1961) suggested the Floodwaters peaked by Day 40 and maintained that level until Day 150.

Furthermore, do the verbs in the Hebrew text imply any oscillation of the waters at any stage during the Flood? Specifically, did the water levels fluctuate vertically at any stage during the Flood, as the geologic record appears to indicate happened (Figures 9 and 10), even during the prevailing stage? And did the waters retreat and advance repeatedly even while they were rising and prevailing?

The geologic record of North America (Figures 6 and 10) consists of six megasequences of sedimentary rock strata separated by unconformities which can be traced and correlated right across the continent (Sloss 1963; Lindberg 1986). These megasequences each begin with transgressive deposition of sediment layers as the ocean waters rose and flooded across the continent, and end with regressive erosion and deposition of sediment layers as the ocean waters receded.

The rise and fall of the ocean waters are depicted in the relative sea level curve in Figures 9 and 10. These figures show that the relative sea level reached its last greatest peak near the end of the Cretaceous, then after some brief fluctuations rapidly fell. In the rock record it also corresponds to the end of deposition of the fifth of the megasequences (the Zuni), the last whose strata extend across the North American continent. It makes sense then to potentially equate the upper Cretaceous sea level peak with Day 150 of the Flood, except that there is relatively much less thickness and volume of rock layers in the geologic record above that level to be accounted for by the two hundred twenty-one days of the subsiding waters of the Flood. This is why Holt (1996) suggested there may be a whole missing section of the rock record at the Cretaceous-Tertiary boundary, which he called the Erodozoic because of the massive erosion that would have occurred as the Floodwaters retreated.

A further intriguing observation from this relative sea level curve is that there was a similar high peaking of relative sea level very early in the geologic record of the Flood at the end of the so-called Cambrian after deposition of the Sauk megasequence (Figures 9 and 10). Indeed, after that peak in the relative sea level so early in the Flood the water levels appear to have fluctuated but dropped progressively, that is relative to land surfaces, until rising again late in the Flood to peak in the so-called late Cretaceous. Of course, there are numerous assumptions involved in constructing this relative sea level curve, and the relative levels of land surfaces would similarly have fluctuated because of the earth movements during the Flood. Nevertheless, if this relative sea level curve is a guide, then this pattern would seem to best equate with the waters of the Flood peaking by Day 40, corresponding to the peak at the end of the so-called Cambrian, and then fluctuating through the following one hundred ten days of the Flood until peaking again on Day 150, equated with the so-called late Cretaceous.

This then begs the question as to whether this interpretation of the rising and falling of the relative sea level (i.e., the Floodwaters) and the corresponding transgressive and regressive sedimentation within these transcontinental megasequences of rock layers can be sustained by the Hebrew text of the Genesis Flood account. To suggest that the relative sea level progressively dropped after initially peaking at the end of the Cambrian until it reached a similar relative level as today by the Jurassic potentially threatens the Ark with possible grounding before the Floodwaters peaked in the Cretaceous and the mountains of Ararat had formed.

At least there is a general consensus as to where in the geologic record represents the beginning of the Flood. The Precambrian-Cambrian boundary is marked by an erosional unconformity in most places around the globe that is consistent with the initial catastrophic transgression of the Floodwaters over the continent(s). Many have also recognized that some of the uppermost Precambrian (upper Neoproterozoic) sediments were catastrophically deposited with fossils of unique shallow marine nearshore creatures that are likely the initial Flood deposits, coinciding with the break-up of the pre-Flood supercontinent Rodinia (see **Chapter 6**).

However, the location of the Flood/post-Flood boundary is still very much debated—see **Chapter 7**). Ultimately, multiple factors have to be considered in order to achieve a consensus. Tertiary sedimentation was definitely more localized as the relative sea level fell rapidly, but some of that sedimentation could equally have resulted from local post-Flood catastrophic flooding due to very heavy rainfall events (Vardiman 2003). Mountain-building also occurred in the Tertiary, which could be consistent with the mountain tops rising and becoming visible above the Floodwaters as they retreated and subsided (Gn 8:5).

Resolving the location of the Flood/post-Flood boundary requires dealing with all these factors and more (e.g., the fossils and the descendants from the animals on the Ark (see **Chapter 7**) in the light of any clues that can be gleaned from the Hebrew text of the Genesis Flood account. Specifically, do the verbs in the Hebrew text imply any oscillation of the waters during the receding stage of the Flood? Did the waters retreat and advance repeatedly even while they were receding? Thus there is much Hebrew scholars can contribute to further our understanding of the geologic record of the Flood.

8. Conclusion

Right from the dawn of history God expected man to use his endowed abilities to investigate and understand the workings of his earthly home so as to wisely utilize its resources. But man rebelled against his Creator, and the earth was filled with wickedness and violence, so God sent the Flood to cataclysmically destroy, cleanse, and reshape the earth (Gn 6:11–13). Thus all efforts to understand the world's geology today must take into account the devastating effects of the Flood, as described by God in the Hebrew text of the book of Genesis.

Sadly, man's efforts to understand the formation of the earth's rock layers have repeatedly abandoned the explanation provided by God's eyewitness testimony of the earth's creation and subsequent judgment by the Flood. Instead, just as the Apostle Peter warned (2 Pt 3:3–6), men have chosen to explain the earth's past formation as only due to the geologic processes and their rates of operation that we observe today. This has been encapsulated as the maxim "the present is the key to the past," which is in reality the belief in the uniformity of natural processes through all of time, or more simply, uniformitarianism. Yet there have always been those who have remained faithful to God's Word being their absolute authority.

The latter half of the twentieth century saw a revival of Flood geology among Bible-believing Christian scholars and scientists, including geologists. Much effort is now focused on building a coherent, robust Flood model for the world's geology.

The current consensus is that the record of the Flood's beginning, when "the fountains of the great deep" were broken up and "the windows of heaven" were opened (Gn 7:11), can be seen in some uppermost Precambrian strata consisting of debris deposited by catastrophic avalanches around the margins of the pre-Flood supercontinent, and at the widespread erosional unconformity marking the Precambrian/Cambrian boundary in the geologic "column." This erosional unconformity was produced by the catastrophic transgression of the ocean (Flood) waters as the relative sea level dramatically rose to flood the land surfaces, depositing a megasequence of rock layers with entombed creatures, for example, across North America. The relative sea level then seems to have fluctuated, so that the Floodwaters retreated then advanced several times, progressively depositing further megasequences of fossil-bearing sediment layers.

Debate continues over the location of the Flood/post-Flood boundary. The highest relative sea level was achieved just prior to the Cretaceous/Tertiary boundary in the geologic record, marked also by what secularists term the last major extinction of life, after which the relative sea level dropped dramatically to around today's level. All are agreed the only Ice Age (the "Pleistocene") was post-Flood. Some would thus place the Flood/post-Flood boundary just at the Pliocene/Pleistocene boundary, some identify it as close to above the Cretaceous/Tertiary boundary, whereas others would place it somewhere in between within the Tertiary, perhaps coinciding with end of deposition of the last of the megasequences which blankets North America.

The need now is for the chronology of the Flood and the Floodwaters' actions to be more clearly understood from the Hebrew text of the Genesis Flood account. In particular, did the Floodwaters peak on Day 40 and then maintain that level until Day 150, or did they only peak on Day 150? And did the Floodwaters fluctuate in their actions and oscillate in their levels both in their prevailing and receding stages? Thus there is much Hebrew scholars can contribute to further our understanding of the geologic record of the Flood.

References

Austin, S. A., J. R. Baumgardner, D. R. Humphreys, A. A. Snelling, L. Vardiman, and K. P. Wise. 1994. Catastrophic plate tectonics: A global Flood model of earth history. In *Proceedings of the third International Conference on Creationism.* Ed. R. E. Walsh, 609–621. Pittsburgh, PA: Creation Science Fellowship.

Austin, S. A., and K. P. Wise. 1994. The pre-Flood/Flood boundary: As defined in Grand Canyon, Arizona and eastern Mojave Desert, California. In *Proceedings of the third International Conference on Creationism.* Ed. R. E. Walsh, 37–47. Pittsburgh, PA: Creation Science Fellowship.

Barrick, W. D. 2008. Noah's Flood and its geological implications. In *Coming to grips with Genesis.* Ed. T. Mortenson, and T. H. Ury, 251–281. Green Forest, AR: Master Books.

Barrick, W. D., and R. Sigler. 2003. Hebrew and geologic analyses of the chronology and parallelism of the Flood: Implications for interpretation of the geologic record. In *Proceedings of the fifth International Conference on Creationism.* Ed. R. L. Ivey Jr., 397–408. Pittsburgh, PA: Creation Science Fellowship.

Berry, W. D. N. 1968. *Growth of a prehistoric timescale: Based on organic evolution,* 11–25. San Francisco, CA: W. H. Freeman and Company.

Brand, L. 1997. *Faith, reason, and earth history.* Berrien Springs, MI: Andrews University Press.

Brand, L. 2009. *Faith, reason and earth history.* 2nd ed. Berrien Springs, MI: Andrews University Press.

Clark, H. W. 1946. *The new diluvialism.* Angwin, CA: Science Publications.

Coffin, H. G. 1983. *Origin by design.* Hagerstown, MD: Review and Herald Publishing Association.

Coffin, H. G., R. H. Brown, and R. J. Gibson. 2005. *Origin by design.* Rev. ed. Hagerstown, MD: Review and Herald Publishing Association.

Darwin, C. 1859. *On the origin of species by means of natural selection, or the preservation of favoured races in the struggle for life.* London, England: J. Murray.

Davidson, J. P., W. E. Reed, and P. M. Davis.1997. *Exploring earth: An introduction to physical geology.* Upper Saddle River, NJ: Prentice-Hall, Inc.

Holmes, A. 1965. *Principles of physical geology.* London, England: Thomas Nelson and Sons.

Holt, R. D. 1996. Evidence for a late Cainozoic Flood/post-Flood boundary. *Creation Ex Nihilo Technical Journal* 10.1: 128–167.

Hutton, J. 1788. Theory of the earth: or an investigation of the laws observable in the composition, dissolution, and restoration of land on the globe. *Transactions of the Royal Society of Edinburgh* 1: 109–304.

Hutton, J. 1795. *Theory of the earth, with proofs and illustrations.* 2 Vols. Edinburgh, Scotland: W. Creech.

Lindberg, F. A. 1986. *Correlation of stratigraphic units of North America (COSUNA): Correlation charts series.* Tulsa, OK: American Association of Petroleum Geologists.

Lyell, C. 1830–1833. *Principles of geology.* 3 vols. London, England: J. Murray.

Morris, H. M. 1993. *History of modern creationism.* 2nd ed. Santee, CA: Institute for Creation Research.

Mortenson, T. 2004. *The great turning point: The church's catastrophic mistake on geology—before Darwin.* Green Forest, AR: Master Books.

Palmer, T. 1999. *Controversy—Catastrophism and evolution: The ongoing debate.* New York, NY: Kluwer Academic/Plenum Publishers.

Playfair, J. 1802. *Illustrations of the Huttonian theory of the earth.* London, England: Cadell and Davies, and Edinburgh, Scotland: William Creech.

Sigler, R., and C. V. Wingerden. 1998. Submarine flow and slide deposits in the Kingston Peak Formation, Kingston Range, Mojave Desert, California: Evidence for catastrophic initiation of Noah's Flood. In *Proceedings of the fourth International Conference on Creationism.* Ed. R. E. Walsh, 487–501. Pittsburgh, PA: Creation Science Fellowship.

Sloss, L. L. 1963. Sequences in the cratonic interior of North America. *Geological Society of America Bulletin* 74: 93–114.

Snelling, A. A. 2009. *Earth's catastrophic past: Geology, Creation and the Flood.* Dallas, TX: Institute for Creation Research.

Snelling, A. A. 2010. The geology of Israel within the biblical creation-Flood framework of history: II. The Flood rocks. *Answers Research Journal* 3: 267–309.

Vaccari, E. 2001. European views on terrestrial chronology from Descartes to the mid-eighteenth century. In *The age of the earth: From 4004 BC to AD 2002.* Ed. C. L. E. Lewis, and S. J. Knell, Special Publication 190, 25–37. London, England: The Geological Society.

Vail, P. R., and R. M. Mitchum Jr. 1979. Global cycles of relative changes of sea level from seismic stratigraphy. *American Association of Petroleum Geologists Memoir* 29: 469–472.

Vardiman, L. 2003. Hypercanes following the Genesis Flood. In *Proceedings of the fifth International Conference on Creationism.* Ed. R. L. Ivey Jr., 17–28. Pittsburgh, PA: Creation Science Fellowship.

Wald, G. 1954. The origin of life. *Scientific American* 191.2: 44–53.

Walker, T. 1994. A biblical geologic model. In *Proceedings of the third International Conference on Creationism.* Ed. R. E. Walsh, 581–592. Pittsburgh, PA: Creation Science Fellowship.

Walker, T. 2011. Charts of biblical geologic model, retrieved from http://biblicalgeology.net/images/stories/resources/geological_model_1.pdf.

Whitcomb, J. C., and H. M. Morris. 1961. *The Genesis Flood: The biblical record and its scientific implications.* Phillipsburg, NJ: Presbyterian and Reformed Publishing Company.

Whitmore, J. H., and P. Garner. 2008. Using suites of criteria to recognise pre-Flood, Flood and post-Flood strata in the rock record with application to Wyoming (USA). In *Proceedings of the sixth International Conference on Creationism*. Ed. A. A. Snelling, 425–448. Pittsburgh, PA: Creation Science Fellowship and Dallas, TX: Institute for Creation Research.

Whitmore, J. H., and K. P. Wise. 2008. Rapid and early post-Flood mammalian diversification evidence in the Green River Formation. In *Proceedings of the sixth International Conference on Creationism*. Ed. A. A. Snelling, 449–457. Pittsburgh, PA: Creation Science Fellowship and Dallas, TX: Institute for Creation Research.

Wingerden, C. V. 2003. Initial Flood deposits of the western North American cordillera: California, Utah and Idaho. In *Proceedings of the fifth International Conference on Creationism*. Ed. R. L. Ivey, Jr., 349–357. Pittsburgh, PA: Creation Science Fellowship.

CHAPTER 6

Geophysical Issues: Understanding the Origin of the Continents, their Rock Layers and Mountains

Andrew A. Snelling

> ***Analogy and Orientation.*** *If a ship is to successfully make landfall and safely arrive at its destination harbor, the ship's captain must have a good knowledge of the coastline and topography surrounding the intended port. Knowing how the landscape formed also informs of dangers, such as potential eruptions from the volcano that is adjacent to the harbor entrance, or potential tsunamis from nearby undersea earthquakes! Maps and charts are available with the needed information, so the captain should study those and not just rely on his own observations. Furthermore, observations only at the earth's surface are inadequate to explain how today's mountains and volcanoes formed. Only when we could understand the earth's internal structure was it possible for the plate tectonics model to become the ruling paradigm it is today. But it could never have happened at the snail's pace at which earth movements occur today. In fact, it was a Christian geologist who read God's eyewitness account of earth history and then proposed in 1859 that continental sprint occurred catastrophically during the Flood. So the goal of this chapter is to briefly review the history of ideas about how mountains and volcanoes form, culminating in how knowledge of the earth's interior eventually led to the adoption of the secular slow and gradual plate tectonics model. Furthermore, it will be shown that the catastrophic plate tectonics model has even greater explanatory power than the secular model*

for the geology and geophysics of the Flood event, yet it still requires refinement from further study of the Hebrew text of the Genesis Flood account.

Abstract. In man's quest to understand the way the earth works, what God's Word tells us about the earth's history was ignored. Instead, extrapolating today's slow and gradual geologic processes back into the past to explain how earth movements have produced today's mountains and volcanoes over countless millions of years has taken a stranglehold on almost all geological thinking. Yet it was a Bible-believing geologist who in 1859 proposed that a pre-Flood supercontinent was catastrophically ripped apart into today's continents which sprinted into their current positions all during the biblical global Flood. Ignored, slow and gradual continental drift was proposed early in the twentieth century by secular geologists. It was new knowledge of the earth's internal structure that led to a new understanding of how the earth operates. Nevertheless, only the catastrophic plate tectonics model for the Flood event can explain how the ocean waters rose to flood the continents, how the fossil-bearing sedimentary layers were rapidly deposited, and how and when the mountains formed and volcanoes erupted due to plate collisions. But while deciphering the chronology of the Flood, there are remaining questions about what the Hebrew text might suggest with regards to the timing of the "fountains of the great deep," the rainfall from the "windows of heaven," and the rising of the mountains, including the mountains of Ararat on which the Ark landed, as well as the actions of the Floodwaters, during both their prevailing and abating stages.

Outline

1. Introduction
2. Some Historical Background
3. The Earth's Internal Structure
4. Isostasy: The Principle of Equal Balances
5. Why the Continents are Above Sea Level
6. Implications for the Tectonics of the Flood
7. Discussion: Where to from Here?
8. Conclusion

1. Introduction

The earth's mountains have always presented challenges to mankind. Not only are they places of beauty, but places of formidable challenges—to climb, explore, and cross them, and to explain how they formed. They are often made up of folded rock layers containing fossils, or sometimes of crystalline metamorphic rocks and granites. It is immediately evident that great forces were at work in the past to buckle rocks and transform these rock layers. And the presence of fossils of marine creatures in many of them signifies the ocean waters must have once covered today's land surfaces before the buckling and transformation subsequently happened.

Tectonics is the branch of geology dealing with the broad architecture of the outer part of the earth, that is, the regional assembling of structural and deformational features, the study of their mutual relations, origin, and historical development (Neuendorf, Mehl, and Jackson 2005). It involves the study of the internal structure of the earth and how the movements of rock materials beneath the earth's surface have generated the various features we see at the earth's surface today. The objective of such study is to understand why the continents and ocean basins are where they are today and how they developed and were constructed in the past. In the process, the aim is to understand the earthquakes generated by earth movements, why volcanoes are found where they are, and why mountains are where they are and how they developed.

2. Some Historical Background

The first attempts to formalize a system of correlating strata regionally were made just after the middle of the eighteenth century. Nicolaus Steno had demonstrated in 1669 that the oldest stratum is at the bottom of any sequence of strata, because the layers are sequentially and progressively deposited on top of one another. Johann Lehmann (1756) applied this superposition principle on a wide scale in northern Germany to establish the order of his three main classes of "mountains" (Dunbar and Rodgers 1957; Berry 1968; Boggs 1995). Distinguished by the rocks from which they are composed, he considered them to represent three different periods of deposition, from oldest to youngest:

1. "Mountains" formed at the formation of the earth and consisting of crystalline rock with steep and unsystematic layering;
2. "Mountains" formed during Noah's Flood and consisting of non-crystalline rocks with regular, horizontal, or near horizontal layers of fossiliferous sediments; and
3. "Mountains" formed since the Flood by local events (earthquakes, volcanic eruptions, flooding by rivers and the sea) and consisting of unconsolidated materials.

This early classification of mountains also recognized that some mountains had been built by volcanic eruptions, and that earthquakes were related to movements of rock masses within the earth and at the earth's surface. But little was then understood regarding the internal constitution of the earth, except it was presumed to be hot, as deduced from the molten rock that spewed from volcanoes and then cooled and hardened as new rock layers. Given that volcanic eruptions and earthquakes were intermittent, it was assumed earth movements in the past had likewise been intermittent, slow, and gradual. It was such observations that were used by James Hutton (1788 and 1795) and Charles Lyell (1830–1833) to persuasively argue that the earth's geology had only been shaped in the past by the same slow and gradual processes we see operating today, so that it was unnecessary to invoke the catastrophic global biblical Flood.

The earth's crust had typically been pictured as dynamic and capable of rapid vertical and horizontal motions on local, regional, and global scales, especially during the global scale catastrophic upheaval of the Genesis Flood. However, as a result of the influence of Hutton (1788 and 1795) and then Lyell (1830–1833), theories of gradualism increased in popularity, so past ideas of geologic processes during the Genesis Flood were replaced with ideas of constancy of present gradual physical processes. Ideas of global-scale and rapid crustal dynamics were replaced by ideas of local erosion, deposition, extrusion, intrusion, and crustal fixity, with only imperceptibly slow vertical subsidence and uplift being possible. So complete was the success of gradualism in geology as promoted by Lyell (in particular) that ideas of Flood geology were nowhere to be found among English-speaking scientists of the world by 1859.

One of the last holdouts for Flood geology was a little-known work published by Antonio Snider-Pellegrini (1859), ironically enough at the same time as the publication of Darwin's *On the Origin of Species*. Intrigued by the reasonably good fit between landmasses on either side of the Atlantic Ocean, Snider proposed that the earth's crust was composed of rigid plates which had rapidly moved horizontally with respect to one another. Snider argued that the description in Genesis 1:9–10 of God creating the dry land on the third day of the Creation Week implied that since the waters were gathered together into one place, the dry land may also have been in one place and therefore as a supercontinent (Figure 1). He thus proposed that this supercontinent broke apart at the commencement of the Flood, and that the horizontal divergence to the present configuration of continents had been rapid, occurring during the Flood. Snider may thus have been the first to propose some of the main elements of modern conventional plate tectonics theory, except he envisaged the plate movements occurring rapidly in the context of catastrophic Flood geology.

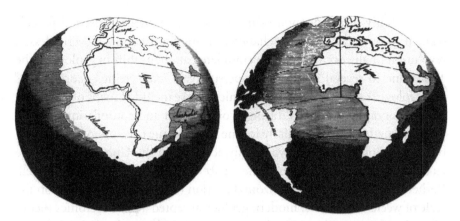

Figure 1. Antonio Snider-Pellegrini's depiction of how a pre-Flood supercontinent was catastrophically ripped apart at the initiation of the Flood and how today's continents sprinted into their present positions as the Atlantic Ocean basin was formed.

Snider's outrageous idea did not receive any serious attention, in large measure because the scientific world at that time was focused on debating Darwin's revolutionary theory on the origin of species and the biological evolution of life culminating in man. Besides, it was tacitly assumed without question that if interchanges between the continents and the ocean basins had to be postulated, the movements involved could hardly be other than vertical, because the earth's crust was believed to be horizontally fixed. So Snider's work was forgotten, and not even acknowledged when the suggestion that there might have been lateral displacements of the continental masses on a gigantic scale was again proposed by F. B. Taylor in the USA (1908) and by Alfred Wegener in Germany (1910). For several years they developed their unorthodox hypotheses quite independently. It was not until Wegener published his famous book on the subject in 1915 that the possibility of continental drift began to be widely discussed. His picture of the world in so-called Carboniferous times was somewhat similar to Snider's, and for this supercontinent he proposed a name Pangaea (from the Greek meaning "all earth").

It seems that a substantial amount of the early twentieth century opposition to continental drift and plate tectonics was due to the fact that geologists were still firmly predisposed to believe that the earth's crust was horizontally fixed. It was the catastrophist school of geology that first proposed plate tectonics (in 1859), and it was the gradualist school that was the first major opponent to plate tectonics. To support his case for continental drift Wegener marshaled an imposing collection of facts and opinions, some of his evidence being undeniably cogent. However, following the lead of many influential geophysicists, most geologists were reluctant to admit the possibility of continental drift, because no recognized natural process seemed to have the remotest chance of bringing it about. Nevertheless, a revolution finally occurred with a complete paradigm shift in geology in the 1960s due to several lines of data persuasively "converting" geophysicists and geologists to embrace plate tectonics. These included maps of the ocean floor topography produced during World War II and compilations of new paleomagnetic data, particularly for the rocks on the ocean floors. However, by the time plate tectonics was finally accepted in the United States in the late 1960s, gradualism had become a part of plate tectonics theory as well. Rather than Snider's rapid horizontal motion (or continental sprint) on the scale of weeks or months, modern geology accepted a plate tectonics theory of gradual horizontal motion (or continental drift) on the scale of tens to hundreds of millions of years.

3. The Earth's Internal Structure

Before we can understand and explain how Snider's idea of catastrophic continental sprint during the Flood has been vindicated and developed further, there are a few basic observations about the earth's structure and the composition and behavior of its outer crust that need to be grasped. The first consideration has to be an understanding of the earth's internal structure. Although the earth's average radius is 3967 mi (6371 km), the deepest drill-holes have only penetrated 9–12 mi (15–20 km) into the crust, the earth's outer "skin." Thus, most of our knowledge of the earth's interior has been derived from analyses of seismic waves, principally generated by earthquakes, and to a lesser extent from studies of the earth's magnetic and gravity fields (Davidson, Reed, and Davis 1997). Seismic waves in rock are similar to sound waves in air. After being generated by an earthquake, itself caused by rock movements, seismic waves travel through the earth so that they can be used to probe its interior in a way similar to our use of x-rays to examine the internal anatomy of an organism.

The speed of seismic waves depends on two material properties, in particular the density of the rocks they are passing through (Davidson, Reed, and Davis 1997). At the earth's surface, a rock is denser than water, but is less dense than aluminum. Deep within the earth, however, rock densities become even greater than the density of aluminum as measured at the earth's surface because of the great pressures in the interior. If a rock is subjected to increasing pressure, its volume decreases while its mass remains the same. Therefore, its density increases, since the density of the material is defined as the ratio of its mass to its volume. Rocks at depth within the earth are compressed by the weight of the rock above them. On the other hand, when a rock is heated it expands. So because its mass remains the same, its density must decrease. Measurements down drill-holes indicate that temperatures increase with increasing depth within the earth. Thus if rocks within the earth were subjected only to increasing temperatures, we would expect their densities to decrease with depth. However, rocks are also subject to pressure changes, and increasing pressure increases the density of a rock within the earth to a greater extent than increasing temperature reduces it. Therefore, the density of rock increases with depth (Figure 2).

The zones making up the internal structure of the earth are depicted in Figure 2. Densities within the earth depend on the rock types as well as on the temperatures and pressures (Davidson, Reed, and Davis 1997). Sedimentary rocks at the surface are the least dense, with a density of about 125 lbs/cubic foot ($2.0 \, g/cm^3$). In contrast, igneous rocks have densities of about 169 lbs/cubic foot ($2.7 \, g/cm^3$). The low densities of sedimentary rocks are mainly due to the rocks' pore spaces—the minute gaps between the rock grains that are filled with gas, water, or other fluids. In the mantle, pressure increases the density of mantle material from about 206 lbs/cubic foot ($3.3 \, g/cm^3$) in the upper mantle to about 344 lbs/cubic foot ($5.5 \, g/cm^3$) at the core-mantle boundary. Olivine is thought to be the dominant mineral in the upper mantle, extending to a depth of 255 mi (410 km). At that depth, the mineral structure is unstable and it changes to one that is more compact. Further changes in mineral structure occur at discrete depths, such as 379 mi (610 km), within the mantle. These changes, which were inferred to exist by observing the behavior of seismic waves, are referred to as phase transitions. At the bottom of the mantle the density then jumps to 625 lbs/cubic foot ($10 \, g/cm^3$) in the outer core at the transition between the silicate rocks of the mantle and the iron of the core. Finally, the density increases to approximately 813 lbs/cubic foot ($13 \, g/cm^3$) in the inner core at the earth's center.

In the field of medicine, a computer can generate a three-dimensional image of the internal structure of the human head. This is accomplished by transmitting information to the computer from x-ray detectors placed around the head. Seismic tomography performs essentially the same task for geology—generating a three-dimensional image of the earth's interior (Davidson, Reed, and Davis 1997). This technique uses earthquakes (or explosions) as transmitters and seismometers as detectors. Rather than obtaining a one-dimensional velocity profile through the earth as shown in Figure 2, we can build a three-dimensional seismic velocity image of the interior of the earth.

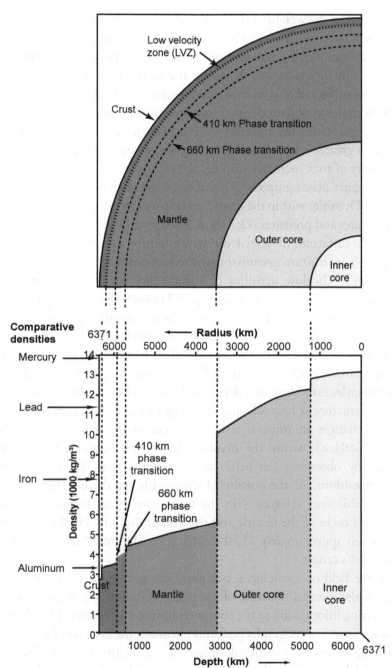

Figure 2. Density as a function of depth within the earth (after Davidson, Reed, and Davis 1997). Sudden increases in the density of the earth's interior occur at the base of the crust, at the mantle-phase transitions, at the mantle-core boundary, and at the inner core boundary. Densities of some common materials (at the earth's surface) are shown for comparison.

Below the crust at any given depth, the earth is fairly homogeneous. In fact, we can compare it with an onion in which each layer has an average seismic velocity and these velocities differ from layer to layer. Seismic tomography searches for the smaller, more subtle variations within each layer, called velocity anomalies, localized regions in the earth having velocity differences from the average values at those depths. In the crust, low-velocity anomalies are associated with heat and magma (molten rock) beneath the volcanoes. Low-velocity anomalies are also associated with crust that has been intruded by hot mantle rocks, such as in continental rift zones. In the mantle, low velocity anomalies are associated with both continental rift zones and mid-ocean spreading ridges, and upwelling convection currents. Thus the behavior of seismic waves clearly provides useful information on the density and material properties of the earth's interior.

4. Isostasy: The Principle of Equal Balances

Early in the nineteenth century, George Airy carried out a survey of India. The surveyors attempted to calculate the gravity due to the Himalayan Mountains and used the law of gravity to estimate the pull of that mass of mountains on a plumb bob (a suspended weight). They were greatly surprised to find that the measurements gave significantly lower numbers (seventy times less) than expected from applying the law of gravity to the protruding mass of mountains (Davidson, Reed, and Davis 1997). Airy surmised that the explanation must be that the mountains were underlain by a low-density root protruding into the high-density mantle. This was an early formulation of the concept of isostasy—the great mass of a mountain that extends above the earth's surface is compensated by a low-density mass in the mountain's underlying crustal root.

The best way to understand the concept of isostasy is to consider a simple model. Imagine several blocks of wood of different thicknesses floating in a tank of water (Figure 3). These blocks float because wood is less dense than water, and the thicker blocks protrude higher above the surface of the water than do the thinner blocks. At the same time, however, the thicker blocks also extend deeper into the water than do the smaller blocks; they are more deeply submerged to compensate for their larger size. The submerged part of a block can be imagined to be the root of that floating block.

Now consider the vertical column of rock beneath a mountain. The weight of the rock applies a load to the earth at the base of the column. If such a load is applied for a sufficiently long time, it will cause the mantle below it (and in some cases the lower crust) to flow until a balance exists between the crustal load and the flotation forces of the mantle. The amount of crust that extends into the mantle is called the crustal root. The crust has a lower density than the mantle, so the crust is therefore analogous to the lower-density wood floating in the water (Figure 3). Here though the crustal blocks can be thought of as floating on the mantle. In the upper mantle, temperatures become sufficiently high for the rock to behave like a fluid. The depth at which this occurs is known as the depth of compensation. Material above this depth acts like a solid floating in the fluid mantle. In fluids at a given depth the pressures are isostatic or equal. The pressure is given by the weight of the overlying rock. Thus the principle of isostasy states that the weight (solid and fluid) per unit area is the same in any column of material above the depth of compensation.

A floating block of wood or a mountain range is said to be in isostatic equilibrium when it is neither sinking nor rising (Figure 4). Now imagine placing a block of wood in honey. Initially, the block will not be in isostatic equilibrium until sufficient time has passed for it to sink to the level of isostatic equilibrium. Likewise, a mountain may be either rising or falling, depending on whether its current elevation is below or above the elevation needed for it to be in isostatic equilibrium.

Thus the mass of a mountain above sea level is compensated for by the mountain's underlying crustal root. Furthermore, a mountain is in isostatic equilibrium if it is neither rising nor sinking. However, if rapid erosion of a mountain occurred to substantially reduce its elevation, then the mountain would have to rise until it again reached isostatic equilibrium. Similarly, wherever the eroded sediments were rapidly deposited in an adjoining basin, then that land area would become heavier and so would sink until it again reached isostatic equilibrium. Such considerations are highly relevant to what was occurring late in the Flood and soon thereafter, because of the shifting of materials during the catastrophism of the Flood and the rapid erosion and continuing deposition as the Floodwaters retreated and the land surfaces were reestablished after the Flood.

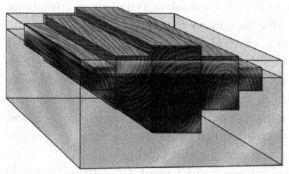

Figure 3. The principle of isostasy. The larger blocks of wood floating in the tank of water have a proportionately larger submerged "root," which supports the portion extending above the water's surface. The force of buoyancy depends on how much of the block is submerged.

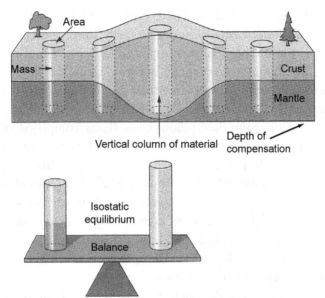

Figure 4. The principle of isostasy (after Davidson, Reed, and Davis 1997). The depth of compensation is the point within the earth where the flow occurs to ensure that the pressure is the same, or isostatic, everywhere. The weight per unit area in each vertical column of material above this depth must be the same.

Thus it would be predicted that large vertical earth movements, or vertical tectonics, would have been a dominant feature during the closing stages of the Flood and in the immediate post-Flood period. The evidence for such vertical tectonics late in the Flood can be seen in the Basin and Range Province of the U.S. Southwest, where the topography alternates between parallel mountain ranges and deep valleys consisting of depositional basins in between them. Huge tectonic adjustments produced vertical movements of thousands of feet along parallel faults defining blocks of the earth's crust between them. Similarly, the observation that the Himalayas are still rising is consistent with their formation only recently at the end of the Flood. And the same principle applies to the observation that parts of Scandinavia are still rising as a result of the removal of the thick ice sheet that "weighed" that land area down only recently in the post-Flood Ice Age.

5. Why the Continents Are Above Sea Level

Why then does continental crust (the crust of the continents) rise above sea level, whereas oceanic crust (the crust of the ocean floors) is submerged? Similarly, why do some plateaus stand 2–4 mi (3–6 km) above sea level, whereas the mean elevation of land is less than 0.6 mi (1 km)? The answers to these questions are obtained by understanding differences in structure and content between oceanic crust and continental crust, and then applying the principle of isostatic equilibrium (Davidson, Reed, and Davis 1997).

The structure of the oceanic crust is well-known from both drilling studies and from ophiolites, fragments of oceanic crust that have been added to the continental crust in collision zones. The oceanic crust is basaltic in composition and is on average only 4.4 mi (7 km) thick (Figure 5). The uppermost portion comprises pillow lavas (lavas comprised of bulbous pillow-shaped structures), basalts erupted under water onto the ocean floor, covered by a thin veneer of deep-sea sediments. This overlies, and is interbedded with, a sheeted dike complex, which is a series of subvertical dikes intruding the sediments and volcanics. Beneath the sheeted dike complex, and in fact the source of it, is gabbro (the coarse-grained intrusive equivalent of basalt) and mantle peridotite. This layered structure seems to occur rather consistently throughout the ocean basins, and is directly related to the processes that formed the oceanic crust.

In contrast, even though much more is known about the geology of the surface of the continents, how the continental crust formed is still the focus of much further study. The composition of the continental crust is much more variable than its predominantly basaltic oceanic counterpart. On average, the crust is made of much less dense material, approximately of granitic to andesitic composition. There is actually a gradation in many regions of the continental crust, from low-density, silica-rich granitic rocks near the surface to silica-poor basaltic rocks in the lower crust. In terms of actual rock types, ninety-five percent of the continental crustal volume comprises igneous and metamorphic rocks (Figure 5). Sedimentary rocks, however, cover most of the continental surface. The absence of sedimentary rocks deep in the crust is caused by increases in pressures and temperatures, which inevitably transform sedimentary rocks that existed at the surface into metamorphic rocks as they are buried deeper. On average, the continental crust is 18 mi (30 km) thick, but of course the thickness varies and is thicker under mountains because of their crustal roots (Figure 5).

We can determine the mean elevation above sea level of the continents from the principle of isostasy (Davidson, Reed, and Davis 1997). The mean depth of the ocean floors is about 2.4 mi (3.8 km) below sea level, and the mean thickness of the oceanic crust is 4.4 mi (7 km) (Figure 5). The effective depth of compensation, the depth at which both continents and ocean basins are in isostatic equilibrium, is 18.7 mi (30 km) below sea level, although the actual depth of compensation is deeper, in the upper mantle. If the mean elevation above sea level of the continents equals x mi, then the principle of

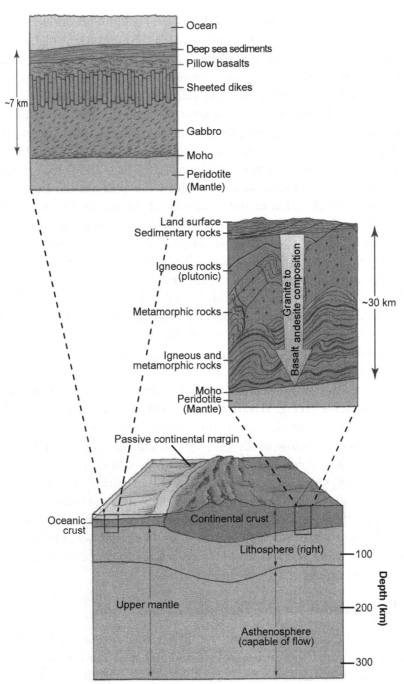

Figure 5. Typical structures—thickness, rock types, and nature of deformation—of both continental and oceanic crust and lithosphere (the outer relatively rigid layer of the earth comprising the crust and the uppermost mantle) (after Davidson, Reed, and Davis 1997).

isostasy requires that an 18.6 mi (30 km) + x mi column of continental crust must have the same weight per unit area as a 2.3 mi (3.8 km) high column of water plus a 4.3 mi (7 km) thick column of oceanic crust plus a 12 mi (19.2 km) thick column of oceanic mantle (2.4 + 4.4 + 12 = 18.6 mi or 3.8 + 7 + 19.2 = 30 km). Isostatic equilibrium dictates that the weight per unit area in each column of material must be the same. When the densities of 178 lbs/cubic foot (2.85 g/cm^3) for the continental crust, 187.5 lbs/cubic foot (3.0 g/cm^3) for the oceanic crust, and 206 lbs/cubic foot (3.3 g/cm^3) for the mantle are taken into account and the two 18.7 mi (30 km) high columns of continental crust and oceanic crust (plus water, plus mantle) are equated, then the mean elevation of the continents above sea level or $x \approx$ 2624 ft (800 m). This is in reasonable agreement with the known average continental elevation of 2755 ft (840 m) above sea level, given the approximate values used for the thicknesses and densities. Thus the fact that oceanic crust and continental crust are in isostatic equilibrium explains why the continents ride atop the mantle above sea level. The effect is slightly accentuated when the slightly greater density of oceanic crust compared with that of the continental crust is also taken into account.

This distribution of elevations for the surface of the earth is illustrated in Figure 6 (Davidson, Reed, and Davis 1997). There is a bimodal distribution of elevations above and below the sea level across the earth's surface, with the average elevation of continental crust being about 2755 ft (840 m) above sea level, whereas the oceanic crust lies on average about 2.4 mi (3800 m) below sea level. Even though the continental crust is 18.7 mi (30 km) thick it has an overall lower density compared to the oceanic crust which is thinner at 4.4 mi (7 km) thick, but which has a higher overall density. The principle of isostasy thus accounts for why the continents float on the mantle beneath them at a higher average elevation than the ocean basins, which are made up of denser oceanic crust. This same information can be shown as a cumulative percentage of the earth's surface that lies above a given elevation (Figure 6).

6. Implications for the Tectonics of the Flood

There can be no question that the Flood was a cataclysmic upheaval that reconstituted the earth's geology and reshaped the earth's surface. A crucial observation is that today we find marine creatures such as corals and clams buried in sediments deposited by water and fossilized in rock layers that stretch right across continents (Snelling 2008a, 2008b). The significance of this is not as immediately evident as it should be until it is

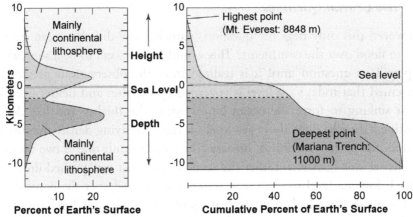

Figure 6. Distribution of elevations across the surface of the earth (after Davidson, Reed, and Davis 1997). *Left:* Percentage of the earth's surface corresponding to a given elevation above or below sea level. There is a bimodal distribution (two "peaks") with average continents at about 2755 ft (840 m) above sea level, and average oceans 12,591 ft (3800 m) below. *Right:* The same information shown as the cumulative percentage of the earth's surface that lies above a given elevation. This can be thought of as a hypothetical cross section from the highest point to the lowest point on the earth's surface.

further observed that whereas corals and clams normally live on the shallow ocean floors surrounding the continents, they are in fact primarily buried in the sedimentary rock layers spread across the continents, and not in sediment layers spread across the ocean floors. Indeed, apart from the thin veneer of deep-sea sediments blanketing the deep ocean floors, the oceanic crust beneath consists of basalt lavas, dikes (intrusive vertical sheets), and intrusive gabbros (Figure 5). Furthermore, these same marine fossil-bearing sedimentary rock layers are found in some of the continents' highest mountains. Obviously the ocean waters in the past had to have flooded over the continents, carrying these marine creatures plucked up from where they lived on the shallow ocean floors and carried with sediments to be deposited up on and across the continents, a clear description of what one would expect to find as a result of the global cataclysmic Flood described in Genesis 7:19–20, when all the high hills under the whole of the heaven, and the mountains, were covered by water.

6.1   Two Crucial Questions
6.2   From Gradualistic to Catastrophic Plate Tectonics
6.3   How Plate Tectonics Works
6.4   How the Ocean Waters Rose to Flood the Continents
6.5   The Origin of the Mountains
6.6   Whither the Pre-Flood Supercontinent

6.1 *Two Crucial Questions*

However, this only begs the question, namely, how did the ocean waters rise to flood over the continents? This would at first seem to be a somewhat supercilious question until it is realized from the observations previously presented that today's sea level is governed by the thin and denser oceanic crust sinking to form the ocean basins while the thicker and less dense continental rocks float above sea level on the underlying denser mantle, as enunciated in the principle of isostasy. There is thus only one of two options to answer this question. Either the continental crust was pushed down or sank below sea level so the ocean waters could flood over the continents, or the ocean floor had to be pushed up or rise so that sea level also rose, enabling the ocean waters to flood over the continents.

A second question, which at first is not obvious but which is related to the first question, is why are there no marine fossil-bearing sedimentary layers spread across the ocean floors between the continents where they outcrop today? Or to phrase this second question another way, why does the oceanic crust have the structure it has today, being thinner and of a different composition to continental crust? The first obvious answer is that today's oceanic crust was not there when the marine fossil-bearing sedimentary layers were deposited across the continents, because today's oceanic crust is in fact younger than those marine fossil-bearing transcontinental sedimentary rock layers. Although he did not realize it at the time, this is a direct corollary to the proposal made by Snider in 1859 that the continental crust had originally at creation been all in one place on the earth's globe as a supercontinent, which was then catastrophically split apart so that the continental fragments rapidly sprinted horizontally across the globe during the Genesis Flood into their positions today.

6.2 *From Gradualistic to Catastrophic Plate Tectonics*

When Wegener in 1915 also observed the jigsaw puzzle fit of the continents around and across today's Atlantic Ocean basin and proposed the supercontinent Pangaea, he also noted, as had Snider, that these transcontinental sedimentary rock layers that today are on different continents lined up with one another in continuous belts (Figure 7). Among the best known examples of these transcontinental sedimentary rock layers that are aligned across and between today's continents were the Carboniferous coal beds of the Northern Hemisphere, which today stretch through 180° of longitude from the Appalachians of North America through

England and western Europe to the Urals of Russia and beyond, and the supposedly glacially produced Permian (the conventional geologic age period 251–299 millions of years ago) strata of the Southern Hemisphere continents. Ongoing field investigations have also recognized further correlations revealed by closing the Atlantic Ocean basin to join the continents either side of it back together again, such as the alignment of the Appalachians of North America with the Caledonian mountain range of Europe (the United Kingdom and Scandinavia), and the Paraná, Etendeka, and North Atlantic flood basalts (Figure 8). Thus this supercontinent reconstruction implies that these transcontinental strata and mountain ranges correlated between today's resulting continents are older than the oceanic crust of the Atlantic Ocean basin between them.

As noted earlier, a revolution finally occurred with a complete paradigm shift in the 1960s to persuasively "convert" geophysicists and geologists to embrace the plate tectonics model for the configuration of today's continents. It was maps of the ocean floor topography produced during World War II and compilations of new paleomagnetic data (the magnetic

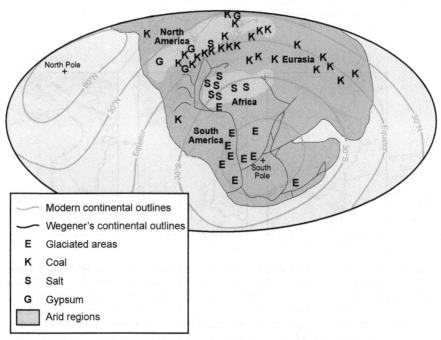

Figure 7. Wegener's reconstruction of continents supposedly 300 million years ago, based on the distribution of glacial features (implying polar regions), the presence of coal (interpreted as the tropics), and the presence of salt, gypsum, or sand deposits (interpreted as deserts).

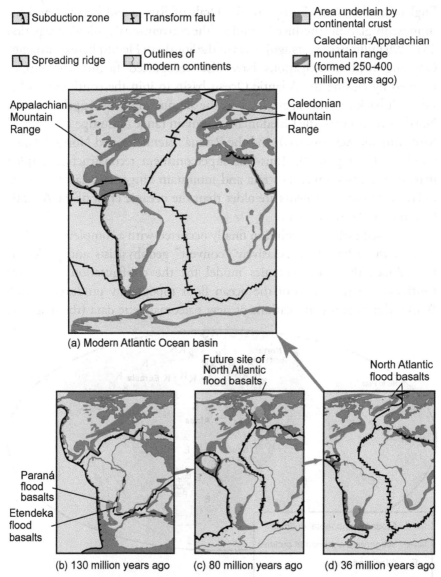

Figure 8. The opening of the Atlantic Ocean basin (after Davidson, Reed, and Davis 1997). (a) The modern Atlantic Ocean and surrounding continents. (b) A continental reconstruction of supposedly 130 million years ago. The South Atlantic has begun to open, although opening of the Central Atlantic is well under way, and the Paraná and Etendeka flood basalts have already erupted. The North Atlantic has not started to open. (c) The Atlantic as it looked supposedly 80 million years ago. The ocean basin separating Africa, South America, and North America has developed and widened. The rift between northern Europe and North America (Greenland) has yet to develop. The position of the rifting of supposedly 60 million years ago is indicated by the future location of the North Atlantic flood basalt province. (d) By supposedly 36 million years ago the North Atlantic has opened and separated the North Atlantic flood basalt province.

imprints in rocks because of the earth's magnetic field), particularly for the rocks on the ocean floors, which convinced them. However, gradualism was also embraced so that the modern plate tectonics model includes Wegener's gradual horizontal motion (or continental drift) of the continental plates on the scale of tens to hundreds of millions of years, rather than Snider's rapid horizontal motion (or continental sprint) on the scale of weeks or months during the year-long global cataclysmic Genesis Flood.

Nevertheless, in pioneering research by creationist geophysicist John Baumgardner, numerical simulations were used to model the rapid and catastrophic large-scale tectonics associated with the Genesis Flood based on the conventional gradualistic plate tectonics model (Baumgardner 1986, 1990, 1994a). He found, however, that once the process of subduction (the process of one plate descending beneath another) started, as the oceanic crust abutting the continental crust at a continental margin detached and began to be thrust under and sink (or subduct) under the edge of the continental plate, the heat generated by friction overcame that friction so that the descending oceanic crustal plate sank faster (Baumgardner 1994b). The further resulting friction generated more heat which overcame that friction and caused the subduction to occur even faster. This feedback loop that produced accelerating subduction is called thermal runaway and led to runaway subduction, with the descending oceanic crustal plate in his computer simulations reaching speeds of meters per second. Baumgardner's work on the geophysics of the Flood thus led to the proposal of a catastrophic plate tectonics model for the geology of the Genesis Flood (Austin et al. 1994; Baumgardner 2003; Snelling 2009). Therefore, Snider's original proposal of continental sprint during the Genesis Flood has been vindicated, with the addition of a mechanism to drive the catastrophic plate motion while the Floodwaters overwhelmed the continents depositing their sediment and fossil loads.

6.3 *How Plate Tectonics Works*

According to conventional gradualistic plate tectonics, the earth's surface is currently divided into plates that in the past moved slowly relative to one another, and are still moving slowly today (Figure 9). Most of these plates currently consist of continental crust "floating" high above sea level on the mantle underneath, but are attached on the same plate to denser oceanic crust that has sunk below sea level and also rides along with the continent in the same plate floating on the mantle. These plates move relative to one another around their common boundaries in one of three ways.

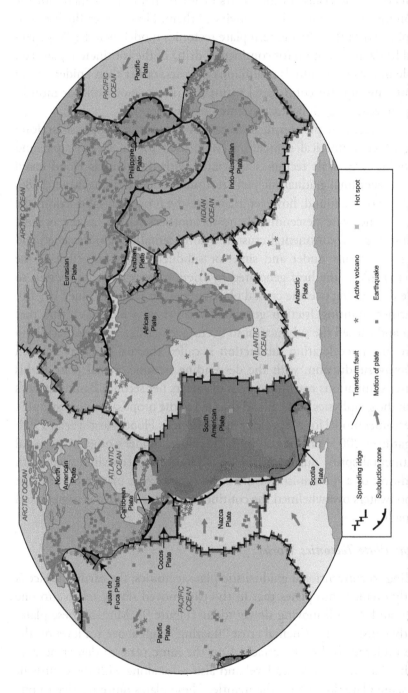

Figure 9. A map of the earth's lithospheric plates, the boundaries of which are defined by subduction zones, spreading ridges, or transform faults (faults with lateral or horizontal ground movements) (after Davidson, Reed, and Davis 1997). The map also shows hot spots, active volcanoes (not submarine ones), and areas of abundant seismic activity.

As best represented down the center of the Atlantic Ocean basin, there are mid-ocean ridges in every ocean basin where rifting is occurring due to magma rising from the upper mantle. The extrusion (discharge at the earth's surface) of lavas in the central rift zones along the mid-ocean ridges is forcing the oceanic crust either side of them apart and generating new oceanic crust as the lavas cool. It is the upwelling of this magma and the lower density of the newly extruded warm lavas and new oceanic crust which results in these mid-ocean ridges rising to become the long mountain chains stretching through today's ocean basins. This process has been called sea-floor spreading, and it adds new oceanic crust to the trailing edges of the two plates that are being pushed apart along each section of these mid-ocean ridges, which stretch for tens of thousands of miles through all today's ocean basins (Figure 9).

The second way in which the plates move relative to one another at their margins is where oceanic crust is being subducted under the continental crust of the continents, or as in a few places, under oceanic crust adjoining the continents. Adjacent to these subduction zones are volcanic arcs. These arcs are produced where oceanic crust is subducted, because at depth melting occurs on the upper surface of the subducting oceanic crust and in the mantle above due to water and friction. The melted rock, or magma, produced being less dense rises to erupt at the surface through volcanoes, which are often aligned in an arc at the earth's surface. This is the explanation for the eruptions of volcanoes in the Andes of South America and Mount St. Helens and its neighboring volcanoes in the U.S. Pacific Northwest.

The last of the three modes of plate interactions is where plate edges slide past one another along a major fault zone. The most well-known example is the San Andreas Fault of southern and central California, where the Pacific Plate is sliding past the North American Plate (Figure 9). All of these plate motions and the accompanying volcanic activity are responsible for generating earthquakes.

The sinking oceanic crust being subducted pushes aside the mantle it is sinking into. This movement of mantle material sets off flow in a convection cycle within the full width of the mantle, the return flow rising to the base of the crust in the rift zones of the mid-ocean ridges. It is this convective flow in the mantle which is the driving force that Baumgardner simulated in his demonstration of how catastrophic plate tectonics during the Flood would have worked. Full details of the catastrophic plate tectonics model are provided in Austin et al. (1994), Baumgardner (2003), and Snelling (2009).

It is envisaged that the reference in Genesis 7:11 to the "breaking up of all the fountains of the great deep" is a description of the rifting all around the earth in the pre-Flood ocean basins and across the pre-Flood supercontinent. Into these rift zones hot molten rock (magma) rose, also generating supersonic steam jets that carried entrained (included) ocean water high into the atmosphere so that it fell back to the earth as intense global rain ("the windows of heaven were opened"). At the same time, the oceanic crust adjoining the continental crust at the margins of the pre-Flood supercontinent was disrupted and began to be subducted. As a consequence, the plates began moving and accelerated to many feet (meters) per second "sprinting."

6.4 *How the Ocean Waters Rose to Flood the Continents*

It is these simultaneous actions that provide the only viable mechanism for explaining how the ocean waters rose up over the continents carrying their sediment and fossil loads and depositing them upon and right across the continents in marine fossil-bearing transcontinental sedimentary rock layers. There is no known mechanism as to how the less dense continental crust of the continents could have been pushed down to allow the ocean waters to flood over the continents. The only exception would have been along the subduction zones, where the subducting oceanic crust also depressed the continental crustal margins. Otherwise, the rising magma along the mid-ocean ridges began generating new oceanic crust.

This new warm oceanic crust was also less dense, so as indicated before, it rose along the mid-ocean ridges, displacing the ocean water above. Because the catastrophic upwelling (upwards movement within the upper mantle) of magma rapidly generating new oceanic crust produced rapid sea-floor spreading, the new oceanic crust being warmer even as it spread away from the mid-ocean ridges expanded, and therefore pushed up the water column above. The net result was that the sea level would have been raised by almost a mile (1.5 km) (Figure 10) (Snelling 2008a). This rapidly rising sea level would have resulted in a surge of water moving towards the continental margins. This surge would have been compounded by the tsunamis generated by the earthquakes produced by the magma upwelling into the mid-ocean ridges and by the subduction along the subduction zones, along which the continental margins were being depressed. The net result would be that the marine life on the shallow ocean floor fringing the continental margins would have been swept by the surging ocean water and tsunamis along with sediments scraped from the ocean floor up onto the continents.

There the marine creatures would be buried as the sediments were deposited and then fossilized in the sedimentary rock layers that progressively spread right across the continents as the waters of the Flood eventually covered the whole earth. When the new oceanic crust cooled and sank, the sea level fell again, thus leaving the marine fossil-bearing transcontinental sedimentary rock layers now exposed on the continents, even in today's mountains.

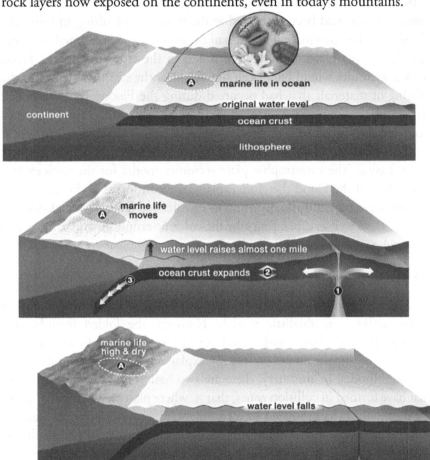

Figure 10. *Top:* Marine creatures obviously live in the ocean (A). For these creatures to be deposited on the continents, the sea level had to rise. *Middle:* The ocean crust is heated and expands. 1. During the Genesis Flood, molten rock was released from inside the earth and began replacing the original ocean crust. The ocean crust was effectively replaced by hot lavas. 2. Because of the hot molten rock, the ocean crust became less dense and expanded. 3. The molten rock displaced and pushed the original ocean crust below the continent. (A) The sea level rose more than 3500 ft (1067 m), and marine creatures were carried onto the continent, buried in sediments, and fossilized. *Bottom:* Toward the end of the Flood, the ocean crust cooled and the ocean floor sank. As the waters drained off the continents, the sea level would have fallen, leaving marine fossils (A) above sea level on the continents (after Snelling 2008a.)

Thus the catastrophic plate tectonics model alone explains how the sea level rose in order for the ocean waters to rise up and flood over the continents. There is no known mechanism that would force the continental crust of the continents to sink while pushing against the isostatic equilibrium established with the mantle beneath on which the continental crust floats. Vertical tectonics would only have come into play once the pre-Flood supercontinent had been disrupted at the initiation of rifting to begin the Flood and after continental sprint had begun with the horizontal tectonics that shifted the plates thousands of miles. In the latter part of the Flood vertical tectonics would have been significant as the earth readjusted to the shifting of materials that had occurred during the Flood. The continental crust and the continents readjusted to their new topographic loadings (the "weights" of crustal thicknesses in different topographic features on the earth's surface) and the oceanic crust cooled and sank to form the new ocean basins. The catastrophic plate tectonics model for the geology and geophysics of the Flood therefore explains the continents and ocean basins that we see today, and the distribution of volcanoes and earthquakes today (Figure 9), as well as explaining why the volcanic eruptions and earthquakes occur when and where they do.

6.5 The Origin of the Mountains

It is the origin of the mountains that has always been difficult to explain in conventional gradualistic models. However, the folded fossil-bearing sedimentary rock layers and crystalline metamorphic rocks and granites in today's mountain ranges are readily explained by the catastrophic plate tectonics model. In summary, there are two basic types of mountain belts that have formed in collision zones, that is, where plates have collided. There are mountain belts produced by a continental plate colliding with another continental plate, and mountains produced by a continental plate colliding with an oceanic crust plate.

The best known example of the first basic type of mountain belt is the Himalayas. They resulted from the collision of the leading edge of the Indian Plate as it moved northward with its load of marine fossil-bearing sedimentary layers and collided with the edge of the Eurasian Plate. In the collision zone marine fossil-bearing sedimentary rock layers were crumpled and buckled, forcing the folded strata upwards to form the Himalayan Mountains. The heat and pressure of the collision also caused melting to produce magmas that were intruded and cooled to become granites, with some accompanying metamorphism. So the Himalayas were not there prior to the Flood, but were instead produced as a consequence of the Flood, as evidenced by the folded marine fossil-bearing sedimentary layers that they consist of.

The best example of the second basic type of mountain belt is the Andes of South America. In that type of collision zone the Nazca Plate is colliding with the South American Plate. The Nazca Plate's oceanic crust is being subducted under the continental margin of the South American Plate. The continental crust at the edge of the South American Plate was pushed down into the mantle against the isostatic forces of the mantle as the oceanic crust of the subducting Nazca Plate plunged into the mantle beneath the continental margin of the South American Plate. Marine fossil-bearing sediment layers accumulating on the continental margin progressively in an accretionary wedge (the wedge of sediments on the edge of a continental plate trapped in a collision zone) were buckled by the force of the collision between these two plates. Sediments carried by the subducting plate down into the mantle under the edge of the South American Plate began to melt due to the heat, pressure, and water, along with melting of some of the mantle above between the subducting plate and the continental crust of the South American continent above. This molten rock being less dense rose to erupt as andesitic lavas (lavas of slightly different composition to basalt named after the Andes) through volcanoes in the mountains forming above, melting some of the continental crust on the way upwards to also produce granite intrusions. As the plate motion slowed and isostatic forces worked to reestablish isostatic equilibrium, the depressed continental crust of the South American continental margin began to rise so that the mountain belt formed along the collision zone. Thus the buckled marine fossil-bearing sedimentary rock layers, extruded volcanic layers, and intruded granites rose to form today's Andes Mountains, with their still-active volcanoes.

6.6 *Whither the Pre-Flood Supercontinent*

There is one further crucial observation that has significant ramifications for the geology and geophysics of the Flood. The Appalachian Mountains on the North American Plate consist of folded marine fossil-bearing sedimentary rock layers that were buckled to high elevations before being eroded so deeply that the crystalline metamorphic rocks and granite intrusions in the deep core of this mountain belt are now exposed in the Blue Ridge. In the reconstruction by both Snider and Wegener of the Pangaea supercontinent, the Appalachian Mountains had already formed. This observation implies that there had to have been a collision along this Appalachian collision zone of earlier plates carrying marine fossil-bearing sediment layers. Since these marine fossil-bearing sediment layers had to also have been deposited during the Flood, this in turn implies that there was an earlier phase of plate movements during the Flood, those plates combining to form the Pangaea supercontinent. Thus the Pangaea supercontinent was not the pre-Flood supercontinent, but merely a transitory reassembly of plates during the Flood that subsequently split apart during the later phase of the Flood as the Atlantic Ocean and other ocean basins opened up and the present configuration of continents and younger mountain belts and later collision zones were produced.

On today's North American Plate the subsequently formed younger mountain belts are seen to the west—the Rocky Mountains first, followed by the Sierra Nevadas during the last phase of subduction of the Pacific Plate under the North American Plate (Figure 9), which is still ongoing today. Though these later mountains are also formed from the buckling of marine fossil-bearing sedimentary rock layers and are intruded by granite plutons, the youthfulness of these mountain belts compared to the Appalachians is due to both their higher elevations (having experienced less erosion) and their contained marine fossil-bearing sedimentary rock layers having been deposited higher up (and therefore later) in the rock record of the Flood, compared to the sedimentary rock layers found in the Appalachians.

The earlier supercontinental configuration that would therefore approximate to the pre-Flood supercontinent appears to be that called Rodinia. Confirming this conclusion is the observation that some of the initial Flood deposits plot geologically and geographically around some of the margins of the reconstructed Rodinia supercontinent (Austin and Wise 1994; Sigler and Wingerden 1998; Wingerden 2003). Furthermore, the Rodinia supercontinent realigns pre-Flood rock units that are today found in continental crust fragments incorporated into today's various continents. Thus the catastrophic plate tectonics model for the Flood would begin with the break-up of the Rodinia supercontinent at the initiation of the Flood. The first phase of continental sprint produced the Pangaea supercontinent as a transitory continental reconfiguration during the Flood, followed by the break-up of that Pangaea supercontinent with further continental sprint later in the Flood. Today's configuration of continents arrived at their present positions as the plates decelerated in the closing stages of the Flood.

This model discounts the suggestion by some that the break-up of Pangaea occurred after the Flood as a result of the Peleg division due to the Babel judgment (Gn 10:25; 11:1–9) (e.g. Northrup 1990). On the one hand, the context in Genesis 10 of this earth division with respect to Peleg is the division of peoples according to their families. Genesis 11 elaborates on this division as due to the confusion of languages at Babel according to families who were assigned the different areas on the earth's surface that they then migrated to. (This is, of course, one of three possible interpretations other than the tectonic one. The other two are halving of lifespans in succeeding generations and the beginning of the digging of canals in Mesopotamia.) On the other hand, if this were a reference to continental sprint as a result of the cleaving of a post-Flood Pangaea supercontinent, the tectonic upheaval with the resulting earthquakes and tsunamis would have produced the same devastation of life on the earth's surface as occurred during the Flood itself. However, there is no record in the Scriptures of such devastation. On the contrary, life continued on after Babel, with Nimrod establishing his kingdom, along with the rise of the Babylonian and Egyptian empires.

7. Discussion: Where to from Here?

It needs to be emphasized that the catastrophic plate tectonics model for the geology and geophysics of the Flood is still only a model subject to further testing against the evidence and further refinement. However, at the present time it is a good working model that is able to explain not only the geological and geophysical data that the conventional gradualistic plate tectonics model does, but also observations that the conventional model cannot explain. The catastrophic plate tectonics model is based on the assumptions that the basic core-mantle-oceanic crust-continental crust structure of the earth was established at the time of the earth's creation during the Creation Week, that there was a pre-Flood supercontinent, and that these are allowed for by the Hebrew text of Genesis 1. This assumption is consistent with the pre-Flood rocks that are still preserved and exposed today at the earth's surface.

Furthermore, there are still details of the operation of the model that need elucidation and refinement by what can be gleaned from the Hebrew text of the Flood account in Genesis 6–9. In particular, it is essential to know whether the Hebrew expression "the fountains of the great deep" can be correctly identified as describing the initiation of the Flood by the catastrophic rifting of the pre-Flood oceanic crust and the continental crust of the pre-Flood supercontinent with the rapid eruption of upwelling magmas from the mantle that also produced supersonic steam jets along thousands of miles of what became mid-ocean ridges and continental rift zones, respectively, all around the globe. Similarly, it needs to be confirmed whether the Hebrew expression "the windows of heaven were opened" is an allowable and accurate description of the triggering of the global torrential rainfall from the ocean water shot up into the upper atmosphere entrained in the supersonic steam jets which erupted from the great deep as fountains through the rifting of the oceanic and continental crust.

Once the catastrophic plate tectonics were thus initiated, the computer modeling studies (Baumgardner 1986, 1990, 1994a, 1994b, 2003) indicate the plates so produced accelerated to the many feet-per-second movements of continental sprint. As the Flood event then progressed, continuing rifting, subduction, sliding laterally, and subsequent collisions at the plate boundaries interacted with and upon the rapidly accumulating thick megasequences of fossil-bearing sediment layers swiftly deposited on and across the continents by the rising, advancing, and fluctuating Floodwaters to produce volcanoes and volcanic eruptions which added lava flows and volcanic ash beds within the sedimentary megasequences, and mountain belts of folded, deformed, and uplifted strata. These huge accelerating earth movements and stupendous volcanic eruptions generated devastating earthquakes which produced enormous tsunamis. Coupled with the rising sea level due to the rising new, rapidly formed, warm, and therefore less dense, sea floor, and the almost twice daily tidal fluctuations which increasingly resonated around the globe as total inundation occurred (Clark and Voss 1990), these tsunamis would have surged and swept landwards, crashing there with catastrophic erosional and depositional consequences. The supercontinent Pangea was produced as a transitory stage within the Flood event, before it rifted apart and today's continents sprinted into their present positions, the plates rapidly decelerating as the Flood came to a close.

If "the fountains of the great deep" were associated with the catastrophic rifting of both oceanic and continental crust that resulted in continental sprint, then the stopping of the fountains on Day 150 of the Flood, as implied by the statements in Genesis 7:24–8:3, would seem to indicate that the rifting and plate movements must have started to decelerate from that time onwards through to the end of the three hundred seventy-one day Flood event. On the same Day 150, the Genesis account states (Gn 8:4) that the Ark ran aground on "the mountains of Ararat."

This raises three issues. First, these mountains are not necessarily related to the present Mt. Ararat, a huge dormant volcano, in spite of the claims of the Ark being sighted and found there (Hodge 2012). Second, when the Ark ran aground on these mountains they may likely have still been rising up through the Floodwaters to "snag" the Ark and then continued rising to their subsequent final height, which would explain how this running aground happened while the Floodwaters were at their peak. And third, whichever of today's mountains were the biblical mountains of Ararat, the biblical region of Urartu (Ararat) includes mountains which formed late in geologic history as a result of the collision of the Eurasian, African, and Arabian plates meeting along and associated with the Anatolian Fault, and which are part of an area that is still tectonically active today. Taken together, this would imply that at least the start of this collision and mountain-building episode had to coincide with Day 150 of the Flood (Barrick and Sigler 2003; Barrick 2008), which in turn would seem to make Day 150 equate to about the upper Cretaceous of the geologic record, which matches other indicators, such as the apparent peaking of the relative sea level (see **Chapter 5**) in accordance with the Genesis account.

If this correlation is correct, then there is less of the geologic record to fit into the remaining two hundred twenty-one days of the Flood (the rest of the upper Cretaceous through to the Pliocene at most), which would tend to push the Flood/post-Flood boundary higher up into the Tertiary before the post-Flood Ice Age commenced with the Pleistocene. On the other hand, considering the Tertiary fossils and their relationships to extant animals (see **Chapter 7**), being descended from the Ark occupants who had to thus rapidly migrate across the globe to be then fossilized by local catastrophes on other continents, would seem to place constraints on how high in the Tertiary the Flood/post-Flood boundary can be placed. This in turn squeezes less geology into the period of the subsiding and retreating Floodwaters and the drying out of the land surface from Day 150 until the end of the three hundred seventy-one day Flood event. However, this latter factor could vary from continent to continent, as it is possible that the Floodwaters only fully retreated from the different continents at different times, due to the different vertical isostatic readjustments.

As a corollary, the continued mountain-building after Day 150 when the Ark ran aground on the mountains of Ararat makes sense of the statement in Genesis 8:5 that seventy-four days later, as the Floodwaters continued to subside and retreat, the tops of surrounding mountains were seen (Barrick and Sigler 2003; Barrick 2008). In other words, the surrounding mountains could have been forming and rising during those seventy-four days, rather than just the Floodwaters' level dropping, so that they then appeared above the Floodwaters on Day 224. It may well be that those surrounding mountains subsequently continued to rise so that today they are higher than the biblical mountains of Ararat on which the Ark landed. This in turn also means that the biblical mountains of Ararat may never have attained a great height above today's sea level. This makes sense, in that one of the problems with the Ark supposedly being atop the modern Mt. Ararat is the lack of oxygen at its 16,854 ft (5137 m) summit, making it impossible for the Ark's occupants to have survived up there while waiting for months to alight, not to mention the long hazardous journey down that mountain's sides!

Thus there is much that could yet be gleaned from the Hebrew text of the Genesis Flood account which might elucidate some of these issues. It needs to be explored as to whether the descriptive applications of "the fountains of the great deep" and the rainfall from the "windows of heaven" to the catastrophic plate tectonics model's mechanisms for initiating the Flood, the rifting of the crust and ocean waters being lifted skywards by supersonic steam jets, are allowed by the Hebrew text. Then in deciphering the chronology of the Flood, it needs to be determined whether "the fountains of the great deep" and the rainfall from "windows of heaven" were both stopped on Day 150, along with the Ark running aground on the mountains of Ararat on the same day. And additionally there are the questions of what the Hebrew text might suggest with regards to the rising of the mountains and the actions of the Floodwaters, during both their prevailing and abating stages. In this process the Hebrew text must be studied carefully according to its word usage in context uninfluenced by our modern perceptions of what the words and the text might mean so that the Hebrew then constrains our Flood modeling rather than the other way around.

8. Conclusion

The Bible refers to the hills and the mountains, some of which emitted smoke (Ps 144:5), and also to earthquakes when the ground trembles (Ps 104:32). Man's quest to understand the way the earth works to produce mountains, volcanoes, and earthquakes is of course motivated by practical concerns, but also by the appetite for knowledge. However, as what God's Word tells us about the earth's history was ignored, ideas of extrapolating today's slow and gradual geologic processes back into the past to explain how earth movements have produced today's mountains and volcanoes over countless millions of years have taken a stranglehold on almost all geological thinking.

Nevertheless, it was a Bible-believing geologist who in 1859 proposed that a pre-Flood supercontinent was catastrophically ripped apart into today's continents which sprinted into their current positions all during the biblical global Flood. Ignored, slow-and-gradual continental drift was proposed early in the twentieth century by secular geologists. For the next fifty years that idea was spurned by geophysicists, because they could not envisage a mechanism, but in the 1960s a revolution in thinking turned the tables so that slow-and-gradual plate tectonics is now entrenched orthodoxy.

Knowledge of the earth's internal structure is essential to our understanding of how the earth operates. Seismic waves generated by earthquakes have been the primary means of determining the density differences between and within the crust, mantle, outer core, and inner core. Velocity anomalies are associated with heat and magma beneath volcanoes and in rift zones, as well as with upwelling convection currents in the mantle. Isostasy, or the principle of equal balances, shows how the mass of a mountain above sea level is compensated for by the mountain's underlying crustal root, that is, the earth's crust is thicker "floating" on the mantle beneath where the topography is higher. This explains why sea level is where it is, the denser (heavier) oceanic crust sinking in the mantle to make the ocean basins, while the less dense continental crust rises above sea level.

Today we find shallow marine creatures buried and fossilized in sedimentary rock layers deposited rapidly by water right across continents and even in high mountains, so in the past the ocean waters must have flooded the continents. Only the revived and numerically modeled catastrophic plate tectonics model for the Flood event can explain how the ocean waters rose to flood the continents, how and where the fossil-bearing sedimentary layers were rapidly deposited, and how and when the mountains formed due to plate collisions. The catastrophic rifting of the pre-Flood ocean floor and supercontinent occurred when the "fountains of the great deep" were broken up. Upwelling magma produced supersonic steam jets that entrained ocean water, carrying it up into the atmosphere from where it fell as intense global rain ("the windows of heaven" were opened). The new warm ocean floor produced along the rift zones was less dense and rose, pushing up the sea level to flood the sprinting continental plates, which were moving at many feet per second due to the concurrent runaway subduction of old, cold ocean floor. Melting at depth in subduction zones fed stupendous volcanic eruptions above at the surface.

There are remaining questions about what the Hebrew text might suggest with regards to the rising of the mountains and the actions of the Floodwaters, during both their prevailing and abating stages. In deciphering the chronology of the Flood, it needs to be confirmed whether "the fountains of the great deep" and the rainfall from the "windows of heaven" were both stopped on Day 150, along with the Ark running aground on the mountains of Ararat on the same day. Answers to these questions have implications for the timing of deceleration of plate movements as the Floodwaters subsided and final plate collisions produced today's youngest mountains, including the mountains of Ararat and other nearby mountains, and for correlating the geologic and fossil records with the biblical account of the ending of the Flood event.

References

Austin, S. A., J. R. Baumgardner, D. R. Humphreys, A. A. Snelling, L. Vardiman, and K. P. Wise. 1994. Catastrophic plate tectonics: A global Flood model of earth history. In *Proceedings of the third International Conference on Creationism*. Ed. R. E. Walsh, 609–621. Pittsburgh, PA: Creation Science Fellowship.

Austin, S. A., and K. P. Wise. 1994. The pre-Flood/Flood boundary: As defined in Grand Canyon, Arizona and eastern Mojave Desert, California. In *Proceedings of the third International Conference on Creationism*. Ed. R. E. Walsh, 37–47. Pittsburgh, PA: Creation Science Fellowship.

Barrick, W. D. 2008. Noah's Flood and its geological implications. In *Coming to grips with Genesis*. Ed. T. Mortenson, and T. H. Ury, 251–281. Green Forest, AR: Master Books.

Barrick, W. D., and R. Sigler. 2003. Hebrew and geologic analyses of the chronology and parallelism of the Flood: Implications for interpretation of the geologic record. In *Proceedings of the fifth International Conference on Creationism*. Ed. R. L. Ivey Jr., 397–408. Pittsburgh, PA: Creation Science Fellowship.

Baumgardner, J. R. 1986. Numerical simulation of the large-scale tectonic changes accompanying Noah's Flood. In *Proceedings of the first International Conference on Creationism*. Ed. R. E. Walsh, C. L. Brooks, and R. S. Crowell. Vol. 2, 17–30. Pittsburgh, PA: Creation Science Fellowship.

Baumgardner, J. R. 1990. 3-D finite element simulation of the global tectonic changes accompanying Noah's Flood. In *Proceedings of the second International Conference on Creationism*. Ed. R. E. Walsh, and C. L. Brooks. Vol. 2, 35–45. Pittsburgh, PA: Creation Science Fellowship.

Baumgardner, J. R. 1994a. Computer modeling of the large-scale tectonics associated with the Genesis Flood. In *Proceedings of the third International Conference on Creationism*. Ed. R. E. Walsh, 49–62. Pittsburgh, PA: Creation Science Fellowship.

Baumgardner, J. R. 1994b. Runaway subduction as the driving mechanism for the Genesis Flood. In *Proceedings of the third International Conference on Creationism*. Ed. R. E. Walsh, 63–75. Pittsburgh, PA: Creation Science Fellowship.

Baumgardner, J. R. 2003. Catastrophic plate tectonics: The physics behind the Genesis Flood. In *Proceedings of the fifth International Conference on Creationism*. Ed. R. L. Ivey Jr., 113–126. Pittsburgh, PA: Creation Science Fellowship.

Berry, W. D. N. 1968. *Growth of a prehistoric timescale: Based on organic evolution*, 28–31. San Francisco, CA: W. H. Freeman and Company.

Boggs, S. Jr. 1995. *Principles of sedimentology and stratigraphy*. 2nd ed., 4–5. Upper Saddle River, NJ: Prentice Hall.

Clark, M. E., and H. D. Voss. 1990. Resonance and sedimentary layering in the context of a global Flood. In *Proceedings of the second International Conference on Creationism*. Ed. R. E. Walsh, and C. L. Brooks, 55–63. Pittsburgh, PA: Creation Science Fellowship.

Davidson, J. P., W. E. Reed, and P. M. Davis. 1997. *Exploring earth: An introduction to physical geology*. Upper Saddle River, NJ: Prentice-Hall, Inc.

Dunbar C. O., and J. Rodgers. 1957. *Principles of stratigraphy*, 289–290. New York, NY: John Wiley & Sons, Inc.

Hodge, B. 2012. Has Noah's Ark been found? In *How do we know the Bible is true?* Ed. K. A. Ham, and B. Hodge. Vol. 2, 175–187. Green Forest, AR: Master Books.

Hutton, J. 1788. Theory of the earth: or an investigation of the laws observable in the composition, dissolution, and restoration of land on the globe. *Transactions of the Royal Society of Edinburgh* 1: 109–304.

Hutton, J. 1795. *Theory of the earth, with proofs and illustrations*. 2 vols. Edinburgh, Scotland: W. Creech.

Lyell, C. 1830–1833. *Principles of geology*. 3 vols. London, England: J. Murray.

Neuendorf, K. E., J. P. Mehl, Jr., and J. A. Jackson, eds. 2005. *Glossary of geology*. 5th ed., 659. Alexandria, VA: American Geological Institute.

Northrup, B. E. 1990. Identifying the Noahic Flood in historical geology, part two. In *Proceedings of the second International Conference on Creationism*. Ed. R. E. Walsh and C. L. Brooks. Vol. 2, 181–88. Pittsburgh, PA: Creation Science Fellowship.

Sigler, R., and C. V. Wingerden. 1998. Submarine flow and slide deposits in the Kingston Peak Formation, Kingston Range, Mojave Desert, California: Evidence for catastrophic initiation of Noah's Flood. In *Proceedings of the fourth International Conference on Creationism*. Ed. R. E. Walsh, 487–501. Pittsburgh, PA: Creation Science Fellowship.

Snelling, A. A. 2008a. High and dry sea creatures. *Answers* 3.1: 92–95

Snelling, A. A. 2008b. Transcontinental rock layers. *Answers* 3.3: 80–83.

Snelling, A. A. 2009. *Earth's catastrophic past: Geology, creation and the Flood*. Dallas, TX: Institute for Creation Research.

Snider-Pellegrini, A. 1859 (early release 1858). *La création et ses mystères dévoilés*. Paris, France: A. Frank et E. Dentu.

Wingerden, C. V. 2003. Initial Flood deposits of the western North American cordillera: California, Utah and Idaho. In *Proceedings of the fifth International Conference on Creationism*. Ed. R. L. Ivey Jr., 349–357. Pittsburgh, PA: Creation Science Fellowship.

CHAPTER 7

Paleontological Issues: Deciphering the Fossil Record of the Flood and Its Aftermath

Andrew A. Snelling

Analogy and Orientation. *The sea floor is not only littered with shipwrecks, but also with the remains of ship's crews and passengers. Divers can explore and investigate such remains, but unless they also have historical records based on eyewitness testimony, they cannot fully identify all the remains and piece together their original relationships to one another and how it all happened. So it is with the fossils found in the earth's geologic record. Their order of appearance has been interpreted by investigators, ignoring the only eyewitness historical record available, God's Word, as reflecting an evolutionary progression of life. Thus the goal of this chapter is to show how the sequence of fossils in the earth's stacked rock layers is instead better understood as recording the burial order of the Genesis Flood, including a progression in the burial of pre-Flood ecological zones and biomes, and the mobility and behavior of vertebrates who temporarily escaped leaving behind footprints as the Floodwaters rose up over the continents and finally buried them. Furthermore, because debate continues over where in the record marks the Flood/post-Flood boundary, due to many fossils higher in the record matching their extant post-Flood descendants from the Ark survivors, it is discussed how Hebrew text studies are thus needed to not only elucidate the Flood's chronology, including the timing of the Floodwaters' peaking, but to provide insights on the waters' actions responsible for accumulating the fossil record.*

Abstract. The fossils scattered through the strata sequence of the geologic record are found in a discernible order. They are thus usually interpreted as a record of the evolution of creatures that lived and died through millions of years while the rock layers were slowly being deposited. However, according to the biblical framework for earth history, the rock record preserved the burial order of the Genesis Flood, starting with the burial of shallow marine invertebrates exclusively at the onset of this cataclysmic upheaval, followed by the progressive destruction of pre-Flood ecological zones and biomes as the waters gradually inundated all land surfaces around the globe. Superimposed on this general order are the evidences of the mobility and behavior of vertebrates, many of whom to varying degrees could temporarily escape the rising Floodwaters, some leaving behind their tracks and footprints before their bodies were eventually buried. Debate continues over where in the record marks the Flood/post-Flood boundary, because higher in the record many fossils match their extant post-Flood descendants from the Ark survivors. But there is a marked paleontological and erosional discontinuity that either marks that boundary or corresponds to the massive erosional waning of the Floodwaters after their peaking on Day 150. Hebrew text studies are thus needed to not only elucidate the Flood's chronology, including the timing of the Floodwaters' peaking, but to provide insights on the waters' actions responsible for accumulating the fossil record.

Outline

1. Introduction: The Fossil Record
2. The Reality of the Fossil Record
3. Interpreting the Fossil Record
4. Burial Order of the Flood
5. Pre-Flood Ecological Zoning and Biomes
6. Behavior and Mobility of Vertebrates
7. The Flood/post-Flood Boundary
8. Discussion: Where to from Here?
9. Conclusion

1. Introduction: The Fossil Record

Fossils are the remains, traces, or imprints of plants or animals that have been preserved in the earth's near-surface rock layers at some time in the past (Neuendorf, Mehl, and Jackson 2005). Indeed, fossils are the remains of dead animals and plants that were buried in layers of sediment that later hardened to sedimentary rock strata. So the fossil record is hardly "the record of life in the geologic past" that so many scientists incorrectly espouse, assuming a long prehistory for the earth and life on it. Instead, it is a record of the deaths of countless billions of animals and plants.

Most people have been led to believe that the fossil record is "exhibit A" for evolution. This is because most geologists insist, and thus it is taught in almost all of the world's education systems, as well as being presented in most museums and through the media, that the sedimentary rock layers were deposited gradually over vast eons of time during which animals lived, died, and then were occasionally buried and fossilized. So when these fossilized animals (and plants) are found in the earth's rock sequences in a particular order of first appearance, such as animals without backbones (invertebrates) in lower layers followed progressively upward by fish, then amphibians, reptiles, birds, and finally mammals, it is concluded, and thus almost universally taught, that this must have been the order in which these animals evolved during those vast eons of time.

However, in reality, it can only be dogmatically asserted that the fossil record is a record of the order in which animals and plants were buried and fossilized. After all, it is not usually emphasized that many of the animals that first appear buried in great profusion in the lowest layers of the fossil record, in particular the shallow-water marine invertebrates, are found in great profusion right through the fossil record, and many are still living today, unchanged from their fossil ancestors. Indeed, the shallow-water marine invertebrates (brachiopods, bivalves, gastropods, corals, echinoderms, crustaceans, cephalopods, etc.) account for the vast majority by number, estimated at ninety-five percent (Wise 1994a), of fossils preserved in the strata record.

Furthermore, the vast eons of time are unproven and unprovable, being based on assumptions about how quickly sedimentary rock layers were deposited in the unobserved past. Instead, there is overwhelming evidence that most sedimentary rock layers were deposited rapidly (Ager 1973, 1993; Austin 1994). Indeed, the impeccable state of preservation of most fossils requires the animals and plants to have been very rapidly buried, virtually alive, by vast amounts of sediments before decay could destroy delicate details of their appearance and anatomy.

There is another consideration that is often overlooked. There is only one thing we can be absolutely certain of when we find animals and plants fossilized together. They didn't necessarily live together in the same environment or even die together, but they were certainly buried together, because that's how we observe them today! We did not observe the animals and plants living together in some ecological environment in the past, but we observe them buried together today in the sedimentary layers of the geologic record. This is not to say that in some instances some of the fossils found buried together may represent animals and plants that did once live together, even if other creatures were also buried with them.

2. The Reality of the Fossil Record

Some biblical creationists believe that the fossil record, as depicted in geologic column diagrams (Figure 1), does not represent reality. Such an assessment is usually based on the unfortunate claim that the geologic column is only theoretical, having been constructed by matching up rock layers from different areas of the world that contain similar fossils, as if that were the only criterion being used for such correlations. They also believe that the rock layers were arranged based on an assumed evolutionary order of the contained fossils, so they conclude that the whole concept of the geologic column and the order of rock layers and their contained fossils must be totally rejected (Walker 1994).

Contrary to such claims, it is possible to walk across various regions of the earth and observe that the rock layers and the fossils contained in them generally match what is depicted in the widely accepted geologic column diagrams. It is true that the complete geologic record is hardly ever, if at all, found in any one place on the earth's surface. Usually several or many of the strata in local sequences are missing compared to the overall geologic record, but usually over a given region there is a more complete preservation of the record via correlation and integration. However, quite commonly there is little or no physical or physiographic evidence of the intervening period of erosion or non-deposition of the missing strata systems, suggesting that at such localities neither erosion nor deposition ever occurred there.

Yet this is exactly what would be expected to be found today based on the biblical account of the Genesis Flood and its implications. Indeed, if the waters of the Flood progressively rose to cover the earth, then we would expect that the sediments carried by the rising Floodwaters as they swept across the continents would have deposited sediment layers, rapidly burying animals and plants in them, right across the continents. Due to the results of the fieldwork of numerous geologists over many decades, details of the local strata sequences at different locations around the world have been carefully compiled from physical observations and via boreholes drilled in the search for minerals and oil. Careful correlations of strata of the same rock types at the same relative levels in the local strata sequences have then been made between local areas, and then from region to region, often by direct physical means, so that the robustness of the overall strata sequence of the geologic record, and the fossil content and order contained within it, has been clearly established. Indeed, it is now well recognized that there are at least six thick sequences of fossil-bearing sedimentary strata, known as megasequences,

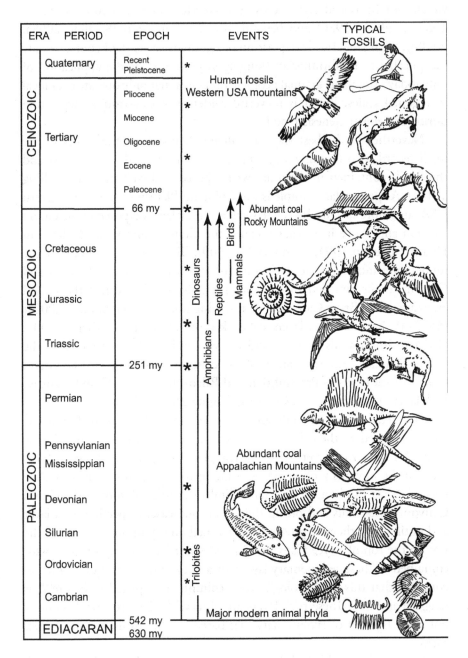

Figure 1. The geologic "column" as it appears in many textbooks, showing its standard named subdivisions. The alleged geologic timescale for some of the key strata boundaries, and some of the representative fossils found in the rock record, are also shown. The asterisks mark the locations of alleged "mass extinctions."

which can be traced right across the North American continent (Sloss 1963; Lindberg 1986) and beyond to other continents (Snelling 2008a, 2010b). Such global-scale deposition of sediment layers is, of course, totally inexplicable to uniformitarian (long-ages) geologists by the application of only today's slow-and-gradual geologic processes that only operate over local to regional scales. But it is powerful evidence of catastrophic deposition during the global Genesis Flood.

Nevertheless, the best way to evaluate claims about the reality of the fossil record is to examine a geographic region where the rock layers and the fossils contained in them are well-exposed and well-studied (Snelling 2010a). A spectacular example is the Colorado Plateau of the southwestern USA, and more specifically, the sequence of rock layers exposed in the Grand Canyon and above it in what is called the Grand Staircase, as depicted in Figure 2 (Austin 1994; Brand 1997, 2009). This diagram shows how the topography moves progressively upwards from the bottom of the Grand Canyon to the rim and then through a series of cliffs called the Grand Staircase to the Bryce Canyon area at the highest elevation. Some 15,000 ft (4572 m) of sedimentary layers are stacked on top of one another—5000 ft (1524 m) in the walls of the Grand Canyon and 10,000 ft (3048 m) in the Grand Staircase. The standard geologic column diagram labels the Grand Canyon rock layers as Precambrian and Paleozoic, and the Grand Staircase rock layers as Mesozoic and Cenozoic (Figure 2).

Full details about the individual sedimentary rock layers, including the names assigned to them for easy reference, are provided in Figure 2. The names for these rock layers represent real places and patterns of occurrences that can be obviously observed by walking in and around this area. Any keen observer can literally hike (and climb) from the bottom of the Grand Canyon up its walls and on up the Grand Staircase, inspecting each layer and noting how they are progressively stacked on top of one another all the way to the top of Bryce Canyon. One does not have to rely on the fossils contained in these sedimentary layers, or any evolutionary assumptions, to conclude that this local geologic strata column, as depicted in Figure 2, is tangible and real. These rock layers are observable data, so this diagram is not some figment of evolutionary bias based on the fossil content of their rocks.

Having now established the physical reality of this local column of rock layers, it must be concluded that the fossils contained in these rock layers are also a valid record of the order that creatures were progressively buried in this region within each successive sedimentary layer. If there is a clear order

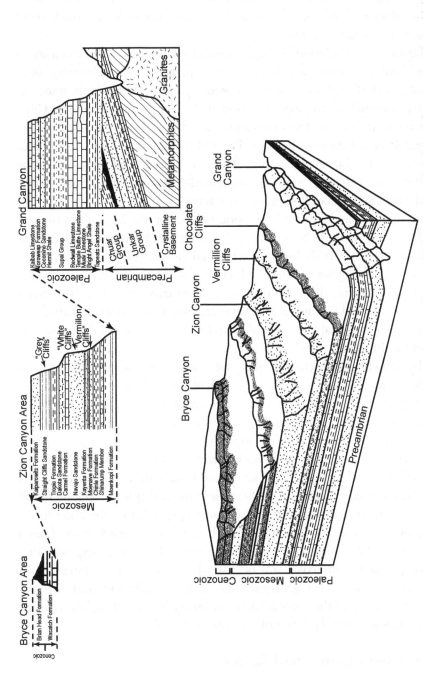

Figure 2. The succession of named rock layers making up wide areas of the Colorado Plateau, from the Grand Canyon sequence (right) upwards and northwards (moving to the left) through the colored cliffs of the Grand Staircase to Zion Canyon and then Bryce Canyon.

of sedimentary layers, then we would expect to be able to look at the fossils contained in each of these layers and thus find the order in which these animals and plants were buried.

Figure 3 is a tabulation listing the fossils found in each of the main layers in the Grand Canyon-Grand Staircase rock sequence (Beus and Morales 2003; Snelling 2010a). The fossils listed in bold represent the first appearance of that type of fossil. A careful examination of this list reveals the order in which creatures were buried. The first major megascopic fossils, apart from the stromatolites and trace fossils in the Precambrian Chuar Group are trilobites and traces in the Tapeats Sandstone, followed by other shallow-water marine invertebrates in the overlying and sequentially deposited Cambrian Bright Angel Shale and Muav Limestone. The remains of fish are then found in the overlying Temple Butte Limestone before the fossilized footprints of vertebrates appear in the Supai Group. It is not until the Mesozoic Moenkopi Formation that the body fossils of terrestrial and freshwater vertebrates are found, and only higher still in the Moenave Formation are fossilized reptiles found, such as crocodiles and dinosaurs. Note that throughout this strata sequence fossilized marine invertebrates are found. Also note that after first appearing in this local fossil record, vertebrates are then found consistently higher up through the rock sequence.

These highlighted details from Figure 3 should now be compared against Figure 1, which is a conventional depiction of the geologic and fossil records, showing the first appearances of animals and plants during accumulation of the rock record. Ignoring that these first appearances are interpreted conventionally as implying when these animals and plants supposedly first lived rather than being simply a burial order, it can be readily seen that the comparison is a close match. The lowest layers in both fossil records contain only shallow-water marine invertebrates and the first fish remains are found in the Devonian. Vertebrate trackways next appear before the body fossils of reptiles higher in the sequence. Thus, because the Grand Canyon-Grand Staircase fossil record is real, being found in this local strata sequence that can be physically observed, and because the fossil record summarized in the conventional global geologic column is virtually identical, we can safely conclude that the latter is based on reality. We can therefore base our interpretation of the fossil record on a physical reality.

3. Interpreting the Fossil Record

If most sedimentary rock layers were deposited rapidly, a proposition the evidence is consistent with, then the total sequence of fossil-bearing sedimentary rocks in the geologic record could have been deposited rapidly over a radically shorter period of time than conventionally claimed, so that a catastrophic global Flood represents a viable explanation of the fossil

BRIAN HEAD FORMATION	terrestrial and freshwater vertebrates, invertebrates, and plants
WASATCH FORMATION	terrestrial and freshwater vertebrates, invertebrates, and plants
KAIPAROWITS FORMATION	terrestrial and freshwater vertebrates, invertebrates, and plants
STRAIGHT CLIFFS FORMATION	marine and freshwater invertebrates; freshwater, marine, and terrestrial vertebrates
TROPIC FORMATION	marine plants, vertebrates, and invertebrates
DAKOTA SANDSTONE	terrestrial plants, vertebrates and invertebrates; marine invertebrates
CARMEL FORMATION	marine invertebrates and vertebrates, and algae
NAVAJO SANDSTONE	terrestrial reptiles, plants, and invertebrate trace fossils; dinosaur tracks
KAYENTA FORMATION	terrestrial plants and vertebrates; dinosaur tracks
MOENAVE FORMATION	freshwater fish, crocodiles, dinosaurs, and reptile tracks
CHINLE FORMATION	terrestrial plants and freshwater invertebrates
MOENKOPI FORMATION	marine invertebrates; terrestrial and freshwater vertebrates, invertebrates, and plants; trace fossils
KAIBAB LIMESTONE	brachiopods, bryozoans, sharks, nautiloids, fish, sponges, trilobites, crinoids, trace fossils, and microfossils
TOROWEAP FORMATION	bivalves, gastropods (molluscs), cephalopods, brachiopods, bryozoans, crinoids, corals
COCONINO SANDSTONE	vertebrate and invertebrate tracks, and trace fossils
HERMIT SHALE	trace fossils (trackways, burrows) and plants
SUPAI GROUP	trace fossils (vertebrate trackways, burrows), brachiopods, foraminifera, and plants
REDWALL LIMESTONE	bivalves, cephalopods, brachiopods, corals, bryozoans, crinoids, trilobites, fish teeth, foraminifera, and algae
TEMPLE BUTTE LIMESTONE	corals, fish scales, crinoids, stromatoporoids, brachiopods, gastropods, microfossils, and trace fossils
MUAV LIMESTONE	trilobites, brachiopods, sponges, gastropods, algal structures
BRIGHT ANGEL SHALE	brachiopods, molluscs, sponges, echinoderms, gastropods, trilobites, trace fossils (tracks, burrows)
TAPEATS SANDSTONE	trace fossils (tracks, burrows) and trilobites
CHUAR GROUP	stromatolites, algae, microfossils, and trace fossils
UNKAR GROUP	none

Figure 3. The order of creatures buried and fossilized in the Grand Staircase's rock layers. This tabulation lists the types of fossils found in each rock layer. The fossils in bold text represent the first appearance of that type of fossil (after Snelling 2010a).

record (Snelling 2008b). Thus when this evidence is placed in a biblical framework for earth history, the animals and plants buried and fossilized in the sedimentary rock layers would have all lived at about the same time, and then have been rapidly buried progressively and sequentially during the global Genesis Flood cataclysm.

If as Bible-believing Christians we are going to interpret the evidence in the fossil and geologic records within the biblical framework of earth history, then having established that we all have the same evidence (fossils and rocks), we also need to remember that we all start with presupposed assumptions. Whereas conventional geologists assume and believe that the origin and evolution of life has occurred over vast eons during gradual accumulation of the rock record, biblical creationists assume God's Word provides a literal historical eyewitness account of the earth's early history that only encompasses thousands of years, beginning with God creating the earth, the solar system, stars and galaxies, and everything in them in six normal days. At the end of that Creation Week, God declared everything He had created and made was "very good" (Gn 1:31). It is then clear from Genesis 1–3, Romans 5:12, 8:20–22, and 1 Corinthians 15:21–22 that the good world God created was subsequently severely marred by death as a result of Adam's sin. Because the animals were created as vegetarians (Gn 1:29–30) and the whole creation was subsequently impacted with corruption and death due to the Fall, there could have been no animal fossils in the rocks at the end of the Creation Week. Indeed, fossilization under present-day conditions is exceedingly rare, so evolutionary geologists applying "the present is the key to the past" have a real problem in explaining how the vast numbers of fossils in the geologic record could have formed. Thus, the global destruction of all the pre-Flood animals and plants by the year-long Flood cataclysm alone makes sense of the fossil and geologic records.

It is important to note that in the geologic record there are very thick sequences of rock layers found below the main strata record containing prolific fossils which are either totally devoid of fossils or only contain very rare fossils of micro-organisms and minor invertebrates. Within the biblical framework of earth history, these strata would therefore have to have been formed prior to the Flood, principally during the latter part of the Creation Week, during and subsequent to God making the dry land on Day 3. The conditions necessary for the wholesale destruction of animal and plant life and their burial in water-deposited sediment layers would have only been available after the Creation Week during the cataclysmic Flood year. However, a few fossils may also have formed since the Flood due to localized, residual catastrophic depositional events.

In the upward progression of strata the fossils of a particular type of animal or plant may stop occurring in the record and there are no more fossils of that animal or plant in the strata above. If there are also no living representatives of that animal or plant today, then that particular creature or plant is regarded as having become extinct. There are, in fact, many animals and plants that are now extinct. We only know they once existed because of their fossilized remains in the geologic record. Perhaps the most obvious and famous example is the dinosaurs.

There are distinctive levels in the fossil record where vast numbers of animals (and plants) are believed to have become extinct. Evolution has claimed that all these animals (and plants) must have died, been buried, and become extinct all at the same time. Since this pattern is seen in the geologic record all around the globe, they call these distinctive levels in the fossil record mass extinctions. Furthermore, because something must have happened globally to wipe out all those animals (and plants), the formation of these distinctive levels in the fossil record are called mass extinction events. However, in the context of catastrophic deposition of the strata containing these fossils, this pattern would be a preserved consequence of the Flood.

There are some seventeen of these so-called mass extinction events in the fossil record as recognized by evolutionary geologists, from the late Precambrian up until the late Neogene, "just before the dawn of written human history." However, only eight of those are classed as major mass extinction events. The most talked about of these is the end-Cretaceous mass extinction event, because that's when the dinosaurs are supposed to have been wiped out, along with about a quarter of all the known families of animals. However, the end-Permian mass extinction event was even more catastrophic, because seventy-five percent of amphibian families and eighty percent of reptile families were supposedly wiped out then, along with seventy-five to ninety percent of all pre-existing species in the oceans.

Evolutionary geologists are still debating the cause of these mass extinction events. The popularized explanation for the end-Cretaceous mass extinction event is that an asteroid hit the earth, generating choking dust clouds and giant tsunamis that decimated the globe and its climate. A layer of clay containing a chemical signature of an asteroid in several places around the globe is regarded as one piece of evidence, and the 124 mi (200 km) wide Chicxulub impact crater in Mexico is regarded as the record of the culprit. However, at the same level in the geologic record are the massive remains of catastrophic outpourings of staggering quantities of volcanic lavas over a large part of India, totally unlike any volcanic eruptions experienced in recent human history. Furthermore, volcanic dust has a similar chemical signature to that of an asteroid. And even more enormous quantities of volcanic lavas are found in Siberia at the same level in the geologic record that coincides with the end-Permian mass extinction event.

On the other hand, in the global watery cataclysm described in Genesis there would be simultaneous wholesale destruction of animals and plants across the globe. The tearing apart of the earth's crust when "the fountains of the great deep burst open" would have released stupendous outpourings of volcanic lavas on the continental scale found in the geologic record. And there can be no doubt from the impact craters found at different levels in the geologic record around the globe that asteroids and meteors also wreaked havoc when they slammed into the earth during the same global Flood (Spencer 1998; Snelling 2012). The resultant "waves" of destruction are thus easily misinterpreted as mass extinction events, when these were just stages of the single, year-long, catastrophic global Flood.

It is also significant that some fossilized animals and plants once thought to be extinct have in fact been found still alive, thus demonstrating the total unreliability of the evolutionary timescale. The last fossilized coelacanth (a fish) is supposedly sixty-five million years old. Living coelacanths were found in 1938 and many times more since then, so this begs the question as to why no coelacanths were fossilized during those supposed sixty-five million years? The Wollemi pine's last fossil is supposedly150 million years old, but identical living trees were found in 1994 (Snelling 2006). The recent burial and fossilization of these animals and plants, and the extinction of many other animals and plants, during the single global biblical Flood thus makes better sense of all the fossil and geologic evidence.

4. Burial Order of the Flood

The geologic and fossil records are clearly consistent with huge masses of water-transported sediments rapidly burying and thus fossilizing countless multitudes of animals and plants on a global scale during the global Genesis Flood cataclysm (Snelling 2008b, 2009). Thus the vertical order in which the fossils are found in the geologic record can be interpreted validly as the order in which animals and plants were buried during the biblical Flood. The first fossils in the record are of marine animals exclusively. It is only higher in the strata record that fossils of land animals are found. This is consistent with the Flood beginning in the ocean basins when "the fountains of the great deep burst open," and the ocean waters would have then flooded over the continents. How else would there be marine fossils in sedimentary layers stretching over large areas of the continents? Added to this, the "floodgates of heaven" were simultaneously opened, and both volcanism and earth movements would have accompanied these upheavals.

The vast majority by number of fossils preserved in the strata record of the Flood are the remains of shallow-water marine invertebrates (brachiopods, bivalves, gastropods, corals, echinoderms, crustaceans, cephalopods, etc.) (Wise 1994a). In the lowermost fossiliferous strata (Cambrian, Ordovician, Silurian, and Devonian) the contained fossils are almost exclusively shallow-water marine invertebrates, with fish and amphibian fossils only appearing in progressively greater numbers in the overlying higher strata (Stanley 1989; Cowen 2000). The first fish fossils are found in Ordovician strata and in Devonian strata are found amphibians and the first evidence of continental-type flora. It is not until the Carboniferous (Mississippian and Pennsylvania) and Permian strata higher in the geologic record that the first traces of land animals are encountered.

Because the Flood began in the ocean basins with the breaking up of the fountains of the great deep, strong and destructive ocean currents were generated by the upheavals and moved swiftly landward, scouring the sediments on the ocean floor and carrying them and the organisms living in, on, and near them. These currents and sediments reached the shallower continental shelves, where the shallow-water marine invertebrates lived in all their prolific diversity. Unable to escape, these organisms would have been swept away and buried in the sediment layers as they were dumped where the waters crashed onto the land surfaces being progressively inundated farther inland. As well as burying these shallow-water marine invertebrates, the sediments washed shoreward from the ocean basins would have progressively buried fish, then amphibians and reptiles living in lowland, swampy habitats, before eventually sweeping away the dinosaurs and burying them next, and finally at the highest elevations destroying and burying birds, mammals, and angiosperms (flowering plants).

Moving water also hydrodynamically selects and sorts particles of similar sizes and shapes. Together with the effect of specific gravities of the respective organisms, this would have ensured deposition of the supposedly simple marine invertebrates in the first-deposited strata that are now deep in the geologic record of the Flood. The well-established "impact law" states that the settling velocity of large particles is independent of fluid viscosity, being directly proportional to the square root of particle diameter, directly proportional to the particles' sphericity, and directly proportional to the difference between particle and fluid density divided by fluid density (Krumbein and Sloss 1963). Moving water, or moving particles in still water, exerts "drag" forces on immersed bodies which depend on the above factors. Particles in motion will tend to settle out in proportion mainly to their specific gravity (or density) and sphericity.

It is significant that the marine organisms fossilized in the earliest Flood strata, such as the trilobites, brachiopods, etc., are very "streamlined" and quite dense. The shells of these and most other marine invertebrates are largely composed of calcium carbonate, calcium phosphate, and similar minerals which are quite heavy (heavier than quartz, for example, the most common constituent of many sands and gravels). This factor alone would have exerted a highly selective sorting action, not only tending to deposit the simpler (that is, the most spherical and undifferentiated organisms) first in the sediments as they were being deposited, but also tending to segregate particles of similar sizes and shapes. These could have thus formed distinct faunal "stratigraphic horizons" with a complexity of structure of deposited organisms, even of similar kinds, increasing progressively upward in the accumulating sediments.

It is quite possible that this could have been a major process responsible for giving the fossil assemblages within the strata sequences a superficial appearance of "evolution" of similar organisms in the progressive succession upward in the geologic record. Generally, the sorting action of flowing water is quite efficient, and would definitely have separated the shells and other fossils in just the fashion in which they are found, with certain fossils predominant in certain stratigraphic horizons, and the supposed complexity of such distinctive, so-called "index" fossils increasing in at least a general way in a progressive sequence upward through the strata of the geologic record of the Flood.

Of course, these very pronounced "sorting" powers of hydraulic action are really only valid generally, rather than universally. Furthermore, local variations and peculiarities of turbulence, environment, sediment composition, etc. would be expected to cause local variations in the fossil assemblages, with even occasional heterogeneous combinations of sediments and fossils of a wide variety of shapes and sizes, just as we find in the complex geologic record.

In any case, it needs to be emphasized that so-called "transitional" fossil forms that are true "intermediates" in the strata sequences between supposed ancestors and supposed descendants according to the evolutionary model are exceedingly rare, and are not found at all among the groups with the best fossil records (shallow-marine invertebrates like mollusks and brachiopods) (Wise 2002). Indeed, even evolutionary researchers have found that the successive fossil assemblages in the strata record invariably only show trivial differences between fossil organisms (variations within the created kinds), the different fossil groups with their distinctive body plans appearing abruptly in the record, and then essentially staying the same (stasis) in the record (Eldridge and Gould 1972; Gould and Eldridge 1977, 1993).

In some areas, distinctive sequences of sedimentary strata with their contained fossil assemblages would be deposited, and in other areas entirely different strata sequences with different fossil assemblages would be deposited, depending on the source areas and directions of the water currents transporting the sediments. Some strata units would have been deposited over wider areas than others, with erosion in some areas but continuous deposition in others, even when intervening strata units were deposited elsewhere. Thus, as a result of the complex interplay of currents, waves, and transported sediments with their entombed organisms, a variety of different types of sedimentary rocks and strata sequences would have been laid down directly on the pre-Flood strata sequences and the crystalline basement that probably dates back to the Creation Week itself. Thus the pattern of deposition of the strata sequences and their contained fossils is directly consistent with the strata record the Flood would be expected to produce. In contrast, by using the present to interpret the past, evolutionary geologists have no more true scientific certainty of their version of the unobservable, unique historic events which they claim produced the geologic record.

Therefore, since the general order of the strata and their contained fossil assemblages is not generally in dispute, then that order in the strata sequences still must reflect the geological processes and their timing responsible for the formation of the strata and their order. Furthermore, if the order in the fossil record does not represent the sequence of the evolutionary development of life, then the fossil record must be explainable within the context of the tempo of geologic processes burying these organisms in the sediment layers during the global Flood cataclysm. Indeed, both the order of the strata and their contained fossils could well provide us with information about the pre-Flood world, and evidence of the progress of different geologic processes during the Flood event. Thus a number of factors have been suggested to explain the burial order in the fossil record in terms of the Flood processes, rather than over the claimed long ages. The hydrodynamic selectivity of moving water and its sorting ability has already been highlighted as one factor, but there is also the issue of the pre-Flood biogeography.

The conventional explanation of the fossil order is, of course, progressive evolutionary changes over long periods of time. But this explanation runs into a huge challenge. Evolution predicts that new groups of creatures would have arisen in a specific order. But if we compare the order that these creatures first appear in the actual fossil record, as opposed to their theoretical first appearance in the predictions, then over ninety-five percent of the fossil record's "order" can best be described as random (Wise 1992).

On the other hand, if these organisms were buried by the Floodwaters, the order of first appearance should be either random, due to the sorting effects of the Flood, or reflect the order of ecological burial. In other words, as the Floodwaters rose, they would tend to bury organisms in the order that they were encountered, so the major groups should appear in the fossil record according to where they lived, and not when they lived. This is exactly what we find, in both the fossil record within a region such as the Grand Canyon-Grand Staircase region, or within the overall global fossil record.

5. Pre-Flood Ecological Zoning and Biomes

If we look at today's living biology, we find that across mountain ranges such as the Sierra Nevada of California, or in a traverse from the South Rim of the Grand Canyon down to the Colorado River, there are distinct plant and animal communities in different life or ecological zones that are characteristic of the sub-climates at the different elevations. Thus, we observe cacti growing in desert zones at lower elevations (such as at the bottom of the Grand Canyon) and pines growing in alpine zones (such as at the South Rim of the Grand Canyon) rather than growing together. Therefore, just as these life/ecology zones today can be correlated globally (all deserts around the world have similar plants and animals in ecological communities or biomes), so too some fossil zones and fossil communities (biomes) may be correlated globally within the geologic record of the Flood.

Thus it has been suggested that there could well have been distinct biological communities (biomes) and ecological zones in the pre-Flood world that were spatially and geographically separated from one another, so that they were then sequentially inundated, swept away, and buried as the Floodwaters rose. This ecological zonation model for the order of fossils in the geologic record (Clark 1946) would argue that the lower fossiliferous layers in the strata record must therefore represent the fossilization of biological communities at lower elevations and/or warmer climates, while higher layers in the geologic record must represent fossilization of biological communities that lived at higher elevations and thus cooler temperatures (Figure 4). Indeed, based on the already established observation above that the earliest fossils in the record are shallow-water, bottom-dwelling marine invertebrates, this ecological zonation model could be extended to encompass the shallow ocean floor as the first ecological zone or biological community to be buried and fossilized in the lowest layers at the beginning of the Flood (Coffin 1983; Coffin, Brown, and Gibson 2005).

Based on the vertical and horizontal distribution of certain fossil assemblages in the strata record, it has been concluded therefore that the pre-Flood biogeography consisted of distinct and unique ecosystems which were destroyed by the Flood and did not recover to become reestablished in the post-Flood world of today. These included a floating-forest ecosystem consisting of unique trees called lycopods of various sizes that contained large, hollow cavities in their trunks and branches and hollow root-like rhizomes, with associated similar plants (Figure 5). It also included some unique animals, mainly amphibians, which lived in these forests that floated on the surface of the pre-Flood ocean (Wise 2003b, 2008a). Spatially and geographically separated and isolated from this floating-forest ecosystem were stromatolite reefs adjacent to hydrothermal springs in the shallow waters at the edges of the continental shelves making up a hydrothermal-stromatolite reef ecosystem (Figure 6) (Wise 2003a, 2008b). These stromatolite reefs may

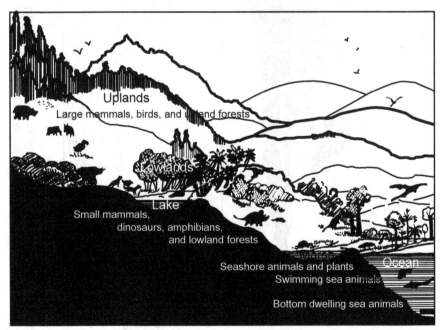

Figure 4. Diagrammatic presentation of likely ecological zonation in the pre-Flood world as proposed by Clark (1946), illustrating how animals and plants could then be buried in a roughly predictable order by the rising Floodwaters (after Coffin 1983).

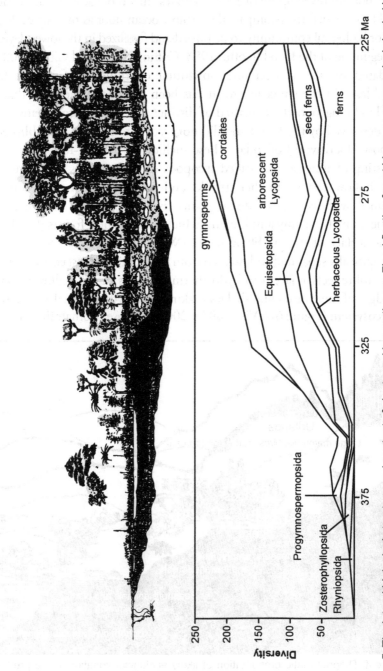

Figure 5. The lateral biological structure and content of plants making up the pre-Flood floating forest biome as progressively buried in the fossil record (from left to right) by the rising Floodwaters, instead of through the supposed millions of years (after Wise 2003b).

have formed a barrier-like elongated mound that protected the pre-Flood continental shoreline from the open ocean, enclosing an extensive shallow-water lagoon that was home to other biological communities, including the rare and now extinct Ediacaran and Tommotian faunas.

In the warmer climates of the lowland areas of the pre-Flood land surfaces, dinosaurs may have lived where gymnosperms (naked seed plants) were abundant, while at higher elevations inland in the hills and mountains where the climate was cooler, mammals and humans may have lived among vegetation dominated by angiosperms (flowering plants) (Wise 2002). Thus these gymnosperm-dinosaur and angiosperm-mammal-man ecosystems (or biomes) were spatially and geographically separated from one another on the pre-Flood land surfaces. In Genesis chapter 2, the river coming out of the Garden of Eden is described as dividing into four rivers, which may imply the Garden of Eden (with its fruit trees and other angiosperms, mammals, and man) was at a high point geographically, the rivers flowing downhill to the lowland swampy plains bordering the shorelines where the gymnosperms grew and the dinosaurs lived. This would explain why, as far as we currently know, we do not find human and dinosaur fossil remains together in the geologic record, yet we find dinosaurs and gymnosperms only fossilized together, and angiosperms only fossilized with mammals higher in the record separate from the dinosaurs and gymnosperms.

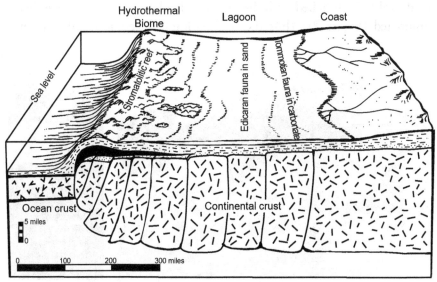

Figure 6. Diagrammatic representation of the offshore position at the edge of the continental crust and margin of the pre-Flood hydrothermal biome consisting of a stromatolite reef built above upwelling hot water springs. The barrier-like reef enclosed a shallow-water lagoon area that was "home" to the rare and now extinct Ediacaran and Tommotian faunas (after Wise 2003a).

It can therefore be argued that in a general way the order of fossil "succession" in the geologic record would reflect the successive burial of these pre-Flood biological communities as the Floodwaters rose up onto the continents (Figure 7). The Flood began with the breaking up of the fountains of the great deep (the breaking up of the pre-Flood ocean floor) (Austin et al. 1994), so that there would have been a sudden surge of strong ocean currents and tsunamis picking up sediments from the ocean floor and moving landward as the margins of the pre-Flood supercontinent started to also collapse (Austin and Wise 1994) that would first of all have overwhelmed the stromatolite reefs in the shallow seas fringing the shorelines. This destruction of the protected lagoons between the stromatolite reefs and the shorelines by the collapsing of the continental margins and these severe storms would have then caused the strange animals that probably were unique to these stromatolite reefs and the adjacent lagoons to be buried and thus preserved in the lowermost fossil strata (the conventional uppermost Neoproterozoic layers) directly overlaying the burial of the stromatolites.

Increasing storms, tidal surges, and tsunamis generated by earth movements, earthquakes, and volcanism on the ocean floor would have resulted in the progressive breaking up of the floating-forest ecosystem on the ocean surface, so that huge rafts of vegetation would have been swept landward to be beached with the sediment load on the land surfaces being inundated (Figure 7). Thus the floating-forest vegetation and associated

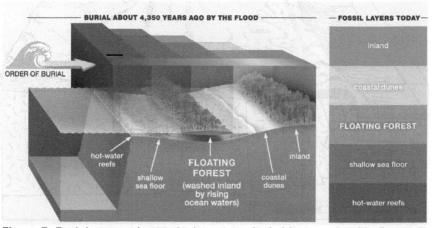

Figure 7. Rock layers and entombed creatures buried in a progressive sequence by the Flood as the waters swept from the ocean and rose up onto the land, leaving behind the pile of rocks and fossils we see today. The hot-water reefs and floating forest were two of the unique ecosystems buried by the Flood and now preserved in the fossil record (after Wise 2008a).

animals would have been buried higher in the strata record of the Flood, well above the stromatolites and the strange animals that lived with them, and above all the shallow-water marine invertebrates and fish fossils. Only later, in the first one hundred fifty days of the Flood, as the waters rose higher across the land surfaces, would the gymnosperm-dinosaurs ecosystem of the lowlands be first swept away and buried, followed later by the angiosperm-mammal-man ecosystem that lived at higher elevations inland. People would have continued to move to the highest ground to escape the rising Floodwaters, and so would not necessarily have been buried with the angiosperms and mammals. Thus the existence of these geographically separated distinct ecosystems in the pre-Flood world could well explain this spatial separation and some of the order of fossilization in the geologic record of the Flood.

6. Behavior and Mobility of Vertebrates

There is another reason why it is totally reasonable to expect that vertebrates would be found fossilized higher in the geologic record than the first invertebrates. Indeed, if vertebrates were to be ranked according to their likelihood of being buried early in the fossil record, then we would expect oceanic fish to be buried first, since they live at the lowest elevation (Brand 1997, 2009). However, in the ocean the fish live in the water column and have greater mobility, unlike the invertebrates that live on the ocean floor and have more restricted mobility, or are even attached to a substrate. Therefore, we would expect the fish to only be buried and fossilized subsequent to the first marine invertebrates.

Of course, fish would have inhabited waters at all different elevations in the pre-Flood world, even up in mountain streams, as well as the lowland, swampy habitats, but their ranking is based on where the first representatives of fish are likely to be buried. Obviously, the fish in the oceans would be the first fish to be affected by the onset of the Flood, whereas those in habitats on the land would be affected subsequently as the Floodwaters progressively invaded their habitats. Thus is it hardly surprising to find that the first vertebrates to be found in the fossil record, and then only sparingly, are marine fish fossils in Ordovician strata. Subsequently, marine fish fossils are found in profusion higher up in the Devonian strata, often in great "fossil graveyards" indicating their violent burial.

A second factor in the ranking of the likelihood of vertebrates being buried is how animals would react to the Flood. The behavior of some animals is very rigid and stereotyped, so they prefer to stay where they are used to living, and thus would have had little chance of escape. Adaptable animals would have recognized something was wrong, and thus would have made an effort to escape. Indeed, many land vertebrates today are known for their ability to sense imminent danger, for example, earthquakes before they actually happen, resulting in them immediately fleeing the danger zone. Fish are the least adaptable in their behavior, while amphibians come next, and they are then followed in adaptability order by reptiles, birds, and lastly, the mammals.

The third factor to be considered is the mobility of the land vertebrates. Once they become aware of the need to escape, how capable would they then have been of running, swimming, flying, or even riding on floating debris? Amphibians would have been the least mobile, with reptiles performing somewhat better, but not being equal to the mammals' mobility, due largely to their low metabolic rates. However, birds, with their ability to fly, would have had the best expected mobility, even being able to find temporary refuge on floating debris on the surface of the Floodwaters.

These three factors would tend to support each other. If they had worked against each other, then the order of vertebrates in the fossil record would be more difficult to explain. However, since they all do work together, it is realistic to suggest that the combination of these factors could have contributed significantly to producing the general sequence we now observe in the fossil record.

In general, therefore, the land animals and plants would be expected to have been caught somewhat later in the period of the rising Floodwaters and buried in the sediments in much the same order as that found in the geologic record, as conventionally depicted in the standard geologic column. Thus, generally speaking, sediment beds burying marine vertebrates would be overlaid by beds containing fossilized amphibians, then beds with reptile fossils, and finally, beds containing fossils of birds and mammals. This is essentially in the order of:

1. Increasing mobility, and therefore increasing ability to postpone inundation and burial;
2. Decreasing density and other hydrodynamic factors, which would tend to promote later burial; and
3. Increasing elevation of habitat and therefore time required for the Floodwaters to rise and advance to overtake them.

This order is essentially consistent with the implications of the biblical account of the Flood, and therefore it provides further circumstantial evidence of the veracity of that account. Of course, there would have been many exceptions to this expected general order, both in terms of omissions and inversions, as the water currents waxed and waned, and the directions changed due to obstacles and obstructions as the land became increasingly submerged and more and more amphibians, reptiles, and mammals were overtaken by the waters.

Other factors must have been significant in influencing the time when many groups of organisms met their demise. As the catastrophic destruction progressed, there would have been changes in the chemistry of seas and lakes from the mixing of fresh and salt water, and from contamination by leaching of other chemicals. Each species of aquatic organism would have had its own physiological tolerance to these changes. Thus, there would have been a sequence of mass mortalities of different groups as the water quality changed. Changes in the turbidity of the waters, pollution of the air by volcanic ash, and/or changes in air temperatures, would likely have had similar effects. So whereas ecological zonation of the pre-Flood world is a useful concept in explaining how the catastrophic processes during the Flood would have produced the order of fossils now seen in the geologic record, the reality was undoubtedly much more complex, due to these many other factors.

There is also another interesting pattern in the fossil record related to the behavior and mobility of animals, and especially the land vertebrates, which confirms what we would expect from a global Flood, rather than from long evolutionary ages for the accumulation of the rock and fossil records. We would expect many larger animals to survive in the Floodwaters initially, even if they were picked up and carried along in the water currents and tried to float or even swim. Before being lifted up by the Floodwaters and swept away many creatures, such as dinosaurs, would have left behind tracks, trails, or even footprints in the sediment surfaces they had been scurrying or running across, so they would leave behind those tracks and trails in the accumulating sediment layers as they tried to escape the rising waters. As they got swept away, incoming sediments would bury their trails and tracks, fossilizing them. As water levels fluctuated, with the rising and falling of the tides, and the passing of water surges and tsunamis, some animals would find themselves again on exposed sediment surfaces and thus leave behind more trails and tracks. But those carried along in the Floodwaters would eventually become exhausted and die, so their bodies would quickly get buried in the sediments deposited by the next water surge. In other words, we would predict that sometimes the trails, tracks, or footprints of animals would be found preserved in the fossil record lower in the sequence than their body fossils. On the other hand, if long evolutionary ages transpired while the rock record slowly accumulated, then we would expect animals to leave their footprints, die, and become buried more or less at the same levels in the strata, as perhaps only inches or a few feet thickness of sediments would be expected to have accumulated during their lifetimes.

So what do we find? In general we find the tracks, trails, and footprints of animals in strata layers long before we find their buried bodily remains fossilized in rock layers higher up in the rock and fossil sequence. This is especially the case with the limbed vertebrates (Brand and Florence 1982) (Figure 8). What is true in the overall global fossil record is also true in the fossil record of regions such as that of the Grand Canyon-Grand Staircase (Figures 2 and 3). In the Cambrian Tapeats Sandstone, at the base of the regional rock and fossil record of the Flood, are fossilized tracks of trilobites left behind as they scurried across the surface of one of the multiple sand beds making up that overall unit. However, the fossilized remains of the bodies of the trilobites do not appear until higher up in the sequence, in the zone where the Tapeats Sandstone transitions into the overlying Bright Angel Shale. Similarly, the fossilized footprints of amphibians and reptiles are found in various places and at different levels in the Pennsylvanian Supai Group, and Permian Hermit Shale and Coconino Sandstone, much lower in the strata sequence than where the fossilized bodies of amphibians and reptiles are first found in the Triassic Moenkopi Formation. This sequential

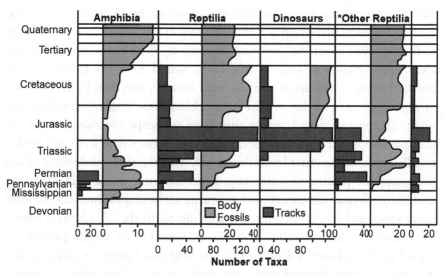

Figure 8. The stratigraphic distribution of fossil amphibian and reptile (including dinosaur) tracks and body fossils (after Brand and Florence 1982).

separation of these fossilized footprints from their fossilized amphibian and reptile makers in the rock record is entirely reasonable in the context of the Genesis Flood, because it would only be days or a few weeks at most between when the animals left their footprints and when the animals subsequently died, and were buried and fossilized. On the other hand, in the long evolutionary ages scenario for the slow accumulation of the sediment layers, the bodies of the amphibians and reptiles would have been buried and fossilized between 20 million and 70 million years after those same amphibians and reptiles supposedly left behind their footprints!

There is a final related example. There is other evidence of normal behavior of animals during deposition of the sedimentary strata sequence. On several continents, sometimes on several to many successive sedimentary layers, abundant fossilized dinosaur eggs in apparent "nests" have been found, sometimes containing fossil embryos. Those who insist the successive layers with repeated dinosaur eggs and "nests" have taken millions of years to form insist they are the required proof. However, no one has ever observed dinosaurs building nests and laying eggs. What we do know is that many dinosaurs were actively walking and running across newly deposited sediment surfaces on which they laid eggs. These were animals that were under considerable stress of continually having to find dry land on which to escape destruction by the Floodwaters. Having retained their eggs within their bodies, perhaps until the eggs were almost ready to hatch, like some modern reptiles do, as their time approached the female dinosaurs would have been desperate to find places to lay their eggs. So as soon as there was a suitable land surface available exposed above the Floodwaters, they would have simply found somewhere to lay their eggs together in what could be interpreted as nests. However, within hours the next inflow of sediments rapidly buried those "nests" and the eggs within them. Those female dinosaurs not yet ready to lay eggs would have been picked up in the next surge of Floodwaters depositing those sediments, only to find their feet again when the next sediment surface was subsequently exposed as the water level dropped again, where they could lay their eggs. Some eggs may have even hatched during these brief intervals. But the preservation of the eggs and newly-hatched babies required catastrophic burial. Thus successive horizons of fossilized dinosaur "nests" and eggs do not require the elapse of large amounts of time, and are thus also consistent with Flood deposition of the sediments, rather than accumulation over long ages. Eventually of course the dinosaurs themselves became exhausted, died, and their bodies were buried in sediment layers in the same strata sequences, but higher up than where they had previously laid their eggs.

7. The Flood/post-Flood Boundary

There is almost unanimous agreement as to where the evidence for the Flood begins in the geologic record. It has been proposed that the pre-Flood/Flood boundary would be associated with five geologic discontinuities in the strata record—a mechanical-erosional discontinuity, a time or age discontinuity, a tectonic discontinuity, a sedimentary discontinuity, and a paleontological discontinuity (Austin and Wise 1994). The Precambrian/Cambrian boundary in the geologic record is the closest fit to all five of these discontinuities, although in some locations the uppermost Precambrian (Neoproterozoic) strata would appear to represent the results of the tectonic upheaval marking the beginning of the Flood (Sigler and Wingerden 1998; Wingerden 2003). In the Grand Canyon, the fossil evidence also points to a latest Precambrian breccia unit (the Sixtymile Formation) being associated with this boundary, below which are the remains of a grown-in-place stromatolite reef that was on the pre-Flood ocean floor (Wise and Snelling 2005). With the profusion of megascopic shallow-water marine invertebrate fossils that start appearing in the geologic record in the Cambrian just above its boundary with the Precambrian, there is thus almost universal agreement that those fossil-bearing sedimentary strata are among the first deposits of the Flood (Austin et al. 1994).

On the other hand, when it comes to what point in the geologic record constitutes the boundary between the Flood and post-Flood strata, there has been much discussion, but little consensus has been reached (Snelling 2009). The Scripture account of the Flood indicates that by Day 314 the waters of the Flood were dried up from off the earth, and the face of the ground was dry (Gn 8:13). However, it wasn't until after another fifty-seven days that the earth was dried (Gn 8:14) and Noah was then instructed to leave the Ark, taking his family and also all the animals with him. Perhaps these extra fifty-seven days were necessary to also allow plants to become reestablished across the ground so that the Ark's cargo would have food to eat when it was finally discharged. Nevertheless, while this extra fifty-seven days of drying would have meant the ground where Noah and the animals alighted from the Ark and surrounding areas was dry and stable enough to be inhabitable, it does not necessarily mean that all residual geologic activity had ceased everywhere else around the globe, nor that the Floodwaters had entirely receded from all other land areas. Thus there could still have been residual localized catastrophic geologic activity elsewhere on the globe producing further fossil-bearing sedimentary layers of localized extent, and there could similarly have been residual volcanic activity and topographic features still forming and being eroded.

Whitcomb and Morris (1961) regarded the Tertiary strata as final Flood deposits, with the mountain-building coinciding with the upper Tertiary strata representing the time at the end of the Flood when the mountains rose and the valleys sank, so that the Floodwaters drained off the earth (Ps 104:7–9). More recently, there are those who would still argue for the Flood/post-Flood boundary being at the Tertiary/Quaternary boundary in the geologic record (Holt 1996; Oard 1996, 2007). However, when early geologists were grouping various strata and categorizing them with respect to the Flood, rocks were labelled as Primary or Primitive, Secondary, Tertiary, and Quaternary, equating to pre-Flood, Flood, post-Flood, and Ice Age, respectively. These major subdivisions and their names became "enshrined" in the geologic column, the Tertiary and Quaternary labels surviving to the present. Thus traditionally the Cretaceous/Tertiary boundary was regarded as the Flood/post-Flood boundary. Austin et al. (1994) maintained that the Cretaceous/Tertiary boundary in the geologic record appeared to correspond to the Flood/post-Flood boundary because from a qualitative assessment of geological maps worldwide it appeared that boundary marked the termination of global-scale erosion and sedimentation, where the types of rock strata changed from being worldwide or continental in character in the Mesozoic, to local or regional in the Tertiary, as would be expected once the Floodwaters retreated off the continents.

A number of other key parameters have been used to determine where in the geologic record the Flood/post-Flood boundary likely occurs. Among the parameters Holt (1996) investigated were the volumes of sediments deposited globally in the geologic record for each of its main subdivisions, from the Cambrian to the Present. He found that the largest volume of sedimentation would appear to have occurred with deposition of the Cretaceous and Tertiary strata. However, such an analysis could be heavily biased because of the erosion and reworking of earlier deposited sedimentary strata. His estimates of sediment volumes in the earlier part of the strata record were based only on the strata that have been preserved in the record, there being no way of quantifying what volumes of strata have been eroded away and redeposited as later strata. Nevertheless, the huge disproportionate volumes of Cretaceous and Tertiary strata, compared to the Cambrian-Jurassic (inclusive) geologic record, is consistent with these strata having been deposited during the mountain-building phase at the end of the Flood, when the uplift was exposing the new land surface and the resultant catastrophic run-off was occurring as the waters of the Flood drained off the continents into the present ocean basins. It is likely that this erosion and sedimentation resulted from the run-off of the Floodwaters continuing as it tapered off in the early post-Flood period, while Noah, his family, and the animals were reestablishing themselves on the new land surface. Thus placement of the Flood/post-Flood boundary at the Cretaceous/Tertiary boundary on an overall global scale would still seem to be feasible, except in those places where marine sedimentation continued on into the Tertiary, before the ocean waters retreated, such as in Israel where Snelling (2010b) therefore placed the end of the Flood around the Oligocene/Miocene (Paleogene/Neogene) boundary in that local strata record.

What then about the Flood/post-Flood boundary being as high in the geologic record as the Tertiary/Quaternary strata boundary, compared with being lower down at the Cretaceous/Tertiary strata boundary? One strong argument against a Tertiary/Quaternary Flood/post-Flood boundary is that the Pleistocene strata immediately above that boundary represent the record of the post-Flood Ice Age, which did not commence immediately after the Flood ended, but instead required at least a century to be fully initiated (Oard 1990). The Flood ending at the end of the Cretaceous, instead, provides time for the Tertiary strata to have accumulated in the first century of the post-Flood era before the onset of the Pleistocene Ice Age. Nevertheless, it is the details in the fossil record which are the major areas in contention with the placement of the Flood/post-Flood boundary at the Cretaceous/Tertiary boundary.

Of particular relevance is the observation that subsequent to the burial of the fossils found in the uppermost Cretaceous strata, all of the large reptiles, including the dinosaurs became extinct (Figure 8), along with pterosaurs and the swimming reptiles such as plesiosaurs, ichthyosaurs, and others, as well as many types of marine invertebrates. On the other hand, whereas mammal and bird fossils are rarely found in Cretaceous and earlier strata, mammal and bird fossils are abundant, more common, and diverse in Tertiary strata (Figure 9). Indeed, the fossils of mammals are used as index fossils to define the various biostratigraphic stages in Tertiary strata, and to correlate those strata between sedimentary basins on all the continents. Furthermore, in ascending the sequence of Tertiary strata, the numbers of contained fossils of fish, amphibians, reptiles, birds, and mammals, and indeed also many of the invertebrate fossils, that are identical to their modern counterparts increase (Figures 10 and 11, after Brand 1997), implying a lineage connection between the fossil and living populations. In fact, the subdivisions of the Tertiary geologic record were originally determined by Charles Lyell on the basis of the percentages of extant mollusk fossils (Berry 1968).

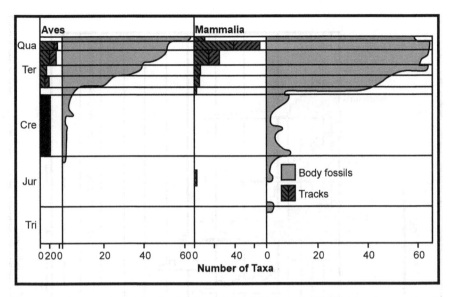

Figure 9. The stratigraphic distribution of fossil bird and mammal tracks, and body fossils (after Brand and Florence 1982).

This is supported in two ways. First, a large number of mammal families have their fossil record and modern distribution limited to only one continent. For example, kangaroos are only found in Australia, and so are their fossils, in upper Tertiary strata. It hardly makes sense to suggest that the kangaroo fossils represent kangaroos buried within the Flood, and that the extant kangaroos are thus only back in Australia after having traveled there from the Ark after the Flood. On the contrary, it is logical that the kangaroo fossils represent kangaroos that were buried by local catastrophes after the kangaroos traveled to Australia from the Ark after the Flood. Thus, the upper Tertiary strata containing kangaroo fossils must be post-Flood, and the Flood/post-Flood boundary is therefore farther down in the strata record. Second, it is within the Tertiary strata that we find stratomorphic series of mammal fossils that have been interpreted as representing post-Flood intrabaraminic diversification (Wise 1994b, 1995). Confirmation of this comes from a baraminological analysis of nineteen fossil equid (horse) species, which found that they all belonged to a single monobaramin ("created kind") (Cavanaugh, Wood, and Wise 2003). The earliest of these fossil equids is found in Eocene strata, so since these fossil equids are apparently related to one another genetically as a stratomorphic series, they can be interpreted as rapid post-Flood genetic diversification.

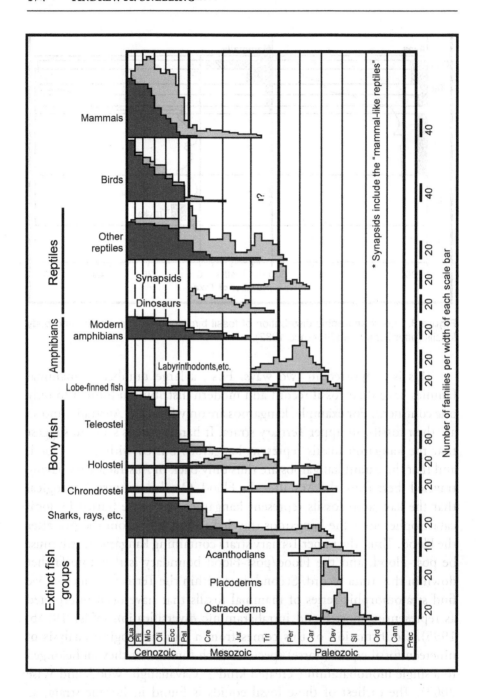

Figure 10. The stratigraphic distribution of major groups of vertebrates and plants in the fossil record, showing the distribution of extant (darker gray) and extinct (lighter gray) forms, and the stratigraphic ranges of dinosaur families (adapted from Brand 1997).

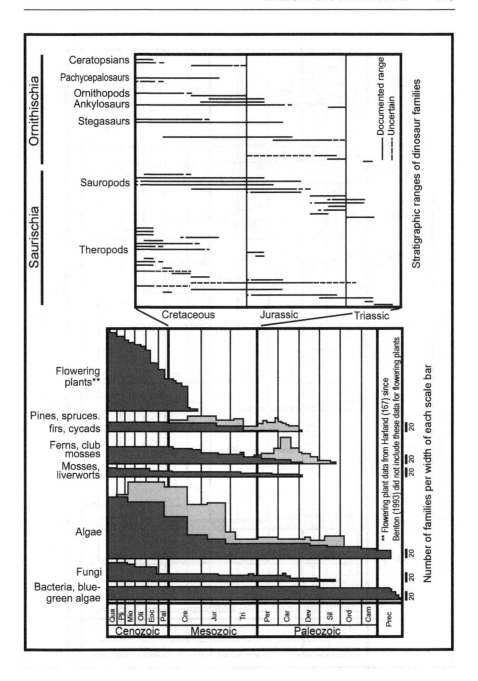

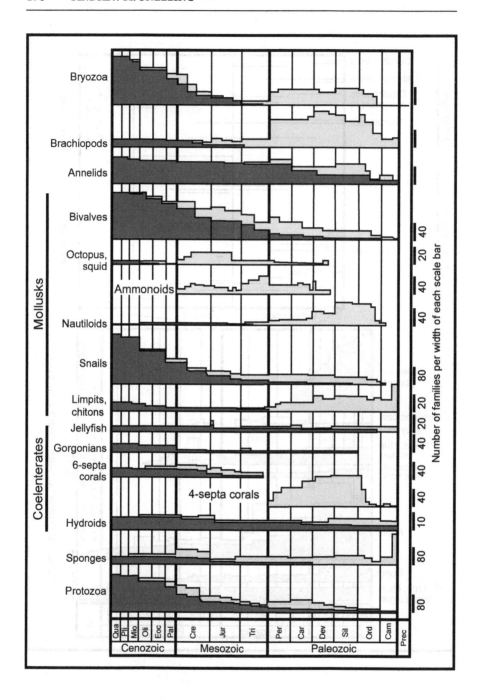

Figure 11. The stratigraphic distribution of major groups of invertebrate animals in the fossil record, showing the distribution of extant (darker gray) and extinct (lighter gray) forms (adapted from Brand 1997).

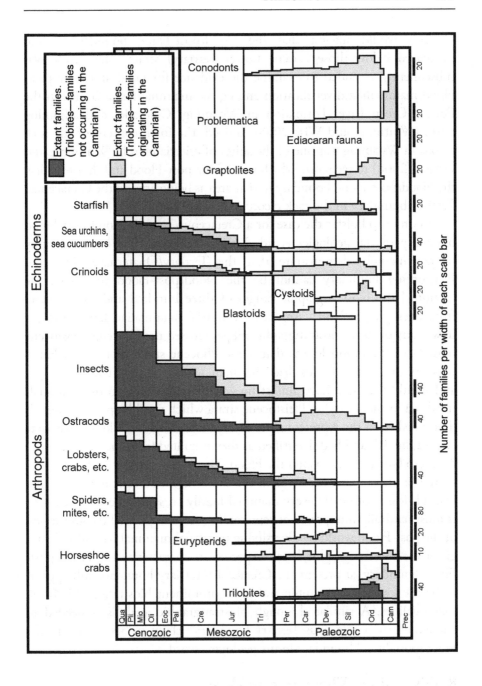

This would suggest that the Flood/post-Flood boundary should be placed below those Eocene (lower Tertiary) strata. That study was subsequently extended to examine the evidence for rapid and early post-Flood mammalian diversification among the mammal fossils buried in the Eocene Green River Formation in Wyoming, Colorado, and adjoining states (Whitmore and Wise 2008). Indeed, the fossil content of the rock record in Wyoming was one of the suites of criteria used by Whitmore and Garner (2008) to recognize which strata were post-Flood and thus establish the Flood/post-Flood boundary in that area as being around the Cretaceous/Tertiary boundary in the rock record.

In order to bolster the case for a Cretaceous/Tertiary Flood/post-Flood boundary in the geologic record, Ross (2012) has used biostratigraphy to convincingly demonstrate that the Tertiary/Quaternary (Pliocene/Pleistocene) boundary cannot be the Flood/post-Flood boundary. He examined the biostratigraphic ranges of three hundred and three genera from twenty-eight North American terrestrial mammalian families to see how many of those biostratigraphic ranges crossed the Pliocene/Pleistocene boundary. The rationale was that if the Pliocene strata represented Flood deposits the mammals fossilized in them would be pre-Flood mammals and should therefore have almost no genetic connection to the mammals fossilized in the overlying Pleistocene strata which would represent animals descended from the representatives of each of the mammal kinds that were aboard the Ark and had diversified as they migrated from the mountains of Ararat to North America after the Flood. The data he presented do not show there is a biostratigraphic break at the Pliocene/Pleistocene boundary, and instead, fossils of nearly every mammal family cross that boundary, which is most naturally interpreted as representing time-sequential recolonization of the post-Flood world by diversifying terrestrial mammal baramins. Thus, given the biostratigraphic break expected to characterize the Flood/post-Flood boundary, at present the Cretaceous/Tertiary boundary still appears to be the lowest stratigraphic and most prominent biostratigraphic break that qualifies. A similar thorough biostratigraphic analysis is needed to strengthen the Cretaceous/Tertiary boundary's claim to best represent the Flood/post-Flood boundary in the geologic record.

8. Discussion: Where to from Here?

Old Testament scholars generally divide the chronology of the Flood into two periods—the one hundred fifty days when the Floodwaters were prevailing, and the subsequent two hundred twenty-one days when the

Floodwaters were subsiding (Barrick and Sigler 2003; Barrick 2008). Most would therefore regard Day 150 as the time when the Floodwaters reached their maximum height, having totally inundated the earth and wiped out all land-dwelling, air-breathing animals. In this view some have suggested that the first forty days of intense global rain raised the Floodwaters to the level where on Day 40 they lifted up the Ark from off the ground, so that for the next one hundred ten days it floated freely across the surface of the Floodwaters.

This issue of when the Floodwaters reached their peak before then seeming to subside and drain off the newly emerging land surfaces is crucial, because it would mark the complete decimation of all land-dwelling, air-breathing life. This in turn has implications for what animals might be expected to be fossilized in the rock record at this point during the Flood. If the peak height of the Floodwaters was instead reached on Day 40 of the Flood, rather than Day 150, and then the waters were sustained at that peak level until Day 150 before they then began to subside, then we might expect that it would be hard for land-dwelling, air-breathing animals swept away by the Floodwaters to survive in the Floodwaters for long beyond Day 40. Again, this has implications for when during the Flood the land-dwelling, air-breathing animals would have been buried and fossilized in the rock record, and therefore for our ability to identify which levels in the rock and fossil records represent Days 40 and 150 of the Flood catastrophe.

There are a number of relevant considerations here that can be gleaned from the rock and fossil records. First is the relative sea level during accumulation of the geologic record, as determined by how much of the earth's surface was covered while the various rock layers were being deposited. This relative sea level curve is depicted in Figures 9 and 10 of **Chapter 5**. These figures show that the relative sea level reached its last greatest peak near the end of the Cretaceous, then after some brief fluctuations rapidly fell. It makes sense then to potentially equate the upper Cretaceous sea level peak with Day 150 of the Flood, except that there is relatively much less thickness and volume of rock layers in the geologic record above that level to be accounted for by the two hundred twenty-one days of the subsiding waters of the Flood. This is why Holt (1996) suggested there may a whole missing section of the rock record at the Cretaceous-Tertiary boundary, which he called the Erodozoic because of the massive erosion that would have occurred as the Floodwaters retreated. Nevertheless, the end of the Cretaceous is very significant in the fossil record, because it marks the last major global mass extinction event that is alleged to have wiped out the dinosaurs and many other land-dwelling and sea-dwelling creatures. In the rock record it also corresponds to the end of deposition of the fifth of the megasequences (the Zuni), the last whose strata extend across the North American continent.

A further intriguing observation from this relative sea level curve is that there was a similar high peaking of relative sea level very early in the geologic record of the Flood at the end of the so-called Cambrian after deposition of the Sauk megasequence (**Chapter 5**, Figures 9 and 10). Indeed, after that peak in the relative sea level so early in the Flood the water levels appear to have fluctuated but dropped progressively, that is relative to land surfaces, until rising again late in the Flood to peak in the so-called late Cretaceous. Of course, there are numerous assumptions involved in constructing this relative sea level curve, and the relative levels of land surfaces would similarly have fluctuated because of the earth movements during the Flood. Nevertheless, if this relative sea level curve is a guide, then this pattern would seem to best equate with the waters of the Flood peaking by Day 40, corresponding to the peak at the end of the so-called Cambrian, and then fluctuating through the following one hundred ten days of the Flood until peaking again on Day 150, equated with the so-called late Cretaceous.

This scenario raises other intriguing questions. If the Floodwaters peaked after the first forty days, by which time the Sauk megasequence had been deposited right across what is now the North American continent and beyond (Snelling 2010b), then where were the animals that were buried and fossilized in subsequent overlying rock layers living after that peaking of the global inundation? The first land-dwelling, air-breathing animals are not found fossilized until higher in the rock sequences in approximately the so-called Pennsylvanian and above, and these are in rock sequences stacked on top of the Cambrian Sauk megasequence. If the land-dwelling, air-breathing animals were swept away by the rising Floodwaters during the first forty days of the Flood while the Sauk megasequence was being deposited across North America, then unless they had other places to go, or lived in other places, they would have had to survive in the Floodwaters while they fluctuated over the subsequent one hundred ten days until all such life was finally extinguished and/or buried by the time of the late Cretaceous peaking of the relative sea level. We do of course know that some creatures did survive in the Floodwaters and found places to leave behind their footprints in temporarily exposed wet sediment surfaces higher up in the rock layer sequences as the Flood progressed from Day 40 onwards. So clearly, all land-dwelling, air-breathing animals were not dead by Day 40 of the Flood, even if there was a peaking of the relative sea level at that time. But even then it is unclear whether all land surfaces all around the earth were inundated at that peaking of relative sea level on Day 40, when all the land-dwelling, air-breathing animals were yet to be buried and fossilized over the coming weeks and months higher in the rock layer sequences deposited by the continually fluctuating and rising Floodwaters until Day 150. Yet some creatures were not fossilized until the last major extinction at the very end of the Cretaceous as the water levels were dropping, although many of those could have been the carcasses of drowned animals.

There are pre-Flood rocks exposed today at some of the continental land surfaces, such as in the Pilbara and Yilgarn cratons of Western Australia and the Superior craton of Canada. We have no way of knowing whether these areas once had Flood rocks covering them, which were then completely eroded away by the retreating Floodwaters, or whether these are pre-Flood remnants that were just further eroded by the Floodwaters. If the latter were the case, then these could have been areas that were still above relative sea level well into the Flood where animals could have survived until the earth was totally inundated on Day 150.

Thus the fossil record leaves us with many unanswered questions. Not only might some of these be elucidated by ongoing original research and lateral thinking, but light could well be shed on them from an ongoing study of the Hebrew text of the Flood account. Critical to this is determining when the Floodwaters peaked and whether the text indicates at what point all animals "in whose nostrils is the breath of life" perished. Additionally, understanding the nuances of some of the Hebrew verbs describing the action of the Floodwaters would help us fit the pieces of the puzzle together to explain the fluctuating water levels responsible for deposition of the megasequences across the continents and the successive burial of different ecosystems as the Flood progressed.

9. Conclusion

The Apostle Peter wrote a warning, that just as surely as God judged the world the first time by a water cataclysm, so coming soon the next time God will judge by fire (2 Pt 3:6–7). God could have used the Floodwaters to obliterate all trace of the pre-Flood world and its biosphere. Instead, He allowed the Floodwaters to progressively destroy the pre-Flood world and to progressively bury the creatures and plants that inhabited it as a reminder of His judgment on man's rebellion and sin, and as a warning of the next coming fire judgment.

The fossil record is thus preserved for our instruction. There is much to be gleaned from it regarding the pre-Flood biosphere, and regarding the passage and behavior of the Floodwaters. As discussed, when viewed as the burial order of the Flood, the fossil record preserves not only jumbled masses of broken and fossilized creatures in graveyards within sedimentary layers spread right across the continents, but the buried remains of pre-Flood ecological zones and whole biological communities (called biomes) that must have been spatially separated in the pre-Flood world by geography and elevation. Even the behavior and mobility of many creatures are preserved in the fossilized tracks, traces, and footprints at various levels in the rock record, being remnants of their activities as the Floodwaters advanced and fluctuated.

However, there are many questions still to be resolved, some of which require insights that only the Hebrew text of the Genesis Flood account might provide. It is crucial we know the chronology of the Flood, and specifically when did the waters peak, before then presumably starting to wane from Day 150 onwards. Furthermore, can the Hebrew words describing the Floodwaters and their actions give us clues to aid our interpretation of the fossil record, specifically, could many creatures have survived in the Floodwaters for some time after being swept away, perhaps even clinging to or floating on debris, and when was all life presumably extinguished? It is the expectation of Bible-believing palaeontologists that the ongoing study of the BH text will provide new aids to our understanding of the lessons in the fossil record God has provided for our instruction.

References

Ager, D. V. 1973. *The nature of the stratigraphical record*. London, England: Macmillan.

Ager, D. V. 1993. *The new catastrophism: The importance of the rare event in geological history*. Cambridge, England: Cambridge University Press.

Austin, S. A., ed. 1994. *Grand Canyon: Monument to catastrophe*, 21–56. Santee, CA: Institute for Creation Research.

Austin, S. A., J. R. Baumgardner, D. R. Humphreys, A. A. Snelling, L. Vardiman, and K. P. Wise. 1994. Catastrophic plate tectonics: A global Flood model of earth history. In *Proceedings of the third International Conference on Creationism*. Ed. R. E. Walsh, 609–621. Pittsburgh, PA: Creation Science Fellowship.

Austin, S. A., and K. P. Wise. 1994. The pre-Flood/Flood boundary: As defined in Grand Canyon, Arizona and eastern Mojave Desert, California. In *Proceedings of the third International Conference on Creationism*. Ed. R. E. Walsh, 37–47. Pittsburgh, PA: Creation Science Fellowship.

Barrick, W. D. 2008. Noah's Flood and its geological implications. In *Coming to grips with Genesis*. Ed. T. Mortenson, and T. H. Ury, 251–281. Green Forest, AR: Master Books.

Barrick, W. D., and R. Sigler. 2003. Hebrew and geologic analyses of the chronology and parallelism of the Flood: Implications for interpretation of the geologic record. In *Proceedings of the fifth International Conference on Creationism*. Ed. R. L. Ivey Jr., 397–408. Pittsburgh, PA: Creation Science Fellowship.

Berry, W. D. N. 1968. *Growth of a prehistoric timescale: Based on organic evolution*, 103–114. San Francisco, CA: W. H. Freeman and Company.

Beus, S. S., and M. Morales, eds. 2003. *Grand Canyon geology*. 2nd ed., 39–75, 90–221. New York, NY: Oxford University Press.

Brand, L. R., and J. Florence. 1982. Stratigraphic distribution of vertebrate fossil footprints compared with body fossils. *Origins* 9: 67–74.

Brand, L. R. 1997. *Faith, reason, and earth history*. Berrien Springs, MI: Andrews University Press.

Brand, L. R. 2009. *Faith, reason and earth history*. 2nd ed. Berrien Springs, MI: Andrews University Press.

Cavanaugh, D. P., C. T. Wood, and K. P. Wise. 2003. Fossil equidae: A monobaraminic stratomorphic series. In *Proceedings of the fifth International Conference on Creationism*, ed. R. L. Ivey Jr., 143–153. Pittsburgh, PA: Creation Science Fellowship.

Clark, H. W. 1946. *The new diluvialism*. Angwin, CA: Science Publications.

Coffin, H. G. 1983. *Origin by design*. Hagerstown, MD: Review and Herald Publishing Association.

Coffin, H. G., R. H. Brown, and R. J. Gibson. 2005. *Origin by design*. Rev. ed., as used in Chapter 5, page 130. Hagerstown, MD: Review and Herald Publishing Association.

Cowen, R. 2000. *History of life*. 3rd ed. Oxford, England: Blackwell Scientific Publications.

Eldridge, N., and S. J. Gould.1972. Punctuated equilibria: An alternative to phyletic gradualism. In *Mammals in paleobiology*. Ed. T. J. M. Schopf, 82–115. San Francisco, CA: Freeman, Cooper and Company.

Gould, S. J., and N. Eldridge. 1977. Punctuated equilibria: The tempo and mode of evolution reconsidered. *Paleobiology* 3: 115–151.

Gould, S. J., and N. Eldridge. 1993. Punctuated equilibrium comes of age. *Nature* 366: 223–27.

Holt, R. D. 1996. Evidence for a late Cainozoic Flood/post-Flood boundary. *Creation Ex Nihilo Technical Journal* 10.1: 128–167.

Krumbein, W. C., and L. L. Sloss. 1963. *Stratigraphy and sedimentation*. 2nd ed., 198. San Francisco, CA: W. H. Freeman and Company.

Lindberg, F. A. 1986. *Correlation of stratigraphic units of North America (COSUNA): Correlation charts series*. Tulsa, OK: American Association of Petroleum Geologists.

Neuendorf, K. E., J. P. Mehl, Jr., and J. A. Jackson, eds. 2005. *Glossary of geology.* 5th ed., 251. Alexandria, VA: American Geological Institute.

Oard, M. J. 1990. *An Ice Age caused by the Genesis Flood.* El Cajon, CA: Institute for Creation Research.

Oard, M. J. 1996. Where is the Flood/post-Flood boundary in the rock record? *Creation Ex Nihilo Technical Journal* 10.2: 258–278.

Oard, M. J. 2007. Defining the Flood/post-Flood boundary in sedimentary rocks, *Journal of Creation* 21.1: 98–110.

Ross, M. R. 2012. Evaluating potential post-Flood boundaries with biostratigraphy— the Pliocene/Pleistocene boundary. *Journal of Creation* 26.2: 82–87.

Sigler, R., and C. V. Wingerden. 1998. Submarine flow and slide deposits in the Kingston Peak Formation, Kingston Range, Mojave Desert, California: Evidence for catastrophic initiation of Noah's Flood. In *Proceedings of the fourth International Conference on Creationism.* Ed. R. E. Walsh, 487–501. Pittsburgh, PA: Creation Science Fellowship.

Sloss, L. L. 1963. Sequences in the cratonic interior of North America. *Geological Society of America Bulletin* 74: 93–114.

Snelling, A. A. 2006. *Wollemia nobilis*: A living fossil and evolutionary enigma. *Impact* #394. Santee, CA: Institute for Creation Research.

Snelling, A. A. 2008a. Transcontinental rock layers. *Answers* 3.3: 80–83.

Snelling, A. A. 2008b. Doesn't the order of fossils in the rock record favor long ages? In *The New Answers Book 2.* Ed. K. A. Ham, 341–354. Green Forest, AR: Master Books.

Snelling, A. A. 2009. *Earth's catastrophic past: Geology, Creation and the Flood.* Dallas, TX: Institute for Creation Research.

Snelling, A. A. 2010a. Order in the fossil record. *Answers* 5.1: 64–68.

Snelling, A. A. 2010b. The geology of Israel within the biblical Creation-Flood framework of history: 2. The Flood rocks. *Answers Research Journal* 3: 267–309.

Snelling, A. A. 2012. Did meteors trigger Noah's Flood? *Answers* 7.1: 68–71.

Spencer, W. R. 1998. Catastrophic bombardment surrounding the Genesis Flood. In *Proceedings of the fourth International Conference on Creationism.* Ed. R. E. Walsh, 553–566. Pittsburgh, PA: Creation Science Fellowship.

Stanley, S. M. 1989. *Earth and life through time.* 2nd ed. New York, NY: W. H. Freeman and Company.

Walker, T. B. 1994. A biblical geologic model. In *Proceedings of the third International Conference on Creationism.* Ed. R. E. Walsh, 581–592. Pittsburgh, PA: Creation Science Fellowship.

Whitcomb, J. C., and H. M. Morris. 1961. *The Genesis Flood: The biblical record and its scientific implications.* Phillipsburg, NJ: Presbyterian and Reformed Publishing Company.

Whitmore, J. H., and P. Garner. 2008. Using suites of criteria to recognise pre-Flood, Flood and post-Flood strata in the rock record with application to Wyoming (USA). In *Proceedings of the sixth International Conference on Creationism.*

Ed. A. A. Snelling, 425–448. Pittsburgh, PA: Creation Science Fellowship and Dallas, TX: Institute for Creation Research.

Whitmore, J. H., and K. P. Wise. 2008. Rapid and early post-Flood mammalian diversification evidence in the Green River Formation. In *Proceedings of the sixth International Conference on Creationism*. Ed. A. A. Snelling, 449–457. Pittsburgh, PA: Creation Science Fellowship and Dallas, TX: Institute for Creation Research.

Wingerden, C. V. 2003. Initial Flood deposits of the western North American Cordillera: California, Utah and Idaho. In *Proceedings of the fifth International Conference on Creationism*. Ed. R. L. Ivey Jr., 349–357. Pittsburgh, PA: Creation Science Fellowship.

Wise, K. P. 1992. The fossil record: The ultimate test case for young-earth creationism. *Opus: A Journal for Interdisciplinary Studies* 1991–92: 17–29.

Wise, K. P. 1994a. Quoted in J. D. Morris, *The young earth*, 70. Green Forest, AR: Master Books.

Wise, K. P. 1994b. *Australopithecus ramidus* and the fossil record. *Creation Ex Nihilo Technical Journal* 8.2: 160–65

Wise, K. P. 1995. Towards a creationist understanding of "transitional forms." *Creation Ex Nihilo Technical Journal* 9.2: 216–222.

Wise, K. P. 2002. *Faith, form, and time*, 170–75. Nashville, TN: Broadman and Holman.

Wise, K. P. 2003a. The hydrothermal biome: A pre-Flood environment. In *Proceedings of the fifth International Conference on Creationism*. Ed. R. L. Ivey Jr., 359–370. Pittsburgh, PA: Creation Science Fellowship.

Wise, K. P. 2003b. The pre-Flood floating forest: A study in paleontological pattern recognition. In *Proceedings of the fifth International Conference on Creationism*. Ed. R. L. Ivey Jr., 371–381. Pittsburgh, PA: Creation Science Fellowship.

Wise, K. P. 2008a. Sinking a floating forest. *Answers* 3.4: 40–45.

Wise, K. P. 2008b. Exotic communities buried by the Flood. *Answers* 3.4: 44–45.

Wise, K. P., and A. A. Snelling. 2005. A note on the pre-Flood/Flood boundary in the Grand Canyon. *Origins* 58: 7–29.

PART III

THE VOYAGE BEGINS:

INVESTIGATION

FIRST SECTION

WEIGHING ANCHOR:
CHRONOLOGICAL SCENARIOS
AND TEXT

זֶה ׀ הַיָּם גָּדוֹל וּרְחַב יָדָיִם שָׁם־רֶמֶשׂ וְאֵין מִסְפָּר חַיּוֹת קְטַנּוֹת ־גְּדֹלוֹת׃ ²⁵

שָׁם אֳנִיּוֹת יְהַלֵּכוּן לִוְיָתָן זֶה־יָצַרְתָּ לְשַׂחֶק־בּוֹ׃ ²⁶

This is the sea, great and wide of hands.

There are the moving creatures without number,

Living things, small along with the great.

There the ships go—[and] Leviathan, whom you formed to play in it.

Once more upon the waters, yet once more!

And the waves bound beneath me as a steed

That knows his rider – welcome to their roar!

Swift be their guidance, wheresoe'er it lead!

Though the strained mast should quiver as a reed

And the rent canvas fluttering strew the gale,

Still I must on...

—Byron, from *Childe Harold's Pilgrimage*

CHAPTER 8

Waves of Opinion: The Chronology of the Flood in Literature Past and Present

Lee Anderson Jr.

Analogy and Orientation. *Anyone who has ever been in a boat on a windy day knows the effect that waves can have on a vessel. In most cases, waves move in predictable patterns and are quite manageable; however, shifting winds and underwater topography can, at times, create waves that are incredibly difficult to sail through. In certain conditions, series of waves may even cross each other, adding an additional level of hazard to sailing.*

The prevailing historical opinions surrounding the chronology of the Flood are very much analogous to waves. Each one is marked to a certain degree by a variety of assumptions concerning the text, Hebrew grammar, and biblical interpretation. Like a ship battling through choppy waters, the modern biblical scholar must navigate through these opinions on the chronology of the Flood, being careful to avoid being swept away by a mere "wave of opinion," that is, an interpretation that may appear to be correct, but is not truly warranted by the biblical text itself. The goal of this chapter is to navigate through each major historical view on the chronology of the Genesis Flood, examining the arguments given by the proponents of each position, and assessing the potential interpretive problems encountered by each view.

Abstract. A thorough study of the chronology of the Genesis Flood requires that diligent attention be given to prior literature on the subject. Literature addressing the Genesis Flood yields a considerable diversity of opinion on the chronology of the event. Liberal scholarship, built upon the fundamentally errant assumptions of the Documentary Hypothesis, posits that the Flood narrative, in its current form, is comprised of two or more sources compiled and integrated by an unknown redactor. This alleged composite narrative supposedly evidences two separate and incompatible chronological schemes (although some attempts at harmonization have been made). Such a view is untenable in light of the logical fallacies inherent to the Documentary Hypothesis, as well as the clear textual evidence attesting to Mosaic authorship. However, conservative scholarship, in adhering to a biblical view of Mosaic authorship, has made only limited efforts to address the difficulties associated with the Flood chronology or to respond to liberal attacks. To date, there remains no consensus among conservative biblical scholars regarding a proper understanding of the chronology of the Flood. Sources from the Reformation era to the present reveal three prevalent positions on the subject, as well as several other minor views. The primary differences between the various positions center upon two main factors: the day on which the Floodwaters peaked, and the duration that peak was sustained. Consideration of the presuppositions and arguments of these positions demonstrates a need for investigation of several issues, including 1) the viability of the commonly-assumed sequentiality of the *wayyiqtol* verb; 2) the timing of the stopping of the Flood mechanisms in relation to the initiation of the assuaging of the Floodwaters; 3) the precise meaning of וַיִּגְבְּרוּ, commonly translated "prevailed," specifically with regard to the common assumption of its use to indicate either the rising or the stagnation of the Floodwaters; and 4) the possibility of chronological disjunction in the Flood narrative and the factors involved in indicating where such instances of chronological disjunction may occur.

Outline

1. Introduction: The Flood, Literature, and the History of Chronological Scenarios
2. An Assessment of Textual Parameters Governing Chronological Scenarios
3. An Analysis of Chronological Scenarios: Arguments and Presuppositions
4. An Observation of Trends in the Chronological Scenarios
5. Conclusion

1. Introduction: The Flood, Literature, and the History of Chronological Scenarios

Any thorough study of the Genesis Flood must be prepared to deal with a near incalculable amount of literature on the subject spanning from ancient times to the present day. The Flood event and the theology presented in the Genesis account have always been of considerable interest to biblical scholars, and mounds of books have been written addressing the various issues contained within the biblical text. Additionally, the last five decades have also seen, at least among young-earth creationists, a renewed consideration of the scientific ramifications of the event (i.e., in relation to hydrology, geology, paleontology, etc.). This, of course, has only led to an increased influx of literature on the Flood narrative.

Given the sheer volume of material already available on the Flood, what could possibly justify the publication of another book on the subject? As already expressed in **Chapter 3**, despite the bulk of literature on the Flood, comparably little attention has been given to chronological issues. Some statistics will be discussed later in this chapter; suffice it to say for the time being, however, that the majority of sources consulted in the research of historical opinion on the chronology of the Flood were devoid of any useful chronological information. Even among the sources that did address chronology, only some provided solid argumentation in support of their respective positions. In short, there is great indifference concerning the Flood's chronology. This is terribly unfortunate.

Biblical scholar Harold Hoehner once stated, "The backbone of history is chronology" (1977, 9). Consequently, to disregard the importance of the chronology of the Genesis Flood is to invite an attack on its historicity. This is precisely what liberal critics have done. Not surprisingly, for those scholars who deny the historicity of the Flood (and, by default, attack the inspiration and authority of the biblical text), one of their major points of argumentation surrounds the alleged confusion of the account's chronology. Having the advantage of hindsight, it seems likely that the force of the liberals' arguments would have diminished greatly had those committed to the authority of Scripture given more careful consideration to the historical and chronological aspects of the text. Martin Luther's statement that certain chronological aspects of the Flood "do not matter" (1958, 152) foreshadowed a general trend in academia that hit full force centuries later. His attitude of indifference toward this pivotal subject was, unfortunately, characteristic of those who inadvertently left the door open for the takeover of theological liberalism.

Despite the general inattentiveness to the issue of chronology, there have been a fairly wide range of opinions on the subject, with multiple chronological scenarios having been proposed. Accordingly, this chapter is designed to serve as a general orientation to the array of views on the subject. Its aim is to provide an analysis of the various views on the chronology of the Flood, examining and assessing their respective arguments. In doing so, this chapter will also serve as a point of reference for some of the studies to be presented in later chapters. It is beyond the scope of this chapter to determine the accuracy of any particular position; that is a part of the purpose of this book as a whole. However, where any position is blatantly deficient in light of the irrefutable statements of Scripture, note will be made.

Prior to examining the arguments for the various positions, however, it is necessary to review certain principles governing the determination of the correct chronological scenario.

2. An Assessment of Textual Parameters Governing Chronological Scenarios

As will be demonstrated, not all views on the chronology of the Flood are equally sound. In order to avoid a metaphorical shipwreck, the navigation of these "waves of opinion" must be guided by certain non-negotiable principles. There are two areas of consideration that must frame this study of the various chronological scenarios: 1) the inspiration, unity, and coherence of the text, and 2) the five fixed dates contained in the text.

    2.1   Inspiration, Unity and Coherence of the Text
    2.2   Five Fixed Dates

2.1 *Inspiration, Unity, and Coherence of the Text*

In order to correctly understand the chronology of the Flood (or, for that matter, to properly interpret any aspect of the Flood narrative), the narrative must be regarded as a coherent unity. All of its parts (clauses, sentences, etc.) are marked by an orderly and logical relationship which affords comprehension of the narrative as a whole. It would seem that this fact ought to be assumed without question; however, with the rise of the Documentary Hypothesis in the nineteenth century and the continued rejection of the Mosaic authorship of the book of Genesis, the coherence of the Flood narrative has come under direct attack.

The Documentary Hypothesis sees in the Flood narrative two (or sometimes more) sources, woven together (rather crudely, some would argue) by a redactor. Ignoring for the moment the incongruence of this vein of liberal scholarship with the indisputably clear claims of the text itself, it must be stated that the attack on Mosaic authorship and the reinterpretation of the narrative in light of its alleged multiplicity of sources has certainly not produced any clarification whatsoever concerning the literary structure, meaning, or purpose of the Flood narrative. Furthermore, it has rendered fruitless any attempt to make sense of the chronological indicators embedded in the narrative. If anything, the Documentary Hypothesis and the subsequent theories of authorship it has spawned have led not to intellectual enlightenment, but to intellectual paralysis in the field of studies focused on Genesis.

What then is a proper approach to the Flood narrative? The Bible presents its own standard for those attempting to study it: "The beginning of wisdom is the fear of the LORD (יְרְאַת יְהוָה), and the knowledge of the Holy One is understanding" (Pr 9:10; cf. 1:7; 15:33; Ps 111:10; Jb 28:28). Including, but extending beyond, a reverent awe toward God, the "fear of the LORD" demands that one listens to, learns, and responds to God's word (Dt 4:10; cf. 8:6). Correctly interpreting any portion of biblical literature thus necessitates that the interpreter heed the Bible's own claims regarding its origin, authorship, accuracy, etc. Because the Bible is divinely inspired (2 Tm 3:16), it is by nature supremely authoritative. Therefore, any effort to understand it must begin by presupposing the accuracy of what it says (cf. Ps 119:160; Jn 17:17). While this logic is arguably circular, it is not fallacious; any supreme standard *must* be inherently authoritative, as there is no higher source of authority to which to appeal (cf. Heb 6:13). By contrast, the abandonment of biblical presuppositions will inevitably lead to futility in seeking to comprehend the Scriptures. More specifically, rejecting Mosaic authorship (contra Ex 17:14; 24:4, 7; 34:27; Nm 33:1–2; Dt 31:9, 11; etc.) and speculating about the proposed sources responsible for the Flood narrative invariably results in confusion about what the narrative is communicating. In short, conclusions concerning the chronology of the Flood must be derived from the text itself; they must not be the product of man's so-called autonomous reasoning, lest they be subject to grave error.

The point is that the text has spoken authoritatively to the fact that the Flood narrative is a single, unified, divinely-inspired account originating from the pen of a single human author. The logical consequence of this fact is that the narrative communicates a coherent chronology: there is one definite sequence of events embedded in the text which the reader must uncover.

On one hand, the unity and coherence of the Flood narrative is to be presupposed on the basis of biblical testimony; on the other hand, the unity and coherence of the Flood narrative may also be corroborated through careful study, being logically demonstrated on the basis of solid evidence. The most important piece of evidence is the Flood narrative's literary structure. Embedded in the Flood narrative is an elaborate chiasm centering on a critical theological feature: God's remembrance of Noah (Gn 8:1a). More specifically, the chronology of the Flood, far from being an unimportant, unconnected aspect of the account, is masterfully woven into the literary structure. Wenham comments,

[E]ven the chronology of the flood story becomes a vehicle for expressing theological ideas. Further, it is a chronology that embraces the whole story, not just parts of it. Thus, the evidence of chronology corroborates that of syntax and literary structure, that the Genesis flood story is a coherent unity. (1978, 345)

Wenham rightly recognizes that the chiastic structure of the Flood (inclusive of its chronological elements) simply could not have been the product of the careless compilation of multiple sources: it evidences order, unity, and coherence.

Accordingly, there is indeed observational data from the literary study of the text that agrees with the text's own claims of being a unified composition by a single author.

2.2 *Five Fixed Dates*

In addition to providing its own defense of inspiration and unity, the text gives precise chronological indicators that serve to guide the interpreter in mapping out the sequence of events contained in the narrative. Five verses present five fixed dates, respectively, which provide a framework for correctly understanding the Flood's chronology:

GENESIS 7:11
In the six hundredth year of the life of Noah, on the seventeenth day of the second month; in that day all the springs of the great deep broke forth and the windows of the heavens were opened.

GENESIS 8:4
And the ark rested on the seventeenth day of the seventh month on the mountains of Ararat.

GENESIS 8:5
And the waters continued to diminish until the tenth month. In the tenth month, on the first day of the tenth month the tops of the mountains appeared.

GENESIS 8:13
And it came to pass in the six hundred and first year, in the first month, on the first day of the month the waters dried up from upon the earth. And Noah removed the covering of the ark, and he looked, and behold, the face of the ground was dried up.

GENESIS 8:14
And in the second month, on the twenty-seventh day of the month, the earth was dry.

It must be stated that there is a wealth of chronological data in the narrative beyond these five fixed dates. However, the five fixed dates are clear statements of chronological fact, largely beyond contestation.[1] Whereas the other chronological information is subject to interpretational challenges (namely the difficulty of determining where to anchor the various chronological indicators in relation to stated dates), the five fixed dates stand independently, needing no other information to anchor them within the narrative's sequence of events.

With the inspiration, unity, and coherence of the Flood narrative already established, it can be stated that any correct understanding of the Flood's chronology must properly take into account these five fixed dates. With only occasional exception, the views encountered by this study depended upon the five fixed dates as a basic framework. However, it was in the chronological matters beyond these dates that considerable differences were noted. Of primary importance (often to the exclusion of other chronological considerations) was the timing of the peak of the Flood. As such, in the following analysis of the various chronological scenarios, the different positions are categorized according to their view on the Flood's peak.

3. An Analysis of Chronological Scenarios: Arguments and Presuppositions

Almost unavoidably in the field of biblical interpretation there will be differences of opinion. Sometimes differences result from things which can be avoided, such as poor scholarship, unwarranted conjecture, etc. While there have been, as with any topic, a few instances where sources have displayed shoddy research, it seems clear that most of the differences in interpreting the chronology of the Flood relate to differences in presuppositions. As already stated, the dividing line between the liberal position and the various conservative views stems from basic differences in foundational assumptions concerning the inspiration, inerrancy, and coherence of the Genesis record. However, within the conservative camp, there is further division due, in part, to differing presuppositions concerning Hebrew grammar.

It is not the point of this work to suggest that there ought to be division between Christians (or, more specifically, biblical creationists) over the chronology of the Flood. However, this presentation of the various views on the chronology ought to provide an impetus among both scholars and

---

1. One caveat remains, which is the matter of the calendar employed by the author (lunar, solar, etc.). However, regardless of precise calendar used, the differences in the dates offered for the five main events are only slight.

laypersons alike to be very careful in their study of the biblical text, to ensure that those presuppositions that they bring to the table are indeed warranted. It is not the goal of this chapter to argue for the superiority of any one position; however, by going over each chronological view in detail, it will inevitably expose the presuppositions inherent to each view. In later chapters, it will be necessary to examine some of these presuppositions so as to determine if they are truly warranted.

3.1   The Liberal Position: A Text in Conflict
3.2   The Conservative Positions: A Text of Complexities
3.3   Summary

3.1 *The Liberal Position: A Text in Conflict*

The liberal position has already been discussed in brief. It is characterized, most prominently, by a wholesale rejection of the unity of the Flood narrative, at least in its original form. Rooted in the Documentary Hypothesis, it argues that the Flood narrative is composed of multiple literary strands pieced together by a later redactor. It is not the point of this chapter to serve as an introduction to the Documentary Hypothesis; however, a basic overview is necessary in order to show the relevant points of contact between the view and the division of the Flood narrative into multiple sources.

In its classic form, the Documentary Hypothesis assumes that Moses did not write the Pentateuch, but rather that it is comprised of at least four sources written centuries after the life of the historical Moses and compiled by a redactor. The four sources generally submitted by the theory include the Jahwist Source (J), the Elohist Source (E), the Deuteronomist Source (D), and the Priestly Source (P). The J source was supposedly written in the ninth century BC by an unknown writer in the Southern Kingdom of Judah. Sections attributed to J include personal biographies (namely those in Genesis), as well as portions containing theology and ethics, but little revolving around sacrifice and rituals. The E source, by contrast, was allegedly the work of an unknown writer in the Northern Kingdom of Judah during the eighth century BC. The focus of the sections attributed to E concern mainly concrete particulars and little of theology. Supposedly, around the mid-seventh century BC, the J and E sources were combined by an unknown redactor to create the source J-E. Shortly thereafter, it is assumed that the D source was composed in Judah perhaps under the supervision of Josiah and the high priest Hilkiah to promote the reforms instituted by Josiah ca. 621 BC. The D source was then worked into the J-E source. Finally, the P source (written in stages beginning in roughly 570 BC to the time of Ezra) was allegedly compiled by the priests. It included the holiness code of Leviticus and puts a distinct emphasis on origins, genealogies, sacrifice, and rituals.

The main lines of reasoning used in support of this classic view include 1) the diversity of divine names, 2) the presence of variations in style, 3) so-called "doublets," and 4) the presence of Aramaisms and other "late words" (i.e., words that occur rarely in the Pentateuch but more commonly in books known to have been written later). Allegedly, this criterion evidences different strands of material underlying the tapestry of the Pentateuch.

Soon after the initial development of the Documentary Hypothesis, scholars began dividing up the Flood narrative into what they thought were its different components. In addition to the normal factors involved, the chronological aspects of the account are commonly viewed as evidencing the supposed multiplicity of sources. N. P. Lemche, for example, argues that "we have dates in the flood story not presupposing the joining of J and P" (1980, 58). It is customarily assumed that the J source presents a shorter Flood with a peak occurring at the end of the period of rain, i.e., on the fortieth day. The P Source, by contrast, supposedly presents a longer catastrophe, a Flood which peaks after a total of one hundred fifty days.

It should be noted that the majority of scholars who hold to multiple sources for the Flood narrative do so on a presuppositional level. In other words, few make it a point to argue for their position. It is assumed that the Documentary Hypothesis has been established beyond contestation and, as such, the division of the Flood narrative into multiple sources need not be defended. This perspective is sorely lacking on multiple levels.

First, the Documentary Hypothesis exhibits a number of fatal flaws, not the least of which is a marked conflict with the explicit statements of the text itself. The Pentateuch uniformly testifies to Mosaic authorship (Ex 17:14; 24:4, 7; 34:27; Nm 33:1–2; Dt 31:9, 11), as does the remainder of the Old Testament (Jo 1:7–8; 8:31–32; 1 Kgs 2:3; 2 Kgs 14:6; 21:8; Ezr 6:18; Neh 13:1; Dn 9:11–13; Mal 4:4). So too, the New Testament directly ascribes authorship of the Pentateuch to Moses (Mt 19:8; Mk 12:26; Jn 5:46–47; 7:19; Acts 3:22; Rom 10:5; Heb 10:28).[2]

Second, the Documentary Hypothesis clearly contradicts the internal evidence of the Pentateuch in relation to historical and cultural details. G. L. Archer (2007, 95–99) mentions the following:

---

2. Even if it is assumed that Jesus and the New Testament writers were merely accommodating themselves to the common view of the time (that Moses wrote the Pentateuch), it is impossible to hold to the Documentary Hypothesis without attributing to them either gross deception or considerable ignorance.

(1) The author of the Pentateuch shows attention to detail in a manner befitting one who actually partook in the incredible events described (e.g., the author's report of the geography of Elim [Ex 15:27], and his description of the appearance and taste of manna [Nm 11:7–8]).

(2) The author of the Pentateuch shows notable acquaintance with life in Egypt (names, language, etc.), such as could only be expected of a resident of Egypt from the time period in question (e.g., the Joseph narrative [Gn 37; 39–50]).

(3) The author of the Pentateuch writes from the perspective of a foreigner to the land of Canaan and as a native to the land of Egypt when referencing the flora, fauna, creatures, and geography of the Promised Land (e.g., Gn 13:10).

(4) The author of the Pentateuch describes in the books of Exodus and Numbers an environment that is unmistakably that of a desert (e.g., Lv 16:10), which is inconsistent with theories on the time and place of writing of the alleged sources J, E, D, and P.

(5) The author of the Pentateuch, namely in the book of Genesis, references archaic customs which did not continue until the alleged time of the writing of J, E, D, or P (e.g., his detailed account of the purchase of a cave in Machpelah [Gn 23] and his assumption of the validity of the oral deathbed will [Gn 49]).

(6) The author of the Pentateuch uses archaic Hebrew words and phrases inconsistent with Hebrew literature known to be of a later time (most notably the spelling of the pronoun "she" with a *waw* instead of a *yodh*). Such bizarre usages cannot be explained apart from the assumption that the text is genuinely ancient.

(7) The author of the Pentateuch arranged the entire work as a progressive whole, evidencing multiple stages of revelation—something utterly inexplicable from the perspective of the Documentary Hypothesis.

Third, the Documentary Hypothesis exhibits a considerable number of obvious logical fallacies. Archer (2007, 91–93) points out many of these, including the nine listed here:

(1) The Documentary Hypothesis is "characterized by a subtle species of circular reasoning; it tends to posit its conclusion (the Bible is no supernatural revelation) as its underlying premise (there can be no such thing as supernatural revelation)."

(2) The Documentary Hypothesis is "allegedly based upon the evidence of the text itself, and yet the evidence of the text is consistently evaded whenever it happens to go counter to the theory" (note, for instance, the roughly two dozen aforementioned references to Mosaic authorship scattered throughout the Old and New Testaments).

(3) The Documentary Hypothesis assumes "that Hebrew authors differ from any other writers known in the history of literature in that they alone were incapable of using more than one name for God; more than one style of writing, no matter what the difference in subject matter; or more than one of several possible synonyms for a single idea; or even more than one theme-type or circle of interest."

(4) The Documentary Hypothesis exhibits subjective bias "in the treatment of the Hebrew Scriptures as archeological evidence. All too frequently the tendency has been to regard any biblical statement as unreliable and suspect, though the very antiquity of the Old Testament (even by the critics' own dating) should commend it for consideration as an archeological document."

(5) The Documentary Hypothesis starts "with the pure assumption . . . that Israel's religion was of merely human origin like any other religion, and that it was to be explained as a mere product of evolution."

(6) The Documentary Hypothesis assumes, in the case of a so-called "discrepancy," that no means of reconciliation exists. Rather, it exploits all such instances so as to "prove" diversity of sources.

(7) The Documentary Hypothesis assumes that "although other ancient Semitic literatures show multiplied instances of repetition and duplication by the same author in their narrative technique, Hebrew literature alone cannot show any such repetitions or duplications without betraying diverse authorships."

(8) The Documentary Hypothesis presumes to date with a high degree of certainty the time of the composition of each of the documents allegedly comprising the Pentateuch despite the absence of any contemporaneous Hebrew literature with which to compare them.

(9) The Documentary Hypothesis assumes most ironically "that scholars living more than three thousand four hundred years after the event can (largely on the basis of philosophical theories) more reliably reconstruct the way things really happened than could the ancient authors themselves (who were removed from the events in question by no more than six hundred or one thousand years, even by the critics' own dating)."

Despite these arguments, the Documentary Hypothesis is still the mode within academia. The glaring question, however, is whether that should remain the case. The Documentary Hypothesis is so incredibly fallacious that none of its tenets can or should be employed in this study.

The majority of the more liberal interpreters (e.g., Driver, von Rad, etc.) see in the Flood narrative the presence of two sources, J and P. However, some, such as Lemche, posit the presence of at least three (1980, 52–62).

The precise number of sources, however, is wholly inconsequential, as the presuppositions are equally flawed in either case. Any attempt to reconstruct the chronology of the Genesis Flood from the standpoint of the presuppositions advanced by the Documentary Hypothesis is doomed to failure because, as the foregoing overview has demonstrated, those very presuppositions are fundamentally errant.

Notably, a few scholars holding to the Documentary Hypothesis have attempted to maintain the consistency of the chronological record. For example, both F. H. Cryer (1985) and L. M. Barré (1988) strive to reconcile the two allegedly differing records comprising the Flood narrative.[3] However, the fact remains that any attempt to study the chronology of the Flood from the perspective of the Documentary Hypothesis will ultimately result in futility. A correct chronological view simply cannot be discovered by employing errant presuppositions.

Consequently, can anything at all be learned from the arguments of those holding to the Documentary Hypothesis? The answer needs to be a cautious "yes." While the ultimate *conclusions* of the liberal interpreters may be subject to considerable error, that does not mean that all of their *observations* are invalid. They are correct in that some of the chronological information in the Flood narrative is complicated, and may even appear contradictory. For example, on one hand, Genesis 7:12 indicates that rain fell upon the earth for forty days; on the other hand, Genesis 7:24 states that the waters "prevailed" for a total of one hundred fifty days. While the liberal interpreters have erred in their conclusion that these verses represent separate, incompatible chronological outlooks, it must be admitted that such seeming chronological contradictions are truly challenging to reconcile (at least when examined from the standpoint of the traditional perspective

---

3. These efforts fall markedly short in their attempt to produce a usable chronology. In their respective works, neither Cryer nor Barré presume to be studying an actual historical record. Cryer concludes that the dates listed in reference to the Flood comprise two overlapping methods of tracking duration, which are in harmony with each other (1985, 254). That being said, he argues that the dates are purely arithmetical and schematic; he does not attempt to relate the system to the event, nor does he postulate how the dates work in relation to the peak of the Flood or the assuaging of the waters. Barré likewise seeks to reconcile the two alleged sources, arguing that the Floodwaters rose for the totality of the initial one hundred fifty days and that the beginning of the decrease was not until Genesis 8:3 (thus, the sequentiality of the *wayyiqtol* is assumed). Genesis 7:19 is taken to mark the midpoint of the first one hundred fifty days, whereas Genesis 8:5 is taken to mark the midpoint of the second one hundred fifty day set. As a result, Barré's chart (1988, 12) shows a high level of structure, with the high point directly in the middle of the Flood (after one hundred fifty days), but it fails to take into account the fact that it is a real event being described.

on Hebrew grammar). The interpreter must not naïvely assume that the Flood narrative is laid out in an overly simplistic and straightforward fashion devoid of any intricasies. The answer to the perceived difficulties, however, is not to attribute alleged contradictions to flaws in the authorship of the narrative, but rather to humbly admit that there is still much in the biblical text that remains beyond the comprehension of even the most skilled modern scholar, and then to forge ahead in careful study, employing appropriate tools and methods in an effort to determine how seemingly contradictory statements in the text do in fact fit together.

3.2 The Conservative Positions: A Text of Complexities

Opposed to the liberals' presuppositional conjecture that the Flood narrative presents an incoherent chronology, conservative expositors and theologians have seen in the Flood narrative a complex chronological structure that presents the progression of a catastrophic event from its beginning, to its climax, to its end. In this perspective, as already discussed, the five fixed dates (Gn 7:11; 8:4, 5, 13, 14) are viewed as major markers which serve to highlight the most important events and tie them to an absolute chronology. Beyond these fixed dates, however, there are a variety of different interpretations of the Flood's chronology, each with a different view on the Flood's peak and the ensuing decline of the water's level.

A comprehensive study of the chronology of the Genesis Flood necessitates that each of these views be traced back to its origin. However, after embarking on this task, it soon became evident that the sheer bulk of the literature was prohibitive to the discussion of so general a topic. Instead, it has proved prudent to discuss in the present chapter the various prevailing modern views. It is the goal of the members of this collaborative study to discuss at length the origin of these views in a later volume (for at least three of the views can be traced back to the dawn of the Reformation or earlier, suggesting that they may be very old indeed). For the purposes of the present chapter and its discussion of modern views on the subject, the modern era is defined as the period of roughly five centuries since the advent of the Reformation triggered by Luther's writings in 1517. Although this date may seem a somewhat arbitrary division between "modern" and "pre-modern" works, it serves to allow this chapter to view as a collective whole all the writings since the time of Luther's unfortunate statement about the chronology of the Flood (see page 191) and determine how pervasive such an attitude is within modern research. Additionally, the simple fact remains that if the Reformation is not considered a reasonable divider between modern and pre-modern works, there remains no other monumental event in the history of the church (at least within the last several hundred years) to serve as an effective marker. Thus, this division is both strategic and practical.

3.2.1 Position 1: Peak at One Hundred Fifty Days
3.2.2 Position 2: Peak at Forty Days
3.2.3 Position 3: Peak at Forty Days Sustained until One Hundred Fifty Days
3.2.4 Alternative Positions

3.2.1 Position 1: Peak at One Hundred Fifty Days

By far the most common position among conservative scholars on the chronology of the Flood is that the peak occurred on the one hundred fiftieth day. Indeed, sources promoting this view account for well over twenty percent of those consulted in this study. Before proceeding on to a consideration of the presuppositions and arguments employed by this position, however, it is only fair to note that a large portion of the sources which hold to this view offered no reasoned defense of the position. (Into this category fall a number of lighter, devotionally oriented commentaries on the book of Genesis, as well as, more surprisingly, heftier, well-respected works by A. P. Ross, along with B. K. Waltke and C. J. Fredricks.) Accordingly, as with any subject, in the overall evaluation of the different views on the Flood's chronology, it must be understood that the correctness of a position does not relate directly to the quantity of the sources backing it.

Undoubtedly, the most comprehensive work taking this view on the Flood's chronology is that of W. D. Barrick and R. Sigler, and it is therefore the intent of this chapter to carefully survey the arguments they present and the assumptions they hold. Other notable works backing this view include those of M. Kline, K. A. Mathews, H. M. Morris, and C. Westermann, as well as (despite their noticeable bent toward the viability of the Documentary Hypothesis) J. Skinner and G. J. Wenham (for details on these works, see **Appendix A**).

Barrick and Sigler hold that the first forty days of the Flood are included in the one hundred fifty days of "prevailing" and are followed by two hundred twenty-two days of subsidence. Plainly evident in this chronological scheme is the assumption that the *wayyiqtol* verb form is to be understood as strictly sequential. Their idea that the Ark was unmoved until the fortieth day of the Flood is rare; however, the idea represents the inevitable conclusion of the consistent application of the understanding of the sequentiality of the *wayyiqtol*. Barrick and Sigler remark (2003, 403),

There are two main phases: 150 days of prevailing waters and 221 days of receding waters. The ark was lifted off the earth on the 40th day. After this the waters kept rising until the Antediluvian (pre-Flood) mountains were submerged. Then all land-dwelling, air-breathing creatures were destroyed. By the end of the 150th day only those in ark [sic] were left (7:23).

Similarly, within this perspective, the rain continued for one hundred fifty days, not forty. In support of this view, they argue (2003, 401),

Based on a misunderstanding of 7:4, it is a common misconception that rain (and the whole Flood for that matter) ceased after 40 days. In reality the detailed account of the Flood in 7:11–24 is an expansion of the generalized prophecy of 7:4. It is sequential also: that all life would be destroyed at some point after the 40th day as clearly revealed in 7:11–24. Neither the single verse (7:4) nor the detailed expansion (7:11–24) claim that rain would cease after 40 days. Just as Flood models based upon isolated key word studies are mistaken, so are geologic models based on 7:4 alone.

Barrick and Sigler are not the only ones who maintain that the rain continued beyond the fortieth day of the Flood. Also holding to a peak on the one hundred fiftieth day, H. F. Vos (1982, 317) writes more concisely, "It poured for 40 days and nights, during which time the waters rapidly covered the earth. Evidently, it continued to rain lighter for another 110 days, making a total of 40 + 110 or 150 days of rain (7:24; cf. 8:4)." Such a perspective is also very popular among those arguing for a peak on the fortieth day that was then sustained until the one hundred fiftieth day (see, for instance, the work by A. Heidel, listed in the **Appendix A**). Thus, a second major presupposition is evident: namely, that Genesis 7:12 (cf. 7:4) does not argue for a cessation of the rain after the fortieth day.

In consistency with this perspective, the water is viewed as continuing to rise after the initial forty days. In support of this, וַיִּגְבְּרוּ in 7:17b is taken to mean "increased," and relates to the increase following the forty days. Thus, the general succession of events during the first one hundred fifty days of the Flood can be viewed as follows:

From day 1 torrential rain and flooding caused the water level to increase and rise. On the 40th day the water level was sufficient to lift the ark off the ground surface (Genesis 7:17).... After this, the waters increased greatly so that the ark floated freely on the water surface (7:18). Then the waters continued to rise and all the pre-Flood mountains were covered (7:19–20). After the highest regions became submerged, all flesh (all land-dwelling, air-breathing creatures) died (7:21). The significance of the first 40 days (7:12, 17) is with raising the ark off the ground surface, not when the rain stopped and not when the land creatures died. (Barrick and Sigler 2003, 401)

Specifically concerning the peak of the Flood, Barrick and Sigler state, "Genesis 8:1 marks the turning point in the Flood. When the mechanisms cease at the end of 150 days, the writer describes a constant back and forth motion of the waters as they return to a relatively stable state over the course of the following 165 days" (2003, 402). Arguing that the Flood mechanisms did indeed function until the one hundred fifieth day of the catastrophe, they write (2003, 406),

> Genesis 8:2 provides one of the principal contributions of the text to the chronology of the Flood. That text describes the reversal of the mechanisms that were first activated in 7:11. If language has any meaning, there can be little doubt that the biblical record presents a full 150 days in which the dual sources (rain and submarine 'fountains') continued to provide water for the flooding process.

They later state, "As indicated, the level kept rising until some day between the 40th and 150th day. The level began falling at the end of the first 150 days" (2003, 404). Of importance to young-earth paleontologists they conclude, "All land-dwelling, air-breathing creatures died by the 150th day of the Flood" (2003, 405).

Barrick and Sigler further assume that Genesis 8:1–4 is to be understood sequentially and that Genesis 8:6 is referring to forty days of progression in the event rather than serving as a summary (2003, 403). Of the time following the peak, they note,

> The second mention of 150 days in 8:3 is a reference back to the same 150 days in 7:24. The turning point in the Flood is marked in 8:1. The waters began to abate at the end of the 150th day. The waters subsided just enough to allow the ark to land on high ground—in the mountains of Ararat. This occurred at some unknown hour during day 151. The tops of the mountains emerged on day 225 (8:5). After this, a more narrow perspective of the earth's condition ensues—the perspective from Noah's viewpoint. Before 8:5 the language of the narrative is global. After the mountains appear, Noah waits 40 days. Then he sends out the birds over the next 4 weeks. The dove returned with the olive leaf on the 280th day, and did not return after it was released on the 287th day. On day 315, Noah observed that the ground surface was drying up. The earth is declared to be dry on day 371. (Barrick and Sigler 2003, 403)

This paragraph presents a perspective similar to the general line of argumentation set forth by most proponents of a peak on the one hundred fiftieth day. The very fact that Genesis 7:24 states that the waters "prevailed" for a period of one hundred fifty days is commonly understood as a closed-case argument for the rising of the Floodwaters for the totality of that period. Genesis 8:3 is often treated in a similar fashion (see in **Appendix A** the works by J. J. Davis, L. D. Edwards, A. H. Finn, A. Fuller, H. Gunkel, V. P. Hamilton [1990], J. MacArthur, K. A. Mathews, T. C. Mitchell, H. M. Morris, J. R. Rice, M. F. Unger, G. J. Wenham, and others).

In evaluation of this view, the following questions deserve to be asked: 1) Is it warranted to view the *wayyiqtol* as inherently sequential? 2) Can it be determined whether the rain (and/or other Flood mechanisms) continued beyond the fortieth day? And 3) What is the precise meaning of וַיִּגְבְּרוּ, commonly translated "prevailed"? Does it necessarily indicate that the water level was rising? The remaining chapters of this work will serve to investigate these questions.

3.2.2 Position 2: Peak at Forty Days

A minority position, but by no means lacking in careful argumentation, is the view that the peak of the Flood occurred on the fortieth day and was followed immediately by the recession of the waters. Despite being underrepresented in the modern era by comparison to the preceding view, proponents of this position have argued their case well from multiple angles. This view is perhaps best defined in terms of its differences from the preceding view. First, rather than assuming the strict sequentiality of the *wayyiqtol* (and thus of the chronological progression of the narrative as a whole), this view tends to see the Flood narrative as containing instances of chronological disjunction, with the driving purpose in the order of the narrative being thematic or theological as opposed to chronological. Second, this view understands (based upon such verses as Gn 7:12, 17, etc.) that the rain and other Flood mechanisms ceased at the end of the initial forty days. Third, this view rejects the notion that וַיִּגְבְּרוּ indicates an increase of the water level. It presumes only that Genesis 7:24 is a general reference to the continuing might of the Floodwaters.

Writing on the first of these issues in the first half of the twentieth century, U. Cassuto argued that the Flood narrative was not strictly sequential. According to his view, Genesis 8:1, although rightly understood as marking the centermost point of an elaborate chiastic structure, is not to be regarded as the chronological center of the event. Accordingly, the events described early in chapter 8 did not take place chronologically following the "prevailing" of the Floodwaters on the one hundred fiftieth day (Gn 7:24); rather, the section of text beginning in Genesis 8:1 reverts to an earlier point—in Cassuto's estimation, the fortieth day of the catastrophe. Commenting on Genesis 8:2, he wrote,

[A]nd this took place, of course, at the end of the forty days of rain. To understand these verbs (remembered, were closed, etc.) as pluperfects (He had already previously remembered, [the fountains] had already previously been closed, etc.) is certainly incorrect and not in keeping with Hebrew idiomatic usage, as we saw above in similar cases. The interpretation here must follow the same lines as the explanation we advanced regarding the relationship between the story of Creation and the story of the Garden of Eden. The preceding paragraph tells how the waters prevailed upon the earth, and this episode forms the theme of that paragraph up to the end; whereas this new paragraph deals with a different topic—the first stage of the deliverance of the survivors—and commences the narration of this story from the beginning, although the commencement antedates the conclusion of the episode described above. (Cassuto 1997, 99–100)

In consistency with this perspective, when commenting on the mechanism bringing about the recession of the water, he noted, "The blowing of the wind must be regarded as taking place immediately after the forty days of rain" (Cassuto 1997, 101). He also argued,

Only 150 days after the commencement of the Flood was the abatement of the waters noticed; till then their might alone was felt, as was stated earlier (vii 24). Their decrease became apparent through the fact that the ark came to rest on the mountains (v. 4). Until the ark came to a halt, Noah saw only water and sky, and it was not possible for him to sense that the level of the waters was steadily falling. But the stopping of the ark made him aware that the waters had decreased to an appreciable extent. (Cassuto 1997, 102–03)

Cassuto's position, though lacking in popularity, has nonetheless garnered recent support. Significantly, R. B. Chisholm has argued in defense of a peak on the fortieth day of the Flood, contending that a major shift in the theme of the narrative indicates a backward movement in the chronological setting. He writes,

Genesis 8:1 provides another example of the flashback technique. After a description of the devastating effects of the Flood and Noah's isolation (7:17–24), the theme shifts to God's concern for Noah and the removal of the waters (8:1). In 7:17–24 the waters are described as prevailing over the earth for 150 days, but in 8:1–5 the focus is on their receding between the fortieth and one hundred and fiftieth days. As the theme shifts from judgment to renewal, the scene shifts back to the fortieth day of the Flood, when God began the process whereby he caused the waters to recede. (Chisholm 2003, 67–68)

Although his comments dealing with the chronology of the Flood are brief, D. Kidner is particularly helpful in further detailing this position, specifically in how Genesis 7 relates to Genesis 8. Unfortunately, he does not take a clear stand on the issue, but his comment would lead one to suspect that he favored a peak on the fortieth day,

> [I]t seems more likely... that, in true Semitic style, chapter 7 rounds off its account of the first phase, namely the forty days and their continuing effects, by summing its duration (150 days); then chapter 8 describes the second phase, that of deliverance, starting from its logical beginning in the stopping of the forty days' downpour (8:2), but noting the intermediate period that elapsed before the grounding of the ark (8:3). (Kidner 1967, 99)

Accordingly, it is plainly evident that there are legitimate alternatives to the assumption of the strict sequentiality of the narrative.[4]

Similarly, contrary to the preceding position, this view rejects the notion that the rain continued beyond the fortieth day of the Flood. Such a stance is evident in the previous excerpts from Cassuto, as well as in the works of C. Burton and (despite his favorable view of the Documentary Hypothesis) H. Alford. Necessarily coupled with such a perspective is the fact that this position rejects the idea that וַיִּגְבְּרוּ (i.e., "prevailed"; lit. "were mighty") indicates any kind of increase in the water level. In fact, in this perspective, in the one hundred ten days following the torrential rains, the waters would have, if anything, declined rather than increased. Commenting on the word "prevailed," R. P. Smith wrote on Genesis 7:24,

> The rains lasted forty days; for one hundred and ten days more they bore up the ark, and then it grounded. But though still mighty, they had by this time "abated" (see chap. Viii. 3), inasmuch as, instead of covering the hills to a depth of nearly four fathoms, the ark now had touched dry land. (Smith 1885, 133–34)

Cassuto likewise observed on Genesis 7:24,

> The verb *prevailed* connotes here a continuing state: the power of the water upon the earth continued a hundred and fifty days, and did not decline in appreciable measure till after this period, which comprise... the tremendous downpour of rain for forty days followed by another hundred and ten days. The word מְאֹד *meʼōdh* ["greatly," "mightily"] is not used here as in *vv.* 18–19; hence the reference is not to the peak of the waters' strength but to their power in general. (Cassuto 1997, 97)

4. This is not to say that sequentiality is altogether discarded. For instance, Cassuto noted on Genesis 8:6 regarding the chronological reference to "the end of forty days," "This is equal to the duration of the Flood; thus the numerical harmony continues. Forty days after the date mentioned in the previous verse was the *tenth* day of the eleventh month, which corresponds to the *tenth* day of the second month, when God spoke for the first time to Noah" (Cassuto 1997, 106).

While it is true that this position avoids some of the assumptions of the previous view, an honest evaluation must ask at least the following questions: 1) What definitive textual evidence exists that the rain and other mechanisms driving the Flood ceased after the fortieth day? Also, 2) can it be convincingly demonstrated that the narrative as a whole does indeed contain instances of chronological disjunction, i.e., that the events described in the account occurred in a different sequence than that in which they are presented? If so, 3) what is the purpose of the (re)arrangement of the events in the text? These are the issues to be investigated in the subsequent chapters.

3.2.3 Position 3: Peak at Forty Days Sustained until One Hundred Fifty Days

This position on the chronology of the Flood has much in common with each of the preceding conservative views. Old Testament scholars C. F. Keil and F. Delitzsch succinctly describe the position in their commentary:

> The words of ver. 17, "and the flood was (came) upon the earth for forty days," relate to the 40 days' rain combined with the bursting forth of the fountains beneath the earth. By these the water was eventually raised to the height given, at which it remained 150 days (ver. 24).... [T]he water was rising for 40 days, and remained at the highest elevation for 150 days.(Keil and Delitzsch 1976, 146)

Based upon this description, it is debatable whether this view ought to be classified separately from the preceding position. In fact, the view might be considered something of a hybrid between the other two major conservative positions, although, in terms of its general assumptions, it more closely parallels the view which holds to a peak on the fortieth day rather than that which holds to a peak on the one hundred fiftieth day. Indeed, it is sometimes difficult to make a distinction. Note, for instance, that the aforementioned comment by Cassuto on Genesis 7:24 seems to indicate that he may have favored the notion that the Floodwaters remained relatively close to their peak level until the end of the initial one hundred fifty days. This was also the view of N. M. Sarna. Although he did not comment on the chronology of the Flood per se, he did offer comment on what he believed to be the case concerning the one hundred fifty day marker of Genesis 7:24:

> This verse may introduce the next chapter or close the preceding. In the latter case it would be rendered, "The waters swelled on the earth..." one hundred and fifty days. That is, exactly five months of thirty days each. The waters drained away so slowly and imperceptibly that they appeared to remain at their maximum height for this length of time. (Sarna 1989, 56)[5]

---

5. This may suggest that Sarna's views would align most closely with the acceptance of a peak at forty days, followed by a period of the waters being stagnate. However, there is not enough commentary to deduce this with certainty.

The means by which the waters were sustained at their maximum height is debated by proponents of this position. Some, such as A. Heidel (1949, 245–48), posit that after the initial forty days of relentless downpour, the rain continued at a more moderate rate for the next one hundred ten days. Whether the rain did indeed continue throughout the entire course of the Flood's initial one hundred fifty days is a question that must be subjected to careful textual analysis. However, at this point, a distinction must be made between this view and the previous position arguing for a peak on the one hundred fiftieth day. Whereas the former view *requires* the continuation of rain and/or the other Flood mechanisms beyond the fortieth day, this view simply *allows* for such a possibility. An increase in the water level would necessitate some kind of driving force; however, the mere stagnation of the Floodwaters—with the water level neither substantially increasing or decreasing—makes no such demand, although it would not inherently preclude that option. Consequently, the following question must be asked: Does the text of the Flood narrative at any point preclude the continuance of the Flood mechanisms (rain, etc.) beyond the initial forty days? If not, does the text in any way hint that they did indeed do so?

In terms of the history of this position, it can be said that this is a relatively old view, dating at least to the earliest days of the Reformation, if not earlier. Among the reformers themselves, John Calvin was a notable proponent of this view.[6] Statistically speaking, of the conservative sources consulted by this study, this position is significantly more popular than position 2 (which holds to a peak on the fortieth day followed by the immediate assuaging of the waters) but still ranks well behind position 1 (which holds to a peak on the one hundred fiftieth day). As for the assumptions made by this view, they are essentially the same as those made by position 2, with the exception that it does not necessarily argue that the Flood mechanisms ceased upon the fortieth day. Furthermore, some still posit that the account is strictly sequential (contra Cassuto and Chisholm). For instance, in the groundbreaking work *The Genesis Flood*, J. C. Whitcomb and H. M. Morris (1961, 4) write:

> Now some commentators have assumed that the waters continued to rise
> during the 150 days that the waters "prevailed upon the earth," because

---

6. Calvin's position is unusual, in that he argues that the peak occurred on the fortieth day of the Flood, but preferred not to include those initial forty days of rain within the one hundred fifty days mentioned in Genesis 8:3. He says, "But I make this distinction, that until the fortieth day, the waters rose gradually by fresh additions; then that they remained nearly in the same state for one hundred and fifty days; for both computations make the period a little more than six months and a half [*sic*]" (Calvin 1979, 277–78).

"the windows of the heavens were stopped, and the rain from heaven was restrained (8:2) only after the end of the 150-day period (8:3). This is certainly a possible interpretation of the text, but it is better to conclude with Leupold that the Flood attained its maximum depth after the first forty days and continued to maintain this level for an additional 110 days before beginning to assuage (7:24, 8:3). Our basis for assuming this is found in 7:4 and 7:12, where we read that the rains came "upon the earth forty days and forty nights"; and in 7:17 where we are told that "the flood was forty days upon the earth." Most of "the waters which were above the firmament" (Gen 1:7) must have fallen through "the windows of heaven" during the first period of forty days; and although the "windows of heaven" were not stopped for another 110 days (8:2), the rainfall during this second period may have contributed only to the maintaining of the Flood at its maximum height.

Likewise assuming the straightforward sequentiality of the narrative, A. Snelling (2009, 20–21) arrives at a similar conclusion, positing that the peak was attained after only forty days, but that the Flood mechanisms remained active until the one hundred fiftieth day, which served to at least sustain the water level throughout that period. Consequently, it is all the more evident that the factors involved with the assumption of sequentiality need to be analyzed. Conversely, it must also be determined if the Flood narrative permits for instances of chronological disjunction and, if so, where such disjunctions may occur.

3.2.4 Alternative Positions

Aside from the three main views on the Flood's chronology already discussed, there are at least four other minor views. Admittedly, the works in which these views were advocated, taken together, represent less than three percent of the volumes researched by this study. Nevertheless, they have been included for the sake of completeness.

(1) H. Stigers presents a chronological scheme which, though differing little from the third major position listed above, is genuinely distinct, as demonstrated by the fact that he does not maintain that the peak was necessarily maintained until the one hundred fiftieth day of the Flood. Stigers clearly states that the rain lasted for forty days, which brought about the "prevailing" of the Floodwaters for a total of one hundred fifty days. In his view, the Flood's peak necessarily occurred somewhere *between* these two points (though he does not specify precisely where). Commenting on Genesis 8:3, he posits that the section is similar to a "flashback"

(cf. Chisholm); he maintains that it overlaps with the general period described in Genesis 7:24. He writes, "Verse 3 describes what some have considered the retreat of waters on the earth, but just as well might it describe a gradual shutting off of the rains, as happens now. This agrees with 7:24, indicating that the abatement period is to be included in the 150 days, but that it occupies at least part of the 110 days" (1976, 111). In sum, therefore, Stigers presumes neither a long nor short recession, and is content to assume that there was a gradual tapering off of the torrential activity providing for a peak somewhere in between days forty and one hundred fifty. Admittedly, however, Stigers presents his view in somewhat vague fashion and offers little defense.

(2) Supporting a very old and little-known position, in his introduction to the Pentateuch, V. P. Hamilton defended a peak on the one hundred ninetieth day of the Flood (which was contrary to the position he espoused in his earlier commentary on Genesis), noting, "Again, does the text indicate an inconsistency in the duration of the flood, forty versus 150 days? Was not the actual downpour forty days and nights, followed by five months (150 days) of rising water until the water level peaked?" (2005, 71). The fact that Rashi in the Middle Ages promoted the same view in his commentary on Genesis (1949, 70–71) places Hamilton in good company. However, the fact remains that the text of the Flood narrative nowhere suggests that the one hundred fifty days of "prevailing" (Gn 7:24) are *in addition to* the previously-mentioned forty days of rain (Gn 7:12). Thus, Hamilton's position contends that the events of Genesis 7:24ff. commence at the close of the period of rain. It assumes an incredibly rigid (if not unnatural) understanding of sequentiality.

(3) Loosely related to Hamilton's view is that of J. G. Murphy. Murphy, somewhat arbitrarily, held to a peak on the ninety-fifth day of the Flood, defending his position with the following formula:

$$\frac{40 \text{ days of rain} + 150 \text{ days of "prevailing"}}{2}$$

= an approximate date for the peak at the 95th day.

Accordingly, he saw forty days of heavy rain, followed by (in Gn 7:17–24), "…the prevalence of the waters. The forty days are now completed. And at the end of this period the ark had been afloat for a long time" (1998, 215–16). On the one hundred fifty day period mentioned in Genesis 7:24, he wrote, "These, and the 40 days of rain, make 190 days, about six lunar months and 13 days.... The waters may be said to prevail as long as the ark had its full draught of water. It is probable they were still rising during the first half of the hundred and fifty days, and then gradually sinking during the other half" (1998, 217). Later, on Genesis 8:1–3, he argued, "The waters commence their retreat. And God remembered Noah. He is said to remember him when he takes any step to deliver him from the waters" (1998, 219). Murphy obviously held that the *wayyiqtol* verb form served to mark sequentiality. On other chronological elements in the account he wrote, "The incessant wind and violent showers had continued for six weeks. It is probable the weather remained turbid and moist for some time longer" (1998, 219) and, "At the end of the hundred and fifty days the prevalence of the waters begins to turn into a positive retreat" (1998, 220). These statements show that he saw a contrast between the one hundred fifty day period of "prevailing" (during which time he seems to assume a progressive tapering off of the rain and moderate recession) and the period of noticeable assuaging thereafter. Unfortunately, Murphy's view is subject to the same difficulties as that of Hamilton. Furthermore, it is entirely arbitrary, as there is no way to prove either scientifically or textually that the Floodwaters continued to rise until the ninety-fifth day or that the time of the rising of the waters was equal to that of the receding of the waters. To put it bluntly, even if this view is accurate, it remains outside of the realm of what it provable.

(4) The final alternative view on the chronology of the Flood is set forth in a little-known work by D. Fasold, who argues that the Flood was actually three hundred ten days long, as based upon a ten month, thirty day-per-month calendar (1988, 51). Notably, Fasold ignores the five fixed dates, which renders his view completely untenable. Like the chronological views maintained by those backing the notion of conflicting sources in the Flood narrative, Fasold's view is flawed at a fundamental level, abandoning the most basic biblical constraints.

3.3 *Summary*

This study has presented a total of eight different views on the chronology of the Flood. Of these, two are untenable due to direct conflict with the biblical presuppositions governing this study. The remaining positions (particularly the three major views espoused by conservative scholars) are deserving of careful evaluation in the following chapters of this book. Before doing so, however, it is necessary to discuss some general trends observed in the preceding overview of chronological scenarios on the Flood.

4. An Observation of Trends in the Chronological Scenarios

Having set forth the various views on the chronology of the Genesis Flood, it is worth considering some of the general observations that have been made during the course of the research for this chapter. When research for this chapter began, it was determined that careful attention needed to be given to two factors that were presumed to play a role in a given interpreter's understanding of the Flood's chronology: 1) the text considered (whether the Hebrew Text or a translation), and 2) the author's stance on the authorship of the book of Genesis (i.e., whether Genesis was written by Moses as the Scripture itself claims, or was the product of multiple sources combined through a long period of redaction).

Not surprisingly, the latter of these two factors proved to be a major issue. Most of the sources consulted that adhered to the Documentary Hypothesis, if they commented on the chronology of the Flood at all, inevitably regarded the chronology to be undecipherable, the product of at least two accounts that were fused together, each one with its own distinct chronological system. A few interpreters (e.g., Wenham, Westermann) did try to reconcile the allegedly disparate chronological indicators, but most were reluctant to attempt any kind of harmonization. (By contrast, all but a few of those who held to any of the major conservative positions tended to hold to the traditional view on the authorship of Genesis.)

The other factor, remarkably, turned out to be virtually inconsequential. While those who backed the Documentary Hypothesis were commonly, by virtue of their education and discipline, adept in BH, their knowledge of the Hebrew language did not contribute noticeably to their understanding of the Flood's chronology. So too, among conservative interpreters, there were no discernible trends among those who worked from the Hebrew text as opposed to those who did not. The fact that one of the arguments for a peak on the one hundred fiftieth day was tied directly to a commonly taught view in Hebrew grammar (i.e., the sequentiality of the *wayyiqtol*) seemed, in fact, to be of little consequence. A far more prevalent argument for a peak on the one hundred fifieth day stemmed from a cursory reading of Genesis 7:24, which was appealed to by those working from English translations, as well as those working from the Hebrew text.

Aside from these factors, two noteworthy observations were made: 1) in sources dealing with the Genesis Flood, there has been a considerable lack of attention given to chronological issues; and 2) among sources that do discuss chronological issues, there is often a general failure to carefully examine the text in its entirety.

4.1   Overall Lack of Attention to Chronology
4.2   General Failure to Examine the Text

4.1 *Overall Lack of Attention to Chronology*

In overviewing the various views on the chronology of the Genesis Flood in modern literature, over one hundred sixty sources were consulted. Sources consulted included a wide array of commentaries on the book of Genesis (ranging from devotional works for laymen to technical works aimed at scholars), as well as Old Testament introductions, Bible encyclopedias, journal articles, etc. Of these, slightly less than half gave any consideration to the chronology embedded in the Flood narrative. In fairness, this statistic deserves a bit of explanation, as not all sources should be viewed equally. As can be expected, many of the commentaries that declined to comment on the chronology of the Flood were of a more devotional flavor; however, this fact is not universally true, as there were at least a modest number of lengthier expositional or detailed exegetical commentaries that overlooked the issue as well (see sources listed in **Section 6** of **Appendix A**). Even among those sources which did comment on chronological issues, many gave it only brief discussion relative to the amount of material concerning the Flood in general.

While it is not the intent of this chapter to in any way disparage or downplay the notable efforts made by such individuals as Barrick and Sigler, Cassuto, and others to resolve the chronology of the Flood, the obvious fact remains that the issue has certainly not been given a proper treatment. It seems that too many expositors have taken to heart Luther's attitude expressed in his statement that the chronological aspects of the Flood do not matter. In examining the text of the Flood narrative, they have overlooked the wisdom articulated in Hoehner's remark that chronology is the "backbone" of history. While it may not be the intent of every individual writing on the Flood to discuss the chronology of the Flood at length, the fact that over half of the sources consulted by this study failed to say anything at all is a sad testimony to the fact that biblical scholarship often fails to give even brief attention to things which the omniscient God saw fit to include in the holy text. On the contrary, every word of Scripture deserves attention, especially where it concerns an issue that has (like the chronology of the Flood) been used as fodder for the liberals' attacks on the authorship and authority of the text.

4.2 *General Failure to Examine the Text*

A second observation made during the course of this study concerns a general failure to carefully examine the text of the Flood narrative in attempting to decipher the chronology. It has already been demonstrated that liberal scholarship tends to superimpose on the text a preconceived notion of two (or three) contradictory chronological schemes rather than seeking to deduce from the text itself the grand sequence of events. Beyond this, however, the thoroughgoing trend among conservatives arguing for a particular position on the chronology of the Flood has been to center the argument on only one or two verses. For example, among those who argued for a peak on the one hundred fiftieth day of the cataclysm, several simply referenced Genesis 7:24 without giving any further thought to the issue. If this verse was indeed an unambiguous, clinching argument however, there should be no competent Bible scholars expressing views to the contrary. Moreover, as the preceding overview has demonstrated, this is clearly not the case.

The point is that the chronology of the Flood needs to be approached seriously. It is obviously a topic of contention between the liberal and conservative camps and has, unfortunately, been employed more than once in the liberal attack on the inspiration and authority of Scripture. Therefore, conservative scholarship would do well to treat the Flood's chronology as more than a mere side issue, making diligent effort to examine it from all angles, looking at the totality of the narrative and taking into account all its features—whether grammatical, linguistic, etc.—in order to gain a more definitive, holistic picture not only of the chronology of the event, but also of how the recording of that chronology is used within the broader scope of the narrative to aid in the communication of important theological information (see **Chapter 14, Section 2**).

5. Conclusion

As the preceding material demonstrates, the Genesis Flood has certainly not received the careful attention that it deserves in order to deduce the precise sequence of events it describes. Nevertheless, even where rigorous study has lacked, there has been no shortage of opinion on the matter. In one sense it is good that the discussion has been kept alive. At the same time, however, it is regrettable that there are so many different positions on the subject, commonly stated without defense and sometimes resting on assumptions that may not be provable. In view of the current state of research on the topic, in what direction is further study on this issue to proceed? Clearly, while there need not be dissention between those holding to different perspectives on the matter (provided they fall within the parameters allowed by a biblical view of the authorship, inspiration, and authority of the Genesis text), it is downright unscholarly to presume that all views are equally valid and that no further research is warranted. Thus, in concluding this overview of the literature on the chronology of the Flood, this chapter will look at specific areas in need of continued, deeper study.

5.1   The Need for a Methodological Approach in the Determination of the Chronology of the Flood

5.2   The Need for Continued Research

5.1 *The Need for a Methodological Approach in the Determination of the Chronology of the Flood*

This overview of the differing positions on the chronology of the Flood has uncovered a variety of assumptions on which those respective positions are based, as well as a number of arguments that are commonly employed. In order to properly and conclusively identify which view truly conforms best to the textual evidence, it is necessary to examine each of the assumptions underlying the different perspectives to determine if they are indeed sound. It is also necessary to assess the validity of each of the major arguments. In particular, as has been demonstrated in the previous sections, the following needs to be considered:

(1) Is the *wayyiqtol* verb form to be understood as inherently sequential? Does its presence throughout the Flood narrative indicate strict sequentiality in the progression of events? (If the *wayyiqtol* verb form is not an indication of sequentiality, it will be necessary to demonstrate what elements [whether grammatical, pragmatic, etc.] can be employed to determine the sequence of events described in the narrative.)

(2) Can it be determined whether the rain (and/or other Flood mechanisms) continued beyond the fortieth day? More precisely, do the verbs involved with announcing the turning on and shutting off of the Flood mechanisms provide any indication that they may have continued at either an equal or reduced pace beyond the initial forty days of the Flood?

(3) What is the precise meaning of וַיִּגְבְּרוּ, commonly translated "prevailed"? Can it be determined whether it may indicate either a rising or a stagnation of the water level?

(4) Can it be convincingly demonstrated that the Flood narrative contains instances of chronological disjunction? (If so, it will be necessary to demonstrate, in a reasoned, non-arbitrary fashion, where such chronological disjunctions occur and determine how great of an impact they bear on the progression of the narrative.) Furthermore, what purpose might such instances of chronological disjunction serve?

It is the aim of the following chapters to address the following questions and more. **Chapter 10** will address the alleged sequentiality of the *wayyiqtol*. **Chapter 11** will look at temporal progression as it relates to individual verbs. **Chapter 12** will investigate what other factors play a role in the determination of sequence, investigating temporal progression on the macro-level. **Chapter 13** will then look at temporal progression on the broadest level. **Chapter 14** will follow by examining how theme tracing may be employed in the segmentation of Hebrew narrative with the goal of determining any location(s) wherein chronological disjunction may be present. Only once these issues are evaluated will it be possible to gain a more certain perspective on the chronology of the Genesis Flood.

5.2 *The Need for Continued Research*

Although this chapter has taken a careful look at the various modern views on the chronology of the Flood in the literature, it still remains to be considered how each of these views developed. Further research on this topic must be conducted in order to determine the origin of each view. While the antiquity of a position does not determine its correctness, an understanding of the historical circumstances in which each view developed may aid in providing a better understanding of each view, inclusive of their respective assumptions and arguments. Consequently, in the second installment of this study, attention will be given to tracing the history of each of the main conservative views and delineating, if possible, what other arguments for these views have been employed in the pre-modern era.

A second, related issue to be addressed is that of the calendar. By comparison to other factors, the calendar employed in the Flood narrative is of less significance to the determination of chronology. (Notably, it has but little bearing on the precise date of the peak. Unlike other factors, which could indicate a peak after either the initial forty days of rain, or after the long period of the "prevailing" of the waters—i.e., a factor of over three and one half months—the calendar employed in the narrative would make a difference of, at most, only a few days. The alteration in the length of the total Flood event would likewise be a matter of days.) Nevertheless, for the sake of completeness, it will be necessary to consider the different calendars that *may* have been utilized in the narrative and, if possible, determine which was the most likely choice of the biblical author.

Appendix A: Bibliography of Sources Consulted on the Chronology of the Flood in Literature Past and Present

This appendix lists the bibliographical information for each source consulted in the writing of this chapter. Sources are categorized according to the view taken by the author. Sources with particularly insightful, extensive, or otherwise valuable argumentation are marked with a dagger (†).

A1. Chronological Perspectives Influenced by the Documentary Hypothesis

The following sources hold (often on the basis of pure supposition in accordance with the Documentary Hypothesis) that the Flood narrative is comprised of two or more sources. Almost invariably, it is argued that these sources are in conflict and beyond reconciliation, thereby rendering discussion of the actual chronology pointless. It is important to note that this list does not represent all sources which promote some variant of the Documentary Hypothesis. There are included in the other sections of this bibliography a number of sources that subscribe to multiple authors for the book of Genesis. However, due to attempts at harmonization or other factors, these sources concluded upon one of the other positions on the chronology of the Flood.

†Barré, L. M. 1988. The riddle of the Flood chronology. *Journal for the Study of the Old Testament* 41: 3–20.

Buttrick, G. A., ed. 1962. *The interpreter's dictionary of the Bible: An illustrated encyclopedia*. Vol. 2. New York, NY: Abingdon Press.

†Cryer, F. H. 1985. The interrelationships of Gen 5, 32; 11, 10–11, and the chronology of the Flood (Gen 6–9). *Biblica* 66: 241–261.

Delitzsch, F. 1978. *A new commentary on Genesis*. Vol. 1. Trans. S. Taylor. Minneapolis, MN: Klock and Klock Christian Publishers. (Orig. pub. 1899).

Driver, S. R. 1926. *The book of Genesis*. 12th ed. London, England: Methuen and Company.

Elliot, R. H. 1961. *The message of Genesis*. Nashville, TN: Broadman Press.

Gibson, J. C. L. 1981. *Genesis*. Vol. 1. Edinburgh, Scotland: The Saint Andrew Press.

Hable, N. C. 1988. The two Flood stories in Genesis. In *The Flood myth*. Ed. A. Dundes. Berkeley, MA: University of California Press.

Harland, J. P. 1996. *The value of human life: A study of the story of the Flood (Genesis 6–9)*. Leiden, Netherlands: Brill.

Hastings, J., ed. 1963. *Dictionary of the Bible*. Rev. ed. New York, NY: Charles Scribner's Sons. (Orig. pub. 1899).

Kraft, C. F. 1964. *Genesis: Beginnings of the biblical drama*. New York, NY: The Methodist Church.

†Lemche, N. P. 1980. *The chronology in the story of the Flood*. *Journal for the Study of the Old Testament* 18: 52–62.

Romanoff, P. 1931. A third version of the Flood narrative. *Journal of Biblical Literature* 50: 304–07.

Ryle, H. E. 2001. *The book of Genesis*. Cambridge, England: Cambridge University Press.

Ska, J. L. 2006. *Introduction to reading the Pentateuch*. Trans. S. P. Dominique. Winona Lake, IN: Eisenbrauns.

Ska, J. L. 2009. *The exegesis of the Pentateuch: Exegetical studies and basic questions*. Tübingen, Germany: Mohr Siebeck.

Vawter, B. 1956. *A path through Genesis*. New York, NY: Sheed and Ward.

Von Rad, G. 1973. *Genesis: A commentary*. Trans. J. H. Marks. Philadelphia, PA: Westminster.

Wenham, G. J. 1987. *Genesis 1–15*. Word biblical commentary 1. Waco, TX: Thomas Nelson.

Worcester, E. 1901. *The book of Genesis in light of modern knowledge*. New York, NY: McClure, Phillips and Company.

A2. Chronological Models Holding to a Peak at One Hundred Fifty Days

The following sources adhere to a peak for the Flood on the one hundred fiftieth day. Typical arguments given center on 1) the assumption that וַיִּגְבְּרוּ in Genesis 7:24 indicates the rising of the water level, and/or 2) that Genesis 8:3ff. must necessarily be read sequentially, and/or 3) that the *wayyiqtol* verb form is inherently sequential.

†Barrick, W. D., and R. Sigler. 2003. Hebrew and geologic analyses of the chronology and parallelism of the Flood: Implications for interpretation of the geologic record. In *Proceedings of the fifth International Conference on Creationism*. Ed. R. L. Ivey Jr., 397–408. Pittsburgh, PA: Creation Science Fellowship.

Brayford, S. 2007. *Genesis*. Septuagint commentary series. Leiden, Netherlands: Brill.

Bush, G. 1851. *Notes, critical and practical, on the book of Genesis: Designed as a general help to biblical reading and instruction*. Vol. 1. New York, NY: Ivison, Phinney, Blakeman and Co. (Orig. pub. 1838).

Carroll, B. H. 1937. *Studies in Genesis*. Nashville, TN: Convention Press.

Davis, J. J. 1975. *Paradise to prison: Studies in Genesis*. Grand Rapids, MI: Baker Book House.

Douglas, J. D., ed. 1980. *The illustrated Bible dictionary*. Vol. 1. Downers Grove, IL: Inter-Varsity Press.

Edwards, L. D. 2006. *The twelve generations of the creation: A physician's perspective of the book of Genesis*. Longwood, FL: Xulon Press.

Erdman, C. R. 1950. *The book of Genesis: An exposition*. New York, NY: Fleming H. Revell Company.

Finn, A. H. n.d. *The Creation, Fall, and Deluge*. London, England: Marshall Brothers.

Fuller, A. 1836. *Expository discourses on the book of Genesis interspersed with practical reflections*. London, England: Thomas Tegg and Son.

Gunkel, H. 1997. *Genesis: A translation*. Macon, GA: Mercer Library of Biblical Studies. (Orig. pub. 1910).

Hamilton, V. P. 1990. *The book of Genesis: Chapters 1–17*. New international commentary on the Old Testament. Grand Rapids, MI: William B. Eerdmans Publishing Company.

Hocking, D. 1989. *The rise and fall of civilization: From Creation through the Flood*. Portland, OR: Multnomah Press.

Kikawada, I. M., and A. Quinn. 1985. *Before Abraham was: The unity of Genesis 1–11*. Nashville, TN: Abingdon Press.

Kline, M. 1970. Genesis. In *The new Bible commentary*. Rev. ed. D. Guthrie, et al. Grand Rapids, MI: William. B. Eerdmans Publishing Co.

Lange, J. P. 1960. *A commentary on the Holy Scriptures: Genesis*. Trans. P. Schaff. Grand Rapids, MI: Zondervan. (Orig. pub. 1864).

Louth, A., ed. 2001. *Genesis 1–11*. Ancient Christian commentary on Scripture: Old Testament 1. Downers Grove, IL: Inter-Varsity Press.

Luther, M. 1958. *Luther's commentary on Genesis*. Vol. 1. Trans. J. T. Mueller. Grand Rapids, MI: Zondervan Publishing House.

MacArthur, J., ed. 2006. *The MacArthur Bible commentary*. Nashville, TN: Thomas Nelson.

Mathews, K. A. 1996. *Genesis 1–11:26*. The new American commentary. Nashville, TN: Broadman and Holman Publishers.

McGee, J. V. 1975. *Genesis*. Vol. 1. LaVerne, CA: El Camino Press.

Mitchell, T. C. 1982. Flood. In *New Bible dictionary*. 2nd ed. Ed. J. D. Douglas. Wheaton, IL: Tyndale House Publishers.

Morgenstern, J. 1965. *The book of Genesis: A Jewish interpretation*. New York, NY: Schocken Books.

Morris, H. M. 1976. *The Genesis record: A scientific and devotional commentary on the book of beginnings*. Grand Rapids, MI: Baker Book House.

Pfeiffer, C. F. 1958. *The book of Genesis: A study manual*. Grand Rapids, MI: Baker Book House.

Rice, J. R. 1975. *In the beginning: A verse-by-verse commentary on the book of Genesis*. Murfreesboro, TN: Sword of the Lord Publishers.

Ross, A. P. 1983. Genesis. In *The Bible knowledge commentary: Old Testament*. Ed. J. F. Walvoord, and R. B. Zuck. Colorado Springs, CO: David C. Cook.

Ross, A. P. 1996. *Creation and blessing: A guide to the study and exposition of Genesis.* Grand Rapids, MI: Baker Books.

Schrader, S. R. 1982. Genesis. In *The liberty Bible commentary.* Ed. J. Falwell. Nashville, TN: Thomas Nelson.

Skinner, J. 1910. *Genesis.* International critical commentary. Edinburgh, Scotland: T. and T. Clark.

Spencer, W. R., and M. J. Oard. 2004. The Chesapeake Bay impact and Noah's Flood. *Creation Research Society Quarterly* 41: 206–215.

Unger, M. F. 2002. *Unger's commentary on the Old Testament.* Chattanooga, TN: AMG Publishers.

Vos, H. F. 1982. Flood. In vol. 2 of *The international standard Bible encyclopedia.* Rev. ed. Ed. G. W. Bromiley. Grand Rapids, MI: William B. Eerdmans Publishing Company.

Waltke, B. K., and C. J. Fredricks. 2001. *Genesis: A commentary.* Grand Rapids, MI: Zondervan.

†Wenham, G. J. 1978. The coherence of the Flood narrative. *Vestus Testamentum* 28: 336–348.

†Westermann, C. 1984. *Genesis 1–11: A commentary.* Trans. J. J. Scullion. Minneapolis, MN: Augsburg.

A3. Chronological Models Holding to a Peak at Forty Days

The following sources assert that the Flood achieved its peak on the fortieth day, which marked the end of the period of rain. This position tends to avoid the assumption that the Flood narrative is purely sequential.

Alford, H. 1979. *Genesis and part of Exodus: A revised version with marginal references and an explanatory commentary.* Minneapolis, MN: Klock and Klock Christian Publishers. (Orig. pub. 1872).

Burton, C. 1845. *Lectures on the deluge and the world after the Flood.* London, England: Hamilton, Adams, and Co.

†Cassuto, U. 1997. *A commentary on the book of Genesis, part II—from Noah to Abraham.* Trans. I. Abrahams. Jerusalem, Israel: The Magnes Press.

†Chisholm, R. B., Jr. 2003. History or story? The literary dimension in narrative texts. In *Giving the sense: Understanding and using Old Testament historical texts.* Ed. D. M. Howard Jr., and M. A. Grisanti. Grand Rapids, MI: Kregal Publications.

Hartley, J. E. 2000. *Genesis* (The new international biblical commentary). Peabody, MA: Hendrickson Publishers.

†Smith, R. P. 1885. *The first book of Moses, called Genesis.* London, England: Cassell and Company, Limited.

Ussher, J. 2003. *The annals of the world.* Revised and updated by L. Pierce, and M. Pierce. Green Forest, AR: Master Books. (Orig. pub. 1654).

A4. Chronological Models Holding to a Peak at Forty Days and Sustained Until the One Hundred Fiftieth Day

The following sources defend a mediating position, which states that the peak of the Flood was reached on the fortieth day and was then sustained until the one hundred fiftieth day. The defense of this position commonly rests on a cursory reading of Genesis 7:24. Most proponents assume, in agreement with a number of the supporters of a peak on the one hundred fiftieth day, a continuation of rain (at least to a milder degree) until the one hundred fiftieth day.

Aalders, G. C. 1981. *Genesis*. Vol. 1. Trans. W. Heynen. Grand Rapids, MI: Zondervan Publishing House.

†Calvin, J. 1979. *Commentaries on the first book of Moses called Genesis*. Trans. J. King. Grand Rapids, MI: Baker Book House. (Orig. pub. 1948).

Eveson, P. 2001. *The book of origins: Genesis simply explained*. Darlington, England: Evangelical Press.

Froede, C. R. Jr. 1994. Sequence stratigraphy and creation geology. *Creation Research Society Quarterly* 31: 138–147.

†Heidel, A. 1949. *The Gilgamesh epic and Old Testament parallels*. 2nd ed. Chicago, IL: Phoenix Books.

†Keil, C. F., and F. Delitzsch. 1976. *Commentary on the Old Testament*. Vol. 1. Trans. J. Martin. Grand Rapids, MI: William B. Eerdmans Publishing Company. (Orig. pub. 1878).

Kramer, F. 1970. The biblical account of the Flood. In *Rock strata and the biblical record*. Ed. P. A. Zimmerman. Saint Louis, MO: Concordia Publishing House.

†Leupold, H. C. 1942. *Exposition of Genesis*. Vol. 1. Grand Rapids, MI: Baker Book House.

Pfeiffer, C. F., H. F. Vos, and J. Rea, eds. 1975. *Wycliffe Bible encyclopedia*. Vol. 1. Chicago, IL: Moody Press.

Rehwinkel, A. M. 1994. *The Flood in light of the Bible, geology, and archeology*. Saint Louis, MO: CPH. (Orig. pub. 1951).

†Snelling, A. A. 2009. *Earth's catastrophic past: Geology, Creation and the Flood*. Vol. 1. Dallas, TX: Institute for Creation Research.

Stolee, H. J. 1937. *Genesis: Outline and notes for Bible classes*. Minneapolis, MN: Augsburg Publishing House.

†Whitcomb, J. C., and H. M. Morris. 1961. *The Genesis Flood: The biblical record and its scientific implications*. Phillipsburg, NJ: Presbyterian and Reformed Publishing Company.

Young, E. J. 1964. *An introduction to the Old Testament*. Grand Rapids, MI: William B. Eerdman's Publishing Company.

A5. Alternative Chronological Models

The following sources hold alternative views of the Flood's chronology, some of which are simply implausible (e.g., Fasold). Others represent only slight divergences from one of the aforementioned major positions (e.g., Stigers).

Fasold, D. 1988. *The ark of Noah.* New York, NY: Wynwood Press.

Hamilton, V. P. 2005. *Handbook on the Pentateuch.* Grand Rapids, MI: Baker Academic.

Murphy, J. G. 1998. *A critical and exegetical commentary on the book of Genesis.* Eugene, OR: Wipf and Stock Publishers. (Orig. pub. 1847).

†Stigers, H. 1976. *A commentary on Genesis.* Grand Rapids, MI: Zondervan Publishing House.

A6. No Explicitly Stated Position

The following sources promote no definite view on the chronology of the Flood (or are too vague to determine if their authors take a definitive position) even though they are commentaries or other specialized material that devote a considerable degree of attention to the Genesis Flood. Some, however, are still quite valuable in their comments on the text as it relates to chronology (e.g., Currid, Kidner, and Sarna).

Adar, Z. 1990. *The book of Genesis: An introduction to the biblical world.* Jerusalem, Israel: The Magnes Press.

Alexander, T. D. 2002. *From paradise to the Promised Land: An introduction to the Pentateuch.* 2nd ed. Grand Rapids, MI: Baker Academic.

Alter, R. 2004. *The five books of Moses: A translation with commentary.* New York, NY: W. W. Norton and Company.

Arnold, B. T. 1998. *Encountering the book of Genesis: A study of its content and issues.* Grand Rapids, MI: Baker Books.

Atkinson, D. 1990. *The message of Genesis 1–11: The dawn of creation.* Downers Grove, IL: Inter-Varsity Press.

Ault, W. U. 1976. Flood (Genesis). In vol. 2 of *The Zondervan pictorial encyclopedia of the Bible.* Ed. M. C. Tenney. Grand Rapids, MI: Zondervan.

Bailey, L. R. 1989. *Noah: The person and the story in history and tradition.* Columbia, SC: University of South Carolina Press.

Barnhouse, D. G. 1970. *Genesis: A devotional exposition.* Vol. 1. Grand Rapids, MI: Zondervan.

Barton, J., and J. Muddiman, eds. 2001. *The Oxford Bible commentary.* Oxford, England: Oxford University Press.

Blenkinsopp, J. 1965. *From Adam to Abraham: Introduction to sacred history.* Glen Rock, NJ: Paulist Press.

Blenkinsopp, J. 2004. *Treasures old and new: Essays in the theology of the Pentateuch.* Grand Rapids, MI: William B. Eerdmans Publishing Company.

Boice, J. M. 1982. *Genesis: An expositional commentary*. Vol. 1. Grand Rapids, MI: Zondervan Publishing House.

Bonar, H. 1875. *Earth's morning: Or, thoughts on Genesis*. New York. NY: Robert Carter and Brothers.

Brodie, T. L. 2001. *Genesis as dialogue: A literary, historical, and theological commentary*. Oxford, England: Oxford University Press.

Brueggemann, W. 1982. *Genesis: A Bible commentary for teaching and preaching*. Atlanta, GA: John Knox Press.

Bull, B., F. Guy, and E. Taylor, eds. 2006. *Understanding Genesis: Contemporary Adventist perspectives*. Riverside, CA: Adventists Today Foundation.

Candlish, R. S. 1956. *Commentary on Genesis*. Vol. 1. Grand Rapids, MI: Zondervan Publishing House. (Orig. pub. 1868).

Coates, C. A. 1920. *An outline of the book of Genesis*. London, England: Paternoster Square.

†Currid, J. D. 2003. *A study commentary on Genesis*. Vol. 1. Webster, NY: Evangelical Press.

Davidson, R. 1973. *Genesis 1–11*. The Cambridge Bible commentary. Cambridge, England: Cambridge University Press.

Dods, M. 1901. *The book of Genesis: With introduction and notes*. New York, NY: A. C. Armstrong and Son. (Orig. pub. 1888).

Drew, E. 1939. *Studies in the book of Genesis*. Paterson, NJ: Lont and Overkamp Publishing Company.

Ellison, H. L. 1999. Genesis. In *The new international Bible commentary*. Ed. F. F. Bruce. Grand Rapids, MI: Zondervan.

Evans, W. 1916. *The book of Genesis*. New York, NY: Fleming H. Revell Company.

Exell, J. S. 1960. *Genesis*. The biblical illustrator 1. Grand Rapids, MI: Baker Book House.

Filby, F. A. 1970. *The Flood reconsidered: A review of the evidences of geology, archeology, ancient literature and the Bible*. Grand Rapids, MI: Zondervan Publishing House.

Fretheim, T. E. 1994. Genesis. In vol. 1 of *The new interpreter's Bible*. Ed. L. E. Keck. Nashville, TN: Abingdon Press.

Fritsch, C. T. 1978. *The book of Genesis*. The layman's Bible commentary. Atlanta, GA: John Knox Press.

Gaebelein, A. C. 1912. *The book of Genesis*. New York, NY: Our Hope Publication Office.

Gigot, F. E. 1901. *Special introduction to the study of the Old Testament, part 1: The historical books*. Rev. ed. New York, NY: Benziger Brothers.

Gowan, D. E. 1988. *From Eden to Babel: A commentary on the book of Genesis 1–11*. Grand Rapids, MI: William. B. Eerdmans Publishing Company.

Graham, J. R. 1955. *A philosophy of Scripture (cosmology): A connected commentary on the book of Genesis*. Butler, IN: The Higley Press.

Gray, J. M. 1910. *The great epochs of sacred history and the shadows they cast*. New York, NY: Fleming H. Revell Company.

Gutzke, M. G. 1975. *Plain talk on Genesis.* Grand Rapids, MI: Zondervan.

Hart-Davies, D. E. 1932. *The genesis of Genesis.* New York, NY: Fleming H. Revell Company.

Hobbs, H. H. 1975. *The origin of all things: Studies in Genesis.* Waco, TX: Word Books.

Hopkins, J. 1936. *Talks on the book of Genesis.* Vol. 1. Los Angeles, CA: The Pioneer Press.

Hughes, R. K. 2004. *Genesis: Beginning and blessing.* Wheaton, IL: Crossway Books.

Jamieson, R., A. R. Fausset, and D. Brown. 1961. *Commentary, practical and explanatory, on the whole Bible.* Grand Rapids, MI: Zondervan. (Orig. pub. 1871).

†Kidner, D. 1967. *Genesis.* Tyndale Old Testament commentary series 1. Downers Grove, IL: Inter-Varsity Press.

Kselman, J. S. 2000. Genesis. In *The Harper Collins Bible commentary.* Ed. J. L. Mays. San Francisco, CA: Harper San Francisco.

Larsson, G. 2000. Remarks concerning the Noah-Flood complex. *Zeitschrift für die Alttestamentliche Wissenschaft* 112: 75–77.

Leibowitz, N. 1981. *Studies in Bereishit (Genesis), in the context of ancient and modern Jewish Bible commentary.* Jerusalem, Israel: Alpha Press.

Mackintosh, C. H. 1959. *Notes on the book of Genesis.* New York, NY: Loizeaux Brothers. (Orig. pub. 1880).

Maclaren, A. 1906. *The book of Genesis.* New York, NY: A. C. Armstrong and Son.

McCall, T. S., and Z. Levitt. 1978. *The Bible Jesus read is exciting!* Garden City, NY: Doubleday-Galilee.

Miller, P. D., Jr. 1978. *Genesis 1–11: Studies in structure and theme. Journal for the Study of the Old Testament* supplement series. Sheffield, England: University of Sheffield Department of Biblical Studies.

Monro, M. T. 1966. *Thinking about Genesis.* Chicago, IL: Henry Regnery Company.

Neil, W., ed. 1962. *Harper's Bible commentary.* New York, NY: Harper and Row, Publishers.

Niles, D. T. 1958. *Studies in Genesis.* Philadelphia, PA: The Westminster Press.

Owens, J. J. 1978. *Analytical key to the Old Testament: Genesis.* San Francisco, CA: Harper and Row, Publishers.

Parker, J. 1896. *The people's Bible—vol. 1: The book of Genesis.* London, England: Hazell, Watson and Viney.

Pieters, A. 1943. *Notes on Genesis: For ministers and serious Bible students.* Grand Rapids, MI: William B. Eerdmans Publishing Company.

Pink, A. W. 1922. *Gleanings in Genesis.* Chicago, IL: Moody Press.

Plaut, W. G. 1974. *The Torah: A modern commentary—vol. 1: Genesis.* New York, NY: Union of American Hebrew Congregations.

Purkiser, W. T., ed. 1955. *Exploring the Old Testament.* Kansas City, MO: Beacon Hill Press.

Robertson, F. W. 1877. *Notes on Genesis.* London, England: Henry S. King and Company.

Rogerson, J. W. 1991. *Genesis 1–11*. Sheffield, England: JSOT Press.

Rogerson, J. W., R. W. L. Moberly, and W. Johnstone. 2001. *Genesis and Exodus*. Sheffield, England: Sheffield Academic Press.

Rooker, M. F. 2001. The Genesis Flood. *Southern Baptist Journal of Theology* 5.3: 58–74.

Rosscup, J. n.d. *Genesis*. Sun Valley, CA: The Master's Seminary.

Roy, A. 1996. Fountains of the great deep: The primary cause of the Flood. *Creation Research Society Quarterly* 33: 18–21.

Sailhamer, J. H. 1990. Genesis. In vol. 2 of *The expositor's Bible commentary*. Ed. F. E. Gæbelein. Grand Rapids, MI: Zondervan.

Sarna, N. M. 1966. *Understanding Genesis: The heritage of biblical Israel*. New York, NY: Schocken Books.

†Sarna, N. M. 1989. *Genesis: The traditional Hebrew text with the new JPS translation*. JPS Torah commentary. Philadelphia, PA: Jewish Publication Society.

Schaeffer, F. A. 1973. *Genesis in space and time*. Glendale, CA: G/L Publications.

Speiser, E. A. 1964. *Genesis: Introduction, translation, and notes*. The Anchor Bible 1. Garden City, NY: Doubleday and Company.

Spurrell, G. J. 1887. *Notes on the Hebrew text of the book of Genesis*. Oxford, England: Clarendon Press.

Stedman, R. C. 1978. *The beginnings*. Waco, TX: Word Books.

Thielicke, H. 1961. *How the world began: Man in the first chapters of the Bible*. Trans. J. W. Doberstein. Philadelphia, PA: Muhlenberg Press.

Thomas, W. H. G. 1946. *Genesis: A devotional commentary*. Grand Rapids, MI: William. B. Eerdmans Publishing Company.

Trumbull, C. G. 1926. *Genesis and yourself: The book of beginnings speaks to the world of today*. Philadelphia, PA: The Sunday School Times Company.

Tsumura, D. T. 1994. Genesis and ancient Near Eastern stories of creation and Flood: An introduction. In *I studied inscriptions from before the Flood; Ancient Near Eastern, literary, and linguistic approaches to Genesis 1–11*. Ed. R. S. Hess, and D. T. Tsumura. Winona Lake, IN: Eisenbrauns.

Turner, L. A. 2000. *Genesis*. Sheffield, England: Sheffield Academic Press.

Unfred, D. W. 1986. Flood and post-Flood geodynamics: An expanded earth model. *Creation Research Society Quarterly* 22: 171–79.

Van Wijk-Bos, J. W. H. 2005. *Making wise the simple: The Torah in Christian faith and practice*. Grand Rapids, MI: William B. Eerdmans Publishing Company.

Vawter, B. 1977. *On Genesis: A new reading*. Garden City, NY: Doubleday and Company.

Walker, T. 1994. A biblical geologic model. In *Proceedings of the third International Conference on Creationism*. Ed. R. E. Walsh, 581–592. Pittsburgh, PA: Creation Science Fellowship.[7]

---

7. Walker's work on the Flood's chronology is too indefinite to justify classifying it under the heading of a distinct chronological perspective. He holds rather arbitrarily to a peak on the sixtieth day of the deluge; however, he admits the need for modification to his view depending upon the actual time of inundation. Interestingly, Walker contends that the rain stopped on the fortieth day (585–86), leaving one to wonder why he saw a need for an additional twenty days prior to the initial subsiding of the Flood.

Walton, J. H. 2001. *Genesis*. The NIV application commentary. Grand Rapids, MI: Zondervan.

Watson, D. C. C. 1988. *Myths and miracles: A new approach to Genesis 1–11*. Sunnybank, Australia: Creation Science Foundation.

Westermann, C. 1976. *Handbook to the Old Testament*. Trans. and ed. R. H. Boyd. Minneapolis, MN: Augsbugh Publishing House.

Whitelaw. T. 1950. *Genesis: Exposition and homiletics*. The pulpit commentary 1. Ed. H. D. M. Spence. Grand Rapids, MI: William. B. Eerdman's Publishing Company.

Williams, P. 2001. *From Eden to Egypt: Exploring the Genesis themes*. Epsom, England: Day One Publications.

Woodson, L. 1974. *The Beginning: A study of Genesis*. Wheaton, IL: Victor Books.

Wright, C. H. H. 1859. *The book of Genesis in Hebrew*. London, England: Williams and Norgate.

Yates, K. M. 1962. Genesis. In *The Wycliffe Bible commentary*. Ed. C. F. Pfeiffer, and E. F. Harrison. Chicago, IL: Moody Press.

Youngblood, R. F. 1991. *The book of Genesis: An introductory commentary*. Grand Rapids, MI: Baker Book House.

Appendix B: Statistics on Sources Consulted on the Chronology of the Flood in Literature Past and Present

This appendix lists the statistical data relevant to the sources consulted in the writing of **Chapter 8**: Waves of Opinion: The Chronology of the Flood in Literature Past and Present.

Out of a total of one hundred sixty-eight sources discussing the Genesis Flood, only eighty-one sources (roughly forty-eight percent) took a definitive stance on a particular chronological perspective. Over half of the sources written on the Genesis Flood neglect to give any reasonable attention to chronological matters.

Of the eighty-one sources that did comment on chronology, twenty (nearly one-fourth) held that the Flood narrative is comprised of a compilation of source material and that the chronological perspectives of these sources are in conflict. Thirty-six sources (roughly forty-four percent) argued for a peak on the one hundred fiftieth day of the Flood; seven (nine percent) argued for a peak on the fortieth day of the Flood; and fourteen (seventeen percent) maintained that the peak was attained on the fortieth day and sustained until the one hundred fiftieth day. Additionally, four sources (five percent) held to some form of alternative perspective on the Flood's chronology.

Examination of Chronology

□ Position Stated   ■ No Position Stated

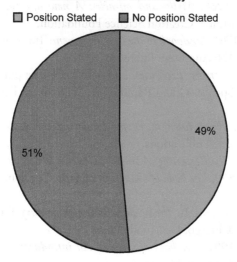

Comparison of Chronological Perspectives

■ Documentary Hypothesis; Sources in Conflict
□ Peak on the 150th Day
■ Peak on the 40th Day
■ Peak on the 40th Day; Sustained until the 150th Day
■ Alternative Models

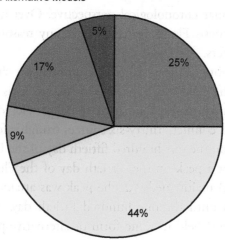

References

Archer, G. L. 2007. *A survey of Old Testament introduction*. Rev. ed. Chicago, IL: Moody Bible Institute.

Barré, L. M. 1988. The riddle of the Flood chronology. *Journal for the Study of the Old Testament* 41: 3–20.

Barrick, W. D., and R. Sigler. 2003. Hebrew and geologic analyses of the chronology and parallelism of the Flood: Implications for interpretation of the geologic record. In *Proceedings of the fifth International Conference on Creationism*. Ed. R. L. Ivey Jr., 397–408. Pittsburgh, PA: Creation Science Fellowship.

Calvin, J. 1979. *Commentaries on the first book of Moses called Genesis*. Trans. J. King. Grand Rapids, MI: Baker Book House. (Orig. pub. 1948).

Cassuto, U. 1997. *A commentary on the book of Genesis, part II—from Noah to Abraham*. Trans. I. Abrahams. Jerusalem, Israel: The Magnes Press.

Chisholm, R. B. Jr. 2003. History or story? The literary dimension in narrative texts. In *Giving the sense: Understanding and using Old Testament historical texts*. Ed. D. M. Howard Jr., and M. A. Grisanti. Grand Rapids, MI: Kregal Publications.

Cryer, F. H. 1985. The interrelationships of Gen 5, 32; 11, 10–11, and the chronology of the Flood (Gen 6–9). *Biblica* 66: 241–261.

Fasold, D. 1988. *The ark of Noah*. New York, NY: Wynwood Press.

Hamilton, V. P. 2005. *Handbook on the Pentateuch*. Grand Rapids, MI: Baker Academic.

Heidel, A. 1949. *The Gilgamesh epic and Old Testament parallels*. 2nd ed. Chicago, IL: Phoenix Books.

Hoehner, H. W. 1977. *Chronological aspects of the life of Christ*. Grand Rapids, MI: Academie Books. (Orig. pub. 1973).

Keil, C. F., and F. Delitzsch. 1976. *Commentary on the Old Testament*. Vol. 1. Trans. J. Martin. Grand Rapids, MI: William B. Eerdmans Publishing Company. (Orig. pub. 1878).

Kidner, D. 1967. *Genesis*. Tyndale Old Testament commentary series 1. Downers Grove, IL: Inter-Varsity Press.

Lemche, N. P. 1980. The chronology in the story of the Flood. *Journal for the Study of the Old Testament* 18: 52–62.

Luther, M. 1958. *Luther's commentary on Genesis*. Vol. 1. Trans. J. T. Mueller. Grand Rapids, MI: Zondervan Publishing House.

Murphy, J. G. 1998. *A critical and exegetical commentary on the book of Genesis*. Eugene, OR: Wipf and Stock Publishers. (Orig. pub. 1847).

Rashi. 1949. *The Penteteuch and Rashi's commentary: A linear translation into English (Genesis)*. Compiled by Rabbi Abraham Ben Isaiah, and Rabbi Benjamin Sharfman. Brooklyn, NY: S. S. and R. Publishing Company.

Sarna, N. M. 1989. *Genesis: The traditional Hebrew text with the new JPS translation*. JPS Torah commentary. Philadelphia, PA: Jewish Publication Society.

Smith, R. P. 1885. *The first book of Moses, called Genesis*. London, England: Cassell and Company, Limited.

Snelling, A. A. 2009. *Earth's catastrophic past: Geology, creation and the Flood*. Vol. 1. Dallas, TX: Institute for Creation Research.

Stigers, H. 1976. *A commentary on Genesis*. Grand Rapids, MI: Zondervan Publishing House.

Vos, H. F. 1982. Flood. In vol. 2 of *The international standard Bible encyclopedia*. Rev. ed. Ed. G. W. Bromiley. Grand Rapids, MI: William B. Eerdmans Publishing Company.

Wenham, G. J. 1978. The coherence of the Flood narrative. *Vestus Testamentum* 28: 336–348.

Whitcomb, J. C., and H. M. Morris. 1961. *The Genesis Flood: The biblical record and its scientific implications*. Phillipsburg, NJ: Presbyterian and Reformed Publishing Company.

CHAPTER 9

Charting the Textual Waters: Textual Issues in the Chronology of the Genesis Flood Narrative

Drew G. Longacre

Analogy and Orientation. A wise captain procures and studies nautical charts for a voyage to avoid treacherous waters and to determine the proper course. In the same way, responsible critical examination of the biblical writings must be based on a thorough examination of the text itself. One of the most prominent textual problems in the Genesis Flood narrative is its chronology, so any volume attempting to evaluate the chronology of the narrative cannot avoid the text-critical task. This chapter meets that demand by evaluating the textual variants relating to the chronology of the Genesis Flood narrative.

Abstract. Any sophisticated analysis of the Genesis Flood chronology requires close investigation of the text to be studied. The ancient witnesses vary widely in their chronological details, making adjudication between these variants a necessary prerequisite for properly understanding the chronology. This chapter lists and evaluates all the textual problems related to the Genesis Flood chronology as the foundation for this volume's treatment of the chronological issues.

Outline

1. Introduction

Chronological details are very prominent in the Genesis Flood narrative, as any reader can immediately recognize. What the average reader may not realize, however, is that these details are also extraordinarily controversial. Nearly every element of chronological information in the narrative is contested, either by ancient manuscripts and commentators or by modern scholars. In order to study the chronology of the Genesis Flood narrative, scholars must first wade through this confusion to ensure that the chronological data used as the foundation for the study are the most accurate possible.

The textual commentary in this chapter stems from the results of a broader investigation into the entire text of the Genesis Flood narrative. The full critical text is included as an appendix for further scholarly consideration. Unfortunately, due to limitations of space, I was not able to include the entire textual commentary justifying all of the conclusions indicated. I have included in this chapter a simplified introduction dealing only with details important for understanding the chronological issues, and full scholarly discussion has been reserved for a separate introduction to the critical text in the appendix. Readers should consult the appendix for detailed discussions about the editions collated, textual characteristics of the given witnesses, and important details more pertinent to the critical text than the Flood chronology.

1.1   Textual Criticism
1.2   Textual Witnesses
1.3   Variant Apparatuses
1.4   Symbols
1.5   Abbreviations

1.1 *Textual Criticism*

Over millennia of copying the biblical text, occasionally scribal errors or intentional interventions into the text gave rise to incorrect readings in biblical manuscripts. One goal of textual criticism is to work back from these manuscripts as nearly as possible to the earliest text of the literary works to which they attest. Textual critics do this first by examining and comparing ("collating") the readings of all the surviving ancient manuscripts. In cases where there are differences, they then evaluate the variants based on the strength of their manuscript support and the probable directions of change to determine which readings are most original. This process is essential for studying any ancient text which survives in handwritten copies, as does the Bible.

1.2 *Textual Witnesses*

The text of the Genesis Flood narrative can be found in many different textual witnesses. I have included here a simplified introduction to the major textual witnesses. See the appendix for further explanation.

    1.2.1 The Masoretic Text (MT)
    1.2.2 The Samaritan Pentateuch (SP)
    1.2.3 The Dead Sea Scrolls
    1.2.4 The Greek Septuagint (LXX)
    1.2.5 The Syriac Peshitta (Syr.)
    1.2.6 The Aramaic Targums (Targs.)
    1.2.7 The Latin Vulgate (Vulg.)
    1.2.8 The Other Sources

1.2.1 The Masoretic Text (MT)

The Masoretic text (MT) is the text preserved in the medieval Jewish manuscripts, which serves as the foundation for most critical texts and translations of Genesis. Its text for the Pentateuch is very conservative and well-preserved, and it shows little evidence of intentional revision.

1.2.2 The Samaritan Pentateuch (SP)

The Samaritan Pentateuch (SP) is the text preserved in medieval Samaritan manuscripts. Its text for the Pentateuch gives evidence of being heavily revised, modernized, expanded, and harmonized to alleviate perceived problems. In the Flood narrative, however, it reads very closely with the MT.

1.2.3 The Dead Sea Scrolls

4Q252 (4QCommentary on Genesis A). 4Q252 is by far the most important witness to the Genesis Flood narrative surviving at Qumran. It dates approximately to the second half of the first century BC (Brooke 1996, 190). The literary genre of 4Q252 remains hotly debated, but it clearly retells the story of the Flood narrative in a very condensed form, focusing on the chronologically significant elements of the story. Its chronological data are key readings for determining the original chronology of the Genesis Flood narrative. 4Q252 explains how, in its author's opinion, the chronology of the Flood fits with the three hundred sixty-four day schematic-solar calendar commonly attested in the Qumran documents. It does so by restating the chronological details of the Flood narrative (closely following the MT and SP with one important exception), making explicit details left implicit in Genesis, and showing how the dates and time periods cohere perfectly (to the day, as 4Q252 takes pains to point out) when reckoned according to the three hundred sixty-four day calendar. Whether 4Q252 has rightly understood the calendar of the Genesis Flood narrative or not, its intention is clear enough.

   4Q254a (4QCommentary on Genesis D). 4Q254a is a commentary on the Genesis Flood narrative that is preserved only in fragmentary form. It can be dated to the end of the first century BC or the beginning of the first century AD (Brooke 2002, 235). The text is extremely fragmentary and does not follow the biblical text closely, so it is generally of little text-critical value. It does, however, preserve one date, which may be extraordinarily important for the chronology of the Flood.

1.2.4 The Greek Septuagint (LXX)
The Septuagint (LXX) is the late third century BC Greek translation of Genesis. Its text gives evidence of being heavily revised, expanded, and harmonized to alleviate perceived problems. In the Flood narrative its chronology differs greatly from the MT, SP, and Dead Sea Scrolls. The LXX was revised many times in antiquity to align it more closely with the MT. It was also translated into many additional languages.

1.2.5 The Syriac Peshitta (Syr.)
The Peshitta (Syr.) is the Syriac translation of Genesis from the Hebrew. It is a minor version and attests to the dates in the MT and SP.

1.2.6 The Aramaic Targums (Targs.)
The Targums (Targs.) are Aramaic translations of Genesis. Targ. Onkelos became the authoritative translation in rabbinic Judaism. Targs. Neofiti and Pseudo-Jonathan present alternative translations. Different fragments of Aramaic translations were also found in a genizah (manuscript burial chamber) in Cairo. The Samaritans also preserved an Aramaic Targ. These are minor versions and attest to the dates in the MT and SP.

1.2.7 The Latin Vulgate (Vulg.)
The Vulgate (Vulg.) is the Latin translation of Genesis by Jerome. It is a minor version, but it does have significant chronological readings.

1.2.8 The Other Sources
A number of other ancient literary works and commentaries have been cited for their chronological data. The second century BC Jewish retelling of Genesis and Exodus named Jubilees (*Jub.*) is one of the more significant. Variant data in the writings of the ancient Jewish scholars Philo and Josephus also figure prominently.

1.3 *Variant Apparatuses*

An apparatus listing all the variant readings in ancient manuscripts and commentators precedes the discussion for each problematic reading in the textual commentary. Occasionally, conjectural emendations are also noted when deemed significant enough.

Preferred readings are listed first, concluded by a right bracket]. Rejected variants are then listed in descending order of preferability, separated by a single vertical line |. Hebrew text in the apparatus does not have vocalization, accentuation, or any other Masoretic accoutrements in addition to the consonantal text.

Each variant is listed first in Hebrew, either according to Hebrew manuscripts or as reconstructed from the ancient versions. Where Hebrew witnesses with only minor differences of orthography attest to the same reading, they are normally cited together without distinction according to the editor's preferred orthography. I also include an English translation of each variant for the aid of any lay readers.

Where Hebrew variants are retroverted from versional readings without Hebrew-language attestation, the apparatus utilizes a three-tiered system of notation to indicate levels of reliability of the reconstructions. Where, in the end, variants are considered to be unquestionably translational in nature or inner-versional corruptions with no viable claim to being a Hebrew reading, I have marked the reconstruction as merely diagnostic with a superscripted asterisk *. A superscripted question mark ?, in contrast, indicates a reconstruction that could plausibly be explained either as due to translation style or reflecting a different Hebrew text in the version's *Vorlage*, the Hebrew manuscript from which it was translated. Reconstructions that almost certainly reflect a variant Hebrew *Vorlage* (or at least a misreading of a Hebrew text) are cited as Hebrew variants without additional annotation. I have also included the major versional evidence in its versional forms for ease in checking proposed reconstructions, should those with the requisite knowledge so desire.

The supporting witnesses for each variant (specified by the symbols defined in **Subsection 1.4** and abbreviations listed in **Subsection 1.5**) follow the Hebrew readings in five tiers. First, the Hebrew witnesses are cited (𝔐 𝔴 4Q252 etc.). Second, the primary ancient versions are cited in alphabetical order (𝔊 𝔖 𝔗 𝔙), followed by the respective versional texts cited in parentheses. Third, significant ancillary witnesses that attest to the text are cited (*Jub.* etc.). Fourth, daughter versions translated from the Septuagint are cited in alphabetical order when they disagree with the Septuagint in alignment with major textual witnesses (Aeth Arab Arm La Pal Syh etc.). Fifth, any ancient commentators who differ in chronological details are cited. In cases where versional readings could potentially be interpreted as supporting more than one reading but not another reading, they are listed at the end of the list after bidirectional arrows ↔ followed by the potentially supported readings separated by forward slashes / (e.g., ↔ מאות ששה/מאות שש 𝕲 [τῷ ἑξακοσιοστῷ]). For proposed Hebrew readings that are conjectural emendations without significant manuscript support, supporting scholars have been cited. Whenever it becomes important to cite individual manuscripts or groups of manuscripts in disagreement with the preferred reading of the witness with which they are normally associated, this is indicated by a superscripted MS or MSS after the symbol for the witness from which they differ. Additional notes after all of the supporting witnesses indicate yet other witnesses to be considered that may have a bearing on understanding the variant, but do not directly support it.

The apparatus uses English words and abbreviations for explanatory notes rather than Latin. A full listing of the English abbreviations can be found on the abbreviations page.

1.4 *Symbols*

𝕲	Septuagint
𝔐	Masoretic text
οἱ λ'	οἱ λοιποί
𝔪	Samaritan Pentateuch
𝔖	Syriac
𝕿	Targum
𝕿ᶜ	Cairo Geniza Targum fragment(s)
𝕿ᴶ	Targum Pseudo-Jonathan
𝕿ᴺ	Targum Neofiti
𝕿ᴼ	Targum Onkelos
𝕿ˢ	Samaritan Targum(s)
𝔙	Vulgate
>	indicates direction of change
+	adds
↔	may support multiple variants against another
]x[	brackets marking the limits of extant text *x*
*	marks a literal reconstruction of a variant created in the act of translation or an inner-versional variant
?	marks a reconstruction of a variant created either in the act of translation or textual variation in the Hebrew
ẋ	combining dot above marks a partially-preserved or uncertain letter
vacat	space intentionally left blank in a manuscript
x̄	combining overline marks letters used as numbers

1.5 *Abbreviations*

Aeth	Ethiopic
Arab	Arabic
Arabic Frag.	
to Pent.	*Arabic Fragments to the Pentateuch*
Arm	Armenian
Hebr. Quaest.	*Hebraicae Quaestiones in Libro Geneseos*
Jub.	Jubilees
La	Old Latin
La[M]	text of Ambrose divergent from the Italian text
LXX	Greek Septuagint
MS(S)	Manuscript(s)
MT	Masoretic text
OT	Old Testament
Pal	Palestinian-Syriac
Quaest.	
in Gen.	*Quaestiones in Genesim*
SP	Samaritan Pentateuch
Syr.	Syriac Peshitta
Syh	Syrohexapla
Targ(s).	Aramaic Targum(s)
te	text of an edition
Vulg.	Latin Vulgate

2. Textual Commentary on the Chronological Variants from Genesis 6:5–9:17

7:11 שש מאות *six hundred* 𝔐 4Q252 I 3, ↔ שש מאות/השש מאות 𝕲 (τῷ ἑξακοσιοστῷ) 𝕾 (ܫܬܡܐܐ) 𝕮ᴼᴺᶜ (שית מאה) 𝖁 (*sescentesimo*)] השש מאות *the six hundred* ṃ, ↔ שש מאות/השש מאות 𝕲 (τῷ ἑξακοσιοστῷ) 𝕾 (ܫܬܡܐܐ) 𝕮ᴼᴺᶜ (שית מאה) 𝖁 (*sescentesimo*) | אחת ושש מאות* *six hundred and one* 𝕲ᴹˢˢ (τῷ ἑνὶ [πρώτῳ 𝕲ᴹˢˢ] καὶ ἑξακοσιοστῷ) Aethᴹˢˢ.

Wevers (1993, 93) explains that some manuscripts have the Flood beginning on the six hundred first year, probably rationalizing that the Flood must have happened in the year after the one mentioned in 7:6. Both the MT and SP readings are identical in meaning, but the MT reading is stylistically preferable. The syntax of the SP with the article preceding the numerals is quite rare, particularly in the earlier books. The SP, then, is likely to reflect a later reading.

7:11 השני *the second* 𝔐 ṃ 4Q252 I 4 𝕲 (τοῦ δευτέρου) 𝕾 (ܕܬܪܝܢ) 𝕮ᴼᴺᶜ (תנינא) 𝖁 (*secundo*)] השביעי* *the seventh* Armᵗᵉ Philo *Quest. in Gen.* ii.17, 31.

This minor variant probably reflects an attempt to locate the Flood in a given season, rather than any viable textual difference (cf. Lewis 1968, 49). The Armenian may be influenced by Philo.

7:11 בשבעה עשר יום *on the seventeenth day* 𝔐 ⅏ 4Q252 I 4 (בשבעה) בשבעה) 𝕮ᴺᶜ (בשבעת עשרה יומא) 𝕮° (ܒܫܒܥܣܪ) S (ⅉ καὶ ī) 𝔊ᴹˢˢ (עשר בשבע עסר יום) 𝕮ᴶ (עשר יומין) 𝕮ˢ⁽ᴹˢ⁾ (בשבעסר יום) 𝕮ˢ⁽ᴹˢˢ⁾ (בשבסרי יומין) 𝔙 (*septimodecimo die*) Arab Syh *Jub.* 5:23] בשבעה ועשרים² *on the twenty-seventh* 𝔊 (ἑβδόμῃ καὶ εἰκάδι) Philo *Quest. in Gen.* ii.17, 31, 33 Josephus *Antiquities* i.81, cf. *Book of Adam and Eve* iii.7.

The dates given in 7:11; 8:4, 14 have been the center of intense controversy throughout the textual history of the Genesis Flood narrative, as well as in modern times. The textual evidence for these three dates is extremely complicated. For the date of the beginning of the Flood, given in 7:11, the MT, SP, 4Q252, Syr., Vulg., all the Targs., an early Greek revised reading, and Jubilees 5:23 attest to בשבעה עשר יום "on the seventeenth day," whereas the LXX is alone in attesting to בשבעה ועשרים (יום) "on the twenty-seventh (day)." For the date of the Ark's setting aground, given in 8:4, the MT, SP, 4Q252, Syr., all the Targs., and an early Greek revised reading attest to בשבעה עשר יום "on the seventeenth day," whereas the LXX and Vulg. attest to בשבעה ועשרים (יום) "on the twenty-seventh (day)." For the date of the end of the Flood, given in 8:14, the MT, SP, LXX, Syr., Vulg., and all the Targs. attest to בשבעה ועשרים (יום) "on the twenty-seventh (day)," whereas 4Q252, Jubliees 5:31, a number of significant Greek manuscripts and families (L 58 *b d* 54 59), and perhaps 4Q254a attest to בשבעה עשר יום "on the seventeenth day." Thus both the seventeenth and twenty-seventh are attested for all three dates, and with no consistent pattern.

Traditionally, the dates of the MT have been accepted without much defense, and critical scholars have set out to explain the redactional relationships of the MT dates on the basis of various source theories. The LXX is known for intentionally altering dates, and Jubilees' late rediscovery, complex transmissional history, and characteristic looseness with regard to the biblical chronology did not engender much respect for its readings. But the discovery of the Dead Sea Scrolls has inaugurated a new age of inquiry, providing ancient Hebrew manuscript evidence for variant readings once thought impossible. There has been within the past few decades a reinvigorated methodological discussion on the contested dates of the Flood narrative, with scholars divided between rational and mechanical explanations.

The source of the controversy stems from a number of unique characteristics of the numbers. The MT and SP date the full course of the Flood from 600.2.17 (the seventeenth day of the second month of the sixtieth year of Noah's life) to 601.2.27, or one year and ten days.[1] Jewish exegetical traditions, however, state that the Flood lasted exactly one year (e.g., 1 Enoch 106:15; 4Q252 II 4–5; Philo *Quaest. in Gen.* ii.33; *Genesis Rabbah* 28:8; 30:6; 33:7; 34:1; Origen *Homilies on Genesis* ii.1–2), which is also the length preserved in various formulations in the LXX, 4Q252, and Jubilees. This raises the possibility that the witnesses to the biblical text may have been influenced by the parallel exegetical tradition. Furthermore, it is an interesting and often-noted phenomenon that the additional ten days in the MT and SP are also the same number of days as the difference between a lunar year (three hundred fifty-four days) and the schematic-solar year of many Second Temple Jewish works (three hundred sixty-four days),[2] which has given rise to many theories that seek to explain the differing dates as rational attempts to convert the Flood chronology from one calendar to another. In this case, the many textual witnesses that state that the Flood lasted exactly one year correctly recognize that the Flood of the MT and SP (reckoned according to the lunar calendar) lasted one lunar year plus ten days (or one full three hundred sixty-four day schematic-solar year), and so converted the dates to an equivalent year-long span of time according to the schematic-solar calendar (Zipor 1997, 207–08). Or conversely, the original length of the Flood was one three hundred sixty-five day solar year, and the MT and SP converted the dates to the lunar calendar by adding the eleven necessary days beyond the lunar year of three hundred fifty-four days (Lemche 1980, 55).

But another complicating factor has been noted in recent years by scholars who believe that some or all of the differing dates may have accidental scribal causes at their root, rather than intentional alterations and calendar conversions. The Hebrew בשבעה עשר יום "on the seventeenth day" is graphically very similar to (יום) בשבעה ועשרים "on the twenty-seventh (day)," the easy accidental interchange of which could potentially have led

---

1. One year and eleven days if counted inclusively. The simplified format (600.2.17) has been utilized in this chapter instead of the more explicit format (600y 2m 17d) used for the rest of the book because of its particularly frequent occurrence in this chapter.

2. A similar situation, though less precise, obtains with the standard solar calendar of three hundred sixty-five day years, in some systems modified with an additional intercalated day every fourth year. The eleven (or twelve?) additional days of this solar calendar can only be reconciled with the ten additional days of MT and SP if one is prepared to conjecture a shift from an inclusive reckoning of the dates to an exclusive system in the conversion process. Nevertheless, this link with the three hundred sixty-five day solar year is often asserted.

to the diversity of attested dates.[3] Thus, numerous scholars have proposed
that the solution to the complex web of variant dates can be discerned by
reversing the process of scribal error and textual corruption without recourse
to proposals of extensive revisions and reworking of the biblical chronology
in the textual witnesses. The battle lines have been drawn, and scholars
remain divided on the best way out of this quandary.

Critical resolution of the contested dates of the Flood narrative requires
a well-formulated methodological approach. First, this approach must not
unduly manipulate the textual data to bolster personal theories about the
redactional significance of the given dates. A proper understanding of the
significance of the dates must derive inductively from the established critical
text, rather than by forcing the text to fit into predetermined patterns
foreign to the original text. Redaction criticism must be in conversation
with textual criticism, but it should not be allowed to dominate it. Second,
this approach must reflect a balanced treatment of the various textual
witnesses, without granting inordinate authority to one or another witness.
Variant witnesses from the MT must be given due consideration without an
ideological bias in favor of the MT, and the same applies to all witnesses.
Third, this approach must be broadly informed, adjudicating between all
the various types of proposals based on their relative merits, rather than
granting a priori preference for one over the other. Critical scholars must
be willing to consider both accidental and intentional causes (or some
combination of the same) without necessary methodological preference for
one over the other, and they should generally prefer solutions that require
the most economical combination of accidental and intentional errors over
solutions with extreme compounding of layers of complexity *ad absurdum*.
And fourth, because these three dates exhibit identical interchanges of
numerals in the textual witnesses, potentially entail chronological problems,
and probably influenced one another, they should be treated together as a
complex of three interrelated dates. Solutions should be preferred which best
explain not only the variants for each individual date considered in isolation,

---

3. 17 > 27 requires בשבעה עשר יום > בשבעה עשריום (word misdivision) >
בשבעה עשרים (haplography of יו) > בשבעה ועשרים (secondary addition of ו) > בשבעה
ועשרים (יום) (secondary addition of יום or dittography of ים as יום). 27 > 17 requires
בשבעה ועשר > בשבעה ועשרים (omission of יום by haplography) > בשבעה ועשרים (יום)
(dittography of י as וי) > בשבעה ועשר יום (word misdivision) > בשבעה עשר יום
(secondary omission of ו). Broken down as such, the changes in both directions may at first
seem extraordinarily unwieldy, but all of the alterations are natural, common, and are likely
to have occurred simultaneously. Therefore, the complete change from בשבעה עשר יום to
בשבעה עשרים (יום) or vice versa is text-critically quite feasible.

but also all of the dates in the variously attested chronologies considered in combination. As such there are eight possible combinations of the dates in 7:11, 8:4, and 8:14 that could feasibly be proposed as original. Each of these will be systematically evaluated in ascending order of probability in an attempt to thoroughly exhaust the textual possibilities.

600.2.27–600.7.27–601.2.17 Original

In this scenario the original combination is not preserved in any extant witnesses. It could easily explain the LXX, with the last date changed either accidentally or to make the Flood last one year, but it fails to account for the other witnesses. It is extremely unlikely that the MT and SP would change all three dates by any cause, and only slightly less improbable that 4Q252 and Jubilees would change the first two. Thus, this combination of dates should be rejected.

600.2.17–600.7.27–601.2.17 Original

If this combination of dates were original, then the original would not be consistently retained in any extant sources. This is extremely unlikely, however, because this solution does not adequately explain any of the textual witnesses. It is most inexplicable that the MT and SP would change the last two dates in opposite directions, whether accidentally or intentionally. Finding the identical change for the second date in 4Q252 and Jubilees raises further suspicions. Likewise, it is quite difficult to explain why the LXX would have changed the first and third dates. It is true that the Vulgate supports the second date, but this reading is probably of little value. As such, this combination of dates should be rejected.

600.2.27–600.7.17–601.2.17 Original

In this combination as well, the original would not be preserved. Josephus apparently does attest to the first two dates, but his dates do not cohere well and may be problematic (*Antiquities* i.81, 90). This solution accords well with the dates of 4Q252 and Jubilees, as the first date could have been changed accidentally, to make the Flood last one year, or even more likely to correct the perceived chronological problem that 2.27 to 7.17 (according to any calendar) is less than the required one hundred fifty day period. But the other textual witnesses are more difficult to explain. The LXX would have had to have changed the second (to account for the one hundred fifty day period) and third dates (accidental or to make the Flood last one year), but this is somewhat stretched. And it is even more difficult to explain the reversal of the first and third dates in the MT and SP, so this solution should be rejected.

600.2.27–600.7.17–601.2.27 Original

This combination of dates is not preserved in any witnesses, though Josephus apparently does attest to the first two dates (*Antiquities* i.81, 90). It does, however, have some explanatory power. The MT and SP would have then changed the first date either accidentally or to allow sufficient room for the one hundred fifty day period between the beginning of the Flood and the setting aground of the Ark (somewhat more likely for the SP than the MT). The LXX can also quite plausibly be said to have changed the second date either accidentally or, more likely, to allow room for the same one hundred fifty day period. Only 4Q252 and Jubilees remain problematic for this view. Identical accidental corruptions in the first and third dates do not seem plausible. It could be said that the first date was changed to account for the one hundred fifty day period and that the third date was secondarily altered to retain the year-long length of the Flood, but this could have been much more easily accomplished by altering the second date instead as in the LXX. The 4Q252 and Jubilees dates could then only be explained on the supposition of a prior accidental error for either the first or third dates, followed by secondary corrections either to account for the one hundred fifty day period or to make the Flood last one year. While this is possible, this solution is rejected because of its lack of attestation and the difficulty in accounting for 4Q252 and Jubilees.

600.2.27–600.7.27–601.2.27 Original

The dates preserved in the LXX can claim significant ancient testimony,[4] but they cannot adequately explain the origin of the variant readings. The situation with the MT and SP is very difficult, as they are unlikely to have accidentally changed both the first and second dates. It is even more implausible that they would have intentionally changed both dates, as it would have artificially prolonged the Flood past one year with no apparent reason.[5] If the second date were accidentally changed, however, the first date may have been altered to allow for the one hundred fifty day period between the beginning of the Flood and the setting aground of the Ark. But the dates in 4Q252 and Jubilees are even more inexplicable on the presupposition of the originality of the LXX.

---

4. Philo's chronology is somewhat confused on the months in which these dates occur, but the key events all occur on the twenty-seventh of the month (*Quaest. in Gen.* ii. 17, 29, 31, 33, 45, 47; cf. Lewis 1968, 49–50; Zipor 1997, 208). Josephus apparently agrees with the LXX on the first date (twenty-seventh, *Antiquities* i.81), but with the MT, SP, and 4Q252 on the second date (seventeenth, *Antiquities* i.90). He does not give the third date. Because his dates do not cohere well with the one hundred fifty day period, it is possible that there is a problem with the dates in the transmission of Josephus' works, though we cannot be sure.

5. It would be far too speculative and historically dubious to propose that they somehow intended to convert an original (or Priestly) solar calendar into a lunar calendar (contra Vogt 1962). Such a proposal would also encounter the same problems with other proposals of calendar conversion mentioned below.

Only an exceedingly complicated and multi-leveled series of accidental and intentional changes could explain the complete inversion of all three dates. The LXX dates are rejected, then: they inadequately account for the origin of the dates in the MT, SP, and the ancillary sources.

600.2.17–600.7.17–601.2.17 Original

The combination of dates preserved in 4Q252 and Jubilees (recently gaining supporters and to date the most strongly argued alternative to the dates of the MT and SP) implies that the MT and SP would have changed the end date of the Flood. E. Vogt (1962, 213, 215) proposes that this change may have been directed against the Priestly calendar (having originally all three dates as the seventeenth), to undermine the symbolic significance he sees in the seventeenth if reckoned according to the Priestly calendar. This significance for the dates is not textually substantiated, however, and no textual decisions should be grounded in it. More likely is his proposal (215), which Hendel follows (1995; 1998, 54–55), that the MT and SP changed the third date from בשבעה עשר יום "on the seventeenth day" to בשבעה ועשרים יום "on the twenty seventh day" accidentally. Zipor (1997, 208–09) has objected that the exact nature of the change is actually much more complicated than simple dittography, but the proposed change is certainly text-critically feasible.[6]

Hendel adduces support for his text-critical explanation by further comparison with the LXX. He notes that, not only does the LXX have the twenty seventh for each of the three readings, but in each case it does not have an equivalent for the Hebrew יום. He concludes that the literal translation

---

6. Zipor incorrectly claims that Hendel "overlooks" the copulative ו in his reconstruction, because Hendel clearly recognizes this complication (1995, 78; 1998, 55), even though he does at times simplify his instructions. As noted before, the interchange between seventeen and twenty-seven requires בשבעה עשר יום > בשבעה עשריום (word misdivision) > בשבעה עשרים (haplography of יו) > בשבעה ועשרים (secondary addition of ו) > בשבעה ועשרים יום (secondary addition of יום or dittography of ים as יום). Instead, Hendel (1995, 78) suggests dittography of יום at the beginning of the process, which led secondarily to the same end result via a similar process. Another somewhat unlikely scenario he notes is that יום could have been written defectively as ים as is occasionally found in some Hebrew inscriptions (Siloam, Samaria, Lachish, Arad), though it is never thus written in the Hebrew Bible (77). This somewhat complex interchange could quite easily be made in one single step in the copying process. For instance, a scribe reading a manuscript with a small space between עשר and יום could have easily mistaken it for עשרים upon a quick reading and unconsciously substituted the proper formula including ו and יום to arrive at בשבעה ועשרים יום. The complexity of each individual alteration viewed independently cannot be used to negate the possibility of the interchange as a whole. Thus, Hendel's text-critical solution cannot be easily dismissed, but must be seriously considered. Indeed, as will be discussed below, it is doubtful that all of the diverse textual evidence can be adequately explained without appeal to this or the reverse scribal error on some level.

style of the LXX in Genesis would lead us to expect an equivalent in these locations as well. Hendel is correct that the LXX in Genesis consistently translates the Hebrew word יוֹם.[7] His statement rings somewhat hollow, however, when weighed against the fact that these three dates are the only similar date formulae with יוֹם in the MT of Genesis (Rösel 1998a, 592).

The limited pool of data demands the consideration of date formulae throughout the entire Pentateuch. When this is done, the LXX is seen to agree with the MT and SP in the presence or absence of the word "day" twenty-four of thirty-two times.[8] The LXX includes a "day" not present in MT only in Leviticus 23:5, but here the SP agrees with the LXX. In only five instances (Gn 7:11; 8:4, 14; Ex 12:6; Lv 23:34) do MT and SP have the word "day," when it is not found in the LXX. This additional data substantially confirms the conclusion that the LXX generally literally translates the Hebrew word יוֹם, including in date formulae. However, it also provides two additional counter-examples where it is not present, just as in the Flood narrative dates.[9] In the end, the evidence is probably inconclusive on whether the LXX would have left יוֹם untranslated, but it is certainly difficult to find any evidence for an LXX tendency to omit the word "day" for "idiomatic reasons" (contra Wevers 1993, 93; Zipor 1997, 209; Rösel 1998a, 592; 1998b, 69).[10]

---

7. Of the one hundred fifty-two instances of "day" in the MT, it is always translated ἡμέρα or σήμερον in Genesis, except 3:8; 14:1; 18:1; 25:7; 26:1, 8, 15 (which are translated idiomatically), 26:18 (which is anomalous), and the date formulae in 7:11; 8:4, 14.

8. Present: Ex 12:18; 16:1; Lv 23:6, 39; Nm 9:3, 5, 11; 28:16, 17; 29:12; 33:3. Absent: Ex 12:3; Lv 16:29; 23:24, 27, 32; 25:9; Nm 1:1, 18; 10:11; 29:1, 7; 33:38; Dt 1:3. Ex 40:2, 17 are anomalous cases of little value.

9. The one example of disagreement between MT and SP/LXX (Lv 23:5) may open the door to the idea that even these two counter-examples, however, could be explained as textual variants in the *Vorlage* of the LXX, rather than characteristic of the LXX translation style. It is also interesting that both of these counter-examples are isolated occurrences in chapters where there is in the MT, SP, and LXX otherwise identical alternation between dates with and dates without an explicit יוֹם, which further shows the literalistic tendencies of the LXX with regard to the date formulae. In the Genesis Flood narrative alone is there a consistent pattern of LXX omission of an equivalent for יוֹם, and text-critical explanations may account for these anomalies.

10. In light of the above results, the onus is on those who would explain away the omission of "day" as translational to prove their case. For one, they should identify precisely which idiomatic reasons would have led to leaving it untranslated, along with supporting evidence, rather than simply making the vague assertion. What evidence can be adduced that the word was redundant and unnecessary in Greek, as opposed to Hebrew (per Zipor 1997, 209)? They must also explain why these idiomatic reasons do not appear to have been operative throughout the rest of the Pentateuch. Even granting the harmonizing tendency of the LXX (per Rösel 1998a, 592), what could these passages be harmonized to? To 8:5 and 8:13, which lack יוֹם? But both of these refer to the first of the month, which normally lacks יוֹם (even in the LXX), while Hendel (1995, 77) argues that numbers in the teens consistently have יוֹם. And how likely is the harmonizing tendency of the LXX to lead to the *omission* of the words, when most of its characteristic harmonizations in the Flood narrative are *additive*? The stylistic question is incredibly complex and cannot easily be brushed over by those who see no significance in the omission of "day" in the LXX.

Since the LXX has the same formula for the date of the end of the Flood as it does for the beginning of the Flood and the setting aground of the Ark, Hendel has concluded that a similar alteration from the seventeenth to the twenty-seventh as is present in 7:11 and 8:4 likely also occurred in 8:14 (1995, 77). The LXX is then seen as the intermediate link between the date 601.2.17 of 4Q252 and Jubilees and the 601.2.27 of the MT and SP, so בשבעה עשר יום (original, 4Q252, Jubilees) > בשבעה ועשרים יום (LXX) > בשבעה ועשרים יום (MT, SP). While the LXX text is certainly not an actual precursor to the MT and SP text, it is reasonable to cite it as illustrative of an intermediate stage of the process that would lead eventually to the text of the MT and SP.

One particular weakness in Hendel's argumentation is his failure to address alternative possibilities. For instance, the process he proposes is completely reversible without loss of feasibility, as in בשבעה ועשרים יום (original, MT, SP) > בשבעה ועשרים (LXX) > בשבעה עשר יום (4Q252, Jubilees). So even if Hendel has identified one possible solution to the variants in 8:14, he has not established that his is the only—or even preferred—solution. His only argument in support of his proposed direction of corruption against other possibilities is the parallel situation in 7:11 and 8:4, but this alone is far from compelling. Hendel himself recognizes that it is exceedingly improbable that all three dates in the LXX would have been independently changed by accidental means in exactly the same way, so his analogy with 7:11 and 8:4 cannot stand.[11] There are, then, multiple possible explanations of the LXX data from a text-critical perspective.

At this point, methodology becomes paramount. Hendel has concluded that his proposed direction of change best accounts for the variant readings extant for 8:14. But what he has not done is consider the date in 8:14 as part of a complex of three interrelated dates (Zipor 1997, 209). The solution to be preferred should rather be best able to explain not only the origin of the variant readings in 8:14 viewed as an isolated textual problem, but also the origin of the complete dating systems in the extant witnesses viewed

---

11. He states for instance, "It would seem likely that in G (or proto-G) the misreading of one phrase influenced or contaminated the other two by assimilation, rather than the same error occurring in each verse independently" (1995, 78). If only one instance of this text-critical interchange led to the corruption of the other two dates in turn, then the process of the creation of the date scheme in the LXX necessarily becomes much more complicated. Just as it is very unlikely that all three changes were independently made, it is almost as difficult to explain how one accidental error could have led to the subsequent corruption of two other dates, unless one resorts to complex rational alterations. In that case, the parallels between 7:11; 8:4, 14 have absolutely no validity in arguing for the direction of change proposed by Hendel.

as coherent wholes. It is not sufficient to explain the origin of the variants for each individual date independently, but an adequate answer to the problem must also explain how each of the affected dates influenced the other dates within each witness. When viewed as a complex whole as such, Hendel's proposal performs poorly. His solution for 8:14 may provide a possible origin for all the variant dates in 8:14, but on the supposition of an original chronology with the dates of 4Q252 and Jubilees, there is no good explanation for the complete threefold transformation of the LXX date system.[12] The LXX, therefore, would seem to belie Hendel's solution.

Somewhat less complicated, but still quite significant, is the date structure of 4Q252 and Jubilees. Because these two witnesses are ancillary sources, rather than biblical texts, some have objected that they are unreliable guides to reconstructing the original dates. Rösel claims, for instance, that 4Q252 expands and reworks the dates according to its preferred three hundred sixty-four day calendar, and as such, he easily dismisses its end date for the Flood (1998a, 592; so also Brooke 1998, 16–17). But this claim is only half true. It is correct that 4Q252 expands the chronology of the biblical text substantially by adding new dates and even identifying the days of the week for the events according to its calendar. But in every case, these additional dates are derived from contextual indicators of time intervals found in the Genesis text, rather than invented. 4Q252 extrapolates additional chronological information from the data implicit in the biblical text, but in no certain case does it "rework" any of the dates found in its textual *Vorlage*. Rather, with extraordinary precision, 4Q252 reproduces the chronological information found in the MT and SP (with the exception of the contested end date) within the perspective of its three hundred sixty-four day calendar perfectly.[13]

---

12. Probably the most likely explanation would be that the third date was changed to the twenty-seventh accidentally (as in the MT and SP), the first date was then changed to make the Flood last one year, and then the second date was changed to account for the one hundred fifty day period between 7:11 and 8:4. But this compounding of three layers of complexity renders this and any other possible explanations of the LXX dates highly problematic.

13. The same is true of 4Q252's treatment of the days of the week. In every case they are derived from the application of the three hundred sixty-four day calendar to the dates of the biblical text, even if 4Q252 may have understood the days to have had symbolic significance. Never are the dates invented or altered to have significant events occur on certain days of the week. It is true that in 4Q252 the Flood ends and begins on the same day, but that is a necessary phenomenon in the three hundred sixty-four day calendar. Additionally, Noah opens the window, each dove is sent out, and the land is finally dried out on the first of the week. This may at first seem significant until it is realized that 601.2.27 in the 4Q252 calendar would have occurred on the fourth day of the week, which is the second equally repetitive day, with the waters continuing to decrease, the mountaintops appearing, Noah's removing the cover, and the waters drying off the face of the earth. By changing the dates, 4Q252 would then have gained very little. Additionally, it seems too great a coincidence that (of all the possible dates that could have been on the first of the week in the 4Q252 calendar) the date chosen would correspond exactly to identical interchanges in other witnesses and which so easily beg text-critical explanations.

Besides the utter lack of evidence for 4Q252's supposedly characteristic reworking of the dates of the MT and SP, the rhetorical aims of the document render such reworking highly unlikely. To claim that 4Q252 is converting the chronology of the Flood reckoned in lunar months in the MT and SP into terms of its schematic-solar calendar (so García Martínez 1998, 106) misunderstands the intent of the author, as evidenced by three points. First, even though it clearly propounds a three hundred sixty-four day schematic calendar, 4Q252 gives no explicit indication of an intentional conversion between calendars. Second, while lowering the date to the seventeenth would give an equivalent total length of the Flood (three hundred sixty-four days) in the three hundred sixty-four day calendar, a true calendar conversion would also require the alteration of all the intermediate dates in the Flood narrative, but 4Q252 does not do this. It is impossible that a calendar text which analyzes the chronology of the Flood as precisely as 4Q252 could make such a facile mistake. And third, to argue that the author of 4Q252 is engaged in converting a biblical lunar calendar into a schematic-solar calendar undermines his actual argument. Such a conversion would implicitly admit that the original biblical calendar is lunar, against his preferred schematic-solar calendar, and so would undermine his case for the originality of the schematic-solar calendar. 4Q252 intends to prove, by precise calculations and full expansion of the biblical data, that the biblical chronology is best explained when fit into the three hundred sixty-four day calendar, and thus his calendar is the correct one (Lim 1992, 292).[14] Noah (or at least Moses), according to 4Q252, must have used the three hundred sixty-four day calendar. To engage in intentional calendar conversion would be to admit defeat in the calendar wars of Second Temple Judaism, where the biblical text was to be the authoritative guide to calendrical practice.[15] 4Q252, therefore, cannot be explained by recourse to intentional calendar conversion.

---

14. Regarding the only apparent contradiction between the biblical and 4Q252 calendar, Lim notes, "It is also possible that the Qumran commentator was conscious of the discrepancy between his own reckoning of the dates with the solar calendar and the biblical chronology, but the convergence of the biblical data with his own dates elsewhere would have suggested to him that one hundred fifty days and 17/VII were referring to the two different events of the end of the mighty waters and the coming to rest of the ark." Thus, 4Q252 has removed the potential contradiction by not equating the one hundred fifty days with the five months. This may not satisfy modern scholars attempting to identify the original calendar of the biblical text, but it did satisfy the author of 4Q252.

15. Hendel (1995, 75) makes a similar argument for Jubilees, stating that it viewed Genesis as the warrant for its calendar.

The conclusion that must be drawn from this discussion is that the author of the work to which 4Q252 attests must have had a Hebrew-language textual *Vorlage* that read the date 601.2.17 in 8:14. This variant biblical text must be taken seriously and accounted for in any reconstruction without simply disregarding it because of its preservation in ancillary documents. That said, this 4Q252 date is probably corrupt, contra Hendel, since it cannot adequately explain the rise of the LXX date scheme. Either the text was intentionally revised to make the Flood last one year, or more likely, the original date of the twenty-seventh was corrupted accidentally to the seventeenth. Whatever explanation is preferred, the date 601.2.17 seems to be secondary.

4Q254a also seems to agree with the date 601.2.17 for the end of the Flood. Its text is fragmentary at this point and somewhat uncertain, but there are good contextual indicators that it agrees with 4Q252. Fragment 3, line 1 reads ב[שבעה עשר לחודש ". . . on the seventeenth of the month . . . ," and line 2 reads נוח יצא מן התבה למועד ימים ימימה [°° ". . . Noah went forth from the Ark at the annual appointed time." First, the proximity of the two lines fits the conclusion well, despite the missing connecting text. Second, the missing connection could very easily be reconstructed by analogy to similar phrases in 4Q252, which puts Noah's exit from the Ark on the seventeenth of the month. And third, this close relationship with 4Q252 is bolstered by their common reference to the annual appointed time at which Noah exits the Ark (perhaps the Feast of Shavuot/Weeks, according to Brooke 2002, 239). Alternatively, the gap could be filled with the land drying on 2.17, with Noah exiting the Ark at a later date as apparently in Jubilees. In all likelihood, however, 4Q254a attests to the same tradition as 4Q252, which places the end of the Flood and exit from the Ark on 601.2.17 (Brooke 2002, 236). This common reading shows that 4Q252 and 4Q254a are not idiosyncratic and innovative documents, but rather preserve a strong tradition at Qumran which cannot be lightly brushed off.

The situation with the book of Jubilees is similar. Hendel notes that Jubilees 5:31 gives the end date for the Flood when the earth was dry as 2.17, just as 4Q252. Others have pointed out, however, that Jubilees is not a simple support for the 4Q252 date, because it also cites the date 2.27 in 5:32 as the day Noah opened the Ark and let the animals out, thus managing to incorporate both competing traditions in its retelling in typical midrashic fashion (Zipor 1994, 388; 1997, 209; Rösel 1998a, 592). Because Jubilees is given to reworking the chronological information of the biblical text (unlike 4Q252), it is exceedingly difficult to tell whether Jubilees' 2.17 end date is based on a textual tradition or newly invented to make the Flood last one year in accord with contemporary exegetical traditions (cf. Van Ruiten 1998, 71). On either explanation, the 2.17 date is suspect as discussed above, and Jubilees also clearly attests to the 601.2.27 date of the MT, SP, and LXX.

Jubilees' older age and popularity at Qumran raises the possibility that the final date in 4Q252 (and 4Q254a?) may actually have been dependent upon Jubilees' date (cf. VanderKam 1998, 399). This could easily explain the source of the date 601.2.17 (and, hence, undermine its textual viability), and so is worthy of consideration. There are a number of major problems with this view, however. First, 4Q252 closely follows the data given in the biblical text, never otherwise including the innovative data of Jubilees. Second, 4Q252 actually disagrees with Jubilees in its final date. 4Q252 says that Noah exited the Ark on 601.2.17 after exactly one year. Jubilees, however, says only that the earth was dry on the seventeenth, delaying Noah's exit from the Ark until first of the next month (6:1). Thus 4Q252 cannot be directly dependent upon Jubilees. If Jubilees was indirectly the source of the 4Q252 reading, it could only have done so by influencing the biblical tradition on which 4Q252 was based. Whether the date 601.2.17 was influenced by Jubilees or was inherited by Jubilees, it is still secondary.

In sum, the proposal that 4Q252 and Jubilees preserve the original end date of the Flood is untenable, not because it lacks textual support, but because it fails adequately to account for the full diversity of date schemes extant in the textual witnesses. Hendel has proposed a viable explanation for the variant dates in 8:14 viewed in isolation, but his proposed solution cannot easily explain the origin of the entire LXX date structure. This solution, therefore, must be rejected in favor of a solution that better accounts for all the attested chronological systems.

600.2.17–600.7.27–601.2.27 Original

This combination is preserved only in the Vulg., which is not likely to testify to the original for this problem. The anomalous second date in the Vulg. rather probably stems from a Septuagintal reading or a corrupt Hebrew manuscript. The LXX could be easily explained from this perspective by accidental corruption of the first date or else revision to make the Flood last one year. The MT and SP could be explained by accidental corruption of the second date. 4Q252 and Jubilees are somewhat harder to explain, however, changing both the second and third dates. The third date could potentially be explained as changed to make the Flood last one year, but the second date would require the same accidental corruption as in the MT and SP, as it is unlikely that it would have been assimilated to match the first and third dates in these sources.

Horst Seebass provides another angle in support of the originality of the twenty-seventh date of the Ark's setting aground in the LXX and Vulg. (in his Genesis commentary, cited in Rösel 1998a, 592; not available to the editor). He notes that 2.17 to 7.17 in a lunar calendar with months of twenty-nine or thirty days is less than one hundred fifty days, leaving the Ark setting aground while the water is still prevailing. If the Ark does not set aground until the 7.27, then the water has seven or eight days after the one hundred fifty day period of prevailing to recede the fifteen cubits necessary for the Ark to land on the mountain. While Seebass succeeds in resolving a potential chronological problem in the MT and SP text, his solution is not entirely compelling. His strict reckoning on the basis of the lunar calendar neglects the fact that the 2.17 to 7.17 period is apparently to be identified with the one hundred fifty day period consisting of five thirty-day months, a correspondence which is not likely to be coincidental (Mundhenk 1994, 208–09; Rösel 1998a, 593). Otherwise, the one hundred fifty days may have been intended as a round number. Seebass' argument is thus invalidated, and the argument for the current solution is limited to the aforementioned discussion. Najm and Guillaume (2004) also support this position, but their arguments are forced in their attempt to prove the existence of the Priestly calendar in the Flood narrative. They prefer the LXX dates 600.2.27 and 600.7.27,[16] because this seven-month period of "re-creation" is supposed to parallel the seven days of creation in Genesis 1. They can only arrive at this conclusion, however, by selectively explaining away the one hundred fifty day period as a later insertion to conform the Flood narrative to the three hundred sixty-five day Egyptian calendar (twelve months × thirty days + five additional days) and speculating about a suspension of time in P, yielding a chronological gap in its account. Their theory should not, therefore, be determinative for our textual decision here. Though this combination of dates does provide somewhat viable explanations for all the variants, it is rejected for its lack of valuable attestation and the preferability of yet another solution.

600.2.17–600.7.17–601.2.27 Original

After thorough examination of all the possible combinations of dates, the one here deemed most probable is that preserved in the MT, SP, Targs., and Syr. This solution is preferred because it has substantial textual support, provides the most simple and natural explanation of the origins of all the variants, and accords well with the known characteristics of the various textual witnesses.

---

16. And inexplicably, they seem to misread the LXX date of the beginning of the Flood as 600.2.17, thus wrongly supposing they are in agreement with the LXX at this point as well.

On this supposition, 4Q252 (and 4Q254a) and Jubilees are easily explicable along the lines mentioned above. Jubilees 5:32, in fact, does attest to the final date proposed here, and its 2.17 in 5:31 is quite possibly an original invention. Even if the 5:31 reading is based on a textual tradition it is still to be rejected either as an attempt to conform the length of the Flood to the year of contemporaneous exegetical tradition or accidental textual corruption. 4Q252 was shown to attest to an authentic textual variant, but it too likely arose either from exegetical revision, or more likely, scribal error. As shown above, textual corruption in the direction of בשבעה ועשרים יום (original, MT, SP) > בשבעה עשר יום (4Q252, Jubilees) is equally as feasible as the reverse, so the answer to the question of the direction of textual change must be determined by comparison of the multiple complexes of dates as wholes.

The LXX is only slightly more difficult to explain, since it requires two textual changes. Nevertheless, given the textual diversity, every possible solution must proffer at least two changes in at least one source, so this cannot be used to negate the solution proposed here. Additionally, if any source is to have undergone substantial revision, the known propensity of the LXX for rational revisions makes it quite a likely candidate. It is possible, but not likely, that the LXX dates can be explained either entirely by accidental or entirely by intentional changes of the dates of the beginning of the Flood and the setting aground of the Ark.[17] Even better, the sequence of changes most likely to have led to the LXX dates is that the first date (7:11) would have been accidentally altered to read the twenty-seventh, and the second date (8:4) would then have been intentionally changed to account for the

---

17. These two identical accidental corruptions are unlikely to have occurred entirely independently. Probably the best explanation with recourse purely to intentional alterations is that the LXX could have changed the first date to make the Flood last one year and then changed the second date to allow room for the one hundred fifty day period before the Ark set aground. The second date would then have been changed to solve the perceived chronological problem of not having enough time between 600.2.27 and 600.7.17 for the one hundred fifty days, rather than some vague concern with matching dates or symmetry (contra Larsson 1983, 405). While this solution is quite possible, it is questionable whether the LXX would have changed the first date with the sole purpose of making the Flood last one year. Nothing in the text states that the Flood lasted one year, so the LXX would have no reason to revise the text in this way. The change of the second date to account for the one hundred fifty day period would be solving an apparent chronological problem in the text, which is common enough in the LXX (cf. 2:2; 8:5?), but no such contradiction would lead the LXX to correct the first date to make the Flood last one year. In fact, the initial act of altering the first date is also the act which would create the problem for the LXX and require further revision. Additionally, if it were the intention of the LXX to make the Flood last one year, it could have been done much more simply and without creating the chronological problems if the third date had been altered as in 4Q252. It is worth considering whether the LXX could have revised the first date solely to bring it into conformity with extra-biblical exegetical tradition, but a simpler solution may be available.

one hundred fifty day period between the start of the Flood and the setting aground of the Ark (cf. Rösel 1998a, 591–92).

Only the absence of the word "day" in the LXX dates noted by Hendel requires further explanation, if indeed it is not due to idiomatic causes. If בשבעה עשר יום (original, MT, SP) became בשבעה ועשרים (LXX), the absence of the word "day" in 7:11 is easily explicable as resulting from word misdivision. The second date in 8:4, when intentionally altered to read בשבעה ועשרים, would quite naturally have omitted the word יום in parallel fashion, perhaps assuming the original בשבעה עשר יום was incorrectly divided. As for the third date in 8:14, the יום was probably omitted either by haplography or intentionally for consistency under the influence of the first two dates. While it is not characteristic of the LXX to assimilate together adjacent date formulae with alternating presence and absence of יום, the fact that the dates in 7:11 and 8:4 are otherwise identical in number and form is reason enough to propose such assimilation here.

As mentioned above, the Vulg. reading in 8:4 is probably influenced by a Septuagintal reading or a corrupt Hebrew manuscript and is unlikely to retain the original in this case. Alternatively, perhaps this date was moved back to make room for the one hundred fifty day period according to a three hundred sixty-four day or three hundred sixty-five day calendar.

This solution accounts for all of the variant chronologies with only one level of change, except for the LXX, which is likely to reflect more substantial revision in this instance. All the data can be easily accounted for with an economical combination of accidental and intentional alterations. The explanations for the origins of each variant chronology accord well with the tendencies of each witness. And this solution also has the strongest manuscript support of all the various possibilities. As such, we can conclude that the MT, SP, Targs., and Syr. probably preserve the original dates of the beginning of the Flood (7:11), setting aground of the Ark (8:4), and the end of the Flood (8:14).

8:3 מקץ חמשים 4Q252 I 8 מקץ חמשים/מקצה חמשים ↔ , 𝔐 *after (1)50* מקצה חמשים
מסוף (. . .) 𝕮ᴼᴶ (... כהل ←, מ) S (ممحبم ...) 𝕾 (μετὰ πεντήκοντα) 𝕲 (ובסוף חמשים)
after מקץ חמשים [(*post... quinquaginta*) 𝕧 (לסוף ... וחמשין) 𝕮ᴺᶜ (וחמשין)
(μετὰ 𝕲 (ובסוף חמשים) 4Q252 I 8 מקץ חמשים/מקצה חמשים ↔ , ممح *(1)50*
πεντήκοντα) 𝕾 (ممحبم ...) 𝕮ᴼᴶ (וחמשין) 𝕮ᴺᶜ (מסוף ...) לסוף
וחמשין) 𝕧 (*post... quinquaginta*) | מקץ החמשים *after the (1)50* Eißfeldt.

The textual decision here is quite difficult. The SP reads מקץ, which is the normal spelling for the temporal expression "after . . ." (in the Pentateuch:

Gn 4:3; 8:3[SP], 6; 16:3; 41:1; Ex 12:41; Num 13:25; Dt 9:11; 14:28[SP]; 15:1; 31:10). The MT, however, reads מקצה, which is normally spatial in orientation in the Pentateuch. In the Pentateuch מקצה introduces a temporal expression in only two places, both of them contested by the SP (Gn 8:3[MT]; Dt 14:28[MT]).

Eißfeldt (1969) has proposed the quite plausible emendation that the additional ה on the unusual form of the MT arose from word misdivision, and that the ה was originally attached to the following numeral leaving מקץ החמשים ומאת יום "after *the* one hundred fifty days" with an anaphoric article explicitly identifying these one hundred fifty days as the one hundred fifty days of 7:24. The SP's lack of the ה in either position is then explained as haplography of הח. Thus, the standard form מקץ is preferred and the loss of the ה preceding the numeral is explained as resulting from normal scribal error. Though Eißfeldt's conjecture does explain the origin of all the extant variants and rightly emphasizes the parallel between 7:24 and 8:3, it remains improbable for two reasons. First, even where temporal מקץ introduces periods of time, an article is never elsewhere used before the numerals to make the anaphoric reference explicit (e.g., Ex 12:41; Dt 9:11; Jgs 11:39; 2 Chr 8:1; Is 23:15, 17; Ez 29:13). In 7:10, the article (translated literally by the LXX) is used before the units of time, rather than the numeral. Second, this disagreement between the MT מקצה and SP מקץ also occurs in Deuteromony 14:28 (which cannot be explained as here), which means that 8:3 cannot be treated as an isolated incident, but must be examined as part of a pattern of differences between the MT and SP. These variants are best explained from the perspective of the tendencies of the given witnesses.

There are two possibilities for explaining the differences between the MT and SP. By far the more common spelling for the introduction of the temporal clause is מקץ (Gn 4:3; 8:3[SP], 6; 16:3; 41:1; Ex 12:41; Nm 13:25; Dt 9:11; 14:28[SP]; 15:1; 31:10; Jgs 11:39; 2 Sm 14:26; 15:7; 1 Kgs 2:39; 17:7; 2 Chr 8:1; Est 2:12; Is 23:15, 17; Jer 13:6; 34:14; 42:7; Ez 29:13), whereas the spelling מקצה for the temporal clause seems to be more common in the later books (Gn 8:3[MT]; Dt 14:28[MT]; Jo 3:2; 9:16; 2 Sm 24:8; 1 Kgs 9:10; 2 Kgs 8:3; 18:10; Ez 3:16; 39:14). This could indicate that the SP retains the original forms in Gn 8:3 and Dt 14:28 and that the MT reflects later modernized forms. This proposed MT modernization, however, is not convincing for three reasons. First, it would have been uncharacteristic of the tradition, in contrast to the normal modernizing tendencies of the SP. Second, it would have been entirely inconsistent, only affecting two of the potential instances. And third, it would have been inexplicable, as the form

מקצה is in fact still the less common form in the later books. It is more likely that the SP standardized the two variant forms in the MT to the more common מקץ, as in all the other examples in the MT (Wenham 1987, 153). Though stylistically inconsistent, the longer orthography is preferred. There is no difference in meaning between the orthographic variants.

8:4 השביעי *the seventh* 𝔐 ᴤ 4Q252 I 10 𝕲 (τῷ ἑβδόμῳ) 𝕾 (ܫܒܝܥܐ) 𝕿ᴼᴺ (שביעיא) 𝒱 *(septimo)*] העשירי* *the tenth* Hippolytus *Arabic Frag. to Pent.* Gn 8:1.

A quote attributed to Hippolytus seems to confuse this date with the following one in 8:5 (Lewis 1968, 190).

8:4 בשבעה עשר יום *on the seventeenth day* 𝔐 ᴤ 4Q252 I 10 (שבעה עשר) 𝕿ᶜ (עשר יומין בשבעת) 𝕿ᴺ (בשבעת עשרא יומא) 𝕿ᴼ (ܟܒܬܣܪܐ) 𝕾 (ܐܘܣܪ̈ܐ) [יו]ם בשבסרי יומין) 𝕿ˢ⁽ᴹˢ⁾ (בשבעסר יום) 𝕿ˢ⁽ᴹˢˢ⁾ יום (בשבעת עשר [יומא] 𝕿ᴶ (בשבע עסר) οἱ λ' *(septimo decimo)* Syh Josephus *Antiquities* i.90] ועשרים בשבעה *on the twenty-seventh* 𝕲 (ἑβδόμη καὶ εἰκάδι) Philo *Quest. in Gen.* ii.31, 33, cf. 𝒱 *(vicesima* [+ *et* 𝒱ᴹˢ] *septima die) Book of Adam and Eve* iii.9 | בשבעה ועשרים יום² *on the twenty-seventh day* 𝕲ᴹˢˢ (ἑβδόμη καὶ εἰκάδι ἡμέρᾳ) 𝒱 *(vicesima* [+ *et* 𝒱ᴹˢ] *septima die)* Arab, cf. *Book of Adam and Eve* iii.9 | יום עשר מחבש* *on the fifteenth day* 𝕾ᴹˢ (ܟܬܣ̈ܥܘܐ) | ועשרים* *twenty(-seventh month)* 𝕲ᴹˢ (καὶ εἰκάδι) | באחד* *on the first* Hippolytus *Arabic Frag. to Pent.* Gn 8:1.

See the discussion on the chronology at 7:11 for explanation of the interrelated dates in 7:11; 8:4, 14. Lewis (1968, 190) notes that a supposed quote from Hippolytus seems to confuse this date with the following date in 8:5. A few other minor variants are obvious corruptions.

8:5 העשירי *the tenth* 𝔐 ᴤ 4Q252 I 11 (הע[שירי) 𝕲 (δεκάτου) 𝕾 (ܕܥܣܪ̈) 𝕿ᴼᴺᶜ (עשיראה) 𝒱 *(decimum)*] השביעי *the seventh* 𝔐ᴹˢ.

A single medieval manuscript reads "seventh" instead of "tenth," probably under the influence of the other dates.

8:5 בעשירי *on the tenth* 𝔐 ᴤ 𝕲ᴹˢˢ (ἐν δὲ τῷ δεκάτῳ μηνί) 𝕿ᴼᴺᶜ (בעשיראה) 𝒱 *(decimo enim mense)* 𝕾 (ܒ- ... ܚܡܣܝܢ) Pal Syh *Jub.* 5:30 Philo *Quest. in Gen.* ii.32, cf. 4Q252 I 11 (חדש [הע]שירי) Hippolytus *Arabic Frag. to Pent.* Gen 8:1] בעשירי באחד² or בעשתי עשר² *on the eleventh* 𝕲 (ἐν δὲ τῷ ἑνδεκάτῳ μηνί) *Book of Adam and Eve* iii.10 | בהעשירי *on the tenth* ᴤᴹˢ | בעשירי* *on the tenth* 𝔐ᴹˢ | omit בעשירי* *on the tenth* 𝔐ᴹˢ 4Q252 I 11.

All the ancient versions except for the LXX agree with the MT and SP. Jubilees likewise agrees with this date. So does 4Q252, though it rewords and simplifies the date formula to avoid the redundancy of the MT's and SP's mentions of the tenth month.

The textual critic is initially struck by the somewhat difficult construction of the MT and SP, the two-fold (MT and SP) or three-fold (LXX) repetition of the word "month," and the reality that the following numeral (1), if added to the numeral here in the MT and SP (10), equals the numeral in the LXX (11). But while there may be a connection between these data and the attested forms, it is actually quite difficult to reconstruct a textual explanation for the difference in readings. There is no feasible explanation for how the text of the MT and SP could have been accidentally corrupted from a reading "eleventh" via normal scribal practices. The LXX could be related to the MT and SP in one of four ways.

The first possible explanation depends on the reconstruction of a variant Hebrew *Vorlage* for the LXX. Noting the possible influence of the following numeral, Hendel proposes that the LXX read in its parent text בעשירי באחד באחד לחדש for the MT and SP בעשירי באחד לחדש. The additional באחד of the LXX *Vorlage* would then have arisen from dittography of the single באחד in the MT and SP (1998, 138). But a serious problem with this reconstruction is that the proposed reading for the LXX *Vorlage* is intolerable and incomprehensible Hebrew. While it is not uncommon for the number "eleven" to be formed by combining the numerals "one" and "ten" (32:23; 37:9; Dt 1:2; Jo 15:51; 1 Kgs 6:38; 2 Kgs 9:29; 23:36; 24:18; 2 Chr 36:5, 11; Jer 52:1; Ez 30:20; 31:1), the numeral "one" is always written before the numeral "ten" as in אחד עשר. Even worse is the fact that the additional ב separating the numerals "ten" and "one" makes this chain of three prepositional phrases utter nonsense. It is most unlikely that such a horrendous construction could long survive in a Hebrew manuscript tradition or that the LXX translators would translate such a phrase as they did. Dittography, then, cannot adequately explain the LXX reading.

The second possible reconstruction of a variant Hebrew *Vorlage* for the LXX is בעשתי עשר (חדש). The "month" at the end could have been written explicitly (as in Dt 1:3) or else supplied in translation (as in 8:13). This construction (and related forms) is a normal way of expressing the number "eleven" (Ex 26:7, 8; 36:14, 15; Nm 7:72; 29:20; Dt 1:3; 2 Kgs 25:2; 1 Chr 12:14; 24:12; 25:18; 27:14[2×]; Jer 1:3; 39:2; 52:5; Ez 26:1; 40:49; Zec 1:7). While this is a much more feasible Hebrew reading, there is no possible accidental textual explanation for the difference from the reading of the MT and SP. If this reading ever existed in the Hebrew, the textual differences must be explained as rational alterations.

The third possible explanation is that the reading ἐν δὲ τῷ ἑνδεκάτῳ μηνί of the LXX according to the critical editions does not accurately reflect the original LXX translation, but arose from secondary corruption within the LXX textual tradition. Whereas the difference between the two dates is almost impossible to explain on a Hebrew level as simple scribal error, it is significantly more likely in the Greek. The interchange between an original δεκάτῳ "tenth" and a corrupt ἑνδεκάτῳ "eleventh" would have been relatively simple in Greek (perhaps influenced by the graphically similar preceding ἐν δὲ τῷ). Proponents of this explanation could also point to a very popular variant (groups *b d t* and scattered representatives of groups *O′C″fsy*) within the Greek textual tradition that must be quite early.[18] Wevers concludes that the Greek variant "tenth" arose from an early correction towards the MT, which gained a strong showing in the tradition (Wevers 1993, 103), but it is difficult to preclude the possibility of inner-versional corruption at this point.

The fourth possible relationship between the Greek and Hebrew texts is that the LXX variant does not reflect an accurate translation of a Hebrew *Vorlage* at all, but instead is an intentional alteration of the numbers on the part of the translators.

Thus, if the LXX variant reflects a Hebrew *Vorlage* or revision by translation, the differences would then have to be explained as conscious rewriting of the numerals in one direction or another. Vogt has argued that the date of the LXX should be preferred on the basis of intrinsic evidence (1962, 215–16). According to him, the redactor of the Flood narrative harmonized the J and P traditions by adding the forty days (8:6a) to the twenty-one days of the sending of the dove to arrive at exactly the sixty-one days between 600.11.1 (the first day of the eleventh month of the sixtieth year of the life of Noah) and 601.1.1 (8:13) in the Priestly calendar. He either found the date 11.1 in his text or else created it for the correspondence with his preferred intervals. According to Vogt, the progression indicated in the LXXs "the water decreased until the tenth month, and on the eleventh month on the first day of the month the mountaintops appeared" also seems more natural than that of the MT and SP. The words העשירי בעשתי עשר (LXX) could have later been corrupted to העשירי בעשירי (MT and SP) or intentionally changed by the MT and SP traditions in order to read the date

---

18. In this respect, the testimony of Philo against the texts of Wevers and Rahlfs may be particularly significant, since he is elsewhere dependent upon the LXX dates.

of the beginning of the season (10.1). He cites as evidence Jubilees 6:25–27, which specifically emphasizes all of the beginnings of the seasons (1.1; 4.1; 7.1; 10.1; 1.1). With this new date, the sixty-one days of the raven and the dove do not fit any more into the calculation and are thus omitted entirely from Jubilees.

Most scholars have not been convinced by Vogt's arguments, however, for a number of compelling reasons. First, his proposal for accidental corruption from עשתי עשר בעשתי to העשירי בעשירי to העשירי בעשירי would be excessively complicated and improbable (contra Najm and Guillaume 2004). Second, the MT and SP biblical texts betray no obvious interest in aligning dates with the beginnings of the seasons as is clearly the case in the later Second Temple literature. Third, if the biblical author did not use the "Priestly" calendar as has been proposed, but rather a lunar calendar, it is quite likely that the LXX's 600.11.1 to 601.1.1 would only leave room for sixty days (inclusive), and thus the LXX dates would actually create a chronological problem, rather than a proper correspondence between the dates and spans of time. Even if five epagomenal days were added at the end of a year of twelve thirty-day months, the precise correspondence between the LXX dates and time spans would still be destroyed. Vogt's argument rests very heavily on the questionable assumption of a "Priestly" calendar, which is shown to be quite dubious by the correspondence between the one hundred fifty days (7:24; 8:3) and five months (7:11; 8:4). And fourth, a more plausible explanation is readily apparent.

As in 2:2 (and probably also 8:4), the LXX (or one of its predecessors) may have sensed here a potential chronological problem with overlapping and conflicting temporal information and intentionally altered the text to alleviate the perceived difficulty (Wevers 1993, 103). The LXX would then have understood the phrase "continued receding until the tenth month" to imply the continuing recession of the waters in the tenth month, a period of time which would extend beyond the 600.10.1 date of the MT and SP. This would then have presented a problem in sequence, which the LXX would have fixed by moving the date back one month, so that the mountaintops appear only after the water recedes during the tenth month. They may also have been influenced by the correspondence between the sixty-one days of waiting and sending of the birds and the dates 11.1 and 1.1 (Larsson 1983, 405; 2000, 75), but this is uncertain.

On the basis of either mechanical or rational explanations, therefore, the date of the LXX critical editions appears to be secondary. This means that the MT and SP timespans mentioned between 8:5 and 13 do not correspond to the dates given in 8:5 and 13. There is approximately a month of time between the dates of the MT and SP that is unmentioned in the time intervals given for the forty days of waiting and the twenty-one days for the sending of the dove (Larsson 1983, 405; 2000, 75). This is not a problem, in that no unambiguous indication is given as to how much time elapsed between the opening of the window and the sending out of the raven or between the sending of the final dove and the drying of the water from the earth. The function of the ויהי plus temporal clause in 8:13 of indicating a section break and resetting the temporal reference frame should also caution scholars about too quickly assuming that the given time spans are meant as a complete account of the time between the date in 8:5 and the date in 8:13. Since the text never makes that connection, there is no problem when the MT and SP dates leave time unmentioned. The date formula of the MT and SP in 8:5 is perfectly understandable and paralleled with similar date structures elsewhere (Ez 1:1; 8:1; 20:1; 29:1; 31:1; 33:21; 45:25; Hg 1:15; 2:1, cf. 2 Chr 3:2), and it should be preferred.

8:8 beginning of verse 𝔐 𝔰𝔪 𝔊 𝔖 𝔗^ON 𝔳] add ויחל נח שבעת ימים *And Noah waited seven days* Ball Eißfeldt.

The phrase ויחל עוד שבעת ימים אחרים in 8:10 (assuming that that text is rightly established) probably implies that a previous period of seven days had transpired which is not explicitly mentioned in any of the extant witnesses. Eißfeldt supplies an explicit reference to these seven days of waiting here between the sending out of the raven and the dove, the most likely location for such a phrase. There is, however, no obvious mechanism for the omission of this sentence, if it is original. Additionally, there is no manuscript evidence supporting this longer expression. While the emendation would clearly resolve a tension in the text, it is also feasible that the seven days of waiting were originally implicit in the text of Genesis, so it would be dubious to emend the text in lieu of manuscript evidence favoring the emendation.

8:10 אחרים *other* 𝔐 𝔰𝔪 4Q252 I 15 ([א]חרים[) 𝔊 (ἑτέρας) 𝔖 (ܐܚܪܢܐ) 𝔗^ON (אוחרנין) 𝔳 (*aliis*)] omit אחרים* *other* 𝔊^MSS Aeth Arm Pal.

This word is potentially problematic in that it may imply a previous period of seven days not mentioned in any of the extant texts. Wevers notes that a popular Greek variant omits ἑτέρας to mitigate this apparent inconsistency (1993, 105), though the same omission is also found for the identical expression in 8:12, which may mean that it was omitted rather as syntactically redundant. Barré proposes removing אחרים, because it is problematic for his reconstruction of P's chronology. In his words, "The addition could have been made unconsciously through a scribal error. The fact that vv. 10 and 12 begin with the same four words may have caused the eye to jump momentarily to v. 12 from which the suspect word was copied. Or the addition may have been made intentionally by a redactor who sought to integrate the raven and dove episodes. But whatever may have been the cause, it is clear that its presence is problematic. And when the word is removed, we are left with a chronology that is perfectly integrated" (1988, 10–11). Barré's claims, however, are very poorly supported in the manuscript tradition, and his main concern is to remove a problematic element for his source-critical theory, which is methodologically objectionable and does not do justice to the text. Additionally, the back-reference in v. 10 involves not only this word אחרים, but also the previous word עוד, and it is unlikely that any sort of scribal error in this verse would account for the two extraneous words. Others have proposed adding וייחל נח שבעת ימים "And Noah waited seven days" at the beginning of 8:8 to give an explicit prior seven-day time frame to explain the back-referencing terminology of v. 10 (Eißfeldt 1969). There is no clear mechanism, however, for how this phrase could have dropped out of all the extant witnesses. Despite this very real tension, it would be hazardous to propose such emendations without good manuscript support when the archetypal text for all the witnesses is indeed comprehensible on the implicit assumption of a seven-day period between the sending of the raven and the dove in vv. 7 and 8 and there is no obvious mechanism to explain the origin of the reading of the witnesses.

8:13 באחת *on the first* 𝔐 𝔪 𝔊 (ἐν τῷ ἑνί) 𝔖 (ܐܚܕܐ) 𝔗ON (וחדא) 𝔙 (*primo*)] בשבע* *on the seventh Book of Adam and Eve* iii.11.

This minor variant is clearly secondary and confused.

8:13 באחד *on the first* 𝔐 𝔪 𝔊 (μιᾷ) 𝔖 (ܚܕ) 𝔗ON (בחד) 𝔙 (*prima die*)] בשתים* *on the second Book of Adam and Eve* iii.11.

This minor variant is clearly secondary and confused.

8:14 השני *the second* 𝔐 𝔪 𝔊 (τῷ δευτέρῳ) 𝔖 (ܕܬܪܝܢ) 𝔗ON (תנינא) 𝔙 (*secundo*)] השביעי* *the seventh* 𝔊MS (ἑβδόμῳ) Armte Philo *Quest. in Gen.* ii.33, 47.

Philo's chronology is quite confused with regard to the months and probably reflects concerns about locating the Flood within a preferred season, rather than any viable textual variant (Lewis 1968, 49–50). One Greek manuscript may have been influenced by the following Greek word in the LXX.

8:14 בשבעה ועשרים יום *on the twenty-seventh day* 𝔐 𝔪 𝔖 (ܟܬܒܬ ܡܚܡܫܐ) 𝔗° (בשבעה ועסרין) 𝔗ˢ (בעשרין ושובעא יומין) 𝔗ᴶ (בעשרין ושבעא יומא) 𝔙 יום) 𝔙 (*septima et vicesima die*) Laᴹ Philo *Quest. in Gen.* ii.33, 47 *Book of Adam and Eve* iii.11, cf. *Jub.* 5:32] בשבעה ועשרים ˀ *on the twenty-seventh* 𝔊 (ἑβδόμῃ καὶ εἰκάδι) 𝔗ᴺ (בעשרין ושבעה) | בשבעה עשר יום *on the seventeenth day* 4Q252 II 1 *Jub.* 5:31 𝔊ᴹˢˢ (ἑπτακαιδεκάτῃ ἡμέρᾳ), cf. 4Q254a 3 1 בעשרים שבעה בעשרים ועשרים יום [ב] | שבעה עשר vacat עשר vacat לחודש *on the twenty-seventh on the twentieth and twentieth day?* 𝔐ᴹˢ.

See the discussion at 7:11 on the interrelated dates 7:11; 8:4, 14. A number of Greek manuscripts were apparently glossed with the date from Jubilees (see comments on the following variant).

8:14 end of verse 𝔐 𝔪 𝔊 𝔖 𝔗ᴼᴺ 𝔙] add לחדש פתח (יום) ובשבעה ועשרים התבה (את)ˀ *and on the twenty-seventh of the month he opened the Ark* 𝔊ᴹˢˢ (καὶ ἑβδόμῃ καὶ εἰκάδι τοῦ μηνὸς ἀνέῳξεν τὴν κιβωτόν) *Jub.* 5:32.

A significant number of important Greek manuscripts (L 58–426 b d 346 54 59) add this additional event and place it on the twenty-seventh day of the month. The same manuscripts (except 426 and 346) also read the seventeenth for the previous date in 8:14, when the land dried up. Many of these manuscripts (58–426 d 54 59; supported also by 392, a marginal insertion in the mixed codex 55, and secondary insertions into 17'–72'–82–135, which are closely related to 58–426) also read an additional date in 8:19 not attested in other biblical witnesses.[19] It has long been noticed that these readings align, strangely enough, with the dates given in the book of Jubilees (Dahse 1908, 7–10; VanderKam 1989, 36). Jubilees 5:32, for instance, states, "On its twenty-seventh (day) he opened the Ark and sent from it the animals, birds, and whatever moves about." The combination of the dates 601.2.17 and 601.3.1 is also unique to Jubilees, apart from these Greek manuscripts.

Dahse (1908, 7–10) argues that these mansucripts reflect an early recension that preserves the original dates of the Flood narrative in agreement with Jubilees, but against the other biblical witnesses, which are deemed to have truncated the narrative by removing some dates and selecting the middle of the three dates for the end of the Flood. He also presumes that this early Greek recension would have originally read 600.2.17 as the start

---

19. L is not extant at 8:19. The manuscripts cited generally read all three dates from Jubilees. Some manuscripts do not consistently read each of the dates, but the core evidence for all three readings is strong.

of the Flood on the basis of Jubilees. The result of the abbreviation of the Hebrew text as found in the other witnesses, according to Dahse, is that the Flood no longer lasts exactly one year, betraying a problem with the resulting text. Thus, Jubilees and this Greek recension preserve the earliest chronology of the Genesis Flood narrative.

This is unlikely, however, for a number of reasons. First, none of the manuscripts reads the date 600.2.17 for the start of the Flood that Dahse supposes they must have originally had in agreement with Jubilees, but instead they all agree with the LXX date 600.2.27. While this theoretically could be the result of partial correction towards the LXX, the lack of coherence between the readings of Jubilees and the Greek texts does not engender confidence in Dahse's proposal. Second, the numerous marginal insertions and inconsistencies between closely-related manuscripts better fit patterns of secondary interpolations than preservation of earlier texts. Third, the lack of an explicit subject of the opening of the Ark raises suspicions about the plus (Wevers 1993, 108). Fourth, the Greek texts are unlikely to reflect the Old Greek translation of Genesis from the third century BC, since the earliest manuscripts, the ancient versions, and the preponderance of the evidence of the tradition agree with the texts of Rahlfs and Wevers against the dates in these Greek manuscripts. Fifth, there is no good explanation for the origin of the texts of the other biblical witnesses on the supposition of the originality of the dates of Jubilees and these Greek texts. To say that they conflated the three dates and retained the middle one is not to explain why they might have done so. There is no feasible cause for the direction of change proposed by Dahse. And sixth, the origin of the dates is easily explicable on the supposition that they are the original creation of the author of Jubilees. As discussed above (see comment on the significant variant in 7:11), Jubilees may either have created the date 601.2.17 or inherited it from a corrupt Hebrew biblical tradition, but its double date 601.2.17 and 601.2.27 seems to reflect the midrashic conflation of two competing traditions. The date 601.3.1 was almost certainly invented by the author of Jubilees to create a parallel between the Noahic covenant, the giving of the law at Sinai, and the Feast of Weeks, all of which were supposed to occur in the third month (*Jub.* 6:10–22; cf. Ex 19:1). Not only does this explanation fit the rhetorical aims of Jubilees perfectly, but it is also paralleled by many similarly invented dates in the Flood narrative (e.g., *Jub.* 6:23–27).

Thus, it is far more likely that the dates found in Jubilees and some Greek texts were invented by the author of Jubilees than that they preserve the original chronology of the Genesis Flood narrative. This being the case, we must conclude that at some point[20] a Greek manuscript (or multiple manuscripts?) was glossed with additional information from the Greek translation of Jubilees, which was subsequently incorporated into the text somewhat inconsistently.[21]

8:19 end of verse 𝔐 𝔪 𝔊 𝔖 𝔗^ON 𝔇] add באחד לחדש השלישי˙ *on the first of the third month* 𝔊^MSS (ἐν μιᾷ τοῦ μηνὸς τοῦ τρίτου [πρώτου 𝔊^MSS]) *Jub.* 6:1.

As in 8:14 (see the previous comment for detailed discussion), some Greek manuscripts add an additional date from Jubilees, which says that Noah exited the Ark on the first day of the third month. This date was invented by Jubilees, and probably made its way into the biblical manuscript tradition when a Greek manuscript (or manuscripts?) was glossed with information from Jubilees.

3. Conclusion

After thorough examination of the chronological data from a text-critical perspective, a number of conclusions should be highlighted. For the five fixed dates, I have argued that the MT and SP have preserved the archetypal chronology. The LXX chronology appears to have been significantly altered through a combination of accidental scribal errors and intentional revisions to alleviate perceived chronological problems. The final date of 4Q252 and Jubilees is either an accidental error or intentional reworking of the date for exegetical reasons. The additional dates from Jubilees have no claim to being original, but stem from a rewriting of the Genesis account. For minor chronological details, the ancient versions are largely in agreement, and I have not accepted any of the proposed emendations to these details. Occasional differences found in later ancillary works are generally the result of confusion, rather than viable variant texts. Thus, for the chronologically significant variants, the MT and SP texts have been preferred throughout. While I have not advocated any novel dates or chronologies, I have provided a detailed defense of the MT and SP dates

20. L is dated to the fifth to sixth centuries, giving us the latest possible date for the insertion of the additional dates into the Greek tradition.

21. Thanks to Kristin De Troyer and Johannes Magliano-Tromp for their helpful critical comments on this question in response to my oral presentation "The Many Chronologies of the Genesis Flood Narrative: An Exercise in Evaluating Interrelated Variants" at the Second Annual St. Andrews Graduate Conference for Biblical and Early Christian Studies on 9 June, 2012.

against a number of solutions which prefer alternate chronologies. The most important conclusion to be drawn from this is that the dates found in the MT and SP should probably be the starting points in an investigation of the chronology of the Genesis Flood narrative.

Appendix: A Critical Edition of the Hebrew Text of the Genesis Flood Narrative (Genesis 6:5–9:17)

A1.   Introductory Concerns
A2.   Critical Text and Apparatus (Genesis 6:5–9:17)
A3.   Conclusion

A1. Introductory Concerns

The following introductory comments are intended to explain the methodology and format of the edition to aid the reader in utilizing its information. Unfortunately, because of space limitations, I have not been able to include the textual commentary defending the conclusions underlying the critical text.

A1.1   Text and Vocalization
A1.2   Apparatus
A1.3   Textual Witnesses
A1.4   Symbols
A1.5   Abbreviations

A1.1 *Text and Vocalization*

The purpose of this edition is to present a critical text of the Genesis Flood narrative (Gn 6:5–9:17) that, in my opinion, best approximates the original Hebrew text of the narrative in the completed literary form that gave rise to the archetype of all extant textual witnesses, as opposed to the hypothetical reconstruction of prior source materials so prevalent in traditional analysis (e.g., the commentaries of Skinner 1930; Von Rad 1972; Gunkel 1997). Accordingly, I present the text as a single narrative intended to be read as a coherent literary whole. Furthermore, this stance implies that I make no appeal to equally "original" competing readings or different, irreconcilable literary editions, but instead seek to adjudicate between variants, in every case aiming at a single initial text, as indicated by the textual evidence for the passage.

The base electronic copy text has been taken from the Westminster Leningrad Codex via BibleWorks 7 with modification. The text is an eclectic, critical text, so the base text has been emended to the preferred readings in every case. Given the high degree of uncertainty on questions of orthography, this edition makes no systematic attempt to reconstruct an original orthography, though defective spellings are normally preferred. Versification is given according to the consistent pattern in the major editions and translations. The many proposals to rearrange verses and sections of text (normally on analogy with Ancient Near Eastern parallels) have little merit and are not included in this edition.

Tiberian Masoretic vocalization has been included as a reading aid only, with no implication as to the editor's preferred pronunciation. The vowels have been taken from the Westminster Leningrad Codex from BibleWorks 7 with minor modifications per Dotan (2001) at 6:16 and 7:23. The Masoretic pointing has been omitted when a non-Masoretic text variant is preferred and when multiple reasonable readings are possible given an ambiguous consonantal text. The edition does not indicate Masoretic accents or *maqqephs*.

A1.2 *Apparatus*

Variant readings are noted in a single apparatus. Generally, the types of variants cited are limited to semantically-significant variants with at least a potential claim to being genuine Hebrew variants, though at times important versional differences are included, even when they are considered unlikely to be traced back to a different Hebrew *Vorlage*. Such extensive annotation is helpful not only for determining the oldest text, but also for understanding the history of interpretation of the passages in view. Occasionally, conjectural emendations are also noted when deemed significant enough. The apparatus does not enumerate, however, many supposed glosses or radical emendations that have been proposed to eliminate without good text-critical merit stylistic discrepancies considered inconvenient by certain source critics.

Variants in the apparatus are linked to their location in the text with lettered footnotes. The superscripted Latin letters follow the lexeme for single-word variants. For multi-word variants, two identical letters precede the initial lexeme and follow the final lexeme. For instances of transposition, two identical letters mark both the preferred and variant locations. For additions and omissions, the letters are placed where the variants occur, at times preceding words when the variants precede the lexeme, and at other times following words when the variants follow the lexeme.

Preferred readings are listed first, concluded by a right bracket]. Rejected variants are then listed in descending order of preferability, separated by a single vertical line |. Each entry in the apparatus is concluded by a period. Hebrew text in the apparatus does not have vocalization, accentuation, or any other Masoretic accoutrements in addition to the consonantal text.

Each variant is listed first in Hebrew, either according to Hebrew manuscripts or as reconstructed from the ancient versions. Where Hebrew witnesses with only minor differences of orthography attest to the same reading, they are normally cited together without distinction according to the editor's preferred orthography.

Despite the extraordinary difficulties inherent in reconstructions from translations, every versional variant deemed significant enough for inclusion in the apparatus is given a potential reconstruction. I am convinced that every semantically-significant versional variant must be thoroughly evaluated by consideration of the reading on three different horizons: 1) whether the variant is likely to have arisen from inner-versional corruption or reflects the original text of a version; 2) whether the variant is likely to have arisen due to factors involved in translating from the source language to the target language; and 3) whether the variant is likely to reflect a Hebrew reading differing from all known Hebrew witnesses. This third horizon demands that diagnostic reconstructions be proposed for each difference and be compared to the known Hebrew readings to determine the likelihood that the differences could attest to viable Hebrew variants. A variant can only be rejected as translational with confidence when the probability that the difference arose in the process of translation (due to grammatical facilitation, stylistic concerns, literary aims, exegetical or theological purposes, etc.) is significantly greater than the probability that the difference reflects a Hebrew text that differs from all other known Hebrew readings.

Where Hebrew variants are retroverted from versional readings without Hebrew attestation, the apparatus utilizes a three-tiered system of notation to indicate levels of reliability of the reconstructions. Where, in the end, variants are considered to be unquestionably translational in nature or inner-versional corruptions with no viable claim to being a Hebrew reading, the reconstruction is followed by a superscripted asterisk *. A superscripted question mark ?, in contrast, indicates a reconstruction that could plausibly be explained either as due to translation style or reflecting a different Hebrew text in the version's *Vorlage*. Reconstructions that almost certainly reflect a variant Hebrew *Vorlage* (or at least a misreading of a Hebrew text) are cited as Hebrew variants without additional annotation. For ease in checking proposed reconstructions, the edition includes the major versional evidence in its versional forms as well.

The supporting witnesses for each variant follow the Hebrew readings in five tiers. First, the Hebrew witnesses are cited (𝔐 𝔪 4Q252 etc.). Second, the primary ancient versions are cited in alphabetical order (𝔊 𝔖 𝔗 𝔙), followed by the respective versional texts cited in parentheses. Third, ancillary witnesses that attest to the text are cited (*Jub.* etc.). Fourth, pre-hexaplaric recensions of the Septuagint are cited (α′ σ′ θ′). Fifth, daughter versions of the Septuagint are cited in alphabetical order when they disagree with the Septuagint in alignment with major textual witnesses (Aeth Arab Arm Bo La Pal Sa Syh etc.). And sixth, occassionally ancient commentators are cited for significant variants. In cases where versional readings could potentially be interpreted as supporting more than one reading but not another reading, they are listed at the end of the list after bidirectional arrows ↔ followed by the potentially supported readings separated by forward slashes / (e.g., ↔ הבשר/בשר 𝔙 [*caro*]). For proposed Hebrew readings that are conjectural emendations without significant manuscript support, supporting scholars have been cited from critical commentaries and text-critical works. Whenever it becomes important to cite individual manuscripts or groups of manuscripts in disagreement with the preferred reading of the normal witness with which they are associated, this is indicated by a superscripted ^MS or ^MSS after the symbol for the witness from which they differ. Additional notes after all of the supporting witnesses indicate yet other witnesses to be considered that may have a bearing on understanding the variant, but do not directly support it.

The apparatus uses English words and abbreviations for explanatory notes rather than Latin. A full listing of the English abbreviations can be found on the abbreviations page.

A1.3 *Textual Witnesses*

This section is intended to provide introductory comments on the textual character of each of the major witnesses and how they are treated in the edition.

A1.3.1   The Masoretic Text
A1.3.2   The Samaritan Pentateuch
A1.3.3   The Dead Sea Scrolls
A1.3.4   The Greek Septuagint
A1.3.5   The Syriac Peshitta
A1.3.6   The Aramaic Targums
A1.3.7   The Latin Vulgate
A1.3.8   The Other Sources

A1.3.1 The Masoretic Text

The text of the Masoretic text (MT) has been collated from the Leningrad Codex (Freedman et al. 1998), Second Rabbinic Bible (Goshen-Gottstein 1972), and the collations of Kennicott (1776) and De Rossi (1784). Its consonantal text is extraordinarily stable in this passage with only late, minor, secondary variants and differences in *matres lectiones* extant in the manuscripts. These medieval variants, with Moshe Goshen-Gottstein (1967), are not normally listed other than in such exceptional cases as when they have significant attestation, align with the readings of other witnesses, or pertain to chronology.

The MT of the Genesis Flood narrative is a very well-preserved and conservative text displaying very little evidence of interpretive expansions, linguistic modernizations, explicating plusses, harmonizing assimilations, or other intentional revisions. The rare plusses relative to the Septuagint (LXX) (e.g., 7:6?, 14, 22; 8:17; 9:10) are often considered secondary glosses, but a number of observations raise questions as to the validity of this approach. First, in each case the MT is always supported by the Samaritan Pentateuch (SP) and any Qumran manuscripts attesting to that passage. There is no case where a significant Hebrew manuscript reading opposes a major MT plus; only the LXX ever has significant minuses relative to the MT. It would be unlikely for the entire extant Hebrew tradition to have been corrupted with sufficiently early secondary glosses, while at the same time the LXX escaped the same kind of glossing. Second, while the LXX betrays a consistent and purposeful tendency towards harmonistic plusses relative to the MT, the MT plusses do not form a consistent pattern that can be categorized as a tendency in the tradition. Instead, the MT plusses are isolated and sporadic occurrences with little more in common with one another than that they all expand on the meaning of other phrases in the context. Third, the MT plusses are usually repetitive and syntactically awkward. While this may be understandable on the supposition of scribal glosses, it also presents difficulties, because scribes would have been unlikely to mechanically incorporate such syntactical oddities into the text with such regularity. Fourth, in most cases, there is no obvious reason why a gloss would have been added in the first place, since the meanings are already clear and do not appear to require further explanation, such that nothing would be gained by adding the unnecessary and seemingly purposeless glosses. Fifth, the MT plusses are often more difficult and confusing than the phrases they are supposed to explain. Sixth, it is easily understandable in each case why a scribe or translator would be tempted to abbreviate and simplify the repetitive and awkward structure of the MT to alleviate difficulties. Such revision is characteristic of the LXX text throughout, which makes its consistently easier readings suspect. Seventh, in at least one case (9:10) LXX abbreviation may have left its mark in the form of syntactical revision, as the LXX πᾶσι τοῖς θηρίοις τῆς γῆς probably conflates the two readings בכל חית הארץ and לכל חית הארץ (contra Hendel 1998, 57 and most commentators, who wrongly treat this situation as a simple MT plus). Eighth, in each case the MT plusses neatly fit Genesis' style of repetition, recapitulation, and categorical overlap as it expands on other statements with somewhat different forms. And ninth, there are few objective criteria by which to distinguish original appositional phrases from later scribal glosses, so—in lieu of reliable textual evidence for glossing—it is extremely hazardous to omit potential glosses from the critical text. For these reasons, this edition treats the significant MT plusses relative to the LXX in a fairly conservative manner and argues that the MT does not give much evidence of secondary glossing.

A1.3.2 The Samaritan Pentateuch

The text of the Samaritan Pentateuch (SP) has been collated from the editions of Von Gall (1918), Giron Blanc (1976), and Kennicott (1776). Its text is likewise relatively stable, and minor variants are not normally listed but in such exceptional cases as when they have significant attestation, align with the readings of other witnesses, or pertain to chronology.

The SP of the Genesis Flood narrative is closely aligned with the MT on most significant readings. It commonly differs from the MT, however, in minor details, most of which are clearly secondary. The SP text, for instance, is characterized by linguistic modernizations, smoothing out of difficult syntax, and other intentional revisions. It occasionally shows harmonistic tendencies, but not to the same extent as the Septuagint.

A1.3.3 The Dead Sea Scrolls

There are a large number of scrolls found at Qumran which speak of Noah and/or the Flood. García Martínez (1998) and Bernstein (1999) offer good overviews of these numerous references in the literature. Unfortunately, however, many of these texts are of very little text-critical value for the Hebrew text of Genesis, even though they have much to say about early Jewish interpretations of Noah and the Flood. For this reason, I have chosen only to include non-biblical manuscripts when they have readings considered potentially significant for determining the text of the Flood narrative. Scrolls are cited according to their standard sigla using numerals instead of abbreviated names. Fragmentary non-biblical scrolls citations are given in the following format: fragment number with an Arabic numeral (when appropriate), column number with a Roman numeral (when appropriate), and line number with an Arabic numeral, so for example, 3 II 4 cites fragment 3, column 2, line 4, of a given scroll.

Biblical Manuscript. *6Q1 (6QpaleoGenesis)*–6Q1 is the only biblical manuscript of the Genesis Flood narrative surviving in the manuscripts found in the Judean Desert and has been collated from the editions of Baillet (1962) and Ulrich (2010). It is written in a paleo-Hebrew script which can be dated approximately to the second half of the second century BC (Lange 2009, 54). Its text is preserved only in a very fragmentary state for Genesis 6:13–21 and does not allow for much text-typological analysis, though it does occasionally witness to particular textual problems.

Non-Biblical Compositions. *1Q19 (1QNoah)*–1Q19 (and 19[bis]) is a composition about Noah from the end of the first century BC, which was collated from the edition of Batsch (2008). It is very fragmentary and does not follow the biblical text closely, but there are occasional noteworthy points of connection, such as a likely quote of Genesis 6:12.

1Q20 (1QGenesis Apocryphon)–1Q20, otherwise known as the Genesis Apocryphon, has a few points of connection with the text of the Genesis Flood narrative, but its usefulness is rather limited. Its text has been examined from the editions of Schattner-Rieser (2008) and Machiela (2009).

4Q252 (4QCommentary on Genesis A)–4Q252 is by far the most important witness to the Genesis Flood narrative surviving at Qumran. It has been collated from the editions of Brooke (1996), Lim (1992), and Trehuedic (2008). The manuscript is written in an early formal Herodian script which may be dated approximately to the second half of the first century BC (Brooke 1996, 190). Its orthography is substantially fuller than the MT and SP texts. Brooke (1998) points out a number of similarities between 4Q252 and the LXX, but he consistently underappreciates the periphrastic nature of 4Q252. On substantial textual differences, it is much closer to the MT for the text of the Flood narrative. The literary genre of 4Q252 remains hotly debated, but it clearly retells the story of the Flood narrative in a very condensed form, focusing on the chronologically significant elements of the story. Its text is greatly abbreviated and often loosely paraphrased from the biblical text, so it is generally of little text-critical value. Phrases reworked within the context of the manuscript are, therefore, not normally cited in the apparatus. On the other hand, its chronological data are key readings for determining the original chronology of the Genesis Flood narrative. 4Q252 explains how, in its author's opinion, the chronology of the Flood fits with the three hundred sixty-four day schematic-solar calendar commonly attested in the Qumran documents. It does so by restating the chronological details of the Flood narrative (closely following the MT and SP with one important exception), making explicit details left implicit in Genesis, and showing how the dates and time periods cohere perfectly (to the day, as 4Q252 takes pains to point out) when reckoned according to the three hundred sixty-four day calendar. Whether 4Q252 has rightly understood the calendar of the Genesis Flood narrative or not, its intention is clear enough.

4Q254a (4QCommentary on Genesis D)–4Q254a is a commentary on the Genesis Flood narrative that is preserved only in fragmentary form. Its text has been collated from Trehuedic (2008) and Brooke (2002). Its script is a developed Herodian formal hand dated to the end of the first century BC or the beginning of the first century AD (Brooke 2002, 235). The text is extremely fragmentary and does not follow the biblical text closely, so it is generally of little text-critical value. It does, however, preserve one date, which may be extraordinarily important for the chronology of the Flood.

4Q370 (4QAdmonition Based on the Flood)–4Q370 is an early admonition in light of the Flood dated to the first century BC, which was collated from the edition of Legrand (2008). It does not follow the biblical text closely, but it does occasionally provide significant textual evidence with its biblical references.

4Q422 (4QParaphrase of Genesis-Exodus)—4Q422 contains a paraphrase of the Flood narrative with numerous textually valuable phrases. Its text has been cited from the edition of Elgvin and Tov (1994).

4Q464 (4QExposition on the Patriarchs)—4Q464 is an exposition about several important events in the lives of the patriarchs with occasional connections to the Flood narrative. Its text has been collated from the edition of Eshel and Stone (1995).

4Q577 (4QText Mentioning the Flood)—4Q577 is an unidentified text with an explicit mention of the Flood and numerous linguistic parallels to the biblical text. Since the context of its readings is not entirely known, it can generally only be cited as secondary support for readings found in the text, but at times its readings can be enlightening. Its text has been cited from the edition of Puech (1998).

A1.3.4 The Greek Septuagint
The text of the Greek Septuagint (LXX) has been collated from the editions of Wevers (1974a) and Rahlfs (1935), with variants cited from Wevers' edition. These critical editions are in general agreement about the original text of the LXX, differing only occasionally and on minor details. Because of the relative weight of the LXX text, most semantically significant variations are cited in the apparatus. Variant Greek manuscripts and ancient daughter versions of the LXX are only cited when they disagree with the text of the editions, and then usually only when they have significant attestation or they align with readings of other witnesses.

The LXX translation style is ordinarily quite literal, but it is given to occasional modifications such as grammatical facilitations to Greek syntax and style, smoothing out anthropomorphisms, simplification of difficult or redundant texts, internal harmonization, and exegetical clarification. The text of the LXX is helpful at numerous points in correcting text corrupted by accidental scribal mistakes, but it is generally manifestly secondary to a text very similar to the MT and SP on a number of levels. There are many cases where the LXX reading can easily be explained on the basis of a text like the MT and SP, where at the same time it would be impossible to come up with any reasonable explanation for the MT and SP reading on the basis of an original text in line with the LXX.

Often in the LXX, for example, there is clearly assimilation to other, similar passages, when the MT and SP retain original diversified forms. In contrast, the reverse situation is extremely rare. The LXX has, accordingly, significantly more plusses relative to the MT and SP than the reverse, and most of these plusses are easily explained by assimilation, but impossible to explain otherwise. Sometimes the LXX harmonization is clearly made in translation, and other times it clearly operates on the level of the Hebrew *Vorlage*, but most often one cannot decide whether a given harmonization occurred in the *Vorlage* or translation.

Occasionally, syntactical difficulties are smoothed over in the LXX, but not in the MT, as when third person self-references to God in divine speech (common and acceptable in Classical BH) are rendered with first person pronouns. It is quite common for the LXX also to revise the syntax of a difficult, complex, or redundant sentence in the MT.

These differences are so extensive and so consistently to be weighed in favor of a text very similar to the MT that it is impossible not to see the LXX as generally secondary to a text like the MT and the product of substantial revising and harmonizing activity.

Two major issues, however, are significantly more complicated in evaluating the LXX witness. First is the question of the rare MT and SP plusses relative to the LXX. These are often interpreted as evidence for glosses in the MT and SP traditions, but as shown above (see **A1.3.1 The Masoretic Text**), this approach is questionable. These LXX minuses may in fact be better explained within the context of the revisionistic tendencies of the LXX as attempts to abbreviate redundant texts and simplify difficult linguistic problems in the MT and SP texts.

The second major issue is the drastic differences in the divine names between the LXX and the other sources. The common LXX conflate name κύριος ὁ θεός = יהוה אלהים seems to be continued from earlier parts of Genesis, whereas the MT and SP reversion to the shorter titles in the Flood narrative is probably more original. Even these latter two witnesses disagree not infrequently, however. While there will, perhaps, always be an element of doubt about the original divine names used, the LXX revisionist characteristic may be operative on this level as well, flattening out the terminological diversity found in the other witnesses.

A1.3.5 The Syriac Peshitta

The text of the Syriac Peshitta (Syr.) was collated from the edition of de Boer and the Peshitta Institute (1977), and significant variants are listed when they have a viable claim to reflect Hebrew texts or align with other witnesses. The translation is relatively literal with only minor accommodations to Syriac syntax for introductory formulas for direct speech, redundant pronoun usage, prepositional equivalents, etc. The Syr. is closely aligned with the MT, though occasionally it shows the possible influence of LXX readings.

A1.3.6 The Aramaic Targums

The text of Targum (Targ.) Onkelos was collated from the edition of Sperber (1992), with reference to the explanatory notes of Aberbach and Grossfield (1982) and Drazin and Wagner (2006). Onkelos is normally quite literal, but examples of characteristic translational modifications are generally not cited as variants. A few examples of such would be interchanges in number and definiteness, rendering of all divine names as ", substitution of synonymous roots, periphrastic treatments of anthropomorphisms, explicating translations like "men of the house" for the Hebrew "house," and clear exegetical, halakhic, and midrashic elements.

The text of Targ. Neofiti was collated from the edition of Grossfeld (2000), which shows a number of differences with Diez Macho's edition (1968). Marginal notes and textual commentary were also considered from McNamara (1992). In addition to the translational characteristics noted from Onkelos, Neofiti also exhibits a number of double translations which are not cited as variants (e.g., 6:6, 8). Given the state of manuscript Neofiti 1, numerous emendations have been made to Neofiti indicated by an equal sign (e.g., "text = emendation"). When Neofiti essentially agrees with Onkelos, it is usually cited with Onkelos under the preferred orthography of Onkelos from Sperber's edition.

The text of the Fragment Targs. has been collated from Klein's edition (1980), and the text of the Cairo Genizah Targs. has likewise been collated from Klein (1986). The text of Targ. Pseudo-Jonathan has been cited from Rieder's edition (1974) only occasionally for its potential worth in attesting to earlier Palestinian Targ. texts. Likewise, I have only cited the Samaritan Targ. texts from Tal's edition (1980) on rare occasions when deemed appropriate. The Targ. texts hosted by the Comprehensive Aramaic Lexicon (<http://cal1.cn.huc.edu/>, accessed throughout the summer of 2011) were also consulted for comparison with the other editions. All of the Targs. are closely aligned with their respective Hebrew traditions (MT and SP respectively).

A1.3.7 The Latin Vulgate

The text of the Latin Vulgate (Vulg.) has been collated from the edition of Weber and Gryson (2007). Inner-versional variants are not normally cited, unless they are semantically significant, have significant attestation, and are aligned with readings found in other witnesses. While still being a fairly literal translation, the Vulgate text of the Genesis Flood narrative characteristically exhibits extensive formal alterations due to concerns of Latin syntax and literary style, such as differences in word order, changing parts of speech, omitting possessive pronouns, replacing unnecessary identifications of obvious referents with pronouns, inconsistent word choice for translational equivalents, supplying implicit lexemes, and omitting or variously translating connective ıs. The Vulg. is closely aligned with the MT, though it occasionally may show the influence of LXX readings.

A1.3.8 The Other Sources

The only other major work systematically collated is that of Jubilees. Unfortunately no fragments of the Flood narrative section of Jubilees were found at Qumran, so scholars are entirely reliant on the editions of Charles (1902) and, more importantly, VanderKam (1989), both based on the Ethiopic text of the book, translated from the Greek translation of the Hebrew. Jubilees substantially reworks the biblical text within its calendrical arrangement of biblical history. Nevertheless, there is often sufficient overlap with the biblical phrases to use it as an ancillary source for text-critical purposes, particularly on questions of chronology.

A number of other secondary works are occasionally cited when appropriate according to their standard reference details, though they have not been considered worthy of more in depth treatment for the purposes of this edition. I was alerted to many of these readings by the detailed work of Lewis (1968), but I double-checked all of the references. Philo has been cited from the edition of Yonge (1854–55), Josephus from the edition of Niese (1888), Jerome from the edition of Hayward (1995), Hippolytus from the edition of Roberts and Donaldson (1868), and *The Book of Adam and Eve* from the edition of Malan (1882).

A1.4 *Symbols*

α'	Aquila
𝕲	Septuagint
𝕲^W	Wevers (1974a) critical text

𝕲ᴿ	Rahlfs *Septuaginta* (1935) critical text
𝕲ᴿ⁽ˢ⁾	Rahlfs *Septuaginta* (1935) critical text
𝕲ᴿ⁽ᴳ⁾	Rahlfs *Genesis* (1926) critical text cited from Wevers (1974a)
𝔐	Masoretic text
𝔐ᴷ	*Kethib*
𝔐ꟴ	*Qere*
οἱ λ' οἱ	λοιποί
𝖚	Samaritan Pentateuch
𝖚ⱽᴳ	Von Gall (1918) critical text
𝖚ᴳᴮ	Giron Blanc (1976) critical text
𝖚ᴷᴺ	Kennicott (1776) critical text
σ'	Symmachus
𝕾	Syriac
𝕿	Targum
𝕿ᶜ	Cairo Geniza Targum fragment(s)
𝕿ᶠ	Fargment Targum
𝕿ᴶ	Targum Pseudo-Jonathan
𝕿ᴺ	Targum Neofiti
𝕿ᴼ	Targum Onkelos
𝕿ˢ	Samaritan Targum(s)
θ'	Theodotion
𝖁	Vulgate
=	equals
>	omits
+	adds
~	transposition
↔	may support multiple variants against another
]x[	brackets marking the limits of extant text *x*
÷	obelus
※	asterisk
*	marks a literal reconstruction of a variant created in the act of translation or an inner-versional variant
?	marks a reconstruction of a variant created either in the act of translation or textual variation in the Hebrew
ẋ	combining dot above marks a partially-preserved or uncertain letter
vacat	space intentionally left blank in a manuscript
x̄x̄	combining overline marks *nomina sacra* or letters used as numbers

A1.5 *Abbreviations*

| Aeth | Ethiopic |
| ap | variant according to an apparatus in an edition |

Arab	Arabic
Arabic Frag. to Pent.	*Arabic Fragments to the Pentateuch*
Arm	Armenian
BDB	Brown, Driver, and Briggs (1996)
begin	beginning of the verse
Bo	Bohairic
CD	Cairo Genizah Damascus Document
Co	Coptic
conj	conjecture
end	ending of the verse
GKC	Gesenius, Kautzsch, and Cowley (1910)
HALOT	*Hebrew and Aramaic Lexicon of the OT,* Köhler and Baumgartner (1994–2000)
Hebr. Quaest.	*Hebraicae Quaestiones in Libro Geneseos*
in loc	in its location in the critical text
Jub.	Jubilees
La	Old Latin
La^E	European text
La^I	Italian text
La^K	Cyprian and Pseudo-Cyprian
La^M	text of Ambrose divergent from La^I
La^S	Spanish text
La^X	translations from the Greek Jubilees or Psuedo-Philo
LXX	Greek Septuagint
mg	marginal reading
MS(S)	Manuscript(s)
MT	Masoretic text
OT	Old Testament
Pal	Palestinian-Syriac
Quaest. in Gen.	*Quaestiones in Genesim*
Sa	Sahidic
SP	Samaritan Pentateuch
Syr.	Syriac Peshitta
Syh	Syrohexapla
Targ(s).	Aramaic Targum(s)
te	text of an edition
transp	transpose
und	under
Vulg.	Latin Vulgate

A2. Critical Text and Apparatus (Genesis 6:5–9:17)

6:5 וַיַּ֤רְא יְהוָה֙ᵃ כִּ֥י רַבָּ֛הᵇ רָעַ֥ת הָאָדָ֖ם בָּאָ֑רֶץ וְכָל־יֵ֙צֶר֙ מַחְשְׁבֹ֣ת לִבּ֔וֹᶜ רַ֥קᵈ רַ֖ע
כָּל־הַיּֽוֹם׃ᶠ ⁶ וַיִּנָּ֣חֶם יְהוָ֔ה כִּֽי־עָשָׂ֥ה אֶת־הָֽאָדָ֖ם בָּאָ֑רֶץ וַיִּתְעַצֵּ֖בᵇ אֶל־לִבּֽוֹ׃ ⁷ וַיֹּ֣אמֶר
יְהוָ֗הᵃ אֶמְחֶ֨ה אֶת־הָאָדָ֤ם אֲשֶׁר־בָּרָ֙אתִי֙ מֵעַל֙ פְּנֵ֣י הָֽאֲדָמָ֔ה מֵֽאָדָם֙ עַד־בְּהֵמָ֔ה
עַד־רֶ֖מֶשᵇ וְעַד־עֹ֣וף הַשָּׁמָ֑יִם כִּ֥י נִחַ֖מְתִּי כִּ֥י עֲשִׂיתִֽם׃ ⁸ וְנֹ֕חַ מָ֥צָא חֵ֖ן בְּעֵינֵ֥י יְהוָֽה׃ᵃ

6:9 אֵ֚לֶּהᵃ תּוֹלְדֹ֣ת נֹ֔חַ נֹ֗חַ אִ֥ישׁ צַדִּ֛יק תָּמִ֥יםᵇ הָיָ֖ה בְּדֹֽרֹתָ֑יוᶜ אֶת־הָֽאֱלֹהִ֖יםᵈ
הִֽתְהַלֶּךְ־נֹֽחַ׃ ¹⁰ וַיּ֥וֹלֶד נֹ֖חַᵃ שְׁלֹשָׁ֣ה בָנִ֑ים אֶת־שֵׁ֖םᵇ אֶת־חָ֥ם וְאֶת־יָֽפֶת׃ᶜ

6:5 ᵃ יהוה 𝔐 𝔪 𝕲ᴹˢ (κύριος) 𝔖 (ܡܪܝܐ) Arab] ᵃיהוה אלהים 𝕲 (κύριος ὁ θεός) |
אלהים 𝔐ᴹˢ 𝕲ᴹˢ (ὁ θεός) 𝑽 (Deus). |
ᵇ רבה 𝔐 𝔪 4Q422 II 1 𝑽 (multa)] רבתה* 𝕲 (ἐπληθύνθησαν) 𝔖 (ܘܣܓܝܐܬ)
(סגיאת) 𝕮ᴺˢ (סגת) | רבת 𝔐ᴹˢ.
ᶜ לבו 𝔐 𝔪 𝕲 (ἐν τῇ καρδίᾳ αὐτοῦ) 𝔖 (ܕܠܒܗ) 𝕮° (ליביה), cf. 4Q370 I 3 (לבם) 𝕮ᴺ
(לבהון) 𝕲ᴹˢˢ (ἐν τῇ καρδίᾳ) 𝑽 (cordis).
ᵈ רק 𝔐] רק* 𝑽 𝔖. omit (לחד = לחד) 𝕮ᴺ (לחוד) 𝕮° (ἐπιμελῶς) 𝕲.
ᵉ text 𝔐 𝔪 𝕲 𝕮ᴼᴺ 𝑽 𝔖] add מנעריו* 𝕲ᴹˢˢ (ἐκ νεότητος [+ αὐτοῦ 𝕲ᴹˢ Sa]) Aeth Laᴷ Sa.
ᶠ⁻ᶠ כל היום 𝔐 𝔪 𝕮ᴼᴺ (כל יומא) 𝑽 (omni tempore)] כל יום* 𝔖 (ܟܠ ܝܘܡ) כל יום
𝕲 (πάσας τὰς ἡμέρας).
6:6 ᵃ יהוה 𝔐 𝔪 𝕲ᴹˢ (ὁ' κύριος) 𝔖 (ܡܪܝܐ) אלהים 𝕲 (ὁ θεός) | אלהים יהוה* 𝕲ᴹˢˢ
(κύριος ὁ θεός) | omit יהוה* 𝑽 (eum).
ᵇ⁻ᵇ אל לבו 𝔐 𝔪 𝕲ᴹˢˢ (ἐν τῇ καρδίᾳ αὐτοῦ) 𝔖 (ܕܠܒܗ) 𝕮ᴺᶠ (עם לבה) ά (πρὸς
καρδίαν αὐτοῦ)] omit אל לבו* 𝕲.
6:7 ᵃ יהוה 𝔐 𝔪 𝔖 (ܡܪܝܐ) אלהים 𝕲 (ὁ θεός) | יהוה אלהים * 𝕲ᴹˢˢ (κύριος ὁ θεός)
| omit יהוה* 𝑽.
ᵇ⁻ᵇ עד רמש 𝔐 𝔪 𝕮ᴼᴺ ועד רמש] ועד ריחשא 𝔐ᴹˢˢ 𝔖 (ܥܕܡܐ ܠܪܚܫܐ) ומרמש*
𝕲 (καὶ ἀπὸ ἑρπετῶν) | מרמש* 𝑽 (a reptili).
ᶜ ועד 𝔐 𝕮ᴼᴺ (ועד) 𝔖 (ܘܥܕܡܐ) עד 𝔐ᴹˢ 𝔪 𝕲' (ἕως) 𝑽 (usque ad).
6:8 ᵃ יהוה 𝔐 𝔪 𝔖 (ܡܪܝܐ) 𝑽 (Domino)] יהוה אלהים* 𝕲 (κυρίου τοῦ θεοῦ) | אלהים*
𝕲ᴹˢˢ (τοῦ θεοῦ).
6:9 ᵃ אלה 𝔐 𝔪 𝕲ᴹˢˢ (αὗται) 𝔖ᴹˢˢ (ܗܠܝܢ) 𝕮ᴼᴺ (אילן) 𝑽 (hae) Aethᴹˢˢ Bo] ואלה' 𝕲
(αὗται δέ) 𝔖 (ܗܠܝܢ).
ᵇ תמים 𝔐 𝕲 (τέλειος) 𝕮ᴼᴺ (שלים), cf. Ben Sira 44:17] ותמים 𝔪 𝕲ᴹˢˢ (καὶ τέλειος)
𝔖 (ܘܓܡܝܪ) 𝑽 (atque perfectus) Laᴱ.
ᶜ בדרתיו 𝔐 𝔪 𝔖 (ܒܕܪܘܗܝ) 𝕮° (בדרוהי) 𝕮ᴺ (בדרוי) 𝑽 (in generationibus suis)] בדרו*
(ב)דׄורי 𝕲 (ἐν τῇ γενεᾷ αὐτοῦ) 𝕮ᴺᵐᵍ (בדרה), cf. 7:1 𝕮ᶠ to 6:8 (בדריה) 4Q422 II 2a
| בדרכיו conj.
ᵈ⁻ᵈ ואת האלהים 𝔐 𝔪 𝕲 (τῷ θεῷ) 𝕮° (בדחלמא דיוי) 𝕮ᴺ (קדם ייי)] ואת האלהים'
𝔖 (ܘܐܠܗܐ ... ܗ).
ᵉ נח 𝔐 𝔪 𝕲 (Νωε) 𝔖 (ܢܘܚ) 𝕮ᴼᴺ (נח)] omit נח* 𝕲ᴹˢˢ 𝑽 Aeth Arab Laᴱ.
6:10 ᵃ נח 𝔐 𝔪 𝕲 (Νωε) 𝔖 (ܢܘܚ) 𝕮ᴼᴺ (נח)] omit נח* 𝕲ᴹˢˢ 𝑽 Aethᴹˢˢ.
ᵇ⁻ᵇ את חם 𝔐 𝔪 𝕲 (τὸν Χαμ) 𝕮ᴼᴺ (ית חם) 𝑽 (Ham)] ואת חם 𝔐ᴹˢˢ 𝔪ᴹˢˢ 𝔖 (ܘܠܚܡ).
ᶜ⁻ᶜ ואת יפת 𝔐 𝔪 𝕲ᴹˢ (καὶ τὸν Ιαφεθ) 𝔖 (ܘܠܝܦܬ) 𝕮ᴼᴺ (וית יפת) 𝑽 (et Iafeth) Aeth
Pal] את יפת 𝕲 (τὸν Ιαφεθ) 𝑽ᴹˢˢ (Iafeth).

¹¹ וַתִּשָּׁחֵת הָאָרֶץ לִפְנֵי הָאֱלֹהִיםᵃ וַתִּמָּלֵא הָאָרֶץ חָמָס: ¹² וַיַּרְא אֱלֹהִיםᵃ אֶת
הָאָרֶץ וְהִנֵּה נִשְׁחָתָה כִּי־הִשְׁחִית כָּל־בָּשָׂר אֶת־דַּרְכּוֹ עַל־הָאָרֶץ: ¹³ וַיֹּאמֶר
אֱלֹהִיםᵃ לְנֹחַ קֵץ כָּל־בָּשָׂר בָּא לְפָנַי כִּיᵇ מָלְאָה הָאָרֶץ חָמָס מִפְּנֵיהֶם ᶜוְהִנְנִי
מַשְׁחִיתָם אֶת־הָאָרֶץᶜ: ¹⁴ עֲשֵׂהᵃ לְךָ תֵּבַת עֲצֵי־גֹפֶר קִנִּיםᵇ תַּעֲשֶׂה אֶת־הַתֵּבָה
וְכָפַרְתָּ אֹתָהּ מִבַּיִת וּמִחוּץ בַּכֹּפֶר: ¹⁵ וְזֶה אֲשֶׁר תַּעֲשֶׂה אֹתָהּᵃ שְׁלֹשׁ מֵאוֹת אַמָּה
אֹרֶךְ הַתֵּבָהᵇ חֲמִשִּׁיםᶜ אַמָּה רָחְבָּהּᵈ וּשְׁלֹשִׁים אַמָּה קוֹמָתָהּᵉ: ¹⁶ צֹהַרᵃ תַּעֲשֶׂה
לַתֵּבָה וְאֶל־אַמָּה תְּכַלֶּנָּה מִלְמַעְלָה ᵇוּפֶתַח הַתֵּבָהᵇ בְּצִדָּהּ תָּשִׂים תַּחְתִּיִּם שְׁנִיִּםᶜ

6:11 ᵃ האלהים 𝔐 ሠ 𝔊 (τοῦ θεοῦ) 𝔖 (ܐܠܗܐ) 𝔙 (Deo)] 𝔊ᴹˢˢ (κυρίου
τοῦ θεοῦ) Sa | יהוה* 𝔖ᴹˢ (ܡܪܝܐ) 𝔙ᴹˢˢ (Domino).

6:12 ᵃ אלהים 𝔐 ሠ 𝔊ᴹˢˢ (ὁ θεός) 𝔖 (ܐܠܗܐ) 𝔙 (Deus)] יהוה אלהים* 𝔊 (κύριος ὁ
θεός).

6:13 ᵃ אלהים 𝔐 ሠ 𝔊 (ὁ θεός) 𝔖 (ܐܠܗܐ)] יהוה אלהים* 𝔊ᴹˢˢ (κύριος ὁ θεός) Aeth Laᴵ
Sa Syh etc. | omit אלהים* 𝔊ᴹˢ 𝔙 Laˢ.
ᵇ כי 𝔐 ሠ 𝔊 (ὅτι) 𝔖 (ܡܛܠ) 𝔗ᴼ (ארי) 𝔗ᴺ (ארו')] omit כי* 𝔙.
ᶜ⁻ᶜ והנני משחיתם מאת הארץ 𝔐ᴹˢ 𝔗ˢ (ס) את הארץ Gunkel Zipor] והנם משחית(י)ם
את הארץ Eißfeldt Graetz Procksch Westermann | (ואנא מחבל לון מן ארעא)
והא אנא מחבלהון 𝔗ᴼᴶ (ܣܝ ܐܢܐ ܡܚܒܠ ܐܢܐ ܠܗܘܢ ܡܢ) 𝔖 ሠ 𝔐 את הארץ
ᵉγὼ καταφθείρω αὐτοὺς καὶ τὴν γῆν) 𝔗ᴺ (והא אנ' מחבל יתהון וית ארעא |
משחיתם מן הארץ 𝔐 והנני משחיתם מן הארץ Olshausen Stade | Kittel | (עם ארעא
הנני Ball | והנני משחית אתם ואת הארץ Budde | כי (הם) משחיתם את הארץ
והנני משחיתים את הארץ Eerdmans | ሠᴹˢˢ והנני משחיתם את
דרכו על הארץ 𝔐ᴹˢ.
6:14 ᵃ עשה 𝔐 ሠ, ↔ עשי/עשה 𝔊ᴹˢˢ (ποίησον) 𝔖 (ܥܒܕ) 𝔗ᴼᴺ (עיביד) 𝔙 (fac) Pal] עשי*
ሠᴹˢˢ, ↔ עשי/עשה 𝔊ᴹˢˢ (ποίησον) 𝔖 (ܥܒܕ) 𝔗ᴼᴺ (עיביד) 𝔙 (fac) Pal | ועשה* or לכן
עשה* 𝔊 (ποίησον οὖν).
ᵇ קנים 𝔐 ሠ 𝔊 (νοσσιάς) 𝔖 (ܡܕܝܪܐ) 𝔗ᴼ (מדורין) 𝔗ᴺ (כמדורונים) 𝔙 (mansiunculas)]
קנים קנים Philo Quaest. in Gen. ii.3 Budde Delitzsch Dillmann Eißfeldt Gunkel Lagarde
Olshausen Procksch Skinner Westermann.
6:15 ᵃ אתה 𝔐 ሠ 𝔖 (ܠܗ) 𝔗ᴼᴺ (יתה) 𝔙 (eam) Sa] את התבה 𝔊 (τὴν κιβωτόν).
ᵇ⁻ᵇ ארך התבה 𝔐 ሠ 4Q254a 1-2 2 (אר[ך] התבה) 𝔊 (τὸ μῆκος τῆς κιβωτοῦ) 𝔖
(ܐܘܪܟܗ ܕܩܒܘܬܐ) 𝔗ᴼᴺ (אורכא דתיבותא) 𝔙 (longitudo arcae)] ארכה* 𝔊ᴹˢˢ (αὐτῆς [>
αὐτῆς > 𝔊ᴹˢˢ Laᴱ Sa]) Aeth Laᴱ Sa.
ᶜ וחמ[שים] 𝔐 𝔗ᴼᴺ (חמשין) 𝔙 (quinquaginta)] וחמשים ሠ 4Q254a 1-2 (וחמשים) 𝔊
(καὶ πεντήκοντα) 𝔖 (ܘܚܡܫܝܢ).
ᵈ רחבה 𝔐 ሠ 4Q254a 1-2 3 𝔖 (ܦܬܝܗ) 𝔗ᴼᴺ (פותיה) Aeth Arab Pal Syh] הרחב* 𝔊 (τὸ
πλάτος) 𝔙 (latitudo).
ᵉ ק]ומתה] 𝔐 ሠ 6Q1 (ק[ומתה) 𝔊 (τὸ ὕψος αὐτῆς) 𝔖 (ܪܘܡܗ) 𝔗ᴺ (רומה) 𝔗ᴼ (רומ')]
הקומה* 𝔊ᴹˢˢ (τὸ ὕψος) Laˢ Arm Sa.
6:16 ᵃ צהר 𝔐 ሠ 𝔗ᴼ (ניהור) 𝔗ᴺ (בית נהור) 𝔙 (fenestram)] צבר² 𝔊 (ἐπισυνάγων) |
וצהר 𝔖 (ܨܗܪܐ).
ᵇ⁻ᵇ ופתח התבה 𝔐 ሠ 𝔊ᴿ ᴹˢˢ (τὴν δὲ θύραν τῆς κιβωτοῦ) 𝔖 (ܘܬܪܥܐ ܕܩܒܘܬܐ) 𝔗ᴼᴺ
(ותרעא דתיבותא) 𝔙 (ostium autem arcae) Laᴵ] ופתחה* or ופתח* 𝔊ᵂ ᴹˢˢ (τὴν δὲ θύραν)
Aeth Laˢ ופתחה* 𝔊ᴹˢ (τὴν δὲ θύραν αὐτῆς) Arab Pal Sa.
ᶜ שנים 𝔐 ሠ 𝔊 (διώροφα) 𝔗ᴼᴺ (תנינין) 𝔙 (cenacula)] ושנים 𝔖 (ܘܬܠܬܐ).

וּשְׁלִשִׁיםᵈ תַּעֲשֶׂהᵇ׃   17 וַאֲנִי הִנְנִי מֵבִיא אֶת־הַמַּבּוּל מַיִםᵃ עַל־הָאָרֶץ לְשַׁחֵתᵇ
כָּל־בָּשָׂר אֲשֶׁר־בּוֹ רוּחַ חַיִּים מִתַּחַת הַשָּׁמָיִם כֹּל אֲשֶׁר־ᶜבָּאָרֶץ יִגְוָע׃ 18 וַהֲקִמֹתִי
אֶת־בְּרִיתִי אִתָּךְ וּבָאתָ אֶל־הַתֵּבָה אַתָּה וּבָנֶיךָᵃ וְאִשְׁתְּךָᵃ וּנְשֵׁי־בָנֶיךָ אִתָּךְ׃
19 וּמִכָּל־הָחַיᵇ מִכָּל־בָּשָׂר שְׁנַיִםᵈ מִכֹּל תָּבִיא אֶל־הַתֵּבָה לְהַחֲיֹת אִתָּךְ זָכָר וּנְקֵבָה
יִהְיוּᶠ׃ 20 מֵהָעוֹףᵃ לְמִינֵהוּ וּמִן־הַבְּהֵמָה לְמִינָהּ מִכֹּלᶜ רֶמֶשׂ הָאֲדָמָה לְמִינֵהוּᵉ
שְׁנַיִםᶠ מִכֹּל יָבֹאוּ אֵלֶיךָᵍ לְהַחֲיֹותᵍ׃ 21 וְאַתָּה קַח־לְךָ מִכָּל־מַאֲכָל אֲשֶׁר יֵאָכֵלᵃ
וְאָסַפְתָּ אֵלֶיךָᵇ וְהָיָה לְךָ וְלָהֶם לְאָכְלָה׃ 22 וַיַּעַשׂ נֹחַ כְּכֹל אֲשֶׁר צִוָּה אֹתוֹ אֱלֹהִיםᵇ
כֵּן עָשָׂהᶜ׃   7:1 וַיֹּאמֶר יְהוָהᵃ לְנֹחַᵇ בֹּא־אַתָּה וְכָל־בֵּיתְךָ אֶל־הַתֵּבָה כִּי־אֹתְךָ

שלשים 6Q1 [𝔐 ᵐ 𝔊 (καὶ τριώροφα) 𝔖 (ܘܬܠܝܬܐ) 𝔗ᴼᴺ (ותליתאין) 𝔙 (et tristega)] ᵈ
(שלשי[ם]).

6:17 ᵃ מים 𝔐 ᵐ 𝔊 (ὕδωρ) 𝔖 (ܡܝܐ) 𝔗ᴼ (מיא) 𝔗ᴺ (דמיא) 𝔙 (aquas)] omit מים Gunkel Westermann.

ᵇ לשחת 𝔐 ᵐ] להשחית.

ᶜᶜ כל אשר 𝔐 ᵐ 𝔗ᴼ (כל ד) 𝔗ᴺ (כל מה די) 𝔙 (universa quae)] וכל אשר 𝔐ᴹˢˢ 𝔊 (καὶ ὅσα ἐάν) 𝔖
(ܘܟܠ ד).

6:18 ᵃᵃ ובניך ואשתך 𝔐 ᵐ 6Q1 ובניך ואשתך 𝔊 (καὶ οἱ υἱοί σου καὶ ἡ γυνή σου) 𝔖 (ܘܒܢܝܟ)
𝔗ᴼᴺᶜ (ובנך ואתתך) 𝔙 *ואשתך ובניך] 𝔐ᴹˢ 𝔊ᴹˢˢ (*ובנ]יך אשתך) 𝔙 (et filii tui uxor tua) |
(καὶ ἡ γυνή σου καὶ οἱ υἱοί σου) Aeth Sa.

6:19 ᵃ text 𝔐 ᵐ 𝔖 𝔗ᴼᶜ 𝔙 Aethᴾ Syh (καὶ ἀπὸ πάντων τῶν κτηνῶν καὶ ἀπὸ πάντων τῶν ἑρπετῶν
und ÷)] add המש ומכל הבהמה ומכל 𝔊 (καὶ ἀπὸ πάντων τῶν κτηνῶν καὶ ἀπὸ πάντων τῶν
ἑρπετῶν).

ᵇ החי 𝔐 ᵐ 𝔖 (ܕܚܝ) 𝔗ᴼᴶ (דחי) 𝔗ᴺ (חייא) ᵐ החיה 𝔊 (τῶν θηρίων) 𝔗ᶜ (חיתה) α΄ (ζῷων) σ΄ (ζῷων).

ᶜᶜ ומכל בשר 𝔐 𝔖 𝔗ᴼ (מכל ביסרא) 𝔗ᴺᶜ (מן כל בשרא) 𝔙 (universae carnis)] ומכל מכל בשר
מן כל בשרא 𝔗ᴺᶜ ומכל הבשר, cf. 𝔗ᴼ (מכל ביסרא) 𝔖 (וכל אפן פאשׁרא סרקם) | ומכל בשר 𝔐ᴹˢˢ 𝔊² (καὶ ἀπὸ πάσης σαρκός).

ᵈ שנים 𝔐 ᵐ 𝔗ᴼᴺᶜ (תרין) 𝔙 (bina)] שנים שנים 𝔊 (δύο δύο) 𝔖 (ܬܪܝܢ ܬܪܝܢ).

ᵉ מכל 𝔐 ᵐ 𝔊 (ἀπὸ πάντων) 𝔗ᴼ (מכולא) 𝔗ᴺᶜ (מן כולא)] omit *מכל 𝔙.

ᶠ יהיו 𝔐 𝔊 (ἔσονται) 𝔖 (ܢܗܘܘܢ) 𝔗ᴼᴺᶜ (יהון)] והיה 𝔗ᴺ | omit *יהיו 𝔙.

6:20 ᵃ מהעוף 𝔐, ↔ ᵐ מן העוף/מהעוף 𝔐ᴹˢˢ (ἀπὸ τῶν πετεινῶν) 𝔖 (ܡܢ ܦܘܚܕ) 𝔗ᴼᶜ (מעופא) 𝔗ᴺ
(מן עופא) 𝔙 (de volucribus) Sa Syh] מן העוף/מהעוף, ↔ ᵐ מן העוף 𝔖ᴹˢˢ (ἀπὸ τῶν πετεινῶν) 𝔙 (de volucribus) Sa Syh] מכל העוף ᵐ (ἀπὸ πάντων τῶν
ὀρνέων τῶν πετεινῶν).

ᵇ ומן 𝔐 ᵐ 𝔊ᴹˢˢ (καὶ ἀπό) 𝔖 (ܘܡܢ) 𝔗ᴼᴺᶜ (ומן) 𝔙 (et de) Syh] ומכל 𝔊 (καὶ ἀπὸ πάντων) 𝔖ᴹˢ
(ܘܡܟܠ).

ᶜ ומכל 𝔐ᴹˢˢ ᵐ 𝔊 (καὶ ἀπὸ πάντων) 𝔖 (ܘܡܟܠ ܕܠܡ) 𝔗ᴼ⁽ᴹˢˢ⁾ᴶ (ומכל) 𝔗ᴺ (ומן כל) 𝔙 (et ex omni)] מכל ומכל
(מן כל) 𝔗ᶜ (מכל) ᵐ 𝔗ᴼ (מכל).

ᵈ רמש 𝔐 𝔊ᴹˢˢ (τῶν ἑρπετῶν τῶν ἐπί) 𝔖 (ܘܐܒܐ) 𝔗ᴼᴺ (ריחשא) 𝔗ᶜ (רמסה) 𝔙 (reptili)
Arm Bo Laᴷ Syh] הרמש הרמש רמש על | 𝔊 (τῶν ἑρπετῶν τῶν ἑρπόντων ἐπί) אשר רמש על הרמש.

ᵉ למיניהם 𝔐 ᵐ 𝔖 (ܠܓܢܣܝܗܘܢ) 6Q1 למינהו 𝔗ᴺ⁽ᵐᵍ⁾ᶜ* (כατὰ γένος αὐτῶν) 𝔗ᴺ⁽ᵐᵍ⁾ᶜ* (למי]ניהם) 𝔊² (κατὰ γένος αὐτῶν) 𝔗ᴺ⁽ᵐᵍ⁾ᶜ* (למינהון)
𝔗ᴼ (לזנוהי) 𝔗ᴺ (למינה) 𝔙 (secundum genus suum).

ᶠ שנים 𝔐 ᵐ 𝔗ᴼᴺᶜ (תרין) 𝔙 (bina), cf. 6Q1 (] שנים] שנים שנים 𝔊 (δύο δύο) 𝔖 (ܬܪܝܢ ܬܪܝܢ).

ᵍ אליך 𝔐 ᵐ 𝔊 (πρὸς σέ) 𝔗ᴼᴺ (לותך)] *אתך 𝔖 (ܠܘܬܟ) 𝔗ᴺ⁽ᵐᵍ⁾ (עמך) 𝔙 (tecum), cf. 𝔊 (μετὰ σοῦ) |
𝔗ᶜ *אל התבה = לתיבותא (לתיבותיה).

ʰ text 𝔐 ᵐ 𝔊ᴹˢˢ 𝔖 𝔗ᴼᴺᶜ] add אתך זכר ונקבה 𝔊 (μετὰ σοῦ ἄρσεν καὶ θῆλυ), cf. 𝔖 (ܠܘܬܟ)
𝔗ᴺ⁽ᵐᵍ⁾ (עמך) 𝔙 (tecum).

6:21 ᵃ יאכל 𝔐 ᵐ 𝔖 (ܡܬܐܟܠ) 𝔗ᴼ (מתאכיל) 𝔗ᴺᶜ (יתאכל) 𝔙 (mandi possunt)] *תאכלו 𝔊 (ἔδεσθε).

ᵇ אליך 𝔐 ᵐ 𝔊 (πρὸς σεαυτόν) 𝔖 (ܠܘܬܟ) 𝔗ᴼᴺᶜ (לותך) 𝔙 (apud te)] *אליו 𝔊ᴹˢˢ (πρὸς ἑαυτόν).

6:22 ᵃ ככל 𝔐 ᵐ 𝔖ᴹˢˢ (ܟܠ) 𝔗ᴼᶜ (כבל), cf. 4Q577 4 6 [כ]כבל] *כל 𝔊 (πάντα) 𝔖 (ܟܠ) 𝔗ᴺ (כל).

ᵇ אלהים 𝔐 ᵐ 𝔊ᴹˢˢ (ὁ θεός) 𝔖ᴹˢˢ (ܐܠܗܐ) 𝔙 (Deus) Pal] יהוה אלהים 𝔊 (κύριος ὁ θεός) | יהוה* 𝔙ᴹˢ
(Dominus).

ᶜᶜ כן עשה 𝔐 ᵐ 𝔊 (οὕτως ἐποίησεν) 𝔖 (ܗܟܢܐ ܥܒܕ) 𝔗ᴼᶜ (כן עבד) 𝔗ᴺ (כדין עבד)] omit 𝔙.

7:1 ᵃ יהוה 𝔐 𝔊ᴹˢˢ (κύριος) 𝔖ᴹˢˢ (ܡܪܝܐ) 𝔙 (Dominus) Laˢ] אלהים 𝔐ᴹˢˢ ᵐ 𝔊ᴹˢˢ (ὁ θεός) 𝔖 (ܐܠܗܐ)
Arab Armᵃᵖ | יהוה* אלהים 𝔊 (κύριος ὁ θεός).

ᵇ לנח 𝔐 ᵐᴹˢ] אל נח ᵐ.

רָאִיתִי צַדִּיק לְפָנַי בַּדּוֹר הַזֶּה׃ 2 מִכֹּל[a] הַבְּהֵמָה הַטְּהוֹרָה תִּקַּח[b] לְךָ שִׁבְעָה שִׁבְעָה
[c]אִישׁ וְאִשְׁתּוֹ[c] וּמִן הַבְּהֵמָה אֲשֶׁר לֹא טְהֹרָה הִוא[d] שְׁנַיִם[e] [f]אִישׁ וְאִשְׁתּוֹ[f]׃ 3 [a]גַּם
מֵעוֹף הַשָּׁמַיִם[b] שִׁבְעָה שִׁבְעָה זָכָר וּנְקֵבָה[c] לְחַיּוֹת[d] זֶרַע עַל פְּנֵי[e] כָל[f] הָאָרֶץ׃ 4 כִּי
לְיָמִים עוֹד שִׁבְעָה אָנֹכִי[a] מַמְטִיר עַל הָאָרֶץ אַרְבָּעִים יוֹם וְאַרְבָּעִים לָיְלָה וּמָחִיתִי
אֶת כָּל הַיְקוּם אֲשֶׁר עָשִׂיתִי מֵעַל פְּנֵי[b] הָאֲדָמָה[c]׃ 5 וַיַּעַשׂ נֹחַ [a]כְּכֹל אֲשֶׁר[a] צִוָּהוּ
יְהוָה[b]׃ 7:6 וְנֹחַ בֶּן שֵׁשׁ מֵאוֹת שָׁנָה וְהַמַּבּוּל הָיָה מַיִם[a] עַל הָאָרֶץ׃ 7 וַיָּבֹא נֹחַ
[a]וּבָנָיו וְאִשְׁתּוֹ[a] וּנְשֵׁי בָנָיו אִתּוֹ אֶל הַתֵּבָה מִפְּנֵי מֵי הַמַּבּוּל׃ 8 [a]מִן[b] הַבְּהֵמָה הַטְּהוֹרָה

7:2 [a] מכל 𝔐 ⅏ 𝔊^{MSS} (ἀπὸ δὲ πάντων) 𝔗^{OC} (מכל) 𝔗^{N} (מן כל) Arm Syh] ומכל? 𝔖 (ܘܡܢ ܟܠܗ) | ומן? 𝔊 (ἀπὸ δὲ).
[b] תקח 𝔐 ⅏ 𝔖 (ܣܒ) 𝔗^{ONC} (תיסב) 𝔙 (*tolle*)] תביא* 𝔊 (εἰσάγαγε).
[c-c] איש ואשתו 𝔐] זכר ונקבה ⅏ 𝔊? (ἄρσεν καὶ θῆλυ) 𝔖* (ܕܟܪܐ ܘܢܩܒܬܐ) 𝔗^{ONJ}* (דכר ונוקבא) 𝔗^{C}* (דכר וזוגה) 𝔙* (*masculum et feminam*).
[d] הוא 𝔐, ↔ היא/הוא 𝔗^{O} (והי) 𝔗^{NC} (הוא), cf. 𝔊^{MSS} (ὄντων) 𝔖 (ܗܘܬ)] היא 𝔐^{MSS} ⅏, ↔ היא/הוא 𝔗^{O} (-והי) 𝔗^{NC} (הוא), cf. 𝔊^{MSS} (ὄντων) 𝔖 (ܗܘܬ) | omit הוא* 𝔊 𝔙.
[e] שנים 𝔐 𝔗^{ONC} (תרין)] שנים שנים ⅏ 𝔊 (δύο δύο) 𝔖 (ܬܪ̈ܝܢ ܬܪ̈ܝܢ) 𝔙 (*duo duo*).
[f-f] איש ואשתו 𝔐] זכר ונקבה ⅏ 𝔊? (ἄρσεν καὶ θῆλυ) 𝔖* (ܕܟܪܐ ܘܢܩܒܬܐ) 𝔗^{ONJ}* (דכר ונוקבא) 𝔗^{C}* (דכר וזוגה) 𝔙* (*masculum et feminam*).
7:3 [a] גם 𝔐 ⅏^{MSS} 𝔖^{MS} (ܐܦ) 𝔗^{ON} (אף) 𝔗^{C} (להוד)] וגם ⅏ 𝔖 (ܘܐܦ) 𝔙 (*sed et*).
[b] text 𝔐 𝔊^{MSS} 𝔖 𝔗^{ONC} 𝔙 Syh (τῶν καθαρῶν und ÷)] add הטהור ⅏ 𝔊 (τῶν καθαρῶν) 𝔖^{MSS} (ܕܕܟܝܐ).
[c] text 𝔐 ⅏ 𝔖 𝔗^{ONC} 𝔙 Syh (καὶ ἀπὸ κτλ. after ÷)] add ומהעוף אשר לא טהור הוא שנים שנים זכר ונקבה? 𝔊 (καὶ ἀπὸ [+ πάντων 𝔊^{MSS}] τῶν πετεινῶν [+ τοῦ οὐρανοῦ 𝔊^{MSS}] τῶν μὴ καθαρῶν δύο δύο ἄρσεν καὶ θῆλυ).
[d] לחיות 𝔐 ⅏^{MSS}] להחיות ⅏.
[e] פני 𝔐 ⅏ 𝔖 (ܐܦܝ) 𝔗^{ONC} (אפי) 𝔙 (*faciem*)] omit פני* 𝔊.
[f] כל 𝔐 ⅏ 𝔊 (πᾶσαν) 𝔖 (ܟܠܗ) 𝔗$^{OCN(mg)}$ (כל) 𝔙 (*universae*)] omit כל* 𝔗^{N}.
7:4 [a] אנכי 𝔐 ⅏ 𝔊 (ἐγώ) 𝔖 (ܐܢܐ) 𝔗^{ONC} (אנא) 𝔙 (*ego*)] omit אנכי* 𝔊^{MS} Syh (ἐγώ und ÷) La^{S} Aeth^{MSS}.
[b] פני 𝔐 ⅏ 𝔊 (προσώπου) 𝔖 (ܐܦܝ) 𝔗^{ON} (אפי) 𝔙 (*superficie*)] פני כל* 𝔊^{MSS} (προσώπου πάσης).
[c] text 𝔐 ⅏ 𝔊 𝔖 𝔗^{ONC} 𝔙] add מאדם עד בהמה? 𝔊^{MSS} (απο α̅ν̅ο̅υ̅ εως κτηνους [+ και απο ερπετων εως πετεινον του ουρανου 𝔊^{MS}] Arab).
7:5 [a-a] ככל אשר 𝔐 ⅏ 𝔗^{O} (ככל ד) 𝔗^{C} (ככל מה די), cf. 4Q577 4 6 (]כ̇כול א[)] כל אשר* 𝔊 (πάντα ὅσα) 𝔖 (ܟܠ ܕ) 𝔗^{N} (כל מן די) 𝔙 (*omnia quae*) | כאשר* Aeth^{MS} Arab.
[b] יהוה 𝔐 ⅏ 𝔖 (ܡܪܝܐ) 𝔙 (*Dominus*) Sa] יהוה אלהים? 𝔊 (κύριος ὁ θεός) | אלהים* 𝔊^{MS} (ὁ θεός).
7:6 [a] מים 𝔐 ⅏ 𝔊 (ὕδατος) 𝔖 (ܡܝܐ) 𝔗^{ON} (מיא) 𝔗^{C} (מיין) 𝔙 (*aquae*)] omit מים* 𝔊^{MSS} Eißfeldt Gunkel Hendel Maurer McCarter Westermann.
7:7 [a-a] ובניו ואשתו 𝔐 ⅏ 𝔊 (καὶ οἱ υἱοὶ αὐτοῦ καὶ ἡ γυνὴ αὐτοῦ) 𝔖 (ܘܒܢܘܗܝ ܘܐܢܬܬܗ) 𝔗^{ON} (ובנוהי ואתתיה) 𝔗^{C} (ובנוי ונשוי)] ובניו אשתו* 𝔙 (*et filii eius uxor eius*) | ואשתו ובניו* Aeth^{MSS} Bo.
7:8 [a-a-a] ומן העוף in loc 𝔐 ⅏ 𝔊^{MSS} (καὶ ἀπὸ τῶν πετεινῶν) 𝔖 (ܘܡܢ ܦܪܚܬܐ) 𝔗^{ONC} (ומן עופא) 𝔙 (*et de volucribus*) Syh] transp ומן העוף to begin? 𝔊$^{WR(S)}$ (καὶ ἀπὸ τῶν πετεινῶν) | transp ומכל העוף to begin* 𝔊$^{R(G)}$ (καὶ ἀπὸ πάντων τῶν πετεινῶν).
[b] מן 𝔐 ⅏ 𝔗^{ONC} (מן) 𝔙 (*de*)] ומן? 𝔊 (καὶ ἀπὸ) 𝔖 (ܘܡܢ).

וּמִן הַבְּהֵמָה אֲשֶׁר אֵינֶנָּה טְהֹרָה וּמִן הָעוֹף[a] וְכֹל[c] אֲשֶׁר[d] רֹמֵשׂ עַל[d] הָאֲדָמָה:
[9] שְׁנַיִם שְׁנַיִם[a] בָּאוּ אֶל[b] נֹחַ אֶל הַתֵּבָה זָכָר וּנְקֵבָה כַּאֲשֶׁר צִוָּה[c] אֱלֹהִים[d] אֶת נֹחַ:
7:10 וַיְהִי לְשִׁבְעַת הַיָּמִים וּמֵי[a] הַמַּבּוּל[b] הָיוּ עַל הָאָרֶץ: [11] בִּשְׁנַת[a-a] שֵׁשׁ מֵאוֹת[a-a]
שָׁנָה לְחַיֵּי נֹחַ בַּחֹדֶשׁ הַשֵּׁנִי[b] בְּשִׁבְעָה עָשָׂר יוֹם[c-c] לַחֹדֶשׁ הַזֶּה[d] בַּיּוֹם[d-d] הַזֶּה נִבְקְעוּ כָּל[e]
מַעְיְנֹת תְּהוֹם רַבָּה[f] וַאֲרֻבֹּת[g] הַשָּׁמַיִם נִפְתָּחוּ: [12] וַיְהִי הַגֶּשֶׁם עַל הָאָרֶץ אַרְבָּעִים
יוֹם וְאַרְבָּעִים לָיְלָה:
7:13 בְּעֶצֶם הַיּוֹם הַזֶּה בָּא נֹחַ וְשֵׁם[a] וְחָם[b] וָיֶפֶת[c] בְּנֵי נֹחַ וְאֵשֶׁת נֹחַ וּשְׁלֹשֶׁת נְשֵׁי

---

[c] וכל 𝔐 𝕮[ONC] (וכל) 𝔐[MS] 𝖆 𝕲 (καὶ ἀπὸ πάντων) 𝕾 (حذ حل) 𝖁 (et ex omni) | מכל 𝖆[MS]
𝖁[MSS] (ex omni) | ומן] 𝕲[MSS] (καὶ ἀπὸ) Aeth[MS] Arab Co.

[d-d] אשר רמש על 𝔐 𝖆 𝕾 (حل حدد) 𝕮[ON] (דרחיש על) 𝕮[c] (דרחיש על) 𝖁 (quod
movetur super)] רמש אשר על רמש or רמש על or 𝕲 (τῶν ἑρπετῶν τῶν ἐπὶ) | הרמש על
הרמש על *𝕲[MSS] (τῶν ἑρπετῶν τῶν ἑρπόντων ἐπὶ) Arab Arm Co Pal.

7:9 [a] שנים 𝔐 𝖆 CD 5.1 𝕲 (δύο) 𝕾 (ترين) 𝕮[ONC] [ושנים] 𝖁 (et duo).

[b] אל 𝔐 𝖆 𝕲 (πρός) 𝕮[O(MS)C] (לות) 𝕮[JS(MS)] (ל-) 𝖁 (ad)] את 𝕾 *حدر 𝕮[ONS(MS)] (עם).

[c-c-c] את נח in loc 𝔐 𝖆 𝕲[MSS] (τῷ Νωε) 𝕾 (لنح) 𝕮[ONC] (ית נח) 𝖁 (Noe) Aeth[MSS] Arab]
אתו or ‍ו- transp before אלהים 𝕲 (αὐτῷ).

[d] אלהים 𝔐 𝕲 (ὁ θεός) 𝕾 (محلها) 𝖁 (Deus) Aeth[MSS] Arab] יהוה 𝔐[MS] 𝖆 𝕲[MS]* (κύριος)
𝖁[MSS]* (Dominus) | יהוה אלהים 𝕲[MSS] (κύριος ὁ θεός) Arm Bo.

7:10 [a] ומי 𝔐 𝖆 4Q252 I 3? (ומי) 𝕲 (καὶ τὸ ὕδωρ) 𝕾 (محدها) 𝕮[ONFC] [ומי] 𝕲[MS]* (τὸ
ὕδωρ) 𝖁 (aquae) Aeth Bo.

[b] המבול 𝔐 𝖆 𝕲 (τοῦ κατακλυσμοῦ) 𝕾 (دلافدا) 𝕮[O] (טופנא) 𝕮[NF] (דמבולא) 𝕮[c]
(מבולה), cf. 4Q370 1 I 8 (המבול) 4Q422 II 4 (המ‍בול) 4Q464 5 II 3? (המבול) מבול](ה[מ‍בול]
4Q252 I 3.

7:11 [a-a] שש מאות 𝔐 4Q252 I 3, ↔ השש מאות/שש מאות 𝕲 (τῷ ἑξακοσιοστῷ) 𝕾
(دلاددا) 𝕮[ONC] (שית מאה) 𝖁 (sescentesimo)] השש מאות 𝖆, ↔ שש מאות/השש
אחת 𝕲 (τῷ ἑξακοσιοστῷ) 𝕾 (دلاددا) 𝕮[ONC] (שית מאה) 𝖁 (sescentesimo) | מאות
מאות 𝕲 (τῷ ἑξακοσιοστῷ) 𝕾 (دلاددا) *ושש מאות 𝕲[MSS] (τῷ ἑνὶ [πρώτῳ 𝕲[MSS]] καὶ ἑξακοσιοστῷ) Aeth[MSS].

[b] השני 𝔐 𝖆 4Q252 I 4 𝕲 (τοῦ δευτέρου) 𝕾 (دلائ) 𝕮[ONC] (תנינא) 𝖁 (secundo)] *השביעי
Arm[te] Philo Quest. in Gen. ii.17, 31.

[c-c] בשבעה עשר יום 𝔐 𝖆 4Q252 I 4 (בשבעה עשר) 𝕲[MSS] (ζ καὶ ῑ) 𝕾 (دحمديام) 𝕮[O]
בשבעסר 𝕮[S(MS)] (בשבסרי יומין) 𝖁 (בשבעה עשר יומין) 𝕮[NC] (בשבעת עשרה יומא)
בשבעה ועשרים 𝕮[S(MS)] (יום) 𝖁 (בשבע עסר יום) 𝖁 (septimodecimo die) Arab Syh Jub 5:23]
𝕲 (ἑβδόμῃ καὶ εἰκάδι) Philo Quest. in Gen. ii.17, 31, 33 Josephus Antiquities i.81, cf. Book
of Adam and Eve iii.7.

[d-d] ביום הזה 𝔐 𝖆 𝕲 (τῇ ἡμέρᾳ ταύτῃ) 𝕾 (حمادا مددا) 𝕮[O] (ביומא הדין) 𝕮[NC] (היך)
𝖁 *ביום ההוא 4Q252 I 4 | [ומן יומא הדין](זמן יומא הדין omit הזה הזה ביום* 𝖁.

[e] כל 𝔐 𝖆 4Q252 I 5 𝕲 (πᾶσαι) 𝕾 (حل) 𝕮[ONC] (כל) 𝖁 (omnes)] omit כל* 𝔐[MS] 𝕲[MSS]
Arab Pal Sa.

[f] רבה 𝔐 𝖆 4Q252 I 5 𝕲[MSS] (τῆς πολλῆς) 𝕾 (ودا) 𝕮[ONC] (רבה) 𝖁 (magnae) Arm Syh (τῆς
πολλῆς und ※ Jub 5:24] omit רבה 𝕲, cf. 4Q370 I 4 תהמות twice without adjective).

[g] וארבת 𝔐 𝖆 4Q252 I 5 𝕲 (καὶ οἱ καταρράκται) 𝕾 (مددا) 𝕮[ON] (וכוי) 𝕮[c] (וחרכי)
𝖁 (et cataractae), cf. 4Q370 I 5 (וארבות)] *כל ארבות 4Q370 I 4.

7:13 [a] ושם 𝔐 𝕾 (محد) 𝕮[ONC] (ושם) 𝖁 (et Sem) Aeth] שם 𝔐[MSS] 𝖆 𝕲 (Σημ) 𝖁[MS] (Sem).
[b] וחם 𝔐 𝕾 (محد) 𝕮[ONC] (וחם) 𝖁 (et Ham) Aeth Pal] חם 𝔐[MS] 𝖆 𝕲 (Χαμ) 𝖁[MS] (Ham).
[c] ויפת 𝔐 𝖆 𝕲[MSS] (καὶ Ιαφεθ) 𝕾 (مددا) 𝕮[ONC] (ויפת) 𝖁 (et Iafeth) Aeth Pal] יפת 𝕲
(Ιαφεθ).

בָנָיו אִתָּם[d] אֶל הַתֵּבָה׃ 14 הֵמָּה[a] וְכָל הַחַיָּה[b] לְמִינָהּ[c] וְכָל הַבְּהֵמָה לְמִינָהּ[d] וְכָל
[e]הָרֶמֶשׂ הָרֹמֵשׂ[e] עַל הָאָרֶץ לְמִינֵהוּ[f] וְכָל הָעוֹף לְמִינֵהוּ [g]כֹּל צִפּוֹר כָּל כָּנָף[g]׃ 15 וַיָּבֹאוּ[a]
אֶל[b] נֹחַ אֶל הַתֵּבָה [c]שְׁנַיִם שְׁנַיִם[c] מִכָּל הַבָּשָׂר[d] אֲשֶׁר בּוֹ רוּחַ חַיִּים׃ 16 וְהַבָּאִים
[a]זָכָר וּנְקֵבָה[a] מִכָּל בָּשָׂר בָּאוּ כַּאֲשֶׁר צִוָּה אֹתוֹ[b] אֱלֹהִים[bc] וַיִּסְגֹּר יְהוָה[d] בַּעֲדוֹ[ef]׃
7:17 וַיְהִי הַמַּבּוּל אַרְבָּעִים יוֹם[a] עַל הָאָרֶץ וַיִּרְבּוּ הַמַּיִם וַיִּשְׂאוּ אֶת־הַתֵּבָה
וַתָּרָם מֵעַל הָאָרֶץ׃ 18 וַיִּגְבְּרוּ הַמַּיִם וַיִּרְבּוּ מְאֹד עַל הָאָרֶץ[a] וַתֵּלֶךְ הַתֵּבָה עַל

---

[d] אתם 𝔐 ⅏ 𝔖[MS] (ܥܡܗܘܢ) 𝔗[OC] (עימהון) 𝔗[N] (עמהו') 𝔙 (*cum eis*)] אתו? 𝔐[MS] 𝔊 (μετ' αὐτοῦ) 𝔖 (ܥܡܗ) 𝔗[N(mg)J] (עמה).

7:14 [a] המה 𝔐, ↔ הם/המה 𝔊[MSS] (αὐτοί) 𝔖 (ܗܢܘܢ) 𝔗[ON] (אינון) 𝔗[C] (הנון) 𝔙 (*ipsi*) Arm Sa[MS] Syh (αὐτοί und ※)] הם ⅏, ↔ הם/המה 𝔊[MSS] (αὐτοί) 𝔖 (ܗܢܘܢ) 𝔗[ON] (אינון) 𝔗[C] (הנון) 𝔙 (*ipsi*) Arm Sa[MS] Syh (αὐτοί und ※) | omit המה* 𝔊.

[b] החיה 𝔐 ⅏ 𝔊 (τὰ θηρία) 𝔖 (ܚܝܘܬܐ) 𝔗[OC] (חיתא) 𝔙 (*animal*)] חית הארץ* 𝔊[MSS] (τὰ θηρία τῆς γῆς) Arab.

[c] למינה 𝔐 ⅏ 𝔊 (κατὰ γένος) 𝔖 (ܠܓܢܣܗ) 𝔗[O] (לזנה) 𝔗[NC] (למינה) 𝔙 (*secundum genus suum*)] למינהם? 𝔊[MSS] (κατὰ γένος αὐτῶν) Arab Sa[MS] Syh (αὐτῶν und ※).

[d] למינה 𝔐 ⅏ 𝔊 (κατὰ γένος) 𝔖 (ܠܓܢܣܗ) 𝔗[O] (לזנה) 𝔗[NC] (למינה) 𝔙 (*in genus suum*) Syh (αὐτοῦ und ※)] למינהם* 𝔊[MSS] (κατὰ γένος αὐτῶν) Arm Sa[MS].

[c-e] הרמש הרמש 𝔐 ⅏ 𝔊 (ἑρπετὸν κινούμενον) 𝔖 (ܪܚܫܐ ܕܪܚܫ) 𝔗[ON] (ריחשא דרחיש) 𝔗[C] (רמסה דרמס)] הרמש* 𝔙 (*quod movetur*).

[f] למינהו 𝔐 ⅏ 𝔊 (κατὰ γένος) 𝔖 (ܠܓܢܣܗ,) 𝔗[O] (לזנוהי) 𝔗[N] (למינוהי) 𝔗 (ליזניה) 𝔙 (*in genere suo*) Syh (αὐτοῦ und ※)] למינהם* 𝔊[MSS] (κατὰ γένος αὐτῶν) 𝔗[C] (למינהון) Arm Sa.

[g-g] כל צפור כל כנף 𝔐 ⅏ 𝔊[MSS] (πᾶν ὄρνεον πᾶν πτερωτόν) 𝔗[OJ] (כל ציפר כל דפרח) 𝔗[S] (כל עוף כל טעאס) Syh (πᾶν ὄρνεον πᾶν πτερωτόν und ※), cf. 4Q370 I 6 (צפור כל] וכל כנף)] omit כל צפור כל כנף* 𝔊 | כל צפור וכל כנף? 𝔙 (*universae aves omnesque volucres*) | צפור וכל כנף? 𝔖 (ܘܟܠ ܕܦܪܚ ܘܟܠ ܕܛܐܣ) 𝔗[N] (וכל דפרח וכל דטייס) | וכל צפור כנף* 𝔊[MSS] (καὶ πᾶν ὄρνεον πτερωτόν) 𝔗[C] (וכל צפר דטאיים), cf. Deut 4:17.

7:15 [a] ויבאו 𝔐 𝔊[MSS] (καὶ εἰσῆλθον) 𝔗[ONC] (ועלו) 𝔙[MS] (*ingressaeque sunt*) Syh] באו? 𝔊 (εἰσῆλθον) 𝔖 (ܥܠܘ) 𝔙 (*ingressae sunt*).

[b] אל 𝔐 ⅏ 𝔊 (πρός) 𝔗[O(MS)CJ] (לות) 𝔗[S(MS)] (-ל) 𝔙 (*ad*)] את* 𝔖 (ܥܡ) 𝔗[ONS(MS)] (עם).

[c-c] שנים שנים 𝔐 ⅏ 𝔊 (δύο δύο) 𝔖 (ܬܪܝܢ ܬܪܝܢ) 𝔗[ONC] (תרין תרין)] שנים ושנים* 𝔙 (*bina et bina*) | שנים ⅏[MS].

[d] הבשר 𝔐, cf. 𝔗[ONC] (בסרא)] בשר ⅏, cf. 𝔊 (σαρκός) 𝔖 (ܒܣܪ).

7:16 [a-a] זכר ונקבה 𝔐 𝔊 (ἄρσεν καὶ θῆλυ) 𝔖 (ܕܟܪܐ ܘܢܩܒܬܐ) 𝔗[ON] (דכר ונוקבא) 𝔙 (*masculus et femina*)] זכר ונקבה זכר ונקבה ⅏.

[b-b] אתו in loc 𝔐 ⅏ 𝔊[MSS] (αὐτῷ) 𝔖 (ܗ-) 𝔗[O] (יתיה) 𝔙 (*ei*)] את נח transp after אלהים? 𝔊 (τῷ Νωε) | את נח in loc* 𝔊[MSS] (τῷ Νωε) Syh | אתו transp after אלהים* 𝔗[N] (יתיה).

[c] אלהים 𝔐 ⅏ 𝔊 (ὁ θεός) 𝔖 (ܐܠܗܐ) 𝔙 (*Deus*)] יהוה אלהים * 𝔊[MSS] (κύριος ὁ θεός) Aeth[MSS] Arab | יהוה* 𝔊[MSS] (κύριος) 𝔖[MS] (ܡܪܝܐ) Bo Sa[MS].

[d] יהוה 𝔐 ⅏ 𝔖 (ܡܪܝܐ) 𝔙 (*Dominus*) Bo] יהוה אלהים? 𝔊 (κύριος ὁ θεός) | אלהים* 4Q422 II 5 (אל).

[e] בעדו 𝔐 ⅏ 𝔖 (ܒܐܦܘܗܝ,) 𝔙 (*eum*)] בעדם 4Q422 II 5 | מ]חוץ* 4Q464 5 II 1, cf. 𝔊 (ἔξωθεν αὐτοῦ) *Jub* 5:23.

[f] text 𝔐 ⅏ 𝔖 𝔗[ONF]] add את התבה* 𝔊 (τὴν κιβωτόν) | add את הפתח* 𝔙 (*de foris*) 𝔗[J] (ית תרעא).

7:17 [a] text 𝔐 ⅏ 𝔊[MSS] 𝔖 𝔗[ONC] 𝔙 Syh (καὶ τεσσαράκοντα νύκτας und ÷)] add וארבעים לילה? 𝔊 (καὶ τεσσαράκοντα νύκτας).

7:18 [a] הארץ 𝔐 ⅏ 𝔊 (τῆς γῆς) 𝔖 (ܐܪܥܐ) 𝔗[ONC] (ארעא) *Jub* 5:26] פני הארץ* 𝔙 (*superficie terrae*).

פְּנֵי[b] הַמָּיִם׃ [19] וְהַמַּיִם גָּבְרוּ מְאֹד מְאֹד [a]עַל הָאָרֶץ ויכסו[a] כָּל הֶהָרִים הַגְּבֹהִים[b]
אֲשֶׁר תַּחַת כָּל[c] הַשָּׁמָיִם׃ [20] חֲמֵשׁ עֶשְׂרֵה אַמָּה מִלְמַעְלָה גָּבְרוּ[a] הַמָּיִם ויכסו
הֶהָרִים[b]׃ [21] וַיִּגְוַע כָּל בָּשָׂר הָרֹמֵשׂ עַל הָאָרֶץ בָּעוֹף וּבַבְּהֵמָה וּבַחַיָּה[a] וּבְכָל[b]
הַשֶּׁרֶץ הַשֹּׁרֵץ עַל הָאָרֶץ וְכֹל[c] הָאָדָם׃ [22] כֹּל[a] אֲשֶׁר [b]נִשְׁמַת רוּחַ[b] חַיִּים בְּאַפָּיו
מִכֹּל[c] אֲשֶׁר בֶּחָרָבָה מֵתוּ׃ [23] וימח[a] אֶת[b] כָּל הַיְקוּם אֲשֶׁר [c]עַל פְּנֵי[c] הָאֲדָמָה
מֵאָדָם [d]עַד בְּהֵמָה עַד רֶמֶשׂ וְעַד עוֹף[d] הַשָּׁמַיִם וַיִּמָּחוּ מִן הָאָרֶץ וַיִּשָּׁאֶר
אַךְ נֹחַ וַאֲשֶׁר אִתּוֹ בַּתֵּבָה׃ [24] וַיִּגְבְּרוּ[a] הַמַּיִם עַל הָאָרֶץ חֲמִשִּׁים וּמְאַת יוֹם׃

8:1 וַיִּזְכֹּר אֱלֹהִים אֶת נֹחַ[a] וְאֵת כָּל הַחַיָּה וְאֶת כָּל הַבְּהֵמָה[b] אֲשֶׁר אִתּוֹ בַּתֵּבָה
וַיַּעֲבֵר אֱלֹהִים רוּחַ עַל הָאָרֶץ וַיָּשֹׁכּוּ הַמָּיִם׃ [2] וַיִּסָּכְרוּ מַעְיְנֹת תְּהוֹם וַאֲרֻבֹּת

---

[b] פני 𝔐 ⅏ 𝔖 (ܐܦܝ) 𝔗[ONC] (אפי) *Jub* 5:26] omit פני* 𝔊 𝔙.

7:19 [a-a] על הארץ ויכסו 𝔐 ⅏ 𝔊 (ἐπὶ τῆς γῆς καὶ ἐπεκάλυψεν) 𝔖 (ܥܠ ܐܪܥܐ ܘܐܬܟܣܝܘ) 𝔗[OJ] (על ארעא ואיתחפיו) 𝔗[NC] (על ארעא ואתכסון) 𝔙 (*super terram opertique sunt*)] עד החדש החמישי באחד לחדש יכסו Barré.

[b] הגבהים 𝔐 ⅏[VG MS] 𝔊 (τὰ ὑψηλά) 𝔖 (ܪ̈ܡܐ) 𝔗[ONC] (רמיא) 𝔗[S(MSS)] (ראמיה) 𝔗[S(MSS)] (שחקיה) 𝔙 (*excelsi*)] הגבחים ⅏[MSS].

[c] כל 𝔐 ⅏ 𝔊[MSS] (παντός) 𝔖 (ܟܠ) 𝔗[ONC] (כל) 𝔙 (*universo*)] omit כל? 𝔊.

7:20 [a] גברו 𝔐 ⅏ 𝔖 (ܥܫܢܘ) 𝔗[O] (תקיפו) 𝔗[N] (איתגברו) 𝔗[C] (אתגברו) α′ (ἐνεδυναμώθη) σ′ (ἐπεκράτησεν)] גבהו? 𝔊 (ὑψώθη), cf. 𝔙 (*altior fuit*).

[b] ההרים 𝔐 ⅏ 𝔖 (ܛܘܪ̈ܐ) 𝔗[ONC] (טוריא) 𝔙 (*montes*) Syh (πάντα und ÷)] כל ההרים הגבהים (> כל 𝔊[MS] 𝔖[MSS])? 𝔊 (πάντα τὰ ὄρη τὰ ὑψηλά) 𝔖[MSS] (ܛܘܪ̈ܐ ܪ̈ܡܐ), cf. *Jub* 5:26 | כל ההרים* 𝔊[MSS] (πάντα τὰ ὄρη) Arab Arm Bo Pal Sa[MS] Syh (πάντα und ÷).

7:21 [a] ובחיה 𝔐 ⅏ 𝔊 (καὶ τῶν θηρίων) 𝔖 (ܘܒܚܝܘܬܐ) 𝔗[OJC] (ובחיתא) 𝔙 (*bestiarum*)] ובכל החיה* 𝔗[N] (ובכל חיתא).

[b] ובכל 𝔐 ⅏ 𝔖 (ܘܒܟܠܗ) 𝔗[ONC] (ובכל) 𝔙 (*omniumque*)] וכל? 𝔊 (καὶ πᾶν).

[c] וכל 𝔐 ⅏ 𝔊 (καὶ πᾶς) 𝔖 (ܘܒܟܠܗܘܢ) 𝔗[ONC] (וכל)] כל ⅏[MSS] 𝔙 (*universi*).

7:22 [a] כל 𝔐 ⅏ 𝔖 (ܟܠ) 𝔗[ONC] (כל)] וכל* 𝔊 (καὶ πάντα) 𝔖[MSS] (ܘܟܠ) 𝔙 (*et cuncta*).

[b-b] נשמת רוח 𝔐 ⅏ 𝔖 (ܢܫܡܬܐ ܕܪܘܚܐ) 𝔗[OC] (נשמת רוח) 𝔗[N] (נשמה דרוח)] נשמת* 𝔊 (πνοὴν) 𝔙 (*spiraculum*) Budde Gunkel Hendel.

[c] מכל 𝔐 ⅏ 𝔖 (ܡܢ ܟܠ) 𝔗[OJ] (מכל) 𝔗[N] (מן כל) 𝔙] וכל* 𝔊 (καὶ πᾶς) 𝔗[C] (וכל).

7:23 [a] וימח 𝔐 ⅏ 𝔊 (καὶ ἐξήλειψεν) 𝔖 (ܘܥܛܐ) 𝔗[O] (ומחא) 𝔗[NJ] (ושיצי) 𝔙 (*et delevit*)] וימחי ⅏[MSS].

[b] את 𝔐 ⅏ 𝔖 (ܠ) 𝔗[ONCJ] (ית), cf. 𝔊 𝔙] omit את 𝔐[MSS].

[c-c] על פני 𝔐 ⅏ 𝔊[MSS] (ἐπὶ προσώπου τῆς γῆς) 𝔖 (ܥܠ ܐܦܝ) 𝔗[ONC] (על אפי) Aeth Arab Bo Pal] על פני כל? 𝔊 (ἐπὶ προσώπου πάσης τῆς γῆς) | על* 𝔙 (*super*).

[d-d] עד בהמה עד רמש ועד עוף 𝔐 𝔗[OCJ] (עד בעירא עד ריחשא ועד עופא)] עד בהמה עד רמש עד עוף 𝔐[MSS] ⅏ 𝔗[N] (עד בעירה עד ריחשא עד עוף), cf. 𝔙? (*usque ad pecus tam reptile quam volucres caeli*) | עד בהמה ועד רמש ועד (ה)עוף? 𝔊 (ἕως κτήνους καὶ ἑρπετῶν καὶ τῶν πετεινῶν) | ועד בהמה ועד רמש ועד עוף 𝔐[MS] 𝔖? (ܘܒܥܝܪܐ ܠܪܚܫܐ ܘܒܥܝܪܐ ܠܐܢܫܐ ܘܒܥܝܪܐ ܠܦܪܚܬܐ) | ועד בהמה עד רמש ועד עוף 𝔐[MSS].

7:24 [a] ויגברו 𝔐 ⅏ 4Q252 I 7 𝔖 (ܘܥܫܢܘ) 𝔗[O] (ותקיפו) 𝔗[N] (ואתגברו) 𝔗[C] (ואתגברון) 𝔙 (*obtinueruntque*)] ויגבהו* 𝔊 (ὑψώθη).

8:1 [a] text 𝔐 ⅏ 𝔊 𝔖 𝔗[OFCJ] 𝔙] add ואת בניו* 𝔗[N] (וית בנוהי).

[b] text 𝔐 ⅏ 𝔊[MSS MS] (καὶ πάντων τῶν πετεινῶν καὶ πάντων τῶν ἑρπετῶν und ÷) 𝔖[MS] 𝔗[ONFC] 𝔙 Aeth] add ואת כל (ה)עוף ואת כל (ה)רמש? 𝔊 (καὶ πάντων τῶν πετεινῶν καὶ πάντων τῶν ἑρπετῶν) | ואת כל (ה)עוף? 𝔊[MSS] (καὶ πάντων τῶν πετεινῶν) 𝔖 (ܘܠܟܠܗ ܦܪܚܬܐ) Arm Bo.

הַשָּׁמַיִם וַיִּכָּלֵא[a] הַגֶּשֶׁם מִן־הַשָּׁמָיִם: [3] וַיָּשֻׁבוּ הַמַּיִם מֵעַל הָאָרֶץ הָלוֹךְ וָשׁוֹב[a]
וַיַּחְסְרוּ הַמַּיִם[b] מִקְצֵה[cc] חֲמִשִּׁים וּמְאַת יוֹם: [4] וַתָּנַח הַתֵּבָה בַּחֹדֶשׁ הַשְּׁבִיעִי[a]
בְּשִׁבְעָה עָשָׂר יוֹם[b] לַחֹדֶשׁ עַל הָרֵי אֲרָרָט[c]: [5] וְהַמַּיִם הָיוּ הָלוֹךְ[a] וְחָסוֹר[a] עַד
הַחֹדֶשׁ[b] הָעֲשִׂירִי[c] בָּעֲשִׂירִי[d] בְּאֶחָד לַחֹדֶשׁ נִרְאוּ רָאשֵׁי הֶהָרִים:

8:6 וַיְהִי מִקֵּץ אַרְבָּעִים יוֹם וַיִּפְתַּח[a] נֹחַ אֶת חַלּוֹן[b] הַתֵּבָה אֲשֶׁר עָשָׂה: [7] וַיְשַׁלַּח
אֶת הָעֹרֵב[a] וַיֵּצֵא[b] יָצוֹא וָשׁוֹב[b] עַד יְבֹשֶׁת הַמַּיִם מֵעַל הָאָרֶץ: [8] וַיְשַׁלַּח אֶת הַיּוֹנָה

8:2 [a] ויכל[𝕸 ויכלא �samar.

8:3 [a-a] הלוך ושוב[𝕸 𝕲' (πορευόμενον ... ἐνεδίδου [> ἐνεδίδου 𝕲^MSS Aeth Arab]) 𝕾 (ܐܙܠ)
(ܡܗܦܟ) 𝕮^OJ (אזלין ותיבין) 𝕮^N (אזלין וחזרין = אזלין וחסקין) 𝕮^C (אזלין וחזרין) 𝒱 (euntes et
redeuntes)] הלכו ושבו ܜ samar.

[b] המים 𝕸 ܜ samar 4Q252 I 9' 𝕲 (τὸ ὕδωρ) 𝕾 (ܡܝܐ) 𝕮^ONC (מיא)]] omit *המים 𝕲^MSS MS (τὸ ὕδωρ und +) 𝒱
Arab.

[cc] (ובסוף חמשים) 𝕲 (μετὰ 4Q252 I 8 מקצה חמשים/מקץ חמשים, ↔ מקצה חמשים
πεντήκοντα) 𝕾 (ܡܢ ܟܠܗ ... ܚܡܫܝܢ) 𝕮^OJ (מסוף ... וחמשין) 𝕮^NC (לסוף ... וחמשין) 𝒱 (post ...
quinquaginta)] 𝕲 (ובסוף חמשים) 4Q252 I 8 מקצה חמשים/מקץ חמשים, ↔ ܜ מקץ חמשים
(μετὰ πεντήκοντα) 𝕾 (ܡܢ ܟܠܗ ... ܚܡܫܝܢ) 𝕮^OJ (מסוף ... וחמשין) 𝕮^NC (לסוף ... וחמשין) 𝒱 (post
... quinquaginta) | מקץ החמשים Eißfeldt.

8:4 [a] השביעי 𝕸 ܜ samar 4Q252 I 10 𝕲 (τῷ ἑβδόμῳ) 𝕾 (ܫܒܝܥܐ) 𝕮^ON (שביעיא) 𝒱 (septimo)]
*העשירי Hippolytus Arabic Frag. to Pent. Gen 8:1.

[b-b] בשבעת עשרא 𝕮^O (ܫܒܥܣܪ̈ܐ) 𝕾 (יו]ם שבעה עשר 𝕸 ܜ samar 4Q252 I 10 בשבעה עשר יום
בשבעסר) 𝕮^S(MSS) (בשבסרי יומין) 𝕮^N (בשבעת עשר יומין) 𝕮^C (בשבעת עשר [יומא) 𝒱 (יומא
בשבעה ועשרים) 𝕮^S(MSS) (בשבע עסר יום) oi λ' (septimo decimo) Syh Josephus Antiquities i.90]
𝕲 (ἑβδόμῃ καὶ εἰκάδι) Philo Quest. in Gen. ii.31, 33, cf. 𝒱 (vicesima [+ et 𝒱^MS] septima die) Book of
Adam and Eve iii.9 | בשבעה ועשרים יום 𝕲^MSS (ἑβδόμῃ καὶ εἰκάδι ἡμέρᾳ) 𝒱 (vicesima [+ et 𝒱^MS]
septima die) Arab, cf. Book of Adam and Eve iii.9 | בחמש עשר יום 𝕾^MS *(ܚܡܫܬܥܣܪ̈ܐ)
ועשרים 𝕲^MS (καὶ εἰκάδι) | באחד Hippolytus Arabic Frag. to Pent. Gen 8:1.

[c] אררט 𝕸 𝕲' (Ἀραράτ)] הררט ܜ samar 4Q252 I 10 (הורט) 1Q20 X 12 (הורט).

8:5 [a-a] הלוך וחסור 𝕸 4Q252 I 11 𝕲 (πορευόμενον [> πορευόμενον 𝕲^MSS La^I Pal Sa^MS]
ἠλαττονοῦτο) 𝕾 (ܐܙܠ ... ܚܣܪ) 𝕮^ONC (אזלין וחסרין) 𝒱 (ibant et decrescebant)] הלכו וחסרו ܜ samar.

[b] החדש 𝕸 4Q252 I 11, cf. 𝕲 (τοῦ ... μηνός) 𝕾 (ܝܪܚܐ) 𝕮^ONC (ירחא) ܜ samar חדש.

[c] העשירי 𝕸 ܜ samar 4Q252 I 11 (העש]ירי) 𝕲 (δεκάτου) 𝕾 (ܥܣܝܪܐ) 𝒱 (decimum)] עשיראה 𝕮^ONC
השביעי 𝕸^MS.

[d] העשירי 𝕸 ܜ samar 𝕲^MSS (ἐν δὲ τῷ δεκάτῳ μηνί) 𝕮^ONC (בעשיראה) 𝒱 (decimo enim mense) 𝕾
(ܒܥܣܝܪܐ....) Pal Syh Jub 5:30 Philo Quest. in Gen. ii.32, cf. 4Q252 I 11 (חדש העש]ירי) Hippolytus
Arabic Frag. to Pent. Gn 8:1] בעשירי באחד or עשר בעשתי 𝕲 (ἐν δὲ τῷ ἑνδεκάτῳ μηνί) Book
of Adam and Eve iii.10 ܜ samar בעשיר 𝕸^MS | בעשיר 𝕸^MS] omit *בעשירי 𝕸^MS 4Q252 I 11.

8:6 [a] ויפתח 𝕸 ܜ samar 𝕲^MSS (καὶ ἠνέωξεν) 𝕮^ONC (ופתח) 𝕲 *פתח (ἠνέωξεν) 𝕾 (ܦܬܚ) 𝒱 (aperiens).

[b] חלון 𝕸 ܜ samar 𝕲 (τὴν θυρίδα) 𝕮^OJ (כות) 𝕮^CN(mg) (חרכה) 𝕾 (ܟܘܬܐ) 𝒱 (fenestram), cf. Jerome Hebr.
Quaest. 8:6] תרעא) 𝕮^N (תרעא), cf. Jerome Hebr. Quaest. 8:6.

8:7 [a] text 𝕸 ܜ samar 𝕲^MSS MS (verse und +) 𝕾 𝕮^ONC 𝒱 Arm Syh (τοῦ ἰδεῖν εἰ κεκόπακεν τὸ ὕδωρ und ÷)] add
(לראות הקלו המים) 𝕲 (τοῦ ἰδεῖν εἰ κεκόπακεν τὸ ὕδωρ).

[b-b] וחזר והוה אזיל 𝕮^C (והוה נפק וחזר ונפק מיפק ותאיב) 𝕮^N (ונפק נפק וחזר נפק וחזר) 𝕮^O (והוה נפק וחזר
יצא יצוא ושוב ܜ samar 4Q254a 3 4, (ויצא יצוא ושוב 𝕸 ויצא יצוא ושב) 𝒱 (egrediebatur et revertebatur), cf. Syh (οὐχ und ÷)]
cf. 4Q254a 3 5 יצא יצא ושו]ב[𝕾 (οὐχ und ÷) | ויצא יצא ושב ܜ samar, cf. Syh (οὐχ und ÷) | יצא
יצוא ולא שב 𝕲 (καὶ ἐξελθὼν οὐχ ὑπέστρεψεν) 𝕾 (ܘܠܐ ܗܦܟ > ܢܦܩ] 𝕾^MS (ܗܦܟ ܘܠܐ ܢܦܩ).

[c] מעל 𝕸 ܜ samar 𝕲 (ἀπὸ) 𝕾 (ܡܢ) 𝕮^ONC (מעל) 𝒱 (super)] *מעל פני 𝕲^MSS (ܡܢ ܐܦܝ).

8:8 [a] begin 𝕸 ܜ samar 𝕲 𝕾 𝕮^ON 𝒱] add ויחל נח שבעת ימים Ball Eißfeldt.

מָֽאתֹו[b] לִרְאֹות הֲקַלּוּ הַמַּיִם מֵעַל פְּנֵי הָֽאֲדָמָֽה׃ [9] וְלֹא־מָצְאָה[a] הַיֹּונָה מָנֹוחַ לְכַף
רַגְלָהּ וַתָּשָׁב אֵלָיו אֶל־הַתֵּבָה כִּי־מַיִם[b] עַל־פְּנֵי[c] כָל־הָאָרֶץ וַיִּשְׁלַח יָדֹו[d] וַיִּקָּחֶהָ
וַיָּבֵא אֹתָהּ אֵלָיו אֶל־הַתֵּבָֽה׃ [10] וַיָּחֶל[a] עֹוד שִׁבְעַת יָמִים אֲחֵרִים[b] וַיֹּסֶף שַׁלַּח[c] אֶת־
הַיֹּונָה מִן־הַתֵּבָֽה׃ [11] וַתָּבֹא אֵלָיו הַיֹּונָה[a] לְעֵת עֶרֶב וְהִנֵּה עָלֵה[b] זַיִת טָרָף בְּפִיהָ
וַיֵּדַע נֹחַ כִּי־קַלּוּ הַמַּיִם מֵעַל[b] הָאָֽרֶץ׃ [12] וַיִּיָּחֶל[a] עֹוד שִׁבְעַת יָמִים אֲחֵרִים[b] וַיְשַׁלַּח[c]
אֶת־הַיֹּונָה וְלֹא־יָסְפָה שׁוּב[d] אֵלָיו עֹֽוד׃

8:13 וַֽיְהִי בְּאַחַת[a] וְשֵׁשׁ־מֵאֹות שָׁנָה[b] בָּֽרִאשֹׁון[c] בָּֽאֶחָד[d] לַחֹדֶשׁ חָֽרְבוּ
הַמַּיִם מֵעַל[e] הָאָרֶץ וַיָּסַר נֹחַ אֶת־מִכְסֵה הַתֵּבָה[f] וַיַּרְא וְהִנֵּה חָֽרְבוּ[g] פְּנֵי
הָֽאֲדָמָֽה[g]׃ [14] וּבַחֹדֶשׁ הַשֵּׁנִי[a] בְּשִׁבְעָה[b] וְעֶשְׂרִים יֹום[b] לַחֹדֶשׁ[b] יָבְשָׁה הָאָֽרֶץ׃

[b] *(מ) אחריו [[מן לוותה]] (παρ' αὐτοῦ) 𝕾 (ܡ) 𝕮[o] (מלותיה) 𝕮[NC]
(ὀπίσω αὐτοῦ) 𝔙 (post eum) | omit ותאם 4Q252 I 14.
8:9 [a] מצאה 𝔐 ܢ 4Q252 I 15] מצא ܢ[MSS].
[b-b] על פני 𝔐 ܢ 𝔊[MSS] (ἐπὶ προσώπῳ) 𝕾 (ܥܠ ܐܦܝ) 𝕮[o] (על אפי) 𝕮[N] (על אפיה ד) Aeth[MS] Arab
Bo Sa[MS]] על כל פני 𝔊 (ἐπὶ παντὶ προσώπῳ) | על[> 𝔙 (super).
[c] כל 𝔐 ܢ 𝔊 (πάσης) 𝕾 (ܟܠܗ) 𝕮[o] (כל) 𝕮[N] (דכל) 𝔙 (universam)] omit כל* 𝔊[MSS] Aeth Arab Arm
Pal Sa[MS].
[d] את ידו 𝔐 ܢ] ܢ.
8:10 [a] וַיָּחֶל BDB Bowling Budde Dillmann Eißfeldt HALOT Hendel Holzinger Olshausen
Skinner Westermann Wevers, cf. 𝔊 (καὶ ἐπισχών) 𝕾 (ܘܦܫ) 𝕮[OJ] (ואוריך) 𝔙 (expectatis) 8:12] ויחל
𝔐 ܢ 4Q252 I 15 𝕮[O(MS)N] (ושרי).
[b] אחרים 𝔐 ܢ 4Q252 I 15 [[א]]חרים 𝔊 (ἑτέρας) 𝕾 (ܐܚܪܢܐ) 𝕮[ON] (אוחרנין) 𝔙 (aliis)] omit
אחרים* 𝔊[MSS] Aeth Arm Pal.
[c] שלח 𝔐 ܢ] לשלחה 4Q252 I 16.
8:11 [a] עלה 𝔐, cf. 𝔊 (φύλλον) 𝕾 (ܛܪܦܐ) 𝕮[o] (טרף) 𝕮[N] (עלה) 𝔙 (ramum)] עלי ܢ 4Q252 I 16.
[b] מעל 𝔐 ܢ 4Q252 I 18 𝔊 (ἀπό) 𝕮[o] (מעל) 𝕮[N] (מעלוי) 𝔙 (super)] מעל פני ܢ? 𝕾 (ܡܢ ܐܦܝ)
(.
8:12 [a] ויחל 𝔐, cf. 𝔊 (καὶ ἐπισχών) 𝕾 (ܘܦܫ) 𝕮[OJ] (ואוריך) 𝔙 (expectavitque)] ויחל 𝔐[MSS] ܢ
𝕮[NF(MS)] (ושרי), cf. 8:10.
[b] אחרים 𝔐 ܢ 4Q252 I 18? (אחר)ים 𝔊 (ἑτέρας) 𝕾 (ܐܚܪܢܐ) 𝕮[o] (אוחרנין) 𝕮[N] = חרינין
𝔙 (alios)] omit אחרים* 𝔊[MSS] Aeth Arm.
[c] וישלח 𝔐 𝔊[MSS] (ἐξαπέστειλεν) 𝕾 (ܘܫܕܪ) 𝕮[ON] (ושלח) 𝔙 (et emisit) Arab Pal Sa[MS], cf.
4Q252 I 18? ([וישל]ח)] ויסף שלח 𝔊 (πάλιν ἐξαπέστειλεν), cf. 8:10.
[d] שוב 𝔐 ܢ | לשוב | 4Q252 I 19, cf. 4Q252 I 21 (שוב).
8:13 [a] באחת 𝔐 ܢ 𝔊 (ἐν τῷ ἑνί) 𝕾 (ܒܚܕ) 𝕮[ON] (וחדא) 𝔙 (primo)] בשבע* Book of Adam and Eve iii.11.
[b] text 𝔐 ܢ 𝔊[MSS] 𝕾 𝕮[ON] 𝔙] add נח לחיי 𝔊 (ἐν τῇ ζωῇ τοῦ Νωε), cf. 4Q252 II 1 (לחיי נח).
[c] בראשון 𝔐 ܢ 𝕮[o]] בחדש הראשון | בקדמאה] 𝔊 (τοῦ πρώτου μηνός) 𝕮[N] (בירחא קדמיא) 𝔙 (primo
mense), cf. 4Q252 I 21 בחדש הראשון | (חוש ܟܟ)ܒ 𝕾 (בחדש הראשון).
[d] באחד 𝔐 ܢ 𝕮[ON] (בחד) 𝔙 (prima die)] בשתים* Book of Adam and Eve iii.11.
[e] מעל 𝔐 ܢ 4Q252 I 21 𝔊 (ἀπό) 𝕾 (ܡܢ) 𝕮[o] (מעל) 𝕮[N] (מעלוי) 𝔙 (super)] מעל פני* 𝔊[MSS] (ἀπὸ προσώπου)
Arab Arm La[M] Syh.
[f] text 𝔐 ܢ 𝔊[MSS] 𝕾 𝕮[ON] 𝔙 Bo Syh] add עשה אשר* 𝔐[MS] 𝔊 (ἣν ἐποίησεν) Arm (ἣν ἐποίησεν und ※)?.
[gg] (אפיה דארעא) 𝔙 𝔐 ܢ 4Q252 I 22? (פני האדמה)] 𝕾 (ܐܦܝ ܐܪܥܐ) 𝕮[o] (אפי ארעא) 𝕮[N] (אפי) 𝔐 𝕾
(superficies terrae)] 𝔊 (τὸ ὕδωρ ἀπὸ προσώπου τῆς γῆς).
8:14 [a] השני 𝔐 ܢ 𝔊 (τῷ δευτέρῳ)] 𝕮[ON] (תניא) 𝕾 (ܬܢܝܢܐ) 𝔙 (secundo)] השביעי* 𝔊[MS] (ἑβδόμῳ) Arm[te]
Philo Quest. in Gen. ii.33, 47.
[b-b] בעשרין ותשבעא 𝕮 (בעשרין ושבעא יומא) 𝕾 (ܒܟܕܟܬܐ ܬܘܒܥܬܐ) 𝕮[o] בשבעה ועשרים יום 𝔐 ܢ 𝕾
[(בשבעה ועסרין יום) 𝔙 (septima et vicesima die) La[M] Philo Quest. in Gen. ii.33, 47 Book of Adam and Eve
iii.11, cf. Jub 5:32] (יומך 4Q252 II 1 Jub 5:31 𝔊[MSS] (ἑπτακαιδεκάτῃ ἡμέρᾳ), cf. 4Q254a 3 1 לחודש vacat עשר vacat שבעה [ב]
בעשרים שבעה בעשרים ועשרים יום 𝔐[MS]. 𝔊 (ἑβδόμῃ καὶ εἰκάδι) 𝕮[N] (בעשרין ותשבעה) בשבעה עשר יום | 𝔊 בשבעה ועשרים
[c] text 𝔐 ܢ 𝔊 𝕾 𝕮[ON] 𝔙] add התבה (את) לחדש (יום) ועשרים ובשבעה* 𝔊[MSS] (καὶ ἑβδόμῃ καὶ

8:15 וַיְדַבֵּר[a] אֱלֹהִים[b] אֶל נֹחַ לֵאמֹר׃ 16 צֵא מִן הַתֵּבָה אַתָּה וְאִשְׁתְּךָ וּבָנֶיךָ
וּנְשֵׁי בָנֶיךָ אִתָּךְ׃ 17 כָּל[a] הַחַיָּה אֲשֶׁר אִתְּךָ [b]מִכָּל בָּשָׂר בָּעוֹף וּבַבְּהֵמָה
וּבְכָל הָרֶמֶשׂ הָרֹמֵשׂ עַל הָאָרֶץ[b] הוצא[c] אִתָּךְ [d]וְשָׁרְצוּ בָאָרֶץ[d] ופרו ורבו
עַל הָאָרֶץ׃ 18 וַיֵּצֵא נֹחַ [a]וּבָנָיו וְאִשְׁתּוֹ[a] וּנְשֵׁי בָנָיו אִתּוֹ׃ 19 כָּל[a] הַחַיָּה[b]
[c]כָּל הָרֶמֶשׂ וְכָל הָעוֹף כֹּל רוֹמֵשׂ[c] עַל הָאָרֶץ לְמִשְׁפְּחֹתֵיהֶם יָצְאוּ מִן הַתֵּבָה׃[d]

8:20 וַיִּבֶן נֹחַ מִזְבֵּחַ לַיהוָה[a] וַיִּקַּח מִכֹּל הַבְּהֵמָה הַטְּהֹרָה וּמִכֹּל הָעוֹף הַטָּהֹר וַיַּעַל
עֹלֹת בַּמִּזְבֵּחַ׃ 21 וירח[a] יְהוָה[b] אֶת רֵיחַ הַנִּיחֹחַ וַיֹּאמֶר יְהוָה[c] אֶל לִבּוֹ לֹא אֹסִף
[d]לְקַלֵּל עוֹד[d] אֶת הָאֲדָמָה [e]בַּעֲבוּר הָאָדָם[e] כִּי יֵצֶר לֵב הָאָדָם [f]רַע מִנְּעֻרָיו וְלֹא

εἰκάδι τοῦ μηνὸς ἀνέῳξεν τὴν κιβωτόν) *Jub* 5:32.

8:15 [a] וידבר 𝔐 ⅏ 𝔖 (ܘܡܠܠ) 𝔗[ON] (ומליל) 𝔙 (*locutus est autem*)] ויאמר? 𝔊 (καὶ εἶπεν).

[b] אלהים 𝔐 ⅏ 𝔖 (ܐܠܗܐ) 𝔙 (*Deus*)] יהוה אלהים? 𝔊 (κύριος ὁ θεός).

8:17 [a] כל 𝔐 𝔗[ON] (כל) 𝔙 (*cuncta*)] וכל ⅏ 𝔊 (καὶ πάντα) 𝔖 (ܘܟܠ).

[b-b] מכל בשר בעוף ובבהמה ובכל הרמש הרמש על הארץ 𝔐 ⅏ 𝔖[MSS] (ܡܢ ܟܠ ܒܣܪ ܦܪܚܬܐ ܘܒܒܥܝܪܐ ܘܒܟܠܗ ܪܚܫܐ ܕܪܚܫ ܥܠ ܐܪܥܐ) 𝔗[O] (מכל ביסרא בעופא ובבעירא ובכל ריחשא דרחיש על ארעא) 𝔗[N] (מן כל בשרא בעופא ובבעירא ובכל רחשא דרחש על ארעא) 𝔙 (*ex omni carne tam in volatilibus quam in bestiis et in universis reptilibus quae reptant super terram*)] מכל בשר בעוף ובבהמה וכל הרמש הרמש על הארץ ⅏[MSS] | וכל בשר בעוף ובבהמה וכל הרמש הרמש על הארץ? 𝔊 (καὶ πᾶσα σὰρξ ἀπὸ πετεινῶν ἕως κτηνῶν καὶ πᾶν ἑρπετὸν κινούμενον ἐπὶ τῆς γῆς) | מכל בשר ועוף ובהמה וכל הרמש הרמש על הארץ* 𝔖 (ܡܢ ܟܠ ܒܣܪ ܘܦܪܚܬܐ ܘܒܥܝܪܐ ܘܟܠܗ ܪܚܫܐ ܕܪܚܫ ܥܠ ܐܪܥܐ).

[c] הוצא 𝔐[K] ⅏[VG]] הוציה ⅏ | היצא 𝔐[Q MSS].

[d-d] ושרצו בארץ 𝔐 ⅏ 𝔊[MSS MS (καὶ ἕρπετε ἐπὶ τῆς γῆς und ※)] (καὶ ἕρπετε ἐπὶ τῆς γῆς) 𝔖 (ܘܬܘܠܕܘ ܒܐܪܥܐ) 𝔗[ON] (ויתילדון בארעא) 𝔙 (*et ingredimini super terram*) Arm Syh (καὶ ἕρπετε ἐπὶ τῆς γῆς und ※)] omit ושרצו בארץ? 𝔊.

8:18 [a-a] ובניו ואשתו 𝔐 ⅏ 𝔊[MSS] (καὶ οἱ υἱοὶ αὐτοῦ καὶ ἡ γυνὴ αὐτοῦ) 𝔖[MSS] (ܘܒܢܘܗܝ ܘܐܢܬܬܗ) 𝔗[ON] (ובנוהי ואתתיה) 𝔙 (*et filii eius uxor illius*)] ואשתו ובניו? 𝔊 (καὶ ἡ γυνὴ αὐτοῦ καὶ οἱ υἱοὶ αὐτοῦ) 𝔖 (ܘܐܢܬܬܗ ܘܒܢܘܗܝ).

8:19 [a] כל 𝔐 𝔗[ON] (כל)] וכל ⅏ 𝔊 (καὶ πάντα) 𝔖 (ܘܟܠܗ) 𝔙 (*sed et omnia*).

[b] text 𝔐 ⅏ 𝔖[MS] 𝔗[ON]] add וכל הבהמה? 𝔊 (καὶ πάντα τὰ κτήνη) 𝔖 (ܘܟܠܗ ܒܥܝܪܐ) 𝔙 (*iumenta*).

[c-c] כל הרמש וכל העוף כל רומש 𝔐 𝔖[MS] (ܘܟܠܗ ܪܚܫܐ ܘܟܠܗ ܦܪܚܬܐ ܘܟܠ ܕܪܚܫ) 𝔗[OJ] (כל רחשא וכל עופא כל דרחיש) 𝔗[N] (כל רחשא וכל עופה וכל [וכל] 𝔐[MSS] [ܘܟܠ] 𝔖[MS] (וכל) 𝔐[MSS] דרחש)] וכל העוף וכל הרמש הרמש ⅏ 𝔊 (καὶ πᾶν πετεινὸν καὶ πᾶν ἑρπετὸν κινούμενον) 𝔗[S(MS)] (וכל עופה וכול רמסה דרמס) 𝔗[S(MS)] (וכל קמצה וכול הרמס רומיסה) | וכל העוף וכל הרמש* 𝔖 (ܘܟܠܗ ܦܪܚܬܐ ܘܟܠ ܪܚܫܐ) | וכל הרמש הרמש* 𝔙 (*et reptilia quae repunt*).

[d] end 𝔐 ⅏ 𝔊 𝔖 𝔗[ON] 𝔙] add באחד לחדש השלישי* 𝔊[MSS] (ἐν μιᾷ τοῦ μηνὸς τοῦ τρίτου [πρώτου 𝔊[MSS]]) *Jub* 6:1.

8:20 [a] ליהוה 𝔐 ⅏ 𝔊[MSS] (τῷ $\overline{\kappa\omega}$) 𝔖 (ܠܡܪܝܐ) 𝔙 (*Domino*) La[X] Arab] לאלהים? 𝔊 (τῷ θεῷ) | ליהוה אלהים* 𝔊[MSS] ($\overline{\kappa\omega}$ τῷ θεῷ) Sa.

8:21 [a] וירח 𝔐 ⅏[VG MSS]] ויריח ⅏[MSS].

[b] יהוה 𝔐 ⅏ 𝔊[MSS] (κύριος) 𝔖 (ܡܪܝܐ) 𝔙 (*Dominus*) La[E] Syh (ὁ θεός und ÷)] יהוה אלהים? 𝔊 (κύριος ὁ θεός).

[c] יהוה 𝔐 ⅏ 𝔖 (ܡܪܝܐ) Sa Syh (ὁ θεός und ÷) α′ (κύριος) σ′ (κύριος) θ′ (κύριος)] יהוה אלהים? 𝔊 (κύριος ὁ θεός) | omit יהוה* 𝔙.

[d-d] לקלל עוד 𝔐 𝔊[MSS] (τοῦ καταράσασθαι ἔτι) 𝔗[O] (למלט עוד) 𝔗[N] (למלט תוב) Syh] עוד לקלל 𝔐[MSS] ⅏ 𝔊? (ἔτι τοῦ καταράσασθαι) 𝔖? (ܬܘܒ ܠܡܠܛܗ) 𝔙? (*ultra maledicam*).

[e-e] בעבור האדם 𝔐 ⅏ 𝔖 (ܡܛܠ ܒܢܝ ܐܢܫܐ) 𝔗[O] (בדיל חובי אינשא) 𝔗[N] (בגלל בר נשא) 𝔙 (*propter homines*)] בעבוד(ת) האדם 𝔊 (διὰ τὰ ἔργα τῶν ἀνθρώπων).

[f] text 𝔐 ⅏ 𝔊[MSS] 𝔖 𝔗[ON] 𝔙 Aeth Arab Co Syh] add רק? 𝔊 (ἐπιμελῶς).

אֹסִף עוֹד לְהַכּוֹת [g]אֶת כָּל חַי[g] כַּאֲשֶׁר עָשִׂיתִי׃ 22 עֹד[a] כָּל יְמֵי
הָאָרֶץ זֶרַע וְקָצִיר וְקֹר[b] וָחֹם וְקַיִץ[c] וָחֹרֶף [d]וְיוֹם וָלַיְלָה[d] לֹא יִשְׁבֹּתוּ׃
9:1 וַיְבָרֶךְ אֱלֹהִים אֶת נֹחַ וְאֶת בָּנָיו וַיֹּאמֶר לָהֶם פְּרוּ וּרְבוּ וּמִלְאוּ
אֶת הָאָרֶץ׃[a] 2 וּמוֹרַאֲכֶם וְחִתְּכֶם[a] יִהְיֶה עַל כָּל חַיַּת הָאָרֶץ[b] וְעַל כָּל
עוֹף הַשָּׁמָיִם בְּכֹל[c] אֲשֶׁר תִּרְמֹשׂ הָאֲדָמָה וּבְכָל דְּגֵי הַיָּם בְּיֶדְכֶם נִתָּנוּ[d]׃
3 כָּל[a] רֶמֶשׂ אֲשֶׁר [b]הוּא חַי[b] לָכֶם יִהְיֶה לְאָכְלָה כְּיֶרֶק עֵשֶׂב נָתַתִּי לָכֶם
אֶת כֹּל[c]׃ 4 אַךְ בָּשָׂר בְּנַפְשׁוֹ דָמוֹ[a] לֹא תֹאכֵלוּ׃ 5 [a]וְאַךְ אֶת[a] דִּמְכֶם[b]
לְנַפְשֹׁתֵיכֶם אֶדְרֹשׁ מִיַּד כָּל חַיָּה[c] אֶדְרְשֶׁנּוּ[d] [e]וּמִיַּד הָאָדָם מִיַּד אִישׁ אָחִיו[e]

[g-g] את כל חי 𝔐 ⅏ 𝔖 (ܠܟܠ ܚܝ) 𝔗[O] (ית כל דחי) 𝔗[N] (ית כל חייא) 𝔙 (*omnem animantem*) Syh (σάρκα und ÷)] את כל בשר חי* 𝔊 (πᾶσαν σάρκα ζῶσαν).
8:22 [a] עד 𝔐 ⅏ 𝔊[MSS] (ἔτι) 𝔖 (ܘܡܟܝܠ) 𝔗[OFJ] (עוד) 𝔗[N] (מן כדון) Syh] omit עד* 𝔊 𝔙 *Jub* 6:4.
[b] וקר 𝔐 𝔖[MSS] (ܘܩܘܪܐ) 𝔗[O] (וקורא) 𝔗[N] (וקריר) 𝔗[F] (וצינתא)] קר or קור ⅏ 𝔊 (ψῦχος) 𝔖 (ܩܘܪܐ) 𝔙 (*aestus*) *Jub* 6:4.
[c] וקיץ 𝔐 𝔗[O] (וקיטא) 𝔗[N] (וקיט)] קיץ ⅏ 𝔊 (θέρος) 𝔖 (ܘܩܝܛܐ) 𝔙 (*aestas*) *Jub* 6:4 | קץ ⅏[MSS].
[d-d] ויום ולילה 𝔐 𝔊[MSS] (καὶ ἡμέρα καὶ νύξ) 𝔗[OF] (וימם ולילי) 𝔗[N] (ואימממא ולילי) Aeth[MS] α′ (καὶ ἡμέρα καὶ νύξ) σ′ (καὶ ἡμέρα καὶ νύξ)] יומם ולילה ⅏ 𝔊 (ἡμέραν καὶ νύκτα) 𝔖 (ܐܝܡܡܐ ܘܠܠܝܐ) *Jub* 6:4, cf. 𝔗[OF] (וימם ולילי) 𝔗[N] (ואימממא ולילי) | לילה ויום* 𝔙 (*nox et dies*).
9:1 [a] end 𝔐 ⅏ 𝔊[MSS] 𝔖 𝔗[ON] 𝔙 Syh (καὶ κατακυριεύσατε αὐτῆς und ÷)] add וכבשה? or ורדו בה? 𝔊 (καὶ κατακυριεύσατε αὐτῆς).
9:2 [a] וחתכם 𝔐, ↔ וחתתכם/וחתתכם 𝔊[MSS] (καὶ ὁ φόβος ὑμῶν) 𝔖 (ܘܕܚܠܬܟܘܢ) 𝔗[ON] (ואימתכון) Arab Bo Pal *Jub* 6:5] וחתתכם ⅏, ↔ וחתכם /וחתתכם 𝔊[MSS] (καὶ ὁ φόβος ὑμῶν) 𝔖 (ܘܕܚܠܬܟܘܢ) 𝔗[ON] (ואימתכון) Arab Bo Pal *Jub* 6:5 | והחת* 𝔊 (καὶ ὁ φόβος) 𝔙 (*ac tremor*).
[b] text 𝔐 ⅏ 𝔊[W R(S)] 𝔖 𝔗[ON] 𝔙] add ועל כל בהמת הארץ* 𝔊[R(G) MSS] (καὶ ἐπὶ πᾶσι[ν] τοῖς κτήνεσι[ν] τῆς γῆς) Syh (καὶ ἐπὶ πᾶσι[ν] τοῖς κτήνεσι[ν] τῆς γῆς und ÷).
[c] בכל 𝔐 ⅏[VG MSS] 𝔗[ON] (בכל) 𝔙 (*cum universis*)] ובכל ⅏[MSS] 𝔊 (καὶ ἐπὶ πάντα) 𝔖 (ܘܥܠ ܟܠ).
[d] נתנו 𝔐 𝔗[O] (מסירין) 𝔗[J] (יתמסרון) 𝔙 (*traditi sunt*) 𝔖 (ܢܫܬܠܡܘܢ)] נתתיו ⅏ | נתתי 𝔊 (δέδωκα) 𝔗[N] (מסרת) *Jub* 6:6.
9:3 [a] כל 𝔐 ⅏ 𝔗[ON] (כל)] וכל? 𝔊 (καὶ πᾶν) 𝔖 (ܘܟܠ) 𝔙 (*et omne*).
[b-b] הוא חי 𝔐 ⅏ 𝔊 (ἐστιν ζῶν) 𝔖 (ܕܚܝ) 𝔗[OJ] (דהוא חי) 𝔙 (*et vivit*)] בו רוח חיים* 𝔗[N] (דאית ביה נשמה דחיין).
[c] כל 𝔐, cf. 𝔖 (ܟܠ)] הכל ⅏, cf. 𝔊 (τὰ πάντα) 𝔗[ON] (כולא).
9:4 [a] דמו 𝔐 ⅏ 𝔊 (αἵματι) 𝔖 (ܒܕܡܗ) 𝔗[O] (דמיה) 𝔗[N] (אדמ') 𝔙 (*sanguine*) *Jub* 6:7 1Q20 XI 17] omit דמו Ball Eißfeldt Gunkel Holzinger Sievers Zimmerli.
9:5 [a-a] ואך את 𝔐 ⅏[VG] 𝔊 (καὶ γάρ) 𝔖 (ܘܒܪܡ) 𝔗[O] (וברם ית) 𝔗[N] (ולחוד ית)] ואת ⅏[GB KN].
[b] דמכם 𝔐 ⅏ 𝔊 (τὸ ὑμέτερον αἷμα) 𝔖 (ܕܡܟܘܢ) 𝔗[O] (דמכון) 𝔗[C] (אדמכון) *Jub* 6:7] דם* 𝔊[MS] (τὸ αἷμα) 𝔗[N] (אדם) 𝔙 (*sanquinem*) Aeth Arab Co.
[c] חיה 𝔐 𝔊 (τῶν θηρίων) 𝔖 (ܚܝܘܬܐ) 𝔗[OCN(mg)] (חיתא) 𝔙 (*bestiarum*) α′ (ζῴων) σ′ (ζῴων)] חי ⅏, cf. 𝔗[N] (חיא).
[d] אדרשנו 𝔐 ⅏ 𝔊 (ἐκζητήσω αὐτό) 𝔖 (ܐܬܒܥܝܘܗܝ) 𝔗[O] (איתבעיניה) 𝔗[NC] (אתבע יתיה)] omit אדרשנו* 𝔙.
[e-e] ומיד האדם מיד איש אחיו 𝔐 𝔊[MSS MSS (ἐκ χειρὸς ἀνδρός und ※)] (καὶ ἐκ χειρὸς ἀνθρώπου ἐκ χειρὸς ἀνδρὸς ἀδελφοῦ) Aeth[MSS] Arm Syh (ἐκ χειρὸς ἀνδρός und ※) 𝔗[O] (ומיד אינשא מיד גבר דישוד ית דמא דאחוהי) 𝔗[J] (ומידא דאינשא מיד גבר דישוד ית דמא דאחוי)] ומיד האדם מיד איש 𝔐[MSS] 𝔗[N] (ומלות בר נשא ומלוות אחוי דבר נשא) | ומיד איש אחיו מיד האדם 𝔐[MSS] | מיד האדם מיד איש ואחיו ⅏ 𝔗[N(mg)] (מן לוות ברי אנשא מן לוות גבר ואחוי) | ומיד האדם 𝔗[S(MS)] (מן אד אנשה מיד גבר ותלימה) 𝔗[S(MS)] (מן אד אנשה מן אד גבר ואחיו) | מיד האדם ומיד איש ואחיו 𝔐[MSS] 𝔙 (*et de manu hominis de manu viri et fratris eius*) | מיד איש ואחיו 𝔐[MS] 𝔖 (ܘܡܢ ܐܝܕܐ ܕܐܢܫܐ ܘܡܢ ܐܝܕܐ ܕܓܒܪܐ ܘܐܚܘܗܝ) 𝔗[C] (מן יד בר נשא ומן יד גבר ואחוי) 𝔗[S(MS)] (מן אד אנשה ומן אד אנש ואחיו) | ומיד האדם ומיד איש ואחיו 𝔖[MSS] (ܘܡܢ ܐܝܕܐ ܕܐܢܫܐ ܘܡܢ ܐܝܕܐ ܕܓܒܪܐ ܘܐܚܘܗܝ) | ומיד אדם אחיו? or ומיד איש אחיו? 𝔊

אֶדְרֹשׁ אֶת נֶפֶשׁ הָאָדָם: ⁶ שֹׁפֵךְ דַּם הָאָדָם[a] בָּאָדָם דָּמוֹ[b-b] יִשָּׁפֵךְ כִּי בְּצֶלֶם
אֱלֹהִים עָשָׂה[c] אֶת הָאָדָם: ⁷ וְאַתֶּם פְּרוּ וּרְבוּ[a-a] שִׁרְצוּ בָאָרֶץ[b-b] וּרְדוּ בָהּ:
8:9וַיֹּאמֶר אֱלֹהִים[a] אֶל נֹחַ וְאֶל בָּנָיו אִתּוֹ לֵאמֹר: ⁹ וַאֲנִי[a] הִנְנִי מֵקִים אֶת בְּרִיתִי אִתְּכֶם
וְאֶת זַרְעֲכֶם אַחֲרֵיכֶם: ¹⁰ וְאֵת כָּל נֶפֶשׁ הַחַיָּה אֲשֶׁר[a] אִתְּכֶם בָּעוֹף[b] וּבַבְּהֵמָה[c] וּבְכָל
חַיַּת הָאָרֶץ[d] אִתְּכֶם[e] מִכֹּל יֹצְאֵי הַתֵּבָה[f-f] לְכֹל חַיַּת הָאָרֶץ: ¹¹ וַהֲקִמֹתִי אֶת בְּרִיתִי
אִתְּכֶם וְלֹא יִכָּרֵת[a-a] כָּל בָּשָׂר עוֹד[b] מִמֵּי הַמַּבּוּל[b] וְלֹא יִהְיֶה עוֹד מַבּוּל[c] לְשַׁחֵת[c] הָאָרֶץ[d]:

___

(καὶ ἐκ χειρὸς ἀνθρώπου ἀδελφοῦ [+ αὐτοῦ 𝕲^MSS MS (αὐτοῦ und ※) Aeth^MSS Arab Arm Syh (αὐτοῦ
und ※)]).

9:6 ᵃ האדם 𝔐 ‭ﬡ‬ 𝕲^MS (τοῦ ἀνθρώπου) S (ܐܢܫܐ) 𝕮^O (דאינשא)] אדם ‭ﬡ‬^MSS 𝕲
(ἀνθρώπου) 𝕮^NC (דבר נש).

ᵇ⁻ᵇ באדם דמו 𝔐 ‭ﬡ‬ 𝕲^MS (ἐν ἀνθρώπῳ αἷμα [ἀντὶ τοῦ αἵματος αὐτοῦ 𝕲^MS]) S (ܐܢܫܐ
בהמה) 𝕮^NC (ממימר דיניה דמיה) ... אדמיה) Syh (ἐν ἀνθρώπῳ und ※
(על ידי בר נש) 𝕯 (sanguis illius). | דמו[?] or דמו באדת[?] 𝕲 (ἀντὶ τοῦ αἵματος αὐτοῦ) | דמו[?]
Jub 6:8] ’בדמו[?] or דמו[?] or באדת דמו 𝕲 (ἀντὶ τοῦ αἵματος αὐτοῦ).

ᶜ *ברא 𝕮^NC עשיתי 𝕲 (ἐποίησα) | עשיתי 𝕯 (factus est) Jub 6:8] עשה 𝔐 ‭ﬡ‬ 𝕮^O (עבד) S (ܥܒܕ)
(ברא).

9:7 ᵃ⁻ᵃ ושרצו בארץ 𝔐 𝕮^O] שרצו בארץ ‭ﬡ‬ S (איתילדו בארעא) 𝕮^C (שרוצו בארעה)
(ܐܪܥܐ ܘܐܬܝܠܕܘ) 𝕮^N (ואתילדון בארעא) 𝕲 (καὶ πληρώσατε τὴν *ומלאו את הארץ
γῆν) | *וישרצו בארץ ומלאו אתה 𝕯 (et ingredimini super terram et implete eam).

ᵇ⁻ᵇ ורדו בה 𝕲^MSS (καὶ κατακυριεύσατε αὐτῆς) Arab Pal Sa Ball Eißfeldt Gunkel Hendel
Kittel Nestle Skinner Speiser Westermann, cf. 1Q20 XI 16 (ושלט בכולהון)] ורבו בה 𝔐
(בגווה וסגון),‭ﬡ‬ 𝕲^WR (καὶ πληθύνεσθε ἐπ᾽ αὐτῆς) S (ܘܣܓܘ ܒܗ) 𝕮^OC (וסגו בה) 𝕮^N
cf. 𝕯 (et implete eam) | omit בה 𝕯 | *ורבו בה Jub 6:5.

9:8 ᵃ אלהים 𝔐 ‭ﬡ‬ 𝕲 (ὁ θεός) S (ܐܠܗܐ) 𝕯 (Deus)] *יהוה אלהים 𝕲^MSS (κύριος ὁ θεός)
Arab Arm Sa.

9:9 ᵃ ואני 𝔐 ‭ﬡ‬ 𝕲^MSS (καὶ ἐγώ) 𝕮^ONC (ואנא)] *אני 𝕲 (ἐγώ) S (ܐܢܐ) 𝕯 (ego).

9:10 ᵃ אשר 𝔐 ‭ﬡ‬ S (-ܕ) 𝕮^O (ד-) 𝕮^N (די) 𝕮^C (דאית) 𝕯 (quae)] omit אשר ‭ﬡ‬^MS 𝕲.

ᵇ בעוף 𝔐 𝕲 (ἀπὸ ὀρνέων) 𝕮^ONC (בעופא)] ’ובעוף S (ܘܒܥܘܦܐ), cf. 𝕯 (tam in
volucribus).

ᶜ ובבהמה 𝔐^MSS ‭ﬡ‬ 𝕲 (καὶ ἀπὸ κτηνῶν) S (ܘܒܒܥܝܪܐ) 𝕮^O(MSS)NCP, cf. 𝕯
(quam in iumentis)] בבהמה 𝔐 𝕮^O (בבעירא).

ᵈ⁻ᵈ ולכל ובכל חיתא ד] 𝕮^NC (ובכל חית) ובכל חית 𝔐 ‭ﬡ‬ S-(ܘܒܟܠ ܚܝܘܬ) 𝕮^O
(ובחית *ובחית or *ואת כל חית 𝕲 (καὶ πᾶσι τοῖς θηρίοις), cf. לכל חית הארץ | 𝕯 (et
pecudibus) Aeth^MSS Sa.

ᵉ אתכם] 𝕮^ONC (עמכון)] omit אתכם* 𝕲^W MSS MS (ὅσα μεθ᾽ ὑμῶν und ※) 𝕯 Aeth^MSS Arm (ὅσα
μεθ᾽ ὑμῶν und ※) Syh (ὅσα μεθ᾽ ὑμῶν und ※) | *אשר אתכם 𝕲^R (ὅσα μεθ᾽ ὑμῶν) S
(ܕܥܡܟܘܢ).

ᶠ⁻ᶠ לכל] לכל חית הארץ 𝔐 ‭ﬡ‬ 𝕲^MSS (πᾶσι ζῴοις τῆς γῆς) 𝕮^O 𝕮^NC (לכל חית ארעא
ΑΓΜ Syh (πᾶσι ζῴοις τῆς γῆς und ※)] omit לכל חית הארץ 𝕲 S^MS, *לכל חית הארץ* (חיתא דארעא
cf. 𝕯 (πᾶσι τοῖς θηρίοις τῆς γῆς) | ’ולכל חית הארץ S (ܘܒܟܠ ܚܝܘܬ ܐܪܥܐ
(et universis bestiis terrae).

9:11 ᵃ⁻ᵃ כל בסרא עוד) 𝕮^N) כל בשר עוד 𝔐 𝕲 (πᾶσα σάρξ ἔτι) S (ܒܣܪܐ ܟܠ) 𝕮^OC
(כל בשר תוב[?] 𝕯 (ultra ... omnis caro). | עוד כל בשר ‭ﬡ‬ S^MSS (ܒܣܪܐ ܟܠ)

ᵇ מבול 𝔐 𝕲^MS (κατακλυσμός) 𝕮^NC (מבול) Arab, ↔ מבול/המבול 𝕯 (diluvium) La^M]
מבול מים S^? 𝕮^O? (טופנא), ↔ מבול/המבול 𝕯 (diluvium) La^M | המבול 𝕲 S² (ܡܒܘܠܐ)
(κατακλυσμὸς ὕδατος).

ᶜ להשחית] 𝔐 ‭ﬡ‬^MS] לשחת 𝔐.

ᵈ הארץ 𝔐 ‭ﬡ‬ S (ܐܪܥܐ) 𝕮^ONC (ארעא) 𝕯 (terram) Jub 6:4] כל הארץ 𝕲 (πᾶσαν τὴν
γῆν).

9:12 וַיֹּאמֶר אֱלֹהִים[ba] זֹאת אוֹת הַבְּרִית אֲשֶׁר אֲנִי נֹתֵן בֵּינִי וּבֵינֵיכֶם וּבֵין כָּל
נֶפֶשׁ חַיָּה[c] אֲשֶׁר אִתְּכֶם לְדֹרֹת[d] עוֹלָם: 13 אֶת קַשְׁתִּי נָתַתִּי בֶּעָנָן וְהָיְתָה לְאוֹת
בְּרִית בֵּינִי וּבֵין הָאָרֶץ: 14 וְהָיָה בְּעַנְנִי עָנָן[a] עַל הָאָרֶץ[a] וְנִרְאֲתָה[b] הַקֶּשֶׁת[c] בֶּעָנָן:
15 וְזָכַרְתִּי[a] אֶת בְּרִיתִי אֲשֶׁר בֵּינִי[b] וּבֵינֵיכֶם וּבֵין כָּל נֶפֶשׁ חַיָּה[c] בְּכָל[e] בָּשָׂר[dc] וְלֹא
יִהְיֶה עוֹד הַמַּיִם לְמַבּוּל לְשַׁחֵת[f] כָּל בָּשָׂר: 16 וְהָיְתָה הַקֶּשֶׁת[a] בֶּעָנָן וּרְאִיתִיהָ[b] לִזְכֹּר[c]
בְּרִית עוֹלָם[d] בֵּין[d] אֱלֹהִים וּבֵין כָּל נֶפֶשׁ חַיָּה[e] בְּכָל בָּשָׂר אֲשֶׁר עַל הָאָרֶץ:
17 וַיֹּאמֶר אֱלֹהִים[a] אֶל נֹחַ זֹאת אוֹת הַבְּרִית אֲשֶׁר הֲקִמֹתִי אֲשֶׁר בֵּינִי וּבֵין כָּל בָּשָׂר
אֲשֶׁר עַל הָאָרֶץ:

9:12 [a] אלהים 𝔐 𝔴 𝔊[MSS] (ὁ θεός) 𝔖 (ܐܠܗܐ) 𝔙 (Deus) La[X]] [b]יהוה אלהים 𝔊 (κύριος)
ὁ θεός) | יהוה[b]* 𝔊[MSS] (κύριος).
[b] text 𝔐 𝔴 𝔗[ONC] 𝔙 La[X]] add [b]לנח or אל נח 𝔊 (πρὸς Νωε) 𝔖 (ܠܢܘܚ).
[c] חיה 𝔐 𝔊 (ζώσης), cf. 𝔗[C] (דחייא) החיה 𝔴, cf. 𝔖 (ܚܝܬܐ) 𝔗[ONJ] (חיתא).
[d] לברית 𝔗[C] (לדרי) 𝔙 (in generationes)] לדרת 𝔐 𝔴 𝔊 (εἰς γενεάς) 𝔖 (ܠܕܪ̈ܐ) 𝔗[ONJ]
(לקיים).
9:14 [a-a] על הארץ 𝔐 𝔴 𝔊 (ἐπὶ τῆς γῆς) 𝔖 (ܥܠ ܐܪܥܐ) 𝔗[ONJ] (על ארעא)] בשמים[a]*
𝔙 (caelum).
[b] ונראתה 𝔐 𝔴 𝔊[MSS] (καὶ ὀφθήσεται) 𝔖 (ܘܬܚܙܐ) 𝔗[NC] (ותתחזי) ותתחמי[b]]
נראתה[b]* 𝔊 (ὀφθήσεται) 𝔙 (apparebit).
[c] הקשת 𝔐 𝔴 𝔊[MSS] (τὸ τόξον) 𝔖 (ܩܫܬܐ) 𝔗[ONC] (קשתא) Bo Syh] קשתי[b] 𝔊 (τὸ
τόξον μου) 𝔙 (arcus meus).
9:15 [a] וזכרתי 𝔐 𝔴 𝔊 (καὶ μνησθήσομαι) 𝔖[MSS] (ܘܐܬܕܟܪ) 𝔗[O(MS)N] (ודכירנא) 𝔗[OJ]
(ואדכר)] זכרתי[b]* 𝔖 αζαρ or אזכר 𝔖 (ܘܐܬܕܟܪ) 𝔙 (et recordabor).
[b] ביני 𝔐 𝔴 𝔊 (ἀνὰ μέσον ἐμοῦ) 𝔖 (ܒܝܢܝ) 𝔗[ONCJ] (בין מימרי)] omit 𝔙[b]*.
[c] חיה 𝔐 𝔊 (ζώσης) 𝔗[N] (חיה), cf. 𝔗[C] (דחייא) החיה 𝔴, cf. 𝔖 (ܚܝܬܐ) 𝔗[OJ]
(חיתא).
[d] text 𝔐 𝔊 𝔗[ONC] 𝔙] add אשר אתכם 𝔴 𝔖 (ܕܥܡܟܘܢ).
[e] בכל 𝔐 𝔴 𝔊 (ἐν πάσῃ) 𝔗[ON] (בכל)] ובין כל 𝔖 (ܟܠ ܢܦܫ) | 𝔙 (quae ...
vegetat).
[f] לשחית 𝔴 | להשחית 𝔴[MSS].] לשחת 𝔐 𝔴[MSS].
9:16 [a] הקשת 𝔐 𝔴 𝔊[W MSS] (τὸ τόξον) 𝔖 (ܩܫܬܐ) 𝔗[ONC] (קשתא) 𝔙 (arcus) Bo Sa[MS]]
קשתי[b] 𝔊[R MSS] (τὸ τόξον μου) 𝔙[MSS] (arcus meus).
[b] וראיתיה 𝔐 𝔊[MSS] (καὶ ὄψομαι αὐτήν) 𝔖 (ܘܐܚܙܝܗ) 𝔗[O] (ואחזינה) 𝔗[NC] (ואמחי)
ותה) 𝔗[S(MS)] (ואחזיה) 𝔙 (et videbo illum) Aeth Syh] וראיתה 𝔴, cf. 𝔊[MSS] (καὶ ὄψομαι
αὐτῷ) 𝔖 (ܘܐܚܙܝܗ) 𝔗[O] (ואחזינה) 𝔗[NC] (ואמחי יתה) 𝔗[S(MS)] (ואחזיה) 𝔙 (et videbo
illum) Aeth Syh | וראיתי[b]* 𝔊 (καὶ ὄψομαι) 𝔗[N] (ואחזי) | וראית 𝔴[MSS] 𝔗[S(MS)]
(ותתחזי).
[c] לזכר 𝔐 𝔊 (τοῦ μνησθῆναι) 𝔗[O(MSS)J] (למדכרה) 𝔗[C] (למדכר) 𝔗[N] (למדכרה)
(לאדכרה) 𝔙 (et recordabor)] לאזכרה 𝔖 (ܠܡܬܕܟܪܘ) 𝔗[O] (לדוכרן) 𝔗[S(MSS)] (לדכר)
(לאדכרה).
[d-d] בין מימרא 𝔐 𝔴 𝔊[MSS] (ἀνὰ μέσον τοῦ θ̄ῡ) 𝔖 (ܒܝܬ ܐܠܗܐ) 𝔗[ONC]
דיי) 𝔙 (inter Deum) Aeth[-MS]] ביני[d]* 𝔊 (ἀνὰ μέσον ἐμοῦ).
[e] חיה 𝔐 𝔊 (ζώσης), cf. 𝔗[C] (דחיה) החיה 𝔴, cf. 𝔖 (ܚܝܬܐ) 𝔗[O] (חיתא) 𝔗[N] חיה.
9:17 [a] אלהים 𝔐 𝔴 𝔊 (ὁ θεός) 𝔖 (ܐܠܗܐ) 𝔙 (Deus)] יהוה אלהים[b]* 𝔊[MSS] (κύριος ὁ
θεός) Arm[ap] Sa[MS] | יהוה[b]* 𝔊[MSS] (κύριος).

A3. Conclusion

In this critical edition, I have endeavored to reconstruct as nearly as possible the most original Hebrew text of the Genesis Flood narrative with a full inventory of text-critical tools. Unfortunately, due to spatial limitations, I was not able to give detailed defense of all the decisions, but a number of general conclusions are worthy of note. All of the witnesses were easily related to a common archetypal text, which I generally presume closely to approximate this ideal original. The commonly-used Masoretic text has been shown to be generally reliable, but the ancient versions and occasional conjectural emendations were at times helpful in achieving a purer critical text. Throughout the study the results have been instructive for understanding the nature of the ancient texts and versions as well as the variety of interpretations given to the Flood narrative over time. Perhaps most significantly, the dates of the Masoretic text and Samaritan Pentateuch were deemed original, but detailed evaluation of the variants has shed much light on the nature of the calendrical systems and chronological revisions that influenced the transmission of the text of the Genesis Flood narrative. I hope that this critical text will serve as an accurate text and that the apparatus would be a helpful resource for all those who intend to study the Flood narrative in detail.

References

Aberbach, M., and B. Grossfeld. 1982. *Targum Onkelos to Genesis: A critical analysis together with an English translation of the text.* New York, NY: KTAV Publishing House.

Baillet, M. 1962. 1. Genèse en écriture Paléo-Hébraïque. In *Les 'petites grottes' de Qumrân,* Discoveries in the Judaean Desert 3. Ed. M. Baillet, J. T. Milik, and R. de Vaux, 105–06. Oxford, England: Clarendon.

Ball, C. J. 1896. *The book of Genesis: Critical edition of the Hebrew text printed in colors exhibiting the composite structure of the book with notes.* Leipzig, Germany: Hinrichs.

Barré, L. M. 1988. The riddle of the Flood chronology. *Journal for the Study of the Old Testament* 41: 3–20.

Barthélemy, D., A. Schenker, and J. A. Thompson. 1979. *Preliminary and interim report on the Hebrew Old Testament text project, Vol. 1: Pentateuch.* 2nd rev. ed. New York, NY: United Bible Societies.

Batsch, C. 2008. Histoire des Géants et de Noé (1QNoah): 1Q19—1Q19bis. In *La Bibliothèque de Qumrân 1: Torah—Genèse.* Ed. P. André, K. Berthelot, and T. Legrand, 249–255. Paris, France: Les Éditions du Cerf.

Baxter, W. 2006. Noachic traditions and the *Book of Noah. Journal for the Study of the Pseudepigrapha* 15.3: 179–194.

Ben-Dov, J., and S. Saulnier. 2008. Qumran calendars: A survey of scholarship 1980–2007. *Currents in Biblical Research* 7: 124–168.

Bernstein, M. J. 1999. Noah and the Flood at Qumran. In *The Provo International Conference on the Dead Sea Scrolls: Technological innovations, new texts, and reformulated issues.* Ed. D. W. Parry, and E. Ulrich, 199–231. Leiden, Netherlands: Brill.

Brooke, G. J. 1996. 252. 4QCommentary on Genesis A. In *Qumran Cave 4, Vol. XVII: Parabiblical texts, part 3.* Discoveries in the Judean Desert 22. Ed. G. Brooke et al., 185–207. Oxford, England: Clarendon.

Brooke, G. J. 1998. Some remarks on 4Q252 and the text of Genesis. *Textus* 19: 1–25.

Brooke, G. J. 2002. Commentary on Genesis D. In *The Dead Sea Scrolls: Hebrew, Aramaic, and Greek texts with English translations, Vol. 6B, Pesharim, other commentaries, and related documents.* Ed. J. H. Charlesworth, 235–39. Tübingen, Germany: Mohr Siebeck.

Brown, F., S. Driver, and C. Briggs. 1996. *The Brown-Driver-Briggs Hebrew and English Lexicon.* Peabody, MA: Hendrickson.

Cassuto, U. 1964. *A commentary on the book of Genesis.* Trans. I. Abrahams. Jerusalem, Israel: Magnes Press.

Charles, R. H. 1902. *The book of Jubilees or The little Genesis.* London, England: Adam and Charles Black.

Cryer, F. H. 1985. The interrelationships of Gen 5, 32; 11, 10–11 and the chronology of the Flood (Gen 6–9). *Biblica* 66.2: 241–261.

Dahse, J. 1908. Textkritische studien I–II. *Zeitschrift für die alttestamentliche Wissenschaft* 28: 1–21, 161–173.

Delitzsch, F. 1888. *A new commentary on Genesis.* Trans. S. Taylor. Leipzig, Germany: T. & T. Clark. Repr. Klock and Klock, 1978.

de Boer, P. A. H., et al., eds. 1977. *The Old Testament in Syriac according to the Peshitta Version, Vol. 1: Genesis.* Leiden, Netherlands: Brill.

De Rossi, G. B. 1784. *Variae lectiones Verteris Testamenti librorum.* Vol. 1. Parma, Italy: Ex Regio Typographeo.

Díez Macho, A. 1968. *Neophyti 1: Targum Palestinense MS de la Bibliotheca Vaticinia, Vol. 1.* Madrid, Spain: Consejo Superior de Investigaciones Científicas.

Dillmann, A. 1897. *Genesis critically and exegetically expounded.* Trans. Wm. B. Stevenson. Edinburgh, Scotland: T. & T. Clark.

Drazin, I., and S. M. Wagner. 2006. *Onkelos on the Torah: Understanding the Bible text, Genesis.* Jerusalem, Israel: Gefen Publishing House.

Driver, S. R. 1926. *The Book of Genesis with introduction and notes.* Enlarged ed. London, England: Methuen & Co.

Ehrlich, A. B. 1908. *Randglossen zur hebräischen Bibel: Textkritisches, Sprachliches und Sachliches, Vol. 1: Genesis und Exodus.* Leipzig, Germany: Hinrichs.

Eißfeldt, O. 1969. *Liber Genesis: Biblia Hebraica Stuttgartensia.* Stuttgart, Germany: Deutsche Bibelgesellschaft.

Elgvin, T., and E. Tov. 1994. 422. 4QParaphrase of Genesis and Exodus. In *Qumran Cave 4, Vol. XIV: Parabiblical Texts, Part 2*. Discoveries in the Judaean Desert 19. Ed. J. VanderKam, J, Fitzmyer, et al., 417–441. Oxford, England: Clarendon.

Eshel, E., and M. Stone. 1995. 464. 4QExposition on the Patriarchs. In *Qumran Cave 4, Vol. VIII: Parabiblical Texts, Part 1*. Discoveries in the Judaean Desert 13. Ed. J. VanderKam, E. Tov, et al., 215–230. Oxford, England: Clarendon.

Feldman, A. 2007. The reworking of the biblical Flood story in 4Q370. *Henoch* 29: 31–50.

Feldman, A. 2009a. The Flood story according to 4Q422. In *The dynamics of exegesis and language at Qumran*. Ed. D. Dimant, and R. Kratz, 55–77. Tübingen, Germany: Mohr Siebeck.

Feldman, A. 2009b. 1Q19 (the book of Noah) reconsidered. *Henoch* 31.2: 284–306.

Freedman, D. N. et al., eds. 1998. *The Leningrad Codex: A facsimile edition*. Grand Rapids, MI: Eerdmans.

García Martínez, F. 1998. The interpretation of the Flood in the Dead Sea Scrolls. In *Interpretations of the Flood*. Ed. F. García Martínez, and G. P. Luttikhuizen, 86–108. Leiden, Netherlands: Brill.

Gesenius, W. 1910. *Gesenius' Hebrew Grammar*. 2nd English edition. Ed. A. E. Cowley, and E. Kautzsch. Oxford, England: Clarendon Press.

Ginsburg, C. D. 1908. *Pentateuchus*. London, England: Sumptibus Societatis Bibliophilorum Britannicae et Externae.

Giron Blanc, L.-F. 1976. *Pentateuco Hebreo-Samaritano: Genesis. Edición crítica sobre la base de Manuscritos inéditos*. Textos y Estudios 15. Madrid, Spain: Instituto Arias Montano.

Glessmer, U. 1993. Antike und moderne Auslegungen des Sintflutberichtes Gen 6–8 und der Qumran-Pesher 4Q252. *Theologische Fakultät Leipzig, Forschungsstelle Judentum, Mitteilungen und Beiträge* 6: 3–79.

Goshen-Gottstein, M. 1967. Hebrew biblical manuscripts: Their history and their place in the HUBP edition. *Biblica* 48: 243–290.

Goshen-Gottstein, M. 1972. *Biblia Rabbinica: A reprint of the 1525 Venice edition*. 2 vols. Jerusalem, Israel: Makor Publishing.

Graves, M. 2003. The origins of *Ketiv-Qere* readings. *TC: A Journal of Biblical Textual Criticism* 8. Accessed November 25, 2011. http://www.reltech.org/TC/v08/Graves2003.html#fnref1.

Grossfeld, B. 2000. *Targum Neofiti 1: An exegetical commentary to Genesis*. New York, NY: Sepher-Hermon Press.

Gunkel, H. 1997. *Genesis*. Trans. M. Biddle. Macon, GA: Mercer University Press.

Hamilton, V. P. 1990. *The book of Genesis: Chapters 1–17*. New International Commentary on the Old Testament. Grand Rapids, MI: Eerdmans.

Hayward, C. T. R. 1995. *Saint Jerome's Hebrew questions on Genesis*. Oxford, England: Clarendon Press.

Hendel, R. S. 1995. 4Q252 and the Flood chronology of Genesis 7–8: A text-critical solution. *Dead Sea Discoveries* 2.1: 72–79.

Hendel, R. S. 1998. *The text of Genesis 1–11: Textual studies and critical edition.* New York, NY: Oxford University Press.

Joosten, J. 2010. Hebrew, Aramaic, and Greek in the Qumran Scrolls. In *The Oxford Handbook of the Dead Sea Scrolls.* Ed. T. H. Lim, and J. J. Collins, 351–374. Oxford, England: Oxford University Press.

Kennicott, B. 1776. *Vetus testamentum Hebraicum, cum variis lectionibus.* Oxonii, England: E Typographeo Clarendoniano.

Kittel, R. 1905. *Biblia Hebraica.* Lipsiae, Germany: Hinrichs.

Klein, M. L. 1980. *The Fragment-Targums of the Pentateuch according to their extant sources.* Rome, Italy: Biblical Institute Press.

Klein, M. L. 1986. *Genizah manuscripts of Palestinian Targum to the Pentateuch.* 2 Vols. Cincinnati, OH: Hebrew Union College Press.

Koffi, E. 1998. There is more to 'and' than just conjoining words. *Bible Translator* 49.3: 332–343.

Köhler, L., and W. Baumgartner. 1994–2000. *The Hebrew and Aramaic lexicon of the Old Testament.* Rev. W. Baumgartner and J. J. Stamm. Trans. M. E. J. Richardson. Leiden, Netherlands: Brill.

Kutscher, E. Y. 1974. *The language and linguistic background of the Isaiah Scroll. 1QIsaa.* Studies on the texts of the Desert of Judah 6. Leiden, Netherlands: Brill.

Larsson, G. 1977. Chronological parallels between the Creation and the Flood. *Vetus Testamentum* 27.4: 490–92.

Larsson, G. 1983. The chronology of the Pentateuch: A comparison of the MT and LXX. *Journal of Biblical Literature* 102.3: 401–09.

Larsson, G. 1998. More quantitative Old Testament research? *Zeitschrift für die alttestamentliche Wissenschaft* 110.4: 570–580.

Larsson, G. 2000. Remarks concerning the Noah-Flood complex. *Zeitschrift für die alttestamentliche Wissenschaft* 112: 75–77.

Legrand, T. 2008. Homélie sur le déluge. 4QAdmonition based on the Flood—4Q370. In *La Bibliothèque de Qumrân 1: Torah—Genèse.* Ed. P. André et al., 283–89. Paris, France: Les Éditions du Cerf.

Lemche, N. P. 1980. The chronology in the story of the Flood. *Journal for the Study of the Old Testament* 18: 52–62.

Lewis, J. P. 1968. *A study of the interpretation of Noah and the Flood in Jewish and Christian literature.* Leiden, Netherlands: Brill.

Lim, T. H. 1992. The chronology of the Flood story in a Qumran text (4Q252). *Journal of Jewish Studies* 43: 288–298.

Machiela, D. A. 2009. *The Dead Sea Genesis Apocryphon: A new text and translation with introduction and special treatment of columns, 13–17.* Leiden, Netherlands: Brill.

Maher, M. 1992. *Targum Pseudo-Jonathan: Genesis, translated, with apparatus and notes.* The Aramaic Bible 1B. Collegeville, MN: Liturgical Press.

Malan, S. C. 1882. *The book of Adam and Eve: Also called the conflict of Adam and Eve with Satan, a book of the early Eastern church, translated from the Ethiopic, with notes from the Kufale, Talmud, Midrashim, and other Eastern works.* London, England: Williams and Norgate.

McCarter, P. K. Jr. 1986. *Textual criticism: Recovering the text of the Hebrew Bible.* Philadelphia, PA: Fortress Press.

McNamara, M. 1992. *Targum Neofiti 1: Genesis, translated, with apparatus and notes.* The Aramaic Bible 1A. Collegeville, MN: Liturgical Press.

Mundhenk, N. 1994. The dates of the Flood. *Bible Translator* 45.2: 207–213.

Najm, S., and P. Guillaume. 2004. Jubilee calendar rescued from the Flood Narrative. *Journal of Hebrew Scriptures* 5. Accessed 25 December 2011. http://www.arts.ualberta.ca/JHS/Articles/article_31.pdf.

Niese, B. 1888. *Flavii Josephi opera: Antiquitatum iudaicarum.* Berolini, Germany: apud Weidmannos.

Oswalt, J. 1980. גבר. In *Theological wordbook of the Old Testament.* Ed. R. L. Harris, G. L. Archer, and B. K. Waltke, 310. Chicago, IL: Moody Press.

Palache, J. L. 1959. *Semantic notes on the Hebrew lexicon.* Leiden, Netherlands: Brill.

Peters, D. M. 2008. *Noah traditions in the Dead Sea Scrolls: Conversations and controversies of antiquity.* Atlanta, GA: Society of Biblical Literature.

Petersen, D. 1976. The Yahwist on the Flood. *Vetus Testamentum* 26: 438–446.

Puech, É. 1998. 577. 4QTexte mentionnant le Déluge. In *Qumrân Grotte 4: Vol. XVIII,* Discoveries in the Judaean Desert 25. Ed. É. Puech, 195–203. Oxford, England: Clarendon.

Rahlfs, A. 1935. *Septuaginta, id est Vetus Testamentum Graece iuxta LXX interpretes.* Stuttgart, Germany: Deutsche Bibelgesellschaft.

Rieder, D. 1974. *Pseudo-Jonathan. Targum Jonathan ben Uzziel on the Pentateuch.* Jerusalem, Israel: Salomon's Printing Press.

Roberts, A., and J. Donaldson. 1868. *Ante-Nicene christian library. Vol. VI. Hippolytus, Bishop of Rome.* Edinburgh, Scotland: T. & T. Clark.

Rösel, M. 1998a. Die chronologie der Flut in Gen 7–8: keine neuen textkritischen Losungen. *Zeitschrift für die alttestamentliche Wissenschaft* 110.4: 590–93.

Rösel, M. 1998b. The text-critical value of Septuagint-Genesis. *Bulletin of the International Organization of Septuagint and Cognate Studies* 31: 62–70.

Sarna, N. M. 1989. *Genesis.* The JPS Torah commentary. Philadelphia, PA: Jewish Publication Society.

Schattner-Rieser, U. 2008. Histoire des Patriarches (1QApocryphe de la Genèse ar)—1QapGen/1Q20; 6Q19. In *La Bibliothèque de Qumrân 1: Torah—Genèse.* Ed. P. André, K. Berthelot, and T. Legrand, 319–387. Paris, France: Les Éditions du Cerf.

Schrader, L. 1998. Kommentierende Redaktion im Noah-Sintflut-Komplex der Genesis. *Zeitschrift für die alttestamentliche Wissenschaft* 110.4: 489–502.

Skinner, J. 1930. *A critical and exegetical commentary on Genesis.* 2nd ed. International Critical Commentary. Edinburgh, Scotland: T. & T. Clark.

Soisalon-Soininen, I. 1987. *Studien zur Septuaginta-Syntax.* Ed. Y. Blomstedt. Helsinki, Finland: Suomalainen Tiedeakatemia.

Speiser, E. A. 1964. *Genesis.* The Anchor Bible. Garden City, NY: Doubleday & Co.

Sperber, A. 1992. *The Bible in Aramaic, Vol. 1: The Pentateuch according to Targum Onkelos.* Leiden, Netherlands: Brill.

Spurrell, G. J. 1887. *Notes on the Hebrew Text of the book of Genesis.* Oxford, England: Clarendon Press.

Stone, M. E., A. Amihay, and V. Hillel, eds. 2010. *Noah and his book(s).* Leiden, Netherlands: Brill.

Tal, A. 1980. *The Samaritan Targum of the Pentateuch, Vol. 1.* Texts and studies in the Hebrew language and related subjects 4. Tel-Aviv, Israel: Tel-Aviv University.

Trehuedic, K. 2008. Commentaires de la Genèse A-D (4QCommentary on Genesis A-D)—4Q252—4Q253—4Q254—4Q254a. In *La Bibliothèque de Qumrân 1: Torah—Genèse.* Ed. P. André, K. Berthelot, and T. Legrand, 299–317. Paris, France: Les Éditions du Cerf.

Tov, E. 1981. *The text-critical use of the Septuagint in biblical research.* Jerusalem, Israel: Simor.

Ulrich, E. 2010. *The biblical Qumran Scrolls: Transcriptions and textual variants.* Leiden, Netherlands: Brill.

VanderKam, J. C. 1988. Jubilees and Hebrew texts of Genesis-Exodus. *Textus* 14: 71–85.

VanderKam, J. C. 1989. *The book of Jubilees.* Scriptores Aethiopici 88. Louvain, Belgium: In aedibus E. Peeters.

VanderKam, J. C. 1998. Authoritative literature in the Dead Sea Scrolls. *Dead Sea Discoveries* 5.3: 382–402.

Van Ruiten, J. T. A. G. M. 1998. The interpretation of the Flood story in the book of Jubilees. In *Interpretations of the Flood.* Ed. F. García Martínez, and G. P. Luttikhuizen, 66–85. Leiden, Netherlands: Brill.

Vogt, E. 1962. Note sur le calendrier du Déluge. *Biblica* 43: 212–16.

Von Gall, A. F. 1918. *Der hebräische Pentateuch der Samaritaner.* Giessen, Germany: Töpelmann.

Von Mutius, H.-G. 2000. Neues zur textkritik von Genesis 6,17 und 7,6 aus Judaistischer sicht. *Biblische Notizen* 104: 38–41.

Von Rad, G. 1972. *Genesis.* Rev. ed. Trans. J. H. Marks. Philadelphia, PA: Westminster Press.

Waltke, B., and M. O'Connor. 1990. *An introduction to biblical Hebrew syntax.* Winona Lake, IN: Eisenbrauns.

Weber, R., and R. Gryson, eds. 2007. *Biblia Sacra Vulgata.* 5th ed. Stuttgart: Deutsche Bibelgesellschaft.

Wenham, G. J. 1987. *Genesis 1–15.* Word biblical commentary 1. Waco, TX: Word Books.

Werman, C. 1995. The Flood story in the book of Jubilees. *Tarbiz* 64.2: 183–202.

Westermann, C. 1984. *Genesis 1–11*. Trans. J. J. Scullion. Minneapolis, MN: Augsburg.

Wevers, J. W. 1974a. *Genesis*. Septuaginta: Vetus Testamentum Graecum 1. Göttingen, Germany: Vandenhoeck & Ruprecht.

Wevers, J. W. 1974b. *Text history of the Greek Genesis*. Mitteilungen des Septuaginta-Unternehmens 11. Göttingen, Germany: Vandenhoeck & Ruprecht.

Wevers, J. W. 1993. *Notes on the Greek text of Genesis*. Atlanta, GA: Scholars Press.

Willet, A. 1632. *Hexapla in Genesin, that is, a Sixfold Commentarie on Genesis: Wherein six severall translations, that is, the Septuagint, and the Chalde, two Latine, of Hierome, and Tremlius, two English, the Great Bible, and the Geneva Edition are compared, where they differ, with the Originall, Hebrew, and Pagnine, and Montanus interlinearie interpretation*. London, England: Thomas Man, Paul Man, and Ionah Man.

Wright, C. H. H. 1859. *The book of Genesis in Hebrew with a critically revised text, various readings, and grammatical and critical notes*. London, England: Williams and Norgate.

Yonge, C. D. 1854–55. *The works of Philo Judaeus, the contemporary of Josephus*. London, England: Henry G. Bohn.

Zipor, M. A. 1991. A note on Genesis VI 13. *Vetus Testamentum* 41: 366–69.

Zipor, M. A. 1994. Notes sur les chapitres I à XVII de la Genèse dans la Bible d'Alexandrie. *Ephemerides Theologicae Lovanienses* 70.4: 385–393.

Zipor, M. A. 1997. The Flood chronology: Too many an accident? *Dead Sea Discoveries* 4.2: 207–210.

Zipor, M. A. 2002. Some notes on the Greek text of Genesis in the common editions. *Bulletin of the International Organization of Septuagint and Cognate Studies* 35: 121–26.

Zlotowitz, M. 1986. *Genesis: A new translation with a commentary anthologized from Talmudic, Midrashic, and Rabbinic sources*. 2nd ed. The Artscroll Tanach Series. Brooklyn, NY: Mesorah Publications.

PART III

THE VOYAGE BEGINS: INVESTIGATION

SECOND SECTION

GETTING UNDER WAY:
ASCERTAINING TEMPORAL SEQUENTIALITY IN NARRATIVE

Suddenly wind hit full and the canvas bellied out
and a dark blue wave, foaming up at the bow,
sang out loud and strong as the ship made way,
skimming the whitecaps, cutting toward her goal.

—Homer, from *The Odyssey* (Trans. Robert Fagles)

CHAPTER 10

The Charybdis of Morphology: The Sequentiality of *Wayyiqtol?*

Thomas Laney Stroup

Analogy and Orientation. In Greek mythology, there were two sea monsters known as Charybdis and Scylla. Charybdis was cursed to gulp and spout out large volumes of water, creating a deadly whirlpool for passing ships, and Scylla was cursed with the form of a six headed dragon that would snatch as many sailors as it could from any ships that came within reach. These two monsters would sit opposite each other and threaten ships that had to pass between them. The later Aeneid equated these two monsters with a whirlpool and a rocky outcropping off the coast of Italy somewhere in the Strait of Messina. Stray too close to the one, and the ship would be overturned and swallowed up by the whirlpool; but stray too close to the other, and the ship would be dashed against the rocks.

The study of the wayyiqtol *in Hebrew scholarship operates in much the same way. With the advent of text linguistics, Hebrew scholars have moved away from many of the mistakes of older theories of the Hebrew verbal system. In doing so, however, many have swung too close to the early methods of text linguistics, confusing correlation with causation, and have lost the crucial bearings of Comparative Semitics. Both errors have contributed to the unfortunate perpetuation of the assumption of the sequentiality of the* wayyiqtol, *which has not only distorted our understanding of the Hebrew verbal system, but also thrown off course many proposed chronologies of the Flood.*

To avoid this same fate, we must conduct a careful consideration of the strengths and weaknesses of the various theories of the Hebrew verbal system, a careful reconsideration of the Comparative Semitic evidence for the meaning of the wayyiqtol, *and a cautious reinvestigation of the synchronic evidence purported to indicate temporal sequentiatilty. And only a corrected understanding of the* wayyiqtol *can take us safely through these straits.*

Abstract. The majority of Hebrew scholars to date have asserted that the primary function of the *wayyiqtol* is to indicate some form of sequence, whether temporal or logical. In doing so, however, they have ignored the evidence of Comparative Semitics, overlooked the problem of dischronologization, and mistakenly perpetuated the erroneous assumptions of Ewald and S. R. Driver's aspect theory. This has not only distorted our understanding of the Hebrew verbal system, but also hindered the study of the Flood account.

Outline

1. Introduction
2. The Theories of the Hebrew Verbal System
3. The Origins of the *Wayyiqtol*
4. The Problem of Dischronologization
5. Conclusion

1. Introduction

The issue that lies at the heart of this study is the meaning of the *wayyiqtol*, an indicative verb form within the Hebrew verbal system. The majority of Hebrew scholarship to date has held that the primary function of the *wayyiqtol* is to indicate some form of sequence, whether temporal (Ewald 1870, 18–19; Green 1872, 128; S. R. Driver 1892, 80–88; Kennet 1901, 39–40, 43; Gesenius et al. 1910, 326; Niccacci 1990, 62–71; Waltke and O'Connor 1990, 547; Joüon and Muraoka 1993, 387; Gibson 1994, 95; Endo 1996, 272; Gentry 1998, 13; Goldfajn 1998, 124; Li 1999; Van der Merwe et al. 2002, 165; Heller 2004, 85; Moomo 2004, 175, 218–221; Williams 2007, 75; Kahn 2009, 191), or logical (e.g., S. R. Driver 1892, 82; Waltke and O'Connor 1990, 547).[1] In practice, this means that for any uninterrupted sequence of *wayyiqtols* in a Hebrew narrative, each successive

---

1. Both historically and practically speaking, temporal sequence is undoubtedly the primary function of the two (see **Sections 2.3** and **4.3.2**). However, the present chapter will address them equally insofar as it is possible for the sake of argument.

wayyiqtol should generally represent a successive point in time, as well, unless indicated otherwise.[2] This assumption can be depicted as follows:

W = *wayyiqtol*

T = Time

$$W_1 \quad W_2 \quad W_3 \quad W_4$$
$$T_1 \quad T_2 \quad T_3 \quad T_4$$

If true, this assumption creates several problems for the study of the Flood narrative. First, if one assumes the temporal sequence of the *wayyiqtols* in Genesis 7:17 and 18, then one must admit a much slower onset of the Flood, with the Ark remaining on the ground until the fortieth day.[3] This contrasts with the sudden and the catastrophic nature of the Flood pictured elsewhere in Scripture (Mt 24:37–44; Lk 17:26–35; 2 Pt 3:4–10). Second, if one assumes the temporal sequence of the *wayyiqtols* in Genesis 7:17–24, then one must admit a total of at least one hundred ninety days before the Ark comes to rest on a mountain. This is forty days too long, given the fixed dates in 7:11 and 8:4.[4] And third, if one assumes the temporal sequence of the *wayyiqtols* in Genesis 7:7, 7:13, and 7:15, then one must explain how Noah and his family could have entered the Ark as many as three (Gn 7:7, 7:13, and 7:15) or four (7:5) times. In fact, the prima facie evidence of the latter two issues has driven many scholars to conclude that the Flood narrative must have been derived from two or more contradictory sources, roughly pieced together by a later editor (rather than being composed by Moses).[5]

---

2. Although many grammarians will allow for potential breaks in time sequence on a case-by-case basis, often resorting to logical sequence as an explanation, each of the *wayyiqtol* forms is still assumed to indicate temporal sequence unless there is obvious and incontrovertible evidence otherwise. In other words, the *wayyiqtol* is still "guilty until proven innocent" (see **Section 4.3.2**).

3. Barrick, for example, comments that "these 40 days were the period of time required for the ark to become seaborne" (Barrick 2008, 263).

4. In addition, if one were to assume the strict temporal sequence of all of the time periods given in the course of the narrative, there would be a total of $40 + 40 + 150 + 150 + 40 + 7 + 7 = 434$ days in the Flood (Gn 7:12, 17, 24; 8:3, 6, 10, 12), a time period which is about 70 days too long, given the fixed dates of Gn 7:11 and 8:14.

5. "It has been widely agreed for over a century that the flood narrative has been composed by combining two sources known as J and P. The reasons for believing that more than one source has been used are, not only that God is sometimes referred to as Elohim and sometimes as Yahweh, but there is much duplication and even contradiction" (Emerton 1987, 401).

As the present study will demonstrate, however, these apparent contradictions are due not to any error on the part of the biblical authors (not to mention the issue of multiple authorship), but to the erroneous assumption of the sequentiality of the *wayyiqtol*. And secondly, the temporal sequence of the individual events of the Flood narrative depends not on the presence or absence of the *wayyiqtol*, but on other contextual and linguistic factors, several of which will be explored in the following chapters.

To defend this assertion, and to prepare the way for the following chapters, the present chapter will explore three areas of study in relation to the meaning of the *wayyiqtol*. First, it will consider the merits and weaknesses of the various theories of the Hebrew verbal system. This will orient the reader to the broader issues at hand, introduce the various methodologies that have been applied to the study of the *wayyiqtol* thus far, trace the origins, where evident, of the assumption of the sequentiality of the *wayyiqtol* (both temporal and logical), and provide a basis for a reconsideration of the meaning of the *wayyiqtol* in general. Second, it will consider the evidence from Historical and Comparative Semitics for the origins of the Hebrew *wayyiqtol*. This will provide the crucial control of diachronic analysis that has been neglected in many recent studies of the *wayyiqtol*, and provide a more solid basis for the conclusions to be reached regarding the meaning of the *wayyiqtol*. And third, it will consider the problem of dischronologization, and its implications for the meaning of the *wayyiqtol*. This will present the evidence against the temporal sequentiality of the *wayyiqtol*, highlight the underlying problem with both the temporal and logical sequentiality of the *wayyiqtol*, and demonstrate the need in modern studies for a better understanding of the *wayyiqtol* and the Hebrew verbal system as a whole.

In the process, these sections will present the following three conclusions. First, the temporal sequentiality of the *wayyiqtol* can be traced to the erroneous assumptions of Ewald and Driver's aspect theory of the Hebrew verbal system.[6] Second, the temporal sequentiality of the *wayyiqtol* does not align with any given theory of its Proto-Semitic origins. And third, the temporal sequentiality of the *wayyiqtol* does not align with actual usage in the OT.

---

6. This is not to say that the Hebrew verbal system does not exhibit any sort of verbal aspect, as the use of the *yiqtol* in past tense narrative clearly demonstrates. Rather, it is only to say that the specific reasoning of Ewald and Driver which lead them to assert the temporal sequentiality of the *wayyiqtol*, and their theory of the Hebrew verbal system as a whole has since been disproven by the discoveries of Historical and Comparative Semitics. For further details, see **Section 2.3**, as well as **Section 3.2.2**.

2. The Theories of the Hebrew Verbal System

The present chapter will first explore the various merits and weaknesses of the Hebrew Verbal System (hereafter, referred to as HVS). As mentioned in the introduction, this will orient the reader to the broader issues at hand, introduce the various methodologies that have been applied to the study of the *wayyiqtol* thus far, trace the origins, where evident, of the assumption of the sequentiality of the *wayyiqtol* (both temporal and logical), and provide a basis for a reconsideration of the meaning of the *wayyiqtol* in general.

2.1 Introduction
2.2 The Tense Theory (c. 1235—1827)
2.3 The Aspect Theory (1827—1910)
2.4 The Historical-Comparative Semitics Theory (1910—1990)
2.5 The Text Linguistics Theory (1990—Present)
2.6 Summary

2.1 *Introduction*[7]

The central problem of the HVS is the relationship between the four indicative verb forms: *qatal, yiqtol, wᵊqatal* , and *wayyiqtol*. Arranged in terms of Hebrew morphology, these verb forms appear to constitute a two-way opposition, the first being a division between the *qatal* forms and the *yiqtol* forms, and the second being a division between the natural forms and the converted forms. These oppositions result in a two-way cross classification as pictured below.[8]

	Natural Forms	Converted Forms
qatal forms	*qatal*	*wᵊqatal*
yiqtol forms	*yiqtol*	*wayyiqtol*

It is generally understood that the difference in meaning between the *qatal* and the *yiqtol* is one of either aspect or tense. The difference in meaning between the natural forms and the converted forms (i.e., why there is a need for the converted forms when we already have the natural forms), however, is still a matter of debate. In other words, the vertical opposition (between the *qatal* forms and the *yiqtol* forms) is fairly clear; the horizontal opposition, however (between the natural forms and the converted forms), has posed more of a problem.

---

7. For an excellent discussion of this and similar issues involved in the study of the HVS, see also Cook (2002, 74–79).

8. Please note that the present discussion does not endorse this description, nor the terminology "converted forms"; these are used purely for the sake of discussion in order to orient the reader to the problems that the various theories of the HVS have attempted to resolve.

Further complicating the issue is that whether speaking of tense, aspect, or some other opposition between the *qatal* forms and the *yiqtol* forms, contrary to expectation, the converted form that most resembles the *qatal* in meaning appears to be the *wayyiqtol*, while the converted form that most resembles the *yiqtol* in meaning is the *wᵉqatal*. This means that whatever the opposition between the natural forms and the converted forms, the correspondence in meaning (represented by the arrows) appears to be switched for the converted forms.

	Natural Forms	Converted Forms
qatal forms	*qatal*	*wᵉqatal*
yiqtol forms	*yiqtol*	*wayyiqtol*

These complications have resulted in a number of theories of the HVS, and a long history of interpretation (Mettinger 1974, 73–79; McFall 1982; Van der Merwe 1987; Waltke and O'Connor 1990, 458–475; Smith 1991, 1–6; Endo 1996, 1–26; Hatav 1997, 10–24; Cook 2002, 79–143; Heller 2004, 3–24). These proposals include the tense theory, the aspect theory, the Comparative Semitics theory, and various forms of the text linguistics theory. These theories and their explanations of the HVS will be explored below.

2.2 The Tense Theory (c. 1235–1827)⁹

The earliest theory of the HVS to be proposed was the tense theory. During the period of c. 1235 to 1827,¹⁰ the majority of scholars held that the *waw* prefix of the *wayyiqtol* somehow converted the future tense of the *yiqtol* to the past, making it equal in tense to the *qatal*. Likewise, they postulated that the *waw* prefix of the *wᵉqatal* converted the past tense of the *qatal* to the future, making it equal in tense to the *yiqtol*.¹¹ The following chart and examples illustrate this theory:

	Natural Forms	Converted Forms
past tense	*qatal*	waw + *yiqtol* (*wayyiqtol*)
future tense	*yiqtol*	waw + *qatal* (*wᵉqatal*)

9. For general discussion regarding the tense theory, see (McFall 1982, 17–20; Waltke and O'Connor 1990, 458–461; Smith 1991, 2; Hatav 1997, 11–12; Cook 2002, 79–82; Heller 2004, 3–5).

10. For dating purposes, we will use David Kimchi's *Mikhlol* as the starting point for this period, and Ewald's grammar as the endpoint. Although Kimchi was not the first person to propose the tense theory, his work constituted the first comprehensive Hebrew grammar of post biblical times, and remained the primary Hebrew grammar up until the publication of Ewald's grammar in 1827 (McFall 1982, 7).

11. See McFall (1982, 7–13) for examples.

Qatal—Past tense

GENESIS 1:1

בְּרֵאשִׁית **בָּרָא** אֱלֹהִים אֵת הַשָּׁמַיִם וְאֵת הָאָרֶץ׃

In the beginning God created (*qatal*)
the Heavens and the Earth.

Wayyiqtol—Past tense

GENESIS 1:3

וַיֹּאמֶר אֱלֹהִים יְהִי אוֹר **וַיְהִי־אוֹר**׃

And God said (*wayyiqtol*),
"Let there be light."
And there was (*wayyiqtol*) light.

Yiqtol—Future tense

GENESIS 2:17

וּמֵעֵץ הַדַּעַת טוֹב וָרָע לֹא **תֹאכַל** מִמֶּנּוּ כִּי בְּיוֹם אֲכָלְךָ מִמֶּנּוּ מוֹת
תָּמוּת׃

"But from the tree of the knowledge of good and evil you shall not eat
(*yiqtol*), for in the day that you eat of it you shall surely die (*yiqtol*)."

Wᵉqatal—Future tense

GENESIS 3:4–5

וַיֹּאמֶר הַנָּחָשׁ אֶל־הָאִשָּׁה לֹא־מוֹת תְּמֻתוּן׃⁵ כִּי יֹדֵעַ אֱלֹהִים כִּי בְּיוֹם
אֲכָלְכֶם מִמֶּנּוּ **וְנִפְקְחוּ** עֵינֵיכֶם **וִהְיִיתֶם** כֵּאלֹהִים יֹדְעֵי טוֹב וָרָע׃

Then the serpent said to the woman, "You shall surely not die, for God
knows that in the day that you eat from it, your eyes will be opened
(*wᵉqatal*) and you shall be (*wᵉqatal*) like God, knowing good and evil."

The tense theory offered a simple explanation for the switch in meaning between
the natural forms and the converted forms, and explained most occurrences
of these verb forms quite readily.[12] Consequently, the tense theory dominated
Hebrew grammar studies from the thirteenth through the seventeenth century.[13]

---

12. McFall demonstrates the initial statistical weight of the tense theory in his appendices,
where the RSV translates 14,202 of the 14,972 *wayyiqtols* in the past tense (McFall 1982, 186–87).

13. "This solution dominated the grammars, writings, and commentaries of Christian
Hebraists until the grammars of Lee and Ewald broke new ground in 1827" (McFall 1982, 17).

By the eighteenth century, however, a growing number of scholars had
begun to note exceptions to the theory, including occurrences of *yiqtol* and
wᵉqatal in the past tense, and even some occurrences of *qatal* and *wayyiqtol*
in the future tense,[14] casting doubt on the reliability of the tense theory.[15] In
addition, many had begun to doubt the idea altogether that the *waw* prefix
could somehow convert the tense of the verb forms. McFall records the
humorous but revealing protest of Johann Simones (McFall 1982, 13), "God
himself can not change a past into a future." These difficulties eventually led
to the demise of the tense theory and gave way to the aspect theory instead.[16]

2.3 The Aspect Theory (1827–1910)[17]

In 1827, Ewald published a new idea in his Hebrew grammar, suggesting
that perhaps the primary difference between the *qatal* and *yiqtol* verb forms
was not tense, but aspect. For this theory, Ewald proposed that the *qatal*
was perfective in aspect, indicating complete action, and the *yiqtol* was
imperfective in aspect, indicating incomplete action (Ewald 1870/1891,
1–13). Since the majority of complete actions lie in the past, and the majority
of incomplete actions lie in the present or future, the aspect theory explained
both the appearance of tense within the Hebrew verbal system, and the
occasional exceptions to this appearance. The following chart illustrate this
theory and shows its advantages over the tense theory:

	Natural Forms	Converted Forms
perfect (usually past tense)	qatal	wᵉqatal
imperfect (usually, present or future tense)	yiqtol	wayyiqtol

Yiqtol and *wᵉqatal* occuring in past tense

GENESIS 2:6

וְאֵד יַעֲלֶה מִן־הָאָרֶץ וְהִשְׁקָה אֶת־כָּל־פְּנֵי־הָאֲדָמָה׃

And a mist was going (*yiqtol*) up from the Earth, and
watering (*wᵉqatal*) the whole surface of the ground.

Qatal and *wayyiqtol* occuring in future tense (from McFall 1982, 18)

---

14. For examples, see McFall (1982, 18–19).

15. For further discussion of the problems of the tense theory, see McFall (1982, 18–21).

16. For further discussion of the demise of the tense theory, see McFall (1982, 13–14).

17. For general discussion regarding the aspect theory, see (McFall 1982, 43–56, 61–77; Waltke and O'Connor 1990, 461–66; Smith 1991, 2–3; Endo 1996, 2–10; Cook 2002, 82–93; Heller 2004, 8–17).

ISAIAH 9:5

כִּי־יֶ֣לֶד יֻלַּד־לָ֗נוּ בֵּן֙ נִתַּן־לָ֔נוּ וַתְּהִ֥י הַמִּשְׂרָ֖ה עַל־שִׁכְמ֑וֹ וַיִּקְרָ֣א שְׁמ֗וֹ פֶּ֠לֶא
יוֹעֵץ֙ אֵ֣ל גִּבּ֔וֹר אֲבִיעַ֖ד שַׂר־שָׁלֽוֹם׃

For a son is born (*qatal*) to us; a son is given (*qatal*) to us. And the
government shall be (*wayyiqtol*) upon his shoulders. And his name will
be called (*wayyiqtol*) Wonderful Counselor, Almighty God, Eternal
Father, Prince of Peace.

This idea worked well for the natural forms. However, it encountered
a challenge with the *wayyiqtol*: if indeed the *wayyiqtol* were imperfective
in aspect like the *yiqtol*, then one would expect it to be used primarily
of the future, as well. However, despite its proposed imperfective aspect,
grammarians still found it to be used primarily of the past.

To account for this anomaly, Ewald proposed that since each successive
action in a past tense narrative modifies the previous in a sense, they are
always seen as in progress, and therefore take the imperfective aspect of the
wayyiqtol (1870, 20):

> But as, in creation, through the continual force of motion and progress,
> that which has become, and is, constantly modifies its form for something
> new; so, in thought, the new advance which takes place (*and thus . . .,*
> *then . . .*) suddenly changes the action which, taken by itself absolutely,
> would stand in the perfect, into this tense, which indicates becoming—the
> imperfect.

And for the future usage of the *wᵉqatal*, he explained that just as the past
events might be seen as progressing, future events might be seen as advancing
toward "full and complete existence," and therefore take the perfective aspect
of the *wᵉqatal* (Ewald 1870, 22):

> As, therefore, in the combination previously explained, the flowing
> sequence of time or thought causes that which has been realized, and exists,
> to be regarded as passing over into new realization; so, in the present case,
> it has the effect of at once representing that which is advancing towards
> realization, as entering into full and complete existence.

In other words, the reason that past tense narrative is often expressed by a
single *qatal* followed thereafter by *wayyiqtols*, and future tense narrative by
a single *yiqtol* followed thereafter by *wᵉqatals*, is that the converted forms
in each case complement the preceding natural forms. Accordingly, Ewald
named the *wayyiqtol* "the relatively progressive imperfect" (1870/1891, 19),
and the *wᵉqatal* "the relatively progressive perfect" (1870/1891, 22).

S. R. Driver altered Ewald's explanation of the *wayyiqtol* slightly, proposing that the reason that the *wayyiqtol* was still used primarily of the past tense was that the action of each *wayyiqtol* could be viewed as "nascent," i.e. proceeding out of the previous action (1892, 71). Accordingly, S. R. Driver termed the *wayyiqtol* the "*waw consecutive*," proposing the translation, "and he proceeded to say" (1892, 72).

Thus, Ewald and S. R. Driver introduced the idea of temporal sequentiality in order to reconcile the usage of the converted forms with their aspect theory of the Hebrew verbal system.[18]

Observing, however, that there were still exceptions to this explanation, S. R. Driver added the idea of logical sequentiality to account for those instances "in which no temporal relation is implied at all" (Driver 1892, 82). However, he did not provide any explanation or justification for doing so as he and Ewald had for the idea of temporal sequence.

In summary, the aspect theory held two major advantages over the tense theory. First, it explained why each of the different verb forms could be used on occasion for different tenses. And second, it offered an improved explanation for the switch in meaning between the natural and the converted forms, namely the ability to indicate a temporal succession of events. Because of these advantages, the aspect theory quickly replaced the tense theory and became the dominant theory of the HVS through the end of the century. In fact, its adoption was so complete that the *qatal* and *yiqtol* have continued to be referred to as the "perfect" and "imperfect" forms well into recent times. By the beginning of the twentieth century, however, other discoveries had come into play that undermined these assumptions, and casted doubt on the place of the aspect theory as the comprehensive explanation of the HVS.

2.4 The Historical-Comparative Semitics Theory (1910[19]–1990[20])[21]

With the discovery of other Semitic languages, scholars began to look outside

---

18. Although there were elements of the idea of temporal sequentiality in preceding scholars like the relative tense theory (McFall 1982, 21–24), Ewald and S. R. Driver were the first to argue for it extensively, and to incorporate it full force into the theory of the HVS.

19. The date for the beginning of the Comparative Semitics theory is taken from the publication of Hans Bauer's study *Die tempora im Semitischen* (1910). Although work in Comparative Semitics had begun as early as the 1850s (McFall 1982, 87), Hans Bauer is generally recognized as the first major practitioner (McFall 1982, 93–94; Waltke and O'Connor 1990, 466–67; Endo 1996, 11–13; Hatav 1997, 14–15; Heller 2004, 6–7).

20. See the beginning date of the text linguistics theory for explanation.

21. For general discussion regarding the Comparative Semitics theory, see (Mettinger 1974, 70–73; Mcfall 1982, 87–175; Waltke and O'Connor 1990, 466–470; Smith 1991, 4–12; Endo 1996, 11–18; Cook 2002, 93–109; Heller 2004, 6–8).

of Hebrew to neighboring languages for the meaning of Hebrew words and syntax. This effort has produced many fruitful studies, particularly in the area of Hebrew morphology (Blau 2010, 1–5). In addition, these studies have demonstrated that the *wayyiqtol* is not a converted form of the *yiqtol*, as previously thought under the tense and aspect theories, but an older and separate verb form evidenced in other Semitic languages. And by implication, they have suggested that it is not the *waw* prefix that effects a transformation in meaning between the *yiqtol* and the *wayyiqtol*, but the different origins of these separate verb forms.

More will be said on this topic in **Section 3**. For the sake of the present survey, however, two of the early studies that contributed most significantly to this particular discovery were G. R. Driver's *Problems of the Hebrew verbal system* (1936), and Robert Hetzron's The evidence for perfect **y'aqtul* and jussive **yaqt'ul* in Proto-Semitic" (1969). Based on his knowledge of Comparative Semitics, G. R. Driver proposed that the jussive, the *wayyiqtol*, and the *yiqtol* came from three different origins: a jussive *yaqtul*, a preterite *yaqtul*, and an imperfect *yaqtulu* respectively (1936, 32). In further support of G. R. Driver's observations, Robert Hetzron proposed that the preterite *yaqtul* and the jussive *yaqtul* in Proto-Semitic could be distinguished by accentual differences, the *wayyiqtol* coming from *y'aqtul* and the jussive coming from *yaqt'ul* (Hetzron 1969).[22]

This discovery demonstrated that despite their apparent similarities in Hebrew morphology, the Hebrew verb forms should not be considered as a two-way cross classification, but as separate and independent verb forms, and that the attempt to derive the meaning of the *wayyiqtol* from the *yiqtol* in accordance with their Hebrew morphology was entirely mistaken. In addition, this discovery further redressed the uneasiness many had felt regarding the idea that the *waw* prefix could somehow alter the meaning of the verb forms (McFall 1982, 13). As a result, the Comparative Semitics theory discredited both the tense and aspect theories as comprehensive explanations of the HVS.

However, because Comparative Semitics was limited to discussions of the origins of the individual verb forms rather than the internal logic of the HVS, it has never offered a fully working theory of the HVS. In essence, one might say that Comparative Semitics broke the previous theories of the HVS, but was not able on its own to reassemble them. As a result, although the observations of Comparative Semitics were acknowledged as important and most grammarians

---

22. There is some debate on this point. See **Section 3.2** for details and **Sections 3.3** and **3.4** for summary and evaluation.

attempted to incorporate them into their grammars, the aspect theory remained the working theory of the HVS until the advent of text linguistics.

2.5 The Text Linguistics Theory (1990[23]–Present)[24]

The proposals of text linguistics were revolutionary, and its impact on the study of Hebrew has been incalculable. Whereas the tense and aspect theories assumed the need to reconstruct a logically consistent model of the HVS, text linguistics countered that actual usage and meaning may not necessarily follow such a model. And whereas the Comparative Semitics theory proposed that verbs should be understood in terms of their origins, text linguistics proposed that one has to understand language solely in terms of its usage.

These proposals come from two principles of modern philology. First, language is arbitrary. In other words, words and syntax do not always follow internal logic or historical developments. Therefore, one cannot limit the meaning of language by its origins (*contra* the Comparative Semitics theory), by its internal morphology (*contra* the tense and aspect theories), or by any other principle. Rather, and second, language is conventional. In other words, ultimately the only thing that matters in communication is what the speaker and the hearer have agreed that a word means. Now this does not mean that there is, therefore, no hope of understanding the Hebrew verbal system, much less language in general; rather, it simply means that the key to understanding the meaning of a word or verb form is to observe its conventional usage. Thus, whereas Comparative Semitics is diachronic (deriving the meaning of a word from its development *through* time), text linguistics is synchronic (looking solely at the conventional usage of a word *at that point* in time).

---

23. It is difficult to fix a specific end date for the Historical-Comparative Semitics theory, or a specific beginning date for the text linguistics theory. In reality, the work in Historical and Comparative Semitics has continued through the present, though not as well known as it was in the early 1900s. See for example, the works of Joshua Blau, John Huehnergard, and the late Anson Rainey listed in **Section 3.2**. In addition, Van der Merwe comments that work had begun in text linguistics as early as the late 1960s (Van der Merwe 1987, 161).

The matter under consideration here is the shift in the balance of priority from Comparative Semitics to text linguistics. Since the first major Hebrew grammar to reflect this shift was Waltke and O'Connor's *Introduction to Biblical Hebrew Syntax* (1990), the present survey will use its date of publication as the start of this period.

24. For general discussion regarding the text linguistics theory of the HVS, see (Niccacci 1990, 19; Van der Merwe 1994, 13–49; Endo 1996, 18–26; Cook 2002, 132–143; Heller 2004, 17–24).

On the one hand, text linguistics has freed Hebrew scholars from the need to limit the Hebrew verbal system to one single principle, whether tense or aspect. As Endo observes (1996, 26), "different approaches (i.e. aspectual, historical-comparative, and discourse approaches) may not be necessarily antithetical." In fact, rather than limiting verbal systems to tense or aspect, linguists in general now work with the TAM (Gentry 1998; Cook 2002; 2012) or even a TAMP (Harmelink 2011) rubric, recognizing that a verbal system may exhibit a combination of tense, aspect, modality, and pragmatics.[25]

On the other hand, most Hebrew scholars are now accustomed to noting "uses" of the different Hebrew verb forms based on a purely synchronic analysis of their observed usage in the OT, without explaining them in terms of either their internal morphology or their external origins (Gentry 1998, 8). As a result, many Hebrew grammars consist simply of long lists of different uses, without any justification besides the examples that appear to support them (Heller 2004, 18–19). Using this logic, many continue to affirm a modified form of the aspect theory, and may even admit insights from Comparative Semitics, but only where they agree with the conventional uses they observe.

With the advent of text linguistics, the assumption of the sequentiality of the *wayyiqtol* in particular has taken an interesting turn. Because Comparative Semitics had already challenged the aspect theory (which had incorporated the temporal and logical sequentiality of the *wayyiqtol* into the HVS), and because text linguistics technically freed Hebrew scholars from the need to postulate distinctions in meaning between the *qatal* and the *wayyiqtol* (which had necessitated the idea of temporal sequentiality under the aspect theory in the first place), one might expect that text linguistics would have dispensed with the idea of the sequentiality of the *wayyiqtol*, especially given S. R. Driver's seemingly ad hoc inclusion of logical sequentiality to explain the instances "in which no temporal relation is implied at all" (1892, 82). However, rather than dispensing with the idea of temporal sequentiality, it has thus far affirmed it based on the proposed conventional usage of the *wayyiqtol* within OT narrative (Waltke and O'Connor 1990, 547–551). In other words, they argue that since the great majority of *wayyiqtols* in the OT appear to exhibit temporal sequentiality, this must be a distinctive "use" of the *wayyiqtol* within the HVS (Li 1999).

---

25. For a listing of further examples, see Cook's discussion (2002, 144–162).

2.6 *Summary*

In summary, the study of the Hebrew verbal system has undergone several major periods: the tense theory, the aspect theory, the Comparative Semitics theory, and the text linguistics, theory. Throughout the history of interpretation, the main question has been the relationship of the converted forms (the *wayyiqtol* and the *wᵉqatal*) to the natural forms (the *qatal* and the *yiqtol*). The tense system proposed that the *waw* prefix of the *wayyiqtol* and the *wᵉqatal* converted the tense of these verb forms to match the opposing tense of the natural forms. The aspect theory asserted that the converted forms retained the aspect of the corresponding natural forms, but were nonetheless used with the opposing natural forms to communicate temporal or logical sequence due to their ability to complement the action of the natural forms. The Comparative Semitics theory countered that the *wayyiqtol* and *yiqtol* verb forms come from entirely different origins, and therefore are completely unrelated in meaning. And the text linguistics theory countered all of the above, proposing that the meanings of the verb forms should not be defined by either their origins or their internal logical consistency, but by conventional usage. As a result, the majority of Hebrew scholarship today operates under the assumptions of the text linguistics theory, focusing solely (or at least primarily) on conventional usage.

And regarding the temporal sequentiality of the *wayyiqtol*, this survey demonstrates three things: first, Ewald and S. R. Driver introduced the temporal sequentiality of the *wayyiqtol* in order to reconcile the past usage of the *wayyiqtol* with their aspect theory of the HVS; second, S. R. Driver added the idea of logical sequentiality to account for the instances "in which no temporal relation is implied at all" (Driver 1892, 82), but did not include any further reasoning for doing so; and third, since the particular aspect theory of the HVS that Ewald and S. R. Driver proposed has been superseded by Comparative Semitics and text linguistics, the primary data now supporting the proposed temporal and logical sequentiality of the *wayyiqtol* is its assumed usage in the OT under the text linguistics theory.

3. The Origins of the *Wayyiqtol*

Having explored the various theories of the HVS, the present chapter will now consider the diachronic evidence from Historical and Comparative Semitics for the origins of the Hebrew *wayyiqtol*. As mentioned in the introduction, this will provide the crucial control of diachronic analysis that has been neglected in many recent studies, and provide a more solid basis for the conclusions to be reached regarding the meaning of the *wayyiqtol*.

3.1 *Introduction*

As mentioned above, there is a general agreement that the original Proto-Semitic form of the *wayyiqtol* was separate from that of the *yiqtol*, but scholars still differ on whether it was separate from that of the jussive verb form, homonymous with that of the jussive verb form, or the same verb form altogether in Proto-Semitic. In addition, there is even less agreement on what sort of oppositions might have existed between these and other potential verb forms of the Proto-Semitic verbal system. And lastly, there is little explanation for how the *wayyiqol* might have come to assume its present place in the HVS.

One of the reasons for this situation is undoubtedly the paucity of data that Comparative Semitics has had to work with in comparison with the other sciences. As Thomas O. Lambdin purportedly remarked to his students, "I don't know if you've noticed it, but we work with no data in this field" (Huehnergard 1987, ix). Another reason may be the shift away from diachronic studies to synchronic studies under the influence of the text linguistics theory.

Whatever the case, scholars are beginning to understand the importance of diachronic analysis again, bringing about a renewed emphasis on Comparative Semitics. While there is no doubt that meaning is indeed conventional (hence the need for synchronic analysis), convention is rarely without reason, and therefore if a proposed meaning is correct, then it should be possible to validate that proposed meaning in terms of its origins.

For example, if a foreigner were to ask an American tourist what the word "cheese" means when taking a picture, one could simply reply, "That's what we say when we want someone to smile." This reply may be correct, but it is hardly sufficient to satisfy one's curiosity, or to explain why the word "cheese" was chosen rather than some other one. With a little more thought, however, one might note that the long *e* sound causes a person to widen their smile and show their teeth (as opposed to the word "choose"). The *s* at the end ensures that one's mouth remains open for the longest time possible (as opposed to the words "cheap" or "chief"). And finally, the initial *ch* ensures that people will not be caught with their mouth closed if the picture is snapped too early (as opposed to the words "peas" or "bees"). This additional information not only satisfies the foreigner's curiosity, but also confirms to him the accuracy of the explanation.

In a similar manner, it is possible to assert that the *wayyiqtol* functions as the backbone of Hebrew narrative,[26] or that the *wayyiqtol* is sequential on the basis of synchronic analysis. However, if these explanations are correct, then it ought to be possible to demonstrate the derivation of these meanings by means of diachronic analysis, as well. Now whether one will ever be fully able to demonstrate this derivation is another question due to the limited data and lack of native speakers available today. However, even where a full explanation is not possible due to limitations of data, a correct explanation ought to at least align within the parameters of what is known.

In recognition of this importance, recent studies in linguistics have reintroduced a Saussurean term recognizing the interrelationship of diachronic and synchronic analysis called panchronic analysis. As Sadler explains (2007, 33),

> In the last decade or so, more scholars have called attention to the relevance of grammaticization in the understanding of synchronic linguistic behavior (e.g. Heine et al. 1991; Matsumoto 1998; Suzuki 1998; Ohori 1998; Horie 1998). These studies document evidence that synchronic phenomena or syntactic variation can be accounted for by examining diachronic processes and that synchrony and diachrony are interrelated. The interrelated nature of synchrony and diachrony is thematized in Heine et al. (1991, 258), who call it PANCHRONY, referring to "phenomena exhibiting simultaneously a synchronic-psychological and a diachronic relation."

Several recent Hebrew scholars, as well, have begun to link the synchronic and diachronic analysis of the *wayyiqtol*;[27] however, a full accounting for the origins of the *wayyiqtol*, and the various discussions surrounding it, has yet to be made.

The present section seeks to lay the groundwork for a panchronic analysis by exploring anew the origins of the *wayyiqtol*. To do so, it will first trace the discussion to date on the origins of the *wayyiqtol*. Second, it will summarize the current theories regarding the origin of the *wayyiqtol* listing the arguments for and against them. And third, it will evaluate the strengths and weaknesses of these various theories based on the available evidence at this time.

*Note: The following material is included for the sake of comprehensiveness to evidence the conclusions stated in **Section 3.4**. However, due to the technical nature and specialized vocabulary of the following, non-Hebraists are welcome to skip ahead to **Section 3.3** or **3.4**.*

26. For the common phrase "backbone of Hebrew narrative," see Murphy's *Pocket Dictionary for the Study of Biblical Hebrew* (2003).

27. See for example Cook (2002, 193–94) and Alexander Andrason (2011). Andrason applies the same methodology to the *yiqtol*, as well (2010).

3.2 Literature[28]

3.2.1 Bauer 1910—*Die tempora im Semitischen: Ihre entstehung und ihre ausgestaltung in den einzelsprachen*

Bauer is commonly recognized as the first person to offer a full critique of the HVS based on the evidence of Comparative and Historical Semitics. He proposed that the HVS had originally consisted of one timeless verb form, *yaqtul*, which also functioned as the jussive, imperative, and the infinitive (G. R. Driver 1936, 9–10), while the long form *yaqtulu* arose second within the relative clause (G. R. Driver 1936, 10), and the suffixed conjugation arose last from the affixing of pronominal elements to the nominal forms (G. R. Driver 1936, 10–11). In Bauer's analysis, the *yaqtulu* form largely took over the present and future tenses in Proto-Semitic, leaving the *yaqtul* along

---

28. Please note that the following discussion is not intended to endorse any specific theory over another, but simply to present the arguments advanced thus far for and against the various theories for the origins of the *wayyiqtol*. Evaluation of these discussions will be presented in **Section 3.3** and summarized in **Section 3.4**.

with its other functions as primarily a past tense verb form. In addition, the *qatal* encroached on the past tense function of the *yaqtul* in BH, leaving it only the jussive, infinitive, and the imperative functions. However, it still retained a special usage as the past tense verb form for Hebrew narrative, i.e. the *wayyiqtol*.[29]

3.2.2 G. R. Driver 1936—*Problems of the Hebrew verbal system*

In response to Bauer's hypothesis, G. R. Driver posited that the original verb forms included *ya'qtul,* a narrative tense, *yaqtu'l* or *ya'qtulu,* a future tense, and *yaqtul* (no stress given), the jussive mood (G. R. Driver 1936, 26–31, 112–124). Thus, he agreed with Bauer that the basic origins of the *wayyiqtol* and *yiqtol* forms were separate, but posited that the origins of the jussive form were separate, as well (though often indistinguishable), from the narrative tense.[30]

As evidence for the distinction between the *yiqtol* and *wayyiqtol,* G. R. Driver postulated that the shorter form of the *wayyiqtol* with penultimate stress evidenced by the weak verb forms with the accent on the first syllable (e.g. *wayyi'bn*), were actually the original form, and go back to the short form *ya'qtul* (G. R. Driver 1936, 89–91).[31] Thus, he departed from his father S. R. Driver's proposal that the *wayyiqtol* was a conversion of the *yiqtol* imperfect, asserting instead that the long form of the *wayyiqtol* was a later analogical assimilation to the *yiqtol* internal to Hebrew (G. R. Driver 1936, 85–86).

3.2.3 Moran 1960—Early Canaanite *yaqtula*

In 1960, William Moran, a giant in the study of the Amarna letters, entered the discussion from his expertise on the Old Canaanite. Although he himself did not comment on the *wayyiqtol* directly, he laid the basis for Rainey's discovery of the *yaqtul* in the Amarna letters (to be discussed below).

Concerning the *yaqtula,* Bauer had already posited the existence of the *yaqtula* verb form as a later cohortative form based on its presence in Ugaritic, but to date no other evidence for this verb form had been found, and even the *yaqtula* of Ugaritic was seemingly random in its distribution (Moran 1960, 1). Moran, however, suggested that evidence for this *yaqtula* verb form might be found in the Amarna letters.

---

29. "*[Y]aqtul* after as before remained the tense proper to narration" (G. R. Driver 1936, 14).

30. G. R. Driver remarks that it was "in many cases in form indistinguishable from or confused with the preterite and imperfect tenses." (G. R. Driver 1936, 124).

31. More will be said on this under the analysis of Robert Hetzron's article in **Section 3.2.3**.

Until the time of his writing, the cases of *yaqtula* in the Amarna letters had been considered Akkadian ventives.[32] However, Moran demonstrated that roughly two-thirds of these *yaqtula* verb forms express either wish or purpose (1960, 2–7). With this observation, he asserted that this coherence in usage cannot be explained by the Akkadian ventive (Moran 1960, 8–12), but matches instead the usage of the Hebrew jussive (Moran 1960, 15). Moran suggested from this that the *–a* may evidence a true *yaqtula* verb form exhibiting a cohortative meaning, rather than the Akkadian ventive as had been previously supposed.

Although this analysis added weight to Bauer's theory, it is important to note that Moran himself did not offer his full support in this article to Bauer. In addition, it is curious to note that he completely ignored G. R. Driver's study. Thus, although his observations offered evidence potentially in favor of Bauer's theory, he appears to have acted more as an independent investigator, simply offering his expert opinion from his own observations on the Amarna letters.

3.2.4 Hetzron 1969—The evidence for perfect **y'aqtul* and jussive **yaqt'ul* in Proto-Semitic

In *Problems of the Hebrew Verbal System*, G. R. Driver had suggested that there were three separate Proto-Semitic origins for the *wayyiqtol*, jussive, and the *yiqtol* verb forms, corresponding to their Proto-Semitic counterparts as follows:

Hebrew	Proto-Semitic
wayyiqtol	ya'qtul
yiqtol	yaqtu'l or ya'qtulu
jussive	yaqtul

However, he did not propose any accentual differences for the last of these three Proto-Semitic forms. This left the jussive form of Proto-Semitic often "indistinguishable" from the narrative tense (G. R. Driver 1936, 123).

Building on G. R. Driver's theory, Hetzron affirmed the separate origins of the *wayyiqtol*, *yiqtol*, and jussive forms in Proto-Semitic, but countered that the jussive form and the narrative form of Proto-Semitic could be distinguished from each other by stress. In his reconstruction, the three Proto-Semitic forms are as follows (Hetzron 1969, 2):

---

32. The Akkadian ventive is a morpheme that was added to the end of finite verbs in Akkadian to indicate motion in the direction of the speaker or the addressee. See Huehnergard (2011, 133–34).

Hebrew	Proto-Semitic
wayyiqtol	*y'aqtul*
yiqtol	*yaqt'ulu*
jussive	*yaqt'ul*

Regarding the origins of these forms, Hetzron proposed that the *wayyiqtol* and the jussive forms were the original, and that the future tense *yaqt'ulu* likely derived from the jussive (though this is not the main point of his article and does not enter into his evidence) (1969, 2).

To argue this proposal, Hetzron deduces evidence from Akkadian, Ge'ez (also referred to as Ethiopic), and Hebrew, and coordinates his findings with classical Arabic. For Akkadian, Hetzron postulates an early, Proto-Akkadian opposition between the optative *liprus* (equivalent of the jussive *yaqt'ul*), and the perfect *iprus*, where the derivation of *liprus* from the previous merger of *lu + iprus* ("may he separate") contrasts with the phrase *lu iprus* ("he separated indeed") where the words remained separate. As Hetzron argues, one possible reason that the optative particle contracted with *lu* into *liprus*, whereas the asseverative *lu* and *iprus* ("he separated indeed") remained uncontracted in Proto-Akkadian, could be that the optative *liprus* ("may he separate") was formed from *lu + ipr'us* with final stress, allowing for the contraction of the initial vowel with *lu*, while phrases like *lu iprus* ("he separated indeed"), were formed from *lu + 'iprus* with initial stress, preventing the contraction of the initial vowel.

For Ge'ez, Hetzron argues from the peculiar form of the perfect conjugation *yebe* from the verb *bhl*. Normal explanations have proposed that this is simply an irregular form, and that the *h* and *l* simply dropped off the word. Hetzron, however, counters that there is no known process that would cause the *h* and the *l* to drop off like this, and therefore there must be a better explanation for the *y*. He proposes instead that the prefixed *y–* is a remnant form of an old prefix perfect in Ge'ez, and that the fronted stress on the fictitious construction **yebeluh* is likely what caused both the *h* to drop off, and possibly even the *l* to "palatize" to *y*, and then to monophthongize with *ey>e*.

For Hebrew, Hetzron attempts to demonstrate that the short forms of the *wayyiqtol* had to have come from a different origin than the short form of the jussive. As he states, "We are trying to prove here that the prefix-forms used after *waw* conversive are neither descriptively nor historically identical with the jussive" (Hetzron 1969, 9). He argues these points in three steps:

(1) Between the prefix and the suffix forms, the prefix forms must have come first. This is evident from the fact that the *wᵊqatal* forms represent both the imperfect and the jussive without distinction between the two, and therefore must have been a later development.

(2) The *wayyiqtol* has nothing to do with sequentiality, and is merely the "sentence-initial" perfect. Likewise, the *way-* prefix has nothing to do with the *waw* conjunction. Hetzron suggests that it is rather more likely a shortened form of *wayhi* in accord with Michaelis' theory in 1745.

(3) "The prefix-forms used after waw conversive are not jussive or imperfect, but a survival of the old prefix-perfect that was distinguished from the jussive by stress" (Hetzron 1969, 10).

The latter is the point that he takes up in this article. As Hetzron demonstrates, there is a difference in the stress and vocalization between the *wayyiqtol*, *yiqtol*, and jussive forms of II-ו/י verbs (Hetzron 1969, 9–11):

Function	Form
yiqtol	יָשִׂים
jussive	יָשֵׂם
wayyiqtol	וַיָּשֶׂם

Similarly, the *qal* of a I-ו/י verb shows a difference between the *wayyiqtol* form and the other two forms:

Function	Form
yiqtol	יֵרֵד
jussive	יֵרֵד
wayyiqtol	וַיֵּרֶד

Based on these differences, Hetzron proposed that "the stress-opposition between the prefix-perfect and the jussive is genuine, i.e., Proto-Semitic" (1969, 13). To reinforce this explanation, Hetzron uses the process of elimination to demonstrate that no other theories can explain these differences. This includes S. R. Driver's theory of the "retrocession of the tone" due to the heavy *way* prefix (Hetzron 1969, 10–11), Bauer and Leander's postulate of an archaism in the stress (Hetzron 1969, 11), and the phenomenon of *nasig aḥor* (Hetzron 1969, 12). And finally, Hetzron notes that most exceptions to this difference can be explained in terms of syllable structure (1969, 16).

And lastly for Arabic, Hetzron speculates that the use of the negative particle *lam* used to negate the perfect may be related to the separate origins of the perfect and the jussive in Arabic, as well. However, Hetzron admits that this is offered only as possible confirmatory evidence.

Regarding the significance of this evidence, it is important to note, that the weight of Hetzron's evidence lies not in any one language, but in the combination of the three. Regarding the use of this evidence, Hetzron himself comments (1969, 3),

> If we had the testimony of one language only, it would be much less conclusive. The oppositions to be presented below could also have other historical explanations, and attributing them to stress, further claiming that this stress is not a secondary development but an archaism, would be merely a piece of guesswork, an hypothesis as good as any other. Yet when we have the converging evidence of three languages, each belonging to another branch of Semitic and thus representing a very wide range, we cannot but accept that the present hypothesis is relatively the best.

3.2.5 Finley 1981—The *WAW*-consecutive with "imperfect" in biblical Hebrew: Theoretical studies and its use in Amos

Finley affirmed the basic proposal of Hetzron, Moran, and Bauer that the *wayyiqtol* had a separate origin from the ordinary imperfect (1981, 242). In fact, he added an additional evidence in favor of this proposal which he develops in this article, i.e. that the prefix form without the *waw* prefix, but otherwise identical in form to the *wayyiqtol*, can be found in older Hebrew poetry exhibiting a past tense usage (e.g. Ex 15; Ps 8; Am 2:9–12).[33] This further redressed the notions of the former tense and aspect theories that the *waw* of the *wayyiqtol* somehow converted the meaning of the *yiqtol*, and affirmed the idea that it was the separate origins of these verb forms that had given rise to their differences in meaning. He states the important principle, as well, hereto assumed: "Divergence of form would lend support to a theory of divergence of function" (Finley 1981, 242).

Beyond this point, Finley follows Bauer, proposing that the *yaqtul* had originally functioned as a perfect participle, and *qatala* as a present participle, which later reversed in function (1981, 243). Against Hetzron, he limits the distinctions between the *yaqtul* and *yaqtulu* verb forms to consonants and vowels (excluding stress) (1981, 246). And lastly, he follows Moran's work in proposing three main verb forms for Old Canaanite: the *yaqtul*, *yaqtulu*, and *yaqtula* verb forms (1981, 245).

---

33. "Finally, a form of the imperfect without the conjunction is used in early Hebrew poetry in contexts with no imperfect functions associated with it" (Finley 1981, 242).

3.2.6 Revell 1984—Stress and the *WAW* "consecutive" in biblical Hebrew

In 1984, Revell countered Hetzron's assertion that the accentual differences between the *wayyiqtol, yiqtol,* and jussive forms reflect separate Proto-Semitic origins for these verb forms. To do so, he argued that the differences between the Hebrew weak verb forms that Hetzron identifies can be explained in terms of the Masoretic sound rules, rather than Proto-Semitic vestiges. As Revell states, "The stress patterns of MT clearly reflect a prior stage at which words ending in vowels had penultimate stress, while those ending in consonants had final stress. The pattern is much too regular, even in *waw* consecutive forms, to permit the argument that they did not conform to it" (1984, 444).

3.2.7 Rainey 1986—The ancient Hebrew prefix conjugation in the light of Amarnah Canaanite

Building on the work of Moran, his predecessor in the Amarna letters, Rainey proposed an entire West Semitic verbal system. This verbal system contained a short form, a long form, and a suffixed *nun* form, each with an indicative form and an injunctive form distinguished by their final vowel (either −*u* or −*a*). This proposal falls neatly into a two-way cross-section as follows:

Indicative	Injunctive
preterite *yaqtul*	jussive *yaqtul*
imperfect *yaqtulu*	volitive *yaqtula*
energic *yaqtuluna*	energic *yaqtulana*

As a result, Rainey opposes Hetzron's argument, concluding that both the *wayyiqtol* and the jussive came from fully homonymous *yaqtul* forms, undifferentiated by accent. Rainey opposes Hetzron on his analysis of the *waw* prefix, as well, siding with Revell in his assessment that the peculiar form is simply a result of gemination and lengthening internal to the Hebrew language (Rainey 1986, 6). In fact, he omits Hetzron's study entirely from his bibliography, including Finley and Revell's studies instead.

Regarding the origins of the jussive form, Rainey suggests with Bergsträsser that the jussive was probably a development from the imperative (1986, 5). And regarding the special narrative usage of the *wayyiqtol,* he suggests that as the suffix conjugation was introduced, the *wayyiqtol* became more and more restricted, being used only rarely in poetry, and becoming the narrative tense in Hebrew narrative.[34]

---

34. "In prose the *yaqtul* has been restricted to the role of a narrative past tense expressing a sequence of actions" (Rainey 1986, 5).

Regarding methodology, Rainey identifies the key used by both he and Hetzron in distinguishing the origins of the *wayyiqtol* and the *yiqtol* based on differences in the weak verbs (1986, 5):

> The method adopted here for defining the syntactic functions of the biblical Hebrew prefix conjugation is that employed by H. J. Polotsky (1965: 4–6) for Classical Egyptian, viz. the use of variants in the weak verbs as a key for establishing semantic categories. The known morphological distinctions, especially those between the long and short forms of second and third weak roots, have their respective syntagmas. Once these are defined in terms of semantic function, they become the criteria for defining strong verb forms which, in biblical Hebrew, have lost their outward differences that had distinguished the syntactic functions in the older Canaanite dialects.

Rainey's major contribution in his estimate, though, is the discovery of the significance of the prefixed forms with and without the *nun*. He argues that "the imperfects with energic *nun* before the suffix are survivals of the indicative energic with *–un(n)a* found in the Canaanite of the Amarnah letters," noting that Blau reached the same conclusion independently in 1978 (Rainey 1986, 11; citing Blau 1978).

3.2.8 Greenstein 1988—On the prefixed preterite in biblical Hebrew

Rainey's 1986 article on the Ancient Hebrew verbal system prompted a panel discussion at the 1987 National Association of Professors of Hebrew meeting. The papers from the panelists were subsequently revised and published together in the 1987 issue of *Hebrew Studies*. The first of these articles was Greenstein's "On the prefixed preterite in biblical Hebrew" (Greenstein 1988).

On the one hand, Greenstein praises Rainey's proposal that there were two homonymous *yaqtul* verb forms, one a preterite form and one a jussive (Greenstein 1988, 7), and lists additional evidences for this proposal. First, he notes that it could explain certain anomalies where a *yiqtol* in Hebrew follows the word אז (e.g. Ex 15:1), suggesting that these might actually be cases of the *yaqtul* form rather than the *yaqtulu* form (Greenstein 1988, 8). Second, he notes that it explains why the *wayyiqtol* would otherwise appear to be built on the jussive form, a phenomenon that does not make sense apart from the existence of a homonymous preterite *yaqtul* (Greenstein 1988, 8–9). And third, regarding Rainey's specific proposal of an energic *nun* form for the jussive and indicative categories, he notes that this could explain why the *wayyiqtol* form never takes the energic *nun* pronominal suffixes in Hebrew (Greenstein 1988, 10; cf. Ex 19:19 with 1 Sm 7:9).

On the other hand, Greenstein offers several critiques. First, he raises doubt whether there is really a semantic difference between the energic *nun* pronominal suffixes and the normal pronominal suffixes. For example, in Exodus 15:2, he notes that וְאַנְוֵהוּ "is parallel to and for all intents and purposes of the same tense and mood as וַאֲרֹמְמֶנְהוּ" (Greenstein 1988, 12). Second, Greenstein notes, "The very existence of a *yaqtul* preterite in Ugaritic is open to serious doubt" (Greenstein 1988, 13). Third, Greenstein notes that in addition to prefixed verb forms with past tense meaning, there are also apparently suffixed verb forms with future tense meaning, indicating that the problem of one form being used for the other tense is not unique to the prefixed forms (Greenstein 1988, 14). In other words, while Rainey's theory provides an elegant solution to the prefixed forms being used on occasion for the past tense, one should question whether there might be a greater underlying issue that might explain the usage of both the prefixed forms and the suffixed forms for the opposite tense.

Based on this observation, Greenstein offers his own theory that the tense of the verbs is determined not by the forms, but by the "*contrast or opposition of the forms,*" in the context of the sentence (Greenstein 1988, 14). He concludes this analysis with a quote from McFall (Greenstein 1988, 16; citing McFall 1982, 70): "Hebrew does not have any means of distinguishing between punctual, durative, iterative, habitual, and other aspectual distinctions morphologically." Whether this applies to tense, as well, though, Greenstein does not argue.

3.2.9 Huehnergard 1988—The early Hebrew prefix-conjugations

Huehnergard lists several points of disagreement with Rainey. First, Huehnergard suggests that it would be better to view the two homonymous *yaqtul* verb forms proposed by Rainey as a single verb form with two functions, i.e. both a preterite and a jussive function (Huehnergard 1988, 20).

Second, he suggests that Rainey overstates the matter in claiming that the Hebrew verbal system consisted entirely of tenses rather than aspect, a claim which he grants was likely made to counterbalance the prevalence of the widespread assumptions of the aspect theory. Instead, he suggests that a more balanced approach would be to recognize that "in *most* languages the expression of these two categories is intertwined throughout the verbal system, with some forms perhaps connoting primarily aspect and others primarily tense" (Huehnergard 1988, 20–21).

Third, he suggests that rather than *yaqtulu* being marked for the indicative mode alone, that it too may have functioned for both modes. This would make *yaqtul* and *yaqtulu* the two primary verb forms of Proto-

Semitic, with *yaqtul* as the "perfective or punctional form, temporally a specific past," and *yaqtulu* the "imperfective or durative form, temporally a future" (Huehnergard 1988, 22). Huehnergard bases this proposal on the apparent modal function of the *yaqtulu* equivalents in the apodoses of the casuistic laws of the Mosaic law and the Laws of Hammurabi (Huehnergard 1988, 22).

And finally, Huehnergard mentions the alternative view of Kuryłowicz which merits consideration that both the perfective *yatul* and imperfective *yaqtulu* were primary forms in Proto-Semitic (Kuryłowicz 1973), along with a response by Andras Hamori (1973).

3.2.10 Zevit 1988—Talking funny in biblical Henglish and solving a problem of the *yaqtul* past tense

Zevit's disagreement with Rainey is twofold. First, he argues that the Hebrew verbal system marks tense not aspect, and that the terms "perfect" and "imperfect" ought to be discarded altogether with reference to the prefixed and suffixed conjugations.[35] And second, Zevit suggests that the *yaqtul* past and the *yaqtul* present-future in BH had to be distinguishable somehow, and suggests that this distinguishing feature must have been accent.[36]

And lastly, regarding the *waw* prefix of the *wayyiqtol*, Zevit comments that since "the *yaqtul* form occurs regularly in poetry without this conjunction," "[i]ts attestation both with and without the *waw* is significant in that it enables us to discount the *waw* as marking the time reference of the following verb" (Zevit 1988, 27).

3.2.11 Rainey 1988—Further remarks on the Hebrew verbal system

In the same issue, Rainey delivers several answers to Greenstein's, Huehnergard's, and Zevit's critiques. First, Rainey declines Greenstein's offer of additional proof in the use of the prefix conjugation with אז, noting that only 1 Kings 8:1 occurs in the short form which would be equivalent to the *yaqtul* (Rainey 1988, 35). Second, Rainey responds to Greenstein's example of two different verbs in Exodus 15:2, one without the energic *nun* and one with the energic *nun*, by suggesting that both should be understood as injunctive, falling on the right hand side of his paradigm, and therefore Greenstein's analysis is inapplicable to the issue of the preterite *yaqtul* (Rainey 1988, 36). Third, Rainey counters Zevit's remarks regarding tense by noting that the past

35. "The verbal system of biblical Hebrew does not mark aspect. It does not indicate whether an action is complete or incomplete; hence the terms 'perfect' and 'imperfect,' as they are usually employed in discussions of Hebrew, are simply misapplied and misleading (cf. Blau 1971, 24–26)" (Zevit 1988, 26).

36. "The difference between *yaqtul* past and *yaqtul* present-future in biblical Hebrew seems to have been in the accent" (Zevit 1988, 28).

durative action for the *yaqtulu* had been demonstrated by Moran beyond all doubt (Rainey 1988, 36).[37] And fourth, in response to Greenstein's doubts that the *yaqtul* preterite can be definitively identified in Ugaritic, Rainey reexamines Greenstein's examples to demonstrate further evidence for the six forms of his verbal system in Ugaritic (Rainey 1988, 37).

And finally, Rainey provides a helpful summary of the place and significance of his and others' research in the discovery of the Semitic verbal system as follows (Rainey 1988, 41):

> If scholars had given proper attention to the discoveries of Lambert (1903) and Bauer (1912) and to the summary views of Beer (1914, 1916), and Bergsträsser (1929), they could have arrived at a proper understanding of the Hebrew verbal system. The syntactical analysis of the Byblos El-Amarna letters by W. L. Moran (1950, 1951, 1960) demonstrated that Canaanite was the antecedent of biblical Hebrew. The addition to Moran's verbal system, the demonstration of the preterite (Rainey 1971, 1975a), rounded out the picture.

3.2.12 Rainey 1990—The prefix conjugation patterns of early Northwest Semitic

In this article, Rainey does not produce any new arguments. However, he does provide a valuable elucidation of the process of study for the Amarna letters used in his 1986 and 1988 proposals (Rainey 1990, 407):

> It must be clearly stated for the outsider that almost no true Canaanite verb forms appear in these texts. The conjugation patterns are only discernible to the extent that the scribes applied West Semitic prefixes and suffixes to a stem taken from the set of forms available for a particular Akkadian verb. Most of these West Semitic morphemes were noted by scholars at the turn of the century. However, they seldom penetrated behind the Akkadian screen to the real West Semitic thought processes at work.

3.2.13 Rainey 1991–1993—Is there really a *yaqtula* conjugation pattern in the Canaanite Amarna tablets?

In a surprising article, Rainey revisited the conclusions of his mentor Moran on the issue of the Canaanite *yaqtula*. Contrary to Moran's conclusions (1960), Rainey demonstrated that all of the cases of the *–a* suffix in the Amarna letters can indeed be explained as Akkadian ventives, rather than needing to be explained as the jussive *yaqtula* (Rainey 1991–1993, 115).

---

37. Note that this is only a problem for those who would argue that the HVS marks tense only. Zevit's original remarks seem to imply that there might be room for Hebrew to mark aspect within a tense system (Zevit 1988, 26)

To counterbalance this evidence, however, Rainey asserts that the jussive *yaqtula* is still evident in the Arabic subjunctive and the Hebrew cohortative (Rainey 1991–1993, 116). In addition, he suggests that the reason that the Canaanite scribes may have used the Akkadian ventive so frequently in contexts with a jussive meaning may have been precisely "*because it was homophonous* with a *yaqtula* in their native tongue (Rainey 1991–1993, 116).

3.2.14 Goerwitz 1992—The accentuation of the Hebrew jussive and preterite

In 1992, Goerwitz added a second attempt to Revell's (1984) to refute Hetzron's proposals (1969) of a separate jussive *yaqtul* and preterite *yaqtul* form differentiated by stress. Against Hetzron's proposal that the jussive form had come from a Proto-Semitic *yaqtu'l*, Goerwitz countered, "The only way to account for the complete disappearance of the final radical in III-ו/י jussives is to posit that, in addition to being endingless, the final syllable was also unstressed" (Goerwitz 1992, 199). And in answer to Hetzron's evidence from the observation that the *wayyiqtol* and jussive forms of II-ו/י verbs in Hebrew often have different vowels, Goerwitz proposes that rather than the penultimate stress on these verb forms being original, there had to have been both a shift in stress towards the ultimate, followed by a retraction of stress on certain *wayyiqtol* forms back towards the penultimate (Goerwitz 1992, 202). On this basis, Goerwitz asserts that both the jussive and the preterite had to have come from a penultimate stress form, i.e. the *ya'qtul*, making them identical in Proto-Semitic.

3.2.15 Sasson 1997—Some observations on the use and original purpose of the *waw* consecutive in old Aramaic and biblical Hebrew

In 1997, Sasson published an article attempting to explain the usage of the *wayyiqtol* for past tense Hebrew narrative. In his article, Sasson proposed that the reason the *wayyiqtol* came to be used for past tense narrative in Hebrew was because of its association in Old Aramaic with epic and war related texts (Sasson 1997, 117). The evidence for this suggestion comes from the observation that the Zakkur and Tell Dan inscriptions are the only Old Aramaic texts known to include the equivalent of the *wayyiqtol* verb forms (Sasson 1997, 112–14). Sasson's outdated proposals of the imperfect aspect of the *wayyiqtol* had to be corrected by Muraoka and Roglund (Muraoka and Roglund 1998), but his suggestion still merits consideration.

3.2.16 Rainey 2003—The *yaqtul* preterite in Northwest Semitic

In his final article, Rainey reexamined the evidence in the Northwest Semitic languages for the preterite *yaqtul*. In the process, he produced an impressive catalogue of evidence for a preterite *yaqtul* from the Old Canaanite, Ugaritic, Hebrew, Moabite, Old Byblian, and Southern Old Aramaic (i.e. the Zakkur and Tel Dan inscriptions).

3.2.17 Blau 2010—Phonology and morphology of biblical Hebrew

In his masterpiece on the phonology and morphology of BH (2010), Blau makes several important proposals regarding the *wayyiqtol*. First, Blau proposes that the *way-* prefix of the *wayyiqtol* is the same as the conjunctive *waw* (*contra* Hetzron 1969), the *pathach* being due to the penultimate accent of the *wayyiqtol* forms, and the doubling of the prefix being due to pretonic gemination (2010, 152). In support of this theory, Blau notes the parallel occurrence of the vowel under the conjunctive *waw* in the phrase יוֹמָם וְלַיְלָה (e.g. Jo 1:8), where the penultimate accent on the word לַיְלָה causes the usual *shewa* under the conjunctive *waw* to lengthen to a *qamets* (2010, 152).

Second, Blau demonstrates that in close context, the *qatal* and the *wayyiqtol* forms (as well as the *yiqtol* and *wᵉqatal* forms) are often completely interchangeable in meaning. As examples, he lists Genesis 1:27 and Leviticus 26:33, reproduced below (Blau 2010, 190):

GENESIS 1:27

וַיִּבְרָא אֱלֹהִים | אֶת־הָאָדָם בְּצַלְמוֹ בְּצֶלֶם אֱלֹהִים בָּרָא אֹתוֹ זָכָר
וּנְקֵבָה בָּרָא אֹתָם:

So God created (*wayyiqtol*) the man in his image. In the image of God he created (*qatal*) him. Male and female he created (*qatal*) them.

LEVITICUS 26:33

וְאֶתְכֶם אֱזָרֶה בַגּוֹיִם וַהֲרִיקֹתִי אַחֲרֵיכֶם חָרֶב וְהָיְתָה אַרְצְכֶם שְׁמָמָה
וְעָרֵיכֶם יִהְיוּ חָרְבָּה:

I will scatter (*yiqtol*) you among the gentiles, and I will unsheathe (*wᵉqatal*) after you the sword. Your land will become (*wᵉqatal*) desolate, and your cities will be (*yiqtol*) a waste.

Third, based on these observations, Blau proposes that the difference between the *qatal* and the *wayyiqtol* was simply one of word order, rather than aspect, sequentiality, or other distinction (Blau 2010, 190): for the normal order of Verb, Subject, Object (VSO) where the *waw* conjunction is desired, one would use the *wayyiqtol*; however, where the *waw* conjunction was not desired, e.g. when fronting either the subject or the object (SVO or OVS), then one would use the *qatal*. Blau explained this same principle in his earlier Hebrew grammar, as well: "The tenses with consecutive *waw* (*wayyqtl, weqtl*) are used whenever the syntactic environment permits the use of *waw copulative*; otherwise the simple tenses (*qtl, yqtl*)" (1976, 86).

And finally, Blau holds that the *wayyiqtol* derives from the *yaqtul* verb form (Blau 2010, 195), and proposes with Bauer and Bergsträsser that this *yaqtul* verb form originally carried both the jussive and the preterite meaning in Proto-Semitic (Blau 2010, 195).

3.2.18 Summary

Collating the various arguments in the discussion above, it is evident that there are essentially three different theories regarding the origins of the Hebrew *wayyiqtol*. First, Bauer, Huehnergard, and Blau suggest that both the *wayyiqtol* and the jussive originated from the same Proto-Semitic *yaqtul* verb form, and that the *yaqtul* verb form carried both of these functions in Proto-Semitic. Second, G. R. Driver and Rainey suggest that there were two fully homonymous (and therefore indistinguishable) *yaqtuls* in Proto-Semitic, one functioning as the preterite, and one functioning as the jussive. And third, Hetzron and Zevit agree with G. R. Driver and Rainey that there were indeed two *yaqtuls* in Proto-Semitic, one functioning as the preterite and one functioning as the jussive, but further assert that these could be distinguished by accent, the accent of the preterite falling on the first syllable (*ya'qtul*) and the accent of the jussive falling on the second (*yaqtu'l*).

In favor of the first is Huehnergard's demonstration that both the *yaqtul* and the *yaqtulu* verb forms have an indicative and a modal function (contra Rainey's verbal system where the *yaqtula* is the modal equivalent of the *yaqtulu*). Also in favor of the first is the recognition that many times, the same form performs more than one function even in other languages (e.g., in English, "Arise," can be the present, the imperative, or the infinitive). In favor of the second is the neatness of Rainey's Old Canaanite verbal system. And in favor of the third, is Hetzron's attempt to demonstrate a difference in accent between the two forms based on the collective evidence of Ugaritic, Ethiopic, and the weak verbs in Hebrew. Also in favor of the third, Zevit comments that two verb forms this diverse in function ought to be distinguishable in form, as well. Against Hetzron's argument, however, are two responses. Revell argues that these differences in accent can be explained in terms of internal Masoretic accentual rules, and therefore do not necessitate explanation outside of the Hebrew language. And Goerwitz argues that Hetzron's proposed derivation of the jussive from a Proto-Semitic *yaqtuʾl* cannot account for the loss of the final syllable on the jussive forms of III-ה verbs.

Regarding the path that the *wayyiqtol* took from the *yaqtul*, there are several options, as well. First, if one accepts Bauer and Blau's hypothesis, then the *yaqtul* first gave up its future tense meaning to the *yaqtulu* verb form, and then gave up its place as the primary past tense verb to the suffix forms, retaining only the jussive meaning and the specialized past tense usage in narrative. Second, if one accepts Kuryłowicz's theory noted by Huehnergard, where there was originally both a *yaqtul* and a *yaqtulu* form, then the *yaqtul* only had to shed its modal usage before giving up its place as the primary past tense form to the suffix forms and assuming its specialized past tense usage in Hebrew narrative. And third, if one accepts either Rainey or Hetzron's theory, then the *wayyiqtol* is a direct descendant from the preterite *yaqtul*, initially functioning as the primary past tense verb (in opposition to the *yiqtol*), but later giving up this function to the *qatal*, retaining only its special narrative usage.

And last, there are essentially two theories regarding the specific significance attained to by the *wayyiqtol* in Hebrew. First, Revell proposes that the *wayyiqtol* acquired the sense of an epic or war story genre as it was edged out by the suffix tense. And second, Blau and Hetzron propose that rather than becoming a special narrative form per se, the *wayyiqtol* was simply retained as the sentence-initial (Hetzron) or, more precisely, the *waw*-initial (Blau) past tense form.

3.3 Evaluation

As demonstrated above, the discussion regarding the origins of the *wayyiqtol* can be divided neatly into three separate but interrelated questions: first, the verb form from which it descended; second, the path it took to reach the *wayyiqtol* in Hebrew; and third, the final significance it attained to in the Hebrew language.

3.3.1 The Origins of the *Wayyiqtol*
3.3.2 Path from the *Yaqtul*
3.3.3 Final Place in the Hebrew Language

3.3.1 The Origins of the *Wayyiqtol*

Regarding the origins of the *wayyiqtol*, there are three issues to consider. The first is the place of Rainey and Moran's conclusions in discussions of Proto-Semitic. The second is the debate over form and function. And the third is the strength of Hetzron's theory.

(1) *Canaanite vs. Proto-Semitic.* As noted above, the chief disagreement between Rainey and Hetzron over the origins of the *wayyiqtol* is whether the preterite *yaqtul* could be distinguished from the proposed jussive *yaqtul*. In one sense, however, both Rainey and Hetzron could be right, as they are discussing two different periods of the language. Specifically, Hetzron's theory concerns the possible free stress period in Proto-Semitic, while Rainey's observations come from the Old Canaanite of the Amarna letters. Thus, if there were a difference between the preterite and jussive *yaqtul* in Proto-Semitic, one would not expect to find it in the Amarna letters, since the free stress system had been eliminated by then. Therefore, Rainey is right in his observation that they are indistinguishable *in Old Canaanite*, a possible ancestor of Hebrew; however, his data does not necessarily exclude Hetzron's theory that the two forms could have been distinguishable in Proto-Semitic.

(2) *Form vs. Function.* Another area of confusion in the debate, not counting Hetzron's theory, is the question of whether there were two *yaqtul* forms for the two different functions (i.e. the preterite and the jussive) (as proposed by Rainey) or a single *yaqtul* form for all of these functions (as proposed by Huehnergard and Blau). In reality, though, the debate is nothing more than an issue of semantics. If one divides verbs by form, then there was a single form that performed both functions. However, if one divides verbs by function, then there were two indistinguishable verbs performing two separate functions.

In Greek, for example, there is a similar debate over the form and function of the cases. While there is one form for the genitive and the ablative functions in classical and *koine* Greek, there are two forms in its ancestor and sister languages. Similarly, while there is one form for the dative, locative, and instrumental form in Classical and *koine* Greek, there are three forms in its ancestor and sister languages. Thus, while some grammarians hold to a five-case system based on form, others hold to an eight-case system based on function.

Therefore, not including Hetzron's theory, the question of whether there were one or two *yaqtul*s is a matter of perspective regarding form and function. In this matter, the present study is inclined to hold to the form theory, and accept Huehnergard's proposal of a single *yaqtul*. This is further strengthened by Huehnergard's demonstration that the *yaqtulu* could be used in a modal sense, as well.

(3) *The Strength of Hetzron's Theory.* The discussion, then, comes down to the strength of Hetzron's theory. If his evidence is sufficient to demonstrate an accentual difference between the two functions of the *yaqtul* in Proto-Semitic, then there must have been two different forms with two different functions. If, however, his evidence is not sufficient, then there must have been a single form for both functions.

Hetzron's evidence from Akkadian is admittedly weak since it relies not on an actual phonetic difference, but on a potential phonetic difference created by Hetzron as a test for his theory. For example, it could be that the *lu* for *lu iprus* simply did not yield itself syntactically to contraction as the *lu* in *liprus* did. If however, there were two existing forms of *liprus*, one optative and one indicative, which could be distinguished in some way by accent, then his theory would be strengthened. Similarly, Hetzron's evidence from Ge'ez is likewise tentative without further investigation, since it is based on an argument from silence. If one were to discover a *known process* which could explain the apocopation of the *h* in *blh* to *yebe*, then this evidence would be discredited. And Hetzron's evidence from Arabic is given, by his own admission, as merely possible confirmatory evidence.

Hetzron's strongest evidence, then, comes from the I-י and II-ו/י weak verbs in Hebrew. In contrast with his evidence from Akkadian, Hetzron's analysis demonstrates a real phonetic difference between the jussive and *wayyiqtol* forms, and suggests that the reason for this phonetic difference may be that they are derived from two separate forms in Proto-Semitic. And if the phonetic differences can be attributed to different origins in Proto-Semitic, then one may assume that there were different forms for the preterite and the jussive *yaqtul* forms that they have descended from (as evidenced by other Semitic languages, including Akkadian, Ugaritic, Canaanite, etc.).

Although Revell challenged Hetzron's theory, there are several problems with his argument. First, Revell does not deal adequately with the different forms of the I-י and II-ו/י weak verbs. In Section 13.2, where an explanation would be expected of the distinct stress of the *wayyiqtol* form of the hollow roots, he omits it altogether (Revell 1984, 442). Second, Revell suggests that the peculiar form of the *waw* prefix was initially evident only in 3ms forms of III-ה verbs (the apocopation of the ה placing the accent on the penultimate syllable, and the vowel under the *waw* lengthening to accommodate it), but then spread by analogy to all forms of the *wayyiqtol*, both weak and strong. This requires one to postulate two stages otherwise unknown to explain the wayyiqtol forms of the III-ה verbs. Third, even if one were to accept Revell's proposal of these two stages, it still does not explain why the *pathach* would have been retained in the second stage rather than being lost with the loss of the penultimate accent.[38] Fourth, instead of explaining the accentual differences of the II-ו/י verbs (which is Hetzron's central point), he dismisses them as exceptions to his system (cf. section 6; Revell 1984, 439). And fifth, this explanation lies clearly outside of the bounds of the Hebrew accentual system within which Revell proposes to explain their forms (Revell 1984, 444).

Contrary to Revell's assertion, therefore, both he and Hetzron propose anterior developments to explain the accentual differences of the *wayyiqtol*; the difference is simply that Revell proposes a late internal Hebrew development, whereas Hetzron proposes an early Proto-Semitic distinction. Therefore, Revell's theory is not to be preferred for simplicity over Hetzron's. To the contrary, the assumption that the initial accent and the *waw patach* spread by analogy from the III-ה weak verb *wayyiqtol* form to all of the other *wayyiqtol* forms, both strong and weak, is highly capricious. In addition, Revell's theory is still inadequate to explain *why* the I-י and II-ו/י are accented on the first syllable rather than on the second as their respective jussives forms are.

Goerwitz's challenge is more substantial. If indeed the apocopation of the final ה on the jussive form of III-ה verbs would have required a penultimate stress on the jussive *yaqtul* verb form, then Hetzron's proposal of a Proto-Semitic *yaqtuʾl* for the origins of the Hebrew jussive becomes more difficult. As Goerwitz comments, however, this criticism does not necessarily rule out Hetzron's theory; it merely pushes back his proposed free stress system to an earlier period of Proto-Semitic prior to the penultimate stress period (Goerwitz 1992, 203). The real question, then, is the number and order of linguistic changes that occurred between Proto-Semitic and BH. Blau, the clear leader in this field, proposes five stages of development from the Proto-Semitic to the Hebrew stress system, the second of which is the period of penultimate stress, and none of which include such a free stress system (2010, 144–153). However, a full discussion of this field is beyond the scope of the present study.

In conclusion, although Hetzron's data from Akkadian and Geʾez is somewhat tenuous, his evidence from Hebrew remains the least complicated explanation for the accents and vowels of the I-י and II-ו/י *wayyiqtol* forms at present. Other evidence, however, indicates the likelihood of a penultimate stress system rather than a free stress system in Proto-Semitic. This does

---

38. Revell cites *bammʾe* as an example, but does not explain its derivation.

not necessarily rule out Hetzron's conclusions, but it does complicate them beyond the scope of the present study.

3.3.2 Path from the *Yaqtul*

The path taken by the *wayyiqtol* from the *yaqtul* is simply a function of the original nature of the *yaqtul* form. If one believes there was a separate preterite form of the *yaqtul*, whether distinct from the jussive *yaqtul* (Hetzron and Zevit) or not (Rainey), then the *wayyiqtol* is a direct descendant of this verb form. If one holds that there were originally both a *yaqtul* and a *yaqtulu* form in Proto-Semitic, both having an indicative and a jussive meaning (Huehnergard), then it is a two-step process: first, the introduction of the suffix forms encroached on the preterite function of the *yaqtul*, and then the *yaqtul* form split into the jussive form and the *wayyiqtol* forms in Hebrew. If, however, one holds that the *yaqtul* was the primary Proto-Semitic verb form serving all tenses and the jussive form (Bauer and Blau), then it is a three-step process: first, the introduction of the *yaqtulu* form confined the *yaqtul* to the past tense; second, the introduction of the suffix forms encroached on the preterite function of the *yaqtul*; and third, the *yaqtul* form split into the jussive form and the *wayyiqtol* forms in Hebrew.

3.3.3 Final Place in the Hebrew Language

Regarding the final place of the *wayyiqtol* in the HVS, there are three options. First, the traditional theory is that the *wayyiqtol* is the consecutive past tense form. Second, Sasson proposes that the *wayyiqtol* became the narrative tense by means of its usage in epic and war story texts. And third, Blau and Hetzron propose that the *wayyiqtol* was simply the *waw*-initial past tense form.

(1) *Consecutive (Traditional).* Of the three options, the consecutive is the least likely, as there is no explanation for how or why the *yaqtul* would have assumed this function in Hebrew, nor any proponent who advances such a theory. Thus, although it may be valid from a synchronic perspective to say that it is the consecutive form (although this too, will be challenged below), it must be admitted that there is no diachronic explanation for how it might have become the consecutive form.

(2) *Epic (Sasson).* Sasson's proposal improves on the traditional theory by offering a viable diachronic explanation for the usage of *wayyiqtol* in past tense narrative. However, there are several problems with Sasson's theory, as well. First, his proposed timeline (Sasson 1997, 126) conflicts clearly with the biblical data, as the *wayyiqtol* is used prevalently in narrative as early as

Moses and as late as Nehemiah. Second, his explanation of the use of the *wayyiqtol* in Hebrew narrative nowhere accounts for the use of the *wayyiqtol* in everyday speech unless we assume that the actual words of historical figures were recast by the narrator in this epic style (e.g. Gn 12:19; 16:5; 20:13; 24:39–48). And third, his explanation of the *wayyiqtol* does not account for the analogous development of the *wᵊqatal* verb form, as there was clearly no such need for an equivalent epic future tense.

(3) Waw-*initial Past Tense Form (Blau and Hetzron).* The final explanation proposed by Blau and Hetzron is that the *wayyiqtol* simply functioned as the *waw*-initial past tense form in Hebrew, and that its prevalent usage in Hebrew narrative was only a consequence of the normal VSO word order. As Blau notes, this explanation accounts for the interchangeability of the *qatal* and the *wayyiqtol* forms, and explains the analogous development of the *wᵊqatal* as the *waw*-initial future tense form.

Though he disagrees with Blau and Hetzron that the *qatal* and the *wayyiqtol* were fully interchangeable in meaning, Joosten also lists examples in line with Blau's theory, and insightfully documents several of the specific syntactical constraints that would necessitate the *qatal* in place of the *wayyiqtol* due to word order (Joosten 2012, 41–45). These include occurrences with לֹא (e.g., Gn 37:4), occurrences with an adverbial phrase of time (e.g., Gn 2:25–26), and occurrences where an object or adverbial is fronted (e.g., Gn 1:5; Ex 20:21). This lends further support to Blau and Hetzron's proposals.

3.4 *Summary*

In summary, the discussion to date regarding the origins of the *wayyiqtol* has reached a consensus that the *wayyiqtol* is a descendant of the Proto-Semitic preterite *ya'qtul*, unrelated in origin to the *yiqtol* in any way. Whether there was another distinct verb form for the jussive, i.e. a *yaqtu'l* form, depends on the order and number of linguistic changes that occurred between the Proto-Semitic and Hebrew stress systems. If there was such a distinct form, then the *wayyiqtol* is a direct descendant of this Proto-Semitic preterite *ya'qtul*; if not, then the Proto-Semitic *ya'qtul* simply split into the jussive and *wayyiqtol* forms in BH. Regarding the final place of the *wayyiqtol* in the HVS, the best explanation at present is Blau and Hetzron's proposal that the *wayyiqtol* was simply the normal *waw*-initial past tense verb form. And regarding the temporal sequentiality of the *wayyiqtol*, this survey demonstrates that there is no given theory of the origins of the *wayyiqtol* that aligns with the assumption of its sequentiality, whether temporal or logical.

4. The Problem of Dischronologization

Having explored the various theories of the HVS, and documented the discussion to date regarding the origins of the *wayyiqtol*, the present chapter will now consider the problem of dischronologization, and its implications for the meaning of the *wayyiqtol*. As mentioned in the introduction, this will present the synchronic evidence against the temporal sequentiality of the *wayyiqtol*, highlight the underlying problem with the sequentiality of the *wayyiqtol* (both temporal and logical), and demonstrate the need in modern studies for a better understanding of the *wayyiqtol* and the Hebrew verbal system as a whole.

4.1   Studies of Dischronologization
4.2   Examples of Dischronologization
4.3   Extent of Dischronologization
4.4   The Underlying Issue
4.5   Summary

4.1 *Studies of Dischronologization*

Beginning with W. J. Martin in 1968, several Hebrew scholars have begun to notice and catalogue occurrences of a phenomenon which Martin termed "dischronologization." As Martin defines it, dischronologization refers to "the seemingly random dispersal of events as set forth in certain narratives" (Martin 1968, 179). Because his focus lay more in historiography in general than in the specific function of the *wayyiqtol*, Martin did not specifically discuss the role of the *wayyiqtol* with regard to sequentiality; however, among his examples of dischronologization, Martin included several that consisted of the *wayyiqtol*, raising the question of its temporal sequentiality.

In 1971, David Baker, a student of Martin's, expanded upon Martin's work by distinguishing between cases where dischronologization occurs as the result of the *qatal* (a function already well established within the Hebrew verbal system), and those where it occurs with the *wayyiqtol*. In his M.A. thesis, Baker documented thirty-seven examples of the pluperfect *wayyiqtol*, where a *wayyiqtol* refers to previous events out of sequence from the main story line. As a result of these studies, Baker concluded that it is not the verb forms themselves which indicate sequentiality or dischronologization, but "the context and the situation" of the verb (Baker 1971, 54).

After lying dormant for a while, the idea was picked up again by E. J. Revell (1985) and Randall Buth (1994). Both utilized the evidence for dischronologization to explain several biblical narratives where source critics had denied single authorship based on the repetition and breaks in time sequence that they exhibit.

In 1994, in a brief article primarily devoted to the discussion of the advantages of Noam Chomsky's transformational grammar, David Washburn used the supposed sequentiality of the *wayyiqtol* as an example of the consequences of the failure to distinguish between syntax and semantics. In this article Washburn argues that the *wayyiqtol* is a simple "declarative" verb form (1994, 27) that is only made sequential by "the semantics of the word in question" and "the surrounding context" (1994, 29).

In 1995, C. John Collins published an article proposing several useful criteria for the identification of dischronologization in BH narrative (1995, 127–28), and attempting to demonstrate the rhetorical strategy involved in these kinds of dischronologization (1995, 129–140). Collins' article provides an excellent survey of the previous literature on the topic, as well (1995, 122–27).

In 2004, Brian Harmelink devoted a section of his dissertation on *wayhi*, published in 2011, to the meaning of the *wayyiqtol* (2011, 108–135). Under his proposed TAMP rubric (tense, aspect, modality, and pragmatics), Harmelink suggests that "sequentiality is an important feature of the *wayyiqtol*, but not *the* defining characteristic" (2011, 113).

John Cook joined the discussion with two articles in 2004 and 2009 (Cook 2004, 2009). In these articles, Cook discerns the underlying problem in the argument for the sequentiality of the *wayyiqtol*: modern studies have confused the concept of correlation with causation. As Cook argues, just as it would be "erroneous for us to attribute temporal succession to the English Simple Past form" simply because it most often lends itself to temporal sequence in past tense English narrative, so also it is "mistaken" for us to attribute temporal succession to the Hebrew *wayyiqtol* simply because it functions as the primary verbal form of past tense Hebrew narrative (Cook 2009, 10). Thus, although there may indeed be a strong correlation between the *wayyiqtol* and temporal sequentiality in the OT (though exactly how strong will be questioned below), this correlation is simply a consequence of the use of the *wayyiqtol* as the narrative verb form (Cook 2004, 264; 2009, 10).

In addition to his two articles above, Cook's recent volume, *Time and the Biblical Hebrew Verb* (2012), collects and applies his previous articles to his dissertation on the TAM (tense, aspect, and modality) theory of the Hebrew verbal system, further challenging the temporal sequentiality of the *wayyiqtol* (2012, 289–297), and demonstrating that temporal sequentiality comes not from the *wayyiqtol*, but from the various modes of discourse in BH narrative (Cook 2012, 312–338). This idea will be further explored in **Chapter 13**.

And lastly, Jan Joosten has taken up the issue of sequentiality with his long awaited publication, *The Verbal System of Biblical Hebrew* (2012). In this treatise, Joosten defines the *wayyiqtol* as an indicative preterite (2012, 161), and explains its apparent correlation with sequentiality (as Cook does) as a consequence of its prominent use in narrative discourse (2012, 164). In addition, Joosten insightfully groups the dischronologizations evident in Hebrew narrative into several categories, including idiomatic expressions, contemporaneous events, overlapping time frames, backtracking, anticipatory, and iterative processes (2012, 166–175).

4.2 Examples of Dischronologization

The following sample includes fifteen of the clearest examples of dischronologization garnered from the sources above and supplemented by independent observation. For a full database of examples of dischronologization investigated to date including fifty examples rated "probable" or higher, see appendix.

4.2.1   Esau's Soup—Gn 25:34
4.2.2   Jacob's Love—Gn 29:18
4.2.3   Jacob's Wedding Night—Gn 29:21–25
4.2.4   Joseph's Dream—Gn 37:5
4.2.5   Jacob's Blessing—Gn 48:12–17
4.2.6   Manna in the Ark—Ex 16:33–34
4.2.7   The Crossing of the Jordan—Jo 4:10–12
4.2.8   The Bochim Incident—Jgs 2:1, 4–6
4.2.9   The Battle of Benjamin—Jgs 20:35, 36
4.2.10 Saul's Doom—1 Sm 28:20
4.2.11 Ishbosheth's Murder—2 Sm 4:5–7
4.2.12 The Taking of Rabbah—2 Sm 12:26–29
4.2.13 Jezebel's Letter—1 Kgs 21:8–9
4.2.14 Ahab's Death—1 Kgs 22:34–37
4.2.15 The Moabite Stone

4.2.1 Esau's Soup—Genesis 25:34

After selling his birthright to Jacob for a piece of bread and a pot of stew, Esau, in complete disregard for the implications of his actions, "ate and drank and rose and went his way" (Gn 25:34, ESV). The *wayyiqtol* chain reads as follows: (*wayyiqtols* in bold, verses in brackets):

GENESIS 25:34

וַיַּעֲקֹב נָתַן לְעֵשָׂו לֶחֶם וּנְזִיד עֲדָשִׁים וַיֹּאכַל וַיֵּשְׁתְּ וַיָּקָם וַיֵּלַךְ וַיִּבֶז עֵשָׂו
אֶת־הַבְּכֹרָה:

1   Now Jacob gave to Esau some bread and lentil stew.
2   And he **ate**,
3   and he **drank**,
4   and he **rose**,
5   and he **went**.
6   And Esau **despised** the birthright.

There are two dischronologizations in this verse. The first is the overlap of lines 2 and 3. A strictly sequential reading would require that Esau devoured all of the food immediately (perhaps because of his famished state) before giving thought to his drink. However, the usage of this same phrase elsewhere in the OT in reference to normal meals, and particularly to prolonged feasts, demonstrates that it refers to the usual activity of eating and drinking throughout a meal (Gn 24:54; 26:30; Ex 24:11; Jgs 9:27; 19:4, 6, 21; etc.).

The second dischronologization is the statement, "And Esau despised the birthright" (line 6). A strict temporal sequence would suggest that Esau only despised his birthright after he left Jacob. However, the narrative itself seems to suggest that the despising of his birthright was in the act of selling it to Jacob in verses 32–33, and in his heedless consumption of the bread and stew that he had bought with it in verse 34. It is best explained therefore as a summary statement of Esau's actions.

4.2.2 Jacob's Love—Genesis 29:18

Genesis 29 records Jacob's arrival in Padan-Aram to seek his wife from his mother's relatives. Upon his arrival there, Jacob, struck by the beauty of the shepherdess Rachel, moved the large stone from the mouth of the well, watered Laban's flock for her, kissed her, and then related to her his kinship. Hearing of Jacob's deeds, Laban invited him forthwith into his home, and after a month of feasting together, he asked Jacob what he should repay him in exchange for watching his flocks. At this juncture, the text records:

GENESIS 29:18

וַיֶּאֱהַב יַעֲקֹב אֶת־רָחֵל

And Jacob **loved** Rachel.

A strictly sequential reading of the *wayyiqtol* would suggest that Jacob's love for Rachel was a split second decision made only after a month of feasting at Laban's house. However, given the events in the narrative leading up to this point, the narrative seems to imply that Jacob's love for Rachel was a true "love at first sight," and a love that had prompted his subsequent actions. Therefore, this *wayyiqtol* describes a pre-existing and continuing state, rather than a sequential event.

4.2.3 Jacob's Wedding Night—Genesis 29:21–25

The narrative of Genesis 29 continues with Jacob requesting Rachel's hand in marriage from Laban in exchange for seven years of labor. Laban tricked Jacob, however, by giving him Leah instead of Rachel, with the design of forcing him to work another seven years for Rachel, as well. Jacob discovered this surprise the morning after his wedding night: "And in the morning, behold, it was Leah!" (Gn 29:25). The *wayyiqtol* chain reads as follows:

GENESIS 29:21–25

21 וַיֹּאמֶר יַעֲקֹב אֶל־לָבָן הָבָה אֶת־אִשְׁתִּי כִּי מָלְאוּ יָמָי וְאָבוֹאָה אֵלֶיהָ:

22 וַיֶּאֱסֹף לָבָן אֶת־כָּל־אַנְשֵׁי הַמָּקוֹם וַיַּעַשׂ מִשְׁתֶּה:

23 וַיְהִי בָעֶרֶב וַיִּקַּח אֶת־לֵאָה בִתּוֹ וַיָּבֵא אֹתָהּ אֵלָיו וַיָּבֹא אֵלֶיהָ:

24 וַיִּתֵּן לָבָן לָהּ אֶת־זִלְפָּה שִׁפְחָתוֹ לְלֵאָה בִתּוֹ שִׁפְחָה:

25 וַיְהִי בַבֹּקֶר וְהִנֵּה־הִוא לֵאָה וַיֹּאמֶר אֶל־לָבָן מַה־זֹּאת עָשִׂיתָ לִּי

1 [21] And Jacob **said** to Laban, "Give me my wife, for my days are finished, so that I may go in to her."
2 [22] And Laban **gathered** all the men of the place
3 And he **made** a feast
4 [23] And when it **was** evening,
5 He **took** Leah his daughter
6 And he **brought** her to him
7 And he **went in** to her
8 [24] And Laban **gave** Zilpah his maidservant to Leah his daughter to be her maidservant.
9 [25] And when it **was** the morning, behold it was Leah.
   And he **said** to Laban, "What is this you have done to me?"

The problem, of course, is the giving of Zilpah. A strictly sequential reading of the *wayyiqtol* would suggest that in addition to the disturbance of waking up in the morning to find Leah instead of Rachel, Jacob's wedding night (lines 7 and 8) was further by Laban presenting Zilpah to Leah in the middle of the night (line 8).[39] More likely, the timing of the giving of Zilpah was inconsequential to the timeline of Jacob's wedding night, being inserted here for other reasons.

4.2.4 Joseph's Dream—Genesis 37:5

Genesis 37:5, 6 recounts the story of Joseph's dream that he told to his brothers

Genesis 37:5, 6

5 וַֽיַּחֲלֹ֤ם יוֹסֵף֙ חֲל֔וֹם וַיַּגֵּ֖ד לְאֶחָ֑יו וַיּוֹסִ֥פוּ ע֖וֹד שְׂנֹ֥א אֹתֽוֹ׃ 6 וַיֹּ֖אמֶר אֲלֵיהֶ֑ם שִׁמְעוּ־נָ֕א הַחֲל֥וֹם הַזֶּ֖ה אֲשֶׁ֥ר חָלָֽמְתִּי׃

1   [5] And Joseph **dreamed** a dream,
2   And he **told** it to his brothers,
3   And they **hated** him even more.
4   [6] And he **said** to them, "Listen to this dream which I have dreamed."

The wooden translation of these *wayyiqtols* highlights an obvious dischronologization: lines 2 and 3 record that Joseph told his brothers his dream, and that they hated him for it. Verse 6, however, records Joseph's actual words that he spoke in telling them this dream. Thus, lines 1 and 3 refer to the same event and time, while line 2 refers to a later event and time. This same phenomenon is repeated in Genesis 37:9.

4.2.5 Jacob's Blessing—Genesis 48:12–17

Genesis 48:12–17 records the details of Jacob's blessing of Ephraim and Manasseh. During this blessing, Jacob played one final trick by crossing his arms and placing each hand on the head of the opposite boy before pronouncing the blessing. The *wayyiqtol* chain reads as follows.

Genesis 48:12–17

12 וַיּוֹצֵ֨א יוֹסֵ֥ף אֹתָ֛ם מֵעִ֥ם בִּרְכָּ֖יו וַיִּשְׁתַּ֥חוּ לְאַפָּ֖יו אָֽרְצָה׃ 13 וַיִּקַּ֣ח יוֹסֵף֮ אֶת־שְׁנֵיהֶם֒ אֶת־אֶפְרַ֤יִם בִּֽימִינוֹ֙ מִשְּׂמֹ֣אל יִשְׂרָאֵ֔ל וְאֶת־מְנַשֶּׁ֥ה בִשְׂמֹאל֖וֹ מִימִ֣ין יִשְׂרָאֵ֑ל וַיַּגֵּ֖שׁ אֵלָֽיו׃ 14 וַיִּשְׁלַח֩ יִשְׂרָאֵ֨ל אֶת־יְמִינ֜וֹ וַיָּ֣שֶׁת עַל־רֹ֣אשׁ אֶפְרַ֗יִם וְה֣וּא הַצָּעִ֔יר וְאֶת־שְׂמֹאל֖וֹ עַל־רֹ֣אשׁ מְנַשֶּׁ֑ה שִׂכֵּל֙ אֶת־יָדָ֔יו כִּ֥י מְנַשֶּׁ֖ה הַבְּכֽוֹר׃

---

39. One could argue that Laban's presenting of Zilpah did not involve physically bringing her and handing her to Leah, but simply a designating of her to be given to Leah. The question remains, however, why Laban would have waited until the middle of the night to make this designation.

¹⁵ ... וַיְבָ֣רֶךְ אֶת־יוֹסֵ֘ף וַיֹּאמַ֒ר

¹⁷ וַיַּ֣רְא יוֹסֵ֗ף כִּֽי־יָשִׁ֨ית אָבִ֧יו יַד־יְמִינ֛וֹ עַל־רֹ֥אשׁ אֶפְרַ֖יִם וַיֵּ֣רַע בְּעֵינָ֑יו
וַיִּתְמֹ֣ךְ יַד־אָבִ֗יו לְהָסִ֥יר אֹתָ֛הּ מֵעַ֥ל רֹאשׁ־אֶפְרַ֖יִם עַל־רֹ֥אשׁ מְנַשֶּֽׁה׃

1 [12] And Joseph **pulled them off** of his knees
2 And he **bowed down** with his face to the ground.
3 [13] And Joseph **took** the two of them, Ephraim with his right hand
   to the left hand of Israel, and Manasseh with his left hand to the right
   hand of Israel.
4 And he **brought them near** to him.
5 [14] And Israel **stretched out** his right hand
6 and **placed** it on the head of Ephraim, who was the younger, and his
   left hand on the head of Manasseh, crossing his hands (for Manasseh
   was the firstborn).
7 [15] And he **blessed** Joseph
8 And he **said** . . .
9 [17] And Joseph **saw** that his father placed his right hand on the head
   of Ephraim
10 And it **was evil** in his eyes
11 And he **grasped** the hand of his father to switch it from the head of
   Ephraim to the head of Manasseh.

There are two frequently overlooked problems with a strictly sequential reading of this text. First, it records that Joseph placed his father's hands on his sons' heads (line 3) after bowing down with his face to the ground (line 2). And second, it provides no explanation why Joseph would have waited until after his father had pronounced the blessing (lines 7 and 8) to attempt to correct the placement of his hand (lines 9–11). A more likely explanation, and one better reflecting Jacob's skill in trickery, is that Joseph brought his sons forward (lines 3 and 4), Joseph bowed his head with his sons to the ground (line 2), Jacob crossed his hands (with their heads bowed to the ground) and laid them on their heads (lines 5 and 6), Jacob delivered his blessing (lines 7 and 8), and *then* Joseph looked up to find that his father had played one final trick (lines 9–11). If this interpretation is correct, a better translation might read as follows:

> [12] Then Joseph **pulled them off** of his knees, and he **bowed down** with his face to the ground. [13] Now Joseph **had taken** the two of them, Ephraim with his right hand to the left hand of Israel, and Manasseh with his left hand to the right hand of Israel, and **brought** them near to him. [14] But Israel **stretched** out his right hand and **placed** it on the head of Ephraim, who was the younger, and his left hand on the head of Manasseh, crossing his hands (for Manasseh was the firstborn). [15] And he **blessed** Joseph, and **said** . . .

[17] Then Joseph **saw** that his father had placed his right hand on the head of Ephraim, and it was **evil** in his eyes. He **grasped** the hand of his father to switch it from the head of Ephraim to the head of Manasseh.

4.2.6 Manna in the Ark—Exodus 16:33–34

On the way to Mount Sinai, the LORD commanded Moses and Aaron to store away some of the newly given manna as a memorial of the LORD's provision for future generations. The *wayyiqtol* chain reads as follows:

EXODUS 16:33–34

33 **וַיֹּאמֶר** מֹשֶׁה אֶל־אַהֲרֹן קַח צִנְצֶנֶת אַחַת וְתֶן־שָׁמָּה מְלֹא־הָעֹמֶר מָן וְהַנַּח אֹתוֹ לִפְנֵי יְהוָה לְמִשְׁמֶרֶת לְדֹרֹתֵיכֶם:

34 כַּאֲשֶׁר צִוָּה יְהוָה אֶל־מֹשֶׁה **וַיַּנִּיחֵהוּ** אַהֲרֹן לִפְנֵי הָעֵדֻת לְמִשְׁמָרֶת:

[33] And Moses **said** to Aaron, "Take a pot and put in it a full omer of manna, and place it before the LORD to be kept for your descendants"
[34] Just as the LORD commanded Moses, so Aaron **placed** it before the ark to be kept.

The curious problem with this text is that the Israelites did not yet have the Ark. The next mention of the Ark, in fact, is in Exodus 25:16, and the building of it is not initiated until Exodus 37:1. Therefore, the *wayyiqtol* in Exodus 16:34 actually jumps ahead in time sequence.[40]

4.2.7 The Crossing of the Jordan—Joshua 4:10–12

There are a number of dischronologizations in Joshua 3:1–4:24, one of which is found in 4:12. The *wayyiqtol* chain reads as follows:

JOSHUA 4:10–12

10 ... **וַיְמַהֲרוּ** הָעָם **וַיַּעֲבֹרוּ**:

11 **וַיְהִי** כַּאֲשֶׁר־תַּמּוּ כָל־הָעָם לַעֲבוֹר **וַיַּעֲבֹר** אֲרוֹן־יְהוָה וְהַכֹּהֲנִים לִפְנֵי הָעָם:

12 **וַיַּעַבְרוּ** בְּנֵי־רְאוּבֵן וּבְנֵי־גָד וַחֲצִי שֵׁבֶט הַמְנַשֶּׁה חֲמֻשִׁים לִפְנֵי בְּנֵי יִשְׂרָאֵל כַּאֲשֶׁר דִּבֶּר אֲלֵיהֶם מֹשֶׁה:

[10] ... The people **crossed over quickly**.
[11] And **when** all the people had finished crossing over, the Ark of the LORD and the Priests **crossed over** in the presence of the people.
[12] And the sons of Reuben and the sons of Gad and the half of the tribe

---

40. Cassuto actually suggests that verses 31–36 constitute five notes "on matters connected with the manna, which belong mainly to a period subsequent to the episode related above" (Cassuto 1967, 199).

of Manasseh **crossed over** armed in the presence of the sons of Israel, just as God had commanded Moses.

As the translation above demonstrates, a strictly sequential reading of the *wayyiqtols* suggests that the tribe of Reuben, the tribe of Gad, and the half tribe of Manasseh crossed over after the Priests. Joshua 3:17, however, states that the priests stood in the midst of the Jordan until everyone had crossed over, and 4:18 records that the waters rushed down again as soon as they stepped out of the water. Therefore, Reuben, Gad, and Manasseh had to have crossed over with the main body of the Israelites before the priests came up out of the water. This places the events of verse 12 prior to the events of verse 11.

4.2.8 The Bochim Incident—Judges 2:1, 4–6

After the failed conquests reported in the first chapter of Judges, the second chapter of Judges opens with the appearance of the Angel of the LORD at Bochim, and his rebuke to the Israelites there for their disobedience in failing to drive out the Canaanites:

JUDGES 2:1–6

וַיַּ֣עַל מַלְאַךְ־יְהוָ֗ה מִן־הַגִּלְגָּ֜ל אֶל־הַבֹּכִ֛ים פ וַיֹּ֫אמֶר... ⁴ וַיְהִ֗י כְּדַבֵּ֞ר מַלְאַ֤ךְ
יְהוָה֙ אֶת־הַדְּבָרִ֣ים הָאֵ֔לֶּה אֶל־כָּל־בְּנֵ֖י יִשְׂרָאֵ֑ל וַיִּשְׂא֥וּ הָעָ֛ם אֶת־קוֹלָ֖ם
וַיִּבְכּֽוּ: ⁵ וַֽיִּקְרְא֛וּ שֵׁם־הַמָּק֥וֹם הַה֖וּא בֹּכִ֑ים וַיִּזְבְּחוּ־שָׁ֖ם לַיהוָֽה: פ ⁶ וַיְשַׁלַּ֤ח
יְהוֹשֻׁ֙עַ֙ אֶת־הָעָ֔ם וַיֵּלְכ֧וּ בְנֵֽי־יִשְׂרָאֵ֛ל אִ֥ישׁ לְנַחֲלָת֖וֹ לָרֶ֥שֶׁת אֶת־הָאָֽרֶץ:

[1] Now the Angel of the LORD **went up** from Gilgal to Bochim, and he **said** . . . [4] And **when** the Angel of the LORD spoke these words to all of the Israelites, the people **lifted** up their voice and they **wept**. [5] And they **called** the name of that place Bochim, and they **sacrificed** there to the LORD. [6] And Joshua **sent away** the people, and the Israelites **went** each to his inheritance to take possession of the land.

There are three problems here that require explanation. First, verse 6 repeats Joshua's command from Joshua 23:1–13 to go and take possession of the land, the report of which is already given in Judges 1:1–36. Second, the very thing for which the Angel of the LORD rebukes the Israelites in Judges 2:1–3 was their failure to fulfill Joshua's commission repeated here in Judges 2:6. Third, and most importantly, Judges 1:1 records that Joshua had died before any of these events took place, either the failed conquests reported in Judges 1:1–36 or the appearance of the Angel of the LORD at Bochim.[41]

---

41. These dischronologizations will be further explored in **Chapter 13**.

4.2.9 The Battle of Benjamin—Judges 20:35, 36

There are a number of dischronologizations in Judges 20, as well, the most noticeable of which occurs in the middle of verse 36. The *wayyiqtol* chain reads as follows:

JUDGES 20:35–36

³⁵ וַיִּגֹּף יְהוָה| אֶת־בִּנְיָמִן לִפְנֵי יִשְׂרָאֵל וַיַּשְׁחִיתוּ בְנֵי יִשְׂרָאֵל בְּבִנְיָמִן
בַּיּוֹם הַהוּא עֶשְׂרִים וַחֲמִשָּׁה אֶלֶף וּמֵאָה אִישׁ כָּל־אֵלֶּה שֹׁלֵף חָרֶב:
³⁶ וַיִּרְאוּ בְנֵי־בִנְיָמִן כִּי נִגָּפוּ וַיִּתְּנוּ אִישׁ־יִשְׂרָאֵל מָקוֹם לְבִנְיָמִן כִּי
בָטְחוּ אֶל־הָאֹרֵב אֲשֶׁר שָׂמוּ אֶל־הַגִּבְעָה:

1 [35] And the LORD **defeated** Benjamin before Israel
2 And the sons of Israel **destroyed** 25,100 men in Benjamin on that day, all of which could draw the sword.
3 [36] And the sons of Benjamin **saw** that they had been defeated.
4 And the men of Israel **gave** ground to Benjamin because they trusted in the ambush which they had set against Gibeah.

As the narrative continues, verses 37–48 give a second account of the battle of Benjamin. However, this second account begins without warning in the middle of verse 36 (line 4), continuing on with the *wayyiqtol* chain as usual.

In this case, a strictly sequential reading of the *wayyiqtol* chain is completely irreconcilable with the narrative. This has led several scholars to suggest that Judges 20 consists of two "crudely combined" accounts of the same event (Soggin 1981, 293–94). More likely, however, the narrative simply circles back to relate the battle in further detail.

4.2.10 Saul's Doom—1 Samuel 28:20

Near the end of Saul's life, alienated from the LORD and facing his final battle with the Philistines, Saul sought out the assistance of a medium at Endor to help him communicate with the deceased prophet Samuel in search of some reassurance that he might be spared. At Samuel's reply, the narrative records Saul's despairing reaction:

1 SAMUEL 28:20

וַיְמַהֵר שָׁאוּל וַיִּפֹּל מְלֹא־קוֹמָתוֹ אַרְצָה וַיִּרָא מְאֹד מִדִּבְרֵי שְׁמוּאֵל גַּם־
כֹּחַ לֹא־הָיָה בוֹ כִּי לֹא אָכַל לֶחֶם כָּל־הַיּוֹם וְכָל־הַלָּיְלָה:

Then Saul **fell instantly** with his full height to the ground. He **feared** greatly at the words of Samuel. And there was no strength in him, for he was unable to eat bread all day or all night.

There are two dischronologizations in this verse. First, the two *wayyiqtols* וַיְמַהֵר (*to hurry, or do quickly*) and וַיִּפֹּל (*to fall*) form an idiomatic expression, where the first verb modifies the second verb adverbially. In this construction, both verbs work together to describe the same event, ruling out the possibility of temporal sequence. And second, the *wayyiqtol* וַיִּרָא expresses the preexisting and continuing state that caused Saul to fall in the first place. Therefore, it overlaps in time with the preceding *wayyiqtols*, as well as the subsequent narrative of his battle with the Philistines.

4.2.11 Ishbosheth's Murder—2 Samuel 4:5–7

2 Samuel 4:5–7 recounts the story of Ishbosheth's murder. The *wayyiqtol* chain reads as follows:

2 SAMUEL 4:5–7

5 וַיֵּלְכוּ בְּנֵי־רִמּוֹן הַבְּאֵרֹתִי רֵכָב וּבַעֲנָה וַיָּבֹאוּ כְּחֹם הַיּוֹם אֶל־בֵּית אִישׁ בֹּשֶׁת וְהוּא שֹׁכֵב אֵת מִשְׁכַּב הַצָּהֳרָיִם:

6 וְהֵנָּה בָּאוּ עַד־תּוֹךְ הַבַּיִת לֹקְחֵי חִטִּים וַיַּכֻּהוּ אֶל־הַחֹמֶשׁ וְרֵכָב וּבַעֲנָה אָחִיו נִמְלָטוּ:

7 וַיָּבֹאוּ הַבַּיִת וְהוּא־שֹׁכֵב עַל־מִטָּתוֹ בַּחֲדַר מִשְׁכָּבוֹ וַיַּכֻּהוּ וַיְמִתֻהוּ וַיָּסִירוּ אֶת־רֹאשׁוֹ וַיִּקְחוּ אֶת־רֹאשׁוֹ וַיֵּלְכוּ דֶּרֶךְ הָעֲרָבָה כָּל־הַלָּיְלָה:

1	[5] And the sons of Rimmon the Beerothite, Rechab and Baanah, **went.**
2	And they **entered** into the house of Ishbosheth during the heat of the day.
3	Now he was lying on his couch at noon.
4	And behold, they entered into the midst of the house to take wheat.
5	[6] And they **struck** him.
6	And Rechab and Baanah fled.
7	[7] And they **entered** into the house.
8	And he was lying on his couch, with his bed in the middle of the room.
9	And they **struck** him.
10	And they **killed** him.
11	And they **cut off** his head.
12	And they **took** his head.
13	And they **went** ...

The problem occurs at verse 7. Lines 1 through 6 already record that Rechab and Baanah went, entered in, and struck Ishbosheth; however, line 7 reverts to the same verb as line 2 in this sequence and states again that they went in and struck him. As with the battle of Benjamin, the difficulty of this dischronologization has led some to suggest that the problems may be due to a later attempted harmonization of two separate accounts.[42] As with the example above, however, a more likely explanation is that the narrator is simply circling back to expand upon the details of Ishbosheth's death in verses 5–6.[43]

4.2.12 The Taking of Rabbah—2 Samuel 12:26–29

2 Samuel 12:26–29 records the details of Israel's capture of Rabbah. The *wayyiqtol* chain reads as follows:

2 SAMUEL 12:26–29

^{26} וַיִּלָּ֤חֶם יוֹאָב֙ בְּרַבַּ֣ת בְּנֵ֣י עַמּ֔וֹן וַיִּלְכֹּ֖ד אֶת־עִ֥יר הַמְּלוּכָֽה: ^{27} וַיִּשְׁלַ֥ח יוֹאָ֛ב מַלְאָכִ֖ים אֶל־דָּוִ֑ד וַיֹּ֗אמֶר נִלְחַ֣מְתִּי בְרַבָּ֔ה גַּם־לָכַ֖דְתִּי אֶת־עִ֥יר הַמָּֽיִם: ^{28} וְעַתָּ֗ה אֱסֹף֙ אֶת־יֶ֣תֶר הָעָ֔ם וַחֲנֵ֥ה עַל־הָעִ֖יר וְלָכְדָ֑הּ פֶּן־אֶלְכֹּ֤ד אֲנִי֙ אֶת־הָעִ֔יר וְנִקְרָ֥א שְׁמִ֖י עָלֶֽיהָ: ^{29} וַיֶּאֱסֹ֥ף דָּוִ֛ד אֶת־כָּל־הָעָ֖ם וַיֵּ֣לֶךְ רַבָּ֑תָה וַיִּלָּ֥חֶם בָּ֖הּ וַֽיִּלְכְּדָֽהּ:

1   [26] Joab **fought** against Rabbah of the sons of Amon.
2   And he **captured** the royal city.
3   [27] And Joab **sent** messengers to David.
4   And he **said**, "I have fought against Rabbah, and I have taken the city of water."...
5   [29] And David **gathered** all of the people.
6   And he **went** to Rabbah.
7   And he **fought** against it.
8   And he **captured** it.

The first verse of this section records that Joab fought against Rabbah and

---

42. "These verses have created considerable problems for the exegetes. It is possible that we have here not only a textual corruption (in v. 6) but also a conflation of two alternative accounts" (Anderson 1989, 70).

43. "The circumstances of Ish-Bosheth's death are highlighted by repeating them with expansions in vs. 7" (Bergen 1996, 316). "As the thread of the narrative was broken by the explanatory remarks in ver. 6, it is resumed here by the repetition of the words וַיָּבֹאוּ וגו'" (Keil and Delitzsch 1956, 310).

took the city (lines 1 and 2).[44] The next verse, however, records that Joab sent messengers to David prior to capturing the city, telling him to come out and lead the charge to take the city (lest he take the fame at David's expense) (lines 3 and 4). And verses 29–31 record that David, taking Joab's advice, gathered his army and journeyed to Rabbah where he "fought" and "took" (same verbs as in verse 1) the city for himself (lines 5–8). A strictly sequential reading of the *wayyiqtol* would require that they captured the city of Rabbah twice (lines 2 and 8). More likely, though, verses 27–31 constitute an expansion upon the introductory encapsulation of verse 26. One might render the effect of this encapsulation as follows:

> Now Joab fought against Rabbah of the Ammonites and took the royal city (i.e. their capital). *During this conquest,* he sent messengers to David,

---

44. There are two place names in these verses that are significant for the interpretation of the *wayyiqtol* in verse 26b: "the royal city" in verse 26b, and "the city of water" in verse 27. If "the royal city" refers to a subdivision of Rabbah (perhaps synonymous with "the city of water"), then the statement that Joab captured "the royal city" in verse 26b poses no difficulty for the sequentiality of the *wayyiqtol*. If it refers to the city as a whole, however, then verse 26b is out of sequence as shown.

Anderson suggests that the "the royal city" and "the city of water" refer to a fortification outside the city which guarded the city's water supply (Anderson 1989, 168). However, the use of the term מלוכה ("royal") for fortifications is nowhere attested in the OT.

McCarter and Bergen suggest that "the royal city" referred to the royal subdivision of the city of Rabbah, (much like עיר דוד [the City of David] refers to a subdivision of Jerusalem), which also happened to contain the water supply (McCarter 1984, 312; Bergen 1996, 376). However, it is questionable whether the royal subdivision of the city would have been in the same quarter as the water supply, since it is unlikely that the king would have lived in any position except the most secure one (Barton 1908, 147).

One could argue that "the royal city" (v. 26b) and the "city of water" (v. 27) refer to two different subdivisions of Rabbah that Joab captured before summoning David. If this were the case, then perhaps Joab had taken both the cistern at the northern end of the city, as well as the entire north to south "upper citadel", leaving only the "lower citadel" to the east (cf. the diagram in Harrison 2008). However, there is no explanation why Joab would have reported only the capture of the water supply to David (v. 27), and his message seems to indicate that the city remained otherwise intact for David to capture (1 Sm 12:28).

Finally, S. R. Driver suggests that the term "the royal city" (v. 26a) refers to Rabbah itself as the capital of Ammon, hence its importance to Joab's conquest, and the reason for the king's presence there (v. 30), while "the city of water" refers to a distinct subdivision that guarded the water supply (S. R. Driver, 1913, 293). Thus, Joab's capture of "the city of water" refers to his weakening of the city's defenses (after which he summoned David), but Joab's capture of "the royal city" in verse 26 still refers to his conquest of Rabbah as a whole. Barton notes the existence of a large cistern at the northern end of the city, and notes that both Antiochus III and Herod the Great exploited just such a water system in taking the city (Barton 1908, 148–49). Therefore, Driver's identification of "the royal city" (v. 26a) as a synonym for the city of Rabbah is the best option at present, both textually and archaeologically.

saying, "I have fought against Rabbah, and I have taken their water supply . . .".

4.2.13 Jezebel's Letter—1 Kings 21:8–9

1 Kings 21:8–9 records Jezebel's malicious scheme to murder Naboth. The *wayyiqtol* chain reads as follows:

1 KINGS 21:8–9

8 **וַתִּכְתֹּב** סְפָרִים בְּשֵׁם אַחְאָב **וַתַּחְתֹּם** בְּחֹתָמוֹ **וַתִּשְׁלַח** הַסְּפָרִים אֶל־
הַזְּקֵנִים וְאֶל־הַחֹרִים אֲשֶׁר בְּעִירוֹ הַיֹּשְׁבִים אֶת־נָבוֹת׃
9 **וַתִּכְתֹּב** בַּסְּפָרִים לֵאמֹר ...

1   [8] So she **wrote** letters in Ahab's name.
2   And she **sealed** them with his seal.
3   And she **sent** the letters to the elders and to the nobles who lived in the city with Naboth.
4   [9] And she **wrote** in the letters saying....

Verse 8 records a simple sequence of events: Jezebel wrote her letters, sealed them, and sent them. However, verse 9 records that she wrote in the letters, too. Unless one supposes that she chased down, reopened, and rewrote the letters, a strictly sequential reading of the *wayyiqtol* is irreconcilable with the narrative.

4.2.14 Ahab's Death—1 Kings 22:34–37

1 Kings 22:34–37 recounts the circumstances of Ahab's death. The *wayyiqtol* chain reads as follows:

1 KINGS 22:34–37

34 וְאִישׁ מָשַׁךְ בַּקֶּשֶׁת לְתֻמּוֹ **וַיַּכֶּה** אֶת־מֶלֶךְ יִשְׂרָאֵל בֵּין הַדְּבָקִים וּבֵין
הַשִּׁרְיָן **וַיֹּאמֶר** לְרַכָּבוֹ הֲפֹךְ יָדְךָ וְהוֹצִיאֵנִי מִן־הַמַּחֲנֶה כִּי הָחֳלֵיתִי׃
35 **וַתַּעֲלֶה** הַמִּלְחָמָה בַּיּוֹם הַהוּא וְהַמֶּלֶךְ הָיָה מָעֳמָד בַּמֶּרְכָּבָה נֹכַח
אֲרָם **וַיָּמָת** בָּעֶרֶב **וַיִּצֶק** דַּם־הַמַּכָּה אֶל־חֵיק הָרָכֶב׃
36 **וַיַּעֲבֹר** הָרִנָּה בַּמַּחֲנֶה כְּבֹא הַשֶּׁמֶשׁ לֵאמֹר אִישׁ אֶל־עִירוֹ וְאִישׁ אֶל־
אַרְצוֹ׃
37 **וַיָּמָת** הַמֶּלֶךְ **וַיָּבוֹא** שֹׁמְרוֹן **וַיִּקְבְּרוּ** אֶת־הַמֶּלֶךְ בְּשֹׁמְרוֹן׃

1   [34] A certain man drew his bow at random, and he **struck** the king of Israel between the scale armor and the breastplate.[45]
2   And he **said** to his chariot driver, "Turn your hand, and take me from the host, for I am wounded."

---

45. Translation of these two terms taken from the ESV.

3   [35] And the battle **continued** that day.

4   And the king was propped up in his chariot opposite Aram.

5   And the king **died** in the evening.

6   And the blood of the wound **flowed out** into the inside of the chariot.

7   [36] And the cry (to retreat) **passed through** the host just as the sun was setting, saying "Every man to his city, and every man to his country."

8   [37] And the king **died**.

9   And he **entered into** Samaria.

10   And they **buried** the king in Samaria.

As the outline above demonstrates, lines 1–4, 7, 9, and 10 proceed in perfectly sequential order. Lines 5 and 8, though, create a problem: line 5 recounts that Ahab died before the retreat, while line 8 records that he died afterwards. In addition, line 6 places Ahab's bleeding after his death; however, if Ahab had bled to death, as the nature of his wound and the length of his survival suggest, then more likely the blood would have continued flowing into the chariot from the time of his wound until sometime after his death. A strictly sequential reading of the *wayyiqtol* is therefore irreconcilable with the narrative. More likely, verse 37 simply resumes the mention of Ahab's death in verse 35, recounting Ahab's death and burial in fuller detail. And verse 36 simply relates the additional detail that his blood had flowed out into the chariot at the pertinent place in the narrative in order to background the fulfillment of Elijah's prophecy that the dogs would lick up his blood (v. 38).

4.2.15 The Moabite Stone

The Moabite stone recounts King Mesha's conquest of Israel and revenge on Omri's house for his previous oppressions of Moab. Buth's translation of this narrative is provided below (Buth 1994, 145–46), with the *wayyiqtols* underlined as above:

1   (As for) Omri king of Israel,

2   and he **tormented** Moab many days,

3   for Kemosh was angry with his land.

4   And his son **succeeded** him,

5   and he too **said,**

6   "I will torment Moab."

7   It was in my time that he said this.

8   And I **got the victory** over him and his house

9   and Israel perished forever.

10   And Omri **conquered** the land of Mahdeba.

11   And he **dwelt** in it during his days and half of the days of his son, forty years.

12   And Kemosh **returned** it in my days.

13   And I **built** Baal-maon

14   And I **made** the water-works in it . . .

Lines 1–3 describe Omri's oppression of Moab, lines 4–5 relate his son's succession and determination to do the same, and lines 6–9 record King Mesha's victory over Omri's son. However, lines 10–11 revert without warning to describe Omri's conquest and reign over Moab again, and lines 12–14 repeat and expand upon the events of line 8. Thus, lines 10–14 exhibit a break in time sequence from lines 1–9.

4.3 *Extent of Dischronologization*

As Collins observes (Collins 1995, 131), other scholars have indeed noted many of these same examples of dischronologization; however, rather than incorporating these examples into their grammatical description of the *wayyiqtol,* they have explained them away by categorizing them as introductory formulae, summary formulae, epexegetical comments, idiomatic hendiadys, or other special categories (S. R. Driver 1892; 81–88; Waltke and O'Connor 1990, 549–553; Andrason 2011, 25–27), the most widely applied being the category of "logical succession" (Waltke and O'Connor 1990, 547). Therefore, in order to strengthen the case for dischronologization, and to demonstrate the need for a reexamination of the meaning of the *wayyiqtol* as a whole, we will briefly explore these proposed explanations.

    4.3.1 Limited to Cases of Source Redaction?
    4.3.2 Explainable in Terms of Logical Sequentiality?
    4.3.3 Limited to Introductory and Summary Statements?
    4.3.4 Limited to Simultaneous Actions?
    4.3.5 Limited to Isolated Examples of Some Combination of the Above?

4.3.1 Limited to Cases of Source Redaction?

First, some have attempted to explain dischronologization in terms of source redaction criticism. This explanation argues that the reason for these occasional breaks in chronology is that the final editors of the OT failed to smooth over the chronological seams of the different sources when they combined the sources together into a single document. Driver, for example, asserts, "Some of these apparent instances have arisen, doubtless, from the manner in which the Hebrew historical books are evidently constructed, distinct sections, often written by different hands, being joined together without regard to *formal* unity" (S. R. Driver 1892, 88).[46]

In addition to the inherent problems of source redaction criticism, there are three problems with this assertion. First, many of the examples above occur in the middle of the narratives, rather than at the seams. Thus, the story of Esau's soup, Jezebel's letter, Jacob's love, or Jacob's wedding night, in particular, would be difficult to explain in terms of source redaction criticism. Second, the extra-biblical example of the Moabite Stone eludes explanation in terms of source redaction criticism completely since we have the original in stone (quite literally). And third, contrary to Driver's argument that dischronologizations evidence a lack of unity or coherence, as **Chapter 13** will demonstrate, a skilled narrator will frequently employ such dischronologizations intentionally to accomplish the purposes of his narrative.

4.3.2 Explainable in Terms of Logical Sequentiality?

Second, some have suggested that in cases where temporal sequentiality does not hold true, there is still a logical sequentiality that justifies the general sequentiality of the *wayyiqtol* (e.g., S. R. Driver 1892, 81; Waltke and O'Connor 1990, 549–551). While this could possibly allow for many of the dischronologizations above, in practice, it still asserts that the *wayyiqtol* must exhibit temporal sequence unless indicated otherwise. Thus, rather than providing for a neutral investigation of the *wayyiqtol* on a case by case basis, it holds the *wayyiqtol* to be, as it were, "guilty until proven innocent." Therefore, although strictly speaking the matter of logical sequentiality is not the primary target of the present discussion, in order to deal thoroughly with the matter of temporal sequentiality one must discuss this issue, as well.

There are several problems with this assertion. First, the characteristic of logical sequence is not well defined. While Waltke and O'Connor's initial definition and examples suggest that logical sequence refers specifically to the idea of "logical entailment" such that each action proceeds causally out of the previous action (Waltke and O'Connor 1990, 547), their continuing discussion includes the categories of epexegesis, simultaneous uses, pluperfect uses, and others with the justification that they still exhibit progression of thought. As a result, the validity of this explanation depends

---

46. See also Soggin and Anderson's comments mentioned above regarding the example of the Battle of Benjamin (Soggin 1981, 293–94) and Ishbosheth's murder (Anderson 1989, 70).

on what is meant by the term logical sequence. If logical sequentiality means that each successive action depends causally on the previous action, then one would still be hard pressed to explain all of the above examples of dischronologization as cases of logical sequence. If, on the other hand the term logical sequence refers simply to progression of thought in a narrative, then this property is non-unique to the *wayyiqtol*, as other Hebrew verbal forms may exhibit it, as well. In fact, as long as the author of a text is coherent, one can generally expect his statements to exhibit logical sequence, regardless of the language or verb forms in use. Therefore, one might even suggest that the term "logical sequence" as used in this way refers more to the mental coherence of the author than the grammatical properties of the *wayyiqtol*.

Second, even Waltke and O'Connor admit that some uses of the *wayyiqtol* do not fit the category of logical sequence. On page 551, for example, even though they categorize the epexegetical use as logical sequence, they admit that the epexegetical use does not succeed the prior one "either in time or as logical consequence" (Waltke and O'Connor 1990, 551).

And third, the lack of any justification or explanation for logical sequentiality in its initial proposal by S. R. Driver (see **Section 2.3**), causes one to wonder whether the idea of logical sequence would have developed on its own apart from the idea of temporal sequence, or whether it was developed simply as an ad hoc hypothesis to defend the idea of temporal sequence against such so-called exceptions.

4.3.3 Limited to Introductory and Summary Statements?

Third, some admit that there are cases of dischronologization in the OT, but claim that these are limited to introductory or summary statements, which behave differently from the mainline narrative, and thus do not reflect on the normal meaning of the *wayyiqtol* (e.g. Waltke and O'Connor 1990, 550).

There are two problems with this assertion. First, as noted above, many of the examples of dischronologization fall not at the seams of the narrative, but in the center. Esau's soup, Jezebel's letter, Jacob's love, and Jacob's wedding night, in particular contradict the claim that these can be limited to introductory and summary statements. And second, even if dischronologization could be limited to introductory and summary statements, the mere categorization of these instances does not negate the fact that the *wayyiqtol* can express dischronologization, nor does it give any reason why the *wayyiqtol* could not be used to express dischronologization elsewhere.

4.3.4 Limited to Simultaneous Actions?

Likewise, some have suggested that dischronologization can be limited to cases of simultaneous action (Waltke and O'Connor 1990, 551). This suggestion argues that it is not that the *wayyiqtols* occur out of sequence; it is just that when two or more simultaneous actions need to be related, that the *wayyiqtols* can be stacked together in the time sequence to relate two or more simultaneous events.

There are two problems with this assertion. First, while this suggestion might explain the cases of Esau's soup, Jacob's love, and possibly even Jezebel's letter, it does not explain cases where dischronologization involves not just simultaneous actions, but actual reversals in time sequence. And second, as with the argument above, even if dischronologization could be limited to cases of simultaneous actions, the mere categorization of these instances would not negate the fact that two or more successive *wayyiqtols* can overlap in time sequence, nor does it give any reason why the *wayyiqtol* could not be used for larger cases of overlap, either (e.g. the taking of Rabbah, where the introductory *wayyiqtol* overlaps with the rest of the explanatory *wayyiqtols* in the narrative).

4.3.5 Limited to Isolated Examples of Some Combination of the Above?

In reality, rather than positing one comprehensive explanation for dischronologization, most proponents of temporal sequentiality assert that dischronologization may be limited on a case by case basis to any one of the above or other explanations as applicable. This position permits one to answer each example piecemeal, without having to justify any single answer throughout. For Esau's soup and Jezebel's letter, for example, one could apply the category of simultaneous action. For the taking of Rabbah, the death of Ahab, and the Moabite stone, one could apply the category of introductory and summary statements. For Ahab's bleeding and Jacob's love, one could apply the category of logical sequentiality. And for the murder of Ishbosheth and the Battle of Benjamin, one could apply the category of source redaction criticism.

However, there are several problems with this approach. First, as the discussion thus far has demonstrated, far from explaining away dischronologization, each of these explanations actually admits the existence of dischronologization. Second, far from isolating these examples of dischronologization, the sum total of these so-called exceptions actually demonstrates the breadth of dischronologization that the *wayyiqol* can express. Third, there are still several examples above that elude any of these explanations. These include Jacob's wedding night, Jacob's blessing, the placing of the manna in the Ark, the battle of Benjamin, the crossing of the Jordan River, and the Moabite Stone. Fourth, generally speaking, the more scattered the defender's response, the weaker his actual position. And fifth, if anything can be learned from Comparative Semitics, or even outside sciences, it is the exceptions, not the norm, that are frequently the key to interpreting a matter. Therefore, to explain away the exceptions is to throw away the key to understanding the true nature of the *wayyiqtol*.

4.4 *The Underlying Issue*

Even aside from these examples of dischronologization, however, there is an underlying issue with the assertion of sequentiality in the Hebrew verbal system, both temporal and logical: the confusion of correlation and causation. As Cook has noted (2004, 248), "discourse studies have too often made the gratuitous leap from correlation to causation in their analyses." In formal terms, this is known as the logical fallacy of *cum hoc ergo propter hoc*.

To illustrate the problem with this reasoning, David Fischer in *Historians' Fallacies* observes that from the year of 1840 up through the time of his writing, every President elected in a year ending in zero died while in office—William Henry Harrison (1840), Abraham Lincoln (1860), James A. Garfield (1880), William McKinley (1900), Warren G. Harding (1920), Franklin D. Roosevelt (1940), and John F. Kennedy (1960) (Fischer 1970, 168). Naturally, the superstition in this reasoning is readily apparent, and presidents Ronald Reagan (1980) and George W. Bush (2000) have since put this theory to rest. However, it nonetheless illustrates an important point: "Correlation by itself can never establish a cause" (Fischer 1970, 168).

Of course, the issue is slightly more complicated than this, and the fallacy of *cum hoc ergo propter hoc* does not mean that the use of statistical analysis is always equally spurious or unscientific. As Fischer goes on to observe, "If X and Y occur together with perfect regularity, X may be the cause of Y, or Y may be the cause of X, or Z may be the cause of X and Y, or there may be merely a coincidence" (Fischer 1970, 168). In other words, there can still be causation where there is correlation; the question is simply which event causes which. These options, along with the precondition of regularity, can be enumerated as follows:

1. If X and Y occur together with perfect regularity . . .
2. X may be the cause of Y,
3. Y may be the cause of X,
4. Z may be the cause of X and Y,
5. Or the correlation may be merely a coincidence.

In similar manner, the fallacy of *cum hoc ergo propter hoc* does not mean that the use of statistics is invalid for the study of semantics in Hebrew grammar (contra Cook 2012, 184); rather, it simply means that more careful investigation must be performed to discern the precise link between the correlation of the form and the meaning being observed. Now, due to cultural barriers, class distinctions, geographical separations, dialectical differences, psycho-linguistic factors, artistic license, and the general imperfection of human speech, it is admittedly doubtful that any study of a language will ever achieve "perfect regularity" in its analysis of a form like the *wayyiqtol*. However, the goal is still to find the explanation that provides the closest correlation possible, and to discover the underlying causes that best account for the variations in the data in question.

As this methodology applies to the text linguistic study of the *wayyiqtol*, the present chapter has addressed the assumption that the *wayyiqtol* indicates temporal sequence (2) by challenging the regularity of this correlation (1). However, it does not necessarily hold that the remaining correlation between the *wayyiqtol* and temporal sequence is merely coincidental (5). Rather, as **Chapter 13** will demonstrate, it suggests that there is an underlying reason for the frequent correlation of the *wayyiqtol* with temporal sequence (as well as the exceptions), namely the way that narrative works (4). And lastly, further study of the specific semantics involved is needed, but there may still be a sense in which the *wayyiqtol* lends itself to the expression of temporal sequence due to the *waw* conjunction prefixed to it (3).[47] The point at present is simply that the *wayyiqtol* does not necessarily indicate temporal sequence.

4.5 Summary

In summary, there are a number of recent scholars since Martin (1968) who have begun to document and discuss examples of dischronologization, i.e., the occurrence of *wayyiqtols* out of temporal sequence. These examples of dischronologization demonstrate that even within the methods of the present text linguistics theory, the temporal sequentiality of the *wayyiqtol* does not align with actual usage in the OT. Various explanations have been proposed to account for these so called exceptions, but to the contrary, the sum total of these exceptions demonstrates the extent of dischronologization that the *wayyiqtol* can and does communicate. In addition, the lack of

---

47. Our sincere thanks to Stephen A. Kaufman, whose comments were instrumental in prompting this distinction and clarification (personal communication, October 22, 2012).

perfect regularity in the correlation between the *wayyiqtol* and temporal sequentiality suggests that there is more likely an underlying cause for this frequent correlation (as well as the exceptions), namely the way that narrative works. And lastly, there may still be a sense in which the *wayyiqtol* does *lend itself* to temporal and logical sequence due to the *waw* conjunction prefixed to it; the point at present is simply that the *wayyiqtol* does not necessarily indicate temporal sequence.

5. Conclusion

In conclusion, the present chapter has presented three evidences against the temporal sequentiality of the *wayyiqtol*. First, it has shown that the idea of temporal sequentiality can be traced to the erroneous assumptions of Ewald and S. R. Driver's aspect theory. Second, it has shown that the assumption of the temporal sequentiality of the *wayyiqtol* does not align with any given theory of the origins of the *wayyiqtol*. And third, it has shown that even within the methods of the present text linguistics theory, the temporal sequentiality of the *wayyiqtol* does not align with actual usage in the OT. On this basis, it asserts that the assumption of the temporal sequentiality of the *wayyiqtol* is mistaken, and that the various terms used to describe it as such (e.g. *waw*-consecutive, *waw*-relative, *waw*-correlative) are inaccurate.

In addition, although a full discussion is beyond the scope of the present chapter, it suggests with Blau that a more probable explanation for the meaning of the *wayyiqtol* (based on an incorporation of the diachronic evidence thus far) is that it functioned simply as the *waw*-initial past tense verb form (Blau 2010, 152, 190). And, it suggests with Joosten (2012, 164) and Cook (2004, 264; 2009, 10; 2012, 312–338) that its frequent correlation with temporal sequentiality is simply a consequence of its usage as the main verb form of past tense BH narrative. This will be explored further in **Chapter 13**.

And for the purposes of the present study, the present chapter submits that the temporal sequence of the individual events of the Flood narrative depends not on the presence or absence of the *wayyiqtol*, but on other contextual and linguistic factors. As Baker notes, temporal sequentiality is not to be sought in the *wayyiqtol*, but in "the context and the situation" of the verb (Baker 1971, 54). These and other factors will be explored in the following three chapters.

Appendix: Probability of Discronologization

The following is a catalogue of proposed dischronologizations that have been discussed to date, evaluated for probability on a scale of 1–5. This probability is assigned as follows:

1 = highly improbable
2 = improbable
3 = inconclusive
4 = probable
5 = highly probable

Where other grammatical constructions that can affect temporal sequence are involved (i.e. a *wayhi*, a disjunctive *waw*, or a non-verbal clause), this has been noted instead of the probability, as these examples do not provide a pure sample of the dischronologization of the *wayyiqtol*. Those discussed for the first time in the present work are listed as Stroup, and those discussed as examples in **Section 4.2** are printed in bold.

Reference	Probability	Source
Gn 2:18, 19	4	Buth 1994, 148–49; Collins 1995, 135–140
Gn 6:11	4	Joosten 2012, 168
Gn 7:22, 23	5	Joosten 2012, 168
Gn 18:10	4	Joosten 2012, 169
Gn 19:24–29	Involves a *wayhi*	Baker 1971, 63
Gn 25:1	5	Joosten 2012, 168
Gn 25:34	5	Cook 2004, 259; Cook 2012, 290; Joosten 2012, 169
Gn 29:11,12	2	Baker 1971, 70
Gn 29:14b–18	4	Cook 2004, 263; Cook 2012, 290
Gn 29:21–25	4	Baker 1971, 71; Collins 1995, 132; Cook 2004, 262; Cook 2012, 296
Gn 29:28–30	4	Baker 1971, 71; Cook 2004, 262; Cook 2012, 296
Gn 32:25–26	3	Joosten 2012, 170
Gn 34:13–14	5	Joosten 2012, 167
Gn 35:6, 15	4	Baker 1971, 72
Gn 37:5–6	5	Joosten 2012, 174
Gn 45:15	4	Joosten 2012, 169
Gn 48:12–17	4	Stroup
Ex 2:10	4	Baker 1971, 89
Ex 6:2	4	Cook 2004, 259; Cook 2012, 291
Ex 14:6-8	2	Baker 1971, 73–74
Ex 16:21	4	Joosten 2012, 174

Ex 16:34	5	Stroup
Ex 19:1,2	3	Baker 1971, 61; Cook 2012, 295
Nm 12:2	4	Joosten 2012, 169
Nm 13:17	4	Cook 2004, 259
Dt 5:22	5	Joosten 2012, 173
Jo 2:3–4	2	Joosten 2012, 171
Jo 2:15, 16	3	Martin 1968, 182; Baker 1971, 57; Cook 2004, 259; Cook 2012, 290
Jo 2:23, 24	4	Cook 2004, 259
Jo 4:10–12	5	Stroup
Jo 8:3,4	4	Baker 1971, 74–75; Cook 2004, 259
Jo 13:15, 24, 29	4	Baker 1971, 75–78
Jo 18:8	5	Baker 1971, 79–80; Collins 1995, 123
Jgs 2:1–6	5	Stroup
Jgs 3:9, 10	4	Revell 1985, 426
Jgs 3:19–20	2	Revell 1985, 426
Jgs 4:16–21	Involves a disjunctive waw	Revell 1985, 426
Jgs 8:35–9:6	4	Revell 1985, 426
Jgs 11:29–32	4	Revell 1985, 426–27
Jgs 11:36, 37	1	Revell 1985, 427
Jgs 12:8–12	5	Washburn 1994, 32–33
Jgs 14:14–17	2	Revell 1985, 427; Buth 1994, 144–45
Jgs 20:31–39	3	Revell 1985, 427–433; Buth 1994, 143, 150–51
Ru 1:6–7	5	Cook 2012, 289
1 Sm 7:13	2	Baker 1971, 80–81
1 Sm 8:3	5	Joosten 2012, 174
1 Sm 9:26	1	Baker 1971, 81–82
1 Sm 14:24	3	Collins 1995, 135
1 Sm 17:11, 13	4	Baker 1971, 60
1 Sm 18:11	4	Joosten 2012, 169
1 Sm 26:4	2	Baker 1971, 90
1 Sm 28:20	5	Joosten 2012, 168
2 Sm 4:1–3	Involves a relative clause	Baker 1971, 84–85
2 Sm 4:4	Involves a disjunctive waw	Martin 1968, 182; Baker 1971, 59–60
2 Sm 4:7	5	Baker 1971, 85; Washburn 1994, 34–35; Collins 1995, 133
2 Sm 11:2	3	Joosten 2012, 170
2 Sm 11:17	4	Cook 2004, 259
2 Sm 11:18–19	4	Joosten 2012, 172
2 Sm 12:26–29	5	Martin 1968, 181; Baker 1971, 54–55
2 Sm 13:28	4	Baker 1971, 85–87

2 Sm 13:34	5	Baker 1971, 87; Collins 1995, 133–34
2 Sm 23:12	4	Joosten 2012, 171
1 Kgs 7:14	Involves a non-verbal clause	Baker 1971, 62
1 Kgs 9:14	4	Baker 1971, 59
1 Kgs 11:14–22	Involves a *wayhi*	Martin 1968, 184; Baker 1971, 57–59; Collins 1995, 124; Joosten 2012, 172
1 Kgs 18:1–5	Involves a disjunctive *waw*	Martin 1968, 185; Baker 1971, 56–57; Cook 2004, 260; Cook 2012, 293
1 Kgs 18:24	5	Joosten 2012, 167
1 Kgs 18:26–36	2	Revell 1985, 426
1 Kgs 19:6	5	Joosten 2012, 168
1 Kgs 21:8, 9	5	Baker 1971, 87-88; Collins 1995, 123
1 Kgs 22:34–37	5	Baker 1971, 88-89; Cook 2004, 260; Cook 2012, 295
2 Kgs 6:4–5	Involves a *wayhi*	Joosten 2012, 170
2 Kgs 6:29	3	Baker 1971, 90–91
2 Kgs 7:6, 7	Involves a disjunctive *waw*	Baker 1971, 94–95
2 Kgs 7:17–19	Involves a *wayhi*	Baker 1971, 92; Collins 1995, 123
2 Kgs 13:14–14:16	Involves a disjunctive *waw*	Baker 1971, 63–70; Cook 2004, 260; Cook 2012, 291
2 Kgs 17:7ff	Involves a *wayhi*	Baker 1971, 95–99
Is 39:1	4	Buth 1994 147; Collins 1995, 126
Moabite Stone 9a–n	5	Buth 1994, 145–46; Collins 1995, 126B–27

References

Anderson, A. A. 1989. *2 Samuel*. Dallas, TX: Word Books, Publisher.

Andrason, A. 2010. The panchronic *yiqtol*: Functionally consistent and cognitively plausible. *Journal of Hebrew Scriptures* 10. http://www.jhsonline.org/Articles/article_138.pdf (accessed 8/27/2011).

Andrason, A. 2011. Biblical Hebrew *wayyiqtol*: A dynamic definition. *Journal of Hebrew Scriptures* 10, Article 8. http://www.jhsonline.org/Articles/article_155.pdf (accessed on 8/27/2011).

Baker, D. W. 1971. *The consecutive non-perfective as pluperfect in the historical books of the Hebrew Old Testament (Genesis–Kings)*. M.A. thesis, Temple University, Philadelphia.

Barrick W. D. 2008. Noah's Flood and its geological implications. *Coming to Grips with Genesis*. Ed. T. Mortenson, and T. H. Ury. Green Forest, AR: Master Books.

Barton, G. A. 1908. On the Reading 2, עיר המים Sam. 12:27. *Journal of Biblical Literature* 27.2: 147–152.

Bauer, H. 1910. Die tempora im Semitischen: Ihre entstehung und ihre ausgestaltung in den einzelsprachen. *Beiträge zur Assyriologie und Semitischen sprachwissenschaft VIII*, 1. Ed. F. Delitzsch and P. Haupt. Leipzig, Germany: J. C. Hinrichs'sche Buchhandlung. Berlin, Germany:

Bergen, R. D. 1996. *1, 2 Samuel.* Nashville, TN: Broadman & Holman Publishers.

Bergsträsser, G. 1983. *Introduction to the Semitic languages: Test specimens and grammatical sketches.* Trans. and ed. P. T. Daniels. Winona Lake, IN: Eisenbrauns.

Blau, J. 1971. Marginalia Semitica 6: The problem of tenses in biblical Hebrew. *Israel Oriental Studies* 1: 24–26.

Blau, J. 1976. *A grammar of biblical Hebrew.* Wiesbaden, Germany: Otto Harrassowitz.

Blau, J. 2010. Phonology and morphology of biblical Hebrew. Trans. M. O'Connor. *Linguistic Studies in Ancient West Semitic* 2. Winona Lake, IN: Eisenbrauns.

Buth, R. 1994. Methodological collision between source criticism and discourse analysis: The problem of "unmarked temporal overlay" and the pluperfect/nonsequential wayyiqtol. In *Biblical Hebrew and discourse linguistics.* Ed. R. D. Bergen, 138–154. Dallas, TX: Summer Institute of Linguistics.

Cassuto, U. 1967. *A commentary on the book of Exodus.* Trans. I Abrahams. Jerusalem, Israel: Central Press.

Collins, C. J. 1995. The *wayyiqtol* as "pluperfect": When and why. *Tyndale Bulletin* 46: 117–140.

Cook, J. A. 2002. *The biblical Hebrew verbal system: A grammaticalization approach.* Ph.D. diss., University of Wisconsin-Madison.

Cook, J. A. 2004. The semantics of verbal pragmatics: Clarifying the roles of *wayyiqtol* and *weqatal* in biblical Hebrew prose. *Journal of Semitic Studies* 49.2: 247–273.

Cook, J. A. 2009. *Reconsidering the so-called vav-consecutive.* Linguistics and biblical Hebrew section, Society of Biblical Literature Annual Meeting, New Orleans. http://ancienthebrewgrammar.files.wordpress.com/2010/05/recvavcons.pdf (accessed on 6/29/2012).

Cook, J. A. 2012. *Time and the biblical Hebrew verb: The expression of tense, aspect, and modality in biblical Hebrew.* Winona Lake, IN: Eisenbrauns.

Driver, G. R. 1936. *Problems of the Hebrew verbal system.* Edinburgh, Scotland: T. & T. Clark.

Driver, S. R. 1892. *A treatise on the use of the tenses in Hebrew and some other syntactical questions.* 3rd ed. Oxford, England: Clarendon Press.

Driver, S. R. 1913. *Notes on the Hebrew text and the topography of the books of Samuel.* 2nd ed. Eugene, OR: Wipf and Stock Publishers.

Emerton, J. A. 1987. An examination of some attempts to defend the unity of the flood narrative in Genesis. *Vetus Testamentum* 37.4: 401–420.

Endo, Y. 1996. *The verbal system of classical Hebrew in the Joseph story.* Assen, Netherlands: Van Gorcum & Comp.

Ewald, H. 1870/1891. *Syntax of the Hebrew language of the Old Testament.* Trans. J. Kennedy. Edinburgh, Scotland: T. & T. Clark.

Finley, T. J. 1981. The *WAW*-consecutive with "imperfect" in biblical Hebrew: Theoretical studies and its use in Amos. In *Tradition and testament.* Ed. J. S. Feinberg, and P. D. Feinberg, 241–262. Chicago, IL: Moody Press.

Fischer, D. H. 1970. *Historians' fallacies: Toward a logic of historical thought.* New York, NY: Harper & Row, Publishers.

Gentry, P. 1998. The system of the finite verb in classical biblical Hebrew. *Hebrew Studies* 39: 7–39.

Gesenius, W., E. Kautzsch, and A. E. Cowley. 1910. *Gesenius' Hebrew grammar.* Oxford, England: Clarendon Press.

Gibson, J. C. L. 1994. *Davidson's introductory Hebrew grammar-syntax.* 4th ed. Edinburgh, Scotland: T&T Clark.

Goerwitz, R. L. 1992. The accentuation of the Hebrew jussive and preterite. *Journal of the American Oriental Society* 112.2: 198–203.

Goldfajn, T. 1998. *Word order and time in biblical Hebrew narrative.* Oxford, England: Clarendon Press.

Green, W. H. 1872. *A grammar of the Hebrew language.* 3rd ed. New York, NY: John Wiley and Son.

Greenstein, E. L. 1988. On the prefixed preterite in biblical Hebrew. *Hebrew Studies* 29: 7–17.

Hamori, A. 1973. A note on *yaqtulu* in East and West Semitic. *Archiv Orientální* 41: 319–324.

Harmelink, B. L. 2011. *Exploring the syntactic, semantic, and pragmatic uses of* ויהי *in biblical Hebrew.* Dallas, TX: SIL International, Inc.

Harrison, T. P. 2002. The Amman Citadel: An archaeological biography: "Rabbath of the Ammonites." *Archaeology Odyssey* (Mar/Apr):10–19. Accessed on 4/17/2014. http://members.bib-arch.org/publication. asp?PubID=BSAO&Volume=5&Issue=2&ArticleID=4.

Hatav, G. 1997. *The semantics of aspect and modality: Evidence from English and biblical Hebrew.* Amsterdam, Netherlands: John Benjamins Publishing Company.

Heller, R. 2004. *Narrative structure and discourse constellations: An analysis of clause function in biblical Hebrew prose.* Winona Lake, IN: Eisenbrauns.

Hetzron, R. 1969. The evidence for perfect **y'aqtul* and jussive **yaqt'ul* in Proto-Semitic. *Journal of Semitic Studies* 14.1: 1–21.

Heuhnergard, J. 1987. Tribute in *Working with no data: Semitic and Egyptian studies presented to Thomas O. Lambdin.* Ed. D. M. Golomb, ix-xii. Winona Lake, IN: Eisenbrauns.

Huehnergard, J. 1988. The early Hebrew prefix-conjugations. *Hebrew Studies* 29: 19–24.

Huehnergard, J. 2011. *A grammar of Akkadian.* 3rd ed. Winona Lake, IN: Eisenbrauns.

Joosten J. 2006. The disappearance of iterative WEQATAL in the biblical Hebrew verbal system. In *Biblical Hebrew in its northwest Semitic setting: Typological and historical perspectives.* Ed. S. E. Fassberg and A. Hurvitz, 135–147. Winona Lake, IN: Eisenbrauns.

Joosten, J. 2012. *The verbal system of biblical Hebrew: A new synthesis elaborated on the basis of classical prose.* Jerusalem, Israel: Simor Ltd.

Joüon, P., and T. Muraoka. 1993. *A grammar of biblical Hebrew*. Reprint of first ed., with corrections. Rome, Italy: Editrice Pontificio Istituto Biblico, 1996.

Kahn, L. 2009. *The verbal system in late enlightenment Hebrew*, vol. 55. Studies in Semitic Languages and Linguistics. Ed. A. D. Rubin, T. Muraoka, and C. H. M. Versteegh. Leiden, Netherlands: Brill.

Kuryłowicz, J. 1973. *Studies in Semitic grammar and metrics*. London, England: Curzon Press Ltd.

Li, T. 1999. *The expression of sequence and non sequence in Northwest Semitic narrative prose*. Ph.D. diss., Hebrew Union College, Cincinnati.

Martin, W. J. 1968. "Dischronologized" narrative in the Old Testament. *Vetus Testamentum* 17: 179–186.

McCarter, K. P. Jr. 1984. II Samuel: A new translation with introduction, notes, and commentary. In vol. 9 of *Anchor Bible*. Ed. W. F. Albright, and D.N. Freedman. Garden City, NY: Doubleday.

McFall, L. 1982. *The enigma of the Hebrew verbal system: Solutions from Ewald to the present day*. Sheffield, England: The Almond Press.

Mettinger, T. N. D. 1974. The Hebrew verbal system: A survey of recent research. *Annual of the Swedish Theological Society* 9: 64–84.

Moomo, D. O. 2004. *The meaning of the biblical Hebrew verbal conjugation from a crosslinguistic perspective*. Ph.D. diss., University of Stellenbosch.

Moran, W. L. 1960. Early Canaanite *yaqtula*. *Orientalia* 29: 1–19.

Muraoka, T. and M. Roglund. 1998. The *waw* consecutive in Old Aramaic? A rejoinder to Victor Sasson. *Vetus Testamentum* 48: 99–104.

Murphy, T. J. 2003. *Pocket dictionary for the study of biblical Hebrew*. Downers Grove, IL: InterVarsity Press.

Niccacci, A. 1990. *The syntax of the verb in classical Hebrew prose*. Trans. W. G. E. Watson. Sheffield, England: Sheffield Academic Press.

Rainey, A. F. 1986. The ancient Hebrew prefix conjugation in the light of Amarnah Canaanite. *Hebrew Studies* 27: 4–19.

Rainey, A. F. 1988. Further remarks on the Hebrew verbal system. *Hebrew Studies* 29: 35–42.

Rainey, A. F. 1900.The prefix conjugation patterns of early Northwest Semitic. In *Lingering over words: Studies in ancient Near Eastern literature in honor of William L. Moran*. Ed. T. Abusch, J. Huehnergard, and P. Steinkeller, 407–420. Atlanta, GA: Scholars Press.

Rainey, A. F. 1991–1993. Is there really a *yaqtula* conjugation pattern in the Canaanite Amarna tablets? *Journal of Cuneiform Studies* 43–45: 107–118.

Rainey, A. F. 2003. The *yaqtul* preterite in Northwest Semitic. In *Hamlet on a hill: Semitic and Greek studies presented to Professor T. Muraoka on the occasion of his sixty-fifth birthday*. Ed. M. F. J. Baasten, and W. T. Van Peursen, 395–407. Dudley, MA: Uitgeverij Peeters en Departement Oosterse Studies.

Revell, E. J. 1984. Stress and the *WAW* consecutive in biblical Hebrew. *Journal of the American Oriental Society* 104.3: 437–444.

Revell, E. J. 1985. The battle with Benjamin (Judges XX 29–48) and Hebrew narrative techniques. *Vetus Testamentum* 35.4: 417–433.

Sadler, M. 2007. *Grammar in use across time and space: Deconstructing the Japanese dative subject construction.* Philadelphia, PA: John Benjamin's Publishing Co.

Sasson, V. 1997. Some observations on the use and original purpose of the *waw* consecutive in old Aramaic and biblical Hebrew. *Vetus Testamentum* 47: 111–127.

Smith, M. S. 1991. The origins and development of the waw-consecutive: Northwest Semitic Evidence from Ugarit to Qumran. In vol. 39 of *Harvard Semitic Studies.* Atlanta GA: Scholars Press.

Soggin, J. A. 1981. *Judges: A commentary.* Trans. J. S. Bowden. Philadelphia, PA: The Westminster Press.

Van der Merwe, C. H. J. 1987. A short survey of major contributions to the grammatical description of old Hebrew since 1800 AD. *Journal of Northwest Semitic Languages* 13: 161–190.

Van der Merwe, C. H. J. 1994. Discourse linguistics and biblical Hebrew grammar. In *Biblical Hebrew and discourse linguistics.* Ed. R. D. Bergen, 138–154. Dallas, TX: Summer Institute of Linguistics.

Van der Merwe, C. H. J., J. A. Naude, and J. H. Kroeze. 2002. *A biblical Hebrew reference grammar.* Sheffield, England: Sheffield Academic Press.

Waltke, B. K., and M. O'Connor. 1990. *An introduction to biblical Hebrew syntax.* Winona Lake, IN: Eisenbrauns.

Washburn, D. L. 1994. Chomsky's separation of syntax and semantics. *Hebrew Studies* 35: 27–46.

Williams, R. J. 2007. *Williams's Hebrew syntax.* Rev. and expanded by J. C. Beckman. Toronto, Canada: University of Toronto Press.

Zevit, Z. 1988. Talking funny in biblical Henglish and solving a problem of the *yaqtul* past tense. *Hebrew Studies* 29: 25–33.

CHAPTER 11

The Verbal Tiller: Lexical Semantics of Verbs as a Factor in Sequentiality—Temporal Progression at the *Micro-level*

Kai M. Akagi

Analogy and Orientation. Every form of transportation fundamentally requires a system of navigation to control movement. Each morning many commuters control the movements of their vehicles by means of pedals, a gear shifter, and a steering wheel. Within the human body, signals from the brain cause muscles to contract and relax to control movement, allowing the body to advance forward, backward, and to the side while walking from place to place. In a ship, the tiller serves a vital navigational function, whether controlled manually or through a steering wheel. The ship moves according to the will of the helmsman as he directs the ship to port or starboard by using the tiller to shift the rudder.

The movements of narrative consist of movements in time. From the broadest level of the complete story to every smaller division of the discourse, narratives portray temporal relationships of states and occurrences. These relationships include those explicitly portrayed between sentences, as by phrases such as "The next day...," "Four years later...," or even, "Then they lived happily ever after," to the more implicit relationships in time between sentences as they appear in order. However, as tracing the control of movement in a ship leads to one of its small and simple parts, the tiller, tracing the control of movement in narrative leads to individual verbs and the phrases in which they appear.

Abstract. In the field of lexical semantics, situation aspect involves an important set of temporal properties of verb phrases and plays a significant role in dictating the relationships of states and events in narratives. Situation aspect has received relatively little attention in the BH literature. Through the variables of dynamicity, telicity, and durativity, a system of seven situation-aspect classes results for the examination of verb phrases. When combined with a system of mapping between basic- and derived-level situations and observations concerning the correspondence between situation aspect classes and temporal relationships between situations in narratives, this system provides a means for analysis of temporal relationships from clause to clause, that is, at the ***micro-level*** of narrative, in BH and cross-linguistically.

Outline

Abbreviations

ACC [in glosses]	accusative
ACC [elsewhere]	accomplishment
ACH	achievement
ACT	activity
BH	Biblical Hebrew
DAT	dynamic aspect tree
DIR	directional
DO	direct object
F	feminine
GEN	genitive
GER	gerund
HON	honorific
ILS	individual-level state
INF	infinitive
M	masculine
NOM	nominative
NP	noun phrase
pl	plural
PP	prepositional phrase
PREP	preposition
PRES	present

RVC	resultative verb complement
sg	singular
SEM	semelfactive
SLS	stage-level state
TOP	topical
QC	quantifying complement
VOC	vocative
VP	verb phrase

1. Introduction

It is hardly possible to overestimate the importance of the verbal elements of language. Among the parts of speech, the verb plays a uniquely dominating role in portraying the occurrence of events, describing circumstances, ascribing attributes, and making identification. In a narrative, verbs depict the events of the story and illustrate the conditions during which they occur. Consequently, the temporal properties of verbs and verb phrases (VPs) require attention in determining temporal relationships, such as temporal sequence, between these events and conditions. Language users are often conscious of some temporal properties of verbs and VPs, particularly those marked formally. Depending on the language, these may include distinctions of tense and viewpoint aspect (see below) as well as those marked through the use of temporal adverbs or adverbial phrases. BH formally marks temporal properties and relationships through temporal adverbs and verbal inflexion. However, additional temporal properties of the events and circumstances verbs and VPs describe are a function not of formal marking but of the semantic significance of individual verbal lexemes with their accompanying modifiers. Among these properties are those of situation aspect.

While tense concerns the relative placement of situations in time, whether past, present, or future, aspect concerns the internal temporal properties of situations as verbs and VPs represent them.[1] Two classes of aspect receive primary attention in linguistic literature: viewpoint aspect (also called grammatical aspect or *Aspekt*) and situation aspect (also called lexical aspect or *Aktionsart*).[2] The former class encompasses formally marked distinctions

---

1. As a matter of clarification due to variations in terminology and usage, throughout I use "event" to refer to dynamic occurrences portrayed by verbs and VPs, "state" to refer to non-dynamic, that is, stative, conditions, and "situation" as a broad term encompassing both.

2. Some linguists, particularly in the field of Slavic linguistics, use the term *Aktionsart* to refer to a subcategory of morphologically marked distinctions of aspect rather than to situation aspect. In this field, see Wolfgang Klein (1995) for a discussion of aspect in Russian.

and refers to the speaker or writer's portrayal of temporal properties according to viewpoints relative to situations. Such distinctions include that between 'perfective' and 'imperfective' aspect, as between "Mary ate" and "Mary was eating" in English. This distinction features prominently in Slavic languages and Mandarin Chinese, to provide examples, through morphological inflection and aspectual particles respectively. Situation aspect refers to temporal properties of situations due to inherent semantic properties of verbs, along with their accompanying modifiers. Two phrases, such as "Jim ran" and "Jim stopped," although syntactically identical, may portray situations with different temporal properties. The former portrays an event taking place over a duration of time and without any indication of a stopping point inherent in the expression; the latter represents an event as taking place only at a moment in time.[3]

Analysis of situation aspect of verbs and VPs in a narrative assists in determining the variety of temporal natures and relationships of the situations they depict. Obviously, two non-durative events may temporally relate to one another in fewer ways than two durative events. The former may only occur in sequence (either immediately or with an intervening interval of time) or concurrently. The latter may occur with a greater variety of overlapping or non-overlapping relationships and with one event either constituent or non-constituent of the other.

Linguistic studies of situation aspect and related fields, particularly since the 1950s and increasing with profusion in the past two decades, provide bases and models for developing a systematic methodology for analyzing situation aspect in BH narrative. The application of such a methodology to a particular narrative (in the case of the proposed study, that of the Genesis Flood) may then increase the clarity with which modern readers may understand temporal relationships as authorially intended and as original readers would have understood them.

1.1.   Importance of Analysis of BH Situation Aspect
1.2.   Chapter Overview

---

3. Susan Rothstein (2008, 1) offers the following explanation of the distinction between these two kinds of aspect: "Lexical aspect concerns those properties of event structure which are determined by what are traditionally called 'content words,' the meanings of verbs themselves and the modifiers which modify these verbs, and as such lexical aspect usually (in English type languages at least) has focused on structural properties of events expressed by VP internal material. Grammatical aspect focuses on operations on event structure introduced by (in English) VP external material, often functional elements such as inflections, auxiliary verbs and possibly zero-inflectional elements."

1.1 *Importance of Analysis of BH Situation Aspect*

Despite the proliferation of studies of situation aspect in linguistics since the mid-twentieth century and despite the ongoing discussion of the nature of the verbal system in BH,[4] situation aspect in BH has received little attention. Studies addressing it most often have not significantly related it to temporal relationships of situations. F. W. Dobbs-Allsopp (2000, 21 n. 1) speaks of situation aspect as a function of language "which students of Biblical Hebrew have generally ignored." Robert Binnick (2006) includes only a handful of such studies among the one hundred twelve entries on Hebrew from all periods in his extensive bibliography. The most significant studies are those by Galia Hatav (1989), Stuart Alan Creason (1995), Ernst Jenni (2000), and Dobbs-Allsopp (1995, 2000). Ronald S. Hendel (1996) discusses the distinction between stativity and dynamicity but, although he elaborates some morphologically marked difference between event structures across the stems of BH, does not otherwise apply situation aspect classes to BH. Jenni (1994) mentions verbs which may carry either a stative or inchoative sense and considers a third class of aspect, phasal aspect. Nevertheless, a breach remains for the construction of a systematic method for analyzing temporal relationships of situations in BH.

Studies outside of BH have examined the relationship of situation aspect to temporal overlap and progression in narrative. Alice G. B. ter Meulen, beginning with ter Meulen (1997) and Jerry Seligman and ter Meulen (1995), significantly relates situation aspect to the temporal relation of events to one another in English narrative and offers a system of representation, Dynamic Aspect Trees (DATs), drawn from mathematical tree diagrams. Ter Meulen's observations indicate that aspectual properties of events, particularly telicity, often correspond to particular temporal relations between events in the absence of opposing presupposed knowledge or explicit indicators to the contrary. With the sufficiently demonstrated inability of the Hebrew *wayyiqtol* form to serve as a consistent indicator of temporal relationships in narrative (see **Chapter 10** by Stroup on the *wayyiqtol* form), reinforced by the general cross-linguistic acknowledgement that morphology alone does

---

4. The following quote provides one expression of the proliferation of works on the topic: "It has often been hotly disputed among philologists working on particular languages whether their languages were 'tense' or 'aspect' languages; for example, the controversy over Hebrew, Arabic, and other Semitic languages fills a whole library" (Hans-Jürgen Sasse 2002, 210). For an extensive recent treatment to the Hebrew verbal system, see Jan Joosten (2012). See **Chapter 10** by Stroup for a summary of approaches to the BH verbal system with particular focus on the *wayyiqtol* form.

not establish temporal sequence, the significance of the role of situation aspect for temporal relationships of narrative events requires consideration.

1.2 *Chapter Overview*

This study attempts to propose a methodology for the analysis of lexical semantics, particularly situation aspect, in BH as it relates to temporal relationships of situations in the Genesis Flood narrative. Presenting this proposal will begin by introducing the theory of situation aspect and assessing developments relevant to the study of temporal sequence, particularly since Zeno Vendler (1957, 1967). This will include developing a system of classification and considering the role of modifiers and other VP elements for situation aspect. Presentation of the two-level mapping of classes at the lexical and situation levels derived from Zhonghua (Richard) Xiao and Anthony McEnery (2002, 2004a, 2004b) and studies of the relationship of situation aspect to temporal sequence and its representation from ter Meulen (1997) will follow in order to combine these with the classification system in a methodology for analyzing BH. Finally, limitations of the proposed methodology will be explained, the method will be applied in a simplified fashion to a short sample of BH narrative, and the verbs and VPs from the Genesis Flood narrative requiring analysis will be listed in anticipation of a more complete analysis of that narrative in the future.

2. Relevant Research of Situation Aspect Theory and Proposed Modifications

2.1   Overview
2.2   Studies of Situation Aspect Theory Outside of BH and Proposed Modifications
2.3   Studies of Situation Aspect in BH

2.1 *Overview*

The extent of aspect research, particularly during the past two decades, requires a selective treatment of the literature. Others, such as Sasse (2002), Johan van der Auwera and Hana Filip (2008), and Binnick (2006), have offered more thorough summaries or bibliographies. Since our purpose here is to propose a method for analyzing temporal relationships in BH, a discussion of theory relating most closely to development of such a method must suffice. Filip (2011) provides an excellent overview of current theoretical discussion of situation aspect.

2.2 Studies of Situation Aspect Theory Outside of BH and Proposed Modifications

2.2.1 Vendlerian Classification
2.2.2 Modified Situation Aspect Classification and Additional Categories
2.2.3 Modifiers, Aspectual Class, and VP Aspect Diagnostics
2.2.4 Aspectual Class Mapping between Verbs and VPs
2.2.5 Ter Meulen and Temporal Relations in Discourse

2.2.1 Vendlerian Classification

Although Aristotle is generally acknowledged as the first to articulate distinctions between classes of situation aspect,[5] Zeno Vendler's seminal article "Verbs and Times" (1957, 1967) proposed four classes of verbs according to situation aspect which have provided the foundation for the majority of subsequent research.[6] Vendler labeled his classes of verbs "state terms," "activity terms," "achievement terms," and "accomplishment terms," defining them according to a set of three distinctions. He first distinguished between terms denoting processes and those not denoting processes in time. His system then proposed that those in the former category may include an

5. Aristotle's classification of *kinēsis* and *energeia* in a discussion of ontology in the *Metaphysics* anticipated later event structure classification. In this discussion, *kinēsis* denotes that which may be said to have occurred (the Greek perfect form) while taking place (the Greek present form), in contrast to *energeia*. This distinction does not appear in a linguistic discussion but rather while addressing potentiality and actuality, the realization of states of being or actions in reality. Although a *kinēsis* had a "limit" (*peras*), Aristotle's "limit" does not fully correspond with later concepts of telicity. *Kinēsis* and *energeia* more closely correspond to Vendler's (1957, 1967) later distinction between events and states. The relevant section from the *Metaphysics* (*Metaphysics* Θ, 6, 1048b [IX. vi. 7–10]) as it appears in the *Loeb Classical Library* is as follows:

Ἐπεὶ δὲ τῶν πράξεων ὧν ἔστι πέρας οὐδεμία τέλος ἀλλὰ τῶν περὶ τὸ τέλος, οἷον τὸ ἰσχναίνειν [ἢ ἰσχνασία αὐτό], αὐτὰ δὲ ὅταν ἰσχναίνῃ οὕτως ἐστὶν ἐν κινήσει, μὴ ὑπάρχοντα ὧν ἕνεκα ἡ κίνησις, οὐκ ἔστι ταῦτα πρᾶξις, ἢ οὐ ταλεία γε· οὐ γὰρ τέλος· ἀλλ᾽ ἐκείνη <ἣ> ἐνυπάρχει τὸ τέλος καὶ [ἡ] πρᾶξις. οἷον ὁρᾷ ἅμα <καὶ ἑώρακε,> καὶ φρονεῖ <καὶ πεφρόνηκε,> καὶ νοεῖ καὶ νεονόηκε· ἀλλ᾽ οὐ μανθάνει καὶ μεμάθηκεν, οὐδ᾽ ὑγιάζεται καὶ ὑγίασται. εὖ ζῇ καὶ εὖ ἔζηκεν ἅμα, καὶ εὐδαιμονεῖ καὶ εὐδαιμόνηκεν· εἰ δὲ μή, ἔδει ἄν ποτε παύεσθαι, ὥσπερ ὅταν ἰσχναίνῃ· νῦν δ᾽ οὔ, ἀλλὰ ζῇ καὶ ἔζηκεν.   Τούτων δὴ <δεῖ> τὰς μὲν κινήσεις λέγειν, τὰς δ᾽ ἐνεργείας. πᾶσαν ἀρ κίνησις ἀτελής, ἰσχνασία μάζησις βάδισις οἰκοδόμησις· αὗται δὴ κινήσεις, καὶ ἀτελεῖς γε. οὐ γὰρ ἅμα βαδίζει καὶ βεβάδικεν, οὐδ᾽ οἰκοδομεῖ καὶ ᾠκοδόμηκεν, οὐδὲ γίγνεται καὶ γέγονεν, ἢ κινεῖται καὶ κεκίνηται· ἀλλ᾽ ἕτερον καὶ κινεῖ καὶ κεκίνηκεν· ἑώρακε δὲ καὶ ὁρᾷ ἅμα τὸ αὐτό, καὶ νοεῖ καὶ νεονόηκεν. τὴν μὲν οὖν τοιαύτην ἐνέργειαν λέγω, ἐκείνην δὲ κίνησιν.

6. The 1967 essay differs only minimally from the 1957 version. Quotations here are from the 1967 version.

inherent terminal point (accomplishment terms) or lack one (activity terms), and that those in the latter subdivide into instantaneous terms (achievement terms) and those with duration (state terms).

Subsequent writers have sought to refine these four categories (see the discussion of some of these efforts below), which may be expressed according to the variables of dynamicity, telicity (presence of an inherent endpoint), and durativity as follows:[7]

[− dynamic][− telic][+ durative]	state terms
[+ dynamic][− telic][+ durative]	activity terms
[+ dynamic][+ telic][− durative]	achievement terms
[+ dynamic][+ telic][+ durative]	accomplishment terms

Since Vendler, the four classes have been referred to simply as 'states,' 'activities,' 'achievements,' and 'accomplishments.' Further general refinements include the recognition that classification of situation aspect involves the classification of how verbs and VPs represent states and events, rather than necessarily the nature of events in reality, and the emphasis that classification must focus either on verbs themselves or complete VPs. While Vendler recognized the latter, he only minimally develops how modifying elements within VPs relate to situation aspect classes. The former receives ample demonstration through the possibility of describing a single event in reality by means of two expressions utilizing different classes of VPs, as in the following two sentences from Smith (1997, xiv):

(1) a. The bird flew.
    b. The bird was in flight.

These sentences do not indicate whether or not they describe the same occurrence in reality, but nothing prevents their reference to the same bird at the same time in the same action of flight. However, the sentences offer VPs of two different classes: the former displays an activity, the latter a state.

For clarity, the following sentences, drawing example verbs and VPs from Vendler (1967, 107), provide two of each of the four classes as illustrations:[8]

---

7. See, e.g., Carlota Smith (1997, 19–20), Robert D. Van Valin, Jr. (2005, 33), and Dobbs-Allsopp (2000) for the form of representation given here. Dobbs-Allsopp uses these exact variables while Van Valin attempts greater precision through classification according to four variables: ± static, ± dynamic, ± telic, ± punctual. See below for further discussion of Van Valin's system. Smith's are identical, but she prefers to express [± dynamic] by the corresponding opposite value of the variable [± static].

8. Since my primary concern is the analysis of situation aspect and its significance for temporal relations in narrative, English examples throughout will primarily appear in the English past tense.

(2)   a. John loved somebody.
      b. John wanted something.
      c. John ran.
      d. John pulled a cart.
      e. John won the race.
      f. John lost an object.
      g. John painted the picture.
      h. John played a game of chess.

In (2a–b), which display states, the VPs express non-dynamic durative conditions. By contrast (2c–d), alike in their properties to (2a–b) except in that they express processes and are thus dynamic, provide examples of activities. While we may expect that John eventually stopped both running and pulling due to increasing fatigue, the VPs themselves do not include inherent endpoints and are thus atelic. Addition of phrases such as "for half an hour" or "to the lake" would, however, through the endpoints which they would contribute to the newly constructed VPs, change the class of these VPs from activity ([+ dynamic][− telic][+ durative]) to accomplishment ([+ dynamic][+ telic][+ durative]).

When John won the race and lost an object (2e–f), however, these events, at least in their portrayal, occurred and ended at a moment and are thus non-durative, telic processes, that is, achievements. No part of John's running the race was winning the race except for the moment he passed the finish line, and no series of events leading up to John's loss of the object was his losing of that object until the moment of its loss. Finally, for John to paint the picture (2g) portrays John as engaged in this process over time leading to a culmination allowing for his action to be expressed as completed: "John painted the picture." This VP is durative, since the painting itself took place over a duration of time [in contrast to the moment of winning in (2e), yet also telic in that the completion of the picture represents the inherent endpoint of the VP.]

The capacity of an additional temporal phrase to (2c–d) to change the classes of these VPs from activities to accomplishments draws attention to the problem of corresponding modification of state VPs. In (2a–b), while John's state of loving someone may result in him taking actions to express that love, and while John's love unfortunately may end, "loving" itself is not dynamic since the verb does not express a process, and the VP does not in itself show whether or not his love will end. These VPs thus clearly fall within the category of states. However, a modification of the VP in (2a) resulting in an inherent endpoint, such as the addition of "for three years," should correspondingly change the class of the VP. States, as a class, are atelic by definition, and the original Vendlerian system does not account for a class of [– dynamic][+ telic][+durative]. While pioneering in its categories, this system left room for refinement in this respect and others. Following decades have, therefore, resulted in a proliferation of applications and modifications of this system, as well as attempts to offer alternatives.

2.2.2 Modified Situation Aspect Classification and Additional Categories

Although Vendler's article only applied his categories to situation aspect in English, they have provided a general means of classification cross-linguistically. Smith's important *The Parameter of Aspect* (1991, 1997), for example, utilizes modified Vendlerian classification in the consideration of English, French, Russian, Mandarin Chinese, and Navajo.[9] While recognizing distinctions in the classes of aspect and its expression in differing languages, Smith was able to write, "The concepts of aspect play a role in all languages, so far as we know. The aspectual systems of different languages are strikingly similar" (1997, 13). A few arbitrarily selected examples further displaying the variety of languages in which situation aspect has received attention are Koyukon Athabaskan (Melissa Axelrod 1993), Finno–Ugrian languages (Eeva Kangasmaa-Minn 1984), Mandarin Chinese (Jian Kang 2001; Smith 1990; 1994), and Japanese (Wesley M. Jacobsen 1984). Van Valin (2005, 32) notes studies of Bribri, Croatian, Georgian, Hausa, Icelandic, Italian, Japanese, Korean, Lakhota, Mparntwe Arrernte, Sama, Tagalog, Tepehua, and Yatye. Demonstration of the cross-linguistic validity of situation aspect theory lies not only in the number of languages to which linguists have applied it, but also in the variety of languages families in which it has proven functional.

Returning to discussion of classes of situation aspect in order to propose a system of classification, the three variables of dynamicity, telicity, and durativity, each with a positive or negative value, may combine to form eight arrangements as follows:[10]

---

9. Her discussion of Navajo does not apply these categories in the same immediate fashion possible with the other languages due to its composite verb structure. Nevertheless, situation aspect analysis remains possible, and the distinctions of the Navajo verb system allow for greater precision in categories.

10. I am here limiting discussion to the "inner event" of situation aspect (telicity and changes in state), and thus not covering the matters of agents and causation in event structure (see Carol Tenny and James Pustejovsky 2000, 7). While agentivity and causation would require attention in a thorough discussion of aspect, they cannot receive attention here since they do not relate as directly to the temporal nature of VPs and the relationships between them.

[– dynamic] [– telic] [– durative]	Ø
[– dynamic] [– telic] [+ durative]	atelic state
[– dynamic] [+ telic] [– durative]	point state
[– dynamic] [+ telic] [+ durative]	transitory state
[+ dynamic] [– telic] [– durative]	semelfactive
[+ dynamic] [– telic] [+ durative]	activity
[+ dynamic] [+ telic] [– durative]	achievement
[+ dynamic] [+ telic] [+ durative]	accomplishment

These eight arrangements divide into two groups corresponding to event types and state types according to the value of the dynamicity variable. Realization of a situation (either event or state) type requires at least one positive value such that the combination [– dynamic] [– telic] [– durative] represents a null value. This null combination cannot obtain since a positive telicity value involves a change of state at the end of the situation, either as the cessation of an event type leading into a new state or the cessation of a state such that another state obtains through the cessation of the first. The combination of [– telic] and [– durative] would indicate a class which neither occupies a duration of time nor occupies a transition point in time (that is, has an endpoint) to a new state. The combination of negative values of telicity and durativity in the semelfactive event class ([+ dynamic] [– telic] [– durative]) remains a possibility since the positive dynamicity value indicates a dynamic event, although an event which occupies only a conceptual point in time and results in no state change. Negative values for all variables would involve no duration of a condition ([– durative]) in which nothing happens ([– dynamic]) and no ending point at which a change of state ([– telic]) occurs.[11] This seems to represent an impossibility.[12] Therefore, I propose a system taken from these eight arrangements with only seven situation classes: three state types and four event types. Each of these will be discussed in turn.

Elimination of the null value combination results in three combinations with negative dynamicity values, corresponding to three state types: atelic state, point state, and transitory state. Of these three, the atelic state

---

11. Thorough discussion of the nature of telicity and a precise definition falls outside of the scope of this study. Hana Filip and Susan Rothstein (2006) offer a thoughtful recent treatment.

12. Mari Broman Olsen (1997) also labeled this combination as null and presented it as unattested. She explains the unattested nature of the null combination on the basis of the absence of a temporal "nucleus," a term taken from Alice F. Freed (1979), who divides the events into three constituent parts: onset, nucleus, and coda. In private correspondence, ter Meulen suggested that this combination might represent auxiliary verbs or the copula.

([– dynamic][– telic][+ durative]) represents Vendler's original "state term." Examples include the following:[13]

(3) a. The sky was blue.
   b. John is tall.
   c. Mary is angry.
   d. גָּבַהּ מִכָּל־הָעָם
      be tall-3MsgQATAL than-all-GEN the-people
      "He was taller than all the people," 1 Sm 9:2.
   e. יָרֵא אֶת־בֵּית אָבִיו וְאֶת־אַנְשֵׁי הָעִיר
      be afraid-3MsgQATAL ACC house-GEN father-GEN-3Msg and-
         ACC men-GEN the-city
      "He was afraid of his father's house and the men of the city," Jgs 6:27.

Readers familiar with the distinction between 'individual-level states' and 'stage-level states' will notice that I have included examples of both in the category of atelic states. Discussions of state frequently differentiate these two classes, which I will discuss further below. For now distinguishing these two classes by the more inherent nature, and thus generally longer or permanent duration, of the former (e.g. "John is tall") in contrast to the generally expected temporary nature of the latter (e.g. "Mary is angry") shall suffice. Due to the concern in this study with temporal duration and relationships between VPs, which relate closely to telicity values, I would like to define classes of states in the system for analysis according to the variable combinations rather than other semantic features, and so do not place these VPs in separate aspectual classes.

The second class, the point state ([– dynamic][+ telic][– durative]), occurs least frequently among the three classes of states. William Croft (2009) recognized this class of state and offered the label "point state." This class, although non-dynamic, inherently lacks duration and so maintains, as it were, for only a point in time. Statements identifying precise times of day provide examples of point states, such as, "It is eight o'clock." Olsen (1997, 50–53), not aware of examples of this combination, considers it unattested, explaining its absence through the lack of a temporal "nucleus" composed of positive dynamicity or durativity values.

---

13. The method of glossing in the examples essentially follows that of Van Valin (2005). For simplicity I have not indicated the stems of Hebrew verbs and the gender and number morphemes of nouns. The number and gender of nouns, where relevant, will be evident in examples from translation and context. I have labeled the Hebrew indicative verbs as QATAL, YIQTOL, WEQATAL, and WAYYIQTOL according to form. For readers unfamiliar with the BH verbal system, see **Chapter 10** for an introduction.

Transitory states ([– dynamic][+ telic][+ durative]) occur frequently, but the literature on states often does not specifically identify them. Croft (2009) used the same term for one of his three classes of states but defines it differently. Transitory states appear similar to atelic states but have an expressed inherent endpoint, usually through the addition of a limiting temporal phrase to what would otherwise be an atelic state. Again referencing the distinction between individual-level states and stage-level states, this transformation is only possible for the latter, but the reason for this difference in behavior does not lie in an aspectual difference. Note the ordinary infelicity of (4c), in which a limiting temporal phrase appends to what would otherwise be an individual state expression, although (4c) may be possible in certain fictional contexts, such as a fantasy in which a person's height may suddenly change, as in Lewis Carroll's *Alice in Wonderland*.[14] A similar transformation from point states to transitory states is not possible since a durative expression would contradict the inherently non-durative base to which it would be added, as (4d) shows.

(4) a. John was angry for an hour.

   b. שָׁקְטָה הָאָרֶץ עֶשֶׂר שָׁנִים
      be peaceful-3FsgQATAL the-land ten years
      "The land was at peace for ten years," 2 Chr 13:23.

   c. Mary was tall for two years.

   d. It was 5:15 p.m. for two hours.

---

14. This observation suggests that the ability of individual-level states or stage-level states to take limiting temporal expressions and even the distinction between the two types of states derive from world knowledge. Angelika Kratzer (1995), in an extended discussion of the differences in nature and behavior of these kinds of states, asserts consistently with this observation that "if a distinction between stage-level and individual-level predicates is operative in natural language, it cannot be a distinction that is made in the lexicon of a language once and for all. If I dyed my hair every other day, my property of having brown hair would be stage-level. Usually we think of having brown hair as an individual-level property, though, since we don't think of persons dying their hair capriciously . . . We now know that there may be some problems with such classifications. This being said, we will make use of the convenient classifications just the same" (1995, 125–26). Beyond this single division between stage-level and individual-level, some states, due to their semantic nature, ordinarily obtain for relatively short durations, whereas others obtain for long durations. Chungmin Lee's discussion of the felicity of a temporal adverbial with states of different semantic kinds in Korean illustrates the point: "The *toŋan* adverbial is highly compatible with sensation and attitude verbs; sensation may begin, continue for any length of time and then terminate and attitude may be subject to control. Emotive verbs are less compatible with short period or specific time point adverbials, since the state of emotion has a rather long period of time to continue and has less clear starting and ending points than sensation. . . . The *toŋan* adverbial is less compatible with appearance or inherent nature description verbs, since their states have no clear beginning and ending points and usually continue for a comparatively long period of time" (Lee 1982, 571).

In light of this division of states into three kinds according to the variable combinations above, the distinction between individual-level states and stage-level states requires discussion. The aspectual definition of these two classes among linguists is not uniform. As shown below, Xiao and McEnery's (2002, 2004a, 2004b) framework for relating the classification of individual verbs with that of VPs plays a significant role in the methodology which I propose. They recognize these two classes and utilize this split of states as the basis for classifying states. The distinction between the two does not originate with Xiao and McEnery and lies in whether a state is inherent to that which it is predicated at the time for which it is predicated. Xiao and McEnery (2004a, 57) cite Greg N. Carlson (1977) as offering the same distinction between two classes of predicates.[15] The nomenclature of individual-level states and stage-level states may be slightly misleading, since it derives from Carlson's examples predicating "properties" and "stages" to people in derived examples and the term "individual" does not in this sense necessarily refer to a person. The terms nevertheless suffice as a means of differentiation.

Although Xiao and McEnery (2004a, 57–58) associate the distinction with the length of the duration of a state (individual-level states lasting longer than stage-level states), Carlson (1977, 448) rightly dismisses this means of defining the two classes, demonstrating its inconsistency by examples. Xiao and McEnery better explain the difference by presenting a stage-level state as one which "describes the current behaviours or stages of an individual," and an individual-level state as one which "describes the inherent dispositions or properties of an individual" (2004a, 59). As a result, and contrary to diagnostics often proposed for recognizing states (see, for example, the stative tests mentioned in David R. Dowty 1979), verbs generally describing stage-level states may appear as imperatives or progressives (Xiao and McEnery 2004a, 57–59). Unfortunately the latter explanation by Xiao and McEnery still lacks precision since "current behaviours" may derive from "inherent

---

15. Carlson himself draws from Gary Lee Milsark's (1974) distinction between "property" and "state" predicates, which correspond to individual-level states and stage-level states. Milsark provides "imprecise" definitions of them as follows: "Properties are those facts about entities which are assumed to be, even if they are not in fact, permanent, unalterable, and in some sense possessed by the entity, while states are conditions which are, at least in principle, transitory, not possessed by the entity of which they are predicated, and the removal of which causes no change in the essential qualities of the entity" (1974, 212). Milsark recognizes that the classes to which predicates belong do not attach strictly to the particular lexemes used but rather are flexible according to specific instances of the predications. To use one of his examples, "sick" may be predicated as either a property or a state (1974, 212–13).

dispositions or properties" of an individual. Furthermore, the aspectual distinction they propose between individual-level states and stage-level states presents problems for analysis and classification. Xiao and McEnery (2004a, 59) represent individual-level states and stage-level states as sometimes differing in dynamicity, classifying the former as [– dynamic] and the latter as [± dynamic]. They perceive stage-level states as sometimes [+ dynamic] due to their association with dynamic actions. However, this seems to collapse the aspect of states with that of actions with which they are associated. Lauri Carlson (1981), whom Xiao and McEnery cite, also attempts to divide the class of states into "states" and "dynamics" according to the ability of the latter to appear in the progressive. Frank Vlach (1981) attempts to define progressives as statives, collapsing the categories together. However, although progressives and statives resemble each other in certain features of behavior, identifying the former as a subcategory of the latter does not account for the occasional appearance of stative verbs as progressives.

Olsen (1997) similarly presents these two classes of states according to an aspectual distinction. She considers individual-level states as "always true of an individual," while stage-level states "have an inherent end, that is, telicity" (1997, 48). Dobbs-Allsopp follows Olsen in his discussion of BH statives. Due to his understanding of the distinction of the categories as lying in temporariness or permanence, he also considers stage-level states telic (2000, 25). The problem of distinguishing the two classes according to duration has already been mentioned. Additionally, stage-level states, even if often associated with states ordinarily holding for a shorter duration than those associated with individual-level states, do not inherently express the presence of an endpoint according to the usual understanding of telicity. The classification of stage-level states as telic by Olsen and Dobbs-Allsopp departs from the characterization of this class in Smith (1997) and Xiao and McEnery (2004a).

Contrary to the presentation of two classes of states by these writers, the difference between individual-level states and stage-level states, while semantic, is not aspectual. According to the variables of dynamicity, durativity, and telicity (as well as result and boundedness, if Xiao and McEnery's additional variables, discussed below, are recognized), the two classes should be understood identically. Strictly speaking, the two categories of states do not represent two different classes of aspect, but rather subcategories of one aspectual class according to a different domain. Smith (1997), who follows Carlson (1977), correctly does not present the two classes of states as differing in aspect, recognizing them as identical according to the three variables relating to aspect. The usefulness of maintaining a distinction between them lies not in recognizing an aspectual difference, but rather in assisting the identification of states, since the distinction explains how some verbs ordinarily denoting states may appear as progressives and imperatives in some languages, as well as in recognizing two levels of predication.[16]

With respect to the distinction in dynamicity Xiao and McEnery perceive between the two classes of states, while a dynamic event may demonstrate that a particular state holds, the dynamicity of the event does not become part of the state itself. An ordinarily stative verb appearing as an imperative asks its object to enter a particular state, to remain in that state, or to enter that state and to act in accordance with it. Entering the state involves a dynamic change of state, an achievement perhaps, and thus is not a state itself, and acting in accordance with a state likewise involves a dynamic event, most likely an activity.

Thus, and as already noted, the class of atelic states ([– dynamic] [– telic] [+ durative]) may include both individual-level and stage-level states. "John is tall" and "Mary is angry," which correspond respectively to an individual-level state and a stage-level state, therefore fall into identical aspectual classification. Considering VPs such as the latter, although these often are considered temporary in nature as stage-level states, as atelic maintains consistency in the analysis of telicity across states and event types. A comparison with corresponding predicates in activity VPs provides illustration:

(5) a. John was tall.
    b. Martin was angry.
    c. The earth rotated.
    d. Mary ran.

(5c) and (5d) both clearly display activities, and neither represents a telic expression according to any standard definition of telicity. Aspectually, the two VPs are identical, although one is more "inherent" than the other. I propose that the semantic distinction between an individual-level state, such as that in (5a), and a stage-level state, such as that in (5b), is of the same nature; and thus, not an aspectual distinction. Addition of a temporally limiting expression presents little difficulty to a stage-level state, such as in (5b), or what could be called a 'stage-level activity,' (5d), since these are expected to hold only temporarily. However, the same expression attached to (5a) or (5c) seems problematic:

16. See Kratzer (1995) and Gennaro Chierchia (1995) for more on stage-level and individual-level predication.

(6) a. John was tall for an hour.
    b. Martin was angry for an hour.
    c. The earth rotated for an hour.
    d. Mary ran for an hour.

Note, however, that the property of a state as stage-level does not allow for any limiting temporal expression, but only that which world knowledge allows. Thus, "Mary ran for an hour" presents no problem, while "Mary ran for three thousand hours" seems problematic unless understood to express a cumulative number of hours which Mary ran over an extended period of time rather than a single uninterrupted period of continual running. This is not a linguistic problem, but rather a conflict with world knowledge.[17]

While works addressing situation aspect in BH receive greater attention below, this discussion provides opportunity for a few comments concerning the distinction between two classes of statives in BH in Dobbs-Allsopp (2000). Dobbs-Allsopp associates the distinction between individual-level states and stage-level states from Smith (1991) and Olsen (1997) with Hebrew morphological distinctions: "The...twofold division of States according to the thematic vowel of the perfect suggests that derivational morphology also signals (or may have at one time) finer levels of categorization of States. The grammars often distinguish between the small class of permanent statives (with an original *u* as the thematic vowel of the perfect) and the larger class of temporary statives (with an original *i* thematic vowel in the perfect), which correspond respectively to the individual-level and stage-level States" (2000, 25). In addition to the problem of associating the distinction between the two classes with permanency which Carlson (1977, 448) demonstrates, associating the two classes of states with morphology does not provide a reliable means for recognition. The classes differ semantically, and formal features of a verb may or may not reflect this semantic distinction. Some Hebrew statives even appear formally identical to non-stative verbs, such as *Qal* אהב (*'hb*), "to love."

I will take the liberty here of attempting some suggestions to account for the appearance of verbs associated with states as imperatives and progressives and for the seeming dynamic behavior of these verbs. I propose that the association of some states with dynamic events, and thus the ability of some verbs ordinarily denoting states to appear as progressives and imperatives, lies

---

17. By contrast, as ter Meulen observed in private correspondence, the addition of an *in*-adverbial for time, such as "in an hour," would be linguistically problematic for these examples (except in the accomplishment reading of 6c, which would, nevertheless, describe a very short day!).

in a semantic distinction between states relating to disposition, volition, and behavior and those which do not. While perhaps not ideal labels, 'operative states' and 'inert states' may describe the two categories respectively.

My differentiation represents a subtle modification of Xiao and McEnery's classification of stage-level and individual-level states according to whether states are those of "the current behaviors or stages of an individual" or of "inherent dispositions or properties of an individual." While states associated with "current behaviors" always fall into the operative state category, so also do those of "inherent dispositions." "Stages" and "inherent properties" of an individual may fall into either category.

Additionally, the beginning or end of a state, regardless of its semantic significance, allows for progressive or imperative usage due to the dynamicity involved in the change into or out of that state, regardless of the fact that the state itself is not dynamic. This beginning or end may be only perceptual and not actual, as apparent from Dowty's observation that certain verbs may appear in the progressive when "describing stationary objects that momentarily come into the observer's view," as in his example, "When you enter the gate to the park there will be a statue standing on your right, and a small pond will be lying directly in front of you" (1979, 175).

The following sentences may assist to illustrate the relationship between an operative state and associated dynamic events:

(7) a. I love my wife.
    b. Οἱ ἄνδρες, ἀγαπᾶτε τὰς γυναῖκας.
       The-MplNOM/VOC husbands-NOM/VOC love-2plPRES-
       IMPERATIVE the-FplACC wives-ACC
       "Husbands, love your wives," Eph 5:25.
    c. Jim started loving his wife.
    d. After Mary's admirer moved away, she felt like he stopped
       loving her.
    e. Mack seemed like a nice guy: he was being kind to people around
       him, loving his wife and kids, and working hard.

The first example, (7a), declares that a particular state holds. This sentence presents no difficulties since the stative appears as a non-progressive indicative. In the quotation from Paul in (7b), however, the same verb appears as an imperative. The command is to enter or maintain a state associated with actions, as elaborated in the instructions which follow in the passage concerning the manner (self-sacrifice) in which husbands should love their wives. Through the command to enter and maintain or to maintain the state, the imperative thus also logically commands the actions which accompany that state.[18] Example (7c) expresses entrance into a state associated with dynamic actions. If Jim said to his wife, "I've started loving you," but did not practice any actions evidencing that love, his actions would falsify his claim. Sentences (7c), (7d), and (7e) together illustrate the role of viewpoint for felicitous progressive readings. When paired with an aspectual verb such as "started" in (7c) or "stopped" in (7d), focus lies on the beginning or end of a state, leading to felicitous progressive readings. Even a state classified as an individual-level state by Xiao and McEnery (2004a, 57) and often not appearing as a progressive (due to its usually "non-operative" nature according to my explanation) may appear as one when accompanying an aspectual verb, as in the sentence, "Johnny started being tall shortly after his fourteenth birthday." (7e), although not explicitly stating an end of Mack's "loving his wife and kids," also views the "loving" internally or with attention to an endpoint. Readers of the sentence expect that perhaps something happened which brought into question the characterization of Mack being "a nice guy."

Ik-Hwan Lee, Jong-Do Kim, and Kyung-Ae Choi (1988, 88–95) approach a similar semantic distinction to the one I propose between operative states and inert states through the concept of intention in their attempt to resolve the 'imperfective paradox'[19] and account for the use of progressives with states. However, the use of a progressive form with a verb ordinarily denoting a state does not always arise from the intention of an agent or other party. The disposition or the state associated with behavior which the progressive expresses may lack intention, as the following examples demonstrate:

(8) a. Jim is being a fool.
    b. Mary continues being discouraged in spite of her friend's efforts to cheer her up.

In (8a), Jim may not intend to be a fool, but he is currently acting in accordance with the state, "be a fool." In (8b), Mary probably does not intend to be discouraged and would like to cheer up, but for some reason her friend has not been successful in addressing the cause of her discouragement.

18. Subsequent to writing this discussion of (7b), I discovered that Olsen (1997, 155) offered the same example to illustrate a state verb with an activity interpretation.

19. 'Imperfective paradox' refers to the difference in entailment between activities and accomplishments. "John was running" necessarily means that "John ran"; however, using an often cited example, to say that someone was "drawing a circle" does not entail that the person "drew a circle." Dowty coined the term "imperfective paradox"; see Dowty (1977; 1979, 133–38) for discussion and an early attempted explanation.

To an extent, when a stative verb may appear in a form used for progressives is language dependent. In Japanese, for example, stative verbs very frequently appear in the *te-iru* and *te-ita* forms, which respectively may denote present progressives and past progressives of activities, rather than in the forms used for simple present and simple past activities. However, this results from the breadth of the use of the *te-iru* and *te-ita* forms, and statives in these forms are not necessarily progressive in function. The following provide illustrations of these forms:

(9) a. *neko wa hashite-iru.*
    cat TOP run-GER-PRES
    The cat is running.

  b. *kanojo wo aishite-imasu ka.*
    3F ACC love-GER-PRES-HON QUESTION
    Do you love her?

  c. *sore wo shitte-iru.*
    that ACC know-GER-PRES
    (I/you/he/she/they) know(s) that.

  d. Sumisu-san no inu ga shinda koto wo shinjite-ita.
    Smith-HON GEN dog NOM die-PAST NOMINALIZER ACC
    believe-GER-PAST
    (I/you/he/she/they) believed that Smith's dog died. [but see discussion below]

  e. mado ga aite-iru.
    window NOM open-GER-PRES
    The window is open.

(9a) illustrates the progressive function of the present *te-iru* form with an activity. However, *te-iru* and *te-ita* do not correspond to English progressives in (9a–c). In these cases, the Japanese *te-iru* and *te-ita* forms become simple forms in English rather than the problematic "is loving," "is knowing," and "was believing." Simple present forms replacing the *te-iru* forms in (9b) and (9c) would in some contexts serve as futures. The sentences in (9d) in the two languages are not entirely equivalent in that the use of the *te-ita* form in the Japanese sentence makes clear that, although the subject "was believing" that Smith's dog died, the subject no longer believes this. This could be expressed through extension in English to "(I/you/he/she/they) believed that Smith's dog died but stopped believing that" or "(I/you/he/she/they) used to believe that Smith's dog died." When used for achievements, the *te-iru* and *te-ita* forms frequently function as resultatives, as in (9e).

Turning to the possibility of stative verbs in imperative forms, the same verbs from (9d), due to their semantic nature as "operative" verbs in the subcategory of cognitive statives, may appear as imperatives in both languages:

(10) a. *watashi wo shinjinasai*
          1sg ACC believe-IMPERATIVE
          Believe me!
      b. *kono hon no kotoba wo shinjinasai*
          this book GEN word ACC believe-IMPERATIVE
          Believe the words of this book!

A more thorough consideration of how the *te-iru* and *te-ita* forms in comparison with the simple Japanese verb forms lies outside the scope of this discussion.

To conclude the discussion of states, Croft's (2009) distinction of three state types similar to the three in my system should be mentioned. He labels his three types "transitory states," "inherent states," and "point states." He defines the former two according to temporary or inherent nature according to the common definition of stage-level states and individual-level states, and thus not in accordance with a consistent concept of telicity across states and events. However, his "point states" are identical to those in my system.

Leaving states and proceeding to classes of events, the three variables of dynamicity, telicity, and durativity yield four classes: semelfactive, activity, achievement, and accomplishment, all of which, with the exception of semelfactive, appeared in the original Vendlerian system. Smith (1991, 1997) offered the most significant and widely recognized additional category supplementing Vendler by defining the semelfactive. According to the three variables above, this class receives the representation [+ dynamic][– telic] [– durative].[20] VPs of this class "are single-stage events with no result or outcome. . . . Typical examples are [knock at the door], [hic-cup], [flap a wing]. Semelfactives are the simplest type of event, consisting only in the occurrence" (1997, 29). Lauri Carlson (1981) earlier recognized a similar class, "momentaneous," which he considered differing from achievements in that VPs associated with achievements may appear in the progressive. However, Smith considered the repeated occurrences of events which semelfactives denote as multiple-event activities, and such a progressive could express a multiple-event activity. A semelfactive VP could describe a single knock, whereas an activity VP would better describe continued knocking. Not all analysts have defined semelfactives in the same manner, since some would consider VPs describing the repetition of actions as in this class. However, Smith's definition has received general acceptance (see, e.g. Sara Thomas Rosen 2003; Van Valin 2005; Croft 2009). The specification of a limit for the multiple occurrences of a semelfactive action,

---

20. Smith's expression utilizes [– static] for [+ dynamic].

whether a temporal or quantificational limit, may be expressed as part of an accomplishment VP. The following examples illustrate a semelfactive event, a multiple-event activity involving iteration of a semelfactive, and an accomplishment consisting of limited iteration of a semelfactive:

(11) a. John sneezed.

   b. עֲטִישֹׁתָיו תָּהֶל אוֹר
   sneezing-GEN-3Msg flash-3FsgYIQTOL light
   "His sneezing flashes light," Jb 41:10 (Eng. 18).

   c. וַיְזוֹרֵר הַנַּעַר עַד־שֶׁבַע פְּעָמִים
   sneeze-3MsgWAYYIQTOL the-young-man until seven times
   "And the young man sneezed seven times," 2 Kgs 4:35.

The next class, activities ([+ dynamic] [− telic] [+ durative]), requires little discussion beyond that above in the definition of Vendler's original classes. Activities are [− telic] and thus do not express any inherent endpoint. Both ongoing processes and iterations over the course of a duration fall under this category. As already noted, the latter includes the repeated occurrence of what would be semelfactives if occurring singly.

(12) a. וַיִּתְהַלֵּךְ חֲנוֹךְ אֶת־הָאֱלֹהִים
   walk-3MsgWAYYIQTOL Enoch with the-God
   "And Enoch walked with God," Gn 5:24.

   b. וַיְהִי כְּדַבְּרָהּ אֶל־יוֹסֵף יוֹם יוֹם וְלֹא־שָׁמַע אֵלֶיהָ
   be-3MsgWAYYIQTOL as-speak-INF-3Fsg to Joseph day by
       day and-not listen-3MsgQATAL to-3Fsg
   "As she spoke to Joseph day by day, he did not listen to her," Gn 39:10.

Croft (2009) argues for the existence of two kinds of activities differing in whether they result in lasting qualitative change, labeling them "directed activities" and "undirected activities." In his examples, "the soup is cooling" represents a directed activity, and "she's dancing" represents an undirected activity (2009, 152). He credits Jennifer Hay, Christopher Kennedy, and Beth Levin (1999) for making this distinction, although their discussion concerns the aspectual nature of 'degree achievements' (discussed below) rather than classes of activities. Recognition of the difference between activities resulting in qualitative change from those which do not provides a helpful distinction, although one not directly relevant to the time of events. Therefore, for the purposes of this study, activities will represent a single aspectual class. When reference to qualitative change is necessary, I will use Croft's labels. Most often, whether a VP denotes an activity resulting in qualitative change or an "undirected activity" is readily apparent from the context in which the VP appears.

The combination [+ dynamic][+ telic][– durative] represents the achievement class of events. These events, as [– durative], are conceptually instantaneous, but they differ from semelfactives in that there are telic and thus include an end-point transition to a new state. Examples appear below:

(13) a. וַיָּמָת יָאִיר וַיִּקָּבֵר בְּקָמוֹן
die-3MsgWAYYIQTOL Jair buried-3MsgWAYYIQTOL in-Kamon
"And Jair died and was buried in Kamon," Jgs 10:5.

   b. עַד יְפַלַּח חֵץ כְּבֵדוֹ
until pierce-3MsgYIQTOL arrow liver-GEN-3Msg
"Until an arrow cuts through his liver," Prv 7:23.

Croft (2009), collapsing all non-durative events into the category of achievements, recognizes three sub-types of achievements corresponding to his three state types: reversible achievement, irreversible achievement, and cyclic achievement. The last of these he identifies as identical to the semelfactive. His distinction between the reversible achievement and the irreversible achievement concerns whether or not they result in states which may be reversed, providing "the door opened" as an example of the former and "the window shattered" as an example of the latter (2009, 152). The distinction between the two involves the same kind of semantic distinction as that between stage-level states and individual-level states as commonly defined: one is expected to last whereas the other is not. However, aspectually the two classes are identical; both classes identically represent the combination of variables [+ dynamic][– durative][+ telic].

Finally, accomplishments ([+ dynamic][+ telic][+ durative]) refer to those events with both a positive durativity value and a positive telicity value. Although conceptually taking place over time, they lead to a final end-point. The combination of these two positive variables results in the distinctive behavior of accomplishments of the progressive not entailing the simple past. Thus, using a common illustration, "John was drawing a circle" does not mean that "John drew a circle," while, in the case of an activity, "John was running" entails "John ran." This behavior represents an often cited diagnostic distinguishing activities and accomplishments (see, e.g., Dowty 1979, 57). Related is the use of an anticipatory progressive of a verb associated with an achievement. In this case, the progressive again does not entail the simple past. For example, "John was dying" does not entail "John died" if, say, the ambulance reached him on time and his emergency surgery was successful. Croft (2009) again offers subcategories, distinguishing two classes of "performances" differing with regard to the nature of qualitative change occurring during the duration of the process. Both involve a final, lasting change of state. He explains, "An accomplishment is a directed activity that is temporally bounded by its inception and completion phases (hence, three phases are here profiled). A run-up achievement is an undirected activity that is temporally bounded, since the process is not a measurable gradual change to the resulting state" (2009, 153). However, his example of a run-up achievement, "Help! He's dying!" (2009, 153), represents what I have here referred to as an anticipatory progressive of an achievement.[21]

A VP may or may not specify the duration of an accomplishment, and an accomplishment may involve either a uniform process with a final endpoint or a series of progressing stages terminating in a final culmination:

(14) a. אַרְבָּעִים שָׁנָה הָלְכוּ בְנֵי־יִשְׂרָאֵל בַּמִּדְבָּר
forty year walk-3plQATAL sons-GEN Israel in-the-wilderness
"For forty years the sons of Israel walked in the wilderness," Jos 5:6.

b. וַיִּבֶן שְׁלֹמֹה אֶת־הַבַּיִת
build-3MsgWAYYIQTOL Solomon ACC the-house
"And Solomon built the house," 1 Kgs 6:14.

In (14a), a limiting temporal adverbial phrase, "forty years," provides an endpoint to the conceptually uniform process of walking, whereas Solomon's building of the temple in (14b) involved progression through many stages of building activity, culminating in the completion of construction.

An additional label, although of a different category, requiring mention for the present study is 'degree achievements,' a term coined in Dowty (1979) for achievements which allow durational adverbs, such as "cool" and "lengthen." He explains, "A sentence like *The soup cooled for ten minutes* should be analyzed as saying that for each time *t* within an interval of ten minutes duration, there is some resolution of the vagueness of the predicate *cool* by which *the soup is cool* is true at *t* but not true at − 1" (1979, 90, italics in original). Verbs of this kind present a unique set of challenges, and the distinction of aspectual classes according to conceptual paths in Joost Zwarts (2008) provides greater consistency in the definition of degree achievements than previous accounts of their nature. The kind of verb associated with degree achievements, however, does not consistently relate to a particular aspectual class, contrary to Dowty's presentation of them as a sub-class of achievements. Kate Kearns (2007) proposes three ways in which such

---

21. In BH, the *futurum instans* use of the participle is another form of anticipatory progressive.

verbs, also known as deadjectival verbs, may function: processes (iteration of achievements), achievements, or accomplishments. How one of these verbs functions in a particular instance depends upon available readings from the semantic nature of the VP and context. Although this study largely does not use Zwarts's model (discussed immediately below), his account of degree achievements, supplemented as necessary due to the ability of these verbs to denote different aspectual classes, may assist recognizing them.

Two recent alternative models which nevertheless result in similar categories to those in my system are those of Zwarts (2008) and Croft (2009). Zwarts has offered a recent alternative means of deriving situation aspect classes, but notably with essentially Vendlerian classes resulting. Zwarts presents events according to positions and movement in conceptual space in a manner analogous to description of location and movement in physical space through the use of prepositions. Zwarts (2005) earlier discussed prepositions according to spatial paths by utilizing an algebra of paths, and Zwarts (2006) anticipated application to all events through considering the spatial paths of movement verbs and conceptual paths of degree achievements, providing the basis for developing his model of event structures. This model classifies event structures according to the variables of cumulativity and reversibility, resulting in four classes of dynamic events: transitions, progressions, cycles, and continuations. Transitions involve a change from one state into another, and thus are non-reversible (reversing a transition could only involve a different change of state, specifically the corresponding opposite) and non-cumulative (the completion of a state change would not allow for further progression along the conceptual path since the goal would have already been reached, and no conceptual intervening space exists between the two states). Cycles represent reversible, non-cumulative events, that is, events which begin and end in the same state with an intervening departure into another state, but without intervening space between the two states allowing for mediate positions. By contrast, a progression, as a cumulative, non-reversible event, allows for an infinite number of positions along a conceptual path. The occurrence of such an event involves a change in position along the path; however, movement in one direction on the path does not prevent the further occurrence of an event denoted in the same manner involving further movement in the same direction (cumulativity). Finally, events which are reversible and cumulative receive the label "continuations." These consist of the iteration of cycles or other reversible movement in conceptual space occurring in a non-uniform manner.

As Zwarts notes, these classes correspond to classes derived from an essentially Vendlerian system. Transitions correspond to telic events (achievements and accomplishments), progressions to degree achievements, cycles to semelfactives, and continuations to activities. He accounts for states at the end of his articles by presenting them as corresponding to locative prepositions. As already noted, his explanation of degree achievements offers greater consistency for classification but still requires supplementation due to the semantic flexibility of deadjectival verbs.

Croft (2009) provides another recent alternative means of classification, to which several references have already appeared above. This system involves distinctions of points, lines, and arrows on two dimensional axes of time and qualitative state. This results in three kinds of states (transitory, inherent, and point), three kinds of achievements (reversible achievement, irreversible achievement, and cyclic achievement [semelfactive]), two activities (directed [change of state] and undirected [no change of state]), and two "performances" (accomplishment and "runup achievement"). He also proposes a three-dimensional representation of aspectual relations of events, allowing for the distinction in the aspect of an event for each participant. Thus, in his example, "Jane dried the plate," Jane's transitive action of drying represents an undirected (i.e., not producing a change of state in the participant) activity (since it results in no change of state in Jane even though durative), whereas the aspect of the event for the plate is an accomplishment. In ordinary classification, this event represents only an accomplishment. Jane had not dried the plate until the end point of the drying process, and thus "dried the plate" here serves as telic and durative, differing from Dowty's degree achievement only in telicity. For our purposes, this distinction between aspectual classes for participants in a single event need only receive consideration when the change of state in an agent or instrument requires special note, either because it may be easily overlooked or because it bears particular relevance for discussion of the sequence or nature of occurrences in texts analyzed. Change of state in patients are most often obvious in transitive verbs denoting accomplishments and so do not require further comment.

The above discussion has considered each of the seven classes resulting from the combination of positive and negative values for each of the three standard aspectual variables (dynamicity, telicity, and durativity) and some recent approaches to situation aspect offering alternative frameworks. Additional variables in the essentially Vendlerian classification systems of Creason (1995), Van Valin (2005), and Xiao and McEnery (2002, 2004a,

2004b) now require special comment. The studies of these writers hold particular significance since the first represents the most extensive treatment of situation aspect in BH to date and the two-level mapping model of Xiao and McEnery provides an integral part of the methodology I propose for the analysis of BH. Van Valin (2005) relates less directly to the study at hand but nevertheless provides a recent and widely-read presentation of a Vendlerian-based system from a leading syntactician contributing to the field of aspectual studies.

Creason's system for BH presents four variables ([± point] [± durative] [± change] [± telic]) resulting in seven classes of non-complex situations as follows:

[+ point] [– change]	state
[– point] [– durative] [– change] [– telic]	semelfactive
[– point] [– durative] [+ change] [– telic]	atelic achievement
[– point] [– durative] [+ change] [+ telic]	telic achievement
[– point] [+ durative] [– change] [– telic]	unchanging activity
[– point] [+ durative] [+ change] [– telic]	changing activity
[– point] [+ durative] [+ change] [+ telic]	accomplishment

Durativity and telicity in this system follow the common explanations. Although Creason defines the [± point] variable according to whether evaluation of the situation described at a temporal point allows determining its truth value,[22] the value of the point variable corresponds to the opposite dynamicity value in other modified Vendlerian systems. All [– point] situations correspond to [+ dynamic] situations and vice-versa, just as all [+ point] situations correspond to [– dynamic] (stative) situations.

Creason seeks to distinguish the positive value of his [± change] variable from the change of state involved in telicity, although it encompasses such change. A [+ change] value also does not correspond to movement along Croft's qualitative change axis since it includes change involved in uniform processes (e.g., "John walked"). Creason provides the following definition: "a situation involves change if, at the end of the situation, one of the participants is different with respect to some physical property (such as solidity vs. liquidity) or with respect to its location (such as being on one part of a street or another)" (1995, 51). However, Creason proceeds to

---

22. "A + POINT situation is one which consists of undifferentiated moments in time rather than stages. The truth value of a sentence referring to such a situation can be evaluated at a point in time. A – POINT situation is one which consists of stages rather than undifferentiated moments in time. The truth value of a sentence referring to such a situation must be evaluated over an interval of time" (1995, 44–45; see also esp. 39–42).

provide examples of situations with positive change values which involve a more inclusive definition: "learning a foreign language" and "falling in love" (1995, 52). The precise nature of the kind of change involved in the [± change] variable unfortunately seems unclear in Creason's discussion.

Although Creason attempts to distinguish his [± change] variable from the change of state involved in telicity, in the case of non-durative events he gives negative telicity values to VPs ordinarily considered telic, such as "noticed a misprint" and "recalled Bill's nickname" (1995, 59–60). He attempts to distinguish between telic and atelic events on the basis of the felicity of modifying the former with "finish" and the latter with "stop," although he observes that the former is only possible for [+ durative] events. This results in a confusing analysis of the sentence "Bill stopped noticing the fly" as a [+ durative] and [– telic] event involving the cessation of iteration (1995, 61–62). This deviates from standard concepts of telicity and seems to contradict Creason's own definition of telicity, which states that "situations which have an inherent terminus or an inherent goal to which they are directed are telic" (1995, 56). The manner in which a non-durative event could involve a change of state resulting from its momentaneous occurrence without involving an inherent endpoint therefore remains unclear, appearing to render the atelic achievement class illegitimate.

In the case of durative events, Creason presents VPs ordinarily considered states (those in "The ball remained on the table" and "Fred stayed at home") as unchanging activities ([– point][+ durative][– change][– telic]) (1995, 53). His statement that "these situations are clearly – POINT (the truth value of the sentences must be evaluated over an interval)" draws attention to the inadequacy of the [± point] variable as a converse alternative to the [± dynamic] variable. Although all states obtain at a moment in time, so also do the above cited examples of unchanging activities, regardless of whether their truth values may be evaluated observationally at a temporal point. While the verbs in these particular VPs, "stay" and "remain," are associated with duration, this does not prevent their classification as statives. They are states semantically requiring duration, as all transitory states are semantically by nature durative and all point states non-durative. While a legitimate distinction between activities involving qualitative change and those which do not exists, it is that between Croft's directed and undirected activities, a distinction different from that which Creason proposes between activities with positive and negative change values. As a result, the [± change] variable, since it seems inconsistent and involves changes of different classes in different instances, may be absorbed into the [± telic] variable and perhaps also the

[± dynamic] variable and non-aspectual semantic distinctions. The [± point] variable also does not appear to provide a necessary converse alternative to the traditional [± dynamic] variable, so the original three variables remain sufficient.

Van Valin (2005) also presents a four variable system: [± static][± dynamic][± telic][± punctual]. This system includes six primary situation types (one state and five event types), each with a corresponding causative. Two of the variables serve exact converse relationships to original Vendlerian variables: the static variable is the converse of the Vendlerian dynamic variable, and the values of the punctual variable correspond to the opposite Vendlerian duration values. The new variable in Van Valin's system, therefore, is the dynamicity variable, despite comparison of the initial appearance of this system with Vendler's. Van Valin concisely defines his dynamicity variable as "[referring] to whether the situation involves action or not" (2005, 33), elaborating that "the fact that these verbs can be modified by adverbs like *violently, vigorously, actively, strongly* and *energetically*" demonstrates presence of action (2005, 33). The six situation types in this system are as follows:

[+ static][– dynamic][– telic][– punctual]	state
[– static][+ dynamic][– telic][– punctual]	activity
[– static][– dynamic][+ telic][+ punctual]	achievement
[– static][± dynamic][– telic][+ punctual]	semelfactive
[– static][– dynamic][+ telic][– punctual]	accomplishment
[– static][+ dynamic][+ telic][– punctual]	active accomplishment

The [± dynamic] value for the semelfactive represents the possibility of some semelfactive verbs to occur with the dynamicity adverbs.

As in Creason's system, no distinction between sub-classes of states appears. Van Valin does not define what kind of action results in a positive dynamicity value. Certainly some achievement VPs are ordinarily conceived of as denoting action, such as the following:

(15) a. John kissed Mary.
     b. Jenny slapped Sam.
     c. Brutus stabbed Caesar.

Some of the adverbs Van Valin associates with the presence of action may even occur with these VPs with little difficulty, as in a modification of (15b) to "Jenny slapped Sam violently." While the modified VP allows for either an achievement reading or a durative, iterative reading, the presence of action remains clear in both. The inability of the particular adverbs Van

Valin mentions to modify his classes with negative dynamicity values seems to stem in some cases from the negative punctual values (positive Vendlerian durativity values) of some common verbs with which these adverbs may appear (such as, e.g., "run," "drive," "fight") rather than the absence of action. While certainly the absence of action would preclude modification by one of those adverbs, the presence of action must also sometimes pair with duration. This requirement, however, derives from the adverb appearing in a VP which is already necessarily durative.

Eliminating the dynamicity value from Van Valin's system results in only one duplicate variable combination, [– static][+ telic][– punctual], shared by the accomplishment and active accomplishment. The only difference between these two classes is whether they involve "action." While this distinction between accomplishment and active accomplishment might at first seem to suggest an aspectual difference, it does not involve relationship to time or change of state, or even agency and causation, elements of the "outer event" (see Tenny and Pustejovsky 2000, 7). Therefore, it does not represent an aspectual difference and need not receive consideration in the classification of situation types. The presence of action could as easily distinguish between types of achievements, also aspectually identical with each other; in addition to the "active" achievements above, the following would provide examples of "inactive" achievements:

(16) a. I realized that I had forgotten my wallet.
      b. Their friendship was broken when he received the letter.

In light of this discussion, Van Valin's dynamicity variable need not receive consideration in the methodology I propose, leaving again, three variables: static, telic, and punctual, each equivalent or converse of the three Vendlerian variables. Since I am here limiting discussion to the "inner event" of situation aspect (telicity and changes in state) and thus not attempting to cover agency and causation in event structure (see Tenny and Pustejovsky 2000, 7), the corresponding causative situation types in Van Valin's system also need not receive consideration.

Finally, Xiao and McEnery (2002, 2004a, 2004b) utilize a series of five variables for the distinction of aspectual classes, adding [± bounded] and [± result] to the three variables from Vendler. The telic, bounded, and result variable relate to one another in that [+ result] entails [+ telic] and [+ telic] entails [+ bounded] (and therefore [+ result] also entails [+ bounded]). They describe the result variable by explaining, with examples from Mandarin,

... a verb is assigned the value [+ result] if its meaning includes a reference to a changing point at which the final spatial endpoint denoted by the verb starts holding (cf. Moens 1987: 140). While an achievement verb and an accomplishment verb both have a final spatial endpoint, they differ in that the former indicates the success of achieving that endpoint (e.g. *yingqiu* 'to score (a goal)') but the latter does not (e.g. *xiexin* 'letter-writing'). In other words, both verb classes involve a result, but they do so in different ways. While an achievement encodes a result itself, an accomplishment only implies a result and the implied result has to be made explicit by the NP or PP arguments of the verb. (Xiao and McEnery 2004a, 48)

Only achievements are [+ result]. Even with this variable dismissed, however, achievements are uniquely [+ dynamic] [–durative] [+ telic] (see chart on 2004a, 59), so the result variable does not uniquely distinguish any one situation class from others. Additionally, as highlighted by the imperfective paradox, accomplishments do entail results except in the progressive.[23] To use the example of "letter-writing":

(17)   a.   George wrote a letter.
       b.   George was writing a letter.

Although (17a) presents an accomplishment, it entails the result of George's completion of the letter. (17b) in isolation ordinarily allows for either the completion of the letter or only its partial completion, and thus does not entail the result.

The [± bounded] variable results from distinguishing between the presence or absence of a final spatial endpoint (telicity) and a final temporal endpoint (boundedness), the presence of the former entailing the latter but not vice-versa (Xiao and McEnery 2004a, 45–47, 49–52). To quote their own example,

... as the situation *walk to school* is delimited spatially (i.e. a specified distance), it must be bounded temporally (e.g. it usually takes John ten minutes to cover the distance). However, if John walked for only three minutes today, the situation became bounded temporally. In this case, the temporally bounded situation does not have a final spatial endpoint. In our model, the feature [± bounded] refers to the presence or absence of a final temporal endpoint while the feature [± telic] is related to a final spatial endpoint. (Xiao and McEnery 2004a, 51)

---

23. Studies including further discussion of the imperfective paradox which seek to resolve some of the difficulties it presents include Dowty (1979); Lee et al. (1988); Takashi Suzuki (1995); and ter Meulen (1997, 59–60).

While the semantic distinction is helpful, it does not result in distinguishing between separate classes even in the model which Xiao and McEnery present. The example of John's walk, while lacking a final spatial endpoint, only lacks such an endpoint due to the termination of the situation at a prior temporal endpoint. The realization of the spatial endpoint associated with the situation represents only a potential; both kinds of endpoint (temporal and spatial) occur simultaneously in every case where both are realized.[24] Since this study concerns the classification of the situations denoted by VPs and not potential situations, and since it primarily concerns temporal relationships, the distinction between the two kinds of endpoint is not necessary.

With the additional variables of Van Valin, Creason, and Xiao and McEnery unnecessary for the present study, analysis may proceed utilizing the three variables of dynamicity, telicity, and durativity.[25] Degree achievements (deadjectival verbs) may also be distinguished as a unique category, although one of another kind due to its aspectual flexibility in accordance with the above discussion. To review, the three variables combine in eight ways providing one null set and seven situation types. Of the seven situation types, three are states (atelic state, point state, transitory state) and four are events (semelfactive, achievement, activity, accomplishment).

2.2.3 Modifiers, Aspectual Class, and VP Aspect Diagnostics

Since the method I am proposing for the analysis of VPs in BH narrative requires considering verbal lexemes accompanied by various modifiers, the effect of modifiers on aspectual class and the manner in which they may assist the process of classification must be mentioned. A universally recognized feature of the situation aspect of VPs concerns the effect of the presence of modifiers on aspectual class. Verkuyl (1972) and Dowty (1979) represent two significant and often cited studies discussing the role of such modifiers. Verkuyl avoids the Vendlerian terminology, distinguishing three classes of aspect, "durative," "momentaneous," and "terminative," which correspond to activities, achievements, and accomplishments respectively. Verkuyl's study does not primarily concern determining the aspectual class

24. Ilse Depraetere (1995) similarly distinguishes between an inherent or "intended" temporal endpoint and an achieved actual temporal boundary. The former she labels "telicity" and the latter "boundedness." This allows for maintaining classes across non-progressive and progressive forms.

25. Freed (1979) also proposes an additional class, "series," but does not derive it from additional variables. Her "series" class consists of the continual or habitual iteration of events of other dynamic classes.

of VPs by means of diagnostics, but rather how to account for the manner in which differences in aspect arise in relation to verbs in VPs and various modifications. He ultimately reduces the distinction between durative and non-durative aspects to the ability of modification by means of durational adverbials.

Verkuyl's analysis cannot receive a thorough presentation here. He depicts VPs as composed of nodes of various kinds resulting in a final aspectual class. Durative aspect, for him, occurs in instances of "unspecified quantity of x" NP (noun phrase) or QC (quantifying complement) with a VP with a "subcategorial node such as MOVEMENT, AGENTIVE, PERFORM, TAKE, ADD" (1972, 96). The first element of this formula, the "unspecified quantity of x" NP, draws attention to the effect of associated nouns. An "unspecified quantity" derives from an indefinite mass noun or plural, whereas a "specified quantity," as the label indicates, refers to a singular count noun or, in some cases, to a definite mass or plural count noun.[26] The following examples provide a sample of how the categories of NPs may relate to situation aspect:

(18) a.   I ate an apple.
     b.   I ate the apple.
     c.   I ate apples.
     d.   I ate the apples.
     e.   I drank water.
     f.   I drank the water.

These six examples illustrate categories of NPs in a VP and common relations of these categories to situation aspect. (18a), (18b), and, in some cases, (18d) and (18f) present specified quantity NPs, and (18c) and (18e) offer unspecified quantity NPs. In (18a), the indefinite article specifies the quantity of the NP as a single apple. The resulting aspect therefore does not represent Verkuyl's "durative" class (an activity), being telic instead. Rather, it is an accomplishment, or Verkuyl's "terminative" class. Where the indefinite article is replaced by a number (e.g., "I ate three apples"), the modification would produce the same result since the quantity would remain specified. In (18b), the NP again specifies the quantity as a single apple with the same resulting aspectual class as (18a). Definiteness thus does not modify aspectual class in the case of singular count nouns.

---

26. See Rothstein (2010) for a recent semantic account of count nouns and their distinction from mass nouns. Rothstein demonstrates the invalidity of homogeneity, cumulativity, and nature in reality as differentiating between these classes of nouns.

The following two examples, (18c) and (18d), however, show that definiteness may affect the aspectual class of plural nouns, although it does not always do so. (18c), through its "bare plural," provides no indication of the number of apples eaten, so the VP includes no inherent endpoint to my eating of apples, whether two apples, twenty, or more. The aspectual class of the VP in (18c) would therefore be Verkuyl's "durative" class (an activity). In the case of (18d), although the NP is plural, the definite article specifies the quantity as that of a particular set or group of apples which the speaker or author references, expecting the audience to understand the reference. Whether the audience knows the exact number of apples or not, the VP most often portrays the number of apples as limited and thus specifies them. The final two examples demonstrate the similar distinction between indefinite and definite mass nouns: "water" in (18e) represents a mass noun with no specification of quantity; "the water" in (18f), while not indicating the exact amount of water in question, may specify the quantity by means of definiteness. However, the presence of a definite object mass noun does not necessarily indicate the telicity of a VP. The article may specify the source or identity of an unspecified quantity of water. For example, after mention of water in a reservoir and water in a bucket, a narrative may continue by stating that an individual went to the reservoir and drank "the water." While this certainly would not mean that the person was thirsty enough to drain the reservoir dry, it also does not specify how much water the person drank. The definiteness of the direct object in this case identifies the mass noun without specifying its quantity. The same applies to (18d) in certain contexts, though less commonly. Not all mass nouns appear in singular forms, as James D. McCawley's (1979, 172) examples of "clothes" and "guts" in English illustrate. מַיִם, "water," represents an important example from BH.

Consistent with the above observations, Filip (2004) draws attention to the fact that the definite article does not inherently function to specify quantity. However, a specified quantity may be referred to anaphorically through use of the article. Thus the article with a mass or plural noun may refer to either a specified or unspecified quantity, depending on context. Furthermore, the presence or absence of an object altogether, if one of specified quantity, also may relate to aspectual class:

(19) a. I ate.
      b. I ate an apple.
      c. וַיֹּאכְלוּ וַיִּשְׁתּוּ הוּא וְהָאֲנָשִׁים אֲשֶׁר־עִמּוֹ
          eat-3MplWAYYIQTOL drink-3MplWAYYIQTOL 3Msg and-
          the-men who with-3Msg

"And they ate and drank, he and the men who were with him,"
Gn 24:54.

d. יֹאכְלוּ הַכְּלָבִים אֶת־בְּשַׂר אִיזָבֶל

eat-3MplYIQTOL the-dogs ACC flesh-GEN Jezebel
"The dogs will eat the flesh of Jezebel," 2 Kgs 9:36.

In (19a) the VP "ate" is telic and durative, and thus represents an activity, while "ate an apple" in (19b), through the presence of a specified quantity NP, is telic and thus an accomplishment. (19c) and (19d) provide corresponding sentences from BH. All of the examples above have concerned NPs functioning as direct objects (DOs) in VPs. However, Verkuyl also provides examples in which the specified quantity or unspecified quantity of subject, indirect object, or other NPs also impact aspectual class. Such instances may be recognized without difficulty. Erhard W. Hinrichs (1985) provides an extensive treatment of the nature of NPs in relation to situation aspect and considers the parallels between the structure of NPs and VPs.

The second element of Verkuyl's formula, a VP with a "subcategorial node such as MOVEMENT, AGENTIVE, PERFORM, TAKE, ADD," concerns the presence of a VP allowing for an atelic reading when combined with an unspecified quantity NP or QC. VPs, in Verkuyl's conception, are compound in nature, such that "the mechanism underlying the composition of an underlying V is combined with a complex set of categories of a nominal nature and pertaining to quantity" (1972, 98). This set includes the elements of prepositional phrases, the presence and nature of objects, and other features of VPs.

Without a thorough explanation of the nature and legitimacy or illegitimacy of each of the particular nodes Verkuyl mentions, the principle of VP composition assists conceptually in explaining changes in aspectual behavior when various elements are added or removed from VPs. For example, a prepositional phrase expressing an endpoint, whether temporal (e.g., "until three o'clock," "for ten days," "until she couldn't any longer") or spatial (e.g., "to the store") require telicity, and alter otherwise atelic VPs to become telic. I suggest that "specified extent (temporal, spatial, or another kind)" parallels the Verkuyl's "specified quantity," similarly requiring telicity in VPs.[27] However, specified extents may also require durativity and even cause the transformation of VPs otherwise ordinarily non-durative to durative VPs. Examples from English and Hebrew may illustrate:

---

27. Dowty (1979, 185) similarly summarizes: "We have noted the syntactic means by which an activity verb can be converted to an accomplishment (addition of a 'goal' prepositional phrase or extent phrase) and how an accomplishment can be converted into an activity (by the presence of a 'bare plural')."

(20) a. David considered the purpose of his life.

    b. David considered the purpose of his life for three days.

    c. Julia ran as fast as she could.

    d. Julia ran as fast as she could until she reached the closing doors of the store.

    e. Burt coughed.

    f. Burt coughed all night.

    g. וְיָשַׁבְתָּ עִמּוֹ יָמִים אֲחָדִים
       stay-2MsgWEQATAL with-3Msg days few
       "And stay with him a few days."

    h. וְיָשַׁבְתָּ עִמּוֹ יָמִים אֲחָדִים עַד אֲשֶׁר־תָּשׁוּב חֲמַת אָחִיךָ
       stay-2MsgWEQATAL with-3Msg days few until when
         return-3FsgYIQTOL rage-GEN brother-GEN-2Msg
       "And stay with him a few days until your brother's rage goes away," Gn 27:44.

    i. וַיָּרָץ לִפְנֵי אַחְאָב
       run-2MsgWAYYIQTOL before Ahab
       "And he ran before Ahab."

    j. וַיָּרָץ לִפְנֵי אַחְאָב עַד־בֹּאֲכָה יִזְרְעֶאלָה
       run-2MsgWAYYIQTOL before Ahab until go-2Msg
         Jezreel-DIR
       "And he ran before Ahab as far as you go to get to Jezreel,"
       1 Kgs 18:46.

    k. וַיְהִי הַגֶּשֶׁם עַל־הָאָרֶץ
       be-3MsgWAYYIQTOL the-rain upon the-earth
       "And the rain was upon the earth."

    l. וַיְהִי הַגֶּשֶׁם עַל־הָאָרֶץ אַרְבָּעִים יוֹם וְאַרְבָּעִים לָיְלָה
       be-3MsgWAYYIQTOL the-rain upon the-earth forty day
         and-forty night
       "And the rain was upon the earth forty days and forty nights,"
       Gn 7:12.[28]

---

28. The translation of וַיְהִי (*wayᵉhî*) as stative "was" in (20k–l), while differing from many modern English translations, reflects the necessity of classifying this verb as a state type in this context. While Hebrew stative verbs display flexibility between stative ([– dynamic]) and inchoative ([+ dynamic][– durative]) readings, the specified duration of forty days and nights in the VP does not allow for an inchoative reading. Inchoatives are achievements according to situation aspect class. Since achievements are non-durative, they cannot occur throughout a duration except iteratively. Rain repeatedly "becoming" over the course of forty days is nonsensical in this context and is contrary to a natural reading of this verb.

A dynamic verb provides better idiom in some languages. Luther ("und kam ein Regen auf Erden, vierzig Tage und vierzig Nächte") as well as many modern English translations, for example, thus express the presence of rain more naturally in their target languages by means of a dynamic verb. However, some translations still retain the stative from Hebrew as I have done here, such as the Latin Vulgate ("et facta est pluvial super terram quadraginta diebus et quadraginta noctibus"), Geneva Bible ("And the raine was vpon the earth fourtie days and fourtie nightes"), and, perhaps following the Geneva Bible, King James Version.

Although the aspectual transformations I have mentioned thus far would seem to stem from syntax, aspectual changes cannot be reduced to syntax alone. This is most obvious in the definition of situation aspect in distinction from viewpoint aspect in which the former concerns semantic distinctions not dictated by form. Dowty (1986) emphasizes this point. Contrasting himself with Verkuyl, he presents the analysis of aspectual class as a matter of semantics rather than syntax and observes that the relegation of analysis of syntax merely results in moving semantic analysis a further step to the syntactic modifications. Ultimately, the aspectual class in which a reader or listener will place a VP upon hearing it will depend not only on features of the VP, but also on elements of extra-sentential context and world knowledge. "In certain cases," Dowty states, "the intended aspectual class of a sentence is determined in part by the hearer's real world knowledge; i.e. this knowledge is needed to disambiguate sentences that are potentially ambiguous in aspectual class" (1986, 40). As a simple example, upon hearing a sound in the other room, a friend may ask me, "What was that?" In this case, I may respond with the semelfactive, "George coughed." However, in response to, "I heard George isn't feeling well and didn't sleep. What did he do all night?" I could respond with an activity identical in form.[29]

Often the proper aspectual classification of a VP will be readily event from its obvious semantic nature. However, while still taking into account the primacy of semantics, particular syntactic features may demonstrate to which class a VP belongs. Dowty (1979) presents an extensive list of diagnostics for the aspectual classes used up to the time of his writing. However, he recognizes problems or inconsistencies within some of them and reduces his list to ten tests besides those distinguishing states and events. Van Valin (2005, 35–38) similarly offers a more recent and concise list of six tests using his six-class system, though notably with many exceptions. I will mention only two of the most commonly cited diagnostics for aspectual class and then mention the relationship of aspectual class to scale structure.

Perhaps the most often referenced diagnostic of telicity, and one included in the lists of both writers, is that of in- and for- adverbials. This diagnostic is generally recognized and concerns the requirement of durativity for the felicity of for-adverbials in a VP. That is, a situation cannot obtain for an extent of time unless that situation is durative. For-adverbials are distinct

---

29. One could even argue that "all night" specifies an extent of time, making the VP an accomplishment. However, "all night" does not necessarily imply termination of the event, so I have chosen to analyze the VP as an activity which may have continue into the next day.

from *in*-adverbials in that the former are not associated with terminations of situations and therefore only occur with otherwise atelic situations (although the specification of an extent of time by means of the adverbial introduces an endpoint, transforming an otherwise atelic situation into a telic situation). The semantically equivalent temporal expression in BH is the unmarked (no preposition) inclusion of an extent of time, whether general or specified.

(21) a. Morgan walked through the woods for an hour.

b. Clark seemed like a strange man for his entire life.

c. וַיֵּשְׁבוּ שָׁם שְׁלֹשֶׁת יָמִים
stay-3MplWAYYIQTOL there three days
"And they stayed there three days," Jos 2:22.

d. שִׁבְעַת יָמִים תֹּאכַל מַצֹּת
seven days eat-2MsgYIQTOL unleavened bread
"Seven days you will eat unleavened bread," Ex 13:6.

Both Dowty and Van Valin list *for*-adverbials as possible with activities and states (although, as already noted, such an addition would, through specification of extent, make these VPs telic, transforming them, in my model, into accomplishments and transitory states, respectively).

In-adverbials are associated with terminations of situations. Van Valin allows them only for accomplishments whereas Dowty recognizes their occurrence with both telic event classes, accomplishment and achievements. As adverbials associated with termination, *in*-adverbials in English therefore occur appended to accomplishments or, at times, with achievements understood as occurring at the end of an unstated preceding duration (as in, "John arrived at the station in one hour"; "arrived" is an achievement, but the *in*-adverbial shows the duration of an unstated event [John's traveling] preceding its occurrence). BH may use the ל preposition appended to a specified duration of time in the same way:

(22) a. וַיְקַדְּשׁוּ אֶת־בֵּית־יְהוָה לְיָמִים שְׁמוֹנָה
sanctify-3MplWAYYIQTOL ACC house-GEN YHWH in (לPREP)-days eight
"And they consecrated the house of YHWH in eight days,"
2 Chr 29:17.

b. וַתִּשְׁלַם הַחוֹמָה בְּעֶשְׂרִים וַחֲמִשָּׁה לֶאֱלוּל לַחֲמִשִּׁים וּשְׁנַיִם יוֹם
be completed-3FsgWAYYIQTOL the-wall on(בPREP)-ten and-five in(לPREP)-Elul in (לPREP)-fifty and-two day
"And the wall was completed on the fifteenth of Elul, in fifty-two days," Neh 6:15.

This kind of *in*-adverbial differs from the use of "in" to specify a limited duration during part or all of which a situation obtains, as in "My birthday is *in* July," "She was working for a travel agency *in* her senior year of college," "He won four competitions *in* the 1990s." The בְ preposition marks the equivalent in BH, as well as the equivalent of *on*-adverbials marking more specific time:

(23) a. בְּרֵאשִׁית בָּרָא אֱלֹהִים אֵת הַשָּׁמַיִם וְאֵת הָאָרֶץ

in(בPREP)-beginning create-3MsgQATAL God ACC the-heaven and-ACC the-earth

"In the beginning, God created the heaven and the earth," Gn 1:1.

b. בַּשָּׁנָה הַתְּשִׁעִית לְצִדְקִיָּהוּ מֶלֶךְ־יְהוּדָה בַּחֹדֶשׁ הָעֲשִׂרִי בָּא נְבוּכַדְרֶאצַּר מֶלֶךְ־בָּבֶל וְכָל־חֵילוֹ אֶל־יְרוּשָׁלַם

in(בPREP)-the-year the-ninth to-Zedekiah king-GEN Judah in (בPREP)-the-month the-tenth come-3MsgQATAL Nebuchadnezzar king-GEN Babylon and-all army-3Msg to Jerusalem

"In the ninth year of Zedekiah, king of Judah, in the tenth month, Nebuchadnezzar, king of Babylon, came with all his army to Jerusalem," Jer 39:1.

c. וַיְהִי בִּימֵי שְׁפֹט הַשֹּׁפְטִים וַיְהִי רָעָב בָּאָרֶץ

be-3MsgWAYYIQTOL in (בPREP)-days-GEN judge-INF the-judges be-3MsgWAYYIQTOL famine in-the-land

"In the days when the judges were judging, a famine was in the land," Ru 1:1.

The use of the latter sort of in-adverbial with a VP does not itself serve as an aspectual diagnostic. As the examples above demonstrate, any kind of situation may obtain within a duration, whether it does so only for a conceptual point in time within that duration, for a shorter duration of time within it, or for the duration's full extent.

Another diagnostic worth mentioning due to general consistency and frequent mention concerns the progressive's entailment of the simple past, or, quoting Dowty's form, "*x is φing* entails *x has φed*."[30] This diagnostic distinguishes between activities and accomplishments. It holds a positive value for the former but a negative value for the latter due to the impossibility of expressing an accomplishment in the simple past without inclusion of its terminal point. An action intended to be one such as would ordinarily be associated with an accomplishment might have begun, allowing for the use of a progressive to denote the occurrence of its duration, but interrupted. Illustrating by means of

---

30. See Winter (2006, 2) for a recent mention of this diagnostic as a test of telicity.

404   Kai M. Akagi

the most often cited example, "was drawing a circle" does not necessarily entail "drew a circle," since the process of drawing may have been interrupted prior to its completion. By contrast, the progressive of a VP generally denoting an activity, such as, "John was running," necessarily entails "John ran."

Finally, Winter (2006), modifying diagnostics involving the use of "almost" from Dowty (1979) and extending the work of Carmen Rotstein and Yoad Winter (2004) on adjectives, observes that "an open/closed scale structure of an adjective directly leads to an a/telic temporal structure (respectively) of the corresponding verb" (2006, 3).

2.2.4 Aspectual Class Mapping between Verbs and VPs

For the present study, in addition to recognizing how various modifiers affect aspectual class, a systematic means of mapping the aspectual classes of individual verbs to the class of VPs in which they occur is necessary. This need arises from the methodology of analysis of VPs in BH narrative, an analysis which will involve classifying VPs in which particular verbal lexemes occur across a corpus of BH as a means for classifying the aspectual class of the VPs in which these same lexemes occur in the Genesis Flood narrative. It will, therefore, involve moving from the aspectual class of VPs to "neutral" aspectual classes of verbs to, thirdly, the aspectual class of VPs containing instances of those verbs.

Xiao and McEnery (2002, 2004b) provide such a model, demonstrating cross-linguistic viability through application to corpus data from Mandarin Chinese and English. Their studies provide a "two-level model" of situation aspect distinguishing between classes of verbal lexemes and situation types of clauses. For their analysis, they propose a "neutral context" for the determination of classes at the lexical level. In their corpus languages, they define as follows:

> In English, for example, a neutral context is a simple clause in which (a) the verb is in the past tense, (b) the object is syntactically and semantically a singular countable noun and should only be present if it is obligatory, i.e., with a necessarily transitive verb, and (c) viewpoint aspect must be simple . . . . In Chinese, a neutral context is similar except that there is no tense requirement and a perfective viewpoint aspect is preferable. These restrictions are imposed to avoid the possible influences of other sentential elements (e.g., arguments, adjuncts and viewpoint aspect) on verbs. (Xiao and McEnery 2002, 13)

For BH, an analogous "neutral context" may result from (a) a verb in the *wayyiqtol* form, corresponding to elements (a) and (c) for English, and (b) the same requirement for objects as for English and Chinese. Thus וַיִּשְׁבְּרֵהוּ, "and he broke it," (Jer 28:10) provides a neutral context, fulfilling the requirements of *wayyiqtol* form and the presence of a singular object, due to the transitivity of *qal* שׁבר (*šbr*).

In their complete system, Xiao and McEnery (2004b) distinguish three levels of situation aspect: those of the "nucleus," "core," and "clause" ("nucleus," "situation," and "full sentence" in Xiao and McEnery 2002). According to their own explanation, "the nucleus deals with predicates. The core deals with predicates and arguments. The clause deals with predicates, arguments and non-arguments" (2004b, 342). They also distinguish between a "basic-level" and "derived-level," which are the two levels of primary concern for this study. The "basic-level" concerns VPs without any modifiers affecting aspectual class, whereas the "derived-level" concerns VPs with all accompanying modifiers. This division between "basic-level" and "derived-level" may occur at the nucleus, core, and clause levels. Smith (1997, 18) earlier offered the concept of a "basic-level" and "derived-level," defining them as follows: "The basic level of categorization is always available for a verb constellation. The derived level requires adverbial or other information from context." Using the five variables of their classification system discussed above and these situation levels, Xiao and McEnery present a series of twelve mapping rules for their analysis of English and Mandarin Chinese, which appear in Xiao and McEnery (2004b) as follows:

Rule 1: $\text{Verb}_{[-telic/\pm bounded]} + \text{RVCs} \Rightarrow \text{Derived Verb}_{[+result/+telic]}$

Rule 2: $\text{Verb}_{[-telic/\pm bounded]} + \text{reduplicant} \Rightarrow \text{Derived Verb}_{[+bounded]}$

Rule 3: $\text{NP} + \text{Verb}_{[+/-telic]} \Rightarrow \text{Core}_{[+/-telic]}$

Rule 4: $\text{NP} + \text{Verb}_{[-telic]} + \text{NP} \Rightarrow \text{Core}_{[-telic]}$

Rule 5: $\text{NP} + \text{Verb}_{[+telic]} + \text{NP}_{[+/-count]} \Rightarrow \text{Core}_{[+/-telic]}$

Rule 6: $\text{NP} + \text{Verb}_{[-telic]} + \text{PP}_{[Goal]} \Rightarrow \text{Core}_{[+telic]}$

Rule 7: $\text{Core}_{[-bounded]} + \textit{for-PP/from} \ldots \textit{to} \Rightarrow \text{Clause}_{[+bounded]}$

Rule 8: $\text{Core}_{[+telic]} + \textit{for-PP/from} \ldots \textit{to} \Rightarrow \text{Clause}_{[-telic]}$

Rule 9: $\text{Core}_{[\pm bounded]} + \text{temporal quantifier} \Rightarrow \text{Clause}_{[+bounded]}$

Rule 10: $\text{Core}_{[+telic]} + \text{progressive} \Rightarrow \text{Clause}_{[-telic]}$

Rule 11: $\text{Core}_{[-result]} + \textit{de}\text{-construction} \Rightarrow \text{Clause}_{[+result]}$

Rule 12: $\text{Core}_{[-result]} + \textit{ba/bei}\text{-construction} \Rightarrow \text{Clause}_{[+result]}$

"RVCs" in Rule 1 are "resultative verb complements," that is, "verb complements that indicate the resultant state or phase of the situation denoted by their preceding verbs in resultative compounds" (Xiao and McEnery 2004b, 17). "Marie pulled her hand **free**" (2004b, 18, bold type in original) provides an example of an RVC in English.

Modification of this set of rules may provide a corresponding set for the analysis of BH. Each rule may receive discussion in turn. The first two rules concern the construction of the nucleus. In light of a three-variable ([± dynamic][± telic][± durative]) rather than the five-variable system of Xiao and McEnery and the collapsing of telicity and boundedness in the latter into the single variable of telicity (on which, see above), Rule 1 may be reduced to

$$\text{Verb}_{[\pm\text{telic}]} + \text{RVCs} \Rightarrow \text{Derived Verb}_{[+\text{telic}]}$$

This rule only concerns the effects of adding RVCs; the presence of an RVC indicates telicity. Rule 2 concerns the use of verb reduplication for delimitative meaning in Chinese. Since BH does not utilize a corresponding construction, this rule is unnecessary for analysis of BH.

Rules 3 through 6 address additions to the nucleus to form the core. In each, the NP preceding the Verb in the statement of the rule represents a subject NP whereas the NP following the verb expresses an object NP, regardless of actual language syntax. These rules apply without modification to BH as they do to English and Chinese, although Rule 6 does not apply to Chinese since Chinese does not have prepositional phrases expressing a goal distinct from locative or directional prepositional phrases.

In Rule 7, the telicity variable replaces the boundedness variable, resulting in the form

$$\text{Core}_{[-\text{telic}]} + \textit{for-PP/from} \ldots \textit{to} \Rightarrow \text{Clause}_{[+\text{telic}]}$$

This rule concerns the addition of a prepositional phrase limiting the process of an atelic core and restates the diagnostic concerning *for*-adverbials mentioned above. Thus, the atelic core "John ran" becomes telic with the addition of a phrase such as "from his house to the store" or "for an hour." Rule 8, however, expresses the temporal limitation of the process of an accomplishment. The addition of a limiting prepositional phrase may express the failure of the completion of an accomplishment. As far as the presence of a temporal endpoint, however, the addition of such a limiting prepositional phrase does not remove a temporal endpoint, but only places a breach between an expressed actual temporal endpoint and a potential temporal endpoint occurring at the completion of the accomplishment. To illustrate, "John ran the marathon" expresses a telic accomplishment. However, the addition of a phrase such as "for twenty minutes" indicates that John did not complete the marathon and the expected completion of the core accomplishment was never reached. Perhaps John was injured at this point in the race and had to stop running. "John ran the marathon for twenty minutes" therefore divides between the expressed actual temporal endpoint (twenty minutes following the beginning of the race) and the potential endpoint at the completion of the core accomplishment, that is, John's successful completion of the marathon. Xiao and McEnery note that this rule does not always apply (2002, 27). Per discussion above concerning telicity and boundedness in the system of Xiao and McEnery, this rule will not be used in this form for the analysis of BH. According to the definition of telicity above, the limiting phrase retains telicity, although moving the time of the endpoint's occurrence. However, the addition of the prepositional phrase forces durativity, such that the rule may be modified as follows:

$$\text{Core}_{[+\text{telic}]} + \textit{for}\text{-PP}/\textit{from}\ldots to \Rightarrow \text{Clause}_{[+\text{durative}][+\text{telic}]}$$

As for Rules 1 and 7, telicity replaces boundedness in Rule 9 so that it becomes

$$\text{Core}_{[\pm\text{telic}]} + \text{temporal quantifier} \Rightarrow \text{Clause}_{[+\text{telic}]}$$

"Temporal quantifier" here refers to exact specification of a number of occurrences. Rule 10 maintains its original form:

$$\text{Core}_{[+\text{telic}]} + \text{progressive} \Rightarrow \text{Clause}_{[-\text{telic}]}$$

This rule expresses the effect of the progressive to make telic situations atelic, whether through expressing the continuing process of a single-event process or iteration: "the progressive functions to trigger a situation type shift and coerce a telic situation into a derived activity at the full sentence level." Thus "the little boy jumped" is telic whereas "the little boy was jumping" is atelic. Rules 11 and 12 are language specific rules for Chinese and therefore do not apply to BH.

Through this modification and elimination, nine rules thus result for the analysis of BH from Xiao and McEnery's original twelve rules:

Rule 1: $\text{Verb}_{[\pm\text{telic}]} + \text{RVCs} \Rightarrow \text{Derived Verb}_{[+\text{telic}]}$

Rule 2: $\text{NP} + \text{Verb}_{[+/-\text{telic}]} \Rightarrow \text{Core}_{[+/-\text{telic}]}$ (from original Rule 3)

Rule 3: $\text{NP} + \text{Verb}_{[-\text{telic}]} + \text{NP} \Rightarrow \text{Core}_{[-\text{telic}]}$ (from original Rule 4)

Rule 4: $\text{NP} + \text{Verb}_{[+\text{telic}]} + \text{NP}_{[+/-\text{count}]} \Rightarrow \text{Core}_{[+/-\text{telic}]}$ (from original Rule 5)

Rule 5: $\text{NP} + \text{Verb}_{[-\text{telic}]} + \text{PP}_{[\text{Goal}]} \Rightarrow \text{Core}_{[+\text{telic}]}$ (from original Rule 6)

Rule 6: $\text{Core}_{[-\text{telic}]} + \textit{for}\text{-PP}/\textit{from}\ldots to \Rightarrow \text{Clause}_{[+\text{telic}]}$ (from original Rule 7)

Rule 7: $\text{Core}_{[+\text{telic}]} + \textit{for}\text{-PP}/\textit{from}\ldots to \Rightarrow \text{Clause}_{[+\text{durative}][+\text{telic}]}$ (from original Rule 8)

Rule 8: $\text{Core}_{[\pm\text{telic}]} + \text{temporal quantifier} \Rightarrow \text{Clause}_{[+\text{telic}]}$ (from original Rule 9)

Rule 9: $\text{Core}_{[+\text{telic}]} + \text{progressive} \Rightarrow \text{Clause}_{[-\text{telic}]}$ (from original Rule 10)

These nine rules provide the means for mapping between the basic and derived levels of VPs to allow for consistency in analyzing the manner in which particular verbal lexemes are used.[31]

A short sample from BH narrative may help tò illustrate the function of these rules.

(24) a.   וַיָּבֹאוּ עַד־גֹּרֶן הָאָטָד אֲשֶׁר בְּעֵבֶר הַיַּרְדֵּן וַיִּסְפְּדוּ־שָׁם מִסְפֵּד גָּדוֹל
וְכָבֵד מְאֹד וַיַּעַשׂ לְאָבִיו אֵבֶל שִׁבְעַת יָמִים:

come-3MplWAYYIQTOL until threshing floor-GEN the-Atad
which in-opposite the-Jordan lament-3MplWAYYIQTOL
there mourning great and-heavy very make-3MsgWAYY
IQTOL to-father-GEN-3Msg mourning seven days
"And they came to the threshing floor of Atad, which was across
the Jordan, and they lamented there with a great and very
weighty mourning ceremony, and they mourned for his
father seven days," Gn 50:10.

This verse contains three VPs:

---

31. Xiao and McEnery (2004b, 359) present the following matrix of situation classes at the basic and derived levels. Obviously, this matrix is different from the basis for my analysis of BH due to its different set of variables and situation types, as noted in discussion above. The situation type abbreviations are as follows: ILS = individual-level state, SLS = stage-level state, ACC = accomplishment, ACT = activity, SEM = semelfactive, ACH = achievement.

Situation type		[±dyn]	[±dur]	[±bnd]	[±telic]	[±result]
ILS	Basic	−	+	−	−	−
	Derived	−	+	+	−	−
SLS	Basic	±	+	−	−	−
	Derived	±	+	+	−	−
ACC		+	+	+	+	−
ACT	Basic	+	+	−	−	−
	Derived	+	+	±	−	−
SEM	Basic	+	−	±	−	−
	Derived	+	+	±	−	−
ACH	Basic	+	−	+	+	+
	Derived	+	+	+	+	+

Xiao and McEnery (2004b, 359–360) offer samples from Chinese with English for each of the situation types in this table. Below I provide their examples, adding similar examples from BH with English translation. As indicated in the discussion of aspect classification systems above, I do not agree in all cases with Xiao and McEnery's classification of the VPs. Special thanks to Wei Li for her very kind assistance in providing minor modification to the Chinese examples, including the addition of tone markings to facilitate reading of the transliteration for readers familiar with Mandarin Chinese. To assist linguists unfamiliar with Chinese, I have retained Xiao and McEnery's groupings into word units rather than separating the transliteration of each Chinese character.

1. וַיָּבֹאוּ עַד־גֹּרֶן הָאָטָד אֲשֶׁר בְּעֵבֶר הַיַּרְדֵּן

come-3MplWAYYIQTOL until threshing floor-GEN the-Atad which in-opposite the-Jordan

"And they came to the threshing floor of Atad, which was across the Jordan."

2. וַיִּסְפְּדוּ־שָׁם מִסְפֵּד גָּדוֹל וְכָבֵד מְאֹד

lament-3MplWAYYIQTOL there mourning great and-heavy very

"And they lamented there with a great and very weighty mourning ceremony."

3. וַיַּעַשׂ לְאָבִיו אֵבֶל שִׁבְעַת יָמִים

make-3MsgWAYYIQTOL to-father-GEN-3Msg mourning seven days

"And he made mourning for his father for seven days."

VP (1) contains a PP$_{[Goal]}$, a prepositional phrase expressing a goal (עַד־גֹּרֶן הָאָטָד אֲשֶׁר בְּעֵבֶר הַיַּרְדֵּן, "to the threshing floor of Atad, which was across the Jordan"). The VP is telic. According to Rule 5 above (corresponding to Xiao and McEnery's Rule 6), NP + Verb$_{[-telic]}$ + PP$_{[Goal]}$ ⇒ Core$_{[+telic]}$. Thus, while the complete VP is telic, removal of

Situation aspect class	Xiao and McEnery (2004b) examples	BH examples
Basic ILS	tā ài Mǎlì 'He loved Mary.'	וַיֶּאֱהַב גַּם־אֶת־רָחֵל מִלֵּאָה '(and) Jacob loved Rachel' (Gn 29:18)
Derived ILS	tā ài Mǎlì ài-le sān-nián 'He loved Mary for three years.'	וַיִּרְאוּ יְמֵי־חַיָּיו תְּשָׁם־תְּאָ וְאָרֶץ 'They feared Moses all the days of his life' (Jos 4:14)
Basic SLS	Yuēhàn hěn shēngqì 'John was angry.'	טִפְשׁוֹהִי תּוּכְלָם טֹקְשֵׁתוֹ '(and) the kingdom of Jehoshaphat was quiet' (2 Chr 20:30)
Derived SLS (basic SLS ⇒ derived SLS)	Yuēhàn shēng-le yí-gè xiǎoshí de qì 'John was angry for an hour.'	סִיָּוֶשׁ רֶשַׁע יָרְאָה הַטְּמֵא וַיָּמְיָב 'in his days the land was peaceful for 10 years' (2 Chr 13:23)
Basic activities	tā tuī-le yí-liàng chē 'He pushed a cart.'	סֶהֱבִיאָ בִּקְעֵי־תָא לְאַרְשִׁי־יָגֵב וְאַשִּׁיִן '(and) the sons of Israel carried Jacob their father' (Gn 46:5)
Derived activities	tā tuī chē tuī-le yí-gè xiǎoshí 'He pushed the cart for an hour.' (basic ACT ⇒ derived ACT) tā xiě lùnwén xiě-le yí-gè xiǎoshí/tā zài xiě lùnwén 'He wrote his thesis for an hour/was writing his thesis.' (ACC ⇒ derived ACT)	וַיִּבְכּוּ אֹתוֹ מִצְרַיִם שִׁבְעִים יוֹם '(and) Egypt mourned for him for 70 days" (Gn 50:3). (basic ACT ⇒ derived ACT)
Basic semelfactives	dēngtǎ shǎn-le yí-xià 'The beacon flashed once.'	
Derived semelfactives (basic SEM ⇒ derived SEM)	tā késòu ké-le wǔ fēnzhōng/sān-cì/zài késòu 'He coughed for 5 minutes/three times/was coughing.'	סִימְעַף עַבְשׁ־דֵע רַעֲנֵה רְרוֹזָיֵ '(and) the young man sneezed seven times' (2 Kgs 4:35)
Accomplishments	tā xiě-le yì-fēng xìn 'He wrote a letter.'	בְּאוֹי־לֹא רְפַס דָוִד בִּתְכִיוֹ '(and) David wrote a letter to Joab' (2 Sm 11:14)
Basic Achievements	tā bǎ chábēi dǎ-pò-le 'He broke the cup.'	וַהֲרֵבְשֵׁיִן '(and) [Hananiah] broke it' (Jer 28:8)
Derived achievements (basic ACH ⇒ derived ACH)	tā zhùyì-dào-le wénzhāng zhōng de sān-chù cuòwù 'He noticed three errors in the paper.'	סִיָּדֵכָה וּרֲבְשֵׁיִן '(and) they broke the jars' (Jgs 7:20)

the PP$_{[Goal]}$ presents the atelic core וַיָּבֹאוּ, "And they came."[32] The VP represents an accomplishment with an activity core.

VP (2) specifies location and contains an accusative indicating the means of lamentation. However, it does not contain any elements from the nine rules relating to situation aspect. The aspect at both the basic and derived levels is the same. וַיִּסְפְּדוּ, "And they lamented," is dynamic, does not express any endpoint, and expresses a durative action. VP (2) therefore may be analyzed as an activity.

VP (3) consists of a basic transitive verb with accompanying object (וַיַּעַשׂ . . . אֵבֶל, "And he made mourning"), an aspectually neutral prepositional phrase (לְאָבִיו, "for his father"), and a limiting temporal phrase functioning as a *for*-PP. Rules 4 and 6 both come into play in the consideration of VP (3). עָשָׂה, "make," may take either [+ count] or [– count] nouns as objects. However, according to Rule 4 (corresponding to Xiao and McEnery's Rule 5) the addition of a mass or [– count] object NP results in the atelic core וַיַּעַשׂ אֵבֶל, "And he made mourning." By Rule 6 (corresponding to Xiao and McEnery's Rule 7), the addition of the *for*-PP, שִׁבְעַת יָמִים, "for seven days," causes the entire VP to become telic. VP (3), therefore, being durative, dynamic, and telic, represents an accomplishment.

2.2.5 Ter Meulen and Temporal Relations in Discourse

The foregoing material has considered the aspectual properties of individual verbs and VPs. I first presented a system of classification and secondly discussed theory concerning what various features of VPs indicate concerning aspect along with a means of mapping between aspectual classification between a "basic" (neutral context) level and a "derived" level with additional modifiers. One more component remains necessary for constructing a methodology for the analysis of situation aspect in BH narrative. This final element will come as the answer to the question of how situation aspect affects temporal relationships between VPs. This question begins to approach the field of logical semantics and discourse relations, which Boyd will address at length in **Chapter 12**. I shall devote most of the following discussion to the work of ter Meulen, from whose work I will draw for the methodology for analyzing BH.

A correlation between the order of event presentation in narrative and the portrayed temporal relationships between VPs has received recognition by many writers, and some have noted the role of situation aspect in directing

---

32. Since finite BH verbs contain the person, gender, and number of their subjects, it is not possible to present the nucleus of a BH verb without a subject as in English.

such relationships. However, these studies often offer less specificity than ter Meulen. As early as Dowty (1986), Dowty affirmed a relationship between aspectual class and the temporal relationships of VPs. In his construal, a second sentence dictates its relationship to a previous sentence through the telicity of the second's VP: achievements and accomplishments follow events mentioned immediately before, while states and achievements, and all classes in the progressive, present temporal simultaneity with previous sentences. However, in each of the examples Dowty offers as illustration, the first VP is an achievement ("entered the president's office"), so his discussion does not consider other possible variations. While significant as recognition that situation aspect plays a role for temporal relationships between VPs, Dowty's presentation is incomplete and imprecise. Dowty further correctly recognized exceptions due to overriding discourse relations, although without using the term: "this . . . is the 'default case' to be followed when neither time adverbials nor entailments and implicatures of the discourse itself give clues to the ordering of events" (1986, 58). He presents a few examples as illustrations of variation from this "default," all of which may be identified as cases of elaboration.

Marc Moens and Mark Steedman (1987), in another early study, presented events as "nuclei" within or following which subsequently related events take place. For them, "a nucleus is defined as a structure comprising a culmination, an associated preparatory process, and a consequent state" (1987, 3–4). This culmination is associated with telicity. While they do not discuss each of the relationships between VPs of differing aspectual classes, they identify VPs as either denoting complete nuclei or nuclei which are decomposed by subsequently related events. A complete nucleus is followed, as context and world knowledge permit, by a subsequent event. However, a subsequently related event may decompose a nucleus if it relates another event within the nucleus of the first event. They notably draw attention to the possibility of merely implying the existence of a subsequently related event. Although they do not use the terms of logical semantics, such a structure corresponds to the discourse relation of elaboration.

Other studies observing at least a general correspondence between the ordering of VPs in a narrative and a narrative's portrayal of the order of their occurrence include Suzanne Fleischman (1990), who notes iconicity as often primary within narrative. Terence Parsons (2002) recognizes the distinction between the manner in which states and events relate to narrative progression. However, his presentation does not distinguish between aspectual classes of events and merely states in a generally manner that events advance temporal reference while states do not. Co Vet (1995) considers only agentivity in the structure of events in connection with temporal relationships.

In the field of psycholinguistics, Rolf A. Zwaan (1996) presents experimental data on reading time for English narratives containing explicit temporal shifts which provide support for the observation that readers naturally attribute temporal succession according to the succession of events as they appear in narrative texts (the "iconicity assumption"). He includes in his conclusion that "When readers read a narrative, their default assumption is that successively reported events occurred successively and contiguously. However, specific lexical (e.g., time adverbials) or grammatical (tense) information may function as a processing cue to the reader to override the strong iconicity assumption, deactivate the current time interval, and set up a new one" (1996, 1205). Zwaan does not specifically address the effect of situation aspect on the formulation of mental timelines during the reading of narrative texts. Keisuke Ohtsuka and William F. Brewer (1992) earlier offered a study predicting and demonstrating the priority of the iconicity assumption through delay in reading speeds for non-iconic texts, and Jean M. Mandler and Marsha S. Goodman (1982) noted iconic ordering as "canonical" for some elements within stories. Silvia P. Gennari (2004), also from a psycholinguistic approach, cites effects of situation aspect on perception of temporal relationships but only considers the division between states and events, primarily between main and subordinate clauses.

To return to the work of ter Meulen, ter Meulen (1997) and Seligman and ter Meulen (1995) offer a means for graphically representing the temporal relationships of situations in past time English narrative which they designate Dynamic Aspect Trees (DATs). The means of constructing DATs, however, lies in a theory of the perception of temporal relationships between situations in narrative such that the placement of each situation in a DAT correlates fundamentally to aspectual class, barring any contrary dictates of explicit temporal adverbial expressions or logical semantics. A summary presentation of DATs with discussion of differences in kinds of states and a brief comparison of DATs and Discourse Representation Theory also appears in ter Meulen (2000). Kiyong Lee discusses DATs as one semantic representational system which includes temporal relationships in Lee (2004). Lee's discussion presents DATs in a general manner in this study applying representational systems to English and Korean, suggesting their applicability cross-linguistically.

Basic DAT construction involves the formation of a tree displaying temporal relationships in a manner resembling a mathematical tree diagram. From an initial node, each additional non-stative event appears in the tree as a further node, either vertically, indicating temporal inclusion, or horizontally, ordinarily indicating temporal succession. Two kinds of nodes appear in DATs: "holes" (nodes representing events which may temporally encompass other events) and "plugs" (nodes which restrict the "flow" of events, resulting in temporal succession). In terms of aspectual class, "holes" correspond to activities and "plugs" to achievements in the simple past tense (thus, the tense for which this kind of analysis applies notably corresponds to Xiao and McEnery's "neutral context"). Accomplishments, which ter Meulen (1997) refers to as "filters," may function either as "holes" or "plugs," depending on what follows in the narrative.

When events appear in a narrative following a filter, those events may either relate subsequent events, in which case the filter functions as a plug, or describe events composing that which the filter itself describes. Ter Meulen explains:

> The start of an event described as a filter precedes the start of any event described by subsequent clauses, but the end of the event described as a filter is preceded by the end of any described part of it. In that sense, filters serve as semantic objects incorporating information about the (partly) simultaneous subevents. This allows us to infer from the two filter descriptions *Jane climbed Mont Blanc. She walked up to the base camp* that her starting to climb Mont Blanc must have preceded her starting to walk up to the base camp and that the end of that walk to the camp must have preceded the end of the climb. (Ter Meulen 1997, 10; italics in original)

Stative situations (ter Meulen does not subcategorize states as in the above classification system and so only discusses the stative aspectual class [– dynamic] [– telic] [+ durative], the "atelic state" in my system), "stickers," append to current or following nodes, depending on whether a plug or hole, respectively, appears as the current node. States/"stickers" last as long as they are able given the introduction of new narrative material, and information contradictory to one sticker will not necessarily cancel other stickers already present (see 1997, 68). In a complete DAT for past narrative, a plug representing the present and a hole denoting past time serve as the initial two nodes. Seligman and ter Meulen consider progressive and past perfect English expressions to represent states and therefore treat them as such in the construction of DATs: "Sentences expressed in the simple past have a dynamic content determined largely by their aspectual class. The use of progressive and perfective aspect modifies this function, because both past-progressive and past-perfect sentences describe state-types" (1995, 294).[33] Other studies proposing or accepting a stative classification of progressives include Takashi Suzuki (1995) and Vlach (1981); Rosen (2003) seems to accept this classification as well. Although I distinguished between statives and progressives above in the discussion of statives, that distinction does not contest their similarity of behavior in this respect.

Ter Meulen notes that world knowledge and explicit indications of temporal relations as well as *compatibility* and discourse relations contrary to temporal sequence, such as cause, may overrule the significance of aspectual class for the temporal relationships between situations in a narrative (see esp. ter Meulen 1997, 3–4, 14–16, 47–50). Boyd will discuss the various discourse relations in BH narrative vis-à-vis temporal relations in narrative in **Chapter 12**. Importantly, ter Meulen also recognizes that narrative may present ambiguities, and multiple DATs may possibly result from the same narrative text, depending on alternative interpretations which a single text may allow: "There may be choice points at which the interpreter may decide to accept or reject certain inferences or interpretations, based on information that is not contained in the text itself…This means that the DAT construction rules do not constitute a deterministic algorithm—that is, there is not always a unique next step in the construction" (2000, 155). The potential for such ambiguity must remain inescapable, and the reader does not benefit as a listener in conversation through the ability to question and clarify ambiguities. In the consideration of texts, therefore, analysts must recognize and note where ambiguities exist.

Below are two concise sets of rules from ter Meulen (1997, 51) for DAT construction:

---

33. Joseph P. Magliano and Michelle C. Schleich (2000) present the results of psycholinguistic experiments demonstrating frequent perception of temporal inclusion of perfective viewpoint VPs following a progressive viewpoint VP. They only tested, however, the perception of temporal relationships resulting from reading a series of sentences with perfective viewpoint aspect VPs following key sentences in the experiments with either a progressive or perfective aspect VP without regard to the situation aspect in the VPs which follow the key sentences. They also do not address the perception of the temporal relationships between the VPs in the key sentences and those which precede them.

Rules for DAT representation of aspectual classes

1. Sticker rule

   If the new information is a state-type, append the type as a sticker to the current node, if it is a plug, and append it to the next node, if the current node is a hole.

2. Hole rule

   If the new information is an activity-type, introduce a new hole, make it the current node, and label it with the new type.

3. Filter rule

   If the new information is an accomplishment-type, introduce either a hole or a plug, make it the current node, and label it with the new type.

4. Plug rule

   If the new information is an achievement-type, introduce a plug, make it the current node, and label it with the new type.

5. Filler rule

   If the extension of the DAT resulting from applying rules 1–4 is inconsistent, then plug the closest dominating node necessary to remove the inconsistency, make it the current node, and reapply the rules.

Update Rules for DATs

1. Hole update

   If the current node is a hole, represent the new node as its child.

2. Plug update

   If the current node is a plug, represent the new node as its sister.

Although the concern of the present study lies in temporal relationships between VPs more than in the manner of representing them graphically, simple DATs may help in illustrating the role of situation aspect for these relationships as ter Meulen has observed them. Ter Meulen (1997, 47) provides the following sample paragraph:

(25) a. Jane felt ill. She sat down, attempted to decipher the message, and looked at her watch. She sighed. It was not even noon yet.

A. G. ter Meulen provides two DATs for this sample:[34]

---

34. The notation for complete DATs labels each node with a "relation" (often the simple verb itself); the objects of the relation, represented by letter variables in the manner of an algebra as in proposition calculus; parameters; and polarity. See ter Meulen (1997), chapter 2.

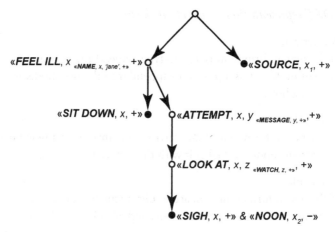

Figure 1.1.

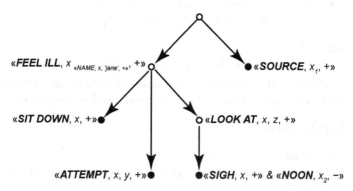

Figure 1.2.

The first sentence presents an activity VP, and thus appears as a hole for "feel ill" according to the hole rule. The next VP, "sat down," again obviously appears as an achievement, resulting in a plug, but the third, "attempted to decipher the message," in ter Meulen's analysis, represents an accomplishment, allowing for two possible interpretations given that following information is compatible with either a hole or plug interpretation. The possibility of these two interpretations results in the difference between Figure 1.1, where the hole interpretation includes Jane's looking at her watch and sighing as temporally within her attempt to decipher the message, and Figure 1.2, where Jane only looks at her watch and sighs following the cessation of her attempt. The final two nodes illustrate again an activity and an achievement as hole and plug, respectively, and the latter of the two nodes also includes the stative information "it was not even noon yet" appended as a sticker.

Ter Meulen's observations concerning the association of situation aspect with temporal relations in a narrative provide a helpful means for analyzing the portrayed time of VPs in texts. They provide the basis for analysis in the methodology I present for BH. However, as she acknowledges, the rules are not airtight, and analysis of any given text requires consideration of context, world knowledge, and other possible discourse relations. A complete account of the temporal relationships between VPs requires consideration of discourse relations in logical semantics. The associations between particular temporal relationships and aspectual classes ter Meulen recognizes generally obtain within the "narration," but at times may also obtain within the "elaboration" and "background," relations of Alex Lascarides and Nicholas Asher (1993), Asher and Lascarides (1997), and Lascarides, Asher, and Jon Oberlander's (1992).

Also from the field of logical semantics, *compatibility* and *incompatibility* of situations in a narrative play a role in directing analysis and may override ter Meulen's basic rules. Seligman and ter Meulen observe:

> Under certain circumstances, the current node may jump to one of its ancestor-holes, turning it into a plug in the process. This happens when the text either explicitly describes the end of the event depicted by the ancestor hole, or else describes an event which is incompatible with the continued growth of the tree. From a logical point of view, this is the most difficult mechanism we face, because of destructive character and its dependence on semantic notions, like "incompatability." (1995, 296–97)

Reasons that ter Meulen's set of rules generally obtain within narrative discourse units, except in the case of temporal reversal, lie partially in semantics and partially in the nature of situation presentation in the narrative genre. A durative event (whether "hole" or "filter") would more frequently be elaborated by other events, allowing for the "elaboration" discourse relation, than a non-durative event. The former, taking place over time, more likely would contain distinguishable, constituent sub-events. Other discourse relations, such as consequence or contrast, require different understandings of temporal relationships; once these receive recognition during the process of analysis, however, DATs may still serve the purpose of representation. Furthermore, more specific discourse relations take precedence over less specific relations when possible, resulting in the precedence of other discourse relations, such as explanation, over narration.[35] Consideration of

---

35. The precedence of a default with greater specificity is known as the Penguin Principle: $\varphi \to \psi, \psi > \chi, \varphi > \neg\chi, \varphi \mathrel{|\approx} \neg\chi$. The name derives from its common verbal formulation: penguins are birds, birds normally fly, penguins normally do not fly, Tweety is a penguin, so Tweety does not fly. The particular representation of the Penguin Principle here is from Lascarides and Asher (1993).

other relevant factors, such as those from logical semantics and discourse analysis, however, escape the field of lexical semantics and lie outside the scope of this chapter. Later chapters will consider them in detail.

Since the system of aspectual classification I present above includes classes in addition to the four original Vendlerian classes, some additional rules must supplement ter Meulen's procedure for analysis. Among dynamic situations, only one additional class, the semelfactive, appears in the classification system. Semelfactives resemble achievements in all respects except in that they do not result in lasting change and therefore have negative telicity values. However, they still lack durativity, occurring at a conceptual point in time, and therefore behave temporally like achievements in narrative. Semelfactives therefore function as "plugs." The two additional stative classes, the transitory state and point state, however, combine elements from different categories in ter Meulen's system. Her states append as "stickers" to previous DAT nodes and last as long as they remain compatible with new nodes. As statives, point states and transitory states similarly append to other nodes. A transitory state, however, functions as a sort of "filter sticker." Due to the positive telicity and durativity values of a transitory state, it may temporally encompass situations denoted by following VPs in a narrative, or these situations may follow the transitory state's completion. Point states also function as a sort of "sticker," but, due to their negative durativity value, they cannot last to cover any situations subsequent in time. Therefore, they often only append to a single situation and do not obtain for any situations which a narrative lists subsequently. In the case that a point state appends to a durative event, say, an accomplishment, the point state only obtains for a moment during of the duration of the accomplishment, most likely the point of its initiation or completion. The possibility remains, however, that a point state may append to a durative event and an additional non-durative event which the durative event encompasses. For, example, a point state may append to an accomplishment and to an achievement following (in the order of the narrative but not temporally) that accomplishment. In the practice of analysis, point states and their temporal relationships to other VPs usually present little difficulty. Ter Meulen (1997) recognizes that different kinds of stickers exist, stating that some states are "more permanent" and others "transient." I hope to increase precision through use of the three classes of states defined above.

With a system of classification, a means for mapping situation classes between "neutral contexts" and derived contexts of verbal lexemes, and a set of rules concerning the association of situation types and narrative temporal relationships, the three elements necessary for developing a methodology for the analysis of BH are available. Following a brief consideration of studies of situation aspect in BH below, I will present the steps of this methodology and a sample.

2.3 *Studies of Situation Aspect in BH*

Before presenting the steps of my method for analysis, studies of situation aspect in BH may receive brief attention. As noted above, situation aspect in BH has received relatively little attention. Some works have focused on BH statives and have included note of the flexibility of BH stative verbs to present either stative or inchoative (achievement) readings and of some non-stative verbs to offer either ingressive or non-ingressive readings. These studies include Jenni (1994), which focuses on the verb חדל (*ḥdl*), and Dobbs-Allsopp (1995), which considers קום (*qûm*). The former lists several examples, including נשא (*nśʾ*) in Judges 8:28, "lift up," compared with 1 Samuel 2:28, "carry," (Jenni 1994, 127–28). Hendel (1996), as noted above, considers the distinction between stativity and dynamicity. However, although he discusses some differences between event structures across the stems of BH, he does not otherwise apply situation aspect classes to BH. Most recently, Joosten (2012) has noted situation aspect as important for the study of BH in his work on the function of the verbs forms in BH.

Hatav (1989) represents an interesting early study which considers temporal relationships between VPs. Hatav seeks to define an "endpoint property," related to telicity but distinct from it. She uses this endpoint property in determining when situations may appear in the sequential timeline of narrative, presenting achievements and accomplishments as always on the sequential timeline of narrative but states and activities as flexible. She also combines these proposals with theory concerning the function of BH verb forms such that she asserts that the *qatal* of a stative verb appears for stative aspect whereas *wayyiqtol* indicates an inchoative function. This final observation has not received general support.

Cristo H. J. van der Merwe (1997), although summarizing a variety of means of conveying temporal relations in BH, does not mention situation aspect. Concerning simultaneity, he writes that "a general principle applying to the syntactic constructions used in these cases is that *wayyiqtol* and *weqatalti* sequences are avoided" (1997, 52). However, he does not provide demonstration of this statement nor account for its sufficiency only as "a general principle."

Creason (1995), Jenni (2000), and Dobbs-Allsopp (2000) emerge as three of the most significant considerations of situation aspect in BH. Dobbs-Allsopp dedicates his study to a consideration of BH stative verbs, focusing on their flexibility for offering stative, inchoative (or other kind of change-of-state), or dynamic readings. He presents situation aspect as the key to understanding these various possible readings and attempts to explain when stative verbs appear with each. He notes several possible indications of Hebrew stative verbs used dynamically: 1) modification by הלך (hlk), "to go," in the participle of infinitive absolute forms; 2) the presence, in some cases, of a direct object or oblique subject; 3) the presence of an effected object; 4) control frames, such as indications of agency (as may be indicated by an imperative (see discussion above concerning statives verbs appearing in the imperative), instrumental clauses, and purpose clauses; 5) the appearance of the stative in a participle, and thus often progressive, form; 6) periphrastic constructions with היה (hyh), "to be," possibly including the use of היה with a non-participle form of a stative;[36] and 7) modification by aspectual verbs, including קום, "to stand, get up," שוב (šûb), "to return," and יסף (ysp), "to add." I will not discuss each of these in turn here. I agree that these generally provide helpful means for recognizing dynamic uses of BH stative verbs, but see my discussion of kinds of statives and the appearance of statives as imperatives and progressives above.

The same article presents narrative sequence and "punctiliar frames" as resulting in inchoative significance of statives. As indicators of the former, Dobbs-Allsopp includes particles, conjunctions, and conditionals requiring sequence. He also includes the use of the *wayyiqtol* form. Stroup discussed this verb form at length in **Chapter 10** of this volume. While stative verbs in the *wayyiqtol* form may often function as inchoatives, where these inchoations temporally occur relative to other situations in the narrative requires consideration of more than merely the use of the *wayyiqtol* form (as Dobbs-Allsopp implicitly indicates by his statement that *wayyiqtol* may denote logically rather than temporally sequential events). In the proposed study, the duration of states entered through these inchoations at times may receive some consideration in the analysis of narrative temporal relations as well. Even when a stative appears with an inchoative sense, the resultant

---

36. Although Dobbs-Allsopp provides several examples of similar constructions of היה with a verbal adjective (in all except one case ירא (yr'), "be afraid," he only offers one with a true verb, 2 Kgs 17:25, in which a *qatal* form of ירא ("to be afraid") follows a temporal clause beginning with וַיְהִי. See **Chapter 15** by Longacre in this volume for a discussion of the use of וַיְהִי in BH narrative.

state may continue while other events occur in a narrative. With regard to punctiliar frames, they may, as Dobbs-Allsopp states, indicate inchoation. However, the inclusion of point states in the classification system I have proposed allows for another possibility. Statives in punctiliar frames must be considered individually to determine whether they denote point states or inchoation.

Jenni (2000) attempts to associate Hebrew verb stems with Vendler's situation classes. He presents causatives, and thus the *Hiphil* stem, as denoting accomplishments and the *Piel*, when it has corresponding causative *Qal* or *Hiphil*, as denoting achievements. While a blanket association of causatives with accomplishments does not seem possible, Jenni provides a helpful statistical demonstration that some observations concerning the *Hiphil* and *Piel* stems generally obtain. Stative verbs, when changed to the *Hiphil* stem, denote causative accomplishments, but they function as factitive achievements when changed to *Piel*. Related to this, verb roots already associated with accomplishments outside of the *Hiphil* do not appear in the *Hiphil* stem. Similarly, achievement verbs rarely appear with the same root in the *Piel* stem, and accomplishment verbs become achievements verbs in their corresponding *Piel* forms. Finally, verbs of movement and transitive activity verbs do not appear in corresponding *Piel* forms.

The most extensive study of situation aspect in BH is Creason (1995). I have discussed his classification system for situation aspect above. The remainder of this dissertation discusses participants and thematic roles (the relationships of entities denoted, particularly by nouns, in a sentence to the actions or states denoted by verbs, i.e., agent, patient, etc.), as well as "complex situations," and voice.[37] These other areas of study, while relating to some degree to this study, fall outside of its scope and focus and therefore do not require detailed consideration here. By "complex" situations, Creason refers to a situation which "entails a subsidiary causal event . . . In other words, a complex situation is composed of two subsituations, one of which causes the other" (1995, 168). For example, a fientive *piel* involves a dynamic situation, such as an achievement, which initiates a stative situation. However, nearly any situation could be further subdivided. Certainly the majority if not all dynamic situations lead to the stative situations denoted by perfect expressions; for example, "Joan hit Mary" results in the statives

37. I use the term "voice" here in an inclusive manner, encompassing distinctions between active, middle, and passive, and therefore refer both to Creason's discussion of "voice" as a distinction between active and passive and "double status situations" (situations denoted by middle voice expressions).

situations of "Mary has been hit" and "Joan has hit Mary." Our concern here is classification of primary situations and analysis of their temporal relationships in narrative, so subsituations, although at times relevant, can only receive secondary attention. I will not discuss in detail further division of event structures, including the constituent states and events of the "basic" event types. These receive reference in Pustejovsky (2000), Seungho Nam (2000), and Suzuki (1995), among other studies, in addition to Creason.

This series of studies evidences promising, though small, attention to situation aspect in BH and hopefully anticipates the further application of situation aspect theory to the study of BH. As noted above, among them a breach remains for the construction of a systematic means for analyzing temporal relationships of situations in BH. It is hoped that the discussion in this study and its proposed methodology may provide a step toward filling that breach.

3. A Methodology for the Analysis of Situation Aspect and Temporal Relationships in BH Narrative

In the final portion of this study, I would like to combine the above theoretical material to form a methodology for the analysis VPs in BH narrative. This methodology will combine my proposed classification system for situation aspect, observations concerning the relationship of modifiers and other VP elements to situation class along with the mapping rules between neutral and derived contexts, and ter Meulen's principles for determining temporal relationships between VPs on the basis of situation aspect. Following a description of the methodology, I will present a small sample of its application, mention limitations, and discuss the application of this methodology to the Genesis Flood narrative.

    3.1   Steps in a Methodology for Analysis of BH
    3.2   Limits of Aspectual Analysis for Establishing Temporal Relationships in Narrative
    3.3   An Illustration of the Application to BH Narrative

3.1 Steps in a Methodology for Analysis of BH

The proposed methodology consists of four steps which receive discussion in turn below:

1. Identify a VP for analysis and isolate its verb.
2. Classify all VPs in which the same verbal lexeme occurs within the corpus (or portion of the corpus) by means of the diagnostics and situation aspect flowchart, noting all relevant accompanying elements in the sentences and their properties, then map this classification to the "neutral" context of the verb through the set of mapping rules.

3. Using the data from step (2), classify the VP under analysis by mapping from the class of the verb in "neutral" context to the class of the complete VP in its narrative context.

4. Repeat for the next VP in the narrative, and identify the likely temporal relationship between the two VPs through the aspectual theory on which DAT relies, constructing DATs as desired.

Step (1) needs little further explanation, involving only the identification of a VP and its verb. This is the briefest step among the four. Such identification merely involves the recognizing, for example, "compare" as the verb in the VP of "Shall I compare thee to a summer's day?", or, in Hebrew, וַיִּיצֶר, "And he formed," as the verb in וַיִּיצֶר יְהוָה אֱלֹהִים מִן־הָאֲדָמָה כָּל־חַיַּת הַשָּׂדֶה וְאֵת כָּל־עוֹף הַשָּׁמַיִם, "And YHWH God formed every living thing of the field and every bird of the sky from the ground" (Gn 2:19).

Most time in applying the methodology for analysis will be spent on Step (2). Following the isolation of a verb in Step (1), a sufficient sample of the use of this verb from the corpus must be observed. For some common verbs, a limited corpus within BH, such as the Pentateuch, may provide a sufficient sample, but for many the analyst must examine the entire BH corpus. At times, the sparsity of a particular verb's use in BH may require examination of corresponding verbs in cognate languages with the qualification that cognate languages may not use cognate verbs in precisely the same manner as BH. Each instance of a verb may be entered into a chart listing relevant contextual information, such as the presence of adverbial modifiers (including prepositional phrases) and objects and the number and countability of subjects and objects. The classification system offered above may serve to classify both the VPs and, through the use of the mapping rules, the isolated verb in each VP according to a neutral context. By this means, two classes may result from analysis of each VP: the class of the VP and the class of its isolated verb in neutral context. In some cases these two classes will be the same.

Various elements and properties of VPs relating to situation aspect class received mention above. Some of the relevant properties may be included in a flow chart to assist in the process of classifying each VP. The flow chart in the appendix provides a sample of the kind which may be constructed from the definitions of the situation classes, the diagnostics, and observations from Xiao and McEnery's mapping system. Although some parts of the flow chart classify on the basis of the presence of certain elements in VPs or morphology, others necessarily merely depend on the semantic value of lexemes, and thus appear as questions concerning "inherent" semantic nature. For the purposes of this study, in the use of the flow chart, distinction of mass and count nouns through the absence of occurrences in the corpus with explicit individuation, as through specification of number, the lack of attestation of both singular and plural forms, and intuition may serve as sufficient.[38]

Although any individual verbal lexeme may display semantic diversity and thus represent multiple event structures through various usages, consideration of a large number of occurrences of each lexeme will reveal its common use or uses when mapped to neutral context and thus the event structure(s) it most often represents. Often a lexeme will much more frequently represent a particular event structure rather than another in a given syntactical construction, and, when a lexeme does display significant flexibility in the kinds of event structures it represents, often clear contextual indicators will make one possibility far more likely in a given context. Therefore, while semantic diversity of lexemes might seem to present a significant difficulty to the method proposed, in practice few ambiguous examples will be encountered. Vendler himself observed, "There is a very large number of verbs that fall completely, or at least in their dominant use, within one of these categories" (1967, 107). Similarly, at times the isolation of a verb must take into account that the verb may appear in a compound expression in which a preposition immediately following the verb modifies the semantic value of the expression.

The third step involves use of the mapping rules in reverse of Step (2). In the absence of any overriding features of the context in which the original VP appears, these rules may map the most common (or most likely given contextual use) class of the isolated verb to the class of the VP with all of its constituent elements. The VP will belong to one of the seven aspectual classes; at times ambiguity may require analysis of surrounding VPs before a final decision is reached.

Step (4) proceeds from the classification of VPs to identifying the temporal relationships between VPs. As the analyst classifies a series of VPs, the manner in which the VPs relate to each other in time may emerge through ter Meulen's rules for temporal relationships of aspectual classes. DATs, or similar representation systems, may serve to portray these relationships visually.

---

38. See Rothstein (2010) for a recent semantic account of count nouns and their distinction from mass nouns. Rothstein demonstrates the invalidity of homogeneity, cumulativity, and nature in reality as differentiating between these classes of nouns.

3.2 *Limits of Aspectual Analysis for Establishing Temporal Relationships in Narrative*

The methodology above provides a tool toward the analysis of temporal relationships in narrative, whether in BH or other languages. However, a series of limitations, some of which have received attention above, must be mentioned.

3.2.1. Subjectivity
3.2.2. Lack of Examples for Some Verbs and the Limitations of Cognate Research
3.2.3. Semantic Diversity of Individual Lexemes
3.2.4. Levels of Sequentiality and Micro-Sequence vis-à-vis Larger Narrative Units
3.2.5. Logical Semantics and Other Discourse Relations in Narrative

3.2.1 Subjectivity

Despite the various diagnostics for identifying the aspectual class of VPs, often VPs lack diagnostic elements which can indicate aspectual class with complete certainty. The analyst must often decide, from the available data, which class seems most appropriate for a VP. Decisions must often result at least partially from intuition and the knowledge of verbs of similar nature in the language under consideration and in other languages. In the analysis of BH and other dead languages, the analyst suffers from the further disadvantage of having no native speakers available for consultation.

The two possible DATs from the same text which appear as samples above provide an illustration of how narrative texts do not always provide sufficient information for determining precise temporal relationships between VPs. Clarifying all temporal relationships with precision often goes beyond the intentions of speakers and writers. Analysts must often choose between more than one possibility, although alternatives may be mentioned. Seligman and ter Meulen (1995, 315, n. 16) note: "We should remember that texts are ambiguous, and so are not directly amenable to logical analysis. We should first mark them in a way that disambiguates." At times interpretive decisions must result from "world knowledge," "common knowledge," and the coherence and *compatibility* of elements in a narrative, but subjectivity plays a role in determining even these. Again, ter Meulen (1997, 60) writes, "In having to explain just how an action must be structured in order to be considered 'normal,' issues of culture, causality, control, and social values are raised that a semantic theory should not have to answer," and, with reference to the constructions of DATs, "Coherence of information is a notoriously slippery concept, for it requires a better understanding of what topics are that speakers give information about and how speakers signal a change of topic" (1997, 79).

Nevertheless, in spite of how much subjectivity may enter into the process of analysis, readers and listeners routinely make many accurate intuitive decisions concerning the temporal relationships of events in narratives with little thought to the process. The method proposed will only increase the level of precision in making these decisions.[39]

3.2.2 Lack of Examples for Some Verbs and the Limitations of Cognate Research

Another limitation for the proposed methodology involves the lack of examples of the use of some verbs. This limitation has received mention in the discussion of the second step of the method. The BH corpus provides only a very limited sample of the use of some verbs, presenting difficulty to observing common use according to particular aspectual classes. Subjectivity of interpretation increases with decrease in sample size. Furthermore, some verbs, which may be used in varying ways, may not clearly evidence the variety of their use in a very small sample of use. Cognate languages may be consulted, as in traditional BH lexicography, but the analyst must always keep in mind that a cognate language may not use a related verb in precisely the same manner as BH. Speakers of two languages may immediately appreciate the difference in usage between related terms in those languages, but such differences are often difficult to determine in the study of BH vis-à-vis its cognate languages.

3.2.3 Semantic Diversity of Individual Lexemes

Care must be taken in the process of analysis to consider the possible semantic diversity of individual verbal lexemes. Vendler himself referenced this diversity at the beginning of his seminal article as he presented his goal as descriptive

---

39. To reiterate and elaborate the point made in the previous sentence, this is not to suggest that texts always require this sort of analysis for readers to understand them in many respects accurately and thoroughly. The general progression of the narrative and its theological import were readily accessible to the ancient reader and are so to the modern reader without consideration of this kind of linguistic analysis. The concern of this study, however, is that of precise temporal relationships. Even in this respect, the original readers, as native speakers and readers of the language in which the texts were delivered to them, would have been able to know intuitively what the author wished to communicate and what the author refrained from clarifying. The need for a more precise means of analysis is amply demonstrated by the divergent views concerning the chronology of the Genesis Flood narrative in the literature, as shown in Anderson's survey in **Chapter 8**.

rather than "to give rules about how to use certain terms" (1967, 98). An individual lexeme may communicate different event structures due not only to the factors of verbal predicates mentioned above, such as transitivity and intransitivity or the inclusion of a temporal modifier, but also due to the possibility of single terms having multiple meanings within the same syntactic structures.

Rosen notes problems this presents in Rosen (1996) and Rosen (2003). Referencing Rosen (1996) in the latter, she writes,

> In Rosen (1996), I pointed out various problems with attempts to classify verbs into lexical semantic groups; much of the criticism there is relevant to event classification efforts as well. My most telling criticism consisted of verbs that seemed to belong to one semantic class as used in one sentence, but to a different semantic class as used in another. The same problem afflicts event classification efforts: Many verbs cannot be assigned rigidly to one and only one event class; their behavior is variable and context dependent. (2003, 327)

In spite of these problems, however, the semantic flexibility of any given term does not extend infinitely. Often one or two meanings will predominate when a verb's use throughout a corpus is considered, demonstrating the likelihood that a given instance of a verb will follow one use or another. Vendler, noting this same limitation, nevertheless concluded, as noted above, "There is a very large number of verbs that fall completely, or at least in their dominant use, within one of these categories" (1967, 107).

3.2.4 Levels of Sequentiality and Micro-Sequence vis-à-vis Larger Narrative Units

Another limitation of the proposed methodology concerns its applicability only to temporal relations at the *micro-level*, that is, from VP to VP within small narrative units. Narratives often have much greater structural sophistication than merely presenting situations either simultaneously or in temporal sequence. While this ordering may predominate within a small narrative unit, other units may take the story of the narrative to a series of events taking place simultaneously in another setting, may offer flashbacks, or may deviate from this kind of ordering in a number of other ways. Other chapters of this volume seek to address temporal relationships in narrative at higher levels, both between small narrative units and over entire discourses. I will not seek to discuss this further here but only refer the reader to those other chapters.

3.2.5 Logical Semantics and Other Discourse Relations in Narrative

Since this chapter principally lies within the field of lexical semantic study, I have only mentioned briefly matters of logical semantics and other discourse relations which a speaker or writer may use in constructing a narrative. Other logical relationships between VPs may exist besides those assumed in the proposed method for analysis. This method must be combined with a rigorous examination of logical relationships in order to thoroughly explain narrative temporal relationships between VPs with accuracy. Two examples of logical relationships which this method cannot handle with precision are (1) when a VP presents the cause of a preceding VP and (2) when a series of VPs describe simultaneous events or provide an elaboration of a previous VP out of temporal order. The following examples illustrate:

> (26) a. Jonathan fell flat on his face in the middle of the sidewalk. He slipped on a banana peel.
> b. A ferocious spider leapt from behind the couch. Bert uttered a yell, Max jumped out the window, Wendy shed a tear, Bob gasped, and Fred curled up on the floor.

In the first example, the second VP presents the cause of the first, but the two situations appear in the narrative in reverse temporal order. In (26b), the first VP about the spider describes an event with several consequences. While the text is ambiguous, its most likely interpretation involves the actions of each of our arachnophobic friends taking place simultaneously (i.e., should we really expect that Bob waited for Max to jump out the window before he gasped?). The possibility even exists that Fred curled up before Wendy's tear. At times events may appear according to order of some kind of prominence and reverse temporal order to some degree. For example, in the evening when a person asks about the day of his or her spouse, the answer is not likely to consist of an ordered narrative of events from early that morning until that time in the evening. Rather, it is likely to begin with what is most prominent in the mind of the speaker, either because it occurred most recently or is the most significant in some way, and then proceed through the occurrence of various other events of lesser significance.

VPs may relate to each other logically in additional ways, not always amenable to analysis strictly according to the rules taken from ter Meulen above. Ter Meulen recognizes this limitation, however, as suggested by earlier references, and also notes the importance of **compatibility**, coherence, and "commonsense reasoning" in her discussions.[40] This and the other limitations

---

40. In addition to the above references, see, e.g., ter Meulen (1997, 48–49, 56, 77).

in this series, although requiring consideration, do not render the above method useless. When they are kept in mind, portions of narrative in which they prevent accurate analysis may usually receive recognition easily.

3.3 *An Illustration of the Application to BH Narrative*

A sample of how VPs may be classed and how to analyze their temporal relationships to each other in BH narrative appears below, principally for illustrating the fourth step of the method. Rather than examining the use of verbs throughout the corpus, as in the second step above, I have abbreviated the process. Below the sample, a table lists the verb of each principal VP with a suggested classification and comments concerning classification and mapping between the classification of the VPs in the narrative and their respective verbs in neutral context. The sample text comes from Genesis 2:18–23. This passage contains eleven *wayyiqtol* verbs presenting the story of the narrative. Additionally, one *qatal* form appears in a contrastive disjunctive clause in verse 20.

18 וַיֹּאמֶר יְהוָה אֱלֹהִים לֹא־טוֹב הֱיוֹת הָאָדָם לְבַדּוֹ אֶעֱשֶׂה־לּוֹ עֵזֶר כְּנֶגְדּוֹ:

19 וַיִּצֶר יְהוָה אֱלֹהִים מִן־הָאֲדָמָה כָּל־חַיַּת הַשָּׂדֶה וְאֵת כָּל־עוֹף הַשָּׁמַיִם וַיָּבֵא אֶל־הָאָדָם לִרְאוֹת מַה־יִּקְרָא־לוֹ וְכֹל אֲשֶׁר יִקְרָא־לוֹ הָאָדָם נֶפֶשׁ חַיָּה הוּא שְׁמוֹ:

20 וַיִּקְרָא הָאָדָם שֵׁמוֹת לְכָל־הַבְּהֵמָה וּלְעוֹף הַשָּׁמַיִם וּלְכֹל חַיַּת הַשָּׂדֶה וּלְאָדָם לֹא־מָצָא עֵזֶר כְּנֶגְדּוֹ:

21 וַיַּפֵּל יְהוָה אֱלֹהִים תַּרְדֵּמָה עַל־הָאָדָם וַיִּישָׁן וַיִּקַּח אַחַת מִצַּלְעֹתָיו וַיִּסְגֹּר בָּשָׂר תַּחְתֶּנָּה:

22 וַיִּבֶן יְהוָה אֱלֹהִים אֶת־הַצֵּלָע אֲשֶׁר־לָקַח מִן־הָאָדָם לְאִשָּׁה וַיְבִאֶהָ אֶל־הָאָדָם:

23 וַיֹּאמֶר הָאָדָם זֹאת הַפַּעַם עֶצֶם מֵעֲצָמַי וּבָשָׂר מִבְּשָׂרִי לְזֹאת יִקָּרֵא אִשָּׁה כִּי מֵאִישׁ לֻקֳחָה־זֹּאת:

18 And YHWH God said, 'It is not good for the man to be alone. I will make for him a helper corresponding to him.' 19 And YHWH God formed from the ground all the animals of the field and all the birds of the sky, and he brought them to the man to see what he would call each, and whatever the man called the being of an animal, that was its name. 20 And the man named all the livestock and birds of the sky and all the animals of the field, but for Adam he did not find a helper corresponding to him. 21 And YHWH God made a deep sleep fall on the man, and he slept. And he took one of his ribs and shut its place with flesh. 22 And YHWH God built the

rib which he took from the man into a woman, and he brought her to the man. 23 And the man said,

> "This is, this time,
> Bone from my bones,
> And flesh from my flesh!
> This will be called 'Woman,'
> For she was taken from man."

(1)	וַיֹּאמֶר "he said" (2:18)	accomplishment	[+ durative] due to time required for the utterance; [+ telic] since the action of the VP finishes with the completion of the utterance. Narrative context equivalent to neutral context.
(2)	וַיִּצֶר "he formed" (2:19)	accomplishment	[+ durative] due to the semantic nature of the verbal lexeme (see, e.g., use in Is 44:9; 59:6; Jer 1:5) and the presence of a plural direct object; [+ telic] due to the requirement for completion of the action in order for the VP to have taken place. Narrative context maps to accomplishment in neutral context.
(3)	וַיָּבֵא "he brought" (2:19)	accomplishment	[+ durative] due to the semantic nature of the verbal lexeme and the presence of a plural direct object; [+ telic] due to the presence of a direct object of specified quantity ("all"). Narrative context maps to accomplishment in neutral context.
(4)	וַיִּקְרָא "he called" (2:20)	accomplishment	[+ durative] due to the presence of a plural direct object; [+ telic] due to the semantic nature of the verbal lexeme and presence of a direct object of specified quantity ("all"). Narrative context maps to achievement in neutral context.
(5)	מָצָא "he found" (2:20)	achievement	[– durative] due to its use expressing negatively the conclusion of the preceding actions associated with the man seeing and naming the various animals. [+ telic] due to completion as part of the semantic nature of the verb. Narrative context maps to accomplishment in neutral context.
(6)	וַיַּפֵּל "he caused to fall" (2:21)	achievement	[– durative] due to the semantic nature of the verb (as presented, no intermediate state between sleep and non-sleep exists). Narrative context equivalent to neutral context.
(7)	וַיִּישָׁן "he slept" (2:21)	activity	[+ durative] due to the semantic nature of the verb and the clear indication that a sequence events in the narrative takes place during the duration of this verb; [– telic] due to the absence of any specified endpoint. Narrative context equivalent to neutral context.

(8)	וַיִּקַּח "he took" (2:21)	achievement	[– durative] due to semantic nature of the verb. Narrative context equivalent to neutral context.
(9)	וַיִּסְגֹּר "he closed up" (2:21)	achievement	[– durative] due to semantic nature of the verb, the absence of intermediate stages of "closedness," and no indication of duration. Narrative context equivalent to neutral context.
(10)	וַיִּבֶן "he built" (2:22)	accomplishment?	Although the action of "building" would in reality require duration under ordinary circumstances, a narrative could possibly portray the action as momentaneous. However, this narrative does not include any indication of an instantaneous reading, so the more common accomplishment reading takes priority, meaning the action is [+ durative]. It is also [+ telic] not only due to the semantic nature of the verb, but also the clear indication of an endpoint: the complete formation of the woman. In this narrative, the classification of this verb as achievement or accomplishment does not alter analysis of temporal relationships. Narrative context maps to identical class in neutral context.
(11)	וַיְבִאֶהָ "he brought her" (2:22)	accomplishment	"Bring," while clearly durative by nature, does not itself indicate an endpoint. However, the VP contains a prepositional phrase expressing a goal, and thus an endpoint: אֶל־הָאָדָם, "to the man." Narrative context maps to activity in neutral context.
(12)	וַיֹּאמֶר "he said" (2:23)	accomplishment	Same as (1) above. Narrative context equivalent to neutral context.

Consistency with Genesis 1 would demand that the second VP (the forming of the animals) occurred prior to the first VP or that it denotes the creation of additional animals specifically for the purpose of receiving names from the man. In the former case, logical semantics may provide reason for the mention of this action at this point in the narrative, and this presents the only likely discrepancy between a construction of temporal relationships based on strictly following the rules derived from ter Meulen and the ordering of events as the author intended. Recognition of this discrepancy can only result from comparison with the Creation account in Genesis 1, in which the creation of animals precedes the creation of human beings. Represented as DATs, the temporal relationships in this piece of narrative would appear as follows in Hebrew and English from considering this passage in isolation:[41]

---

41. I have provided parentheses with indications of NPs, abbreviated some of the VPs, and omitted the source node for a more concise representation.

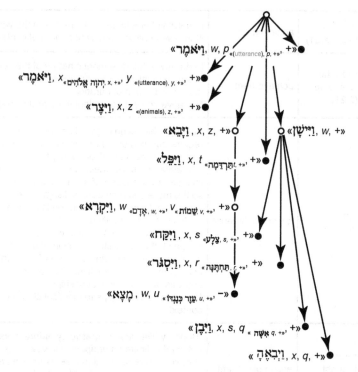

Figure 2.1.

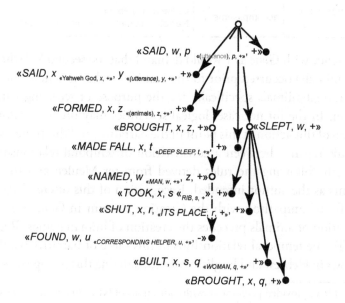

Figure 2.2.

Notice how the DATs account for the overlap of the simultaneity of God bringing the animals to the man and the man's naming of the animals. They also clearly display the series of events taking place during the man's sleep. The penultimate VP becomes a hole due to the knowledge that the man would not have uttered his poem about the woman in his sleep. Whether the man woke up following God making the woman and before God brought her to him, or only after God brought her to him, is not clear from the narrative; either is possible. The DATs above represent the latter possibility.

4. Analysis of the Genesis Flood Narrative

According to the purpose of the project of which this study is a part, the above material may serve as a means for analyzing the VPs in the Genesis Flood narrative and the temporal relationships between them. Such analysis, when combined with the other proposed studies of this project, will assist in constructing a complete chronology of the Genesis Flood from the Hebrew text.

Verbs for Analysis
Comments from Preliminary Analysis of the Flood Narrative

4.1 *Verbs for Analysis*

The Flood narrative represents the primary element of the third *tol^edot* in the *tol^edot* structure of Genesis. This *tol^edot* extends from 6:9 through 9:29 and contains two hundred twenty-five occurrences of verbs.[42] While a thorough consideration of the narrative would require an analysis of all of the verbs, a study concerned specifically with the chronology of the Flood event enjoys a much smaller scope. The Flood itself begins in 7:6 and 7:11 and ends with Noah's observation in 8:14. For the purposes of chronology, lexical semantic analysis need not attempt to establish the order of events in 7:6 or 7:11; the former merely records the age of Noah at the initiation of the Flood event, and the latter describes in slightly more detail the same, fixing it to a specific date. The entrance into the Ark in 7:13–16 by Noah, his family, and the animals serves as a repetition of the same event recorded in 7:7–9 (which concerns macrostructure rather than relationships between VPs at the *micro-level*). Therefore, the sequence of verbs for principal analysis falls

---

42. Obtained through the search *@v* using the WTM database (Groves-Wheeler Westminster Morphology and Lemma Database, 2010, version 4.14 [Chestnut Hill, PA: Westminster Theological Seminary]) of BibleWorks for Windows and subtracting from the total resulting number in Gn 6–9 the 23 verbs which occur in 6:1–8.

between 7:17 and 8:14. This range contains only sixty-five occurrences of verbs. 8:6–12 includes a tight relative chronology for which micro-sequence is clear and therefore need not be considered in a lexical semantics study to establish micro-sequence between clauses. 8:13 and 8:14 likewise do not require analysis because of their inclusion of fixed dates, as do 8:4 and 8:5. Therefore the primary analysis may be limited to verbs from 7:17 through 8:3, a range including only twenty-eight verbs. Although the roots רמש (*rmś*), "crawl" and שרץ (*šrṣ*), "swarm" each occur once among these twenty-eight verbs in 7:21, they are substantival participles denoting particular kinds of life killed by the Flood and are therefore irrelevant for establishing sequence. There are, then, twenty-six verbs of eighteen roots in 7:17 through 8:3 which serve in predicates denoting events which must be analyzed in terms of situation aspect. *Wayyiqtol* forms require principal attention due to their role in presenting the story line of the narrative. The following table lists the eighteen verb roots and where they each occur:

היה (*hyh*) "be"	7:17	מחה (*mḥh*) "blot out"	7:23 (2)
רבה (*rbh*) "be many"	7:17, 18	שאר (*š'r*) "remain"	7:23
נשׂא (*nś'*) "lift/carry"	7:17	זכר (*zkr*) "remember"	8:1
רום (*rûm*) "be high"	7:17	עבר (*'br*) "pass over"	8:1
גבר (*gbr*) "be powerful"	7:18, 19, 20, 24	שכך (*škk*) "recede"	8:1
הלך (*hlk*) "go"	7:18, 8:3	סכר (*skr*) "stop up"	8:2
כסה (*ksh*) "cover"	7:19, 20	כלא (*kl'*) "restrained"	8:2
גוע (*gw'*) "expire"	7:21	שׁוב (*šûb*) "return"	8:3 (2)
מות (*mt*) "die"	7:22	חסר (*ḥsr*) "lack"	8:3

The semantic force of some of these verbs must receive consideration through traditional lexicographical study due to variations in interpretation or rarity of occurrence in the BH corpus. Specifically, the verbs גבר (*gbr*), ישׁב (*yšb*), חסר (*ḥsr*), חרב (*ḥrb*), and שכך (*škk*) require such examination.

4.2 *Comments from Preliminary Analysis of the Flood Narrative*

The presentation of the results of a thorough analysis of the VPs in the Genesis Flood must await subsequent publication. Some brief comments concerning preliminary study of VPs at a very significant portion of the Flood narrative may receive mention, however. 7:17–18 offers a description of the Flood on the earth and resulting incidents. These two verses contain a chain of seven *wayyiqtol* verbs. Notably, preliminary analysis through examination of the use of verbs through the BH corpus demonstrates the stativity or durativity of some of the key verbs in this chain, indicating likely temporal overlap of situations the VPs describe. Specifically, in 7:17, the Ark rose and "became high over the earth" within the temporal boundaries of the first two VPs in the verse, those describing the forty days of the *Mabbûl* and the abundance of water. The VPs in 7:18 all allow temporal overlap.

More clarification and detail of the chronology of the Flood events will emerge from thorough application of this method. Additionally, the study above and its application of its method or others derived from it will serve to expand the study of BH as it represents the application of areas of semantic theory in the consideration of BH for the first time.

5. Concluding Summary

In summary, I have attempted in this chapter to present a methodology for the analysis of situation aspect in BH narrative as it relates to temporal relationships between VPs. This methodology draws from the work of linguists primarily outside of Hebrew studies, in which consideration of situation aspect has largely been neglected. After introducing the foundational theory of situation aspect as pioneered in its most common form by Vendler, I proposed a system of seven aspectual classes. This system retains the three original Vendlerian event types while adding Smith's semelfactive class for a total of four event types. It also distinguished three state types: atelic, point, and transitory. A discussion of state types, contrasting the types I proposed with the more common distinction between individual-level and stage-level states, and interaction with other classification systems followed.

The final three sections of background theory began to focus more directly on BH narrative. From Xiao and McEnery's system of mapping between different situation aspect at various levels, I proposed a "neutral context" for BH verbs, analogous to their "neutral contexts" for English and Chinese, along with a set of nine rules for mapping between the situation class of verbs in neutral contexts and in contexts with additional modifiers. I then presented ter Meulen's representation system for temporal relations in discourse, DATs, with its rules for construction. With the system of classification I proposed earlier, a means for mapping situation classes between "neutral" contexts and derived contexts adopted from Xiao and McEnery, and ter Meulen's work on temporal relations in discourse, the three elements necessary for developing a methodology for the analysis of BH were present. I concluded the presentation of background theory by mentioning some previous studies of situation aspect in BH.

The presentation of the method for analysis described a four-step process incorporating the theoretical material already described. Identification of limitations for the method, particularly those of subjectivity, ambiguity, and a limited corpus, followed, along with an illustration of the method through a simplified sample application to Genesis 2:18–23. The method applies for BH narrative generally and I hope may also be adopted for application cross-linguistically. However, in view of the goal of the present project to investigate the chronology of the Genesis Flood, the final section of the chapter isolated the verbs within that narrative for which the method I proposed must be applied and mentioned some preliminary results from its initial application. A thorough presentation of results must await a later publication.

References

Aristotle. 1933. *The metaphysics I.* Loeb Classical Library. Trans. H. Tredennick. London, England: William Henemann.

Asher, N., and A. Lascarides. 1997. Lexical disambiguation in a discourse context. In *Lexical semantics: The problem of polysemy.* Ed. J. Pustejovsky, and B. Boguraev, 69–108. Oxford, England: Oxford University Press.

Axelrod, M. 1993. *The semantics of time: Aspectual categorization in Koyukon Athabaskan.* Lincoln, NE: University of Nebraska Press.

BibleWorks for Windows. 2007. CD-ROM, version 7.0. Norfolk, VA: BibleWorks.

Binnick, R. 2006. The project on annotated bibliography of contemporary research in tense, grammatical aspect, aktionsart, and related areas. http://www.utsc.utoronto.ca/~binnick/TENSE/Bibliography.html (accessed September 6, 2012).

Carlson, G. N. 1977. A unified analysis of the English bare plural. *Linguistics and Philosophy* 1: 413–457.

Carlson, L. 1981. Aspect and quantification. In *Tense and aspect.* Ed. P. J. Tedeschi, and A. Zaenen, 31–64. Syntax and Semantics Vol. 14. New York, NY: Academic Press.

Chierchia, G. 1995. Individual-level predicates as inherent generics. In *The generic book.* Ed. G. Carlson, and F. Pelletier, 176–223. Chicago, IL: University of Chicago Press.

Creason, S. A. 1995. Semantic classes of Hebrew verbs: A study of *Aktionsarten* in the Hebrew verbal system. PhD diss., University of Chicago.

Croft, W. 2009. Aspectual and causal structure in event representations. In *Routes to language development: Studies in honor of Melissa Bowerman.* Ed. V. Gathercole, 139–166. Mahwah, NJ: Lawrence Erlbaum.

Dahl, Ö. 1981. On the definition of the telic–atelic (bounded–nonbounded) distinction. In *Tense and aspect.* Ed. P. J. Tedeschi, and A. Zaenen, 79–90. Syntax and Semantics Vol. 14. New York, NY: Academic Press.

Depraetere, I. 1995. On the necessity of distinguishing between (un)boundedness and (a)telicity. *Linguistics and Philosophy* 18: 1–19.

Dobbs-Allsopp, F. W. 1995. Ingressive *qwm* in biblical Hebrew. *Zeitschrift für Althebraistik* 8: 31–54.

Dobbs-Allsopp, F. W. 2000. Biblical Hebrew statives and situation aspect. *Journal of Semitic Studies* 45: 21–53.

Dowty, D. R. 1977. Toward a semantic analysis of verb aspect and the English 'imperfective' progressive. *Linguistics and Philosophy* 1: 45–77.

Dowty, D. R. 1978. *A guide to Montague's PTQ*. Bloomington, IN: Indiana University Linguistics Club.

Dowty, D. R. 1979. *Word meaning and Montague grammar: The semantics of verbs and times in generative semantics and in Montague's PTQ*. Synthese Language Library Vol. 7. Dordrecht, Netherlands: D. Reidel.

Dowty, D. R. 1986. The effects of aspectual class on the temporal structure of discourse: semantics or pragmatics? *Linguistics and Philosophy* 9: 37–61.

Dowty, D. R. 1991. Thematic Proto-roles and argument selection. *Language* 67: 547–619.

Dowty, D. R., R. E. Wall, and S. Peters. 1981. *Introduction to Montague semantics*. Synthese Language Library Vol. 11. Dordrecht, Netherlands: D. Reidel.

Filip, H. 2004. The telicity parameter revisited. Paper presented at SALT XIV, Semantics and Linguistic Theory, Cornell University, Ithaca. http://plaza.ufl.edu/hfilip/filip.salt14.pdf (accessed April 10, 2012).

Filip, H. 2011. Aspectual class and Aktionsart. In vol. 2 of *Semantics: An international handbook of natural language meaning*. Ed. K. von Heusinger, C. Maienborn, and P. Porter, 1186–1217. Handbücher zur Sprach- und Kommunikationswissenschaft 33. Berlin, Germany: De Gruyter Mouton.

Filip, H., and S. Rothstein. 2006. Telicity as a semantic parameter. In *Formal approaches to Slavic linguistics 14 (The Princeton Meeting)*. Ed. J. Lavine, S. Franks, Tasseva-Kurktchieva, and H. Filip, 139–156. Ann Arbor, MI: Slavic Publications.

Fleischman, S. 1990. *Tense and narrativity: From medieval performance to modern fiction*. Austin, TX: University of Texas Press.

Freed, A. F. 1979. *The semantics of English aspectual complementation*. Synthese Language Library Vol. 8. Dordrecht, Netherlands: D. Reidel.

Gennari, S. P. 2004. Temporal references and temporal relations in sentence comprehension. *Journal of Experimental Psychology: Learning, Memory, and Cognition* 30: 877–890.

Hatav, G. 1989. Aspects, Aktionsarten, and the time line. *Linguistics* 27: 487–516.

Hay, J., C. Kennedy, and B. Levin. 1999. Scalar structure underlies telicity in "degree achievements." In *Proceedings from Semantics and Linguistic Theory IX*. Ed. T. Matthews, and D. Strolovitch, 127–144. Ithaca, NY: Cornell University.

Hendel, R. S. 1996. In the margins of the Hebrew verbal system: situation, tense, aspect, mood. *Zeitschrft für Althebraistik* 9: 152–181.

Hinrichs, E. W. 1985. A compositional semantics for Aktionsarten and NP reference in English. PhD diss., Ohio State University.

Jacobsen, W. M. 1984. Lexical aspect in Japanese. In *Papers from the parasession on lexical semantics.* Ed. D. Testen, V. Mishra, and J. Drogo, 150–161. Chicago, IL: Chicago Linguistic Society.

Jenni, E. 1994. Lexikalisch-semantische Strukturunterschiede: Hebräisch *HDL*— deutsch "aufhören/unterlassen." *Zeitschrift für Althebraistik* 7: 124–132.

Jenni, E. 2000. Aktionsarten und Stammformen im Althebräischen: Das Pi'el in verbesserter Sicht. *Zeitschrift für Althebraistik* 13: 67–90.

Joosten, J. 2012. *The verbal system of biblical Hebrew: A new synthesis elaborated on the basis of classical prose.* Jerusalem Biblical Studies Vol. 10. Jerusalem, Israel: Simor Ltd.

Kang, J. 2001. Perfective aspect participles or telic Aktionsart markers? Studies of the directional verb compounds. *Journal of Chinese Linguistics* 29: 281–339.

Kangasmaa-Minn, E. 1984. Tense, aspect and Aktionsarten in Finno-Ugrian. In *Aspect bound: A voyage into the realm of Germanic, Slavonic and Finno-Ugrian aspectology.* Ed. C. de Groot, and H. Tommola, 77–93. Dordrecht, Netherlands: Foris Publications.

Kearns, K. 2007. Telic senses of deadjectival verbs. *Lingua* 117: 26–66.

Kehler, A. 2002. *Coherence, reference, and the theory of grammar.* Standford, CA: CSLI Publications.

Klein, W. 1995. A time-relational analysis of Russian aspect. *Language* 71: 669–695.

Kratzer, A. 1995. Stage-level and individual-level predicates. In *The generic book.* Ed. G. Carlson, and F. Pelletier, 125–175. Chicago, IL: University of Chicago Press.

Landman, F. 2008. 1066: On the differences between the tense-perspective-aspect systems of English and Dutch. In *Theoretical and crosslinguistic approaches to the semantics of aspect.* Ed. S. D. Rothstein, 107–166. Linguistics Aktuell Vol. 110. Amsterdam, Netherlands: John Benjamins.

Lascarides, A., and N. Asher. 1993. Temporal interpretation, discourse relations and commonsense entailment. *Linguistics and Philosophy* 16: 437–493.

Lascarides, A., N. Asher, and J. Oberlander. 1992. Inferring discourse relations in context. In *Proceedings of the 30th annual meeting of the Association of Computational Linguistics (ACL92)*, 1–8. Newark, Delaware, June 1992. Stroudburg, PA: Association for Computational Linguistics.

Lascarides, A., and J. Oberlander. 1997. Temporal coherence and defeasible knowledge. Draft. http://homepages.inf.ed.ac.uk/alex/papers/thlx.pdf (accessed September 6, 2012).

Lee, C. 1982. Aspects of aspect in Korean. *Linguistic Journal of Korea* 7: 570–582.

Lee, I., J. Kim, and K. Choi. 1988. Progressive aspect and perfection in situation semantics. In *Seoul papers in formal grammar theory II: Proceedings of the fifth Korean-Japanese Joint Workshop: August 18–21, 1986; In honor of Professor Hyung-Yul Kang*, 77–98. Seoul, South Korea: Hanshin Publishing Company.

Lee, K. 2004. Processing and representing temporally sequential events. In *Proceedings of the 18th Pacific Asia Conference on Language, Information and Computation*. Ed. H. Masuichi, T. Ohkuma, K. Ishikawa, Y. Harada, and K. Yoshimoto, 9–14. Tokyo, Japan: Logico-Linguistic Society of Japan. http://hdl.handle.net/2065/554 (accessed September 6, 2012).

Magliano, J. P., and M. C. Schleich. 2000. Verb aspect and situation models. *Discourse Processes* 29: 83–112.

Mandler, J. M., and M. S. Goodman. 1982. On the psychological validity of story structure. *Journal of Verbal Learning and Verbal Behavior* 21: 507–523.

McCawley, J. D. 1979. Lexicography and the count-mass distinction. In *Adverbs, vowels, and other objects of wonder*, 165–173. Chicago, IL: University of Chicago Press.

Milsark, G. L. 1974. Existential sentences in English. PhD diss., Massachusetts Institute of Technology.

Moens, M., and M. Steedman. 1987. Temporal ontology in natural language. In *Proceedings of the 25th Annual Meeting of the Association for Computational Linguistics*, 1–7. Morristown, New Jersey. Stroudsburg, PA: Association of Computational Linguistics.

Nam, S. 2000. A typology of locatives and event composition in English. *Language Research* 36: 689–714.

Ohtsuka, K., and W. F. Brewer. 1992. Discourse organization in the comprehension of temporal order in narrative texts. *Discourse Processes* 15: 317–336.

Olsen, M. B. 1997. *A semantic and pragmatic model of lexical and grammatical aspect*. Outstanding Dissertations in Linguistics. New York, NY: Garland Publishing.

Parsons, T. 2002. Eventualities and narrative progression. *Linguistics and Philosophy* 25: 681–699.

Pustejovsky, J. 2000. Events and the semantics of opposition. In *Events as grammatical objects: The converging perspectives of lexical semantics, logical semantics and syntax*. Ed. C. Tenny, and J. Pustejovsky, 445–482. Stanford, CA: CSLI Publications.

Rosen, S. T. 1996. Events and verb classification. *Linguistics* 34: 191–223.

Rosen, S. T. 2003. The syntactic representation of linguistic events. In *The second Glot International state-of-the article book: The latest in linguistics*. Ed. L. Cheng, and R. Sybesma, 323–365. Studies in Generative Grammar 61. Berlin, Germany: Mouton de Gruyter.

Rothstein, S. 2008. Introduction. In *Theoretical and crosslinguistic approaches to the semantics of aspect*. Ed. S. Rothstein, 1–10. Linguistik Aktuell 110. Amsterdam, Netherlands: John Benjamins.

Rothstein, S. 2010. Counting and the mass/count distinction. *Journal of Semantics* 27: 343–397.

Rotstein, C., and Y. Winter. 2004. Total adjectives vs. partial adjectives: Scale structure and higher-order modifiers. *Natural Language Semantics* 12: 259–288. http://www.phil.uu.nl/~yoad/papers/RotsteinWinter.pdf (accessed September 5, 2012).

Sasse, H. 2002. Recent activity in the theory of aspect: Accomplishments, achievements, or just non-progressive state? *Linguistic Typology* 6: 199–271.

Seligman, J., and A. ter Meulen. 1995. Dynamic aspect trees. In *Applied logic: How, what and why; logical approaches to natural language*. Ed. L. Pólos, and M. Masuch, 287–320. Synthese Library Vol. 247. Dordrecht, Netherlands: Kluwer Academic Publishers.

Smith, C. S. 1990. Event types in Mandarin. *Linguistics* 28: 309–336.

Smith, C. S. 1991. *The parameter of aspect*. Studies in Linguistics and Philosophy. Vol. 43. Dordrecht, Netherlands: Kluwer Academic.

Smith, C. S. 1994. Aspectual viewpoint and situation type in Mandarin Chinese. *Journal of East Asian Linguistics* 3: 107–146.

Smith, C. S. 1997. *The parameter of aspect*. Studies in Linguistics and Philosophy. Vol. 43. 2nd ed. Dordrecht, Netherlands: Kluwer Academic.

Suzuki, T. 1995. Aspectual verbs in Japanese. In *The Proceedings of the 1994 Kyoto Conference: A festschrift for Professor Akira Ikeya*, 103–112. Tokyo, Japan: Logico-Linguistic Society of Japan. http://hdl.handle.net/2065/11844 (accessed September 6, 2012).

Tenny, C., and J. Pustejovsky. 2000. A history of events in linguistic theory. In *Events as grammatical objects: The converging perspectives of lexical semantics and syntax*. Ed. C. Tenny, and J. Pustejovsky, 3–37. Stanford, CA: CSLI Publications.

ter Meulen, A. G. B. 1997. *Representing time in natural language: The dynamic interpretation of tense and aspect*. Cambridge, MA: MIT Press. (Orig. pub. 1995.)

ter Meulen, A. G. B. 2000. Chronoscopes: the dynamic representation of facts and events. In *Speaking of events*. Ed. J. Higginbotham, F. Pianesi, and A. C. Varzi, 151–168. Oxford, England: Oxford University Press.

Winter, Y. 2006. Closure and telicity across categories. Extended version. http://www.phil.uu.nl/~yoad/papers/WinterTelicity-extended.pdf (accessed February 8, 2012).

van der Auwera, J. and H. Filip. 2008. (Tense), aspect, mood and modality—an imperfect 2008 state of the art report. In *Unity and diversity of languages*. Ed. P. van Sterkenburg, 201–214. Amsterdam, Netherlands: John Benjamins.

van der Merwe, C. H. J. 1997. Reconsidering biblical Hebrew temporal expressions. *Zeitschrift für Althebraistik* 10: 42–62.

van Eijck, J., and H. Kamp. 1997. Representing discourse in context. In *Handbook of logic and language*. Ed. J. van Benthem, and A. ter Meulen, 179–237. Amsterdam, Netherlands: Elsevier.

Van Valin, R. D., Jr. 2005. *Exploring the syntax-semantics interface*. Cambridge, England: Cambridge University Press.

Vendler, Z. 1957. Verbs and times. *Philosophical Review* 66: 143–160.

Vendler, Z. 1967. Verbs and times. *Linguistics in philosophy*, 97–121. Ithaca, NY: Cornell University Press.

Verkuyl, H. J. 1972. *On the compositional nature of the aspects.* Foundations of Language Supplement Series Vol. 15. Dordrecht, Netherlands: D. Reidel.

Vet, C. 1995. The role of Aktionsart in the interpretation of temporal relations in discourse. In *Temporal reference, aspect and actionality, Volume 1: Semantic and syntactic perspectives.* Ed. P. M. Bertinetto, V. Bianchi, J. Higginbotham, and M. Squartini, 295–306.Torino, Italy: Rosenberg & Sellier.

Vlach, F. 1981. The semantics of the progressive. In *Tense and aspect.* Ed. P. J. Tedeschi, and A. Zaenen, 271–292. Syntax and Semantics Vol. 14. New York, NY: Academic Press.

Xiao, Z., and A. McEnery. 2002. Situation aspect as a universal aspect: Implications for artificial languages. *Journal of Universal Language* 3: 139–177. http://eprints.lancs.ac.uk/54/1/jul_paper.pdf. (accessed July 1, 2011).

Xiao, R., and T. McEnery. 2004a. *Aspect in Mandarin Chinese: a corpus-based study.* Studies in Language Companion Series Book 73. Amsterdam, Netherlands: John Benjamins.

Xiao, Z., and A. McEnery. 2004b. A corpus-based two-level model of situation aspect. *Journal of Linguistics* 40: 325–363.

Zwaan, R. A. 1996. Processing narrative time shifts. *Journal of Experimental Psychology: Learning, Memory, and Cognition* 22: 1196–1207.

Zwarts, J. 2005. Prepositional aspect and the algebra of paths. *Linguistics and Philosophy* 28: 739–779.

Zwarts, J. 2006. Event shape: Paths in the semantics of verbs. Paper presented at the Workshop on Geometrical Structure in Event Concepts, University of Konstanz, October 7–8, 2004. http://www.hum.uu.nl/medewerkers/j.zwarts/research.htm (accessed February 9, 2012).

Zwarts, J. 2008. Aspects of a typology of direction. In *Theoretical and crosslinguistic approaches to the semantics of aspect.* Linguistics Aktuell. Vol. 110 Ed. S. Rothstein, 79–105. Amsterdam, Netherlands: John Benjamins.

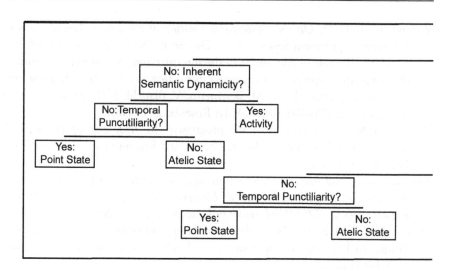

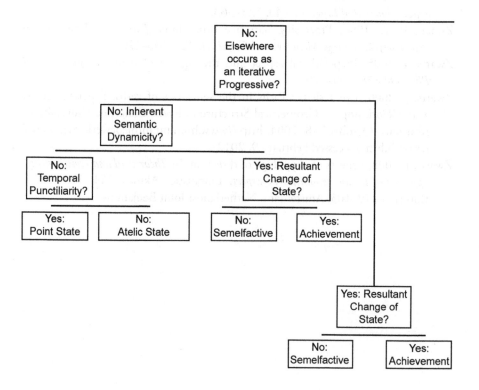

Situation Aspect Flow Chart

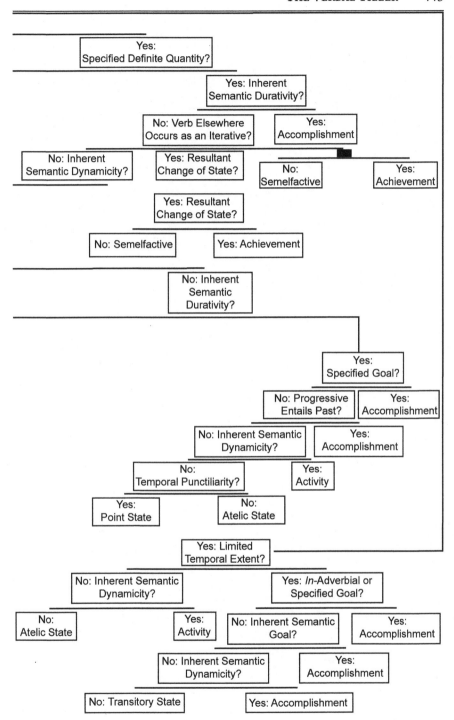

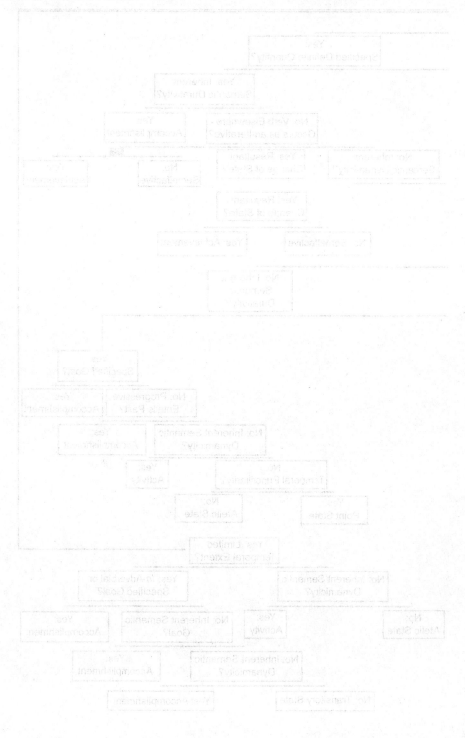

CHAPTER 12

Tacking with the Text:
The Interconnection of Text, Event, and Time
at the *Macro-level*

Steven W. Boyd

Analogy and Orientation. Every four years since 1851 yachtsmen from around the world compete in the prestigious America's Cup, testing the design of their boats and skill in besting a tireless adversary, the wind. This sailing race proves not only the sheer speed of the boats but also challenges the ability of the crews to steer them on a prescribed course against the wind. This is accomplished by a technique called tacking, in which boats cross and re-cross the direction of the wind, but move inexorably forward at speed. Such is the nature of texts and time.

In order to understand the chronology of the Genesis Flood within the larger linguistic context of temporal sequence in narrative in general (inside and outside the Bible), we must concentrate on the verbs (or verb phrases) in the text, considering the following factors pertaining to them: the order of verbs in the text (textual sequence); the individual verbs (or verb phrases) themselves with respect to the states or events the verbs depict (eventualities); the interactions among the verbs or verb phrases in a text (coherence relations); and the time/times in which said eventualities are located.

It is tempting to represent verbs in sequence, interacting with one another, with a chain-link model. This is in essence, a simple one: each link is a verb connected with the verb preceding it and following it. So far so good for a model of the verbal structure of a minimal text—fairly obvious. But what of the eventualities depicted by these three verbs? And what of the temporal dimension connected with each? The time links can be in a different order from the text links. So the chain-link model is too confining, too rigid, and too inflexible to explain temporal sequencing adequately—as we will show below. The chronology of the Flood is more than a sum of the temporal sequence of the chain of eventualities represented by the chain of verbs in the Flood narrative, which is ascertained from the temporal sequence of each link. The text-time interaction is much more fluid and free and therefore more suitably represented by the analogy of sailing.

Temporal sequence in narrative in general—and in the Flood narrative in particular—is controlled by the eventualities represented by verbs and verb phrases, because each eventuality takes place at an instant or during an interval of time. The temporal sequence connected with the eventualities is a given (by which I mean that it is part of reality; and, hence, unalterable), but it is unknown to us except through the text. The textual order also is a given. And although only the verbs of a text are accessible to us, they so closely represent the eventualities that they seem to define the temporal sequence of a text. The verbs or the links between verbs, representing the eventualities and the eventuality sequence, respectively, do this by redirecting the reader in time, just as the wind affects the course of the boats competing for the cup. The ship is the reader moving through the text, windblown by the temporal vagaries of the eventualities he encounters and their interactions with each other. The wind can blow from astern, from ahead, or from the side, moving the ship forward, backward, or sideways, respectively. The reader must adjust the sails so as to hold a steady course, which is maintaining a correct understanding of the correspondences between text and time. It is easy to be blown off course if the reader is unaware of the direction of the wind. And yet with skillful seamanship the reader can move the ship forward as he encounters the wind in the text. So, as we move through a text, time can advance, stop, or be displaced backward.

Thus, in order to ascertain the chronology of the Genesis Flood, or any other narrative for that matter, we must study the complicated nature of the interaction between the verbs of the text, the eventualities they represent, and the time in which the latter took place.

Abstract. Recognizing that *wayyiqtol* is the predominant verb form in BH narrative, and for all intents and purposes its presence is *necessary* to convey linear temporal sequence of simple past, but is *not sufficient* to indicate linear temporal progression in *wayyiqtol* chains, a better method of ascertaining temporal sequence is offered—which is to be coupled with the insight gained from the semantics at the **micro-level** (situation aspect, Akagi's **Chapter 11**)—namely, considering the semantic relations that obtain at the **macro-level** (that is the semantic relations between verbs or verb phrases), comprising: **coherence relations**, which indicate that time advances with *wayyiqtol* in *Serialation* and *Result* but not in *Cause, Explanation, Elaboration (and similar relations), Contrast,* and *Background*; **compatibility** of states or events, the lack of which necessarily displaces them temporally (although not necessarily linearly); **connectedness** (attachments and detachments); and **temporal continuity vs. discontinuity**.

Outline

Symbols

$\rightarrow$	implies
$\mapsto$	is sent to
$\neg$	not
$\wedge$	and
$\vee$	or
$\cap$	intersection
$\in$	element of
$\forall$	for all
$\exists$	there exists
$\emptyset$	empty set
$<$	precedence (in **Subsection 3.4**)
$\sqsubseteq$	inclusion
O	overlap
$\supset\subset$	abutment
$=$	superposition (when referring to temporal intervals)

1. Issues Pertaining to the Temporal Dimension of Texts: A Bird's Eye View

In **Chapter 4** above we proposed a heuristic set of *coherence relations*: *Serialation, Result* (and its polar opposites, *Cause* and the similar relation, *Explanation*), *Elaboration* (and its congeners, *Summary* and *Restatement*, etc.), *Comparison/Contrast,* and *Background.* This set of *coherence relations* pertains to only one of the four factors mentioned above—the interactions between proximate verbs/clauses. But curiously the study of *coherence relations* has not been overly concerned—if at all—with *compatibility* versus *incompatibility*, which we showed above can be decisive. This is probably due to its obviousness as a factor in the temporal profile of texts. In any case, we hope to address this evident lacuna in a modest way below.

It is necessary therefore to expand our analysis to include this important factor and to add the issues of the arrangement of the states or events in the text, and the temporal attachment of states or events. All in all then we will look at six issues pertaining to the temporal dimension of texts: the arrangement of the states or events in the text, the advancement of time within them, the advancement of time between them,[1] the temporal displacement of them, the temporal attachment of them, and the possibility of temporal discontinuity of them.

[In order to explore and elucidate the sometimes recondite issues connected with verbs, eventualities, and time in the biblical text, we will look at a series of contrived texts, involving the shenanigans of three

---

1. Obviously this is the purpose of this chapter. I will be unfolding this throughout the chapter, but the following are very helpful: Lascarides and Asher (1993); Seligman and ter Meulen (1995); ter Meulen (1995); Kehler (1999, 2004); Lee (2004); Asher and Vieu (2005); and Stenning, Lascarides, and Calder (2006). In particular, Asher and Vieu offer four tests to determine whether a *coherence relation* is *coordinate* (temporal progression) or *subordinate* (progression is broken) (2005, 599–604). Also notable is Seligman and ter Meulen's temporal reasoning analysis of a Batman story, in which they look for changes of reference in a narrative (288–293). Or in other words: is the narrative continuing its description of a specific situation or has it gone on to refer to a new situation? For a further illustration of temporal reasoning see the semantic analysis of an original story, Winter Storm, in **Appendix B**, which uses a modified version of Seligman and ter Meulen's dynamic aspect tree (DAT) analysis. See Akagi's **Chapter 11** for specifics on DAT.

If a criticism can be leveled against the countless otherwise-excellent analyses of temporal sequence that are found in the literature, it would be that scholars tend to focus either on the *micro-level* of situational aspect (atelic states, etc.; activities, achievements, etc.) or on the *macro-level* of *coherence relations*. Few have integrated the two. Seligman and ter Meulen in collaboration and ter Meulen in her monograph and papers are notable exceptions, to whom can be added Hinrich's effort (1986). We will return to his analysis in **Section 4**.

fictional schoolboys, Al, Bob, and Carl, on the playground, with A, B, and C being the verbs depicting the escapades of these three, respectively, and the eventualities depicted by them. And then we will apply what we have learned from these heuristic texts to the biblical text. Also hereafter we will employ the term **eventualities** as inclusive of both states and events. The latter will only refer to dynamic eventualities in the balance of the chapter.] The rest of this section is organized as follows:

1.1   Arrangement of VPs
1.2   Advancement within VPs
1.3   Advancement between VPs
1.4   Displacement of VPs
1.5   Attachment of VPs
1.6   Discontinuity of VPs
1.7   Synopsis

1.1 *The Arrangement of the Eventualities: The Temporal Order of the Eventualities Represented by the Verbs*

The first issue to be examined is the temporal order of the eventualities. Are they necessarily in the same order as the verbs? The answer is no, not always. In fact, in only one of the six possible distinguishable sequences of the eventualities depicted by a chain of just three verbs with the same morphology does their temporal order mirror the verb order.[2] Or we could look at it from the other side: do the verbs follow the sequence of eventualities? If they do, the text is said to be iconic.[3]

By way of an illustration consider the six texts in (1) below, which are the six ways of expressing the same sequence of three eventualities: A (Al pushed Bob), which caused B (Bob fell down), and subsequently in response caused C (Carl ran off to tell the teacher).

(1)   a.   Al pushed Bob. He fell down. Carl told the teacher.
       b.   Bob fell down. Al pushed him. Carl told the teacher.
       c.   Al pushed Bob. Carl told the teacher. When he got to his feet, Bob punched Al.

---

2. For three verbs a, b, c, we are looking at the possible orders abc, acb, bac, and so forth. The number of distinguishable sequences of n objects (in our case, verbs) taking m at a time is the permutations of n objects taking m of them at a time, which is $n!/(n-m)!$. For our case, it is the permutations of three objects taking three at a time, which is $3!/0!$, that is $3 \times 2 \times 1 = 6$.

3. This is a term introduced by Charles Sanders Peirce, a pioneer in the field of semiotics, for signs that look like what they signify. For example the Georgia-Pacific paper company at one time designing their logo so that "G" and "P" were juxtaposed to look like a tree. When a text advances as time advances in the eventualities represented in the text, the text is iconic. For more on Peirce's seminal work see (Atkin 2010).

    d. Bob fell down. Carl told the teacher. Al pushed Bob.
    e. Carl told the teacher. Al pushed Bob. He fell down.
    f.   Carl told the teacher. Bob fell down. Al pushed him.

In (1a) the textual order of the verbs depicting the eventualities is ABC. Since the sequence of verbs in the text mirrors the sequence of eventualities, this text is iconic. (Incidentally, all the other texts in (1) are non-iconic, and the eventualities are said to be dischronologized.)

    Symbolically, iconicity can be expressed as a pair of two inequalities as follows:

$$p(B)-p(A) > 0 \qquad\qquad\qquad (i)$$

$$t(B)-t(A) > 0 \qquad\qquad\qquad (ii)$$

where p is the linear position in the text and t is the time of the eventuality depicted by the verb.

    It might be helpful to visually depict what is meant by iconicity. Such a visualization is in Figure 1 below. Notice that the sequence of three verbs is in line with the sequence of the three eventualities in A, but not in B.

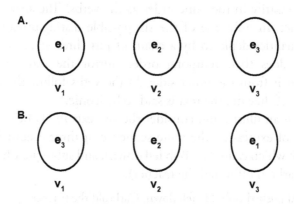

Figure 1. A. Iconic Text versus B. Non-Iconic Text.

Now what does "time of the eventuality" mean? In reality, the "pushing" and "falling" each took place over an interval of time, with the intervals being juxtaposed or overlapping. Consequently, the time from the beginning of the *push* until the end of the *fall* is the difference of the time of the end of the "falling" and the time of the beginning of the "pushing." If there is no overlap of the time intervals and their intersection is not the empty set, this difference is the sum of the two intervals. There is also the likely occurrence, that for at least part of the time the "pushing" and "falling" were simultaneous. And finally there is the possibility—although probably not in this case—that the intervals are separated from one another, such as the desired result in skeet shooting: *Max shot the gun. The clay pigeon shattered*, or perhaps an even better example because of the obvious time delay between verbs, *After sizing up his thirty foot putt, the golfer carefully but smartly* **stroked** *the ball and it* **fell** *into the cup for a birdie to the evident approval of the gallery.*

Furthermore, because the "pushing" caused the "falling" and the verb depicting the former precedes the verb depicting the latter, this text is a parade example of the **coherence relation** *Result*. Moreover, since presumably the combination provided the circumstances for the "telling"—Carlton would not have tattled on Alwyn if the latter were innocent; that would have been a miscarriage of justice. Clearly he was provoked to action by the contumelious deed of the latter. Nevertheless, Carl was not compelled to act; his reporting was not unavoidable. Provocation was necessary but **not** sufficient.[4] So this is an example of *Serialation*.

Our starting point was the eventuality sequence. But what if we only have the text and are trying to ascertain the eventuality sequence? *Result* is still the most likely **coherence relation** in (1a). Then what? Can we prove that a text with *Result* is iconic? By definition *Result* is A caused B, with A coming first in the textual sequence, that is $p(A) < p(B)$, or $p(B)-p(A) > 0$. Moreover, because of the nature of physical processes and the fact that *Result* requires the time of the cause to precede the time of the caused, $t(B)-t(A) > 0$. So, equations (i) and (ii) are satisfied, that is, the text is iconic.

On the other hand, in (1b) above the order is BAC. A still caused B, but in the text the result is placed before the cause, that is $p(B)-p(A) < 0$. This creates a delay in the information supplied by the text: we do not know why Bob fell, but then we are told. The **coherence relation** evidenced here is variously termed *Cause* or *Explanation*. But were not the true order of eventualities known to us, we could have understood (1b) to be iconic, with the possible but improbable scenario that after Bob fell (for some unknown reason—perhaps he tripped over his shoelaces), Al pushed him out of the way of a careening, oncoming bicycle, and Carl reported Al's heroics to the teacher.

A visualization, which contrasts both *Result* and *Serialation* with *Cause* is in Figure 2.

---

4. For a more complete discussion of the important distinction between a *necessary* condition and a *sufficient* condition, see **Sub-subsection 2.2.2 Paragraph 1**.

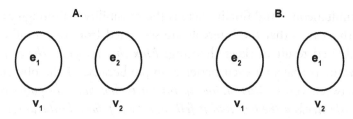

Figure 2. *Contrast* between A. *Result* and B. *Cause*.

In (1c) the order is ACB. The reader's first impression is that Carl's response was due to the "pushing." But "when he got to his feet" implies that Bob had been on the ground, and Bob's action against Al further implies that the latter was responsible for him being there. It is at this point that the reader knows that the "pushing" led to the "falling," and that Carl could have been responding to both.

(1d)'s textual order is BCA, with the cause of Bob's fall held in abeyance until the third sentence.

In (1e) it is CAB, and in (1f) CBA. In these last two what follows "Carl told the teacher" is essentially Carl's report.

Nevertheless, in most cases texts are iconic, due to narrative's tendency for temporal linerarity.[5]

1.2 *Temporal Advancement within Eventualities: The Lexical Semantics of Individual Verbs*

A second factor in the temporal sequence of eventualities is the type of verbs sequenced, with the focus being on the temporal profile *within* the verb phrase. This is known variously as semantic aspect, situation aspect, lexical aspect, and lexical semantics. Akagi has discussed this in detail in **Chapter 11**; but, for the sake of looking at all the factors, consider the following narrative:

(2) a. Al sat daydreaming.
     b. Bob waved his hand in front of his face.
     c. Carl just walked away.

The verb in (2a) fits in the eventuality category of transitory state. In these verbs time is at a standstill. Bob's waving in (2b) could have occurred at the beginning of Al's daydreaming, in the middle, or at the end. The same could be said about Carl's walking away in (2c). In terms of time, Bob and Carl's actions occurred during the time interval when Al was staring vacuously into space.

Besides verbs representing states, there are those representing activities, achievements, accomplishments, and semelfactives. An example of each of these is in (3), in the given order:

---

5. See fn 22 for details.

(3) a. Al climbed.
    b. Bob lost his grip on the top bar of the swing set.
    c. Carl built a fort out of discarded boxes.
    d. Al sneezed extra loud as soon as the teacher started her lesson.

1.3 *The Advancement of Time between Eventualities: The Nature of Time Advance in Texts*

The third factor to be considered is time advance between the eventualities represented by consecutive verb phrases. This takes us to the next level of the temporal property of texts. I want to introduce at this point an important concept, which I call *necessary temporal advance* (NTA). NTA is present if an eventuality sequence *demands* that time move forward, that is for two eventualities A and B, represented by two verbs, if $p(B)–p(A) > 0$ then $t(B)–t(A) > 0$. So, an iconic text exhibits NTA.

Let me illustrate using Al, Bob, and Carl again. In the three non-state eventualities, arranged in six different orders in (1), time either advances or retreats but does not stand still. Consider, however, the following text in which it does:

(4) a. Al climbed to the top of the monkey bars.
    b. Bob and Carl helped him.

In this case Bob and Carl's actions neither preceded nor followed Al's, but rather overlapped with his.[6] So time does not advance in the second sentence. And in terms of the text, the second sentence elaborates on the first.[7] This can only obtain if the eventuality represented by the first verb took place over a time interval rather than at a point of time.

A second scenario, which exhibits temporal stasis is illustrated in (5) and (6) below:

(5) a. Al climbed the monkey bars.
    b. Bob swung on the swings.
    c. Carl balanced himself on the see-saw.
    d. The boys played hard at recess.

(6) a. The boys played hard at recess.
    b. Al climbed the monkey bars.
    c. Bob swung on the swings.
    d. Carl balanced himself on the see-saw.

---

6. This example introduces two of the binary relations that occur between eventualities: **precedence** and **overlap**. For a discussion of their properties see van Benthem (1984, 1991); Dünges (1998) and **Sub-subsection 3.4.2 Paragraph 2** and **Sub-subsection 3.4.3 Paragraph 3**).

7. The ***coherence relation*** *Elaboration* and its congeners, *Restatement* and *Summary*, are discussed below in **Sub-subsection 2.2.2 Paragraph 4**.

(5d) is a summary of the three sentences, (5a), (5b), and (5c). In this case the text goes from the specific to the general. Moreover, the first three eventualities of (5) occurred during a time interval, which is best described as the minimum temporal superset, which contains the three temporal intervals, corresponding to the three eventualities. It does not matter if these intervals overlap or not. In addition, this temporal superset is itself identical to or a subset of the temporal interval "recess."

(6a) is what I call an *Introductory Encapsulation* of the eventualities specified in (6b), (6c), and (6d).[8] Here the text goes from general to specific. In terms of time, this is similar to (5), but in reverse. (6a) is the starting time interval, "recess," when the boys played. All the last three eventualities in (6) occurred during this interval. Again it does not matter if the intervals in which these eventualities took place overlap or not.

Two types of *Elaboration, Summary* and *Introductory Encapsulation* can be seen in Figure 3.

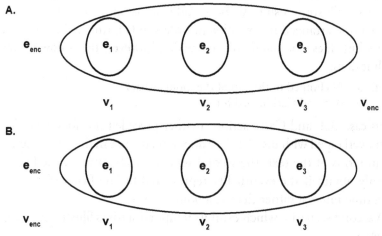

Figure 3. *Elaboration* types contrasted. e_{enc} is the encapsulating eventuality.
A. *Summary.* The encapsulating verb, v_{enc}, follows the encapsulated verbs, as in (5) above. Note that 1, 2, and 3 are (5a), (5b), and (5c), respectively.
B. *Introductory Encapsulation.* The encapsulating verb precedes the encapsulated verbs, as in (6) above. Note that 1, 2, and 3 are (6b), (6c), and (6d), respectively.

8. Kamp and Rohrer give an example of climbing a mountain: so and so climbed a certain mountain in the Alps, which is followed by a description of the stages of that climb (1983). Lascarides and Asher offer the example of I. Guy had a wonderful evening; II. He had a fantastic meal; III. He ate salmon; IV. He consumed a lot of cheese; V. He won a dancing competition (1993, 439). Obviously, II and V are subsumed under I; and III and IV are subsumed under II. Asher and Vieu use the same example with some slight changes (2005). They also cogently observe that this phenomenon is like paragraph structure, in which a topic sentence is followed by developmental details (592). Seligman and ter Meulen discuss the phrase "The Dark Knight . . . patrolled the dark night" as follows: "This event will likely take some time; presumably we are going to be told more about what happened while Batman patrolled the streets" (1995). The story does so: describing all the eventualities that occurred during that patrolling period (291).

For a number of examples in biblical texts see **Sub-subsection 2.2.2 Paragraph 4.**

For a third scenario in which time does not advance, consider the following texts:

(7) a. Bob and Carl went to recess as usual.
     b. Al had to stay in the classroom for misbehavior.

It is obvious that the relation for these texts is *Contrast*,[9] because Bob and Carl were at recess; whereas, Al was not. In addition, these texts show us that time does not advance in *Contrast*: Bob and Carl were at recess while Al was not at recess. It could be argued that examples like (5a) and (5b) (reproduced here as (8) for convenience) also evince *Contrast*. (5c) could be added, but it is not necessary, because the reasoning would be the same.

(8) a. Al climbed the monkey bars.
     b. Bob swung on the swings.

But this differs from (7), in that the **coherence relation** between (8a) and (8b) is not *necessarily Contrast*.

And finally consider the following situation involving two of the boys riding on a see-saw:

(9) a. Bob went slowly down.
     b. Carl went slowly up.

These sentences represent simultaneous eventualities, but the linear constraint of text requires that the sentences be textually sequential.

1.4 *The Temporal Displacement of Eventualities: Incompatibility, The Preventer of Simultaneity of Eventualities*

A fourth factor comprises **incompatibility** (or **compatibility**, its opposite) and the prevention of simultaneity effected by the former, which leads to the temporal displacement of eventualities.[10] Exploiting our three friends again, consider (5a), (5b), and (5c), which is repeated here as (10) for convenience:

(10) a. Al climbed the monkey bars.
      b. Bob rode on the swings.
      c. Carl balanced himself on the see-saw.

These verbs in these sentences are either connected or not. The text could be iconic: Al's climbing followed by Bob's swinging and finished up by Carl's teeter-tottering. Or not: although Bob could have swung after Al climbed,

---

9. Discussed in **Sub-subsection 2.2.2 Paragraph 3**.
10. Discussed in **Subsection 2.3**.

he could have swung while Al climbed. Similarly with Carl's activity: he could ride on the see-saw after Bob swung or while Bob swung; after Al climbed or while he climbed. The reason for these different possibilities is that the three actions performed by three individuals are not mutually exclusive. They can occur simultaneously; they can occur sequentially. But if a text contained these same three verbs in sequence, with only one of the boys doing all three, as in (11) below, temporal sequence is a necessity.

(11) a. Al climbed the monkey bars.
      b. Al swung on the swings.
      c. Al balanced himself on the see-saw.

With other verbs one referent performing three actions simultaneously is not a problem, as in (12) below:

(12) a. Al ran.
      b. Al pumped his arms.
      c. Al whistled.

In these three sentences above simultaneity is not only possible but probable. The decisive factor is ***compatibility*** of verbal actions.

1.5 *The Temporal Attachment of Eventualities Represented by the Verbs in a Text*

A fifth factor influencing temporal sequence is the temporal attachment of a given verb in a chain to others.[11] Consider the quite instructive, more extensive text of six sentences in (13):

(13) a. The boys played hard during recess.
      b. They climbed the monkey bars.
      c. They swung on the swing set.
      d. They rode the see-saw.
      e. They trudged back to their classroom.
      f. They ran home eagerly.

What we note here first is that the sentences (13b), (13c), and (13d) are an elaboration of (13a), as in (6) above, and therefore, that the eventualities took place within the interval of time in which (13a) occurred, known as "recess." We note, second, that they are not necessarily in temporal order. "They" could refer to a collective idea: the boys moving as a group from one playground apparatus to another. But it could just as easily refer to a scenario such as in (5) and (6), with the boys taking turns on the equipment.

---

11. See **Subsection 2.4** for complete discussion.

A third observation is that the sentences temporally connect with one another at different levels. (13e) is not part of the elaboration of (13a). And so instead of time not moving past the end of recess, it resumes its advance at this point. So (13e) is attached to (13a) temporally, albeit not by textual juxtaposition. And by the same reasoning, we can see, fourth, that (13f) temporally and textually follows (13e). A fifth observation is that neither (13b), (13c), nor (13d) could follow (13e) and produce a coherent text—monkey bars, swings, and see-saws are not in the classroom!

1.6 *The Possibility of Temporal Discontinuities in Text*

The sixth and final factor is the potential presence of temporal discontinuities in texts, in the form of breaks or even lacunae.[12] Imagine our three friends as a team of successful lawyers, Alwyn, Robert, and Carlton, reminiscing about their boyhood days, as in (14) below:

(14) "'Al pushed Bob and he fell' were the exact words Carl told the teacher," Alwyn chuckled. "I can still remember how much trouble I got into because Carl tattled to the teacher." Carlton pretended to look insulted. "But Carl didn't see me slug you when I got up," Robert laughed. Carlton feigned shock, "I can't imagine you doing such a thing."

1.7 *Synopsis*

Above we introduced in a more or less cursory fashion the six factors which influence the flow of time in narrative. The first concerns the arrangement of the verb phrases in the text, recognizing that although the eventualities could have been reported in different orders from the temporal sequence in which they happened, the order in a text is a *given*. Nevertheless, our goal is always to get to the correspondence between the sequence of eventualities and the order in the text. The second comprises the semantic characteristics of *individual* verbs, what we term the **micro-level**. The third, fourth, and fifth are the semantic relationships *between* verbs, what we term the **macro-level**, defined by **coherence relations**; the possibility, or not, of simultaneity, which is controlled by **compatibility**; and the place of attachment of verbs to one another, i.e. **connection**, respectively. And the sixth concerns

---

12. For discussion and biblical examples, see **Subsection 2.5**. Anderson in **Chapter 14** identifies potential locations of temporal discontinuity in the Flood narrative, employing methodology developed by Floor in his 2004 dissertation. Also see Stroup's **Chapters 10** and **13** for more examples of such dischronologizations and a discussion of the possible reasons for them.

chronological *continuity*, specifically the possible presence, or not, of chronological discontinuities, and the purposes of the larger narrative, which might cause this.

Factor one need not be further explored, because the word order is a given in a text. Moreover, inasmuch as factor two, the temporal profile of individual verbs or VPs, was the subject of a careful study by Akagi in **Chapter 11**, we do not need to go into it any further either. But the rest of the factors require a careful perusal to see how they determine temporal progression in real texts. To that end in our discussion below we will furnish precise definitions, present BH texts, which evidence these factors at work, and analyze the same for their temporal profile.

2. Issues Pertaining to the Semantic Relationships between Verbs/Eventualities: A Closer Look

The outline of this section is as follows:

2.1   Introduction
2.2   *Coherence relations* in Discourse
2.3   *Compatibility/Incompatibility* and Temporal Displacement
2.4   Attachment and Temporal Dislocation
2.5   Textual Breaks and Temporal Discontinuity
2.6   Concluding Summary

2.1 *Introduction*

As stated above, there are six factors which affect temporal sequence in texts. The focus of this chapter is chiefly on the careful elucidation of the theoretical aspects and application to BH texts of the third, fourth, and fifth of these, on what we have called above, the *macro-level*, which comprises the relationships between verbs/clauses. We will also look at the sixth, which we call the *mega-level*, but only as far as the presence of temporal discontinuities are concerned. Stroup will explore the motivations for these and take up this subject in general in much greater detail in **Chapter 13**.

2.2 *Coherence relations in Discourse*

In order to understand temporal sequence effected at this level, we must first define and illustrate *coherence relations* in general, which occur between verbs/clauses, and then propose, define, and illustrate the set of *coherence relations*, which we will employ for our analysis of biblical texts. We will proceed as follows:

2.2.1 *Coherence relations* Defined
2.2.2 *Coherence relations* Proposed
2.2.3 Summary

2.2.1 *Coherence relations* Defined

The concept of *coherence relations* stems from the assumption that texts are coherent and cohesive. We assume texts are coherent and try to explain the connections between proximate portions of text accordingly. Before we can explore the concept of discourse coherence, we must understand its distinction from textual cohesion. To that end this sub-subsection breaks down as follows:

- Cohesion versus Coherence: Distinguished
- Cohesion versus Coherence: Differences Illustrated

(1) *Cohesion versus Coherence: Distinguished.* Both *cohesion* and *coherence* are important properties of discourse.[13] And although they are usually interrelated and interdependent, they need not be so (as we will show below): both can exist without the other. As a starting point for our discussion, consider how the two are clearly distinguished by Louwerse and Graesser (2005, 216–18):[14] the term *cohesion* applies "to the **surface structure** of the text"; *coherence* "to the **concepts** and relations underlying its meaning." They also refer to *cohesion* as "continuity in **word and sentence** structure"; but, *coherence* as "continuity in **meaning** and context." A third way they differentiate the two is "discourse-as-product" (cohesion) vis-à-vis "discourse-as-process" (coherence). They expand on this contrast as follows:

> *Coherence* can be reserved for the **conceptual** relationships that comprehenders use to construct a coherent mental representation accommodated by what is said in the discourse. *Cohesion* is limited to the **linguistic markers** that cue the comprehender on how to build such coherent representations.[15]

The difference then between the two is clear and is reminiscent of the distinction between lower order and higher order held by medieval rabbis in their analyses of BH poetry. *Cohesion* is the former; concerned with the

---

13. Both are widely discussed in the literature; and from disparate disciplines: linguistics, artificial intelligence, mathematic logic, language acquisition, etc. The following is just a sampling: (Graesser, McNamara, and Louwerse 2003; Graesser et al. 2004 ; Hobbs 2004; Kehler 2004; Louwerse et al. 2004; McNamara et al. 2010).

14. The following discussion on the distinction between these draws on their discussion. The bold-face emphasis is mine.

15. Ibid.

surface features of discourse. *Coherence* is the latter; concerned with concepts and deeper levels of meaning.

Both cohesion and coherence can occur locally (our **macro-level**) and globally (our **mega-level**). The former concerns both types of relations between adjacent sentences; the latter—those on the scene, episode, or even the entire narrative level.

Also both can be evinced in grammar (syntax, morphology, and atypicalities [to bring out emphases]) and semantics. Commenting on this aspect of the interrelatedness of cohesion and coherence, Louwerse and Graesser state, ". . . cohesion cues activate vocabulary-driven (pre-grammatical, knowledge-based) and grammar-driven (syntax-based) coherence" (2005).

At a finer level there are three markers of textual cohesion, to which we can objectively appeal to measure the cohesiveness of a text. We must further distinguish those that are *exophoric* (the expressions refer to the world outside the text), those that are *endophoric* (the connections are inside the text alone), and those that are both. The first marker is the presence of conjunctions. These work on the local level, between adjacent sentences, and are strictly *endophoric*. They are further broken down into sub-classes, which are either extensive or adversative: additive, temporal, and causal.

The second marker is co-reference, which occurs when words or groups of words point to the same extra-linguistic referent; thus, making them more or less equivalents of each other; and, thus, substitutes of each other. Moreover, because they refer to the outside world, they are *exophoric*; but, in addition, because they refer to each other inside the text, they are *endophoric* as well.

The most common "co-referencers" are personal pronouns, which can either look backward to an antecedent (anaphoric) or look forward to a post-cedent (cataphoric). Other substitutes are articles, demonstratives, repetitions, restatements, paraphrases, summaries, synonyms, hypernyms, hyponyms, antonyms, and even ellipsis.

The third marker is the presence of comparisons (or superlatives).

Now that we have explained the difference between cohesion and coherence by examining their respective definitions, we will further clarify their distinctions through the series of illustrations which follow.

(2) *Cohesion versus Coherence: Differences Illustrated.* That connection (or set of connections), which allows a minimal discourse (two verb clauses) to be sensible on a conceptual level, constitutes the **coherence relation** in such a two-sentence text. Consider the following two-sentence discourse: *The reading lamp went on in the corner of the room. Al sat down with his book.*

Apart from additional information we can only speculate as to what caused the lamp to turn on. In fact, we do not necessarily need to know the cause of its illumination. On the other hand, we must resolve the connection between the lamp going on and Al sitting down to read if we understand this mini-discourse to be coherent.

The most likely explanation of the sequence of eventualities concerning Al is that he turned on the lamp so that he could read his book. Another likely possibility in this fictional world is that Zelda, Al's wife, saw him with a book in his hand heading for his favorite chair and turned the light on for him. A third plausible, but less likely, scenario is that the lamp has a proximity detector or timer, which went on automatically. On the other hand if the second sentence had been, *Al went outside to mow the lawn*, we have to work a lot harder to produce a cogent reading; nevertheless, we instinctively do so: introducing an unseen character and unheard dialogue—perhaps Zelda reminding him that work (mowing the lawn) comes before pleasure (reading his book); or imagining that the lamp's going on was some kind of signal for him to begin his chores. In any case, we can come up with a reasonable relationship between the two utterances. But, if the second sentence had been *Al wanted to show off to Zelda the plain-looking rocks in his collection vibrantly fluorescing under the black-light he was carrying*, we might despair of understanding the connection. Why would Al deliberately *minimize* the visual effect of the glowing stones, by having a reading lamp on, if his purpose is to boast about the display? As a matter of fact we would expect Al to turn off the lamp to *maximize* the effect. Consequently, we might pronounce such a text incoherent.

Notwithstanding our final pair of utterances above, it is difficult *not* to establish coherence. Even incohesiveness does not preclude it. As Toolan (2011) observes, a discourse need not be cohesive to be coherent.[16] Arguably,

---

16. Toolan comments on the two important studies of Halliday and Hasan (1976) and de Beaugrande and Dressler (1981). On the former he says: "Halliday & Hasan's (1976) study of cohesion in English is often cited as a pioneering enquiry into the key resources in a language for underpinning textual coherence, indeed for the creation of genuine text. They look chiefly at inter-sentential grammatical mechanisms (e.g. means of co-reference via personal and indefinite pronouns, projecting of relatedness via retrievable ellipsis, use of sense-conveying sentential conjunctions), and they also comment, less systematically, on how texts display coherence by elaborate means of lexical collocation and association" (2011).

On the latter he observes: "De Beaugrande & Dressler (1981) remains an important and still influential overview of text structure which delineates seven standards of "textuality": (a) **cohesion** (mutually connected elements of the surface text); (b) **coherence** (the configuration of concepts and relations which underlie the surface text); (c) **intentionality** (instrumentalizing of cohesion and coherence according to the producer's intention); (d) **acceptability** (use or relevance of the cohesive and coherent text to the receiver); (e) **informativity** (degree to which the occurrences of the text are (un)expected or (un)known); (f) **situationality** (relevance of a text to a situation); (g) **intertextuality** (presupposed knowledge of one or more previous texts)" (2011) [The emphasis is mine].

according to our discussion above, all the discourses above are lacking in cohesion if not entirely devoid of it. Add to these two more. First, Brown and Yule's (1983) parade example of the dialogue a couple has after the doorbell rings. One says, "There is the bell." The other replies, "I'm in the bath." This exchange is clearly incohesive: there are no syntactic, lexical, or even anaphoric connections between the two utterances. But, just as clearly, it is coherent. As competent speakers of English we understand that the first utterance is intended to mean "There is someone at the door. You need to answer the door." The second person, realizing this, responds, conveying that she cannot answer the door by stating the circumstances preventing her from doing so, without explicitly stating that she cannot do so.

And the following anecdotal example is of a similar stripe. A man asked his wife, "Why is the chandelier so bright?" Her reply: "I had a hole in my sweater." On the one hand, these two utterances are obviously, entirely incohesive. But, on the other hand, they form a coherent whole, because it just so happens that the chandelier has a dimmer switch, which she turned up to give her more light so that she could darn her sweater.

We can extract more from the first example. Can we change the second utterance to make the discourse cohesive but incoherent? Yes, but we have to work hard at it. If she were to say, "Then ring it," there would be lexical cohesion and pronominal anaphora with respect to the locutionary meaning of his utterance, at the expense of its illocutionary meaning. What about incohesive and incoherent? If she were to say, "Then paint it," there is only pronominal anaphora. But if she were to say, "Andrew Johnson was the first President to be impeached" even the anaphora is removed, thereby rendering the discourse both incohesive and incoherent.

Having—hopefully—clearly delineated cohesion vis-à-vis coherence, we may now turn to propose the set of ***coherence relations***, which we will use for the balance of this study.

2.2.2 *Coherence Relations* Proposed

Numerous theories have been advanced to explain the semantic relationships within texts, which make them coherent.[17] Moreover, the number of ***coherence relations*** that have been proposed to explain all texts varies

---

17. The three major theories are ***Rhetorical Structure Theory*** (Mann and Thompson 1986, 1988); ***Discourse Representation Theory*** (Kamp 1981; Kamp and Reyle 1993); and ***Segmented Discourse Representation Theory*** (Lascarides and Asher 1993). These last two have collaborated together and with others on a number of papers on this subject.

widely.[18] In addition, which *coherence relations* are required for coherence and their definitions is debated.[19] Even their labeling has not reached a consensus.[20]

In spite of the variegated and uncertain state of this discipline, the *coherence relations* that obtain between verbs/clauses remain an essential factor in any analysis of temporal sequence. The set of *coherence relations* we proffer here—as stated in **Chapter 4**—is neither minimalist nor maximalist. Nor do we claim that it can explain all possible interactions between verbs; however, it bears resemblance to other sets and will be more than adequate for our purposes. Each of these needs to be defined, explained, qualified,

---

18. Hovy and Maier catalogued all the various different efforts to define the set of discourse relations up to that time (1992). They noted that sets of *coherence relations* widely ranged from zero to thirty members; hence "parsimonious to profligate" in the title of their paper. Two appendices consist of an index of all the *coherence relations* and the proponents for each and a list of scholars with the set of relations for each.

19. Since (Hovy and Maier 1992), there have been no shortage of new taxonomies of *coherence relations* proposed. (Lascarides and Asher 1993) build on the relations of (Hobbs 1985), employing a system of defeasible logic with the creative inference names "defeasible modus ponens," "the penguin principle," "the Nixon diamond" and "Dudley Doorite." Moser and Moore argue that the intentionality theory (Grosz and Sidner 1986) and Rhetorical Structure Theory (Mann and Thompson 1988) are "essentially similar in what they say about how speakers' intentions determine a structure of their discourse" (1996, 409). Knott proposes a very large taxonomy (1996). (Knott and Mellish discuss the following properties of relations from this taxonomy: *semantic* and *pragmatic*; *positive* and *negative polarity*; *conditionality*; *unilateral* vs. *bi-lateral*; *causal* and *inductive*; *cause* and *result-driven*; *anchor-based* and *counterpart-based*; *presupposed* and *non-presupposed*; *hypothetical* and *actual* [1996].) Marcu and Echihabi posit 'contrast', 'cause-explanation-evidence', 'condition', and 'elaboration' (2002, 3). (Kehler 2004) built his understanding on Hume's *Resemblance, Contiguity* in time or place, and *Cause* or *Effect* (1748). (Quotations from the philosophers are from the *Stanford Encyclopedia of Philosophy*, http://plato.stanford.edu/.) Kehler credits (Hobbs 1990) with this idea. (Hobbs 2004, 734) said that the relations are 'causal', 'similarity', or 'figure-ground' relations. (Taboada and Mann 2006, 14–16) support the thirty relations advocated by the latest offering of Mann from the RST website (2005), an expansion from the twenty-four proposed by (Mann and Thompson 1988). Similarly, (Taboada 2006, 26). Soria has three: 'additive', 'consequential', and 'contrastive', with a thorough discussion of each (2005, 1–4). Sporleder and Lascarides use 'contrast', 'result', 'summary', 'continuation', 'explanation' (2007, 8, 11, 12) and (2005). Sporleder has the same set (2007, 3–5). Blair-Goldensohn, McKeown, and Rambow model 'cause' and 'contrast' (2007). Pitler et al. 2008 propose 'expansion', 'comparison', 'contingency', and 'temporal' (2008). Subba and di Eugenio have 'causal', 'elaboration', 'similarity', 'temporal', 'other' (2009). Asher and Vieu look at 'elaboration', 'narration', 'explanation', and 'result' (2005).

20. Others refer to *coherence relations* as 'rhetorical relations', 'discourse relations', or 'conjunctive relations'. They are different labels for the same text-linguistic semantic relations. Hovy and Maier refer to these all in general as "intersegmental relations" (1992, 4).

illustrated with biblical texts (and where necessary with contrived texts), and related to temporal sequentiality—a task to which we now turn. The heuristic set we will use and is discussed below is as follows:[21]

- *Serialation*
- *Result/ Cause (Explanation)*
- *Contrast/ Comparison*
- *Elaboration*

(1) Serialation. This is a term I have coined for the most common **coherence relation** in narrative. Called elsewhere *occasion, continuation, contiguity, consequential,* and even *narrative,* this relation obtains where the state that exists after (because of?) the first verbal action *provides the **circumstances*** for the second verbal action to take place but ***not the sufficient cause,*** that is, the first action does not compel the second action. Following this idea a bit further, we can look at this **coherence relation** in terms of *necessary* and *sufficient* conditions, which we will now define.

Suppose that *c(ause)* causes *e(ffect)* in some way or another. *Necessary cause* is defined as follows: *c* is a *necessary cause* of *e* if the presence of *e* requires *c,* but the presence of *c* does not require *e.* For example in the paired sentences, *John turned off the lamp. The room became dark,* the darkness of the room requires that the lamp be off, but the lamp being off does not necessarily mean that the room will be dark; it could be daylight with the windows open. More generally, a *necessary* relationship between one eventuality and the next obtains when an *e(ffect)* cannot occur unless *c(ause)* has occurred; but, the converse, if *c* has occurred, then *e will* occur, is *not* the case.

Sufficient cause occurs when the presence of *c* ensures *e,* but the presence of *e* does not require *c.* Consider the following sentences: *Mugford (a dog) bumped the table. The coffee spilled from the cup filled to the brim.* The jostling of the table by the dog was enough to cause the coffee to spill, but other happenings could have caused this—an earthquake, for instance.

---

21. I will not be discussing *Background* below, because the three states, the atelic state, the point state, and the transitory state, have been thoroughly covered by Akagi in **Chapter 11.** Furthermore, since *Backgound* is a state, it is non-dynamic, either atelic or telic, and either durative or not. Thus, it corresponds with all the event types except for its non-dynamicity, which is not a factor in temporal sequence. When it is an atelic state, it is atelic and durative: the same as an **activity.** When it is a point state, it is telic and non-durative: the same as an **achievement.** And when it is a transitory state, it is telic and durative: the same as an **accomplishment.** In terms of temporal progression, therefore, states behave as events and thus do not need to be treated separately. See **Sub-subsection 4.2.2** for the differences between states and events with respect to the instants or intervals in which they occur.

A *necessary and sufficient* cause is one in which the presence of *c* requires *e* and vice-versa. An example would be: *The temperature dropped precipitously far below zero. The surface of the pond quickly froze,* because freezing requires cold temperatures and cold temperatures freeze standing water. Or in other words, the only way to quickly freeze water is to rapidly lower the temperature below freezing.

It is important that the difference between *necessary* and *sufficient* be clearly understood. Let me explain it in an entirely different context: in terms of the difference between a rectangle and a square. It is *necessary* that a quadrilateral (a closed [no breaks], convex [all points on line segments connecting two points on the figure are within its interior] four-sided figure) have four right angles to be a square, but that is not enough to *guarantee*—this is the meaning of *sufficient*—that it will be a square, because all rectangles have four right angles, but not all are squares. The figure must meet the additional requirement that all of its sides are the same length for it to be a square. Similarly, the condition that a quadrilateral have four equal sides is *necessary* for it be a square, but not *sufficient*, because a rhombus has four equal sides but its opposing angles are either obtuse (greater than a right angle) or acute (less than a right angle). We must add the requirement that the quadrilateral have right angles or equal angles to ensure that it is a square. Thus, we can state the following necessary and sufficient condition for a quadrilateral to be a square: *a quadrilateral is a square if and only if* (iff) *it has equal sides and equal angles.* In fact, extending these ideas beyond quadrilaterals allows us to define any regular polygon (a closed, convex multi-sided figure) as follows: *a polygon will be regular* iff *it has equal sides and equal angles.*

Serialation exhibits the following causal character: in a two eventuality chain, the occurrence of the first is *necessary* for the second to happen, but it is not *sufficient* to guarantee that the second will happen. On the one hand *Serialation* is a **necessary only** relation. On the other hand *cause-and-effect*— what we will call *Result*—is a **necessary and sufficient** relation.

For clarification consider the following example: *John went to the grocery store. He bought some milk.* In the eventualities referred to in this pair of sentences, going to the grocery store does not cause the buying of milk. John could have gone to the grocery store and bought bread instead, or, for that matter, nothing. But being at the grocery store provided the necessary circumstances for the milk to be bought. In fact, all other things being equal, John could not have bought milk unless he went to the grocery store, because according to our experience, milk normally cannot be bought any other way (although it can be purchased directly from dairy farmers and used to be from the milkman). Had John gone to the hardware store, he could not have purchased milk there; thus, the juxtaposition with *"bought some milk,"* is likely incoherent. The coherence of the discourse could be rescued by the understanding that the buying of the milk happened at a later time, at another place, or he happened to run into the milkman there. Conversely, if the first sentence remains unaltered and the second sentence is changed to *He bought a pneumatic nailer,* the new pair might or might not be incoherent— coherence is salvageable in a way similar to the previous example.

With *Serialation* the eventualities depicted by the verbs are in the same order as the verbs. With respect to time, the start of the second eventuality follows the start of the first eventuality. We must couch temporal sequence in these terms, because the first verb could be the initiation of a state that continues past the second event, such as in *Ned fell asleep. Kara tiptoed across the floor so as not to wake him.*

Biblical Hebrew narrative is characterized, and can even be identified, by the prevalence of *wayyiqtol* verb forms, which often occur in chains, with no other finite verb forms between sequential *wayyiqtols* in one link. Moreover, it is undeniable that in BH, the text is frequently iconic: text and time (that is the timeline of the eventualities depicted in the text) have the same linear sequence, as was discussed in **Subsection 1.1** and seen in Figure 1. But does the mere *linking* of the *wayyiqtols,* that is, their *syntactic* relationship, determine their *temporal* relationship? The answer is: no. As Stroup has shown in **Chapter 10,** sequential *wayyiqtols* do not necessarily represent temporally sequential eventualities. Consequently, temporal sequence must be determined semantically. This concurs with general linguistic theory, that, temporal sequence is to be ascertained semantically, not syntactically (that is, by verb order).

What then is the explanation for the frequent occurrence of textual iconicity in BH narrative? It is two-fold. First, it is because the nature of narrative is to trace the main story line,[22] moving forward through time,

---

22. Paul Ricoeur—as usual—has a pithy comment to the point: "My first working hypothesis is that ***narrativity and temporality are closely related***—as closely as, in Wittgenstein's terms, a language game and a form of life. Indeed, ***I take temporality to be that structure of existence that reaches language in narrativity and narrativity to be the language structure that has temporality as its ultimate referent. Their relationship is therefore reciprocal***" (1980, 169) [emphasis mine].

In addition, Zwaan, Madden, and Stanfield cogently observe: "Comprehenders assume that the order in which events are reported in language matches their chronological order. This is known as the iconicity assumption (Dowty 1986; Fleischman 1990). Narrative deviations from chronological order are possible only because a default order exists; the default serving as a baseline from which all else can be compared and understood" (2001).

For further details see Fleischman (1990); Kehler (1999); Lee (2004).

and, as is well known, the chain of *wayyiqtols* forms this "backbone" for BH narrative. And, second, *Serialation* is a common **coherence relation** in BH narrative—although the other **coherence relations** occur as well.

To demonstrate how *Serialation* works in *wayyiqtol* chains we will look at Genesis 12:7–9, in which there are eight *wayyiqtol* independent clauses in a row. This text's *wayyiqtol* chain furnishes seven fine examples of potential *Serialation*. In the following analysis and hereafter in this chapter we will engage in what Alice ter Meulen refers to as "temporal reasoning."[23]

[Please note: in this and all subsequent examples in the chapter, *wayyiqtols* are bold-face in the text and the translation, and are supplied with superscripted letters for convenience in the translation, so that the reader can easily identify the verb referred to in the commentary. The layout of the examples are text, followed by translation, then commentary.]

GENESIS 12:7–9

וַיֵּרָא יְהוָה אֶל־אַבְרָם וַיֹּאמֶר לְזַרְעֲךָ אֶתֵּן אֶת־הָאָרֶץ הַזֹּאת וַיִּבֶן שָׁם
מִזְבֵּחַ לַיהוָה הַנִּרְאֶה אֵלָיו:
8 וַיַּעְתֵּק מִשָּׁם הָהָרָה מִקֶּדֶם לְבֵית־אֵל וַיֵּט אָהֳלֹה בֵּית־אֵל מִיָּם וְהָעַי
מִקֶּדֶם וַיִּבֶן־שָׁם מִזְבֵּחַ לַיהוָה וַיִּקְרָא בְּשֵׁם יְהוָה:
9 וַיִּסַּע אַבְרָם הָלוֹךְ וְנָסוֹעַ הַנֶּגְבָּה:

YHWH ᵃ**appeared** to Abram and ᵇ**said** to him, "To your seed I will give this land." He ᶜ**built** there an altar to YHWH, who had appeared to him. He ᵈ**moved** from there to the mountains east of Bethel. He ᵉ**pitched** his tent with Bethel on the west and Ai on the east. He ᶠ**built** there an altar to YHWH. He ᵍ**called** on the Name of YHWH. Abram ʰ**journeyed** continually toward the Negev.

The question that must be asked to establish *Serialation* is: does the first verb provide the occasion for the second, that is, its *necessary* cause, without being its *sufficient* cause? Verbs **(a)** and **(b)** appear to be in this category: YHWH's appearing certainly provides the occasion for Him to speak but does not constrain Him to do so. On the other hand, the relation between verbs **(b)** and **(c)** is not so clear cut: it could be *Serialation*, but perhaps *Cause/ Result* would be a better analysis, because YHWH's speech to Abram likely motivated him to build an altar and offer a sacrifice of thanksgiving and devotion. **(c)** and **(d)** exhibit *Serialation*. "From there" makes that plain. **(d)** and **(e)** exhibit the same **coherence relation**. Abram cannot pitch his tent in

23. Personal communication.

another place until he moves to that place. Moving to that place however does not *cause* him to *pitch his tent* there, although in a sense it does cause him to pitch his tent *there*. With (e) and (f) the case is the same only more so: why would pitching his tent cause him to build an altar, except indirectly—it was his custom to build an altar, thereby sanctifying the place and devoting himself, after he established his presence at a place. The same obtains for (f) and (g). The altar that resulted from his building of it allowed him to offer sacrifices of devotion on it, which in turn permitted him to call upon the Name of YHWH, but did not *cause* him to do so. And finally let us consider the **coherence relation** evinced between (g) and (h). It is not immediately obvious in what way Abram's calling upon the Name of YHWH occasioned, let alone, caused, his further journeying. We might engage in some creative historiography, that at the time Abram had called on YHWH, He had revealed to him that he should journey toward the Negev, but this is not in the text and remains what it is: *plausible* speculation, but speculation nevertheless. A better approach is to abandon trying to link (h) with (g) and instead link it to the complex of eventualities that occurred after Abram's move to the location between Bethel and Ai: tent pitching, altar building, and calling upon YHWH. Once he had accomplished what he wanted to do at this location it was time for him to journey on. Understood this way (h)'s relationship is with the state effected by (e). Thus, *Serialation* obtains in this case. Moreover, this last pairing is instructive as to the temporal sequence in *Serialation*. Finally, by connecting (h) to (e) rather than the immediately preceding verb, (g), we have serendipitously considered the concept of attachment, which will be the topic of **Subsection 2.4**.

Having considered the **coherence relation** which manifests the *necessary only* condition, we now move on to the **coherence relation** which adds the *sufficient* condition, *Result*.

(2) *Result/Cause*. This is a relation in which the second verb or clause is the result/cause of the first verb. *Cause* is different from *Explanation* (also called *Solutionhood*).[24] The former answers the question *what*? The latter answers *why*? Nevertheless, they are not necessarily mutually exclusive, as the following example illustrates: "As for them, they did not know that Joseph was hearing [and understanding], because an interpreter was between them" (Gn 42:23). Why did Joseph's brothers not know that he was hearing their belated confessions? Only because they assumed he could not understand

---

24. Hovy and Maier classify these as "ideational relations" (1992); whereas, Taboada subsumes them under the rubric "subject matter relations" (2006).

them. Why did they assume this? Because he was using an interpreter. But also it could be said that the presence of the interpreter caused Joseph's brothers to think that he could not understand them. Therefore they spoke in an unguarded manner.

Result is illustrated by *John turned off the light. It was pitch black.* The first sentence implies that the light originally was on and the initial state therefore could not be darkness. The darkness was the state that ensued when and because the light was turned off. This is quite different from the relation *Background*, as in the following: *The basement was dark. John cautiously descended the stairs*, in which the initial state persists during the second action.

Because of the complexity of this part of the sub-subsection, we supply the following outline to assist the reader:

- o   Historical Survey
- o   Current Theories
- o   A Biblical Illustration: The Story of Joseph
- o   *Result* versus *Serialation* in *Wayyiqtol* Chains

(a) Toward a Definition of *Cause*: Historical Survey. For the examples above, we employed *commonsense judgment* to ascertain whether *Result* or *Cause* obtained or not. But ideally we would prefer a rigorous methodology to do this. To that end we need to survey the history of the study of the concept of causation more closely.[25] We start with **PLATO**: ". . . everything that becomes or changes must do so owing to some cause; for nothing can come to be without a cause" (*Timaeus* 28a). But by "cause" he means *formal* cause, that is, the eternal, changeless forms which effect the realization of accidents. **ARISTOTLE** understood three additional types: *material, efficient,* and *final.* We can elucidate their distinctiveness by considering Moses' theme from the soundtrack of *The Ten Commandments.* The *material* cause is the sonic frequencies, represented by the musical notes on the score. The *efficient* cause is who or what is responsible for the theme, the composer who wrote the music, Elmer Bernstein. The *final* cause is the purpose for which he wrote the theme, to musically reinforce Moses' presence on the screen. Only the second of these, efficient cause, was developed in the intellectual history of causation.

The **STOICS** introduced to the understanding of causation the ideas of *regularity* and *necessity*: that every eventuality had a cause and every event, invariably, effected the same result given the same circumstances.

---

25. The following is based on Hulswit's own online abridgment of chapter one of his book (2002). The undesignated quotations are his words of analysis. Quotations from philosophers are from Hulswit as well and are fully documented there.

In the Middle Ages the SCHOLASTICS divided efficient cause into *primary* and *secondary*, God, the originator of being and created persons or things, and the originators of change or motion, respectively. THOMAS AQUINAS further divides secondary into "tight" and "loose," depending on whether or not the circumstances of the cause are a factor in necessitating the effect. Moreover, he said, "For, as nature is, so is its action; hence, given the existence of the cause, the effect must necessarily follow" (*SCG* II: 35.4). And, ". . . the power of every agent which acts by natural necessity is determined to one effect; that is why all natural things happen in the same way, unless there be an obstacle; while voluntary things do not" (*SCG* II: 23.2). By this, Thomas meant "that things belonging to the same type act similarly in similar causal circumstances." By "relating efficient causality to natural necessity, and natural necessity to law-like behavior, Aquinas would have a major impact on the development of the modern conception of causality." But Aquinas—as did other Scholastics— maintained that efficient causation was the transmission of form: "the natural thing necessarily tends to its end in accordance with the power of its form." For example fire transfers its form to wood, so that the wood becomes fire.

The METAPHYSICAL and EMPIRICAL PHILOSOPHERS, who postdated the Renaissance, rejected the Aristotelian and Scholastic fourfold concept of causation and understood causation in a mechanical sense. Among the former RENÉ DESCARTES argued: "Let another, if he likes, imagine in this piece of wood the Form of fire, the Quality of heat, and the Action which burns it as things altogether diverse; for my part I, who fear I shall go astray if I suppose there to be more in it than I see must needs be there, am content to conceive in it the movement of its parts." To him efficient causes were particularizations of the general laws of nature.

For THOMAS HOBBES all effects came from causes, "all the effects that have been, or shall be produced, have their necessity in things antecedent" (1655); and what is more, causes necessitate effects, "it cannot be conceived but that the effect will follow" (1655).

BARUCH SPINOZA refined the concept of causation, introducing the idea of *logical* necessity, that *effects* logically necessitate *causes* and *causes* logically necessitate *effects*: "From a given determinate cause an effect necessarily follows; and, on the other hand, if no determinate cause be given it is impossible that an effect can follow" (1677).[26]

---

26. It is interesting to note that the second half of Spinoza's comment resembles the counterfactual understanding of causation that is dominant today.

Among the empiricists both **JOHN LOCKE** and **SIR ISAAC NEWTON** developed unusual concepts of causation, which did not contribute to our modern understanding. In fact the latter asserted that the law-like behavior of bodies in motion and causation were mutually exclusive. But **DAVID HUME** articulated the concept of causation, upon which modern theories are based or against which modern theories adversely react.

Hume summarized the state of knowledge of causation of his day as comprising three factors, *contiguity, priority,* and *necessity*; and then, challenged the last of these, which he considered the most important. He argues that it cannot be conclusively established, but is only reasoned inductively because of the string of previous instantiations without exception, in which a particular cause produced an effect (for instance, a burning match igniting paper to which it is touched), "There are no objects, which by the mere survey, without consulting experience, we can determine to be the causes of any other; and no objects, which we can certainly determine in the same manner not to be the causes" (Hume 1748). According to Hume two things are involved: the *constant conjunction* of the putative cause and putative effect and the *connection* that is made between them in our minds because of these exceptionless pairings. In modern theory the first of these is considered to be a necessary condition for causation to be inferred. On the other hand, his ideas that constant conjunction is a sufficient condition for causation to be inferred, is not correct: correlation does not imply causation.

IMMANUEL KANT recognized that Hume's concept of causation was devastating[27] and argued that cause and effect was an a priori concept connected with reason:

> If we thought to escape these toilsome enquiries by saying that experience continually presents examples of such regularity among experiences and so affords abundant opportunity of abstracting the concept of cause, and at the same time of verifying the objective validity of such a concept, we should be overlooking the fact that the concept of cause can never arise in this manner. *It must either be grounded completely a priori in the understanding, or must be entirely given up as a mere phantom of the brain.* For this concept makes strict demand that something, A, should be such that something else, B, follows from it necessarily and in accordance with an absolutely universal rule. Appearances do indeed present cases from which a rule can be obtained according to which something usually happens, but they never prove the sequence to be necessary. To the synthesis of cause

27. The existence and determination of causes and effects is a fundamental tenet of empirical science. For a thorough analysis of Kant's strident response to Hume see De Pierris and Friedman (2008).

and effect there belongs a dignity which cannot be empirically expressed, namely, that the effect not only succeeds upon the cause, but that it is posited through it and arises out of it. *This strict universality of the rule is never a characteristic of empirical rules; they can acquire through induction only comparative universality,* that is, extensive applicability. If we were to treat pure concepts of understanding as merely empirical products, we should be making a complete change in [the manner of] their employment (1781/87, emphasis mine).

Furthermore, Kant understood that cause-effect relationships establish an objective order in time—a realization particularly germane to the study of temporal sequence in text. He thereby rejected Hume's understanding that we first perceive temporal order between eventualities and then assign cause and effect to them accordingly.

JOHN STUART MILL—also, contra-Hume—reintroduced the concept of necessary cause with his idea of *unconditionalness*:

If there be any meaning which confessedly belongs to the term necessity, it is unconditionalness. That which is necessary, that which must be, means that which will be, whatever supposition we may make in regard to all other things. The succession of day and night evidently is not necessary in this sense. It is conditional on the occurrence of other antecedents. That which will be followed by a given consequent when, and only when, some third circumstance also exists, is not the cause, even though no case should ever have occurred in which the phenomenon took place without it. (Mill 1874)

Mill also elucidated five methods for detecting evidence of a cause-effect relationship (1843; Kemerling 2011).[28] The first is *agreement*, that is, similar effects stem from similar causes: "If two or more instances of the phenomenon under investigation have only one circumstance in common, the circumstance in which alone all the instances agree, is the cause (or effect) of the given phenomenon." The second is *difference*, that is, all other things being equal, different effects stem from different causes: "If an instance in which the phenomenon under investigation occurs, and an instance in which it does not occur, have every circumstance in common save one, that one occurring only in the former; the circumstance in which alone the two instances differ, is the effect, or the cause, or an indispensable part of the cause, of the phenomenon." The third is a combination of these: "If two or more instances in which the phenomenon occurs have only one

---

28. The quotes in the following paragraph are by Mill.

circumstance in common, while two or more instances in which it does not occur have nothing in common save the absence of that circumstance: the circumstance in which alone the two sets of instances differ, is the effect, or cause, or a necessary part of the cause, of the phenomenon." The fourth is *concomitant variation*, that is, a direct correlation can be established between two things, because the degree of a variable effect is proportional to the degree of a variable cause: "Whatever phenomenon varies in any manner whenever another phenomenon varies in some particular manner, is either a cause or an effect of that phenomenon, or is connected with it through some fact of causation." The fifth is *residues*, that is, if in the case of the existence of a complex nexus of potential causes and a complex of potential effects all the causes and effects are accounted for except for one pair, this last must be a cause-effect pair. In other words, if by a process of elimination all other causes are excluded, whatever is left must be the cause: "Deduct from any phenomenon such part as is known by previous inductions to be the effect of certain antecedents, and the residue of the phenomenon is the effect of the remaining antecedents."

Modern theories of causation build on the theories sketched above, to one degree or another. So we are now poised to consider the current theories.

(b) Toward a Definition of *Cause*: Current Theories. Transitioning to survey the modern theories of causation, we will consider four major rubrics in our discussion: REGULARITY THEORIES, PROBABILISTIC THEORIES, MANIPULATION THEORIES, and COUNTERFACTUAL THEORIES.

REGULARITY THEORIES are more or less the refinement of Hume's concept of concomitant regularity. In this approach causes are examined logically and grouped into *necessary, sufficient, necessary and sufficient, contributory,* and *INUS* types. The last—an acronym for the cause in question—is *I*nsufficient by itself to cause the effect, but is a *N*on-redundant part of a nexus of causes, which is *U*nnecessary but *S*ufficient for the occurrence of the effect—a concept originated by Mackie (1974).

The fourth type is *contributory cause*. This is seen whenever modifying the cause modifies the effect, such as a volume control on an amplifier connected to a tuner.

Mackie argues that most causes are *INUS conditions*, as defined above. A good illustration of this type is the example used above for necessary cause: *John turned off the lamp; The room became dark.* By itself "turning off the lamp" does not make a room dark, because there are other sources of light besides a lamp—the sun, for instance. So for *turning off a lamp* to be able to plunge a room into darkness requires a cluster of circumstances to be in place: there are no windows in the room, or, if there are, their shutters are closed, or the sun must be down, the moon must not have risen yet (or be a moonless light), and the room must be shielded from any street lights. If all other sources of light are eliminated, then and only then will turning off the one remaining source of light, the lamp, produce darkness.

In PROBABILISTIC THEORIES c is not assumed to definitively cause e, but rather makes it more likely that it occurs.[29] It is asserted that imperfect regularities (ala Hume), irrelevance, asymmetry, and spurious regularities demand this approach.

Imperfect regularity means that a cause does not always produce the effect. For example, turning off a lamp does not always darken a room—it might be daytime, or the other circumstances discussed under regularity theories might obtain.

Irrelevance occurs when an action preceding an effect does not contribute to it. This is exemplified quite well in the habit of many Major League Baseball players always going through a little ritual before each pitch, which likely has nothing to do with their getting a hit.

The *asymmetry* of cause and effect, that is, causes temporally precede effects, was codified very clearly by Hume. But philosophers ask why this polarity obtains? They are unsatisfied to merely stipulate the temporal directionality; they want a theory that explains it.

Spurious regularities are correlations that are falsely attributed to causes. Suppose that in a given location every time it snows heavily at night, snow plows and salt trucks are immediately dispatched, and schools close the next day. According to Hume's understanding the invariable conjunction of snow plows being on the streets with the schools closing suggests that the former causes the latter. This, naturally, is incorrect and a parade example of *cum hoc ergo propter hoc*, "with this therefore because of this." In fact, rather than snow plows causing the closing of schools, they are the very things most likely to effect their reopening!

Probabilistic theory is meant to address the above-mentioned potential problems with regularity. The theory is formulated as follows:

$$P(e|c) \rightarrow P(e|\neg c) \qquad \text{(iii)}$$

That is, the probability that e will occur given that c has occurred is higher than the probability that e will occur without c having occurred first.

---

29. See Williamson (2010) and Hitchcock (2012) for a thorough treatment of this topic.

But inferring cause from correlations using probability is difficult because of the complexity of the relationships between two potential causal *relata*.

Hans Reichenbach was the first to develop a comprehensive theory of probabilistic causation. In so doing he made three major contributions by introducing three original concepts: *screening off*, *common cause*, and *fork asymmetry*. The first occurs when the probability of *e* occurring given that both *a* and *c* occur is the same as the probability of *e* occurring given that only *c* occurs. In such a case Reichenbach said that *c* "screens off" *a* from *e*, formulated as follows:

$$P(e \mid a \wedge c) = P(e \mid c) \qquad \text{(iv)}$$

This can happen in two ways: if *c* is a necessary intermediate step between *a* and *e*; or if *c* is a common cause (see below) of both *a* and *e*.

Both types of screening off can be used to identify spurious causation, as in the following. As for the first way, suppose a building has a double door: a normal-weight, outer door with a combination lock and a heavy, inner, security door with a key lock with a vestibule between them. To gain entry to the offices within (*e*) requires that the proper combination be input to open the outer door's combination lock (*a*) and that the proper key be selected from a ring of keys hung next to the inner door to open it (*c*). An alarm will go off if the wrong key is chosen. If two thieves, John and James, gain access to the vestibule by different means, John by having stolen the combination and James with a crowbar, they have the same probability for picking the right key to get in. Thus, getting through the first door has nothing to do with getting into the building.

And as for the second way, let us return to the snow storm example above. Although without fail the snow plows roll out before the schools close, they do not cause the schools to close, because the two come from a common cause, the snow storm.

Reichenbach's second major contribution was generalizing examples as those above into what he called the "Common **Cause** Principle": if two eventualities are correlated, but neither is the cause of the other, that is,

$$P(a \wedge e) \to P(a) \times P(e) \qquad \text{(v)}$$

then they result from a common cause satisfying the following conditions:

$$0 < P(c) < 1 \qquad \text{(vi)}$$
$$P(a \wedge e \mid c) = P(a \mid c) \times P(e \mid c)$$
$$P(a \wedge e \mid \neg c) = P(a \mid \neg c) \times P(e \mid \neg c)$$
$$P(a \mid c) \to P(a \mid \neg c)$$
$$P(e \mid c) \to P(e \mid \neg c)$$

His third contribution is his 'asymmetrical forks theory'. His theory assumes that a cause temporally precedes its effect, but he wanted to establish a probabilistic basis for such asymmetry. He assumed two eventualities a and e were correlated. If a third eventuality c is related to them such that it satisfies the conditions in (vi), he called the triad a *conjunctive fork*. There are three types of forks. If c occurs temporally before the other two and no eventuality meeting the conditions temporally follows the two, the fork is said to be *open to the future*. Conversely, if c follows rather than precedes and no eventuality satisfying the conditions precedes, the fork is *open to the past*. Finally, he called the scenario in which c precedes the two, d follows them, and both satisfy the conditions, a *closed fork*. Then Reichenbach proposed that the direction from cause to effect was that in which *open forks* predominate. Of course, in the real world they do; thus, causes precede effects.

A possible analogy for Reichenbach's conjunctive forks theory is from baseball. Suppose men are on second and third base, because a third batter hits a flair to shallow center. They had been on first and second, because of successive base hits. Of course the man was initially on second, because the man who had stood on first moved him over with a hit. So these are correlated. Furthermore, they only move to third and second, because the third man first got his hit. Now suppose they are on third and second. Could something that occurred after they were at third and second cause them to be at these bases? For instance . . . the man (a slow runner) crossing the plate after they reached third and second? Surely, it is the other way around. Moreover, baseball is a game of statistics. Every player has an on-base percentage. The probability of two players on base would be the product of their on-base percentages. The probability of so and so getting a hit with men on base is known as well. So the conditions might be met. But now we must leave the diamond and return to the outside world.

It is the purpose of all probabilistic theories of causation to express the cause and effect relationship exclusively in terms of probabilities. Thus, ideally, the goal is to arrive at an expression in which c is the cause of e is on the left side of an *iff* condition, and only probabilities involving these are on the right side. This equation should be read: the probability that c causes e is P.

The theory has progressed from Reichenbach's foundation and has become quite esoteric; and, thus, in its details is beyond the scope of this chapter.[30]

---

30. Williamson (2010) surveys the approaches of Good and Suppes and discusses the counterexamples to probabilistic theory of causation in terms of the Causal Markov Condition.

The conception of MANIPULATION THEORIES is fairly straightforward: if *c* is a cause of *e*, then as *c* changes, *e* changes. We are seeking its converse: if *e* changes as *c* changes, then *c* is the cause of *e*.[31] For example, let us say we have a simple electrical circuit, comprising a battery, a variable resistor, and a light bulb. As we increase the resistance the brightness of the bulb decreases. Conversely, as we decrease the resistance the bulb gets brighter. This simple experimental setup allows us to deduce that the battery and the light coming from the bulb are causally connected. Or does it? This type of understanding is criticized by philosophers as being dependent on human agency. But it is not too hard to modify the resistor to remove the human element. So for heuristic purposes, suppose we attach a weight to the resistor control, which moves the resistor depending on the pitch of the resistor. If we take our little apparatus on board a ship, the bulb will change brightness as the ship rocks with the waves—with no human agency.

To meet the objections raised by scholars, Pearl (2000) developed a variation on this concept called intervention theory. Essentially, rather than a modification of *c*, it is a discussion of what happens to *e* at the cessation of *c*. To carry forward the electrical circuit analogy from above, in this case it would be a switch instead of a resistor.

Finally, we look at COUNTERFACTUAL THEORIES of causation.[32] Although the study of this concept did not begin in earnest until the twentieth century, Hume—quite surprising in light of his arguments that cause is nothing more than constant conjunction—gave us the following early definition of counterfactual causation:

> We may define a cause to be an object followed by another, and where all the objects, similar to the first, are followed by objects similar to the second. Or, in other words, where, if the first object had not been, the second never had existed." (1748, Section VII).

Counterfactual causation should not be confused with contrary-to-fact conditional, such as: *If I were outside the earth's atmosphere [in fact, I am*

31. See Williamson (2011a) and (2011b) and Woodward (2012) for a fuller treatment.
32. Menzies (2009) has a very thorough and understandable discussion of counterfactual causation. He traces Lewis' modification of his theories in response to preemption scenarios proposed. He interacts with the latest approach, which is a structural equation analysis of counterfactual causation based on Pearl (2000). Some interesting studies not mentioned by Menzies are the entertaining *The Prince of Wales Problem for Counterfactual Theories of Causation*, in which it is argued that counterfactual theories of causation "cannot accommodate cause by omission . . . "; Richard Scheines' *Causation*; Francis Longworth's 2006 dissertation at the University of Pittsburgh, *Causation, Counterfactual Dependence and Pluralism*; and L. Paul's *Counterfactual Theories of Causation*.

not], I would need a spacesuit. To elucidate the difference, let me continue with this celestial illustration. Suppose for the sake of argument that the following conditional is true: *If I am outside the earth's atmosphere [c], then I need a spacesuit [e].* The counterfactual would be: *If I am **not** outside the earth's atmosphere [not c], then I do **not** need a spacesuit [not e].* The classic articulation of this theory by David Lewis is *c* is the necessary and sufficient cause of *e if and only if* both of the following obtain:

$$\text{if } c \text{ (is true) [the eventuality } c \text{ occurs]},$$
$$\text{then } e \text{ (is true) [the eventuality } e \text{ will occur]} \quad \text{(vii)}$$

$$\text{if not } c \text{ (the eventuality } c \text{ does not occur)},$$
$$\text{then not } e \text{ (the eventuality } e \text{ will not occur)} \quad \text{(viii)}$$

A convenient, symbolic shorthand for this is

$$c \text{ is the cause of } e \text{ iff } c \to e \wedge \neg c \to \neg e. \quad \text{(ix)}$$

From our illustration, if being outside of the earth's atmosphere implies that I am in a spacesuit and not being outside of the earth's atmosphere implies that I am not in a spacesuit, then being outside of the atmosphere is the necessary and sufficient cause of needing a spacesuit or adopting Lewis' terminology: needing a spacesuit is *casually dependent* on being outside of the earth's atmosphere.

Of the many biblical examples of *contrary-to-fact conditionals*, the following are a sampling: "Thus YHWH said, 'If the heaven above can be measured and the foundations of the earth can be searched below, also I will reject the seed of Israel for everything which they have done,' the utterance of YHWH" (Jer 31:37). Since said measuring and searching even in our day and age is impossible, this is a contrary-to-fact conditional. Others are Jeremiah 31:35–36, which concerns the contrary-to-fact faltering of the sun, moon, and stars, and the waves of the sea; and 33:20, the contrary-to-fact altering of the timing of day and night.

Of examples of *counterfactuals*, perhaps the most striking is the parallel destinies of Israel outlined in Leviticus 26 and Deuteronomy 28: if Israel is faithful to YHWH, He will bless them (they will be blessed in myriads of ways). The counterfactual is that if they are not faithful to Him, He will curse them (they will be cursed in the same ways). The truth of both of these is evident throughout Israel's history, which proves that Israel's wellbeing is casually dependent on their faithfulness to YHWH.

Since we are trying to determine whether or not *c* caused *e,* both which have occurred, the first condition ((vii) above) is trivially met. The focus then is on the second condition ((viii) above), the *irrealis* condition: if *c* had not happened, then *e* would not have happened either. Although intuition suggests that this approach to determining causation would be valid, and scholars originally thought it would prove more promising than the regularity theory of Hume, updated by Mackie, it has suffered the onslaught of many scenarios posited to the contrary.[33] Chief among these are the preemptions. It has also been accused of circularity: what constitutes cause has been used to determine counterfactuality.

Let me illustrate by a contrived example. Suppose there is such a competition as tandem skeet shooting, in which two shooters with single-barreled shotguns have an opportunity to hit a given clay pigeon. Shooters alternate going first. They may pass or shoot. In this imaginary sport points are awarded according to how many targets are hit (two points per target), deducted according to how many shots are fired, and no penalty is imposed for a pass. Obviously, the only way to get points is to shoot; conversely, it is the only way to lose points.

If the first shooter passes or does nor shoot for some other reason, the second may pass or shoot. If he does the former, the team nets zero points for the round. If he does the latter and hits the target, the team gains one point for the round. But if he misses, the team loses a point.

If the first shooter shoots and hits, the team gets one point (two for the hit; minus one for the shot)—provided that the second shooter has not shot. If he has, the team gets no points for the round. If the first shoots and misses, the team loses a point; but, the second shooter still has a chance to hit the target. If he does, he gets two points for the hit, but because his is the second shot, the team breaks even for the round. If he too misses, the team loses two points for the round. On the other hand, if he passes, the team has lost only one point, the miss of the first shooter.

The above possibilities put the second shooter on the spot. Should he shoot or not if the first misses? If he shoots and misses, the team will lose an additional point for the round. If he hits the target, the team will break even: a difference of two points from the first scenario. Consequently, second shooters adopt two different strategies—wait to see if the target is hit, then shoot if there has been a miss—risky, because the target might ground by

---

33. Ibid., for a description of these. The most notable are "the two assassins," "Billy and Suzy throwing rocks," "to shock or not to shock," "who saved the king's life: the poisoner or the bodyguard with an antidote that is lethal if it does not encounter a poison?"

then—or shoot a split second after the first shooter. Suppose, further, that both shooters are dead shots and ordinarily never miss; but, this time, the first has a broken hand. The umpires, knowing this, assume that the second shooter would not shoot unless he thought the first shooter was going to miss.

This example is replete with counterfactual situations. One scenario is that the first shooter hits the target and the second does not shoot. Here shooter one clearly caused the target to be hit, but if he had not shot and neither had the second shooter, the target would have escaped. Nevertheless, the second shooter was ready to shoot and would have hit the target had he shot. The target would be hit either way. Who caused the target to be hit? Intuition would tell us that it was shooter one. But shooter two could have hit the target as well if the counterfactual that shooter one had missed or did not shoot had occurred, prompting shooter two to shoot. This leads to the strange result that according to the second condition above (viii) shooter one was not the cause of the destruction of the target, when in fact he was, or that shooter two caused the target to be hit, when he had not even shot. This is called the *problem of early preemption*.

Now suppose that shooter two did not wait, but shot just after the first. His shot would have hit the target, but because the first shooter's shot hit the target, demolishing it, the second shooter's shot passed through the air where the target would have been. Who caused the target to be hit? Again, common sense tells us that shooter one did. But had he not shot, would the target not have been hit? Yes. So, according to condition two above (viii), shooter one did not cause the target to be hit—an obviously wrong conclusion. On the other hand, if shooter two had not shot, given that shooter one missed the target or did not shoot, the target would not have been hit. And then by (viii) shooter two is the cause of the target being hit. Very strange!

Proponents of the counterfactual theory of causation have made various modifications to salvage it, only to have them subjected to additional hypothetical scenarios. This web of stroke and counterstroke is too complicated to go into here. Rather, without embracing a particular position and being fully aware of its pitfalls, I will apply the basic idea of counterfactuality to the convoluted turns in the story of Joseph, establishing causality within it by posing a series of questions of the form: what if had not been . . .? By this exercise I hope to model how cause and effect between the eventualities recounted in Scripture might be determined by counterfactual analysis.

(c) Towards a definition of *Cause*: A Biblical illustration; The Story of Joseph (Genesis 37:2–50:26). Let us first look at the big picture, starting at the end of the story, to ask our FIRST question: would Jacob and his family have gone down to Egypt—to be later miraculously delivered from subsequent Egyptian slavery—had not Joseph been the de facto pharaoh of Egypt? Probably not. And yet they had to, not primarily to survive the famine, as Joseph surmised (although this was the immediate purpose), but rather in the LORD's larger purpose, in order to be removed from pervasive, pernicious Canaanite corruption, which threatened the Messianic line. Moreover, they had to be positioned for the later exodus.

This leads to the SECOND question: would Joseph's brothers have gone down to Egypt had there not been a famine? Again—probably not. In fact, they seemed singularly oblivious to their peril, frozen by indecision-induced shock, and were only awakened from their somnolence and paralysis by the urging of their father. A related THIRD question is: would they have gone back had not the famine continued? Definitely not: as Judah made very clear to his father.

Since condition one (vii) is vacuously true for all three above, according to condition two (viii) of counterfactuals, we have established that the famine and Joseph's stature in Egypt caused Jacob to relocate his family to Egypt.

A FOURTH question pertains to how Joseph came to be in this position of authority: would Joseph have come to the attention of pharaoh had his chief of the cupbearers not mentioned him to him? As an inmate in the pharaoh's prison but not sentenced to be there at his behest, he would have not even known he was there let alone who he was. So, counterfactually this high official's recommendation of Joseph caused him to be brought up before pharaoh. This provokes a FIFTH question: would pharaoh have made Joseph second in command of Egypt had he not been convinced of his abilities to which the chief cupbearer testified and he himself had witnessed (Joseph's prescience in connection with God [or from pharaoh's perspective, the gods] and his weighed advice); and had his magicians and their congeners not failed (or been reluctant) to interpret his dreams? Almost certainly not. Consequently, these things are causes as well.

This moves us to the SIXTH question, which concerns how the cupbearer came to have the stated opinion of Joseph's abilities: would he have risked reminding the typically capricious pharaoh of his imprisonment in the course of recommending Joseph to him had he not been convinced that Joseph could not only help pharaoh but himself as well? Obviously not. He would not wish to incur pharaoh's wrath a second time. The outcome may not have been as salutary for him as at the first. A related SEVENTH question arises: would he have been convinced of Joseph's abilities had he not lived out the fulfillment of the former's predictions, his restoration to pharaoh's favor and the demise of the hapless chief baker? Same answer. Witness how he ascribed to Joseph, not pharaoh, the effecting of the disparate dispositions of himself and the chief baker: "Just as he interpreted for us, thus it was: *me* he returned to my office; *him* he impaled" (Gn 41:13).

But how did these high officials of pharaoh come into contact with Joseph? This prompts an EIGHTH question: would they have done so had Joseph not been in the prison and assigned to be their aid? No. Joseph would have been busily engaged in managing the estate of the pharaoh's chief of the bodyguards and would have had no occasion to visit the prison. Moreover, Joseph was designated as their assistant because his master was aware of his abilities and wanted the best for some of his fellow officials. So, a NINTH question naturally is: would Potiphar have trusted Joseph with such responsibility had he not had the utmost confidence in him? Certainly not.

Of course this brings us to the questions surrounding Joseph's imprisonment. From above we can see that his imprisonment in the pharaoh's prison was essential for the unfolding of God's plan. This was quite a downward turn for Joseph, due to no fault of his own, but to the wantonness of Potiphar's wife, scornful (but perhaps hopeful of seducing him in the future) for being rejected. Consequently, she accuses Joseph in an ambiguous way. The text only says that Potiphar was angry at what his wife said. Notably, it does not say that he was angry at *Joseph*. The TENTH question then is: would Joseph have been thrown into the pharaoh's personal prison had not circumstances worked out this way? And a corollary to this is the ELEVENTH question: would Potiphar have merely incarcerated Joseph had he thought that he had attempted to rape his wife, in spite of the fact that he knew her lascivious tendencies? The answer to both these questions is: no.

As we continue to trace back the necessary chain of eventualities to the beginning of the story, we must now consider the attempted seduction of Joseph. Two questions suggest themselves. The first, our TWELFTH question is: would Potiphar's wife have lusted after Joseph had he not been handsome of form and appearance and had the responsible position he had? Likely not. And second, our THIRTEENTH question: would she have had the opportunity to see him at all if he had not been in the house? The answer of course is: no. We see here that it was necessary for Joseph to be promoted as he was so that she would desire him and scheme to get him. Given this reasoning, the FOURTEENTH question is obvious: if Potiphar had not promoted Joseph would the eventualities have happened as they did? No. Furthermore, concomitant with this are two more (the FIFTEENTH question): if YHWH had not caused Potiphar to prosper as he gave responsibility to Joseph would he have promoted him? And, the SIXTEENTH question: if YHWH had not orchestrated matters so that Joseph was assigned to the house would Potiphar have given Joseph responsibility in the house? Virtually impossible.

We all know how Joseph came to be a slave of Potiphar, but now let us consider the matter counterfactually. Joseph's brothers with Reuben absent sold him into slavery rather than killing him. This moves us to ask the SEVENTEENTH question: if the Egypt-bound caravan of Ishmaelites/Midianites had not come along when it did, would Joseph's brothers have sold him into slavery and not carried out their initial murderous intentions? The text leaves Joseph in a pit and his brothers sitting and eating lunch, while apparently deliberating over how they will do him in and blame his death on a wild animal when they espy a caravan in the distance. There seems to be no indication that the brothers heeded their oldest brother Reuben's pleas. Perhaps they sensed as we do that he had an ulterior motive: to rescue the boy and return him to his father, thereby ingratiating himself to him (which he needed after violating his father's concubine). There also seems to be no indication that the other brothers had considered any other plan than violence. It is likely therefore that the appearance of the caravan gave Judah a new idea of how they could get rid of Joseph without killing him. And with Reuben gone, ostensibly to figure out how to rescue Joseph, the brothers acted quickly. In short, the answer to question seventeen is: no.

What gave the brothers the opportunity to act as they did is that they were far away from their father. In addition, they had moved from the original location where Jacob had sent them. Curiously, it was a certain *man*, who, finding Joseph ineptly wandering about looking for his brothers (not the picture of a confident, self-assertive supervisor at all!), directed him to them. Did this *man* know what awaited Joseph? We must ask this in that he reminds us of another *man* who showed up out of nowhere and wrestled with Jacob through the night. Furthermore, he seems very well informed as to the plans of strangers. Did he just happen to overhear them? In any case, this moves us to frame the EIGHTEENTH question: if the *man* had not told Joseph the new location of his brothers (regardless of how he found out about this) would Joseph have encountered his brothers at all? Clearly, not. To this query we must add another the NINETEENTH question—this time concerning Jacob: if he had not sent Joseph after his sons to check up on them would the subsequent eventualities have obtained? I think not. Finally, we must ask a question coming from a frightful thought. What is this? The text does not say that Jacob sent his sons to Shechem. Rather, they went to Shechem to shepherd his flock there—an uncharacteristically industrious action on their part. Was this to lure Joseph away from his father, knowing that Jacob did not trust them and would follow his customary practice of sending Joseph to find out what they were up to? If so—and I suspect so—this was a very sinister move on their part. And surprisingly, Jacob was not suspicious. Here then is the TWENTIETH question: if the brothers had not gone to Shechem, would there have been an opportunity for the brothers to do anything to Joseph? Not in Jacob's presence, which means they had to get him away from their father.

Now we come to the beginning of the story and must examine an account of misguided favoritism, overweening pride, jealousy building toward hatred, and a normally shrewd man inexplicably oblivious of what is going on between his sons, namely, the details of what brought Joseph's brothers to the point of wanting to kill him and finally selling him into slavery. The text traces ten movements:

1. Jacob's initial favoritism of Joseph
2. the former appointing the latter to supervise (the text allows for "shepherd") the rest of his sons
3. Joseph informing on his brothers
4. the brothers hatred of Joseph because Jacob loved him more than them
5. Joseph arrogantly (because he knew what the dream foretold) relating his first dream to his brothers (what it portended for them they correctly understood)
6. their hateful resolve in return
7. Joseph even more arrogantly reporting his second dream of domination, this time also over his father and acting mother (Rachel had died more than a decade earlier) to both his brothers and, quite impertinently, to his father (!)
8. Jacob's weak rebuke
9. the heated envy and jealousy of his brothers
10. the ambivalence of Jacob

Each of these has a similar counterfactual question connected to it: what if had not happened this way? Would the next movement have taken place? The answer seems to be: no.

In summary, the answer to all of the questions is: no. So, these eventualities and the twenty discussed above establish a cause and effect chain, which had to be exactly as it was. The eventualities of the Joseph story take the family on a wild ride, with unexpected twists and turns, but rather than these eventualities careened down through time, seemingly unstoppable and nevertheless somehow accomplishing YHWH's purpose; they are careering down through time, unstoppable but under His control, orchestrated by Him to accomplish His purposes.

This concludes our cursory examination of the various theoretical understandings of cause and effect. Having bridged the gap between theory and application by examining the Joseph story, we now turn to consider how these concepts can inform our understanding of the semantic relations between verb/verb phrases in the Hebrew text. Our particular focus will be on *wayyiqtol* sequences.

(d) *Cause* versus *Serialation* within *Wayyiqtol* Chains. *Result* is not an uncommon *coherence relation* in *wayyiqtol* sequences. It is clearly seen at the creation of man; the creation of woman; and the temptation, Fall, and its aftermath. Furthermore, in these early texts it is theologically crucial to distinguish *Serialation* and *Result*. We will look at each of these three blocks separately, starting with Genesis 2:7, with the *wayyiqtols* in bold-face and continuing the *ad seriatim* designations of the verbs begun in the text above.

THE CREATION OF MAN; THE PLANTING OF THE GARDEN; THE
PLACEMENT OF MAN IN THE GARDEN (GENESIS 2:7–15)

וַיִּיצֶר יְהוָה אֱלֹהִים אֶת־הָאָדָם עָפָר מִן־הָאֲדָמָה **וַיִּפַּח** בְּאַפָּיו נִשְׁמַת
חַיִּים **וַיְהִי** הָאָדָם לְנֶפֶשׁ חַיָּה:

[8] **וַיִּטַּע** יְהוָה אֱלֹהִים גַּן־בְּעֵדֶן מִקֶּדֶם **וַיָּשֶׂם** שָׁם אֶת־הָאָדָם אֲשֶׁר יָצָר:

[9] **וַיַּצְמַח** יְהוָה אֱלֹהִים מִן־הָאֲדָמָה כָּל־עֵץ נֶחְמָד לְמַרְאֶה וְטוֹב לְמַאֲכָל
וְעֵץ הַחַיִּים בְּתוֹךְ הַגָּן וְעֵץ הַדַּעַת טוֹב וָרָע:

[10] וְנָהָר יֹצֵא מֵעֵדֶן לְהַשְׁקוֹת אֶת־הַגָּן וּמִשָּׁם יִפָּרֵד וְהָיָה לְאַרְבָּעָה
רָאשִׁים:

[11] שֵׁם הָאֶחָד פִּישׁוֹן הוּא הַסֹּבֵב אֵת כָּל־אֶרֶץ הַחֲוִילָה אֲשֶׁר־שָׁם הַזָּהָב:

[12] וּזֲהַב הָאָרֶץ הַהִוא טוֹב שָׁם הַבְּדֹלַח וְאֶבֶן הַשֹּׁהַם:

[13] וְשֵׁם־הַנָּהָר הַשֵּׁנִי גִּיחוֹן הוּא הַסּוֹבֵב אֵת כָּל־אֶרֶץ כּוּשׁ:

[14] וְשֵׁם הַנָּהָר הַשְּׁלִישִׁי חִדֶּקֶל הוּא הַהֹלֵךְ קִדְמַת אַשּׁוּר וְהַנָּהָר הָרְבִיעִי
הוּא פְרָת:

[15] **וַיִּקַּח** יְהוָה אֱלֹהִים אֶת־הָאָדָם **וַיַּנִּחֵהוּ** בְגַן־עֵדֶן לְעָבְדָהּ וּלְשָׁמְרָהּ:

YHWH God [i]**formed** the man out of dust from the ground. He [j]**blew** into his nostrils living breath. He [k]**became** a living being. YHWH God [l]**planted** a garden in Eden in the east. He [m]**placed** there the man that He had formed. YHWH God [n]**caused to sprout** from the ground every tree praiseworthy in appearance and good for food [[about the tree of life and the knowledge of

good and evil and the rivers of Eden]].[2:15] YHWH God °**took** the man and
ᵖ**caused him to rest** in the Garden of Eden to work it and keep it.

The relation between (**i**) and (**j**) is clearly *Serialation*: YHWH's action in (**i**)
did not cause Him to do (**j**) but provided the occasion for it. On the other
hand YHWH's action in (**j**) *caused* (**k**).

The relationship of (**l**) to the previous *wayyiqtols* is not immediately
obvious. But after we consider the role the garden plays in the larger narrative
(see Stroup's **Chapter 13** for an expansion of this), we recognize the garden
has no purpose or reason for existence apart from YHWH's purposes for man.
The praiseworthiness of its trees and the fact that they were edible were for *his*
appreciation and provided *his* food, respectively. Moreover, both of these will
figure prominently in his temptation and Fall. Thus, the **coherence relation**
in question is *Serialation*. Why this and not *Result*? Because the quickening of
man did not *cause* YHWH to plant the garden, in exclusion of all possible other
things He might have done. It did however furnish the circumstances, which
according to YHWH's plan and purposes, made the garden necessary.

Now let us consider (**l**) and (**m**). Certainly, YHWH's planting of the
garden did not *cause* Him to place man there. But it is equally certain that
YHWH could not place man in a garden that did not exist. The planting of the
garden brought it into a state of existence, which could then be acted upon
by Him: placing man there. Hence, this is a case of *Serialation*. But, which
came first: the garden or the man? If we assume the text is iconic, we will say
that man was created first. But if so, where did YHWH place man when He
created him? To be sure there could have been an intermediate place, but
it is more reasonable that YHWH created the garden first. Why then is the
creation of man reported first? I would answer: to show his preeminence in
the created order.

With (**n**) we encounter two quandries: where is it connected in addition
to the usual how is it connected? At first glance it seems that it is not
connected to (**m**) but rather to (**l**): the report of placement of man appears
to interrupt the logical flow from the planting of the garden to causing trees
to grow. But the larger narrative will prove that this conclusion is too hastily
drawn. What matter the trees, their appearance, their consumability, and the
identification of the two special trees without man being there? Furthermore,
the literary device of interchange in the text (man garden man garden man)
invites us to compare or contrast the two. Looked at from these perspectives
(**n**) is connected to (**m**), but this does not negate that, as observed, it is also
connected to (**l**). How is it connected? According to the argument above the
coherence relation between (**m**) and (**n**) is more than just *Serialation*. YHWH's

placing man in the garden is the *reason* He caused the trees to grow, and so forth. And what **coherence relation** links (l) and (n)? (Delayed) *Elaboration*—which we will examine closely in **Paragraph 4** of this sub-subsection.

Wayyiqtols (o) and (p) come after a hiatus of five verses evincing disjunctive constructions (clauses not beginning with verbs, which give background or parenthetic information) describing the rivers of the garden, and coupled together are a recapitulation of 2:8b. It is not a mere repetition of it, however. It has three significant differences/additions: the addition of לקח (*lqḥ*) "take" or "receive"; the change from שׂים (*śîm*) "give" or "place" to the *Hiphil* (causative) of נוח (*nûḥ*) "rest"; and man being given a dual purpose for being in the garden. In order to properly understand the import of these changes, we must understand what they meant to Moses' readers. This will take us afield of **coherence relations** for a while, but it will be worth it, as the brief departure will pay a handsome dividend in understanding. Indeed, without these excurses we will misunderstand the text, because we would have failed to grasp the richness of these roots; and, as a result, we would analyze its **coherence relations** incorrectly.

The first of these roots draws our attention in that (o) is not needed for the restatement of 2:8b. Prompting the question: why is it here? The root is very common in both senses of the term, occuring 976 times in BH (BibleWorks 7.0), and usually considered to be rather prosaic. But not here. Appearing here for the first time in BH, it introduces the theme of YHWH's intimate relationship with His creature who is to reflect Him. Consequently, it figures prominently in the succeeding narrative: positively in the creation of the woman and the institution of marriage (2:21–23), YHWH taking Enoch (5:24), and Noah taking in the dove (8:9); negatively at the Fall and its aftermath (3:6, 19, 22, 23), the murder of Abel (4:11), Lamech (in Cain's line) taking wives (4:19), and the fallen angels taking wives (6:2).

The second change is also intriguing. Here we ask different questions: why the change? Why is there recapitulation at all? The replacement root נוח (*wayyiqtol* [p]) means "rest," which is a powerful theme in Scripture as a whole from its first mention, here, through Isaiah 28:12 (twice), Christ's powerful invitation (Mt 11:28–29), and up to the ten occurrences in Hebrews 3–4, which refer back to Psalm 95:11, which in turn goes back to Israel's recalcitrance at Kadesh Barnea, which precipitated the wilderness wanderings. The verb occurs once more in Genesis 1–11: the verb used to describe the grounding of the Ark (8:4). As YHWH caused man to rest in the first place he would occupy after He created him, so the Ark came to rest on the first place to be occupied after the un-creation/re-creation of the world, which YHWH effected by the Flood. But it is the proper name derived from this root, which dominates the primeval history, *Noah*. His name occurs thirty-nine times in his genealogy (which includes the Flood narrative and its aftermath), twice in chapter 10, twice in Isaiah 54:9, twice in Ezekiel 14 as one of the three most virtuous men, and back to genealogical status in 1 Chronicles 1:4. In the New Testament he is mentioned as part of the Messianic line in the Lukan genealogy of Christ (3:36), twice in the Olivet Discourse as the quintessential picture of apathy before judgment (Mt 24:37–38; Lk 17:26–27), in the hall-of-fame of faith (Heb 11:7) and twice in the Petrine corpus (1 Pt 3:20; 2 Pt 2:5). And finally, the third change established man's purposeful existence.

Equipped with this understanding of (o) and (p), we are now positioned to discuss their *coherence relations*. As a verb freighted with the concepts of marriage and intimacy, (o) is connected to the manner of the creation of man, the planting of the garden, the placing of man there, and the purposeful fructification of the garden: all artful, personal, intimate, and purposeful acts of the Creator toward man. At the same time the description of the garden is replete with superlatives, showing the beauty, splendor, and wonder of the place where YHWH placed man—what a gift for the one He would take. Looked at from this perspective, we realize that YHWH's planned "taking" is the *reason* for what comes before. In this case the second verb is the *cause*, not the *result* of the first verb. This is the inverse of *Result*. This is *Cause*.

This type of *coherence relation* between verb clauses and the eventualities they represent is determined from the *intention* of one of the participants in the sequence of eventualities depicted in the account *to achieve a certain result*. Consequently, the participant does what he does in *anticipation* of the particular eventuality occurring—as when a couple expecting their first child prepares in advance for the blessed homecoming of their yet-to-be-born child by buying a crib, baby clothes, stroller, and so forth. I call the analogous manifestation of this scenario in discourse an *anticipated result coherence relation* (*ARCR*), which incorporates the anticipated result causing an eventuality (*ARC*); the anticipated result being readied for by that same eventuality (*ARR*); and the realization of the anticipated result (*RAR*). In returning to the domestic illustration, the last two would be the preparation of the child's birth followed in time by the birth and the bringing-home of the baby. This can be generalized to succeeding verbs (V_1 and V_2) in text, representing initial and final eventualities, respectively, with *ARC*, *ARR*, and *RAR* working together to produce the following verb sequence/eventuality sequence/time profile: *first*, the anticipation of the final eventuality (represented by V_2), which causes the initial eventuality (represented by V₁); *second*, the occurrence of the initial eventuality (represented by V₁), which prepares for the final eventuality (represented by V₂); and, *third*, the occurrence of the final eventuality (V₂). The effect of the presence of an *ARCR* in a text is that the verb depicting the anticipated eventuality follows the verb depicting the preparation for that event; and, the anticipation of the eventuality represented by the second verb is the cause for the eventuality represented by the first verb, even though the realization of the eventuality represented by the second verb succeeds that of the eventuality represented by the first verb. The latter, for **(o)** is the *realization* of the "taking" following the planting and preparation of the garden. The keyword here is "prepared." So, in this sense **(o)** relates to the previous as *Serialation*. The analysis of **(p)** follows naturally. Because YHWH took, in the sense we have outlined above, of course He wanted to give man a place of rest—and still does (Mt 11:28–29; and the ten passages in Hebrews 3–4). And, so, this is another instance of *Result*. But this is not all. Since **(p)** is a recapitulation of **(m)**, it is also an instance of *Elaboration*.

THE CREATION OF THE WOMAN (GENESIS 2:18–23)

וַיֹּ֨אמֶר֙ יְהוָ֣ה אֱלֹהִ֔ים לֹא־ט֛וֹב הֱי֥וֹת הָֽאָדָ֖ם לְבַדּ֑וֹ אֶֽעֱשֶׂהּ־לּ֥וֹ עֵ֖זֶר כְּנֶגְדּֽוֹ׃

וַיִּצֶר֩ יְהֹוָ֨ה אֱלֹהִ֜ים מִן־הָֽאֲדָמָ֗ה כָּל־חַיַּ֤ת הַשָּׂדֶה֙ וְאֵת֙ כָּל־ע֣וֹף הַשָּׁמַ֔יִם וַיָּבֵא֙ אֶל־הָ֣אָדָ֔ם לִרְא֖וֹת מַה־יִּקְרָא־ל֑וֹ וְכֹל֩ אֲשֶׁ֨ר יִקְרָא־ל֧וֹ הָֽאָדָ֛ם נֶ֥פֶשׁ חַיָּ֖ה ה֥וּא שְׁמֽוֹ׃

וַיִּקְרָ֨א הָֽאָדָ֜ם שֵׁמ֗וֹת לְכָל־הַבְּהֵמָה֙ וּלְע֣וֹף הַשָּׁמַ֔יִם וּלְכֹ֖ל חַיַּ֣ת הַשָּׂדֶ֑ה וּלְאָדָ֕ם לֹֽא־מָצָ֥א עֵ֖זֶר כְּנֶגְדּֽוֹ׃

וַיַּפֵּל֩ יְהֹוָ֨ה אֱלֹהִ֧ים ׀ תַּרְדֵּמָ֛ה עַל־הָאָדָ֖ם וַיִּישָׁ֑ן וַיִּקַּ֗ח אַחַת֙ מִצַּלְעֹתָ֔יו וַיִּסְגֹּ֥ר בָּשָׂ֖ר תַּחְתֶּֽנָּה׃

וַיִּ֩בֶן֩ יְהֹוָ֨ה אֱלֹהִ֧ים ׀ אֶֽת־הַצֵּלָ֛ע אֲשֶׁר־לָקַ֥ח מִן־הָֽאָדָ֖ם לְאִשָּׁ֑ה וַיְבִאֶ֖הָ אֶל־הָֽאָדָֽם׃

וַיֹּאמֶר֮ הָֽאָדָם֒ זֹ֣את הַפַּ֗עַם עֶ֚צֶם מֵֽעֲצָמַ֔י וּבָשָׂ֖ר מִבְּשָׂרִ֑י לְזֹאת֙ יִקָּרֵ֣א אִשָּׁ֔ה כִּ֥י מֵאִ֖ישׁ לֻֽקְחָה־זֹּֽאת׃

YHWH God ⁹**said,** "The man being alone is not good. I will make for him a helper corresponding to him." YHWH God ʳ**formed** from the ground [[all the animals and birds]]. He ˢ**brought** (each) to the man to see what he would name it [[These would be their names]]. The man ᵗ**called out** names [[for all the animals and birds]]. But as for Adam, he did not ᵘ**find** a helper corresponding to himself. YHWH God **caused to** ᵛ**fall** on the man a deep slumber. He ʷ**slept.** He ˣ**took** one of his ribs. He ʸ**closed up** the flesh in its place. YHWH God ᶻ**built** the rib that He had taken into a woman. He ᵃᵃ**brought** her to the man. The man ᵃᵇ**said** "[[his poetic rejoicing over her and naming of her]]."

The first verb in this block, **(q)**, is a verb introducing the internal speech of YHWH, His thoughts. We can tell that He is not talking to the man, because he is talking about the man. The subsequent speech is a continuation in a sense of a larger speech, which begins with YHWH's commands and prohibitions to the man whom He has taken and caused to rest in the garden to accomplish specific tasks and whom he will test in regards to eating from the trees of the garden. This is His first speech to man. By nature, the prohibition, ". . . but from the tree of the knowledge of good and evil, you must not eat from it . . .," contains a negative particle, as does the silent continuation of the speech: ". . . is not good." This quality of continuation unaffected by causation suggests that we are looking at *Serialation*. But is this all? And is this even right? Let us consider again the relationship of **(q)** with the previous verses from the purview of the content of the internal speech: the problem is that the man being alone is not good; the solution is the making of a helper corresponding to him. This prompts two related questions: why is man being alone not good? And how does the presence of a helper address the problem of man's aloneness? The conventional approach to answering these questions is to see YHWH's evaluation in Genesis 2:18 as the beginning of a new section on the inauguration of marriage. Although this analysis is *possible*, it semantically severs the pronouncement from the previous verse; thereby, potentially introducing incoherence. I am persuaded that a better approach—the key to answering these questions—is to connect YHWH's evaluation of the man's situation with the man's responsibilities (2:15) and the dire consequences of violating the prohibitions (2:18). The helper then is not to be just a general helper for the man but more: a helper in *those specific areas the text indicates he will need help*. Seen from this perspective, it is clear that we are looking at *Result* here.

At this point, as readers, we expect, because of the urgency of the situation, YHWH to make the helper. Even more—we expect that YHWH would *want* to make the helper immediately. But, literarily, He does not. And, historically, He did not. Why not? In **coherence relations** terms, we expect the relation between **(q)** and **(r)** to be *Result*—but, it is not. This is called *violation of expectation*.[34] Instead YHWH tasks the man with naming

---

34. (Kehler 2004, 247–48). Originally coined by (Hobbs 1990). This obtains when the reader expects Q because of P, but instead the text has ¬Q. The example given by Kehler is: "George [Bush] wanted to satisfy the right wing of his party, but he refused to introduce an initiative to allow government funding for faith-based charitable organizations." Also see **Sub-subsection 2.2.2 Paragraph 3** for full discussion and biblical examples, among which, particularly striking is Haman not being allowed to impale Mordecai as he desperately and hatefully wanted to do.

the land animals and birds. Why this? How is this connected with providing the man a helper for the purposes outlined above? More so than with straightforward *Result* and *Cause*, *violation of expectation* and its counterpart, *denial of preventer*,[35] stops us in our tracks. We cannot go on until the why-and-how questions are answered. And we will do so after we step sideways to examine the merits of that old canard concerning the putative contradiction between the order of creation here (supposedly, man before animals) and in Genesis 1:20–27 (animals before man),[36] which arises because of this very *violation of expectation*.

Their[37] argument (to which I comment within square brackets) goes something like this: The order of creation in Genesis 1:20–27 is creatures of the water and birds *before* land animals and man, because the former were created on the fifth day and the latter, on the sixth day [so far, so good]. Moreover, according to Genesis 1:24–27, God created man *after* the animals [interpreting all the *wayyiqtols* as marking temporal sequentiality]. But [supposedly] Genesis 2:19 recounts the creation of land animals and birds as occurring after (not before) the creation of man, which is recounted in Genesis 2:7. Thus, they posit a contradiction.

Their argument for the temporal sequence of 2:7 and 2:19 is a logical syllogism. Their major premise is the categorical proposition that all sequential *wayyiqtols* represent temporally sequential eventualities. Their minor premise is that the *wayyiqtols* in 2:7 and 2:19 are sequential. The logically valid conclusion they draw is that these *wayyiqtols* represent temporally sequential eventualities. But is this deduction *sound*? It would be, if both premises were *true*, but the major premise is *not*: that sequential *wayyiqtols* represent temporally sequential eventualities is an unfounded assumption. Consequently, the deduction is unsound. These sequential *wayyiqtols* do not necessarily represent temporally sequential eventualities. This text therefore is not necessarily saying that the creation of the animals followed the creation of man. We can see then that our understanding that sequential *wayyiqtols* do not necessarily indicate temporally sequential eventualities obviates resorting to allegory or some other halting explanation,

---

35. (Kehler 2004, 248). This situation occurs when the reader does *not* expect Q, because of P, but instead the text has Q. An example using the President again is: "George refused to introduce an initiative to allow government funding of faith-based charitable organizations even though he wanted to satisfy the right wing of his party." Again, see **Subsubsection 2.2.2 Paragraph 3** for more. The parade example is Haman being forced to honor Mordecai, which is the last thing he would have wanted to do.

36. *Passim.* This is a standard argument advanced to disprove the historical reliability of the text.

37. "Their" is not specific; it refers to the propounders of the argument in general.

which is the common response to the argument outlined above. Nevertheless, the different order here can be explained. In 1:20–25 the creation of the animals is not connected to the creation of man, as if they were created for an independent purpose apart from man. But that is not the case here. In this chapter, in which man is at the center—as opposed to chapter one, in which creation of man, male and female, is the climax of creation—the order makes it clear that YHWH created the animals for man, so that he could rule over them and dominate them. His naming of them is his first act of asserting his authority over them as king of the earth.

But, unfortunately, this new understanding does not help us answer the questions posed above. What *does* is to recognize that albeit the creation and subsequent naming of the animals appears from a linguistic perspective to be a *violation of expectation*, further thought proves it not to be; rather, it is an essential part of YHWH preparing man to receive his helper. Why is this so? For two reasons. First, he needs to be confirmed as king of the earth, with the animals as his subjects, because his helper will rule with him as queen and at the same time be under his authority. Second, YHWH created man to be an independent free agent. He wanted man to draw his own conclusions and make his own decisions; He did not want to make his decisions for him. So, rather than YHWH telling man that he needed a helper, He took man through a process, which would convince him that he needed a helper. The narrator says, "But as for Adam, he did not find [obviously, among the animals] a helper corresponding to himself." Moreover, Adam's reaction to seeing her, "This one, at last, bone from my bones and flesh from my flesh . . .," indicates that he was looking for one corresponding to himself.

The *coherence relations* for the next seven verbs are quite straightforward. Because Adam did not find a helper corresponding to himself, YHWH now begins the process of providing the helper for him. In the narrative, YHWH actually provides the helper in (aa); whereas, verbs (v) through (z) prepare for this presentation. All along YHWH's ultimate goal was to present the helper to the man. So, all of YHWH's previous actions following His speech, in which He declared that He was going to make a helper corresponding to him (2:18), therefore, were required to accomplish this goal. Thus, (aa) is to (v)–(z) an *Anticipated Result* **coherence relation**.

Putting the man into a deep sleep was the first step in this preparation, making the **coherence relation** between verb (v) and the previous verbs *Result*. The relation between (w) and (v) is also obvious: "He fell asleep" following "YHWH God caused a deep sleep to fall" is *Result*. Now that Adam was asleep, YHWH could perform the surgery. Thus, (w) provides the occasion, but not the cause, for **(x)**. Clearly, this is *Serialation*. The next **coherence relation** is *Result*, because the surgery necessitated closing the flesh afterwards **(y)**. "YHWH God built a woman" **(z)** is connected to taking the rib **(x)** (not to closing up the flesh **[y]**), by *Serialation*; in that circumstances, not cause, are provided by the first verb. The second to last **coherence relation** pertains to "brought her to the man"**(aa)**, which was YHWH's ultimate *purpose*, as if He were saying, "Adam, here is the helper you need. I made her for you." So this is *ARCR*, as mentioned above. Finally, there is Adam's *reaction* in **(ab)**, a spontaneous eruption of joy, which is a striking example of *Result*.

The Fall and its Aftermath (Genesis 3:1–8)

וְהַנָּחָשׁ הָיָה עָרוּם מִכֹּל חַיַּת הַשָּׂדֶה אֲשֶׁר עָשָׂה יְהוָה אֱלֹהִים **וַיֹּאמֶר**
אֶל־הָאִשָּׁה   אַף כִּי־אָמַר אֱלֹהִים לֹא תֹאכְלוּ מִכֹּל עֵץ הַגָּן:

2 **וַתֹּאמֶר** הָאִשָּׁה אֶל־הַנָּחָשׁ מִפְּרִי עֵץ־הַגָּן נֹאכֵל:

3 וּמִפְּרִי הָעֵץ אֲשֶׁר בְּתוֹךְ־הַגָּן אָמַר אֱלֹהִים לֹא תֹאכְלוּ מִמֶּנּוּ וְלֹא תִגְּעוּ
בּוֹ פֶּן־תְּמֻתוּן:

4 **וַיֹּאמֶר** הַנָּחָשׁ אֶל־הָאִשָּׁה לֹא־מוֹת תְּמֻתוּן:

5 כִּי יֹדֵעַ אֱלֹהִים כִּי בְּיוֹם אֲכָלְכֶם מִמֶּנּוּ וְנִפְקְחוּ עֵינֵיכֶם וִהְיִיתֶם כֵּאלֹהִים
יֹדְעֵי טוֹב וָרָע:

6 **וַתֵּרֶא** הָאִשָּׁה כִּי טוֹב הָעֵץ לְמַאֲכָל וְכִי תַאֲוָה־הוּא לָעֵינַיִם וְנֶחְמָד הָעֵץ
לְהַשְׂכִּיל וַתִּקַּח מִפִּרְיוֹ וַתֹּאכַל וַתִּתֵּן גַּם־לְאִישָׁהּ עִמָּהּ וַיֹּאכַל:

7 **וַתִּפָּקַחְנָה** עֵינֵי שְׁנֵיהֶם **וַיֵּדְעוּ** כִּי עֵירֻמִּם הֵם **וַיִּתְפְּרוּ** עֲלֵה תְאֵנָה **וַיַּעֲשׂוּ**
לָהֶם חֲגֹרֹת:

8 **וַיִּשְׁמְעוּ** אֶת־קוֹל יְהוָה אֱלֹהִים מִתְהַלֵּךְ בַּגָּן לְרוּחַ הַיּוֹם **וַיִּתְחַבֵּא** הָאָדָם
וְאִשְׁתּוֹ מִפְּנֵי יְהוָה אֱלֹהִים בְּתוֹךְ עֵץ הַגָּן:

Now the serpent was shrewder than any wild animal, which YHWH God had made. He [ac]**said** to the woman, "Did God really say, 'You shall not eat from any tree of the garden'?" The woman [ad]**said** to the serpent, "From the fruit of the trees of the garden we may eat. But from the fruit of the tree which is in the middle of the garden, God said, 'You shall not eat from it, nor touch it lest you die.'" The serpent [ae]**said** to the woman, "You will not certainly die, because God knows that when you eat from it, your eyes will open and you will be as God, knowing good and evil." The woman [af]**saw** that the tree was good for food, and that it was desirable to the eyes and praiseworthy for prudence leading to success. She [ag]**took** from its fruit. She [ah]**ate**. She [ai]**gave** also to her husband with her. He [aj]**ate**. The eyes of the two of them [ak]**opened**. They [al]**knew** that they were naked. They [am]**sewed** fig leaves. They [an]**made** wraps for themselves. They [ao]**heard** the sound of YHWH God walking in the garden in the wind of the storm.[38] The man and his wife [ap]**frantically hid** from YHWH God amongst the trees of the garden.

This text comprises fourteen *wayyiqtols*, which relate the tragic account of what Milton called *Paradise Lost*. The first three verbs of this block are *wayyiqtols* from אמר (*'mr*), "say," introducing three speeches: the serpent's question to the woman (ac); followed by her answer (ad); and finally the serpent's response (ae). The remaining eleven *wayyiqtols* represent actions, culminating with the man's defiant act in eating from the forbidden tree (aj) and its aftermath.

This text evokes many questions—only some of which admit answers. Why did the serpent address the woman rather than the man? Why did she offer the fruit to him after she had disobeyed? And, tragically, why did he eat? Why did the man permit the interaction to continue, when he heard the woman give arguably erroneous answers? Why were her answers incorrect at all? Why did the man not stop her from taking and eating the fruit?

---

38. "In the wind of the storm" is not the usual understanding of the Hebrew here. רוּחַ הַיּוֹם only occurs in this text. The usual rendering is something like "cool of the day." I will return to considering the merit of this usual understanding, but first I want to argue for the superiority of the former translation, which is based on a compelling idea suggested by M. Tsevat in a classroom setting at Hebrew Union College–Jewish Institute of Religion. Tsevat argued that the Hebrew is unusual, if the words are understood in the usual way. "Wind of the day"—whatever that might mean—does not seem to fit the context of YHWH coming in judgment, which immediately commenced after He confronted the sinful pair. Tsevat proposed that יוֹם is not "day," but a homonym supported by an Akkadian cognate *ūm(u)*, which means "storm." There is much to recommend this theory. First, it is a lexical possibility. There are three homonyms in Akkadian *ūm(u)* A, "day"; *ūm(u)* B, "storm," and *ūm(u)* C, "mythical lion" (*Akkadisches Handwörterbuch* (AHw), 1420). AHw cites texts in which *ūm(u)* B is used of demons. Moreover, it is frequently connected with the gods. Second, the phonological correspondence is correct. Inasmuch as *ūm(u)* A appears in BH as יוֹם, supports the idea that *ūm(u)* B would appear in BH as יוֹם. Third, it fits better in the context. Here is where I would like to give a word or two on the usual rendering of this text vis-à-vis Tsevat's idea. The man and woman's reaction to hide themselves fits better with a reaction of terror, knowing that YHWH is coming to judge them than that He is just out for a pleasant stroll in a time of the day when the wind is blowing, cooling off the day. The usual translation also appears anachronistic and geographically misplaced, drawing on ideas of the weather patterns in the eastern Mediterranean, which produce cooling winds in the evening at higher elevations. But let us not forget that Moses was a Hebrew raised as an Egyptian—trained to be pharaoh. His people lived in Egypt. Would they have even understood an eastern Mediterranean meteorological reference? Would Moses have used one as a result?

Only the first of these questions can be addressed by an analysis of **coherence relations**. By approaching the woman and manipulating her to the point that not only did she disobey YHWH but also provided the opportunity for her husband to do so as well, the serpent turned the hierarchy YHWH had designed on its head. His created order was Himself–man–woman–animals. The serpent inverted this to animal–woman–man–God, and even more diabolically, turned the one whom YHWH had created to help man *not* to sin into the one who helped him *to* sin—seemingly, a momentary, devilish victory.

When taken as a whole then, we can see in this block of verses that although the man's disobedience to YHWH's prohibition **(aj)** follows a sequence of seven *wayyiqtols*, in particular, **she gave (ai)**, we do not have here a case of mere *Result*. In the largest sense the serpent's nefarious purpose to have the man disobey **(aj)** is an *Anticipated Result* **coherence relation**, which caused him to approach the woman in the first place.

We begin with the three speeches. The nature of dialogue is that interlocutors respond to each other in sequence; thereby, producing an interchange structure. But whether the speech-response is *Serialation* or *Result* depends upon the *content* of each speech. On the one hand, if a speech triggers a response, if the listener feels compelled to respond, if he has no choice but to respond, its content is the *cause* of that response; hence, the **coherence relation** is *Result*. If, on the other hand, the listener does not feel compelled, but rather chooses to answer, being in no way forced to (implying that he had a choice), the speaker merely creates the circumstances to which the listener chooses to respond, in which case the **coherence relation** is *Serialation*.

The response is not always another speech. It can also be silence, action brought on by the speech (**[af]** through **[ai]**), or something entirely unrelated. Our concern here is the nature of the second of these applied to the chain of eventualities related in this text. Is the action caused (that is, no choice) or chosen (but not compelled)? The answer to this question determines culpability. If it is the former, then culpability is questionable; if the latter, guilt is established. In this text therefore *Result* or *Serialation* is crucial!

We have already considered the first speech above, recognizing that it was designed to end up in the man's disobedience. To this we can add that it also would have been a vital part of the serpent's scheme that he not force the man to disobey so that he had no choice but to eat. Rather, his eating must be entirely a free choice. Anything else would jeopardize the plan.

The serpent most skillfully worked to achieve his desired end. He deceived the woman. He provoked her to answer. He lied to her. He told her half-truths. She believed him rather than YHWH. She ate. She gave. He now had the man where he wanted him: caught between choosing YHWH or choosing his wife. But the Evil One could go no further. He had to wait for man to choose. Not knowing the future he had to wait and see if his plan had worked . . . . All creation held its breath . . . . He ate . . . . All creation groaned and continues to . . . . Everything changed . . . . Death began its reign . . . . And YHWH initiated His plan for restoration.

In light of the discussion above the **coherence relations** are clear. Since the serpent's question (ac) was so outrageously false, it *caused* the woman to respond (ad). This is *Result*. Of course her response did not cause him to dissemble (ae); rather, his initial question (ac) and his response (ae) were *caused by the anticipated result* of the fall of the man (aj). The woman's reaction to the serpent's response is interesting, because only the last idea she realized, "that [the fruit] was praised for making one successful," echoed the serpent's words; the first two things she realized derived from her own observations. But she would not have been thinking along these lines at all had the serpent not launched his verbal attack on her. Although, he did not compel her to think this way, which clearly would be *Result*; his deception, nevertheless, is responsible for producing a mindset in her (a mental circumstance as it were), which was inclined to questioning, distrust, and disobedience. Hence, I think that the **coherence relation** in question is *Serialation*. This brings us to her taking and eating. The mindset conveyed in (af) *caused* her to take (ag) in order that she could eat (ah). This ensemble of eventualities therefore is another example of *Anticipated Result*. But her next action, "she gave to her husband who was with her" (ai) is most perplexing. Why did she do this?

Prescinding from the real possibility that this was an irrational action—it certainly was wicked and cruel—and assuming that she had a motive, what might it have been? I suggest here two. The first of these could have come from her analysis of what had *not* happened after she had eaten of the fruit of the forbidden tree: she had not died. Thinking that nothing had happened to her when she ate, she might have reasoned that since the tempter's words, "You shall not certainly die," were apparently true, the rest of what he had intimated was apparently true also, namely that God was holding them back from being equal to Him. Moreover, since she had eaten, according to what the serpent had said, she was now as God—and she wanted this for her husband. The second possibility was that when nothing happened, she remembered the serpent had said, ". . . when you

[mp] eat . . . ." That is, the transformation would not occur until *both* ate. She had to get her husband to eat in order for her to become as God. Both of these are examples of *Anticipated Result* of the "eye opening" (**ak**) that the serpent had assured them would come.

Now we come to the terrible words, "he ate" (**aj**). The connection to the previous verb is only *Serialation*: her giving did not *compel* him to eat; rather, it provided the opportunity to eat. Why did he eat? In short, he chose her over God.

This brings us to the aftermath of the Fall, leading up to YHWH's confrontation of the man. This involves six verb phrases. The ***coherence relation*** linking the first of these, "the eyes of the two of the them opened," (**ak**) with the preceding verbs is obviously *Result*, because their eyes would not have opened had the man not eaten. It is not just *Serialation*, because the man's eating of the forbidden fruit *necessarily* effected the change in man.

The ***coherence relation*** for the second of these verb phrases, "they knew that they were naked," (**al**) is not as straightforward, because we must first determine what the *Niphal* of פקח (*pqh*) "eyes) opened" (**ak**) in the previous VP means. Consequently, we must briefly survey the usage of this root.

Of the twenty-one occurrences of the root, three occur in the *Niphal* (here; Gn 3:5; Is 35:5) and pertain to becoming sighted, whereas before there had been no sight (ethical in the Genesis 3 passages; physical in the Isaiah); the rest are in the *Qal*. Only two of these, the account of Elisha raising the Shunammite's son from the dead (2 Kgs 4:35) and the wealthy man opening his eyes after a night of sleep only to find his fortune gone (Jb 27:19), concern actual *opening* of the eyes. The balance refer to YHWH enabling the physically blind to see (Ps 146:8; Is 42:7), restoring the sight of those supernaturally blinded (2 Kgs 6:20 [twice]), giving the ability to see what was not seen before (Gn 21:19), or permitting a glimpse into the supernatural realm (2 Kgs 6:17 [twice]); to YHWH inspecting and evaluating a man (Jb 14:3) and overseeing and protecting His people (2 Kgs 19:16; Is 37:17; Jer 32:19; Zec 12:4; Dn 9:18); to a man enjoined to be alert (Prv 20:13); and strangely enough, once, to the ability to hear (Is 42:20).

In light of the above overview, the verb phrase in question in context means that the pair entered into a state with the potential of a certain type of sightedness, which they had not been in before.

This sightedness was not physical. Before the Fall, having eyes, they would have seen that they were naked compared to the other land animals and birds: the former covered with fur; the latter, with plumage. They might have wondered why, but it did not affect them: they had no shame.

What this text says is that they *knew* that they were *naked*. Stating the obvious—it does not say this earlier. Moreover, the earlier text does not say that they could not *see* that they were naked—they certainly could. And although it does not say that they did not *know* that they were naked, did they? In sum, no comment at all is made about their perception of their condition; rather, it is recounted as a fact. But after the Fall knowledge was tainted by suspicion and fear, as can be seen later in the text. What we can deduce from the text and the meaning of פקח is that this knowledge of their nakedness is something they had not had before. This suggests that in this admittedly difficult text, this is a case of *Result*. Notice, furthermore, that the text does not say that they were ashamed of themselves or each other because of this knowledge; nevertheless, this is often inferred. Is this inference sound?

The text states plainly that they were not ashamed of their nakedness before the Fall. Most often it is inferred that after the man ate, however, they were. But in what sense? Certainly, the Fall happened and nakedness as a reality, which produced no shame, was replaced by knowledge of nakedness, which produced a focused effort to cover themselves. Moreover, it is often reasoned that their shame for themselves and of each other moved them to cover themselves. But the text does not say this. What other reason would they have had for wanting to cover themselves? Again the answer is in the text. Although it is possible that their motivation for doing this was to address their shame at their nakedness in and of itself, the text suggests a better alternative. The following question will launch us toward the answer: whom did they think would see their nakedness? The animals? Possibly. Each other? Shame between a husband and wife? Or was it YHWH? I submit that it was the last: they were terrified at the prospect of the inevitable confrontation with their Creator, He whom they had flagrantly defied.

Consider their effort in preparing for this dreaded meeting. "They sewed fig leaves" (**am**) entails that they had the simulacrum of a needle and thread, which they had to manufacture from scratch. They sewed the fig leaves into a type of fig leaf fabric, which could then be made into clothing (**an**) that would cover their nakedness.

What are the ***coherence relations*** revolving around these two verbs? It depends on how the eventuality complex is viewed. Between the two, the fact that the fig leaf fabric was employed to make the tunics, but did not cause them to be made, causes us to realize that this is *Serialation*. But when the two are looked at as a whole, in light of the discussion above, their relation to the surrounding verbs is a classic example of *Anticipated Result*—

the hoped for result being that these coverings would allow them to weather the confrontation.

We now come to the last two verbs of this section. I believe that the following scenario ensued after the fallen pair made their make-shift clothing. No doubt, being fallen, they felt quite pleased with themselves at their accomplishment: two sets of clothing. They had deluded themselves into thinking that they would be able to proudly stand when YHWH came. But then they heard the sound of YHWH God coming in the wind of the storm (**ao**), and all their false bravado evaporated. When the man and his wife recognized that the confrontation was at hand, their expectation of the coverings being some kind of shield for them, was dashed by a terrifying reality: YHWH God was coming to judge them. As a result they hid themselves among the trees of the garden (**ap**). The verb, being in the *Hithpael*, speaks of the thoroughness born out of desperation with which they attempted to do this.

What is the *coherence relation* in this case? At first glance it seems that this is *Result*, because their fear when they heard YHWH coming caused them to hide. But they did not have to hide. It appears therefore in the final analysis that this is *Serialation*.

Serialation and its congener, *Result*, are the most common **coherence relations** in BH narrative, because the nature of narrative is to trace a plot, which unfolds in time. And because *wayyiqtols* carry this narrative, most often they convey *these* relations. Furthermore, they come first in the clause or sentence, thus establishing the normative word order in BH of verb-subject-object. But if the verb is negated or a referent other than that represented by the verb is fronted, it is emphasized (contrasted with others like it) and the verb is changed to *qatal*. Notwithstanding, *wayyiqtol* can express a turn in the story as well. It is in these contexts that the **coherence relation** *Contrast* is to be found. And, thus, it is to consider its proclivities that we shift our focus. And as we will see below, with this **coherence relation**, time does not progress.

(3) *Contrast (also Concession and Qualification)/Comparison.* This many-monikered relation is included as a separate **coherence relation** in most proposed sets; although it is *Serialation* or *Result/Cause* with a different semantic polarity.[39] It is an additive relation, not advancing the narrative any further, but clarifying it. Often in texts its presence

---

39. On positive and negative polarity in **coherence relations** see (Knott and Mellish 1996, 17–20).

is indicated by such adversatives as "but" or "nevertheless" or such concessives as "although" or "even though." But even if a text lacks these explicit markers, the following definition allows it to be identified: a VP raises expectations in the reader, which are contradicted or violated by the next VP. Thus, *Contrast* combines *Serialation* or *Result/Cause* with either *violation of expectations* or *denial of preventer*. In order to understand *Contrast*, then, we must both revisit the concepts of the former pair (introduced above) and dig much deeper into the concepts of the latter. These are our two goals in the discussion below.

Genesis 44:30 furnishes a parade example of *violation of expectation*. Joseph wanted to exhibit an impassive front before his brothers (in order to prolong the charade to accomplish his purposes—whatever they were); *nevertheless* (no explicit marker of this is in the text), when he saw his full brother, he rushed away from all of his brothers in an emotional state. An example of the *denial of preventer* comes from the grand irony in the Book of Esther, when Haman was forced to personally give the highest honors to Mordecai, whom he hated and wanted to kill.

In the following two sub-subsections we will intertwine the two goals mentioned above in the following way:

o   *Contrast* Explained: *Cause* and Effect Frustrated
o   *Contrast* Illustrated: Mordecai, Haman, Esther and the King

(a) *Contrast* Explained: *Cause* and Effect Frustrated. We must take a closer look at causality, because if it can be established, then the temporal flow is established as well: the time of the cause is before that of the effect, regardless of whether the cause precedes or follows the effect in the text, with the **coherence relations** of *Result* and *Cause*, respectively.

To aid us in our exploration of causality, we introduce at this point the concept of *necessary temporal precedence*, which will be developed in the course of the analysis. A second concept we will need for our analysis is *triggering*.

Aristotle understood four types of causes: material, formal, efficient, and final. But for our purposes we will look at causality in terms of seven contingencies: CAPABILITY, OPPORTUNITY, TELEOLOGY (purpose), MORALITY, PERMISSION, CONSEQUENCES, and REASONABLENESS.

Of these capability and opportunity are indispensable for human-centered actions to occur, that is, something cannot happen unless someone has the capability to do it or the opportunity to do it. But although these are *necessary*, they are not *sufficient*.

If an action is at cross purposes to the human agent (but this can be overcome by external forces), considered immoral by him (although he can do the action in spite of this), permission to do it is denied to him (he can defy the prohibition), consequences are deemed too grave, or the action is seen as unreasonable, then the action will not happen unless there is intervention and interdiction from outside.

In the discussion below we are looking at eventualities that are linked with verbs: Eventuality 1 and Eventuality 2. We will delve into these seven factors, which can frustrate cause and effect. To help us do so, we will enlist the aid of the playground trio as needs be.

CAPABILITY may be defined as follows: Eventuality 2 *cannot* happen until Eventuality 1 occurs. This is further divided into two types: Eventuality 1 triggers Eventuality 2, and Eventuality 1 does not necessarily trigger Eventuality 2.

The first type is that in which Eventuality 1 triggers Eventuality 2. Consider the following examples:

(15) a. Eventuality 1—Lightning; Eventuality 2—Thunder
      b. Eventuality 1—Release a weight; Eventuality 2—Weight falls
      c. Eventuality 1—YHWH opens the eyes of Elisha's servant;
          Eventuality 2—The servant sees the chariots of fire (2 Kgs 6:17b).

Example (15c) is particularly striking, because the servant's consternation in being surrounded by the Aramean forces, recorded in the biblical text, makes it clear that he could not see the supernatural realm.

The second type is that in which Eventuality 1 does not necessarily trigger Eventuality 2. The following is an example involving the boys:

(16) a. Eventuality 1—Severe thunderstorm;
      b. Eventuality 2—The boys run into the school building, but they might choose (foolishly) to continue to play.

The assumption here is that the boys will not run into the school building unless they are forced to do so, and even under the threat of a dangerous thunderstorm might still refuse to abandon their play. The factors that preventuality Eventuality 2 from happening are this factor and the six others listed below.

Let us examine these frustrating-factors more closely. For the sake of argument let us suppose that the boys want to irritate the girls and make them scream. They know that if they wrap the swings around the top bar, the girls will scream and cry. This scenario is depicted in the following sentence divided into *cause* (17a) and *effect* (17b).

(17)   a.   Whenever the boys wrap all the swings around the top bars,
     b.   the girls scream and then cry when they see it.

Since this is the boys' goal (or purpose), they will want to wrap the swings. And if they effect this accomplishment, being untouched by chivalry, gallantry, or charity, they will stand around and laugh at the girls' predicament. But any of the seven factors could frustrate their diabolical scheme. The first of these is capability: do the boys have the physical strength to fling the swings up with sufficient force to wrap them around the top bar? No matter how determined they are to do this, if they do not possess the capability to do it, it will not happen.

To elucidate OPPORTUNITY let us further assume for the sake of argument that the little urchins have enough strength to wrap the swings. Are the girls doomed? Not at all! The boys could be blocked by the frustrating-factor of opportunity. For instance, they might never get the chance to carry out their scheme, because either a teacher or a security guard is on duty at all times at the playground, precluding the possibility of a short period of time in which they would be unsupervised, which would be necessary to carry out their prank.

PURPOSE is the causality factor, which can be forced from the outside. Someone can be forced against his will *to do something he does not want to do* or be forced against his will *not to do something he wants to do*. An example of the first would be the boys being forced to let the girls play on each piece of playground equipment first. An example of the second would be the teacher making the boys get off the swings to give the girls their turn. These two types of duress explain the following two pairs of sentences rather than the boys being imbued with chivalry and gallantry.

(18)   a.   The boys always arrive at the playground first.
     b.   But the girls always get first choice on the equipment there.

(19)   a.   The boys let the girls play on the swings
     b.   Even though they wanted to monopolize them for the entire recess.

The first pair (18) exhibits *violation of expectation:* we expect the boys, not the girls, to get first dibs on the swings, monkey bars, etc. The second pair (19) evidences *denial of preventer,* because the first sentence refers to behavior contrary to that in keeping with the wishes expressed in the second sentence.

Also note the reversal with respect to purpose and reality. The school principal and teachers tell the students that when the bell rings, signifying the end of recess, that they must return to their classrooms. Schematically this scenario is as follows:

(20) a. Eventuality 1—The school bell rings.
   b. Eventuality 2—The boys trudge into the school building.

So, because the principal and teachers want them to return to their classes, they ring the bell. Or in other words the desire for Eventuality 2 to occur causes a desire for Eventuality 1 to occur, because it is known that ontologically Eventuality 1 causes Eventuality 2.

We now consider CONSEQUENCES. Returning to our story about the ignoble efforts of the three boys to overcome the series of contingencies in order to pull their prank—the lads are committed to their task—we posit that our incorrigible trio is quite analytical. They carefully weigh the pros and cons of their coup. Is the few minutes of unbridled mirth at the girls' expense worth the certain severe punishment, which will ensue from all quarters? And being normal boys, they conclude it is.

We define REASONABLENESS as Eventuality 2 likely will not happen until Eventuality 1 happens, but it could. As for the story . . . at the point of no return, a consideration of the reasonableness of the dastardly deed they are about to carry out gives them pause. Might something else cause the girls to cry, without them having to take the risk? But after long and careful deliberation of the small probability of that happening, they throw caution to the wind and it is full steam ahead.

Now turning to MORALITY let us suppose that there is no security guard. What then? If in the unlikely eventuality our three miscreants develop even a modicum of scruples and heed their beleaguered and seared consciences, the girls will be spared. But no such luck for these hapless victims to be.

PERMISSION may be defined as Eventuality 2 not being *allowed* to happen until Eventuality 1 occurs.

There are two versions of this causality factor. The first is when Eventuality 1 necessarily triggers Eventuality 2 as in the following example:

(21) a. Eventuality 1—Al completed writing sentences on the board.
   b. Eventuality 2—Al ran out to the playground.

In the above case, Al, having committed some infraction, was obligated to write sentences on the board rather than to go to recess. As soon as he completed writing the sentences, he was permitted to go outside.

But there is a second version of this factor: Eventuality 2 happens without the trigger of Eventuality 1. In the example above illustrating the first version we met a compliant Al, but below we meet a recalcitrant Al.

(22) a. Eventuality 1—Al had not completed writing his sentences by the time his teacher had been called to the principal's office.
      b. Eventuality 2—Al bolted out the door and ran out to the playground, ignoring his returning teacher's protests.

And finally, let us illustrate this factor by applying it to the swing wrapping plot. The plot has been uncovered and the boys have been strictly forbidden to follow through with their intentions. Less determined rascals would be thwarted at this point, but our three are made of sterner stuff and press on undaunted.

(b) *Contrast* **Illustrated: Haman, Mordecai and the King: A Grand Illustration of Violation of Expectation and Denial of Preventer.** The striking biblical text that comes to mind, evincing the seven factors discussed briefly above is the cause and effect among Ahaseurus, the king, Mordecai, and Haman in the Book of Esther. Haman's resentment towards Mordecai, because he would not show him obeisence, grew into a hatred that drove him to ask the king's permission to execute him, but instead Haman was forced to honor his enemy. This is a perfect example of *violation of expectation* from Haman's point of view. From the king's point of view, on the other hand, Haman was the instrument to carry out his will, the honoring of Mordecai for uncovering a plot against his life. At the same time the king's will forces Haman to do the thing he would last want to do: parade around on the king's richly caparisoned horse a royally garbed Mordecai, whom he hates and has plotted to kill, and to proclaim, "This is what will be done for the man the king delights to honor" (Est 6:11). This is a classic example of *denial of preventer.*

So, it is now time to leave the imaginary heuristic world of the third graders and enter the stark reality of Israel in exile under Persian rule, the milieu of the Book of Esther. This book portrays the providence of God working for His people amidst the intrigues and machinations of the Persian court. And in the process, provides us with an extended text in which the various issues concerning all of the seven factors briefly discussed above, but chiefly, *purpose*, are strikingly displayed. We prescind then from the playground scenarios (to which we will return later) and take an extended look at the twenty-one stages of cause and effect involving the interactions of the king, Haman, Mordecai and others, recorded in Esther 6:1–11.

The FIRST stage takes place in the king's chambers and in his thoughts. He cannot sleep. He knows how boring the official chronicles of his reign are. So he thinks about the ontological cause and effect as follows:

(23) a. When the chronicles are read to me,
      b. I fall asleep.

Because he wants to fall asleep, this causes him to have the chronicles read to him, as stated below.

(24) a. I want to fall asleep.
      b. So, I will have the chronicles read to me.

But in a *violation of expectation* the following, the SECOND stage, happens instead:

(25) a. The chronicles are read to him.
      b. He does not fall asleep but becomes even more alert.

The THIRD stage is

(26) a. He is awake.
      b. He hears the account of Mordecai uncovering the plot against him.

The FOURTH stage has the same setting. It unfolds as follows:

(27) a. The king hears about Mordecai uncovering the plot against him.
      b. He thinks, Mordecai is worthy of honor, because he uncovered a plot against my life.

Notice for the FIFTH stage the following cause and effect in the king's thoughts:

(28) a. Mordecai is worthy of honor, because he uncovered a plot against my life.
      b. Mordecai must be honored.

Connected with this are the king's thoughts of the SIXTH stage:

(29) a. I wonder: have I honored Mordecai?
      b. I must ask my servant.

The SEVENTH stage is the interchange between the king and his servant:

(30) a. The king's question: Has Mordecai been honored?
      b. The servant's answer: No.

The EIGHTH stage takes place in the king's mind as follows:

(31) a. Mordecai is worthy of honor, because he uncovered a plot against my life.
      b. I want to honor Mordecai.

The NINTH stage—in the king's mind—is subsequently

(32) a. I want to honor Mordecai immediately but need an idea of how best to do it.
      b. I need to talk to one of my advisors, who can suggest how this should be done.

In the TENTH stage the king reasons

(33) a. I need to talk to an advisor now.
      b. I wonder if one of them is around?

In the ELEVENTH stage he continues

(34) a. I wonder if one of them is around?
      b. I will ask my servant.

The TWELFTH stage is a question and answer between the king and his servant

(35) a. Question: "Who is in the court?"
      b. Answer: "Haman."

The THIRTEENTH stage brings Haman into the analysis

(36) a. The king's thoughts: Hmmm . . . Haman. He will do.
      b. Let him come in.

The FOURTEENTH stage is the king's question to Haman and the latter's subsequent thoughts, with Haman ignorant of stages one through thirteen:

(37) a. Question: Haman, what should be done for the man that the king delights to honor?
      b. Haman's conceited thought: I am more worthy of honor than any other official of the king.

The FIFTEENTH stage shows this conceit developing into a delusion of grandeur in Haman's mind:

(38) a. I am more worthy of honor than any other official of the king.
      b. The king must want to honor me.

Furthermore, in the SIXTEENTH stage Haman reasons that a public ceremony would honor him. And since he wants (39b) below to happen, he wants (39a) below to happen.

(39) a. A ceremony to be performed for him.
      b. He will be honored.

But, even more, Haman is not satisfied with just being honored; he wants the highest honor that can be bestowed. Moreover, he knows the following cause and effect, the SEVENTEENTH stage:

(40) a. An extremely elaborate ceremony to be performed for him.
       b. He will receive the highest honors.

Since Haman wants (40b), the highest honors for himself, he is caused to ask himself: "What is the most extreme ceremony I can conceive of to give myself the maximum honor?"—which pertains to (40a). Then the EIGHTEENTH stage ensues, Haman's answer and the king's response:

(41) a. Haman describes the elaborate ceremony.
       b. The king's approval of the idea and his orders.

In the NINETEENTH stage we are back in Haman's mind. No doubt initially he is thinking the following as he listens to the king's orders:

(42) a. The king approved my idea, because he wants it to be carried out immediately.
       b. I will be honored in a spectacular ceremony.

Haman told the king how an honoree of the king should be treated, thinking that he was that person and would be so honored. But his reverie is short-lived and abruptly interrupted with the stunning reality of what the king has *actually* said. This is the TWENTIETH stage:

(43) a. You must honor Mordecai, the Jew, in the way you described.
       b. Haman's thoughts: I am not to be honored; Mordecai is. And not only that—I am the one who must honor Mordecai, the man who refused to honor me, with the highest honors I planned for myself.

Finally, there is the TWENTY-FIRST stage:

(44) a. Haman performs an elaborate ceremony to honor Mordecai according to the king's command.
       b. His sworn enemy, Mordecai, receives the highest honors.

In summary, in a dramatic turn of irony, Haman is forced to honor the one he never wanted to honor (because he hated him for not honoring him); Haman was compelled to shamefully humble himself before the one who refused to humble himself to him. This is a classic example of *denial of preventer*.

With this great example we conclude our perusal of *Contrast*. So now we turn to investigate another additive **coherence relation**, *Elaboration*.

(4) *Elaboration/Restatement/Summary.* These relations are frequently included in **coherence relation** sets. It is also referred to as 'additive', 'expansion', and 'resemblance'.

Elaboration, which is always wedded to a preceding *Introductory Encapsulation,* may be defined as follows: given two text segments, the second expands on the first (the *Introductory Encapsulation*) by specifying it in greater detail or in other words, in the following ways: set to member; process to step; whole to part; object to attribute; abstract to instance; and general to specific (Hovy and Maier 1992, 9). *Restatement* and *Summary* go in the opposite direction: member to set; part to whole, and so forth.

An artificial example of *Elaboration* is

(45) a. John wrote an email to his friend.
      b. He booted up his computer,
      c. opened his browser,
      d. went to the college webpage,
      e. moused down to "email",
      f. entered his password,
      g. clicked on "new",
      h. typed out a message,
      i. and sent it.

In this sequence of verbs, "wrote an email" is an *Introductory Encapsulation,* elaborated by the verbs following it.[40] That is, all the eventualities depicted by the verbs after "wrote an email" are parts of the overall event of emailing. Now, on to not a few biblical examples, which unmistakably exhibit these types of **coherence relations**.

To assist the reader we offer the following outline for the discussion below:

o   Examples of *Elaboration*
o   Examples of *Restatement*
o   Examples of *Summary*

(a) Examples of *Elaboration.* We begin with Genesis 37:5–8, because it is a parade example of *Elaboration* and its congeners, *Restatement* and *Summary.*

JOSEPH BOASTS OF HIS DREAMS TO HIS BROTHERS;
THEIR REACTION (GENESIS 37:5–8)

וַיַּחֲלֹם יוֹסֵף חֲלֹום וַיַּגֵּד לְאֶחָיו וַיּוֹסִפוּ עוֹד שְׂנֹא אֹתֽוֹ׃

------

40. The CCRG suspects that Genesis 7:17a, "The Flood was on the earth for forty days," is such an *Introductory Encapsulation,* with the subsequent verses elaborating the particulars.

⁶וַיֹּ֣אמֶר אֲלֵיהֶ֔ם שִׁמְעוּ־נָ֖א הַחֲל֥וֹם הַזֶּ֖ה אֲשֶׁ֥ר חָלָֽמְתִּי׃

⁷וְ֠הִנֵּה אֲנַ֜חְנוּ מְאַלְּמִ֤ים אֲלֻמִּים֙ בְּת֣וֹךְ הַשָּׂדֶ֔ה וְהִנֵּ֛ה קָ֥מָה אֲלֻמָּתִ֖י וְגַם־
נִצָּ֑בָה וְהִנֵּ֤ה תְסֻבֶּ֙ינָה֙ אֲלֻמֹּ֣תֵיכֶ֔ם וַתִּֽשְׁתַּחֲוֶ֖יןָ לַאֲלֻמָּתִֽי׃

⁸וַיֹּ֤אמְרוּ לוֹ֙ אֶחָ֔יו הֲמָלֹ֤ךְ תִּמְלֹךְ֙ עָלֵ֔ינוּ אִם־מָשׁ֥וֹל תִּמְשֹׁ֖ל בָּ֑נוּ וַיּוֹסִ֙פוּ֙ עוֹד֙
שְׂנֹ֣א אֹת֔וֹ עַל־חֲלֹמֹתָ֖יו וְעַל־דְּבָרָֽיו׃

Joseph **dreamed** a dream. He **told** [it] to his brothers. They **hated** him even more.

He **said** to them, "Please listen to this dream, which I have dreamed. [[Joseph describes his dream at this point; their reaction]]; They **hated** him even more because of his dreams and because of his words.

Verse five describes the entire interaction between Joseph and his brothers regarding his first dream from a bird's eye view: 1) he dreamt, 2) then he told them his dream, 3) and then they reacted. This verse then is an *Introductory Encapsulation*—but, with the somewhat unusual characteristic of having parts. Then verses six and seven retrace 2) and 3), furnishing many more details: Joseph—no doubt, relishing being able to lord it over his brothers yet again—describing the contents of his dream, which in turn evokes his brothers' furious reaction: "Shall you indeed reign over us?; you shall NEVER even RULE over us!"[41] This is followed by a repetition (or *Restatement*) of 3) with additional words of explanation, "because of his dreams and because of his words," making it a summary statement for the whole.

JOSEPH'S COMMANDS TO HIS SERVANTS CONCERNING
HIS BROTHERS (GENESIS 42:25)

וַיְצַ֣ו יוֹסֵ֗ף וַיְמַלְא֣וּ אֶת־כְּלֵיהֶם֮ בָּר֒ וּלְהָשִׁ֤יב כַּסְפֵּיהֶם֙ אִ֣ישׁ אֶל־שַׂקּ֔וֹ וְלָתֵ֥ת
לָהֶ֛ם צֵדָ֖ה לַדָּ֑רֶךְ וַיַּ֥עַשׂ לָהֶ֖ם כֵּֽן׃

Joseph **commanded** [his servants] and they **filled** their vessels with grain and [he commanded] to return each man's silver to his sack and to give them provisions for the journey. So he **did** for them thus.

After the first *wayyiqtol* of verse twenty-five, the text does not straightforwardly tell us what Joseph commanded his servants. Instead

---

41. The usual way of translating y אִם x הֲ is "x or y?" Thus, here: "Shall you indeed reign over us or rule over us?" But this seems to be an insipid translation in light of the fact that the text says that they hated him even more. It is better to understand אִם as introducing a negative oath, which is not only permissible but preferable in that it conveys the fury of the brothers, goaded on by Joseph, which is according to the tenor of the narrator's account.

we can infer his orders to them. It seems that the strategy of the narrator was not to mention the mundane command, which is deducible from the servants' subsequent action (the second *wayyiqtol*)—it must have been something like, "Fill the vessels of these men!"—but rather, to highlight with infinitive constructs the *unusual* commands to return their silver and to provision them. Also, we note that the text does not report the carrying out of these commands. Nor does it need to: obedience to the orders of the second in command in Egypt is a given. The final *wayyiqtol* is a summary statement of what Joseph's servants did at his behest: those commands not recorded, but compliance to them is recorded; and those commands recorded, but compliance to them is not recorded but assumed. There is obviously no temporal progression with this final *wayyiqtol*.

JOSEPH'S INSTRUCTIONS TO THE HEAD OF HIS HOUSE TO FILL HIS BROTHERS' SACKS WITH GRAIN, TO RETURN THEIR SILVER, AND TO GIVE BENJAMIN HIS SILVER GOBLET (GENESIS 44:1–2)

וַיְצַ֞ו אֶת־אֲשֶׁ֣ר עַל־בֵּיתוֹ֮ לֵאמֹר֒ מַלֵּ֞א אֶת־אַמְתְּחֹ֤ת הָֽאֲנָשִׁים֙ אֹ֔כֶל כַּאֲשֶׁ֥ר יוּכְל֖וּן שְׂאֵ֑ת וְשִׂ֛ים כֶּֽסֶף־אִ֖ישׁ בְּפִ֥י אַמְתַּחְתּֽוֹ׃
²וְאֶת־גְּבִיעִ֞י גְּבִ֣יעַ הַכֶּ֗סֶף תָּשִׂים֙ בְּפִי֙ אַמְתַּ֣חַת הַקָּטֹ֔ן וְאֵ֖ת כֶּ֣סֶף שִׁבְר֑וֹ וַיַּ֕עַשׂ כִּדְבַ֥ר יוֹסֵ֖ף אֲשֶׁ֥ר דִּבֵּֽר׃

And he **commanded** the one who was over his house: "Fill the sacks of the men with food according to what they are able to carry and place each man's silver in the mouth of his sack. And my goblet, the silver goblet, you must place in the mouth of the sack of the youngest along with the silver for his grain." So he **did** according to the word of Joseph, which he had spoken.

This is another interesting text within the Joseph narrative. Unlike the incident recorded in Genesis 42:25, here we are given the complete contents of Joseph's commands, which follows the first *wayyiqtol*. It is instructive to examine this incident from the perspective of his *major domo*. As that man considered how Joseph had shown special favor toward a group of men he had formerly accused of being spies—no doubt he had supervised the carrying out of Joseph's orders in regards to the regaling of the men (inviting them to his house, dining with them, arranging them in a certain order at the table, and even becoming inebriated with them)—he must have been amazed at Joseph's orders. Not the first two of course. They were consistent with the special attention he had given the men (related earlier in the chapter). But giving his special cup as a gift to the youngest man, was a different matter. He had clearly most favored (the five-fold portion having been given to Benjamin) this man, but to give him his divining cup? At this point the man thinks that the cup is an extraordinary gift. He has no inkling that this is meant to frame him. In any case, the second *wayyiqtol* records his carrying out all these orders.

JOSEPH'S INSTRUCTIONS TO THE HEAD OF HIS HOUSE
TO OVERTAKE HIS BROTHERS AND TO ACCUSE THEM
OF STEALING HIS CUP (GENESIS 44:4–6)

הֵ֣ם יָצְא֣וּ אֶת־הָעִיר֮ לֹ֣א הִרְחִיקוּ֒ וְיוֹסֵ֣ף אָמַ֗ר לַֽאֲשֶׁ֤ר עַל־בֵּיתוֹ֙ ק֚וּם רְדֹ֣ף
אַחֲרֵ֣י הָֽאֲנָשִׁ֔ים וְהִשַּׂגְתָּם֙ וְאָמַרְתָּ֣ אֲלֵהֶ֔ם לָ֛מָּה שִׁלַּמְתֶּ֥ם רָעָ֖ה תַּ֥חַת
טוֹבָֽה:
5 הֲל֣וֹא זֶ֗ה אֲשֶׁ֨ר יִשְׁתֶּ֤ה אֲדֹנִי֙ בּ֔וֹ וְה֕וּא נַחֵ֥שׁ יְנַחֵ֖שׁ בּ֑וֹ הֲרֵעֹתֶ֖ם אֲשֶׁ֥ר
עֲשִׂיתֶֽם:
6 **וַיַּשִּׂגֵ֑ם וַיְדַבֵּ֣ר** אֲלֵהֶ֔ם אֶת־הַדְּבָרִ֖ים הָאֵֽלֶּה:

They [the brothers] went out of the city. They had not gone far when Joseph said to the one who was over his house, "Pursue immediately after the men, overtake them, then say to them, 'Why have you repaid evil in place of good? Surely this is from what my master drinks. Moreover, he himself assuredly divines by this. You have acted in an evil way in what you have done.'" So he **overtook** them and **spoke** to them these words.

As we analyze this text, we will continue to do so from the viewpoint of Joseph's *major domo*. If he was amazed at Joseph's first set of orders (Gn 44:1–2), these must have completely befuddled him. He had thought that the cup was an extraordinary present, but now he realized it was to frame the youngest man, whom clearly his master had most favored.

GOD'S SPEECH TO MOSES (EXODUS 6:2)

וַיְדַבֵּ֥ר אֱלֹהִ֖ים אֶל־מֹשֶׁ֑ה **וַיֹּ֣אמֶר** אֵלָ֖יו אֲנִ֥י יְהוָֽה:

God **spoke** to Moses and **said** to him, "I am YHWH."

Certainly, the second *wayyiqtol*, וַיֹּ֣אמֶר, does not indicate any temporal progression; it is introducing the particulars of what YHWH spoke (the first *wayyiqtol*, וַיְדַבֵּ֥ר).

MOSES INSTRUCTIONS TO ISRAEL CONCERNING
THE BLASPHEMER (LEVITICUS 24:23)

וַיְדַבֵּ֣ר מֹשֶׁ֗ה אֶל־בְּנֵ֣י יִשְׂרָאֵ֔ל וַיּוֹצִ֣יאוּ אֶת־הַֽמְקַלֵּ֗ל אֶל־מִחוּץ֙ לַֽמַּחֲנֶ֔ה
וַיִּרְגְּמ֥וּ אֹת֖וֹ אָ֑בֶן וּבְנֵֽי־יִשְׂרָאֵ֣ל עָשׂ֔וּ כַּֽאֲשֶׁ֛ר צִוָּ֥ה יְהֹוָ֖ה אֶת־מֹשֶֽׁה׃

Moses **spoke** to the sons of Israel. Then they **brought out** the curser
outside of the encampment. Then they **stoned** him with stones. Hence,
the Sons of Israel _did_ just as YHWH had commanded Moses.

As in Genesis 42:25, which was discussed above, the text does not tell us
what Moses spoke, but we know from the previous verses what YHWH
had commanded be done, and moreover, we can infer it from what the
text reports the people did. As far as the temporal signature of this text is
concerned, our interest centers on the last verbal phrase, "Hence, the sons
of Israel _did_ . . . ." The verb is not a _wayyiqtol_, but a _qatal_ [italicized in the
text; italicized and underscored in the translation]; nevertheless, its temporal
sequence with respect to the previous verb is instructive. This is a summary
statement. There is no new eventuality being reported here: the referent of
"did" is the same referent as that of the two preceding verb phrases. Thus,
there is no temporal progression here.

MOSES' INSTRUCTIONS TO THE SPIES (NUMBERS 13:17FF)

וַיִּשְׁלַ֤ח אֹתָם֙ מֹשֶׁ֔ה לָת֖וּר אֶת־אֶ֣רֶץ כְּנָ֑עַן וַיֹּ֣אמֶר אֲלֵהֶ֗ם עֲל֥וּ זֶה֙ בַּנֶּ֔גֶב
וַעֲלִיתֶ֖ם אֶת־הָהָֽר׃
18 וּרְאִיתֶ֥ם אֶת־הָאָ֖רֶץ מַה־הִ֑וא וְאֶת־הָעָם֙ הַיֹּשֵׁ֣ב עָלֶ֔יהָ הֶחָזָ֥ק הוּא֙
הֲרָפֶ֔ה הַמְעַ֥ט ה֖וּא אִם־רָֽב׃
19 וּמָ֣ה הָאָ֗רֶץ אֲשֶׁר־הוּא֙ יֹשֵׁ֣ב בָּ֔הּ הֲטוֹבָ֥ה הִ֖וא אִם־רָעָ֑ה וּמָ֣ה הֶֽעָרִ֗ים
אֲשֶׁר־הוּא֙ יוֹשֵׁ֣ב בָּהֵ֔נָּה הַבְּמַֽחֲנִ֖ים אִ֥ם בְּמִבְצָרִֽים׃
20 וּמָ֣ה הָ֠אָרֶץ הַשְּׁמֵנָ֨ה הִ֜וא אִם־רָזָ֗ה הֲיֵֽשׁ־בָּ֥הּ עֵץ֙ אִם־אַ֔יִן וְהִ֨תְחַזַּקְתֶּ֔ם
וּלְקַחְתֶּ֖ם מִפְּרִ֣י הָאָ֑רֶץ וְהַ֨יָּמִ֔ים יְמֵ֖י בִּכּוּרֵ֥י עֲנָבִֽים׃

Moses sent them to spy out the land of Canaan. And he said to them, "Go
up here into the Negev, then go up into the hill country. See the land,
what it is, and what the people who dwell in it are like. Are they strong
or are they weak? Whether they are few or many. And what is the land in
which they dwell: is it good or bad? And what are the cities like in which
they dwell? Are they in camps or in fortifications? And what of the soil: is
it rich or poor? Are there any trees in it or not? Strengthen yourselves and
take some of the fruit of the land." (Now the days were the days of the first
fruits of the grapes.)

Clearly, he gave them this long charge concerning their mission as he sent them out, or before he sent them out, not afterwards. They would not have been there after he sent them. If, on the one hand, sending is a process, the text elaborates on this process. Part of the process is the charge. If on the other hand, it is an instantaneous event, it must follow the charge. To put it another way, the charging occurred during the time period of the sending or preceded it. In addition, for the former way of understanding, although Moses' actions of sending and speaking are compatible, and thus, not constrained to happen at different times, the linearity of texts requires this verbal sequence; for the latter way, the verbs are in reverse temporal order.

The Return of Joshua's Men Sent to Reconnoiter Jericho (Joshua 2:23)

וַיָּשֻׁבוּ שְׁנֵי הָאֲנָשִׁים וַיֵּרְדוּ מֵהָהָר וַיַּעַבְרוּ וַיָּבֹאוּ אֶל־יְהוֹשֻׁעַ בִּן־נוּן
וַיְסַפְּרוּ־לוֹ אֵת כָּל־הַמֹּצְאוֹת אוֹתָם:

Then the two men **returned**. They **descended** from the hill country, **crossed** [the Jordan], **came** to Joshua bin Nun and **recounted** to him everything which had happened to them [[lit. "found them"]].

The first sentence above (first *wayyiqtol*) leaves the men safe in the camp of Israel on the plains of Moab across from Jericho. The second *wayyiqtol* takes us back in time, expanding on their journey back to their camp in Transjordan, starting with their descent from their hiding place for three days in the hill country above Jericho. The third *wayyiqtol* relates their subsequent crossing of the Jordan. The fourth is their eventual coming before Joshua to give their report. The three actions represented by last three of these *wayyiqtols* occurred within the time span of the eventuality depicted by the first *wayyiqtol*, וַיָּשֻׁבוּ, "returned." The final *wayyiqtol* in the above text conveys the giving of this report.

Joshua Orders an Ambush to be Set against Ai (Joshua 8:3–4)

וַיָּקָם יְהוֹשֻׁעַ וְכָל־עַם הַמִּלְחָמָה לַעֲלוֹת הָעָי וַיִּבְחַר יְהוֹשֻׁעַ שְׁלֹשִׁים אֶלֶף
אִישׁ גִּבּוֹרֵי הַחַיִל וַיִּשְׁלָחֵם לָיְלָה:
4 וַיְצַו אֹתָם לֵאמֹר רְאוּ אַתֶּם אֹרְבִים לָעִיר מֵאַחֲרֵי הָעִיר אַל־תַּרְחִיקוּ
מִן־הָעִיר מְאֹד וִהְיִיתֶם כֻּלְּכֶם נְכֹנִים:

Joshua and all the men of war **arose** to go up to Ai. Joshua **chose** thirty thousand men, the best warriors and **sent** them at night. He **commanded** them, "Look, you are going to set an ambush for the city. Do not be very far from the city. And all of you be ready."

The pertinent issue for us in these verses is the temporal sequence—or lack thereof—between the third and fourth *wayyiqtols*. Here we see Joshua sending men on a mission, as Moses did earlier (Numbers 13:17ff). The second verb differs from that in the Numbers passage, but the reasoning is the same—save one additional thought. The necessary secrecy, which had to obtain to have a successful ambush, precludes—I think—the idea that Joshua shouted the orders to the ambushers after they left to position themselves. Thus, the text here cannot be iconic.

JOSHUA'S INSTRUCTIONS TO THE DELINQUENT TRIBES ABOUT THEIR LAND ALLOCATION (JOSHUA 18:2–10)

וַיִּוָּתְרוּ בִּבְנֵי יִשְׂרָאֵל אֲשֶׁר לֹא־חָלְקוּ אֶת־נַחֲלָתָם שִׁבְעָה שְׁבָטִים:

3 **וַיֹּאמֶר** יְהוֹשֻׁעַ אֶל־בְּנֵי יִשְׂרָאֵל עַד־אָנָה אַתֶּם מִתְרַפִּים לָבוֹא לָרֶשֶׁת אֶת־הָאָרֶץ אֲשֶׁר נָתַן לָכֶם יְהוָה אֱלֹהֵי אֲבוֹתֵיכֶם:

4 הָבוּ לָכֶם שְׁלֹשָׁה אֲנָשִׁים לַשָּׁבֶט וְאֶשְׁלָחֵם וְיָקֻמוּ וְיִתְהַלְּכוּ בָאָרֶץ וְיִכְתְּבוּ אוֹתָהּ לְפִי נַחֲלָתָם וְיָבֹאוּ אֵלָי:

5 וְהִתְחַלְּקוּ אֹתָהּ לְשִׁבְעָה חֲלָקִים יְהוּדָה יַעֲמֹד עַל־גְּבוּלוֹ מִנֶּגֶב וּבֵית יוֹסֵף יַעַמְדוּ עַל־גְּבוּלָם מִצָּפוֹן:

6 וְאַתֶּם תִּכְתְּבוּ אֶת־הָאָרֶץ שִׁבְעָה חֲלָקִים וַהֲבֵאתֶם אֵלַי הֵנָּה וְיָרִיתִי לָכֶם גּוֹרָל פֹּה לִפְנֵי יְהוָה אֱלֹהֵינוּ:

7 כִּי אֵין־חֵלֶק לַלְוִיִּם בְּקִרְבְּכֶם כִּי־כְהֻנַּת יְהוָה נַחֲלָתוֹ וְגָד וּרְאוּבֵן וַחֲצִי שֵׁבֶט הַמְנַשֶּׁה לָקְחוּ נַחֲלָתָם מֵעֵבֶר לַיַּרְדֵּן מִזְרָחָה אֲשֶׁר נָתַן לָהֶם מֹשֶׁה עֶבֶד יְהוָה:

8 **וַיָּקֻמוּ** הָאֲנָשִׁים **וַיֵּלֵכוּ** **וַיְצַו** יְהוֹשֻׁעַ אֶת־הַהֹלְכִים לִכְתֹּב אֶת־הָאָרֶץ לֵאמֹר לְכוּ וְהִתְהַלְּכוּ בָאָרֶץ וְכִתְבוּ אוֹתָהּ וְשׁוּבוּ אֵלַי וּפֹה אַשְׁלִיךְ לָכֶם גּוֹרָל לִפְנֵי יְהוָה בְּשִׁלֹה:

9 **וַיֵּלְכוּ** הָאֲנָשִׁים **וַיַּעַבְרוּ** בָאָרֶץ **וַיִּכְתְּבוּהָ** לֶעָרִים לְשִׁבְעָה חֲלָקִים עַל־סֵפֶר **וַיָּבֹאוּ** אֶל־יְהוֹשֻׁעַ אֶל־הַמַּחֲנֶה שִׁלֹה: 10 **וַיַּשְׁלֵךְ** לָהֶם יְהוֹשֻׁעַ גּוֹרָל בְּשִׁלֹה לִפְנֵי יְהוָה **וַיְחַלֶּק**־שָׁם יְהוֹשֻׁעַ אֶת־הָאָרֶץ לִבְנֵי יִשְׂרָאֵל כְּמַחְלְקֹתָם: פ

And seven tribes **remained** among the Sons of Israel who had not allocated their inheritance.

So, Joshua **said** to the sons of Israel, "How long will you be lax about entering into possessing the land that YHWH, the God of your fathers, has given to you? Appoint for yourselves three men per tribe in order that I might send them, that they might immediately go all about the land and write out [a description of] it for the purpose of their inheritance, and then come to me. Then they will allocate it into seven portions/Then it will be allocated into seven portions [[the latter understands the masculine plural *w*ᵊ*qatal* to have a dummy subject; and, thus, to be a passive]]. Judah will stand according to its border in the Negev. And the House of Joseph will stand according to their border in the north. But as for you, you will write out the land into seven portions. Then you will bring [the results] to me here. Then I will throw the lot for you here before YHWH, our God. But the Levites have no portion amongst you, because the priesthood of YHWH is their inheritance. Also, Gad, Reuben, and half of the tribe of Manasseh received their inheritance on the other side of the Jordan eastward, which Moses, the servant of YHWH, had given to them."

Then the men **went** immediately. And Joshua **commanded** those who went to write out the land: "Go all around in the land, write it out, and return to me. Then, here I will throw [[different root]] the lot for you before YHWH at Shiloh."

So, the men **went**, **traveled** through the land and **wrote** it out upon a scroll by [its] cities into ten portions. Then they **came** to Joshua, to the camp at Shiloh. And Joshua **threw** [[same root as previous]] the lot for them at Shiloh before YHWH.

So, Joshua **apportioned** there the land for the sons of Israel according to their allotments.

I have split up the text above into its natural divisions. The first is strictly a narrative, giving the background for the rest of the text: there is a problem: seven tribes had not yet determined—let alone claimed—their portions of the land. The second part of the text is Joshua's reaction to their delinquency, his speech to them, comprising a preliminary rebuke, followed by commands for them to survey the remaining land, divide it into seven parts and return to him, at which time he would cast lots to determine each tribe's allotment. And inasmuch as it was Joshua's *reaction*, the circumstances detailed in the first part of the text were its cause. Thus, Joshua's first speech is an example of *Result*; and, temporally follows his realization of the tribes' laxness. The third section of text recounts in narrative prose the surveyors' response to Joshua's command (they went, as he had earlier ordered them); and a second speech, Joshua's instructions to them as he dispatched them (very similar to what he said before), which would have preceded their actual leaving. The fourth section of the text begins with a restatement of the first part of the third section: "the men went"—consequently, there is no time advance—and continues with the record of the compliance of the men sent out by Joshua and of Joshua's actions on their behalf. The fifth section could be part of the fourth, but I set it off by itself as a summary of the whole. The redundant re-lexicalization of Joshua's name in the last section corroborates this analysis. And, furthermore, it then ties in nicely with the first section: the problem has been solved. In either case (part of the fourth or a separate fifth) casting lots is part of the apportionment process, so there is no temporal progression from "threw" to "apportioned."

THE PHILISTINES GATHER FOR BATTLE (1 SAMUEL 17:1)

וַיַּאַסְפוּ פְלִשְׁתִּים אֶת־מַחֲנֵיהֶם לַמִּלְחָמָה וַיֵּאָסְפוּ שֹׂכֹה אֲשֶׁר לִיהוּדָה וַיַּחֲנוּ בֵּין־שׂוֹכֹה וּבֵין־עֲזֵקָה בְּאֶפֶס דַּמִּים:

The Philistines **gathered** their camp for battle. They **amassed** at Sokoh, which belongs to Judah, and **camped** between Sokoh and 'Azekah in Ephes Dammim.

It is clear from both the immediate and extended context what this text describes: the staging of the Philistines in the Valley of Elah to fight against the forces of Saul. The first *wayyiqtol* gives us a general *Introductory Encapsulation*: the Philistines gathered together their forces to engage in battle. The second and third *wayyiqtols* give us the particulars of the location of their camp, with the third further specifying the place beyond what the second does. The result is general, followed by specific, followed by even more specific. The elaboration is spatial: it concerns the circumstances of the event; it does not break down the eventuality into sub-eventualities. In this case, the second obviously occurred within the same time interval in which the first happened. And, the third happened within this interval as well. Consequently, there is no temporal progression represented by the textual sequence.

JOAB'S REPORT TO DAVID ABOUT THE IMMINENT CAPTURE OF RABBAH OF AMMON (2 SAMUEL 12:27)

וַיִּשְׁלַח יוֹאָב מַלְאָכִים אֶל־דָּוִד וַיֹּאמֶר נִלְחַמְתִּי בְרַבָּה גַּם־לָכַדְתִּי אֶת־עִיר הַמָּיִם:

Joab **sent** messengers to David. And he **said**, "I have fought against Rabbah. I have even captured the city of the water [[likely, the city's water supply complex]]."

The pertinent issue in this text is whether "he" refers to Joab giving the message to be conveyed to David, with an ellipsis more or less like the following, *And he said to them, 'you will say to the king...'*, one of the messengers as the mouthpiece for Joab, or the messengers collectively speaking as him. If it is the first of these—which I believe to be the most likely scenario, albeit it is ambiguous—then this is another case of the recounting of a message given to messengers, which textually follows the recounting of them being sent. We know that the giving of a message cannot occur after the messenger has left. The latest it can occur with respect to the sending is that it happened at the same time; to suggest that the message was shouted to them after they left, which would have to be the case if this text were iconic, strains credulity. Thus, again, the temporal order of the *wayyiqtols* is reversed from their order in the text. So there is no temporal progression in the text. On the contrary, it is likely that there is temporal *regression*.

On the other hand, if is the second or third possibility, there would be *Serialation* (or possibly even *Result*).

NINEVEH'S RESPONSE TO JONAH'S MESSAGE (JONAH 3:5–8)

וַיַּאֲמִינוּ אַנְשֵׁי נִינְוֵה בֵּאלֹהִים וַיִּקְרְאוּ־צוֹם וַיִּלְבְּשׁוּ שַׂקִּים מִגְּדוֹלָם וְעַד־
קְטַנָּם:

6 וַיִּגַּע הַדָּבָר אֶל־מֶלֶךְ נִינְוֵה וַיָּקָם מִכִּסְאוֹ וַיַּעֲבֵר אַדַּרְתּוֹ מֵעָלָיו וַיְכַס
שַׂק וַיֵּשֶׁב עַל־הָאֵפֶר: 7 וַיַּזְעֵק וַיֹּאמֶר בְּנִינְוֵה מִטַּעַם הַמֶּלֶךְ וּגְדֹלָיו לֵאמֹר
הָאָדָם וְהַבְּהֵמָה הַבָּקָר וְהַצֹּאן אַל־יִטְעֲמוּ מְאוּמָה אַל־יִרְעוּ וּמַיִם אַל־
יִשְׁתּוּ: 8 וְיִתְכַּסּוּ שַׂקִּים הָאָדָם וְהַבְּהֵמָה וְיִקְרְאוּ אֶל־אֱלֹהִים בְּחָזְקָה
וְיָשֻׁבוּ אִישׁ מִדַּרְכּוֹ הָרָעָה וּמִן־הֶחָמָס אֲשֶׁר בְּכַפֵּיהֶם

The men of Nineveh **believed** in God. They **called** for a fast and **wore** sackcloth, from the greatest of them to the least of them.

The matter **reached** the king of Nineveh. He **arose** from his throne, **removed** his robe from himself, **covered** himself with sackcloth, and **sat** on ashes. He **cried out** and **said**, "In Nineveh from the decree of the king and his great ones [[formal introduction of the decree to follow]]: '[[decree begins here]] Let neither man nor domestic animal (cattle and flocks) taste anything or graze, and water let them not drink. Let man and domestic animal cover themselves with sackcloth and cry forcefully to God. And let each turn back from his evil way and from the violence which is in their hands'."

This text can be analyzed in two non-mutually exclusive ways: either verses six through eight are an explanation of the origin of the fast proclamation or they are an elaboration of it. And since they are non-contradictory, both could obtain. For all three possibilities, the actions recorded in verses six through eight were anterior to that reported in verse five. But, the structure of the elaboration is not so simple: it applies to only the second and third *wayyiqtol*, not the first; and, the italicized portion above is not part of the elaboration.

(b) Examples of *Restatement*

ABRAHAM JOURNEYS TO THE LAND OF CANAAN WITH SARAI,
LOT, AND THE REST OF HIS HOUSEHOLD (GENESIS 12:4–5)

וַיֵּ֣לֶךְ אַבְרָ֗ם כַּאֲשֶׁ֨ר דִּבֶּ֤ר אֵלָיו֙ יְהֹוָ֔ה וַיֵּ֥לֶךְ אִתּ֖וֹ ל֑וֹט וְאַבְרָ֗ם בֶּן־חָמֵ֤שׁ שָׁנִים֙ וְשִׁבְעִ֣ים שָׁנָ֔ה בְּצֵאת֖וֹ מֵחָרָֽן:

⁵ וַיִּקַּ֣ח אַבְרָם֩ אֶת־שָׂרַ֨י אִשְׁתּ֜וֹ וְאֶת־ל֣וֹט בֶּן־אָחִ֗יו וְאֶת־כָּל־רְכוּשָׁם֙ אֲשֶׁ֣ר רָכָ֔שׁוּ וְאֶת־הַנֶּ֖פֶשׁ אֲשֶׁר־עָשׂ֣וּ בְחָרָ֑ן וַיֵּצְא֗וּ לָלֶ֙כֶת֙ אַ֣רְצָה כְּנַ֔עַן וַיָּבֹ֖אוּ אַ֥רְצָה כְּנָֽעַן:

Abram **went** just as YHWH had spoken to him. And Lot **went** with him. Now Abram was seventy-five years old when he went out of Haran. Abram **took** Sarai, his wife, Lot, the son of his brother, and all their possessions, which they had acquired, and every person, whom they had acquired in Haran. And they **went out** to go to the land of Canaan. And they **entered** the land of Canaan.

This text exhibits *Restatement* in the following way. The second VP with *wayyiqtol*, "And Lot went with him," is reprised in the third VP with *wayyiqtol*, "And Abram took Sarai, his wife, and *Lot*, the son of this brother" [emphasis, mine]. What is the purpose of the repetition? It might be providing clarification: that Lot went because Abram took him; he did not go on his own. In addition, it establishes the importance of Lot to Abram. He was *not obligated* to take Lot; but, could it be that he *wanted* to take him as a possible heir, in light of the fact that Sarai was barren? At any rate, the eventuality of Lot having been taken by Abram is the *very same eventuality* as Lot having gone with him. So, obviously, there is no temporal progression here. Moreover, the eventuality is further examined in the text in the fourth main clause. Its *wayyiqtol* is plural, because Abram did not go out of his country by himself; he took his whole household (including Sarai and Lot) with him. But it is still looking at the same event. Again, therefore, time does not advance.

THE ACCOUNT OF THE DEATH OF URIAH THE HITTITE
(2 SAMUEL 11:17)

וַיֵּצְאוּ אַנְשֵׁי הָעִיר וַיִּלָּחֲמוּ אֶת־יוֹאָב וַיִּפֹּל מִן־הָעָם מֵעַבְדֵי דָוִד וַיָּמָת גַּם
אוּרִיָּה הַחִתִּי:

The men of the city **came out** and **fought** with Joab. Some of the people
from the servants of David **fell**. Also, Uriah the Hittite **died**.

The text above, although short, is extremely poignant, as we will see below,
and must be examined in some detail to understand its import. The first two
wayyiqtols give us the circumstances of a report of the fatalities afflicted on
the army of Israel by the inhabitants of the besieged city of Rabbah, who
staged a counterattack against Joab's forces surrounding the city in a desperate
effort to break the siege. These verbs are an *Introductory Encapsulation* of a
peculiar type for the details supplied farther on in the text in a report of the
battle, which was given to David (2 Sm 11:23–24). Although in speech,
rather than in narrative, and occurring at a later time than the eventualities
recounted, this description clearly functions as an *Elaboration,* taking us
back to the time of the battle.

This brings us to the next two *wayyiqtols.* It is the narrator's account
of the death of a few and the death of one. Why is the death of *this* man
singled out? We know the answer from the larger context of the story. Uriah
refused to have conjugal relations with his wife—and thereby cover up
David's adultery and impregnation of her—while his fellow soldiers were
on the battlefield. Uriah viewed it as a matter of loyalty. His integrity is
boldly sketched; David's lack thereof is most apparent. And thus, in David's
mind Uriah must die, so that he could hastily marry his widow and disguise
her pregnancy. Never mind that this would be snuffing out a life. He was a
threat.

So, David asked Joab to arrange for Uriah's death by having his forces
withdraw from him in the heat of the battle, allowing him to be overwhelmed
and killed (2 Sm 11:15). Joab must have wondered why the king wanted
this man dead. Notwithstanding his puzzlement, in loyal obedience to his
liege's nefarious orders, he placed the noble Hittite at the point of the attack
(16). But not even ruthless Joab could bring himself to carry out such a
callous act as the second order. Nevertheless, conveniently for David, gallant
Uriah did die as part of the vanguard in the siege of Rabbah.

We also are acquainted with the rest of the story. David married Uriah's
widow, and seemed to have gotten away with his sin by staging a successful
cover-up—with men, that is; not with God. A Divine reckoning was coming.

Supplied with this background, we now look at the temporal profile of the eventualities recorded here. Our focus is on the third and fourth *wayyiqtols*. The former reports the casualties sustained in the battle: "some of the servants of David." We cannot swoop by this verb on the way to the next without the following comment: David's orders not only cost Uriah his life but other loyal servants of David as well! With the latter *wayyiqtol*, the text zooms in on one of those loyal servants who gave their lives fighting for their king, namely, Uriah, in a classic *Restatement* of general to specific, with the curt (only four Hebrew words) grim report: "Also, Uriah the Hittite died." Why this repetition in this way? It is because a driving emphasis in the immediate context and the larger as well is loyalty versus disloyalty. Loyal Uriah, loyal Joab, disloyal David. How loyal was Uriah the Hittite, husband of Bathsheba, loyal servant but hapless threat to a monarch who thought himself to be unaccountable and unassailable? So loyal, in fact, that he bore without question the missal containing his death warrant—he was no fool, the significance of David's bizarre antics in Jerusalem was transparent[42]—to the battle lines and put it into the hands of his commander. This way too he could demonstrate loyalty to his king, who had been disloyal to him—to protect the latter from himself as it were, at the cost of his life. His loyalty is in stark contrast to David's treachery, for that is what it was. He ordered a murder for personal gain. In short, the better man died. The Scripture is not finished with this bald statement; more must be said. And so it does, launching into Joab's report to his king of the results of the battle—including Uriah's death—in the following verses [which we will look at below]. As to the temporal profile of this text, Uriah's death is part of the death of the rest, and occurred therefore within the same time span as theirs. Hence, there is no temporal progression between the last two verbs of the text.

JOAB'S REPORT TO DAVID ABOUT THE BATTLE (2 SAMUEL 11:18–21)

וַיִּשְׁלַ֖ח יוֹאָ֑ב וַיַּגֵּ֣ד לְדָוִ֔ד אֶֽת־כָּל־דִּבְרֵ֖י הַמִּלְחָמָֽה׃

וַיְצַ֥ו אֶת־הַמַּלְאָ֖ךְ לֵאמֹ֑ר כְּכַלּוֹתְךָ֗ אֵ֚ת כָּל־דִּבְרֵ֣י הַמִּלְחָמָ֔ה לְדַבֵּ֖ר אֶל־הַמֶּֽלֶךְ׃ 19

וְהָיָ֗ה אִֽם־תַּעֲלֶה֙ חֲמַ֣ת הַמֶּ֔לֶךְ וְאָמַ֣ר לְ֔ךָ מַדּ֛וּעַ נִגַּשְׁתֶּ֥ם אֶל־הָעִ֖יר 20 לְהִלָּחֵ֑ם הֲל֣וֹא יְדַעְתֶּ֔ם אֵ֥ת אֲשֶׁר־יֹר֖וּ מֵעַ֥ל הַחוֹמָֽה׃

---

42. See Meir Sternberg's fascinating and insightful analysis of the narrative of David trying to manipulate Uriah to have conjugal relations with his wife (in *The Poetics of Biblical Narrative: Ideological Literature and the Drama of Reading*.)

מִי־הִכָּה אֶת־אֲבִימֶלֶךְ בֶּן־יְרֻבֶּשֶׁת הֲלוֹא־אִשָּׁה הִשְׁלִיכָה עָלָיו פֶּלַח 21
רֶכֶב מֵעַל הַחוֹמָה **וַיָּמָת** בְּתֵבֵץ לָמָּה נִגַּשְׁתֶּם אֶל־הַחוֹמָה וְאָמַרְתָּ גַּם
עַבְדְּךָ אוּרִיָּה הַחִתִּי מֵת:

Joab **sent** [a messenger] and **told** David the complete account of the
battle. He **commanded** the messenger, "When you finish speaking the
complete account of the battle to the king, if the anger of the king should
arise, and he should say to you, 'Why did you fight so near the city?! Surely
you know that they shoot from the wall! Who struck Abimelek, son of
Jerubbeshet? Surely a woman threw upon him a millstone from the wall;
and he died at Tebets. Why did you draw near the wall?!' Then you will say,
'Also, your servant, Uriah the Hittite, died.'"

The first two *wayyiqtols* are an *Introductory Encapsulation*, explaining that
Joab sent a messenger to David, who gave him the complete report of the
battle in which Uriah died. Consequently, what follows is an *Elaboration*,
but of a different kind: rather than giving us details of the report itself (a few
of these come later in verses 24–25), we are looking at details of secondary
instructions to the messenger of how he should respond to the king if he were
to react to a certain section of it in a particular way—which, no doubt, was
given to him before he was sent to the king. So this is a temporal flashback
from the later time of the reporting to the earlier time of the sending.

The second *wayyiqtol* clause suggests that it was a complete report, as do
Joab's words, "When you finish speaking the complete account of the battle
to the king," as well as the narrator's comment in verse twenty-two. And
although we are not privy to the contents of the report, we can infer from
the king's potential objections, that a portion of the report, not surprisingly,
listed casualties, which are to be expected in war. This time however, they
included those incurred because of a highly questionable strategy, which
went against historical precedent, the deployment of his troops near the
wall of the city. Joab suspected that David would be angry at him and
perplexed—given the fact that he was a general who knew military history—
that he had ordered an assault near the wall. This implies that in compliance
with David's orders to put Uriah into the thick of the battle in order that
he would be killed, Joab ordered an elite unit, which included him, into
a dangerously exposed position. (We will learn in verses twenty-three and
twenty-four that Joab was not that foolish or cavalier with his men.) So,
in anticipation of David's justifiable ire and what he suspected he might
likely say, Joab gave further orders that he knew would mollify the king:
"Then you will say, 'Also, your servant, Uriah the Hittite, died'." According

to verse twenty-two, the messenger gave the report verbatim to David [also an *Introductory Encapsulation*]. This is followed in verses twenty-three and twenty-four by an *Elaboration* of a portion of that report, which comprised the details of the elite unit's contribution to the battle, they pushed the enemy back to its gate, but suffered casualities in the process—including one in particular, Uriah. It appears that the messenger gave the last detail without waiting for the king's objections. It turns out—not unexpectedly, because David had schemed to effect this outcome—that he did not object to this section of the report.

ELISHA'S PROPHECY TO THE KING'S OFFICER AND ITS FULFILLMENT
(2 KINGS 7:1–2; 17–20)

[For the convenience of the reader, in the text and the translation below the prophecies are italicized; the circumstances in question are in a gray font; and what happened to the officer is highlighted in gray. The fulfillment of all these and their recounting is within braces.]

וַיֹּ֣אמֶר אֱלִישָׁ֗ע שִׁמְע֖וּ דְּבַר־יְהוָ֑ה כֹּ֣ה׀ אָמַ֣ר יְהוָ֗ה כָּעֵ֤ת׀ מָחָר֙ סְאָה־סֹ֣לֶת בְּשֶׁ֔קֶל וְסָאתַ֥יִם שְׂעֹרִ֛ים בְּשֶׁ֖קֶל בְּשַׁ֥עַר שֹׁמְרֽוֹן׃

² וַיַּ֣עַן הַשָּׁלִ֡ישׁ אֲשֶׁר־לַמֶּלֶךְ֩ נִשְׁעָ֨ן עַל־יָד֜וֹ אֶת־אִ֣ישׁ הָאֱלֹהִים֮ וַיֹּאמַר֒ הִנֵּ֣ה יְהוָ֗ה עֹשֶׂ֤ה אֲרֻבּוֹת֙ בַּשָּׁמַ֔יִם הֲיִהְיֶ֖ה הַדָּבָ֣ר הַזֶּ֑ה וַיֹּ֙אמֶר֙ הִנְּכָ֣ה רֹאֶ֣ה בְּעֵינֶ֔יךָ וּמִשָּׁ֖ם לֹ֥א תֹאכֵֽל׃

¹⁷ וְהַמֶּ֡לֶךְ הִפְקִ֣יד אֶת־הַשָּׁלִישׁ֩ אֲשֶׁר־נִשְׁעָ֨ן עַל־יָד֜וֹ עַל־הַשַּׁ֗עַר {וַיִּרְמְסֻ֧הוּ הָעָ֛ם בַּשַּׁ֖עַר וַיָּמֹ֑ת} כַּאֲשֶׁ֤ר דִּבֶּר֙ אִ֣ישׁ הָאֱלֹהִ֔ים אֲשֶׁ֣ר דִּבֶּ֔ר בְּרֶ֥דֶת הַמֶּ֖לֶךְ אֵלָֽיו׃

¹⁸ וַיְהִ֗י כְּדַבֵּר֙ אִ֣ישׁ הָאֱלֹהִ֔ים אֶל־הַמֶּ֖לֶךְ לֵאמֹ֑ר *סָאתַ֣יִם שְׂעֹרִ֣ים בְּשֶׁ֗קֶל וּסְאָה־סֹ֙לֶת֙ בְּשֶׁ֔קֶל יִהְיֶה֙ כָּעֵ֣ת מָחָ֔ר בְּשַׁ֖עַר שֹׁמְרֽוֹן׃*

¹⁹ {וַיַּ֨עַן הַשָּׁלִ֜ישׁ אֶת־אִ֣ישׁ הָאֱלֹהִים֮ וַיֹּאמַר֒ וְהִנֵּ֣ה יְהוָ֗ה עֹשֶׂ֤ה אֲרֻבּוֹת֙ בַּשָּׁמַ֔יִם הֲיִהְיֶ֖ה כַּדָּבָ֣ר הַזֶּ֑ה} וַיֹּ֙אמֶר֙ {הִנְּךָ֤ רֹאֶה֙ בְּעֵינֶ֔יךָ וּמִשָּׁ֖ם לֹ֥א תֹאכֵֽל׃}

²⁰ וַיְהִי־ל֖וֹ כֵּ֑ן {וַיִּרְמְס֨וּ אֹת֥וֹ הָעָ֛ם בַּשַּׁ֖עַר וַיָּמֹֽת׃}

Elisha **said**, "Hear the word of Y_HWH_; thus, Y_HWH_ has said, '*At this time tomorrow a seah of flour for a shekel; two seahs of barley for a shekel in the gate of Samaria.*'" The officer upon whose hand the king leaned **answered** the man of God and said, "If at this moment Y_HWH_ was about to make apertures in heaven, could this thing be?" He [Elisha] **said**, "*You are about to see it with your eyes, but from it you shall not eat.*"

The king **appointed** the officer upon whose hand he leaned **to supervise** at the gate. {And the people **trampled** him at the gate and he **died**}, just as the man of God had spoken, which he had spoken when the king came down to him.

It was as the man of God had spoken to the king, {"*Two seahs of barley for a shekel; a seah of flour for a shekel will be at this time tomorrow in the gate of Samaria.*" And the officer **answered** the man of God and said, "If at this moment YHWH was about to make apertures in heaven, could this thing be?" He [Elisha] **said**, {"*You are about to see it with your eyes, but from it you shall not eat.*"}

It was to him that way: {the people **trampled** him at the gate and he **died**}.

The above is a remarkable case of *Restatement*. Both of Elisha's predictions and the circumstances which prompted the second of these are recalled in their entirety, almost verbatim, to show that what happened was a fulfillment of prophecy. What happened to the king's officer is also repeated.

The first prophecy was that the price of food would dramatically drop the next day. This could only happen—of course—if there were a sudden unexpected windfall of food for the city. But the city was in the grip of a deadly famine, brought on by a prolonged siege of the Aramean army. As readers we wonder. So did the king's officer. But questioning the word of the man of God had fatal consequences for him. This leads us to the second prophecy concerning those consequences. The second prophecy was Elisha's response to the disbelieving sarcastic comment of the king's officer: that the latter would see the famine broken but would not eat any of the food. This smacks of being a riddle: how can you see food but not eat it? We find out as the story unfolds. Lepers found the camp of the besieging Arameans abandoned, because YHWH had caused them to hear the sound of a massive army approaching, upon which they had panicked and fled, leaving all their supplies. After gorging themselves for a while on the Arameans' food, the lepers were struck with their need to inform the city—which they did. The king thought it was a trap, sent scouts to verify their story, and found it to be true. The starving people rushed through the gate to plunder the Aramean camp, trampling to death the king's officer in the process. The relating of the death of the king's officer frames the portion of the text evincing the fulfillment of both Elisha's prophecies. Of course, the officer's demise is a fulfillment in itself. The *wayyiqtols* translated "answered," "said," "trampled," and "died" recur in the text, referring to exactly the same incidents as when used the first time and to exactly the same times.

(c) Examples of *Summary*

ASSESSMENT OF ESAU'S ACTIONS (GENESIS 25:34)

וְיַעֲקֹב נָתַן לְעֵשָׂו לֶחֶם וּנְזִיד עֲדָשִׁים **וַיֹּאכַל וַיֵּשְׁתְּ וַיָּקָם וַיֵּלַךְ וַיִּבֶז** עֵשָׂו
אֶת־הַבְּכֹרָה:

As for Jacob, he gave Esau bread and lentil stew. And he [Esau] **ate** and
drank, **arose** and **went**. So, Esau **despised** his birthright.

Stroup has discussed this verse above and pointed out the obvious fact that
Esau did not wait until he had eaten all the stew before he had anything
to drink. Indeed, most likely he alternated between eating and drinking as
we do, given that the two actions represented by the first two *wayyiqtols* are
compatible. On the other hand, the third and fourth *wayyiqtols* are most
likely not compatible with the first two, and thus must occur after them
in time, even though one can imagine a scenario with Esau still chomping
on his food and carrying a wineskin from which he frequently takes a deep
draught as he runs off, not giving a single thought to what he has lost in
exchange for fleeting gratification. The fifth *wayyiqtol* is altogether different
from the rest. It is summary assessment of what Esau has done. Thus, time
does not advance.

SUMMARIES OF DURATIONS OF MINOR JUDGESHIPS (JUDGES 12:11B–12)

וַיִּשְׁפֹּט אֶת־יִשְׂרָאֵל עֶשֶׂר שָׁנִים: 12 **וַיָּמָת** אֵלוֹן הַזְּבוּלֹנִי **וַיִּקָּבֵר** בְּאַיָּלוֹן
בְּאֶרֶץ זְבוּלֻן:

And he **judged** Israel seven years. Then Elon, the Zebulonite **died** and **was
buried** in Ayyalon in the land of Zebulun.

This happens to be the formulaic ending of the account of Elon's judgeship,
but each of the three accounts of the minor judges from this portion of the
Book of Judges, ends in the same formulaic way with three *wayyiqtols*: the
first is a summary statement of how many years the judge judged, differing
from the others only in his length of tenure; the second, reporting his death;
and the third, recording his burial in such and such a place. Each first
wayyiqtol encompasses that judge's entire rule and thus does not evince any
temporal progression.

SAMSON'S WEEPING PHILISTINE WIFE (JUDGES 14:16–17)

16 וַתֵּבְךְּ אֵשֶׁת שִׁמְשׁוֹן עָלָיו וַתֹּאמֶר רַק־שְׂנֵאתַנִי וְלֹא אֲהַבְתָּנִי הַחִידָה
חַדְתָּ לִבְנֵי עַמִּי וְלִי לֹא הִגַּדְתָּה וַיֹּאמֶר לָהּ הִנֵּה לְאָבִי וּלְאִמִּי לֹא הִגַּדְתִּי
וְלָךְ אַגִּיד:
17 וַתֵּבְךְּ עָלָיו שִׁבְעַת הַיָּמִים אֲשֶׁר־הָיָה לָהֶם הַמִּשְׁתֶּה וַיְהִי בַּיּוֹם
הַשְּׁבִיעִי וַיַּגֶּד־לָהּ כִּי הֱצִיקַתְהוּ וַתַּגֵּד הַחִידָה לִבְנֵי עַמָּהּ:

The wife of Samson **wept** upon him. She **said**, "You only hate me; you do not love me. A riddle you told to the sons of my people, but me you did not tell." Then he **said** to her, "Indeed, my father and my mother I have not told; and you I should tell?" She **wept** upon him the seven days that constituted their feast. Finally, on the seventh day he **told** her, because she had pressured him [so]. Then she **told** the riddle to the sons of her people.

Because her countrymen invited to the wedding feast for Samson and herself threatened to immolate her if she did not find out the secret of Samson's riddle, Samson's wife, instead of telling her husband of their intimidation, determined to pry the secret out of him. She tried to move him with her tears (the first *wayyiqtol*) and to break his resolve with baseless charges that his unwillingness to tell her the secret showed that he hated her (the second *wayyiqtol*). His retort to her that since he had not even told his parents, why should he tell her (the third *wayyiqtol*), indicates that he resisted her efforts at first. Although a man should trust his wife with secrets more than he does his parents—and thus his reply to her evinces a basic misunderstanding of marriage—his misgivings about her loyalty to him vis-à-vis to her countrymen were apparently not misplaced, seeing that she betrayed him as soon as she knew the secret (the seventh *wayyiqtol*). One could ask: why did she not seek his help? Instead she resolutely pursued her campaign of tears and false accusations for their entire wedding celebration week (the fourth *wayyiqtol*) until he broke under her ceaseless barrage and told her the secret (the sixth *wayyiqtol*). The fourth *wayyiqtol* is a summary of the first three, the same cycle repeating itself over and over again for seven days.

2.2.3 Summary

In light of all the various perspectives on *coherence relations*, we could have approached the subject from many angles; used different, more, or fewer categories; and furnished other and certainly more biblical examples. In no stretch of the imagination have we examined all of the occurrences of any of the categories. But hopefully we have a better understanding of how they work in the BH text, particularly with respect to temporal sequence.

The set of **coherence relations** we chose (*Serialation, Result/Cause, Contrast,* and *Elaboration*) seems well represented in BH narrative and provides not a few examples of dischronologized *wayyiqtol*. We can further say that time progresses in the first two, but not in the second two.

Now we must move on to consider what might be perhaps the most decisive factor in determining temporal progression in a text, the **compatibility** or **incompatibility** of eventualities.

2.3 Compatibility/Incompatibility and Temporal Displacement

This subsection is organized as follows:

2.3.1 Introduction
2.3.2 Biblical Examples
2.3.3 Summary

2.3.1 Introduction

As discussed above, the **compatibility** versus **incompatibility** of the eventualities represented by the VPs in a text is a decisive factor in determining the temporal profile of that text, specifically with regard to the possibility of the simultaneity or non-simultaneity of the eventualities. **Compatibility** and *simultaneity* go hand in hand. *Compatible eventualities* means those that *can* occur simultaneously; but they are not constrained to do so. This requires us then to understand the concept of simultaneity.

If we posit that an eventuality occurs over an interval of time, simultaneity is overlap—however small—of these intervals. Most often in our discussion below we will employ common nomenclature, such as *at the same time, concurrent,* or *contemporaneous,* referring when we do so to overlapping time intervals, but only employing the latter more cumbersome verbiage when necessary.

Compatible eventualities can occur simultaneously (although are not constrained to be so); incompatible cannot. But even so, the linear character of text (word follows word) requires that concurrent eventualities be recounted sequentially. In this case, textual sequentiality does not mirror reality: the text cannot be iconic. On the other hand, if eventualities are incompatible, the time the eventualities occurred must be different: the **incompatibility** of eventualities displaces the time of the eventualities. And, in this case, the sequentiality can be iconic, but not necessarily so: the polarity of the text could be reversed as in *Bob fell. Al pushed him.* It is up to the reader to use temporal reasoning to deduce whether or not the eventualities did indeed happen at the same time.

In the texts below, I will argue that the eventualities described were either certainly simultaneous or likely so.

2.3.2 Biblical Examples

JACOB COOKING; ESAU ARRIVES (GENESIS 25:29)

וַיָּ֥זֶד יַעֲקֹ֖ב נָזִ֑יד **וַיָּבֹ֥א** עֵשָׂ֛ו מִן־הַשָּׂדֶ֖ה וְה֥וּא עָיֵֽף׃

Jacob **was cooking** a stew. Esau **came** in from the field. (Now he was exhausted.)

My translation of the first *wayyiqtol* clause as "Jacob was cooking a stew," reflects my perception of this event. From common knowledge we understand that Esau could have arrived while Jacob was cooking the stew. Both *cooking* and *arriving* can happen at the same time.

Then the question must be asked: why was Jacob's cooking not grammaticalized as an infinitive construct with prefixed בְּ or כְּ, ("when" and "when and because," respectively)? My answer is that this would subordinate the cooking to the arriving, which is not what the author wanted to convey. Nor did he want to contrast the two, which probably would have been done with the second clause being disjunctive with *qatal* instead of conjunctive with *wayyiqtol*. All of this *may* suggest that sequential *wayyiqtols* are required to represent the occurrence of equally sentient, simultaneous eventualities, which are not meant to be contrasted.

BALAAM'S SHE-ASS CRUSHES HER MASTER'S FOOT (NUMBERS 22:25)

וַתֵּ֣רֶא הָאָת֗וֹן אֶת־מַלְאַ֣ךְ יְהוָה֮ וַתִּלָּחֵץ֮ אֶל־הַקִּיר֒ וַתִּלְחַ֛ץ אֶת־רֶ֥גֶל בִּלְעָ֖ם אֶל־הַקִּ֑יר **וַיֹּ֖סֶף** לְהַכֹּתָֽהּ׃

The she-ass **saw** the Angel of YHWH. She **pressed** against the wall and **pressed** Balaam's foot against the wall. Then he **struck** her again.

The verse above furnishes a parade example of simultaneous actions constrained to be sequential in the text because of its physical linearity. The second and third *wayyiqtols* clearly refer to the same event. There is no other possibility. Simultaneity might be debatable for the other examples in this sub-subsection, but not this one. Even the roots for the two are the same; although, the stems differ. The first is a *Niphal*; the second is a *Qal*. The *Niphal* in this verse is a verb of physical motion: to move next to something or squeeze against something—in this case, the wall.[43] In English

---

43. The *Niphal* is a verb of motion; but, not usually physical motion. Usually the subject-experiencer-referent moves from one *state* to another; but, occasionally—as in this case—it can refer to physical motion. I elucidated these ideas in my dissertation and argued from the *Niphal*'s attested diatheses that it has medio-passive voice. Indeed, I discussed this verse in particular.

translations this idea has been rendered in a number of different ways, often with a pseudo-reflexive (adding "herself"): "thrust herself against" (GNV; KJV), "pushed herself" (NKJ), "pushed against" (ESV), "pressed herself against" (TNK), "pressed close to" (NIV), "scraped against" (NJB, NRS), and so forth. At any rate, the text looks at the same eventuality from different perspectives: hers and his. From hers, she moved as close as she possibly could to the wall to avoid the menacing Angel of YHWH. From his, one of his dangling feet—because he was straddling her—was between her side and the wall. And so it was crushed, pressed, pinched, scraped, etc. against the wall.

GOLIATH AND DAVID RUN TOWARDS EACH OTHER (1 SAMUEL 17:48)

וְהָיָה כִּי־קָם הַפְּלִשְׁתִּי **וַיֵּלֶךְ וַיִּקְרַב** לִקְרַאת דָּוִד **וַיְמַהֵר** דָּוִד **וַיָּרָץ** הַמַּעֲרָכָה לִקְרַאת הַפְּלִשְׁתִּי׃

When the Philistine arose, he **went** and **drew near** to meet David. David **hastened** and **ran** to the battle line to meet the Philistine.

Although it is *possible* that David waited until Goliath had taken his position and then ran to meet him; it is not *plausible*. Most likely David delayed, at most, a split second before running toward Goliath. In other words they were approaching one another at the same time. And yet the physical linearity of texts requires that their respective actions be reported sequentially: two *wayyiqtols* describing Goliath's approach, followed by two *wayyiqtols* for David. In addition, this may support what I said above concerning how simultaneous eventualities having the same level of significance were construed by the author when his purpose was not to indicate contrast.

DAVID DODGING SAUL'S SPEAR (1 SAMUEL 18:11)

וַיָּטֶל שָׁאוּל אֶת־הַחֲנִית **וַיֹּאמֶר** אַכֶּה בְדָוִד וּבַקִּיר **וַיִּסֹּב** דָּוִד מִפָּנָיו פַּעֲמָיִם׃

Saul **hurled** a spear and **said**, "I will transfix David to the wall."[44] But David **dodged** him twice.

---

44. This is the same construction found in Dt 15:17, concerning the servant who does not want to leave his master. The legislation dictated that in such a case the master would mark that servant by piercing his ear at the door (cf Ex 21:6). As was noted by Stephen Geller at Dropsie College, a ב preceeding the word for ear and also preceeding the word for door suggests that the ear is against the door, and that the awl would pass through the ear into the door. Thus here, David was against the wall (already), and Saul hoped to cause his spear to pass through David into the wall.

A little common sense brings light to these eventualities. First of all, Saul certainly did not throw his spear and *then* think his murderous thought. They were simultaneous or the thought preceded the action. But what of David's dodging? Assuming that David knew that Saul usually threw on target, he could not have waited to determine if that was the case, because he was the target! He must have delayed, however, for an instant until Saul released the spear, at which point, the king would have no further control over it. If David had moved too soon, Saul could have just altered his aim. Nevertheless, David did dodge when the spear was in flight towards him. It is like and unlike baseball. The pitcher releases the ball from his fingers first. Saul did the same with his spear. Then the batter—unlike David, who did not want to intercept the projectile from Saul—moves his bat to intercept the projectile. The batter has to hit the ball before it reaches its intended destination, the catcher's mitt, in mid-flight, as it were. But the ball's trajectory is determined by the pitcher (and gravity, and the wind, and possibly other factors) as was Saul's spear. The question is: does throwing an object anticipate hitting an intended target and thus include its trajectory or is it just its release? I believe that the former is the case, as Saul made clear by his thoughts, and certainly what is the goal of pitching.

2.3.3 Summary

Up to this point we have been looking only at consecutive verbs to understand the factors that determine temporal progression. But clearly because of *Elaboration* and *Contrast*, temporal progression can skip over verbs, as we will now show as we consider to which verb a given verb is linked. With this next factor we begin to expand from the immediate context (the **macro-level**) to the larger context of the **mega-level**.

2.4 Attachment/Detachment and Temporal Dislocation

This section breaks down as follows:

> 2.4.1 What is Verbal Attachment?
> 2.4.2 Biblical Examples
> 2.4.3 Summary

2.4.1 What is Verbal Attachment? And Where Do Verbs Attach?

It is a fact that most often verbs attach to the verbs closest to them, but not always. What do we mean by attachment? A verb is attached to another verb if the eventuality corresponding to the second verb is more closely connected (temporally or logically) to the first verb than to other verbs.

Verbs attach to other verbs at the same level, as if in an outline.[45] Verbs can also be connected in this way, that all of them are subsets of another verb. To illustrate these ideas and a number of others we have discussed above consider the following contrived scenario involving our playground trio:

(46)a. The boys had a full day on Saturday
    b. They flew kites
      c. Al brought the kite kits
      d. Bob brought the string
      e. Carl assembled them
      f. They all ran as fast they could so that their kites went up in the air
      g. The wind died down for a few minutes
      h. Al left
      i. The wind picked up again
    j. Al road his bike in the neighborhood
    k. The three went to the shore in the afternoon with their parents, older siblings, and their dogs
      l. They played with their dogs
        m. Al ran with his—or at least tried to
        n. Bob and Carl played fetch with theirs
          o. They threw balls into the water
          p. Their dogs chased them
          q. They brought them back so that they could throw them again
        r. Al joined in with his dog on the fun they were having
      s. Al built a sand castle
      t. Bob and Carl watched their older brothers surf
      u. Al fell asleep
      v. They all fell asleep on the way home
    w. They sleepily climbed up the stairs of their respective houses
    x. They fell into bed
    y. They went to church the next day

I organized this according to its levels using world knowledge of what things naturally go together. But when considered formally, this amounts to recognizing the hierarchy that is in the text; or from Asher and Vieu's (2005, 596–97) perspective: ascertaining where there is coordination (temporal progression occurs[46] versus where there is subordination

---

45. Organizing these eventualities as an outline as I did above, allows us to see the truth of Asher and Vieu's assertion that "discourse has a hierarchal structure" (2005, 591). Also—as they note—coherence relations differ in two more significant ways. First, coordinating relations alter the topic of the discourse; subordinating, do not (596). And, second, subordinating relations can be deleted and still have a coherent text; not so, with coordination (596–97).

46. They consider narration—what we have called *Serialation*—the prototypical *coordinating coherence relation*; whereas, *Elaboration* is the prototypical *subordinating* relation (600).

(no temporal progression). Among the general characterizations of **coherence relations**, which are noted by them, two stand out as the most significant. First, coordinating relations alter the topic of the discourse; subordinating, do not. And second, subordinating relations can be deleted and still have a coherent text; not so, with coordination. Attempting attachments outside of a level leads to temporal confusion and a faulty understanding of a text.

The groupings of (46) are obvious using our understanding of *Serialation, Causation, Contrast, Elaboration,* and **compatibility** (or the lack thereof). The following is a possible analysis: (a) is an *Introductory Encapsulation* for (b) through (x). (y) is not included, because it is not on Saturday. The eventualities (b), (j), (k), (w), and (x) are mutually exclusive activities for Bob and Carl [I am not using "activities" in the technical sense of situation aspect]. They are not *compatible*. But, Al could ride his bike while Bob and Carl flew their kites. Nevertheless, he most likely cannot fly a kite while riding a bike—additionally, he left the kite-flyers. So, for Al, (b), (j), (k), (w), and (x) are *incompatible*. (c) through (i) are an elaboration of (b). (c) and (d) could happen at the same time. (e) cannot happen until (c) and (d) do, but are not caused by them. (e) provides the circumstances for (f), but does not cause it. (g) is not caused by (f); nor does the latter provide the circumstances for the former. Rather, the negation of (g) caused their kites to fly. This is a bit of temporal reversal. (g) causes (h) or at least provides the circumstances for it. (i) would allow the kites to fly again. (j) could happen while Bob and Carl continue to fly their kites, but has nothing to do with kite flying. (k) also is *incompatible* with (b) and (j) and happens later in the day. It is not connected to (j); but rather, is an obvious subset of (a), as are, (b), (w), and (x). (l), (s), (t), (u), and (v) are all subsets of (k) and therefore elaborations of it. (s), (t), (u), and (v) are not *compatible* with (l); but (s) is *compatible* with (t), (t) is *compatible* with (u), even though (s) is not *compatible* with (u). Obviously, (v) is not *compatible* with (l), (s), (t), and (u). (m), (n), and (r) are subsets of (l), for which it is their *Introductory Encapsulation*. Of these (m) and (n) are *compatible*, (n) and (r) are *compatible*; but, (m) and (r) are not compatible. In addition, (o), (p), and (q) are an elaboration of (n) and are temporally in order, since (o) provides the circumstances for (p) and (p) for (q).

The same types of structures obtain in BH narrative, as will be shown in the examples below—and this is usually with *wayyiqtols*. Failure to recognize this can lead to misunderstanding and misinterpretation.

2.4.2 Biblical Examples

We are going to look at three extraordinary examples, in which considering attachment can greatly help in understanding the temporal profile of the text.

ISAAC SENDS JACOB TO PADAN ARAM; ESAU RESPONDS (GENESIS 28:1–10)

וַיִּקְרָא יִצְחָק אֶל־יַעֲקֹב וַיְבָרֶךְ אֹתוֹ וַיְצַוֵּהוּ וַיֹּאמֶר לוֹ
לֹא־תִקַּח אִשָּׁה מִבְּנוֹת כְּנָעַן: ² קוּם לֵךְ פַּדֶּנָה אֲרָם בֵּיתָה בְתוּאֵל אֲבִי
אִמֶּךָ וְקַח־לְךָ מִשָּׁם אִשָּׁה מִבְּנוֹת לָבָן אֲחִי אִמֶּךָ: ³ וְאֵל שַׁדַּי יְבָרֵךְ אֹתְךָ
וְיַפְרְךָ וְיַרְבֶּךָ וְהָיִיתָ לִקְהַל עַמִּים: ⁴ וְיִתֶּן־לְךָ אֶת־בִּרְכַּת אַבְרָהָם לְךָ
וּלְזַרְעֲךָ אִתָּךְ לְרִשְׁתְּךָ אֶת־אֶרֶץ מְגֻרֶיךָ אֲשֶׁר־נָתַן אֱלֹהִים לְאַבְרָהָם:

⁵ וַיִּשְׁלַח יִצְחָק אֶת־יַעֲקֹב וַיֵּלֶךְ פַּדֶּנָה אֲרָם אֶל־לָבָן בֶּן־בְּתוּאֵל הָאֲרַמִּי
אֲחִי רִבְקָה אֵם יַעֲקֹב וְעֵשָׂו:

⁶ וַיַּרְא עֵשָׂו כִּי־בֵרַךְ יִצְחָק אֶת־יַעֲקֹב וְשִׁלַּח אֹתוֹ פַּדֶּנָה אֲרָם לָקַחַת־לוֹ
מִשָּׁם אִשָּׁה בְּבָרֲכוֹ אֹתוֹ וַיְצַו עָלָיו לֵאמֹר לֹא־תִקַּח אִשָּׁה מִבְּנוֹת כְּנָעַן:
⁷ וַיִּשְׁמַע יַעֲקֹב אֶל־אָבִיו וְאֶל־אִמּוֹ וַיֵּלֶךְ פַּדֶּנָה אֲרָם:
⁸ וַיַּרְא עֵשָׂו כִּי רָעוֹת בְּנוֹת כְּנָעַן בְּעֵינֵי יִצְחָק אָבִיו:
⁹ וַיֵּלֶךְ עֵשָׂו אֶל־יִשְׁמָעֵאל וַיִּקַּח אֶת־מָחֲלַת | בַּת־יִשְׁמָעֵאל בֶּן־אַבְרָהָם
אֲחוֹת נְבָיוֹת עַל־נָשָׁיו לוֹ לְאִשָּׁה: ס

¹⁰ וַיֵּצֵא יַעֲקֹב מִבְּאֵר שָׁבַע וַיֵּלֶךְ חָרָנָה:

Isaac ªsummoned Jacob, ᵇblessed him and ᶜcommanded him and ᵈsaid to him, "You must not take a wife from the daughters of the Canaanites. Go immediately to Padan Aram, to the house of Bethuel, the father of your mother, and take for yourself from there a wife from the daughters of Laban, the brother of your mother. May El-Shaddai bless you, make you fruitful and multiply you, and may you/you will become an assembly of peoples. And may He give to you the blessing of Abraham, to you and to your seed along with you, as your possession the land of your sojourning, which God gave to Abraham."

Then Isaac ᵉsent out Jacob. And he ᶠwent to Padan Aram, to Laban, the son of Bethuel the Aramean, the brother of Rebecca, the mother of Jacob and Esau.

Esau ᵍsaw that [[realized that]] Isaac had blessed Jacob and had sent him to Padan Aram to take for himself from there a wife: [that] when he had blessed him, he ʰcommanded him, "You must not take a wife from the daughters of the Canaanites." [that] Jacob [had] ⁱlistened to his father and his mother and [had] ʲgone to Padan Aram.

Then Esau ᵏsaw that [[realized that]] the daughters of the Canaanites were bad in the eyes of Isaac his father.

So Esau [l]**went** to Ishmael and [m]**took** Mahalat, the daughter of Ishmael, the son of Abraham, the sister of Nebayot—besides his (other) wives—for himself as a wife.

And Jacob [n]**went out** from Be'er Sheva, and he [o]**went** to Haran.

This is a very interesting text, which illustrates a number of the points discussed above. First of all, we notice that *wayyiqtols* **(b)**, **(c)**, and **(d)** require **(a)** (it is *necessary*): Isaac could not command or bless Jacob until he had summoned him. Furthermore, **(a)** is not *sufficient* to *cause* **(b)**, **(c)**, and **(d)**; therefore, this is an example of *Serialation*, not *Result*. In either case, time advances. But, we notice that Isaac's actual speech is ordered differently: his directive to Jacob precedes his blessing of him. Thus, the temporal order of these eventualities was probably **a c d b**, which was temporally followed by **e**, and then by **f**.

The narrative then departs for three verses from the main story line, which is of Jacob, to consider Esau's reaction to all that had occurred between his father and his brother, and the latter's leaving on a journey back to their ancestral homeland to find a wife. Since this scene is his *reaction* to all the preceding eventualities, its first verb (*wayyiqtol* **[g]**) is related to the previous scene considered as a whole by either *Serialation* or *Result*. The issue is whether or not the eventualities surrounding the departure of Jacob, were *sufficient* to make Esau think about the significance of all of it to him, in which case the **coherence relation** would be *Result*. But, I doubt it: the record of Esau's thinking is not very flattering to him. Nevertheless, in either case, time marches forward.

This is a scene within the greater narrative, which unfolds as follows so as to report what Esau was thinking after Jacob left. Shortly after Jacob departed for Haran, Esau came to the realization **(g)** of the significance to him of what had happened. He rehearsed in his mind the chain of past eventualities: principally, Isaac's blessing (*qatal* for anterior action), sending (waw + *qatal*—not *w^{e}qatal*—for anterior action), and commanding (*wayyiqtol* **[h]**) Jacob, and the latter's unquestioned and immediate obedience (*wayyiqtols* **[i]** and **[j]**).

From this analysis it is clear that the eventualities depicted by the textual sequence **h i j** were not temporally sandwiched between the eventualities represented by **(g)** and **(k)**. Rather, due to the fact that the sequence is the record of Esau's thoughts about the past, they reprise **(a)** through **(f)**. In addition, this informs us that the main narrative line in this sub-narrative scene is **g k l m**. So **(k)** is temporally connected to **(g)**, not to **(j)**.

We also learn that a sub-narrative, just as the main narrative, has its own narrative line, which is independent of that of the main narrative. And, moreover, this particular sub-narrative has an additional narrative nested within it, which also has its own temporal sequence apart from that of the scene. Indeed, it is following part of the temporal sequence of the main narrative.

The narrative line of this scene resumes with *wayyiqtol* (k). Here we learn that Esau reflected not only on the order of eventualities but also on the kernel of Isaac's words to Jacob: not to take a wife from the Canaanites. He concluded (*wayyiqtol* [k]) from this that he was obliged—as Jacob had set out to do—to address his father's displeasure with the nationality of his wives. *Wayyiqtols* (l) and (m) record his subsequent actions. And with these, this subsection about Esau comes to an end.

At this juncture the text takes up again the story of Jacob with *wayyiqtols* (n) and (o). Obviously, the first of these is not connected to Esau's actions in any way, since it preceded the latter. In fact, it is temporally connected to both (e) and (f), the latter which is the record of Jacob's obedience to his father. (n) is attached to (e) by *Serialation* or even *Result*, in that the eventuality it depicts provided the circumstances for Jacob's going out from Beersheba, if not the impetus for it. (n) is attached to (f) by *Elaboration*, in that it details the beginning of Jacob's journey. Thus, (n) does not temporally advance the account. Furthermore, it functions to reorient the reader to the main narrative by recommencing the story of Jacob's journey when and where it left off before the hiatus of the scene involving Esau.

RAHAB AND THE SPIES (JOSHUA 2:1–22)

וַיִּשְׁלַ֣ח יְהוֹשֻֽׁעַ־בִּן־נ֠וּן מִן־הַשִּׁטִּ֞ים שְׁנַֽיִם־אֲנָשִׁ֤ים מְרַגְּלִים֙ חֶ֣רֶשׁ לֵאמֹ֔ר לְכ֛וּ רְא֥וּ אֶת־הָאָ֖רֶץ וְאֶת־יְרִיח֑וֹ **וַיֵּלְכ֡וּ וַיָּבֹ֩אוּ֩** בֵּית־אִשָּׁ֨ה זוֹנָ֧ה וּשְׁמָ֛הּ רָחָ֖ב **וַיִּשְׁכְּבוּ־שָֽׁמָּה**׃

²**וַיֵּ֣אָמַ֔ר** לְמֶ֣לֶךְ יְרִיח֖וֹ לֵאמֹ֑ר הִנֵּ֣ה אֲנָשִׁ֞ים בָּ֧אוּ הֵ֛נָּה הַלַּ֖יְלָה מִבְּנֵ֣י יִשְׂרָאֵ֑ל לַחְפֹּ֖ר אֶת־הָאָֽרֶץ׃

³**וַיִּשְׁלַח֙** מֶ֣לֶךְ יְרִיח֔וֹ אֶל־רָחָ֖ב לֵאמֹ֑ר ה֠וֹצִ֠יאִי הָאֲנָשִׁ֨ים הַבָּאִ֤ים אֵלַ֙יִךְ֙ אֲשֶׁר־בָּ֣אוּ לְבֵיתֵ֔ךְ כִּ֛י לַחְפֹּ֥ר אֶת־כָּל־הָאָ֖רֶץ בָּֽאוּ׃

⁴**וַתִּקַּ֧ח** הָאִשָּׁ֛ה אֶת־שְׁנֵ֥י הָאֲנָשִׁ֖ים **וַֽתִּצְפְּנ֑וֹ וַתֹּ֣אמֶר ׀** כֵּ֗ן בָּ֤אוּ אֵלַי֙ הָֽאֲנָשִׁ֔ים וְלֹ֥א יָדַ֖עְתִּי מֵאַ֥יִן הֵֽמָּה׃

⁵**וַיְהִ֨י** הַשַּׁ֜עַר לִסְגּ֗וֹר בַּחֹ֙שֶׁךְ֙ וְהָאֲנָשִׁ֣ים יָצָ֔אוּ לֹ֣א יָדַ֔עְתִּי אָ֥נָה הָלְכ֖וּ הָֽאֲנָשִׁ֑ים רִדְפ֥וּ מַהֵ֛ר אַחֲרֵיהֶ֖ם כִּ֥י תַשִּׂיגֽוּם׃

⁶**וְהִ֖יא** הֶעֱלָ֣תַם הַגָּ֑גָה **וַֽתִּטְמְנֵם֙** בְּפִשְׁתֵּ֣י הָעֵ֔ץ הָעֲרֻכ֥וֹת לָ֖הּ עַל־הַגָּֽג׃

7 וְהָאֲנָשִׁים רָדְפוּ אַחֲרֵיהֶם דֶּרֶךְ הַיַּרְדֵּן עַל הַמַּעְבְּרוֹת וְהַשַּׁעַר סָגָרוּ
אַחֲרֵי כַּאֲשֶׁר יָצְאוּ הָרֹדְפִים אַחֲרֵיהֶם:

8 וְהֵמָּה טֶרֶם יִשְׁכָּבוּן וְהִיא עָלְתָה עֲלֵיהֶם עַל־הַגָּג:

9 וַתֹּאמֶר אֶל־הָאֲנָשִׁים יָדַעְתִּי כִּי־נָתַן יְהוָה לָכֶם אֶת־הָאָרֶץ וְכִי־נָפְלָה
אֵימַתְכֶם עָלֵינוּ וְכִי נָמֹגוּ כָּל־יֹשְׁבֵי הָאָרֶץ מִפְּנֵיכֶם:

10 כִּי שָׁמַעְנוּ אֵת אֲשֶׁר־הוֹבִישׁ יְהוָה אֶת־מֵי יַם־סוּף מִפְּנֵיכֶם בְּצֵאתְכֶם
מִמִּצְרָיִם וַאֲשֶׁר עֲשִׂיתֶם לִשְׁנֵי מַלְכֵי הָאֱמֹרִי אֲשֶׁר בְּעֵבֶר הַיַּרְדֵּן לְסִיחֹן
וּלְעוֹג אֲשֶׁר הֶחֱרַמְתֶּם אוֹתָם:

11 וַנִּשְׁמַע וַיִּמַּס לְבָבֵנוּ וְלֹא־קָמָה עוֹד רוּחַ בְּאִישׁ מִפְּנֵיכֶם כִּי יְהוָה
אֱלֹהֵיכֶם הוּא אֱלֹהִים בַּשָּׁמַיִם מִמַּעַל וְעַל־הָאָרֶץ מִתָּחַת:

12 וְעַתָּה הִשָּׁבְעוּ־נָא לִי בַּיהוָה כִּי־עָשִׂיתִי עִמָּכֶם חָסֶד וַעֲשִׂיתֶם גַּם־אַתֶּם
עִם־בֵּית אָבִי חֶסֶד וּנְתַתֶּם לִי אוֹת אֱמֶת:

13 וְהַחֲיִתֶם אֶת־אָבִי וְאֶת־אִמִּי וְאֶת־אַחַי וְאֶת־(אַחְיוֹתַי) [אַחְיוֹתַי] וְאֵת
כָּל־אֲשֶׁר לָהֶם וְהִצַּלְתֶּם אֶת־נַפְשֹׁתֵינוּ מִמָּוֶת:

14 וַיֹּאמְרוּ לָהּ הָאֲנָשִׁים נַפְשֵׁנוּ תַחְתֵּיכֶם לָמוּת אִם לֹא תַגִּידוּ אֶת־דְּבָרֵנוּ
זֶה וְהָיָה בְּתֵת־יְהוָה לָנוּ אֶת־הָאָרֶץ וְעָשִׂינוּ עִמָּךְ חֶסֶד וֶאֱמֶת:

15 וַתּוֹרִדֵם בַּחֶבֶל בְּעַד הַחַלּוֹן כִּי בֵיתָהּ בְּקִיר הַחוֹמָה וּבַחוֹמָה הִיא
יוֹשָׁבֶת:

16 וַתֹּאמֶר לָהֶם הָהָרָה לֵּכוּ פֶּן־יִפְגְּעוּ בָכֶם הָרֹדְפִים וְנַחְבֵּתֶם שָׁמָּה
שְׁלֹשֶׁת יָמִים עַד שׁוֹב הָרֹדְפִים וְאַחַר תֵּלְכוּ לְדַרְכְּכֶם:

17 וַיֹּאמְרוּ אֵלֶיהָ הָאֲנָשִׁים נְקִיִּם אֲנַחְנוּ מִשְּׁבֻעָתֵךְ הַזֶּה אֲשֶׁר הִשְׁבַּעְתָּנוּ:

18 הִנֵּה אֲנַחְנוּ בָאִים בָּאָרֶץ אֶת־תִּקְוַת חוּט הַשָּׁנִי הַזֶּה תִּקְשְׁרִי בַּחַלּוֹן
אֲשֶׁר הוֹרַדְתֵּנוּ בוֹ וְאֶת־אָבִיךְ וְאֶת־אִמֵּךְ וְאֶת־אַחַיִךְ וְאֵת כָּל־בֵּית אָבִיךְ
תַּאַסְפִי אֵלַיִךְ הַבָּיְתָה:

19 וְהָיָה כֹּל אֲשֶׁר־יֵצֵא מִדַּלְתֵי בֵיתֵךְ הַחוּצָה דָּמוֹ בְרֹאשׁוֹ וַאֲנַחְנוּ נְקִיִּם
וְכֹל אֲשֶׁר יִהְיֶה אִתָּךְ בַּבַּיִת דָּמוֹ בְרֹאשֵׁנוּ אִם־יָד תִּהְיֶה־בּוֹ:

20 וְאִם־תַּגִּידִי אֶת־דְּבָרֵנוּ זֶה וְהָיִינוּ נְקִיִּם מִשְּׁבֻעָתֵךְ אֲשֶׁר הִשְׁבַּעְתָּנוּ:

21 וַתֹּאמֶר כְּדִבְרֵיכֶם כֶּן־הוּא וַתְּשַׁלְּחֵם וַיֵּלֵכוּ וַתִּקְשֹׁר אֶת־תִּקְוַת הַשָּׁנִי
בַּחַלּוֹן:

22 וַיֵּלְכוּ וַיָּבֹאוּ הָהָרָה וַיֵּשְׁבוּ שָׁם שְׁלֹשֶׁת יָמִים עַד־שָׁבוּ הָרֹדְפִים וַיְבַקְשׁוּ
הָרֹדְפִים בְּכָל־הַדֶּרֶךְ וְלֹא מָצָאוּ:

Joshua, the son of Nun, secretly ᵃ**sent** from the Shittim two men as spies:
"Go see the land, Jericho." So, they ᵇ**went** and ᶜ**entered** into the house of a
woman, a prostitute, whose name was Rahab. And they ᵈ**lay down** there.

It ᶜ**was said** to the king of Jericho, "Indeed men have come here tonight from the sons of Israel to search out the land." So, the king of Jericho ᶠ**sent** [messengers, [most likely soldiers]] to Rahab: "Bring out the men who came to/into you, who came to your house, because to search out the entirety of the land they have come."

The woman ᵍ**took** the two men and ʰ**hid** them.

And she ⁱ**said**, [[her first dialogue—to the king's messengers]] "Yes, the men/men have come to/into me; but, I do not know from where they have come. And [it] ʲ**was** when the gates were about to close, the men/men went/go out. I do not know to where the men went. Pursue after them quickly! Indeed, you might overtake them!"

She herself had taken them up to the roof and ᵏ**hidden** them in the stalks of flax, which were arranged by her on the roof.

The men pursued after them by the way of the Jordan to the fords. The gate they closed/was closed afterwards, as soon as the pursuers went out after them.

And as for the men [[the Israelites]], before they lay down, she herself came up to them on the roof.

And she ˡ**said** to the men, "[[her second dialogue—to the Israelite men, which includes her confession of faith in YHWH and a request for them to spare her family]]." Then the men ᵒ**said** to her, "[[their first dialogue, a response to her request]]." Then she ᵖ**lowered** them by a rope through a window, because her house was on the inner wall of the city wall. (She was actually dwelling in the city wall.) And she ᑫ**said** to them, "[[her third dialogue—instructions on where to hide]]." Then the men ʳ**said** to her "[[their second dialogue]] . . . . Indeed, we are about to come into the land. This cord of scarlet thread you must tie in the window through which you lowered us . . . ." Then she ˢ**said**, "[[her fourth dialogue]] According to your words, thus [be] it." Then she ᵗ**sent** them away; and they ᵘ**went**. Then she ᵛ**tied** the scarlet cord in the window.

They ʷ**went**, ˣ**entered** into the hill country, and ʸ**stayed** there three days until the pursuers returned [to the city]. The pursuers ᶻ**sought** [them] along every road, but they did not find [them].

There are twenty-six *wayyiqtols* in this text. They are identified by bold superscripted letters in the translation above and will be referred to by bold letters in the discussion below. Twenty-three occur in the narrative; three occur in dialogue. The lettering jumps from (**l**) to (**o**), because (**m**) and (**n**) are in Rahab's second dialogue, which was directed at the Israelite men.

Now let us look at this text rather closely, starting with the most general of questions: how much time did Joshua's men spend in Jericho? It appears that they arrived at night, because some of the men frequenting her house said so: "men have come here tonight" (verse 2). It is likely that they slipped into the city at night to avoid detection. Some of the men at her house must have voiced their suspicions about the strangers: that they were Israelites. Somehow Rahab also knew that they were Israelites. When she heard what the suspicious men were saying, Rahab would have recognized at once that the strangers were in grave danger and so she lost no time in taking them up to the roof and hiding them, knowing that the suspicious men would go to the king immediately that night (hoping for reward). She also would have realized that the king would straightway dispatch soldiers to interrogate her and search her premises. She was right; they said *tonight* when they reported to the king. Also, he did send soldiers. Her foresight and quick actions saved the spies' lives! Immediately after the king's soldiers left her house, she began to make plans to get Joshua's men out of the city. As soon as the pursuing party left the city and the gates closed, she went up to the roof and talked with the men. Then without further ado she lowered them through a window (whether this was an aperture in the wall accessible from the roof or in one of her rooms below, we cannot tell). In conclusion, they only stayed there during one evening and part of that night.

Next let us consider the portions of the text that are iconic. The first four *wayyiqtols* appear to be so. (b) is related to (a) by *Result*; thus, there is temporal progression from (a) to (b). (c) follows (b) by *Serialation*; and, (d) follows (c) the same way. So, there is temporal progression from (a) through (d). But, (e) does not necessarily follow (d). It better follows (c). The arrival of two strangers at night for some reason caught the attention of some of the men visiting Rahab's establishment. And they reported their suspicions to the king—no doubt to ingratiate themselves to him. In addition, (l) and (o) are iconic. It is fairly obvious that Rahab's conversation with the Israelites (verses 9–14) is temporally sequential. She went up to the roof (a second time? [more on this below]) to have the conversation with them. In her speech (introduced by *wayyiqtol* [l]), she pleaded with them to extend the same חֶסֶד (*hesed*) "mercy-grace" to her and her household that she had shown to them. In their first speech (*wayyiqtol* [o], verse 14), they mention this חֶסֶד, which suggests that this speech is a reply to hers, and therefore followed it temporally. The temporal sequentiality of verses fifteen through twenty-one also is evident. *Wayyiqtol* (q) (verse 16) could have either temporally followed, been at the same time, or even preceded *wayyiqtol*

(p) (verse 15). There is nothing that precluded Rahab from speaking to the men before, while or after she lowered them. There would have been enough noise at a brothel to hide her words to them. I tend to think that it was the last. Verse seventeen (introduced by *wayyiqtol* [r]) records the men mentioning the window through which Rahab had lowered them ([p], verse 15). This ties verses sixteen and seventeen together—with normal temporal polarity. As to the four *wayyiqtols* in verse 21, (s) introduces her response to the men's second and final speech (introduced by [r]). With her final words to them she agreed to their terms. Her dismissal of them followed naturally (t). And so they went away (u). Finally, most likely after they left, she tied the scarlet cord in the window (v)—although she could have done so after (s). Thus, it appears that (r) through (v) are in chronological order. Finally, (w), (x), and (y) are in the order established by *Serialation*: they left Jericho (w), entered into the hill country (x) and remained there for three days (y). This leaves the following chronological uncertainties, which we will turn to below: between (d) and (e); between (f) and (g); between (h) and (i); between (o) and (p); between (v) and (w); and between (y) and (z).

In spite of the iconic sections within this text mentioned above, the text is not wholly iconic: it contains significant and glaring dischronologizations involving *wayyiqtols*, which indicate that all of them are not temporally sequential. Striking among them are the four in verses three and four: "(the king of Jericho) ^f sent," "(the woman) ^g took," "(she) ^h hid," and "(she) ^i said [[to the messengers of the king]]." As far as the first two are concerned, it is highly improbable that Rahab excused herself from the king's soldiers without being challenged or followed; went to where the spies had hidden *themselves*, even though the text does not say that they had done this, but only that they had lain down there; spirited them from there (g); and then hid them (h) again. Similarly, it is equally dubious that she, having returned from her clandestine task of treasonous defiance of the king, caught her breath, composed herself and craftily answered the questions of the messengers (i) without being challenged in any way. I submit then that *wayyiqtols* (g) and (h) are not in temporal sequence with (f) and (i), but occurred earlier. Nevertheless, they are here to show where Rahab's allegiance lay: in response to the king, confronted with a choice, even with the death penalty of treason potentially facing her, she chose YHWH, and acted accordingly.

In addition, this text evokes many intriguing questions: those of a general nature and not a few of a temporal nature. We will ask and attempt to answer both. Concerning the former, why did the spies choose to go to a brothel? Answer: it is a place where men come and go without questions—

even strangers. It is a place active at night. It is a place with rooms, where they could hide out. It is a place where men would not be as guarded in their talk as at other times; and, so, Joshua's men could find out the latest "news." It was a place loud and noisy at all times, ideal for hiding necessary quiet exchanges between themselves. They also might have noticed that it was located on the wall, convenient if they had to escape.

Moreover, what of her response to the king's men? It is an audacious, brilliant blend of ambiguity, half-truths, outright lies, and misdirection. She took full advantage of what these men thought of her because of her occupation and made use of the ambiguity of the Hebrew root בוא (*bô'*), which can mean "enter" in the usual sense or "enter into" as a reference to sexual intercourse, seizing their miscues and turning them on them. Thus, her reply to them in verses four and five, has several possible double entendres. Was she pretending to misunderstand their questions, coquettishly answering them that of course men came to her (or is she saying, came *into* her—she being a prostitute) and she did not know where they came from and where they were going when they left; or was she knowingly lying, because she *was* referring to the spies and claiming to have no knowledge of them? She was so skillful in her language that it is impossible for us to tell which it is, and neither could the king's men. Her demeanor and clever speech caught them so off-guard that when they perceived that she was no longer toying with them, they believed her lies.

Furthermore, *where* did Joshua's men lay down (**d**)? We do not know from verse one. It is not out of the realm of possibility that they rented a room. Nevertheless, there is another plausible answer. Verse eight reads, "before they lay down, she herself came up to them on the roof." Could this be a reprise of the earlier mention, filling in the information gap left by verse one?

Finally, how did it happen that the nationality of the spies became known? More to the point, how did she know? They certainly would not have announced their nationality—even in a brothel! Did their accents betray them? Their clothes? Their furtiveness? Or did YHWH reveal it to her? We do not know. But somehow she knew. And, unfortunately, others did, and informed the king.

As far as temporal questions are concerned, first: do *wayyiqtols* (**h**) and (**k**), two different roots meaning "to hide," refer to the same eventuality or to separate eventualities? The latter is highly unlikely. This would require that Rahab hid the men twice, once in some location undisclosed in the text and then on the roof. Second: when did her hiding of the men take place? As soon as they came into her house? After she suspected that their presence was known? As stated above, most likely she hid them before the soldiers came. She suspected that the latter would search for them through all the rooms, but probably not on the roof. She even made provision for that by hiding them under the flax stalks. But her speech to the soldiers was cogent enough that apparently they did not search but acted on her advice to pursue after the men. This means that the time of verse six was before that of verse two, if not earlier. Third: what is the temporal sequence of the eventualities in verses six, seven, and eight? All three verses begin with a noun or independent personal pronoun (ipp), which are followed in the first two by *qatals*. In verse eight, the pronoun is a *casus pendens*, which is resumed by the *yiqtol* following טֶרֶם, (*ṭerem*) "before." In verse six the ipp is redundant, indicating emphasis and contrast, "she *herself*," making it clear that she had hid them herself and not had one of her prostitutes do it. The eventualities of verse seven, the pursuit sent out after the spies, temporally follows verse five, but—question four— where is it temporally located with respect to verse eight? We will return to this later. The fifth question is: what is the temporal sequence of verses eight and nine? It might seem that this is easily answered, since obviously her reason for going up to the roof was to talk with the men, the verses are in chronological order. But that would be too hasty of a conclusion. The answer depends on when she went up to the roof and how many times. We know that she went up *before* the king's men came, to take the spies up there and hide them. That she would have taken them up there to hide them while or after the soldiers were there is impracticable, as we argued above. This drives us back to reexamine verse six, which apparently does not record the same eventuality as that in verse eight. The former recounts her taking them up onto the roof to hide them. But according to this verse, they were already there. Moreover, she speaks about her valorous actions on their behalf as being in the past. Aware of the suspicions that the presence of the men had aroused and suspecting that her house would therefore be under surveillance, she would not have risked another trip to the roof unless she knew there was no possibility that the spies would be discovered. This situation only could have obtained after the pursuers left and the gates were closed. This then was her second trip to her roof. Thus, we have an answer to question four; but what of question five: what is the temporal relation of this visit to the roof and her speech? Could she have given this speech earlier when she took them up to the roof? To answer these related questions we must first deal with question six: where are the two temporally sequential blocks of verses nine through fourteen (group one) and fifteen through twenty-one (group two) located in the narrative at large?

Let us look at the latter grouping first, because there are clear temporal relations, which can be observed. By the same reasoning used to answer question four, Rahab would not and could not have lowered the men from her window if there were soldiers snooping around her house. This also must have happened after she encouraged the king's men to leave the city, because she lied that the men had gone out of the city. Observing that the direction of the pursuit was eastward,[47] toward the Jordan, she warned the Israelites to go in the opposite direction, westward into the mountains (introduced by *wayyiqtol* [q], verse 16). Thus, the eventualities reported in these verses temporally follow those of verse seven.

As to the former grouping, this depends on a seventh question: do the eventualities of verse fifteen temporally follow those of verse fourteen, joining the two blocks into one? The answer is: yes. The spies' speech in verses seventeen through twenty depends on Rahab's words in verses twelve through thirteen, in particular their words "this oath of yours, which you have caused us to swear" (verse 17). Looking at it another way, the two blocks of verses are incompatible: the eventualities reported could not have occurred at the same time—except, perhaps (p) and (q). So, the blocks must be in one chronological order or the other: verses nine through fourteen must either precede or follow fifteen through twenty-one. The spies' reference to the oath that she convinced them to give requires that grouping two temporally follows grouping one. This means that *wayyiqtols* (l) and (o) though (v) are in chronological order, and the verses form one block. Given the fact that these eventualities occurred in the order of the text, right after each other, and her lowering of Joshua's men through the window had to follow her climb to the roof, all the eventualities (including her speech of verses nine through thirteen) had to follow her second assent to the roof. This is consistent with the additional observations that Rahab's speech temporally locates her second visit after the first one mentioned in verse six, because, as was said above, she referred to her act of mercy and grace as being in the past. Now we have the answers to questions five and six. In summary, the eventualities recorded in verses eight through twenty-one all had to happen after the pursuers had left on a wild goose chase and the gates had closed behind them.[48]

---

47. How was Rahab able to see the direction of the pursuit? City gates normally close at sunset, which Rahab, answering the queries of the king's men, said was about to happen. Either a detachment of soldiers was hastily gathered for the pursuit before the gates closed, or after they had been closed, they were subsequently opened to allow the detachment of soldiers to leave the city, after which they would have been closed again. It would have been twilight. The pursuers would have been visible for about an hour—longer, if there was moonlight. Also, they would have been carrying torches.

48. This could have been the first time the gates closed or the second, depending on which of the two scenarios proposed in the footnote above occurred. I suspect that it was the latter.

This brings us to the last two questions and their temporal and interpretive implications: does *wayyiqtol* (**w**) refer to the same eventuality as (**u**); and where is (**z**) temporally attached, questions eight and nine, respectively? The answer to the first of these is that it obviously refers to the same eventuality and thus is attached to *wayyiqtol* (**t**), not (**v**). I believe that the action is reprised because with verse twenty-one Rahab's interaction with the spies was over. Starting with verse twenty-two they were on their own, even though the connection with her lingered in that they followed her instructions. Finally, *wayyiqtol* (**z**) is temporally attached to the eventualities of verse seven, where the pursuit of the spies is first mentioned, but it continued for the entire time they were hiding in the hill country. Therefore, it follows (**y**) in the text. In addition, it is an appropriate restatement and concluding statement for the Rahab story, epitomizing the failure of the pursuit because of Rahab's courageous intervention.

THE MURDER OF ISHBOSHETH (2 SAMUEL 4:5–7)

וַיֵּלְכ֞וּ בְּנֵֽי־רִמּ֣וֹן הַבְּאֵֽרֹתִ֗י רֵכָ֤ב וּבַֽעֲנָה֙ וַיָּבֹ֙אוּ֙ כְּחֹ֣ם הַיּ֔וֹם אֶל־בֵּ֖ית אִ֣ישׁ בֹּ֑שֶׁת וְה֣וּא שֹׁכֵ֔ב אֵ֖ת מִשְׁכַּ֥ב הַֽצׇּהֳרָֽיִם׃

⁶ וְ֠הֵנָּה בָּ֜אוּ עַד־תּ֤וֹךְ הַבַּ֙יִת֙ לֹקְחֵ֣י חִטִּ֔ים וַיַּכֻּ֖הוּ אֶל־הַחֹ֑מֶשׁ וְרֵכָ֥ב וּבַעֲנָ֖ה אָחִ֥יו נִמְלָֽטוּ׃

⁷ וַיָּבֹ֣אוּ הַבַּ֗יִת וְהֽוּא־שֹׁכֵ֤ב עַל־מִטָּתוֹ֙ בַּחֲדַ֣ר מִשְׁכָּב֔וֹ וַיַּכֻּ֙הוּ֙ וַיְמִתֻ֔הוּ וַיָּסִ֖ירוּ אֶת־רֹאשׁ֑וֹ וַיִּקְחוּ֙ אֶת־רֹאשׁ֔וֹ וַיֵּ֙לְכ֜וּ דֶּ֧רֶךְ הָעֲרָבָ֛ה כׇּל־הַלָּֽיְלָה׃

The sons of Rimmon, the B'erotite, Rekab and Ba'anah, **went** and in the heat of the day **entered** into the house of Ish Boshet. Now he was lying on a couch in the afternoon. There they entered into the middle of the house receiving wheat and **struck** him in the belly. Then Rekab and Ba'anah his brother escaped.

They **entered** the house. Now he was lying on his bed in his bedroom. They **struck** him, **put him to death**, **removed** his head and **took** his head and **went** by the way of the 'Arabah all night.

This is an interesting text in that it appears to be susceptible to two erroneous approaches. The first of these is that it describes the same murder twice and thus should be approached as having gratuitous redundancy because of a careless redactor. The second is that it describes a two-part murder and thus should be approached as if the brothers bungled the job the first time around and had to go back a second time to finish it. But these are only appearances, not reality, as we will show below. Let us look at the text to disabuse ourselves of these incorrect understandings. But first, the cast of characters.

Ishbosheth was the youngest son of Saul, too young, apparently, to have gone into battle with his father against the Philistines. He was a weak ruler, unable to hold onto any territory in Cisjordan and thus ruled from exile in Transjordan. He was also propped up by Abner's strong leadership. When he heard of the latter's death, he lost heart, and all of Israel despaired with him. His murderers are introduced in verse two as captains of raiding parties and Be'erothites (and are thus considered Benjamites). Thus, Ishbosheth's killers were his own men from his own tribe.

The first description (verses 5–6), has three *wayyiqtols*: "went," "entered," and "struck." The second description (verse 7) has six: "entered," "struck," "put to death," "removed," "took," and "went." The first and last, being identical, form an *inclusio*, framing the deed itself with the *going* of sons of Rimmon from Israel to Transjordan (where Ishboshet "ruled" Israel from exile) and their *going* from the scene of the crime back to David (who ruled over Judah from Hebron and would soon rule over all Israel). In addition, the second and third *wayyiqtols* are repeated as the fourth and fifth, forming a skewed chiasm, which serves to highlight the sixth through the eighth. Why these? The *Hiphil* of מות, (*mût*), "to cause to die," refers to an execution, that is, someone is killed who deserves to die. The next verbal clause speaks of beheading, which is how enemies, not kin, were treated. Finally, to take the head to David was to present it to him as his war trophy, an act of war he had not authorized. In short, they treated their king as David had treated Goliath.

David considered Ishbosheth to be an innocent man. As weak as he was and in light of the fact of where he was, he probably did not view him as a threat. Moreover, David most likely thought he would yield to him in time. In addition, they killed an unarmed man while he was asleep—not in battle—the most disgraceful way for a warrior to die and the most cowardly way to kill a man—instead of facing him in battle. The text emphasizes his repose; both accounts record that he was lying down. They killed him in his bedroom, a man's inner sanctum, where his guard is down and he is not expecting treachery. Furthermore, David, by severely dealing with the murderers, proved to the tribes loyal to Saul that he had nothing to do with the heinous act, thereby continuing to build bridges from himself to those tribes.

Now let us look at the text from the perspective of ***coherence relations***. For one thing, the first description leaves details unsaid, which the second supplies. Conversely, the first includes details the second excludes. For another, the author has skillfully employed ***coherence relations*** to achieve a specific purpose.

We can make seven observations on the first account of the murder. First, the account begins with a *wayyiqtol* connected to verse two. Verses three and four are of a parenthetic nature, describing the flight (ברח [*brḥ*]) of the Be'erothites and the flight (נוס [*nûs*]) of Mephibosheth's nanny, who dropped him when he was baby, laming him. The semantic parallelism here is clear. The connection with the two murder accounts is also semantic in that the murderers escaped (מלט [*mlṭ*] in *Niphal*) after their perfidious deed. Second, we note that we do not know from these verses whether or not they killed Ishbosheth. We only know that they stabbed him in the belly. Now, of course, this is usually a fatal blow; but that would be surmise and not certainty. Third, we are at a loss (especially considering that the brothers were his own Benjamite soldiers) as to what was their motive for doing this; only later do we learn what it was. Fourth, their method is a bit foggy. We do know that they entered into Ishbosheth's house at around noon. To perpetrate their crime and get away with it, they had to do it inside, away from any witnesses and those that might try to stop them. It appears that they had no opposition. They must have reasoned—and correctly—that Ishbosheth would likely be indoors at midday and that they could gain admittance to his house either because onlookers would not think it unusual to see men trying to get out of the sun; or—if they were in their military apparel—would not be suspicious of two of the king's men coming to see him. What we do not know is the certain meaning of verse six. There are at least three possibilities, both involving taking wheat, whatever that means (carrying some? picking some up?). We can understand הֵנָּה (*hēnnāh*) as a third feminine plural ipp, meaning that some women (on guard?) took the wheat inside because of the heat, which gave the murderers the chance to slip in; or we can understand it as a locative particle, "here" or "there," in which case the men are the ones entering the house carrying wheat. A third, even more bizarre possibility, is that the two men disguised themselves as women (hence, the third feminine plural ipp) in order to get in. All three are rather strange, supporting the fact that murdering their king in such a fashion is not only wicked but unnatural. A fifth observation is that they found the king sleeping on his bed, obviously unarmed—convenient for skulking murderers. Sixth, they struck him in the belly as Ehud had Eglon—an assassin's blow. And, seventh, the text reports that the brothers escaped. Their names are redundantly relexicalized and fronted for emphasis at this point (to contrast them with heroes), with the result that *qatal* must be used. Thus, this first account gives us the basics: where they killed him, how they killed him, and that they got away, undetected. In fact, no one would have been the wiser had they not carried their gruesome trophy to David.

As far as the temporal profile of this text is concerned, the sequence of three *wayyiqtols* matches that of the eventualities, all exhibiting *Serialation,* and, therefore, temporal progression: *going* to the location provides the circumstances for *entering* the house; *entering* the house provides the circumstances for *striking.* The last verb in the first account is a *qatal,* because of the fronting of the names of the murderers; but, nevertheless, *escaping* also temporally follows the last *wayyiqtol* as *Result,* rather than *Serialation.*

As far as the second account goes, its first *wayyiqtol* (the fourth in the text as a whole) reprises the second of the first account and thus is attached to the very first one, "went." And although it omits the bit about the wheat and that they stabbed him in the belly (this detail is not repeated, because it is in the first account), this account proceeds to give us more details: precisely where the murder happened, what their perspective was on the killing (an execution), the beheading, taking the head, and details of their flight by night. This, then, is an elaboration of the first account. Within this elaboration is the following temporal sequence: progression by *Serialation* (*entered* followed by *struck*); stagnation by *Elaboration* (*struck* followed by *put him to death* [incidently, this is where we find out that they did kill him]); progression by *Serialation* (*put him to death* followed by *removed* his head); progression by *Serialation* (*removed* his head followed by *took* his head); both progression by *Result* (having his head *required* that they go) and regression by *Anticipated Result Cause* (wanting to show it to David— which occurs later in both text and time— required that they go to where he was).

2.4.3 Summary

Above we looked at some striking illustrations of attachment, but the overall temporal range in these passages is small. They are relatively temporally contiguous. This is not always the case, however. Texts can have gaping holes and large jumps in time. We are well on our way to the ***mega-level*** considering the texts below, but will leave the elucidation of the particulars to Stroup in the next chapter. In addition, Anderson discusses the means of identifying temporal discontinuities in **Chapter 14.**

2.5 Continuity/Discontinuity: Significant Dischronologizations

The outline for this subsection is as follows:

2.5.1 Temporal Gaps
2.5.2 Biblical Examples
2.5.3 Summary

2.5.1 Temporal Gaps

We know come to the fourth temporal characteristic of texts: the presence of large temporal gaps, in which the text leaps over spans of time, either backward or forward. The former are often called *flashbacks*. The latter are *foreshadowing*. In the biblical examples that follow these gaps are obvious; but, they are not always so. In such cases, the gaps must be detected through various means, such as Anderson does in **Chapter 14**. The gaps also are divisions in the texts, the depth of the gap determining whether they are separating narratives from narratives, episodes from episodes, scene from scene, or thematic paragraph from thematic paragraph.

2.5.2 Biblical Examples

HADAD'S MOTIVATION FOR OPPOSING ISRAEL (1 KINGS 11:14–22)

וַיָּ֨קֶם יְהוָ֤ה שָׂטָן֙ לִשְׁלֹמֹ֔ה אֵ֖ת הֲדַ֣ד הָאֲדֹמִ֑י מִזֶּ֧רַע הַמֶּ֛לֶךְ ה֖וּא
בֶּאֱדֽוֹם׃

15 וַיְהִ֗י בִּהְי֤וֹת דָּוִד֙ אֶת־אֱד֔וֹם בַּעֲל֗וֹת יוֹאָב֙ שַׂ֣ר הַצָּבָ֔א לְקַבֵּ֖ר אֶת־
הַחֲלָלִ֑ים וַיַּ֥ךְ כָּל־זָכָ֖ר בֶּאֱדֽוֹם׃ 16 כִּ֣י שֵׁ֧שֶׁת חֳדָשִׁ֛ים יָֽשַׁב־שָׁ֥ם יוֹאָ֖ב וְכָל־
יִשְׂרָאֵ֑ל עַד־הִכְרִ֥ית כָּל־זָכָ֖ר בֶּאֱדֽוֹם׃

17 וַיִּבְרַ֣ח אֲדַ֣ד ה֗וּא וַאֲנָשִׁ֤ים אֲדֹמִיִּים֙ מֵעַבְדֵ֣י אָבִ֔יו אִתּ֖וֹ לָב֣וֹא מִצְרָ֑יִם
וַהֲדַ֖ד נַ֥עַר קָטָֽן׃ 18 וַיָּקֻ֙מוּ֙ מִמִּדְיָ֔ן וַיָּבֹ֖אוּ פָּארָ֑ן וַיִּקְחוּ֩ אֲנָשִׁ֨ים עִמָּ֜ם מִפָּארָ֗ן
וַיָּבֹ֣אוּ מִצְרַ֘יִם֮ אֶל־פַּרְעֹ֣ה מֶֽלֶךְ־מִצְרַיִם֒ וַיִּתֶּן־ל֣וֹ בַ֔יִת וְלֶ֖חֶם אָ֣מַר ל֑וֹ וְאֶ֖רֶץ
נָ֥תַן לֽוֹ׃ 19 וַיִּמְצָא֩ הֲדַ֨ד חֵ֜ן בְּעֵינֵ֤י פַרְעֹה֙ מְאֹ֔ד וַיִּתֶּן־ל֣וֹ אִשָּׁ֔ה אֶת־אֲח֖וֹת
אִשְׁתּ֑וֹ אֲח֖וֹת תַּחְפְּנֵ֥יס הַגְּבִירָֽה׃ 20 וַתֵּ֨לֶד ל֜וֹ אֲח֣וֹת תַּחְפְּנֵ֗יס אֵ֚ת גְּנֻבַ֣ת
בְּנ֔וֹ וַתִּגְמְלֵ֣הוּ תַחְפְּנֵ֔ס בְּת֖וֹךְ בֵּ֣ית פַּרְעֹ֑ה וַיְהִ֤י גְנֻבַת֙ בֵּ֣ית פַּרְעֹ֔ה בְּת֖וֹךְ בְּנֵ֥י
פַרְעֹֽה׃ 21 וַהֲדַ֞ד שָׁמַ֣ע בְּמִצְרַ֗יִם כִּֽי־שָׁכַ֤ב דָּוִד֙ עִם־אֲבֹתָ֔יו וְכִי־מֵ֖ת יוֹאָ֣ב
שַׂר־הַצָּבָ֑א וַיֹּ֤אמֶר הֲדַד֙ אֶל־פַּרְעֹ֔ה שַׁלְּחֵ֖נִי וְאֵלֵ֥ךְ אֶל־אַרְצִֽי׃ 22 וַיֹּ֧אמֶר ל֣וֹ
פַרְעֹ֗ה כִּ֠י מָה־אַתָּ֤ה חָסֵר֙ עִמִּ֔י וְהִנְּךָ֥ מְבַקֵּ֖שׁ לָלֶ֣כֶת אֶל־אַרְצֶ֑ךָ וַיֹּ֣אמֶר ׀
לֹ֔א כִּ֥י שַׁלֵּ֖חַ תְּשַׁלְּחֵֽנִי׃

YHWH **raised up** an adversary against Solomon, Hadad the Edomite. He was from the king's seed in Edom.

When David **was** in Edom, when Joab, the commander of the army went up to bury the slain, he **struck** every male in Edom. Indeed for six months Joab and all Israel remained there until he cut off every male in Edom.

Hadad, he and Edomite men, some of the servants of his father, **fled** with him toward Egypt. Now Hadad was a little boy. And they **arose** from

Midian and **entered** Pa'ran. They **took** men with them from Pa'ran and **came** to Egypt to pharaoh, king of Egypt. And he **gave** to him a house. And bread he promised to him and land he gave to him. Hadad **found** favor in the eyes of pharaoh exceedingly. He **gave** to him as a wife the sister of his wife, the sister of Lady Tahpenes. And the sister of Tahpenes **bore** for him Gnubat, his son. And Tahpenes **weaned** him within the house of pharaoh. And Gnubat **was** in the house of pharaoh amongst the sons of pharaoh. Hadad heard in Egypt that David had lain down with his fathers and that Joab, the commander of the army, had died. Then Hadad **said** to pharaoh, "Release me in order that I may go to my country." Pharaoh **said** to him, "Indeed, but what have you lacked with me that now you are seeking to go to your country?" And he **said**, "Nothing. But you certainly must release me."

The temporal gaps are obvious in this text. The time of the eventualities of verse fifteen is late in Solomon's reign, after his third flagrant violation of the Law of the King (Dt 17:14–20)—the prohibition not to multiply wives. The text says that in his pursuit of foreign women he apostasized after their gods as well. As chastisement, YHWH raised up three adversaries against him: Hadad of Edom, Rezon of Aram, and Jereboam, an Ephraimite. The text above is the story of the first of these.

After we are introduced to Hadad of the royal house of Edom, an antagonist to Solomon, the text suddenly jumps backwards in time to the days of David, in order to give us the background of Hadad, in particular why he hated the line of David so much that he rebelled against his son. It was David's policy of genocide against Edom carried out by Joab. Hadad narrowly escaped Joab's sword and fled to Egypt, where he found asylum. The pharaoh showed him preferential treatment: giving him a house, food, land, and even a wife. This last was his greatest favor. He gave him his wife's sister as a wife, who bore him a son. Pharaoh's wife herself weaned the boy and he grew up with pharaoh's sons.

At this point of time, in spite of all the advantages that had accrued and would have continued to do so for himself and for his son if he had stayed in Egypt, when Hadad heard that David and Joab, his great foes, had died, he demanded to be released from pharaoh's court—the time of his vengeance was at hand. And although it could not be directed against his enemy directly, it could be against his son.

The time of the text has taken quite a ride: plunging as it were off a temporal cliff from late in Solomon's reign all the way down to the time of David's reign, then gradually climbing up at the usual temporal rate to the beginning of Solomon's reign and finally, jumping back up to the original time at the beginning of the text.

Interactions between Elijah, Obadiah, and Ahab (1 Kings 18:1–7)

וַיְהִי יָמִים רַבִּים וּדְבַר־יְהוָה הָיָה אֶל־אֵלִיָּהוּ בַּשָּׁנָה הַשְּׁלִישִׁית לֵאמֹר לֵךְ
הֵרָאֵה אֶל־אַחְאָב וְאֶתְּנָה מָטָר עַל־פְּנֵי הָאֲדָמָה: 2 **וַיֵּלֶךְ** אֵלִיָּהוּ לְהֵרָאוֹת
אֶל־אַחְאָב

וְהָרָעָב חָזָק בְּשֹׁמְרוֹן: 3 **וַיִּקְרָא** אַחְאָב אֶל־עֹבַדְיָהוּ אֲשֶׁר עַל־הַבָּיִת
וְעֹבַדְיָהוּ הָיָה יָרֵא אֶת־יְהוָה מְאֹד:

4 **וַיְהִי** בְּהַכְרִית אִיזֶבֶל אֵת נְבִיאֵי יְהוָה **וַיִּקַּח** עֹבַדְיָהוּ מֵאָה נְבִאִים
וַיַּחְבִּיאֵם חֲמִשִּׁים אִישׁ בַּמְּעָרָה וְכִלְכְּלָם לֶחֶם וָמָיִם:

5 **וַיֹּאמֶר** אַחְאָב אֶל־עֹבַדְיָהוּ לֵךְ בָּאָרֶץ אֶל־כָּל־מַעְיְנֵי הַמַּיִם וְאֶל כָּל־
הַנְּחָלִים אוּלַי| נִמְצָא חָצִיר וּנְחַיֶּה סוּס וָפֶרֶד וְלוֹא נַכְרִית מֵהַבְּהֵמָה:
6 **וַיְחַלְּקוּ** לָהֶם אֶת־הָאָרֶץ לַעֲבָר־בָּהּ אַחְאָב הָלַךְ בְּדֶרֶךְ אֶחָד לְבַדּוֹ
וְעֹבַדְיָהוּ הָלַךְ בְּדֶרֶךְ־אֶחָד לְבַדּוֹ: 7 **וַיְהִי** עֹבַדְיָהוּ בַּדֶּרֶךְ וְהִנֵּה אֵלִיָּהוּ
לִקְרָאתוֹ **וַיַּכִּרֵהוּ וַיִּפֹּל** עַל־פָּנָיו **וַיֹּאמֶר** הַאַתָּה זֶה אֲדֹנִי אֵלִיָּהוּ:

[It] **was** many days. Then the word of YHWH came to Elijah in the third year: "Go, show yourself to Ahab in order that I may give rain upon the surface of the ground." So, Elijah **went** to show himself to Ahab.

Now the famine was severe in Samaria. Ahab **summoned** Obadiah, who was over the house.

Now Obadiah exceedingly revered YHWH.

And when Jezebel cut off the prophets of YHWH, Obadiah **took** one hundred prophets, **hid** them, fifty each in a cave, and nourished them with bread and water.

Ahab **said** to Obadiah, "Go through the land to all the water springs and to all the torrent streams. Perhaps we can find grass so that we can keep alive the horses and mules and we will not have to cut off some of the livestock." And they **divided up** the land for themselves to pass through it: Ahab went one way alone; Obadiah went one way alone. When Obadiah **was** on the road, right then and there Elijah came to meet him. And he **recognized** him, **fell** on his face, and **said**, "Is this you, my lord, Elijah?"

This text too leaps about in time. Although explicit temporal phrases such as "and it was many days" and "in the third year," indicate the passage of significant amounts of time, in other places the jumps must be deduced. It was after "many days" in the "third year" (presumably since the drought began) that YHWH commanded Elijah to appear before Ahab so that the drought could be ended.

Sometimes instead of temporal phases there are grammatical indicators. In verse three for instance we find a disjunctive construction (non verb + *qatal*) introducing a parenthetic paragraph, in which we meet Ahab's steward, Obadiah, a man who fears YHWH. The time of the events mentioned here is uncertain at this point in the narrative, but must predate that of the main narrative, which is tracing the movements of Elijah.

Then within this paragraph we jump backward to an even earlier time when Obadiah rescued one hundred true prophets from the clutches of Jezebel. Then the time jumps back to the uncertain time again, as the narrative recounts the efforts of Ahab and Obadiah to save the animals during the famine brought on by the supernaturally imposed drought.

Although time is not mentioned it seems to be passing at the usual rate as the search for fodder for the animals continued. And while Obadiah was so engaged (at the same time Ahab is doing this in another part of the country) he met up with Elijah on his way to appear before Ahab. And so we find ourselves on the timeline of the main narrative, with time and text seemingly marching in step once again.

ELISHA AND JOASH (2 KINGS 13:13–21)

וַיִּשְׁכַּב יוֹאָשׁ עִם־אֲבֹתָיו וְיָרָבְעָם יָשַׁב עַל־כִּסְאוֹ וַיִּקָּבֵר יוֹאָשׁ בְּשֹׁמְרוֹן עִם מַלְכֵי יִשְׂרָאֵל: פ

14 וֶאֱלִישָׁע חָלָה אֶת־חָלְיוֹ אֲשֶׁר יָמוּת בּוֹ וַיֵּרֶד אֵלָיו יוֹאָשׁ מֶלֶךְ־יִשְׂרָאֵל וַיֵּבְךְּ עַל־פָּנָיו וַיֹּאמַר אָבִי אָבִי רֶכֶב יִשְׂרָאֵל וּפָרָשָׁיו: 15 וַיֹּאמֶר לוֹ אֱלִישָׁע קַח קֶשֶׁת וְחִצִּים וַיִּקַּח אֵלָיו קֶשֶׁת וְחִצִּים: 16 וַיֹּאמֶר| לְמֶלֶךְ יִשְׂרָאֵל הַרְכֵּב יָדְךָ עַל־הַקֶּשֶׁת וַיַּרְכֵּב יָדוֹ וַיָּשֶׂם אֱלִישָׁע יָדָיו עַל־יְדֵי הַמֶּלֶךְ: 17 וַיֹּאמֶר פְּתַח הַחַלּוֹן קֵדְמָה וַיִּפְתָּח וַיֹּאמֶר אֱלִישָׁע יְרֵה וַיּוֹר וַיֹּאמֶר חֵץ־תְּשׁוּעָה לַיהוָה וְחֵץ תְּשׁוּעָה בַאֲרָם וְהִכִּיתָ אֶת־אֲרָם בַּאֲפֵק עַד־כַּלֵּה: 18 וַיֹּאמֶר קַח הַחִצִּים וַיִּקָּח וַיֹּאמֶר לְמֶלֶךְ־יִשְׂרָאֵל הַךְ־אַרְצָה וַיַּךְ שָׁלֹשׁ־פְּעָמִים וַיַּעֲמֹד: 19 וַיִּקְצֹף עָלָיו אִישׁ הָאֱלֹהִים וַיֹּאמֶר לְהַכּוֹת חָמֵשׁ אוֹ־שֵׁשׁ פְּעָמִים אָז הִכִּיתָ אֶת־אֲרָם עַד־כַּלֵּה וְעַתָּה שָׁלֹשׁ פְּעָמִים תַּכֶּה אֶת־אֲרָם: ס 20 וַיָּמָת אֱלִישָׁע וַיִּקְבְּרֻהוּ

וּגְדוּדֵי מוֹאָב יָבֹאוּ בָאָרֶץ בָּא שָׁנָה: 21 וַיְהִי הֵם| קֹבְרִים אִישׁ וְהִנֵּה רָאוּ אֶת־הַגְּדוּד וַיַּשְׁלִיכוּ אֶת־הָאִישׁ בְּקֶבֶר אֱלִישָׁע וַיֵּלֶךְ וַיִּגַּע הָאִישׁ בְּעַצְמוֹת אֱלִישָׁע וַיְחִי וַיָּקָם עַל־רַגְלָיו:

Joash **lay down** with his fathers; and, Jereboam sat on his throne. Joash **was buried** in Samaria with the kings of Israel.

Elisha had become sick with his sickness by which he would die. Joash, the king of Israel, **went down** to him, **wept** upon him and **said**, "My father, my father, the chariot of Israel and its horsemen!" Elisha **said** to him, "Take a bow and arrows." So, he **took** to himself a bow and arrows. Then he **said** to the king of Israel, "Mount your hand on the bow." So, he **mounted** his hand. Then Elisha **placed** his hands over the hands of the king and said, "Open the window on the east." So, he **opened** [it]. Then Elisha **said**, "Shoot!" So, he **shot**. And he **said**, "An arrow of victory for YHWH; an arrow of victory against Aram. You will strike Aram at Aphek until [you] finish [them]." Then he **said**, "Take the arrows." So, he **took** [them]. Then he **said** to the king of Israel, "Strike the ground!" So, he **struck** three times and **stopped**. The man of God **was angry** at him and **said**, ". . . to strike five or six times! Then you would have struck Aram until [you] finished [them]. But now, three times you will strike Aram." Then Elisha **died** and they **buried** him.

Moabite raiding parties would come into the land as a year came. Once they were burying a man and indeed they saw a raiding party. So they **threw** the man into the tomb of Elisha and **went**. The man **touched** the bones of Elisha and **came to life** and **stood up** on his feet.

Time jumps seem to be part and parcel of the narratives pertaining to the "prophetic twins," Elijah and Elisha. The bulk of these relate interactions between these prophets and the kings of Israel. Elijah principally confronted and castigated kings; Elisha supported and encouraged them. Consequently, whereas kings feared the appearance of the former and were relieved when he left, kings welcomed the latter and wept when he left. Above we saw one connected with Elijah; here we look at one connected with Elisha. [In the discussion below time words are italicized and boldface so that the movements of time can be clearly seen.]

In the text above, ***time goes off a cliff*** for the king with whom the prophet interacted. In fact, this text starts with the death and burial of the king, namely, Jehoash (the grandson of Jehu), whose son Jereboam II reigned in his stead. According to the pattern in the Book of Kings, we expect that the reign of Jereboam II will now be presented. But this text breaks the pattern, and with ***a dramatic temporal leap*** jumps back to the reign of Jehoash, in particular his dealings with Elisha in the latter's last days. The presentation per se of Jehoash's reign takes only four verses, which is unusually short, but his activities are covered as they pertain to the kings of Judah, in particular, Amaziah. So too here we learn more about Jehoash from this last time he spent with Elisha.

This text records the death and burial of Elisha, but first describes the last interaction between the king and the prophet. The king knew that the prophet was sick and dying. Therefore, he went to him. When he saw him, he wept. Then Elisha placed his hands on those of the king and gave him a series of commands. They were a bit unusual, but Joash did everything Elisha told him to do. The only place he faltered was that he struck the ground only three times with the arrows, but in fairness to him: how was he supposed to know that he was to keep on striking the ground? In any case, after this incident, Elisha died and was buried. But curiously enough there would be one more miracle connected with him.

An unknown period of time passed, but, enough such that Elisha's body had become just his bones.

Some time after this there was a funeral procession, but those carrying the body of the deceased fled and tossed the body into the nearest burial cave when Moabite raiders showed up, which they regularly did *at a particular time of the year*. Then a singular eventuality occurred, which is recorded only here in the Bible—the resurrection of a dead man when his body touched the bones of a dead prophet. As soon as the body of the deceased touched the bones of Elisha, the man came back to life and stood up.

2.5.3 Summary

Although we have only furnished a few examples above, once readers are alert to their presence, many more can be discovered in the biblical text. This is not surprising in light of the fact that biblical narrative accounts are literary; and therefore exhibit such devices as flashback, prolepsis (looking forward in the text), and analepsis (looking backward in the text). But their presence within *wayyiqtol* chains militates against assuming temporal progression for the latter and suggests that the flow of time in BH is much more complicated than was thought.

2.6 *Concluding Summary*

In this chapter so far we have studied four factors, which structure the temporal profile of a narrative: *coherence relations* between VPs; *compatibility* issues constraining *simultaneity*; the role of *connectedness*; and the possibility of temporal *discontinuity*. We founded our analysis of these factors which determine temporal sequence upon a number of assumptions regarding time: its continuity, its polarity, its constituency, etc. It is now time to raise these assumptions to a higher level and confirm them. We need therefore to attempt to better understand—however imperfectly this may be—the philosophy of physical time, our perception of time, and the properties of time. We also need to develop a mathematical model of time. This is not a trivial endeavor; nor can it be short-circuited. We must proceed carefully and thoroughly. Even so our treatment will be all too brief.

3. Issues Pertaining to Time

Outline of the section:

3.1   Introduction
3.2   Types of Time
3.3   Nature of Time
3.4   Model for Time

3.1 *Introduction*

Having defined, explained and copiously exemplified from the Hebrew Bible our heuristic set of **coherence relations**, we now turn to consider their temporal dimension. There are three types of sequences pertinent to this study: *verbs, eventualities,* and *time*. Knowledge of two determines the third. Our study so far has yielded eventuality sequences for each **coherence relation**. The sequence of verbs, which represent the eventualities, is what it is in the text. We expect therefore that we should be able to determine in a more or less straightforward manner the temporal sequences. But this may not necessarily be the case; we might need to take into consideration the situational aspect (Akagi, **Chapter 11**) of the constituent verbs of the textual sequence.

But in order to ascertain the flow of time in BH narrative, we need to have a better understanding of time itself.[49] This section of the chapter will seemingly take us far off course [continuing our sea voyage metaphor] from the biblical texts we have been studying into the heavy seas of the study of the philosophy of time. This is necessary because we must have a fundamental grasp of the nature of time in order to properly comprehend how time works in an historical narrative, such as the Flood account. So hard to starboard.

3.2 *Types of Time*

There are three types of time: 1) physical, real, or public time, which has three properties we exploit, duration, order, and point; 2) phenomenological,

---

49. The following is a synthesis of Markosian (2010) and Dowden (2013).

psychological, or private time, which is our mental perception of time; and 3) perspectival, literary, or narrative time, which is time controlled by an author. We have been exploring this last for most of this paper but will draw everything together in **Section 4**.

    3.2.1 Physical Time
    3.2.2 Phenomenological Time
    3.2.3 Summary

3.2.1 Physical Time

We govern our lives by physical time without knowing what it is. We wear wrist watches, we wake up to alarm clocks, we set timers, we time athletic competitions, and we use calendars and all sorts of day planners. We experience the duration of time. How long to cook a casserole, for instance; that students have fifty-five minutes to take their Hebrew examination. We understand temporal order, that January 2, 2013 is after July 4, 2012 and that George Washington was born before he died. We remember particular times and do things at particular times. Family birthdays. Wedding anniversaries. The time that the faculty meeting begins. What time the class starts. And so forth. Duration, order, and point of time. We can measure time and are aware of the measure of time. How long it takes for a sprinter to run a 100-meter dash we measure in seconds. The winner might only win by hundredths of a second. How long it takes for coffee to cool enough so that it can be drunk, for bread to rise before it can be baked, for grass seed to germinate, and for puppies to be born. But we cannot manipulate real time. "A watched pot never boils" is not true. Nevertheless, as we have seen above an author can manipulate perspectival time.

Exactly what is time? And what are its properties? The study of time is not a trivial study and a number of issues are hotly debated by those philosophers who have studied time: are the past and future as real as the present? does time flow? is tense basic or is tenselessness? does time exist apart from change? is time substantival or relational? is time basic or is it derived? The debate has centered on the issue of whether the ordering of the location of eventualities in time is objective, based on these eventualities having the *objective properties* of presentness, pastness, or futureness, or is it based on *subjective relations*, now, before, and after: that is, whether there is an objective distinction between the present and the past and future or not.[50] Time philosophers thus basically support one of two theories, imaginatively named A and B, forming two camps: those that say that this ordering is

---

50. (Zimmerman 2005); (Fitzgerald n.d.).

objective, and those that say this ordering is by two-place relations (earlier than, later than, etc.); those that say that the present moment is objectively real, and those that say it is not; those that would say that from the perspective of January 3, 2013, the Battle of Hastings (AD 1066) has the *property* of being nine hundred forty-seven years in the past, and those that would say that it occurred nine hundred forty-seven years before the time this sentence was typed. According to the first view, one millennium ago, the Battle of Hastings would have the *property* of being fifty-three years in the future. According to the second camp it would be three years after AD 1063. These camps take their names from McTaggart's influential paper of 1908, in which he introduced the idea of two different ways of looking at time: the A-series and B-series of time.[51] Which theory is correct has profound implications, which will frame and inform our discussion below. On this foundation a theory of narrative time can be built.

This sub-subsection is organized as follows:

- History of the Study of Physical Time
- The Current Discussion

(1) *Time through Time: A Brief History of the Study of Physical Time.* To assist the reader we provide the following outline for this part:

- ○ Aristotle
- ○ Descartes
- ○ Barrow/Newton
- ○ Leibniz
- ○ Kant
- ○ McTaggart

The following subsection deals only with theories on the nature of time itself, not on the perception of time. Now, of course, there were those who insisted that the perception of time is all there is. Chief among these was Augustine, but following hard on his heels was Kant. We postpone our discussion of Augustine until **Sub-subsection 3.2.2**; but, we will take up Kant here, because he interacted with Newton and Leibniz. Having said this, please note that this is a sampling of the various theories. It must also be said that this is not the place to debate their value or validity.

(a) Aristotle. We begin this brief survey with Aristotle, because of his introspection on the concept of change and the ramifications thereof. And

---

51. McTaggart concluded that time was not real, which philosophers of time have recognized to be his worst idea (1908). But in 1927 McTaggart launched the concept of A-series versus B-series of time, an idea which has the framed the debate ever since (1927).

although others who preceded him interacted with this concept as well, they did not do so in the same way. Notably, Parmenides concluded that reality was changeless; whereas, Heraclitus, concluded that the essence of reality was change. Plato, in the *Timaeus* seems to equate time and motion: ". . . And so people are all but ignorant of the fact that time really is the wandering of these bodies [the planets]" (39d).

For Aristotle time is inexorably linked to the measure of motion. But unlike his predecessors, he "abstracted time from motion." This was his innovation. To him motion was change. So, his basic idea was that time is connected to change: "time is the measure of change" (*Physics* Book IV, chapter 12). But he clarified this idea: "time is not change [itself]" (chapter 10), because the rate of time does not change; the rate of change changes: "[change] may be faster or slower" (*Physics,* chapter 10). Thus, time is just the measure of change. Also he believed that time was continuous.

(b) Descartes. Descartes understood time differently, rejecting Aristotle's idea of the continuation of time. He did not think that the corporeal has the innate capacity of duration; God has to re-create the body at each successive moment.

(c) Barrow/Newton. Barrow rejected Aristotle's connection of time with change and movement. Sir Isaac Newton, his greatest pupil, in the Scholium of his *Principia* argued that time and space are a nexus of entities (not substances), an infinitely large container in which eventualities take place, but which is not dependent on them. This view is known as *substantivalism* (some prefer, *absolutism*), which is opposed by the idea of *relationalism,* initially espoused by Leibniz.

(d) Leibniz. Leibniz objected to Newton's understanding of time. He advanced his view in a series of letters between Samuel Clark (who defended Newton's view) and himself. Leibniz insisted that time does not exist apart from the sequence of non-simultaneous eventualities; that in fact this sequence *is* time. His view is known as *relationalism* or *reductionism.* We will delve into the contrast between Newton's view and Leibniz's much more below.

(e) Kant. Kant reacted to both Newton and Leibniz in his *Critique of Pure Reason.* Kant's innovations were often in the form of synthesis. It appears that from the disparate perspectives of British empiricism and French rationalism, he forged the idea that our minds are "wired" to perceive the empirical data. No less did he do this with Newton's concept of the nature of time, absolutism, vis-à-vis Leibniz's, relationalism.

Now what are space and time? Are they actual entities [wirkliche Wesen, Newton's view]? Are they only determinations or also relations of things [Leibniz's view], but still such as would belong to them even if they were not intuited? Or are they such that they belong only to the form of intuition, and therefore to the subjective constitution of our mind, without which these predicates could not be ascribed to any things at all.[52]

Not surprisingly, his approach was to frame the discussion around the mind's perception of reality. As Dowden—I think—has stated it quite well:

Immanuel Kant said time and space are forms that the mind projects upon the external things-in-themselves. He spoke of our mind structuring our perceptions so that space always has a Euclidean geometry, and time has the structure of the mathematical line. Kant's idea that time is a *form* of apprehending phenomena is probably best taken as suggesting that we have no direct perception of time but only the ability to experience things and eventualities *in* time.[53]

(f) McTaggart. We now come to McTaggart's seminal contribution, which has been the substance of the discussion ever since. He maintained that there are two different ways of looking at a sequence of eventualities. One, which he called the 'A-series', is a sequence of temporal positions running from the past through the present to the future. The other, which he called the 'B-series', is to see those positions as going from earlier than through simultaneous with to later than. The *properties* of being past, being present, or being future are called 'A-properties.' The *two-place relations* of earlier than, simultaneous with, and later than are called 'B-properties.' And the corresponding theories are of course called the A-theory of time and the B-theory of time, respectively, and their proponents, A-theorists and B-theorists. The former insist that there is an objective distinction of the present from the past and from the future apart from any other temporal context of an utterance, time, or frame of reference. The B-theorists deny such an objectivity.

There are serious theoretical ramifications depending upon which theory is embraced, A or B: whether the present is all there really is or not; whether time flows or not; whether the truth of an utterance is time dependent or not; whether tense is semantically basic or not; whether reality is fundamentally three dimensional or four dimensional, and whether the time of eventualities is fluid or fixed. The bulk of the discussion below will continue to return to the A versus B issue and its repercussions.

52. (Le Poidevin 2011).
53. (Dowden 2013).

(2) *The Current Discussion: Subsequent A and B Theories*. McTaggart set the table for all subsequent discussion on the nature of time. Because of their basic stand, A or B, time philosophers divide on the following: the status of the present, the flow of time, and the time dependence of truth.[54] To clarify these concepts in our discussion below we will apply them to a real time series: the Battle of Hastings (AD 1066, when William the Conqueror of Normandy defeated King Harold of England), the signing of the Declaration of Independence (AD 1776), the writing of this sentence (THE PRESENT; or if you prefer, the time you are reading this sentence), and a manned mission to Mars (AD 2028?).

Again to assist the reader the following outline is supplied:

o   Does the Present Have Special Status?
o   Does Time Flow?
o   Are the Truth of Propositions Time Dependent?

(a) Does the Present Have Special Status? A-theorists are of three stripes: the *presentists*, *growing blockers*, and *eternalists*. The first say that the present is all that there is, and the past no longer exists; and, that neither does the future, because it is not yet. William is not defeating Harold now, nor is the Declaration being signed, nor is man on Mars or on his way there. Therefore, these eventualities do not exist. The second group would only exclude the Mars mission from existence. The third group would accept the existence of all three, but would say the first two have the property of pastness, whereas the third has the property of futureness.

B-theorists accept the existence of all the eventualities. The first two happened earlier than the writing/reading of this sentence. The last will happen later than the writing/reading of this sentence.

The fundamental question for the theory of time is: does reality imply presentness? In other words, is existence equivalent to the portion of reality accessible to the senses, which is necessarily confined to the present? Or to put it another way: was/is the past real? Did it really happen? Did William defeat Harold? Without question! Did John Hancock sign the Declaration? His bold signature is blazoned below the famous text! And so it goes for all the past. If something is not present, but past, it is past; but, it is still real. Presentness and existence are wholly distinct. As far as the future is concerned, it is real in the sovereign purposes of God, which will come to pass.

---

54. On A-theory (Zimmerman 2005); B-theory, (Oaklander 2004).

One further thought: part of the problem might be linguistic. Many languages use relative spatial locations to refer to temporal realities. In English, the past is *behind* us; the future is *before* us. We say we are looking *back* at the past or looking *forward* to the future. And so it is with sundry languages. Think about, then, what perspective on time is expressed by this. We cannot see what is behind us, but we can see what is in front of us. We might question the existence or reality of what we cannot see or what is not immediately sensible to us. This is not the case however with the Semitic languages. In Hebrew, the same root, קדם, (*qdm*) is used for one of the words for being in front of and the past. And the same root, אחר, (*'ḥr*) is used for being behind and the future. In Hebrew, the past is seen; it is the future, which is not seen. So in a sense, the Hebrew mindset is that we back into the future. And reasoning as above: what we see, what is immediately sensible to us, we deem as real and existing.

(b) Does Time Flow? This is the penultimate topic in terms of its importance. A-theorists would say that in AD 1065 the Battle of Hastings had the property of futureness. In AD 1066 this changed to the property of presentness. And in AD 1067, to the property of pastness. For these theorists this obtains for every eventuality in time. This is the "flow" of time. Time is dynamic.

B-theorists say that this is an illusion, what they call "the myth of passage." Time does not flow. Time is static. All the eventualities are affixed to a time line. No properties change with time. Hence, it is appropriate to refer to the past and the future with "is." The times of events are relative to one another. Of AD 1065, one could say that the time of the Battle of Hastings is later. Of AD 1066 it could be said that the time of the Battle of Hastings is concurrent with this. Of AD 1067 it could be said that the time of the Battle of Hastings is earlier than this. The writing of the Declaration could be described as occurring earlier than my typing of this sentence. And the time of the Mars mission is later than all three: the Battle, the Declaration, and my typing/your reading.

I am going to suggest that reality evinces a blend of these. Time is static in the past, but it might not be in the present and the future. Past eventualities have happened: they were real, but they can longer change in any way, including the time they occurred. Moreover, an eventuality in the present moves into the past, where it then becomes static. But the performer or experiencer of the present eventuality moves from the present into what is the future from the perspective of the present. Eventualities and performers/experiencers move along what might be a static line—whether or not the entire line is static is irrelevant to this argument—and, thus, with respect to these, the line has a relative motion, as when driving, the scenery appears to be moving past.

(c) Are the Truth of Propositions Time Dependent? Now we come to the most interesting question of all: is the truth value of a proposition time dependent or not? In other words, is tense an integral part of truth? A-theorists say, "yes"; B-theorists say, "no." The latter objected to the idea that the truth of a proposition could change with time. Propositions were either true or false; not indeterminate. But there is no denying that many languages have a way of communicating tense. For example, the statement, "William defeated Harold," was not true in AD 1065. It certainly seems to be a time-dependent proposition. B-theorists responded by translating all tensed propositions into tenseless ones. A-theorists claim that the new propositions do not have the same meanings as the originals. And so it goes. We will return to these issues later. Let me sum up the differences in the following table, after which we will look at our mental perception of time:

Metaphysical Categories	A-Theory	B-Theory
Now	Objective	Subjective
Ontology	Presentism or Growing Past	Eternalism or Block Universe Theory
Flow of Time	Real	Illusory
Propositions	Neither true or false when uttered	Either true or false when uttered
Tenses	Semantically Basic: p is v at t, where p is the proposition, v is its truth value, t is the time	Not Semantically Basic: p is v
Ontology of Fundamental Objects	3 dimensional	4 dimensional

3.2.2 Time and Mind: Phenomenological Time

We now turn to our perception of time, or phenomenological time, for that is how we experience and perceive it.[55] Pöppel lists five ways we experience time: duration, non-simultaneity, past and present, change, and order.[56] We will briefly survey those who have reflected on this, consider these five ways, and then turn to contemplate the metaphysical issues involved. The outline for this subsection is as follows:

- Historical Survey
- The Experience of Time
- Metaphysical Issues

55. (Le Poidevin 2011).
56. (Pöppel 1978).

(1) *Historical Survey.* The following made the greatest contributions and this part is organized accordingly:

- ° Aristotle
- ° Augustine
- ° Kant

(a) **Aristotle.** While deliberating on the nature of physical time—although he did not call it that—Aristotle appears to be commenting on phenomenological time, asking, "Whether, if soul (mind) did not exist, time would exist or not, is a question that may fairly be asked; for if there cannot be someone to count, there cannot be anything that can be counted . . ." (*Physics* Book IV, chapter 14). In other words, time requires a being with a mind to be able to count it. Dowden further adds that Aristotle seemed to be reflecting on his question as he qualified it—that it depends on whether time is the conscious numbering of movement or instead is just the capability of movements being numbered were consciousness to exist.

(b) **Augustine.** It will be helpful to begin this discussion with an understanding of how Augustine's approach to the study of time and observations on time greatly differ from Aristotle's. Callahan states:

> Aristotle examines motion and change in nature and finds that time is the number or measure of change. Augustine, looking from the beginning at the way we measure time, wonders how we can measure past and future time, which do not exist, or present time, which, strictly speaking, has no extension. Since a thing must exist in order to be measured, Augustine comes eventually to the conclusion that all time must now exist in the mind. (1958)

Augustine extensively discusses the nature and experience of time in *Confessions* Book XI, concluding that we measure time in our minds. He also appears to be aware of the idea of the existence of time apart from our mental perception of it, but he rejects this idea:

> It is in you, O mind of mine, that I measure the periods of time. *Do not shout me down that it exists [objectively]*; do not overwhelm yourself with the turbulent flood of your impressions. In you, as I have said, I measure the periods of time. (11.27.36) [emphasis mine][57]

How did Augustine arrive at this conclusion? He begins by logically thinking through the nature of the passage of time, asking: what is the past; what is the future; and what is the present? It is only because the present passes into the past that there is a past; and, it is only because that something is coming with respect to the present that there is a future:

---

57. Translation from Albert Outler (1955). Henry Chadwick's 2011 translation is also highly recommended by Augustine scholars. Citation is by book.chapter.section.

Yet I say with confidence that I know that if nothing passed away, there would be no past time; and if nothing were still coming, there would be no future time; and if there were nothing at all, there would be no present time.

But, then, how is it that there are the two times, past and future, when even the past is now no longer and the future is now not yet? But if the present were always present, and did not pass into past time, it obviously would not be time but eternity. (11.14.17)

He then reflects on the nature of eventualities in the past that were present; and the nature of eventualities in the future that are present: neither exists anymore:

But we measure the passage of time when we measure the intervals of perception. But who can measure times past which now are no longer, or times future which are not yet—unless perhaps someone will dare to say that what does not exist can be measured? Therefore, while time is passing, it can be perceived and measured; but when it is past, it cannot, since it is not. (11.16.21)

So, then, if they do not exist, how do we perceive them, since it is plain that we do? Augustine concludes that we perceive the *memory* of them for the past and the *anticipation* of them for the future:

Although we tell of past things as true, they are drawn out of the memory—not the things themselves, which have already passed, but words constructed from the images of the perceptions which were formed in the mind, like footprints in their passage through the senses. . . . [Past and future eventualities] coexist somehow in the soul, for otherwise I could not see them. The time present of things past is memory; the time present of things present is direct experience; the time present of things future is expectation. (11.18.23; 11.20.26)

And he affirms that the memory of the past is in the present:

I measure as time present the impression that things make on you as they pass by and what remains after they have passed by—I do not measure the things themselves which have passed by and left their impression on you. This is what I measure when I measure periods of time. (11.27.36)

(c) **Kant.** Immanuel Kant, in reacting to both Newton and Leibniz's ideas, expressed his concept of time in terms of our "intuiting" time. Furthermore, he appears to convey Aristotle's ideas that time does not exist except in this way:

Or are they [time and space] such that they belong only to the form of intuition, and therefore to the subjective constitution of our mind, without which these predicates could not be ascribed to any things at all?[58]

58. Janiak (2012).

As stated above, his philosophical approach was to frame discussions around the mind's perception of reality. And to repeat Dowden's quote from above: "Immanuel Kant said time and space are forms that the mind projects upon the external things-in-themselves. He spoke of our mind structuring our perceptions."

(2) *The Experience of Time.* We experience time in the following ways, which will be covered below:

- ° Duration
- ° The Specious Present
- ° The Past, the Present, and the Passage of Time
- ° Change
- ° Order

(a) Duration. Our starting point for considering duration is Augustine. He wrestled with the concept of temporal duration, because, according to his analysis, to be able to measure time from the present we would have to start our measurement from the beginning of the period of a temporal interval. This "beginning" is in the past, which, he argued does not exist: "But in what sense is something long or short that is nonexistent? For the past is not now, and the future is not yet" (11.15.18). He continues:

> And yet, O Lord, we do perceive intervals of time, and we compare them with each other, and we say that some are longer and others are shorter. We even measure how much longer or shorter this time may be than that time. And we say that this time is twice as long, or three times as long, while this other time is only just as long as that other. But we measure the passage of time when we measure the intervals of perception. But who can measure times past which now are no longer, or times future which are not yet—unless perhaps someone will dare to say that what does not exist can be measured? Therefore, while time is passing, it can be perceived and measured; but when it is past, it cannot, since it is not. (11.16.21)

An additional problem his contemplation exposes is that we only perceive the present moment, which has no duration. But, would not the present need to have duration to be able to measure duration? And yet it has none:

> If any fraction of time be conceived that cannot now be divided even into the most minute momentary point, this alone is what we may call time present. But this flies so rapidly from future to past that it cannot be extended by any delay. For if it is extended, it is then divided into past and future. But the present has no extension whatever. (11.15.20)

Notwithstanding, we clearly do apprehend the measure of time. What was Augustine's solution to this conundrum? We measure the length of our memory of a temporal interval in the past: "Therefore I do not measure them, for they do not exist any more. But I measure something in my memory which remains fixed" (11.27.35). And further:

> It is in you, O mind of mine, that I measure the periods of time . . . I measure as time present the impression that things make on you as they pass by and what remains after they have passed by—I do not measure the things themselves which have passed by and left their impression on you. This is what I measure when I measure periods of time. Either, then, these are the periods of time or else I do not measure time at all. (11.27.36)

Was Augustine right? In any case, his thoughts on time have informed the discussion since they were penned. One of the keys to his thought is his understanding of the present. And to this issue we now turn.

(b) The Specious Present. Augustine's cogitations on time move us to ask a salient but strange question: how long is the moment when we directly perceive an object with our senses? Salient: because we only directly perceive then. Strange: because a moment is conceptually instantaneous; how can it have any duration? Le Poidevin suggests four possibilities for the specious present (a termed introduced by E. R. Clay but characterized by William James of Harvard):

1. the span of short-term memory;
2. the duration which is perceived, not as duration, but as instantaneous;
3. the duration which is directly perceived—i.e. not through the intermediary of a number of other, perhaps instantaneous, perceptions;
4. the duration which is perceived both as present and as extended in time

Looking at each in turn we can set all but the last aside, for speech would be a hopeless muddle if the hearing of words were simultaneous rather than being spread over an interval. But the reality is that the words are not blurred. Moreover, trying to fix one's eyes to see the wings of a hummingbird, where there is blurring, and the direct perception of duration seems precluded by Augustine's arguments. We are left with a paradox: an interval perceived as both instantaneous and extended. But this is the nature of reality. We perceive motion, which by definition cannot be instantaneous; but, we can only directly perceive the instantaneous.

(c) The Past, the Present, and the Passage of Time. We perceive the past, present, and future and what appears to us be the passage of time in different ways. The first three are real; the fourth might not be. We have the capacity to perceive reality. We do not directly perceive the past with our senses, but as we stated above, this does not preclude its reality. We directly perceive the present. And we perceive the prophetic future by faith. But what of the last, the passage of time? Illusions can appear to be real. The rising moon appears to be much bigger than the moon at its zenith, but in fact, the image is no larger. Yes that which was the future becomes the present, which becomes the past, but the reality is that the times of eventualities are what they are. This leads us to consider a sequence of eventualities, which is the essence of change.

(d) **Change.** We also perceive change. Change is motion: spatial or metaphorical: change of place or change of state. Motion takes time. Depending on how rapidly we receive the information that a change has occurred, we will either distinguish the individual changes or not. And the latter is not limited to fast changes, which appear as a blur. Something can be moving too slow for us to see the changes over a short interval, in which case there does not appear to be any movement at all. This is related to the individual changes being too small. Both of these can be seen in the movement of the hour hand. But if the interval is lengthened out and the initial position is in our memory, we can see that the hour hand has moved. The same thing applies to the rotation of the earth. When we gaze at the stars for a few seconds, to our eyes, they do not appear to move. But in the field of vision of a telescope eyepiece, they certainly do. Order is directional change. How do we perceive this?

(e) **Order.** Order is concerned with the direction of the change, not just the fact of the change. It is a vector, not a scalar. This is a different "kettle of fish" from perceiving the past or even change. This is perceiving different degrees of pastness. *Cause* can help. A cause precedes its effects. But what if there is not cause and effect relation? Mellor suggests that the brain represents time by time. But this has its problems, which we will not go into here. It remains a mystery, but, nevertheless, a reality, the presence of which we have abundantly documented in texts above.

(3) *Metaphysical Issues.* These have been dealt with adequately above. So, we will be content to just define the issues below.

(a) **Reality of Tense.** The issue is this: is tense semantically basic or is it derived? Can we express a tensed proposition without using tense?

(b) **Presentism versus Eternalism.** The issue is this: does the present only exist for us or do the past and future as well? Is the fact that only the present is sensible to us, mean that the past and future do not exist?

(c) **The Temporal Asymmetry of Cause.** The issue is this: why is it that causes always precede effects? This is often called "the arrow of time."

3.2.3 Summary

Having briefly examined the types of time by surveying the historical and current discussions on physical time and phenomenological time, we now turn to consider the ontology of time. For our purposes the relationship between time and eventualities is most crucial and will therefore command our attention.

3.3 The Nature of Time

This subsection on the ontology of time will be broken down in the following way:

    3.3.1 Time and Space
    3.3.2 Time and Cause
    3.3.3 Time and Eventualities
    3.3.4 Time and Truth

3.3.1 Time and Space: The Topology of Time

The topology of time is the properties that time seems to possess, namely: time appears to flow; time appears to be linear; and time can be understood as consisting of instants or intervals. We will briefly touch on the first below, because it has been thoroughly discussed above. The second needs more discussion than given above and the third is entirely new and will be covered under **Subsection 3.4**. Outline of sub-subsection:

- The Flow of Time
- The Shape of Time

(1) *The Flow of Time: "Myth of Passage" versus Dynamic.* We experience the overwhelming impression that time flows. Is this due to the nature of time? Or is it an illusion, "the myth of passage"? To put in a different way: is time dynamic or static?

(2) *The Shape of Time: Linear versus Circular.* I discussed earlier in this chapter and in an earlier chapter the constraint, which the linearity of text places upon simultaneous eventualities. Time too is linear, although some cultures deny it and affirm its circularity. The Hebrew Bible stands out among its contemporaries in presenting eventualities as sequentially moving from the past, through the present to the future along a time line, instead of proceeding in cycles consonant with the seasons. And it is also distinct in advancing the idea that human history will have a culmination, instead of an endless circular sameness. The linearity of time was also held by the Zorastrians and Seneca. Augustine stated that time was a one-way journey

from Genesis to Judgment regardless of the cyclical patterns in nature. Aquinas concurred. Francis Bacon referred to the linearity of time. Newton formulated the idea mathematically and geometrically, representing time by a line. And Leibniz, Locke, and Kant followed suit—the latter maintaining that it was necessarily that.

What is this shape? A single line, non-branching, straight (that is, without curvature, so that it cannot form a closed loop). Does the line have a beginning? That is, is it a ray, rather than a line? Does it have an end as well, making it into a line segment? Theology informs these issues. God created time. So it has a beginning. But does it have an end? Is the eternal state part of time; and, thus the ray never ends?

3.3.2 Time and *Cause*

The relationship between time and cause has been discussed above in **Section 2**, in particular what Aristotle, Hume, and Reichenbach had to say. The issue which piques our interest in this subsection is the so-called "arrow of time," a term coined in 1927 by the British astronomer, Arthur Stanley Eddington, about the unmistakable, seemingly inviolable asymmetry of time.[59] Stated succinctly: why do causes always seem to precede their effects? To be specific, why does a cup of tea always fall off a table, splinter into a million pieces, and spill its contents onto a rug, making a big stain. Why do stains not vanish from rugs, form into drops of tea, broken pieces assemble into a cup, the drops go back into the cup, and the cup with its tea whisk back onto the table? What is most curious is that the quantum mechanics equations, such as the Schroedinger Wave Function, the solutions of which describe reality at the sub-atomic and atomic level, admit time reversals. Furthermore, Maxwell's equations allow for the convergence of electromagnetic waves instead of just their radiation, but such reversals as described above are not observed on the *macro-level*, and as far as we know have never been so. Referred to as the Second Law of Thermodynamics, it is the law of increasing entropy, the endless tendency to disorder. Time's arrow is also manifested on a grand scale in the expansion of the universe. This phenomenon evokes seven questions: 1) Why there is an arrow? 2) Why do the laws of Physics

---

59. Eddington commented that time has a one-way behavior, not shared by space: "Let us draw an arrow arbitrarily. If as we follow the arrow we find more and more of the random element in the state of the world, then the arrow is pointing towards the future; if the random element decreases the arrow points towards the past. That is the only distinction known to physics. This follows at once if our fundamental contention is admitted that the introduction of randomness is the only thing which cannot be undone. I shall use the phrase 'time's arrow' to express this one-way property of time which has no analogue in space" (1928).

not affirm its existence? 3) What is its connection to entropy? 4) Why is it not manifested in micro-processes? 5) Why does entropy increase in the future? 6) What would a physical theory look like, which selects a specific direction for time? 7) What is the relationship between disparate arrows, for example: entropy, cause, radiation, and knowledge?[60] We must let the matter rest for now, but suffice it to say that these questions figure large in the nature of time.

What cannot rest and must be treated now is the altogether-relevant-to-this-study topic of the relationship between time and eventualities.

3.3.3 Time and Eventualities: Substantivalism versus Relationalism
Outline of the sub-subsection:

- Newton
- Leibniz

As promised we will now try to elucidate the Newton-Leibniz debate over the nature of time and space, which has continued in one form or another until the present. This is not merely an arcane issue: splitting academic hairs. Its application will affect the mathematical model of time, which we will endeavor to explain below. But at this point we will concentrate on the two views themselves. We will start with Newton.

(1) *Newton—Absolutism/Substantivalism.* Sir Isaac Newton, the great Cambridge physicist of the seventeenth and eighteenth centuries, was the father of classical mechanics, and perhaps best known for his theories of motion and universal gravitation. He based his theories of physics on a certain *philosophical* perspective on time and space: that space was an entity distinct from the objects in it, and, that time passed whether eventualities occurred in it or not. Consequently, he spoke of absolute space and absolute time, differentiating these from the measurement of these, which he called relative space and time.

Newton's philosophy of time first appears in *De Gravitatione et æquipondio fluidorum,* but its main articulation occurs in a minor section (entitled *Scholium*) of his great work, *Philosophae Naturalis Principia Mathematica* (commonly known by the third word in the title). In this section he writes the following about time:

> Absolute, true and mathematical time, in and of itself and of its own nature, without reference to anything external, flows uniformly and by another name is called duration. Relative, apparent, and common time

---

60. Posed by Dowden (2013).

is any sensible and external measure (precise or imprecise) of duration by means of motion; such a measure—for example, an hour, a day, a month, a year—is commonly used instead of true time.[61]

Newton went beyond his statement on the nature of time to defend his view from the need for the so-called "equation of time" and celestial mechanics, the details of which we will not go into here. Suffice it to say that his view allowed absolute time to remain constant while relative time changed. He argued for the difference between absolute and relative motion by— among other things—his famous, rotating-bucket-of-water illustration [we will return to this later]. In addition, he maintains that it is necessary, not optional, to make the distinction between "true quantities" and "their absolute measure":

> *But because the parts of space cannot be seen, or distinguished from one another by our senses, therefore in their stead we use sensible measures of them.* For from the positions and distances of things from any body considered as immovable, we define all places; and then with respect to such places, we estimate all motions, considering bodies as transferred from some of those places into others. And so, *instead of absolute places and motions, we use relative ones*; and that without any inconvenience in common affairs; *but in philosophical disquisitions, we ought to abstract from our senses, and consider things themselves, distinct from what are only sensible measures of them.*[62]

Furthermore, Newton's laws of classical mechanics themselves evince his ideas about time, assuming that all types of motion (straight line, circular, elliptical, and other trajectories and orbits) happen in space and in time, with time as the main independent variable. Location is time dependent. Velocity is time dependent. Displacement is time dependent. Physicists still use Newton's time-dependent notation today: $\dot{x}$ is the first derivative of x with respect to *time* (the infinitesimal change of the dependent variable x with respect to *time*); $\ddot{x}$ is the second derivative of x with respect to *time* (the infinitesimal change of the first derivative of x with respect to *time*); and, so forth. Even the more generalized theories of classical mechanics, of Lagrange and of Hamilton, have time as an independent variable.

Now on to Leibniz's view.

---

61. The original Latin text can be found at the Newton Project (http://www.newtonproject.sussex.ac.uk).

62. In the Scholium of Newton's *Principia*, which is between the definitions and his laws of motion. Emphasis is mine.

(2) *Leibniz—Relativism/Reductionism.* Leibniz did not respond directly to Newton, but rather to the latter's former student and friend, Samuel Clarke. The occasion for this series of correspondences was a letter Leibniz sent to an acquaintance of his, Caroline of Ansbach, the Princess of Wales, in which he warned her of the danger of Newton's ideas to natural religion:

> Natural Religion it self, seems to decay [in England] very much . . . . Sir Isaac Newton says, that Space is an Organ, which God makes use of to perceive Things by. But if God stands in need of any Organ to perceive Things by, it will follow, that they do not depend altogether upon him, nor were produced by him. Sir Isaac Newton, and his Followers, have also a very odd Opinion concerning . . . .[63]

She responded by contacting her friend, Samuel Clarke, who engaged Leibniz in an exchange of twelve papers, six from each correspondent (Leibniz's first paper is the letter to the princess) from 1715–16. Clarke's arguments are his, not Newton's; but, most likely the latter reviewed and approved them. The idea that Newton was the ghostwriter, however, appears to be unfounded. Most likely, Newton did not respond directly because of the rancor he had for Leibniz, being convinced that the latter had stolen his ideas for the calculus. The acrimony was mutual. And thus, I suspect that the vehemence in Leibniz's papers is directed more at Newton than towards Clarke—although, in that Leibniz was responding to Clarke, they were also directed at him. The papers of both parties passed through the princess's hands. The repartee no doubt would have continued were it not cut short by Leibniz's death. Leibniz wrote in French. The following is Clarke's original translation of 1717 without any modern corrections. Clarke died two years later.

Leibniz advanced the argument of *relationalism*: that there is no such thing as absolute space, motion, or time; rather everything was just related:

> These Gentlemen maintain therefore, that Space is a real absolute Being. But this involves them in great Difficulties; For such a Being must needs {sic} be Eternal and Infinite. Hence Some have believed it to be God himself, or, one of his Attributes, his Immensity. But since Space consists of Parts, it is not a thing which can belong to God.
>
> As for my Own Opinion, I have said more than once, that I hold Space to be something merely relative, as Time is; that I hold it to be an Order of Coexistences, as Time is an Order of Successions. For Space denotes,

---

63. The original was in French. This letter is considered to be the first in the exchange of papers. The Newton Project has Clarke's translations of Leibniz's French originals.

in Terms of Possibility, an Order of Things which exist at the same time, considered as existing together; without enquiring into their Manner of Existing. And when many Things are seen together, one perceives That Order of Things among themselves.[64]

Leibniz had a three-pronged argument against Newton's position: the principle of sufficient reason (PSR); the principal of the identity of indiscernibles (PII); and the principle of indetectible substance. The first of these is: "Nothing happens without a sufficient reason, why it should be So, rather than otherwise."[65] PSR, PII and his relational understanding of time are all evident in the following statement on time by Leibniz:

> The Case is the same with respect to Time. *Supposing any one should ask, why God did not create every thing a Year sooner; and the same Person should infer from thence, that God has done something, concerning which 'tis not possible there should be a Reason, why he did it so, and not otherwise:* The Answer is, That his Inference would be right, *if Time was any thing distinct from Things existing in Time. For it would be impossible there should be any Reason, why Things should be applied to such particular Instants, rather than to others, their Succession continuing the same. But then the same Argument proves, that Instants, consider'd without the Things, are nothing at all; and that they consist only in the successive Order of Things:* **Which Order remaining the same, one of the two States, viz. that of a supposed Anticipation, would not at all differ, nor could be discerned from, the other which Now is** [emphasis, mine: bold italics–PSR; italics–on time; bold–PII].[66]

Leibniz also argued against the idea of absolute space and time from the fact that it is indetectible. If it is a reality, we should be able to detect it. But since we cannot, it is not. He maintains:

> If Space is a property or Attribute, it must be the Property of some Substance. But what Substance will That Bounded empty Space be an Affection or Property of, which the Persons I am arguing with, suppose to be between Two Bodies?

> If infinite Space is Immensity, finite Space will be the Opposite to Immensity, that is, 'twill be Mensurability, or limited Extension. Now Extension must be the Affection of some thing extended. But if That Space

---

64. From Leibniz's third paper, originally titled by Samuel Clarke, *Mr. Leibnitz's Third Paper. being An Answer to Dr. Clarke's Second Reply.*
65. Ibid.
66. Ibid.

be empty, it will be an Attribute without a Subject, an Extension without any thing extended. Wherefore by making Space a Property, the Author falls in with My Opinion, which makes it an Order of things, and not any thing absolute.[67]

Clarke parried each of Leibniz's thrusts. To PSR, he responded that it is due to the arbitrary sovereign will of God. As for PII, he did not concede Leibniz's point that things done at different times are identical, and that space-time is a special kind of property/substance. Although it must be admitted that the last was his weakest defense: he kept on modifying his idea as Leibniz pressed the attack.

At first glance it would appear that Einstein's theories have won the day for relationalism—his concept of inertial reference frames moving at constant velocity, the hallmark of Special Relativity, does away with the idea of absolute space, absolute velocity, and even simultaneity of instants—were it not for Newton's bucket, a thought experiment about a spinning bucket of water.[68]

The essence of the experiment and significance is as follows: Suppose that a bucket of water is suspended from a rope and then set spinning. What

67. Leibniz's fourth paper to Clarke.

68. Andrew Motte's English translation of 1729 from the original Latin: If a vessel, hung by a long cord, is so often turned about that the cord is strongly twisted, then filled with water, and held at rest together with the water; thereupon, by the sudden action of another force, it is whirled about the contrary way, and while the cord is untwisting itself, the vessel continues for some time in this motion; the surface of the water will at first be plain [plana], as before the vessel began to move; but after that, the vessel, by gradually communicating its motion to the water, will make it begin sensibly to revolve, and recede by little and little from the middle, and ascent to the sides of the vessel, forming itself into a concave figure (as I have experienced), and the swifter the motion becomes, the higher will the water rise, till at last, performing its revolutions in the same times with the vessel, it becomes relatively at rest in it. This ascent of the water shows [indicat] its endeavor to recede from the axis of its motion; and the true and absolute circular motion of the water, which is here directly contrary to the relative, becomes known [innotescit], and may be measured [mensuratur] by this endeavor. At first, when the relative motion of the water in the vessel was greatest, it produced no endeavor to recede from the axis; the water showed no tendency to the circumference, nor any ascent towards the sides of the vessel, but remained of a plain [plana] surface, and therefore its true circular motion had not yet begun. But afterwards, when the relative motion of the water had decreased, the ascent thereof towards the sides of the vessel proved [indicabat] its endeavor to recede from the axis; and this endeavor showed [monstrabat] the real circular motion of the water continually increasing, till it had acquired its greatest quantity, when the water rested relatively in the vessel. And therefore this endeavor does not depend upon any translation of the water in respect of the ambient bodies, nor can true circular motion be defined [defineri] by such translation.

we will observe? At first the surface of the water will remain flat, with the sides of the bucket rotating around the mass of water, because of the inertia of the water. This is Newton's first law of motion. At this point the water is rotating with respect to the bucket and vice versa, but the water is not rotating with respect to the earth. After a while, because of surface tension, the water will start to rotate as well until its angular velocity is the same as that of the bucket. It will no longer be moving with respect to the bucket, but the fact that the water will start to go up the sides of the bucket proves that is moving with respect to some absolute reference frame. Newton called this absolute space. Now rotational motion is accelerated motion, with the direction of the velocity changing, rather than the magnitude.

Even Einstein's General Theory of Relativity seems to gulp at Newton's bucket. Substantivalism is still alive.[69] Moreover, common everyday language—not sophisticated linguistics—suggests that in one way or another time is absolute, as in the sentence: *We went to the store on Saturday.* Suppose today is Sunday. Then relationalism would argue that if it were Monday and the utterance were *We went to the store on Sunday*, given that the sequence and span between the going to the store and the time of speaking is the same for both, that they are the same. This is clearly not the case.

We will return to these two views later when we formulate a mathematical model for time, because each must be handled differently. But for the present, however, "Time and Truth" is before us.

3.3.4 Time and Truth: Tensed or Tenseless: Is the Truth of Propositions Dependent on Time?
Although certainly an indispensable aspect of the ontology of time, this issue—for our purposes—was adequately covered above. Moreover, it is not immediately germane to our purpose in this chapter: to elucidate the factors that determine temporal sequence in texts. So we move on to a topic quite germane: exploring a mathematical model for time.

3.4 A Mathematical Model for Time

3.4.1 Introduction
3.4.2 Issues in Developing a Mathematical Model
3.4.3 Temporal Structures
3.4.4 Summary

---

69. On the current state of the debate see Huggett and Hoefer (2009), Rynasiewicz (2012), and the series *Ontology of Spacetime*, begun in 2006, following the First International Conference on the *Ontology* of Spacetime, and continuing as papers published from subsequent conferences.

3.4.1 Introduction

This is a fascinating aspect of this study at large. We have talked already about moments of time, periods of time, overlapping intervals of time, eventualities starting at a certain point of time, overlapping eventualities, etc., knowing that we experience such things. We have assumed their reality for heuristic purposes. For this study, however, we must be much more precise.

We are now going to develop a mathematical model for time, called a temporal structure, to which we can attach eventualities. By this means, we will attempt to make the abstract ideas of the philosophy of time more concrete and more easily processed.

According to van Benthem (1984, 1) the type of tense logic developed by Prior (1967) has lacked mathematical precision. Most often it is *assumed* that time is made up of instants of time (these correspond to mathematical points), which are related to one another by strict precedence (less than or before). But these structures must be built in a systematic way.[70]

3.4.2 Issues in Developing a Temporal Model

To build a temporal structure we must have a set of **elements** (temporal entities) and one or more **binary relations** between the elements, which exhibit certain well defined **properties**. We will take up these and the issue of **the relationship of time to eventualities**, below.

Outline:

- Temporal Elements
- Temporal Relations
- Temporal Properties
- Relationships of Eventualities to Time

(1) *The Temporal Elements.* We must ask what should be the temporal elements: instants (i.e. points) or intervals? We can build intervals from instants—as usual—or we can assume that they are primitives. Constructed from instants, they are a dense ordered set of points, where dense means that there is always a point between any two points. Also the set is convex, meaning that when we move from one point to another we will always pass through points in the set.

Van Benthem shows how temporal structures built on the usual assumptions fare in their ability to yield the well-known properties of time,

---

70. This will be our task, following (van Benthem 1984); (van Benthem 1991); and (Dünges 1998). Also the slightly different approach of Kamp was consulted with profit (1979).

such as linearity. Of interest for our purposes is van Benthem's development of temporal structures, in which he proposes that the temporal elements are intervals instead of points. This is a cogent choice, because we experience intervals of time, because simultaneous eventualities always have an interval when they are both occurring (if they begin and end at exactly the same time, the intervals will be the same as the intervals for both eventualities), and because a point is just the limit of shorter and shorter intervals.[71] It is plain that we will also need instants in our model, because *achievements* [see Akagi's **Chapter 11**] theoretically occur at an instant of time. So if we opt for intervals as our primitive element, we must have some way to derive instants from them.

(2) *The Temporal Relations.* What should the temporal relations be? Our intuition and experience of time informs us that temporal intervals associated with events or states can be *ordered* (preceding or following one another), *simultaneous* (both instants and intervals), *overlapped* (intervals only), *nested* (one interval included within another), and *juxtaposed* (one interval abuts the other).[72] These correspond to the relations of strict **precedence** (hereafter "precedence," unless qualified otherwise), **superposition** (of intervals), **overlap**, **inclusion**, and **abutment**, respectively. Which of these should we use? Should we employ a combination of more than one? It is fairly obvious that we need fewer relations to represent instants than intervals. In fact, one will do: **precedence**. But there is a difference of opinion on intervals, regardless of their origin: **precedence** and **overlap** (Kamp and Reyle 1993), **precedence** and **inclusion** (van Benthem 1984), or **precedence**, **overlap**, and **inclusion** (Dünges 1998).

Having chosen intervals as the temporal element, van Benthem then selects the appropriate relations by which they can interact. He opts for strict **precedence** and **inclusion** (although, he could have chosen **overlap**). The latter is added to accommodate the fact that intervals—unlike points—are extended and therefore, an interval can be entirely contained within another. Moreover, he shows that **overlap** relations can be derived from **inclusion** relations; and, that points can be derived from intervals.

Let us see how these divers temporal relations can be derived from one another. (In the discussion below uppercase letters [X, Y, Z, and V] refer to intervals; lowercase, to instants.) First of all, **precedence** of temporal

---

71. (Van Benthem 1984, 5–10) makes a strong case for starting with intervals rather than points as the primitive temporal element.

72. See Figure 4 below for a visualization of these temporal relations.

intervals (<) can be understood in terms of temporal instants as follows: for intervals X and Y, interval X precedes interval Y *iff* for all instants within X and Y, all those within X precede all those within Y. Formally:

$$X < Y \; \textit{iff} \; \forall t_x \in X \land \forall t_y \in Y, \; t_x < t_y \tag{x}$$

Secondly, both **overlap** (O) and **inclusion** (⊑) can be derived from **precedence**. **Overlap** obtains with two intervals X and Y *iff* they do not precede one another and their intersection is not the empty set (∅). Formally:

$$X O Y \; \textit{iff} \; \neg X < Y \land \neg Y < X \land X \cap Y \neq \emptyset \tag{xi}$$

This is simply affirming that intervals either precede or follow one another or they overlap; and, moreover, that inclusion is a kind of overlap. The final condition is to preclude the possibility of abutment, which is one instant away from being an overlap.

Inclusion occurs with two intervals X and Y *iff* for all instants within X, those instants are within Y. Formally:

$$(X \sqsubseteq Y) \; \textit{iff} \; \forall t_x \in X : t_x \in Y \tag{xii}$$

In this case X is the subinterval of Y. We can define this relation in terms of **precedence** as follows: X is included within Y *iff* for all interval Z, Interval Z precedes interval Y implies interval Z precedes interval X; and Y preceding Z implies X precedes Z. Formally:

$$X \sqsubseteq Y \; \textit{iff} \; \forall Z \; (Z < Y \rightarrow Z < X) \land (Y < Z \rightarrow X < Z) \tag{xiii}$$

Let us see how this excludes all other possibilities save nesting. If the intervals precede one another in either direction, they cannot overlap. If they abut, clearly X is not a subinterval of Y. If the intervals overlapped in such a way that X is not nested in Y, Z could be nested within the overlap portion and therefore would precede Y but not X. The only thing left is X nested in Y.

Thirdly, **overlap** can be derived from **inclusion** and vice versa. Let us examine just the first of these. What is **overlap**? It means that a subinterval of one interval is also a subinterval of the other. And if there is a one subinterval in both, there will be a maximum subinterval in both, which will be the extent of the overlap. Formally:

$$X O Y \; \textit{iff} \; \exists Z \; (Z \sqsubseteq X \land Z \sqsubseteq Y) \tag{xiv}$$

Finally, **abutment** appears to be a limiting case for both strict **precedence** and **overlap**. In fact, **abutment** is type of weak **precedence** (≤), and is—as I stated above—only one instant from **overlap**. How do we distinguish this temporal relation from the others? Informally, **abutment** is two intervals, X and Y, juxtaposed with no "space" in between. In set theory, it is the union of two sets to form a third set, in which the intersection of the first two sets is the empty set. Keeping in mind that these are time intervals, a third way is to recognize that instants $t_{i(\text{initial})}$ through $t_{f(\text{inal})}$ form the endpoints of the first interval and, therefore are elements of it. **Abutment** obtains when $t_f + \Delta t \in Y$, where Δt is a liminal time increment, which we call an instant of time.

(3) *Temporal Properties*. Finally, we need to look at the temporal postulates, which come from these structures. **Precedence, overlap**, and **inclusion** each independently exhibit *symmetry* (or *asymmetry*), *transitivity*, *reflexivity*, *linearity*, *density*, and *convexity*; and when they are combined, they also manifest *monotonicity*, *freedom*, and *atomicity*. Let me explain each of these in turn and then examine their contribution to our overall analysis.

Asymmetry is best understood as the converse of *symmetry*, which is *a* equals *b* implies *b* equals *a*, for the relational operator *equality*. Formally:

$$a = b \rightarrow b = a \qquad \text{(xv)}$$

Obviously, we do *not* have symmetry for strict **precedence** in temporal structures (with instants or intervals): $t_a < t_b$ and $t_b < t_a$ are *not* the same; and $X < Y$ does not imply that $Y < X$. But, **inclusion** can be symmetric if the intervals are identical. Formally,

$$X \subseteq Y \wedge Y \subseteq X \rightarrow X = Y \qquad \text{(xvi)}$$

The same thing applies to **overlap**.

Transitivity of strict **precedence** is fairly simple. We certainly understand it with integers:

$$\forall \text{ integers } i, j, k, i < j < k \rightarrow i < k \qquad \text{(xvii)}$$

The same applies to rational numbers and real numbers. It is similarly straightforward with instants and intervals (see Figure 4). But, how this works with **inclusion** is not as obvious. Nevertheless, the concept can be illustrated simply. Imagine three mayonnaise jars: a small one, a medium sized one, and a large one. If we put the small one inside of the medium size one and then the medium with the small jar inside it into a big jar, clearly the small jar will be inside the large jar. This is the way it is with intervals.

Reflexivity for numbers is also easy to comprehend: for all x in the set of integers, rational numbers or real numbers x R x, where R (a relational operator in a set) is equality; that is, x = x. If on the other hand the relational operator is one of strict precedence (*less than*, or in temporal terms, *before*), then reflexivity does not hold: 3 < 3, for instance, is not true. The same thing applies to instants and to intervals. Both are *irreflexive*. But what of

inclusion? Here our mayonnaise jar analogy fails us. But is not reflexivity simply affirming that x is equal to or within itself? Indeed. This is self-evident. In addition, it is always the case that something overlaps itself.

Linearity is certainly one of the most important properties of temporal relations because of the patently linear nature of time. Applied to the instant structures we will present below, it is as follows: if two instants of time are not the same, the first must follow the second or the second the first. Formally,

$$t_1 \neq t_2 \rightarrow t_1 < t_2 \vee t_2 < t_1 \qquad \text{(xviii)}$$

Density is also an important property. When intervals are defined in terms of instants and not taken as primitives, they are said to be a dense ordered set of instants. Described informally above, here it remains for us to formalize:

$$t_1 < t_2 \rightarrow \exists t' \, (t_1 < t' < t_2) \qquad \text{(xix)}$$

The only further comment that we must make is that the interval must not consist of a finite number of instants. In that case, *density* would not hold.

Monotonicity is a little more complicated. It is fairly comprehensible with functions such as $y = x^3$. A function is monotonically increasing if as x increases, y increases. But in our specific case of set theory—in which *monotonicity* is not nearly as straightforward as with functions—as x is included in y, which precedes z, x precedes z. To illustrate this let us go back in time to the fourth game of the 1926 World Series. Babe Ruth hit three homeruns. Of course the 1926 World Series preceded the 1927 season. And the fourth game was within that Series. Clearly, the fourth game of the 1926 World Series preceded the 1927 season. This is *monotonicity*.

Another interesting property is *conjunctivity*. It comes from the nature of **overlap**. As we said above, in this case, there is a maximum subinterval shared by two intervals. This property states that all subintervals shared by the two intervals will necessarily be nested within the maximum subinterval. As with other second order axioms, the formal structure is too complicated for our purposes.

Moreover, two additional properties are *freedom* and *atomicity*. I will just *describe* the first of these. If two intervals, X and Y, **overlap**, *freedom* is an axiom, which comes from the observation that unless the intervals entirely **overlap** one another, there will be a portion of each interval that is not in the maximum shared subinterval. Therefore, any subinterval in this portion within X will not be a subinterval of Y. And similarly, any subinterval in this portion within Y will not be a subinterval of X. *Atomicity* maintains that intervals are indivisible. I will not comment on this axiom any further at this point.

The last property we will look at is *convexity*. This is simpler than *monotonicity*—as simple as how the shape of a baseball or football differs from that of a donut. Imagine that we take a piece of string and join any two points on one of the two balls or within them. Every point on that piece of string will be within the volume of that ball. Now take the same string and join any two points on or within a donut. Every time the string crosses the hole in the donut, the points crossing the hole are not part of the donut. Therefore, a donut is not a convex set of points. Similarly, a set of intervals with inclusion and strict precedence is a convex set. Formally, we can state *convexity* for the intervals X, Y, X, and V as follows:

$$X < Z < Y \wedge X \sqsubseteq V \wedge Y \sqsubseteq V \rightarrow Z \sqsubseteq V \qquad \text{(xx)}$$

One final word: *density* and *convexity* are similar, in that they both concern an element between two other elements. But they differ in one important aspect and in this way they are somewhat the converse of each other: for the former, the existence of the in-between element is the issue at stake; for the latter, since the in-between element is a given, the issue is: is it in the set?

The result of the above discussion is that we could have a mathematical model of time using intervals as the elements of the temporal structure with the relations of strict **precedence** and **inclusion**.

(4) *The Relationship of Eventualities to Time: Relationalism versus Substantivalism*

(a) **The Two Positions.** We must necessarily revisit the issue of the relationship of eventualities to time on this occasion, because it affects the mathematical model, specifically how eventualities can be mathematically localized in time. If on the one hand, relationalism/reductionalism (hereafter *rr*), the view of Aristotle and Leibniz (that time is nothing more than the measure of change; that time does not exist apart from eventualities; that there is no empty time) is right, then the embedding of an eventuality structure in a temporal structure—although not a trivial task—is fairly straightforward, as we will see below. If on the other hand, substantivalism/absolutism (hereafter *sa*), held by Barrow and Newton (that time is an independent entity; that time is independent of eventualities; that there is empty time) is correct, then the embedding is much more difficult, as we will see.

(b) Effect on the Model. Which view of time is adopted will affect the mathematical model of time in three ways: how time is defined in the model, how instants and intervals are related to the maximum pairwise intersection of eventualities in the model, and how eventualities are embedded in time in the model. We will examine the first and third of these below as we look at the respective temporal structures, but it is important that we look at the second right now. Note the following contrast, due to time being independent of eventualities in *sa*: from the perspective of *rr*, the intersection of all pairwise overlapping eventualities is an *instant*; but, from the perspective of *sa* the intersection of these is an *interval*.

3.4.3 Temporal Structures

We will look at the two fundamental **temporal elements** needed to understand the way eventualities interact with time, *instants* and *intervals*; the structure of **eventualities**; and how the latter is **embedded in time**.[73]

- Instants
- Intervals
- Eventualities
- Embedding

(1) *Instants.* For *rr*, we can define a set of instants, $\mathbf{T}$, with one temporal relation, **strict precedence** ($<$). This set with the given binary relation is an instant structure

$$T = (\mathbf{T}, <) \tag{xxi}$$

which has the following properties (which we call axioms, all defined above): *asymmetry, transitivity, linearity, irreflexivity,* and *density*.[74] For *sa* instants are the limiting case of intervals, if the latter are considered to be the temporal elements.

(2) *Intervals.* We can look at temporal intervals as being constructed from instants or as primitives. If the former, then let us define $\mathbf{I}$ as a *convex* set of instants with the temporal relations of **precedence**, **overlap**, and **inclusion**. Formally,

$$I = (\mathbf{I}, <, \mathrm{O}, \sqsubseteq) \tag{xxii}$$

Within this structure **precedence** is *irreflexive, asymmetric, transitive*; **inclusion** is *transitive, reflexive, asymmetric,* and satisfies *conjunctivity*; and together they are *monotonic*.[75]

---

73. Dünges lays out the strategy for her whole paper in her introduction (1998, 2–5).
74. Ibid., 5–7.
75. Ibid., 7–13.

(3) Eventualities. Now we need to build an eventuality structure from the observations we made above on the way time works in narrative in general and biblical narrative in particular. Since eventualities can follow and precede one another, abut, overlap, and nest in time, our structure will need **precedence, overlap,** and **inclusion.** We will be able to derive abutment from these. So let **E** be the set of all eventualities **e**, then for the structure $E = (E, <, O, \sqsubseteq)$, the following axioms will hold:[76]

for **precedence**	*asymmetry*	$e_x < e_y \nrightarrow e_y < e_x$	(xxiii)
	transitivity	$(e_x < e_y \wedge e_y < e_z) \rightarrow e_x < e_z$	
for **overlap**	*reflexivity*	$e_x O e_x$	
	symmetry	$e_x O e_y \rightarrow e_y O e_z$	
for mixed	*precedence*	$e_x < e_y \nrightarrow e_x O e_y$	
	monotonicity	$(e_x < e_y \wedge e_y O e_z \wedge e_z < e_w) \rightarrow e_x < e_w$	
	linearity	$e_x < e_y \vee e_x O e_y \vee e_y < e_x$	

Furthermore, **inclusion** can be defined in terms of **precedence** as follows: eventuality X is included within eventuality Y *iff* eventuality X preceding eventuality Y implies that eventuality W precedes eventuality X; and eventuality Y preceding eventuality W implies that eventuality X precedes eventuality W. Formally:

$$e_x \sqsubseteq e_y \; iff \; (e_x < e_y \rightarrow e_w < e_x) \wedge (e_y < e_w \rightarrow e_x < e_w) \qquad \text{(xxiv)}$$

And, in addition, **overlap** can be derived from **precedence** as follows: eventuality X overlaps eventuality Y *iff* eventuality X does not precede Y, and eventuality Y does not precede X. Formally:

$$e_x O e_y \; iff \, \neg (e_x < e_y) \wedge \neg (e_y < e_x) \qquad \text{(xxv)}$$

We can make three groups of observations about these axioms. The first group concerns what is there and how—if at all—they differ from temporal structures; and, why? *Asymmetry* and *transitivity* with **precedence** and *linearity* for **mixed** reminds us of the axioms for instant structures, although with the latter, all of these apply to **precedence**. *Linearity* requires further consideration, which will prove instructive. Instants, if they are not the same, must either follow or precede one another: this is *linearity*. But, with eventualities, there is a third possibility: **overlap.** In this way eventualities resemble an interval structure. It is not surprising that eventualities have characteristics of both instants and intervals. *Achievements* (e.g., arrive, win, and die) occur at an instant, whereas other eventualities (*states, accomplishments,* and *activities*) occur over an interval.

---

76. Ibid., 13–17.

The second group of observations involves the axioms, which are missing or modified, and why that might be so. Several of the axioms that hold with temporal structures, do not with eventuality structures, namely: *convexity*, *asymmetry* with **inclusion**, *conjunctivity*, and *freedom*. For the sake of space, we will look only at the first two of these. The first is violated by *semelfactives*,[77] such as *Bob sneezed all day*. We understand that this sentence does not imply that Bob incessantly sneezed without talking, eating, drinking, breathing, etc. Rather, we mean that he sneezed off and on all day. Consequently, Bob's sneezing all day is a summary of the temporally discontiguous individual episodes of his paroxysms of sneezing. And if each of these is made up of two or more sneezes, then each episode itself is a summary. All of this to say that since eventualities can be spaced out in this way, in such cases there are times when there is no eventuality happening. And thus, between sequential but discontiguous eventualities no eventuality is occurring. Consequently, eventuality structures do not have the property of *convexity*.

The second of these—one that is modified—is *asymmetry*. In eventuality structures **inclusion** can exhibit symmetry, because **inclusion** is not strict inclusion ($\sqsubset$). If it were, eventuality structures would be asymmetric. But since precedence is strict precedence, combining this with strict inclusion would exclude the possibility of identity. There must be the possibility of a complete overlap; therefore, **inclusion** cannot be strict inclusion.

The third group comprises modifications of the connection between the relations. As with temporal intervals, **overlap** can be derived from **inclusion**; but, note, that unlike with interval structures, the implication goes in only one direction: there exists an eventuality Z such that eventuality Z precedes eventuality X and eventuality Z preceding eventuality Y implies that eventuality X overlaps eventuality Y. Formally:

$$\exists e_z(e_z \sqsubseteq e_x \wedge e_z \sqsubseteq e_y) \rightarrow e_x O e_y \qquad \text{(xxvi)}$$

Now we turn to rigorously localizing eventualities in time.

(4) *Embedding Eventualities in Time*. To account for the two different theories of space-time, *rr* and *sa*, we must discuss two different approaches to localizing eventualities in time. We will not subject the reader to any of the proofs; these can be found in the literature. We will concentrate on the significance of these constructions—first, those for *rr*.

Outline:

 o Relationalism
 o Substantivalism

---

77. See Akagi **Chapter 11**.

(a) **Relationalism.** The tenet of relationalism most germane for our purposes in this approach, in which time is dependent on eventualities, is that instants are "maximal sets of pairwise overlapping eventualities."[78] Formally, i will be an instant (which is a set) of the eventuality structure, E, if

$$i \subseteq E; \; e_x, e_y \in i \rightarrow e_x O e_y;$$

and if   (xxvii)

$$\mathbf{H} \text{ [a random set] } \subseteq E, \; i \subseteq \mathbf{H}$$

and

$$\forall e_x, e_y \in \mathbf{H}, \; e_x O e_y,$$

then

$$\mathbf{H} \subseteq i.$$

Of course then i and $\mathbf{H}$ are identical sets. Call the set of instants thus defined I(E). This means **e** occurs at i *iff* e∈i. We want to define **precedence** for this set of instants so that instants will be in a given order if and only if there are eventualities, which are elements of these instants, such that the corresponding eventualities are in the same temporal order. Then the instant structure $I(E) = (I(E), <)$ is an instant structure of E, with **precedence** being *asymmetric*, *transitive*, and *linear*.

An interval structure, $I(I(E))$, can be composed from an instant structure, as above, to yield a localization function, such that every eventuality is sent to a set of instants derived from a pre-eventuality structure.[79] Formally:

$$\mathbf{L} : E \rightarrow I(I(E)), \; \mathbf{e} \mapsto \{i \in I(E) \mid e \in i \qquad \text{(xxviii)}$$

The mapping is not necessarily a bijection (one-for-one mapping of every member of the domain to the range). But possibly it is a surjection (at least one member of the domain for every member of the range). In addition, the intervals are not guaranteed to be closed; they might be open at one end or the other or both.

(b) **Substantivalism.** Because this approach assumes the independence of time, the task of embedding eventualities in time is mathematically much more formidable.[80] It requires an intermediate step of constructing pre-localization functions. With good reason, we can assume that eventualities will be localized at intervals, which are convex sets of instants. And the localization

---

78. Dünges (1998, 20–21).
79. Ibid., 20–22.
80. Ibid., 22–31; Kamp (1979).

function will be a relation preserving function (called a *h(omomorphism)*), so that the binary relations (**precedence, overlap**, etc.) in the set of eventualities will be preserved among the intervals to which they are mapped. Formally, let

$$h : E \rightarrow I(T) \text{ be a homomorphism,}$$

that is   (xxix)

$$e_x < e_y \text{ iff } h(e_x) < h(e_y) \wedge e_x Oe_y \text{ iff } h(e_x) Oh(e_y)$$

Also, we want the intersection of the localizations of all eventualities, I, to differ from that of the *rr* approach—in which it was an instant—and instead be an interval. With these things in mind, the pre-localization function with the relations of **precedence** and **overlap** can be defined formally as follows:

$$e_x < e_y \rightarrow L(e_x) < L(e_y); \ e_x Oe_y \rightarrow L(e_x) OL(e_y)$$

and   (xxx)

$$\forall i \in I(E) : \bigcap \{L(e) \mid e \in i\} \neq \emptyset$$

The first expression says that the order of the eventualities determines the order of their temporal localizations. The second expression ensures a correspondence relationship for overlap. And the last expression ensures that the intersection discussed above is an *interval*.

Unlike with *rr*, with *sa* two eventualities can be simultaneous without being identical. Thus, the mapping is not an injection. Nor is it a surjection, which requires that every member of the range be mapped from members of the domain: there can be intervals which are not localizations of eventualities, because in *sa* time is independent of eventualities. Therefore in *sa* there can be *empty instants* into which no eventuality is localized. Let us call the set of empty instants connected with localization E(L). Formally:

$$e \in E \exists t_e \in T \wedge \neg t_e \in L(e)$$ (xxxi)

The two approaches are connected, however by the following observation: that all *ra* localization functions are *sa* pre-localization functions.

It will be important for the development of full-fledged localization functions that we define the **abut** relation for a *sa* pre-localization function. It is in accordance with our intuitive idea of what this should be, namely:

$$e_x \supset\subset e_y \text{ iff } L(e_x) \supset\subset L(e_y)$$ (xxxii)

Since the right side of this expression is just two juxtaposed intervals of time, we know what this means: we have discussed it above. But what of the left side of this expression? It too is not unexpected given a little thought: e_x must precede e_y and no e_w exists to interpose between e_x and e_y.

In order to complete bridging the gap between eventualities and time we will need to work with the concept of equivalence relations and classes. An equivalence relation is a relation between any two members of a set, which is *reflexive*, *symmetric*, and *transitive* and divides it up into separate subsets, so that each member of the set is in only one subset (called equivalence classes). Thus, the intersection of any two such subsets is the empty set. For example, suppose the set is all the people of the world. This would be a set with more than seven billion members. Now let us consider the equivalence relation of common birthdays on this set. This creates a set with only three hundred sixty-five members, which are obviously non-intersecting subsets: everyone is born on only one day of the year. Or suppose that the set is the teams in the National League of Major League Baseball and the equivalence relation between teams is "be in the same division." This would divide up all the teams into three equivalence classes: Eastern, Central, and Western.

The equivalence relation we are interested in is on the instant structure $T = (\mathbf{T}, <)$, but pertains to the pre-localization function as follows: two instants will be in the same equivalence class $[t]$ if and only if they are elements of the localizations of the same eventualities. Formally:

$$t \sim t' \; iff \; \forall e \left(t \in L(e) \leftrightarrow t' \in L(e) \right) \qquad \text{(xxxiii)}$$

and the set of all such equivalence classes is

$$A = \left\{ [t] \mid t \in \mathbf{T} \right\}$$

But it is not enough just to have the set of equivalence relations; we must also have the same binary relation of **precedence** on the set A (call it $<^A$) that is on the set $\mathbf{T}$, and for our purposes it must be *well-defined*; that is, we *want*

$$[t] <^A [t'] \text{ in } A \text{ if } t < t' \text{ in } \mathbf{T} \qquad \text{(xxxiv)}$$

This only obtains when every instant in the equivalence class $[t]$ occurs before every instant in the equivalence class $[t']$. Formally, assuming that $[t] \neq [t']$, the following two conditions will ensure this:

$$t < t', \; t_a \in [t] \rightarrow t_a < t'$$

and   (xxxv)

$$t < t', \; t'_b \in [t'] \rightarrow t < t'_b$$

In which case $t \mapsto [t]$ is a surjective homomorphism from $\mathbf{T}$ to $\mathbf{A}$.

Let me illustrate this considerable abstraction with stars and Major League Baseball. Although, there are billions of galaxies with billions of stars in each, they fall into seven color types: blue, blue-white, white, yellow-white, yellow, orange, and red,[81] which can be looked at as seven equivalence classes

81. Excellent descriptions of each stellar spectral type can be found at http://hyperphysics.phy-astr.gsu.edu/hbase/starlog/staspe.html.

on the relation "stars having the same color." But suppose we define a binary relation of absolute brightness between stars, called $<^{\text{brightness}}$. If every red star were less bright than every orange star, and every orange dimmer than every yellow, and so forth—with blue white always being the brightest; then, the proposed **precedence** relation would be "well-defined." In fact, it is not, because brightness is determined by the mass of the star, not its color! Or falling back on our baseball analogy again, we could only say that the Eastern division is better than the Central, which in turn is better than the Western, if in every game between an Eastern team and a Central team the former wins, and every game between a Central and a Western, the latter loses, and every game between the East and the West, the East prevails. Then the binary relation, "better than," would be *well-defined.*

How does all this help develop a model of time for *sa*? The answer: if the relation $<^A$ is *well-defined* on **A**, then the structure $A = (A, <^A)$ is a *homomorphic contraction* of $T = (T, <)$, into which the instant structure of *rr* can be embedded.

Consequently, we want to determine the necessary and sufficient conditions on $L : E \rightarrow I(T)$, which will guarantee that A is a *homomorphic contraction* of T, that is, that it will be *well-defined.*[82] For this to be the case, we must ensure that the localizations of eventualities are **not** between equivalent instants. This unwanted situation can only obtain if both instants are empty or both not empty. Therefore we desire these instants to not both be empty and not both be non-empty. As for the first *desideratum*, we want our construction to allow for empty instants, but not on both sides of the localizations. Since they can exist, they must either precede or follow localizations of eventualities, because they cannot be within them by definition. Furthermore, if the non-empty sets of instants, which frame a localization of an eventuality are such that they are in different equivalence classes, then the second *desideratum* will be satisfied. So it can be shown that if the following two-part postulate obtains then both these *desiderata* will be satisfied. The first part applies immediately to empty instants but will figure in the second part as well. Formally:

$$E(L) \neq \emptyset \rightarrow E(L) < L(e) \lor L(e) < E(L) \qquad \text{(xxxvi)}$$

And although the second part, which follows, is complicated, it is worth our attention, for it localizes an eventuality by positioning it between intervals of time, which are themselves localizations of other eventualities (underlined for emphasis). Formally:

---

82. According to the topologist, Saburo Matsumoto (in a private conversation), this is the most important and most difficult part of Dünges' paper.

$$\frac{\forall t_x, t_y \left(\exists e_x \left(t_x \in L(e_x) \right) \land \exists e_y \left(t_y \in L(e_y) \right) \land \exists e \left(\{t_x\} < L(e) < \{t_y\} \right) \right) \rightarrow}{\left(\exists e_x (t_x \in L(e_x) \land \neg t_y \in L(e_x)) \lor \exists e_y (t_y \in L(e_y) \land \neg t_x \in L(e_y)) \right)} \text{(xxxvii)}$$

3.4.4 Summary

An important result of this analysis is that it shows that every *rr* localization function is an *sa* localization function. But even more significant is that it shows that eventualities carry along time; and, thus, it is proper to speak of them interchangeably, as we have done so frequently above. In addition, we now have a precise nomenclature and understanding of temporal relations and their connection with eventualities regardless of which theory (*rr* or *sa*) is embraced.

It only remains for us to integrate the temporal signatures of the different types of eventualities with those of the temporal relations between intervals or instants, which we will do in the next section of the chapter.

4. Issues Pertaining to Text, Event, and Time

Outline:

    4.1 Temporal Relations of Temporal Elements in Texts
    4.2 Integration of Temporal Elements with Eventualities in Text

4.1 *Temporal Relations of Temporal Elements in Texts*

From the discussion above we recognize that temporal intervals (or instants) can be related, that is, interact, in four concrete ways (although theoretically this can be reduced, as we will show below): **precedence, inclusion, overlap**, and **abutment**. Furthermore, we have established above that these temporal elements are localizations of eventualities. In addition, we have discussed above the effect of ***compatibility*** on temporal sequence, which in terms of temporal relations, precludes **inclusion** and **overlap**. We have also elucidated above and in an earlier chapter that texts constrain the verbs/VP representing eventualities to be linear. But even more precisely, this linearity is with respect to precedence in textual order, not necessarily in temporal order. This is epitomized by simultaneous eventualities, which must be presented linearly. Moreover, we have shown above that ***coherence relations*** in text can transform the temporal order of eventualities by reversing the normal polarity of time or halting its advance. We have seen that time progresses in *Result* and *Serialation*, but stops in *Elaboration* and *Contrast*. And when result precedes cause in a text, time is reversed. Thus, in a text each interaction can occur in both directions: x can be before y and y before x; x can be included in y, and y in x; x can overlap y (xOy), and y x; x can butt up against y, and vice versa. This yields eight possibilities, to which we must add one more, because x and y can be superimposed and be perfectly contemporaneous. Thus, there are nine ways in all.

How does our model hold up to the actual possibilities? First, xOy can be defined in terms of **inclusion** as follows: there exists an interval z, which is included within both x and y. This potentially reduces the number of temporal relations to three. Moreover, juxtaposition is the limit of **overlap**: zero **overlap** without separation of the intervals. Similarly, **superposition** is the maximum **overlap**. This brings us down to two distinct ways of relating. But this can be reduced to one, in that **inclusion** can be defined in terms of **precedence**: x is included within y means that for all z, z precedes y implies that z precedes x, and y precedes z implies x precedes z. All nine possibilities can be seen in Figure 4, which is a *v*isualization of the *t*emporal *r*elations in *t*ext (VTRT). The following are few simple rules to keep in mind when looking at the visualization: the x eventuality/temporal element is depicted by a blue bar, y by red, and their overlap by purple; for **precedence**, **overlap**, and **abutment**, the priority of a letter means that the temporal interval or instant begins before that of the second; and priority with **inclusion** signifies that the first is nested within the second.

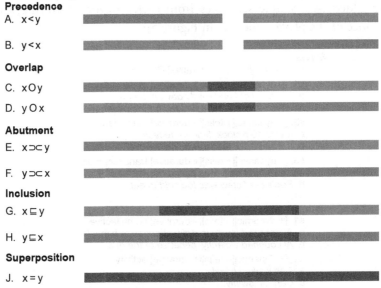

Precedence
A. x < y

B. y < x

Overlap
C. x O y

D. y O x

Abutment
E. x ⊃⊂ y

F. y ⊃⊂ x

Inclusion
G. x ⊑ y

H. y ⊑ x

Superposition
J. x = y

Figure 4. Possible relationships of temporal elements.

The above VTRTs are subject to restrictions and are limited by *coherence relations*. Assuming that these are all attached (as we have discussed above), *incompatibility* would preclude VTRTs C, D, G, H, and J. Also, VTRTs B and D occur when result precedes cause in a text. And VTRTs C, H, and J obtain when the *coherence relation* is either *Elaboration* or *Contrast*.

4.2 *Integration of Temporal Elements with Eventualities in Text*

Outline:

    4.2.1   Eventuality-Temporal Element Configurations
    4.2.2   Discussion

4.2.1 Eventuality-Temporal Element Configurations

To integrate the temporal element profiles in text with eventualities we adopt the model of situational aspect proposed by Akagi in his **Chapter 11**. There are three components that make up each category of situational aspect: dynamicity, telicity, and durativity; each which can be positive or negative. Thus, mathematically speaking there are $2 \times 2 \times 2 = 8$ *theoretically possible* eventuality types. But from a real world perspective, the – dynamic – telic – durative category is *not* possible. So there are only the following seven categories of eventualities: **atelic states**, **point states**, **transitory states**, **semelfactives**, **activities**, **achievements**, and **accomplishments**. They break down by their component structure, with states (– dynamic) separated from events (+ dynamic), as follows in Figure 5 [from Akagi, **Chapter 11** to which I have added two sample sentences from each category, featuring a final appearance of the playground trio in Figure 5]:

States
    [– dynamic][– telic][– durative] Ø
    s1. [– dynamic][– telic][+ durative] atelic state
    a. *It was a cold and windy day on the playground.*
    b. *It was a warm and calm day on the playground.*
    s2. [– dynamic][+ telic][– durative] point state
    a. *It was 10 o'clock, time for recess.*
    b. *It was 10:18, recess was nearly over.*
    s3. [– dynamic][+ telic][+ durative] transitory state
    a. *Bob's beef stew was piping hot.*
    b. *Bob's beef stew was too cold to eat.*

Events
    e1. [+ dynamic][– telic][– durative] semelfactive
    a. *Al sneezed loudly to draw attention to himself.*
    b. *Al coughed violently, because of the dust.*
    e2. [+ dynamic][– telic][+ durative] activity
    a. *Carl walked briskly.*
    b. *Carl ran swiftly.*
    e3. [+ dynamic][+ telic][– durative] achievement
    a. *Bob let go of the bar (and dropped to the ground).*
    b. *Bob dropped the ball.*
    e4. [+ dynamic][+ telic][+ durative] accomplishment
    a. *The boys built a fort from wind-blown boxes.*
    b. *The boys wound the swings up on the top bar.*

Figure 5. Eventuality categories with sample sentences.

Since each of the temporal elements can be a localization of any of these seven, and the former have nine possibilities for a two VP sequence, there are 9×7 = 63 possible temporal configurations in a two VP sequence. But are all of these attested?

4.2.2 Discussion

With the limited purpose of showing how we will proceed in the second book of our metaphorical shiplog, which will document new waters and islets we will have charted by then, we will confine our attention to the three types of states (S1, S2, S3 in Figure 5), determining *compatibility* with any of the *other* eventuality types for both states and events (holding in abeyance *compatibility* within a category). Atelic states can be represented by a ray or a line, because there is no required right hand end point and no necessary indication of the beginning of the state. Transitory states by definition will end: we cannot coherently assert that *Bob's beef stew was piping hot* after it had cooled off. Transitory states are a line segment. Point states, semelfactives, and achievements are a point—the last marking a change of state.

Also we must comment on how states interact with the instants or intervals in which they occur vis-à-vis how events do. Seligman and ter Meulen observe the following contrast: a particular state is in effect for every instant in an interval in which the state persists (1995, 303). We will call this **State Behavior** (*SB*). In addition they assert that for an event the interval in which it occurs extends to the entirety of the event. We will call this **Event Behavior** (*EB*). Let us illustrate how this works with states using the following sentence: *It was cold and windy on the playground that day.* **SB** says that *all* that day it was cold and windy. Now let us look at **EB**, using *The boys built a fort from wind-blown boxes.* **EB** says that the interval in which the boys built extended to the full duration of the event.

Now we must consider the integration of the levels.[83] To do this, we must first peruse the interactions between eventualities in terms of their possible temporal relations (Figure 4), limiting our consideration to those crossing categories, that is, to the "a" sentences in Figure 5. The first three

---

83. Hinrichs does this by discussing the nine temporal pairings that come from the three ways in which time can be indicated in a text: tense morpheme, temporal adverb, and temporal conjunction (1986, 63–64). Then he works his way through these, considering the situational aspect (*Aktionsart*) of the verbs and even the possibility of overlap and inclusion of eventualities—as well as the expected, precedence, of course—in terms of a Reichenbachian-like reference point for tense (64–80). He does not look, however, at *coherence relations*, *compatibility*, *connectivity*, or *discontinuity*.

could be simultaneous (**J**), overlap (**C** and **D**), or nest (**G** and **H**) in both polarities with any other state or event, because the subjects of the three sentences differ. But if the subjects of the three sentences were the same, then *compatibility* issues might arise, depending on the semantics of the individual verbs. As a matter of fact, they do with the accomplishment sample sentence in e4, if "boys" refers to the three. On the other hand it might just as readily refer to three other boys, in which case there is no issue. But are the eventualities viable if paired in the same category?

Second, therefore, we must turn to consider the interaction within the categories. I deliberately composed the "b" sentences above to conflict with their "a" counterparts in regards to *compatibility*. Since the former are just as plausible eventualities as the latter, this proves that interactions within categories are not necessarily compatible. But I could just as easily have composed compatible eventualities within each category. So it obviously depends on the specific pairings.

4.3 Concluding Summary: The Intergration of the Micro-, Macro- and Mega-levels: Application to the Flood Narrative

How will we apply our knowledge of the four factors and their integration with time to BH narrative and the Flood narrative in particular to determining the chronology of the text? By working up from the *micro-level* (individual VPs) through the *macro-level* (relationships between VPs) and on to the *mega-level* and back down again, pursuing a feedback approach to guard against false conclusions. There is no shortcut. Each VP will have to be analyzed, along with its relations with others, with the purpose of the narrative at large kept in mind. We will proceed as follows:

I.   Ascertain the temporal profile of every VP in the narrative in question. Of most importance is the telicity and durativity of each.

II. Ascertain the **coherence relations** between VPs in order to determine where temporal progression is possible. *Serialation* and *Result/Cause* evince temporal progression, *Contrast* and *Elaboration* (and its siblings) do not.

III. Ascertain trouble spots with respect to simultaneity by considering the **compatibility** of connected VPs (usually sequential, but see IV below).

IV. Ascertain the VP **connection** outline. Sequential verbs are not always temporally connected. In such cases, find where the place of attachment is. And, thus, organize the narrative according to its levels of attachment.

V.   Ascertain the locations in the narrative, which could be hiding a temporal **discontinuity**.

5. Final Summation

Confronted with the reality that in not a few instances sequential *wayyiqtols* do not manifest temporal progression, perforce we conclude that it does not mark temporal progression.[84] Rather, it is **necessary** if progression is to be conveyed, but **not sufficient** to ensure that it is. This state of affairs charges us with a task, but also leaves us with a quandary. The task: if *wayyiqtol* does not indicate temporal progression, what does? We have outlined a semantic approach to answering that question. At all levels, *micro*, *macro*, and *mega* the temporal profile of a text is being shaped. We have attempted to clarify this process: on the *micro-level* with seven eventuality types, on the *macro-level* with four *coherence relations*, *compatibility* considerations, issues of *connection*, and *discontinuity*; and on the *mega-level*, the vagaries of which will be unfolded in the next chapter. And as for the quandry: what then is the function of *wayyiqtol* beyond the construal of simple past? Is there a beyond? Armed with a consideration of its origins, its congeners in the other Semitic languages, and its usage in the text, it would prove a worthy study indeed, for another place and another time.

Appendix A:
Sample Texts, Transliteration, and Interlinear Translation

GENESIS 25:34

וַיֵּשְׁתְּ	וַיֹּאכַל	עֲדָשִׁים	וּנְזִיד	לֶחֶם	לְעֵשָׂו	נָתַן	וְיַעֲקֹב
wayyēšt	*wayyō 'kal*	*'ădāšîm*	*ûn°zîd*	*lehem*	*l° 'ēśāw*	*nātan*	*w°ya 'ăqōb*
and/then he drank	and/then he ate	of lentils	and cooked food	bread	to Esau	he gave	and Jacob

And Jacob gave Esau bread and cooked food made from lentils. And/then he **ate**. And/then he **drank**.

הַבְּכֹרָה:	אֶת־	עֵשָׂו	וַיִּבֶז	וַיֵּלַךְ	נָקָם
habb°kōrāh	*'et-*	*'ēśāw*	*wayyibez*	*wayyēlak*	*wayyāqom*
the birthright	(DO marker)	Esau	and/then he despised	and/then he went	and/then he got up

And/then he **got up**. And/then he **went away**. And/then Esau **despised** (his) birthright.

---

84. This is in keeping with the conclusions drawn by ter Meulen and her fellow linguist, Susan Rothstein to sample *wayyiqtol* chains sent to them for their consideration. They said "... [with respect to the] documents analyzing specific Hebrew examples of temporal anaphora .... [it] seems we have a general consensus that w-marking is entirely independent of temporal progression ..." (personal communication). These sample chains are in **Appendix A**.

JOSHUA 2:23–24

מֵהָהָר	וַיֵּרְדוּ	הָאֲנָשִׁים	שְׁנֵי	וַיָּשֻׁבוּ
mēhāhār	wayyērᵉdû	hā ᵃnāšîm	šᵉnê	wayyašūḇû
from the mountain	and/then they went down	the men	two	and/then they returned

And/then the two men **returned**. And/then they **descended** from the mountain.

נוּן	בִּן־	יְהוֹשֻׁעַ	אֶל־	וַיָּבֹאוּ	וַיַּעַבְרוּ
nûn	bin-	yᵉhôšūaʿ	ʾel-	wayyāḇōʾû	wayyaʿaḇrû
Nun	son of	Joshua	to	and/then they came to	and/then they crossed over

And/then they **crossed over**. And/then they **came** to Joshua the son of Nun.

אוֹתָם:	הַמֹּצְאוֹת	כָּל־	אֵת	לוֹ	וַיְסַפְּרוּ־
ʾôṯām	hammōṣᵉʾôṯ	kol-	ʾēṯ	lô	waysappᵉrû-
them	the things which found	all	(DO marker)	to him	and/then they recounted

And/then they **recounted** to him all the things that had happened to them.

הָאָרֶץ	כָּל־	אֶת־	בְּיָדֵנוּ	יְהוָה	נָתַן	כִּי־	יְהוֹשֻׁעַ	אֶל־	וַיֹּאמְרוּ
hā ʾāreṣ	kol-	ʾet-	bᵉyāḏēnû	yᵉhwāh	nāṯan	kî-	yᵉhôšūaʿ	ʾel-	wayyōʾmᵉrû
the land	all	(DO marker)	into our hand	YHWH	he gave	that	Jošua	to	and/then they said

And/then they **said** to Joshua, "YHWH has given into our hand the whole land.

מִפָּנֵינוּ:	הָאָרֶץ	יֹשְׁבֵי	כָּל־	נָמֹגוּ	וְגַם־
mippānênû	hā ʾāreṣ	yōšᵉḇê	kol-	nāmōḡû	wᵉgam-
from before us	the land	the dwellers of	all	they have despaired	and also

And also all those who live in the land have despaired because of us."

JUDGES 1:17–20

הַכְּנַעֲנִי	אֶת־	וַיַּכּוּ	אָחִיו	שִׁמְעוֹן	אֶת־	יְהוּדָה	וַיֵּלֶךְ
hakkᵉnaʿanî	ʾet-	wayyakkû	ʾāḥîw	šimʿôn	ʾet-	yᵉhûḏāʰ	wayyēlek
the Canaanite	(DO marker)	and/then they struck	his brother	Simeon	with	Judah	and/then he went

And/then Judah **went** with Simeon his brother, and/then they **struck** the Canaanite

הָעִיר	שֵׁם־	אֶת־	וַיִּקְרָא	אוֹתָהּ	וַיַּחֲרִימוּ	צְפַת	יוֹשֵׁב
hā ʿîr	šēm-	ʾet-	wayyiqrāʾ	ʾôṯāh	wayyaḥᵃrîmû	ṣᵉpaṯ	yôšēḇ
of the city	name	(DO marker)	and/then they called	it	and/then they destroyed	in Zephath	dwelling

dwelling in Zephath. And/then they **destroyed** it. And/then they **called** the name of the city

גְּבוּלָֽה	וְאֶת־	עַזָּ֥ה	אֶת־	יְהוּדָ֖ה	וַיִּלְכֹּ֣ד	חָרְמָ֑ה׃
gᵊbûlāh	wᵊ'et-	'azzāh	'et-	yᵊhûdāh	wayyilkōd	ḥormāh
its territory	and (+DO marker)	Gaza	(DO marker)	Judah	and/then he captured	Hormah

"Hormah." And/then Judah **captured** Gaza and its territory,

עֶקְר֖וֹן	וְאֶת־	גְּבוּלָ֑הּ	וְאֶת־	אַשְׁקְל֖וֹן	וְאֶת־
'eqrôn	wᵊ'et-	gᵊbûlāh	wᵊ'et-	'ašqᵊlôn	wᵊ'et
Ekron	and (+DO marker)	its territory	and (+DO marker)	Aškelon	and (+DO marker)

and Ashkelon and its territory, and Ekron

וַיֹּ֣רֶשׁ	יְהוּדָ֗ה	אֶת־	יְהוָה֙	וַיְהִ֤י	גְּבוּלָֽהּ׃	וְאֶת־
wayyōreš	yᵊhûdāh	'et-	yᵊhwāh	wayhî	gᵊbûlāh	wᵊ'et-
and/then he took possession	Judah	with	YHWH	and/then he was	its territory	and (+DO marker)

and its territory. And/then YHWH **was** with Judah. And/then he **took possession of**

הָעֵֽמֶק	יֹשְׁבֵ֣י	אֶת־	לְהוֹרִישׁ	לֹ֥א	כִּ֛י	הָהָ֑ר	אֶת־
hā'ēmeq	yōšᵊbê	'et-	lᵊhôrîš	lō'	kî	hāhār	'et-
the valley	dwellers of	(DO marker)	to dispossess	not	because	the mountain	(DO marker)

the mountain because (they were not able) to dispossess the inhabitants of the valley

כַּאֲשֶׁ֣ר	חֶבְר֖וֹן	אֶת־	לְכָלֵ֔ב	וַיִּתְּנ֤וּ	לָהֶ֑ם׃	בַּרְזֶ֖ל	רֶ֥כֶב	כִּֽי־
ka'ᵃšer	ḥebrôn	'et-	lᵊkālēb	wayyittᵊnû	lāhem	barzel	rekeb	kî-
as	Hebron	(DO marker)	to Caleb	and/then they gave	to them	of iron	chariotry	because

because they had iron chariotry. And/then they **gave** Hebron to Caleb as

הָעֲנָֽק׃	בְּנֵ֣י	שְׁלֹשָׁ֖ה	אֶת־	מִשָּׁ֔ם	וַיֹּ֣רֶשׁ	מֹשֶׁ֑ה	דִּבֶּ֖ר
hā'ᵃnāq	bᵊnê	šᵊlōšāh	'et-	miššām	wayyōreš	mōšeh	dibber
of Anak	sons	three	(DO marker)	from there	and/then he dispossessed	Moses	he spoke

Moses **had spoken**. And/then he **dispossessed** the three sons of Anak from there.

2 SAMUEL 4:5–7

כְּחֹ֣ם	וַיָּבֹ֙אוּ֙	וּבַעֲנָ֔ה	רֵכָ֣ב	הַבְּאֵרֹתִ֗י	רִמּ֣וֹן	בְּנֵֽי־	וַיֵּלְכ֞וּ
kᵊḥōm	wayyābō'û	ûba'ᵃnāh	rēkāb	habbᵊ'ērōtî	rimmôn	bᵊnê-	wayyēlᵊkû
at heat	and/then they entered	and Baanah	Rekab	the Beerothite	Rimmon	the sons of	and/then they went

And/then the sons of Rimmon the Beerothite, Rekab and Baanah, **went**. And/then they **entered**, in the heat of

הַצָּהֳרָיִם:	מִשְׁכַּב	אֶת	שֹׁכֵב	וְהוּא	אִישׁ בֹּשֶׁת	בֵּית-	אֶל-	הַיּוֹם
haṣṣohŏrāyim	miškab	'ēt	šōkēb	wᵊhû'	'iš-bōšet	bêt	'el-	hayyôm
midday	bed	(DO marker)	lying	and he	Ish-bosheth	house of	to	the day

the day, into the house of Ish-bosheth. And he was lying on his bed at midday.

וַיַּכֻּהוּ	חִטִּים	לֹקְחֵי	הַבַּיִת	תּוֹךְ-	עַד-	בָּאוּ	וְהֵנָּה
wayyakkūhû	ḥiṭṭîm	lōqᵊḥê	habbayit	tôk	'ad-	bā'û	wᵊhēnnāh
and/then they struck him	wheat	takers of	the house	middle of	as far as	they entered	and there

And there they entered as far as the middle of the house as people getting wheat, [Hebrew text is unusual, LXX markedly different], and they **struck** him

נִמְלָטוּ	אָחִיו	וּבַעֲנָה	וְרֵכָב	הַחֹמֶשׁ	אֶל-
nimlāṭû	'āḥîw	ûbaʿᵃnāh	wᵊrēkāb	haḥōmeš	'el-
they escaped	his brother	and Baanah	and Rekab	the belly	into

into the belly. But Rekab and Baanah his brother escaped.

מִשְׁכָּבוֹ	בַּחֲדַר	מִטָּתוֹ	עַל-	שֹׁכֵב	וְהוּא-	הַבַּיִת	וַיָּבֹאוּ
miškābô	baḥᵃdar	miṭṭātô	'al-	šōkēb	wᵊhû'-	habbayit	wayyābō'û
his bed	in the chamber	his bed	on	lying	and he	the house	and/then they entered

And/then they **entered** the house. And he was lying on his bed in his bedroom.

רֹאשׁוֹ	אֶת-	וַיָּסִירוּ	וַיְמִתֻהוּ	וַיַּכֻּהוּ
rō'šô	'et-	wayyāsîrû	waymîtūhû	wayyakkūhû
his head	(DO marker)	and/then they removed	and/then they put him to death	and/then they struck him

And/then they **struck** him. And/then they **killed** him. And/then they **removed** his head.

הַלָּיְלָה:	כָּל-	הָעֲרָבָה	דֶּרֶךְ	וַיֵּלְכוּ	רֹאשׁוֹ	אֶת-	וַיִּקְחוּ
hallāylāh	kol-	hāʿᵃrābāh	derek	wayyēlᵊkû	rō'šô	'et-	wayyiqḥû
the night	all	the Arabah	way of	and/then they went	his head	(DO marker)	and/then they took

And/then they **took** his head, and/they **went** on the way of the Arabah all night.

2 SAMUEL 17:21–29

וַיַּגִּדוּ	וַיֵּלְכוּ	מֵהַבְּאֵר	וַיַּעֲלוּ	לֶכְתָּם	אַחֲרֵי	וַיְהִי
wayyaggidû	wayyēlᵊkû	mēhabbᵊ'ēr	wayyaʿᵃlû	lektām	'aḥᵃrê	wayhî
and/then they told	and/then they went	from the cistern	and/then they went up	they go	after	and/then was

After they went, they **climbed up** from the cistern. And/then they **went**. And/then they **told**

הַמַּיִם	אֶת־	מְהֵרָה	וְעִבְרוּ	קוּמוּ	דָּוִד	אֶל־	וַיֹּאמְרוּ	דָּוִד	לַמֶּלֶךְ
hammayim	'et-	m°hērā'	w°'ibrû	qûmû	dāwīd	'el-	wayyō'm°rû	dāwīd	lammelek
the water	(DO marker)	quickly	and cross over	get up	David	to	and/then they said	David	to the king

to King David. And/then they **said**, "Get up and cross quickly over the water

אֲשֶׁר	הָעָם	וְכָל־	דָּוִד	וַיָּקָם	אֲחִיתֹפֶל:	עֲלֵיכֶם	יָעַץ	כָּכָה	כִּי־
'ašer	hā'ām	w°kol-	dāwīd	wayyāqom	'aḥîtōpel	'alêkem	yā'aṣ	kākā'	kî-
who	the people	and all	David	and/then he got up	Ahithophel	against you	he advised	thus	because

the water because thus Ahithophel advised against you." And/then David and all the people who

הַבֹּקֶר	אוֹר	עַד־	הַיַּרְדֵּן	אֶת־	וַיַּעַבְרוּ	אִתּוֹ
habbōqer	'ôr	'ad-	hayyardēn	'et-	wayy'abrû	'ittô
the morning	light of	until	the Jordan	(DO marker)	and/then they crossed over	with him

were with him, and/then they **crossed over** the Jordan until the morning light,

וַאֲחִיתֹפֶל	הַיַּרְדֵּן:	אֶת־	עָבַר	לֹא־	אֲשֶׁר	נֶעְדָּר	לֹא	אֶחָד־	עַד־
wa'aḥîtōpel	hayyardēn	'et-	'ābar	lō'-	'ašer	ne'dār	lō'	'aḥad	'ad-
and Ahithophel	the Jordan	(DO marker)	he crossed over	not	who	missing	not	one	until

until not one was missing from those who crossed over the Jordan. And Ahithophel

הַחֲמוֹר	אֶת־	וַיַּחֲבֹשׁ	עֲצָתוֹ	נֶעֶשְׂתָה	לֹא	כִּי	רָאָה
haḥamôr	'et-	wayyaḥ°bōš	'aṣātô	ne'eśtā'	lō'	kî	rā'ā'
the donkey	(DO marker)	and/then he saddled	his advice	done	not	that	he saw

saw that his advice was not performed. And/then he **saddled** a donkey.

וַיְצַו	עִירוֹ	אֶל־	בֵּיתוֹ	אֶל־	וַיֵּלֶךְ	וַיָּקָם
wayṣaw	'îrô	'el-	bêtô	'el-	wayyēlek	wayyāqom
and/then he gave instructions	his city	to	his house	to	and/then he went	and/then he got up

And/then he **got up**. And/then he **went** to his house, to his city. And/then he **gave instructions** [[presumably, an order to humanely kill him]]

אָבִיו:	בְּקֶבֶר	וַיִּקָּבֵר	וַיָּמָת	וַיֵּחָנַק	בֵּיתוֹ	אֶל־
'ābîw	b°qeber	wayyiqqābēr	wayyāmot	wayyēḥānaq	bêtô	'el-
his father	in the grave	and/then he was buried	and/then he died	and/then he was strangled	his household	to

to his household. And/then he was **strangled**. And/then he **died**. And/then he **was buried** in his father's grave.

הַיַּרְדֵּן	אֶת־	עָבַר	וְאַבְשָׁלֹם	מַחֲנָיְמָה	בָּא	וְדָוִד
hayyardēn	'et-	ʿābar	wᵊ'abšālōm	maḥᵃnāymāʰ	bā'	wᵊdāwīd
the Jordan	(DO marker)	he crossed over	and Absolom	Mahanaim	he came	and David

And David came to Mahanaim, but Absolom crossed over the Jordan,

יוֹאָב	תַּחַת	אַבְשָׁלֹם	שָׂם	עֲמָשָׂא	וְאֶת־	עִמּוֹ:	יִשְׂרָאֵל	אִישׁ	וְכָל־	הוּא
yô'āb	taḥat	'abšālōm	śām	ʿᵃmāśā'	wᵊ'et-	ʿimmô	yiśrā'ēl	'îš	wᵊkol-	hū'
Joab	instead of	Absolom	he put	Amasa	and (+DO marker)	with him	Israel	man	and every	he

he and every man of Israel with him. And Amasa Absolom installed instead of Joab

אֲשֶׁר־	הַיִּשְׂרְאֵלִי	יִתְרָא	וּשְׁמוֹ	אִישׁ	בֶן־	וַעֲמָשָׂא	הַצָּבָא	עַל־
'ᵃšer-	hayyiśrᵊ'ēlî	yitrā'	ûšᵊmô	'îš	ben-	waʿᵃmāśā'	haṣṣābā'	'al-
who	the Israelite	Yithra	and his name	man	son of	and Amasa	the army	over

over the army. Amasa was the son of a man named Yithra the Israelite, who

יוֹאָב:	אֵם	צְרוּיָה	אֲחוֹת	נָחָשׁ	בַּת־	אֲבִיגַל	אֶל־	בָּא
yô'āb	'ēm	ṣᵊrûyāʰ	'ᵃḥôt	nāḥāš	bat-	'ᵃbîgal	'el-	bā'
Joab	the mother	Zeruiah	sister of	Nahaš	daughter of	Abigail	to	he went in

had gone in to Abigail, the daughter of Nahash, sister of Zeruiah, the mother of Joab.

דָוִד	כְּבוֹא	וַיְהִי	הַגִּלְעָד: ס	אֶרֶץ	וְאַבְשָׁלֹם	יִשְׂרָאֵל	וַיִּחַן
dāwīd	kᵊbô'	wayhî	haggil'ād	'ereṣ	wᵊ'abšālōm	yiśrā'el	wayyiḥan
David	when came	and/then was	Gilead	land of	and Absolom	Israel	and/then it camped

And/then Israel and Absolom **camped** in the land of Gilead. When David came

עַמִּיאֵל	בֶּן־	וּמָכִיר	עַמּוֹן	בְּנֵי־	מֵרַבַּת	נָחָשׁ	בֶן־	וְשֹׁבִי	מַחֲנָיְמָה
'ammî'ēl	ben-	ûmākîr	ʿammôn	bᵊnê-	mērabbat	nāḥāš	ben-	wᵊšōbî	maḥᵃnāymāh
Ammiel	son of	and Machir	Ammon	sons of	from Rabbah of	Nahaš	son of	and Šobi	to Mahanaim

to Mahanaim, Shobi the son of Nahash of Rabbah of the Ammonites, and Mahir son of Ammiel

יוֹצֵר	וּכְלִי	וְסַפּוֹת	מִשְׁכָּב	מֵרֹגְלִים	הַגִּלְעָדִי	וּבַרְזִלַּי	רְבָד	מִלֹּא
yôṣēr	ûkᵊlî	wᵊsappōt	miškāb	mērōgᵊlîm	haggil'ādî	ûbarzillay	dᵊbār	millō'
potter	and vessels	and bowls	bed	from Rogelim	the Gileadite	and Barzillai	Debar	from Lo-

from Lo-Debar, and Barzillai the Gileadite from Rogelim presented beds, and bowls, and pottery,

וּדְבַשׁ	וְקָלִי:	וַעֲדָשִׁים	וּפוֹל	וְקָלִי	וְקֶמַח	וּשְׂעֹרִים	וְחִטִּים
ûdᵊḇaš	wᵊqālî	wa'ᵃdāšîm	ûpôl	wᵊqālî	wᵊqemaḥ	ûśᵊ'ōrîm	wᵊḥiṭṭîm
and honey	and roasted grain	and lentils	and beans	and roasted grain	and flour	and barley	and wheat

and wheat, and barley, and flour, and roasted grain, and beans, and lentils, and roasted grain, and honey,

אִתּוֹ	אֲשֶׁר־	וְלָעָם	לְדָוִד	הִגִּישׁוּ	בָּקָר	וּשְׁפוֹת	וְצֹאן	וְחֶמְאָה
'ittô	'ᵃšer-	wᵊlā'ām	lᵊdāwid	higgîšû	bāqār	ûšᵊp̄ôt	wᵊṣō'n	wᵊhem'āʰ
with him	who	and to the people	to David	they presented	herd	and cheese	and flocks	and buttermilk

and buttermilk, and flocks, and cheese from cow's milk they presented to David and the people who were with him

בַּמִּדְבָּר:	וְצָמֵא	וְעָיֵף	רָעֵב	הָעָם	אָמְרוּ	כִּי	לֶאֱכוֹל
bammidbār	wᵊṣāmē'	wᵊ'āyēp̄	rā'ēḇ	hā'ām	'āmᵊrû	kî	le'ᵉkôl
in the wilderness	and thirsty	and tired	hungry	the people	they said	because	to eat

to eat because they said, "The people are hungry and tired and thirsty in the wilderness."

1 KINGS 22:34–37

יִשְׂרָאֵל	מֶלֶך	אֶת־	וַיַּכֶּה	לְתֻמּוֹ	בַּקֶּשֶׁת	מָשַׁך	וְאִישׁ
yiśrā'ēl	melek	'et-	wayyakkeʰ	lᵊtummô	baqqešet	māšak	wᵊ'îš
Israel	king	(DO marker)	and/then he struck	in his innocence	on the bow	pulled	and a man

And a man drew his bow without intention, and/then it (an arrow)/he struck the king of Israel

הֲפֹך	לְרַכָּבוֹ	וַיֹּאמֶר	הַשִּׁרְיָן	וּבֵין	הַדְּבָקִים	בֵּין
hᵃp̄ōk	lᵊrakkāḇô	wayyō'mer	hašširyān	ûḇên	haddᵊḇāqîm	bên
turn back!	to his charioteer	and/then he said	the armor	and between	the scales	between

between the scales of his armor, and/then he said to his charioteer, "Turn back

הָחֳלֵיתִי:	כִּי	הַמַּחֲנֶה	מִן־	וְהוֹצִיאֵנִי	יָדְך
hoḥᵒlêtî	kî-	hammaḥᵃneʰ	min-	wᵊhôṣî'ēnî	yādᵊkā
I have been wounded	because	the camp	from	and take me out	your hand

your hand and take me out of the ranks because I am wounded."

הָיָה	וְהַמֶּלֶך	הַהוּא	בַּיּוֹם	הַמִּלְחָמָה	וַתַּעֲלֶה
hāyāʰ	wᵊhammelek	hahû'	bayyôm	hammilḥāmāʰ	watta'ᵃleʰ
and he was	and the king	that	in the day	the battle	and rose

And/then the battle increased on that day, and the king was

וַיָּצֶק	בָּעֶרֶב	וַיָּמָת	אֲרָם	נֹכַח	בַּמֶּרְכָּבָה	מָעֳמָד
wayyīṣeq	bāʿereb	wayyāmot	ʾᵃrām	nōkaḥ	bammerkābāh	moʿᵒmād
And/then it poured out	in the evening	and/then he died	Aram	in front of	in the chariot	stood up

stood up in the chariot opposite Aram. And/then he **died** in the evening, and

בַּמַּחֲנֶה	הָרִנָּה	וַיַּעֲבֹר	הָרָכֶב:	חֵיק	אֶל-	הַמַּכָּה	דַּם-
bammaḥᵃneh	hārinnāh	wayyaʿᵃbōr	hārākeb	ḥêq	ʾel-	hammakkāh	dam-
the ranks	the cry	and/then passed through	the chariot	bottom	to	the wound	blood

the blood of the wound **poured out** on the bottom of the chariot. And/then the cry **passed through** the ranks

אַרְצוֹ:	אֶל-	וְאִישׁ	עִירוֹ	אֶל-	אִישׁ	לֵאמֹר	הַשֶּׁמֶשׁ	כְּבֹא
ʾarṣô	ʾel-	wᵊʾîš	ʿîrô	ʾel-	ʾîš	lēʾmōr	haššemeš	kᵊbōʾ
his land	to	and a man	his city	to	a man	saying	the sun	when went in

when the sun went down, saying, "Every man to his city, and every man to his land!"

בְּשֹׁמְרוֹן:	הַמֶּלֶךְ	אֶת-	וַיִּקְבְּרוּ	שֹׁמְרוֹן	וַיָּבֹא	הַמֶּלֶךְ	וַיָּמָת
bᵊšōmᵊrôn	hammelek	ʾet-	wayyiqbᵊrû	šōmᵊrôn	wayyābōʾ	hammelek	wayyāmot
in Samaria	the king	(DO marker)	and/then they buried	Samaria	and/then he entered	the king	and/then he died

And/then the king **died**, and/then he **entered** Samaria. And/then they **buried** the king in Samaria.

PSALM 78:55–58 [: marks a minor caesura in a poetic line]

נַחֲלָה	בְּחֶבֶל	וַיַּפִּילֵם	גּוֹיִם	מִפְּנֵיהֶם	וַיְגָרֶשׁ
naḥᵃlāh	bᵊḥebel	wayyappîlēm	gôyīm	mippᵊnêhem	waygāreš
an inheritance	by a line	and/then made them fall	nations	from before the	and/then he drove out

And/then he **drove out** nations from before them, : And/then he **allotted** them an inheritance by a line, :

וַיְנַסּוּ	יִשְׂרָאֵל:	שִׁבְטֵי	בְּאָהֳלֵיהֶם	וַיַּשְׁכֵּן
waynassû	yiśrāʾēl	šibṭê	bᵊʾohᵒlêhem	wayyaškēn
And/then they tested	Israel	the tribes of	in their tents	and/then he made dwell

And/then he **made** the tribes of Israel **dwell** in their tents. And/then they **tested**

שָׁמָרוּ:	לֹא	וְעֵדוֹתָיו	עֶלְיוֹן	אֱלֹהִים	אֶת-	וַיַּמְרוּ
šāmārû	lōʾ	wᵊʿēdôtāyw	ʿelyôn	ʾᵉlōhîm	ʾet-	wayyamrû
they kept	not	and his testimonies	Most High	God	(DO marker)	and/then they rebelled

And/then they **rebelled** against God, Most High, : And his testimonies they did not keep.

JONAH 4:1–9

וַיִּתְפַּלֵּל	לוֹ:	וַיִּחַר	גְדוֹלָה	רָעָה	יוֹנָה	אֶל-	וַיֵּרַע
wayyitpallēl	lô	wayyiḥar	gᵉdōlāh	rā'āh	yônāh	'el-	wayyēra'
and/then he prayed	to him	and/then it burned	great	evil	Jonah	to	and/then it was bad

And/then it was **bad** to Jonah as a great evil, and/then he was **angry**, and/then he **prayed**

הֱיוֹתִי	עַד-	דְבָרִי	זֶה	הֲלוֹא-	יְהוָה	אָנָּה	וַיֹּאמַר	יְהוָה	אֶל-
hᵉyôtî	'ad-	dᵉbārî	zeh	hᵃlô'-	yᵉhwāh	'ānnāh	wayyō'mar	yᵉhwāh	'el-
I was	when	my word	this	not (+question marker)	YHWH	Ah!	and/then he said	YHWH	to

to YHWH, and/then he **said**, "Ah, YHWH! (Was) this not my word when I was

אֶל-	אַתָּה	כִי	יָדַעְתִּי	כִי	תַרְשִׁישָׁה	לִבְרֹחַ	קִדַּמְתִּי	כֵּן	עַל-	אַדְמָתִי	עַל-
'el-	'attāh	kî	yāda'tî	kî	taršîšāh	librōaḥ	qiddamtî	kēn	'al-	'admātî	'al-
God	you	that	I knew	because	to Taršiš	to flee	I was in front	thus	upon	my ground	on

on my own turf. Therefore I fled at first to Tarshish, because I knew that you are a

הָרָעָה:	עַל-	וְנִחָם	חֶסֶד	וְרַב-	אַפַּיִם	אֶרֶךְ	וְרַחוּם	חַנּוּן
hārā'āh	'al-	wᵉniḥām	ḥesed	wᵉrab-	'appayim	'erek	wᵉraḥûm	ḥannûn
bad	concerning	and relenting	grace	and great	nose/anger	long	and compassionate	merciful

favoring and merciful God, long of nose [i.e. forebearing], and great in grace, and relenting concerning calamity.

מֵחַיָּי:	מוֹתִי	טוֹב	כִי	מִמֶּנִּי	נַפְשִׁי	אֶת-	נָא	קַח-	יְהוָה	וְעַתָּה
mēḥayyāy	môtî	ṭôb	kî	mimmennî	napšî	'et-	nā'	qaḥ-	yᵉhwāh	wᵉ'attāh
than my life	my death	good	because	from me	my life	(DO marker)	please	take	YHWH	and now

And now, YHWH, please take my life away from me, because my death is better than my life.

יוֹנָה	וַיֵּצֵא	לָךְ:	חָרָה	הַהֵיטֵב	יְהוָה	וַיֹּאמֶר
yônāh	wayyēṣē'	lāk	hārāh	hahêṭēb	yᵉhwāh	wayyō'mer
Jonah	and/then he went out	to you	to burn	be good (+question marker)	YHWH	and/then he said

And/then YHWH **said**, "Is it good for you to be angry?" And/then Jonah **went out**

סֻכָּה	שָׁם	לוֹ	וַיַּעַשׂ	לָעִיר	מִקֶּדֶם	וַיֵּשֶׁב	הָעִיר	מִן-
sukkāh	šām	lô	wayya'aś	lā'îr	miqqedem	wayyēšeb	hā'îr	min-
hut	there	to him	and/then he made	to the city	at east	and/then he sat	the city	from

from the city and/then he **sat** at the east of the city. And/then he **made** a hut for himself there

בָּעִיר:	יִהְיֶה	מַה-	יִרְאֶה	אֲשֶׁר	עַד	בַּצֵּל	תַּחְתֶּיהָ	וַיֵּשֶׁב
bā'îr	yihyeʰ	mah-	yir'eʰ	'ašer	'ad	baṣṣēl	taḥteyhā	wayyēšeb
in the city	it would be	what	he would see	when	until	in the shadow	under	and/then he sat

and/then he **sat** under it in its shade until he saw what would happen in the city.

לִהְיוֹת	לְיוֹנָה	מֵעַל	וַיַּעַל	קִיקָיוֹן	אֱלֹהִים-	יְהוָה	וַיְמַן
lihyôt	lᵉyônāʰ	mē'al	wayya'al	qîqāyôn	'ᵉlōhîm	yᵊhwāh	wayman
to be	to Jonah	from upon	and/then it went up	castor-oil plant	God	YHWH	and/then he appointed

And/then YHWH God **appointed** a castor-oil plant, and/then it **went up** above Jonah to become

הַקִּיקָיוֹן	עַל-	יוֹנָה	וַיִּשְׂמַח	מֵרָעָתוֹ	לוֹ	לְהַצִּיל	רֹאשׁוֹ	עַל-	עַל	צֵל
haqqîqāyôn	'al-	yônāʰ	wayyiśmaḥ	mērā'ātô	lô	lᵊhaṣṣîl	rō'šô	'al-		ṣēl
the castor-oil plant	over	Jonah	and/then he rejoiced	from its harm	him	to save	his head	on		shade

a shade over his head to save him from harm. And/then Jonah **rejoiced** over the castor-oil plant

לַמָּחֳרָת	הַשַּׁחַר	בַּעֲלוֹת	תּוֹלַעַת	הָאֱלֹהִים	וַיְמַן	גְּדוֹלָה:	שִׂמְחָה
lammoḥᵒrāt	haššaḥar	ba'ᵃlôt	tôla'at	hā'ᵉlōhîm	wayman	gᵊḏōlāʰ	śimḥāʰ
on the next day	the dawn	when go	worm	God	and/then he appointed	great	joy

with great joy. And/then God **appointed** a worm when the dawn came on the next day

הַשָּׁמֶשׁ	כִּזְרֹחַ	וַיְהִי	וַיִּיבָשׁ:	הַקִּיקָיוֹן	אֶת-	וַתַּךְ
haššemeš	kizrōaḥ	wayhî	wayyîḇāš	haqqîqāyôn	'et-	wattak
the sun	when rose	and/then it was	and/then it dried up	the castor-oil plant	(DO marker)	and/then it struck

And/then it **struck** the castor-oil plant, and/then it **dried up**. And/then when the sun rose,

עַל-	הַשָּׁמֶשׁ	וַתַּךְ	חֲרִישִׁית	קָדִים	רוּחַ	אֱלֹהִים	וַיְמַן
'al-	haššemeš	wattak	ḥᵃrîšît	qāḏîm	rûaḥ	'ᵉlōhîm	wayman
on	the sun	and/then it struck	scorching	east	wind	God	and/then he appointed

and/then God **appointed** a scorching east wind, and/then the sun **beat down** on

וַיֹּאמֶר	לָמוּת	נַפְשׁוֹ	אֶת-	וַיִּשְׁאַל	וַיִּתְעַלָּף	יוֹנָה	רֹאשׁ
wayyō'mer	lāmût	napšô	'et-	wayyiš'al	wayyit'allāp	yônāʰ	rō'š
and/then he said	to die	his life	(DO marker)	and/then he asked	and/then he became faint	Jonah	head

Jonah's head. And/then he **became faint**, and/then he **asked** to die. And/then he said,

חָרָה־	הַהֵיטֵב	יוֹנָה	אֶל־	אֱלֹהִים	וַיֹּאמֶר	מֵחַיָּי:	מוֹתִי	טוֹב
ḥārā-	hahêṭēḇ	yônā	'el-	'ᵉlōhîm	wayyō'mer	mēhayyāy	môṯî	ṭôḇ
to burn	be good (+question marker)	Jonah	to	God	and/then he said	than my life	my death	good

"My death is better than my life." And/then God **said** to Jonah, "Is it good

מָוֶת:	עַד־	לִי	חָרָה־	הֵיטֵב	וַיֹּאמֶר	הַקִּיקָיוֹן	עַל־	לְךָ
māwet	'ad-	lî	ḥārā-	hêṭēḇ	wayyō'mer	haqqîqāyôn	'al-	lᵉkā
death	until	to me	burning	it does good	and/then he said	the castor-oil plant	concerning	for you

for you to be angry about the castor-oil plant?" And/then he **said**, "It's good for me
to be angry until death!"

Appendix B: Dynamic Aspect Tree Analysis of a Text

Short Story: "Winter Storm"

The menacing clouds barely visible in the vanishing twilight hung low in the northern sky. They were sporadically, but with increasing frequency, brilliantly lit by dramatic lightning. The man looked worriedly out the window at the swiftly approaching storm, unconsciously jiggled his keys, and listened intently to the rumblings of thunder. His wife joined him and sensed his anxiety. He sighed in resignation. "What are you upset about, Honey?'" she asked. Almost as an answer the storm front hit. At first it was just an unusually strong wind, which howled relentlessly. The rain arrived with a particularly powerful downdraft. It drummed on the roof. The storm rapidly grew in intensity. A mighty gust shook the house and rattled the windows. The temperature plummeted. The earlier din steadily diminished to an ominous quieter sound. Wind driven snow stuck to the window in front of the silent couple. The man spoke his thoughts out loud, "It's going to take a while to dig out from this one." He was right. During the night the snow piled up into deep sculpted drifts around the house.

Analysis:

Key: Blue—stative
Green (bud in tree)—atelic activities (directed or undirected)
Red (berry in tree)—telic achievement or accomplishment

The menacing clouds barely visible in the vanishing twilight hung low in the northern sky. They were sporadically, but with increasing frequency, brilliantly lit by dramatic lightning. The man looked worriedly out the window at the swiftly approaching storm, unconsciously jiggled his keys and listened intently to the rumblings of thunder. His wife joined him and sensed his anxiety. He sighed in resignation. "What are you upset about, Honey?" she asked. Almost as an answer the storm front hit. At first it was just an unusually strong wind, which howled relentlessly. The rain arrived with a particularly powerful downdraft. It drummed on the roof.

The storm rapidly grew in intensity. A mighty gust shook the house and rattled the windows. The temperature plummeted. The earlier din steadily diminished to an ominous quieter sound. Wind driven snow stuck to the window in front of the silent couple. The man spoke his thoughts out loud, "It's going to take a while to dig out from this one." He was right. During the night the snow piled up into deep sculpted drifts around the house.

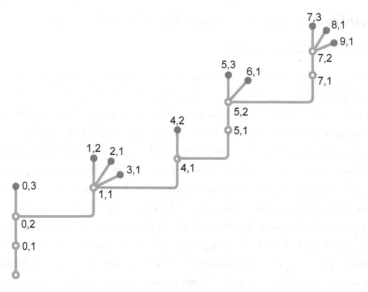

References

Asher, N., and L. Vieu. 2005. Subordinating and coordinating discourse relations. *Lingua* 115.4: 591–610.

Atkin, A. 2010. Peirce's theory of signs. *The Stanford Encyclopedia of Philosophy* (Winter 2010 Edition). Ed. N. Zalta. http://plato.stanford.edu/archives/win2010/entries/peirce-semiotics/>.

Blair-Goldensohn, S., K. McKeown, and O. Rambow. 2007. Building and refining rhetorical-semantic relation models. *Proceedings of the NAACL HLT*, 428–435.

Brown, G., and G. Yule. 1983. *Discourse analysis*. Cambridge, England: Cambridge University Press.

Callahan, J. F. 1958. Basil of caesarea a new source for St. Augustine's theory of time. *Harvard Studies in Classical Philology* 63: 437–454.

de Beaugrande, R., and W. Dressler. 1981. *An introduction to text linguistics.* London, England: Longman.

De Pierris, G., and M. Friedman. 2008. Kant and Hume on causality. *The Stanford Encyclopedia of Philosophy* (Fall edition). Ed. E. N. Zalta. http://plato.stanford.edu/archives/fall2008/entries/kant-hume-causality/.

Dowden, B. 2013. Time. *The Internet Encyclopedia of Philosophy.* http://www.iep.utm.edu/time/.

Dowty, D. 1986. The effects of aspectual class on the temporal structure of discourse: Semantics or pragmatics? *Linguistics and Philosophy* 9: 37–61.

Dünges, P. 1998. *Eventualities in time.* CLAUS Report Nr. 104. Universität des Saarlandes, Computerlinguistik, Saarbrücken, Germany.

Eddington, A. 1928. *The Nature of the Physical World.* Cambridge, England: Cambridge University Press.

Fitzgerald, C. n.d. *A brief history of the A-theory/B-theory debate about time.* http://www.cefitzgerald.com/papers/historyA-B.html.

Fleischman, S. 1990. *Tense and narrativity.* Austin, TX: UT Press.

Graesser, A. C., D. S. McNamara, and M. M. Louwerse. 2003. What do readers need to learn in order to process coherence relations in narrative and expository text? In *Rethinking reading comprehension.* Ed. A. Sweet, and C. Snow, 82–98. New York, NY: Guilford Press.

Graesser, A. C., D. S. McNamara, M. M. Louwerse, and Z. Cai. 2004. Coh-metrix: analysis of text on cohesion and language. *Behavior Research Methods, Instruments, & Computers* 36.2: 193–202.

Grosz, B., and C. Sidner. 1986. Attention, intention, and the structure of discourse. *Computational Linguistics* 12.3: 175–204.

Halliday, M., and R. Hasan. 1976. *Cohesion in English.* London, England: Longman.

Hinrichs, E. 1986. Temporal anaphora in discourses of English. *Linguistics and Philosophy* 9.1: 63–82.

Hitchcock, C. 2012. Probabilistic causation. *The Stanford Encyclopedia of Philosophy* (Winter edition). Ed. E. N. Zalta. http://plato.stanford.edu/archives/win2012/entries/causation-probabilistic/.

Hobbs, J. R. 1985. *On the coherence and structure of discourse.* Stanford, CA: CSLI Publications.

Hobbs, J. R. 1990. *Literature and cognition.* CSLI Lecture Notes 21. Stanford, CA: CSLI Publications.

Hobbs, J. 2004. Abduction in natural language understanding. In *The handbook of pragmatics.* Ed. L. Norn, and G. Ward, 724–741. Malden, MA: Oxford: Blackwell.

Hovy, E., and E. Maier. 1992. *Parsimonious or profligate: How many and which discourse structure relations?* Marina del Rey, CA: University of Southern California, Information Sciences Institute.

Huggett, N., and C. Hoefer. 2009. Absolute and relational theories of space and motion. *The Stanford Encyclopedia of Philosophy* (Fall edition). Ed. E. N. Zalta. http://plato.stanford.edu/archives/fall2009/entries/spacetime-theories/.

Hulswit, M. 2002. *From cause to causation. A Peircean perspective*. Dordrecht, Netherlands: Kluwer Publishers.

Janiak, A. 2012. Kant's views on space and time. *The Stanford Encyclopedia of Philosophy* (Winter edition). Ed. N. Zalta. http://plato.stanford.edu/archives/win2012/entries/kant-spacetime/.

Kamp, H. 1979. Events, instants and temporal reference. In *Semantics from different points of view*. Ed. R. Bäuerle, U. Egli, and A. von Stechow. Berlin, Germany: Springer-Verlag.

Kamp, H. 1981. A theory of truth and semantic representation. In *Formal methods in the study of language, part I*. Ed. J. Groenendijk, T. Janssen, and M. Stokhof, 277–322. Amsterdam, Netherlands: Mathematisch Centrum, University of Amsterdam.

Kamp, H., and C. Rohrer. 1983. Tense in texts. In *Meaning, use and interpretation of language*. Ed. R. Buerle, C. Schwarze, and A. von Stechow, 250–269. Berlin, Germany: Walter de Gruyter.

Kamp, H., and U. Reyle. 1993. *From discourse to logic*. Dordrecht, Boston, London: Kluwer Academic Publishers.

Kehler, A. 1999. *Identifying temporal relations from tense and coherence*. Unpublished paper presented at the Annual Meeting of the Linguistic Society of America, Los Angeles, January 8, 1999.

Kehler, A. 2004. Discourse coherence. In *The handbook of pragmatics*. Ed. L. Horn, and G. Ward, 241–265. Malden, MA: Oxford: Blackwell.

Kemerling, G. 2011. *John Stuart Mill*. http://www.philosophypages.com/ph/mill.htm.

Knott, A. 1996. *A data-driven method for motivating a set of coherence relations*. Ph.D. Diss., Department of Artificial Intelligence, University of Edinburgh.

Knott, A., and C. Mellish. 1996. A data-driven method for classifying connective phrases. (draft) [published as A featured-based account of the relations signalled by sentence and clause connectives. *Journal of Language and Speech* 39.2–3: 143–183.]

Lascarides, A., and N. Asher. 1993. Temporal interpretation, discourse relations and commonsense entailment. *Linguistics and Philosophy* 16: 437–493.

Lee, K. 2004. Processing and representing temporally sequential events. In *Proceedings of the 18th Pacific Asia Conference on Language, Information and Computation*. Ed. H. H. Gao, and M. Dong. Tokyo, Japan: Wasada University.

Le Poidevin, R. 2011. The experience and perception of time. *The Stanford Encyclopedia of Philosophy* (Fall edition). Ed. E. N. Zalta. http://plato.stanford.edu/archives/fall2011/entries/time-experience/.

Louwerse, M., P. McCarthy, D. McNamara, and A. Graesser. 2004. Variation in language and cohesion across written and spoken registers. In *Proceedings of the Twenty-Sixth Annual Conference of the Cognitive Science Society*. Ed. K. Forbus, D. Gentner, and T. Regier, 843–48. Mahwah, NJ: Erlbaum.

Louwerse, M., and A. Graesser. 2005. Coherence in discourse. In *Encyclopedia of Linguistics*. 2 vols. Ed. P. Strazny, 216–18. Chicago, IL : Fitzroy Dearborn.

Mackie, J. 1974. *The cement of the universe: A study of causation*. Oxford, England: Clarendon Press.

Mann, W. 2005. *RST Web Site*. <http://www.sfu.ca/rst>.

Mann, W., and S. Thompson. 1986. Relational propositions in discourse. *Discourse Processes* 9.1: 57–90.

Mann, W., and S. Thompson. 1988. Rhetorical structure theory: Toward a functional theory of text organization. *Text-Interdisciplinary Journal for the Study of Discourse* 8.3: 243–281.

Marcu, D., and A Echihabi. 2002. An unsupervised approach to recognizing discourse relations. *Proceedings of the 40th Annual Meeting of the Association for Computational Linguistics (ACL–2002)*, 368–375. Philadelphia, PA: Association for Computational Linguistics.

Markosian, N. 2010. Time. *The Stanford Encyclopedia of Philosophy* (Winter edition), ed. E. N. Zalta. http://plato.stanford.edu/archives/win2010/entries/time/.

McNamara, D., M. Louwerse, P. McCarthy, and A. Graesser. 2010. Coh-metrix: Capturing linguistic features of cohesion. *Discourse Processes* 47.4: 292–330.

McTaggart, J. 1908. The unreality of time. *Mind* 17.68: 457–474.

McTaggart, J. 1927. *The nature of existence*. Vol. 2. Cambridge, England: Cambridge University Press.

Menzies, P. 2009. Counterfactual theories of causation. *The Stanford Encyclopedia of Philosophy* (Fall edition). Ed. E. N. Zalta. http://plato.stanford.edu/archives/fall2009/entries/causation-counterfactual/.

Moser, M., and J. D Moore. 1996. Toward a synthesis of two accounts of discourse structure. *Computational Linguistics* 22.3: 409–420.

Oaklander, L. 2004. *The ontology of time*. Amherst, NY: Prometheus Books.

Outler, A. 1955. Trans. and ed. *Augustine: Confessions and Enchiridion*. Philadephia, PA: Westminster Press.

Pearl, J. 2000. *Causality*. Cambridge, England: Cambridge University Press.

Pitler, E., M. Raghupathy, H. Mehta, A. Nenkova, A. Lee, and A. Joshi. 2008. *Easily identifiable discourse relations*. Technical Report No. MS-CIS-08-24. University of Pennsylvania.

Pöppel, E. 1978. Time perception. In *Handbook of sensory physiology*, Vol. VIII: Perception. Ed. R. Held, H. Leibowitz, and H.-L. Teuber, 713–729. Berlin, Germany: Springer-Verlag.

Prior, A. 1967. *Past, present and future*. Oxford, England: Clarendon Press.

Ricoeur, P. 1980. Narrative time. *Critical Inquiry* 7.1: 169–190.

Rynasiewicz, R. 2012. Newton's views on space, time, and motion. *The Stanford Encyclopedia of Philosophy* (Winter edition). Ed. E. N. Zalta. http://plato.stanford.edu/archives/win2012/entries/newton-stm/.

Seligman, J., and A. ter Meulen. 1995. Dynamic aspect trees. In *Applied logic: How, what and why?* Ed. L. Pólos, and M. Masuch. Synthese Library, Vol. 247: 287–320. Netherlands: Kluwer Academic Publishers.

Soria, C. 2005. Constraints on the use of connectives in discourse. *Manuscrito No Publicado. Istituto De Linguistica Computazionale (CNR), Pisa, Italia.* pdf.

Sporleder, C. 2007. Manually vs. automatically labelled data in discourse relation classification: Effects of example and feature selection. *LDV Forum* 22.1: 1–20.

Sporleder, C., and A. Lascarides. 2005. Exploiting linguistic cues to classify rhetorical relations. In *Recent advances in natural language processing IV: Selected papers from RANLP 2005* (Current Issues in Linguistic Theory, 157–166). Amsterdam, Netherlands: John Benjamins.

Sporleder C, and A. Lascarides. 2007. Using automatically labelled examples to classify rhetorical relations: An assessment. *Natural Language Engineering* 14.3: 369–416.

Stenning, K., A. Lascarides, and J. Calder. 2006. *Introduction to cognition and communication.* Cambridge, England: MIT Press.

Subba, R., and B. di Eugenio. 2009. An effective discourse parser that uses rich linguistic information. *NAACL '09 Proceedings of Human Language Technologies: The 2009 Annual Conference of the North American Chapter of the Association for Computational Linguistics,* 566–574. Stroudsburg, PA: Association for Computational Linguistics.

Taboada, M. 2006. Discourse markers as signals (or not) of rhetorical relations. *Journal of Pragmatics* 38.4: 567–592.

Taboada, M., and W. Mann. 2006. Rhetorical structure theory: Looking back and moving ahead. *Discourse Studies* 8.3: 423–459.

ter Meulen, A. G. B. 1995. *Representing time in natural language: The dynamic interpretation of tense and aspect.* Cambridge, MA: MIT Press.

Toolan, M. 2011. Coherence. In *The living handbook of narratology,* ed. P. Hühn, J. C. Meister, J. Pier and W. Schmid. http://www.lhn.uni-hamburg.de/article/coherence.

van Benthem, J. 1984. Tense logic and time. *Notre Dame Journal of Formal Logic* 25.1: 1–16.

van Benthem, J. 1991. *The logic of time: A model-theoretic investigation into the varieties of temporal antology and temporal discourse.* 2nd ed. Synthese Library. Dordrecht, Boston, London: Kluwer Academic Publishers.

Williamson, J. 2010. Probabilistic theories of causality. In *The Oxford handbook of causation.* Ed. H. Bybee, C. Hitchcock, and P. Menzies, 185–212. Oxford, England: Oxford University Press.

Williamson, J. 2011a. Mechanistic theories of causality Part I. *Philosophy Compass* 6.6: 421–432.

Williamson, J. 2011b. Mechanistic theories of causality Part II. *Philosophy Compass* 6.6: 433–444.

Woodward, J. 2012. Causation and manipulability. *The Stanford Encyclopedia of Philosophy* (Winter edition). Ed. E. N. Zalta. http://plato.stanford.edu/archives/win2012/entries/causation-mani/.

Zimmerman, D. 2005. The A-theory of time, the B-theory of time, and 'taking tense seriously.' *Dialectica* 59.4: 401–457.

Zwaan, R., C. Madden, and R. Stanfield. 2001. Time in narrative comprehension: A cognitive perspective. In *Psychology and Sociology of Literature, In Honor of Elrud Ibsch. Utrecht Publicatins in General and Comparative Literature 35*, ed. D. H. Schram, and G. J. Steen, 71–86. Amsterdam, Netherlands: John Benjamins.

CHAPTER 13

Reading the Literary Currents:
The Complexity of Hebrew Narrative and
Modes of Discourse—
Temporal Progression at the *Mega-level*

Thomas Laney Stroup

Analogy and Orientation. Around 1769, Benjamin Franklin, having served as a deputy postmaster in New England, was consulted on a significant maritime puzzle: the board of customs at Boston had complained to the lords of the treasury in London that the British packet ships which carried mail from Britain to the colonies were taking about two weeks longer than the Rhode Island merchant ships to cross the Atlantic Ocean. The British packet ships were better manned and traveled nearly the same route, save that the merchant ships landed at Rhode Island instead of New York. Upon looking into the matter, he learned the reason for this delay from a New England whaler: there was a narrow current, now known as the Gulf Stream, that traveled eastward across the Atlantic Ocean that the Rhode Island captains knew to cross over and avoid; the British packet ships, however, unaware of this current, were sailing directly against it, losing as much as seventy miles (about 113 km) a day at some points, and ultimately requiring an extra two weeks in their voyages to America. Having learned the reason for this delay, Benjamin Franklin promptly wrote a letter to the British, advising them of this current and spelling out in detail how they might avoid it in their crossings.

The present story illustrates the value of understanding the currents. Of course the British packet ships were able to reach the colonies eventually, but had they understood the currents, they could have arrived with less time and greater ease. In the same way, an understanding of biblical narrative advances the argument of the previous three chapters by explaining many of the underlying reasons for potential breaks in temporal sequence. As the present chapter will demonstrate, such breaks are ultimately due not to the constraints of the grammar within a language, but to the nature of narrative in general, as well as the underlying strategies and techniques of the narrator. Thus, there are multiple reasons that a narrative will exhibit breaks in temporal sequence, and examples of such breaks abound (even in English).

Abstract. The reigning assumption appears to be that a narrative consists of an ordered sequence of events. As the previous three chapters have suggested, however, the sequence of events in a narrative may not necessarily match the actual sequence of events in real time. The present chapter seeks to bolster their argument by briefly exploring several of the factors that can cause the order of events in a narrative to differ from that of real time. These include levels of complexity, modes of discourse, and the purposes of the narrator.

Outline

1. Introduction
2. Factors that Can Complicate the Time Sequence of a Narrative
3. Application to Dischronologization
4. Conclusion

1. Introduction

The previous three chapters have dealt with the question of how to identify temporal sequence within a text. Their answers, however, lead to a second question: Why would an author record events out of sequence in the first place? The present chapter seeks to bolster the argument of these chapters by explaining why a narrator might record events out of sequence in a narrative, and by demonstrating that, contrary to the general expectation, dischronologization is actually quite common.

In order to make this case, the present chapter will proceed in two simple steps. First, it will discuss the *factors that can complicate the time sequence of a narrative*, whether Hebrew or English. These include the level of complexity, the mode of discourse, and the purposes of the narrator. And second, in order to validate these proposals, it will use this information to explain several of the examples of dischronologization listed in **Chapter 10**.

The present chapter is not by any means intended to provide a full treatment of the techniques of BH narrative. For treatments of this nature, see Alter (1981) Sternberg (1985), Bar-Efrat (1989), Ska (1990), Fokkelman (1995), and Walsh (2009). Nor is it intended to outline a methodology for discerning advances in temporal sequence as the previous two have done. Rather, it simply seeks to demonstrate several of the reasons why an author might record events out of sequence in order to undergird the arguments of the previous three chapters.

2. Factors that Can Complicate the Time Sequence of a Narrative

2.1. *The Level of Complexity*

2.1.1 Introduction

When speaking of narrative, it is useful to distinguish between two levels of complexity in narrative. One level is *simple narrative*, featuring a single protagonist, a single plot, and a single set of events. The other is *complex narrative*, featuring multiple protagonists, multiple plots and subplots, and multiple sets of events. These two levels of complexity will be explored below.

Because a simple narrative has a single set of events to follow, it is generally able to follow this set of events in their actual order of occurrence. As Genette notes, "It is well known that the folk-tale generally keeps a one-to-one correspondence between the "real" order of events that are being told and the order of the narrative..." (Genette 1971, 94). This is especially true when a story is narrated from a first person perspective, as in *Robinson Crusoe*. If one were to place the real order of events and the narrative order of events on a timeline, the two orders would generally match in sequence:

N = Narrative time
T = Real time

N1	N2	N3	N4
T1	T2	T3	T4

Likewise, in simple narratives like the sacrifice of Isaac (Gn 22:1–24), the book of Ruth, or the book of Jonah, the events of the narrative proceed in a more or less one-to-one correspondence with the actual order of their occurrence since the narrator is able to focus on a single set of events for these narratives.

Because a complex narrative has more than one set of events to follow, however, it is obligated to switch back and forth between these different sets of events, and is therefore unable to maintain a one-to-one correspondence between the real order of events and the narrative order of events.

2.1.2 Extra-biblical Example: *The Lord of the Rings*

In J. R. R. Tolkien's *The Lord of the Rings*, for example, the nine companions of the fellowship split apart at the end of the first volume and the beginning of the second, with Frodo and Sam headed to Mordor (Tolkien 1965, 1:396–98), Pippin and Merry being carried off by the Uruk-Hai (Tolkien 1965, 2:404), and Aragorn, Gimli, and Legolas following in pursuit of Pippin and Merry (Tolkien 1965, 2:404). From this point on, *The Lord of the Rings* splits into two interwoven narratives, one following the journey of Frodo and Sam, and one following the rest of the fellowship. In order to follow these two narratives, the second and third volumes, *The Two Towers* and *The Return of the King*, are split into two books, one devoted to each group of companions. Only in chapter 4 of the second book of *The Return of the King*, where Sam awakens from his coma in Gandalf's presence, do the narratives reunite (Tolkien 1965, 3:930). As a result, although the two narratives proceed simultaneously in real time, and various interwoven threads strengthen this effect (e.g., Faramir's sighting of Frodo across the river in chapters 4–6 of the second book of *The Two Towers* and his report of Frodo to Gandalf in chapter 4 of the first book of *The Return of the King*), they have to be narrated separately, with the narrator switching back and forth between each group of companions until they are reunited in *The Return of the King*. Therefore, if one were to place the actual order of events on a timeline, each of the narratives would proceed simultaneously. However, because of the limitations of the narrator in only being able to follow one group at a time, the order of events in the *The Lord of the Rings* does not match the order of events in real time. This may be represented as follows:

N = Narrative time
T = Real time
a = Aragorn, Legolas, Gimili, Pippin, and Merry
b = Frodo and Sam
N1 = The first book of *The Two Towers*
N2 = The second book of *The Two Towers*
N3 = The first book of *The Return of the King*
N4 = The second book of *The Return of the King*

N1   N2   N3   N4

T1a   T1b   T2a   T2b

In addition to these splits, there are several more splits that are not marked by book division. In the first book of *The Two Towers*, Pippin and Merry escape from the Uruk-Hai, and then journey with the Ents to destroy Isengard (chapters 3 and 4). Aragorn, Legolas, and Gimli, however meet up with Gandalf, who tells them that Pippin and Merry are safe, journey to see King Theoden of Rohan, and help him defend Helms Deep (chapters 5–7). After the battle of Helms Deep, Gandalf, Aragorn, Legolas, and Gimli journey to Isengard, where they find Pippin and Merry guarding the premises (chapter 8). In the first book of *The Return of the King*, Gandalf and Pippin journey ahead to Minas Tirith to meet with the Steward of Gondor, and prepare for the siege (chapter 1 and 4). Merry travels with Theoden and the Rohirrim, arriving at Minas Tirith just in time to break the siege (chapters 3 and 5). And Aragorn, Legolas, and Gimli take the path through Dimholt to summon the oathbreakers (chapter 2). None of the switches between these groups are marked by any more than a chapter division, leaving it to the reader to identify its place in real time.

And in addition to these larger breaks in time sequence, there are smaller ones, as well. At the Inn of the Prancing Pony, for example, in *The Fellowship of the Ring*, Tolkien narrates Frodo's disappearance with the ring as follows (Tolkien 1965, 1:157):

> The local hobbits stared in amazement, and then sprang to their feet and shouted for Barliman. All the company drew away from Pippin and Sam, who found themselves alone in a corner, and eyed darkly and doubtfully from a distance. It was plain that many people regarded them now as the companions of a travelling magician of unknown powers and purpose. But there was one swarthy Bree-lander, who stood looking at them with a knowing and half-mocking expression that made them feel very uncomfortable. Presently he slipped out of the door, followed by the squint-eyed southerner.

In this section, several groups of people react at once to Frodo's disappearance, and their reactions may be represented on the narrative timeline as follows:

T1a = The local hobbits stare in amazement
T2a = The local hobbits spring to their feet
T3a = The local hobbits call for Barliman
T1b = The rest of the company in the inn draws away from Pippin and Sam
T2b = The rest of the company regards them as the companions of a traveling magician
T1c = The swarthy Bree-lander makes the hobbits feel uncomfortable
T2c = The swarthy Bree-lander slips out the door

N1	N2	N3	N4	N5	N6	N7
T1a	T2a	T3a	T1b	T2b	T1c	T2c

If viewed in real time, one would likely have seen all three groups of events (a, b, and c), occurring at once, or at least overlapping in sequence. In reality, however, the reader is not even told the precise relation of these groups of events with each other, but left to discern it for himself. In addition, within these sets of events, it is evident that T1b must be simultaneous with T2b, as T2b is stated as the reason for T1b. And at any rate, one would be foolish to think that T3a had to be completed before T1b or even T1c likely commenced.

2.1.3 Biblical Example: Absalom's Conspiracy

Similarly, in the story of David's flight from Absalom (2 Sm 15:7–17:29), there are several different groups of characters, and therefore several different sets of events for the narrator to follow. These groups and their respective sets of events are as follows:

Absalom and his company

- 15:7–12—Absalom conspires against David
- 16:15–17:14—Absalom enters into Jerusalem, defiles David's harem, and takes counsel with Ahithophel
- 17:24b–26—Absalom crosses the Jordan River, and encamps in Gilead

David and his company

- 15:13–23—David crosses the Kidron and dismisses the Ittites
- 15:30, 31—David scales the Mount of Olives, and hears the news of Ahithophel's treachery
- 16:1–14—David meets with Mephibosheth and Shimei
- 17:24a—David reaches Mahanaim

Abiathar and Zadok

- 15:24–29—Abiathar and Zadok offer to bring the Ark

Hushai the Archite

- 15:32–37—Hushai offers to accompany David
- 17:15–22—Hushai sends warning to David

Ahithophel

- 17:23—Ahithophel has himself strangled

In this short narrative, then, there are as many as five different groups of people, and five different sets of events between which the narrator alternates back and forth over the course of the three chapters, the main two being Absalom and David. This produces a number of dischronologizations at the seams of these alternations:

- At the end of 15:23, the narrative records that all Jerusalem was watching and weeping (Qal PA) as David and his men were in the process of crossing (Qal PA) over to the east side of the Kidron Valley. However, verse 24 begins with Abiathar and Zadok waiting outside of Jerusalem to converse with David on the west side of the Kidron Valley.
- 2 Samuel 15:37 records that Hushai returned to Jerusalem just as Absalom was entering the city. Therefore, David could not have crested the Mount of Olives any sooner than an hour or two before Absalom entered into Jerusalem. 2 Samuel 16:15 and 16 resume this narrative with Absalom entering into Jerusalem and Hushai coming out to greet him. In between, however, 16:14 records that David reached the Jordan River and refreshed himself there, a 25 mile (40.23 km) journey from Jerusalem. Therefore, the events of 16:14 had to have occurred much later than the events of 16:15.
- In addition, given the length of the journey from Jerusalem to the Jordan River, the taking of counsel in 16:20–17:14, and most of the sending of warning to David in 17:15–22, undoubtedly took place before David reached the Jordan River in 16:14.
- Another potential dischronologization in the narrative is in 2 Samuel 16:23. This verse records that Absalom entered into David's harem in the sight of all of the people of Jerusalem in accordance with Ahithophel's counsel given in 16:21–22. Ahithophel continues his counsel, however, in 17:1–4, advising that David be pursued to the Jordan that night to catch him while he was weary and before he could cross to the other side. It is possible that Absalom might have entered into his father's harem as his first act in Jerusalem, dismissing his court and summoning them

back afterwards to see what Ahithophel would advise next. However, given the urgency of the situation, it is more likely that 16:21–22 and 17:1–4 constitute a single advisory session, with 16:23 occurring shortly thereafter.

• And lastly, 2 Samuel 17:23 records that Ahithophel had himself strangled once he saw Absalom had rejected his advice. However it records that he first went to his city (Gilo, cf. 15:12) and issued a command to his house; and that afterwards he died and was buried. The narrative does not state how long it took Ahithophel to get to Gilo and command his house, nor how soon after his death they buried him. The point however, is that the narrator does not indicate the chronological sequence of these events to the reader, and they could very well have occurred days later (though probably not past David's return to Jerusalem in 2 Samuel 20:3).

2.1.4 Summary

The principle at play in these examples is the fact that narrative is a linear art (Walsh 2009, 15). Therefore, even though two or more sets of events might occur simultaneously, they have to be narrated separately. As Walsh remarks (Walsh 2009, 62),

> In visual art, a painter can paint a diptych, or put two different scenes on the same canvas (in two different rooms of a house, for example). Or a cinematographer can split his screen to show different events at the same time. Not so the storyteller, who must deliver his story one word at a time.

Therefore, whether simple or complex, any narrative will exhibit breaks in time sequence, and this is simply due to the nature of narrative in general. A painting can be viewed in a moment and processed all at once. A narrative, however, must be told in sequence one word at a time, whether the events it describes occurred in sequence or not. Sometimes the narrator will use keywords to clue his readers into these breaks in time sequence like "meanwhile," "however," or "at that time" (Walsh 2009, 62), but more often than not it is simply left up to the readers to understand and piece together the actual sequence of events on their own.

Sam's comment at the reunion of the two groups in the third volume is instructive in this matter (Tolkien 1965, 3:936). Sam, hearing about all of adventures of the others, and that they had seen "the great Oliphaunt" in his absence, humorously remarks, "Well, one can't be everywhere at once, I suppose." In the same way, the narrator and the reader's attention can only be directed to one thing at a time, and thus the narrator has to trust the readers to piece together the actual sequence of events in their own minds based on the logical relationship that these events exhibit.

2.2 *The Mode of Discourse*[1]

2.2.1 Introduction

In addition to the different levels of complexity explored above, there are also different modes of discourse. In her seminal work, *Modes of Discourse: The Local Structure of Texts* (Smith 2003), Smith sets forth the essential characteristics of five different types of discourse: **Narrative, Report, Description, Information, and Argument**, each with its own distinct properties of situations, temporality, and progression (Smith 2003, 19–21).

Narrative as defined by Smith consists primarily of states and events related to each other dynamically through cause and effect, where the reference time progresses with the narrative. A *Report* likewise consists of states and events (with the addition of general statives), which are related to each other dynamically in time; however, the reference time is related not to the events of the narrative, but to the speech time, stating, for example, what *has* happened, or what is *now* the case. Smith comments further, "The report mode can be recognized quite reliably by the presence of deictic adverbials" (Smith 2003, 108).

In contrast to Narrative and Report, *Description* is static in time, with no indication of temporal progression. Instead, it progresses by "spatial advancement through the scene or object" (Smith 2003, 20). As a result, it consists primarily of states, events, and ongoing events. The *Information* mode is atemporal altogether, consisting primarily of general statives. It progresses with metaphorical motion through the information it conveys. And lastly, the *Argument* mode is atemporal, as well, consisting primarily of facts and propositions, and progressing with metaphorical motion through the argument that it makes.

Smith's proposals suggest several important principles for understanding the time progression of any given text. First, not all text is necessarily temporal (e.g., Information and Argument). Second, even the text that is temporal

---

1. The author received John Cook's work late in the editing process, and was unable to incorporate all of its insights into the present study, but was pleased to discover that Cook has taken much the same approach in his incorporation of Carlota Smith's modes of discourse into his recent volume, *Time and the Biblical Hebrew Verb* (Cook 2012, 312–338).

may not necessarily indicate temporal progression (e.g., Description). And last, even the text that indicates temporal progression may be related to the speaker's time rather than the narrative time, and thus may not necessarily follow a temporal sequence (e.g., Report). In reading a text, therefore, one must question carefully what mode of discourse it belongs to before assuming temporal sequentiality.

In addition, as Smith argues, a text rarely consists of a single mode of discourse throughout; to the contrary, a narrative text in particular will often include smaller passages of other modes of discourse within the larger whole of the narrative (Smith 2003, 8).

> Actual texts are usually not monolithic. In narratives, for instance, the significant unit is the episode: a group of Events and States in sequence that are bound together by a unifying theme. Narrative episodes, however, rarely consist only of sequence. There are also descriptive passages, and perhaps argument as well.

Therefore, Smith's proposals suggest a corollary to the above for smaller portions of text within a larger narrative text: where one can detect characteristics of other modes of discourse in subsections of a larger narrative, those subsections may not necessarily indicate temporal progression either.

2.2.2 Extra-biblical Examples: *The Hobbit*

In the first chapter of *The Hobbit* (Tolkien 1937), for example, one finds a brief section of report embedded within the larger narrative regarding Bilbo's ancestry, and the invention of golf:

> If you have ever seen a dragon in a pinch, you will realize that this was only poetical exaggeration applied to any hobbit, even to Old Took's great-grand-uncle Bullroarer, who was so huge (for a hobbit) that he could ride a horse. He charged the ranks of the goblins of Mount Gram in the Battle of the Green Fields, and knocked their king Golfimbul's head clean off with a wooden club. It sailed a hundred yards through the air and went down a rabbit-hole, and in this way the battle was won and the game of Golf invented at the same moment.

As characterized by Smith, this embedded Report consists of dynamic states and events related causally to each other in time. In contrast to narrative, however, several factors indicate that it is oriented to the speech time. These include the beginning of the narrator's aside ("If you have ever seen"), the frequent changes in tense, the deictic adverbials ("in the Battle of Green

Fields," "in this way," "at the same moment"), and the mention of the modern sport of golf. As a result, although this section progresses temporally, it is oriented to the speech time rather than the narrative time, and thus exhibits gaps and jumps in time sequence. For example, the narrative jumps from the beheading of Golfimbul to the winning of the battle, and all the way to the invention of golf.

Earlier in the same chapter, one finds an elaborate description of Bilbo's hobbit hole:

> It had a perfectly round door like a porthole, painted green, with a shiny yellow brass knob in the exact middle. The door opened on to a tube-shaped hall like a tunnel: a very comfortable tunnel without smoke, with paneled walls, and floors tiled and carpeted, provided with polished chairs, and lots and lots of pegs for hats and coats—the hobbit was fond of visitors. The tunnel wound on and on, going fairly but not quite straight into the side of the hill—The Hill, as all the people for many miles round called it—and many little round doors opened out of it, first on one side and then on another. . . .

As characterized by Smith, this description consists primarily of states, events, and ongoing events, and progresses from the front door into the comfortable hallway. As a result, it is static in time, and progresses spacially rather than temporally.

Also in this chapter is a section consisting of information about hobbits in general, including their bodily features and their habits:

> The mother of our particular hobbit—what is a hobbit? I suppose hobbits need some description nowadays, since they have become rare and shy of the Big People, as they call us. They are (or were) a little people, about half our height, and smaller than the bearded Dwarves. Hobbits have no beards. There is little or no magic about them, except the ordinary everyday sort which helps them to disappear quietly and quickly when large stupid folk like you and me come blundering along, making a noise like elephants which they can hear a mile off. They are inclined to be fat in the stomach; they dress in bright colours (chiefly green and yellow); wear no shoes, because their feet grow natural leathery soles and thick warm brown hair like the stuff on their heads (which is curly); have long clever brown fingers, good-natured faces, and laugh deep fruity laughs (especially after dinner, which they have twice a day when they can get it).

As characterized by Smith, this section consists primarily of general statives. There is some spatial progression in the description of Bilbo's physical features (overlapping with the mode of Description above), but this progression does not extend throughout, especially with regards to the information regarding their ability to disappear quickly, and their eating habits mentioned at the end. As a result, it is atemporal altogether, and proceeds metaphorically through the information it conveys.

And lastly, one can detect numerous examples of Argument in the various asides to the reader. In chapter 9, for example, where Bilbo packs the dwarves into wine barrels to help them escape from the wood elves, Tolkien writes,

> It was just at this moment that Bilbo suddenly discovered the weak point in his plan. Most likely you saw it some time ago and have been laughing at him; but I don't suppose you would have done half as well yourselves in his place. *Of course, he was not in a barrel himself, nor was there anyone to pack him in, even if there had been a chance!*

As characterized by Smith, the italicized portion consists primarily of facts ("he was not in a barrel himself") and propositions ("nor was there anyone to pack him in, even if there had been a chance!"). As a result, it is atemporal, and proceeds metaphorically through its argument.

2.2.3 Biblical Examples: Genesis 6:4 and 1 Kings 15:9–14 (Report); 1 Samuel 14:4–5 (Description); Genesis 4:20–22; Job 1:1–5 (Information); 2 Kings 17:7–23 (Argument)

A good example of Report may be found in Genesis 6:4, just prior to the Flood Narrative. As characterized by Smith, even though the statement includes reference to specific events in time, it is related not to the narrative's timeline, but to the speech time, as indicated by the deictic adverbial "In those days":

GENESIS 6:4

הַנְּפִלִים הָיוּ בָאָרֶץ בַּיָּמִים הָהֵם וְגַם אַחֲרֵי־כֵן אֲשֶׁר יָבֹאוּ בְּנֵי הָאֱלֹהִים
אֶל־בְּנוֹת הָאָדָם וְיָלְדוּ לָהֶם הֵמָּה הַגִּבֹּרִים אֲשֶׁר מֵעוֹלָם אַנְשֵׁי הַשֵּׁם: פ

The Nephilim were on the Earth in those days, and also afterwards, when the sons of God would go into the daughters of men, and they would bear to them the mighty warriors who were men of renown from of old.

A lengthier example (including several *wayyiqtols*) is the summary evaluation of King Asa's reign in 1 Kings 15:9–14 (*wayyiqtols* in bold):

1 KINGS 15:9–14

וּבִשְׁנַת עֶשְׂרִים לְיָרָבְעָם מֶלֶךְ יִשְׂרָאֵל מָלַךְ אָסָא מֶלֶךְ יְהוּדָה:
¹⁰ וְאַרְבָּעִים וְאַחַת שָׁנָה מָלַךְ בִּירוּשָׁלִָם וְשֵׁם אִמּוֹ מַעֲכָה בַּת־אֲבִישָׁלוֹם:
¹¹ וַיַּעַשׂ אָסָא הַיָּשָׁר בְּעֵינֵי יְהוָה כְּדָוִד אָבִיו: ¹² וַיַּעֲבֵר הַקְּדֵשִׁים מִן־
הָאָרֶץ וַיָּסַר אֶת־כָּל־הַגִּלֻּלִים אֲשֶׁר עָשׂוּ אֲבֹתָיו: ¹³ וְגַם| אֶת־מַעֲכָה
אִמּוֹ וַיְסִרֶהָ מִגְּבִירָה אֲשֶׁר־עָשְׂתָה מִפְלֶצֶת לָאֲשֵׁרָה וַיִּכְרֹת אָסָא אֶת־
מִפְלַצְתָּהּ וַיִּשְׂרֹף בְּנַחַל קִדְרוֹן: ¹⁴ וְהַבָּמוֹת לֹא־סָרוּ רַק לְבַב־אָסָא הָיָה
שָׁלֵם עִם־יְהוָה כָּל־יָמָיו:

[9] In the twentieth year of Jeroboam the king of Israel, Asa became king of Judah. [10] He reigned forty-one years in Jerusalem, and the name of his mother was Maacah, the daughter of Abishalom. [11] Asa **did** what was upright in the eyes of the LORD as David his father had done. [12] He **expelled** the cult prostitutes from the land, and **removed** all of the idols that his fathers had made. [13] Even Maacah his mother he **removed** from being queen because she had made an image for the Asherah. Asa **cut down** her image and **burned** it in the Kidron valley. [14] The high places he did not remove; however, the heart of Asa was wholly with the LORD all of his days.

Although there is no explicit indication that the narrator is speaking with reference to the speech time rather than the narrative time (as in Gn 6:4), there are several other clues that indicate that this is also most likely an occurrence of Report. First, there is a summary description bracketing both the beginning and the end of this section, evaluating Asa's obedience to the LORD. These are repetitious, and furthermore overlap with the events in between, negating the possibility of temporal sequence. And second, the particle גַם ("also") in verse 13 suggests that there is a different principle of progression in focus with regards to Asa's actions, namely the easiest to the most difficult, i.e., the removing of his own mother and the burning of her Asherah. These clues suggest that the summary evaluation of Asa's reign proceeds logically, rather than temporally, and that the events therein are more likely related to the speaker's time rather than the narrative time.

A good example of Description is the description in 1 Samuel 14 of the rocks that Jonathan and his armor bearer had to scale to reach the Philistine garrison:

1 SAMUEL 14:4–5 (ESV)

⁴ וּבֵין הַמַּעְבְּרוֹת אֲשֶׁר בִּקֵּשׁ יוֹנָתָן לַעֲבֹר עַל־מַצַּב פְּלִשְׁתִּים שֵׁן־הַסֶּלַע מֵהָעֵבֶר מִזֶּה וְשֵׁן־הַסֶּלַע מֵהָעֵבֶר מִזֶּה וְשֵׁם הָאֶחָד בּוֹצֵץ וְשֵׁם הָאֶחָד סֶנֶה: ⁵ הַשֵּׁן הָאֶחָד מָצוּק מִצָּפוֹן מוּל מִכְמָשׂ וְהָאֶחָד מִנֶּגֶב מוּל גָּבַע: ס

[4] Within the passes, by which Jonathan sought to go over to the Philistine garrison, there was a rocky crag on the one side and a rocky crag on the other side. The name of the one was Bozez, and the name of the other Seneh. [5] The one crag rose on the north in front of Michmash, and the other on the south in front of Geba.

As characterized by Smith, this description consists of states and proceeds spatially from one side of the ravine to the other.

Since descriptions are related primarily through verbless clauses in Hebrew (i.e. with a noun in the subject and an adjective in the predicate), it is rarer to find extended descriptions with the *wayyiqtol*. Shorter ones may be found, however, making use of stative verbs like גבה.

1 SAMUEL 10:23

וַיָּרֻצוּ וַיִּקָּחֻהוּ מִשָּׁם וַיִּתְיַצֵּב בְּתוֹךְ הָעָם וַיִּגְבַּהּ מִכָּל־הָעָם מִשִּׁכְמוֹ וָמָעְלָה:

They ran, and they took him out of there. Then he stood in the midst of the people; *he was taller than any of the people from his shoulders up.*

A good example of Information (also including several *wayyiqtols*) is the description of Job's prosperity at the beginning of the book of Job. The narrative records in Job 1:1–5 (*wayyiqtols* bolded for reference):

JOB 1:1–5 (ESV)

¹אִישׁ הָיָה בְאֶרֶץ־עוּץ אִיּוֹב שְׁמוֹ וְהָיָה הָאִישׁ הַהוּא תָּם וְיָשָׁר וִירֵא אֱלֹהִים וְסָר מֵרָע: ² **וַיִּוָּלְדוּ** לוֹ שִׁבְעָה בָנִים וְשָׁלוֹשׁ בָּנוֹת: ³ **וַיְהִי** מִקְנֵהוּ שִׁבְעַת אַלְפֵי־צֹאן וּשְׁלֹשֶׁת אַלְפֵי גְמַלִּים וַחֲמֵשׁ מֵאוֹת צֶמֶד־בָּקָר וַחֲמֵשׁ מֵאוֹת אֲתוֹנוֹת וַעֲבֻדָּה רַבָּה מְאֹד **וַיְהִי** הָאִישׁ הַהוּא גָּדוֹל מִכָּל־בְּנֵי־קֶדֶם: ⁴ וְהָלְכוּ בָנָיו וְעָשׂוּ מִשְׁתֶּה בֵּית אִישׁ יוֹמוֹ וְשָׁלְחוּ וְקָרְאוּ לִשְׁלֹשֶׁת אַחְיֹתֵיהֶם לֶאֱכֹל וְלִשְׁתּוֹת עִמָּהֶם: ⁵ **וַיְהִי** כִּי הִקִּיפוּ יְמֵי הַמִּשְׁתֶּה **וַיִּשְׁלַח** אִיּוֹב **וַיְקַדְּשֵׁם** וְהִשְׁכִּים בַּבֹּקֶר וְהֶעֱלָה עֹלוֹת מִסְפַּר כֻּלָּם כִּי אָמַר אִיּוֹב אוּלַי חָטְאוּ בָנַי וּבֵרֲכוּ אֱלֹהִים בִּלְבָבָם כָּכָה יַעֲשֶׂה אִיּוֹב כָּל־הַיָּמִים: פ

[1] There was a man in the land of Uz whose name was Job, and that man was blameless and upright, one who feared God and turned away from evil. [2] There were **born** to him seven sons and three daughters. [3] He **possessed** 7,000 sheep, 3,000 camels, 500 yoke of oxen, and 500 female donkeys, and very many servants, so that this man **was** the greatest of all the people of the east. [4] His sons used to go and hold a feast in the house of each one·on his day, and they would send and invite their three sisters to eat and drink with them. [5] And when the days of the feast had **run their course**, Job would **send** and **consecrate** them, and he would rise early in the morning and offer burnt offerings according to the number of them all. For Job said, "It may be that my children have sinned, and cursed God in their hearts." Thus Job did continually.

As characterized by Smith, this section consists primarily of states and generalizing statives, relating what kind of person Job was ("There were born," "he possessed," and "Job would send"). And it advances metaphorically, rather than temporally (like Report) or spatially (like Description), in its demonstration of Job's wealth and his righteousness.

And last, a good example of Argument is the refrain repeated in the book of Judges (Jgs 17:6; 21:25):

JUDGES 17:6

בַּיָּמִים הָהֵם אֵין מֶלֶךְ בְּיִשְׂרָאֵל אִישׁ הַיָּשָׁר בְּעֵינָיו יַעֲשֶׂה׃ פ

In those days there was no king in Israel; *each would do what was right in his own eyes.*

Several factors identify the latter statement as argument. First, the statement "each would do" constitutes a state rather than an event. Second, there is no relation to the timeline of the narrative, as it encompasses the whole period of "in those days." And third, in the context of the book of Judges, chapters 17–21 in particular catalogue the kinds of horrors that were occurring during this period of Israelite history. The refrain, "Each would do what was right in his own eyes," which encompasses these chapters argues the reason for these horrors: the Israelites had failed to follow the warnings of Moses in Deuteronomy to teach the law to their children (Dt 6:6–9) so that they could do what was right in the LORD's eyes (Dt 12:28) (see **Sub-subsection 2.3.3** for further details).

2.2.4 Summary

Smith's study demonstrates that contrary to the general assumption that a narrative always proceeds in temporal sequence, where subsections consisting of other modes of discourse can be detected within that larger narrative, one will often find states and events related to the speaker's standpoint instead of the narrative timeline (Report), states, events, and general statives progressing spatially rather than temporally (Description), or even facts and propositions that are atemporal altogether and progress metaphorically instead of temporally (Information and Argument).

2.3 *The Purposes of the Narrator*

2.3.1 Introduction
2.3.2 Extra-biblical Example: *Uncle Tom's Cabin*
2.3.3 Biblical Example: The Book of Judges
2.3.4 Summary

2.3.1 Introduction

In addition to the differing levels of complexity and the different modes of discourse within a narrative, a narrative can have two or more purposes, as well, and the combination of these purposes can determine which events are included, which events are omitted, and even the order in which the events are conveyed.

For example, when a child reports mistreatment at the hands of another child ("Billy pushed me!"), that child is constructing a narrative. The experienced parent, however, knows to inquire whether there are any other details that were not included in the narrative ("I told him he couldn't play with us"). In addition, even when a child rightfully includes all of the details from the start, the ordering of the events in the narrative will still likely reflect his desire to emphasize the other's fault ("Billy pushed me! I just told him he couldn't play with us."). The reason, of course, is that the child's narrative presents an argument ("I am innocent, he is guilty").

In like manner, a narrative will often have more than one purpose. For some, the only purpose may be to entertain. For most, however, there may be social reform (e.g., *Uncle Tom's Cabin*), behavioral instruction (e.g., *The Berenstein Bears* series), historical documentation (e.g., *J. R. R. Tolkien: A Biography*), or other purposes, and these will inevitably color the narrative, influencing both the details that are included, and the order in which they are told.

More specifically, the skilled narrator will frequently employ specific techniques in narrative in order to serve the various purposes identified above. These include tempo, gapping, suspense, comparison and contrast, characterization, and others that can affect the portrayal of temporal sequence in the narrative.

2.3.2 Extra-biblical Example: *Uncle Tom's Cabin*

Harriet Beecher Stowe begins *Uncle Tom's Cabin* (1852), for example, with the uncomfortable conversation of two men in a parlor. As the conversation progresses, the reader learns that the topic is the potential sale of a faithful slave by a reluctant plantation owner, Mr. Shelby, to an amoral slave trader, Mr. Haley. During this conversation, just as Mr. Haley gains the upper hand in demanding that the sale would require two slaves instead of one, a delightful little boy named Harry peeks into the room, and the reader discovers in the course of his visit that he belongs to Mrs. Shelby's beautiful handmaid, Eliza. The plantation owner expresses his reluctance to sell the boy, but invites the slave trader to return later that night.

In the second and third chapter, the reader learns in retrospect of the blissful marriage of the boy's mother to a handsome, hardworking, and well-educated slave on a neighboring plantation who, despite his faithfulness and his remarkable achievements, had been subjected to mindless drudgery and mistreatment by his envious owner. At last, he had even been told that he would be forced to marry another one of his owner's slaves, and at this final provocation, had determined to run away. Eliza bids him Godspeed, but still places confidence for herself and Harry in the goodness and reassurance of her mistress.

In the fourth chapter, two scenes proceed simultaneously. In *Uncle Tom's Cabin*, a scene of happiness, warmth, and song unfolds among the joyful slaves. At the head of this fellowship is Uncle Tom, the faithful, unsuspecting slave in question of being sold to Mr. Haley. In Mr. Shelby's parlor, however, a cold, heartless scene unfolds, as the remaining scruples of Mr. Shelby bend, being "obliged" to make the deal.

In the fifth chapter, the reader discovers for certain in the course of Mr. Shelby's conversation with his wife that he had sold not only his faithful slave, Uncle Tom, but also Eliza's son, Harry. In addition, the reader discovers through Mrs. Shelby's response that Mr. Shelby had thereby broken faith with Uncle Tom, whom they had promised his freedom on multiple occasions. And lastly, the reader discovers through Mr. Shelby's attempted defense, that the reason he had had to sell both slaves was that he had overstretched his investments, and was in danger of losing the plantation otherwise.

There are several narrative techniques to note in these chapters that serve to highlight and advance the argument of the narrative. First, the narrative begins *in media res* with a close angle lens on the uncomfortable conversation of Mr. Shelby and Mr. Haley. This serves to highlight the debate over the ethics of the decision to be made, and focus the reader on this seemingly innocent, yet dastardly deed that is about to unfold. Second, the narrator masterfully employs a gradual and suspenseful characterization of Mr. Shelby, allowing the reader to experience Eliza's terror, as well as the betrayal of Mrs. Shelby's confidence. Third, the narrator employs flashback to inform the reader of the blissful marriage of Eliza and her husband, and his subsequent mistreatment at his owner's hands, evoking the timely sympathy of the reader. Fourth, the narrator employs comparison and contrast to highlight the cold heartedness of Mr. Shelby's sale of the faithful, joyful, and unsuspecting Uncle Tom. Fifth, the narrator employs ellipsis (also known as gapping) by omitting the detail of whether the boy was included in the sale, leaving the reader to discover it with Mrs. Shelby's wife in the next chapter. And sixth, the narrator employs ellipsis in omitting the true reason for the sale of Uncle Tom and Eliza's son until the fifth chapter, leaving the reader to discover it too with Mrs. Shelby: Mr. Shelby's foolish investments. If there were any doubt before, this final detail serves to clinch Mr. Shelby's guilt and his hypocrisy: that he would sell Tom, and Eliza's son, to make up for his financial imprudence in order to preserve his own comfort.

In regards to temporal sequence, had the narrator simply wanted to retell these events in historical succession, the order of events would likely have proceeded as follows:

T1 = Background Info (Uncle Tom's faithfulness, Eliza and George's marriage, Harry's birth)
T2 = George's mistreatment
T3 = Mr. Shelby's bad investments
T4 = Discussion in the parlor
T5a = The slaves' dinner
T5b = The sale of Uncle Tom
T5c = The sale of Harry
T6 = Mr. Shelby's explanation to Mrs. Shelby

N1	N2	N3	N4	N5	N6
T1	T2	T3	T4	T5(a, b, and c)	T6

The actual order of events in the narrative, however, proceeds as follows:

N1	N2	N3	N4	N5	N6	N7	N8
T4	T1	T2	T5a	T5b	T6	T5c	T3

Using this order, the narrator highlights with particular skill the immanency and tangibility of the guilt of Mr. Shelby in selling not only the unsuspecting Uncle Tom (T5b), but also the innocent Harry (T5c) to his own wife's horror (T6) to recover from his foolish investments (T3).

Therefore, as the story of *Uncle Tom's Cabin* demonstrates, when a narrative serves more than one purpose, the narrator will often employ ellipsis, suspense, characterization, comparison and contrast, flashback, and other techniques, reordering the events in the narrative in order to advance these purposes. For some of these the order is indicated in the text (e.g. George's mistreatment, the contrast of the slave's dinner and the parlor sale), but for others the order is not (e.g. Mr. Shelby's investments), being left instead for the reader to discern and piece together in his own mind.

2.3.3 Biblical Example: The book of Judges

One can note similar rearrangements and gapping in chronology due to the author's argument in the book of Judges. As the opening chapters reveal, the book of Judges is not only a history of the period between the conquest of Canaan and the ministry of Samuel, but a highly focused theological treatise on Israel's failure to drive out the inhabitants of Canaan, and the subsequent dark ages that ensued, the central reason for which may be inferred from the words of Judges 2:10:

JUDGES 2:10

And all that generation also were gathered to their fathers. And there arose another generation after them who did not know the LORD or the work that he had done for Israel.

In other words, in contrast with the command to teach the law of the LORD to their children (Dt 6:7–9) and tell them of all of the works that he had done for them (Dt 6:20–25), the Israelites did not tell them of the works that the LORD had done, or teach his law to their children. As a result, the people of Israel had forgotten the LORD within two generations of entering into Canaan, and did what was right in their own eyes (Jgs 17:6, 21:25), rather than doing what was right in God's eyes (cf. Dt 12:28).

JUDGES 17–21

Central to this argument are the stories of Judges 17–21. As noted above, these chapters are bracketed by the refrain of Judges 17:6 and 21:25: "In those days there was no king in Israel; everyone did what was right in his own eyes." Therefore, the stories of chapters 17–21 support the argument of Judges 2:10 by highlighting the consequences of Israel's abandonment of the LORD.

The first one is the story of the wandering Levite (Jgs 17–18). The story begins with Micah's theft of money from his mother, and Micah's use of this money, with his mother's knowledge and blessing, to make family idols (Judges 17). The narrative progresses with the theft of these idols by the tribe of Dan on their way to their new, self-appointed inheritance, and the traitorous consent of this same wandering Levite to accompany them. The second story (Jgs 19–21) is the mistreatment of a Levite's concubine, including her careless neglect by the Levite, the savagery of the Benjamite city of Gibeah (rivaling that of Sodom and Gomorrah), the near obliteration of the entire tribe of Benjamin in the ensuing civil war, and the kidnapping of the maidens of Jabesh Gilead, organized by the elders of Israel, to preserve the Benjamite tribe.

There are two indications that the events of chapters 17–18 do not occur in chronological sequence with the rest of the book, or even necessarily with the following story of chapters 19–21. First, Judges 5:17 mentions Dan among the northern tribes as early as the defeat of Jabin in Judges 4:1–24. This places the narrative very early on in the book of Judges. Second, the end of this narrative reveals that the wandering Levite was none other than Jonathan, the son of Gershom, the son of Moses (Jgs 18:30). This places it within twenty years at most, of Joshua's death around 1366 BC (Merrill 2008, 166).[2] There is also indication that the events of chapters 19–21 do not occur in chronological sequence with the rest of the book, or even necessarily with the events of chapters 17–18. Just as Moses' grandson Jonathan limits the *terminus ad quem*

---

2. Unfortunately, we do not know the exact year of either Jonathan or Gershom's birth. However, we do know that Gershom was born in Midian (Ex 2:22), and that he was circumcized by the time Moses returned to Egypt (Ex 4:25). This places his birth date at the latest by 1446 BC.

Assuming a maximum age of fifty years for Gershom at the time of Jonathan's birth (and assuming that Gershom was young enough to survive the rebellion at Kadesh Barnea in 1444 BC, then Jonathan would have been born by 1396 BC at the latest. And since Jonathan is described as a young man (נער) in Judges 17:7, and assuming a maximum age of fifty years old for this description (cf. Merrill 2008, 199), the events of Judges 17–18 could not have taken place much later 1346 BC.

of Judges 17–18, Aaron's grandson Phinehas limits the *terminus ad quem* of Judges 19–21 (Jgs 20:28). In this case, however, we know that Phinehas was at least old enough to wield a spear at the time of the conquest (Nm 25:11). Assuming a maximum age of about eighty years old for Phinehas at this time, and an age of no more than twenty at the time of the conquest, then the events of Judges 19–21 could not have taken place much later than 1346 BC.

As a result, rather than following in chronological sequence with the rest of the book, Judges 17–21 functions as a flashback on the period as a whole, saving for last the two greatest calamities that occurred during this period.[3] This is evidenced by the refrain that brackets Judges 17:6–21:25 (discussed above), and the deictic adverbial "in those days" (Jgs 17:6; 18:1; and 21:25) that resets the reference time of these narratives. In addition, the gapping of the mention of Jonathan and Phinehas' names until later on in the narratives (Jgs 18:30; 20:28), and the gradual characterization of Jonathan in particular, increases their shock value, showing how far and how quickly Israel had fallen. Placed at the end of the book and combined together in this way, they highlight the darkness that ensued in the immediate wake of Israel's departure from the LORD.

JUDGES 1:1–2:23

Judges 1:1–2:23 constitutes an introduction to the book, including Judah and Simeon's initial successes in taking their land (Jgs 1:1–20), the disobedience of the rest of the tribes in permitting the Canaanites to live in their lands (1:21–36), the Angel of the LORD's appearance at Bochim (2:1–5), Joshua's death (2:6–10), and an outline of the cycle of the judges (2:11–23). As a result, there are several overlaps in chronology between the introduction and chapters 3–16, as well as several dischronologizations within the different sections of the introduction.

First, if taken in temporal sequence, the *wayyiqtols* in Judges 2:1–6 would require that Joshua dismissed the people after hearing the LORD's indictment at Bochim for failing to drive out the Canaanites (Jgs 2:1–5). However, as Joshua 23:4–13 indicates, Joshua was involved only in the initial conquest of Canaan, charging the Israelites before his death to complete the conquest by driving out the remaining inhabitants.[4] Therefore,

---

3. Another possibility is that these chapters indicate the *kind* of events in general that were taking place in this period. Either one fits with the present analysis.

4. Of course, there are other problems involved here that are not unique to the chronology of Judges 2:1–5, i.e. the question of how the tribes of Israel could have struggled so much to take their inheritance in the book of Judges if Joshua had already defeated the Canaanites in the book of Joshua (cf. Jo 11:23). The most likely answer is that Joshua accomplished the initial destruction of the main armies of the Canaanites in fulfillment of the LORD's promises; the final eradication of the inhabitants, however, was left as a test for the tribes.

he could not have been alive when the Angel of the LORD indicted Israel at Bochim. And Judges 1:1 accordingly places the date of his death prior to the conquests of Judges 1:1–36. Judges 2:6–10, therefore, more likely provides a summary statement of the reason for Israel's disobedience in Judges 2:11–23, contributing to the theological argument of the book (discussed above).

Second, Judges 2:11–23 presents an outline of the cycle of the judges: disobedience (2:11–14), distress (2:15), deliverance (2:16–18), devotion (2:19) and disobedience (2:19). In doing so, it provides a flashforward of chapters 3–16 that serves to link the downward spiral of the Israelites in these chapters to their failure to teach the law to their children in Judges 2:10, further supporting the thesis of the book.

And third, the mention of Caleb's conquest of Hebron in Judges 1:12–15, and 20 represents a potential dischronologization. Joshua 14:1–15 records that Caleb was eighty-five years old when he received the allotment of Hebron from Joshua. Given this age, it is likely that he would have made conquest immediately, and almost certain that he would have made conquest prior to the death of Joshua mentioned in Judges 1:1, his long lived comrade with whom he had spied out the land of Canaan. This indicates that the conquests narrated in 1:1–36 are more likely a summary descriptions of Israel's failure to drive out the inhabitants backgrounding the appearance of the Angel of the LORD in 2:1–6, rather than a chronological narrative of each successive conquest.

Together, these dischronologizations indicate that Judges 1:1–2:23 is not to be taken as a chronological narration of events, but as a summary statement of Israel's failure to take the land (1:1–2:5), a theological treatise for the reason that they abandoned the LORD so quickly thereafter (2:6–10), and an introductory encapsulation of the events to follow in chapters 3–16 (2:11–23).

JUDGES 13–16

Finally, it is well known that the span of years narrated in Judges 13–16 does not fit within the dates for the book of Judges (Merrill 2008, 169). To explain this anomaly, previous studies have had to assume that the judges must have overlapped in their rules, but without any apparent textual justification, and certainly in clear violation of the assumed temporal sequentiality of the *wayyiqtol* (Jgs 3:7, 12; 4:1; 6:1; etc.).

However, having explored the theological argument of the book of Judges, and refuted the assumption of the temporal sequentiality of the *wayyiqtol* (see **Chapter 10**), we are now equipped to understand the reason for this overlap: the purpose of the narrator is not to chronicle the precise history of the book of Judges; rather, it is to show how and why Israel abandoned the LORD, and the dire consequences of their doing so. Therefore, it is not the narrator's concern to provide a reignal synchronization for the judges as in the books of Samuel and Kings (e.g. 1 Kgs 15:1), but to evidence the various cycles of disobedience and deliverance (Jgs 3–16), and to highlight how far and how quickly Israel had fallen (Jgs 17–21).

2.3.4 Summary

These examples demonstrate that where there are purposes, such as theological argument, in a narrative, these purposes will inevitably color the narrative, often resulting in dischronologization of the events in the narrative. More specifically, the skilled narrator will often employ specific techniques in narrative in order to serve its various purposes, including tempo, gapping, suspense, comparison and contrast, characterization, and others that can affect the portrayal of temporal sequence in the narrative.

2.4 *Summary*

The previous three sections have demonstrated that the order in which events are narrated in a narrative will often differ from the actual order in which they occurred, and this can be attributed to one or more of three reasons. First, the complexity of following two or more sets of events in a narrative often requires the narrator to switch back and forth between these sets of events, resulting in numerous breaks in temporal sequence. Due to the linearity of narrative, this applies to smaller instances, as well, where a narrator wishes to indicate simultaneous action, or to momentarily concentrate on several different groups of characters. Second, not all modes of discourse convey events in temporal sequence, and where smaller sections of these modes of discourse are embedded within a narrative, the events therein will often be arranged out of sequence (especially in cases of description). And third, a narrative often possesses more purposes than simply chronicling a precise order of events in time, and in order to accomplish these purposes, narrators will frequently employ various techniques that can affect the portrayal of time in the narrative.

3. Application to Dischronologization

Using the techniques and the principles explored above, the present chapter will now proceed to explain several of the examples of dischronologization presented in **Chapter 10**. This will complete the tie between the two studies, demonstrating why a narrator might narrate events out of their actual sequence, and how this can result in the non-sequential usage of the *wayyiqtol* in BH narrative.

    3.1 Absalom's Flight—2 Samuel 13:23–39
    3.2 Esau's Soup—Genesis 25:34
    3.3 Jacob's Wedding Night—Genesis 29:21–25
    3.4. Manna in the Ark—Exodus 16:33–34

3.1 *Absalom's Flight—2 Samuel 13:23–39*

The first example is Absalom's flight. As demonstrated in **Chapter 10**, there is a potential break in sequence at verse 34 ("But Absalom fled…") as it is unlikely that Absalom would have waited long enough at Baal-Hazor (about a twenty mile (32.2 km) journey from Jerusalem) for the news of his deeds to reach David (v. 30), before fleeing the scene of the murder. This contradicts both the temporal sequentiality of the *wayyiqtol,* and the general assumption that a narrative always relates events in temporal sequence.

In terms of the differing levels of complexity in narrative, however, it is easy to explain. The author is following two different characters at this point, David and Absalom, involving two simultaneous sets of events. Due to the linear nature of narrative, however, he is forced to focus on one set of events at a time. As a result, he has to backtrack to narrate Absalom's flight in verse 34, resulting in a break in time sequence and a dischronologization of the *wayyiqtol.*

3.2 *Esau's Soup—Genesis 25:34*

The second example is Esau's soup. As demonstrated in **Chapter 10**, the narrative states in sequence that he "ate, and he drank, and he rose, and he went, and he despised his birthright." However, a closer study of these terms suggests that he most likely ate and drank at the same time, and that he despised his birthright through these actions, not just at the very end. This contradicts both the temporal sequentiality of the *wayyiqtol,* and the general assumption that a narrative always relates events in temporal sequence.

In terms of the linear nature of narrative, however, it is easy to explain. While a picture allows a viewer to observe everything in a scene at once, a narrative is linear, and thus has to relate the details of the scene one word at a time, whether they occurred in sequence or not, and trust the reader to piece together the order of events in his own mind. In addition, the summary comment, "And Esau despised the birthright," likely functions as an embedded report in the larger narrative, relating the event in reference to the speaker's time instead of the narrative itself. This results in a break in time sequence in the narrative and a dischronologization of the *wayyiqtol*.

3.3 Jacob's Wedding Night—Genesis 29:21–25

The third example is Jacob's wedding night. As demonstrated in **Chapter 10**, the narrative records the information that Laban gave Zilpah as a handmaid to Leah (v. 24) between the events of Jacob going in to his wife (v. 23), and Jacob waking up the next morning to discover that it was Leah (v. 25). This order of events my be illustrated as follows:

Jacob's wedding night

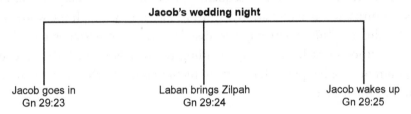

| Jacob goes in | Laban brings Zilpah | Jacob wakes up |
| Gn 29:23 | Gn 29:24 | Gn 29:25 |

Given this order of events, one has to assume that either Laban took the liberty to further disturb Jacob's wedding night, or the narrator took the liberty to insert this additional detail out of sequence.

In terms of the complexity of BH narrative, however, the order of events is easy to explain. The reason that the narrator includes such an odd detail is that this information is actually part of a larger macronarrative that picks up in Genesis 30:1–23: the birth of the nation of Israel. In this narrative, the competition between Leah and Rachel results in the use of their handmaidens Zilpah and Bilhah to birth even more children, resulting in the increase of Jacob's family to the twelve sons that would later become the twelve tribes of Israel. Thus, although verse 24 may be foreign to the micronarrative of Jacob's wedding night, the author knowing that it was essential to the macronarrative of the formation of the nation of Israel, simply inserted this information into the micronarrative at the most convenient point in the narrative. This phenomenon may be depicted as follows:

The Birth of a Nation

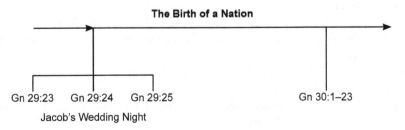

Gn 29:23   Gn 29:24   Gn 29:25   Gn 30:1–23

Jacob's Wedding Night

3.4 *Manna in the Ark—Exodus 16:33–34*

The last example in this chapter is the placing of manna in the ark of the covenant. As demonstrated in **Chapter 10,** Exodus 16:34 states that Aaron placed the manna he gathered before the ark; however, the building of the ark was not initiated until Exodus 37:1. Therefore, 16:34 jumps ahead in time sequence, resulting in a dischronologization of the *wayyiqtol*.

This advancement in time sequence is easy to explain, however, in terms of the author's purpose. The narrator simply has no reason for drawing out the potential plot of Aaron's placing of the manna into the ark. Rather, the narrator recounts this minor sequence of events in summary detail, and then returns to the main narrative of Israel's journey through the wilderness in Exodus 17. This is perfectly permissible in terms of narrative technique, as an author must be selective regarding the details he includes, and the amount of time he spends focusing on them in order to elucidate a coherent plot for the reader.

4. Conclusion

The present chapter brings the previous three chapters full circle. Contrary to the majority opinion of Hebrew scholars, temporal sequence is not determined by the presence or the absence of the *wayyiqtol*. Rather, it is dependent on other contextual factors, including logical relationships, and lexical semantics. As a result, it is not impossible to find occasions where events are narrated out of sequence in BH narrative. To the contrary, given the complexity of BH narrative, the linear nature of narrative in general, the presences of various embedded modes of discourse, the theological agenda of the authors (in addition to the historical and narrative agendas), and the skill par excellence of the biblical authors, one should expect them.

References

Adar, Z. 1959. *The biblical narrative.* Trans. M. Louvish. Jerusalem, Israel: Goldberg's Press.

Alter, R. 1981. *The art of biblical narrative.* New York, NY: Basic Books.

Amit, Y. 2000. *Hidden polemics in biblical narrative.* Trans. J. Chipman. Leiden, Netherlands: Brill.

Amit, Y. 2001. *Reading biblical narratives: Literary criticism and the Hebrew Bible.* Minneapolis, MN: Fortress Press.

Bar-Efrat, S. 2004. *Narrative art in the Bible.* Sheffield, England: Sheffield Academic Press Ltd. (Orig. pub. 1989).

Carpenter, H. 2000. *J. R. R. Tolkien: A biography.* New York, NY: Houghton Mifflin Company.

Cook, J. A. 2012. *Time and the biblical Hebrew verb: The expression of tense, aspect, and modality in biblical Hebrew.* Winona Lake, IN: Eisenbrauns.

Fokkelman, J. P. 1999. *Reading biblical narrative: An introductory guide.* Trans. I. Smit. Leiderdorp, Netherlands: Deo Publishing. (Orig. pub. 1995).

Genette, G. 1971. Time and narrative. In *A la recherché du temps perdu.* In *Aspects of narrative: Selected papers from the English Institute.* Ed. J. Hillis Miller. Trans. P. De Man. New York, NY: Columbia University Press.

Goldfajn, T. 1998. *Word order and time in biblical Hebrew narrative.* Oxford, England: Clarendon Press.

Hatav, G. 1997. *The semantics of aspect and modality: Evidence from English and biblical Hebrew.* Philadelphia, PA: John Benjamin's Publishing Company.

Joosten J. 1997a. The indicative system of the biblical Hebrew verb and its literary exploitation. In *Narrative syntax and the Hebrew Bible: Papers of the Tilburg Conference 1996.* Ed. E. van Wolde. Leiden, Netherlands: Brill Academic Publishers, Inc.

Joosten J. 1997b. Workshop: Meaning and use of the tenses in 1 Samuel 1. In *Narrative syntax and the Hebrew Bible: Papers of the Tilburg Conference 1996.* Ed. E. van Wolde. Leiden, Netherlands: Brill Academic Publishers, Inc.

Merrill, E. H. 2008. *Kingdom of priests: A history of Old Testament Israel.* 2nd ed. Grand Rapids, MI: Baker Academic.

Preminger, A., and E. L. Greenstein, eds. 1986. *The Hebrew Bible in literary criticism.* New York, NY: Ungar Publishing Company.

Ska, J. L. 2000. *"Our fathers have told us": Introduction to the analysis of Hebrew narratives.* Rome, Italy: Editrice Pontificio Istituto Biblico. (Orig. pub. 1990).

Smith, C. 2003. *Modes of discourse: The local structure of texts.* Cambridge, England: Cambridge University Press.

Sternberg, M. 1985. *The poetics of biblical narrative: Ideological literature and the drama of reading.* Bloomington, IN: Indiana University Press.

Stowe, H. B. 1852. *Uncle Tom's cabin.* New York, NY: Houghton Mifflin Company, 1890.

Tolkien, J. R. R. 1998. *The Hobbit.* New York, NY: Houghton Mifflin Company. (Orig. pub. 1937).

Tolkien, J. R. R. 1994. *The Lord of the Rings.* Volumes 1–3. 2nd ed. New York, NY: Houghton Mifflin Company. (Orig. pub. 1965).

Walsh, J. T. 2009. *Old Testament narrative: A guide to interpretation.* Louisville, KY: Westminster John Knox Press.

PART IV

BATTENING DOWN THE HATCHES:

PREPARATION FOR APPLICATION TO THE FLOOD NARRATIVE

...on the starboard bow, was a bank of mist, covering sea and sky, and driving directly for us....there was no time to be lost....It was nothing but "haul down and clew up," until we got all the studding-sails in, and the royals, flying-jib, and mizen top-gallant sail furled, and the ship kept off a little, to take the squall....the first blast showed us that it was not be trifled with. Rain, sleet, snow, and wind, enough to take our breath from us, and make the toughest turn his back to windward! The ship lay nearly over on her beam-ends; the spars and rigging snapped and cracked; and her top-gallant masts bent like whip-sticks....The decks were standing nearly at an angle of forty-five degrees, and the ship going like a mad steed through the water, the whole forward part of her in a smother of foam....we climbed up to windward, and sprang into the weather rigging. The violence of the wind, and the hail and sleet, driving nearly horizontally across the ocean, seemed actually to pin us down to the rigging....our new sails...were as stiff as boards, and the new earings and reef-points, stiffened with the sleet, knotted like pieces of iron wire....we were soon wet through, and it was every moment growing colder. Our hands were soon stiffened and numbed, which, added to the stiffness of everything else, kept us a good while on the yard....The shrouds were now iced over, the sleet having formed a crust or cake round all the standing rigging, and on the weather side of the masts and yards. When we got upon the yard, my hands were so numb that I could not have cast off the knot of the gasket to have saved my life. We both lay over the yard for a few seconds, beating our hands upon the sail, until we started the blood into our fingers' ends, and at the next moment our hands were in a burning heat....We fisted the sail together, and after six or eight minutes of hard hauling and pulling and beating down the sail, which was as stiff as sheet iron, we managed to get it furled....

—Dana, from *Two Years before the Mast*

CHAPTER 14

Sounding the Structural Depths: Theme Tracing and the Segmentation of the Narrative

Lee Anderson Jr.

Analogy and Orientation. Before the advent of sonar, ocean depth was determined by a process called depth sounding. In shallow waters, this was accomplished through the use of simple poles, while deeper waters required the use of weighted sounding lines. Measuring beneath the water's surface was often a necessary practice in uncharted waters to ensure the safety of larger vessels, as running aground in shallow water could incur great damage.

In examining the Genesis Flood account, it is also important to "measure" beneath the text's surface. Some of the clues vital to a correct chronological understanding of the event are not the most evident, but are hidden beneath the surface of the account, that is, the text's most obvious features. The following chapter contains a study directed at tracing the progressive development of the narrative's theme, which is embedded in some of the obvious and not-so-obvious features in the Genesis account. By evaluating the transitions occurring in the thematic structure of the narrative, this study will be able to segment the narrative into smaller units of text. In doing so, it will be possible to gain a better understanding of potential chronological disjunction in the narrative, which will aid greatly in mapping out the chronology of the Flood.

Abstract. The Flood narrative exhibits an elaborate chiastic structure centering on God's remembrance of Noah in Genesis 8:1a. This structure, while quite effective in conveying important theological information, adds a layer of complexity to the Flood narrative that obscures the chronology of the events recorded in the narrative. Because the driving force in the thematic arrangement of the Flood narrative is theological rather than chronological, there remains the possibility that the narrative manifests instances of chronological disjunction. In order to determine where such instances of chronological disjunction may be located, it is necessary to segment the text of the narrative, dividing it into smaller, meaningful textual units (i.e. segments) in accordance with theme, the divisions between those units therefore being marked by transitions in theme. *Theme,* that is, "the developing and coherent core or thread of a discourse in the mind of the speaker-author and hearer-reader, functioning as the prominent macrostructure of the discourse" (Floor 2004, 243) is deduced by examining *theme traces* present in the topic and focus structures contained in each sentence of the narrative. Each segment of text is marked, to some degree and in one or more of a variety of ways, by discontinuities in theme from that of the preceding segment. A single type of discontinuity may serve to mark a minor or subtle break between segments, while a greater number of discontinuities may signal a far more drastic break. The more drastic a given break between segments is, the greater the likelihood that there may exist between those segments an instance of severe chronological disjunction. By tracing the theme of the Flood narrative (Gn 6:9–9:19), it can be determined that the narrative comprises three major episodes (6:9–22; 7:1–24; and 8:1–9:19; respectively), each of which can be further divided into multiple scenes. Analysis of these smaller units of text and the thematic transitions between them reveals several possible instances of chronological disjunction, the most obvious and significant of which occurs at the boundary between two episodes, at the fissure of Genesis 7:24 and 8:1, which is also the very pinnacle of the narrative's chiastic structure. The monumental thematic shift at this point may permit the chronological overlap of the content of the two adjacent episodes, bearing substantial ramifications for the understanding of the chronology of the event.

Outline

1. Introduction: Text Segmentation of Hebrew Narrative

No literary work consists of a mere jumbled mass of meaningless text. Each sentence, clause, and word contributes to a progressively-unfolding message designed to convey the author's point. This is especially true of discourse narrative. Whether the work is a piece of fiction or non-fiction, each unit of text is intended to communicate new information (or, at the very least, further stress known information), thereby further developing what was previously written. So too, each unit of text is designed to add to the reader's growing comprehension of the discourse narrative.

This being stated, there is need to emphasize that each unit of text in a discourse narrative is involved in advancing a central theme. Whether that theme clearly expresses the point(s) that the author desires to convey is a moot point, as is whether that theme can be easily grasped by the reader; every discourse narrative presents a theme. According to Sebastiaan Jonathan Floor (2004, 243), theme can be defined as "the developing and coherent core or thread of a discourse in the mind of the speaker-author and hearer-reader, functioning as the prominent macrostructure of the discourse." Naturally, each unit of text is but a small piece of the whole. The theme of a discourse narrative is drawn from the totality of these pieces. Of course, it must be recognized that some themes are more comprehensive than others. The theme of a book containing discourse narrative is broader than that of each of the individual chapters constituting that same book. Likewise, the theme of each chapter is more comprehensive than that of each individual paragraph contained within the chapter. Consequently, it is fair to speak of some themes as being more local than others. The smaller a unit of text by comparison to the discourse narrative as a whole, the more localized the theme it conveys. As such, the discourse narrative as a whole, though itself advancing an overarching theme, also contains a series of local themes.[1] The transitions in local theme from one unit of text to the next are key to determining where breaks in the narrative may occur.

Accordingly, the purpose of this chapter will be to trace the theme of the Flood narrative, facilitating the segmentation of the text, and differentiating between individual local themes and the more comprehensive themes spanning multiple units of text. In doing so, this chapter will identify thematic breaks in the narrative, which will in turn lead to a greater comprehension of where chronological disjunctions may be located within the Flood narrative.

---

1. Similarly, each unit of text can be divided into increasingly smaller units of text, each containing an increasingly localized theme. For a description of the hierarchy of textual units within discourse narrative, see **Section 3.3**.

1.1 *A Definition of Text Segmentation*

The process of text segmentation is defined simply as breaking a piece of literature into smaller units of text. More specifically, according to the definition set forth by Masao Utiyama and Hitoshi Isahara (2001, 499), it is a matter of dividing documents by "identifying and isolating topics." Each text segment is a homogeneous unit of continuous text that is linked internally (Salton et al. 1996, 55). As Hideki Kozima argues (1993, 286), "A text segment, whether or not it is explicitly marked, as are sentences and paragraphs, is defined as a sequence of clauses or sentences that display local coherence." For the purposes of this chapter, and for the sake of avoiding needless confusion due to the use of overlapping terms, text segmentation will be defined as *the process of dividing a document* (in this case, a discourse narrative) *into meaningful units of text in accordance with transitions in theme.*

1.2 *The Usefulness of Segmentation to the Flood Narrative*

The link between the segmentation of the Flood narrative and the chronology of the Flood event itself is somewhat obscure. Indeed, aiding in the research of biblical chronology is a virtually unexplored avenue in the range of the use of text segmentation. Various models for text segmentation have been proposed and have been used primarily in the field of computer science for purposes such as information retrieval and summarization (Salton et al. 1996, 53; Utiyama and Isahara 2001, 499). Nevertheless, the fact that this is an uncommon application of text segmentation does not negate its usefulness, provided 1) that it is employed according to a rigorous, comprehensive, tested model, and 2) that the conclusions gleaned from it are subject to a set of recognized presuppositions concerning the text itself, and governed by the known limitations of text segmentation.

As previously mentioned, a transition in theme indicates the beginning of a new segment in a discourse narrative. Each new segment of text is therefore marked, to some degree and in one or more of a variety of ways, by discontinuities from the preceding segment.[2] Alexander

---

2. At the risk of circular reasoning, it should be noted that such discontinuities not only reflect thematic breaks between segments in the text, but are highly useful for identifying them.

Nakhimovsky (1988, 38) noted four main types of discontinuities which may occur between two adjoining segments: discontinuities of topic, discontinuities of space and time, discontinuities of figure and ground, and discontinuities of the narrative perspective (cf. Nakhimovsky and Rapaport 1988). Similarly, in building on the work of S. H. Levinsohn, Steven Edward Runge (2007, 126) likewise outlined four different "dimensions" which can promote either continuity or discontinuity within a narrative:

Dimension	Continuity	Discontinuity
Place	Same place or (for motion) continuous change	Discrete changes of place
Time	Events separated by at most only small forward gaps	Large forward gaps or events out of order
Participants	Same cast or gradual changes of cast	Discrete changes of cast
Action	All material of the same type; event, non-event, reported conversation, etc.; Events are in sequence	Changes from one type of material to another and/or the event concerned is NOT the next in sequence

A single type of discontinuity may serve to mark a minor or subtle break between segments, while a greater number of discontinuities may signal a far more drastic break. Generally speaking, the more drastic a given break in a narrative is, the greater the likelihood that there may be severe chronological disjunction in the actual sequence of events described at that point in the narrative. Thus, by segmenting the text of the Flood narrative and by analyzing the thematic breaks between segments, it may be possible to attain a clearer understanding of the chronology embedded in the Flood narrative.

1.3 *The Presuppositions Governing the Segmentation of the Flood Narrative*

Prior to setting forth a model for the segmentation of the Flood narrative, it is necessary to comprehend the presuppositions to which the conclusions of such a study must be subject. A thorough study of the segmentation of the text of the Flood narrative may indeed open the door to a greatly enhanced and more profitable study of the chronology of the Flood—even to the point of possibly overturning certain prior assumptions concerning the event. However, certain presuppositions, namely the unity and the coherence of the text, are non-negotiable and beyond contestation regardless of any new information uncovered though this study of text segmentation.

1.3.1 The Unity of the Text
1.3.2 The Coherence of the Text

1.3.1 The Unity of the Text

The first presupposition that must be considered in this study is the unity of the book of Genesis as a whole and, more specifically, the unity of the text of the Flood narrative. To date, the book of Genesis (as well as the rest of the Pentateuch) has seen over two centuries of attempts to divide it into different source material and, as such, has been the subject of the most speculative dissection known to modern literary study. The classic Documentary Hypothesis with its four main sources (the Jahwist, the Elohist, the Deuteronomist, and the Priestly source) has not left the Flood narrative unscathed. Dozens of contemporary Old Testament scholars have sought to parcel out the various textual units of the Flood narrative to two, if not three, different anonymous authors.[3] (Notably, these attempts have often complicated the study of the meaning of the biblical text itself, therefore severely reducing the usefulness of sources backing the Documentary Hypothesis in the study of the chronology of the Flood.)

Despite its popularity, however, the Documentary Hypothesis is in direct conflict with the claims of the text itself. As the word of God, the biblical text is supremely authoritative (2 Tm 3:16), and its statements supersede any human suppositions (no matter how scholarly) on its authorship. The Pentateuch forcefully testifies that Moses was indeed its author (Ex 17:14; 24:4, 7; 34:27; Nm 33:1–2; Dt 31:9, 11). Similarly, other Old Testament books assume the Mosaic authorship of the Pentateuch (Jo 1:7–8; 8:31–32; 1 Kgs 2:3; 2 Kgs 14:6; 21:8; Ezr 6:18; Neh 13:1; Dn 9:11–13; Mal 4:4). Furthermore, the New Testament affirms that Moses indeed authored the Pentateuch (Mt 19:8; Mk 12:26; Jn 5:46–47; 7:19; Acts 3:22; Rom 10:5; Heb 10:28).[4] In addition to these unmistakably clear claims, there is a mass of weighty internal evidence contained in the Pentateuch which further bolsters the case for Mosaic authorship.[5] As Derek Kidner (1967, 22) aptly stated,

3. For an evaluation of the Documentary Hypothesis in relation to the chronology of the Flood, see **Chapter 8**.

4. Even if it is assumed that Jesus and the New Testament writers were merely accommodating themselves to the common view of the time (that Moses wrote the Pentateuch), it is impossible to hold to the Documentary Hypothesis without attributing to them either gross deception or considerable ignorance.

5. For a comprehensive rebuttal of the Documentary Hypothesis and an explanation of both the textual and historical evidences for the Mosaic authorship of the Pentateuch, see especially chapters 6–13 of Gleason L. Archer's 2007 work, *A Survey of Old Testament Introduction*, rev. ed. (Chicago, IL: Moody Publishers).

"With the study of Genesis *on its own terms*, that is, as a living whole, not a body to be dissected, the impression becomes inescapable that . . . the book itself [is] a unity."

Accordingly, for the purposes of this study of text segmentation, the purported disunity in the origin of the text will not be considered. If breaks between segments fall at locations customarily understood to be seams joining different alleged sources, it is merely a coincidence based upon transitions in theme paralleling shifts in other factors assumed to indicate different sources. Similarly, the conclusions of this study should not be extrapolated to argue for multiple sources in the Flood narrative. Some of the thematic breaks between segments in the Flood narrative are indeed substantial; nevertheless, no matter how severe a transition in theme may be, all the segments contained in the narrative originated from the same author in accordance with the clear and direct claims of the word of God.

1.3.2 The Coherence of the Text

The second presupposition which must frame this study is that the text is coherent. The various segments, though exhibiting breaks in theme, are nonetheless marked by an orderly and logical relationship which affords for the comprehension of the narrative as a whole. This presupposition rests on the former: because the text of the Flood narrative is a unified work rather than a fractured disarray of textual units, coherence can be expected. Therefore, if at any point the text appears incoherent in light of the findings of this study, it is resultant purely from a deficiency in the study, rather than in the text itself.

1.4 *The Limitations of Segmentation*

Just as this study is subject to the boundaries set forth in the two aforementioned presuppositions, it must also be governed by an understanding of two limitations, namely that theme tracing and text segmentation 1) are descriptive in nature, and 2) are subject to the propositional statements contained in the text.

    1.4.1 Descriptive in Nature
    1.4.2 Subject to the Propositional Statements of the Text

1.4.1 Descriptive in Nature

The tracing of a theme throughout the course of a narrative is not an exact science. As Floor (2004, 190) wisely surmises, "For that, the human mind, human communication, and language itself is too complex." That being stated, the ability to discern transitions between local themes in a narrative and thereby divide the text into segments is likewise a delicate matter. Unlike fields such as mathematics, physics, and chemistry, which are, with the exception of miracles, bound by incontrovertible laws that can enable one to make prescriptive statements about what will always be the case under specific circumstances, the study of various facets of linguistics (such as theme tracing and text segmentation) frequently encounters principles which are only generally true. Most rules are subject to the occasional exception.

This is not to say that theme tracing and text segmentation are imprecise or that they cannot yield information helpful in determining the chronology of the Flood. On the contrary, the systematic method of theme tracing and text segmentation proposed by Floor and augmented by the studies on participant reference by Runge is very precise by comparison to mere guesswork. Together, these two works serve to provide a very strong foundation for this study on the segmentation of the Flood narrative. Accordingly, theme tracing and text segmentation are valuable tools, *but only if employed correctly*. The method to be outlined in this study is not so exacting or prescriptive that it can dictate where thematic breaks ought to occur (and thereby, where chronological disjunctions *must* be present). Rather, the method is intended to be descriptive of where thematic breaks exist so that one may thereby discern where chronological disjunctions *may* be present. Stated simply, theme tracing and text segmentation are not tools designed to prove the locations of chronological disjunctions (that is the role of other facets of research in the study of the chronology of the Flood). Rather, theme tracing and text segmentation are tools intended to streamline and facilitate the search for potential chronological disjunctions by identifying the locations in the text subject to thematic transition.

1.4.2 Subject to the Propositional Statements of the Text

The second limitation of theme tracing and text segmentation is that they are bound by the clear propositional statements of the text itself. In the event of a substantial thematic break, there remains the possibility for severe chronological disjunction *only* if it does not conflict with the clear propositional statements of the text. The presence of a thematic break at any given point does not give the interpreter liberty to suggest just any theory regarding chronological disjunction. Rather, any chronological scheme proposed as a result this study's investigation of theme tracing and text segmentation must be in accord with what the text itself has expressly stated concerning chronology, namely the five fixed dates marking the occurrence of specific events (Gn 7:11; 8:4, 5, 13, 14).

Having now established the intent of this study, and having also set forth the presuppositions and limitations to which this study is subject, this chapter will now examine one prior approach to the segmentation of the Flood narrative, and then proceed to introduce the methodology that will guide this study in tracing the theme and segmenting the text of the Flood narrative.

2. An Intuitive Approach to the Segmentation of the Flood Narrative

While this study is the first to subject the Flood narrative to a rigorous, comprehensive model of theme tracing for the purpose of segmenting the text, it does not mark the first time that the Flood narrative has been divided into textual units. The 1949 work by premier Hebraist Umberto Cassuto proposed that the Flood narrative consists of twelve distinct paragraphs,[6] which together constitute two larger groups or "acts." The first six paragraphs (act one) depict, step by step, the acts of divine justice that brought cataclysmic destruction upon the earth, while the remaining six paragraphs (act two) describe the unfolding of divine acts of compassion that brought a renewal of life to the devastated world. He writes,

> The first paragraph (vi 9–12) describes the situation in the world before the Flood: the corruption of all flesh and the righteousness of Noah. The second (vi 13–22) relates that God told Noah of His decision to destroy the earth on account of the wickedness of mankind and enjoined him to build the ark. The third (vii 1–5) tells how God spoke again to Noah, informing him that the time had come for him to enter the ark, for in another seven days the Deluge would come upon the world. The fourth (vii 6–9) records the entrance into the ark of all concerned, in accordance with the divine command. The fifth (vii 10–16) depicts the commencement of the Deluge. The sixth (vii 17–24) narrates how the flood continued and the waters prevailed over the earth. The seventh (viii 1–14) portrays the end of the Flood and the beginning of the return of the world to normality. The eighth (viii 15–17) contains the Divine communication instructing Noah to go forth from the ark. The ninth (viii 18–22) deals with the exit of the occupants from the ark according to the Divine injunction, and with Noah's sacrifice and its favorable acceptance. The tenth (ix 1–7) tells of the blessing God bestowed on Noah and his sons. The eleventh (ix 8–11) announces the covenant that God promised them. The twelfth (ix 12–17) describes the sign that God appointed for the covenant. (Cassuto 1997, 30–31)

6. The paragraphs outlined in Cassuto's work are comparably large textual units that ought not to be confused with a "thematic paragraph" as defined in **Section 3.3**. In most instances, they rank closer to the level of a "scene."

This rough segmentation of the text was achieved through Cassuto's intuitive and masterful grasp of the Hebrew language. While Cassuto employed no linguistic tests to confirm the accuracy of his approach to segmenting the text, his findings were backed by a large number of textual indicators (verbal parallelisms, numerical repetition, etc.) It is significant that he noted 1) a hierarchy of textual divisions, and 2) transitions in the flow of theme between the text segments of the narrative (especially between the primary textual division at the juncture of Genesis 7:24 and 8:1). Perhaps most important though is the fact that his elucidation of the narrative's main textual division is vital to his later proposition of severe chronological disjunction occurring in the narrative.

Before further analyzing Cassuto's views on the presence of chronological disjunction in the Flood narrative, however, it is necessary to illustrate the elaborate chiastic structure running throughout the Flood narrative (see chart). This chiastic structure is also intensified by the strategic organization

A. Transitional Introduction: Noah and His Sons (6:9–10)

   B. The Corruption of All Flesh (6:11–12)

      C. God's Resolution to Destroy the Earth by Flood (6:13–22)

         D. God's Command and Noah's Response: The Entrance of the Ark (7:1–10)

            E. The Beginning of the Flood: The Inundating of the Earth (7:11–16)

               F. The Rising of the Waters (7:17–24)

                  G. God's Remembrance of Noah (8:1a)

               F'. The Recession of the Waters (8:1b–5)

            E'. The End of the Flood: The Drying of the Earth (8:6–14)

         D'. God's Command and Noah's Response: The Exodus from the Ark (8:15–19)

      C'. God's Resolution to Never Again Destroy the Earth by Flood (8:20–22)

   B'. The Covenant with All Flesh (9:1–17)

A'. Transitional Conclusion: Noah and His Sons (9:18–19)

of key numbers used to mark durations of time: seven days (7:4, 10; 8:10, 12), forty days (7:12; 8:6), and one hundred fifty days (7:24; 8:3). This particular way of interpreting the structure clearly points to God's remembrance of Noah (וַיִּזְכֹּר אֱלֹהִים אֶת־נֹחַ) as a matter of utmost theological importance and as the turning point in the narrative (Wenham 1978, 339–340). Here, God's remembrance entails not the recollection of something forgotten, but rather the act of calling something to mind that eventuates in the expression of faithful love combined with timely intervention (Kidner 1967, 92).

While it is true that the chiastic structure running throughout the Flood narrative centers on God's remembrance of Noah in Genesis 8:1, it remains uncertain whether this verse should be regarded as the actual pinnacle of the catastrophe itself, framed chronologically between the two periods of one hundred fifty days mentioned in Genesis 7:24 and 8:3. This is where Cassuto's segmentation of the text is particularly beneficial. Having marked Genesis 8:1 as the principle point of transition between the narrative's two main textual units, Cassuto considered this textual break to manifest severe disjunction in the chronology of the Flood. He comments,

> The meaning is not that He remembered at the termination of the hundred and fifty days mentioned in the previous verse, for we are subsequently told *(v. 2): the fountains of the deep were closed, and the windows of the heavens, and the rain was restrained from the heavens,* and this took place, of course, at the end of the forty days of rain. To understand these verbs (remembered, were closed, etc.) as pluperfects (He had already previously remembered, [the fountains] had already previously been closed, etc.) is certainly incorrect and not in keeping with Hebrew idiomatic usage. . . . The interpretation here must follow the same lines as the explanation we advanced regarding the relationship between the story of Creation and the story of the Garden of Eden. The preceding paragraph tells how the waters prevailed upon the earth, and this episode forms the theme of that paragraph up to the end, whereas this new paragraph deals with a different topic—the first stage of the deliverance of the survivors—and commences the narration of the this story from the beginning, although the comment antedates the conclusion of the episode described above. (Cassuto 1997, 99–100)

In his discussion of the arrangement of Old Testament narrative texts, Old Testament scholar Robert B. Chisholm, Jr. expressed similar thoughts. Intriguingly, he too noted the monumental thematic break between Genesis 7:24 and 8:1. Having described a "flashback" as an arrangement of material that allows for temporal overlay, he writes,

Genesis 8:1 provides another example of the flashback technique. After a description of the devastating effects of the Flood and Noah's isolation (7:17–24), the theme shifts to God's concern for Noah and the removal of the waters (8:1). In 7:17–24 the waters are described as prevailing over the earth for 150 days, but in 8:1–5 the focus is on their receding between the fortieth and one hundred and fiftieth days. As the theme shifts from judgment to renewal, the scene shifts back to the fortieth day of the Flood, when God began the process whereby he caused the waters to recede. (Chisholm 2003, 67–68)[7]

Summarily stated, Cassuto and Chisholm concur that the center of the chiastic structure has nothing to do with the centermost point in the chronology of the Flood itself. The chiastic structure (with Gn 8:1 at its heart) is employed chiefly to illuminate a vital theological truth. In order to grasp the chronology of the event, however, one has to dive beneath the chiastic structure engrained on the narrative's surface. The theme tracing model presented in this chapter will do just that. Through its application, this study will be able to discern whether Cassuto and Chisholm were correct in seeing Genesis 8:1 as marking a major division between two segments in the text. If so, there may be substantial reason to entertain the theory of chronological disjunction at this location.

3. The Methodological Approach to the Segmentation of the Flood Narrative

While the observations of Cassuto and Chisholm are extremely valuable, they remain somewhat speculative. It is important to recognize that their observations are not altogether arbitrary; rather, they are based upon specific textual clues, such as verbal parallelisms and numerical repetition. Nevertheless, such clues are incapable of proving the exact location of transition from one segment of text to the next. Similarly, while the chiastic structure running throughout the narrative is highly useful in that it provides strong evidence for a major thematic break at the center of the narrative (and thus a likely division between two large segments of text), it is substantially less suitable for identifying lesser thematic transitions in other locations and, as previously shown, may actually complicate the charting of the Flood's chronology.

7. Interestingly, as will be discussed later, Chisholm (2003, 65) also notes the presence of at least four other minor chronological disjunctions in the Flood narrative incurred by the use of recapitulation (a form of parallelism in which an earlier statement is both repeated and expanded).

Consequently, in order to overcome these difficulties, a different methodology of text segmentation must be employed—one based upon recognizable linguistic factors that remain constant regardless of the text considered. It is one thing for thematic transitions and divisions between text segments to be proposed on the basis of the peculiarities of the Flood narrative (such as its unique and expansive chiastic structure), but it is a far more significant matter if the same transitions and divisions are identified by a method of theme tracing built upon linguistic principles that has already been tested on other Hebrew narrative texts and proven effective.

In 2004, as the culmination of his studies under leading Hebraist Christo H. J. van der Merwe, Floor proposed in his doctoral dissertation a method of theme tracing based upon information structure (i.e. the interaction between topic and focus in the clauses and sentences constituting a narrative).[8] Building largely on Knud Lambrecht's theory of information structure (1994), Floor was able to set forth a workable and concise model of theme tracing and text segmentation applicable to all Hebrew narrative texts. The final chapter of his work successfully demonstrated the usefulness and precision of the model by applying it to Genesis 17. This chapter will therefore seek to employ the same model in tracing the theme of the Flood narrative.[9] The remainder of this section will set forth a working definition of theme and explain the different indicators involved in identifying it (topic and focus). **Section 4** will then lay out the four-step process involved in theme tracing and apply it to the Flood narrative.

3.1   Preliminary Assumptions Concerning Theme and Theme Tracing
3.2   A Definition of Theme
3.3   Textual Strata: Discourse Segment Hierarchy
3.4   Textual Rifts: The Nature and Location of Theme Shifts
3.5   Textual Clues: Theme Traces
3.6   Textual Building Blocks: Topic and Focus
3.7   Summary: From Topic, Focus and Theme Traces to Text Segmentation

3.1 *Preliminary Assumptions Concerning Theme and Theme Tracing*

Before a useful approach to theme analysis based upon information structure can be laid out, it is imperative that a clear definition of theme be provided.

8. For definitions of topic and focus, see **Sections 3.6.1** and **3.6.2**, respectively.

9. Admittedly, Floor's treatment of participant reference (the analysis of which can aid in the segmentation of the text) was underdeveloped. However, where this study seeks to address participant reference, it will lean heavily on the equally competent work of Runge, (who likewise earned his doctorate under van der Merwe).

In order to do this, it is necessary to briefly summarize the preliminary assumptions regarding theme and theme tracing.

The first basic set of assumptions revolves around the text. In order to successfully trace the theme of a discourse narrative, it must be assumed that the discourse narrative possesses both cohesion and coherence. Cohesion, as Floor defines it, is distinctly grammatical. It can be marked by a variety of surface-level indicators, such as "anaphora, lexical repetition, tense-aspect continuity, frame-setting devices, structural patterning like inclusion and chiasm, and more" (Floor 2004, 236). Many of these indicators—especially lexical repetition and chiasm—are blatantly exhibited in the Flood narrative. Furthermore, the Flood narrative is coherent; it is marked by an orderly and logical relationship which affords for the comprehension of the narrative as a whole. As previously asserted, the coherence of the Flood narrative rests squarely upon the fact that it is a unified whole rather than a fractured disarray of textual units. Coupled with the assumption that the text is a coherent whole, however, it must also be understood that the text consists of multiple pieces forming a hierarchical structure; it is composed of textual/thematic units that are embedded in increasingly higher level units (Floor 2004, 236; cf. **Section 3.3**). Coupled with this is the assumption that a text has levels of "grounding" with regard to information. Whether information is foregrounded (i.e. assigned saliency) or backgrounded, some discrimination of prominence is evident (Floor 2004, 236).

The second set of basic assumptions concerns the presence and nature of theme itself. As mentioned previously, every text has a theme. Floor notes that although the nature of theme is somewhat enigmatic, its presence in a text is beyond contestation. As such, it is guaranteed that theme traces exist within every text, even if they are obscure (Floor 2004, 237). A theme does not stand in isolation; it is accompanied by and intertwined with a macrostructure, that is, "the global organization of a text" which facilitates its comprehension (Kintsch 1998, 67). It must not be taken for granted, though, that only one theme or macrostructure exists in a given discourse narrative; discourse narratives differ in their degree of thematic complexity and may actually possess multiple themes and/or macrostructures (Floor 2004, 236). Finally, despite the enigmatic nature of theme, it must not be regarded as static; rather, theme must be understood as a dynamic entity which unfolds throughout a narrative, as it is progressively illuminated by theme traces (Floor 2004, 237).

3.2 A Definition of Theme

As mentioned earlier in this study, theme can be defined as "the developing and coherent core or thread of a discourse in the mind of the speaker-author and hearer-reader, functioning as the prominent macrostructure of the discourse" (Floor 2004, 243). For the sake of clarification it should be noted that theme is not the equivalent of the primary topic(s) of a unit of text (though primary topic is highly instrumental in illuminating theme). Nor is theme simply that information which is added to the known information in a unit of text (i.e. the information contained in the focus structure; cf. **Section 3.6.2**). As Floor (2004, 240–41) points out, theme is not the same as the plot or the "chronological action line" of a narrative. Furthermore, theme cannot be reduced to a lone macro-word, a single "macro-proposition" (a title statement that captures the complete thematic development of the discourse), or a motif (a recurrent thematic element). Similarly, in relation to biblical texts like the Flood narrative, theme is not identical to the main theological or doctrinal point asserted by a narrative. Each of these aspects may be connected with or have some degree of bearing on the theme of a text, but none alone is adequate to provide a definition of what theme is.

By contrast, *theme is a conceptual entity expressed in language and evidenced by distinct traces in a text.* It possesses a variety of properties. Having defined theme as "the semantic thread providing coherence that is perceived cognitively in the mind of the communicators," Floor (2004, 241) observes, "The thread can consist of one or even multiple microthemes, one or multiple motifs, expressed by one or more macro-words, and expressed by one or more primary topics. More than one title statement can capture the same summary of the discourse." Given the nature of human language, it is simply not possible for the theme of any text to be stated in unequivocal terms. Nevertheless, by analyzing theme traces present in the information structure of a text (in this case a discourse narrative) it is possible to have an *adequate* understanding of the theme of a text requisite to its segmentation.

3.3 Textual Strata: Discourse Segment Hierarchy

Having set forth an understanding of theme, it is necessary to explain the hierarchy of text segments within discourse narrative. Perhaps the easiest way to understand the discourse segment hierarchy is by comparing it to a multilevel outline: The largest units of text are the equivalent of the highest level of the outline; the units of text constituting the largest unit are directly comparable to the second level of the outline; and so on. Both

Floor (2004, 244–45) and Runge (2007, 126) agree that there are four levels of textual units, the largest being the narrative, followed by the episode, the scene, and the thematic paragraph.[10]

    3.3.1 Narrative
    3.3.2 Episode
    3.3.3 Scene
    3.3.4 Thematic Paragraph

3.3.1 Narrative

A narrative is the largest textual unit. Floor notes that a narrative consists of at least one, but more likely several episodes, each with its own topic framework and focus content. He writes,

> In a narrative one expects some hypertopic, that is, a primary topic than is recurring across most if not all the subunits (episodes and scenes) of the narrative. A hypertopic brings coherence between the various episodes, like for example Abraham in the Abraham Narrative (Genesis 12–25) or Noah in the Flood Narrative of Genesis 6–9. The hypertopic is frequently the primary topic in episodes and scenes in the theme units lower down in the hierarchy. (Floor 2004, 244)

In the process of theme tracing and text segmentation, one of the first necessary tasks is to identify the boundaries of the narrative. Genesis 17, the text which Floor used to test and illustrate his model, possesses very clear boundaries. The Flood narrative, by contrast, provides some unique challenges to determining its scope. Does the narrative begin with the birth of Noah in Genesis 5:28, with the Lord's recognition of man's total wickedness in Genesis 6:5, or with the *tol^edot* of Noah in Genesis 6:9? Similarly, does the narrative end with the close of God's declaration of the covenant in Genesis 9:17, or with Noah's death and the conclusion of the *tol^edot* of Noah in Genesis 9:29? The matter is not as simple as it appears. Accordingly, further treatment of the precise boundaries of the narrative will be given in **Section 4.2.**

3.3.2 Episode

The second-largest textual unit is an episode. As opposed to a narrative, an episode has only a single topic framework, rather than several different ones.

---

10. Note that Runge, following R. A. Dooley and S. H. Levinsohn's stratification, prefers the terms "discourse," "thematic unit," "episode," and "development unit," respectively, to represent the four levels of textual units. To these he also adds "clause" as a fifth level (which Floor recognizes, but does not include in his list of textual units). For the sake of avoiding confusion, this study will adopt Floor's titles.

Floor (2004, 244) remarks that while an episode can have more than one spatial and temporal setting, only one set of primary and secondary topics is commented on.

3.3.3 Scene

Just as a narrative is composed of episodes, so too is an episode composed of scenes. Each scene contains a single primary topic and is limited to one set of participants at one time in one place (which dictates that discontinuities of space and time, as noted by Nakhimovsky, occur *between*, rather than *in* scenes). Floor (2004, 244) further notes that scenes can be very short, but have a minimum of "two propositions with a sequentiality relation between them."

3.3.4 Thematic Paragraph

The thematic paragraph is the smallest textual unit above the level of the clause. Floor's description is significant:

> The thematic paragraph must consist of at least one sentence with one primary topic or a topicless sentence focus structure. Although a single proposition can function as a thematic paragraph, normally a thematic paragraph has at least two propositions, with only one primary topic. The units of setting, background comments, digressions, and closures (like summaries or evaluations, both common in Biblical Hebrew narrative) fit into the category of theme paragraphs, not scenes. (Floor 2004, 245)

3.4 *Textual Rifts: The Nature and Location of Theme Shifts*

By the very nature of the discourse segment hierarchy, it stands to reason that there are only two possible locations in which a shift in theme may occur (Floor 2004, 246): either between two textual units at the same level in the hierarchy (e.g. between two scenes within the same episode), or between textual units at different levels in the hierarchy (e.g. between the last scene in one episode and the beginning of the next episode). Floor posits that while divisions between lower units of text are sometimes more obscure (in that there is little syntactic or semantic marking distinguishing the beginning of a new textual unit from the preceding unit), divisions between higher units of text are clearly marked by semantic and (often) syntactic indicators. Runge comes to much the same conclusion in his comments on the study by T. Givón (1984). He writes:

Givón states, "The four unities—or continuities—are more likely to be maintained *within* any particular discourse unit than *across* its boundary with another unit." ... Thus, changes in place, time, participants or action will *naturally* lead the reader to sense a discontinuity in a narrative.[11] The discontinuity, in turn, leads the reader to segment the discourse. Furthermore, Givón claims that the number of discontinuities observed in a given context is directly proportional to the discourse level of the discontinuity in the overall hierarchy of the discourse. In other words, a single discontinuity might indicate a break at a lower level of discourse, while three or more would likely indicate a higher-level discourse boundary. (Runge 2007, 126)

Taken in conjunction with the aforementioned work of Nakhimovsky on the types of discontinuities in narrative, it should be understood that the thematic breaks occurring between textual units located higher in the discourse segment hierarchy manifest a greater degree of discontinuity than do the breaks occurring between textual units at a lower level.

3.5 *Textual Clues: Theme Traces*

The signals embedded in the text that aid in the illumination of the theme are called theme traces. A theme trace may be defined as follows:

[A] clue in the surface form of a discourse, viewed from the perspective of information structure, that points to the cognitive macrostructure or theme of a text. This clue is in the form of (1) a marked syntactic configuration, be it marked word order or marked in the sense of explicit and seemingly "redundant," signaling some thematic sequencing strategy, or (2) some recurring concept(s) signaling some prominence and coherence. (Floor 2004, 255–56)

In accordance with this definition, it should be noted that theme traces, though potentially obscure, are not at all arbitrary. They can be identified with a considerable degree of precision. In relation to how these theme traces actually serve to illuminate the theme of a textual unit, Floor (2004, 247) states, "The basic discourse function of such theme hints or theme

---

11. Note that such changes, however, do not disunify the narrative structure; changes are necessary in order to advance the narrative. This does not mean, however, that all advances made in a narrative are necessarily chronological. So too, disunity does not automatically indicate chronological discontinuity, though it can in certain circumstances.

traces is to mark macro-words, which in turn provide the coherence of the thematic thread." He further observes that, in BH narrative, there are three common types of theme traces embedded in the information structure: 1) marked word-order constructions, 2) seemingly redundant and optional explicit pronominal markings, and 3) the relexicalization of discourse-active or semi-active referents (Floor 2004, 248).[12]

The first type of theme trace deserves additional consideration. What precisely is marked word order? As noted in *A Biblical Hebrew Reference Grammar*, normal sentence word order within BH is verb, followed by the subject, and then the object (van der Merwe, Naude, and Kroeze 1999, 336).[13] Marked word order, then, constitutes a departure from this normal arrangement. In particular, fronting and left-dislocation are often crucial to identifying and tracing theme.[14]

The second type of theme trace (seemingly redundant and optional explicit pronominal marking) needs no further explanation; however, in order to provide added clarification on the third type of theme trace (the relexicalization of discourse-active or semi-active referents) it is necessary to rely upon Runge's study of participant encoding in BH. Runge's study, building on the work of Dooley and Levinsohn, discussed the default encoding of participants in both subject and non-subject contexts. He defines the various contexts as follows:

---

12. Additionally, Floor notes that grammatical elements other than information structure-determined configurations (i.e. discourse markers like הִנֵּה and interclausal connectives like כִּי) can also function as theme traces, though such were not the main focus of his study.

13. Barry L. Bandstra (1992, 123) similarly notes that "Word order is...seen to be one of the most significant syntactic factors which are responsible for maintaining continuity between clauses as well as indicating thematic breaks between paragraphs." Likewise, "Word order in biblical Hebrew narrative must first be defined in terms of an unmarked constituent order, namely V–S–O and V–O. Presence and absence of an explicit noun phrase subject primarily reflect actor discontinuity and continuity respectively."

14. Left-dislocation differs from fronting in that "a constituent stands at the beginning of a clause *and* is taken up again later in the clause by a constituent of the clause (called the resumptive)" (van der Merwe, Naude, and Kroeze 1999, 339). Both syntactic configurations may be illustrated through adaptations to the sentence, "Reginald sat on the chair." The sentence, "On the chair Reginald sat," is an illustration of fronting. Left-dislocation, by contrast, dislocates the fronted element from the main sentence and has an anaphoric resumptive pronoun in the main sentence. An illustration of this configuration is as follows: "As for the chair, Reginald sat on it." Despite the syntactic difference, both fronting and left-dislocation have a similar purpose in illuminating theme. Note that because Hebrew reads right-to-left, left-dislocation speaks of material at the beginning (right) of the sentence. Right-dislocation, to be discussed, refers to material toward the end (left) of a sentence.

Subject Contexts

INT Initial introduction of a brand new participant.

S1 Participant was the subject of the immediately preceding clause.

S1+ Participant was the subject of the immediately preceding clause, and at least one other subject participant is added in the present clause to create a compound subject.

S2 Participant was the addressee of a speech reported in preceding clause.

S3 Participant was in non-subject role other than addressee in preceding clause.

S4 Participant is semi-active/accessible; context is other than those covered in *S1–S3*.

S5 Participant is inactive; context is other than those covered by *S1–S4*.

Non-subject Contexts

INT Initial introduction of a brand new participant.

N1 Participant was in the same non-subject role in the preceding clause.

N2 Participant was the speaker in a speech reported in the preceding clause.

N3 Participant was in a role in the preceding clause other than *N1–N2*.

N4 Participant is semi-active/accessible; context is other than those covered by *N1–N3*.

N5 Participant is inactive; context is other than those covered by *N1–N4*. (Adapted from Runge 2007, 90)

In each of the preceding contexts outlined by Runge, participants are denoted in a variety of ways (e.g. by a full noun phrase, a clitic pronoun, etc.). However, for each context outlined, there is a "default" method of encoding; that is, an expected method of encoding from which a departure (in the form of "overencoding") may be instrumental in identifying theme traces.

Context *INT*, for the purpose of its role in introducing participants, requires 1) the establishment of a primary referring expression for the participant (i.e. the default referring expression used when relexicalizing a participant), and 2) the creation of a semantic connection between the newly activated participant and the discourse context (Runge 2007, 91). Contexts *S1* and *S2*, as well as *N1* and *N2*, require minimal encoding (almost invariably either a clitic pronoun or an independent personal pronoun; Runge 2007, 94–101). On the other hand, contexts *S3–S5*, as well as *N3–N5* all require the use of a full noun phrase in order to reestablish which participant is in view (contexts *S5* and *N5* actually require not only the use of a full noun phrase, but also the reestablishment of the participant's anchoring relation to the discourse; Runge 2007, 102–05).

For the purposes of this study, a consideration of departures from the default encoding of participants in contexts *S1* and *S2*, as well as *N1* and *N2* is primary. As Runge (2007, 121) observes, instances of the overencoding of participants in these contexts (through the use of a full noun phrase) often "function as pragmatic markers to guide the reader in the segmentation of the discourse into discrete development units for easier cognitive processing of the text."[15] However, it must be stated too that not *all* redundant noun phrases involved in the overencoding of participants serve to demarcate the beginning of a new textual unit; they can also be used pragmatically for highlighting purposes (Runge 2007, 124).[16]

Having sketched the various levels of textual units involved in theme tracing, and having also investigated the nature of theme traces, this study will now examine topic and focus (the "building blocks" of information structure), and how they are involved in identifying theme.

3.6 *Textual Building Blocks: Topic and Focus*

In Hebrew narrative, each sentence generally consists of two components: topic (that which the sentence is about; always presupposed or given information) and focus (the element of information that is added to the presupposition of a sentence).[17] Therefore, because each unit of text, from the

---

15. Runge (2007, 144) later notes that overencoding is used, more specifically, to demarcate development units "in contexts of natural continuity, as well as in conjunction with formal markers of discontinuity to demarcate higher-level discourse divisions, viz. thematic units."

16. Runge (2007, 174–75) later identifies two kinds of highlighting: *thematic highlighting* and *cataphoric highlighting*. Thematic highlighting "assigns added prominence to **information** that is crucial to understanding the interpretive point of the story. Thematic highlighting places the spotlight on the added information itself." Furthermore, it can have "the pragmatic effect of reorienting an active or semi-active participant to the discourse based on the anchoring relation specified by the writer/editor." It also can "explicitly indicate the referential center, which prototypically coincides with the current center of attention/ initiating participant." Additionally, thematic highlighting may indicate shifts in point of view, that is, "the vantage point from which the narrative is being recounted."

By contrast, cataphoric highlighting "adds prominence to surprising or important **developments**. Cataphoric highlighting places the spotlight on a following speech or event, *not* on the added information itself." Its main pragmatic effect is to "add prominence to a following speech or event by creating a marked segment which serves to 'slow down' the pace of the narrative."

17. There are certain exceptions to this pattern. For example, presentational sentences contain no topic, as they consist entirely of discourse-new information. Likewise, sentences containing argument focus structures involve presupposed but non-topical information (Floor 2004, 161–62, 166). Normally, however, a sentence includes both elements. It should also be noted that focus information is not *necessarily* discourse-new; it can be already active information that is identified for a particular reason. Again, however, the normal pattern is that focus information is discourse-new.

narrative level down to the thematic paragraph, consists of a conglomeration of sentences, each textual unit likewise consists of two entities: an active discourse topic (or topics), as well as the most salient information about the topic(s) inferred from all the focus data presented in that unit (Floor 2004, 6).[18] Both of these aspects of the textual unit contain clues (i.e. theme traces) vital to tracking the development of a theme throughout the course of a narrative. In particular, the way in which topics are identified, activated, re-activated, and continued throughout a narrative is essential to comprehending theme.

Recalling Floor's definition and the three common types of theme traces in BH narrative, in the following evaluation of topic and focus, it will be necessary to take special note of such things as marked word-order (namely fronting and left-dislocation, but also, on occasion, right dislocation, etc.), the use of full noun phrases, relexicalization, and the use of explicit independent personal pronouns—all of which are vital to a proper assessment of theme (Floor 2004, 263). Such will prove particularly instrumental in the application of the theme tracing model (**Section 4.2**).

    3.6.1 Topic
    3.6.2 Focus

3.6.1 Topic

(1) *Definition.* Topic, basically defined, is the element of a proposition, which the proposition is about. It is "the presupposed referent to which the newly asserted information (the focus) adds" (Floor 2004, 73). In relation to a text, however, it is more appropriate to refer not to the topic of a textual unit, but rather to a *topic expression*. Floor (2004, 73) defines the difference, stating, "Topic is first and foremost a cognitive, pragmatic mental representation, whereas a topic expression is the surface manifestation of that mental representation in spoken and written discourse."

Because a topic expression always involves presupposed information, it is incapable of standing alone within a narrative. A topic must be introduced—identified—by, for example, a topicless presentation sentence (Floor 2004, 73). After a topic has been introduced, topic expressions may be used in two different types of sentences, *topic-comment sentences* (the most frequently-occurring information structure sentence type, usually

---

18. In most cases, there is also some link with the previous textual unit. The opening units of books beginning with discourse narrative (most notably Genesis) are obvious exceptions.

unmarked) and *scene-setting, all topic sentences.* Floor (2004, 74) explains the latter, noting, "Such a sentence (or better, clause) is always a subordinate clause, with no new information asserted. Tail-head constructions fall in this category, where information is repeated as part of the introduction to a subsequent section."

While all topic expressions involve presupposed information, Lambrecht cautions that not every piece of presupposed information is necessarily topical. In order to determine if a piece of presupposed information is genuinely topical, he advises that certain heuristic tests be applied: the *as-for* test and the *about* test. He gives examples of the application of both (Lambrecht 1994, 152):

"As for the children, they went to school," in which "children" is the topic.

"He said about the children that they went to school," in which "children" is the topic.

In the first example, where x is the topic, it can be said, "As for x, y is true." In the second example, where x is the topic, it can be understood, "About x, y is the case." In the instances in which both tests fail to identify a topic, it is to be assumed that the sentence is a marked focus structure (see **Section 3.6.2**). Nevertheless, where a topic expression exists, Lambrecht's tests serve well to rightly identify the topic.

(2) *Types of Topic Expressions.* Not all topic expressions are the same. Floor presents four different types of topics: *primary topics, secondary topics, tail topics,* and *topic frames.* Each of the four types of topic expressions is defined in accordance with the attributes it possesses. These defining attributes include *informational separation, predication, addressation,* and *frame setting.* Informational separation occurs where there is a clear separation in the information structure role of constituents x and y: x is topical and y is focal. Predication occurs where x is the semantic subject and y is the semantic predicate. Addressation occurs where the comment y is "about" topic x; y is relevant to x, regardless of grammatical or semantic relation. Finally, frame-setting occurs where x sets the frame for the interpretation of y (Floor 2004, 75).[19] Notably, various topic expressions may occur with unmarked word-order, marked word-order, or both.

(a) Primary Topics. A primary topic has informational separation in the sense that the sentence is about the primary topic; the focus structure asserts

---

19. For a more detailed examination of these attributes, see J. Jacobs' 2001 publication, "The Dimensions of Topic-Comment," *Linguistics* 39: 645–655.

something about it. It also possesses the attributes of predication (it is typically the semantic subject) and addressation (it is the address of new information). It is not, however, involved in frame-setting (Floor 2004, 78). Floor also notes, "A primary topic is discourse active and accessible, and generally so accessible that only pronominal reference to it is sufficient. Generally, the primary topic is a grammatical subject in biblical Hebrew" (2004, 79). He further argues that a primary topic 1) is either made identifiable in the context of the discourse, or its identity is known and assumed as known from the cognitive text-world; 2) is a referent that has been made discourse active; 3) remains active or continues, through a span of discourse; that is, it remains the topic of a sequence of sentences; and 4) is the pragmatically most salient topic, if there is more than one topic in a proposition (Floor 2004, 79–80).

Primary topics may occur in either unmarked word-order or marked word-order constructions. In unmarked word-order constructions, primary topics are often carried by the pronominal coding in verbs. In such cases, they tend to express both topic continuity and thematic continuity. The primary topic may also appear as a relexicalized referent (Floor 2004, 81).[20] In marked constructions, primary topics appear as nouns and may be fronted or even left-dislocated. Both syntactical configurations tend to indicate changes in topic, and may, at times, signal significant breaks in theme.

(b) *Secondary Topics.* Secondary topics are presupposed, discourse-active topic expressions that are less salient

---

20. Note also Floor's comments on primary topics in various grammatical constructions (2004, 81–83): 1) "In *indicative* clauses, when the subject is eclipsed, the subject is still signaled in the pronominal affix on the verb. Such pronominal referents are primary topics, already identifiable, discourse-active, and presupposed. When the subject is not eclipsed, it can either appear after the verb or in front of the verb." 2) "In *nominal* clauses with a *participle verbal-nominal*, the semantic agent of the verbal event is the primary topic. This semantic agent is either presupposed contextually or made explicit with a pronoun or nominal before the participle. The basic, unmarked word-order of such nominal clauses is *(subject)-participle-complement*... with the explicit subject optional." 3) "In *verbless* clauses, with the basic word-order of *subject-predicate*... the subject is the primary topic." 4) "In clauses with *imperative* verbs, the addressee is presupposed contextually. When an imperative clause is transformed into an indicative clause, the addressee becomes the subject." 5) "*Subject pronominals* are primary topic expressions. They are used as subjects in verbless clauses, or as optional topical expressions in we-X-qatal clauses." And 6) "*Vocatives* are topics as well. Vocatives make explicit the identity of the addressee. A vocative is an extra-clausal element referring to the primary topic or to the secondary topic, depending on the syntactic role of the addressee in the clause proper."

than primary topics and dependent upon the presence of a primary topic in the proposition in which they occur (Floor 2004, 88). They possess addressation, but no other attributes. Floor (2004, 88) argues that "secondary topics differ from primary topics by virtue of being part of the asserted or new information in a sentence, whereas primary topics cannot, by definition, be part of the focus domain." He further notes that secondary topics are always cognitively identifiable and are always discourse active, which implies that they are always cognitively presupposed. Additionally, they are always part of the comment in topic-comment sentence articulations and, grammatically, tend to be either direct objects or indirect objects—though not all objects are secondary topics (Floor 2004, 89–90).

Also like primary topics, secondary topics can appear in both unmarked word-order and marked word-order constructions. In unmarked word-order constructions, they may be expressed by either a fully lexicalized object, by an object suffixed to a verb, or by a suffixed direct object marker (Floor 2004, 90). Secondary topics may also, like primary topics, appear in fronted or left-dislocated constructions. Notably, they are sometimes more difficult to identify in marked word-order constructions since they are in a salient position. However, as long as there is a clearly identifiable primary topic, there is no reason for confusion (Floor 2004, 90–91). Significantly, left-dislocated secondary topics are often instrumental in indicating transitions in theme (Floor 2004, 93).

(c) *Tail Topics.* Tail topics are unique in that they always appear in right-dislocated constructions (Floor 2004, 93). They possess the attributes of information separation and addressation, and, like secondary topics, can appear only in topic-comment sentences along with a primary topic (Floor 2004, 93). Floor argues that tail topics serve to elaborate on primary topics either by providing some additional (but less salient) information about that topic, or by making explicit any information that is already cognitively accessible about that topic. As an example, such is often a function of lists given at the end of sentences (Floor 2004, 93–94).

(d) *Topic Frames.* A topic frame is a presupposed, topical referent that, true to its name, sets a frame for another topic, normally a primary topic. As Floor states, the primary topic is to be interpreted in terms of this framing topic (2004, 95). Typically, a more generic topic sets the frame for a more specific topic (Floor 2004, 96). By virtue of their role, they always appear in marked word-order constructions (i.e. either fronted or left-dislocated; Floor 2004, 97).

(3) *The Function of Topic Expressions in Relation to Theme.* Having clearly defined the various topic expressions in accordance with their attributes, it is necessary to examine their precise function, that is, how they are used in expressing the topic (and, to a degree, the theme) of a discourse narrative. In his study of the thematicity of the four types of topic expressions, Floor (2004, 262–63) sets forth five "information structure strategies" of discourse topics:

1.   Maintaining topic continuity
2.   Introducing topic discontinuity, which includes both topic promotion (from identifiable, inactive or semi-active to active), signaling a theme shift, and topic shift (from one active topic to another active topic), also signaling a theme shift
3.   Topic frame-setting
4.   Topic strengthening by means of topic contrasting (which may involve confirming the identity of a topic, restricting the identity of a topic, or comparing a pair of topics)
5.   Topic deictic orientation (situation or text-world frame-setting), signaling a theme shift

The remainder of this section is designed to demonstrate which topic expressions are used (and in what way they are used) to fulfill these five information structure strategies. In doing so, it will also explain the role of the various topic expressions in aiding in the determination of theme.

(a) Primary Topics. Although all four types of topic expressions can be used in a theme trace role, the primary topic expression is generally the most useful in the illumination of theme. It is the principal carrier of theme and is thematic in both marked and unmarked structures (Floor 2004, 264).

As Floor summarizes, primary topics are used for "topic continuity, topic promotion, topic shift, topic theme announcing, and topic contrasting" (2004, 265). Used for topic continuity, the primary topic is generally introduced by a full noun phrase and then carried by the pronominal coding in the verb. (Although, as already mentioned, overencoding may be used for the purpose of highlighting, and topic continuity may be both signaled and strengthened through relexicalization. Furthermore, in instances of scene change, relexicalization will be employed despite the continuance of the primary topic [Floor 2004, 266, 279].) Used for topic promotion, the primary topic activates a referent (i.e. promotes the referent from merely identifiable or semi-active to discourse active), which simultaneously involves a shift in theme (Floor 2004, 269). Similarly, used for topic shifting, the primary topic signals a new development in the theme of a discourse narrative by transitioning from one discourse-active topic to another. Such a function often occurs in a marked word-order structure (Floor 2004, 272). On the other hand, topic strengthening by means of topic contrasting (which, as previously noted, may be accomplished by confirming the identity of a topic, restricting the identity of a topic, or comparing a pair of topics) involves not a shift in theme, but rather the increase of the thematic status of a given referent (Floor 2004, 275–76).

In view of the fact that this study concerns the Flood narrative, which spans roughly from chapter 6 to chapter 9 of Genesis, it is worth considering Floor's analysis of the rhetorical and syntactic devices used to carry primary topics in Genesis 1–25. He found that the typical devices are, in order of frequency: 1) affixed pronominal references in unmarked word-order clauses, 2) relexicalized nominal references in unmarked word-order clauses, 3) fronted explicit pronouns (often used in signaling a topic shift), 4) fronted/left-dislocated nouns (commonly used for primary topic shift in marked $w^e qatal$ clauses), and 5) double fronted/left-dislocated constructions (used for topic shift; Floor 2004, 279–282). This, then, is a preview of the types of rhetorical and syntactic devices used to carry primary topics that will be encountered in the Flood narrative.

(b) Secondary Topics. Secondary topics, though less significant than primary topics for use in identifying theme, can nonetheless be theme traces. As Floor observes, "When a secondary topic is continuously mentioned, lexicalized or pronominalized in one episode, it gains strength cognitively" (2004, 282). Like primary topics, a secondary topic may be used for topic continuity, in which its "thematic importance increases to the degree that it does not have significant competition besides the primary topic, and to the degree that it is recurring" (Floor 2004, 283). Secondary topics may also be used for topic promotion and topic shifting (mainly through the use of fronting and left-dislocation), both of which constitute shifts in theme, regardless of how minor they may be (Floor 2004, 284–85). Additionally, they may, like primary topics, be used for topic strengthening by means of topic contrasting (Floor 2004, 288).

(c) **Tail Topics.** Floor notes that the thematic role of tail topics is rather unclear. Occurring only rarely, tail topics are often used only for elaboration or to express an afterthought, though they can serve to reinforce the primary topic. In such cases, a tail topic may be thematic (Floor 2004, 290).

(d) **Topic Frames.** Also occurring only rarely, topic frames are used simply to set a frame for another topic (normally a primary topic). In doing so, they can serve as theme traces "in the sense that they cognitively strengthen the topical referent they provide the frame for" (Floor 2004, 290).[21]

3.6.2 Focus

(1) *Definition.* A definition of focus is somewhat more elusive than that of topic. Because not all sentences possess a topic expression, focus cannot be regarded simply as the complement of topic (Lambrecht 1994, 206). However, focus may be defined as:

> [A]n element of information that is ADDED TO, rather than superimposed on, the pragmatic information. . . . The focus of a proposition is seen as the element of information whereby the presupposition and the assertion DIFFER from each other. The focus is that portion of the proposition which cannot be taken for granted at the time of speech. It is the UNPREDICTABLE or pragmatically NON-RECOVERABLE element in an utterance. The focus is what makes an utterance into an assertion. (Lambrecht 1994, 206–07)

Of course, as in relation to topic, focus refers most strictly to a cognitive, pragmatic mental representation; it is expressed using a *focus structure*. Because focus structures involve newly-asserted information, they can best be identified within a sentence by first isolating the topic expression (see Lambrecht's heuristic tests in **Section 3.6.1**). Further criteria for the identification of the different kinds of focus structures are given below.

(2) *Types of Focus Structures.* Just as there are a variety of different types of topic expressions, so too there are multiple types of focus structures: *predicate focus structures, sentence focus structures,* and *argument focus structures.*

---

21. In addition to these four categories of topic expressions, note also *topical deictic orientations.* Not strictly a type of topic expression in their own right, but more precisely a function of topic, they express presupposed information often useful in tracing theme. A topic deictic orientation (also referred to as "text-world frame") is "a presupposed point of departure basic to the subsequent discourse" which functions to "*frame* the theme in the sense of setting its spatio-temporal parameters" (Floor 2004, 293). Not all deictic orientations are topical (some contain brand new information which is, by definition, a part of focus). Deictic orientations are considered topical "when the information contained in such constructions is cognitively recoverable from the context" (Floor 2004, 293).

(a) **Predicate Focus Structures.** As Floor observes, predicate focus structures are the most common in BH narrative and are used in simple topic-comment sentence articulations. The comment portion of such a sentence may involve only the predicate (with the subject, naturally, as the primary topic), or may comprise the predicate plus its complements (Floor 2004, 154).[22]

With the discussion of predicate focus structures, it is necessary to mention the principle of *end-weight*, which may be described as follows:

> [T]he feature of some focus structures that is in accordance with the pragmatic principle that new information tends to be moved towards the end of a sentence. End-weight is an overlay to predicate focus or even sentence focus structures, where one specific constituent right at the end of a sentence receives the additional element of what can be called *focus weight*. (Floor 2004, 182)

The role of end-weight in signaling important macro-words that contribute to an understanding of theme will be discussed later.

(b) **Sentence Focus Structures.** Sentence focus structures, as the name suggests, occur in sentences without a topic expression in which all of the sentence's information is focal. Besides the absence of a topic, sentence focus structures are identifiable by a number of factors including, but not limited to, discontinuity with the preceding discourse, a sentence subject that is irregular (either syntactically or semantically), and—often—irregular or marked word order (Floor 2004, 160). Floor remarks, "Sentence focus structures provide unexpected and discontinuous information, out-of-the-blue information that redirects the thematic development onto a new course" (2004, 305). He further notes, "Sentence focus will sometimes be hard to identify, and one way to reach a sentence focus conclusion is to eliminate any possibility of a predicate focus topic-comment sentence as well as an identificational argument focus structure. If it is not one of the first two, it follows that the proposition may have a sentence focus structure" (Floor 2004, 161).

---

22. Floor further differentiates between "broad predicate focus" and "narrow predicate focus" (2004, 155–59). The former "is where both the verb as the predicator, and its complement(s) are newly-asserted information." By contrast, the latter "is where only the verb is newly-asserted information, or where the predicate does not contain any complements." Though such distinction is important to linguistic studies, it is a less significant matter with regard to theme tracing than are other aspects of information structure.

Sentence focus structures can be further classified as either event/state-reporting sentences or participant presentation sentences. Event-reporting sentences occur in both marked and unmarked word-order constructions, contain a subject that is not presupposed, and often appear at the beginning of textual units to redirect the theme, signal a change in scene and participants, or provide setting or background information (Floor 2004, 161). State-reporting sentences tend to be negative sentences and share information on the state of something that is important to the understanding of the remainder of the discourse narrative (Floor 2004, 162). Participant presentation sentences serve to activate participants in a discourse narrative. Significantly, the *tol^dot* statement in Genesis 6:9 is a prime example of a presentational sentence (Floor 2004, 163).[23]

(c) Argument Focus Structures. Floor (2004, 166) defines the argument of a proposition as "any non-predicate constituent, be it a subject, an object, an indirect object, a spatio-temporal adjunct, a manner adjunct, or qualitative adjunct."[24] Accordingly, argument focus structures appear where the focus is carried by the argument portion of a sentence. Argument focus structures appear in identificational sentences opposite presupposed but non-topical information and almost always occur in marked word-order sentence arrangements (Floor 2004, 166–68). The chief factor which differentiates argument focus structures from the more common predicate focus structures is that predicate focus structures have the verb in focus. In argument focus structures, by contrast, the verb (if applicable) is part of the presupposed information. Admittedly, argument focus structures may prove challenging; nonetheless, Floor (2004, 172) demonstrates that they can be extremely important in that they, as a sub-function of their role in identification, may serve to illuminate newly-asserted theme-announcing macro-words (which occur only in fronted sentence arrangements).

There are a variety of examples of argument focus structures in BH. Perhaps most notably, with the exception of rhetorical questions, all questions asking "Who?" "What?" "When?" "Where?" "Why? and "How?"

---

23. The particle הנה is instrumental for either 1) focusing attention *"on events that are surprising or unexpected for the person addressed or the characters in a story"* or 2) presenting either speakers or "someone or something as available at the moment of speaking" (van der Merwe, Naude, and Kroeze 1999, 330). Significantly, the particle הנה can be used in (and may aid in signaling) sentence focus structures.

24. In strict linguistics terms, only a subject, object, and indirect object are arguments, whereas adjuncts are not considered arguments. However, for the purpose of this chapter, Floor's broader definition will be employed.

are argument focus structures, as they presuppose all information except, of course, the interrogative word (Floor 2004, 169).[25] Other instances of argument focus structures include subjects, objects, prepositional phrases, and spatio-temporal adjuncts fronted before presupposed, but non-topical, information (2004, 169–171).[26]

It is important to note the role that *focus particles* play in marking certain argument focus structures. Floor states that focus particles, which may occur anywhere in a sentence without having an effect on word order, serve to mark their subsequent constituents as focal. Van der Merwe, Naude, and Kroeze (1999, 311) explain: "They are called focus particles because they place a particular focus on the entity or clause that follows them. An outstanding feature of focus particles is that their meaning always indicates that the referent to which they refer *is an addition to or limitation of another referent*." The words אַךְ (indicating limitation), אַף (indicating addition), אֶפֶס (indicating limitation), גַּם (indicating addition), בִּלְתִּי (indicating exclusion), and רַק (indicating limitation) are all considered focus particles (Van der Merwe, Naude, and Kroeze 1999, 311–18).

(3) *The Function of Focus Structures in Relation to Theme.* Like topic expressions, focus structures can be instrumental in illuminating theme. Also like topic expressions, focus structures are employed to accomplish a variety of information structure strategies. Floor (2004, 298–99), building on the work of Lambrecht, recognizes the following functions:

1.   Commenting on topics
2.   Presenting brand-new referents or presenting inactive but identifiable referents
3.   Reporting events that are discontinuous to the flow of the narrative, redirecting the thematic development, and reporting events or states that support the theme: backgrounded anterior or simultaneous events or states

---

25. By virtue of the same reasoning, all direct answers to such questions also contain argument focus structures; they presuppose all information except that which specifically answers the "Who?" "What?" "When?" "Where?" "Why? or "How?"

26. Given the rather difficult nature of this concept, it is useful to provide an example with commentary by Floor. A clear example of an argument focus structure appears in Genesis 24:7 (a fronted prepositional phrase): "To your offspring I will give this land." On this, Floor (2004, 170) writes, "The primary topic is the subject 'I,' meaning God, and the rest of the clause is the predicate. 'Give this land' is presupposed from the context. The fronted argument 'to your offspring' is the focus domain. The fronted element also has the focalised peak of contrastiveness as overlay, contrastiveness here meaning exhaustive listing (or restricted identification): 'to your offspring and them only.'"

4.   Identifying referents and deictic text-world frames
5.   Framing the theme (i.e. announcing what will be thematic)
6.   Identifying theme-announcing macro-words

It is worth noting that, although they are not as obviously thematic as, for example, primary topics, the various focus structures all have some bearing on theme.

(a) Predicate Focus Structures. As the most common type of focus structure, predicate focus structures serve chiefly to comment on primary topics. In the more frequently-occurring unmarked word-order constructions, it tends to have little to do with theme. By contrast, in marked word-order constructions, predicate focus structures tend to be theme traces, serving to stress information which may prove important (Floor 2004, 299). Regardless of markedness, however, end-weight may be used in predicate focus structures to point directly to thematic material (Floor 2004, 301–04). Admittedly, it is largely a matter of context as to whether a word or phrase involved in end-weight is thematic (Floor 2004, 302). However, if particular attention is drawn to a word through the use of end-weight, it is worth investigating as potentially thematic, especially if any other factors in the information structure point to that possibility.[27]

(b) Sentence Focus Structures. As mentioned previously, sentence focus structures may be further classified as either participant presentation sentences or event/state-reporting sentences. The former type, not surprisingly, serve to identify brand new participants. The latter may function to report events that are discontinuous with a discourse narrative's flow of thought, or to report events or states containing background information pertinent to a discourse narrative's storyline (Floor 2004, 305). As Floor points out, there is some degree of overlap between these two types of sentences (2004, 307).

The thematic significance of presentational sentences resides squarely in their role of identifying and promoting new referents. As Floor (2004, 308) states, there are five notable syntactic devices that are employed to achieve this function: 1) verbless clauses, 2) הָיָה clauses, 3) וַיְהִי clauses, 4) תּוֹלְדֹת statements, and 5) הִנֵּה + noun + participle clauses. Because of these syntactic features, presentational sentences are usually difficult to miss.

---

27. Besides end-weight, Floor (2004, 332) states, "Another configuration in commenting sentences is irregular post-verbal word-order, where a specific focus peak is placed on a constituent in an irregular position." For the purpose of tracing the theme of the Flood narrative, however, this study will focus mainly on the more common and more obvious end-weight.

Similarly, the thematic significance of event/state-reporting sentences is directly intertwined with their ability to abruptly introduce wholly new information to the discourse narrative. In doing so, they automatically redirect the theme. Such sentences may feature topicless unmarked word-order *wayyiqtol* clauses. More often, however, marked constructions are employed: *wᵉqatal* clauses, הִנֵּה + *wᵉqatal* clauses, or negative *wᵉqatal* clauses (Floor 2004, 312–16).[28] Naturally, in analyzing such constructions, the use of context is important in determining if all the information they contain is focal.

(c) **Argument Focus Structures.** Despite admitting the need for further research, Floor (2004, 321) contends that, "argument focus structures are normally part of the thematic core of an episode." As mentioned already, argument focus structures are used for two related pragmatic functions: the identification of brand new referents and the illumination of theme-announcing macro-words. As for the role of such structures in aiding in the determination of theme, Floor (2004, 321) argues, "The thematicity of argument focus structures is to be found in the type of sentence articulation in which argument focus structures are found, namely in identificational sentences." The role of focus particles has already been demonstrated. However, it should be noted that fronting may also be used for the purpose of marking identificational argument focus structures.

Where argument focus structures are used specifically to illuminate a theme-announcing macro-word, they cognitively function to announce or frame the theme for the subsequent discourse. In such instances, certain syntactic features may be involved. These features include fronting, cataphoric pronouns (i.e. pronouns that look to the subsequent discourse for their reference), and the prophetic formula כֹּה־ (Floor 2004, 329–332).[29]

---

28. Notably, event/state-reporting sentences are also used to strengthen a topic by sharing background information. For this purpose, anterior *wᵉqatal* clauses are typically used. Additionally, for the sake of reporting simultaneous states or events, both verbless clauses and הנה + participle clauses are commonly employed (Floor 2004, 318–320).

29. Floor's discussion of argument focus structures was considerably more complicated than that on most (if not all) other aspects of information structure. Accordingly, rather than choosing to summarize the totality of his discussion (which would virtually require the duplication of his work), the following application of Floor's model to the Flood narrative takes note of his own identification of argument focus structures. Conveniently, Floor (2004, 170–72) lists a number of the argument focus structures which occur in the book of Genesis, some of which appear within the parameters of the Flood narrative (Gn 6:9, 19; 7:11, 13, 20; 8:5, 6, 12–14; 9:2, 13, 17, 18).

3.7 *Summary: From Topic, Focus, and Theme Traces to Text Segmentation*

The preceding section of the chapter, which has been largely a summary of Floor's masterful work, shows that an understanding of the information structure of a discourse narrative is imperative to fully comprehending its theme. Clearly, not all parts of the information structure are equally instrumental to a determination of theme. For example, primary topic tends to be the major carrier of theme, whereas proportionately fewer theme traces are found in the other topic expressions and focus structures. Nevertheless, as this overview of topic, focus, and theme has demonstrated, all parts of the information structure are useful to some degree in determining the theme of a discourse narrative. Accordingly, an analysis of the entire information structure of the Flood narrative is necessary in order to properly segment the text and thereby determine the potential locations of chronological disjunction.

By taking into account the theme traces found in both the topic expressions and focus structures contained within the text, the following section of this chapter will serve to cogently demonstrate the textual divisions in the Flood narrative. In examining the text, an inventory will be taken of instances of fronting, left- and right-dislocation, end weight, explicit pronouns, focus particles, and spatio-temporal orientations. It will also note recurring topics and potential macro-words. Using these syntactic features as a starting point for the investigation of the information structure, the following section of this chapter will proceed to determine both the boundaries and the theme of each textual unit.

4. An Implementation of Floor's Segmentation Model on the Flood Narrative

Having defined both topic and focus, and having also laid out a summary explanation of how the theme traces found in each are involved in illuminating the theme of a discourse narrative, it is possible to apply Floor's four-step model of theme tracing to the text of the Flood narrative. Before proceeding, a brief explanation of each of the four steps is in order. This overview will serve to link the somewhat abstract, conceptual material discussed in **Section 3** with the practical application of the model to follow.

4.1. An Overview of the Four Steps of Theme-tracing

4.2. An Application of the Four Steps of Theme-tracing to the Flood Narrative

4.1 *An Overview of the Four Steps of Theme-tracing*

Floor's approach to tracing theme within BH narrative (and thereby being able to segment the text) hinges upon two main assumptions. The first, which has already been addressed in this study's introduction, is that a discourse narrative has layers of themes, with more local themes embedded in more expansive themes just as smaller units of text are embedded within larger units. The second is that the lower a unit of text resides in the discourse segment hierarchy, the easier it is to determine its theme, on a relative scale (Floor 2004, 256). The determination of the theme of a narrative, or even an episode, is often a far more difficult task because of the mass of text it contains and the (sometimes divergent) variety of local themes contained within. Accordingly, as Floor summarizes (2004, 256–57), the four-step model of theme tracing can be outlined as follows:

4.1.1 Step 1: Identification of Theme Traces
4.1.2 Step 2: Analysis of the Information Structure of the Theme Traces
4.1.3 Step 3: Determination of the Thematic Units
4.1.4 Step 4: Determination of the Theme
4.1.5 Summary

4.1.1 Step 1: Identification of Theme Traces

The first step involves the identification of any potential theme traces, which may appear in the form of either 1) syntactically marked configurations in the text (e.g. fronting and left-dislocation, as well as, to a lesser degree, right-dislocation, end weight, explicit pronouns, focus particles, and spatio-temporal orientations) or 2) syntactically unmarked but still cognitively prominent configurations, like relexicalization or repetition (i.e. factors that indicate recurring concepts and may signal prominence and coherence).

4.1.2 Step 2: Analysis of the Information Structure of the Theme Traces

The second step involves the analysis of the information structure of the aforementioned potential theme traces and a determination of what information structure strategies are involved. As Floor states, one must "analyze these potential theme traces in terms of the information structure of the proposition it is part of, and in its cognitive context, [and using this] determine (1) the information structure of the relevant propositions and (2) the cognitive strategies it is used for in that specific context" (2004, 256).

4.1.3 Step 3: Determination of the Thematic Units

The third step involves the determination of the individual thematic units "by means of the information structure strategies of the theme traces, as well as by means of text-world orientations and topic continuation spans (for instance, the repetition of topics)" (Floor 2004, 256). This is, simply stated, the application of theme tracing to text segmentation. Based upon the information structure strategies revealed by the theme traces, it can be determined where one thematic unit ends and where another begins. In the application of this model to the Flood narrative in the following section, the discourse segment hierarchy will be mapped down to the level of the scene (to map out each individual thematic paragraph would prove cumbersome in view of the great bulk of text to be covered). Notably, for the unique purposes of this study, the illustration of the divisions between scenes will be sufficient to demonstrate locations of potential chronological disjunction.

4.1.4 Step 4: Determination of the Theme

The final step involves the determination of the local theme of each textual unit by identifying its topic framework and focus content. In the application of this model to the Flood narrative the themes of the various scenes will be presented first; the study will then use the local themes to build upward to the determination of the more expansive themes.

4.1.5 Summary

For the sake of simplicity, in the application of this model to the text of the Flood narrative, step 1 will be discussed first. Steps 2–4 will then be discussed together as they relate to each unit of text. In the interest of space, not every feature of the text's information structure will be discussed in detail; rather, this study will concentrate primarily (though not exclusively) on those features involved in demarcating the boundaries of the various textual units so as to aid in the segmentation of the text and help facilitate the study of the Flood's chronology.

4.2 An Application of the Four Steps of Theme-tracing to the Flood Narrative

Having discussed the role of the various constituents of information structure, as well as the nature and purpose of theme traces, and having also set forth the four steps involved in theme tracing, it is time to apply Floor's model to the text of the Flood narrative.

This necessitates, of course, that the exact parameters of the Flood narrative be clearly determined. As previously mentioned, there is some discrepancy over the exact location of both the beginning and end of the narrative. The earliest possible beginning for the narrative is Genesis 5:28, in which the birth of Noah is recorded. Similarly, the latest possible ending for the narrative is in Genesis 9:29, which records Noah's death. The question then arises, however, whether the material in Genesis 5:28–6:8 and 9:18–29 can rightly be considered a part of the Flood narrative. The material preceding Genesis 6:9, while serving well as a background to the worldwide catastrophe, has little to do with the Flood itself. Correspondingly, the second half of Genesis 9, which records the drunkenness of Noah, bears minimal connection with the Flood. Based upon his paragraph divisions, Cassuto (1997, 30) believed the narrative to span from Genesis 6:9 to 9:17. This opinion is seconded, on the grounds of noted textual divisions, by Robert E. Longacre (1979, 93).

Others have expressed a desire to expand the parameters of the narrative. John H. Sailhamer (2009, 270), for example, argues that the narrative runs from Genesis 6:5 to 9:27, bracketed by the genealogical structure evident in Genesis 5:28–32 and 9:28–29.[30] However, as Longacre points out (1979, 73), it does not seem prudent to propose boundaries for a narrative that overlap Genesis' own *tol'dot* structure (which, in all other instances in Genesis, appears to mark clear textual boundaries).[31] He further notes that such does not make good sense in terms of the structure of the Flood narrative itself. As previously demonstrated, the Flood narrative manifests an incredibly elaborate chiastic structure spanning from Genesis 6:9 to 9:19, with the beginning and end marked specifically by reference to Noah and his sons

---

30. The reason for Sailhamer's seemingly odd division is his underlying belief that the Flood narrative (along with a distinct section of introductory material; i.e. Gn 6:1–4) came to be inserted into the *tol'dot* of Adam by the author/compiler of Genesis. In support of his argument, he contends that the framework of the genealogy in Genesis 5 is carried over into chapter 9 in the record of Noah's death. It should be noted, however, that similarity in form does not automatically support this notion; in fact, the orthodox position of the authorship and unity of Genesis can easily account for the masterful overlapping of multiple structures (i.e. the *tol'dot* structure and the genealogical structure). Sailhamer's view, unfortunately, borders very closely on various theories of source redaction proposed in non-orthodox circles. Summarily, it is to be excluded by the presuppositions governing this study (note **Section 1.3**).

31. Floor's study backs this observation. He writes, "The תלדת statement functions as a title statement for what follows and is as such thematic" (Floor 2004, 311). Accordingly, *tol'dot* should be regarded as the introduction to a thematic unit. The fact that it is the highest level of syntactical division in Genesis is a good indicator that it is likely indicative of a substantial thematic break on the level of a narrative (rather than, for example, a mere scene or thematic paragraph). See also on this issue the work of Jason DeRouchie (2013).

(cf. Wenham 1978, 339). While there seems to be some parallelism between the events preceding and following these boundaries (e.g. Lamech's prayer in Genesis 5:29 and the indication of Lamech's hope realized in Genesis 9:20), they do not appear to fit naturally within the chiastic structure. To force the chiasm beyond its obvious limits would prove both arbitrary and artificial.

This being stated, there clearly arises a question of what to do with Genesis 9:20–29. In view of Floor's definition of the various levels constituting the discourse segment hierarchy, it would appear that this textual unit is too short to be a narrative in its own right. Furthermore, it probably ought not be included in the next narrative (beginning in chapter 10), due to, among other factors, the presence of a *toľdot* statement in Genesis 10:1. What a brief overview of the information structure of Genesis 6–9 reveals, however, is that the narrative does indeed appear to span the entirety of Genesis 6:9–9:29, with key thematic elements bridging the break between Genesis 9:19 and 9:20. Furthermore, it seems that it is most specifically Noah (and, to a lesser degree, his immediate descendants), not the Flood, which binds the narrative together. Taken as a whole, this "Noah narrative" (of which the Flood account is a major component), spans multiple episodes. The Flood account, either directly or indirectly, stretches across all but the last of these episodes. Simply stated, through the use of an expansive chiastic structure, the Flood closely binds together Genesis 6:9–9:19 without severing the final episode from the narrative.

This study therefore proposes Genesis 6:9 and 9:19 as marking, respectively, the beginning and end of the Flood account. These boundaries are only slightly divergent from those delineated by Cassuto and Longacre, and correspond precisely with those proposed by T. D. Alexander (2002, 134–35).[32] Summarily stated, these boundaries recognize the extent of the account's own structure and avoid crossing any obvious syntactical divisions (namely the *toľdot* statement of Genesis 6:9). Moreover, as far as this study is concerned, these boundaries contain within them all of the account's chronologically relevant information. Accordingly, the following multi-step analysis will probe the information structure and theme of Genesis 6:9–9:19, recognizing that the episodes and scenes contained therein do not constitute a narrative in its entirety, but do make up a sufficiently broad basis for this chapter's investigation of the chronology of the Flood.

---

32. Significantly, Alexander (2002, 135) contends that the episode contained in the second half of Genesis 9 begins with the introduction of Noah as a "man of the soil" in 9:20 rather than with the relexicalization of Noah and his sons in 9:18.

4.2.1 Step 1: Identification of Theme Traces

4.2.2 Steps 2–4: Analysis of the Information Structure to Determination of Theme

4.2.1 Step 1: Identification of Theme Traces

The following marked word-order constructions are noted in Genesis 6:9–9:19[33]:

- Clauses containing fronting or left-dislocation in 6:9 (2×), 12, 13 (2×), 14, 15, 16 (4×), 17 (2×), 19 (2×), 20, 21 (2×), 22 (2×); 7:1, 2, 4 (2×), 5, 6, 8–9, 10, 11 (2×), 13, 16, 19, 20, 22; 8:5 (2×), 6, 8, 11, 13, 14, 17, 19, 21, 22; 9:2 (2×), 3 (2×), 4, 5 (3×), 6 (2×), 7, 9, 12, 13, 17 and 19.[34]

- Clauses containing right dislocation in 6:18; 7:1, 13–14, 15, 21, 23; 8:16, 18 and 9:10.

- Clauses containing end-weight in 8:4; 9:2, 3 and 12.

The following explicit pronouns are noted in Genesis 6:9–9:19[35]:

- אֲנִי/אָנֹכִי in 6:17; 7:4; 9:9 and 12

---

33. In order to better analyze the text of the Flood account in a search for marked word-order constructions, this study relied, in part, upon the work of Barry Bandstra (2008, 350–505).

34. As mentioned previously, fronting and left-dislocation differ syntactically. However, for the purposes of this study, they are listed together because they function in similar ways to illuminate theme. Identification of clauses in which either fronting or left-dislocation occurred was achieved primarily through an evaluation of morphology. *Wayyiqtol* and *wᵉqatal* verbs are, by nature, clause initial and thus outside of consideration. Similarly, infinitives need not be considered by virtue of the fact that they may not be used independently of the main verb of a clause. *Yiqtol* and *qatal* verbs, by contrast, occur in disjunctive clauses, which by definition have a fronted element. Participles, likewise, normally occur in clauses where the subject is fronted (van der Merwe, Naude, and Kroeze 1999, 339). In the Flood account, nearly all the instances of fronting and left-dislocation occur in clauses containing *qatal* or *yiqtol* verb forms, or participles (on rare occasion, imperatives were also fronted). It must be noted that negatives, subordinated conjunctions and discourse markers (namely הִנֵּה as well as לָכֵן and עַתָּה) may occupy the preverbal field, but are not considered fronted constituents (van der Merwe, Naude, and Kroeze 1999, 338). Furthermore, it should be stressed that not all cases of fronting or left-dislocation are thematic. Many of the cases listed involve such things as fronted prepositions, demonstrative pronouns, or relative pronouns. As previously demonstrated, the fronted or left-dislocated elements that are of primary importance to determining theme are generally subjects and objects. For the sake of completeness, however, all instances have been listed.

35. Searches for the lexical features listed in this section were conducted using the electronic version of *Biblia Hebraica Stuttgartensia* with Westminster 4.2 Morphology as it appears in Logos Bible Software 3.

- אַתָּה in 6:18, 21; 7:1 and 8:16

- אַתֶּם in 9:7

- הוּא in 9:3 and 18

- הֵמָּה in 7:14

- הוּא in 7:2

The following focus particles are noted in Genesis 6:9–9:19:

- אַךְ in 7:23; 9:4 and 5

- גַּם in 7:3

The following words associated with presentational clauses are noted in Genesis 6:9–9:19:

- הָיָה in 6:9 and 7:6

- וַיְהִי in 7:10, 12, 17; 8:6 and 13

- תּוֹלְדֹת in 6:9[36]

The following recurring topics and potential macro-words are noted in Genesis 6:9–9:19:

- God (אֱלֹהִים) occurs 16 times (6:9, 11, 12, 13, 22; 7:9, 16; 8:1 [2×], 15; 9:1, 6, 8, 12, 16 and 17. Additionally, the Tetragrammaton (יְהוָה) occurs six times (7:1, 5, 16; 8:20 and 21 [2×]).

- Noah (נֹחַ) occurs thirty-one times (6:9 [4×], 10, 13, 22; 7:1, 5, 6, 7, 9 [2×], 11, 13 [3×], 15, 23; 8:1, 6, 11, 13, 15, 18, 20; 9:1, 8, 17, 18 and 19).

- Land/earth (אֶרֶץ) occurs forty-five times (6:11 [2×], 12 [2×], 13 [2×], 17 [2×]; 7:3, 4, 6, 10, 12, 14, 17 [2×], 18, 19, 21 [2×], 23, 24; 8:1, 3, 7, 9, 11, 13, 14, 17 [3×], 19, 22; 9:1, 2, 7, 10 [2×], 11, 13, 14, 16, 17 and 19). Additionally, ground (אֲדָמָה) occurs eight times (6:20; 7:4, 8, 23; 8:8, 13, 21; 9:2).

- Water (מַיִם) occurs twenty-one times (6:17; 7:6, 7, 10, 17, 18 [2×], 19, 20, 24; 8:1, 3 [2×], 5, 7, 8, 9, 11, 13; 9:11 and 15).

---

36. Additionally, in 6:13, 17 and 9:9, the particle הִנֵּה occurs with a first person, common, singular pronominal suffix followed by a participle. Such a construction achieves very nearly the same purpose as the הִנֵּה + noun + participle constructions discussed by Floor (2004, 311).

- Ark (תֵבָה) occurs twenty-six times (6:14 [2×], 15, 16 [2×], 18, 19; 7:1, 7, 9, 13, 15, 17, 18, 23; 8:1, 4, 6, 9 [2×], 10, 13, 16, 19; 9:10 and 18).

- Flood (*Mabbûl*, מַבּוּל) occurs eight times (6:17; 7:6, 7, 10, 17; 9:11 [2×] and 15).

- Day (יוֹם) occurs sixteen times (7:4 [2×], 10, 11 [2×], 12, 13, 17, 24; 8:3, 4, 6, 10, 12, 14 and 22).

- Flesh (בָּשָׂר) occurs fourteen times (6:12, 13, 17, 19; 7:15, 16, 21; 8:17; 9:4, 11, 15 [2×], 16 and 17).

- Covenant (בְּרִית) occurs eight times (6:18; 9:9, 11, 12, 13, 15, 16, 17).

In addition, at least a dozen text-world deictic, spatio-temporal orientations are noted throughout the course of the Flood account (Gn 7:10, 11 [cf. verse 6], 13, 20; 8:3, 4, 5, 6, 10, 12, 13 and 14).[37]

4.2.2 Steps 2–4: Analysis of the Information Structure to Determination of Theme

EPISODE 1, SCENE 1: GENESIS 6:9–10[38]

אֵלֶּה תּוֹלְדֹת נֹחַ נֹחַ אִישׁ צַדִּיק תָּמִים הָיָה בְּדֹרֹתָיו אֶת־הָאֱלֹהִים
הִתְהַלֶּךְ־נֹחַ: [10]וַיּוֹלֶד נֹחַ שְׁלֹשָׁה בָנִים אֶת־שֵׁם אֶת־חָם וְאֶת־יָפֶת:

[9]These are the generations of Noah: Noah was a righteous man; he was unmixed [or *blameless*] in his generation. With God Noah walked. [10]And Noah fathered three sons: Shem, Ham, and Japheth.

The initial scene of the Flood account serves to introduce the main characters involved in the remainder of the narrative. "Noah" (נֹחַ), while still discourse active from the final scene of the previous episode, is relexicalized four times, thereby leaving no doubt regarding the significance of Noah as a theme trace in this scene. The initial *tol*ᵉ*dot* statement functions as a presentational sentence and promotes Noah as the centermost character of the following narrative.[39] The brief verbless clause, followed by the fronted prepositional phrase in the argument focus structure in the middle of verse 9, draw attention to Noah's unimpeachable uprightness. The fronted construction at

37. The majority of these text-world deictic, spatio-temporal orientations are fronted in argument focus structures (Floor 2004, 171, n. 117). Additionally, there is a temporal clause preceding the verb in the poetic statement of 8:22.

38. Hebrew text is taken from the electronic version of *Biblia Hebraica Stuttgartensia* with Westminster 4.2 Morphology as it appears in Logos Bible Software 3. Translation is that of the author.

39. A noted departure from most other *tol*ᵉ*dot* statements in Genesis, the *tol*ᵉ*dot* of Noah actually concerns itself more with Noah himself than with his descendants.

the end of verse 9 likewise presents God (אֱלֹהִים) as the other main character of the narrative. It can therefore be expected that both Noah and God will be mentioned again and that the following drama will revolve primarily around them. Verse 10 contains an unmarked word-order sentence, used for topic continuity (i.e. of Noah, the primary topic), while also introducing Noah's sons through a common predicate focus structure. The boundaries of this scene are clear, being marked at the beginning by the *toľdot* statement, and at the end by the next verse's abrupt transition away from Noah to the state of the world at large. Accordingly, the local theme of this unit can be stated as: *The righteousness of Noah in his generation and his fathering of Shem, Ham, and Japheth.*

EPISODE 1, SCENE 2: GENESIS 6:11–12

וַתִּשָּׁחֵת הָאָרֶץ לִפְנֵי הָאֱלֹהִים וַתִּמָּלֵא הָאָרֶץ חָמָס: ¹²וַיַּרְא אֱלֹהִים אֶת־הָאָרֶץ וְהִנֵּה נִשְׁחָתָה כִּי־הִשְׁחִית כָּל־בָּשָׂר אֶת־דַּרְכּוֹ עַל־הָאָרֶץ: ס

¹¹Now the earth had become corrupt before God, and the earth filled with violence. ¹²And God saw the earth, and it had become corrupt because all flesh had corrupted their way on the earth.

This short scene, devoid of any notable marked constructions, contains four important macro-words that are useful theme traces: earth (אֶרֶץ; 4×), corrupt (שׁחת; 3×), flesh (בָּשָׂר; 1×), and God (2×). The first mention of "earth" in verse 11 marks a shift in both topic and theme. Significantly, the recurring relexicalization of "earth" stands in contrast to the four-fold mention of Noah in the previous scene. Whereas everything described about Noah was positive, the earth is described in indisputably negative terms. The use of the discourse marker הִנֵּה in verse 12 only acts to reinforce this fact. (This, coupled with the corruption of "all flesh," leads to the expectation of the judgment that is yet to unfold.) A minor topic shift occurs mid-scene, with God (the secondary topic in verse 11), promoted to primary topic in the beginning of verse 12. This scene clearly begins with the brief shift in both topic and theme away from Noah in verse 11 and concludes with another shift in theme in verse 13, as the narrative returns to God's interaction with Noah. The local theme of this scene is plainly evident: *The total corruption of earth in the sight of God.*

EPISODE 1, SCENE 3: GENESIS 6:13–16

וַיֹּאמֶר אֱלֹהִים לְנֹחַ קֵץ כָּל־בָּשָׂר בָּא לְפָנַי כִּי־מָלְאָה הָאָרֶץ חָמָס

מִפְּנֵיהֶם וְהִנְנִי מַשְׁחִיתָם אֶת־הָאָרֶץ: ¹⁴עֲשֵׂה לְךָ תֵּבַת עֲצֵי־גֹפֶר קִנִּים
תַּעֲשֶׂה אֶת־הַתֵּבָה וְכָפַרְתָּ אֹתָהּ מִבַּיִת וּמִחוּץ בַּכֹּפֶר: ¹⁵וְזֶה אֲשֶׁר תַּעֲשֶׂה
אֹתָהּ שְׁלֹשׁ מֵאוֹת אַמָּה אֹרֶךְ הַתֵּבָה חֲמִשִּׁים אַמָּה רָחְבָּהּ וּשְׁלֹשִׁים
אַמָּה קוֹמָתָהּ: ¹⁶צֹהַר תַּעֲשֶׂה לַתֵּבָה וְאֶל־אַמָּה תְּכַלֶּנָּה מִלְמַעְלָה וּפֶתַח
הַתֵּבָה בְּצִדָּהּ תָּשִׂים תַּחְתִּיִּם שְׁנִיִּם וּשְׁלִשִׁים תַּעֲשֶׂהָ:

¹³And God said to Noah, "The end of all flesh is coming before Me, for the earth is full of violence because of them. Now indeed I am about to destroy them with the earth. ¹⁴Make for yourself an ark of gopher wood; with compartments you will make the ark and cover it inside and outside with pitch. ¹⁵And this is how you shall make it: three hundred cubits shall be the length of the ark; fifty cubits shall be its width; and thirty cubits shall be its height. ¹⁶A covering you shall make for the ark, and you shall finish it to within a cubit from the top. And the door of the ark you shall put in its side. With a lower, second, and third deck you shall make it.

Returning from the brief interjecting scene describing the condition of the earth at large, the opening clause of this scene contains a relexicalization of both "God" and "Noah." God's statement to Noah in verse 13 includes an obvious case of fronting, a theme trace intended to announce God's planned devastation of the earth. The thematicity of God is reinforced in the final clause of verse 13, in which הִנֵּה appears with a pronoun. The theme, however, moves away from God's planned destruction in verse 14; the Ark (תֵּבָה) appears for the first time within the focus content of the verse. The continued relexicalization of "Ark" (five times in verses 14–16) clearly points to its status as a macro-word and to its thematicity in this scene. The repeated fronting of focus content (i.e. new information about the construction of the Ark) in verse 16 do not detract from the importance of the topical information (i.e. the Ark itself). They do serve, however, to broaden the theme of this textual unit by describing the instructions for the Ark in a significant amount of detail. Whereas the opening of this scene is clearly indicated by the beginning of God's utterance, the end is somewhat more obscure. The abrupt interjection of the fronted first common singular independent personal pronoun followed by הִנֵּה in verse 17, however, provides a thematic break and initiates a transition away from the matter of the construction of the Ark to the proclamation of the coming of the Flood itself. As such, the local theme of this unit can be expressed as: *God's announcement of His intent to destroy the earth and His precise instructions to Noah for the construction of an Ark.*

EPISODE 1, SCENE 4: GENESIS 6:17–22

וַאֲנִ֗י הִנְנִי֩ מֵבִ֨יא אֶת־הַמַּבּ֥וּל מַ֙יִם֙ עַל־הָאָ֔רֶץ לְשַׁחֵ֣ת כָּל־בָּשָׂ֗ר אֲשֶׁר־בּוֹ֙
ר֣וּחַ חַיִּ֔ים מִתַּ֖חַת הַשָּׁמָ֑יִם כֹּ֥ל אֲשֶׁר־בָּאָ֖רֶץ יִגְוָֽע׃ ¹⁸וַהֲקִמֹתִ֥י אֶת־בְּרִיתִ֖י
אִתָּ֑ךְ וּבָאתָ֙ אֶל־הַתֵּבָ֔ה אַתָּ֕ה וּבָנֶ֛יךָ וְאִשְׁתְּךָ֥ וּנְשֵֽׁי־בָנֶ֖יךָ אִתָּֽךְ׃ ¹⁹וּמִכָּל־
הָחַ֙י מִֽכָּל־בָּשָׂ֜ר שְׁנַ֧יִם מִכֹּ֛ל תָּבִ֥יא אֶל־הַתֵּבָ֖ה לְהַחֲיֹ֣ת אִתָּ֑ךְ זָכָ֥ר וּנְקֵבָ֖ה
יִהְיֽוּ׃ ²⁰מֵהָע֣וֹף לְמִינֵ֗הוּ וּמִן־הַבְּהֵמָה֙ לְמִינָ֔הּ מִכֹּ֛ל רֶ֥מֶשׂ הָֽאֲדָמָ֖ה לְמִינֵ֑הוּ
שְׁנַ֧יִם מִכֹּ֛ל יָבֹ֥אוּ אֵלֶ֖יךָ לְהַחֲיֽוֹת׃ ²¹וְאַתָּ֣ה קַח־לְךָ֗ מִכָּל־מַֽאֲכָל֙ אֲשֶׁ֣ר
יֵֽאָכֵ֔ל וְאָסַפְתָּ֖ אֵלֶ֑יךָ וְהָיָ֥ה לְךָ֛ וְלָהֶ֖ם לְאָכְלָֽה׃ ²²וַיַּ֖עַשׂ נֹ֑חַ כְּ֠כֹל אֲשֶׁ֨ר צִוָּ֥ה
אֹת֛וֹ אֱלֹהִ֖ים כֵּ֥ן עָשָֽׂה׃ ס

[17]And I, even I, am about to bring the *Mabbûl,* water upon the earth to destroy all flesh in which is the breath of life from under the heavens. All that is on the earth will perish. [18]But I will confirm my covenant with you, and you shall go into the ark, you and your sons and your wife, and the wives of your sons with you. [19]And from all the living, from all flesh; two from all you shall bring into the ark to keep them alive with you—male and female they shall be. [20]From the flying creatures according to their kind and from the beasts according to their kind; from all creeping things of the ground according to their kind—two from all—they will come to you to keep them alive. [21]And as for you, you shall take for yourself from all food that can be eaten, and you shall gather it to yourself. And it shall be for you and for them for food." [22]And Noah did this; according to all that God commanded him, so he did.

The fourth scene in this episode is initiated by a marked construction containing the independent personal pronoun "I" followed by הִנֵּה. This is an obvious case of overencoding and, as such, is important in the evaluation of theme (cf. Runge 2007, 90–101). The Flood (מַבּוּל) is introduced in verse 17 in a predicate focus structure. Though relexicalized less frequently than some of the other macro-words in the account, it will later prove extremely significant to the theme of the unfolding narrative. The fronted primary topic in the last clause of verse 17 is also thematic and blatantly announces the extent of the destruction God intends to bring about on the earth. God remains the primary topic in verse 18, and "covenant" (בְּרִית) is introduced within the focus content. In a sense, this foreshadows the use of "covenant" as a macro-word in chapter 9. Also occurring in verse 18 is a right-dislocated construction, a tail topic which serves to define precisely the extent of the salvation promised to Noah's family. Noah remains discourse active in verses 19 and 20, wherein marked word-order constructions draw attention to the various living creatures that Noah is to bring into the Ark to save. Additionally, the fronted second person masculine singular independent personal pronoun reaffirms the thematicity of Noah. Finally, in verse 22, the text transitions from the utterance of God to the response of Noah. Too brief to be regarded as a scene by itself, verse 22 stands out as an important thematic paragraph. Though unmarked, the transition incurs a mild shift in topic and is rightly regarded as thematically significant. It also serves to provide a natural end to the scene, summing up the content contained in the previous verses. The thematic boundaries of this scene are clear—especially the end, which constitutes not only the boundary of a scene, but also that of an episode. Taking into account the array of theme traces employed in this scene, the local theme is rather complex, but can be stated as: *God's proclamation of His intent to bring the Flood to destroy all flesh on earth, as well as His resolve to establish His covenant with Noah and his family, along with the living creatures that He instructs Noah to take with him; and Noah's full obedience to God's instruction.* On a larger scale, taking into account the theme traces present in all four scenes spanning Genesis 6:9–22, the global theme of this episode can be expressed as follows: *God's intent to destroy all corrupted flesh on the earth by means of a Flood, while preserving righteous Noah, his family, and a limited number of all living creatures; God's instructions for an Ark intended for the preservation of Noah, and Noah's wholly obedient response to God's instructions.*

EPISODE 2, SCENE 1: GENESIS 7:1–5

וַיֹּאמֶר יְהוָה לְנֹחַ בֹּא־אַתָּה וְכָל־בֵּיתְךָ אֶל־הַתֵּבָה כִּי־אֹתְךָ רָאִיתִי צַדִּיק לְפָנַי בַּדּוֹר הַזֶּה: 2מִכֹּל | הַבְּהֵמָה הַטְּהוֹרָה תִּקַּח־לְךָ שִׁבְעָה שִׁבְעָה אִישׁ וְאִשְׁתּוֹ וּמִן־הַבְּהֵמָה אֲשֶׁר לֹא טְהֹרָה הִוא שְׁנַיִם אִישׁ וְאִשְׁתּוֹ: 3גַּם מֵעוֹף הַשָּׁמַיִם שִׁבְעָה שִׁבְעָה זָכָר וּנְקֵבָה לְחַיּוֹת זֶרַע עַל־פְּנֵי כָל־הָאָרֶץ: 4כִּי לְיָמִים עוֹד שִׁבְעָה אָנֹכִי מַמְטִיר עַל־הָאָרֶץ אַרְבָּעִים יוֹם וְאַרְבָּעִים לָיְלָה וּמָחִיתִי אֶת־כָּל־הַיְקוּם אֲשֶׁר עָשִׂיתִי מֵעַל פְּנֵי הָאֲדָמָה: 5וַיַּעַשׂ נֹחַ כְּכֹל אֲשֶׁר־צִוָּהוּ יְהוָה:

[1]And YHWH said to Noah, "Enter, you and all your household, into the ark, because you I have seen as righteous before Me in this generation. [2]From all the clean beasts you shall take seven pairs, a male and his mate, and from the beasts that are not clean, take two, a male and his mate. [3]Also, from the flying creatures of the skies, take seven pairs, a male and female, to keep their seed alive on the surface of all the earth. [4]For in seven more days I will make it rain on the earth for forty days and forty nights.

And I will wipe out everything alive that I made from upon the surface of the ground." ⁵And Noah did according to all that Yʜᴡʜ commanded him.

This scene, instituting the start of a new episode, presents a more drastic break from the previous scene than do the scenes contained together within an episode. Most significantly, there is great leap forward in time (assumed on the outset from the presence of the completed Ark, even though there is no temporal information given until verse 4). The relexicalization of "God" in verse 1 introduces a new instructive revelation distinct from that given in chapter 6. Once again, God and Noah are the primary players in this scene, with both "Yʜᴡʜ" (יְהוָה) and "Noah" being relexicalized twice each (verses 1 and 5). These references form an inclusio that helps to clearly demarcate the boundaries of this scene. Other theme traces in this scene include a fronted object in verse 2, as well as the focus particle גַּם (indicating addition) in verse 3. Both serve to highlight the types of animals that Noah was responsible for taking on the Ark. The fronted statement in verse 4 is also a theme trace, which indirectly serves to reorient the narrative as to the precise time of God's revelatory speech. The independent personal pronoun "I" in verse 4 functions as the primary topic and draws attention to God as the bringer of the judgment. The boundaries of this scene are evident based in part upon the aforementioned inclusio, and the close of the scene is reinforced by the verbless presentational sentence in verse 6. Also, as in the previous scene, the culminating statement summarizing Noah's full obedience provides natural closure. The local theme of this textual unit can be stated as: *God's instruction for Noah and his family to board the Ark, along with precise numbers of all living creatures (clean and unclean land-dwelling creatures, as well as flying creatures), for the purpose of their preservation; and Noah's full obedience to God's instruction.*

Episode 2, Scene 2: Genesis 7:6–9

וְנֹחַ בֶּן־שֵׁשׁ מֵאוֹת שָׁנָה וְהַמַּבּוּל הָיָה מַיִם עַל־הָאָרֶץ: ⁷וַיָּבֹא נֹחַ וּבָנָיו
וְאִשְׁתּוֹ וּנְשֵׁי־בָנָיו אִתּוֹ אֶל־הַתֵּבָה מִפְּנֵי מֵי הַמַּבּוּל: ⁸מִן־הַבְּהֵמָה
הַטְּהוֹרָה וּמִן־הַבְּהֵמָה אֲשֶׁר אֵינֶנָּה טְהֹרָה וּמִן־הָעוֹף וְכֹל אֲשֶׁר־רֹמֵשׂ
עַל־הָאֲדָמָה: ⁹שְׁנַיִם שְׁנַיִם בָּאוּ אֶל־נֹחַ אֶל־הַתֵּבָה זָכָר וּנְקֵבָה כַּאֲשֶׁר
צִוָּה אֱלֹהִים אֶת־נֹחַ:

⁶Now Noah was six hundred years old when the *Mabbûl* came, water upon all the earth. ⁷And Noah and his sons and his wife and the wives of his sons went in to the ark because of the presence of the waters of the *Mabbûl.*

⁸From the clean beasts and from the beasts that are not clean, and from the flying creatures and all that creeps upon the ground, ⁹two by two they came to Noah, to the ark, a male and a female, as God had commanded Noah.

The scene begins with a verbless topic-comment sentence which announces the age of Noah at the time of the Flood, thereby stressing the thematicity of "Noah." It is followed by an event-reporting הָיָה statement that reintroduces the Flood (identifiable but discourse inactive, having last been mentioned in 6:17). Notably, Noah remains discourse active and prevalent throughout the entire scene. "Ark" proves to be a significant macro-word in this scene, being relexicalized in verses 7 and 9. As for other noteworthy theme traces, a long marked word-order construction (containing a primary topic) consumes the totality of verse 8 and highlights the presence on the Ark of all the land-dwelling and flying creatures, in addition to Noah and his family. While the beginning of this scene is clearly marked, the end is somewhat more obscure, being made evident only by the presence of a וַיְהִי statement in verse 10, which aids in updating the narrative's temporal orientation.[40] The local theme of this scene is: *The boarding of the Ark by Noah and his family, as well as the land-dwelling and flying creatures, to escape the coming Flood.*

EPISODE 2, SCENE 3: GENESIS 7:10–12

וַיְהִי לְשִׁבְעַת הַיָּמִים וּמֵי הַמַּבּוּל הָיוּ עַל־הָאָרֶץ: ¹¹בִּשְׁנַת שֵׁשׁ־מֵאוֹת שָׁנָה לְחַיֵּי־נֹחַ בַּחֹדֶשׁ הַשֵּׁנִי בְּשִׁבְעָה־עָשָׂר יוֹם לַחֹדֶשׁ בַּיּוֹם הַזֶּה נִבְקְעוּ כָּל־מַעְיְנֹת תְּהוֹם רַבָּה וַאֲרֻבֹּת הַשָּׁמַיִם נִפְתָּחוּ: ¹²וַיְהִי הַגֶּשֶׁם עַל־הָאָרֶץ אַרְבָּעִים יוֹם וְאַרְבָּעִים לָיְלָה:

¹⁰When the seven days passed, the waters of the *Mabbûl* came upon the earth. ¹¹In the six hundredth year of the life of Noah, on the seventeenth day of the second month; on this day all the springs of the great deep split open and the windows of the heavens opened. ¹²And the rain came upon the earth for forty days and forty nights.

This short scene contains multiple important theme traces. Introduced by a וַיְהִי statement, verse 10 has all the markings of a presentational sentence intended to announce the passage of the prescribed amount of

---

40. Note that וַיְהִי can also close a text unit, just as it can open one (cf. van der Merwe, Naude, and Kroeze 1999, 333). Alternatively, therefore, in view of the blatant case of extreme fronting in verse 11, it is possible to see this scene as extending through verse 10, with the next scene beginning in verse 11. This shows that the factors governing text segmentation are, as with other linguistic principles, descriptive rather than prescriptive. Notably, this variation has little, if any, effect on the chronology or theology of the passage.

time anticipated in the initial scene of this episode. Significantly, in this role, the initial וַיְהִי statement functions to set the stage for the continued progression of the narrative, introducing the temporal setting of this scene (cf. van der Merwe, Naude, and Kroeze 1999, 332).[41] Along with the relexicalization of "Flood" in a fronted clause, the וַיְהִי statement in verse 10 marks a theme shift away from Noah (mentioned by name four times in the preceding scene) to the Flood itself. An argument focus structure featuring a temporal adjunct appears in verse 11, providing for a precise temporal reorientation in the narrative. The fronted structure appearing in the final clause of verse 11 is somewhat unique. Placing emphasis on one of the methods by which the Flood came upon the earth (i.e. by the "windows of the heavens"), it appears to be the latter half of a poetic verse.[42] The scene's second וַיְהִי statement in the closing verse functions specifically to draw the scene to a conclusion, signaling a state of affairs resultant from and intertwined with the happenings described in the verses immediately preceding it (cf. van der Merwe, Naude, and Kroeze 1999, 333). Contending against the notion that this וַיְהִי statement functions simply as an ordinary verb and that the scene continues in the following verses is the presence of a fronted temporal adjunct in verse 13 and the reversal of the theme away from the Flood itself back to the occupants of the Ark. The theme traces contained in this scene present very powerfully a simple local theme: *The coming of the Flood.*

EPISODE 2, SCENE 4: GENESIS 7:13–16

בְּעֶ֙צֶם֙ הַיּ֣וֹם הַזֶּ֔ה בָּ֣א נֹ֔חַ וְשֵׁם־וְחָ֥ם וָיֶ֖פֶת בְּנֵי־נֹ֑חַ וְאֵ֣שֶׁת נֹ֔חַ וּשְׁלֹ֥שֶׁת נְשֵׁי־
בָנָ֖יו אִתָּ֑ם אֶל־הַתֵּבָֽה: ¹⁴הֵ֜מָּה וְכָל־הַֽחַיָּ֣ה לְמִינָ֗הּ וְכָל־הַבְּהֵמָה֙ לְמִינָ֔הּ
וְכָל־הָרֶ֜מֶשׂ הָרֹמֵ֤שׂ עַל־הָאָ֙רֶץ֙ לְמִינֵ֔הוּ וְכָל־הָע֖וֹף לְמִינֵ֑הוּ כֹּ֥ל צִפּ֖וֹר כָּל־
כָּנָֽף: ¹⁵וַיָּבֹ֥אוּ אֶל־נֹ֖חַ אֶל־הַתֵּבָ֑ה שְׁנַ֤יִם שְׁנַ֙יִם֙ מִכָּל־הַבָּשָׂ֔ר אֲשֶׁר־בּ֖וֹ ר֥וּחַ
חַיִּֽים: ¹⁶וְהַבָּאִ֗ים זָכָ֨ר וּנְקֵבָ֤ה מִכָּל־בָּשָׂר֙ בָּ֔אוּ כַּֽאֲשֶׁ֛ר צִוָּ֥ה אֹת֖וֹ אֱלֹהִ֑ים
וַיִּסְגֹּ֥ר יְהוָ֖ה בַּֽעֲדֽוֹ:

[13]On that very same day, Noah; and Shem, Ham and Japheth, the sons of Noah, and the wife of Noah and the three wives of his sons with them went in to the ark—[14]they and all the living things according to their kind and all the beasts according to their kind and all the creeping things that

---

41. See also Longacre's work in **Chapter 15** of this study.

42. Cassuto (1997, 84) argues that the phrase נִבְקְעוּ֙ כָּל־מַעְיְנֹת֙ תְּה֣וֹם רַבָּ֔ה וַאֲרֻבֹּ֥ת הַשָּׁמַ֖יִם נִפְתָּֽחוּ posesses poetic structure, rhythm, and parallelism, and that it contains distinctly poetic words.

creep on the ground according to their kind, and all the flying creatures according to their kind—every winged creature of every sort. [15]And they came to Noah, to the ark; they came two by two, from all the flesh in which was the breath of life. [16]And those that came, male and female from all flesh, went in as God had commanded them. And YHWH closed the ark behind him.

As previously mentioned, the opening boundary of this scene is marked by an obvious redirection in theme away from the Flood back to the occupants of the Ark; the word מַבּוּל ("Flood") is totally absent. At this point, thematic interchange between scenes begins to become evident. Whereas the scene spanning Genesis 7:6–9 is concentrated primarily on Noah and the others boarding the Ark, the following scene in verses 10–12 devotes its attention to the catastrophe itself. This scene reverts its attention to Noah and the occupants of the Ark, while the following scene again shifts to address the waters of the Flood. Moreover, Chisholm (2003, 65) notes the presence recapitulation that is powerfully employed in this scene. This scene looks back and expands upon the information given in the second scene of this episode (namely verses 7–9). Also, as will be demonstrated, the two scenes contained in verses 17–24 function the same way in relation to the third scene of this episode (verses 10–12), further describing the Flood and the accompanying devastation.

In addition to the fronted temporal adjunct in verse 13, this scene features two right-dislocated tail topics, appearing in verses 13–14 and 15, respectively. Serving to elaborate upon the primary topic, both right-dislocated constructions detail precisely who and what entered into the Ark. Prominent macro-words contributing to the theme of this section include "Noah" (four times), "Ark" (twice), and "flesh" (twice). God/YHWH is also mentioned twice in verse 16. The closing boundary of this scene is clear. Between verse 16 and the end of the episode, there is a major thematic shift away from both God and the occupants of the Ark: Noah is mentioned passively only once; "God" is not relexicalized at all. By contrast, the Flood itself dominates the theme of the remaining scenes within this narrative (the beginning of which is evidenced, in part, by the וַיְהִי statement in verse 17). Exegetically, the closing of the Ark by God in verse 16 aids in drawing the scene to a fitting conclusion: The occupants of the Ark are closed inside and the narrative redirects its attention to the events outside the closed door. The local theme of this textual unit is: *The boarding of the Ark by Noah and his family, as well as pairs of all land-dwelling and flying creatures; and God's act of closing the Ark.*

EPISODE 2, SCENE 5: GENESIS 7:17–20

וַיְהִי הַמַּבּוּל אַרְבָּעִים יוֹם עַל־הָאָרֶץ וַיִּרְבּוּ הַמַּיִם וַיִּשְׂאוּ אֶת־הַתֵּבָה וַתָּרָם
מֵעַל הָאָרֶץ: ¹⁸וַיִּגְבְּרוּ הַמַּיִם וַיִּרְבּוּ מְאֹד עַל־הָאָרֶץ וַתֵּלֶךְ הַתֵּבָה עַל־פְּנֵי
הַמָּיִם: ¹⁹וְהַמַּיִם גָּבְרוּ מְאֹד מְאֹד עַל־הָאָרֶץ וַיְכֻסּוּ כָּל־הֶהָרִים הַגְּבֹהִים אֲשֶׁר־
תַּחַת כָּל־הַשָּׁמָיִם: ²⁰חֲמֵשׁ עֶשְׂרֵה אַמָּה מִלְמַעְלָה גָּבְרוּ הַמָּיִם וַיְכֻסּוּ הֶהָרִים:

[17]And the *Mabbûl* was upon the earth for forty days. And the waters increased and lifted up the ark, and it rose up from upon the earth. [18]And the waters were powerful, and they increased greatly upon the earth. And the ark went upon the surface of the waters. [19]The waters were exceedingly powerful upon the earth. All the high mountains which were under all the heavens were covered. [20]Fifteen cubits higher the waters were powerful and the mountains were covered.

This scene opens with a וַיְהִי statement announcing the arrival of the Flood. Having dropped out of the picture in the last scene, the *Mabbûl* is now reintroduced as the primary topic to produce a sharp break with the preceding scene. To differentiate between "Flood" and "water" in this scene is probably unjustified, as the water is understood to be that of the Flood (cf. Gn 6:17; 9:11). "Water" is indeed a macro-word and its thematicity is undeniable. It is relexicalized five times in these four verses, fronted in verse 19, and is the primary topic of all the clauses containing it. "Earth" is also a significant macro-word, being mentioned four times in this scene. The other major theme trace in this section is the fronted spatial adjunct in verse 20, which serves to describe the impressive depth of the Floodwaters over the surface of the planet. Concerning the boundaries of this textual unit, it could be argued that verse 17 institutes not only a new scene, but also a new episode. Indeed, there is a notable shift in topic, as well as a marked change in terms of key macro-words (namely "God"/"YHWH," which is absent from 7:17–24). Additionally, there is a definite shift in perspective from inside the Ark to the doomed world outside brought on by God's act of closing the Ark in 7:16. Against this notion, however, is the fact that there is too much thematic similarity between 7:17–24 and some of the preceding material, especially 7:10–12 (note again the use of recapitulation). This being stated, however, the presence or absence of certain internal elements (e.g. important macro-words) thematically binds the two scenes spanning 7:17–24 more closely than they are bound to the other scenes within the same episode. The local theme of this unit can be stated as: *The flooding of the earth for forty days and nights and the great*

power of the water over the surface of the whole earth to a minimum depth of
fifteen cubits.

EPISODE 2, SCENE 6: GENESIS 7:21–24

וַיִּגְוַע כָּל־בָּשָׂר׀ הָרֹמֵשׂ עַל־הָאָרֶץ בָּעוֹף וּבַבְּהֵמָה וּבַחַיָּה וּבְכָל־הַשֶּׁרֶץ
הַשֹּׁרֵץ עַל־הָאָרֶץ וְכֹל הָאָדָם: ²²כֹּל אֲשֶׁר נִשְׁמַת־רוּחַ חַיִּים בְּאַפָּיו מִכֹּל
אֲשֶׁר בֶּחָרָבָה מֵתוּ: ²³וַיִּמַח אֶת־כָּל־הַיְקוּם׀ אֲשֶׁר׀ עַל־פְּנֵי הָאֲדָמָה
מֵאָדָם עַד־בְּהֵמָה עַד־רֶמֶשׂ וְעַד־עוֹף הַשָּׁמַיִם וַיִּמָּחוּ מִן־הָאָרֶץ וַיִשָּׁאֶר
אַךְ־נֹחַ וַאֲשֶׁר אִתּוֹ בַּתֵּבָה: ²⁴וַיִּגְבְּרוּ הַמַּיִם עַל־הָאָרֶץ חֲמִשִּׁים וּמְאַת
יוֹם:

[21]And all flesh that crept on the earth perished: flying creatures and beasts and wild animals, and all the swarming things that swarm on the earth, and all mankind. [22]All in whose nostrils was a breath of the spirit of life, from all that were on dry land, died. [23]And it wiped out everything alive that was on the face of the ground, from mankind to beasts, to creeping things, and to flying creatures of the skies. They were wiped out from the earth. Only Noah remained, and those that were with him in the ark. [24]And the waters were powerful upon the earth for one hundred fifty days.

Rather than being distinguished from the previous scene by any obvious syntactic features, this scene is demarcated by a significant shift in topic. "All flesh" (not discourse active since Gn 7:16) is reactivated and expanded by the right-dislocated tail topic in verse 21. The thematicity of "all flesh" is further supported by a fronted construction in verse 22 and by another right-dislocated construction in the first half of verse 23. Undeniably, the emphasis of this textual unit is set on the total destruction of all non-aquatic life on earth. As an exegetical note, it has been assumed that the third person masculine singular coding of וַיִּמַח relates to God, the last player mentioned in this episode (verse 16), and should be translated "And He wiped out" (Bandstra 2008, 421). However, given the thematic prevalence of the Flood itself, as well as the absence of God throughout the entirety of the preceding scene, it seems more likely that וַיִּמַח should be translated "And it wiped out." Based upon Runge's study of participant encoding in BH (2007, 102–05), if God were intended by verse 23, His name would almost certainly require relexicalization. As for other theme traces in this scene, the focus particle אַךְ (indicating limitation) in verse 23 provides clear contrast between the fate of Noah (expressly mentioned in the final clause of verse 23) and those with him, versus the masses outside the Ark. The concluding sentence of this scene is a theme-closing one; it sums up the devastation brought upon the earth by the Flood. In addition to the considerable discontinuity evident in Genesis 8:1, it serves to indicate the end of both the scene and the episode. The local theme of this textual unit can be expressed as: *The destruction of all flesh (land-dwelling and flying creatures) with the exception of Noah and those with him, and the powerfulness of the Floodwaters for the duration of one hundred fifty days.* Taking into account the theme traces from the larger body of text, the theme of this action-filled episode can be summarized as: *God's instruction for Noah, his family, and pairs of land-dwelling and flying creatures to board the Ark, followed by the actual embarkation of the Ark by Noah and the others, and the closing of the Ark by God; the coming of the Flood, forty days and nights of rain, bringing mighty waters over the surface of the whole earth and causing the destruction of all non-aquatic life, while sparing only Noah and those with him in the Ark.*

EPISODE 3, SCENE 1: GENESIS 8:1–5

וַיִּזְכֹּר אֱלֹהִים אֶת־נֹחַ וְאֵת כָּל־הַחַיָּה וְאֶת־כָּל־הַבְּהֵמָה אֲשֶׁר אִתּוֹ בַּתֵּבָה וַיַּעֲבֵר אֱלֹהִים רוּחַ עַל־הָאָרֶץ וַיָּשֹׁכּוּ הַמָּיִם: ²וַיִּסָּכְרוּ מַעְיְנֹת תְּהוֹם וַאֲרֻבֹּת הַשָּׁמָיִם וַיִּכָּלֵא הַגֶּשֶׁם מִן־הַשָּׁמָיִם: ³וַיָּשֻׁבוּ הַמַּיִם מֵעַל הָאָרֶץ הָלוֹךְ וָשׁוֹב וַיַּחְסְרוּ הַמַּיִם מִקְצֵה חֲמִשִּׁים וּמְאַת יוֹם: ⁴וַתָּנַח הַתֵּבָה בַּחֹדֶשׁ הַשְּׁבִיעִי בְּשִׁבְעָה־עָשָׂר יוֹם לַחֹדֶשׁ עַל הָרֵי אֲרָרָט: ⁵וְהַמַּיִם הָיוּ הָלוֹךְ וְחָסוֹר עַד הַחֹדֶשׁ הָעֲשִׂירִי בָּעֲשִׂירִי בְּאֶחָד לַחֹדֶשׁ נִרְאוּ רָאשֵׁי הֶהָרִים:

¹But God remembered Noah and all the wild animals and all the beasts that were with him in the ark. And God caused a wind to pass over the earth, and the waters abated. ²And the springs of the deep and the windows of heaven closed and the rain from the skies was restrained. ³And the waters receded steadily, and the waters lacked at end of one hundred fifty days. ⁴And the ark rested on the seventeenth day of the seventh month on the mountains of Ararat. ⁵And the waters continued to diminish until the tenth month. In the tenth month, on the first day of the tenth month the tops of the mountains appeared.

Genesis 8:1 begins what is perhaps the most obvious thematic transition in the Flood account. "God," absent from the narrative throughout the last two scenes, is relexicalized in a pivotal statement that constitutes the centermost point of the account's pervading chiastic structure. Everything in the account thus far has been leading up to this climax; from this point on, however, everything in the account moves away from this climax and toward a resolution. In other words, the global theme of the narrative to this point has been preoccupied with preparation for the Flood, followed by the catastrophic destruction of the earth and the life on it. From this point forward, by contrast, the narrative focuses on God's restoration of the earth, the replenishing of life, and God's covenant to never again destroy the earth in the same manner. This drastic thematic shift is substantial enough to establish the beginning of more than just a new scene; it also begins a new episode.

Even viewed apart from the Flood account's chiastic structure, there is ample evidence of thematic transition in Genesis 8:1 and following. In terms of the information structure, the promotion of God to the position of primary topic brings about a highly noticeable topic shift.[43] The seemingly-redundant relexicalization of the word "God" a second time in verse 1 supports its prominence as a macro-word. Theologically speaking, God is sovereign at all times and was certainly in control over every detail of the cataclysm; however, the Flood account in 7:17–24 speaks of the Flood itself (and the water thereof) in language that presents it as the dominant power bringing destruction on the earth. In 8:1, though, the account clearly presents God as the controlling power behind the Flood. "Water" is also an important macro-word, as it is relexicalized four times, once in a fronted construction (verse 5). Additionally, there is the presence of end-weight in verse 4, which proves significant in that it reveals locational information, namely, the resting place of the Ark on the mountains of Ararat. Finally, in the second half of verse 5, there is a fronted temporal adjunct which aids in providing more information regarding the subsiding of the Floodwaters. When both the chiastic structure of the account and the theme traces in the account's information structure are viewed together, the opening boundary of this scene (and episode) is unambiguously clear. The end of the scene is

43. Consideration of this scene-opening statement in light of Runge's observations of the four dimensions (place, time, participants, and action; cf. **Section 1.2**) evidences notable discontinuity. From a theological perspective, God's act of remembrance is not the recollection of forgotten information, but the intervention of God on Noah's behalf. This certainly involves God's act of bringing about the recession of the Floodwaters, but it likely extends beyond that. The catastrophic forces at work during the time of the Flood were such that survival would be impossible apart from God's constant providential—miraculous—protection. This being the case, the statement appears to describe more than just a momentary act of God that occurred *after* the events described in Genesis 7:17–24, but rather the continuous initiative of God *throughout* the whole length of the Flood. If this observation is correct, then the statement "But God remembered Noah . . ." incurs not only a major shift in topic and participants, but also a shift in time and action (factors which may indeed suggest chronological disjunction). Regardless, the thematic shift brought about by this statement is monumental.

only slightly less obvious, as it is signaled by both a וַיְהִי statement and a shift in primary topic to Noah in verse 6. The local theme of this scene can be stated as: *God's remembrance of Noah and His providential act of bringing a recession of the Floodwaters on the earth, so that the Ark ran aground on the mountains of Ararat; and the continued subsiding of the Floodwaters on the earth.*

EPISODE 3, SCENE 2: GENESIS 8:6–12

וַיְהִי מִקֵּץ אַרְבָּעִים יוֹם וַיִּפְתַּח נֹחַ אֶת־חַלּוֹן הַתֵּבָה אֲשֶׁר עָשָׂה: 7וַיְשַׁלַּח אֶת־הָעֹרֵב וַיֵּצֵא יָצוֹא וָשׁוֹב עַד־יְבֹשֶׁת הַמַּיִם מֵעַל הָאָרֶץ: 8וַיְשַׁלַּח אֶת־הַיּוֹנָה מֵאִתּוֹ לִרְאוֹת הֲקַלּוּ הַמַּיִם מֵעַל פְּנֵי הָאֲדָמָה: 9וְלֹא־מָצְאָה הַיּוֹנָה מָנוֹחַ לְכַף־רַגְלָהּ וַתָּשָׁב אֵלָיו אֶל־הַתֵּבָה כִּי־מַיִם עַל־פְּנֵי כָל־הָאָרֶץ וַיִּשְׁלַח יָדוֹ וַיִּקָּחֶהָ וַיָּבֵא אֹתָהּ אֵלָיו אֶל־הַתֵּבָה: 10וַיָּחֶל עוֹד שִׁבְעַת יָמִים אֲחֵרִים וַיֹּסֶף שַׁלַּח אֶת־הַיּוֹנָה מִן־הַתֵּבָה: 11וַתָּבֹא אֵלָיו הַיּוֹנָה לְעֵת עֶרֶב וְהִנֵּה עֲלֵה־זַיִת טָרָף בְּפִיהָ וַיֵּדַע נֹחַ כִּי־קַלּוּ הַמַּיִם מֵעַל הָאָרֶץ: 12וַיִּיָּחֶל עוֹד שִׁבְעַת יָמִים אֲחֵרִים וַיְשַׁלַּח אֶת־הַיּוֹנָה וְלֹא־יָסְפָה שׁוּב־אֵלָיו עוֹד:

[6]And at the end of forty days, Noah opened the window of the ark which he had made. [7]And he sent out a raven, and he went back and forth until the waters dried up from upon the earth. [8]And he sent out a dove from with him to see whether the waters had lessened upon the face of the ground. [9]And the dove found no resting place for the sole of her foot, and she returned to him, to the ark, because water was upon the face of all the earth. And he stretched out his hand and he took her, and he brought her to himself, to the ark. [10]And he waited yet another seven days and he again sent the dove from the ark. [11]And the dove came to him at the time of evening, and there was a freshly plucked leaf of an olive tree in her beak. And Noah knew that the waters had lessened upon the earth. [12]And he waited yet another seven days and he sent out the dove, but she did not return to him again.

Considering its length, the second scene of this episode is surprisingly straightforward. There are no significant marked word-order constructions contributing to the development of the local theme and, apart from "dove" (יוֹנָה), there are no distinctive new macro-words. Noah remains thematic throughout, serving as the primary topic of many of the sentences contained in this scene. The sequence of events contained in this scene is very plainly laid out, employing a long string of *wayyiqtol* verbs. Admittedly, there is ambiguity concerning precisely when the "forty days" specified by the temporal adjunct in verse 6 begin (this remains one of the chronological challenges of the Flood narrative deserving further attention). As previously mentioned, the beginning of the scene is signaled by the presence of a וַיְהִי statement and a shift in topic away from the recession of the water toward Noah. The end of the scene is not apparent until Genesis 8:13, in which another וַיְהִי statement (followed by a fronted temporal adjunct) serves to introduce the next scene. The local theme of this textual unit is: *The sending out of the raven and then the dove by Noah, as well as the indications provided by the dove of the gradual recession of the water from the surface of the earth.*

EPISODE 3, SCENE 3: GENESIS 8:13–14

וַיְהִי בְּאַחַת וְשֵׁשׁ־מֵאוֹת שָׁנָה בָּרִאשׁוֹן בְּאֶחָד לַחֹדֶשׁ חָרְבוּ הַמַּיִם מֵעַל הָאָרֶץ וַיָּסַר נֹחַ אֶת־מִכְסֵה הַתֵּבָה וַיַּרְא וְהִנֵּה חָרְבוּ פְּנֵי הָאֲדָמָה: ¹⁴וּבַחֹדֶשׁ הַשֵּׁנִי בְּשִׁבְעָה וְעֶשְׂרִים יוֹם לַחֹדֶשׁ יָבְשָׁה הָאָרֶץ: ס

¹³And in the six hundred and first year, in the first month, on the first day of the month the waters dried up from upon the earth. And Noah removed the covering of the ark, and he saw [that] the surface of the ground was dry. ¹⁴And in the second month, on the twenty-seventh day of the month, the earth was [completely] dry.

This short scene begins, like the preceding one, with a וַיְהִי statement. The first fronted temporal adjunct serves to reorient the narrative chronologically, indicating the passage of time since the sending out of the birds in the former scene. There is emphasis on the drying of the earth, with the verb "dried up" (חָרְבוּ) occurring twice in verse 13. (יָבֵשׁ, a verb with a similar meaning, also occurs once in verse 14, functioning to indicate what was apparently the *complete* drying of the earth.) Verse 13 also marks the first time that dry land has been beheld by human eyes for over ten months. It is the touching of two vastly different worlds—that of Noah, protected in the Ark, and that of the devastated planet, ravaged by the Flood. The use of fronting in verse 14 provides another update in the time frame of the Flood account. Despite the fact that verse 14 relates more closely to the events of the following scene (verses 15–17) chronologically, it is, in terms of theme, more directly connected to verse 13. The end of the scene is more subtle, not evident until the speech-introducing phase and the relexicalization of "God" in verse 15. The local theme of this scene is: *The drying of the water from the ground, which is beheld by Noah, and the total drying of the earth.*

EPISODE 3, SCENE 4: GENESIS 8:15–17

וַיְדַבֵּר אֱלֹהִים אֶל־נֹחַ לֵאמֹר: ¹⁶צֵא מִן־הַתֵּבָה אַתָּה וְאִשְׁתְּךָ וּבָנֶיךָ וּנְשֵׁי־

בָּנֶיךָ אִתָּךְ: ¹⁷כָּל־הַחַיָּה אֲשֶׁר־אִתְּךָ מִכָּל־בָּשָׂר בָּעוֹף וּבַבְּהֵמָה וּבְכָל־
הָרֶמֶשׂ הָרֹמֵשׂ עַל־הָאָרֶץ הוצֵא (הַיְצֵא) אִתָּךְ וְשָׁרְצוּ בָאָרֶץ וּפָרוּ וְרָבוּ עַל־
הָאָרֶץ:

¹⁵And God spoke to Noah, saying, ¹⁶"Go out from the ark, you and your
wife and your sons and the wives of your sons with you. ¹⁷All the living
things that are with you, from all flesh: flying creatures, and beasts, and all
the swarming things that swarm on the earth, bring them out with you,
and they will swarm on the earth. Be fruitful, and become numerous on
the earth."

This scene is initiated by a speech-introducing phase and the relexicalization
of "God" in verse 15. "Noah" is also relexicalized in verse 15 and later
mentioned by use of an independent personal pronoun in verse 16. Together,
these theme traces mark a shift in topic away from the earth back to the
two main players in the narrative: God and Noah. This scene, in which
Noah is instructed to leave the Ark, contains the first speech by God since
He commanded Noah to enter the Ark in the first scene of the previous
episode. The content of verses 16 and 17 is also thematically significant.
The right-dislocated tail topic in verse 16 aids in indicating the extent of
God's instruction: Just as Noah entered the Ark with his family, so too were
they to accompany him in his exodus from the Ark. Likewise, the fronted
secondary topic beginning verse 17 serves as theme-supporting information
in that God's instruction was not just for humanity, but also for all the
living creatures that had spent roughly the last year of their lives onboard the
Ark. The scene, having begun with the announcement of God's speech, is
fittingly ended with the close of God's instruction. The topic shift from God
to Noah in Genesis 8:18 also serves to indicate that this scene has reached its
conclusion. In view of the theme traces in this textual unit, its local theme
can be expressed as: *God's instruction for Noah and his family, as well as all
land-dwelling and flying creatures, to come out from the Ark and to repopulate
the earth.*

EPISODE 3, SCENE 5: GENESIS 8:18–20

וַיֵּצֵא־נֹחַ וּבָנָיו וְאִשְׁתּוֹ וּנְשֵׁי־בָנָיו אִתּוֹ: ¹⁹כָּל־הַחַיָּה כָּל־הָרֶמֶשׂ וְכָל־הָעוֹף
כֹּל רוֹמֵשׂ עַל־הָאָרֶץ לְמִשְׁפְּחֹתֵיהֶם יָצְאוּ מִן־הַתֵּבָה: ²⁰וַיִּבֶן נֹחַ מִזְבֵּחַ
לַיהוָה וַיִּקַּח מִכֹּל| הַבְּהֵמָה הַטְּהוֹרָה וּמִכֹּל הָעוֹף הַטָּהֹר וַיַּעַל עֹלֹת
בַּמִּזְבֵּחַ:

¹⁸And Noah and his sons and his wife and the wives of his sons with him
went out. ¹⁹All the living things, all the swarming things, and all the flying

creatures—all that swarms on the earth according to their kinds came out from the ark. [20]And Noah built an altar to YHWH, and he took from all the clean beasts and from all the clean birds and he offered burnt offerings on the altar.

Set off from the previous scene by a shift in primary topic from God back to Noah (and those accompanying him), this scene describes Noah's obedient response to God's instructions given in the preceding verses. As in the previous scene, the right-dislocated tail topic in verse 18 expands upon the primary topic. Just as God instructed, Noah's family—his sons, his wife and his sons' wives—followed Noah out of the Ark. Again, the fronted construction in verse 19 also provides important theme-supporting information, indicating that the animals also participated in the mass exodus in accordance with God's stated desire. The thematicity of Noah continues in verse 20. In what comprises a string of three common topic-comment clauses, he is described as the executor of a sacrificial ceremony. "YHWH" is relexicalized and raised to the level of the secondary topic in verse 20, which leads to a smooth transition into the next scene, where God's gracious response to Noah's sacrifice is described. The local theme of this scene may be easily stated as: *The exodus from the Ark by Noah and his family, as well as all the land-dwelling and flying creatures; and Noah's construction of an altar and sacrificing of an offering to God.*

EPISODE 3, SCENE 6: GENESIS 8:21–22

וַיָּ֣רַח יְהוָה֮ אֶת־רֵ֣יחַ הַנִּיחֹחַ֒ וַיֹּ֨אמֶר יְהוָ֜ה אֶל־לִבּ֗וֹ לֹֽא־אֹ֠סִף לְקַלֵּ֨ל ע֜וֹד אֶת־הָֽאֲדָמָה֙ בַּעֲב֣וּר הָֽאָדָ֔ם כִּ֠י יֵ֣צֶר לֵ֧ב הָאָדָ֛ם רַ֖ע מִנְּעֻרָ֑יו וְלֹֽא־אֹסִ֥ף ע֛וֹד לְהַכּ֥וֹת אֶת־כָּל־חַ֖י כַּֽאֲשֶׁ֥ר עָשִֽׂיתִי׃ [22]עֹ֖ד כָּל־יְמֵ֣י הָאָ֑רֶץ זֶ֡רַע וְ֠קָצִיר וְקֹ֨ר וָחֹ֜ם וְקַ֧יִץ וָחֹ֛רֶף וְי֥וֹם וָלַ֖יְלָה לֹ֥א יִשְׁבֹּֽתוּ׃

[21]And YHWH smelled the soothing scent, and YHWH said to Himself, "Never will I curse again the ground on account of mankind even though the intent of the mind of mankind is evil from his youth; and never again will I strike all life which I have made. [22]From now on, all the days of the earth, seed [time] and harvest, and cold and heat, and summer and winter, and day and night, will not cease."

This scene witnesses another shift in the primary topic, this time away from Noah and back toward God. The Tetragrammaton, having been relexicalized as a secondary topic in Genesis 8:20, appears twice more in verse 21, indicating its role as a macro-word and a theme trace. As an exegetical note, the reason for the use of יְהוָה (as opposed to אֱלֹהִים) is not completely clear, though it almost certainly ties in with the parallelism between the Flood narrative and the record of Creation and the Fall in Genesis 1–3. That being said, however, the long-held liberal argument that these two words mark the contributions of different sources is to be excluded on the basis of the presuppositions framing this study (cf. **Section 1.3**). Furthermore, it should be stressed that, by this point in the narrative, the amazing coherence and complexity of the text is so blatantly obvious that it renders virtually impossible any hypothesis of multiple sources. Nevertheless, the author's use of אֱלֹהִים versus יְהוָה (and vice versa) throughout the Flood narrative is a worthy topic for future study.

Notwithstanding the prominence of יְהוָה, another important macroword emerges in this scene, the particle עוֹד ("again"). The word is repeated twice in verse 21 for the express purpose of emphasizing God's definite resolve to never again curse the ground on account of man or to bring about the total destruction of life on the earth. Besides these key words, the only other notable theme trace which presents itself in this scene is the massive fronted construction in verse 22. This verse is obviously poetic, as betrayed by its use of meter and parallelism. The word עוֹד appears again in the fronted construction, this time stressing the certainty of the continuance of the times and seasons. The initial boundary of this scene is clearly marked by the shift in primary topic and the relexicalization of יְהוָה. By contrast, the end of the scene is not apparent until a shift in the focus content occurs in Genesis 9:1. In view of the aforementioned theme traces, the local theme of this textual unit can be expressed as: *God's reception of the sacrifice and His resolve to never again bring about a curse on the ground because of man, or the total destruction of life on earth; or to permit an interruption of the times and seasons.*

EPISODE 3, SCENE 7: GENESIS 9:1–7

וַיְבָרֶךְ אֱלֹהִים אֶת־נֹחַ וְאֶת־בָּנָיו וַיֹּאמֶר לָהֶם פְּרוּ וּרְבוּ וּמִלְאוּ אֶת־הָאָרֶץ: ²וּמוֹרַאֲכֶם וְחִתְּכֶם יִהְיֶה עַל כָּל־חַיַּת הָאָרֶץ וְעַל כָּל־עוֹף הַשָּׁמָיִם בְּכֹל אֲשֶׁר תִּרְמֹשׂ הָאֲדָמָה וּבְכָל־דְּגֵי הַיָּם בְּיֶדְכֶם נִתָּנוּ: ³כָּל־רֶמֶשׂ אֲשֶׁר הוּא־חַי לָכֶם יִהְיֶה לְאָכְלָה כְּיֶרֶק עֵשֶׂב נָתַתִּי לָכֶם אֶת־כֹּל: ⁴אַךְ־בָּשָׂר בְּנַפְשׁוֹ דָמוֹ לֹא תֹאכֵלוּ: ⁵וְאַךְ אֶת־דִּמְכֶם לְנַפְשֹׁתֵיכֶם אֶדְרֹשׁ מִיַּד כָּל־חַיָּה אֶדְרְשֶׁנּוּ וּמִיַּד הָאָדָם מִיַּד אִישׁ אָחִיו אֶדְרֹשׁ אֶת־נֶפֶשׁ הָאָדָם: ⁶שֹׁפֵךְ דַּם הָאָדָם בָּאָדָם דָּמוֹ יִשָּׁפֵךְ כִּי בְּצֶלֶם אֱלֹהִים עָשָׂה אֶת־הָאָדָם: ⁷וְאַתֶּם פְּרוּ וּרְבוּ שִׁרְצוּ בָאָרֶץ וּרְבוּ־בָהּ: ס

¹And God blessed Noah and his sons and He said to them, "Be fruitful

and become numerous and fill the earth. ²And the fear of you and the terror of you will be upon every living thing of the earth, and upon every flying creature of the skies, and in all that swarms on the ground, and in all fish of the sea. Into your hand they are given. ³Every swarming thing that is alive will be for you for food; as the green plant, I give to you everything. ⁴However, flesh in its life principle, its blood, you shall not eat. ⁵And surely for your blood according to your life principles I will demand [an account]; from the hand of every living thing I will demand it. From the hand of a man, from the hand of each man's brother I will demand [an account] for the life principle of a man. ⁶Whoever sheds the blood of mankind, by mankind shall his blood be shed, for in the image of God He made man. ⁷But as for you, be fruitful and increase; teem on the earth and increase in it."

Genesis 9:1 incurs a shift in theme. "God" is relexicalized as the primary topic, which lends to topical continuity. However, God's speech is no longer a matter of private resolve; He proceeds to direct the remainder of His speech toward Noah and his sons. "Noah" is relexicalized in verse 1 and there then follows a major shift in focus content. The thematicity of Noah and his sons is also indicated near the closure of the scene. The second person masculine plural independent personal pronoun "you" is used in verse 7 in a reiteration of God's opening command, which functions as an inclusio (Floor 2004, 278). It thereby strengthens the thematic significance of Noah and his sons. End-weight is another prominent feature in this scene. On this topic, Floor writes:

> The proposition in verse 2 is a sentence focus structure reporting a state of affairs that is to be. There is no topic, but the addressee (Noah and his descendants) is presupposed. The "heavy," long complement in the sentence makes for an end-weight construction. The activated referents from the end-weight configuration in verse 2 are further strengthened by the fronted construction in verse 3a, "Every moving thing that lives" forming the end-weight information, by way of repetition and summary. The final 'all' [translated above as "everything"] at the end of verse 3 is a case of end-weight and further strengthens the central concept in this passage. (2004, 278)

In addition to the theme traces noted in Floor's observation, it should be stated that the use of fronting abounds in this scene. Verse 2 employs it to stress the new order on the earth: the harmony that previously existed between man and animals will cease to be as it once was, with animals now living in fear of man. Verses 4 and 5 both begin with fronted constructions initiated with the focus particle אַךְ, used to indicate limitation. In verse 4, it is employed with respect to the content of the expression immediately preceding it. Practically stated, though Noah and his descendants are now permitted to eat meat, they are still prohibited from consuming it while the blood of the creature remained in it. All three uses of fronting in verse 5 serve to stress the seriousness of murder: God declares that He Himself will demand an account for the shed blood of any human being. Verse 6 is a concise poetic unit employing unmistakable chiastic parallelism. Designed to emphasize the seriousness of murder by implicitly describing it as the defacing of God's image, it also institutes a stiff penalty for such transgression. Both the beginning and ending boundaries of this section are clearly marked, as the whole scene is bracketed by the aforementioned inclusio. The ending boundary is also strengthened by the relexicalization of both "God" and "Noah" in Genesis 9:8, followed by another shift in focus content. This scene's local theme can be stated as: *God's act of blessing Noah and his sons, and God's command for them to repopulate the earth; as well as God's statement concerning the new order on the earth, including the ordinance permitting the consumption of the meat (though not the blood) of animals, and the ordinance against murder on account of man's standing as a being made in the image of God.*

EPISODE 3, SCENE 8: GENESIS 9:8–17

וַיֹּ֤אמֶר אֱלֹהִים֙ אֶל־נֹ֔חַ וְאֶל־בָּנָ֥יו אִתּ֖וֹ לֵאמֹֽר׃ ⁹וַאֲנִ֗י הִנְנִ֥י מֵקִ֛ים אֶת־בְּרִיתִ֖י אִתְּכֶ֑ם וְאֶֽת־זַרְעֲכֶ֖ם אַחֲרֵיכֶֽם׃ ¹⁰וְאֵ֣ת כָּל־נֶ֣פֶשׁ הַֽחַיָּה֮ אֲשֶׁ֣ר אִתְּכֶם֒ בָּע֧וֹף בַּבְּהֵמָ֛ה וּֽבְכָל־חַיַּ֥ת הָאָ֖רֶץ אִתְּכֶ֑ם מִכֹּל֙ יֹצְאֵ֣י הַתֵּבָ֔ה לְכֹ֖ל חַיַּ֥ת הָאָֽרֶץ׃ ¹¹וַהֲקִמֹתִ֤י אֶת־בְּרִיתִי֙ אִתְּכֶ֔ם וְלֹֽא־יִכָּרֵ֧ת כָּל־בָּשָׂ֛ר ע֖וֹד מִמֵּ֣י הַמַּבּ֑וּל וְלֹֽא־יִהְיֶ֥ה ע֛וֹד מַבּ֖וּל לְשַׁחֵ֥ת הָאָֽרֶץ׃ ¹²וַיֹּ֣אמֶר אֱלֹהִ֗ים זֹ֤את אֽוֹת־הַבְּרִית֙ אֲשֶׁר־אֲנִ֣י נֹתֵ֗ן בֵּינִי֙ וּבֵ֣ינֵיכֶ֔ם וּבֵ֛ין כָּל־נֶ֥פֶשׁ חַיָּ֖ה אֲשֶׁ֣ר אִתְּכֶ֑ם לְדֹרֹ֖ת עוֹלָֽם׃ ¹³אֶת־קַשְׁתִּ֕י נָתַ֖תִּי בֶּֽעָנָ֑ן וְהָֽיְתָה֙ לְא֣וֹת בְּרִ֔ית בֵּינִ֖י וּבֵ֥ין הָאָֽרֶץ׃ ¹⁴וְהָיָ֕ה בְּעַֽנְנִ֥י עָנָ֖ן עַל־הָאָ֑רֶץ וְנִרְאֲתָ֥ה הַקֶּ֖שֶׁת בֶּֽעָנָֽן׃ ¹⁵וְזָכַרְתִּ֣י אֶת־בְּרִיתִ֗י אֲשֶׁ֤ר בֵּינִי֙ וּבֵ֣ינֵיכֶ֔ם וּבֵ֛ין כָּל־נֶ֥פֶשׁ חַיָּ֖ה בְּכָל־בָּשָׂ֑ר וְלֹֽא־יִֽהְיֶ֨ה ע֤וֹד הַמַּ֙יִם֙ לְמַבּ֔וּל לְשַׁחֵ֖ת כָּל־בָּשָֽׂר׃ ¹⁶וְהָיְתָ֥ה הַקֶּ֖שֶׁת בֶּֽעָנָ֑ן וּרְאִיתִ֗יהָ לִזְכֹּר֙ בְּרִ֣ית עוֹלָ֔ם בֵּ֣ין אֱלֹהִ֔ים וּבֵ֙ין֙ כָּל־נֶ֣פֶשׁ חַיָּ֔ה בְּכָל־בָּשָׂ֖ר אֲשֶׁ֥ר עַל־הָאָֽרֶץ׃ ¹⁷וַיֹּ֥אמֶר אֱלֹהִ֖ים אֶל־נֹ֑חַ זֹ֤את אֽוֹת־הַבְּרִית֙ אֲשֶׁ֣ר הֲקִמֹ֔תִי בֵּינִ֕י וּבֵ֥ין כָּל־בָּשָׂ֖ר אֲשֶׁ֥ר עַל־הָאָֽרֶץ׃ פ

⁸And God spoke to Noah and to his sons with him, saying, ⁹"I, even I, am about to confirm My covenant with you, and with your seed after you, ¹⁰and with all the living things that were with you: flying creatures,

beasts, and every living thing of the earth with you—all that came out from the ark—to every living thing of the earth. [11]And I will confirm My covenant with you, and never again will all flesh be cut off by the waters of the *Mabbûl,* and never again will there be a *Mabbûl* to destroy the earth." [12]And God said, "This is the sign of the covenant that I am about to place between me and you and every living thing that was with you, to generations of all time. [13]My bow I hereby set in the clouds and it shall become a sign of the covenant between Me and the earth. [14]And whenever I form clouds above the earth, the bow will appear in the clouds; [15]then I will remember My covenant that is between Me and you and every living thing of all flesh. And never again will the waters of a *Mabbûl* come to destroy all flesh. [16]And the bow will be in the clouds, and I will see it to remember the covenant of perpetuity between God and every living thing of all flesh that is on the earth." [17]And God said to Noah, "This is the sign of the covenant that I hereby confirm between Me and all flesh that is on the earth.

This scene is set apart from the previous one by a notable shift in the focus content (though not in topic). Verse 8 relexicalizes both "God" and "Noah" as the primary and secondary topics, respectively, reestablishing both as theme traces. The thematicity of God is reinforced in verse 9 in which the independent personal pronoun "I" appears in a fronted construction, followed by the discourse marker הִנֵּה. The word "covenant," having not been mentioned since the beginning of the narrative in Genesis 6:17, begins to emerge as an important macro-word that binds together this scene thematically. In verse 10, a long right-dislocated tail topic expands upon the theme, clearly specifying the beneficiaries of God's newly-introduced covenant. In verse 12, topic continuity is maintained as "God" is relexicalized. At this point, a mild thematic shift occurs (though not enough of one to warrant the beginning of a new scene): Having defined the extent of His covenant, God now discusses the sign of His covenant. The use of end-weight in verse 12 specifies for whom God made the sign of His covenant. "My bow" (קַשְׁתִּי) appears as the fronted constituent of an argument focus structure in verse 13. The word appears twice more in this scene (without the pronominal suffix; verses 14 and 16), thereby raising its thematic importance. Also occurring in this scene, and by no means insignificant, is the three-fold relexicalization of "*Mabbûl,*" each time accompanied by God's promise that never again (עוֹד; cf. scene 6) would there be another worldwide flood like this one. Verse 17 once again relexicalizes both "God" and "Noah" and forms an inclusio with verse 8. Similar to the one occurring in the previous scene, this inclusio neatly brackets the textual unit and aids greatly in defining its boundaries. The ending boundary is also reinforced by the rather abrupt change in topic occurring in Genesis 9:18. In light of the theme traces contained in this scene, its local theme can be expressed as: *God's establishment of His covenant with Noah, his descendants, and all life on the earth to never again send a worldwide flood upon the earth to destroy all life; and the sign of God's covenant—His bow—given for all life on the earth.*

EPISODE 3, SCENE 9: GENESIS 9:18–19

וַיִּהְיוּ בְנֵי־נֹחַ הַיֹּצְאִים֙ מִן־הַתֵּבָ֔ה שֵׁ֖ם וְחָ֣ם וָיָ֑פֶת וְחָ֕ם ה֖וּא אֲבִ֥י כְנָֽעַן׃

19שְׁלֹשָׁ֥ה אֵ֖לֶּה בְּנֵי־נֹ֑חַ וּמֵאֵ֖לֶּה נָֽפְצָ֥ה כָל־הָאָֽרֶץ׃

[18]And the sons of Noah, the ones coming forth from the ark, were Shem and Ham and Japheth. (Now Ham was the father of Canaan.) [19]These three were the sons of Noah, and from these was all the earth populated.

In a sense, this scene picks up the flow of the narrative where Genesis 6:10 left off, by mentioning the names of Noah's sons. The relexicalization of "Ham" followed by the use of the independent personal pronoun "he" in the verbless clause contained in the second half of verse 18 serves to state as bluntly as possible that Ham was Canaan's father. This brief topic-comment sentence proves to be extremely important background information for the next episode (Genesis 9:20–29), as well as the remainder of biblical history. The short fronted statement appearing in the latter half of verse 19 summarizes the important fact that the entire earth would be repopulated by the three sons of Noah. As a whole, this brief scene serves to draw to a close the final episode in the Flood account and the remarkable chiastic structure which binds the account together. The local theme of this textual unit is: *The sons of Noah: Shem, Ham, and Japheth, through whom all the earth was populated.* Taking into account the theme traces present in all nine scenes spanning Genesis 8:1–9:19, the global theme of this episode is too expansive to be expressed in a single sentence. Summarily stated, it includes: *God's remembrance of Noah, the recession of the Floodwaters, the grounding of the Ark and the continued subsiding of the Floodwaters; the sending out of the birds by Noah and the eventual drying up of the water from the earth; God's instruction for Noah, his family, and the animals to come out from the Ark and to repopulate the earth; Noah's exodus from the Ark in response to God's instruction and his sacrifice of an offering to God; God's reception of the sacrifice, His resolve to never again destroy all life on earth, and His act of blessing Noah and his sons, followed by His command for them to repopulate the earth; God's statement concerning the new order on the earth (with its provisions regarding eating and murder) and the establishment of His covenant with Noah, his descendants, and all creatures as signified by His bow; and the repopulation of the earth through Noah's three sons.*

5. Conclusion: Segmentation and Its Implications for the Chronology of the Flood

This study has succeeded in analyzing the information structure of the Flood account and tracing the progressive development of the account's theme throughout its numerous scenes. In doing so, this study has determined the location of thematic breaks which facilitated the segmentation of the text into episodes and scenes. In accordance with the stated goal of this study, this process of theme tracing and segmentation has produced an opportunity to gain a clearer understanding of the chronology embedded in the Flood narrative. In particular, this study has identified at least one major chronological gap and two areas of potential chronological disjunction.

The first of these findings, the chronological gap, is fairly obvious and is located at the break between episodes 1 and 2. As noted previously, the assumption in Genesis 7:1 of a completed Ark necessitates a huge leap forward chronologically, from the time of God's initial spoken revelation to Noah in episode 1, to the time of His second spoken revelation to Noah at the beginning of episode 2. Admittedly, there is no textual information to suggest precisely how long this chronological gap with regard to the Ark may have been. Moreover, while this gap is significant in the unfolding of the Flood account, it has no direct bearing on the actual chronology of the cataclysm.[44]

More important to the determination of the chronology of the Flood itself are the locations of potential chronological disjunction. The first instance of potential disjunction spans scenes 2–6 in episode 2. This study has already noted the presence of thematic interchange in these scenes from Noah and the occupants of the Ark (scene 2; Gn 7:6–9), to the Flood (scene 3; Gn 7:10–12), back to Noah and the occupants of the Ark (scene 4; Gn 7:13–16), and then back to the Flood (scenes 5 and 6; Gn 7:17–24). Such thematic interchange depends upon the use of recapitulation. The

---

44. There also remains the possibility of other, smaller chronological gaps in other places in the narrative. For example, there may be a gap of time between the exodus from the Ark and Noah's construction of an altar (Gn 8:18–20). Likewise, there may be a gap between God's reception of Noah's sacrifice and his blessing of Noah and his sons (8:22–9:1). However, unlike the instance occurring between 6:22 and 7:1, nothing in the text suggests that these gaps are substantial.

presence of this technique in these scenes is virtually undeniable in light of the opening statements of these scenes. Only once did Noah actually board the Ark and only once did the Flood actually come upon the earth. Yet these occurrences are reiterated multiple times. It is to be understood, therefore, that scene 4 takes a backwards step in time in order to expand upon scene 2. Similarly, scenes 5 and 6 take a backwards step in time to expand upon scene 3. These instances of recapitulation fit naturally into the narrative and do not create any serious problems for mapping the chronology of the Flood.

Of far more serious consequence to the determination of the Flood's chronology is the other location of potential chronological disjunction. As previously mentioned, the thematic shift from Genesis 7:24 to 8:1 at the height of the account's pervading chiastic structure allows for the *possibility* of a unique situation in the chronological progression of the account. As presented in **Section 2**, Cassuto and Chisholm agreed that Genesis 8:1, while marking the center of the chiastic structure, did not mark the centermost point in the chronology of the Flood itself but reverted to an earlier chronological point (i.e. the fortieth day of the Flood). Had there been seamless thematic progression (i.e. no notable shift in the account's topic or focus content), this possibility would be unlikely. However, as there is a considerable thematic shift occurring at this point, there remains the possibility of major chronological disjunction in which the beginning of episode 3 overlaps the concluding statement of episode 2. Such a theory contradicts none of the clear statements of the text itself and may provide for a more straightforward interpretation of the information in Genesis 8:1–5.

As stated already, the analysis of the account's information structure cannot offer positive *proof* in favor of chronological disjunction; that is the role of some of the other studies within this collaborative endeavor. Nevertheless, this analysis has served its purpose in highlighting where thematic breaks exist and, thus, where chronological disjunction may be present. In doing so, it has helped to lay a foundation for further study on the chronology of the Flood.

References

Alexander, T. D. 2002. *From paradise to Promised Land: An introduction to the Pentateuch*. 2nd ed. Grand Rapids, MI: Baker Academic.

Bandstra, B. 1992. Word order and emphasis in biblical Hebrew narrative: Syntactic observations on Genesis 22 from a discourse perspective. In *Linguistics and biblical Hebrew*. Ed. W. R. Bodine. Winona Lake, IN: Eisenbrauns.

Bandstra, B. 2008. *Genesis 1–11: A handbook on the Hebrew text.* Waco, TX: Baylor University Press.

Cassuto, U. 1997. *A commentary on the book of Genesis, part II: From Noah to Abraham.* Trans. I. Abrahams. Jerusalem, Israel: The Magnes Press.

Chisholm, R. B. Jr. 2003. History or story? The literary dimension in narrative texts. In *Giving the sense: Understanding and using Old Testament historical texts.* Ed. D. M. Howard Jr., and M. A. Grisanti. Grand Rapids, MI: Kregal Publications.

DeRouchie, J. 2013. The blessing-commission, the promised offspring, and the *toledot* structure of Genesis. *Journal of the Evangelical Theological Society* 56.2: 219–247.

Floor, S. J. 2004. *From information structure, topic and focus, to theme in biblical Hebrew narrative.* Ph.D. Diss., University of Stellenbosch.

Givón, T. 1984. *Syntax: A functional-typological introduction.* Vol. 1. Amsterdam, Netherlands and Philadelphia, PA: John Benjamins Publishing Company.

Jacobs, J. 2001. The dimensions of topic-comment. *Linguistics* 39: 645–655

Kidner, D. 1967. *Genesis.* Downers Grove, IL: InterVarsity Press.

Kintsch, W. 1998. *Comprehension: A paradigm for cognition.* Cambridge, England: Cambridge University Press.

Kozima, H. 1993. Text segmentation based on similarity between words. In *Proceedings of the 31st Annual Meeting on Association for Computational Linguistics*: 286–88. Stroudsburg, PA: Association for Computational Linguistics.

Lambrecht K. 1994. *Information structure and sentence form: Topic, focus and the mental representation of discourse referents.* Cambridge, England: Cambridge University Press.

Longacre, R. E. 1979. The discourse structure of the Flood narrative. *Journal of the American Academy of Religion* 47 Supplement: 89–133.

Nakhimovsky, A. 1988. Aspect, aspectual class, and the temporal structure of narrative. *Computational Linguistics* 14.2: 29–43.

Nakhimovsky, A. and W. J. Rapaport. 1988. Discontinuities in narrative. In *Proceedings of the 12th International Conference on Computational Linguistics,* 465–470. Stroudsburg, PA: Association for Computational Linguistics.

Runge, S. E. 2007. *A discourse-functional description of participant reference in biblical Hebrew narrative.* Ph.D. Diss., University of Stellenbosch.

Sailhamer, J. H. 2009. *The meaning of the Pentateuch: Revelation, composition and interpretation.* Downers Grove, IL: IVP Academic.

Salton, G. et al. 1996. Automatic text decomposition using text segments and text themes. In *Proceedings of the seventh ACM Conference on Hypertext*: 53–65. New York, NY: ACM.

Utiyama, M. and H. Isahara. 2001. A statistical model for domain-independent text segmentation. In *Proceedings of the 39th Annual Meeting on Association for Computational Linguistics,* 499–506. Stroudsburg, PA: Association for Computational Linguistics.

Van der Merwe, C. H. J., J. Naude, and J. Kroeze. 1999. *A biblical Hebrew reference grammar.* Sheffield, England: Sheffield Academic Press.

Wenham, G. J. 1978. The coherence of the Flood narrative. *Vetus Testamentum* 28: 336–348.

CHAPTER 15

Navigation Points in Text: Methodological and Linguistic Preliminaries for the Study of the Semantic, Syntactic, and Discourse-Pragmatic Functions of וַיְהִי in Biblical Hebrew Narrative

Drew G. Longacre

Analogy and Orientation. Reading Hebrew narrative has some analogy to maritime navigation in at least one respect. At sea a pilot is guided by buoys strategically placed to mark the proper channels to follow. Similarly, in text, readers are brought along by the narrator through the narrative via numerous temporal navigation waypoints. One of the most significant of these time buoys in Hebrew narrative is the verb וַיְהִי *way°hî, which often marks key points in the temporal flow of the narrative and provides otherwise orientating information to help the reader navigate through the narrative. Because this verb occurs numerous times at key points in the Genesis Flood narrative, understanding its functions will form an integral part of understanding the narrative structure of the text.*

Abstract. Because the Hebrew verb וַיְהִי *way°hî* occurs at a number of key points in the Genesis Flood narrative, any detailed investigation into the information structure of the text must necessarily take account of its role in structuring and advancing the narrative. The following chapter lays down some methodological guidelines and an overview of some of the most important questions about the significance of וַיְהִי by examining key issues concerning lexical-level semantics, sentence-level syntax, paragraph-level syntax, narrative-level structure, and discourse-pragmatic functions.

Outline

1. Introduction
2. Lexical-Level Semantics
3. Sentence-Level Syntax
4. Paragraph-Level Syntax
5. Narrative-Level Structure
6. Discourse-Pragmatic Functions
7. Conclusion

1. Introduction

In order to understand the structure of the Genesis Flood narrative, we must first understand the function of the prominent verb וַיְהִי *way^ehî* in BH narrative. Its linguistic status and pragmatic function in discourse have been the source of intense controversy in recent years, and there is still far from a consensus on what precisely it is and does. Since it occurs at significant points in the Genesis text (7:10, 12, 17; 8:6, 13), this state of affairs poses significant challenges to tracing the information structure of the narrative. For instance, does the וַיְהִי in 7:10 anchor the onset of the Flood to a sequential narrative timeline (in which case the Flood would have come in between at least two separate entrances of Noah into the Ark—cf. 7:7, 13, 15), or is narrative time progression suspended or reversed at points in the narrative? Or do the וַיְהִיs in 7:12 and 7:17 signal the onset of the event(s) they describe (in which case the forty days of flooding would have occurred twice and the waters would not have begun to rise until after the rain had ceased) or do they simply serve to summarize the situation? In order to provide the theoretical background for further linguistic study of וַיְהִי and for applying these results to the examples in the Flood narrative, I will here describe the most important problems and theories associated with וַיְהִי concerning lexical-level semantics, sentence-level syntax, paragraph-level syntax, narrative-level structure, and discourse-pragmatic functions.

2. Lexical-Level Semantics

וַיְהִי is a *Qal*-stem *wayyiqtol*-form third person masculine singular stative verb from the root היה "to be." The *Qal* stem is not particularly controversial, as it is the simple active stem. The significances of all of the other data are, however, extraordinarily contentious. The stative nature of the verb and its *wayyiqtol* form, in particular, are integral to understanding its semantics on the lexical level.

2.1 *Verbal Aspect*

Verbal aspect is a significant factor in determining the nature of וַיְהִי.
Linguists commonly distinguish between two types of verbal aspect (see
Akagi, **Chapter 11** of this volume for more detailed discussion). Viewpoint
aspect refers to the perspective with which an author chooses to portray
the internal time of events, which can ordinarily be classified as perfective
(portraying the verbal event as an undifferentiated whole) or imperfective
(portraying the verbal event with emphasis on its internal constitution).
Situation aspect refers to the semantically inherent temporal nature of the
event itself as it is portrayed by a given verbal lexeme with its modifiers.

Wayyiqtol-form verbs are normally considered to have perfective viewpoint
aspect (e.g., Waltke and O'Connor 1990, 546)—which, I agree, accurately
reflects the standard usage of the form—so we would *prima facie* expect
the same of וַיְהִי (so Longacre 2003, 64). The fact that וַיְהִי is a stative verb,
however, complicates this picture, since many characteristics of stative verbs
are often associated with imperfective viewpoint aspect (Eskhult 1990, 27).
We must, then, factor in the situation aspect of the verb to get a full picture
of its significance. When used with the pure stative nuance "to be" (which
indicates a state of being) the lexeme וַיְהִי inherently describes a durative
(ongoing) state of affairs. In contrast, when the dynamic nuance "to
become" or "to begin to be" (which indicates entrance into a state of being)
is appropriate, it is non-durative. וַיְהִי may, then, have perfective viewpoint
aspect and at the same time refer to events whose temporal nature affects the
semantics of the verb. The semantic distinction between dynamic and pure
stative nuances is important for information structure in Hebrew narrative,
because the former can often function on the main event line of a narrative,
while the latter generally do not, as can be seen in examples (1a-b) and (2)
respectively.

(1) Dynamic

a.　　　　　　　　　　　וַיְהִי הָאָדָם לְנֶפֶשׁ חַיָּה (Gn 2:7)
　　　　　　　　　　　　　*And the man **became** a living being.*

b.

וַיְהִי־אוֹר (Gn 1:3)
*And light **came**
into being.*

(2) Stative

וַיְהִי יוֹסֵף יְפֵה־תֹאַר וִיפֵה מַרְאֶה (Gn 39:6)
*And Joseph **was** handsome in
form and appearance.*

2.2 *Tense Value?*

Some linguists attribute to the *wayyiqtol* verb form a marked tense value, considering it a past tense narrative form or "preterite" (e.g., Cook 2004, 258, 261). Applied to וַיְהִי, Cook argues that BH by default does not use an explicit copula for present tense, but that it does use וַיְהִי for past tense (2012, 309).[1] This claim remains controversial, particularly because of examples of *wayyiqtol-*form verbs in verse which are better understood as non-past, as in example (4) (Waltke and O'Connor 1990, 546, 557). Niccacci (1990, 159), accordingly, argues that וַיְהִי has no tense of its own, but rather continues the tense of its context. The overwhelming number of *wayyiqtol-*form verbs are clearly past tense as in example (3), however, and I am not aware of a single non-past use of וַיְהִי.[2] The tense value of וַיְהִי, or its lack thereof, will relate to the discussion below of the theory which makes וַיְהִי a tense marker (**Subsection 6.1**). The following are examples of *wayyiqtol-*form verbs (according to the Masoretic vocalization), which occur in both past and non-past contexts.

(3) Past *Wayyiqtol*

וַיֹּאכַל הָעָם וַיִּשְׁתַּחֲווּ לֵאלֹהֵיהֶן (Nm 25:2)
*And the people **ate** and **bowed
down** to their gods.*

(4) Non-Past *Wayyiqtol*

אָכְלוּ וַיִּשְׁתַּחֲווּ כָּל־דִּשְׁנֵי־אֶרֶץ (Ps 22:30 [Heb])
*All the rich of the earth **will** eat and **bow down**…*

2.3 *Sequentiality?*

וַיְהִי is commonly assumed to indicate sequential events as in example (5) (Floss 1985, 39–40; van der Merwe 1999, 98, 109), based on the consecutive

---

1. According to Cook, the *qatal form of* היה also indicates past tense, *yiqtol* indicates future tense, and *wᵉqatal* indicates irrealis mood.
2. At least according to Masoretic vocalization. Examples like וַיְהִי in 1 Samuel 10:5 might be seen as exceptions to this, but they are textually dubitable (see **Subsection 2.5**).

theory for *wayyiqtol*-form verbs. Because *wayyiqtol*-form verbs are often considered to be marked for sequentiality or event-line progress, this broad semantic category is then mapped onto וַיְהִי.

This theory will be discussed further under the discourse-pragmatic functions of וַיְהִי (**Subsection 6.4**), but it is sufficient at this point to argue that such sequentiality should not be hastily assumed based on the *wayyiqtol* verbal form of וַיְהִי (Harmelink 2004, 135). The intrinsic sequentiality of *wayyiqtol*-form verbs in general is a highly questionable assertion (see Stroup, **Chapter 10** of this volume), and such event-line consecution should probably be attributed to typical narrative strategy rather than any morphologically marked quality (Cook 2004, 257–261). This counter-argument is bolstered in our case by examples of וַיְהִי which cannot be explained as temporally advancing the narrative, such as flashbacks as in 1 Kings 11:15 and example (6) (Gropp 1995, 200)[3] and frequent examples where וַיְהִי introduces new biblical books (e.g., Joshua, Judges, Ruth, Samuel, Nehemiah, Esther, Ezekiel, Jonah).[4] Thus, even though the majority of uses of וַיְהִי do involve some temporal progression in the narrative, sequentiality does not appear to be an intrinsic property of וַיְהִי, as the following examples show.

(5) Sequential וַיְהִי

> וַיֵּשֶׁב אַבְרָהָם בִּבְאֵר שָׁבַע וַיְהִי
> אַחֲרֵי הַדְּבָרִים הָאֵלֶּה וַיֻּגַּד
> לְאַבְרָהָם (Gn 22:19–20)
> *And Abraham dwelt in Beersheba.*
> *And **after these things, it was***
> ***told** to Abraham . . .*

(6) Non-Sequential וַיְהִי

> וַיִּקְרָא אַחְאָב אֶל־עֹבַדְיָהוּ אֲשֶׁר עַל־
> הַבָּיִת וְעֹבַדְיָהוּ הָיָה יָרֵא אֶת־יְהֹוָה מְאֹד
> וַיְהִי בְּהַכְרִית אִיזֶבֶל אֵת נְבִיאֵי יְהֹוָה
> וַיִּקַּח עֹבַדְיָהוּ מֵאָה נְבִאִים
> וַיַּחְבִּיאֵם (1 Kgs 18:3–4)

---

3. van der Merwe (1999, 101–02, 107, 109, 113) cites numerous other examples of וַיְהִי which he cannot explain on the basis of his own theory of temporal progression (e.g., 1 Sm 1:2; 7:10; 23:26; 2 Sm 3:2; 21:20; 1 Kgs 5:2, 6, 29).

4. Even if some of these examples can be explained by inner-canonical connections, it is unlikely that all of them can be. These are compelling counter-examples, because the first verb in a literary work cannot possibly follow a previous verb temporally and, thus, cannot be marked for sequentiality. van der Merwe (1999, 102), recognizes this difficulty, though he discounts it in the end.

> *And Ahab called Obadiah, who was over his*
> *house. Obadiah feared the* Lord *very much,*
> ***and when Jezebel had been killing*** *the*
> *prophets of the* Lord, *Obadiah **had taken***
> *100 prophets and **hidden** them...*

2.4 *Grammaticalization?*

One further complicating factor at the lexical level is the question of whether וַיְהִי should actually be analyzed as a true verb at all, or whether it is instead a grammaticalized particle. It is possible that some of the usages of וַיְהִי have become so stereotyped that they cease to function as normal Hebrew verbs and take on a life of their own as mere grammatical markers. This may be indicated by the fact that, in many instances, וַיְהִי may play no verbal role in the sentence. Harmelink (2004, 274–77), for instance, argues that וַיְהִי functions like a deictic particle for three reasons: 1) Only וַיְהִי precedes temporal clauses, not other similar forms (see **Subsection 2.5**); 2) וַיְהִי has no explicit subject (see **Subsection 3.3**); and 3) "וַיְהִי has no nominal or adjectival complement in the temporal clause (276)." Others, like Niccacci (1990, 159–160), insist that temporal וַיְהִי retains its verbal nature, rather than being grammaticalized (or in Niccacci's terms "fossilized"). For Niccacci, this means that we must view וַיְהִי as functioning verbally on the narrative level, rather than the sentence level. Endo retains the verbal nature of וַיְהִי by interpreting it as a cleft construction, "And it was when... that..." (1996, 176), and a number of similar explanations will be detailed below. Whether or not וַיְהִי retains its verbal qualities may have a dramatic effect on perceptions of its function.

2.5 *Alternative Forms*

Because of its verbal qualities, וַיְהִי cannot be considered in isolation, but must also be viewed in connection with similar morphological forms (Harmelink 2004, 64–65). In particular other *wayyiqtol* forms of היה "to be" with different person, gender, and/or number should be taken into account (e.g., וַתְּהִי, וַיִּהְיוּ). In this connection, it is interesting to note that no other *wayyiqtol* forms are used to introduce temporal clauses, indicating a specialized usage for וַיְהִי before temporal clauses (Harmelink 2004, 252). Also significant for comparison is the parallel *wᵉqatal* form וְהָיָה, which has a similar range of functions as וַיְהִי, though it is not generally found in the narrative mode of discourse (Harmelink 2004, 451–52). In this regard, exceptions to the standard patterns of ויהי in past contexts and והיה in non-past or habitual-past contexts complicate the picture considerably, if they are indeed sound readings (Bartelmus 1982, 224–25; Endo 1996, 184–86).[5]

2.6 Diachronic Development

Another complicating factor in studying וַיְהִי is the historical development of the Hebrew language. In post-BH, וַיְהִי eventually completely loses its function before temporal clauses. Though וַיְהִי occurs before temporal clauses in biblical books both early and late, some have argued that this function of וַיְהִי is already getting less common in the later biblical books (e.g., Qimron 1986, 72–73; Eskhult 1990, 115–16), which would be important to take into consideration when studying its uses in different books. Compare examples (7) and (8) for possible diachronic development of the language.

(7) Early

וַיְהִי כְּכַלּוֹת שְׁלֹמֹה לְהִתְפַּלֵּל (1 Kgs 8:54)
And when Solomon had finished praying...

(8) Late

וּכְכַלּוֹת שְׁלֹמֹה לְהִתְפַּלֵּל (2 Chr 7:1)
And when Solomon had finished praying...

3. Sentence-Level Syntax

The syntactical role that וַיְהִי plays in sentences has been the topic of a great deal of discussion in recent years, and there are still many points of disagreement. A couple of key questions require further examination.

3.1   Verbal vs. Temporal
3.2   Connection between Temporal וַיְהִי and Temporal Clauses
3.3   Prominence of Fronted Temporal Clauses
3.4   Subjects of Temporal וַיְהִי
3.5   Participants in Temporal Clauses
3.6   Semantic Nature of Temporal Clauses
3.7   Continuation Forms

3.1 Verbal vs. Temporal

The most fundamental distinction to be made when studying וַיְהִי is

---

5. Many וַיְהִי forms (e.g., 1 Sm 10:5; 2 Sm 5:24; 1 Kgs 14:5 [MT]; 1 Chr 14:15; Ru 3:4) are often emended to the more common form וְהָיָה in critical texts, and often not without good reason. 4QSam[a], for instance, reads והיה for the MT ויהי in 1 Samuel 10:5 (Ulrich 2010, 270).

between verbal and temporal syntactical constructions (Harmelink 2004).[6] In verbal constructions, וַיְהִי behaves syntactically as a normal stative verb (or predicate), which indicates the state of being of its syntactic subject. In temporal constructions, however, וַיְהִי serves the special syntactic role of introducing a temporal adverbial clause. The two categories of וַיְהִי behave very differently on nearly every level and so should be carefully distinguished, as in examples (9) and (10).

(9) Verbal

וַיְהִי רָעָב בָּאָרֶץ (Gn 12:10)
And there was a famine in the land.

(10) Temporal

וַיְהִי בִּהְיוֹתָם בַּשָּׂדֶה וַיָּקָם קַיִן (Gn 4:8)
And when they were in the field, Cain rose up...

3.2 *Connection between Temporal* וַיְהִי *and Temporal Clauses*

The sentence-level syntax of temporal uses of וַיְהִי is extraordinarily complex and controversial. In particular, scholars in recent decades have debated the connection between a temporal וַיְהִי and the following temporal clause. Some have argued that וַיְהִי plus a temporal clause should be understood as an independent sentence (with the temporal clause subordinate to וַיְהִי) providing the temporal context for the following events, which might be literally translated "And it happened that...," followed by the following independent sentence "And then..." (Vanoni 1982; Gross 1987, 69, 76–77; Schneider 1993, 79). Similarly, Endo (1996, 176–77) argues that it is a cleft construction, dividing a single sentence into two sections, as in "And it was when... that..." Such understandings may be supported by treating וַיְהִי as a true verb and the formal evidence which normally separates וַיְהִי plus temporal clause from the following verb with a conjunction וֹ, as in examples (11a-b).

---

6. Since on some theories even "temporal" וַיְהִי may retain its verbal properties, the terminology would need to be adjusted accordingly. Cook (2012, 310) prefers to speak of a copular or predicate usage and a discourse usage, which would resolve this tension, but at the same time it would commit oneself to the theory of a discourse-level significance for the usage of וַיְהִי with a temporal clause. Harmelink's descriptive taxonomy has been utilized here, despite its potential difficulties.

(11) Separated by Conjunction

a. וַיְהִי בִּהְיוֹתָם בַּשָּׂדֶה וַיָּקָם קַיִן (Gn 4:8)
And when they were in the
field, (**and**) *Cain rose up...*

b. וַיְהִי כְעָבְרָם וְאֵלִיָּהוּ אָמַר (2 Kgs 2:9)
And when they had crossed
over, (**and**) *Elijah said...*

Others have argued, however, that וַיְהִי plus temporal clause is not an independent sentence at all. Instead, the temporal clause is merely a fronted,[7] temporal adjunct of the following verb, and וַיְהִי is an optional, syntactically disjointed element (Richter 1980, 206; Bartelmus 1982, 102, 114, 213–17; Floss 1985, 39–47, 88–98; Niccacci 1990, 56, 142–4, 158–59; Gropp 1995, 203; van der Merwe 1999, 100; Longacre 2003, 66; Harmelink 2004, 254, 273–75, 425–26; Holmstedt and Cook 2011; Cook 2012, 311). According to this theory, the temporal clause may be shifted from its default position towards the end of the sentence to the beginning to mark it for some sort of prominence (van der Merwe 1999, 93–94), a syntactical construction on which וַיְהִי has no effect. The examples below show temporal clauses in their default position (12) and fronted, where the fronted temporal clauses may (14a-b) or may not (13a-b) be preceded by וַיְהִי.

(12) Default

וַיֵּבְךְ יוֹסֵף בְּדַבְּרָם אֵלָיו (Gn 50:17)
And Joseph wept **when**
they told him.

(13) Fronted

a. בְּלֶכְתּוֹ אֶל־צִיקְלַג נָפְלוּ עָלָיו מִמְּנַשֶּׁה (1 Chr 12:21)
When he went to Ziklag, *some*
of the Manassites joined him.

b. בַּיּוֹם הַשְּׁלִישִׁי וַיִּשָּׂא אַבְרָהָם (Gn 22:4)
On the third day, *Abraham*
lifted up...

---

7. Van der Merwe, Naudé, and Kroeze (1999, 339), classify examples where the temporal adjunct is separated from the main sentence by a ו "dislocated constructions" rather than "fronted," since the intervening conjunction makes for a syntactic disjunction. Nevertheless, they still understand the temporal clause as an adjunct modifying the main verb in the following sentence, so this fine distinction makes little difference in their analysis.

(14) Fronted Plus וַיְהִי

a.   (Neh 1:4) וַיְהִי כְּשָׁמְעִי אֶת־הַדְּבָרִים הָאֵלֶּה יָשַׁבְתִּי
     And when I heard these words, I sat down...

b.   (Gn 4:8) וַיְהִי בִּהְיוֹתָם בַּשָּׂדֶה וַיָּקָם קַיִן
     *And when they were in the
     field,* Cain rose up...

The understanding that וַיְהִי is not integrally connected with its following
temporal clause as an independent sentence, but is instead an optional
element appended to a sentence with a fronted temporal adjunct may be
supported by the arguments that וַיְהִי is functioning as a grammaticalized
marker that cannot be understood as a complete, independent sentence
(see **Subsection 2.4**) or that it is functioning as a verb on a level above
the sentence-level syntax (Niccacci 1990, 159–160). Additionally, counter-
examples where וַיְהִי plus temporal clause is not formally separated from the
following verbs with the conjunction ו may point in this direction.

(15) Not Separated by Conjunction

(Neh 1:4) וַיְהִי כְּשָׁמְעִי אֶת־הַדְּבָרִים הָאֵלֶּה יָשַׁבְתִּי
And when I heard these words, I sat down...

More importantly, there are also a number of often-overlooked examples
where fronted temporal adverbials without וַיְהִי are separated from the
following verbs with the conjunction ו, but yet remain dependent on them,
undermining one of the main arguments in favor of understanding וַיְהִי plus
temporal clause as an independent sentence.

(16) Subordination Despite Separating Conjunction

a.   (Gn 22:4) בַּיּוֹם הַשְּׁלִישִׁי וַיִּשָּׂא אַבְרָהָם
     *On the third day, (and)
     Abraham lifted up...*

b.   (Jgs 11:16) בַּעֲלוֹתָם מִמִּצְרָיִם וַיֵּלֶךְ יִשְׂרָאֵל
     *When they went up from Egypt,
     (and) Israel went...*

c.   (2 Sm 15:10) כְּשָׁמְעֲכֶם אֶת־קוֹל הַשֹּׁפָר וַאֲמַרְתֶּם
     *When you hear the trumpet's sound,
     (and) you shall say...*

d.   וּבְבֹא מֹשֶׁה אֶל־אֹהֶל ... וַיִּשְׁמַע (Num 7:89)
     And when Moses entered the tent..., (and) he heard...

This interpretation is further confirmed by comparison of parallel passages where the temporal clauses preceded by וַיְהִי are clearly understood as subordinate to the following verbs, as in example (17) (Cook 2012, 311).[8]

(17) Subordination in Parallel Passages

a.   (2 Kgs 22:3) שָׁלַח...אֶת־שָׁפָן...עֶשְׂרֵה שָׁנָה וַיְהִי בִּשְׁמֹנֶה
(And) in the eighteenth year..., *he sent Shaphan...*

b.   (2 Chr 34:8) שָׁלַח...אֶת־שָׁפָן עֶשְׂרֵה...וּבִשְׁנַת שְׁמוֹנֶה
(And) in the eighteenth year . . . , he sent Shaphan . . .

If scholars conclude that וַיְהִי is an optional addition to fronted temporal adjuncts, they must then also seek to answer a number of additional questions. They must determine the reasons for this syntactic shift of the temporal clauses into fronted position. And they must also explain the difference between the less common fronted forms without וַיְהִי and the fronted forms with וַיְהִי. The latter question will be further discussed under the consideration of the discourse-pragmatic functions of וַיְהִי (**Section 6**).

3.3 Prominence of Fronted Temporal Clauses

The question of why temporal clauses might be fronted is complicated. Scholars still debate precisely what effect וַיְהִי has on this construction (see **Subsection 6.5**), but most discussions share some similar starting points. As mentioned above, most agree that the default, unmarked position for temporal expressions is at the end of a sentence (Gross 1996, 259; cited in van der Merwe 1999, 93–94).[9] As a consequence of this, shifting the temporal expression to the front of the sentence may be a means of thematically promoting the expression.[10] Some identify this thematic prominence as focus (Endo 1996, 176–78; van der Merwe 1999, 93–94, 110–12), but others prefer to identify it with topic (Floor 2004, 100–04, 293–94; Holmstedt and Cook 2011).[11] Floor (2004,

8. Cook also cites the parallel passages in 1 Kgs 8:54 and 2 Chr 7:1 (see examples (7) and (8) above) as well as 2 Kgs 12:11 and 2 Chr 24:11.

9. van der Merwe (1999, 112) makes the interesting observation that, because the default position places temporal clauses at the end of sentences, fronted temporal clauses might occasionally be misinterpreted as referring to the *previous* sentence, rather than the *following*. In these cases, וַיְהִי may be obligatory to avoid the ambiguity by separating the temporal clause from the preceding sentence.

10. van der Merwe (1999, 94) notes, however, that Gross does not find sufficient evidence for concluding that fronting temporal clauses puts them in a marked word order. If fronting alone is, indeed, not significant enough to mark a temporal clause for thematic prominence, perhaps this marking could be a primary function of וַיְהִי (see **Subsection 6.5**).

11. In terms of information structure, topic, and focus refer to the given information and the additional information respectively. Topic is what the sentence is about, and focus what is said about it. See Floor (2004) for a detailed description of topic and focus in BH.

100–04, 293–94) argues that וַיְהִי plus temporal clause is topic-framing, setting the deictic (spacio-temporal) orientation for the following text.[12]

The precise terminology used by different scholars is conflicting, but their general conclusions are similar. The significance of this thematically promoted structure is generally to update the reference time in the narrative (van der Merwe 1999, 93–97; Floor 2004, 100–04; Cook 2012, 312).[13] Gropp adds the significant qualification, however, that while temporal clauses with בְּ often occur in both default and fronted position, temporal clauses with כְּ are almost exclusively fronted, which must affect our evaluation of their prominence (1995, 209). He understands the significance of the fronting generally as backreferencing to previous events, strengthening the cohesion of the narrative (1995, 185).

3.4 Subjects of Temporal וַיְהִי

Equally as perplexing as the relationship of the וַיְהִי plus temporal clause to the following verb is the question of the subject of the temporal וַיְהִי in such cases. If functioning as a verb, we would naturally expect to find a grammatical subject for any given וַיְהִי, but the nature of the subject is not immediately evident. The facts that temporal וַיְהִי has no obvious, explicit subject[14] and that no other forms of different person, gender, or number are used with temporal clauses (see **Subsection 2.5**) make this a difficult question for those who stress the verbal nature of וַיְהִי. The subject could be understood as impersonal "it" (Longacre 2003, 67–88), the following adverbial element, the following paragraph (Niccacci 1990, 160), or even perhaps non-existent (Harmelink 2004, 276; Cook 2012, 310). The last conclusion fits naturally with theories that take temporal וַיְהִי as a grammaticalized particle (see **Subsection 2.4**).

3.5 Participants in Temporal Clauses

It is also important to note any participants in the temporal clause and compare them with the participants in the following verbal clause in order to understand how the clauses are related (Harmelink 2004, 298–99). The temporal clause

12. I.e., it is topical not in the sense that the sentence is about it, but that it sets "the spatio-temporal framework in which the topics operate" (100).

13. Reference time is the time relative to which events are viewed, as opposed to the event time (when the event itself took place) and the speech time (when the event was narrated) (Declerck 1991, 224–25). For example, in the phrase, "By ten o'clock, I had gone to sleep," the speech time is when I wrote the sentence, the event time is when I went to sleep, and the reference time is ten o'clock, the time before which the event is said to have occurred.

14. I.e., וַיְהִי does not consistently agree in person, gender, and number with any element in the sentence (Harmelink 2004, 158; Cook 2012, 310).

with וַיְהִי may have no active participants, the same participant(s) as the subject(s) of the following verb, different participant(s) from the subject(s) of the following verb, participants inclusive of the subject(s) of the following verb, or participant(s) included among the subjects of the following verb.

3.6 Semantic Nature of Temporal Clauses

Many scholars have also pointed out the importance of examining the semantic nature of the temporal clauses which follow וַיְהִי to understanding its significance. Van der Merwe, for instance, categorizes the temporal clauses into durations of time, frequency of events, and points in time (1999, 96, 103–04). His study of 1 Samuel reveals no instances of וַיְהִי preceding a temporal clause indicating duration[15] and only one frequentative example (1 Sm 18:30).[16] The great majority of examples place events on a timeline, providing either the temporal frame in which the event occurs or the exact point at which it is located. These categories are particularly important for van der Merwe, because they often have different pragmatic distributions and functions. For him, examples indicating the frequency of events tend to anchor a state of affairs onto a timeline (1999, 104, 114). Also, framing temporal clauses (normally introduced by the preposition בְּ) tend to introduce scenes or sub-sections, whereas exact-point temporal clauses (often marked by the preposition כְּ) tend to occur at significant points inside scenes (1999, 114).[17] Examples (18), (19), and (20) demonstrate temporal clauses indicating frequency, time frame, and exact point in time.

(18) Frequency

וַיְהִי מִדֵּי צֵאתָם שָׂכַל דָּוִד (1 Sm 18:30)
And as often as they went out, David succeeded...

(19) Time Frame

וַיְהִי בַּיּוֹם הַהוּא וַיָּבֹאוּ (Gn 26:32)
And on that day, they came...

---

15. Indeed, van der Merwe (1999, 96) says that he has not found any fronted temporal adjuncts referring to the duration of an event in Deuteronomy, Judges, 1 and 2 Samuel or 1 and 2 Kings. He explains this by arguing that durations of time cannot anchor events on a timeline or update the reference time, which is the normal significance he attributes to fronted temporal clauses.

16. He also cites 1 Kgs 14:28; 2 Kgs 4:8; 2 Chr 12:11 as additional frequentative examples outside of his corpus. Compare Is 28:19; Jer 20:8; 31:20; 48:27 as similar examples where וַיְהִי is omitted in dialogue.

17. This corresponds well with what Gropp (1995, 210) says when he claims that temporal clauses with כְּ often initiate narrative material on the main narrative event line, whereas those with בְּ normally initiate off the main line information.

(20) Exact Point in Time

וַיְהִי כְּהַזְכִּירוֹ אֶת־אֲרוֹן הָאֱלֹהִים וַיִּפֹּל (1 Sm 4:18)
And when he mentioned the
ark of God, he fell...

Gropp argues similarly to van der Merwe that כ normally marks a temporal clause for succession (indicating the exact point after which the following event occurs), whereas ב is unmarked for succession, allowing for either succession or temporal overlap with the following event (1995, 205–09; cf. Niccacci 1990, 53).

(21) Succession

a.   וַיְהִי כְּהַזְכִּירוֹ אֶת־אֲרוֹן הָאֱלֹהִים וַיִּפֹּל (1 Sm 4:18)
And when (i.e., immediately after) he
mentioned the ark of God, he fell...

b.   וַיְהִי כְּבוֹאוֹ וַיִּתְקַע בַּשּׁוֹפָר (Jgs 3:27)
And when (i.e., immediately after)
he arrived, he blew the trumpet...

(22) Temporal Overlap

וַיְהִי בַּיּוֹם הַהוּא וַיָּבֹאוּ (Gn 26:32)
An on (i.e., during) that
day, they came...

We should further note the significant point that many fronted temporal clauses contain backreferencing material, or reference to previous information either stated or implied in the preceding text (Gropp 1995, 185; Longacre 2003, 8–67). These references to previous information strengthen the cohesion of the narrative by making explicit connections between paragraphs and narrative units (Gropp 1995, 185). Gropp particularly notes that כ plus an infinitive construct is nearly always backreferencing (1995, 183).

(23) Backreferencing

a.   וַיַּעַבְרוּ שְׁנֵיהֶם בֶּחָרָבָה וַיְהִי כְעָבְרָם
וְאֵלִיָּהוּ אָמַר (2 Kgs 2:8–9)
*And the two of them **crossed over***
*on dry ground. **And when they had***
***crossed over**, Elijah said...*

b.
וַיְהִי אַחַר הַדְּבָרִים הָאֵלֶּה וְהָאֱלֹהִים
נִסָּה אֶת־אַבְרָהָם (Gn 22:1)
And after these things (i.e., the
preceding events), God tested
Abraham…

These backreferences may indicate the direction of temporal motion between
the narrative units they connect, as in examples (24–26).

(24) Anterior

וַיִּקְרָא אַחְאָב אֶל־עֹבַדְיָהוּ אֲשֶׁר עַל־הַבָּיִת וְעֹבַדְיָהוּ הָיָה יָרֵא
אֶת־יְהוָה מְאֹד וַיְהִי בְּהַכְרִית אִיזֶבֶל אֵת נְבִיאֵי יְהוָה וַיִּקַּח
עֹבַדְיָהוּ מֵאָה נְבִיאִים וַיַּחְבִּיאֵם (1 Kgs 18:3–4)
*And Ahab called Obadiah, who was over his house. Obadiah
feared the* LORD *very much,* **and when Jezebel had been killing**
the prophets of the LORD, *Obadiah* **had taken** *100 prophets and*
hidden *them…*

(25) Simultaneous

וַיִּקַּח שְׁמוּאֵל טְלֵה חָלָב אֶחָד וַיַּעֲלֵהוּ עוֹלָה כָּלִיל לַיהוָה
וַיִּזְעַק שְׁמוּאֵל אֶל־יְהוָה בְּעַד יִשְׂרָאֵל וַיַּעֲנֵהוּ יְהוָה וַיְהִי
שְׁמוּאֵל מַעֲלֶה הָעוֹלָה וּפְלִשְׁתִּים נִגְּשׁוּ (1 Sm 7:9–10)
*And Samuel took a suckling lamb and offered it up as a
whole burnt offering to the* LORD. *Then Samuel cried out to
the* LORD *on behalf of Israel, and the* LORD *answered him.
And* **while Samuel was offering** *up the sacrifice, the
Philistines drew near…*

(26) Sequential

וַיֵּשֶׁב אַבְרָהָם בִּבְאֵר שָׁבַע וַיְהִי אַחֲרֵי הַדְּבָרִים
הָאֵלֶּה וַיֻּגַּד לְאַבְרָהָם (Gn 22:19–20)
And Abraham dwelt in Beersheba. And **after**
these things, it was told *to Abraham…*

Gropp makes one final point about fronted temporal adverbials that may
also affect the way we analyze וַיְהִי. Often temporal clauses, by way of
lexical choice and other means, can signal a change in participants' point
of reference, which commonly indicates changes of scene (1995, 197). For
instance, if a participant is first said to go somewhere, his arrival at that
location would imply a new setting.

(27) Introducing New Setting

וַיִּמָּלֵט הַשְּׂעִירָתָה וַיְהִי בְּבוֹאוֹ וַיִּתְקַע בַּשּׁוֹפָר (Jgs 3:26–27)

And he escaped (old vantage point) to Seirah. And when
he arrived (new vantage point), he blew the trumpet...

All of these conclusions may argue that many of the functions commonly attributed to וַיְהִי are actually performed by the following temporal clauses, which would further complicate the question of וַיְהִי's semantic or pragmatic contribution (van der Merwe 1999, 108–09). For all of these reasons we cannot overlook the semantic nature of temporal clauses following temporal וַיְהִי for their influence on the pragmatic distribution of וַיְהִי and the temporal structuring of the text.

3.7 Continuation Forms

Another important question is to ask which forms continue the syntax following the וַיְהִי plus temporal clauses. These clauses can be followed by *wayyiqtol*-form verbs, *qatal*-form verbs, *we-x-qatal*,[18] *we-x-qotel*(?), *yiqtol*-form verbs, *wᵉqatal*-form verbs, or a simple nominal clause, the former three being the most common and the latter four being quite rare. These different continuation forms may entail semantic distinctions and affect the relationships between וַיְהִי plus temporal clauses and the following clauses. For instance, Harmelink concludes that *wayyiqtol* continuation forms give the first event for the given temporal reference frame, whereas *qatal* continuation forms give information anterior to the given temporal reference frame (2004, 439). Gropp argues that some *qatal* continuation forms may narrate events on the main line, whereas *we-x-qatal* do not (1995, 203). Below are examples of the various types of continuation forms.

(28) *Wayyiqtol*

וַיְהִי בִּהְיוֹתָם בַּשָּׂדֶה וַיָּקָם קַיִן (Gn 4:8)

And when they were in
the field, Cain rose up...

(29) *Qatal*

וַיְהִי כְּשָׁמְעִי אֶת־הַדְּבָרִים הָאֵלֶּה יָשַׁבְתִּי (Neh 1:4)

And when I heard these words, I sat down...

(30) *We-x-qatal*

וַיְהִי כְעָבְרָם וְאֵלִיָּהוּ אָמַר (2 Kgs 2:9)

And when they had crossed
over, Elijah said...

---

18. I.e., a conjunction ו with a *qatal*-form verb, separated by a non-verbal element.

(31) *We-x-qotel* (?)

וַיְהִי מִקֵּץ שְׁנָתַיִם יָמִים וּפַרְעֹה חֹלֵם (Gn 41:1)[19]
*And after two full years, **Pharaoh was dreaming**...*

(32) *Yiqtol*

וַיְהִי כִּקְרוֹא יְהוּדִי שָׁלֹשׁ דְּלָתוֹת וְאַרְבָּעָה יִקְרָעֶהָ (Jer 36:23)
And whenever Jehudi would read three or
*four columns, **he would cut it off**...*

(33) *Wᵉqatal*

וַיְהִי...כִּרְאוֹתָם...וּבָא סוֹפֵר (2 Chr 24:11)[20]
And...whenever they would see
*...**the scribe would come**...*

(34) Simple Nominal Clause

וַיְהִי בִּרְאֹתִי וַאֲנִי בְּשׁוּשַׁן (Dn 8:2)
*And when I saw, **I***
***was in Susa**...*

4. Paragraph-Level Syntax

The locations of the וַיְהִי clauses with respect to paragraph divisions is also worthy of consideration. The overwhelming majority of occurrences are found at the beginning of paragraphs, so much so that some scholars have considered temporal וַיְהִי to be primarily a paragraph marker (Gropp 1995, 185; Heller 2004, 434). וַיְהִי can also be found in the middle and at the end of paragraphs, however, as well as in positions which cannot easily be located within a paragraph at all.[21] As might be expected, these paragraph-level positions often correspond to higher level discourse-pragmatic functions. וַיְהִי found at the beginning of paragraphs normally introduces and gives orientation to narrative units. Accordingly, temporal וַיְהִי tends to be found at the beginning of paragraphs, as is orientating verbal וַיְהִי. וַיְהִי found in the middle of paragraphs tends to be verbal and further the story line with dynamic events (van der Merwe, Naudé, and Kroeze 1999, 333). And וַיְהִי found at the end of paragraphs tends to be verbal and summarize preceding content (van der Merwe, Naudé, and Kroeze 1999, 333). Thus, it is clear that proper evaluation of וַיְהִי requires not only analysis of its sentence-level syntax, but also its position on the paragraph level.

---

19. According to the Masoretic vocalization, חֹלֵם is vocalized as a participle, though it is also possible to read this example as a *qatal*-form verb.

20. The syntax for this example is complicated with two parallel infinitives construct introduced by a single וַיְהִי and numerous subordinate clauses, but the example seems sound.

21. E.g., sub-paragraphs and extra-paragraph comments.

In connection with paragraphs, it might also be intriguing to see how the pragmatic distribution of וַיְהִי correlates to Longacre's paragraph types (2003, 81ff.). According to Longacre, paragraphs can be classed into a number of types, each potentially reflecting different distribution patterns:

- **Sequence** (indicating temporal progression)
- **Simple** (including only one preterite)
- **Reason** (indicating a reason)
- **Result** (indicating a result)
- **Comment** (commenting on an event in the story line)
- **Amplification** (amplifying a thesis)
- **Paraphrase** (adding little or no information)
- **Coordinate** (linking by common ideas within paragraphs)
- **Antithetical** (contrasting within the paragraph)

5. Narrative-Level Structure

As an extension of its role on the paragraph level, וַיְהִי is often found at key junctions in the macrostructure of narratives. Ancient Hebrew authors apparently considered וַיְהִי an appropriate transition between major blocks of text and frequently used it accordingly. וַיְהִי is commonly found initiating narratives, episodes, and scenes (Schneider 1993, 79; van der Merwe 1999, 100, 106; Schneider 2001, 245, 260; Longacre 2003, 25; Cook 2012, 310).[22] Because of this, some have come to view temporal וַיְהִי primarily as an episode initiator (Schneider 1993, 81, 86; 2001, 245; Longacre 2003, 25). In this capacity, it would be used to mark major structural divisions in the narrative for the aid of the reader in tracing the information structure.

The question of whether or not וַיְהִי is an episode initiator closely relates to the theoretical discussion of continuity vs. discontinuity below (**Subsection 6.4**), but some preliminary response is in order at this point. One potential problem with this theory is that its pragmatic distribution is inconsistent. Van der Merwe (1999, 107) and Bartelmus (1982, 213), for instance, claim that temporal וַיְהִי can also occasionally be found within and concluding narrative units or in subsections of narrative units. Harmelink (2004, 55, 441–47) likewise points out that since many episodes are not initiated by וַיְהִי and many וַיְהִיs do not initiate episodes, there is no consistent correlation between the two, so episode initiation must be a complex system of which וַיְהִי is only one factor. Of

---

22. Narratives can be divided into distinct episodes, which can further be divided into distinct scenes (van der Merwe 1999, 93; Anderson, **Chapter 14** in this volume).

course, he says, even if such a correlation could be established, we would still have to be cautious about too hastily jumping to causation and a discourse-pragmatic function, since being at the beginning of episodes does not automatically mean that its function is to initiate them. Furthermore, at times, segmentation based purely on the distribution of וַיְהִי may even contradict segmentation based on a more nuanced appreciation of the information structure of the text with all of its contributing components. The episode initiator theory also has difficulties with multiple back-to-back וַיְהִיs clustered together. For all of these reasons, we must be cautious about hastily attributing to וַיְהִי the intrinsic function of an episode initiator, even if it does seem to account for many examples.

6. Discourse-Pragmatic Functions

The reason וַיְהִי regularly occurs in structurally significant positions in narratives is because its typical discourse-pragmatic functions are well-suited to major thematic transitions. A proper evaluation of וַיְהִי must include not only its formal lexical, syntactic, and structural characteristics, but also the practical roles it plays in the development of narratives.

6.1 Past Tense Marker?

וַיְהִי is used (almost?) exclusively in past tense contexts. Because of this, a number of scholars (e.g., Bartelmus 1982, 211–12, 214–18; Eskhult 1990, 31) have argued that וַיְהִי is primarily a past tense marker. Rather than carrying any semantic weight, וַיְהִי would then be used simply to clarify that the following events should be located in the past. This argument may be supported by juxtaposition of וַיְהִי with its generally non-past counterpart וְהָיָה (Harmelink 2004, 437).

There are a number of difficulties with this theory, however (cf. Harmelink 2004, 5, 56). First, in the overwhelming number of cases, the past tense situation is already clear from the co-text, making a disambiguating past tense marker superfluous (cf. Harmelink 2004, 438). Second, it would then be difficult to explain the uneven distribution of וַיְהִי, since some past-tense passages do not have any occurrences and others have multiple occurrences strung together (Harmelink 2004, 437). Third, in those cases where וַיְהִי does indicate a past tense situation, it does not differ from other *wayyiqtol*-form verbs, which can also situate a narrative in the past. And fourth, the past-tense value of וַיְהִי is based on the theory of *wayyiqtol*-form verbs as preterites marked for past tense, which has been questioned by many scholars (see **Subsection 2.2**).

Harmelink (2004, 437–38) offers a compromise explanation that takes וַיְהִי not as a tense marker for the entire narrative, but rather as "one of the components of temporal reference in the text." For him, וַיְהִי does not mark the tense for the whole narrative, but is instead one part of a complex system of temporal reference. He argues that the past-tense value of וַיְהִי is particularly active when preceding atemporal infinitives construct, helping to establish their temporal reference. For him, then, וַיְהִי does not have a unique tense-marking role on the level of the narrative, but at the same time, its tense value is not irrelevant.

6.2 *Narrative Genre Marker?*

וַיְהִי is also used almost exclusively in texts in the narrative genre. Because of this, some scholars (e.g., Niccacci 1990, 33, 48–49) have argued that וַיְהִי is a narrative genre marker. Rather than carrying any semantic weight, וַיְהִי would then be used to clarify that the surrounding text should be understood as narrative.

There are a number of difficulties with this theory, however (cf. Harmelink 2004, 144–46). First, in the overwhelming number of cases, the narrative genre is already clear from the co-text, making a disambiguating narrative genre marker superfluous. Second, in those cases where וַיְהִי does introduce a narrative, it does not differ from other *wayyiqtol*-form verbs, which can also initiate narratives. Third, many narratives do not have וַיְהִי. And fourth, וַיְהִי can, on rare occasions, occur in verse (e.g., Is 12:2). וַיְהִי, then, does not appear to have a unique genre-marking role.

6.3 *Main Event Line vs. Thematic Prominence*

Another theoretical discussion is important for understanding the debate about the role of וַיְהִי in BH narrative and pulling together all of its discourse-pragmatic functions. Discussion on the thematic prominence of וַיְהִיs plus temporal clauses and their role relative to the main event line of the story are integrally related but distinct questions. Terminological confusion in the linguistic literature occasionally conflates these two questions and muddies the waters.

The key culprit is the "background/foreground" distinction, which is used in two distinct ways in the literature. Some linguists use the concept of "background" in contrast to the main event line in the narrative (e.g., Niccacci 1990, 71, 161; Longacre 2003, 57, 79). For them, *wayyiqtol*-form verbs trace the main event line of the story, and other syntactical forms provide "background" information that supports the story line but does not advance it. These scholars differ on whether וַיְהִי as a *wayyiqtol* form of the quintessential stative verb הָיָה "to be" also functions on the main line (Niccacci 1990, 48, 159; van der Merwe, Naudé, and Kroeze 1999, 333 Collins 2009; Cook 2012, 312)[23] or as background information (Longacre 2003, 64; Heller 2004, 444). I would argue that dynamic uses of וַיְהִי more plausibly identify main-line events, whereas stative uses should not be expected to do so (see **Subsection 2.1**).

Other linguists use the concept of "background" in contrast to elements syntactically marked for some sort of thematic prominence, which are said to be in the "foreground" (cf., Floor 2004, 9–11, 228–235). For these scholars, it is complex forms and departures from syntactic norms which are the most noteworthy, and it is in fact the commonplace *wayyiqtol* form which forms the unmarked "background."

I would suggest that both perspectives have merit, but that they are mired in terminological overlap. It is true that the main event line of the story is generally carried along by *wayyiqtol*-form verbs and that other forms tend to provide background, orientating information.[24] It is also true that complex and unusual constructions are syntactically marked to stand out as thematically prominent from the background, unmarked structure. To avoid confusion, I have used the term "orientating" to describe the former notion and "unmarked" to describe the latter. With this distinction clearly made, we are in a better position to judge theories which put וַיְהִי on the main event line of the narrative and/or attach thematic prominence to it. Forms syntactically marked for prominence may be thematically significant

---

23. Cook argues, however, that for discourse/temporal וַיְהִי the question of foreground is moot, "since it simply (re)asserts the temporal reference time" (2012, 312).

24. Though, as will be seen, the actual main line of events is probably much more complicated than simply tracing *wayyiqtol* chains, which should caution us about making hasty assumptions about וַיְהִי and the main line.

and at the same time off the main event line of the narrative. Thus, וַיְהִי clauses may not generally advance the main event line, but still fulfill some important thematic role.

6.4 *Continuity vs. Discontinuity*

One of the biggest points of contention in studies of וַיְהִי is whether it is primarily a marker of continuity or discontinuity. Scholars who advocate continuity rely heavily on the main event line and consecutive theories of the *wayyiqtol* verb form. Niccacci, for instance, argues that וַיְהִי places a fronted temporal clause and following main clause (in his terms, the protasis and apodosis respectively) on the main event line (like other *wayyiqtol*-form verbs), whereas the same construction without וַיְהִי marks a break in a story or a new story or episode (1990, 59–60).[25] Similarly, van der Merwe argues that וַיְהִי almost always occurs in contexts of narrative progression—parallel to his consecutive theory of the *wayyiqtol* verb form—whereas fronted temporal clauses without וַיְהִי tend not to advance the narrative (1999, 109–110; van der Merwe, Naudé, and Kroeze 1999, 331–32).

According to these scholars, the chief function of וַיְהִי is to tie the narrative together for enhanced textuality and cohesion (Niccacci 1990, 60). Thus, for Niccacci, וַיְהִי connects the following events—which would otherwise introduce a break in the narrative—with the main line of the narrative (1990, 59–60; so also Eskhult 1990, 102). For van der Merwe, וַיְהִי anchors a state of affairs to the narrative timeline by continuing the current reference time of the preceding event, and the following temporal clause updates or specifies the reference time (1999, 109–110, 113–14; similarly Cook 2012, 310). וַיְהִי maintains the continuity of the narrative whenever the author needs to update the reference time, which explains why וַיְהִי can occur almost anywhere in the narrative (van der Merwe 1999, 112–13).

A number of responses can be made against these explanations, however. The first is that the theories which underlie them are open to question. I have already discussed the dubious assertion of the intrinsic sequentiality of the *wayyiqtol* verb form above (**Subsection 2.3**), and it is worthy of restatement here. Also, it is unlikely that the main event line of a narrative can be completely reduced to its *wayyiqtol* verb chains. For instance, some non-*wayyiqtol* forms may advance the narrative, such as momentous negation of a *qatal*-form verb (Heller 2004, 437) or *qatal*-form verbs functioning on the main line (e.g., 1 Kgs 19:4). Additionally, not all *wayyiqtol*-form

---

25. Similarly Talstra (1978, 173; cited in Harmelink 2004, 43) states that וַיְהִי distinguishes the main story from the embedded stories.

verbs necessarily advance the narrative (e.g., statives). The verb הָיָה "to be" especially, as the quintessential stative verb, is not likely to advance the main event line of a narrative (at least when used with a purely stative nuance), as Longacre recognizes with his hierarchy of clauses (2003, 64; so also Heller 2004, 444). Observations such as these threaten to undermine the theoretical basis for asserting that וַיְהִי primarily marks continuity or progression on the main line of the narrative. The fact that so many narratives—and even entire biblical books—begin with וַיְהִי also causes many evidential difficulties for this theory, as do examples of flashbacks (such as 1 Kgs 11:15; 18:4) and other texts where no progression is involved.[26]

Other scholars have concluded that וַיְהִי primarily indicates textual discontinuity. Basing their theories on the pragmatic distribution of וַיְהִי in narratives—which is heavily weighted on the beginnings of new textual units—they consider וַיְהִי to be a marker of a new textual unit. Some, for instance, argue that וַיְהִי is primarily a paragraph marker (Gropp 1995, 185; Heller 2004, 434). Others associate וַיְהִי with the beginning of a new narrative unit as an episode initiator (Schneider 1993, 81, 86; 2001, 245, 261; Longacre 2003, 25). For these scholars, וַיְהִי does not signal that a narrative must be connected to a preceding story line, but rather that it is the beginning of a new narrative, episode, scene, or paragraph (see **Section 5**). Narrative connections may be indicated through other means, such as backreferencing temporal clauses (Gropp 1995, 185–86; see **Subsection 3.6**). This explanation has the benefit of being able to explain וַיְהִיs in contexts of both temporal progression and non-progression, as well as examples which are clearly off the main line of narrative events. It may also be supported by Harmelink's (2004, 438–39) assertion that וַיְהִי updates the reference time in conjunction with the temporal clause (see **Subsection 6.5**).

This understanding too is not without its difficulties, however. The theory of discontinuity has difficulty explaining the occurrences of וַיְהִי that occur inside of or at the end of textual units (see **Sections 4** and **5**). The inconsistency of usage is also a problem, as many narrative units are not initiated by וַיְהִי and others have repetitive clusters of וַיְהִיs in close proximity (e.g., Gn 39).

So both continuity and discontinuity theories have significant disadvantages, and we find ourselves torn between the two. We must determine if וַיְהִי is primarily a connective term tying events into the main

---

26. See fn 3 of this chapter for counter-examples admitted by van der Merwe.

narrative (i.e., pointing backwards) or a disjunctive term marking the segmentation of new major narrative units (i.e., pointing forwards), or perhaps some combination of the two.[27]

6.5 *Speaker Deixis*

As has been shown, fronted temporal clauses can occur with or without וַיְהִי, with little or no semantic difference (see **Subsection 3.2**).

(35) Temporal Clauses with and without וַיְהִי

    a.   בַּיּוֹם הַשְּׁלִישִׁי וַיִּשָּׂא אַבְרָהָם (Gn 22:4)
                              On the third day, Abraham
                              lifted up ...

    b.   וַיְהִי בַּיּוֹם הַשְּׁלִישִׁי וַתִּלְבַּשׁ אֶסְתֵּר (Est 5:1)
                              And on the third day,
                              Esther clothed herself ...

If we interpret this situation as meaning that temporal וַיְהִי is optional (rather than mandated by some syntactical principle), then we must explain why וַיְהִי would be included. In addition to the explanations discussed above (past tense marker, narrative genre marker, thematic continuity or discontinuity marker), some have argued that וַיְהִי performs the function of speaker deixis.

Harmelink (2004, 276–77, 440–42), for instance, argues that וַיְהִי aids the reader in following the temporal organization of the text by signalling important temporal references. Thus,

> The proper interpretation of narrative depends on the hearer or reader accessing the same temporal organization with which the text was communicated. One of the cognitive functions of וַיְהִי involves accessing proper temporal reference. (2004, 441)

He further explains,

> [C]ommunicators do not intend all linguistic items they use to perform the same referential function. The function of some items is not strictly referential, but rather is related to the proper cognitive processing of the text. At a cognitive level, וַיְהִי aids the proper temporal interpretation of

---

27. Rocine (2000, 51; cited in Harmelink 2004, 52) views וַיְהִי as a "transition marker," stating that it "is simultaneously a divider and joiner of text. It is a divider in the sense that it marks the onset of a new scene or a new episode or the entrance of a new participant in the story. At the same time it does indeed join the scene or episode it marks to a larger discourse." Harmelink claims that he leaves unclear how exactly it joins the narrative unit to the larger discourse.

the text and contributes to its proper segmentation. The propositional content of the temporal expression is provided by the expressions themselves: after these things, three days later, at the end of ten days, etc. וַיְהִי signals the way in which the temporal expression is intended to connect to its context. Temporal expressions without וַיְהִי are still involved in the temporal organization of the narrative, but the discourse-pragmatic connection differs. (2004, 441–42)

For him, then, while temporal expressions by themselves provide temporal references in the text, וַיְהִי serves especially to mark them as particularly significant for the temporal organization of the narrative, increasing their identifiability to the reader.[28] In accordance with Harmelink's understanding of *wayyiqtol*-form verbs as updating the reference time, וַיְהִי (in conjunction with a following temporal clause) updates the reference time relative to which the following events must be understood (2004, 438–39). A fronted temporal clause without וַיְהִי "still signals a temporal transition in the narrative, but without וַיְהִי there is not the same *deictic* function of establishing this as a new point of reference on the temporal axis" (2004, 446). וַיְהִי is, therefore, a tool to aid the reader to identify when the reference time is being updated. To look back at examples (35a-b), according to Harmelink's theory, the temporal clauses in Genesis 22:4 and Esther 5:1 both signal temporal transitions in their respective narratives, but the latter is explicitly marked for the reader for a role in the temporal organization of its narrative as establishing a new reference time in a way that the former is not.

Harmelink's theory is in direct conflict with that of van der Merwe mentioned above, however. Recall that, for van der Merwe, the temporal clause alone updates or specifies the reference time, and וַיְהִי anchors the state of affairs to the narrative timeline by continuing the current reference time of the preceding event (1999, 109–110, 113–14). וַיְהִי does not signal the updating of the reference time, but rather maintains the continuity of the narrative whenever the author needs to update the reference time (112–13). To look at examples (35a-b) again, according to van der Merwe's theory, the temporal clauses in Genesis 22:4 and Esther 5:1 both update the reference times in their respective narratives, but the latter is explicitly marked for a connection with the preceding narrative in a way that the former is not.

---

28. Endo (1996, 176–78) argues similarly on different linguistic grounds (i.e., וַיְהִי plus temporal clause as a cleft construction, "And it was when…that…"). He claims that such temporal clauses are marked for "thematic and focal prominence."

What should we make of this discussion? It is difficult to see how non-referential וַיְהִי would update the reference time. On the other hand, it is even more difficult to see why וַיְהִי should resume the reference time of the previous narrative (so Harmelink 2004, 438). If temporal וַיְהִי has no referential contribution of its own, I cannot see the need for a reactivation of the previous reference time, just to be immediately updated again without any intervening referential content (contra van der Merwe). This is especially true since many temporal clauses are backreferencing, providing sufficient narrative cohesion in and of themselves (see **Subsection 3.6**). Instead, the significance of temporal וַיְהִי is more naturally determined in combination with its following temporal clause. This explanation also more easily explains examples of narrative-initial temporal וַיְהִי.

It seems clear that the temporal clauses introduced by temporal וַיְהִי are integral to the temporal organization and framing of narratives (Floor 2004, 100–04, 293–94), but the specific role of וַיְהִי in that orientation remains somewhat nebulous and, in my view, requires further testing and refinement. Scholars of the persuasion that וַיְהִי plays a role in framing narratives must show the significance of their observation through detailed analysis and comparison of fronted temporal clauses with and without וַיְהִי, with respect to their precise function in the information structures of Hebrew narratives.

6.6 Discourse-Pragmatic Functions of Verbal וַיְהִי

One common fallacy in linguistic studies of וַיְהִי is the assumption that verbal וַיְהִי does not have any discourse-pragmatic function (e.g., Richter 1980, 206; Niccacci 1990, 159). The primary indication of discourse-pragmatic significance is assumed to be the inability to account for the meaning of a phrase from a purely sentence-level syntactic perspective, and since verbal uses of וַיְהִי present no syntactic or semantic difficulties on the sentence level, there is then no need to look for broader thematic purposes behind them. Most studies, therefore, only consider temporal וַיְהִי from a discourse-pragmatic perspective. But this assumption is unwarranted (Harmelink 2004, 433–35).

I have argued that even verbal uses of וַיְהִי can (and often do) carry discourse-pragmatic significance. In fact, verbal וַיְהִי may have a significantly broader range of pragmatic functions than temporal וַיְהִי, which has an almost exclusively orientating function. Not only does verbal וַיְהִי often have an orientating function, but it also commonly serves to summarize and conclude thematic units, as seen in the examples below (van der Merwe 1999, 100–02; Harmelink 2004, 431–35).

(36) Orientation

וַיְהִי רָעָב בָּאָרֶץ (Gn 12:10)
And there was a
famine *in the land.*

(37) Conclusion

a.

וַיְהִי־כֵן (Gn 1:7)
And it *(i.e., the preceding events)* ***was*** *so.*

b.

וַיָּבֵא יְהוֹנָתָן אֶת־דָּוִד אֶל־שָׁאוּל וַיְהִי לְפָנָיו כְּאֶתְמוֹל (1 Sm 19:7)
And Jonathan brought David to Saul, ***and he was*** *in his presence as before.*

6.7 *Orientation*

The macrosyntactical distribution of וַיְהִי can most naturally be explained by its semantic values and pragmatic functions in Hebrew narratives. One reason that most וַיְהִיs are found at the beginning of narratives, episodes, or scenes, is that the verb היה "to be" is well suited to providing the settings of narrative units.[29] This common orientating function of וַיְהִי is not necessarily due to any perceived discourse-structuring intention on the part of the author, but rather to the semantic nature of the verb היה "to be."[30] וַיְהִי is not the only factor in setting the background for the narrative, but it does help orientate the narrative in a number of ways.

---

29. Van der Merwe (1999, 100–01; van der Merwe, Naudé, and Kroeze 1999, 332–33) makes a distinction between וַיְהִי which introduces a new episode or scene, וַיְהִי which introduces the setting of an episode or scene, and וַיְהִי which occurs in the setting of an episode or scene. The first is normally temporal, whereas the latter two are normally verbal. While the difference between temporal and verbal וַיְהִי is clear, it is not clear to me why it would be helpful to make a distinction between verbal וַיְהִי which occurs within the setting and verbal וַיְהִי which introduces the setting, as the latter still functions to give background information as part of the setting.

30. The main possible exception being temporal וַיְהִי, which is hard to account for semantically.

Participant Presentation. Verbal וַיְהִי and similar verbal forms are often used in their existential sense ("there is/exists") to introduce new referents in a narrative as in example (38) (Schneider 1993, 67; Floor 2004, 309; Harmelink 2004, 210). Referents introduced in this way are normally anarthrous (Harmelink 2004, 210), and they may often be minor characters who are not "thematically enduring" (Floor 2004, 310).

(38) Participant Presentation

וַיְהִי אִישׁ אֶחָד מִן־הָרָמָתַיִם (1 Sm 1:1)
There was a certain man
from Ramathaim…

Situational Setting. Verbal וַיְהִי and similar verbal forms are also often used in their existential ("there is/exists"), equative ("X is" + nominal complement), and descriptive ("X is" + adjectival complement) senses to describe states of affairs as background information (Harmelink 2004, 150–219). When these constructions are used, the situations described often play an important role in the narrative to follow (van der Merwe, Naudé, and Kroeze 1999, 333). Examples (39) to (41) illustrate these types of constructions used for establishing the situational context of the story.

(39) Existential

וַיְהִי רָעָב בָּאָרֶץ (Gn 12:10)
*And **there was** a famine
in the land.*

(40) Equative

וַיְהִי שֶׁם־בְּנוֹ הַבְּכוֹר יוֹאֵל (1 Sm 8:2)
*And the name of his firstborn
son **was Joel**…*

(41) Descriptive

וַיְהִי יוֹסֵף יְפֵה־תֹאַר וִיפֵה מַרְאֶה (Gn 39:6)
*And Joseph **was handsome** in
form and appearance.*

Locative Setting. Verbal וַיְהִי and similar verbal forms are occasionally used in their deictic sense ("X is there") to locate the narrative in its geographical setting (Harmelink 2004, 214–15). Locative indicators may also be added to other usages of the verb הָיָה "to be" to set the location of the scene. Examples (42) to (44) show different ways וַיְהִי can geographically orientate the reader.

(42) Deictic

וַיְהִי־שָׁם בְּבֵית הַסֹּהַר (Gn 39:20)
*And he was **there in the prison**.*

(43) Descriptive

וַיְהִי בְּבֵית אֲדֹנָיו הַמִּצְרִי (Gn 39:2)
*And he was **in the house** of
his master, the Egyptian.*

(44) Existential

וַיְהִי רָעָב גָּדוֹל בְּשֹׁמְרוֹן (2 Kgs 6:25)
*And there was a great
famine **in Samaria***

Temporal Setting. וַיְהִי plays an integral role in setting the temporal background for narratives as well. It does this in one of two ways. First, verbal וַיְהִי and similar verbal forms may be modified by temporal information. Second, and by far the most common, is that temporal וַיְהִי precedes temporal clauses, which locate the following events on a timeline (van der Merwe, Naudé, and Kroeze 1999, 339; see **Subsection 6.5**). Examples (45) and (46) show how both verbal and temporal וַיְהִי can be used to set the temporal reference frame for the narrative.

(45) Verbal וַיְהִי

וַיְהִי רָעָב בִּימֵי דָוִד (2 Sm 21:1)
*And there was a famine **in
the days of David**...*

(46) Temporal וַיְהִי

וַיְהִי בִּימֵי אָחָז...עָלָה רְצִין (Is 7:1)
*And **in the days of Ahaz**...,
Rezin went up...*

6.8 Climax?

Some important studies have concluded that temporal וַיְהִי may also serve to mark significant events in narrative. For instance, van der Merwe (1999, 106–08) argues that it may introduce new scenes or subsections of scenes either at the complication of an episode or at the climax/turning point of an episode. According to him, וַיְהִי plus temporal clauses indicating exact points in time (normally with the preposition בְּ) perform this pragmatic function more often than those which indicate time frames. These uses "signal what triggered a climactic event" (van der Merwe, Naudé, and Kroeze 1999, 332). Examples (47) and (48a-b) occur at significant points in the narratives of which they are a part.

(47) Complication

וַיְהִי בְּעֵת תֵּת אֶת־מֵרַב בַּת־שָׁאוּל לְדָוִד
וְהִיא נִתְּנָה לְעַדְרִיאֵל (1 Sm 18:19 [MT])
And when the time came to give Merab,
the daughter of Saul, to David, she was
given to Adriel...

(48) Climax/Turning Point

a.   וַיְהִי שְׁמוּאֵל מַעֲלֶה הָעוֹלָה וּפְלִשְׁתִּים נִגְּשׁוּ (1 Sm 7:10)
And as Samuel was offering up the sacrifice,
the Philistines drew near...

b.   וַיְהִי כְּהַזְכִּירוֹ אֶת־אֲרוֹן הָאֱלֹהִים וַיִּפֹּל מֵעַל־הַכִּסֵּא
אֲחֹרַנִּית (1 Sm 4:18)
And when he mentioned the ark of God, he
[Eli] fell backwards from his seat...

Others have argued similarly that וַיְהִי may mark significant points in narratives. Winther-Nielsen (1995, 286; cf. also Exter Blokland 1995, 49; both cited from Harmelink 2004, 44–47), for instance, claims that וַיְהִיs may cluster at discourse peaks, as in example (49).

(49) Discourse Peak Cluster

וַיְהִי בַּיּוֹם הַשְּׁבִיעִי וַיַּשְׁכִּמוּ כַּעֲלוֹת הַשַּׁחַר וַיָּסֹבּוּ אֶת־הָעִיר
כַּמִּשְׁפָּט הַזֶּה שֶׁבַע פְּעָמִים רַק בַּיּוֹם הַהוּא סָבְבוּ אֶת־הָעִיר שֶׁבַע
פְּעָמִים וַיְהִי בַּפַּעַם הַשְּׁבִיעִית תָּקְעוּ הַכֹּהֲנִים בַּשּׁוֹפָרוֹת וַיֹּאמֶר
יְהוֹשֻׁעַ אֶל־הָעָם הָרִיעוּ כִּי־נָתַן יְהוָה לָכֶם אֶת־הָעִיר (Jo 6:15–16)
And on the seventh day, they got up at daybreak and, as before,
marched around the city seven times (They only marched around
the city seven times on that day). **And on the seventh time**
around, the priests had blown their trumpets. And Joshua said to
the people, "Shout! For the LORD has given you the city!

It is unlikely that וַיְהִי plus temporal clause has any intrinsic suitability to marking such complication, climax, or discourse peaking. Instead, its climactic pragmatic function is probably secondary to its orientating function, as these examples still provide orientating information for scenes or subsections of scenes. וַיְהִי plus temporal clause simply sets the stage for narrative climax. Similarly, examples of וַיְהִי plus temporal clause in discourse peaks are probably more a function of clustering or other peaking techniques than a specific pragmatic function of the expression itself. Nevertheless, the significant number of examples associated with key events warrants further consideration.

6.9 *Summary*

Normally occurring at the beginning or end of paragraphs, verbal וַיְהִי in particular commonly has the function of summarizing narrative units. When it occurs at the beginning of a paragraph, it serves as introductory encapsulation, giving a proleptic summary of the series of events which are to be expounded by the following sentences. In contrast, when it occurs at the end of a paragraph, it concludes a thematic unit in one of two ways. It can function as a concluding summary by summing up the contents of the narrative unit (Longacre 2003, 78),[31] or it can conclude the narrative unit by stating the results or outcome of the events described in the unit (van der Merwe 1999, 101; van der Merwe, Naudé, and Kroeze 1999, 333; Longacre 2003, 78).[32] These functions are not unique to וַיְהִי (Harmelink 2004, 432), but they are commonly associated with it. These types of summarizing functions are illustrated in examples (50), (51), and (52a-b).

(50) Introductory Encapsulation

וַיְהִי הַמַּבּוּל אַרְבָּעִים יוֹם עַל־הָאָרֶץ (Gn 7:17)
And the flood was on the earth for 40 days
(followed by a detailed account of the flood).

(51) Concluding Summary

וַיְהִי־כֵן (Gn 1:7)
And it (i.e., the preceding events) was so.

(52) Concluding Results
a.

וַיָּבֵא יְהוֹנָתָן אֶת־דָּוִד אֶל־שָׁאוּל וַיְהִי לְפָנָיו כְּאֶתְמוֹל שִׁלְשׁוֹם (1 Sm 19:37)
And Jonathan brought David to Saul,
and he was in his presence as before.

---

31. In Longacre's terms "paraphrase."
32. In Longacre's terms "amplification."

b.   וְאַבְשָׁלוֹם בָּרַח וַיֵּלֶךְ גְּשׁוּר וַיְהִי־שָׁם
                                                       שָׁלֹשׁ שָׁנִים (2 Sm 13:38)
                                          And Absalom fled and went to
                                          Geshur, **and he was there for**
                                          three years.

7. Conclusion

As the preceding discussions have shown, both the semantic nature and
discourse-pragmatic functions of וַיְהִי in BH narratives are extraordinarily
complex and interrelated. Individual scholars' positions on any one of the
above-isolated questions may be influenced by and in turn influence their
answers to other questions in an effort to achieve consistency. And a study of
this nature is further complicated by the fact that scholars' treatment of וַיְהִי
cannot simply be considered in isolation, but must rather be understood
within the context of the various theories of the Hebrew verbal system
of which וַיְהִי is merely one important part.[33] A full appreciation of the
significance of וַיְהִי, therefore, can only be realized in conjunction with the
decipherment of the entire verbal system, an aim which to date still appears
somewhat elusive.

Some things have become increasingly clear, however. For one, the
conventional ways of treating temporal וַיְהִי in particular are woefully
inadequate. Retaining a literalistic rendering such as "And it came to pass"
in our translations does little to tell the reader why the phrase is in the
text and may even mislead the reader with inaccurate referential content.
On the other hand, omitting the literalistic rendering of the phrase in our
translations because of English style fails to alert the reader to its significant
presence in the text. Similarly, designations of וַיְהִי as a tense, genre, or
structural marker—unnecessary in English—may still fail to grasp the full
significance of וַיְהִי. Of the many explanations offered for its presence, few
are unproblematic. Only when the discourse-pragmatic functions of וַיְהִי
are fully analyzed and situated within the context of a reliable theory of
the Hebrew verbal system will we be in position adequately to describe its
role in the information structure of narrative. The studies examined in this
chapter have all contributed to the growing appreciation for the diverse and
significant functions of וַיְהִי, but we are still far from a consensus within
the field of text-linguistics on what it is and what it does. I do not claim
to have given the final answer to these difficult questions, but I hope this

---

33. Thanks to Robert Holmstedt for his comments on a draft of this paper and
particularly for stressing this important caveat.

chapter has at least been successful in bringing together the important questions, theories, taxonomies, and methodological concerns which must be foundational to any future contextual treatment of וַיְהִי.

References

Bartelmus, R. 1982. *HYH. Bedeutung und Funktion eines hebräischen "Allerweltswortes"* zugleich ein Beitrag zur Frage des hebräischen Tempussystems. Arbeiten zu Text und Sprache im Alten Testament 17. St. Ottilien, Germany: EOS Verlag.

Collins, C. J. 2009. The refrain of Genesis 1: A critical review of its rendering in the English Bible. *The Bible Translator* 60.3: 121–131.

Cook, J. A. 2004. The semantics of verbal pragmatics: Clarifying the roles of *wayyiqtol* and *weqatal* in biblical Hebrew prose. *Journal of Semitic Studies* 49.2: 247–273.

Cook, J. A. 2012. *Time and the biblical Hebrew verb: The expression of tense, aspect, and modality in biblical Hebrew*. Winona Lake, IN: Eisenbrauns.

Declerck, R. 1991. *Tense in English: Its structure and use in discourse*. London, England: Routledge.

Endo, Y. 1996. *The verbal system of classical Hebrew in the Joseph story: An approach from discourse analysis*. Assen, Netherlands: Van Gorcum.

Eskhult, M. 1990. *Studies in verbal aspect and narrative technique in biblical Hebrew prose*. Uppsala, Sweden: Almqvist & Wiksell.

Exter Blokland, A. F. den. 1995. *In search of text syntax: Towards a syntactic text-segmentation model for biblical Hebrew*. Amsterdam, Netherlands: VU University Press.

Floor, S. J. 2004. From information structure, topic and focus, to theme in biblical Hebrew narrative. PhD diss., University of Stellenbosch.

Floss, J. P. 1985. Verbfunktionen der Basis *HYY*. *Biblische Notizen* 30: 35–101.

Gropp, D. M. 1995. Progress and cohesion in biblical Hebrew narrative: The function of kĕ-/bĕ- + the infinitive construct. In *Discourse analysis of biblical literature: What it is and what it offers*. Ed. W. R. Bodine, 183–212. Atlanta, GA: Scholars Press.

Gross, W. 1987. *Die Pendenskonstruktion im biblischen Hebräisch*. Studien zum althebräischen Satz 1. St. Ottilien, Germany: EOS Verlag.

Gross, W. 1996. *Die Satzteilfolge im Verbalsatz alttestamentlicher Prosa*. Tübingen, Germany: J. C. B. Mohr (Paul Siebeck).

Harmelink, B. L. 2004. Exploring the syntactic, semantic, and pragmatic uses of וַיְהִי in biblical Hebrew. PhD diss., Westminster Theological Seminary.

Hatav, G. 1997. *The semantics of aspect and modality: Evidence from English and biblical Hebrew*. Philadelphia, PA: John Benjamins.

Heller, R. L. 2004. *Narrative structure and discourse constellations: An analysis of clause function in biblical Hebrew prose*. Harvard Semitic Studies 55. Winona Lake, IN: Eisenbrauns.

Holmstedt, R. and J. Cook. 2011. Genesis 1.1 and topic-fronting before a *wayyiqtol*. Accessed March 5, 2012. http://ancienthebrewgrammar.wordpress. com/2011/11/14/genesis-1-1-and-topic-fronting-before-a-wayyiqtol/.

Isaksson, B., ed. 2009. *Circumstantial qualifiers in Semitic: The case of Arabic and Hebrew*. Abhandlungen für die Kunde des Morgenlandes 70. Wiesbaden, Germany: Harrassowitz.

Longacre, R. E. 2003. *Joseph: A story of divine providence*. 2nd ed. Winona Lake, IN: Eisenbrauns.

Niccacci, A. 1990. *The syntax of the verb in classical Hebrew prose*. Trans. W. G. E. Watson. Sheffield, England: JSOT Press.

Ogden, G. S. 1971. Time, and the verb היה in O.T. prose. *Vetus Testamentum* 21: 451–469.

Qimron, E. 1986. *The Hebrew of the Dead Sea Scrolls*. Harvard Semitic Studies 29. Atlanta, GA: Scholars Press.

Richter, W. 1980. *Grundlagen einer althebräischen Grammatik*. St. Ottilien, Germany: EOS Verlag.

Rocine, B. M. 2000. *Learning biblical Hebrew: A new approach using discourse analysis*. Macon, GA: Smyth and Helwys.

Schneider, W. 1993. Und es begab sich…Anfänge von Erzählungen im biblisch Hebräisch. *Biblische Notizen* 70: 62–87.

Schneider, W. 2001. *Grammatik des biblischen Hebräisch*. Munich, Germany: Claudius.

Talstra, E. 1978. Text grammar and Hebrew Bible. I: Elements of a theory. *Bibliotheca Orientalis* 35: 169–174.

Ulrich, E. 2010. *The biblical Qumran scrolls: Transcriptions and textual variants*. Leiden, Netherlands: Brill.

van der Merwe, C. H. J. 1994. Discourse linguistics and biblical Hebrew grammar. In *Biblical Hebrew and discourse linguistics*. Ed. R. D. Bergen, 13–49. Dallas, Texas: Summer Institute of Linguistics.

van der Merwe, C. H. J. 1999. The elusive biblical Hebrew term ויהי: A perspective in terms of its syntax, semantics, and pragmatics in 1 Samuel. *Hebrew Studies* 40.1: 83–114.

van der Merwe, C. H. J., J. A. Naudé, and J. H. Kroeze. 1999. *A biblical Hebrew reference grammar*. Sheffield, England: Sheffield Academic Press.

Vanoni, G. 1982. Ist die Fügung HYY + Circumstant der Zeit im Althebräischen ein Satz? *Biblische Notizen* 17: 73–86.

Waltke, B. and M. O'Connor. 1990. *An introduction to biblical Hebrew syntax*. Winona Lake, IN: Eisenbrauns.

Winther-Nielsen, N. 1995. *A functional discourse grammar of Joshua. A computer-assisted rhetorical structure analysis*. Stockholm, Sweden: Almqvist and Wiksell.

PART V

ON THE HIGH SEAS:
SUMMATION, APPLICATION,
EXPECTATIONS

CORVINE PERCHED ON THIS FRIGATE'S TALLEST TREE,
SALT SPRAYED D'SPITE THIS BRIG'S CELESTIAL EYRIE,
WHENCE DO WE HAIL? WHITHER THIS CAR'VEL NOW?
AS WRAPPED BY THE SEA, WHAT HEAD THIS SHIP'S PROW?
ROUND YON HORIZON OUR GAZES WE FLING
FROM THIS SPIRE MAST-HEAD WHAT WORDS MORTALS SING?
HARBOR—FAR AFT. NEW LANDS 'FORE THIS BARK BE:
THE TRUTH OF THE TIMES OF NOAH'S GREAT SEA.

CHAPTER 16

The View from Aloft

Steven W. Boyd, Andrew A. Snelling, Thomas L. Stroup,
Drew G. Longacre, Kai M. Akagi, and Lee A. Anderson Jr.

*Analogy and Orientation. In the heyday of wind-powered ocean transportation,
virtually all large vessels had on their mainmast a mast-head. In the earliest
ships it was a crude contraption, simply a large barrel or basket lashed to
the upper portion of the mainmast. However, as technology became more
elaborate, it evolved into a specially-designed railed platform. Provided there
was good weather, the crew member with the responsibility of manning the
mast-head had the ability to see clearly both where the ship had traversed and
the way ahead along the vessel's current heading.*

*In his great American epic, Moby Dick, Herman Melville mentions
another purpose of the mast-head for whale hunting, that of sighting their
catch, and discusses the importance for those who manned the mast-head to
remain vigilant, lest they miss a whale sighting and defeat the purpose of their
voyage. In particular, he warns against the danger of philosophical musings,
which could not only cause the whalers to miss their catch, but also lull the
mast-head stander into a daydream, causing him to plummet to his death.*

*In order to ensure the success of our voyage and avoid the unfortunate
fate of the muser, we must likewise take full account of our surroundings,
and vigilantly maintain the purpose of our voyage. Therefore, having come
to the end of this book, it is time to climb to the dizzying height of the
metaphorical mast-head and survey the course of this study. What do we see
from this lofty perch? From where have we come? How far have we come?
Where will our current heading lead us? And is there any danger ahead—
hidden reefs, cross currents, or squall lines?* [SWB/LAA/TLS/HWB]

Abstract. Yet to be published is a second volume that will detail the final conclusions of this research on the internal chronology of the Flood. And hopefully a third volume on the external chronology of the Flood will follow that. In the meantime, this final chapter will review in brief those issues examined in this book and seek to lay out the charted course for the remainder of the study. Below we will endeavor to tie up all our thoughts with respect to these questions posed above, under the following rubrics: What has been said on these subjects in the past? What have we discovered so far? How will we apply this to the Flood narrative? And, what do we expect to find? [SWB/LAA]

1. Whence Have We Come?

We were moved to challenge the accepted idea that *wayyiqtol* indicates progression because—among other things—the inclusive sequence of nine *wayyiqtols* from Genesis 7:24 to 8:4 is problematic. Verse twenty-four tells us, "The water was powerful upon the earth for one hundred fifty days." The Ark ran aground, however, five months after the Flood began, which—depending on the calendar—is about one hundred fifty days. Yet, seven *wayyiqtols **describing processes*** are in the gap between 7:24 and 8:4. If *wayyiqtol* marks progression, it would seem that the eventualities they represent would take up much more time between 7:24 and 8:4 than is available. How can this be? Understanding the one hundred fifty days as following the forty days of rain is of no help. In fact, it exacerbates the problem. We were left with only one cogent possibility: these *wayyiqtols* do not represent a temporal sequence. But this was a break with the long-held idea that *wayyiqtol does* indicate temporal sequence, because clearly here they do not. This led us to wonder have others questioned the temporal sequence here and in the rest of the Flood narrative? Is this text an exception? How does this affect our understanding of the geology, geophysics and paleontology connected with the Flood? [SWB]

1.1. *Literature*

The analysis of the literature on the Genesis Flood in **Chapter 8** has demonstrated that there has been a considerable lack of attention to the chronological issues related to the Flood. The fact that over one-half of the sources consulted declined to address the chronology at all, coupled with the fact that many of the sources which did comment on the matter addressed it only briefly, is a clear sign that many have rejected the significance of chronology within the broader scope of the narrative. Taking into consideration those who did address chronology, **Chapter 8** has shown that there are at least eight different chronological scenarios proposed for the Flood. Among these, the dominant position held by liberal scholarship is that the Flood narrative is comprised of multiple sources, and that these sources are in conflict and beyond reconciliation with respect to chronology. Conservative scholarship, by contrast, has largely held to one of three major positions which maintain, respectively, that the peak of the Flood: 1) occurred on the one hundred fiftieth day, 2) occurred on the fortieth day, or 3) occurred on the fortieth day and was sustained until the one hundred fiftieth day.

Overview of the accompanying arguments for these chronological scenarios has raised several questions: First, is the *wayyiqtol* verb to be understood as inherently sequential? Does its presence throughout the Flood narrative indicate strict sequentiality in the progression of events? Second, can it be determined whether the rain (and/or other Flood mechanisms) continued beyond the fortieth day? More precisely, do the verbs involved with announcing the turning on and shutting off of the Flood mechanisms provide any indication that they may have continued at either an equal or reduced pace beyond the initial forty days of the Flood? Third, what is the precise meaning of וַיִּגְבְּרוּ (*wayyigbᵉrû*), commonly translated "prevailed"? Can it be determined whether it may indicate either a rising or a stagnation of the water level? Fourth, can it be convincingly demonstrated that the Flood narrative contains instances of chronological disjunction? Furthermore, what purpose might such chronological disjunctions serve? These questions and others have been addressed in later chapters within this book.

Two major issues still remain to be addressed. First, it must be considered how each of these chronological scenarios developed. Further research on this topic must be conducted in order to determine the origin of each view. As mentioned previously, while the antiquity of a position does not determine its correctness, an understanding of the historical circumstances in which each view developed may aid in providing a better understanding of each view, inclusive of their respective assumptions and arguments. Second, further research must investigate the calendar employed in the Genesis Flood account. Admittedly, issues of calendar have minimal bearing on the precise date of the Flood's peak. Unlike other factors, which could indicate a peak after either the initial forty days of rain, or after the long period of the "prevailing" of the waters—i.e. a factor of some one hundred ten days—the calendar employed in the narrative would make a difference of, at most, only a few days. The alteration in the length of the total Flood event would likewise be a matter of days. Still, for the sake of completeness, it will be necessary to consider the different calendars that may have been utilized in the narrative. [LAA]

1.2 *Textual Criticism*

With the text critically established in **Chapter 9**, we have a good starting point for our evaluation of the Genesis Flood narrative and its chronology. As with all critically-reconstructed texts, our conclusions must remain somewhat tentative and open to correction, but at least we will not be caught unaware by difficult textual problems that threaten to undermine our results. Additionally, the arguments adduced for the preferred readings at chronologically-significant points of variation provide a strong case for which information is most likely to reflect the original chronology of the Genesis Flood narrative. Furthermore, the data derived from the collation of ancient manuscripts and versions will be a helpful foundation for our future study about the early history of the interpretation of the Flood narrative in both Judaism and Christianity. [DGL]

2. Where are We? Wither Now?

2.1 *Geological, Geophysical and Paleontological Issues (Chapters 5–7)*

Right from the dawn of history God expected man to use his endowed abilities to investigate and understand the workings of his earthly home so as to wisely utilize its resources. But man rebelled against his Creator, and the earth was filled with wickedness and violence, so God sent the Flood to cataclysmically destroy, cleanse, and reshape the earth (Gn 6:11–13). God could have used the Floodwaters to obliterate all trace of the pre-Flood world and its biosphere. Instead He allowed the Floodwaters to progressively destroy the pre-Flood world and to progressively bury the creatures and plants that inhabited it as a reminder of His judgment on man's rebellion and sin, and as a warning of the next coming fire judgment (2 Pt 3:6–7). Thus all efforts to understand the world's geology today must take into account the devastating effects of the Flood, as described by God in the Hebrew text of the book of Genesis.

Sadly, man's efforts to understand the formation of the earth's rock layers and to understand the way the earth works to produce mountains, volcanoes, and earthquakes have repeatedly abandoned and ignored the explanation provided by God's eyewitness testimony of the earth's creation and subsequent judgment by the Flood. Instead, just as the Apostle Peter warned (2 Pt 3:3–6), men have chosen to explain the earth's past formation as only due to the geologic processes and their rates of operation that we observe today. This has been encapsulated as the maxim "the present is the key to the past," which is in reality the belief in the uniformity of natural processes through all of time, or more simply, uniformitarianism. This philosophy has taken a stranglehold on almost all geological thinking. So today's slow and gradual geologic processes are extrapolated back into the past to explain how earth's movements have produced today's mountains and volcanoes over countless millions of years.

Yet there have always been those who have remained faithful to God's Word being their absolute authority. It was a Bible-believing geologist who in 1859 proposed that a pre-Flood supercontinent was catastrophically ripped apart into today's continents which sprinted into their current positions all during the biblical global Flood. Unaware of this proposal, secular geologists in the early twentieth century proposed slow-and-gradual continental drift instead. For the next fifty years that idea was spurned by geophysicists, because they could not envisage a mechanism for the slow-and-gradual continental drift, but in the 1960s a revolution in thinking turned the tables so that slow-and-gradual plate tectonics is now entrenched orthodoxy. Yet the latter half of the twentieth century also saw a revival of Flood geology among Bible-believing Christian scholars and scientists, including geologists.

Much effort is now focussed on building a coherent, robust Flood model for the world's geology.

The current consensus is that the record of the Flood's beginning, when "the fountains of the great deep" were broken up and "the windows of heaven" were opened (Gn 7:11), can be seen in some uppermost Precambrian strata consisting of debris deposited by catastrophic avalanches around the margins of the pre-Flood supercontinent, and at the widespread erosional unconformity marking the Precambrian/Cambrian boundary in the geologic "column." This erosional unconformity was produced by the catastrophic transgression of the ocean (Flood) waters as the relative sea level dramatically rose to flood the land surfaces, depositing a megasequence of rock layers with entombed creatures, for example, across North America. The relative sea level then seems to have fluctuated, so that the Floodwaters retreated then advanced several times, progressively depositing further megasequences of fossil-bearing sediment layers.

The fossil record is thus preserved for our instruction. There is much to be gleaned from it regarding the pre-Flood biosphere, and regarding the passage and behavior of the Floodwaters. When viewed as the burial order of the Flood, the fossil record preserves not only jumbled masses of broken and fossilized creatures in graveyards within sedimentary layers spread right across the continents, but the buried remains of pre-Flood ecological zones and whole biological communities (called biomes) that must have been spatially separated in the pre-Flood world by geography and elevation. Even the behavior and mobility of many creatures are preserved in the fossilized tracks, traces, and footprints at various levels in the rock record, being remnants of their activities as the Floodwaters advanced and fluctuated.

Knowledge of the earth's internal structure is essential to our understanding of how the earth operates. Seismic waves generated by earthquakes have been the primary means of determining the density differences between and within the crust, mantle, outer core, and inner core. Velocity anomalies are associated with heat and magma beneath volcanoes and in rift zones, as well as with upwelling convection currents in the mantle. Isostasy, or the principle of equal balances, shows how the mass of a mountain above sea level is compensated for by the mountain's underlying crustal root, that is, the earth's crust is thicker "floating" on the mantle beneath where the topography is higher. This explains why sea level is where it is, the denser (heavier) oceanic crust sinking in the mantle to make the ocean basins, while the less dense continental crust rises above sea level.

Today we find shallow marine creatures buried and fossilized in sedimentary rock layers deposited rapidly by water right across continents and even in high mountains, so in the past the ocean waters must have flooded the continents. Only the revived and numerically modelled catastrophic plate tectonics model for the Flood event can explain how the ocean waters rose to flood the continents, how and where the fossil-bearing sedimentary layers were rapidly deposited, and how and when the mountains formed due to plate collisions. The catastrophic rifting of the pre-Flood ocean floor and supercontinent occurred when the "fountains of the great deep" were broken up. Upwelling magma produced supersonic steam jets that entrained ocean water, carrying it up into the atmosphere from where it fell as intense global rain ("the windows of heaven" were opened). The new warm ocean floor produced along the rift zones was less dense and rose, pushing up the sea level to flood the sprinting continental plates, which were moving at meters per second due to the concurrent runaway subduction of old cold ocean floor. Melting at depth in subduction zones fed stupendous volcanic eruptions above at the surface.

Debate continues over the location of the Flood/post-Flood boundary. The highest relative sea level was achieved just prior to the Cretaceous/ Tertiary boundary in the geologic record, marked also by what secularists term the last major extinction of life, after which the relative sea level dropped dramatically to around today's level. All are agreed the only Ice Age (the "Pleistocene") was post-Flood. Some would thus place the Flood/post-Flood boundary just at the Pliocene/Pleistocene boundary, some identify it as close to above the Cretaceous/Tertiary boundary, whereas others would place it somewhere in between within the Tertiary, perhaps coinciding with the end of the deposition of the last of the megasequences which blankets North America.

The need now is for the chronology of the Flood to be more clearly understood from the Hebrew text of the Genesis Flood account. And what might the Hebrew text suggest with regards to the rising of the mountains and the actions of the Floodwaters, both during their prevailing and abating stages? In particular, did the Floodwaters peak on the fortieth day and then maintain that level until the one hundred fiftieth day, or did they only peak on the one hundred fiftieth day? And did the Floodwaters fluctuate in their actions and oscillate in their levels both in their prevailing and receding stages?

It needs to be confirmed what were "the fountains of the great deep" and "windows of heaven," and whether the fountains and the rainfall from the "windows" were both stopped on the one hundred fiftieth day, along with the Ark running aground on the mountains of Ararat on the same day. Answers to these questions have implications for the timing of deceleration of plate movements as the Floodwaters subsided and final plate collisions produced today's youngest mountains, including the mountains of Ararat and other nearby mountains, thus enabling correlation of the geologic and fossil records with the biblical account of the ending of the Flood event.

Can the Hebrew words describing the Floodwaters and their actions also give us clues to aid our interpretation of the fossil record, specifically, could many creatures have survived in the Floodwaters for some time after being swept away, perhaps even clinging to or floating on debris, and when was all life presumably extinguished?

Thus there is much Hebraists can contribute to further our understanding of the geologic and geophysical record of the Flood, with the ongoing study of the BH text providing new aids to our understanding of the fossil record God has left for our instruction. [AAS]

2.2 Grammatical Issues: Sequentiality of Wayyiqtol?

Chapter 10 has challenged the temporal sequentiality of the *wayyiqtol*, presenting three observations against this long held assumption. First, the temporal sequentiality of the *wayyiqtol* can be traced to the erroneous assumptions of Ewald and S. R. Driver's aspect theory. Second, the temporal sequentiality of the *wayyiqtol* does not align with any given theory of the origins of the *wayyiqtol*. And third, the temporal sequentiality of the *wayyiqtol* conflicts with actual usage in the OT. Based on these observations, it concludes that while the *wayyiqtol* may indeed lend itself to temporal sequence due to the conjunctive *waw* prefixed to it, it does not necessarily indicate temporal sequence. In other words, it may be *necessary* (to a degree) for temporal sequence, but it is *not sufficient* for it.

In application to the present study, this demonstrates that the *wayyiqtol* does not function as a reliable indicator of temporal sequence. This opens the door to consider other factors that may contribute to temporal sequence and temporal discontinuity within a text, which are discussed in **Chapters 11–13**. In addition, it opens the door to revisit several apparent contradictions within the Flood narrative, including the length of time before the Ark rose up from the ground (Gn 7:17–18), the differences between the time spans and the fixed dates (Gn 7:11; 8:4), and Noah's repeat entrances into the Ark (Gn 7:7; 7:13; 7:15).

The explanation of what the *wayyiqtol does* indicate awaits an extended study, including a deeper investigation into the origins of the *wayyiqtol* (a diachronic analysis), a fuller investigation into the corpus of its occurrences, both in narrative and in poetry (a synchronic analysis), and a full reconciliation of the two, demonstrating exactly *how* the *wayyiqtol* arrived at its place within the Hebrew verbal system (a panchronic analysis). It is anticipated that such a study would demonstrate that the *wayyiqtol* was indeed a descendant of the proto-Semitic *yaqtul* preterite (whether differentiated from the jussive by accent or not), preserving its past tense meaning, which functioned as the *waw*-initial equivalent of the *qatal*. For the purposes of the present study, however, no further work is needed, as **Chapter 10** serves only to clear the way for the discussions of **Chapters 11–13**. [TLS]

2.3 Exploring the Factors that Determine Temporal Sequence

2.3.1 Assessment

Overwhelmed with numerous examples of non-iconic *wayyiqtol* sequences, we are forced to conclude that the old idea, that *wayyiqtol* indicates progression, is incorrect and requires modification. This realization evokes an obvious question: if *wayyiqtol* does not indicate sequence, what does? This confronted us with a challenge to explore the semantic structure of texts at three levels to discover what determines temporal progression: [SWB]

2.3.2 Temporal Sequence on the *Micro-level*

Chapter 11 considered the role of situation aspect for analyzing time in BH narrative. Through its system of classifying situation aspect and a set of rules for mapping between classes at "neutral" and "derived" contexts, analysts may determine the internal temporal properties of verbs and VPs in BH narrative. Combining this classification system and set of rules with ter Meulen's observations concerning the interrelationship of situation aspect and temporal relationships between VPs, the chapter offered a four-step method for analyzing the likely temporal relationships between VPs in the absence of overriding contradictory discourse relations, world knowledge, and temporal adverbials.

Applying this method to the Genesis Flood narrative will involve simply identifying the relevant narrative verbs from Genesis 6–9 (listed at the end of **Chapter 11**) and recording the results of the method's four steps. By this means, each of the relevant VPs will receive a likely classification, or in some cases a short list of possible classifications. Of particular significance for reading the Flood narrative and establishing its chronology will be the method's identification of where VPs semantically allow for temporal overlap, suggest temporal progression, or may indicate that the narrative's temporal movement is static. While a complete presentation of results and full application of the method must await later publication, initial analysis of some of the verbs from the Flood narrative suggests some conclusions that may result: the following may be mentioned.

A number of key verbs will likely allow for either stative or inchoative (achievement in terms of situation aspect) readings in neutral context, including *Qal* גבר (*gbr*), *Qal* היה (*hyh*), *Qal* חסר (*ḥsr*), *Qal* יבש (*ybš*), and *Qal* רום (*rûm*). *Qal* חרב (*ḥrb*) also will likely allow for both readings, although its predominant use in the Hebrew corpus seems to be inchoative. A similar flexibility between activity and achievement readings for the neutral context of *Qal* נשא (*nś'*) is expected, while *Qal* גוע (*gw'*), *Qal* מות (*mût*), and *Niphal* מחה (*mḥh*) in neutral context likely consistently present achievement readings. It is also anticipated that, while it may represent either activities or states in neutral context, *Qal* רבה (*rbh*) serves primarily to denote activities. If these expectations are correct, some significant implications for the chronology of the Flood will emerge. 7:17–7:18 may describe temporally overlapping stative conditions and activities during the forty days mentioned in 7:17. 7:21–23 may express the death of life on earth four times by means of three verbs, all expressing this death by means of achievements, which may in turn highlight a reason other than temporal advancement or conflation of sources for this repetition, such as theological and narratological purpose. Additionally, *Qal* חרב (*ḥrb*) and *Qal* יבשׁ (*ybš*), both flexible between expressing entrance into a "dry" state as an achievement or the stative condition of "dryness," likely differ semantically in the nature of dryness they denote. Thorough analysis will assist in confirming or disproving these expectations and may reveal further how readers were expected to understand the time of VPs throughout the account. [KMA]

2.3.3 Temporal Sequence on the *Macro-level*

Since our ultimate goal is to determine temporal sequence of the entire Flood narrative, not only must we understand the intra-verbal temporal characteristics, semantics on the *micro-level*, we must also understand the inter-clausal, inter-verbal temporal characteristics, that is, the semantic relationships between verbs or verb phrases (VP). We call this semantics on the *macro-level*. We discussed in **Chapter 12** four factors that influence temporal sequence in texts: *coherence relations*, *compatibility* (or the lack thereof), *connection* (sometimes called attachment), and *continuity* (or its converse *discontinuity*).

As for the first, we chose a set of *coherence relations*, which was in keeping with that found in the literature, with the full realization that we may discover later that this needs to be amended. Our set for now, however, is *Serialation*, *Result/Cause*, *Contrast*, and *Elaboration*. We found that there is temporal progression between VPs when the *coherence relations* are *Serialation* or *Result*, but there is no progression with *Contrast* or *Elaboration*.

Furthermore, we came to realize that *compatibility* is essential for simultaneity to obtain, but it does not compel simultaneity. On the other hand, incompatible eventualities cannot occur at the same time.

Moreover, issues of *connection*, which VPs attach to which VPs, is also important to determining the temporal profile, especially of longer texts such as the Flood narrative.

Finally, there is the possibility of temporal breaks in a text, true temporal *discontinuities*. Usually, texts are continuous, but breaks and jumps can happen, resetting or advancing the narrative clock.

All of these factors will be translated into tests for temporal progression in the second book and applied to the Flood narrative.

I expect that once freed from the constraint of temporally progressive *wayyiqtol*, as we look at the Flood narrative through the lens of semantic structure at all three levels, we will see places in the text where there might not be temporal advance. Genesis 7:17ff is a case in point (there are many others). I suspect that "The *Mabbûl* was on the earth for forty days" is an *Introductory Encapsulation* with the subsequent verses—I do not know how many at this point—elaborating on what happened during those forty days. This means that instead of the eventuality described in the next verse, "the water multiplied," not occurring until after the forty days were complete (the result from taking *wayyiqtol* to be sequential here), it may have been the first thing that happened. I suspect the linear constraint of text causing simultaneous eventualities to be narrated as sequential, could suggest that the very next sentence, "it lifted the Ark," likely occurred at the same time the water was multiplying. Nevertheless, in terms of **coherence relations**, the relations between "multiplying" and "lifting" appears to be *Result*, which would suggest temporal progression. Obviously, many questions remain. I also suspect that the usage of *wayᵉhî* will be temporally determinative in several places: 7:10, 12, 17; 8:6, 13, the time of the onset of the *Mabbûl* (the unique word for the Flood), the duration of the rain, the duration of the *Mabbûl*, the period Noah waited (from what time?) before he sent out the raven, and the date the water was dry and Noah removed the Ark's cover, respectively. [SWB]

2.3.4 Temporal Sequence at the *Mega-level*

Chapter 13 has explored several factors at the narrative level (or *mega-level*) that can influence the portrayal of temporal sequence in a narrative. These include the level of complexity of the narrative, the modes of discourse embedded within the narrative, and the purposes of the author at hand. An additional underlying factor is the linearity of narrative in general, which dictates that a narrative can only portray a single event at a time, regardless of the order (and possible overlap) of its occurrence with other events in the narrative. In doing so, it argues that temporal discontinuity is not an isolated occurrence, but a regular feature of narrative, both English and Hebrew.

In application to the present study, this strengthens the case made in **Chapter 10** against the temporal sequentiality of the *wayyiqtol*, and also helps to explain the potential for temporal discontinuity discussed in **Chapters 11** and **12**. In addition, although the *mega-level* eludes any specific methodology at present due to its complexity (as proposed for the *micro-* and *macro-levels* in **Chapters 11** and **12**), it nonetheless provides a promising source of confirmation for many of the potential temporal discontinuities in the Flood narrative to be identified using these methodologies (as well as those employed in **Chapter 14**), and especially the insertion of Genesis 8:1 at the midpoint of the narrative. Such calls for a literary analysis of the Flood narrative as a whole, with particular attention to the complexity of the narrative, the modes of discourse within the narrative, and the purposes of the author in the narrative.

With regards to the Flood narrative, the *mega-level* has several important implications. First, it is expected that the fixed dates within the narrative belong not to the narrative mode of discourse, but to the report mode. This may help to explain at least one of the supposed repeat entrances of Noah into the Ark (Gn 7:13). Second, it is expected that much of the discussion of the Floodwaters belongs not to the narrative mode of discourse, but to the descriptive mode of discourse (Gn 7:17–24). This may help to explain why the rising of the Ark is likely mentioned out of order with the forty days of rain in Genesis 7:17, 18, as well as the potential temporal overlap between the verbs in 7:17–24 discussed in **Chapter 11**. And third, it is anticipated that the author, Moses, possessed a theological purpose, as well as the narrative and historical, which may explain the reason for the placement of Genesis 8:1 at the midpoint of the narrative rather than at the beginning. [TLS]

2.3.5 Temporal Sequence and Text Segmentation

The study presented in **Chapter 14** has analyzed the information structure of the Flood account and traced the progressive development of the account's theme throughout its numerous scenes. In doing so, it has located significant thematic breaks which are instrumental in the segmentation of the text into smaller units. As anticipated, this process of theme tracing and segmentation has produced an opportunity to gain a clearer understanding of the chronology embedded in the Flood narrative. In particular, **Chapter 14** identified at least one major chronological gap and two areas of potential chronological disjunction.

Understandably, the chronological gap present in the Flood narrative between Genesis 6:22 and 7:1 is of no significance in mapping the chronology of the Flood event. So too, the potential chronological disjunction suggested in part by the obvious thematic interchange in Genesis 7:6–16 is of minimal consequence in resolving any significant chronological issues. However, the other instance of potential chronological disjunction is of notable consequence to understanding the chronology of the Flood event. As mentioned in the chapter, the thematic shift from Genesis 7:24 to 8:1 occurs at the height of the account's pervading chiastic structure and allows for the possibility of a unique situation in the chronological progression of the account. Both Cassuto and Chisholm acknowledge that Genesis 8:1, while marking the center of the chiastic structure, does not mark the centermost point in the chronology of the Flood itself but reverts to an earlier chronological point (i.e. the fortieth day of the Flood). If there had been seamless thematic progression this possibility would be unlikely. However, because there is a substantial thematic shift occurring at this point, there is the possibility of major chronological disjunction wherein the episode beginning at Genesis 8:1 overlaps chronologically with the concluding content of the preceding episode ending in Genesis 7:24. (Thus, the latter episode can be thought of as being akin to a "flashback"; its content chronologically precedes that of the previous block of text.) This theory contradicts none of the clear statements of the text itself and may provide for a more straightforward interpretation of the information in Genesis 8:1–5.

As noted in **Chapter 14**, this kind of analysis of the account's information structure cannot offer positive *proof* in favor of chronological disjunction. Indeed, the other chapters in this book have had a far greater role in that respect. Nevertheless, **Chapter 14**'s analysis has served to highlight where thematic breaks exist and, therefore, where instances of chronological disjunction may be present. It thus bolsters the legitimacy of other elements within this collaborative research endeavor. In doing so, it has also aided in laying a foundation for further study on the chronology of the Genesis Flood. [LAA]

2.3.6 Temporal Sequence and *Wayᵊhî.*

In **Chapter 15** we thoroughly examined the important prerequisites for understanding the semantics and pragmatics of the verb וַיְהִי. With this groundwork laid, we will be in a better position to incorporate וַיְהִי into a viable theory of the verbal system and information structure in BH narrative. This synthesis, in turn, will greatly aid a nuanced reading of the Genesis Flood narrative and an analysis of its chronology. In particular, the five instances of וַיְהִי in the Flood narrative (7:10, 12, 17; 8:6, 13) provide important clues to its arrangement, and we must now carefully evaluate them within the context of our broader treatment of the narrative. [DGL]

3. Concluding Thoughts

It is very appropriate that we bring this book to a close with a look at one last passage, which crystalizes much of what we have said in the book above— and even alludes to the Flood narrative.

We invite the reader's attention to Exodus 24:12–18. In the following translation, the *wayyiqtol* forms are bold-face and lettered sequentially, *qatal* is italicized, and the *way^ehî* is bold and underscored:

> YHWH ^a**said** to Moses, "Come up to me to the mountain and be there in order that I might give to you the stone tablets and the instruction and the commandment, which *I have written* to instruct them." Then Moses and Joshua his attendant ^b**arose**, and Moses ^c**went up** to the mountain of God.
>
> Now to the elders he *had said*, "Stay [[i.e. "wait"]] for us in this place until we return to you. Indeed Aaron and Hur are with you. Whoever has words [[i.e. a legal matter]], let him approach to them."
>
> Moses ^d**went up** to the mountain. A* cloud ^e**covered** the mountain. The weighty Presence of YHWH ^f**tabernacled** upon Mount Sinai. The cloud ^g**covered** it for six days. Then He ^h**called** to Moses on the seventh day from the midst of the cloud.
>
> The appearance of the weighty Presence of YHWH was as a consuming fire on the summit of the mountain to the eyes of the Sons of Israel.
>
> Moses ⁱ**entered** into the cloud and ^j**went up** to the mountain. Moses ^k**<u>was</u>** on the mountain forty days and forty nights.

This is an extraordinary passage in a number of ways beyond the concerns of this volume. Our observations, however, will be confined to the purview of this book. We will mention five.

The first concerns the results from just counting the verb forms. The *wayyiqtol* form occurs eleven times in these seven verses, which are half of the verb forms in the passage. Eight of the eleven non-*wayyiqtol* forms have no temporal impact. Two are participles: one used substantively, "attendant"; the other used adjectively "consuming (fire)." Three are imperatives: "come up," "be," and "stay." One is a cohortative: "in order that I might give," and one is a jussive ("let him approach"). One is an infinitive construct: "(to) instruct them." Only three are finite verb forms (marked for person as well as gender and number): two *qatals* ("I have written" and "he had said") and one *yiqtol* ("we return"). In terms of finite verbs, therefore, eleven out of fourteen are *wayyiqtol*. This is approximately 78.6 percent of the finite verbs. This illustrates how important it is to grasp the temporal properties of *wayyiqtol*—which we have endeavored to do throughout this work—in order to understand the overall temporal profile of a narrative.

---

* This reflects a generic use of the article. If, on the other hand, it is anaphoric, referring back to Ex 19:16, it would be translated "the (cloud)." But this latter alternative is unlikely, in that so much text (five chapters) intervenes between these two occurrences of "cloud."

The second pertains to the **macro-level** of the semantic structure. We note that Moses' ascent of Mount Sinai is mentioned three times, each time using a *wayyiqtol* and each time referring to the same event. Thus, we have **(c)**, the record of what happened (verse 13); **(d)**, a restatement of it (verse 15); and **(j)**, a summary (verse 18)—with the time in the last two not advancing from that of the first. The first of these has the **coherence relation**, *Result*, which is connected with YHWH's command to ascend the mountain. It is not just *Serialation*, because the command of YHWH is *necessary* and *sufficient* to cause Moses to comply. The second is a *Restatement*, also connected to YHWH's command—which, incidentally, resets the time of the narrative, after giving us Moses words to the elders. The third appears to have the relation *Summary*.

The third touches on the interaction between the **macro** and **micro-levels** of the passage. Either in isolation can take us only so far in our analysis of temporal progression; they must be considered together. The ensuing, intertwining complexity of the levels is seen in the following. With respect to the **macro-level**, "covered the mountain" occurs twice, with **(f)**, "tabernacled," sandwiched between, and **(d)**, "(Moses) ascended (the mountain)," preceding its first instantiation. Presumably, the eventuality represented by **(f)**, "tabernacled," occurred after **(e)**, "(a cloud) covered (the mountain)," but nothing precludes it from having happened at the same time as the covering (i.e. the semantic relation between **(e)** and **(f)** is a matter of **compatibility**). And the same remarks apply to the relationship between **(d)** and **(e)**. In any case, the covering provided the circumstances for YHWH's tabernacling but did not *compel* it, suggesting that the **coherence relation** between **(e)** and **(f)** is *Serialation*, not *Result*. But what of **(e)**'s relationship to **(d)**? And **(f)**'s to **(g)**? Is the latter describing the same eventuality as **(e)**? These questions require that we examine the **micro-level** for the possibilities for the innate semantic characteristics of these verbs. We note that **(e)** has three possibilities for its situation aspect: *activity, achievement,* or *atelic state,* depending on whether the situation is being considered at the beginning of the covering process, at the end of the covering process, or a state without a designated endpoint, respectively. And **(g)** refers to either an *accomplishment event* (because it is durative, has an endpoint, i.e. "six days," and might be considered +dynamic) or a *transitory* **state** (because it is durative, has an endpoint, and might be considered –dynamic). Such **micro-level** analysis affects also how these verbs relate to others around them, which means we must revisit the **macro-level**. And so goes the interplay between these two different levels.

The fourth relates to the use of *wayᵊhî* (**k**) to conclude the passage, which appears to be an *Introductory Encapsulation* of the subsequent events recounted in the text: YHWH's order to build the tabernacle and the explicit plan of how to do it.

Finally, the fifth is with respect to the **mega-level**: allusions to the Flood narrative. Three are obvious: forty days and forty nights, covered the mountain, and entered, which speak to the overall purpose of the narrative. There are, in addition, allusions to other passages (for instance, Abraham and Isaac on Mount Moriah).

In summary, this passage illustrates the **micro-level**, the **macro-level**, and the **mega-level** at work. [SWB]

4. *Postscriptum*

We are one-third of the way to our destination: we have developed methodologies which will allow us to ascertain the temporal profile of the Flood narrative. But this narrative will not easily yield its chronology. It is a complex, theologically-weighted narrative. So our voyage ahead is fraught with danger. We expect we will succeed, but we cannot be certain. Even then we will only be two-thirds of the way to our goal. For we seek to determine the external chronology of the Flood, as well, that is, when did the Flood occur with respect to world history? Only then will we have grappled with the chronology of the Flood and won. [SWB]

> Gentle breath of [God] our sails
> Must fill, or else [our] project fails,

(adapted from Shakespeare, *The Tempest*, Act 5, Scene 2, Prospero's address to the audience)

So we pray the LORD will give us

> calm seas, auspicious gales
> And sail so expeditious that shall catch
> [us] far off.

(adapted from Shakespeare, *The Tempest*, Act 5, Scene 1, Prospero's last words to Ariel).

GLOSSARY

abutment. Two **intervals*** of time touching one another without any overlap. The same as **juxtaposition.**

accomplishment. The **situation aspect** class represented by [+ dynamic] [+ telic] [+ durative]. When used in a technical sense refers to a type of situation aspect which obtains when a verb or verb phrase is dynamic, telic (having an inherent endpoint involving a change of **state**), and durative, that is, an action taking place over time with a specified end. For example, "John *built the house*" represents an accomplishment. The action of building requires temporal duration and the completion of the house marks the inherent endpoint of the action.

accretionary wedge. A generally wedge-shaped mass of sediments deformed by earth movements at the boundary between two crustal plates where one plate is being subducted under the edge of the other plate, and is formed when marine sediments, ocean-floor **basalt**s, and rapidly accumulating sediments that have cascaded into the elongated depression or trench formed in the subduction zone, are scraped off the downgoing plate during the process of **subduction.**

achievement. The **situation aspect** class represented by [+ dynamic] [+ telic] [– durative]. When used in a technical sense refers to a type of situation aspect of a verb or verb phrase which obtains when a verb is dynamic, telic (having an inherent endpoint involving a change of **state**), and non-durative. An instantaneous change of state. For example, "Al *won the race*" represents an instantaneous change in state. Al does not win the race unless he breaks the tape at the finish line. An instant before he breaks the tape, the race has not yet been won. An instant after he breaks the tape, it has been won. Another obvious example is "Bob's turtle *died.*"

activity. The **situation aspect** class represented by [+ dynamic] [– telic] [+ durative]. When used in a technical sense refers to a type of situation aspect obtaining when a verb or verb phrase is dynamic, atelic (lacking an inherent endpoint involving a change of **state**), and durative. Examples include, "Mary *ran*" and "Susan *ate apples.*" Neither the actions of running nor eating apples are instantaneous, but both **predicate**s do not inherently indicate endpoints of the actions they describe.

---

* The boldface technical terms which occur within definitions appear as lemmas in the **Glossary.**

Aktionsart. Another term for **situation aspect**; in Slavic linguistics, a subcategory of morphologically marked distinctions in **aspect**.

anaphora/anaphoric. A text-linguistic term in which a portion of a text (a word, phrase, or clause), refers back to something previously mentioned in the text. For example, Naaman is introduced in 2 Kings 5:1. Later in the same verse we find "*he* was…," which refers back to Naaman. Another example is in Psalm 1:4: "Not *so* are the ungodly." *So* refers back to the characterization of the righteous in verses 1–3.

andesitic. Pertaining to, or the composition of, the volcanic rock andesite, which is a dark-colored, fine-grained rock containing small crystals of plagioclase feldspar and one or more of the darker minerals biotite (mica), hornblende, and pyroxene in a groundmass of very tiny crystals generally of the same minerals, named after the Andes Mountains.

angiosperms. Plants with true flowers, in which the seeds are enclosed in an ovary, comprising the fruit. The definition includes grasses, orchids, elms, and roses.

anticipated result. A variety of the **coherence relation, result**, in which the hope of a future result is the motivation for an action in the present. For example, a couple buys a crib knowing that their baby is due in two months.

argument (mode of discourse). One of the five **modes of discourse**. Argument is identical to **information** except that it expresses primarily facts and propositions, rather than just general statives, which seek to persuade the reader to a particular view. Examples of Argument include political speeches or philosophical debates. As such, Argument does not indicate temporal sequence.

argument focus structure. Any **focus structure** comprised of non-**predicate** constituents, including subjects, objects, indirect objects, spatio-temporal adjuncts, manner adjuncts, or qualitative adjuncts.

aspect. The internal temporal **structure** of **situation**s as portrayed by verbs and verb phrases; kinds of aspect include **viewpoint aspect** (grammatical aspect, *Aspekt*), **situation aspect** (lexical aspect, *Aktionsart*), and phasal aspect.

asteroid. One of the many small rocky celestial bodies in orbit around the Sun, most asteroid orbits being between those of Mars and Jupiter. The largest asteroid (Ceres) is more than 600 mi (965.6 km) in diameter, and there are likely ten million or more up to a mile (1.6 km) in diameter, of which nearly 100,000 have currently been discovered.

asymmetry. A property of a binary relation between two elements of a set, where the relation is not true if the elements are reversed. For example, in the set of counting numbers 1 is less than 2, but 2 is not less than 1.

atelic state. A **situation aspect** class traditionally labeled 'state' or 'state term' and represented by [– dynamic][– telic][+ durative]. Examples include, "The leaves *were red*," "She *was short*," and "They *loved each other*." These verb phrases do not describe events, nor to they communicate inherent endpoints to that which they describe.

atomicity. A property of ordered sets in which the elements of the set are indivisible.

attachment. Also called **connection**. The connection of verb to verb, based on the temporal or logical relationship between the eventualities they represent. Consecutive verbs might not be connected.

background. Information that sets the stage for the main story line.

baraminological. Pertaining to baraminology, which is a creationist taxonomic system that classifies animals into groups called "created kinds" or "baramins" (a compound word derived from the transliteration of two BH words), these kinds not being able to interbreed and having no evolutionary relationship to one another, as per the biblical account of creation in Genesis where all creatures and plants were created and then commanded by God to reproduce after their kinds.

basalt/basaltic. Pertaining to, or composed of, the volcanic rock basalt, a dark-colored volcanic rock composed chiefly of plagioclase feldspar and pyroxene, and sometimes includes **olivine**. Basalts are the most prolific volcanic rock, found in extensive lava flows on every continent.

biogeography. The science that deals with the geographic distribution of all living organisms.

biomes. A biological community that characterizes a particular natural region, especially a particular type of vegetation, climatically bounded, which dominates a large geographic area.

biostratigraphic. Pertaining to the distribution of fossils in the **stratigraphic** or rock layer record, and the organization of rock layers into units on the basis of their contained fossils.

bivalves. Invertebrate animals having a shell composed of two distinct and usually movable valves, equal or sub-equal, that open and shut. This is a general term that includes clams, oysters, scallops, and mussels, as well as **brachiopods**.

brachiopods. A group of **bivalves** that are solitary marine invertebrate animals characterized by two bilaterally symmetrical valves that are commonly attached to a substratum (for example, the ocean floor), but may also be free; otherwise known as lamp shells.

breccia. A coarse-grained rock composed of angular broken rock fragments held together by a mineral cement or in a fine-grained matrix, differing from a conglomerate in that the fragments have sharp edges and unworn corners. A breccia may originate as a result of sedimentary processes such as debris accumulation, or explosively in volcanic processes.

Cambrian. The lowest system of rock layers and time period in the **Paleozoic** era of the standard global geologic timescale, conventionally dated as covering the time span 845–541 million years ago, and named after "Cambria," the Roman name for Wales, where rocks of this "age" were first studied.

Carboniferous. A system of rock layers and the time period late in the **Paleozoic** era in the conventional global geologic timescale, covering the conventional time span 299–359 million years ago, and named after its coal-rich deposits in Europe and North America.

cataphoric. The converse of **anaphoric**. A text-linguistic term in which a portion of a text (a word, phrase, or clause) refers forward to something mentioned later in the text. For example, in the ubiquitous expression, "*Thus* says YHWH," *thus* refers to the speech that is to follow.

cause. When referring to **coherence relations**, the relation which obtains when the **eventuality** represented by the second verb of a pair is the cause of the eventuality depicted by the first verb. (See **result** for the coherence relation with reverse temporal polarity.) For example, "Bob fell. Al pushed him."

cephalopods. Marine **molluscs** characterized by a definite head, with the mouth surrounded by part of the foot that is modified into lobe-like processes with tentacles or arm-like processes with hooklets or suckers, or both. An external shell, if present, is univalve and resembles a hollow cone, which may be straight, curved, or coiled, and is divided into chambers connected by a tube (siphuncle). In nearly all present-day cephalopods and their fossil ancestors the shell is internal. Common living cephalopods include octopuses, squids, and cuttlefishes, whereas fossil cephalopods include nautiloids, ammonites, and belemnites.

climax. The high point of a **narrative**.

coelacanth. A member of the suborder of lobe-finned bony fish characterized by a hinged brain-case, conical teeth, and more. This fish supposedly existed during the **Mesozoic**, but survives in its sole living representative called *Latimeria*, found alive off the coast of Southern Africa and subsequently in Indonesian and Japanese waters.

coherence relation. A semantic relationship between the eventualities represented by verbs or verb phrases. For our purposes we have identified four: **serialation, result, contrast,** and **elaboration**. For example in Genesis 1:3 "Let light be" is followed by "and light was." The latter is the result of the former, a fiat of God. So we say that the *coherence relation* is result.

coherence. The systematic or logical connection and consistency in a text derived from the fluidity of its **theme**(s) perceived cognitively in the mind of its communicators and readers. Continuity in meaning and context. Applies to the *concepts and relations underlying the meaning* of a text. *Coherence* is the conceptual relationships that readers use to construct a coherent mental representation accommodated by what appears in a text. (Contrast with **cohesion.**)

cohesion. Continuity in word and sentence structure. Applies to the *surface structure* of a text. *Cohesion* is limited to the linguistic markers that cue the comprehender on how to build coherent representations. (Contrast with **coherence.**)

comparative Semitics. The study of the Semitic languages in comparison with one another to elucidate the phonology, morphology, syntax, etymology, and other aspects of the languages. It is often used interchangeably with **historical and comparative Semitics**.

compatibility. The **situation** when two eventualities can occur simultaneously. For example, in "Al ran and whistled" it is possible for Al to run and whistle at the same time. (Contrast with **incompatibility.**)

conjunctivity. See **Chapter 12, subsection 3.4.**

continental basement. The complex of crystalline rocks that underlie the sedimentary deposits on the continents, extending down to the base of the earth's crust, and usually consisting of igneous and metamorphic rocks, often of **Precambrian** age.

contrast. A **coherence relation** in which the second verb of a pair representing eventualities is either a **violation of expectations** or a **denial of preventer**. Time, therefore, does not advance.

convection. A process of heat transfer involving movements of rock masses or where the flow of waters is around and through heated zones. During convection, warmer, less dense material rises while cooler, denser material sinks. Convection occurs in the earth's mantle and the flow may exert stress to the base of the crustal plates, sometimes affecting their motion.

convexity. In Euclidian space a property of an object, in which for every line between any two points in the object, all the points along the line are in the object. For example, a sphere is a convex set, but a donut is not.

copula. A "to be" verb that joins a subject and its complements.

counterfactual. A theory of causation defined as: if *c* does not occur, then *e* does not occur. For example, in a natural cave, "If you do not turn on your flashlight, then you will not be able to see."

Cretaceous. The uppermost rock system and time period of the **Mesozoic** era in the conventional global geologic timescale, covering the time span of 66–145 million years ago, and named after the Latin word for chalk (*creta*) because of the English chalk beds of this system.

crustaceans. Solitary invertebrates characterized chiefly by jointed appendages and segmented bodies, which also have two pairs of antennae on their heads. Most forms occur in marine environments and are second only to insects in numbers of individuals. Examples include lobsters, shrimps, and crabs.

Dead Sea Scrolls. Scrolls from around the turn of the era discovered at sites across the Judean desert. The finds include both biblical and non-biblical manuscripts and greatly increase our understanding of the early history of the transmission and interpretation of the biblical texts.

deadjectival verb. See **degree achievement.**

default. The typical, **unmarked** way of expressing something.

degree achievement. A term coined by David R. Dowty for verbs which can denote **achievement**s but may appear with durational adverbs; also called **deadjectival verb.** Examples include *cool, shorten,* and *increase.* "The *soup cooled*" describes the occurrence of an event taking place over time and reaching an endpoint (thus, an achievement according to **situation aspect** class), adverbs such as *quickly, gradually,* or *for five minutes* may be appended to the original verb phrase felicitously.

deixis. Deixis refers to when a speaker uses an expression whose meaning can only be inferred based on contextual information. See **exophoric.**

denial of preventer. This is a type of **contrast**, which occurs when the reader does *not* expect Q, because of P, but instead the text has Q. For example, "When Al and Bob were bachelors, Bob liked Zelda a lot. When Al asked him if he would mind if he asked Zelda out for a date—surprisingly—Bob said no." See **violation of expectations**.

density. A continuous set in which between any two points in the set there is a point that is within the set. See **Chapter 12, subsection 3.4**.

description (mode of discourse). One of the five **modes of discourse**. Description differs from **narrative**$_{(2)}$ and **report** in that it is static, and progresses spatially rather than temporally through the discourse. Description can be found frequently within larger narrative sections where the narrative pauses to describe the appearance of a person, place, or thing. As such, it does not exhibit temporal sequence.

detachment. The reverse of **attachment**. A type of relation where the **eventuality** behind the verb is *not* temporally or logically connected either to the eventualities that precede it or to those that follow it.

Devonian. The system of rock layers and the time period of the **Paleozoic** era on the conventional global geologic timescale covering the time span 359–419 million years ago, and named after Devonshire in England where rocks of this system were first studied.

diachronic analysis. The study of language as it develops through time for the purpose of understanding the origins of various words and grammatical constructions. Compare with **synchronic analysis**.

dike. A tabular igneous intrusion that cuts across the bedding of the country rock. It is due to molten rock being squeezed up and along a fracture where it cools into hard rock, often **basalt**.

dinosaurs. Reptiles distinguished especially by features of their pelvic bones that were carnivorous or herbivorous, bipedal or quadrupedal, land-dwelling, and of moderate to very large size. Many examples have been popularized, such as tyrannosaurs, stegosaurs, and *Triceratops*.

dischronologization. A departure in **narrative** sequence, i.e. the order in which a narrative relates a set of events, from temporal sequence, i.e. the actual order in which those events occurred.

discontinuity. Any interruption in sedimentation, whatever its cause or length, being usually a manifestation of non-deposition and accompanying erosion, or a surface separating two unrelated groups of rocks.

discourse-pragmatics. The study of language as communication: how it is used practically to shape a discourse; and how meaning is determined through not only the words themselves but also their contexts.

durativity. The property of a verb or verb phrase concerned with the portrayal of events or **states** as continuing over the course of a specified or unspecified extent of time rather than obtaining instantaneously. While "The ball *flew through the air*" portrays an action, that of flying through the air, taking place over time and thus displays a durative verb phrase, the verb phrase in "The ball *shattered the window*," is non-durative since in its linguistic portrayal the action described occurred instantaneously.

dynamic aspect tree (DAT). A system for graphically representing the temporal relationships of **situation**s in **narrative**$_{(2)}$, developed by Alice G. B. ter Meulen.

dynamicity. The property of a verb or verb phrase concerned with the portrayed occurrence of action. A dynamic verb phrase, such as "The dog *jumped into the pool*," describes action taking place, whereas a non-dynamic verb phrase, such as "The clock *stood on top of the desk*," describes a **state** with no specified action.

echinoderms. Solitary marine bottom-dwelling invertebrates characterized by radial symmetry, an internal skeleton formed of plates or ossicles composed of crystalline calcite (calcium carbonate), and a water-vascular system. Examples include starfishes and sea urchins.

ecological zones. An area or region, or environment, in which certain unique organisms are interrelated to one another in communities or populations that support one another and are together because of the climate, geography, and other environmental factors.

Ediacaran. A system of rock layers and a time period of the conventional global geologic timescale, being the uppermost system and period of the **Neoproterozoic** era and the **Precambrian**, characterized by the earliest well-documented soft-bodied forms of metazoan (multi-cellular animal) life, spanning the conventional time of 541–635 million years ago, and named after the first such fossils discovered in the Ediacaran Hills of South Australia.

elaboration. The **coherence relation** in which eventualities depicted by a group of verbs take place in the same time interval as that of the **eventuality** represented by the verb that precedes the group. For example, "Carl had a great morning [an **introductory encapsulation**]. His wife made the family bacon and eggs. There was little traffic driving into the office. His secretary had a pot of coffee waiting for him. His cranky first client cancelled his appointment." See **introductory encapsulation**.

endophoric. A text-linguistic term in which a portion of a text (a word, phrase, or clause), refers to something within the text.

episode. The second-largest textual unit (following **narrative**$_{(1)}$) in the discourse segment hierarchy, being comprised of a single **topic** framework and commenting on only one set of primary and **secondary topics**.

equids. The horse family or kind (baramin), that is, mammals that include horses, donkeys, zebras, and extinct related animals.

eventuality. The **state** or event represented by a verb.

exophoric. A text-linguistic term in which a portion of a text (a word, phrase, or clause), refers to something outside the text.

filter. A **DAT** node representing an event which may function either as a **hole** or **plug** depending on what follows in a **narrative**$_{(2)}$; filters are the **default** representation of **accomplishments** in the simple past **tense**.

focus. That portion of a proposition which cannot be taken for granted at the time of speech; i.e. the element of information whereby the presupposition and the assertion differ from each other; that which makes an utterance into an assertion. Strictly speaking, focus refers to a cognitive, pragmatic mental representation; it is expressed using a focus structure.

foreground. Information that is more prominent in the story than the **background** information. In a **narrative**$_{(2)}$, the main story line is foreground information; whereas, the time and the place and other ancillary details are background information.

freedom. See **Chapter 12, Subsection 3.4.**

fronting. Moving an expression from its **default** position to the front of the sentence, normally for purposes of promoting it thematically.

gabbro. The coarse-grained intrusive and compositional equivalent of a **basalt**, consisting of interlocking small crystals of plagioclase feldspar and pyroxene, with or without **olivine**, plus several common accessory minerals. It forms when basalt **magma** cools and crystallizes underground, much like a granite cools and crystallizes from a granite magma.

gastropods. Any mollusc that has a body contained in an asymmetric helically-coiled shell with an apex pointing away from the head, which is distinct and can be moved independently of the rest of the body. This includes snails of all varieties and environments with a foot used for creeping and moving.

genre. A type or category of literature marked by certain shared features, which prevent readers or audiences from mistaking it for another kind.

geyser. A type of hot spring that intermittently erupts jets of hot water and steam, often being the result of groundwater coming into contact with rock or steam hot enough to create steam under conditions preventing free circulation.

gloss. An expression which was incorporated into the text (either accidentally or intentionally) after it was originally composed.

grammaticalization. When a usage becomes so commonplace and stereotyped that it ceases to retain its original significance and takes on a meaning of its own.

granitic. Pertaining to, or composed of, granite, which is a coarse-grained intrusive rock in which the mineral **quartz** constitutes ten to fifty percent of the light-colored components, that also include feldspars. Biotite (black mica) and hornblende are often minor constituents. The name comes from the Latin *granum*, "grain." Granites are dominant, widespread crystalline rocks on the continents. One spectacular example is the Yosemite area of California.

gymnosperms. Seed plants in which the seeds are not enclosed by a carpel or modified leaf wall, being borne singularly or in cones. Examples of these so-called naked seed plants include cycads, gingkoes, conifers, and seed ferns.

harmonization. When scribes conformed similar passages to each other to remove potential discrepancies.

Hiphil. The most common derived verb stem in BH, occurring in about thirteen percent of verbs. Morphologically it is characterized by having a preformative *h*, which in regular verbs, is followed by an a-class or i-class vowel. This stem is primarily a causative, and as such, adds a direct object. For example, the stem of the verb (italicized) in "Pharoah *has seen* what God is about to do (direct object)" is *Qal*, but in "God has *caused* Pharaoh (direct object) *to see* what He is about to do (direct object)," the stem is *Hiphil*.

historical and comparative Semitics. The study of the Semitic languages in comparison with one another to determine the relationships between them and to identify their changes over time. It is diachronic in approach, and is usually conducted with reference to the presumable ancestor language of **proto-Semitic**. It depends heavily on **comparative Semitics**, and the term is often used interchangeably with comparative Semitics.

Hithpael. A derived stem in BH, which is morphologically characterized by the doubling of the second consonant of the **root** (or its equivalent) and a preformative *it*. This stem primarily is reflexive of the ***Qal***, but with certain roots it can be reciprocal, with others to act in a certain way, and with yet others iterative action. For example, "to strike oneself," "to look at one another," "to act crazy," and "to walk all around (not in a particular direction)," respectively.

hole. A **DAT** node representing an event which may temporally encompass other events; holes are the **default** representation of activities in the simple past **tense**.

homomorphic contraction. A set derived from another set which has the same properties as the original set. See **Chapter 12, Subsection 3.4** for much more detail.

hydrodynamic. Relating to, or involving the principles of, hydrodynamics, that is, the physics dealing with the motions of fluids, and the forces acting on solid bodies immersed in fluids and in motion relative to them, the principal such fluid being water.

ichthyosaurs. Reptiles that have porpoise-like or shark-like bodies which are adapted for life in the ocean. They are marine reptiles that are extinct.

iconicity assumption. The assumption of readers of texts or hearers of discourse that **situation**s occur in the order they are presented in the absence of explicit indications to the contrary or **incompatibility** of situations.

iconicity. Resemblance of form to meaning; with regard to temporal relationships in **narrative**$_{(2)}$, correspondence between the order **situation**s appear in a narrative and the order in which the narrative presents the occurrence of those situations. Iconicity is a term from Peircian semiotics (the science of signs), which signifies that a word, phrase, clause, or concept resembles what it means. For example in Psalm 29, "the voice of YHWH," which in the psalm refers to thunder, is repeated many times, thereby resembling the rolling peal of thunder.

illocutionary meaning. The intended meaning of an utterance or text, which goes beyond the literal meaning of the utterance or text. For example, the words "It is cold in here," spoken to a classroom of students is meant to convey to the one closest to the door that he should shut the door.

inclusion. A binary relation between two **intervals** or two sets in which one is nested within or contained within the other, respectively. For example, the interval of 2 p.m. to 3 p.m. is included within the interval 1 p.m. to 4 p.m. Or the set {1, 2} is included within the set {1, 2, 3, 4}.

incompatibility. The **situation** when two eventualities cannot occur simultaneously. For example, "Al ran and sat." Al cannot run and sit at the same time. This causes a displacement in the time **intervals** of the two eventualities; they cannot overlap.

indicative (verb). A verb form relating to fact, rather than command, wish, or possibility. For example, "He ate the cake," would be an indicative, but "Please eat the cake," or "He may eat the cake," would be imperative or modal.

individual-level state. A **state** expressing an inherent characteristic or expected to last for an extended period of time due to world knowledge; with regard to **situation aspect**, individual-level states do not differ from **stage-level state**s. "Diamonds *are hard*" and "His hair *is brown*" represent **individual-level state**s.

information (mode of discourse). One of the five **modes of discourse**. Information differs from **description** in that it is not only static, but atemporal altogether (containing no reference to time), and consists primarily of general statives (e.g. a butterfly *has* two wings). A good example of this mode of discourse would be an encyclopedia article, or a world atlas. As such, information does not exhibit temporal sequence.

information structure. The way information is arranged in discourse.

instants. A point of time. For the set-theoretic concept in the mathematical model of time see **Chapter 12, Subsection 3.4**.

intervals. A period of time. For the set-theoretic concept in the mathematical model of time see **Chapter 12, Subsection 3.4**.

intrabaraminic. Pertaining to within a baramin or created kind.

introductory encapsulation. A verb representing an **eventuality** that subsumes a series of eventualities, which elaborate on the whole. For example in Genesis 37:5–7, "Joseph dreamed a dream and told it to his brothers and they hated him even more," is an introductory encapsulation, which is followed by the **elaboration**: "He said to them, 'Please listen to this dream I have dreamed,'" after which he regales them with the content of the dream. See elaboration.

isostasy. The condition of equilibrium, comparable to floating, of different areas and regions of the earth's crust above the mantle beneath. Crustal loading by ice, water, sediments, or volcanic flows leads to isostatic depression or downwarping, whereas removal of rock load by erosion or uplift leads to upwarping. This principle of equal balancing results from the different densities of crustal rocks and affects the earth's topography.

Jubilees. A second century BC retelling of the story of Genesis and Exodus.

Jurassic. The middle system of rock layers and time period of the **Mesozoic** era in the conventional global geologic timescale, covering the time span of 145–201 million years ago, and named after the Jura Mountains between France and Switzerland in which rocks of this supposed age were first studied.

jussive. A third person modal verb form within the Hebrew verbal system used to express a wish or command.

juxtaposition. Two **intervals** of time touching one another without any overlap. The same as **abutment**.

linearity. If x ≠ y, then x < y or y < x. Also, see **Chapter 12, Subsection 3.4**.

locutionary meaning. The literal meaning of an utterance or text. For example, "It is cold in here" is a comment about the temperature in a room.

lycopods. A class of plants with small, scale-like leaves and branching non-woody stems containing soft tissue, and similar root-like **rhizomes** so that these plants preferred boggy conditions or lived in a community that floated on water. Many varieties are extinct, but a living example is the club mosses.

macro-level. Pertaining to the **semantic** relations between verbs or verb phrases.

macrostructure. The way in which a discourse is structured.

macrosyntax. The way words and phrases are connected to the discourse **macrostructure**.

macro-word. A recurring or otherwise syntactically and/or cognitively prominent word commonly involved in announcing and progressing **theme**.

magma. Naturally occurring molten or partially molten rock material generated within the earth and capable of intrusion and extrusion, from which igneous rocks are derived through solidification, crystallization, and related processes.

main event line. The main events in a **narrative**$_{(2)}$ that move the story along. In most cases these events are narrated with ***wayyiqtol*-**form verbs.

Masoretic text. The text preserved in the medieval Jewish manuscripts of the Hebrew Bible.

Masoretic vocalization. The pronunciation indicated in the medieval Jewish reading tradition of the Hebrew Bible by the addition of vowels to the written text. The earliest Hebrew manuscripts do not indicate vowels.

mega-level. Pertaining to the **semantic** relations on the level of the **narrative**$_{(1)}$ as a whole.

megasequences. Very large packages of rock layer sequences conventionally spanning many tens of millions of years that are grouped together because they begin with **transgressive** sequences as the ocean waters rose and covered continents, and end with **regressive** sequences as the ocean waters retreat, so that each whole megasequence was deposited during each single rise and fall of the ocean waters over the continents.

Mesozoic. The era of the conventional global geologic timescale encompassing the rocks that were formed in the time span 66–252 million years ago, and comprises three strata systems and conventional time periods, namely, the **Cretaceous, Jurassic**, and Triassic.

metabolic. Pertaining to metabolism, which is the set of life-sustaining chemical reactions and transformations within the cells of living organisms that allow them to grow and reproduce, maintain their structures, and respond to their environments. These chemical reactions that occur in living organisms include digestion and the transport of substances into and between different cells.

micro-level. Pertaining to the **semantic** characteristics of individual verbs and verb phrases.

minus. When one text has less text than what is found in another text.

Miocene. A series of rock layers and a time epoch of the **Neogene** system and period of the **Tertiary** era of the conventional global geologic timescale, covering the time span of 5.3–23 million years ago.

Mississippian. The lower subsystem of rock layers and the subperiod of the **Carboniferous** system and period of the conventional global geologic timescale, covering the time span of 323–359 million years ago, and named after the Mississippi River valley in which there are good exposures of rocks of this presumed age.

modes of discourse. The five modes of discourse proposed by Carlota Smith. These are **narrative**$_{(2)}$, **report**, **description**, **information**, and **argument**, each of which is defined in this glossary. See **Chapter 13, Subsection 2.2.1** for further discussion.

molluscs. Solitary invertebrates characterized by a non-segmented body that is bilaterally symmetrical and by a radially or biradially symmetrical mantle and shell. Included in this category are **gastropods**, **bivalves**, and **cephalopods**.

monobaramin. A single created kind, from mono (single) and baramin (created kind).

monotonicity. A property pertaining to sets, such that, with functions. If $x < y$, then $f(x) < f(y)$. For its application to set **structures**, see **Chapter 12, Subsection 3.4.**

narrative$_1$ **(unit of text).** The largest textual unit consisting of at least one, but more likely several **episode**s, each with its own **topic** framework and **focus** content. A narrative$_{(1)}$ generally contains a "hypertopic," that is, a **primary topic** that is recurring across most if not all of its constituent parts (episodes and **scene**s). In the Flood narrative, "Noah" is an example of a hypertopic.

narrative$_2$ **(mode of discourse).** One of the five modes of discourse. Narrative consists of **states** and events, related to each other dynamically in time, whose relationships progress as the reader advances through the text. As a result, a narrative usually exhibits temporal sequence. Examples of narrative$_{(2)}$ include the English novel, short stories, and other forms of narrative literature.

Neogene. The upper system of rock layers and time period of the **Tertiary** era of the conventional global geologic timescale, covering the time span of 2.6–23 million years ago.

Neoproterozoic. The youngest era of the Proterozoic eon of the conventional global geologic timescale, covering the time span of 541–1000 million years ago, also being the terminal era of the **Precambrian.**

Niphal. The derived verbal stem in BH, which is characterized by having a preformative *n* in all forms. Approximately 5.65% of verbs are in this stem. *Niphal* conveys middle or passive voice. For example, whereas the **Qal** of a **root** meaning "open," conveys active grammatical voice, as in "he *opened* the door," the *Niphal* would be used for a sentence with middle voice, such as, "the door *opened*." Or, if the root is "bury," the *Qal* would be used in "they *buried* the king," but the *Niphal* would be "the king *was buried.*"

Oligocene. The uppermost series of rock layers and time epoch of the **Paleogene** system and period within the **Tertiary** era of the conventional global geologic timescale, covering the time span of 23–33.9 million years ago.

olivine. An olive-green, grayish-green, or brown common rock-forming mineral in **basalt**s and **gabbro**s and other low-silica igneous rocks. It consists of magnesium and iron bonding together silica structural units and is thus a dense mineral that in its various forms is the major component of the earth's mantle.

ophiolites. Assemblages of dark-colored intrusive and extrusive (volcanic) rocks, widely believed to represent former oceanic crust, and thus ideally consists of a thin sequence of marine sediments overlying **basalt pillow lavas**, overlying a sheeted **dike** complex, underlain by **gabbro**s and **peridotite**s, though the entire sequence is rarely preserved.

Ordovician. A system of rock layers corresponding to a time period of the conventional global geologic timescale, covering the time span of 444–485 million years ago, and named after a Celtic tribe called the Ordovices.

orthography. The spelling practices of a given text.

overlap. When used in a technical sense. A binary temporal relation pertaining to **intervals** in which two (or more) intervals share **instants** of time. For example, the interval 2 p.m. to 3 p.m. is an overlap of the interval 1 p.m. to 3 p.m. with the interval 2 p.m. to 4 p.m., in that both of the latter two intervals share all the instants of the former interval.

Paleogene. The lowest system of rock layers and time period of the **Tertiary** era of the conventional global geologic timescale, covering the time span of 23–66 million years ago.

paleomagnetic. Pertaining to paleomagnetism, the study of natural magnetic properties locked into earth materials (primarily minerals within rocks), reflecting the direction and intensity of the earth's magnetic field in the past when the minerals and rocks formed.

Paleozoic. The era of the conventional global geologic timescale, above the **Precambrian** and below the **Mesozoic**, covering the time span of 252–541 million years ago.

participant. Someone or something involved in a story. Noah is a participant in the Flood **narrative**.

peak (of Flood). The occasion on which the waters of the Flood generated by the various flood mechanisms swelled to their maximum height.

Pennsylvanian. The upper subsystem of rock layers and time subperiod of the **Carboniferous** system and period of the conventional global geologic timescale, covering the time span of 299–323 million years ago, and named after the state of Pennsylvania in which rocks of this supposed age are widespread and yield much coal.

peridotite. A coarse-grained intrusive igneous rock composed chiefly of **olivine** with or without dark-colored minerals such as pyroxenes, amphiboles, or micas, and containing little or no feldspars.

Permian. The uppermost system of rock layers and time period of the **Paleozoic** era of the conventional global geologic timescale, covering the time span of 252–299 million years ago, and named after the province of Perm in Russia where rocks of this supposed age were first studied.

Peshitta. The standard translation of the Bible in the Syriac language, a dialect of Aramaic.

physiological. Pertaining to physiology, which is the scientific study of function in living systems, including how organisms, organ systems, organs, cells, and biomolecules carry out the chemical or physical functions that exist in a living system.

pillow lavas. A general term for those lavas displaying pillow structures (bulbous pillow-shaped masses) and considered to have formed underwater, such as **basalt** lavas being extruded onto the ocean floor.

Pleistocene. The lower series of rock layers and the time epoch of the **Quaternary** system and period of the conventional global geologic timescale, covering the time span of 0.01–2.6 million years ago.

plesiosaurs. Extinct marine reptiles with broad bodies and a short tail, as well as two pairs of large flippers, and often with a long neck. They range in length from six to sixty-six feet (1.8 m–20.1 m) long.

Pliocene. The uppermost series of rock layers and time epoch of the **Neogene** system and period of the **Tertiary** era of the conventional global geologic timescale, covering the time span of 2.6–5.3 million years ago.

plug. A **DAT** node representing an event which does not allow for temporal inclusion of further events and thus results in temporal succession; plugs are the **default** representation of **achievements** in the simple past **tense**.

plus. When one text has additional text not found in another text.

plutons. Deep-seated igneous intrusions, particularly of granites, which when eroded to be exposed at the earth's surface are mapped as individual granite bodies, often many square miles in area and perhaps a few miles in depth.

point state. A **situation aspect** class recognized by William Croft which is non-dynamic but only occupies a conceptual point in time. "It *was 5:32 p.m.*" represents a point state.

Precambrian. A commonly used term to designate all rocks older than the **Cambrian** period of the conventional global geologic timescale. It includes the Archean and Proterozoic eons and conventionally represents ninety percent of geologic time. Within the biblical framework of earth history these rocks largely represent the Creation Week and pre-Flood continental rocks.

precedence. When used in a technical sense a binary relation between two **instants** or **intervals** in which the first occurs before the second. In the case of intervals precedence cannot obtain where there is **overlap** or **inclusion**. For example, for instants, 2 p.m. is before 3 p.m.; for **intervals**, 1 p.m. to 2 p.m. is before 3 p.m. to 4 p.m. For its meaning with ordered sets, see **Chapter 12, Subsection 3.4**.

predicate focus structure. The most common type of **focus structure** in BH **narrative**, used in simple topic-comment sentence articulations.

predicate. A part of speech more commonly called a verb.

primary topic. A **topic** expression possessing informational separation in the sense that the **focus structure** asserts something about it. A primary topic possesses the attributes of predication and addressation, and is discourse active and accessible—generally so accessible that only pronominal reference to it is sufficient. Generally, the primary topic is a grammatical subject in BH.

proto-Semitic. The presumable ancestor language of the Semitic language group. This language is derived from the commonalities between the various Semitic languages for the purpose of explaining their common origins in line with the principles of historical linguistics.

pterosaurs. Extinct reptiles highly adapted to flight and characterized by extreme elongation of the fourth digit of the hand for support of the membranous wing, and by reduction of the hind limbs.

Qal. The ground verb stem in BH. Approximately sixty-nine percent of verb occurrences in BH are in this stem. This stem occurs with active/ transitive (active verbs with a direct object, e.g. "hit"); intrasitive (active verbs of motion, e.g. "ascent") stative transitive (verbs of perception, cognition, and emotion—which take a direct object, e.g. "see"); and stative verbs, e.g. "be heavy."

qatal. An **indicative** verb form within the Hebrew verbal system most often used to express the past **tense**. Compare with the *yiqtol.*

quartz. Crystalline silica, which is the same composition as window glass. After feldspar it is the commonest rock-forming mineral, occurring either in transparent hexagonal crystals (colorless, or colored by impurities) or in crystalline masses. It forms the major proportion of most sands, and has a widespread distribution through igneous (especially **granitic**), metamorphic, and sedimentary rocks.

Quaternary. The uppermost system of rock layers and time period of the Cenozoic era of the conventional global geologic timescale, covering the time span between the present and 2.6 million years ago.

redaction. The process of compiling and editing a work, often based on previous sources.

reflexivity. For a given relational operator where x R x is true, if R is =, then we have reflexivity. If R is <, then x R x is not true.

regressive. Pertaining to the retreat or contraction of the sea from land areas and the consequent evidence of such withdrawal, such as enlargement of areas of deposition in deltas. Also, any change, such as fall of sea level or uplift of land, that brings nearshore, typically shallow-water environments to the areas formerly occupied by offshore, typically deep-water conditions, or that shifts the boundary between marine and non-marine deposition, or between deposition and erosion, or the center of a marine basin.

relationism. A theory from the philosophy of space-time, which asserts that space and time are not absolutes and have no existence independent of the eventualities that take place within them. The foremost proponent of this idea was Leibniz.

report (mode of discourse). One of the five modes of discourse. Report is characterized by **states** and events related to each other dynamically in time. Unlike **narrative**$_{(2)}$, however, the time is viewed with reference to the speaker's time, and therefore may not necessarily exhibit temporal sequence. Examples include news articles, or history textbooks, where events are frequently summed up with reference to the present time rather than given in specific detail in narrative form.

restatement. A **coherence relation**, in which a verb representing an **eventuality** occurring at a particular time, is repeated in a text. For example, "They [The Sons of Israel] *camped* in the wilderness. Israel *camped* there opposite the mountain" (Ex 19:2).

result. A **coherence relation**, in which the **eventuality** represented by the first verb is the necessary and sufficient cause of the eventuality represented by the second verb. Of course the quintessential example is "God said, 'Let light be.' And light was" (Gn 1:3). See **cause** for the coherence relation with reverse temporal polarity.

rhizomes. Underground root-like stems that lie horizontally and that are often enlarged in water to store food.

root. The sequence of consonants (usually three) which carries the meaning of a word in BH. A word comprises a **root** and vowels and/ or consonants. The combination of vowels and/or consonants (called a *pattern*) grammatically modifies the meaning of the root. From one perspective every root generates a cluster of words that have the same meaning but grammatically differ. From another, a group of words that have a common meaning will have the same root. For example, "he wrote," "you will write," "to write," "when writing," "writer," and "written" all have the same root, the sequence of consonants, *k t b*.

Samaritan Pentateuch. The text preserved in the medieval Samaritan manuscripts of the first five books of the Hebrew Bible. The Samaritans and Jewish communities split in the centuries before Christ and independently preserved copies of Scripture.

scene. The third-largest textual unit (following **narrative**$_{(1)}$ and **episode**) in the discourse segment hierarchy, containing a single **primary topic** and limited to one set of **participants** at one time in one place. Scenes can be very short, but are comprised of a minimum of two propositions with a **sequentiality** relation between them.

secondary topic. A presupposed, discourse-active **topic** expression that is less salient than a **primary topic** and dependent upon the presence of a primary topic in the proposition in which it occurs. Secondary topics differ from primary topics by virtue of being part of the asserted or new information in a sentence, whereas primary topics cannot be part of the **focus** domain.

segmentation. The process of dividing a document into meaningful units of text in accordance with a set of predetermined, observable factors, e.g. transitions in **theme**.

seismic waves. A general term for elastic waves produced by earthquakes or generated artificially (by explosions), and includes both body waves that travel through the earth's interior, and surface waves that move across the earth's surface. The released energy travels like sound waves through the earth's rocky materials.

semantics. The study of the intrinsic meaning of words and phrases.

Semitic/BH verb morphology. Every Semitic/BH verb is a combination of two/three separate morphemes (morphological groupings that affect meaning). It always has a **root**, which comprises a sequence of discontiguous consonants (usually three). Furthermore, it always has a **stem**, which comprises a sequence of discontiguous vowels (and four of the stems also have preformative consonants). Lastly, it may contain (but is not required to have) a pronominal element, which may include person (p) (1st ["I" and "we"], 2nd ["you"], 3rd ["he," "she," and "they"]), gender (g) (masculine or feminine), and number (n) (singularly or plural), Pgn is indicated by either suffixes or a combination of suffixes and prefixes.

semelfactive. The **situation aspect** class defined by Carlota Smith represented by [+ dynamic][– telic][– durative]. For example, "Mack *sneezed*." The verb *sneezed* portrays an instantaneous event, and thus is non-durative, but it does not include an inherent endpoint involving a change of **state**.

sentence focus structure. A **focus structure** occurring in sentences without a **topic** expression in which all of the sentence's information is focal and identifiable by factors including, but not limited to, **discontinuity** with the preceding discourse, an irregular sentence subject, and—often—irregular or marked word order. Sentence focus structures can be further classified as either event/**state**-reporting sentences or **participant** presentation sentences.

Septuagint. Septuagint originally referred to the traditional seventy translators of the first Greek translation of the first five books of the Old Testament in the third century BC and, by extension, came to be used of the translation itself. The term is often used to refer to the first Greek translation of each of the books of the Old Testament, even beyond the first five.

sequentiality. The property of expressing temporal or logical sequence.

serialation. A **coherence relation** in which a verb or verb phrase provides the circumstances for the succeeding one but not its cause. In other words the first is necessary for the second to happen, but not sufficient to make it happen. For example in Genesis 14:13 "An escapee *came* and *told* Abram the Hebrew," *came* provides the circumstances for the telling of the news to Abram, but did not compel him to do it.

Silurian. A system of rock layers and a time period of the **Paleozoic** era in the conventional global geologic timescale, covering the time span of 419–444 million years ago, and named after the Silures, a Celtic tribe.

simultaneity. An interaction between two eventualities, which obtains when they can occur at the same time. See **compatibility**.

situation. A condition or occurrence, real or unreal, portrayed linguistically by a verb or verb phrase.

situation aspect. The kind of aspect associated with semantic properties of verbs and verb phrases rather than formal marking. Two verb phrases, such as "The hare *ran the race*." and "The hare *won the race*," although syntactically identical, differ in situation aspect in that their temporal properties differ; the latter verb phrase is telic, that is, includes an inherent endpoint associated with a change of **state** (the state of the hare having won the race), whereas the former is not.

stage-level state. A state expected to last only temporally due to world knowledge; with regard to **situation aspect**, stage-level states do not differ from individual-level **state**s. Examples include "Andrew *was sick with a cold*," and "Joan *was upset about the situation*." The state in both examples would ordinarily be expected to last only temporarily.

stasis. Morphologic (body shape) constancy of a species through a stratigraphically significant conventional time interval, that is, through a significantly large sequence of rock layers.

state. A non-dynamic **situation**; states may be subcategorized according to the system of classification proposed in **Chapter 11** as **atelic states**, **transitory states**, and **point states**, each which is defined in this glossary. An atelic state is durative and atelic (e.g. "Their house *is beautifully nestled between two hills*"); a transitory state, while also durative, is telic, that is, has an inherent endpoint at which the state ceases ("We *were anxious until the package arrived*"); and a point state is non-durative, obtaining only instantaneously, but also telic ("It *was 7:15 p.m. when the gentlemen walked through the door*").

sticker. Stative **situation** information appended to a node in **DAT**.

stratigraphic. Pertaining to stratigraphy, which is the science of rock layers, being concerned not only with the original succession and age relationships of rock layers, but also with their form, distribution, rock composition, fossil content, and geophysical and geochemical properties, that is, with all characters and attributes of rocks as strata, and their interpretation conventionally in terms of environment or mode of origin and geologic history.

stratomorphic series. A series of fossils in successively stacked rock layers that show changes in their morphology or body shape and ornamentation, even though they remain varieties within the same created kind or **monobaramin**, often being conventionally argued as showing the evolution of an organism through gradual changes over time, when in fact there is no change in the body plan so it is just variation within a created kind.

stromatolites. Organo-sedimentary structures produced by sediment trapping, binding, and/or precipitation as a result of the growth and **metabolic** activity of micro-organisms, principally cyanophytes (blue-green algae). Such algal mats on sediment surfaces build these structures that have a variety of growth forms, from nearly horizontal to markedly columnar, domal, or subspherical.

structure. When applied to set theory, it refers to a set with one or more binary relations between the elements of the set. For example, an instant structure is the set of all **instants** of time, which has the property of **precedence**.

subduction. The process of one crustal plate descending beneath another crustal plate. A current example is the eastern edge of the Pacific Plate descending into the mantle underneath the western edge of the South American Plate along the Peru-Chile Trench offshore of Peru and Chile.

substantivalism. A theory from the philosophy of space-time, which asserts that space and time are absolutes. The foremost proponent of this idea was Sir Isaac Newton.

substrate. A substance, base, or nutrient on which, or the medium in which, an organism lives and grows, or the surface to which a fixed organism is attached, such as soil, rocks, the ocean floor, water, and leaf tissues.

summary. A **coherence relation**, in which eventualities depicted by a group of verbs, take place in the same time interval as that of the **eventuality** represented by the verb that follows the group. For example, "Carl's wife made the family bacon and eggs. There was little traffic driving into the office. His secretary had a pot of coffee waiting for him. His cranky first client cancelled his appointment. *Carl had a great morning.*"

superposition. The order in which rocks are placed or accumulated in beds one above the other, the highest bed being the youngest. That is, the process by which successively younger sedimentary rock layers are deposited on lower and older layers.

symmetry. For a given relational operator, if x R y, then y R x. For example, suppose R is =. If x = y, then y = x. But this would not be the case were R to be <. (See **asymmetry**.)

synchronic analysis. The study of language as it exists at a certain point in time with sole attention to actual usage, conducted for the purpose of understanding the contemporary meaning of various words and grammatical constructions. Unlike **diachronic analysis**, it is conducted without reference to previous changes or developments over time that might have contributed to different meanings in the language.

tail topic. A **topic** expression which always appears in right-dislocated constructions and which serves to elaborate on **primary topic**s either by providing some additional (but less salient) information about that topic, or by making explicit any information that is already cognitively accessible about that topic.

Targum. An Aramaic translation of the Old Testament. Several such translations were made around the turn of the era and the centuries following in both Jewish and Samaritan circles.

tectonics. A branch of geology dealing with the broad architecture of the outer part of the earth, that is, the regional assembling of structural or deformational features, a study of their mutual relations, origin, and historical development, involving large-scale earth movements that form mountain ranges and other topographic features, as well as explaining where the continents are today and how they came to be in their positions.

telicity. A semantic ending point; definitions differ concerning whether this endpoint is temporal or spatial. Temporal endpoints may be present for stative **situations**, as in the example "He *was sick for three weeks*," where the adverbial modifier "for three weeks" specifies an endpoint in time. Spatial endpoints may only obtain with dynamic situations, as in the example, "He *ran to the store*," in which "the store" marks a spatial endpoint and the time of the arrival at the store becomes the temporal endpoint of the situation.

temporal discontinuity. A break in the normal flow of time in a **narrative**$_{(2)}$. Time can jump backward (called flashback) or forward before resuming its normal flow.

tense. The grammatical expression of time.

Tertiary. The system of rock layers and era compromising the **Paleogene** and **Neogene** of the conventional global geologic timescale, covering the time span of 2.6–66 million years ago.

textual criticism. The discipline of comparing copies of texts, delineating the history of texts' transmission, and reconstructing earlier forms of the texts.

thematic paragraph. The smallest textual unit above the level of the clause, consisting of at least one sentence with one **primary topic** or a topicless **sentence focus structure**.

thematic prominence. The significance a given expression has in developing the **theme** of a discourse.

theme trace. A signal embedded in the text that aids in the illumination of the **theme**. A theme trace may be, e.g., a marked syntactic configuration or a recurring concept.

theme. The developing and coherent core or thread of a discourse in the mind of the speaker-author and hearer-reader, functioning as the prominent **macrostructure** of the discourse. Theme is not equivalent to the **primary topic**(s) of a unit of text or that information which is added to the known information in a unit of text. Theme is not the same as the plot of a **narrative**$_{(2)}$, nor can it be reduced to a lone **macro-word**, a single macro-proposition, a motif, or in the case of biblical texts, a main theological or doctrinal point asserted by a narrative.

Tommotian. A series of rock layers in Russia that together form a time stage within the lower **Cambrian** time period of the conventional global geologic timescale, as well as referring to the unusual shelly fauna found fossilized in those rock layers.

tomography. A method for finding the velocity distribution for a multitude of observations using combinations of source and receiver locations, used especially with **seismic waves** to give a three-dimensional "picture" of the internal structure of the earth, based on different densities of the rock and other materials and their distribution inside the earth.

topic frame. A type of topic expression: a presupposed, topical referent that sets a frame for another topic, normally a **primary topic**.

topic. The element of a proposition which the proposition is about, i.e. the presupposed referent to which the newly asserted information adds. Within a **narrative**$_{(2)}$, topic is evidenced and advanced by the means of a topic expression.

transgressive/transgression. Pertaining to transgression, which is the spread or extension of the sea over land areas, and the consequent evidence of such advance, such as rock layers deposited unconformably on older rocks, especially where marine deposits are spread far and wide over the former land surface. It also pertains to any change, such as rise of sea level or subsidence of land, that brings offshore, typically deep-water sediments to areas formerly occupied by nearshore, typically shallow-water sediments, or that shifts the boundary between marine and non-marine deposition (or between deposition and erosion) outward from the center of a marine basin.

transitivity. For a given relational operator R, if x R y and y R z, then x R z. For example, for R = < . if x < y and y < z, then x < z.

transitory state. A **situation aspect** class defined in **Chapter 11** of this volume and represented by [− dynamic][+ telic][+ durative]. It may also refer to a **state** type defined by William Croft and corresponding to a **stage-level state**.

transposition. When words are moved (accidentally or intentionally) from one place in a text to another.

trilobites. Marine arthropods characterized by a three-lobed, ovoid to sub-elliptical external skeleton divisible longitudinally into axial and side regions, and transversally into cephalon (head), thorax (middle body), and pygidium (posterior or tail). Such creatures are now extinct and are found only in rock layers assigned to the **Paleozoic**.

tsunami. Gravitational sea-waves produced by any large-scale, short-duration disturbance of the ocean floor, principally by a shallow submarine earthquake, but also by submarine slumps, subsidence, or volcanic eruption. They are characterized by great speed of propagation (up to 600 mph [965.6 kph]), long wavelength (up to 125 mi [201 km]), long period (varying from five minutes to a few hours), and low observable height on the open sea, although they may pile up to heights of 100 ft (30.4 m) or more and cause much damage on entering shallow water along an exposed coast (often thousands of miles from the source). The word is derived from the Japanese for "harbor waves."

unconformities. Substantial breaks or gaps in the geologic record where a rock unit is overlain by another that is not next in the **stratigraphic** or rock layer succession, such as an interruption in the continuity of a depositional sequence of sedimentary rocks or a break between eroded igneous rocks and younger sedimentary rock layers. They result from a change that caused deposition to cease for a period of time, and normally imply uplift and erosion with loss of the previously formed rock record.

uniformitarianism. The assumption that "the geological forces of the past differ neither in kind nor in energy from those now in operation," which was the basis advocated by Charles Lyell for interpreting past phenomena by analogy with modern ones, often expressed in the cliché "the present is the key to the past."

unmarked. The typical way of expressing something that does not suggest any particular added significance. For instance, the phrase "he runs" is a normal, unmarked, simple present verb, whereas the more unusual "he is running" is marked to emphasize the progressive nature of that verb.

(verb) stems. These are for the most part morphological-semantic-syntactic transformations of the simple verbal stems (or grand stem) of the Semitic languages. "Morphological" because they have different vowels from the ground stem, and some stems have preformatives (consonants added in front of the ground form) as well. "Semantic" because they involve a change in meaning. And "syntactic" because they may add or subtract the number of direct objects as compared with the ground stem. BH has seven regular stems: the ground stem (*Qal*) and six derived stems.

viewpoint aspect. The kind of **aspect** marked formally which expresses viewpoints (e.g. internal, external) relative to **situation**s. For example, the difference between the two past time verb phrases, "The koala *ate the eucalyptus*" and "The koala *was eating the eucalyptus*" is one of viewpoint aspect. Languages differ in what kind of marking is associated with differences in **situation aspect**.

violation of expectations. This **situation** obtains when the reader expects Q because of P, but instead the text has *not* Q. For example, "When Bob was in college he liked Zelda a lot, but he never asked her out for a date." (See **denial of preventer**.)

volcanic arcs. Generally curved linear belts of volcanoes and volcanic rocks above a subduction zone along which one crustal plate is descending underneath the edge of another adjoining plate, the **subduction** process causing melting of rocks to produce **magma** that rises to the surface to form volcanoes along the edge of the plate above the subducting plate.

Vulgate. Jerome's Latin translation of the Bible from the late fourth and early fifth centuries AD.

waw. The Hebrew conjunction, usually translatable as "and" or "but" in English. It is prefixed to the *wayyiqtol* as *way-*, and it is prefixed to the *wᵊqatal* as *we-*.

wayyiqtol. A clause-initial **indicative** verb form within the Hebrew verbal system, which is inflected for person, gender, and number. It is most often assumed to indicate temporal sequence, but more likely functions as the *waw*-initial simple past **tense**, forming the "backbone" of a **narrative**$_{(2)}$. Although It is not sufficient to indicate temporal progression, it appears that its presence is necessary for it to be conveyed.

wᵊqatal. A clause-initial **indicative** verb form within the Hebrew verbal system, which functions as a iterative (or habitual) past or future **tense** equivalent of the *wayyiqtol*.

yaqtul. The likely **proto-Semitic** ancestor of the Hebrew *wayyiqtol* and **jussive** verb forms.

yaqtulu. The likely proto-Semitic ancestor of the Hebrew *yiqtol* verb form.

yiqtol. An **indicative** verb form within the Hebrew verbal system most often used to express the future **tense** or past iterative (or habitual) action. Compare with the *qatal*.

INDEXES

INDEXES

Subject Index

AUTHORITIES INDEX

Scripture Index

22:37 349
22:38 349

2 Kings
2:8–9 718
2:9 ... ... 713, 720
4:8 717
4:35 ... ...386, 409, 497
5:1 758
6:4–5 359
6:17 ... ...497, 501
6:20 497
6:25 733
6:29 359
7:1–2 522–523
7:6–7 359
7:17–19 359
7:17–20 522–523
8:3 253
9:29 255
9:36 399
12:11 715
13:13–21 549–550
13:14–14:16 359
14:6 ... ...197, 644
17:7–23 ... ...616, 620
17:17 359
17:25 420
18:10 253
19:16 497
21:8 ... ...197, 644
22:3 715
22:34–37 597–598
23:36 255
24:18 255
25:2 256

1 Chronicles
1:4 488

12:14 256
12:21 713
14:15 711
24:12 256
25:18 256
27:14 256

2 Chronicles
3:2 258
7:1 ... ... 711, 715
8:1 253
12:11 717
13:23 ... ... 377, 409
20:30 409
24:11 ... ... 715, 721
29:17 402
34:8 715
36:5 255
36:11 255

Ezra
1:1 45
3:2 44
6:18 ... ...197, 644

Nehemiah
1:4 ... ... 714, 720
6:15 402
8:1 44
8:3 44
8:8–9 44
13:1 ... ...197, 644

Esther
2:12 253
5:1 ... ... 728, 729
6:1–11 504
6:11.. ... ... .504